PRESTON
LOCAL
STUDIES

THE
LANCASHIRE
LIBRARY

FOR REFERENCE

ONLY

AUTHOR	CLASS J6
	287.541 DIC

TITLE

DICTIONARY of Methodism in Britain
& Ireland

A Dictionary of Methodism in Britain and Ireland

A Dictionary of Methodism
in
Britain and Ireland

edited by

John A. Vickers

EPWORTH PRESS

To
all those members of the Wesley Historical Society
past and present
whose research has contributed to the making of this Dictionary

081252870 Cpp Pf.

0 7162 0534 3

First published 2000
by Epworth Press
20 Ivatt Way
Peterborough PE3 7PG

Typeset by Rowland Phototypesetting,
Bury St Edmunds, Suffolk
Printed in Great Britain by
Biddles Ltd, Guildford and King's Lynn

Preface

Towards the end of his series of short biographies, *Wesleyan Takings*, James Everett wrote: 'We are compelled to close . . . still leaving hundreds unnamed, who, to do justice to each, would lead at once to what is a desideratum in Methodism – a Biographical Dictionary.' It may seem strange that, apart from a few annual volumes of the *Methodist Who's Who* in the early twentieth century, Everett's desideratum remained a pipe dream. On the other hand, the fact that no such work as this *Dictionary* has previously been attempted may simply point to an excess of Methodist angels over fools eager to rush in.

The present work contains many biographical entries such as Everett desired, but is by no means confined to them. Subject entries and outline local histories are also included. The process of selection, however well informed and carefully planned, presents difficulties that may go a long way towards explaining why it has no predecessor. The choice of subject entries presented relatively little problem; but drawing the line between those persons and places to be included and those omitted is not so much a difficult as an impossible aspect of the editorial process. No two individuals would ever agree on exactly where to draw the line through the grey area separating the two extremes. Compiling the list of entries has involved much consultation and much combing of standard histories and other works on Methodism, including the two General Indexes to the *Proceedings* of the Wesley Historical Society.

Many persons are missing from the Dictionary, primarily because of the limited space available, but also because 'worthiness' on its own was not deemed sufficient to justify an entry. Whether or not 'faithful service' is, as the hymn says, a means to 'full salvation', it does not in itself guarantee a place in the record books. One example will suffice. The Rev. James Wood, after 53 years in the ministry and being twice President of the Wesleyan Conference, was described in his obituary as 'preaching the Gospel with great fidelity, earnestness, diligence and success, and exercising the pastoral charge to the edification of all the societies that were placed under his care'. (Would that there were more such paragons!) Yet much the same might be said of many of his ministerial fellows, then and now, and for that very reason he does not stand out enough to justify an entry.

Like all reference books, the *Dictionary* is designed to be no more than a first port of call, giving little more than the essential information, but 'hopefully' leading to a desire for more. Wherever possible, therefore, sources of further information are added at the end of an entry. Unfortunately, books go out of print all too quickly and may be hard to locate except in specialist libraries. To have taken this factor into account would have seriously limited the guidance given on further reading. It has therefore been ignored, but unpublished sources, whether academic theses or manuscript records, have only occasionally been included.

Decisions on the scope of the *Dictionary* had to be taken in the early stages. 'Methodism' is itself an elastic term which has suffered changes of meaning over the years. Here it is used to include not only the non-Wesleyan connexions of the nineteenth century, but Calvinistic as well as Arminian Methodism and such independent stalwarts as the Wesleyan Reform Union and Independent Methodism.

On the other hand, it has been necessary to deal quite selectively with Methodism beyond the British Isles. In the case of overseas Churches which stem from one or other of the British connexions, the focus has been on origins and early developments, rather than on the indigenous Churches which have resulted from earlier missionary activity. In general the *terminus ad quem* has been the achievement of autonomy, though this does not imply any theological or ecclesiological judgment, so much as an acceptance of inescapable limitations of space. Similarly, the most that can be claimed for the choice of missionaries included is that it aims to be a representative selection. Records of missionary wives and of lay missionaries in the MMS Archives are woefully inadequate or non-existent. And as a matter of policy, the indigenous leaders who played a key role in the rise of overseas Methodism, have had to be excluded.

It has not been part of editorial policy to apply positive discrimination in favour of any groups which might be thought to have received less than their due attention in the past. A high proportion of the biographical entries are Wesleyan, not because of preferential treatment, but because throughout the main period of Methodist disunity, 1797–1932, Wesleyan Methodism remained by far the largest of the Methodist bodies. Similarly, though every effort has been made to do justice to the significant contribution of women, they will nevertheless be found to be heavily outnumbered by the other sex. This is, on the one hand, because of the subordinate roles they were accorded through most of the period and on the other because detailed historical evidence is often lacking, despite the strenuous efforts of feminist historians in recent years. Our task has not been to attempt to make bricks without straw or to set new historiographical trends, but merely to reflect and record the fruits of existing research.

Nonetheless, where evidence exists for the significant, though neglected, role of lay persons (of either sex), we have done our best to avoid the predominantly ministerial stance of earlier (especially Wesleyan) generations of Methodist historians. Methodists who made their mark in the wider society (e.g. in such 'secular' spheres as politics, industry or education) have their place; and those who either left Methodism of their own accord or were expelled (whether from membership or from the ranks of the ministry) have not thereby been debarred from these pages. All are part of our history.

A certain number of Anglican clergy and a few Nonconformists, mostly from the eighteenth century, have been included because of their significant relationship to Methodism in its formative years. For convenience, rather than from any sinister ecclesiological motive, the title 'Rev.' is confined to Anglican clergy. Methodist ministers (including the early itinerants) are readily identifiable by the year they were officially deemed to have 'entered the ministry' ('e.m. . . . '), which is appended to their years of birth and death.

As a matter of convenience, members of the same family are sometimes accorded separate entries, but in other cases are grouped together under a single family entry. Where such family entries occur, they are placed *before* any entries on individuals with the same surname (e.g. **Fletcher Family** before **Fletcher, Rev. John William**).

Entries on Methodism in particular localities are supplemented by others surveying in outline each of the ten Registration Divisions into which England was divided in the nineteenth century for the purposes of the population census (and also for the Census of Religious Worship in 1851): London, the South East, the South Midlands, the Eastern Counties, the South West, the West Midlands, the North Midlands, the North West, Yorkshire and the Northern Counties. The Divisions varied greatly in their Methodist significance, but they furnish an opportunity for a much wider survey of the growth and distribution of the movement, including the non-Wesleyan bodies.

A number of abbreviations are used throughout the text and a list of these will be found on pp. 409–11. To avoid undue duplicating of information there is extensive cross-referencing between related entries, indicated in most cases by an asterisk before the key word or phrase in the text. An exception is made in the case of those that occur most frequently, such as 'Methodism' itself and the names of the Wesley brothers, where the asterisk is omitted.

The sources of further information at the end of entries are given in abbreviated form (by author and year of publication or, in the case of standard reference works and periodicals, by title), fuller details being found in the Bibliography on pp. 412ff. In the case of ministers, the date of an obituary in the *Methodist Recorder* (and occasionally in the secular press) is given, but the existence of one in the *Minutes of Conference* is tacitly assumed.

The *Dictionary* would have been a totally impossible project but for the interest and support of a large number of knowledgeable people at every stage of its compilation. These include the Editorial Advisers and others with special knowledge of particular aspects of British and Irish Methodism. Almost without exception contributors were exemplary in fulfilling their commitments and in meeting deadlines. The editor's debt to them (both for their expertise and for their exemplary patience when they found their contributions squeezed into the proverbial pint pot) is incalculable, as is our common debt to past generations of Methodist historians and theologians whose work we have garnered. Individual contributors are identified by the initials at the end of each article and by reference to the list on pp. xi–xii.

It would have been equally impossible to attempt such a project without the benefits of computerization, and in this respect the editor is heavily indebted to his sons Stephen and Michael who, mostly from the other side of the world, gave expert guidance and support, and also to Mrs Sue Gascoigne and her colleagues at the Methodist Publishing House. My appointment to a Senior Research Fellowship at Westminster College, Oxford was of great help in furthering editorial research and I am glad of the opportunity to acknowledge this here. I am also indebted to Margaret Lydamore's expert copy-editing, which has substantially reduced the editorial blemishes and inconsistencies in the text.

It would be folly indeed to claim that such a work as this contains no errors or omissions. Such as they are, they will begin to creep out of the woodwork the moment the book is published – and, indeed, have already begun to do so. The case of Rita Snowden may, all too probably, prove to be a harbinger of many others. Her death as the page proofs were being checked alerted the editor to the fact that she was not, as he had assumed, a New Zealander, but a deaconess from England. So prolific and popular an author would certainly, but for editorial ignorance, have had her niche in the *Dictionary*. The most, therefore, that may be claimed is that all concerned have done their utmost to make the information accurate and reliable and to avoid that repetition of errors already in print which is the hallmark of reference works in general. We can at least echo the words of Wesley himself, in commending his *Complete English Dictionary* (1753) as 'the best English Dictionary in the World': 'Many are the mistakes in all the other English Dictionaries which I have yet seen: Whereas, I can truly say, I know of none in this: And I conceive the reader will believe me; for if I had, I should not have left it there.' The present editor cannot do better than rest his case on the same ground. He will be none the less grateful to those who draw his attention to undetected errors and indefensible omissions, provided they are accompanied by supporting evidence; and these will be taken into account, if not in a second edition, then in the electronic version of the *Dictionary* which is already being planned.

John A. Vickers

Editorial Advisers

Geoffrey E. Milburn

Dr John A. Newton

Dr Henry Rack

John Munsey Turner

Dr Margaret Batty (Scotland)

Dr Owen E. Evans (Wales)

Mrs M. Joy Fox (Overseas Missions)

Graham Slater (Theology)

Dr Norman W. Taggart (Ireland)

Contributors

*Deceased

Anderson, John H., Stoke on Trent (JHA)
Anstey, Ruth, London (RA)
*Backhouse, Barbara, Wearhead, Co.
    Durham (BB)
Batstone, Dr Patricia, Honiton (PB)
Batty, Dr Margaret, Edinburgh (MB)
Beasley, John D., London (JDB)
Beck, Dr Brian E., Cambridge (BEB)
Beckerlegge, Dr Oliver A., York (OAB)
Bennett, W., Amble, Northumberland (WB)
Biggs, Dr Barry J., Foston, Lincs (BJB)
Blanchard, Bernard W., Chirnside,
    Berwickshire (BWB)
Bolitho, Paul, Warwick (PBo)
Bowden, Kenneth F., Bacup (KFB)
Bridge, J. David, Bognor Regis (JDBr)
Butler, David A.R., Bromley (DARB)
Carter, Dr Barbara J., Swindon (BJC)
Carter, David J., Carshalton (DJC)
Carter, Philip L., Bristol (PLC)
Cass, Alan N., Sheffield (ANC)
Champley, Andrew P., Richmond,
    N. Yorks (APC)
Clancy, Eric G., Carlingford (EGC)
Clarke, Ernest A., Dursley (EAC)
Claxton, Cecil, Berwick-upon-Tweed (CC)
Cooke, Sheila M.E., Gloucester (SMEC)
Cooney, D.A. Levistone, Glenageary,
    Co. Dublin (DALC)
Cowin, Frank, Douglas, IOM (FC)
Crawford, Keith E., Witney (KEC)
Crocker, W. John, Stroud (WJC)
Crofts, Bruce D., Bath (BDC)
Crofts, John, Attenborough, Notts (JC)
Dews, D. Colin, Leeds (DCD)

Dolan, John A., Warrington (JAD)
Dunn-Wilson, Dr David, Meru, Kenya (DDW)
Dykes, Eric W., Lytham St Annes (EWD)
*Edwards, Michael S., Redhill (MSE)
English, Dr John C., Baldwin , Kansas (JCE)
Ensor, David, Fovant, Salisbury (DE)
Evans, Dr Owen E., Llanfair PG, Ynys
    Môn (OEE)
*Farrow, Derek R., Christchurch (DRF)
Field, Dr Clive D., Birmingham (CDF)
Forsaith, Peter W., Wootton, Abingdon (PWF)
Fox, M. Joy, High Wycombe (MJF)
Garfoot, John, Kings Lynn (JG)
Gentry, Peter W., Weston-super-Mare (PWG)
*George, A. Raymond, Bristol (ARG)
Graham, Dr E. Dorothy, Birmingham (EDG)
Greet, Dr Kenneth G., Rustington (KGG)
Griffiths, E.H., Rhuddlan, Clwyd (EHG)
Grundy, Donald M., Selston (DMG)
Hargreaves, Dr John A., Halifax (JAH)
Harris, Dr Elizabeth J., London (EJH)
Harris, Jeffrey W., St Albans (JWH)
Hatcher, Dr Stephen G., Tunstall (SGH)
Haydon, Donald G., Flagstaff Hill, S. Australia
    (DGH)
Hempton, Professor David N., Belfast (DNH)
Himsworth, Sheila J., Cambridge (SJH)
Horton, William D., Bury St Edmunds (WDH)
Howdle, Susan R., Leeds (SRH)
Hughes, Dr. Glyn T., Tregynon, Powys (GTH)
Hunt, Martin R., Cardiff (MRH)
Jackson, Michael J., Mansfield (MJJ)
Jakes, Eileen, Ely (EJ)
James, E. Margaret, Wareham (EMJ)
Kerridge, Peter A., York (PAK)
Knighton, Donald G., Aberystwyth (DGK)
Lander, John K., Reigate (JKL)

Le Boutillier, Freda, St Helier, Jersey (FLeB)
Leary, William, Grimsby (WL)
Lee, Geoffrey D., Milton Keynes (GDL)
Lenton, John H., Wellington, Salop (JHL)
Leteve, Edward, Carlisle (EL)
Lewis, I.G.P., Welshpool (IGPL)
Lowes, Mary, Barnard Castle (ML)
Luckcock, Dr Janet L., Dereham (JLL)
McGonigle, Dr Herbert, Manchester (HMG)
McMurray, Nigel, Greenford (NM)
Macquiban, Timothy S.A., Oxford (TSAM)
Milburn, Geoffrey E., Sunderland (GEM)
Moore, Norman, F., Newcastle-upon-Tyne (NFM)
Morris, Dr Geoffrey M., Sprotbrough, Doncaster (GMM)
Myatt, Dorothy F., Cheltenham (DFM)
Newton, Dr John A., Bristol (JAN)
O'Connor, Dr T. Max, Brighton, Australia (TMO)
Parkes, Dr William, Biddulph (WP)
Parsons, R. Keith, Torquay (RKP)
Peck, Albert E., Coventry (AEP)
Phillipps, Donald J., Dunedin, New Zealand (DJP)
Plant, Dr Stephen J., London (SJP)
Pritchard, John R., Croydon (JRP)
Robson, Dr Geoffrey, Derby (GR)
Rodd, Dr Cyril S., Emsworth (CSR)
Roddie, Robin P., Newtownards, Co. Down (RPR)

Rose, E. Alan, Mottram (EAR)
Royle, Dr Edward, York (ER)
Ryan, Donald H., Wolverhampton (DHR)
Scotland, Dr Nigel A.D., Cheltenham (NADS)
Senior, Geoffrey R., Emsworth (GRS)
Shaw, Thomas, Perranporth (TS)
Slater, Graham, Beaumaris (GS)
Smith, C. Hughes, Nottingham (CHS)
Spittal, C. Jeffrey, Bristol (CJS)
Sutcliffe, Peter W., Stockton-on-Tees (PWS)
Taggart, Dr Norman W., Coleraine (NWT)
Thorne, Roger. F.S., Exeter (RFST)
Tranter, Donald B., Oxford (DBT)
Trinder, Dr Barrie, Rothwell (BT)
Tudur, Dr Geraint, Bangor, Gwynnedd (GT)
Turner, J. Munsey, Bolton (JMT)
Valentine, Dr Simon R., Bradford (SRV)
Vanns, Sidney, Newark (SV)
Vickers, Dr John A., Emsworth (JAV)
Vincent, Dr John J., Sheffield (JJV)
Virgoe, Norma, Wymondham (NV)
Wakefield, Dr Gordon S., Lichfield (GSW)
Watthews, Elizabeth, Ipswich (EW)
Webb, Dr Pauline M., London (PMW)
Weetman, Barry, Walsall (BW)
Wellings, Dr Martin, Brackley (MW)
White, Herbert W., Taunton (HWW)
Willavoys, David, Tewkesbury (DW)
Yabaki, Akuila D., Fiji (ADY)

Abercrombie, Richard (1797–1881; e.m. 1836), WMA and UMFC minister, joined the army after Waterloo. In France he was converted and later accompanied Lorenzo Dow to Ireland. He assisted in establishing Methodism in *Gibraltar, but was expelled from WM in 1834 because of his Reform sympathies. He joined the WMA and entered its ministry, superannuating in 1871.

OAB

Aberdeen JW responded to a request from Dr John Memis by sending C. *Hopper in 1759 to preach and form a society and made the first of 14 visits himself in 1761. An octagon chapel was built in Queen Street in 1764. Aberdeen Circuit was formed by 1765. In 1792, during his superintendency, A. *Kilham wrote his 'Trueman and Freeman' address, advocating the extension of lay power in governing the Connexion, and in 1797, when the WM Conference rejected the admission of laymen to the District Meeting, members of the Aberdeen society seceded and were instrumental in founding the Congregational Church in Scotland. There were further losses between 1835 and 1850, mainly of those who wanted more independence. Under V. *Ward the society moved in 1818 to Longacre Chapel (formerly St Andrew's Episcopal Church), which was replaced by the present church in Crown Terrace, designed by James Souttar and still in use. In the mid-nineteenth century there was a remarkable expansion along the Moray coast from Banff to Portgordon, led by James *Turner, a *local preacher of Peterhead.

C. Diack (1901); A. Gammie (1909); W.F. Swift (1947); E. Wilkinson (1972)

MB

Abney House *see* **Hoxton**

Ackworth, John *see* **Smith, F.R.**

Adam, Rev. Thomas (1701–84), rector of Wintringham, Cambs, 1724–84, close friend and correspondent of the Rev. S. *Walker of Truro. His writings included the posthumous *Private Thoughts on Religion*. Like Walker, he urged JW in the 1750s against separating from the Cof E and in 1768 protested that the Methodists were acting 'under a lie, professing themselves members of the Church of England while they licensed themselves as Dissenters'. In July 1772 W was 'surprised and grieved' by his '*Comment on the former part of the Epistle to the Romans*', judging it to be 'the very quintessence of *Antinomianism'.

A. Westoby (1837)

JAV

Adams, John Couch (1819–92), English astronomer, born at Laneast, Cornwall and educated at St John's College, Cambridge, where he was senior wrangler and the first Smith's prizeman. His discovery by mathematical deduction of the existence of the planet Neptune in 1843–45, at the same time as but independently of Leverrier, led to controversy and he refused a knighthood in 1847. He was awarded the Adams Prize and became an FRS in 1849. He was a Fellow of St John's until 1852 and then of Pembroke. From 1859 on he was Professor of Astronomy at Cambridge and from 1861 Director of the Cambridge Observatory. His investigation of lunar theory and Leonid meteors won him a gold medal of the Royal Astronomical Society in 1866. His omnivorous reading included theology and there is a memorial to him in *Truro Cathedral.

DNB

JAV

Adams, Margaret (1799–1822) an early BC itinerant whose ministry resulted in many conversions. Her name appears in the first list of BC itinerants (1819) as stationed at *Truro. She then went to Canworthy Water, but in 1821 ill-health (described as 'scrophula' – probably a form of tuberculosis) forced her superannuation. She took occasional services before retiring to her uncle's home at Hartland, where she died, the first BC female itinerant to 'die in the work' and merit an obituary in the BC *Minutes*.

F.W. Bourne (1905)

EDG

Adams-Acton, John (1830–1910), sculptor, son of a WM mother. Born John Adams at Acton, Middx, he adopted the hyphenated name. He was a prolific sculptor of royalty, statesmen and ecclesiastics and such prominent figures as Dickens and Spurgeon. He exhibited frequently at the Royal Academy. He was the only Protestant to sculpt Pope Leo XIII, also producing the tomb effigy of Cardinal Manning in Westminster Cathedral. Known as 'the Wesleyan sculptor' for his many prominent WM sitters (e.g. J.H. *Rigg, W.F. *Moulton, J. *Farrar, Sir R. *Perks, Sir I. *Holden, and H.H. *Fowler), some of which may be seen at *Wesley's Chapel, he was also responsible for the memorial to JW and CW (1876) in Westminster Abbey, instigated by F.W. *Jobson, and for the bronze statue of JW (1891) in the forecourt of Wesley's Chapel. His two sons Harold and Murray Adams-Acton were also sculptors. His wife Marion (1846–1928) wrote fiction under the name 'Jeanie Hering'.

MR 3 Nov. 1910; *DNB*; A.M.W. Stirling (1954)

PSF

Addyman, John (1808–87; e.m. 1833) and his brother Robert (b.1819) were WM *local preachers in *Leeds who seceded to the *Protestant Methodists before joining the *MNC. John, the first MNC overseas missionary, served in *Canada 1837–45, was Irish President in 1851 and President of the Conference, 1858. His brother Robert, a Leeds cloth merchant and manufacturer, was a Liberal councillor, elected Mayor in 1879.

DCD

Advance and Priority Fund, Connexional, established in 1968, is one of the few which make grants for both property and ministry. It is raised by a levy on proceeds from the sale of property. Where these are to be used immediately for a replacement scheme, the levy is waived. Grants are made for new work of connexional significance, essential and urgent building schemes and the creation and support of priority appointments. The fund is administered by a committee appointed by Conference. Among projects supported by it have been new diaconal appointments made when the *Diaconal Order was re-opened in 1986 and the major refurbishment of *Westminster Central Hall.

PWS

African Methodist Episcopal and **African Methodist Episcopal Zion Churches** are Churches of American origin with several small congregations located in the London area. The AME Church originated in Philadelphia in 1787, when black members separated from St George's ME Church under the leadership of Richard Allen. The denomination was officially organized in 1816 and is the largest of the black Methodist bodies. The AME Zion Church was formed out of John Street ME Church, New York, when black members built Zion Chapel, but maintained close relations with the ME Church until 1821. Both bodies have work in Africa and the Caribbean.

WMC Handbook 1997–2001; D.H. Bradley (1956)

WP

Ainsworth, Percy (1873–1909; e.m. 1896), WM minister, poet and naturalist. A prophetic preacher with a powerful command of language, he held truth to be beauty and beauty, truth. He exercised a forceful social and temperance ministry and actively supported the *Wesley Guild movement. He was an authority on reptiles, a keen sportsman and a gymnastic instructor. His publications included two volumes of sermons, biblical meditations and *Poems and Sonnets* (1910). He died of a fever contracted in the course of his pastoral work.

MR 8 July 1909

WDH

Aitken, Rev. Robert (1799–1873), ordained Anglican priest in 1824, was appointed curate at St George's, Douglas, *IOM and built Eyreton Castle, Crosby, in 1834. He supported the building of a WM chapel at Crosby (1833) and of Castletown WM chapel (1834). In conflict with the Anglican Church, he applied for recognition as a WM minister (1834–35). This was refused, but he was granted the status of *local preacher in the Douglas Circuit. Accused of subversive activities because of his association with Manx WR, he left the Island and supported the WMA in Lancashire. In 1836 he founded the Christian Society in *Liverpool, was re-instated as an Anglican priest and returned to the IOM in 1847. He engaged in evangelistic temperance work in the North of England, was invited to supervise St John's Episcopal Church, *Glasgow, and eventually settled in Pendeen, Cornwall, though still travelling extensively, mostly on temperance crusades.

E.V. Chapman (1982)

FC

Akroyd, Jonathan (1782–1847), son of **James Akroyd** who successfully made the transition from rural yeoman clothier to textile manufacturer. Associated initially with WM, his family became founder members of the MNC cause at Salem, *Halifax in 1797. Jonathan opened a large Sunday School near his mills, employed a home missionary and contributed £2,330 to the new chapel built in 1845. An opponent of factory legislation, he successfully repelled an attack on his mills by plug rioters in 1842 and was a prominent supporter of the Anti-Corn Law League. He dominated the Whig-Liberal leadership in Halifax until his sudden death during the 1847 election campaign. In 1854 his body was reinterred in a sumptuous mortuary chapel built by his son at Haley Hill.

JAH

Alder, Dr Robert (1795–1870; e.m.1816), WM missionary to Nova Scotia and Montreal 1817–28 and a Secretary of the WMMS 1833–51 during a period of vacillating relations between British and *Canadian Methodism. Between 1833 and 1847 he was involved as representative of the WMMS in negotiations over Canadian Methodism's relationship to the MEC and to British Methodism. Seen by his Canadian critics as conservative and autocratic, he nevertheless presided over the first Canadian Conference following Canadian Methodism's return to the British fold in 1847. He received a doctorate from Middletown University. He resigned from the ministry in 1853, obtained Anglican orders and later was Archdeacon of *Gibraltar.

F&H 1

JAV

Allan, Charles Wilfrid (1870–1958; e.m. 1895), WM missionary appointed to Central *China in 1895, where he helped to prepare the Union Version of the Chinese Bible. During World War I he worked with Chinese labourers in France. Returning to China in 1922, he taught at Union Theological College, Changsa and from 1930 served with the Christian Literature Society. Interned by the Japanese 1943–45, he superannuated in 1946. He wrote several books on China,

including *Lives of Chu and Lo* (two Chinese ministers), and edited an enlarged edition of W.H. *Scarborough's *Collection of Chinese Proverbs* (Shanghai, 1926).

MR 22 May 1958

GRS

Allan, Thomas (1774–1845), a London solicitor, born in Malton, was appointed connexional legal adviser in 1803 and was the brain behind the *Committee of Privileges. He came into national prominence in countering the *Sidmouth Bill of 1811, which would have effectively ended *local preaching. Helped by J. *Butterworth and T. *Thompson, Allan produced 700 petitions containing 30,000 signatures and the Bill was 'killed'. He also master-minded the new *Toleration Act of 1812 (52 George III c 155), which was important for all the Free Churches. He drafted a new *Model Deed and advised *Bunting on Mission administration, the education of the preachers and general Conference legislation. Ardently Protestant, he opposed Catholic Emancipation in 1829 and grants to Catholic schools. He was Master of the Haberdashers' Company in 1838. As *local preacher he was content to preach to the poor. He was a much under-estimated figure in the consolidation of WM.

D. Hempton (1996) pp. 109–29; M. Batty (1993)

JMT

Allan Library was given to the WM Connexion in 1884 by Thomas Robinson Allan (1799–1886), barrister son of T. *Allan. It comprised a large and valuable collection of Bibles, liturgical works and Reformation literature, to be situated in London for the use of WM ministers. A Committee of Management was appointed by the Conference in 1885. In 1920 it was sold to the London Library, the proceeds to be used to assist WM ministers and others to be members of that Library. Subsequently the administration of the fund came under the *General Purposes Fund Committee and in 1986 the Charity Commissioners approved a scheme vesting the fund in the *Trustees for Methodist Church Purposes as custodian trustees. The managing trustees (now the Methodist Council) are to apply the income for Methodist Ministers and probationers by assisting in library provision, library subscriptions and travelling expenses in attending libraries for research purposes.

LQR Oct. 1885 pp. 123–36

SRH

Allen, Elizabeth (*c*. 1803–1850) began to take part in services soon after the PM preachers visited her native Kirkoswald. Although her talent for speaking aroused opposition, she became a *local preacher at 21 and an itinerant in 1825. She conducted missions in *Scotland and *Ireland, often in the open air because of the great crowds attracted by the novelty of a woman preacher. She retired on marrying John Vernon of *Macclesfield in 1835, but continued as a local preacher.

PMM 1850; E.D. Graham (1989) p. 1

EDG

Allen, Thomas, DD (1837–1912; e.m. 1859) trained at *Didsbury College for the WM ministry. As Chairman of the Sheffield WM District, 1886–97, he was highly regarded by both civic leaders and working classes. In 1896 he represented WM at the General Conference of the MEC. From 1897 to 1905 he was Chairman of the Birmingham District and Governor of *Handsworth College and was elected President of the Conference in 1900.

MR 22 Aug. 1912

JAV

Allen, William Shepherd, MP (1831–1915), WM *local preacher and circuit steward, born in *Manchester. He became a magistrate and Deputy Lieutenant for Staffordshire and was Liberal MP for *Newcastle-under-Lyme 1865–86. He was opposed to raising the educational requirements for local preachers. He published *Revivalism* (1868), *The Present Position of Wesleyan Methodism* (1871) and *The Itinerant System Considered in Reference to the Future of Wesleyan Methodism and the Forward Movement* (1892).

M. Stenton, vol. 1 (1976); G. Milburn & M. Batty (1995) pp. 77–8

CJS

Alley, James Murdock (1867–1955; e.m. 1886), Secretary of the Irish Conference 1913–21 and General Secretary of the Irish HM Fund 1930–38, was the son of a WM minister, George Alley (1830–1912; e.m. 1852). During his long and influential ministry he occupied most of the responsible posts under the Irish Conference and made an impressive contribution to the development of its administrative departments. He played a large part in shaping the 1915 Parliamentary Statutes which constituted the Statutory Trustees of the MCI. He edited the *Irish Church Record* for most of its 25 years existence.

ICA 26 Nov. 1954; *MR* 13 Jan. 1955

RPR

Allin, Thomas (1784–1866; e.m. 1808), MNC minister who quickly became its leading apologist. Despite a limited formal education, he soon showed himself an outstanding preacher, especially in the defence of orthodoxy. With S. *Hulme he laboured to raise the status of the MNC ministry. He was a resolute opponent of J. *Barker and conducted the trial which led to his expulsion in 1841. He was Corresponding Member of the Annual Committee 1833–48 and Missionary Secretary 1849–60, and was elected President in 1822 and 1846.

S. Hulme (1881); G.J. Stevenson (1884–86) 4 pp. 600–7

EAR

Alsop, Ada (1915–68), celebrated soprano, from *Darlington. She sang in oratorio with all the leading British choirs, recorded with Decca and became widely known through her work on radio and TV and her appearances at the 'Proms'. She and her husband Harry Hayman, who was also her manager, belonged to Elm Ridge Methodist Church, where she sang in the choir and he was choirmaster. In 1951, and again in 1956, she made successful tours of the USA and Canada, arranged by her former minister, A.S. *Leyland, the secretary for ministerial exchanges.

MR 28 June 1951

JAV

America Though the ground had been prepared by G. *Whitefield on his several transAtlantic visits, WM arrived in the American colonies with Irish immigrants in the 1760s. It has been one of the least profitable controversies between northern and southern historians whether priority should be accorded to Robert Strawbridge in Maryland or to Barbara Heck and Philip Embury in New York. The evidence remains inconclusive, but it was with the New Yorkers that contact was made by Captain T. *Webb in 1767 and in response to appeals from New York that the first British itinerants, R. *Boardman and J. *Pilmore, went out in 1769. Others followed, notably F. *Asbury in 1771 and T. *Rankin in 1773. To them, more than to any other preacher, belongs the credit for uniting what had been scattered and isolated societies into an American *connexion, despite the major disruption of the Revolutionary War. The spiritual destitution of his American followers in the wake of that war caused JW in September 1784 to take matters into his own hands and *ordain two of his itinerants, R. *Whatcoat and T. *Vasey, for the American work, with Dr T. *Coke, appointed as Superintendent. The 'Christmas Conference' in Baltimore later that year formally constituted the Methodist Episcopal Church, with Coke and Asbury as its Superintendents (soon to be called 'Bishops' despite W's strong disapproval) and from then on American Methodism, with only fraternal links to the British connexion, grew rapidly in a rapidly developing nation, to become one of the largest Protestant bodies in America and by far the largest member Church in *World Methodism.

C. Atmore (1801) pp. 537–82; F&H 1 pp. 199–255; F.A. Norwood (1974) pp. 61–102; F. Baker (1976); F. Baker in *PWHS* 44 pp. 117–29
                                                        J A V

Anderson, Capt Edward, farmer's son from Kilham on the Yorkshire wolds. After a period working as a shepherd, he went to sea, where he had many escapades, including shipwreck, capture by French privateers and seizure by the press-gang. Converted under the preaching of his brother Henry Anderson (1766–1843; e.m. 1791), WM minister at Pitt Street chapel, *Liverpool, he settled in *Hull, joined the Mill Street PM society and became an anti-slavery advocate and temperance reformer. He was present at the first Mow Cop *camp meeting in 1807 and it was he who raised a flag to direct people to the ground. He wrote a poem *The Life of a Sailor*, which he used at the camp meeting.
                                                        W L

Anderson, Dr George W., FBA, FRSE (1913– ; e.m. 1936)) was born in *Arbroath and educated at St Andrews, *Wesley House, Cambridge and the University of Lund. He was Assistant Tutor at *Richmond College before serving as an RAF chaplain (1941). In 1946 he was appointed OT Tutor at *Handsworth College; in 1956, Lecturer in OT Literature and Theology at St Andrews; and in 1958, Professor of OT Studies at Durham. He moved to the University of Edinburgh in 1962, being successively Professor of OT Literature and Theology and of Hebrew and OT Studies, retiring in 1975. He received the Birkitt Medal for Biblical Studies in 1982. He played a prominent part in both the British and the International OT Societies, being elected President of both. *A Critical Introduction to the OT* (1959) and *The History and Religion of Israel* (1966) are excellent textbooks. He gave the first C. Ryder *Smith Memorial Lecture in 1964 and the *Fernley Hartley Lecture in 1969. His translation of Mowinckel's *He That Cometh* (1956) is notably fluent.
                                                        C S R

Andrews, Charles William (1862–1940; e.m. 1885), scholar and evangclist, one of three ministerial sons of P. Neville Andrews (1833–94; e.m. 1861), was educated at *Kingswood and St Andrews University. He wrote a biography of W. *Bramwell (1909) and was appointed in 1897 to create the highly successful *Bolton Mission. As a Missionary Secretary, 1913–30, he reorganized the work in the *West Indies after the failure of self-government, wiped out its debts and in 1928 bought 'Caenwood' as a centre for ministerial training in Jamaica.

MR 1 Feb. 1940
                                                        J H L

Anglican Clergy The eighteenth century *Church of England became predominantly Erastian and Latitudinarian in reaction against the religious fanaticism of the previous century. Nevertheless, the high church party retained the support of many of the parish clergy (like JW's father) and survived to provide part of the background to the nineteenth-century Oxford Movement.

Most evangelicals were *Calvinistic. The earliest sympathizers and supporters of the Evangelical Revival who had been associated with the *'Holy Club' at Oxford (e.g. J. *Clayton. J. *Hervey, C. *Kinchin) tended to distance themselves from Methodism as it developed under JW's leadership, partly because of his *Arminianism. Some followed *Whitefield or joined the Countess of *Huntingdon. Others became *Moravians. Otherwise sympathetic parish clergy had misgivings about such irregularities as *field preaching and the use of unordained preachers. In the 1750s S. *Walker and T. *Adam joined CW in persuading JW against a formal separation from the Church.

JW was unable to persuade more than one or two to abandon their parish work for an itinerant ministry, though W. *Grimshaw, J. *Berridge and J. *Baddiley were partial exceptions. Even J. *Fletcher confined himself largely to *Madeley. Some of those who joined him on a full-time basis were ones who had been ousted from their parish because of their evangelical leanings (e.g. T. *Coke, J. *Richardson).

Local clergy (who were often also magistrates) sometimes incited the mob against the Methodist preachers, especially if they found themselves the object of criticism for their worldliness or even immorality (e.g. at Wednesbury). Some bishops gave qualified encouragement to the early movement in its early days, but others (e.g. E. *Gibson, G. *Horne, W. *Warburton and notably G. *Lavington) were among its outstanding critics.

In the mid-1760s JW made a determined attempt to form a united front among the evangelical clergy of his acquaintance, but his circular letter of 19 April 1764 brought only three responses.

During the early nineteenth century the evangelical clergy increased their influence, though they were challenged by the rise of Anglo-Catholicism in the wake of the Oxford Movement. Despite the rise of organizations for pan-evangelical activity, Nonconformist hostility to the Established Church tended to antagonize the Evangelical clergy and suspicion of the 'Romanizing' Oxford Movement alienated the Wesleyans. Attacks on Methodism came from such divergent sources as Sydney Smith and E.B. *Pusey. In the twentieth century, although Methodism responded more favourably than the rest of the Free Churches to proposals for intercommunion and union with the Church of England, it is noticeable that a combination of extreme Evangelicals and Anglo-Catholics defeated the union proposals in the House of Clergy in 1969 and 1972.

See also **Anglican-Methodist Conversations**

————

J.H. Whiteley (1939); F. Baker (1970); A.S. Wood (1992); A. Brown-Lawson (1994)

JAV

Anglican-Methodist Conversations In 1946 Archbishop Fisher invited the Free Churches to consider taking episcopacy into their system. Only the Methodists responded positively to this and conversations began in 1955, with 12 Anglicans and 12 Methodists led by Bishop Bell and Dr H. *Roberts. By 1958 they were ready to propose that the two Churches should unite their ministries on an episcopal basis. Their 1963 Report included a strong Methodist 'Dissentient' section, resulting in the formation of groups such as the *'Voice of Methodism' opposed to the proposals, which they saw as a take-over of Methodism, and especially the 'Service of Re-

conciliation' as implying re-ordination. The eventual Scheme of 1968 was accepted by the Methodist Conference, but did not gain the required 75% majority in the Anglican General Synod, either in 1969 or 1972, because of the combined opposition of Evangelicals and Anglo-Catholics. Since then, despite the failure of the 1980 Covenant proposals (involving other Free Churches), there has been some local growing together, e.g. through Local Ecumenical Partnerships (LEPs). A new round of exploratory talks began in the 1990s.

————

R.E. Davies (1979); G.T. Brake (1984) pp. 99–150; J.M. Turner (1985) pp. 194–225; R.E. Davies (1993) pp. 29–42; *Commitment to Mission and Unity* (1996)

JHL

Annesley, Samuel (1620–96), Puritan divine and JW's maternal grandfather, was ordained in 1644 and served as chaplain in the parliamentary Navy. He was appointed rector of Cliffe (Kent) in 1645, but his opposition to Charles I's execution forced him to leave there for London in 1652. In 1653 Richard Cromwell gave him the living of St Giles, Cripplegate. Ejected in 1662, he became the acknowledged leader of Dissent in the City. He continued to minister (not without cost) to a Presbyterian congregation in Spitalfields.

See also **Puritanism; Wesley Family**

————

L. Tyerman (1866); G.J. Stevenson (1876); *PWHS* 45 pp. 29–57

WDH

Annual Assembly, the WMA and UMFC equivalent of 'Conference'. Held annually in July, it had only four *ex officio* members: the President, Secretary, Corresponding Secretary and Connexional Treasurer. The rest, ministers and laymen, were elected by the circuit *quarterly meetings, in the ratio of one per 500 members, up to a maximum of three. The Assembly lasted up to 21 days and dealt with all matters relating to doctrine and discipline, rules and regulations in respect of circuits, chapels, connexional funds, membership and ministerial appointments.

————

E. Askew (1899)

WL

Annuitant Society *see* **Finance, Ministerial**

Antinomianism Though primarily indicating the belief that the justified believer is no longer bound by the moral law, the term can also imply, as in the controversy of 1739–41, to indifference to the due use of the *means of grace. JW vigorously and consistently opposed this view, while the antinomians and some *Calvinists accused him of teaching 'works righteousness'. The paradoxical Wesleyan response to this charge is expressed in CW's couplet: 'Joyful from my own works to cease,/Glad to fulfil all righteousness'. These issues were dealt with especially in the Conferences of 1744, 1745 and 1770. In 1745 W admitted that 'the truth of the Gospel lies within a hair's breadth' of Calvinism and Antinomianism; but in 1770 he emphasized the importance of 'works meet for repentance'. His positive insistence on the pursuit of *holiness as the goal of the Christian life was reinforced by his fear of antinomianism.

See also **Hall, W**; **Wheatley, J.**

W.S. Gunter (1989); R.P. Heitzenrater (1995) pp. 240–1

DJC

Antliff Brothers, PM ministers and scholars. **William Antliff** (1813–84; e.m. 1830) was called into the ministry at 16 and served mainly in the East Midlands and Lancashire. Largely self-educated, he became proficient in the ancient languages, developed into a considerable public speaker and published a number of books, including a life of H. *Bourne. He was awarded a DD by Middletown (Methodist) University, Ct. He was Connexional Editor 1862–67 and became first Principal of the *Sunderland Theological Institute, 1868–81. He was President of the Conference in 1863 and 1865. His brother **Samuel Antliff** (1823–92; e.m. 1840) ministered in East Midland circuits, except for two years (1874–76) in *Australia and *New Zealand. A powerful preacher, lecturer and temperance advocate, he was sent on deputation to *Canada and the USA in 1871. He was President of the British Conference in 1873 and of the New Zealand Conference in 1875. He served as Missionary Secretary 1869–74, Secretary of the General Missionary Committee 1878 and Treasurer of the Mission Fund 1880. As an advocate of improved education, he supported the founding of *Elmfield College and the *Sunderland Theological Institute.

F.H. Hurd (1872) pp. 149–58, 204–15; G.J. Stevenson (1884–86) 5 pp. 748–58; A.Wilkes & J. Lovatt (1942) pp. 79–81

GEM

Appeals to Men of Reason and Religion Although he ignored the more scurrilous attacks in print, JW sometimes felt impelled to defend himself and the Methodist movement against those known, or suspected, to come from eminent critics. The two *Appeals* published in 1743–45 were essential documents for the defence to which he sometimes referred in later controversies. The *Earnest Appeal* of 1743 was shorter and more cogent than its sequel and went through ten editions in his lifetime. The *Farther Appeal*, written at the urging of the 1744 Conference, was in three parts and, though more prolix, reveals him as the eighteenth century academic employing his skills as a logician. He was concerned to deal with false charges regarding the teaching and practice of the Methodists, in response particularly to two recent attacks, *The Notions of the Methodists fully disprov'd* (Newcastle, 1743) and Bishop *Gibson's *Observations upon the Conduct of a Certain Sect* (1744). His defence involved showing the compatibility of his teaching with the *BCP*, the Thirty-nine Articles and the Homilies and justifying the 'irregularities' in his conduct. He was particularly at pains to counter accusations of *enthusiasm, i.e. claims to extraordinary inspiration by the Holy Spirit. In Part II he counter-attacked by declaring the nation to be in a state of apostasy and calling for it to return to Christianity; and in Part III he describes Methodism's response to that situation and its effect in changed lives.

G.R. Cragg (1975) pp. 37–325

JAV

Arbroath Thomas Cherry of Swaledale formed a society in 1768 under the leadership of James Millar, a local mason. JW made the first of nine visits in 1770. He was made a freeman of the burgh in 1772 and preached at the opening of the preaching house known as the 'Totum Kirkie', the only octagon in Scotland still in use, as well as the oldest place of worship in regular use in Arbroath. The 'Lifeboat Window' is a memorial to the crew, drowned in 1953, of whom the captain and two others were members.

MR(W) 1905 pp. 64–6; G.W. Davis (1996)

MB

Arch, Joseph (1826–1919), *trade unionist, born in Barford, Warwicks, received a minimal grounding in the three Rs. Leaving school at 9, he became a bird-scarer, then ploughboy and, in later years commanded a good wage as a contract hedge-cutter. In 1872 he met the need for the co-ordination of local agricultural trade unions in southern counties by organizing the National Agricultural Labourers' Union. By 1874 it had 1,000 branches and 86,214 members. Arch continued as President until its collapse in 1896. He was Liberal MP for North West Norfolk 1885–1900 and served on the Royal Commission on the Aged Poor 1893–94. In his younger days he had been an enthusiastic PM *local preacher. Later his links with Methodism gradually diminished. Both his second marriage and his funeral were held in Barford parish church.

R. Groves (1949); P. Horn (1971)

NADS

Archbell, James (1798–1866; e.m. 1818), missionary in *Southern Africa from the age of 20. After working with B. *Shaw in Leliefontein, he ministered among the Batswana and trekked with the Barolong group as they were forced by tribal warfare and then by scarcity of natural resources to leave Transvaal and settle in Thaba 'Nchu. He published a Tswana grammar and NT, ministered to the Afrikaner Voortrekkers who made Thaba 'Nchu their headquarters in 1836/37 and in 1842 accompanied the British forces who took control of Natal. He built the first church in Durban. Resigning from the ministry in 1847 after a clash with the mission authorities, he later ran a newspaper, founded a bank, served on the first Natal Legislative Council and was repeatedly mayor of Pietermaritzburg.

JRP

Architecture JW's earliest building venture was the *New Room in Bristol (1739, enlarged 1748), intended as a meeting place for the religious societies under his leadership there. The *Foundery in London and the Newcastle *'Orphan House' were multi-purpose buildings, designed as much for community life and social service as for religious fellowship and nurture. The early Methodists often met in homes or on premises, adopted, like the Foundery, from other uses, before aspiring to purpose built preaching-houses (W's preferred term, to distinguish them from Anglican 'chapels' and dissenting 'meeting-houses'). They were expected to go to their parish church for *worship and the *sacraments.

Inspired by Dr John Taylor's new meeting-house in *Norwich, from 1757 JW strongly advocated octagonal chapels. Fourteen were built, beginning with Rotherham (1761) and four have survived: at *Yarm (1764), *Heptonstall (1764),

*Arbroath (1772) and *Taunton (1776, now in secular use). But he also approved of the rectangular plan exemplified in Wren's St James' Church, Piccadilly, as effective for preaching. The opening of *Wesley's Chapel in City Road, London in 1778 marked a new stage in Methodism's development from movement to denomination. Sacramental services had hitherto been held at *West Street Chapel (taken over in 1743 from the *Huguenots). The 'City Road arrangement', with its central pulpit in front of the sanctuary, copied the eighteenth century Anglican 'auditory chapels' – a layout swept away in nineteenth century Anglicanism by the Oxford Movement and surviving in Methodism only at Northbrook Street, Newbury (1838). Other Methodist chapels, including several designed by W. *Jenkins, were modelled on Wesley's Chapel.

The continuing growth of WM prosperity and respectability was expressed in the early nineteenth century in the proliferation of substantial and capacious chapels, classical or Renaissance in style, later to be furnished with impressive rostrums. Local trustees often had a decisive influence on the kind of building they wanted. But the burden of debt, which had become a concern of Conference even in JW's time, was intensified by years of economic depression following the Napoleonic wars, a problem addressed by J. *Crowther Senr and others and eventually by the setting up of a Chapel Committee in 1854.

Early PM was constrained by financial rather than theological or aesthetic factors. Early chapels were built in a vernacular, domestic style, easily adapted, if need be, to secular purposes. Burdensome debts were a particular concern, leading eventually to the establishment of the PM *Chapel Aid Association.

Following the latest Anglican fashion, the mid-nineteenth century saw a revival of Gothic under the influence of F.J. *Jobson and this continued in much simplified form into the twentieth century, with sanctuary and choir stalls in a chancel flanked by pulpit and lectern. By 1873 Gothic was being advocated even in the PM Connexion (in G. Hodgson Fowler's *Manual on Chapel Architecture*). The prolific building programme in the later nineteenth century was partly due to the divisions and rivalries within Methodism and coincided with the period when Victorian eclecticism was the architectural vogue. It left a legacy of buildings of varying architectural quality strewn around the country, mostly the work of architects known only within a narrow area. Exceptions to this included J. *Wilson of *Bath and Sir Banister Fletcher

(St George's, Old Kent Road, London). The *Forward Movement of the 1880s produced a new wave of multi-purpose premises, notably the Central Halls in which the distinction between ecclesiastical and secular architecture was deliberately avoided.

Extensive rebuilding of premises damages or destroyed in World War II was facilitated by generous support from the Joseph *Rank Benevolent Trust. In these post-war years, the influence of the Methodist architect E.D. *Mills was widespread. Architectural styles and building materials have diversified and there has been increasing emphasis on buildings which relate to community use. The flexible arrangement of the 'worship area' often reflects the emphasis of the Liturgical Movement on sacramental worship and increasing congregational participation; while the effect of the *Ecumenical Movement is seen in the number of shared churches.

See also **Chapel Affairs; Metropolitan Wesleyan Chapel Building Fund; Trustees; Watering Places Fund**

F.J. Jobson (1850); E.B. Perkins (1946); G.W.Dolbey (1964); W. Oliver Phillipson (1966); S. Hatcher (1999); annual reports of the Chapel Department and Property Division

BWB/JAV

Archives Until the late twentieth century there was little systematic attempt at ordering the archives and records of the Church, despite its emphasis on the need to produce circuit *preaching plans, schedules and membership returns regularly. In 1955 the Conference appointed a Commission, which recognized the need for depositing local church and circuit records in local record offices rather than keeping archives in safes or sending them all to London. But the first District Archivists were not appointed until 1969. The appointment of the first Connexional Archivist, W.F. *Swift, in 1961 and the establishment of a Centre in Epworth House at City Road, London under the direction of an Archives and History Committee was the start of a period of extensive cataloguing and guidance in the care of archives. Under his successor J.C. *Bowmer, much progress was made despite limited resources, but in 1976 financial constraints led to the decision to transfer the Connexional Archives to the John Rylands University Library, Manchester. Following this move a Connexional Archives Liaison Officer replaced the Connexional Archivist. The archives of the MMS were deposited in the library

of the School of Oriental and African Studies, London. Other Methodist collections are located at *Wesley College, Bristol and major heritage sites.

TSAM

Armagh, the ecclesiastical capital of Ireland. The first society was formed in 1767. JW came seven times between 1767 and 1778 and was forbidden by the sovereign of the city to preach in any public place. William McGeough offered him the use of his private avenue and it is on this site the present Methodist Church stands. The McGeough family later built a mansion, The Argory (now National Trust). CW's son Samuel advised on the installation of an organ in its upper hall.

JWJ

DALC

Armed Forces JW himself was drawn to preach to soldiers and noted their appearance in Methodist societies and congregations with pleasure. They provided him with some of his earliest itinerants, such as J. *Haime and S. *Staniforth. Soldiers (e.g. A. *Armour) were the first to introduce Methodism in a number of other places. In 1769 there was a Methodist society of 32 at *Gibraltar, with the approval and protection of Lord Cornwallis, the garrison Commander. But during the Napoleonic Wars a different attitude prevailed. The drilling of the militia on Sundays posed a question of conscience for Methodists. In 1803 members of the Gibraltar garrison were court-martialled and punished for attending Methodist meetings. The *Committee of Privileges was the outcome of this.

W.H. *Rule was the first to develop the concept of Methodist chaplaincy, first at Gibraltar and later at Aldershot, following the Crimean War. But there was a long struggle before Methodist preachers were permitted to care for Methodist personnel and Methodists themselves allowed to parade for worship at Methodist churches. This was granted in the 1870s by the Royal Navy and in 1881 by the Army. The first Garrison Chapel to be opened was at Aldershot. In 1857 Rule advocated the need for a Soldiers' Home at Aldershot and the first was opened there in 1869 during the time of Joseph Webster (1817–99; e.m. 1847). Similar 'Homes' (known as 'Wesley Houses') were later opened in all important military and naval centres. During World War I PM and UM (but not WM) chaplains worked in conjunction with Baptist and Congregational colleagues in a United Chaplaincy Board. At *Methodist Union a Royal Navy, Army and Royal Air Force Board was established, with a secretary who liaised with the Admiralty, War Office and Air Ministry over the appointment of chaplains.

In World War II some 430 ministers served as chaplains, plus a few Wesley Deaconesses (serving without rank) with the Women's Services. But only in the post-war years have Methodist chaplains been granted the same status as Anglican clergy. In 1998 there were 21 full-time chaplains (including one in Ireland) holding commissions, plus 49 circuit ministers serving as officiating chaplains and 4 as territorial army chaplains. The link between forces chaplaincy and Methodism has been through Home Mission ever since the 1850s.

See also **War**; **Watkins, O.**

MR(W) 1902 pp. 91–3, 1904 pp. 75–8; O.S. Watkins (1906); F. C. Spurr (1915)

JWH

Arminian Bible Christians The BC founder, W. *O'Bryan, was a charismatic but flawed leader. After membership had dropped for two years in succession, he seceded at the Conference of 1829 with a small group of supporters whom he called 'Arminian Bible Christians' (reviving a term originally used by O'Bryan himself, but discarded by 1819). At least three ministers seceded with him, as well as possibly some individual societies and one or two Cornish circuits, but the actual loss was greater – as many as 1,100 members in Cornwall. Documentary evidence for the denomination comprises six preaching plans for 'Tiverton and Kingsbrompton Circuit and 'Tiverton and Chard Missions' and nine class tickets, 1830–1834. Some Meeting House licences for the period have been identified in Devon. In 1835 a deputation to the BC Conference sought a reconciliation and the Minutes refer to their societies, 700 members and heavy debts. The Conference agreed to accept these members and seven unmarried preachers, including one woman. At the following Conference it was reported that 534 members had returned.

F.W. Bourne (1905) pp. 190–4; R.F.S. Thorne in *PWHS* 52.

RFST

Arminian Magazine (later *Methodist Magazine*), was first published in 1778 as part of JW's response to the continuing challenge of *Calvinism by promulgating the gospel of 'universal redemption'. The first issue opened with a life of Arminius. The original intention was to include 'no news, no politics, no personal invective' and 'nothing offensive either to religion, decency, good nature or good manners'. As a handbook of spiritual pilgrimage each issue would have four parts: (1) writings that defended universal redemption; (2) biographies of holy persons; (3) letters and accounts of the experience of pious living persons and (4) poetry explaining and confirming essential doctrines. JW came to see its function increasingly as broader than Arminian propaganda and responded to the charge that it lacked variety by publishing his own sermons and lives of other Methodists beside his preachers. Engravings of many of the itinerants featured as frontispieces. Later issues contained condensations of travel books, accounts of supernatural phenomena and of marvels and 'providences', all designed to show God's presence and activity in the world. After his death some of the contents became more miraculous and strange. Between 1811 and 1870 an abridged edition (known as the 'sixpenny edition') was published. The title was changed to the *Methodist Magazine* in 1798 and in 1822 J. *Bunting added the prefix *'Wesleyan' to distinguish it from those of the other branches of Methodism. In 1913 it became *The Magazine* (of the WM Church), reverting to the title *Methodist Magazine* at the time of the 1932 Union. On the formation of the *Women's Fellowship in 1944 a section devoted to its interests was included. Articles became wider in scope and of more general interest. But in 1969 'the oldest magazine in the world' succumbed to a changing climate and Methodist decline.

See also **Bible Christian Magazine**

L. Tyerman (1878) 3 pp. 280–5; F.H. Cumbers (1956) pp. 52–7

EWD/GSW

Arminian Methodist Connexion originated as a division in the *Derby WM Circuit (hence the alternative name, 'Derby Faith Folk') in January 1832. Strongly revivalistic in nature, it has been characterized as the only secession that occurred on doctrinal grounds. Its members emphasized entire *sanctification and were charged with holding Sandemanian views. Some of the leaders were semi-Pelagian, believing that it was not necessary to pray for faith. Like other revivalist groups, it made use of *women preachers, notably E.A. *Evans. The movement spread into other Northern and Midland counties and at its height numbered about 1,800 members.

It amalgamated with the *WMA in 1837, but several circuits later withdrew, becoming independent, linking with the *WRU or ceasing to exist. Its most notable minister was H. *Breeden.

PWHS 23, pp. 25–8; W. Parkes (1995)

WP

Arminianism describes the Wesleyan emphases on the universality of the offer of salvation and the freedom of individuals to accept or reject it. The Dutch theologian Arminius (1560–1609) challenged the traditional *Calvinist teaching that salvation is available only to the 'elect', i.e. those who are predestined to it and JW certainly studied his writings. It seems, however, that the theological debates of the seventeenth century, in which Archbishop Laud's position was labelled 'Arminian', were a more direct influence. Even so, JW's stance was that of a participant in the eighteenth century revival and should therefore be know as 'Evangelical Arminianism'. 'Universal redemption', espoused in contrast to the Calvinism widespread in contemporary Anglicanism and Dissent, was vigorously propagated in CW's hymns (e.g. 'Father of everlasting grace', *HP* 520), where key words like 'all' and 'general' were emphasized in the original.
See also **Grace**

A.W. Harrison (1937); *LQHR* Oct. 1960; G. Nuttall (1967) pp. 67–79

DJC

Armour, Andrew (d.1828) was born near *Glasgow. Converted as a young soldier in Ireland, he established societies in *Gibraltar and Madras. A gifted linguist, he was posted to Colombo as a Tamil interpreter for the Supreme Court and after discharge from the army became head of a government high school. In 1812 he was licensed to preach in Portuguese and Sinhalese and he welcomed, accompanied and interpreted for the first WM missionaries, who arrived in 1814. In 1821 he took Anglican orders and served as chaplain of St Paul's Church, Colombo.

F&H vol.4 p. 418; vol.5 pp. 58–9; W.J.T. Small (1964) pp. 44–5

JRP

Armstrong, Ernest, MP (1915–96), a typical product of the strong links between Methodism and the Labour Party, was a schoolmaster 1937–52, a headmaster 1952–64, and chairman of the *Sunderland Education Committee 1960–65. He was MP for North West Durham 1964–87 and held posts at the Treasury (1969–70), the Department of Education and Science (1974–75) and the Department of the Environment (1975–9). He was Deputy Speaker from 1981 to 1987. A *local preacher to whom preaching was a vital part of life, he was Vice-President of the 1974 Conference. He wrote, mostly on social issues. From 1982 he was President of the Northern Football League. He handed on his Parliamentary seat to his daughter Hilary Armstrong (b.1945).

Times 10 July 1996; *MR* 1 Aug. 1996; *Who's Who* (1996)

JHL

Armstrong, Walter Henry (1873–1949; e.m. 1899), WM minister, born in King's Cross, London. He had little formal education before training for the ministry at *Didsbury College. He served briefly in Ceylon, then in mission circuits, where he was particularly successful with working men, notably with the Brotherhood at *Bradford, and as an open-air speaker. He became secretary of the London Mission Fund in 1924 and was twice minister of *Wesley's Chapel, where his daughter became curator. He was the first Moderator of the FCFC and a member of the committee it set up to respond to the 1920 Lambeth Appeal. In 1926 he was a leading opponent of *Methodist union, but in 1941 became President of the Conference. He wrote a life of J.A. *Sharp (1932).

JHL

Art Although often characterized as 'philistine' and indifferent to culture, Methodism has in reality enjoyed a steady undercurrent of interaction with the world of the fine arts and there are significant names which can be cited as artists with clear Methodist links.
Many artists have turned their talents to the portrayal of JW and he sat to such important painters of the eighteenth century English School as Hone, Romney and probably Reynolds. He was also sculpted by E. *Wood. In his later years he took a lively, though puritanical, interest in the works of art as well as the architecture of the country houses he visited in his travels. CW was probably more sensitive to the creative life, encouraging J. *Russell, an early RA. Later on, J. *Jackson RA (who provided portraits for the *WMM) was also prominent and J. *Adams-Acton was a noted sculptor. H.P. *Parker (from a UMFC background) was a history and scene painter; J. *Smetham was associated with the Pre-Raphaelites, Burne-Jones and E.J. Poynter

married into the *Macdonald family, and *Van Gogh was briefly associated with Methodism in *Richmond, Surrey. The *Methodist Church Collection of Modern Christian Art is evidence of the Church's appreciation of the era of modern art.

Methodism's Nonconformist ethos has profoundly influenced the work of artists, some (such as F.O. *Salisbury) setting their faces determinedly against the prevailing artistic movements of their time. Others have felt their creativity compromised by Methodist beliefs (and may indeed have been repressed by or outcast from the Church), rejecting or subordinating their faith in order to pursue their art – although its influence can often be discerned in their work. William Etty and Stanley Spencer had Methodist upbringings and Eric Gill's roots were in the *Countess of Huntingdon's Connexion.

With notable exceptions, such as the efforts of successive WM *Book Stewards, Methodism has not had a prominent tradition of patronage of the arts or of artists. Perhaps understandably, more attention has been paid to the architecture and decorative arts of its buildings, including *stained glass; but, as in literature, where hymnody may overshadow other poetic achievements, so the existence of fine churches and church furnishings points to deeper and broader interests in the world of the arts.

See also **Yoxall, J.**

LQHR July 1958

PSF

Arthur, William (1819–1901; e.m. 1838), WM preacher, missionary and author, born in Co. Antrim. He served in Mysore, *India from 1839 until eye trouble forced him to return in 1841. After a period of convalescence, he remained in London, involved in advocating missions, then served in Boulogne and Paris, 1846–49. In 1851 he was appointed a WMMS Secretary. Despite continuing ill-health this enabled him to influence national and international thinking within Methodism and beyond. He was closely associated with the development of the YMCA, the Evangelical Alliance and the first *World Methodist Conferences. He was President of the WM Conference in 1866 and President of *Methodist College, Belfast, 1868–71. His other interests included philosophy, spirituality, Roman Catholicism and politics and he was a gifted linguist. The most influential book in his considerable literary output was *The Tongue of Fire* (1856) on the role and importance of the Holy Spirit. It

ran to 18 editions in three years and was translated into many languages. It has been suggested that Arthur's views on revival and renewal, expounded in person during a visit to *America in 1855 and in the pages of his book, contributed to the gathering pace of revival in America at that time. He died in Cannes in 1901.

G.J. Stevenson (1884–86) 3 pp. 382–96; *MR* 14 March 1901; T.B. Stephenson (1907); N.W. Taggart (1993)

NWT

Arthur Rank Centre was established in 1972 at the National Agricultural Centre, Stoneleigh, Warwicks as a joint venture by the Churches, the Royal Agricultural Society and the *Rank Foundation. It was opened by HM Queen Elizabeth II and dedicated by the Bishop of Coventry. Facilities include Conference and meeting rooms and a library and resource unit. The ecumenical Chaplaincy Centre provides support for the Churches' rural mission and pastoral ministry, partly through the Rural Stress Information Network. Other activities include courses on rural ministry, training opportunities for young people, the Rural Housing Trust and the National Churches Tourism Group.

JAV

Articles of Religion were commonly formulated by reformed Churches to encapsulate what they regarded as the essentials of the faith. The Church of England issued the Thirty-Nine Articles in 1571. In 1784 JW abridged these to twenty-five, in some cases shortening the text, for use by the American Methodists. He omitted Art. 17 'On Predestination' as contrary to his understanding of the Gospel and several others as inessential. The Twenty-Five Articles have remained authoritative in American Methodism, but have not enjoyed the same status in Britain, despite being printed in the 1882 WM *Service Book*. In response to signs of doctrinal laxity among the younger preachers, a set of Articles was prepared by order of the 1806 Conference, but seems never to have been formally adopted. J.H. *Rigg commented in 1904 that the hymns of the Ws, rather than any Articles, were the doctrinal standard for British Methodists.

Articles of Religion . . . 1806 (1897)

DJC

Ashton-under-Lyne was the scene of early preaching by B. *Ingham, J. *Bennet and others, but a permanent society dates only from the 1760s.

A chapel was built in 1781 and JW paid three visits in the 1780s. A. *Kilham spent six weeks there early in 1797 and in August the majority of members joined the newly-formed MNC and retained the chapel. WM never recovered from this secession and the exodus of the followers of J.R. *Stephens in the 1830s. In 1851 the *Religious Census confirmed the MNC as the strongest Methodist body in the town. The MNC Conference met there six times between 1826 and 1906. In 1821 a PM *local preacher, Samuel Waller, was imprisoned for preaching in the open air. The IM church dates from 1819 and the IM Conference met there in 1879.

E.A. Rose in *PWHS* 37 pp. 83–5; E.A. Rose (1967, 1969)

EAR

Ashville College, Harrogate, was founded in 1877 by the UMFC for the sons of middle-class Methodists. Despite its early reputation for sound, broadly based education, by 1905 it had a huge capital debt, unrepaired buildings and only 32 pupils. Its recovery was due to the vision of the Rev. A. *Soothill, headmaster 1905–26. In 1930 it merged, on its own site, with New College, a Baptist foundation in Harrogate whose premises became the Junior School, and in 1932 with *Elmfield College, York. It reverted to full independence in 1976 following the withdrawal of the government's Direct Grant regulations. In 1997 it had 825 boarding and day boys and girls, aged 4–18.

W. Booth (1977)

DBT/EDG

Ashworth, John (1813–75), UMFC *local preacher and philanthropist, started life as a weaver. After attending a WM Sunday School in *Rochdale, where he spent his whole life, he joined the WMA. Determined to serve the labouring classes, in 1848 he formed a ragged school which led ten years later to the 'chapel for the destitute', which he supervised until his death. He was a prolific writer of tracts, notably successive volumes of *Strange Tales from Humble Life*.

A.L. Calman (1875)

OAB

Aspey, Albert (1911–98; e.m. 1934), missionary in *Portugal, born into a UM family in *Leeds and educated at Leeds University and *Hartley Victoria College. From 1955 until retirement in 1984 he was stationed in Oporto, where he became fluent in Portuguese. He founded the Portuguese *Christian Endeavour Union (UPEC) and was involved in ecumenical activities especially through Reconciliation Ecumenical Centre at Figueira da Foz. He was President of the Portuguese Council of Christian Churches in 1971 and fostered relations with the RC Church in the post-Vatican II era. His wife was very active in the Girl Guide movement. In retirement he was honoured by the Portuguese President for his service to the country.

MR 7 Jan. 1999

JAV

Assessments *see* **Finance, Local**

Assistant At the first *Conference, in 1744, all JW's itinerants were called 'Helpers', i.e. of JW himself and the other ordained clergy. Their work was 'in the absence of a minister, to feed and guide the flock'. By 1745 the term 'Assistant' was in use and, as the movement spread, this became the term for the supervising preacher in each circuit, responsible to JW for the other itinerants (called 'Helpers'), for *local preachers, for regulating the societies, making the quarterly *preaching plan and keeping membership lists up to date. After W's death, the term was replaced by *Superintendent.

Minutes, 1744, 1745, 1792

MB

Assurance JW taught (e.g. in the two sermons on 'The Witness of the Spirit') that, according to the NT, it is the privilege of ordinary Christian believers to experience 'the witness of God's Spirit with their spirit that they are children of God' (Rom. 8:26). He claimed that 'this great evangelical truth has been recovered [by the Methodists] which has been for many years wellnigh lost and forgotten.' Assurance has been regarded ever since as one of the key doctrinal emphases of Methodism. W regarded it not only as fully scriptural, but also as confirmed by his own experience at Aldersgate Street and by that of many of his followers. The doctrine was criticized by Bishop J. *Butler and others, who regarded it as conducing to presumptuousness, *enthusiasm and perhaps spiritual pride, and as creating too great a dependence on 'feeling' in the Christian life; hence E.B. *Pusey's later charge that Methodists preached 'justification by feeling'.

W hedged the doctrine with safeguards. He did not regard the experience as necessary to salvation. Moreover, he recognized that it was all too possible to fall from grace, even after an experience of present salvation. In the second of his two sermons on the doctrine (1767) he acknowledged that Christians might have periods of doubt in which the sense of assurance (though not the relationship with God in which it was grounded) was lost. The doctrine may be seen as the logical corollary of belief in 'adoption' as the means of our incorporation into Christ and in the restoration of the divine image in us.

A.S. Yates (1952); C.W. Williams (1960) pp. 102–14; R.L. Maddox (1994)

DJC

Atherton, William (1775–1850; e.m. 1797), WM minister, advocate of missions and of Methodist *day schools, having had the advantage of a Scottish education. Elected President of the Conference in 1846, he was a leading opponent of J. *Bunting. He wrote a Life of Lady *Maxwell (1838). His son, **Sir William Atherton** (1806–64), was called to the bar in 1839 and became a QC in 1851 and MP for *Durham in 1852. A staunch Liberal, he supported the abolition of all religious disabilities. Knighted and appointed Solicitor-General in 1859, in 1861 he became the first Methodist Attorney-General.

DNB

JAV

Atlay, John (b.1736) of Sheriff-Hutton, Yorks, entered the itinerancy in 1763 and from 1773 served as W's *Book Steward (trading from 1785 as a coal-merchant on the side!). He took the side of the *Dewsbury trustees and left the connexion in 1788 to become minister of the estranged congregation there.

L. Tyerman (1878) 3 pp. 552–60; F.H. Cumbers (1956) pp. 93–4

JAV

Atmore, Charles (1759–1826; e.m. 1781), WM itinerant, born at Heacham, Norfolk. He soon became one of JW's 'inner cabinet' and in 1784 was included in the *Legal Hundred. In 1786 W ordained him for work in Scotland, where he opened the first preaching house in *Glasgow in 1787. Eager to continue administering the Sacrament after his return to England, he was one of the younger generation of preachers who pressed

for Methodist autonomy after JW's death. He was a close friend of J. *Pawson and one of his most intimate correspondents. In 1801 he published *The Methodist Memorial*, a volume of short sketches of the 'lives and characters' of Methodist itinerants, together with a short account of American Methodism. He was President of the Conference in 1811.

Extracts from Journal in *WMM* 1845; G.J. Stevenson (1884–86) 2 pp. 212–21; J. Pawson (1994–5)

PSF

Aubrey, Thomas (1808–67; e.m. 1826), Welsh WM minister, from Cefncoedcymer, known as 'Owbre Fawr' ('the Great Aubrey'), was converted and began to preach at 15 while working in an iron mill. He made up for his lack of early education by constant study and became one of the most outstanding preachers, lecturers and statesmen in Welsh WM. He was Chairman of the North Wales District 1854–65. His evangelical zeal introduced a new spirituality that prepared the way for the 1859 Revival. He was a stalwart defender of WM doctrine in the era of theological disputes, and of its Constitution against the *Wesle Bach reformers. By establishing District HM and Chapel Funds and a Jubilee Fund he opened a new chapter of self-supportive independence in Welsh WM. He was a noted *temperance advocate.

S. Davies (1877); *DWB*; *EW* 60 pp. 19, 101 p. 24; *Bathafarn*, 16 (1961) pp. 5–22

EHG

Australia The first WM *class meetings in the penal colony of New South Wales were established in Sydney and Windsor in 1812 by T. *Bowden and E. *Eagar. In 1815 S. *Leigh was sent as the first Methodist preacher, and was given encouragement and support by the Anglican chaplain Samuel Marsden. The work was hindered for a while by dissention between him and his colleagues, notably W *Lawry, whose attitude to the Established Church led to strained relations with Marsden, but recovered under the leadership of J. *Orton and W.B. *Boyce. This became the base for missions in other settlements: Hobart, Tasmania (1820), Melbourne (1836), Adelaide (1837) and Perth (1840). An autonomous Australasian Conference was constituted in 1855 and assumed responsibility for the South Pacific Missions. From 1874, following the pattern of American Methodism, it was a General Conference, meeting every three years, with Annual Conferences for New South Wales and Queensland, Victoria and Tasmania, South Australia and Western Australia, and *New Zealand. The PM work began in South Australia in 1841 and New South Wales in 1844–45 and the first BC preachers began in South Australia in 1849. WM, PM and other non-Wesleyan bodies were united in South Australia in 1900 and elsewhere in 1902, and a General Conference was held in 1904. In 1977 Methodism joined with Congregationalists and Presbyterians to form the Uniting Church in Australia, which is a member of the *WMC.

_____

F&H 3 pp. 13–161; D. Wright & E. Clancy (1993)
                                                              J A V

Autonomous Churches Churches under the auspices of the British Conferences' overseas missions were organized, as at home, into *circuits and *districts. During the nineteenth century those in *France, *Canada, *Australasia and *South Africa became Conferences in their own right – as *American Methodism had been since 1784. A *West Indian Conference (1884–1903) foundered and its Districts reverted to British jurisdiction until 1967. In 1947 the British Methodist Districts in South *India became founder dioceses of the Church of South India. Between 1961 (*Ghana) and 1996 (*Portugal) thirteen autonomous Conferences and two united Churches (North India and *Zambia) were established, leaving only two overseas Districts (The *Gambia and *Togo) under the authority of the British Conference (though with a large measure of de facto self-government).

                                                              J R P

Auxiliary Fund *see* **Finance, Ministerial**

Averell, Adam (1754–1847), an ordained deacon in the (Episcopalian) Church of Ireland. Requested to speak against Methodism, he examined its teaching and found himself in broad sympathy. Eventually he joined the Methodists and was received into full connexion in 1796. Partly on account of being ordained, he rose to a position of leadership. In 1816 he resisted the proposal to allow limited authority to the Irish preachers to administer the *sacraments and was elected President of the *Primitive Wesleyan Methodists in 1818, continuing this role until his death.

_____

C.H. Crookshank (1885–8) passim
                                                              N W T

Bacup *see* **Rossendale**

Baddiley, Rev. John (fl. 1748-*c.* 1765), rector of Hayfield, Derbys., converted in 1748, was described by JW as 'a second *Grimshaw', though he later fell from grace. After reading a volume of W's sermons, he acknowledged his orthodoxy 'by the standards of primitive Christianity' and opened his church to him in April 1755 (and again in 1757). He joined with S. *Walker and T. *Adam in their efforts to dissuade Methodists from separating from the Church.

_____

JWJ; A. Brown-Lawson (1994)
                                                              J A V

Bainbridge, Emerson Muschamp (1817–92), prosperous draper of *Newcastle upon Tyne and staunch pillar of WM. He built up a progressive department store, with associated manufacturing and wholesale activities. He was one of the first lay representatives to the WM Conference in 1878. Keen to promote evangelism, he actively encouraged the visits to England, and the northeast in particular, of Phoebe Palmer in 1859 and Moody and Sankey in 1873. Two of his sons, Cuthbert Bainbridge (1840–72) and Thomas H. Bainbridge (1842–1912) espoused these causes and the latter, influenced by T. *Champness and H.P. *Hughes, had a fine record of religious and philanthropic service.

_____

T.H. Bainbridge (1913); A. & J. Airey (1979); *DBB*
                                                              G E M

Baker, Dr Eric Wilfred (1899–1973; e.m. 1922), son of a *Birmingham City councillor and magistrate, served during World War I but later became a pacifist. Trained for the ministry at *Wesley House, Cambridge, in 1946 he became Secretary of the Methodist *Education Department and concurrently Chairman of the London NE District. During twenty years (1951–70) as Secretary of the Conference he proved to be a superb administrator and an ecumenical statesman. He was President of the Conference in 1959. Among his published works is his Fernley-Hartley Lecture, *The Faith of a Methodist* (1958).

_____

MR 9 July 1959, 27 Sept. 1973; *Times* 24 Sept. 1973
                                                              K G G

Baker, Dr Frank (1910–99; e.m. 1934), leading Methodist historian, was in English circuits until 1959 and, after two years lecturing in religious studies at *Hull Training College, in 1960 joined the staff of Duke University, Durham NC, where he nurtured a whole generation of Wesley scholars. He was four times the winner of the *Eayrs Essay Prize between 1936 and 1948; was Registrar of the *WHS 1943–49 and its Secretary 1946–61; and was Secretary of the British Methodist *Archives Commission 1955–60. He served on the World Methodist Council 1944–60 and as joint secretary of the International (now *World) Methodist Historical Society 1947–60. He was made a Fellow of Methodist History in 1956. He was the chief initiator and Editor-in-Chief of the Wesley Works Project, edited the first two volumes of JW's letters and the (as yet unpublished) Bibliography of W's publications. A prolific writer, his books include *Charles Wesley as Revealed by his Letters* (WHS Lecture, 1948), *William Grimshaw* (1963), *John Wesley and the Church of England* (1970) and *From Wesley to Asbury* (1976). He has been honoured internationally for his outstanding and sustained contribution to Methodist historical studies.

PWHS 47 pp. 154–5; F. Baker (1998b); *MR* 4 Nov. 1999

JAV

Baker, Shirley Waldemar (1836–1903), controversial WM missionary in *Tonga. Born in London, he arrived in *Australia at 16 and became a *local preacher in the Castlemaine district, Victoria. Despite his meagre education and a lack of theological training, he was accepted for missionary service in 1860 and had a colourful career. During 20 years as a missionary he showed himself to be articulate and able in administration, earned the enmity of traders, British officials and the missionary authorities and survived an attempted assassination. The medical knowledge he had acquired benefited mission staff and Europeans as well as Tongans. Defying his recall to Australia in 1879, he became Premier in 1880 under King Tupou I. He gave vigorous support to the Tongans' policy of national independence and in 1885 set up the self-governing Free Wesleyan Church, which did nothing to allay ill-feeling between him and WM leaders like J.E. *Moulton. His pro-German leanings led to a treaty with Germany in 1876, giving recognition to Tonga's status and Tupou's sovereignty. Expelled in 1890, he pursued his business interests in Auckland, *Samoa and Europe, before returning to settle in Ha'apai.

MR 20 Feb. 1997

ADY

Bakewell, John (1721–1819), preacher and hymnwriter, born at Brailsford, Derbys. Converted at 18, he began to preach in 1744. He moved to London, where he became acquainted with the Wesleys, J. *Fletcher and other leading Methodists. He became headmaster of the Royal Park Academy in Greenwich, but resigned in favour of his son-in-law, Dr James Egan (through whom he was related to the *Moulton family) in order to devote himself to evangelism, though without becoming an itinerant. The only one of his hymns to survive into *MHB* and *HP* is 'Hail, thou once despisèd Jesus'. He died at Lewisham and is buried in the graveyard at *Wesley's Chapel.

PWHS 39 pp. 92–3

JAV

Ball, Hannah (1733–92), of High Wycombe, founder of the first *Sunday School in Britain. She was attracted to Methodism by reading the sermons of T. *Walsh. In 1769 she began a class for the ostler children who worked at the inns in High Wycombe. In this work she was encouraged by JW, who regarded her as one of his most trusted and honoured women workers. She was frequently asked to monitor the work of his preachers stationed in Oxfordshire and her advice was sought at times of dispute. She was entrusted with carrying out W's plans to build a chapel in High Wycombe and came to be regarded as one of the main lay leaders of the Methodist people in Oxfordshire.

J. Parker (1839); M.L. Edwards (n.d.) pp. 75–84

PMW

Ball, Mary (1810–60), PM itinerant. Converted at around 10 years old, she became a PM, taught in Sunday School, became a *local preacher at 15 and an itinerant in 1822. She worked unofficially in Belper for 22 months, and was then stationed in *Louth, *Grimsby and *Whitby, but retired on marrying T. Barkworth of Grimsby in 1837, continuing as *local preacher and class leader. She died in February 1860 after much suffering following a mastectomy.

PMM 1860 pp. 329–31; E.D. Graham (1989) pp. 3–4

EDG

Ballard, Dr Frank (1851–1931; e.m. 1873), WM minister, gifted lecturer and debater whose academic versatility included science, philosophy and several languages. At *Headingley College he came under the influence of G.G. *Findlay. Between 1896 and 1901 he served Congregational churches. As 'Christian Evidence Missioner' from 1907 to 1922 he toured the country, using his skills as lecturer and debater to oppose the influence of rationalism and agnosticism. A controversialist rather than a scholar, though without personal acrimony, his many publications included *The Miracles of Unbelief* (1900) and the *Fernley Lecture of 1916, *Christian Reality in Modern Light*.

Times 23 Dec. 1931; *MR* 24 Dec. 1931; WHS(NE), March 1997

JAV

Ballard, Robertson (1892–1982; e.m.), Methodist minister and an outstanding missioner, was educated at *Kingswood School and *Headingley College. He had a distinguished ministry in Central Missions at *Birmingham, Walsall, *Liverpool and *Huddersfield, before being appointed to the London Mission. He served at Old Ford, Sydenham and Bethnal Green, where he took over a downtown cause and established a centre which effectively combined evangelical witness and social outreach. It was written of him that 'he would turn the mangle in the communal kitchen, hold a baby, run for the doctor, do anything for the poor people he loved so unselfishly.'

MR 30 Dec. 1982

PWS

Banbury   JW passed through the town several times during his years at Oxford, but did not return until 1784, when he was offered the Presbyterian meeting house to preach in. He came again in 1790. During that period a society came into existence under the leadership of James Ward, a dyer and a chapel was opened in 1791 at the top of Calthorpe Street. It was replaced by new chapel in Church Lane in 1812 (extended 1818 and 1841). In the mid-nineteenth century Banbury's prosperity as a centre for the manufacture of agricultural equipment was matched by a flourishing local Nonconformity. For many years WM remained politically conservative and until the 1850s was hampered by continuing debt. Then the support of prosperous businessmen (notably W. *Mewburn) transformed the largely working-class congregation to a predominantly middle-class one. Church Lane was replaced in 1865 by the much more impressive gothic church in Marlborough Road (with W.M. *Punshon at the

stonelaying and S.D. *Waddy at the opening). New Sunday School premises were added in 1883. A mission hall in Calthorpe Street, only a short distance from Marlborough Road, flourished between 1903 and 1931, and suburban chapels were built at Grimsbury in 1858 (replaced in 1871 and redeveloped in the 1980s to incorporate an old people's home), Neithrop in 1888, Easington in 1937 and Ruscote in 1957.

Banbury Circuit was formed (from Northampton Circuit) in 1793, though renamed Brackley Circuit between 1797 and 1804. It extended as far as Warwick and Kenilworth.

The first PM preaching in the area was at Chacombe, when Joseph Preston travelled from Witney in 1836. In Banbury a chapel was built in Broad Street in 1839 (extended 1847) and a Banbury Circuit was formed in 1842. PM had local support from both the Baptist and the Congregational ministers. In 1865 they took over the Church Lane premises from the WM, adding schoolrooms in 1898; it closed in 1947. Their more important work was in the villages, especially among the agricultural workers. The Reform movement had little local impact, but a small WR congregation, with no chapel of its own, survived until 1855.

B. Trinder (1965); B. Trinder (1982); *VCH: Oxfordshire* 10 (Oxford, 1972) pp. 108–20; Barrie Trinder in *Cake & Cockhorse* VIII (1982) pp. 207–21

JAV

Band Room Methodists, a group of Revivalist Methodists in *Manchester. In 1798 John Broadhurst, a prosperous draper and member at Oldham Street WM chapel, took out a licence for a meeting house in North Street, which became known as the Band Room. Despite its semi-autonomous character, North Street appeared on the circuit plan and successive superintendents supplied it with preachers. J. *Bunting preached his trial sermon there.

Conflict between the Band Room and the Manchester Circuit arose repeatedly over three issues in particular: (1) failure to submit to the Leaders' Meeting, (2) admission of non-members to class and band meetings and (3) the disorderly character of meetings which were not entirely under the preacher's control. Finally an ultimatum was given – either to conform to WM discipline or separate from the Methodist body. Separation was chosen and the Band Room Methodists constituted themselves as a 'Methodist Independent'

Church in February 1806. By 1808 they had five preaching rooms in Manchester, with 493 members and nine preachers. Many of the original founders returned to WM within a few years, but the new Church joined *IM and its successors continue under that name to the present day.

_____

T.P. Bunting (1859); J.C. Bowmer (1975); *IM Magazine* 1908

JAD

Bands, also known as 'band-societies', were introduced into Methodism in its early days and preceded the organization into *classes. The bands were modelled on what JW saw among the *Moravians at Herrnhut. Men and women, married and single met in separate bands, numbering between five and ten, smaller than the classes. Advocated by JW as one of the 'prudential' means of grace, the bands met weekly to confess their faults to and pray for one another; but W repudiated any comparison with the Roman Confessional. From 1741 admission was by band ticket, distinguished from the *class ticket by the addition of a letter 'b'. In December 1738 (or possibly a year later) he drew up 'Rules of the Band Societies', following these in 1744 by more explicit 'Directions for the Band Societies'. In 1764 he found it necessary to rebuke those who neglected to meet in band, and the searching demands of membership of a band meant that it steadily lost ground to the class meeting as Methodist *discipline was relaxed.

_____

HMGB 1 pp. 217–20, 4 pp. 23–4, 71–2; *PWHS* 161–4

JAV

Banks, Eliza Jane (Sister Jeanie) (1845–1932), daughter of **Matthew Banks** (1798–1878; e.m. 1826), a missionary in the *West Indies. She served as a Sister with P. *Thompson in East London for eight years before transferring to the Wesley *Deaconess Order in 1896. She concentrated on evangelistic work, preaching and conducting many very successful missions from Shetland to Northern Ireland. In 1912 she became the first Wesley Deaconess to superannuate.

_____

E.D. Graham in R. Sykes (1998) pp. 94–102

EDG

Banks, Dr John Shaw (1835–1917; e.m. 1856), pioneer missionary in the Mysore District, *India 1856–65. From 1880–1910 he held the Chair of Theology at *Headingley College. His *Manual of Christian Doctrine* (1887) went

through many editions and among his other publications were the *Fernley Lecture of 1880 on *Christianity and the Science of Religion* and translations of German theological works. He was President of the Conference in 1902 and received a DD from Edinburgh the following year.

_____

MR 22 March 1917

JAV

Banner, Horace H. (1906–74), IM minister with the Unevangelised Fields Mission 1928–72, supported by the IM Connexion. He worked among Amazonian Indians and in 1935 undertook a search for three missing missionaries in the Xingu River and opened up a new area of work with hitherto undiscovered tribes. He and his wife Eva Banner (*née* Tristram) established new mission stations in the region. In 1962 the social and humanitarian aspects of his work were recognized by the Brazilian government and he was awarded honorary citizenship. He translated hymns and Bible portions into Indian languages. In 1997 a NT translation was completed in the Kayapo language, which he had been the first to commit to writing.

_____

S.V. Poultney (1965); *Horace Banner: Outstanding Pioneer* (Wigan 1971)

JAD

Baptism In 1756 JW published *A Treatise on Baptism* largely taken from his father. He believed in the baptismal *regeneration of infants but, as people fall into sin, he preached to adults in general the need for the new birth or *Regeneration. Those who had not been baptized as infants should receive adult baptism, which, if duly received, was a *means of grace. But JW came to see that, though regeneration might sometimes accompany baptism, it might often precede or follow it. At first he (re-)baptized those baptized by ministers who had not been episcopally ordained, but later changed his view on the necessity for this, though still willing to do it conditionally. In 1750 he asserted to the Baptist minister Gilbert Boyce, citing the case of *Quakers, that baptism was not 'necessary to salvation'. In *The Sunday Service of the Methodists* (1784), he considerably modified the Anglican services from the *BCP*, 1662, both for infants and for 'such as are of riper years'. Among other changes he omitted references to godparents and the signation, though the latter was retained in one version of the service for infants. The service for infants reduces but does not eliminate references to regeneration. There were further changes in 1786 and in several subsequent books. Infant baptism is now regarded in Methodism as a sign of *future* regeneration, for which prayer is made.

See also Methodist Service Book; **Sacraments**

LQHR July 1961; A.M. Ward in *LQHR* July 1962 pp. 207–11; B.G. Holland (1970)
ARG

Barber, John (1757–1816; e.m. 1782)), born at Hayfield, Derbys, began life as a farm labourer. Converted on Easter Sunday 1778, he became a *local preacher and at *Macclesfield in 1782 found himself having to preach before JW, who then appointed him to the *Birmingham Circuit. In 1788 W ordained him for the work in *Scotland. Noted for his independence of mind, he was a member of the *Committee of Privileges and was elected President of the Conference in 1807 and again in 1815, being the first President to die in office. He marked a significant shift in Methodist thinking when he declared in 1799 that 'for the weak to be strengthened, the tempted succoured, the wavering confirmed and the children of God fed' was as important as converting sinners.

WMM 1867 pp. 625–6; *Wesley and his Successors* (1895) pp. 73–4
JAV

Barber, Dr William Theodore Aquila (1858–1945; e.m. 1882) son of a WM missionary, was born in Ceylon, grew up in South Africa and was educated at *Kingswood School and Caius College, Cambridge. An accomplished linguist, in 1884 he was sent to Wuchang, *China, to establish a college for higher education. In 1898, after two years as a Mission House Secretary, he succeeded W.F. *Moulton as headmaster of The *Leys School. He was President of the Conference in 1919 and from 1920 to 1929 Principal of *Richmond College. He wrote a life of David *Hill and was *Fernley Lecturer in 1917.

MR 25 Oct. 1945; F. Tice (1966) pp. 118–21
GRS

Bardsley, Samuel (d. 1818; e.m. 1768), born in *Manchester, where he worked as an errand boy for a wine merchant before becoming an itinerant. 'Simple-hearted' and loving, he was highly regarded by JW, who corresponded frequently with him, relied on him for advice and named him as one of the *Legal Hundred. The Rev. David Lloyd (1752–1838) of Llanbister,

author of *Horae Theologicae* (1823) and keen supporter of the CMS, was converted under his preaching. Because of the exigencies of the itinerancy, he was discouraged by both JW and J. *Pawson from marrying his sweetheart Mary ('Molly') Charlton of Manchester (whom JW buried in 1781, calling her 'an Israelite indeed'). He lived to be the senior preacher in the Connexion.

JAV

Barkby, Joseph Thomas (1861–1932; e.m. 1884), PM itinerant, born in Coventry. After training at the Manchester PM Institute, he served mainly in the North and the *IOM. He was General Missionary Secretary, 1918–23 and President of the 1924 Conference; Chairman of the *Chapel Aid Association, 1927–32, Moderator of the FCFC, 1931 and President of the National Council of Evangelical Free Churches, 1932. His wife Maggie Ann was a daughter of Sir W. *Hartley.
GEM

Barker, Joseph (1806–75), fourth son of WM clothiers at Bramley, near Leeds. From early youth he had a hunger for knowledge, but his formal education was confined to a few years at J. *Sigston's Academy. He became a *local preacher, but then joined the MNC and in 1828 became an itinerant. His views became steadily more liberal and radical; he became an enthusiastic teetotaller and in 1841 was expelled from the MNC for rejecting infant baptism. A compulsive communicator, he published over 100 tracts and books. His periodicals and lectures brought him immense popularity, so that his expulsion led to a damaging loss of members, ministers and chapels and the formation of the *'Christian Brethren'. He was, however, a poor organizer and many 'Barkerites' rejoined the MNC. Others followed him into Unitarianism. By 1851, when he emigrated to Ohio, he was virtually a free-thinker. He returned to England in 1860 to edit the secularist weekly *The National Reformer*, but gradually reverted to orthodoxy and became a PM local preacher at Tunstall. His last years were spent in the USA.

J.T. Barker (1880); *DNB*
EAR

Barker, Reginald John (1890–1981; e.m. 1914) was born in Ludlow and trained at *Handsworth College. He was an Army chaplain in Malta before going to the newly-built Tonypandy Central Hall in 1924. He had become a pacifist and socialist and his preaching attracted huge crowds. He founded the Community House Fellowship as a place of retreat and practical activities like boot-repairing for the unemployed. After moving to the *Huddersfield Mission he resigned from the ministry to continue his work with the Fellowship, but was reinstated in 1972. His gifts as preacher, politician, poet writer, musician and mystic enriched the lives of countless people. When the Fellowship was disbanded its assets were entrusted to the *Methodist Peace Fellowship.

KGG

Barlow, James (c. 1821–1887), son and heir of a small mill-owner in Edgworth, Lancs. Against fierce opposition from his employees, he prospered by introducing machinery into his mill. He became Mayor of *Bolton at 46 and had to read the Riot Act in the face of a series of Fenian outrages. The first Chairman and Treasurer of the WM Insurance Company, he remained a devoted and influential Methodist and *temperance advocate. He was an early supporter of *NCH, to which he gave an estate at Edgworth near Bolton to be developed as a training centre for boys.

Methodist Insurance Company (1970) p. 16

JAV

Barnard Castle *see* **Dales Circuit**

Barnstaple JW recorded no visit to this market town and small port in N. Devon, but in July 1745 met the evangelical vicar of St Gennys, G. *Thompson at neighbouring Fremington. In 1758 CW came to visit his niece, Philadelphia (d. 1773), daughter of his brother Samuel, who married the local apothecary Thomas Earle. The first society was formed in 1787. Among the WM chapels designed by the local architect A. *Lauder were Boutport Street (1869) and Newport Road (1911). The BC initially established themselves typically in the adjoining rural parish of Tawstock. Their 1895 Conference met in the Thorne Memorial chapel (1876, enlarged 1892) in Bear Street, named in memory of J. *Thorne.

J.G. Hayman (1871)

RFST

Barr, David, JP (1831–1910), *Birmingham businessman and WM *local preacher, was vice-chairman, treasurer and trustee of the Wesleyan and General Assurance Society. He served the local community in various offices, held office in the local church and circuit and in 1892 was elected to the *LPMAA General Committee,

becoming President in 1906. He instituted a fund and gave a site in Fillongley, near Coventry, to provide seven cottages for necessitous local preachers. His autobiography *Climbing the Ladder* was published in 1910.

WHS(WM) vol.6 no.7; G. Milburn & M. Batty (1995) pp. 209–11

EDG

Barratt, Thomas H. (1870–1951; e.m. 1894), WM minister, a son of the manse, taught at *Woodhouse Grove School before training for the ministry at *Handsworth College. He was Tutor in Pastoral Theology at *Richmond College 1909–16 and at *Didsbury College from 1919, becoming Principal 1925–39. He was a powerful preacher and caring pastor, whose students and congregations benefited from his Celtic inheritance and love of the classics.

MR 22 June 1939, 13 Sept. 1951; W.B. Brash & C.J. Wright (1942) pp. 9–17

EWD

Barrett, Alfred (1808–76; e.m. 1832), WM minister, born at Attercliffe, *Sheffield, Governor of *Richmond College, 1858–68. He was well versed in patristic and systematic theology and moral philosophy, and among his varied publications were lives of Ellen Gribbin, 'the boatman's daughter' (1847), which went through numerous editions, and of the missionary J.H. *Bumby (1852).

WL

Barrett, Dr Charles Kingsley, FBA (1917– ; e.m. 1937) was educated at *Shebbear College, Pembroke College and *Wesley House, Cambridge. In 1942 he became Assistant Tutor at *Headingley College and in 1945 Lecturer in NT at Durham, where he remained until retirement, being appointed Professor of Divinity in 1958. An internationally renowned scholar, elected President of the Society for NT Studies, he was awarded honorary doctorates at Hull, Aberdeen and Hamburg, as well as the Burkitt Medal for Biblical Studies. His early *The Holy Spirit and the Gospel Tradition* (1947) was a landmark in the study of the Spirit in the NT; but his most important work is a series of commentaries, notably on John's Gospel (1955), 1 & 2 Corinthians (1968, 1973), Romans (1957) and Acts (1996). The son of a PM minister, he was one of four Methodists who signed a Dissentient Statement on the *Anglican-Methodist Conversations in 1963.

CSR

Barritt, Mary (Mrs Taft) (1772–1851) came from farming stock, was converted at an early age and became convinced of the importance of communicating her faith to others. Even when her *Superintendent threatened to expel her if she persisted in 'exhorting', she felt impelled to 'obey God rather than men'. She received many invitations and travelled extensively throughout northern England, despite much opposition. A number of her converts became itinerant preachers and missionaries. She attended the Conferences in *Manchester and *Leeds, chiefly to meet itinerants sympathetic to female preaching, and in 1802 married Zechariah Taft (1772–1848), an itinerant very supportive of her work. He encouraged her to preach in spite of the fierce controversy which led to the banning of *women preachers by the 1803 Conference. He wrote three pamphlets on the subject and the two-volume *Biographical Sketches of Holy Women* (1825, 1828). In 1827 Mary published her own account of her work and this, with her subsequent career, shows that she was effectively another itinerant in her husband's circuits.

M. Taft (1827); L.F. Church (1949)

EDG

Barry, John (1792–1838; e.m. 1824), Irish minister, born in Co. Cork. Well educated, he was at first a teacher. He served as a missionary under the WMMS, in Jamaica from 1825 to 1832, in *Canada from 1832 to 1834 and in Bermuda from 1834 to 1836. His colourful ministry was marked by frequent, sometimes unauthorized, travel, social comment, e.g. on behalf of slaves, and eloquent preaching. Talented and touchy, vulnerable to personal criticism and vehement in his prosecution of what he considered just, he attracted much opposition.

N.W. Taggart (1986) pp. 146–67

NWT

Barton, Edgar Charles (1873–1953; e.m. 1898), *Book Steward 1932–48. The son of Henry Sumpter Barton (1836–99; e.m. 1860) and grandson of William Barton (d.1857; e.m. 1826), he was educated at *Woodhouse Grove School and *Richmond College. He served briefly in Malta and the Gold Coast (now *Ghana), then from 1911 to 1922 in the inner-city mission at St John's Square, Clerkenwell, London. After four years as Assistant Book Steward, in 1932 he succeeded J.A. *Sharp and was responsible for the building of Epworth House, City Road, as the headquarters of Methodist *publishing. He played a leading role in the formation of the Religious Group of the Publishers' Association. From 1914 he was Secretary of the First London District, becoming its Chairman in 1932, and in 1935 became the first secretary of the *MCMS.

MR 12 Nov. 1953; F.H. Cumbers (1956) pp. 111–12

JAV

Bastard, Abraham (d.1868), BC *local preacher, of Treligga, St Teath, Cornwall. In his youth fond of hunting, boxing, wrestling, poaching and swearing, he was converted by Betsy Reed, one of the female BC itinerants, and became a class leader, Sunday School teacher and a preacher who used A. *Clarke's *Commentary*. He regularly preached in the open air.

S.L. Thorne (1877)

TS

Batchelor, Mary (*née* Twiddy) (1813–92), daughter of a WM minister, went in 1841 as a teacher to Ceylon (now *Sri Lanka) with the Ladies' Society for Promoting Female Education in China and the East, since the WMMS did not then send single women overseas. In 1842 she married a widower, Peter Batchelor (1809–81; e.m. 1837), who had been a lay missionary with the CMS Press in Madras before serving as a WM missionary in *India (1838–54 and 1857–62), in the Crimea (1856–57) and in South Africa (1862–75). Mrs Batchelor opened a girls' day school in Negapatam and in 1858 her request for women teachers to start a boarding school prompted what in time became *Women's Work. On their return from South Africa, she served on its Committee.

P.M. Webb (1958) pp. 24–31

JRP

Bateman, Rev. Richard Thomas (*c.* 1712–1760), rector of St Bartholomew the Great, Smithfield, London from 1738, also held a Welsh living and seems to have commuted between the two. Born in Haverfordwest, he graduated from Jesus College, Oxford. He was hostile to the evangelical revival until influenced by his curate at Llansyfran, Howell Davies, a convert of H. *Harris. He attended the Conferences of 1747 and 1748. JW preached at St Bartholomew's several times from 1747 on; but their friendship later cooled, perhaps because Bateman was influenced by the Countess of *Huntingdon and attended some of the early meetings of the *Calvinistic Methodist Association.

A.S. Wood (1992) pp. 26–30

JAV

Bateman, Thomas (1799–1897), farmer, land surveyor and PM *local preacher. Brought up an Anglican, he was a Guardian of the Nantwich Union and for 30 years vestry clerk at Wrenbury. He began attending WM services, but under the influence of J. *Wedgwood became PM in 1819. A local preacher from 1822, he pioneered the work in Cheshire and Shropshire. An ally, adviser and companion of H. *Bourne, W. *Clowes and J. Wedgwood, he was a Deed Poll member from 1851 and President of the Conference in 1857 and 1867.

F.H. Hurd (1872) pp. 91–106; G.J. Stevenson (1884–86) 5, pp. 834–43; H. Woodcock (c. 1907) pp. 81–5

DCD

Bath, to which the rich and idle flocked in the eighteenth century, was the social centre of England, renowned for 'Humbug, Follee and Vanitee'. JW first preached there on 10 April 1739 and roundly condemned the frivolity around him. He clashed with the self-styled 'King of Bath', Richard ('Beau') Nash, at the Ham, and in all preached 150 times in the city. The first purpose-built preaching house was in the tawdry Avon Street area. Gradual progress culminated in the opening of New King Street chapel by JW in 1779. It possessed the first organ in any of his chapels. A larger chapel (by J. *Wilson) erected on the site in 1847 was destroyed in the 1942 blitz.

Lady *Huntingdon first visited Bath in 1739 and subsequently built one of her 'safe' chapels (opened 1765) adjacent to her house on the Paragon (now housing the 'Building of Bath Museum'). Here JW preached to socially privileged congregations until the dispute over *Calvinism in the 1770s.

The splendid classical Walcot Chapel in London Road (by W. *Jenkins) was opened in 1816 and has been refurbished to meet modern needs. MHA provides sheltered accommodation for the elderly at Walcot Court, built on its burial ground, and at Stratton House in Park Lane for those needing closer care.

PM activity began in 1828. They bought a house at 4, Westgate Buildings in 1845 which was rebuilt in 1866. A gloomy building, it survived the bombing in World War II, but closed in 1964. After occupying several other places, the UMFC acquired what they renamed Hope Chapel in Lower Borough Walls in 1866 and moved to a new church at Beechen Cliff in 1913.

*Kingswood School has been on Lansdown since its move from Bristol in 1851.

J. Rigg (1848); B. Crofts (ed.) (1990)

BDC

Batty, Thomas (1790–1856), PM itinerant, born near *Hull to a father who had abandoned Catholicism for Methodism and who entertained W. *Bramwell and other preachers in the family home. Thomas served in the Navy when young. Converted in 1813, he became a WM *local preacher, but in 1821 gave allegiance to the PMs and was immediately engaged as an itinerant missioner, opening up large areas of Lancashire and the northern dales. He came to be known as 'the Apostle of Weardale' and laid the foundations for much successful PM work.

J. Petty (1857); *DE*

GEM

Baulkwill, William Robert Kellaway (1860–1915; e.m. 1882), BC minister, connexional treasurer 1902–6, missionary treasurer 1901–8; President of the Conference, 1904. He was Governor of *Shebbear College, 1909–15.

WL

Bavin, Francis, FRSA, FRMetS (1852–1933; e.m. 1874), UMFC minister who, after 25 years in English circuits, became General Superintendent of the UMFC missions in Jamaica and Central America 1898–1907. He sought to establish the Jamaican Church on a self-governing and self-supporting basis. When the UMFC withdrew from the island, he was primarily responsible for the Enabling Act whereby many of the former Methodist Free Churches voluntarily came under the jurisdiction of the WM *Synod. He served on the island's Legislative Council and as a member of the Board of Education had a considerable influence on education throughout the island.

GRS

Baxter, John (d. 1805; e.m. 1785), a government shipwright who went to Antigua in 1778 and, being a *local preacher, became the leader of the society formed by N. *Gilbert at St John's. Within three years it had grown from 30 to 600 members. He was appointed an 'Elder' at the Christmas Conference in Baltimore in 1784 and ordained by T. *Coke the following summer. He was essentially a pioneer worker who, because of his extensive knowledge of the *West Indies, frequently accompanied Coke on his tours of the islands. In 1788 Coke persuaded him to take charge of the Carib mission on St Vincent. Through his efforts a school-house was built, but the enterprise failed, mainly because of political disaffection, fostered by France, among the Caribs. Baxter returned to his work among the Negroes of Antigua and, apart from one year's furlough, spent the rest of his life there.

J.A. Vickers (1969) pp. 99, 149–56

GRS

Baxter, Matthew (1812–93), UMFC minister, formerly PM and WMA. Converted through J. *Flesher, he entered the PM ministry *c.* 1834, but after his *Scarborough circuit became independent, he joined the WMA with them in 1836. In 1842 he went to Kingston, Jamaica for nine years. Back home, he served as *Connexional Editor and *Book Steward 1854–59 and was elected President in 1856. In 1868 he went out to superintend the work in *New Zealand, superannuating there in 1873. His most important publication was *Memorials of Free Methodism* (1856) and with J. *Everett he edited the UMFC hymn-book (1860).

G.J. Stevenson (1884–86) 6 pp. 939–44

OAB

Bayley, Rev. Cornelius (1751–1812), evangelical incumbent of St. James's, *Manchester, born near Whitchurch, Salop. He was educated and taught at Whitchurch Grammar School and from 1773–83 taught at *Kingswood School. He took holy orders, 1780–82 and for a time served as J. *Fletcher's curate at *Madeley. Later he preached in the Manchester Circuit, built a proprietary chapel, St James's, in Manchester (opened 1788) and exercised a highly popular ministry there. Many Oldham Street Methodists were among his hearers, but after 1791 he was estranged by the itinerants' claims to ministerial status and opposed them in his *Questions . . . on the Ministerial Office* (1795). He published a Hebrew Grammar in 1782, for which he was awarded a DD by Aberdeen University. His other writings included a hymn-book and *The Swedenborgian Doctrine of the Trinity Considered* (1785).

DNB; E.A. Rose in *PWHS* 34 pp. 153–8

JAV

Beal, Susannah Gooding (1826–60), the first woman missionary sent overseas by the Ladies' Committee of the WMMS. Born in Dover, she came to London to work in domestic service and became a Sunday School teacher at the King's Cross WM chapel. Later, when she was working as a governess, her minister heard of the plan to send women missionaries overseas and encouraged her to apply. She was sent to *Westminster College for six months' teacher training and in 1859 set sail for Belize in British Honduras. She began working enthusiastically in a school of 130 pupils, but within a few months succumbed to yellow fever.

P.M. Webb (1958) pp. 35–42

PMW

Beales, W. Harold (1886–1967; e.m. 1906), a persuasive preacher, a pacifist and skilful conference leader, held a roving commission with the *HM Department, 1934–40. From 1940 to 1952 he was Warden of the Wesley *Deaconess Order. His most distinctive work was done at *Cambridge (1924–30) where he initiated the *Cambridge Group movement. Undergraduates, dons and local church members met in fellowships (similar to the traditional *class meetings), retreats and projects for Christian action. The movement became 'MethSoc' and spread to other universities and colleges, influencing many future Church leaders.

MR 21 Sept. 1967

WDH

Beard, Thomas, one of W's earliest lay preachers. J. *Bennet's journal indicates that he was preaching in Derbyshire in March 1743. In 1744 he was 'pressed in Yorkshire for preaching, and so sent for a soldier.' While in the army he visited *Scotland, taking every opportunity to exhort. As he remarked: 'Many thought it strange to see a man in a red coat preach.' Soon after regaining his freedom he fell ill at *Newcastle and died two or three days later.

JWJ; C. Atmore (1801)

SRV

Beaty, A. Stanley (1883–1970; e.m. 1906) worked in local government before offering for the ministry. After training at *Headingley College, he spent 20 years (1906–26) in South Ceylon District (*Sri Lanka), chiefly on the tea and rubber estates. He returned in 1930 as Chairman of the District (and of the Provincial Synod) to lead the Church through a period when political independence, coupled with an ongoing Buddhist Revival, called for a radical review of its educational and social activities. He is commemorated in the new Conference headquarters at Colpetty, Colombo. Before retiring in 1952 he was for five years Warden of *Kingsmead College.

MR 11 June 1970

J A V

Beaumont, George (1763–1841), one of the earliest MNC ministers, having first been a *local preacher in *Stockport. He was Secretary of the MNC Conference in 1802. During the Napoleonic period he published a string of radical pamphlets in which he defended *Luddism, attacked landlords, the aristocracy and war; but after a further pamphlet, *The Helmet*, he resigned in 1814 in the face of Conference disapproval. His *Norwich congregation remained loyal to him and he ministered to it as an Independent chapel until his death.

EAR

Beaumont, John (1762–1822; e.m. 1786), WM itinerant, the son of an Anglican farmer from whom he inherited musical talents and a fine singing voice. Encountering the Methodists at the age of 16, he joined them despite parental opposition. He composed over 60 hymn tunes (including 'St Ignatius' to CW's 'All thanks to the Lamb' (MHB 747)) and several anthems. He wrote a *Treatise on . . . the Disease of Melancholy* (1808) and an account of his 'experience and travels' with 'his reasons for composing music'.

J.T. Lightwood (1935) pp. 411–14

J A V

Beaumont, Joseph, MD (1794–1855; e.m. 1813), WM minister, son of John *Beaumont, was educated at *Kingswood School. When precarious health made him anxious about surviving the rigours of the itinerancy, he qualified in medicine. He overcame an inhibiting stammer and was in demand far beyond the Connexion as a preacher and lecturer. He was eloquent in debate and a forceful adversary of J. *Bunting's dominance in Conference and the Connexion. His political and ecclesiastical liberalism led him to plead for greater WM co-operation with both Dissent and the Established Church. Reflecting on JW's equivocal churchmanship, he commented that 'Wesley, like a strong and skilful rower, looked one way, while every stroke of the oar took him in an opposite direction.' In the controversies over *Wesleyan Takings* and the *Fly Sheet, he opposed the expulsion of J. *Everett and others. He used his medical knowledge to argue the physiological case against alcohol and was a founder member of the English *Temperance Society.

G.J. Stevenson (1884–86) 2 pp. 295–306; B. Gregory (1897), passim

EWD

Beckly Trust was set up in 1926 on the suggestion of S.E, *Keeble by the WM layman John Henry Beckly (1864–1932), a partner in a *Plymouth drapery firm and President of the Commercial Travellers' Association in 1912. Educated at *Shebbear College (of which he was later a generous benefactor), he served on the connexional *Sunday School Committee and attended the international Sunday School Conferences in Rome (1907) and Washington, DC (1910) and the COPEC meetings in 1924. Under the terms of the Trust an annual lecture is given during the Methodist Conference 'to set forth the social implications of Christianity and to further . . . the expression of the Christian attitude in reference to social, industrial, economic and international subjects'. The first was given by Sir Josiah *Stamp on *The Christian Ethic as an Economic Factor*. Other early lecturers included the controversial Dean W.R.Inge (1930) and Archbishop William Temple (1943). In addition to the lectures, the Trust has also published series of pamphlets and 'occasional papers'.

MR 29 Dec. 1932, 5 Jan. 1933

J A V

Beckworth, William (1840–1911), PM *local preacher and man of culture, whose parental home was the first PM meeting place in east *Hull, became a leading and influential layman in the Connexion. On moving to *Leeds in 1857, he played a prominent part in establishing the Leeds PM *Sunday School Union, which led to the connexional SS Union, of which he became the first treasurer. In 1871 he was elected to Leeds

School Board on a PM ticket. He gave considerable support to what became *Hartley College and held a number of connexional posts, including African Missions treasurer 1871–75 and joint treasurer with W.P. *Hartley of PM Chapel Aid. He supported J.D. *Thompson when charged with heresy. The owner of a tannery business, he was a Liberal councillor. He wrote a substantial history of Leeds PM, *A Book of Remembrance* (1910).

DCD

Bedford, known for its association with John Bunyan, was visited in 1739 by B. *Ingham and W. *Delamotte and a small society was formed soon afterwards. But the 'nursing father' of Methodism in the town was William Parker (1708–85), a leading citizen who, after parting company with the *Moravians, invited JW to pay the first of his many visits in October 1753. W preached a number of times on St Peter's Green and in 1758 was invited to preach the Assize Sermon in St Paul's Church. Parker was succeeded as leader, after an interval, by William Cumberland (1760–1833), a *local preacher and class leader. The first preaching room was over a hog-stye in the vicinity of the George Inn, which seems to have been replaced by 1763, when JW refers to preaching in the 'new room'. A chapel in Angel Street (1804) was replaced by St Paul's Chapel (1832); altered in 1896, this was the first place of worship in the town to be lit by electricity.

J.M. Anderson (1953)

JAV

Beecham, Dr John (1787–1856; e.m. 1815), WM minister, born at Barnoldby le Beck, Lincs. While in the *Liverpool Circuit he wrote his *Essay on the Constitution of Wesleyan Methodism* (1829; 3rd edn, 1851), a classic statement of the 'high Wesleyan' view of the *Pastoral Office and the idea that the 'living Wesley' is the collective pastorate of the Conference. Beecham was a Secretary of the WMMS from 1831 to 1855 and as secretary for West Africa wrote a book on *Ashantee and the Gold Coast* (1841) which must have relied heavily on the reports of T. B. *Freeman. He played a part in devising constitutions for affiliated Conferences, including *Canada which he visited in 1855. As President of the Conference in 1850, he supported the disciplinary action which lost thousands of members at that time.

W.R. Ward (1972) pp. 149–52

JMT

Beer, Alfred (1874–1963), musician and schoolmaster, born in *Birmingham, the son of a WM minister of the same name (1840–1922; e.m. 1863). He joined the staff at *Kingswood School in 1904, where H.B. *Workman commissioned him to write a number of tunes for Wesley hymns. Five appeared in the 1933 *MHB*. Due to failing eyesight he had to leave Kingswood in 1928, but then served as organist and choirmaster in Minehead and Uxbridge.

PLC

Beet, Joseph Agar (1840–1924; e.m. 1864) was a leading WM exegete and systematic theologian. From 1885 to 1905 he was tutor at *Richmond College. His first major work, a commentary on Romans (1877), was followed by a trilogy on Trinitarian theology and eschatology. After the publication of his *The Last Things* (1897) the orthodoxy of his views on eternal punishment was challenged in Conference, and in 1902 he narrowly avoided losing his chair at Richmond College. Though deeply loyal to WM, he was determined to adapt the tradition to modern insights, and under the influence of the late nineteenth-century *Holiness Movement, he produced an updating of W's teaching on *Christian perfection. A strong individualist, he was a member of the *Legal Hundred, but was never elected President of the Conference. Revered by many of his students, he is perhaps the greatest 'forgotten' theologian of British Methodism.

MR 7 Aug. 1902, 29 May 1924; D.J. Carter in *PWHS* 51 pp. 197–216

DJC

Beetham, Thomas Allen (1906–92; e.m. 1927), WM missionary. As an undergraduate he heard W.J. *Platt speak about the Harris movement in West Africa and immediately offered his services to the WMMS. With first class degrees in Maths and Theology, he was sent to Wesley College, Kumasi in the Gold Coast (now *Ghana) to train teachers, catechists and ministers, soon became its Principal and later oversaw its rapid post-war expansion. He was Africa Secretary of the MMS 1950–60 and of the Conference of British Missionary Societies 1960–67, playing a notable part in the transition to African self-government in church and state. He devised the system which enabled the transfer of authority to autonomous Methodist Conferences and was one of the pioneers of the Islam in Africa Project (now the Programme for Christian-Muslim Relations in Africa).

MR 14 Jan. 1993; T.A. Beetham in *International Bulletin of Missionary Research*, Oct. 1990 pp. 167–71

JRP

Belben, Howard Albert George (1914–99; e.m. 1936), biblical scholar and teacher, was chaplain and lecturer at *Southlands College 1943–47 before spending more than half his ministry at *Cliff College, as Junior Tutor (1947–53), Senior Tutor (1960–65) and Principal (1965–77). He was always ready to introduce new educational methods and his own gifts as a teacher enabled students to realise the contemporary relevance of the Bible. His constant availability for pastoral counselling helped to ensure that the College remained a Christian family, rather than an impersonal institution.

JAV

Belfast was a small town, mostly of thatched houses, when JW visited it in 1756, the first of 11 visits between then and 1789. Its rapid growth as an industrial city in the nineteenth century was accompanied by a similar increase in the number of Methodist members and churches. Another major period of growth followed World War II. *Methodist College was founded in 1868 and *Edgehill College in 1928. The first city mission in Ireland, the Belfast Central Mission, began work in 1888 and continues to redevelop as needs change. The North Belfast Mission, established a few years later, has relocated its work to Newtownabbey. In 1960 Aldersgate House was opened to provide a spiritual and social centre for students at the nearby Queen's University. It also houses the collection of the Irish Branch of the Wesley Historical Society. Student work later moved elsewhere. The increase in membership in Northern Ireland and its decline in the Irish Republic led to the Church's administration being moved to Belfast in 1970 and it now occupies offices in Aldersgate House and neighbouring buildings.

J.W. Jones (1893)

DALC

Bell, George (d.1807), Methodist *enthusiast. A former corporal in the Life Guards, he was converted in 1758 and joined the *Foundery Society, where he became associated with T. *Maxfield. In March 1761 he claimed the gift of

entire *sanctification, including infallibility, and attempted miraculous healings. JW was slow to condemn him or to counteract his influence and he gained the allegiance of many of the *London Methodists. Early in 1763 he and Maxfield left the society, along with about one fifth of the members. His prophesy that the Second Coming would occur on 28th February caused widespread consternation and he was arrested and charged with causing public disorder, with JW belatedly speaking out against his enthusiasm. He represents a minor strand in early Methodism which has been largely played down by its historians.

W.S.Gunter (1989), pp. 217–20; K.G.C.Newport in *MH* Jan. 1997, pp. 95–105

JAV

Bellingham, John Parry (1826–1909; e.m. 1852), PM minister, born at Bickley, N. Yorks, the son of a village schoolmaster and grandson of a blacksmith. His writings on natural science published in the *PMM* and the *Teacher's Assistant* helped to bridge the widening gap between Christian belief and scientific knowledge in the post-Darwin era.

JAV

Bellman, Sir Harold (1886–1963). Joining the Abbey Road Building Society (later the Abbey National) in 1918, he became its Secretary in 1921. In a distinguished career in the building society movement, his chairmanship of the National Association of Building Societies from 1933 and presidency of the International Union of Building Societies, 1934–38 won him international acclaim. He was a governor of *Queenswood School and the L.S.E. and general treasurer of the *NCHO. He supported Ramsay Macdonald in 1931 and was knighted the following year. A voracious reader and prolific author, his autobiography was called *Cornish Cockney*.

Times, June 3 & 10, 1963; *MR* 13 June 1963

JAV

Bemersley The farm at Bemersley Green on the northern boundary of *Stoke-on-Trent was the family home of H. and J. *Bourne from 1788. It was the site of the PM Book Room until it was moved to London in 1843. During this period the connexional printing was done there by James Bourne and for over 20 years PM books, magazines and other printed matter were distributed from this remote farm by cart and canal to all parts of the country.

H.B. Kendall (1906) 2 pp. 1–14; F. Baker in *PWHS* 30 pp. 138–50

JHA

Benin   The Republic of Benin was formerly the French colony of Dahomey. Methodism traces its origins to T.B. *Freeman in the 1840s and spread from the town of Porto Novo. At first part of the Lagos District and then the French West Africa District, it became an autonomous Conference in 1992. It is one of the member Churches of the Evangelical Community for Apostolic Action (CEVAA) which placed a pioneering international Joint Action for Mission team in central Dahomey in the 1960s. The theological college at Porto Novo has for many years served Protestant Churches in Benin, *Côte d'Ivoire, *Togo and elsewhere in the region.

JRP

Bennet, John (1714–59) one of the earliest and most significant of W's lay preachers (not to be confused with the Rev. John Bennet of Laneast, Cornwall). Born near Chinley, Derbyshire, he attended the local Presbyterian chapel, pastored by James Clegg. After a brief time at Findern Academy, *Derby, he became a legal clerk and then a pack-man. Following a dramatic conversion experience at Hayfield in 1742, he became associated with D. *Taylor and B. *Ingham. Joining the Methodists on 15 April 1743 he worked as a lay assistant, establishing a network of religious groups, in Lancashire, Cheshire, Yorkshire and Derbyshire, which became known as 'John Bennet's Round.' He was influential in establishing *Quarterly Meetings and possibly the introduction of annual *Conferences as features of Methodist Connexionalism. On 3 October 1749 he married G. *Murray, a widow apparently already betrothed to JW. Adopting *Calvinistic views, and forming closer links with G. *Whitefield, he openly accused W of preaching 'Popery' and seceded from Methodism in 1752. Supervising the Duke's Alley Chapel in *Bolton, he became the founder of Congregationalism in that town. On obtaining ordination in 1754 he took charge of an Independent Chapel at Warburton, Cheshire, remaining there until his death five years later.

C. Atmore (1801) pp. 49–51; S.R. Valentine (1997)

SRV

Bennett, George *see Primitive Methodist Leader*

Bennis, Elizabeth (*née* Patten) (1725–1802), born into a Presbyterian family in *Limerick, was influenced in her early teens by Aleine's *Alarm to the Unconverted*. One of JW's earliest women helpers in Ireland, she was the wife of Michael Bennis, Master of the Corporation of Sadlers in Limerick. She was actively involved in the growth of Irish Methodism and acted as spiritual adviser to many. She corresponded with JW between 1763 and 1776 and kept him informed of Irish developments. She upheld many dispirited missionaries by her sound and independent advice; notably John Stretton, a layman converted through her in *Waterford and whom she nurtured spiritually and intellectually after he moved to Newfoundland. Late in life she lived in Philadelphia with her son Thomas, who published her correspondence after her death.

JWL; E. Bennis (1809); C.H. Crookshank (1882) pp. 20–30

RPR

Benson, Sir Clarence Irving, CBE (1897–1980), born in *Hull and trained at *Cliff College. On arriving in *Australia in 1916, he was appointed to Cavendish, Western Victoria and in 1926 to Wesley Central Mission, Melbourne, where from 1933 to 1967 he was Superintendent. This enabled him to enter into civic, business and political circles and enhanced his status as Melbourne's leading Methodist minister. As trustee and later chairman of the State Library he helped to extend free library services in Victoria. He pioneered a controversial radio session from 1938 to 1944 and broadcast the Mission's Pleasant Sunday Afternoons, making them a forum for social and community issues. His weekly column 'Church and People' appeared in the *Melbourne Herald* for 50 years. He received a DD from Toronto University in 1939, was President of the Victoria and Tasmania Conference in 1943 and knighted in 1963. An evangelical preacher with a strong following, he also administered a range of innovative community welfare work and residential care. His dominant, conservative personality was frequently misunderstood and criticized from within the Church, but Benson always pointed Melbourne to Christ.

ADB; *ADEB*

TMO

Benson, Joseph (1748–1821; e.m. 1771), WM itinerant, born in Cumberland, where he was educated by a Presbyterian minister. He had some thought of taking Anglican orders; but having encountered the Methodists he travelled to London to meet JW and while still in his teens was appointed classics master at *Kingswood School. In 1769 he enrolled at St. Edmund Hall, Oxford, but within months was appointed 'headmaster' at Lady *Huntingdon's college at *Trevecka. Together with J. *Fletcher he left after nine months because of the renewed dispute between the *Calvinist and *Arminian wings of Methodism. From 1771 to 1800 he served mostly in northern circuits and was a close friend and confidant of JW, with whom he corresponded frequently. A conservative sympathetic to the 'Church Methodists', in 1775 he joined with Fletcher in proposing a scheme to the Conference for keeping the Methodists within the Church by the ordaining of suitably qualified itinerants and by using *Kingswood School to train others for the ministry. In the dispute at *Bristol in 1794 he caused concern to his colleagues by siding with the *New Room trustees in opposing the administration of the Sacrament by the itinerants. He had a high concept of the *Pastoral Office and strongly opposed *Kilham's radicalism, seeing great danger in giving people the power to appoint and dismiss the Preachers. He was twice President of the Conference, in 1798 and 1810. One of the leading Methodist scholars of his time, he produced *A Defence of the Methodists* (against Dr Edward Tatham of Oxford) and *A Farther Defence* (both 1793), a life of Fletcher (1804, frequently reprinted) and a five-volume *Commentary* (1815–18). As *Connexional Editor at the Book Room 1804–21 he gave new life to the *Magazine* and produced a new edition of JW's *Works* in 16 octavo volumes (1809–13). J. *Everett described his life as a 'monotony of greatness'.

J. Macdonald (1822); R. Treffry (1840); G.J. Stevenson (1884–86) 2 pp. 175–87; *SL* vols 5–8 passim

                                                                 EWD/PSF

Bermondsey Settlement, Southwark, was founded by J.S. *Lidgett in 1892, to provide opportunity for the educationally privileged to serve the needs of the local community in a wide range of religious, educational and social activities. An early resident was Dr Alfred Salter, who later became MP for Bermondsey West. Lidgett was Warden for 58 years. The Chailey Heritage Hospital was one of its offshoots. The Settlement closed in 1967, when the South London Mission incorporated some of its activities.

J. Scott Lidgett (1936); J.D. Beasley (1989)
                                                                       JDB

Berridge, Rev. John (1716–93), vicar of Everton, Beds, 1755–93, graduated from Clare Hall, Cambridge. He first met JW in 1758, became more evangelical and made his parish the centre of an itinerant ministry in the East Midlands. Later, under the influence of G. *Whitefield and Lady *Huntingdon, he became a *Calvinist and attacked JW's theology. He preached frequently at Whitefield's Tottenham Court Road Tabernacle. He has been described as 'academically brilliant' and 'more eccentric' than W. *Grimshaw. JW protested at his alterations to his and CW's hymns in his *Collection of Divine Songs* (1760) and he included few of them in his later collection *Sion's Songs or Hymns* (1785). His *Cheerful Piety; or Religion without Gloom* (1792) was frequently reprinted. E. *Hurrell was one of his converts.

Memoir in R. Whittingham (1838); *DNB*; *PWHS* 11 pp. 169–74; C. Smyth (1940) pp. 149–200; A. Brown-Lawson (1994) pp. 63–70

                                                                       JAV

Berwick, Lin (1950–), founder of the Trust that bears her name, has cerebral palsy and is blind. Despite these disabilities, she became a *local preacher, a qualified psychotherapeutic counsellor and homeopath and is a lecturer, writer and broadcaster. She has been honoured for her work for the disabled and in 1977 was the subject of a 'This is Your Life' programme. She has written two autobiographical works, *Undefeated* (1980) and *Inner Vision* (1990). The Lin Berwick Trust provides purpose-built holiday accommodation for people with disabilities and their families and carers.

                                                                       JAV

Berwick-upon-Tweed A small society was formed by Robert Sutty some years before JW paid the first of his 20 visits in July 1748. W preached in the open air and in the Guildhall (Town Hall), where the society seems to have met until the Walkergate Chapel was built in 1797. A Berwick Circuit existed briefly from 1783 to 1789, and then more permanently from 1817. The PM chapel was built in 1829 and the two congregations remained separate until 1920, when the WM and PM societies entered into a voluntary amalgamation. The resulting Berwick PM Circuit, embracing the united Berwick society (worshipping at Walkergate) and village chapels, anticipated *Methodist Union by 11 years.

W.M. Patterson (1909) pp. 363–72; *PWHS* 33 pp. 161–69; *In Wesley's Footsteps: the bicentenary of Berwick Methodist Church 1797–1997* (1997)

                                                                        CC

Bestall, Arthur H., K-i-H (1863–1936; e.m. 1887), pioneer missionary in Burma (now *Myanmar) 1887–1910 and 1920–24. He established the first leper home in Mandalay and was a translator for the BFBS. His son **Alfred Edmeades Bestall** (1892–1986) artist and illustrator, was born in Mandalay and educated at *Rydal School. From 1919 he worked in Fleet Street and became known for his book and magazine illustrations, but especially for the 'Rupert Bear' stories which he wrote and illustrated for many years. There is a permanent exhibition of his work at Rake Court, Milford.

MR 28 June 1962, 10 Dec. 1936, 23 Jan. 1986; G. Perry (1985)

                                                                        JAV

Bett, Dr Henry (1876–1953; e.m. 1899), WM minister and church historian, born at Maidenwell, Lincs. From 1923 he taught Pastoral Theology and Church History at *Handsworth College, where he was affectionately known as 'Uncle Henry'. In 1934 he gave the first WHS Lecture, on the early Methodist preachers, and in 1937 the *Fernley-Hartley Lecture on *The Spirit of Methodism*. He published many other works on history, literature and spirituality and was a frequent contributor to the *Methodist Recorder*. His year as President of the Conference (1940) was a challenging one for a convinced pacifist. His expertise in hymnology issued in *The Hymns of Methodism in their Literary Relations* (1913; 3rd enlarged edition, 1945) and in service on the committee which produced the 1933 *MHB*.

MR 9 April 1953

                                                                        JAN

Bible Christian Magazine, planned by W. *O'Bryan for circulation among the *c.* 5000 members of what became a new Methodist denomination, was first published in 1822 as *The Arminian Magazine* and consisted of 'Extracts and Original Treatises on Universal Redemption'. Both its title and its contents reflected the format and *Arminian stance of the magazine launched by JW in 1778. In an introduction 'To the Reader', O'Bryan recommended it to the members of his societies, some of whom thought that all books other than the Bible were largely useless. It was printed and published by S. *Thorne, first from Stoke Damarel and later from *Shebbear. In 1828, under its new editor J, *Thorne, the title was changed to *Bible Christian Magazine*. He made it his pulpit for his educational, chapel building and missionary enthusiasms as well as for championing teetotalism and nonconformist rights. F.W. *Bourne, editor from 1866 to 1899, with an eye on approaching *Methodist Union, widened its ecumenical coverage, stating its purpose as to chronicle 'whatever takes place that is of concern to the Methodist group of churches'. Despite this, it remained the house journal O'Bryan had intended, as the series on 'Living Friends in Active Circuits' (1901–1903) exemplifies.

                                                                        TS

Bible Christians, a denomination founded in 1815 by W. *O'Bryan, a WM *local preacher turned self-appointed evangelist working in the vicinity of the WM Stratton Mission in north-east Cornwall. Expelled (for the second time) from membership of the St Austell Circuit and failing to gain the approval of the Superintendent of the Stratton Mission for his local evangelizing, on 1 October 1815 he established an independent circuit based on Week St Mary, where the whole society joined with him. Soon afterwards he formed new classes at Launcells and at *Shebbear across the Devon border. This was at Lake Farm, home of the *Thorne family who joined him en masse. The new denomination was still unnamed, but soon became known as the 'Bible Christians', to which *O'Bryan himself sometimes prefixed the adjective 'Arminian' (dropped after 1819). (They were also popularly known as 'Bryanites'.)

Circuits were soon formed and a *quarterly meeting was held on 1 January 1816. The first Conference was held in 1819 at Launceston. The movement was not a break-away from WM, but, like the PM movement, an attempt to return to its roots. O'Bryan himself said that JW was 'ever near' him; the BC Rules of Society were closely modelled on JW's Rules, and when the monthly magazine was begun in 1822 it was, like W's, called the *Arminian Magazine*. As an evangelical mission, the movement followed the WM model, reflected the form of the contemporary Cornish revivals and was, in many ways, an outreach of the 'Great Revival' of 1814. O'Bryan's small army of itinerant preachers, most of them young men and women, went everywhere, usually on foot, to engage in open-air preaching, form societies and eventually build chapels. In this way the movement took root in Cornwall and the West Country and by 1825 had been transplanted from there, though on a smaller scale, to Kent and *London, along the south coast, to the *Channel Islands and South Wales, and was beginning to follow west country migrants to the north of England. Increasingly, the leading figure during this period of expansion was J. *Thorne.

When O'Bryan left the denomination in 1829 he was accompanied by two of the preachers and a few hundred members, who reverted to the name *Arminian Bible Christians. The denomination's spread overseas began with O'Bryan's emigration to *Canada in 1831 and reached the USA in 1845. Back home, in 1907 the BC Church, with over 32,000 members, joined with the *MNC and *UMFC to form the *United Methodist Church.

See also **Overseas Missions**

W. O'Bryan in [BC] *Arminian Magazine* vol.2 (1823–4); F.W. Bourne (1905); R. Pyke (1941); T. Shaw (1965); M.J.L. Wickes (1987)

TS

Bickford, James (1816–95; e.m. 1838), WM missionary, born in Modbury, Devon, the son of a yeoman farmer and brought up an Anglican. Converted at 165, he joined the WM Church. After serving 14 years in the *West Indies, he was posted to *Australia for health reasons, where he served in Victoria 1854–72 (except for two years in Sydney) and then in South Australia, where he was minister at Pirie Street, Adelaide. He was President of the Australasian Conference in 1868 and of the South Australia Conference in 1875. He appealed to the British WM Conference for 'men who know how to save souls, men who can endure toil, sound Wesleyans, conservative yet progressive, with the additional recommendation of culture and superior mental power'. A proud Wesleyan and lukewarm towards Union, he believed the WM ministry to have as much claim to the apostolic succession as any RC or Anglican priest.

DGH

Bideford was visited by JW in 1757. The WM chapel in Allhalland Street (1809) was replaced in 1892 by one in Bridge Street, seating 1,000. Both WM and BC had circuits centred on the town, which was also the centre of a short-lived PM mission from Cornwall in the 1830s and 40s. Perhaps because it was the nearest town to

*Shebbear, four BC Conferences were held there between 1857 and 1885, in their Silver Street chapel of 1844 (replaced in 1913 by the imposing UM chapel in High Street). In 1884 they established *Edgehill College for girls to complement the boys school at Shebbear. The High Street and Bridge Street congregations amalgamated in 1962. A dissident group which joined the WRU ceased in 1981.

J.G. Hayman (1871)

RFST

Bielby, Morwenna Rayson (1907–79), daughter of Arthur Sidney Lyne (1878–1949; e.m. 1902), was a founder member of the *'Cambridge Group' out of which the 'MethSoc' movement developed. Before her marriage she lectured in English at *Southlands College. Her husband was headmaster of *Huddersfield College. She was a *local preacher and was on the Bench in West Yorkshire. She wrote plays on religious themes and was a member of the Religious Drama Society. Her connexional activities included being National President of the *Girls' League and Chairman of the *Women's Fellowship (1969–70). She was actively involved in the Marriage Guidance Council in its early years and was remembered as a great enabler and encourager.

MR 30 Aug. & 27 Sept. 1979

JAV

Bird, Sir Charles Hayward, CBE (1862–1944), UM layman and industrial chemist. On his mother's side he was the grandson of William Butler (1819–1900), founder of an important coaltar works at *Kingswood, Bristol. (Both Birds and Butlers were prominent in Kingswood Methodism.) As a member of *Cardiff City Council for 33 years, alderman for 24 years and Lord Mayor 1910, he took a special interest in the problems of water supply and was created a Freeman in 1923. He sat on the National Food Council and on the Royal Commission on London Squares and was knighted in 1929. He was secretary of the last UM Conference, held in *Kingswood in 1932.

Times 7 Sept. 1944

CJS

Bird, Mark Baker (1807–80; e.m. 1833), WM missionary, born in London and a tailor by trade. After some years in Jamaica, he served in Haiti from 1839 to 1879. In the face of earthquake, fire, debt, civil war and the Missionary Committee in

London, he fought sectarian interests to establish the mission among all classes of society, with education as a major focus. Never afraid to voice his concerns, he became a popular and respected figure because of his commitment to the people of Haiti and his indomitable faith in their future.

MJF

Birkett, William Norman, 1st Baron (1883–1962) was born in Ulverston and educated at Emmanuel College, Cambridge, becoming President of the Union in 1910. Called to the Bar in 1913, he became a Q.C. in 1924, was a Judge of the King's Bench Division 1941–50 and a Lord Justice of Appeal, 1950–57. He gained a high reputation as a persuasive council for the defence, served on the Nuremberg Tribunal and was in much demand as a public speaker. He received several honorary doctorates. His final triumph in the Lords was in the debate over *Manchester's plans to use Ullswater as a reservoir. Though he described himself as a Christian agnostic, he acknowledged his indebtedness to a WM upbringing and to the hymns of I. Watts and CW.

Times, 13 Feb. 1962; *MR* 22 Feb. 1962; H.M. Hyde (1964)

JAV

Birmingham began to develop rapidly from a market town into a manufacturing centre in the second half of the eighteenth century. Methodism began with the preaching of both CW and JW in 1743. JW regularly faced hostile mobs and Steelhouse Lane chapel was badly damaged by the mob soon after opening in 1751. JW opened Cherry Street chapel in 1782 (demolished 1887), preaching to a congregation described by the local press as 'genteel and very numerous'. With encouragement from the Rev. John Riland, evangelical vicar of St. Mary's Church, Methodism was well established by the end of JW's life and during the Priestley riots of 1791 the mob refused to burn down the three chapels (Cherry Street, Bradford Street and Belmont Row) because Methodists were 'Church People'.

Birmingham became the head of a circuit in 1782 and was a regular venue for the WM Conference from 1836 on. *Handsworth Theological College opened in 1880. In addition to moving into the expanding suburbs and rural hinterland, WM endeavoured to meet the needs of the poorest parts of the town centre, with Tract Societies, Town Missionaries in the 1840s and regular open-air preaching. This culminated in the Central Mission whose first Superintendent, from 1887 to 1913, was

F.L. *Wiseman. The impressive Central Hall in Corporation Street was opened in 1903.

The MNC established a society in 1797, took over an Independent chapel in Oxford Street in 1811 and built another in Unett Street in 1838. The WMA opened a chapel at Bath Street in 1839. Both MNC and WMA membership was small until 1850 when, following the *Fly Sheets controversy, WM numbers in Birmingham fell dramatically, resulting in some gains for the MNC, but particularly for the WR and WMA. After some rivalry, the former WR chapel in Rocky Lane, Nechells (1854) became the head of the largest UMFC circuit in Birmingham in the later nineteenth century.

PM never made an impact in Birmingham comparable with its success in the *Black Country. The Balloon Street chapel (1826) broke away from the PM Connexion. Not until 1849 was there a permanent chapel, at New John Street West. The circuit was extensive, but most societies were in rural areas to the south and west, some of which were subsequently incorporated within the city boundaries. *Bourne College opened in 1876 and moved to Quinton in 1882.

The 1851 *Religious Census and a local census in 1892 (covering a larger area than the 1891 city) show the relative strength of the different Methodist bodies:

Chapels:	1851	1892	Sittings:	1851	1892
WM	13	51		7,814	22,454
MNC	3	6		1,388	2,480
UMFC	3	4		870	1,900
(WMA+WR)					
PM	3	18		656	4,410

Both in 1851 and in 1892, total Methodist attendances were greater than those of any other single nonconformist denomination, but the CofE remained by far the strongest both in church accommodation and attendances.

W.C. Sheldon (1903); Conference Handbooks 1931 (WM), 1953

GR

Birstall Chapel Case When the chapel at Birstall, Yorks was rebuilt in 1782, the *trustees included in its deed a clause providing that, after the death of JW and CW, the choice, appointment and removal of preachers should revert to them. JW condemned this as 'Presbyterian' and a threat to the *itinerancy, but was persuaded to sign the deed. He later came to see this as an error on his part. The subsequent Conference decided that, unless the trustees rescinded this provision, a fund should be raised to build a new chapel and settle it 'on the Conference plan'. T. *Coke was sent to negotiate with the trustees, but without success, despite the offer of compensation. The Conference of 1783 took steps to get all the chapels settled on the *Model Deed, but similar disputes occurred later at Dewsbury and North Shields and conflict between the Conference and local trustees continued after JW's death, e.g. at *Bristol in 1794.

L. Tyerman (1878) 3 pp. 373–83; E.B. Perkins (1952) pp. 25–30

SRH

Birtwhistle, Norman Allen (1910–79; e.m. 1940) was born in *Leeds and graduated in Chemistry at Leeds University before serving with the MMS as a teacher in *Nigeria. On returning home in 1940 he trained at *Wesley House, Cambridge and served as a Secretary at the Mission House (1951–58) and as Ministerial Training Secretary (1958–73). In 1973 he became the minister of *Wesley's Chapel during the period of its refurbishment, when the congregation met in St Martin-within-Ludgate. In spite of ill health he travelled widely, raising money for the restoration. He was an artist and author, and wrote several missionary biographies.

MR 22 Feb. 1979

KGG

Bishop, Abraham (d. 1793; e.m. 1791), a native of Jersey, spoke both English and French. Offering for overseas service, he was the first WM missionary to New Brunswick in British North America, where he arrived in September 1791. He began a fruitful ministry in the city of Saint John and the surrounding settlements, but was called to meet the need for a French-speaking missionary in Grenada. Arriving there on 5 January 1793, he purchased a house and converted it into a chapel and threw himself into the work. But on 16 June his ministry was cut short by a fatal bout of fever. A fund established by his will continues to benefit *Channel Island Methodism.

C. Atmore (1801) pp. 51–2; R.D. Moore (1952) pp. 72–3

GRS

Bishop, Mary (Mrs Mills) (fl.1725–90) ran two residential private schools, in *Bath in the 1760s and 70s and later at Keynsham from 1781 to c. 1789. She corresponded with JW for about 15 years and he advised her on the running of her schools. She was also a class and band leader and W consulted her about the state of the society at Bath. She married a widowed Quaker.

JWL vols. 5–7

EDG

Bishop Auckland *see* **Dales Circuit**

Bisseker Brothers Tilden Boyns Bisseker (1877–1966; e.m. 1905) and Harry Bisseker (1878–1965; e.m. 1901), WM ministers born at Handsworth, *Birmingham. Tilden worked for 12 years in his father's business and for some years was organist and choirmaster at Birmingham Central Hall. He trained for the ministry at *Headingley College and served in Burma (now *Myanmar) 1905–12. Harry was educated at King Edward's School, Birmingham and Jesus College, Cambridge. He served as chaplain at The *Leys School and in the London (City Road) Circuit before becoming tutor in NT studies at *Richmond College, 1910–15. From 1919 to 1934 he was Headmaster of The Leys. Both brothers retired on health grounds.

MR 9 Dec. 1995

WL

Bissell, Bert(ie), MBE (1902–98), son of the PM minister Joseph B. Bissell (1869–1931; e.m. 1890), moved to Dudley in 1925 and founded the Vicar Street Young Men's Bible Class, which at times numbered over 300 members and which he led for more than 70 years. Its objective was 'to find men for Christ' and over the years some 18 became ministers and 100 *local preachers. In 1931 he was appointed lay pastor of the Vicar Street church and in 1933 became Dudley's Probation Officer. Consequently the Bible Class became a haven for young men on probation and ex-prisoners on licence. In August 1945 he encouraged members of the class to erect a 'peace cairn' on the top of Ben Nevis and this developed into an international shrine for world peace. He sought to further world peace through the mountaintop concept, by encouraging a number of distinguished climbers to place peace messages on the summits of some of the world's highest peaks. He was awarded the MBE in 1959 and the World Methodist Peace Award in 1987.

MR 12 Nov. 1998; D. Bissell & B. Weetman (1997)

GRS

B(i)urks, Mary (1796–1837) attended an Independent chapel before being converted in *Hull and joining the PMs. She was a PM itinerant from 1822 to 1836. Forced to retire through ill-health, she returned home to East Stockwith, acting as class leader and taking services whenever her health permitted. She was an impressive 6 ft. tall, with a powerful voice and forceful personality and is said to have (unsuccessfully) petitioned the Hull Quarterly Meeting in 1828 to buy her an ass to ride to her appointments!

PMM, 1837; J. Davison (1840); E.D. Graham (1989)

EDG

Black, William (1760–1834; e.m. 1782), pioneer preacher in Nova Scotia, born in *Huddersfield. His family emigrated c.1775. He was converted at a prayer meeting in 1779 and began to preach, though conscious of his lack of theological education. To combat the influence of the New-Light preacher Henry Alline, he began to itinerate in 1781. When he wrote to JW for help, he was advised to look to *American Methodism. In 1783 he organized classes and held services for Loyalist emigrants from New York. He attended the Christmas Conference in Baltimore in 1784 and was ordained by T. *Coke at the Conference in Philadelphia in May 1789 as superintendent for Nova Scotia. In 1791 he visited Newfoundland and reorganized the work there. Despite moves to put him in charge of the work in the *West Indies (1792–3) and in Bermuda (1804), he remained the effective chairman of the Nova Scotia District until his retirement in 1812, at what he recognized as an appropriate time. He is remembered as 'the Apostle of Nova Scotia Methodism'.
See also **Canada**

M. Richey (1839); F&H 1

JAV

Black Country In the rapidly developing industrial area north-west of *Birmingham, Methodism was based on the *Wednesbury society (which nurtured the young F. *Asbury) until the 1760s. By then the early persecution had died down and places such as Dudley and *Wolverhampton, where JW had initially faced violent mobs, developed separate societies. By 1801 there were ten chapels: at Wednesbury, Darlaston, Dudley, Bradley, Bilston, Tipton, Wolverhampton, Sedgley, Oldbury and Walsall. Although JW preached at Cradley, near Stourbridge, in 1770, the southern part of the area

was only gradually incorporated into the Dudley Circuit (formed in 1794). Subsequent evangelism led to the formation of separate Stourbridge (1828), West Bromwich (1811) and Walsall (1835) Circuits.

In 1819 PM established a base at Darlaston with the support of a WM *local preacher. A separate Darlaston Circuit was formed in 1820. During that year T. *Brownsword was briefly imprisoned at *Worcester for open-air preaching at Stourbridge and James Bonser was similarly treated at Stafford for committing the same offence in Wolverhampton. Both WM and PM membership grew rapidly during the first half of the century, especially during the two great cholera epidemics of 1832 and 1849. The PM circuits divided after each epidemic: Dudley separated from Darlaston in 1832, whilst Brierley Hill and West Bromwich circuits were created from these in 1849.

The MNC gained most from the Warrenite controversy in 1835. In Dudley local agitation against the WM Conference was led by a former itinerant John Gordon, who succeeded in detaching several societies from the Dudley and Stourbridge circuits and leading them into the MNC before he himself left to become a Unitarian pastor. In the 1851 *Religious Census the MNC recorded the largest Methodist attendances in the Dudley and Stourbridge registration sub-districts. Nevertheless the MNC did not expand as much as either WM or PM after the 1830s. Together these three Methodist denominations accounted for 44% of the church attendance in the Black Country as a whole – the largest percentage of any denominational group, though the CofE had the largest share in Wolverhampton, Wednesbury and Walsall. Methodism was strongest in Dudley, West Bromwich and the smaller industrialized settlements in and around Oldbury, Tipton, Sedgley and Rowley Regis, with the largest overall attendances also in places like Darlaston, Bilston, Brierley Hill and Halesowen.

J. Hall (1886); A.C. Prat (1891); Conference Handbook 1966

GR

Blackwell, Ebenezer (d. 1782), a London banker, born in *Tewkesbury, was a close friend and correspondent of the Wesleys for over 40 years. JW confided in him on both financial and marital problems and repeatedly exhorted him to avoid worldliness. He gave much financial support to JW's philanthropic activities and was one of the first trustees of *Wesley's Chapel. His country home at Lewisham was one of JW's favourite retreats, where a number of JW's sermons and other writings were prepared and where, in November 1777, he had a cordial meeting with Robert Lowth, Bishop of London and uncle to Blackwell's second wife.

SL passim; SJ 2 pp. 259–60

JAV

Blades, John (*c*. 1750-after 1807), a native of Northumberland who was on trial as an itinerant for a short time in 1778, but broke with JW in 1784 to found the 'Bladites', with societies scattered between *Newcastle and *Whitby. Though joined by some *local preachers, he proved an enthusiast who was discredited in 1788 when predictions of the Day of Judgment proved false. He fled with some of his followers to America, where he was last heard of among the Shakers at Albany, NY in 1807.

WMM 1797 p. 533; L. Tyerman (1878) 3 pp. 536–7; A. Steele (1857) pp. 162–75

JHL

Blatherwick, Douglas Pursey, OBE (1909–73), solicitor and *local preacher in *Newark, educated at *Rydal School. In 1954 he helped P. *Race found the Westminster Laymen's Movement. As Vice-President of the 1956 Conference he was the first to be more than a token lay person, sharing in some of the President's travels and arranging to meet the laity in each District. Convinced that it was wrong for Christians to spend conspicuously in a starving world, he refused an invitation from American Methodists to a dinner at the Hilton. His wife **Ruth Blatherwick** (*née* Quibell) was President of the National *Sunday School Union.

MR 5 July 1956, 6 & 13 Dec. 1973; D.P. Blatherwick (1959); R. Blatherwick (n.d.)

JHL

Bleby, Henry (1809–82; e.m. 1830), born in Winchcombe, Glos, gave memorable missionary service in the *West Indies. In Jamaica 1830–43, he faced fierce persecution on the eve of emancipation, and during a second period in the Caribbean, 1853–78, founded Queen's College, a secondary school in Nassau. Among his numerous publications were accounts of his missionary experiences and discussions of the apostolic succession. He founded a missionary dynasty, with three sons following him into the West Indian work: John Lucas Bleby (1843–82; e.m. 1862); Richard Henry Bleby (1845–91; e.m. 1864) who after service in the West Indies was appointed in 1879 to the English work in Calais; and William H.F. Bleby (1856–1939; e.m. 1876). In the next two generations, Henry Moore Bleby (1871–1951; e.m. 1895) served in Bengal and was instrumental in opening a leprosy settlement and orphanage at Raniganj, and his son Henry Edwin Bleby (1902–1928; e.m. 1923) served in Trichinopoly, extending the Church among the workers on the tea estates in the Anamalai Hills.

MR 3 Jan. 1929, 10 & 17 Aug. 1939, 12 April 1951; H. Bleby (1876); H.M. Bleby (1935)

GRS

Blindell, Sir James (1884–1937) PM layman, was born in *Grimsby of poor parents. Starting at 11 as an errand boy, by 19 he was a shop manager. He soon started his own business as a boot factor and in 1924 formed the company, of which he was managing director, with shops throughout Lincolnshire. He founded the Grimsby Flottergate Benevolent Homes, a Methodist enterprise which he personally supervised. After serving as councillor and alderman, he suddenly entered Parliament as MP for Holland with *Boston. He was knighted in 1934. His promising career was cut short by a fatal car accident in May 1937.

Times, 11 May 1937; MR 13 & 20 May 1937

WL

Blumer, Thomas Rickaby (1860–1937), a *Sunderland shipbuilder whose family worshipped at Dock Street UMFC Chapel. In 1904, assisted financially by his father and by Joseph Lowes Thompson (another shipbuilder and UMFC member), he opened the Thompson Memorial Hall as a base for Christian social work in the riverside working-class community of Monkwearmouth. He soon abandoned his industrial commitments to devote himself entirely to the Hall and was national president of the Brotherhood Movement in 1910.

J. Young (1923)

GEM

Boaden, Edward (1827–1913; e.m. 1849), leading UMFC minister. His early training as a lawyer was put to great use in the WMA ministry. His gifts were early recognized and he was appointed Chapel Secretary in 1864, a post he held, in addition to circuit appointments, for nearly 40 years. He was involved in almost all the developments in the UMFC and was President in 1871; also, in 1907, first President of the UM Conference at the age of 80. He supervised the drafting of the UM *model deed, was a powerful evangelical preacher and composer of hymns, and wrote a biography of R. *Chew (1896).

G.J. Stevenson (1884–86) 6 pp. 998–1007

OAB

Board of Management for Methodist Residential Schools was established by the WM Conference in 1903, initially to administer grants to its boarding schools. Appointed annually by Conference, it is the legal governing body of *Culford, *Edgehill, *Farringtons and Stratford House, *Kent College Canterbury, *Kent College Pembury, Queen's College, *Truro and *Woodhouse Grove schools. While delegating extensive powers to the schools, it retains jurisdiction over the sale and disposal of property, loan negotiations, appointment of Heads and annual reports to Conference.

HMGB 3 pp. 301–2

DBT

Boardman, Richard (c. 1738–82; e.m. 1763), WM itinerant whose early background is unknown. At the *Bristol Conference of 1769, shortly after his wife and only child had died, he and J. *Pilmore offered to go as the first British preachers appointed to *America. On his way to Bristol he had preached at Monyash, Derbys, on 'Jabez was more honourable than his brethren' (I Chron. 4.9).

A young woman, Mary Redfern, found spiritual comfort in the sermon and when she later married William *Bunting in *Manchester called her son Jabez. Boardman's American ministry extended from Philadelphia to New York and into New England. He returned to English and Irish circuits in 1774 and died in *Cork after a seizure which left him blind.

C. Atmore (1801) pp. 58–61; J.P. Lockwood (1881); R.H. Gallagher (1965) pp. 15–17; F. Baker (1976) pp. 86–94

JAV

Böhler, Peter (1712–75), German *Moravian, born at Frankfurt-am-Maine and converted under A.G. Spangenberg. As a Lutheran theological student he met Count *Zinzendorf, became tutor to his son, joined the *Moravians and was ordained a minister. Early in 1738, en route to Georgia, he met J&CW and his conversations with them were a formative influence in their spiritual experience of that year. Moravian principles as expounded by him governed both the *Fetter Lane Society and later on the Methodist societies. He was consecrated a Moravian bishop in 1748, dividing his time between Germany and America. Disenchanted with aspects of Moravianism, JW was estranged from Böhler, but many years later they renewed contact by letter shortly before Böhler died at Fulneck and JW acknowledged his spiritual indebtedness to him.

J.F. Lockwood (1868); DEB

WDH

Bolton A strong Puritan tradition contributed to the success of Methodism, from J. *Bennet's first visits in 1746–47. JW paid at least 24 visits after 1748. A chapel was opened in 1751, where Bennet led a secession following a confrontation with JW in 1752. A new chapel in Ridgway Gates was needed by 1776 and Bolton became the head of a circuit in 1784. The Barlow family were prominent WM benefactors, providing funds for the first *NCH home outside London at Edgworth, north of the town, and the initial stages of T. *Champness's *Joyful News Mission for training lay evangelists, which began in Bolton in the 1880s. A Central Mission, the Victoria Hall, began in 1897 and a second Mission, the King's Hall, was opened in 1907.

During the nineteenth century every branch of Methodism established itself in the town – MNC, UMFC, PM, IM, and there was even a BC chapel. The IM Conference met there 13 times up to 1934.

W. Walker (1863); J. Musgrave (1865); Conference Handbook 1952; D. Tomkins (1997)

EAR

Bolton, Ann ('Nancy') (1743–1822), the eldest child of a Witney baker, became a close friend and correspondent of JW for nearly 30 years. Converted to Methodism at 19, she became a class leader in 1777 and kept a detailed spiritual journal. JW called her 'the sister of my choice' and 'the perfect pattern of womanhood'. He often stayed with her and her brother Edward Bolton, a *local preacher, at Witney and Finstock. She was prone to ill health and Wesley plied her with much spiritual and medical advice. He published over

20 of her letters in the *AM* and left her £100 in his will. Having been dissuaded by JW from an earlier marriage, in 1792 she married George Conibeere of *Gloucester.

J. Banks (1984); M.L. Edwards (n.d.) pp. 100–14

PB

Bond, Dr Robert (1870–1952; e.m. 1894) trained for the WM ministry at *Didsbury College. In 1927 he became Assistant Secretary of the WM Conference and, in 1928, its Secretary. His advocacy of *Methodist Union, combined with his diplomatic skills, contributed to the successful outcome of the union negotiations and he was appointed Secretary of the new Methodist Conference in 1932. He was President of the 1937 Conference and Moderator of the FCFC in 1938. From 1937 to his retirement in 1942 he was Secretary for Connexional Funds.

MR 30 Oct. 1952

WDH

Book of Offices (1936), replacing earlier WM service books dating from 1882, was sub-titled 'the Orders of Service authorized for use in the Methodist Church together with the Order for Morning Prayer'. This last was 'included for the convenience of the Methodist Churches where it is in use'. The other services were authorized by the Conference of 1936 and the book supplied the need for an agreed book of services after *Methodist Union. It included a new Alternative Service for the *Lord's Supper, for those branches of Methodism which had not been accustomed to the traditional full order of Word and Sacrament. This was clearly designed to follow a preaching-service and appealed also to some ex-WMs, but has not survived. The 1936 Book was one of the first Methodist books to include an order for *Ordination of *Deaconesses. It was superseded by *The Methodis Service Book* (1975) and more recently by *The Methodist Worship Book* (1999).

ARG

Book Room *see* **Publishing**

Book Steward JW himself was in sole charge of Methodist *publishing until in 1753 a 'Steward' was appointed to set him free for his evangelism and pastoral oversight. The Steward became managing director of the Publishing House and from 1880 his name appeared on books as publisher. He had to be a minister in full connexion, which meant that he was elected by and had the

full support of Conference. He had a professional publisher as his lay deputy. He also had charge of Methodist *archives until an archivist was appointed to serve at City Road. Similar arrangements were made in other branches of Methodism before the Union of 1932, but the MNC abolished the office in 1893, sharing editorship among several ministers and in PM the office was limited to a five-year period. In all connexions, Book Stewards were responsible to a Book Committee, meeting quarterly. The office was abolished after publishing was re-ordered in 1969, the Steward being replaced by a Chief Executive.

F.H. Cumbers (1956)

GSW

Boot, Jesse, 1st Baron Trent (1850–1931), drug manufacturer and founder of the chain of chemist shops, was born in *Nottingham, where his father, a dedicated Wesleyan preacher, had a herbalist's shop. After his father's death in 1860, he took over the family business and by great application and entrepreneurial flair developed it into a nation-wide chain selling cut-price medicines (increasingly produced from his own factories). He remained a Wesleyan with wide evangelical sympathies and his considerable benefactions included the rebuilding of the Albert Hall, Nottingham (1906–9) and what was to become Nottingham University. A strong Liberal supporter, he received a knighthood in 1909 and was raised to the peerage in 1929.

MR 18 June 1931; S. Chapman (1974)

JAV

Booth, Alan Richard (1911–90; e.m. 1937), noted author and ecumenical leader, was born in *Dublin, read law at Trinity College, Dublin and had his theological training at *Edgehill College. Influenced early on by the SCM, he became one of their staff members, which gave him important contacts. As London Secretary of the WCC Commission on International Affairs, from 1956 to 1970 he was in charge of their UK office and assisted in setting up the Institute for Strategic Studies in 1958. From 1970 to 1975 he was Director of Christian Aid.

MR 8 March 1990

RPR

Booth, George (1840–1926), son of a PM itinerant, born in Hasland, Derbys. He spent most of his life as a pharmacist and medical practitioner in Chesterfield, and was active in the town's religious, social and political life, serving as mayor in 1887. Because of his musical skill and knowledge he was musical editor of several PM hymn-books: the Sunday School books of 1879 and 1901, the connexional *Hymnal* of 1889 and its 1912 *Supplement*.

PWHS 44 p. 44

GEM

Booth, William (1829–1912) was born in *Nottingham, where he was apprenticed to a pawnbroker and became a WM *local preacher, but resigned in order to give himself to open-air evangelism. In the Spalding Circuit and then in London he was associated with *WR, but in 1854 joined the *MNC and was ordained in 1858. His wife Catherine Booth, *née* Mumford (1829–90), was born at Ashbourne, Derbys. They were married at Stockwell MNC chapel in 1855 and she gave him vigorous support and co-operation in his work. During his time as a MNC evangelist, disagreement over where he should be stationed and how he should be used came to a head at the Conference of 1861 and he left the ministry. (That same year both the WM and the PM Conferences debarred the Booths from their chapels.) Their work in East London led to the formation of the Christian Mission, which eventually became the *Salvation Army, and his account of conditions in the East End, *In Darkest England and the Way Out* (1890) had a widespread influence on urban mission.

R. Collier (1965); C. Bramwell-Booth (1970)

JDB

Borlase, Rev. Walter (1694–1776), vicar of Madron, Cornwall. As a local magistrate in 1745 he issued warrants under the vagrancy laws for the arrest of JW and other Methodist preachers suspected of being Jacobites. His brother **Dr William Borlase** (1695–1772), a graduate of Exeter College, Oxford, was rector of Ludgvan and vicar of St Just in Penwith. JW read his *Antiquities, Historical and Monumental . . . of Cornwall* (1754) in 1757. His collections are now in the Ashmolean Museum.

P.A.S. Pool (1986)

JAV

Bosanquet, Mary (Mrs Fletcher) (1739–1815) met with opposition from her well-to-do family because of her religious inclinations and left home at 22, taking lodgings in London. She joined the London society and became involved in the great Methodist revival there in 1761–62. In 1762 she went to live in her own house in Leytonstone where, with S. *Crosby and S. *Ryan, she established a Christian community and began 'to exhort, and to read and expound the scriptures'. In June 1768, partly for financial reasons, the community moved to Cross Hall at Morley, near *Leeds. Mary corresponded with JW, consulting him about her call to preach. Although women preachers were not then permitted among the Methodists, he admitted that she had an 'extra-ordinary call', but stopped short of agreeing to her becoming an itinerant preacher.

On 12 Nov. 1781 she married the Rev. J. *Fletcher of Madeley and they exercised what was effectively a joint ministry. To avoid giving local offence, Mary 'spoke' regularly in the Madeley tithe barn. After her husband's death, she continued her work in Madeley, acting as an unofficial curate to his successor.

H. Moore (1817); Z. Taft (1825); M.L. Edward (n.d.) pp. 85–99

EDG

Boston (Lincs) Although JW paid three visits between 1759 and 1780, it was his preachers who founded the society. A small chapel was erected in 1764 in Wormgate, replaced by another, privately owned, in 1808. Centenary Chapel (1809) was in a new style, with twin towers and a massive colonnade. It was replaced by the present chapel (1911), following a disastrous fire in 1909. Others included a small mission chapel in Hospital Bridge (1870) and the post-Union 'Zion' (1934). Boston WM Circuit, separated briefly from Horncastle in 1795–97, dates from 1812.

PM took root in the town in 1819 through the efforts of two self-appointed roving preachers. A chapel in George Street (1839) was replaced by one in West Street (1866), where the Band of Hope, Sunday School, choir and orchestra and a lending library flourished. Boston also had a strong MNC society, formed in 1828, and under William *Innocent (father of the China missionary) a chapel was built in West Street (1829). A WR group established themselves in Pump Square in 1856, struggled through the 60 years of the UMFC, failed to unite with the local MNC in 1907, but joined the former WM and PM societies in 1947.

MR(W) 1904 pp. 40–3; W. Leary (1972)

WL

Bourne, Frederick William (1830–1905; e.m. 1850), BC minister, born at Woodchurch, Kent. As the chief BC administrator and spokesman in succession to W. *O'Bryan and J. *Thorne, he held many connexional offices between 1860 and 1904, including Connexional Treasurer 1866–1904 and Book Steward and Editor 1869–88. He visited *Australia, *New Zealand, *Canada and the USA in the course of his work and was President of the Conference in 1867, 1875 and 1891. An earnest advocate of *Methodist Union, he was a member of the Ecumenical Methodist Conferences of 1881, 1891 and 1901. He was a tireless worker, much in demand as a special preacher. His publications included *James Thorne* (1895), *The Bible Christians: Their Origins and History* (1905) and a highly popular life of Billy *Bray, *The King's Son* (1871).

G.J. Stevenson (1884–6) 6 pp. 903–12

TS

Bourne, Hugh (1772–1852) and his brother **James Bourne** (1781–1860) were born at Fordhays Farm, *Stoke-on-Trent. In his youth Hugh was a keen reader, including JW's sermons. At the age of 16 Hugh moved to *Bemersley farm and in 1799 was converted at a WM love feast and became a member of the Ridgeway society. Despite his shyness he was pressed to become a preacher and his first sermon, preached out of doors, was in 1801. His neglect of meeting in his appointed *class due to pioneering evangelistic work elsewhere and his involvement with *camp meetings led to his expulsion from the society in June 1808.

His name is linked with that of W. *Clowes as one of the founders of *PM. He was responsible for the printing of the first PM *class ticket in 1811. He became the editor of the *PM Magazine* and later started a Children's Magazine. In 1823 he wrote a short history of the PM movement, drawing on his personal journal. When an annual *Conference was set up, he was its secretary in 1825, 1826 and 1829. He wrote hymns and set up a study and library at Bemersley, which was also used by other PM preachers. From this base he travelled widely, directing and encouraging the various societies. He was largely responsible for the Deed Poll approved by the *Scotter Conference of 1829. In 1844 he went on a tour of the USA and *Canada.

The anxiety that filled his early years, spent on an isolated farm with a drunken and violent father, led to a shyness and awkwardness in making relationships in adult life, and to a lack of confidence about his evangelistic work. This led to considerable tension between him and the more popular *Clowes, fuelled by differences of temperament, geographical distance, Bourne's strong teetotalism and concern over the work in the *Hull Circuit (over which he did not exercise such direct control), and his later mental deterioration. That the PM movement did not fracture is to the credit of both men. The development and survival of a vigorous PM Connexion owed much to his imagination, his originality and practicality, and his organizational ability and insistence on strict discipline.

His brother James spent his early years working on the family farm, but was an advocate of the camp meetings and combined his labours with sporadic preaching tours, walking some weekends upward of 80 miles. He was President of the PM Conference in 1826, 1829 and 1842. He was a signatory to the Deed Poll and as the first *Book Steward looked after the printing press at Bemersley.

J. Walford (1855–7); W. Antliff (1872); F.H. Hurd (1872) pp. 5–36; G.J. Stevenson (1884–6) 5 pp. 657–68; J.T. Wilkinson (1952); *LQHR* Dec. 1952;

WL

Bourne, Moses, JP (1866–1941), PM layman, a powerful pulpit orator, said to have been a collateral descendant of H. *Bourne. He was an associate of and successor to Horace Mansfield MP in both church and business, manager of collieries and other businesses around Swadlincote, Derbys. He was joint secretary of the Million Shillings Fund and treasurer of the committee which bought Mow Cop for the National Trust in 1937. He was elected Vice-President of the PM Conference in 1926 and the second Vice-President after *Methodist Union, and wrote *From a Pilgrim's Scrip* (1927).

MR 13 July 1933, 8 May 1941

JHL

Bourne, Wilfrid Harry (1897–1988; e.m. 1922), born into a BC family at Horsham, was shot through the eye at the Battle of the Somme, but studied at Mildmay College, London and worked for the YMCA before entering the UM ministry. He became well known for a telephone ministry (described in *God Gave Me a Telephone*, Evesham, 1957 and *The Christian Telephone Ministry*, 1962) which brought him as many as 3,500 calls a year and was taken over in 1974 by the Westminster Pastoral Foundation. He broadcast frequently on radio and TV. He also contributed a weekly column to the *Chichester Observer* for 28 years and wrote *Preparation for Christian Healing* (1960).

MR 20 Jan. 1972, 13 Oct. 1988

JAV

Bourne College, *Birmingham In 1876 the Birmingham PM College opened in the city centre, but moved in 1882 to purpose-built premises in Quinton, where T.J.S. *Hooson became its one and only headmaster. The curriculum was wide-ranging, including current affairs and sport. The students were taken on external visits, e.g. to exhibitions, and there were close links with the local PM church. However, as with *Elmfield, the growth of affordable state secondary education and the anticipation of *Methodist Union decimated the numbers and the College was forced to close in 1928. The property was sold and was demolished in 1979.

E.D. Graham (1998) pp. 31–49

EDG

Bowden, Thomas (1778–1834), pioneer WM layman and schoolteacher in Sydney, NSW. Previously Master of the Great Queen Street Charity School, London, he was recommended by J. *Butterworth and William Wilberforce to the Rev. Samuel Marsden, arrived in Sydney in 1812 and took charge of the Charity School there. He formed the first Methodist *class meeting in Sydney on 6 March 1812 and preached to isolated settlers in the country areas. Deeply concerned at the spiritual destitution of the community, he joined with others in addressing a powerful appeal to the British WM Church for a preacher to be sent out. In response, S. *Leigh arrived in 1815. Bowden helped found the Benevolent Society of NSW, the Sunday School Institution and the NSW Auxiliary of the Bible Society.

ADB; *ADEB*

EGC

Bowmer, Dr John Coates (1911– ; e.m. 1935), was educated at Leeds University and *Hartley Victoria College. Following the death of W.F. *Swift he served as Connexional Archivist 1962–76, organizing the *Archives Centre at Epworth House, London and cataloguing the collection before it was moved to *Manchester. He

published *The Sacrament of the Lord's Supper in Early Methodism* (1951), with a sequel covering the years 1792–1960 (WHS Lectures, 1961) and gave the *Fernley Hartley Lecture in 1975, a study of the *pastoral office in WM, published as *Pastor and People*. He was editor of the *Proceedings* of the WHS 1962–80 and the Society's President 1975–80.

JAV

Bowran, John George ('Ramsay Guthrie') (1869–1946; e.m. 1889), PM itinerant and author, was born in *Gateshead and became a pupil teacher before training at the Manchester PM Theological Institute. As a circuit minister, mainly in the north-east, he built large chapels at Middlesborough and Hexham and during an eight-year spell at Middlesborough demonstrated great pastoral and administrative skill in consolidating the effects of the recent revival on Teeside. He was Connexional Editor 1916–21, President of the Conference in 1928 and acting President in 1929 (following his successor's death), a director of the *Chapel Aid Association from 1925 and its chairman, 1939–46. He gave the *Hartley Lecture in 1923 on *Christianity and Culture*. Under his pen name he was a prolific writer of homely stories on people, places and village chapel life in north-east England, beginning with *On God's Lines* (1899), and was a regular contributor to Free Church journals. His eldest son **John Ramsay Guthrie Bowran** (1897–1974), a *local preacher, was a director of the Methodist *Chapel Aid Association, of the General Chapel Committee and of the *Hartley Victoria Committee.

MR 12 Dec. 1946; J.G. Bowran in WHS(NE), nos. 25, 27, 28, 29 (1976–8)

GEM

Boyce, William Binnington (1803–89; e.m. 1829), WM missionary in *South Africa (1830–43) and *Australia (1846–57) and an influential Secretary of the WMMS (1858–76). He was a man of 'decided opinions and disconcerting frankness'. In his first appointment he rapidly published a Xhosa (Kaffir) grammar and acted as advisor to Sir Benjamin D'Urban and as a mediator with the Xhosa chiefs. While General Superintendent of WM missions in Australia he prepared for the autonomy of the Australasian Conference and was its first President (1855 and 1856). In his retirement in Sydney he wrote *The Higher Criticism of the Bible* (1881), a conservative attack on contemporary trends in biblical studies, and *An Introduction to the Study of History* (1884). He was elected a member of the senate of Sydney University. An omnivorous reader, he gave many books to both the University Library and the Wesleyan Theological Institute.

ADB

JRP/EGC

Brackenbury, Robert Carr (1752–1818; e.m. 1784), squire of Raithby Hall (Lincs), was influenced by Methodist preaching in *Hull, met JW in 1776 and travelled with him in England, Scotland and Holland. Sent by W to the *Channel Islands in 1783, he established societies and built chapels in both Jersey and Guernsey. On returning to England in 1790, he continued this work, notably in Portland (Dorset). A modest, educated and generous man, he spent himself for Methodism though he never sought recognition as an itinerant. In 1784 included him in the *Legal Hundred. The work he began was supported by his second wife **Sarah** (née Holland; d. 1847) long after his death. The chapel he built at Raithby (opened by JW in 1779) is still in use and there is now an annual Brackenbury Memorial Lecture.

MR(W) 1901 pp. 94–6; *PWHS* 20 pp. 170–4
WDH

Bradburn, Samuel (1751–1816; e.m. 1774), friend and confidant of JW, whose influence within Methodism continued into the uncertain years after 1791. Known as 'the Demosthenes of Methodism', he was noted for his oratory and wit and was an eloquent preacher, writer and protagonist for Methodism against establishment intolerance. A champion of the poor, he was the founder of the *Manchester *Strangers' Friend Society (1792). Although suspected of political radicalism and of initial sympathy with A. *Kilham, he opposed lay democracy within the Church and supported Kilham's expulsion. His *Are Methodists Dissenters?* (1792) put forward the view (which he claimed to be held by JW) that Methodism was presbyterian in character. In 1792 his wearing of a gown to conduct the opening service of Portland Chapel, *Bristol, was strongly condemned by the *New Room Trustees, who were staunch 'Church Methodists'. He attended the *Lichfield meeting in 1794, which unsuccessfully advocated an episcopal hierarchy for Methodism. His proposal for 'travelling bishops' the following year was also rejected by Conference. His second wife, Sophia Cooke of *Gloucester, had encouraged Robert Raikes to start his Sunday School there. He was President of the Conference in 1799, but in 1802 was censured

and suspended for a year because of over-indulgence in wine at a time of illness and personal stress.

T.W. Blanshard (1870); G.J. Stevenson (1884–86) 2 pp. 188–200
WDH

Bradfield, William (1859–1923; e.m. 1884), WM minister, a native of Kingsclere, studied at *Headingley College. During successive Superintendencies at *Oxford and *Cambridge he established considerable rapport with the students. As both Warden of the Wesley *Deaconess Order (1907–20) and Chairman of the Halifax and Bradford District (1907–23), he worked unstintingly in the interests of *women workers in the Church. His kindly nature and considerable experience was much appreciated by all who encountered him. He wrote a *Life* of T.B. *Stephenson (1913).

MR 11 Jan.1923
EDG

Bradford (Yorks) CW visited the town in 1742, followed by JW in May 1744, when he preached at Little Horton Hall and Sticker Lane. Pioneer preachers included J. *Nelson, J. *Bennet, W. *Grimshaw, W. *Darney and T. *Mitchell. Although Nelson was imprisoned at Ivegate in 1744, the Methodists remained relatively unmolested by the mob and JW had a good relationship with the evangelical incumbent, John Crosse. In 1756 'the Cockpit' was rented as a meeting place. An octagonal chapel built on Horton Road in 1766 was replaced by the Kirkgate chapel in 1811. Eastbrook chapel was opened in 1825. Bradford became head of a circuit in 1769. Later churches included the neo-gothic St John's (1879), with its regular liturgical service and surpliced choir of men and boys, and Eastbrook Hall (1904).

A PM chapel was opened in Manchester Road in 1824, succeeded by Providence chapel and later by the Central Hall. UM established the Bridge Street Circuit in 1836. In 1860 the WR Union was formed at Bethesda Chapel. In 1885 a BC chapel was opened in Toller Lane. The 'Jumping Ranters' held meetings in Wibsey and Dudley Hill. Six WM and four Methodist Conferences have been held in Bradford between 1853 and 1978.

See also **Clough, B.**; **Stamp, W.W.**; **Woodhouse Grove**

W.W. Stamp (1841); S.R. Valentine in *PWHS* 51 pp. 141–54; Conference Handbook 1937, 1950
SRV

Bradford, Joseph (1748–1808; e.m. 1773), an itinerant who was JW's travelling companion 1774–79 and 1787–89 and was entrusted with transcribing his *Journal. In 1785 JW entrusted him with a letter to be read to the Conference after his death, at which Bradford was present. He was President of the 1795 Conference, which adopted the *Plan of Pacification, and again in 1803. His closing years were marred by bodily and mental decay.

JAV

Bradford, Robert, MP (1941–81) Irish minister, was brought up by foster parents in *Belfast after his father deserted the family. He entered the ministry in 1964 and in 1970 was appointed to Suffolk, close to West Belfast's Lenadoon Estate, a flash-point in the early years of Ulster violence. He became involved in politics and when elected Unionist MP for South Belfast in 1974 resigned from the Irish Conference. He held British Israelite views, launched a 'Methodists Awake' campaign attacking the Ecumenical Movement and published anti-Roman Catholic pamphlets. He maintained his standing as a Methodist minister by joining the Missouri Conference of the Methodist Protestant Church. He was assassinated by the IRA in 1981 while on constituency work.

––––––––

N. Bradford (1984)

RPR

Bramwell, William (1759–1818; e.m. 1786), WM minister and evangelist. Although he had little formal education, JW recognized his preaching gifts and he exercised a powerful evangelical ministry, chiefly in the north. His revivalist methods were similar to those of Charles Finney in America and were suspect to the WM establishment. He stressed the efficacy of faithful prayer in winning conversions and looked for an immediate, personal response to his preaching. He encouraged *women to become preachers and (unsuccessfully) opposed moves in the Conferences of 1803 and 1804 to exclude them from this ministry.

––––––––

J. Sigston (1820)

WDH

Branfoot, John (1795–1831; e.m. 1821), early PM itinerant, born near Ripon. He joined the PMs on their arrival in Yorkshire in 1821 and undertook extensive work in their huge *Hull Circuit and its branches. He pioneered many places, including *Sunderland and Tyneside. He died, along with his fellow itinerant John Hewson (Huison) (1793–1831; e.m. 1824), after being struck by coal wagons on the Sunderland-Hetton colliery line in the course of his circuit duties. His son **William Branfoot** (1825–1902) was brought up in Sunderland and became a prosperous businessman on Wearside with interests in coal and shipping. He was very active as a PM lay leader and preacher and in wider evangelical causes. Disaffected by developments in PM, he was a leading figure in the secession of the *Christian Lay Churches in 1877 and became active in *IM nationally.

GEM

Brash, W. Bardsley (1877–1952; e.m. 1901), WM minister educated at *Kingswood School and *Handsworth College. An able scholar, he specialized in English literature and in 1928 was appointed to the chair of English and the English Bible at *Didsbury College. As Principal from 1939 to 1949 he accomplished the difficult task of transferring the College's work from Manchester to *Bristol. He wrote an introduction to *Methodism* (1928), contributed the article on John Wesley to the *ERE* and, to mark the centenary of Methodist *ministerial training, *The Story of our Colleges* (1935).

––––––––

MR 1 May 1952

WDH

Braund, Thomas (1842–1914; e.m. 1863), BC itinerant, born at Milton Damerel, Devon. During semi-retirement because of ill-health from 1879, he found ways of continuing his ministry, including the organization of a travelling lending library in the villages of the *Shebbear Circuit. In 1897, at his instigation, the Conference adopted a course of study on the Bible and Christian doctrine for young people and young *local preachers. He was secretary of the *local preachers' Examination Board from 1907 and President of the Conference in 1899.

TS

Bray, 'Billy' (1794–1868), a Cornish tin-miner, was born near *Truro and lived a profligate life until converted at 28. As a BC *local preacher he was noted for his unconventional and enthusiastic manner, calling himself 'the King's son'. Many of his eccentric sayings and exploits were lovingly recorded. Of the six chapels he built with his own hands, only one (Kerley Downs) survives.

––––––––

F.W. Bourne (1869); C.J. Davey (1979)

JAV

Brearley, Joe (1855–1934), *Halifax business-man of humble origins. He started work at 12 as an errand boy, but by 1872 had opened a small boot and shoe shop, which led to a successful boot-making business occupying the Albert Works, 1894–1931. A staunch member of Eben-ezer PM chapel and active at all levels of the Connexion, he declined to stand as *Vice-President, but in 1911 was a PM representative at the Methodist Ecumenical Conference in Toronto. An advanced Liberal, he served from 1898 on the Halifax borough council (from 1906 as alderman), was chairman of the Licensing Committee and of the local Liberal Party.

Halifax Daily Courier and Guardian 23 & 27 Jan.1934; *PMM* 1924 pp. 768–70

GEM

Bredin, John (1737–1819; e.m. 1769), Irish-born Roman Catholic schoolmaster, rescued from a drink problem by one of the Methodist preachers. He became one of JW's itinerants in Ireland, Scotland, England and the *Channel Islands. He corresponded frequently with W, who admired his preaching, but admonished him for failing to apply Methodist *discipline. Poor health forced him to superannuate in 1792. His most notable achievement was to recognize the potential in A. *Clarke and commend him to JW.

R.H. Gallagher (1960)

EWD

Breeden, Henry (1804–78; e.m. 1831), WM lay revivalist and holiness preacher, who became a WMA (and later UMFC) minister. Born at Southwell, Notts, he came to prominence as the prayer leader and associate of J. *Smith ('Smith of Cudworth') and became the first *Arminian Methodist itinerant in 1832. He was their General Superintendent until they joined the WMA in 1837. He was WMA President in 1848. A very successful evangelist, his *Call to Holiness and Usefulness* (Derby, 1834) went into many editions on both sides of the Atlantic. His semi-Pelagian belief in the human capacity for faith diverged from the general Wesleyan understanding of *grace. He wrote an autobiographical *Striking Incidents of Saving Grace* (1878; reprinted Burslem 1981).

WP

Brennan, Eleanor (1792–1859), born in Douglas, *IOM. When cholera struck in 1832, she helped nurse the sick and move bodies for burial, and cared for orphaned children. She was appointed Matron of the Dispensary *c.* 1841 and of the hospital when it was built in 1850, and was a founder member of the Douglas Dorcas Society. Seven ministers of different congregations joined the long procession at her funeral.

FC

Bretherton, Francis Fletcher (1868–1956; e.m. 1891), WM minister, born in Brixton, London and educated at WM schools in *Taunton and Harrogate and at University College, London, before training for the ministry at *Didsbury College. A founder member of the *WHS, he served from 1919 as its General Secretary and from 1941 as President. His leisure time and retirement years were devoted to Methodist history and he was an expert on JW and the eighteenth century. He built up a network of contacts by correspondence with Methodist historians across the world. His library became the nucleus of the Society's Library, which moved to *Westminster College, Oxford in 1993.

MR 8 March 1956; *PWHS* 30 pp. 101–3

JAN

Brettell, Jeremiah (1753–1828; e.m. 1774), WM itinerant named in the *Deed of Declaration. With his elder brother **John Brettell** (1742–96; e.m. 1771) he spent three years in *Ireland and was JW's travelling companion there. Appointed to *Macclesfield in 1778 he pioneered new soci-eties in spite of local opposition to Methodism and won the approval of JW who, unusually, appointed him to the circuit for a second year.

Atmore (1801) pp. 65–7; *PWHS* 7 p. 17

WDH

Brigden, Thomas E. (1852–1936; e.m. 1880), born in Worthing. A historian of early Methodism, he was a founder member of the WHS and editor of its *Proceedings*. He taught at *Westminster College while stationed in London circuits. He was a keen collector of books, pamphlets and engravings. He collaborated with Bp. J.F. Hurst on the British volumes of his *History of Methodism* (1902) and wrote the chapter on JW in the *NHM*.

MR 26 Nov. 1936; *PWHS* 20 pp. 169–70

JAV

Brighton until the eighteenth century was still the fishing village of Brighthelmstone, but under the patronage of the Prince Regent became both a fashionable resort and a stronghold of evangelicalism and Dissent. JW left it to the Calvinists. G. *Whitefield preached there and Lady *Huntingdon built a chapel in North Street. The first WM society was formed in 1804 by militiamen stationed in the town, together with a carpenter, Edward Be(e)ves, and his employee William Mitchell, and met above stabling in Middle Street. The first chapel in the working-class district of Dorset Gardens was opened by J. *Benson in 1808, known locally as 'the Arminian Chapel'. It was extended several times and given a semi-classical façade, reflecting the gradual rise of its congregation in social status, and was rebuilt in 1884–85. Norfolk Road chapel (1869) gave WM a foothold west of Old Steine. In 1907 under the leadership of E.A. *French, the Dome (formerly royal stables) was rented for a year and the Brighton Mission was launched, with popular Sunday evening services featuring music from an orchestra and choir. Saturday night variety concerts, begun by French and re-introduced in 1976, were supported by many show-biz celebrities and provided both funding and publicity for the Mission. The interior had a major refit in 1934–35. When it was formed in 1807, the Lewes and Brighton Circuit extended as far as Littlehampton and Arundel in the west and Tunbridge Wells to the north-east.

A small BC society was formed in 1823 by members from Kent. The next year a BC evangelist Henry Freeman and two women preachers, Ann Mason and Sarah Willis, began open-air preaching and Andrew *Cory was stationed in the town. A separate circuit was formed in 1827, but the cause struggled in premises taken over from other denominations until Bristol Road chapel was built in 1873, followed by Stanford Avenue in 1898. A PM Brighton Mission was launched in 1836 by William Harland of the Portsmouth Mission. The first preacher was stationed in the town in 1842. A converted building in George Street was succeeded by a purpose-built chapel in 1856. John Parrott in 1862–64 gave the Mission new impetus, despite harassment by the police during open-air preaching. But numbers remained small until W. *Dinnick's 23-year ministry in the circuit (1878–1901). London Road church (1877) was replaced on a new site in 1895; High Street opened in 1886 and Queens Park Road in 1891.

The Churches of Brighton (London, c.1883) II pp. 64–86; L.H. Court (1923); E.W. Griffin (1957); R.C. Swift (1984)

JAV

Brimelow, William (1837–1913), the leading figure in the IM Connexion in the late nineteenth century, was born in *Warrington, but spent most of his life in *Bolton. He was President of the Connexion on four occasions, edited the _IM Magazine_ 1869–96 and wrote _A Free Church and a Free Ministry_ (1883). He formulated much of the administration of the Connexion, prepared its *Model Deed, established the Evangelistic Department on a formal basis and introduced the Ministers' Assistance Fund. He was the prime mover of the Ministers' Education Course which established ministerial training on a connexional basis. Under his influence the denomination finally settled on the name of *Independent Methodist, ending almost a century in which churches had retained various local names.

IM Magazine, July 1913

JAD

Brisco, Thomas (1737–97; e.m. 1751) was an itinerant for _c_. 30 years despite a weak and nervous constitution which he ascribed to poor accommodation and damp beds during his service in Ireland. He had a formative influence on the friend of his schooldays R. *Roberts. JW named him as one of the *Legal Hundred and as a beneficiary in his will. He spent his retirement in *Chester.

C. Atmore (1801) p. 67

JAV

Bristol, the scene of JW's first *field preaching, of his earliest building venture, the *New Room, the first *class meeting and *Watchnight service, and JW's first *ordinations, was a busy port, a centre of the slave trade and second only to London in population. In April 1739 he responded with some hesitation to a summons from G. *Whitefield to support his work there, but Bristol quickly became the second strategic base in his itinerant ministry, especially for the west and south west. Here he had his famous interview with Bishop *Butler in August 1739 and many years later, in 1788, preached by invitation in the mayoral chapel on College Green. It was the location of 18 *Conferences in JW's lifetime.

After his marriage, CW made his home there between 1749 and 1771. In 1779 JW opened a second chapel, in Guinea Street, which became the centre of Methodist work south of the river. It was replaced in 1828 by Langton Street in 1828, a much more pretentious chapel, with one of the earliest Methodist organs (1839) and a Day School (1866) which boasted Dame Clara Butt among its past scholars. It later became part of the Bristol Mission, but was destroyed in World War II. In 1788 JW preached twice in a chapel in Little George Street, in 'the poorest part of the city' near the Old Market. Before it closed late in the nineteenth century, this became the springboard for the Methodist *Sunday School movement and for the work of the *Stranger's Friend Society in Bristol.

To the north of the city centre, Portland Street chapel on Kingsdown, then a fashionable suburb, was opened in 1792, largely through the dedicated efforts of Captain *Webb. It maintained the tradition of Morning Prayer and was the spiritual home of the enterprising G. *Pocock, leader of the *Tent Methodists. When the WR movement of the 1850s decimated Bristol WM, leading to the loss of many members, **local preachers and *class leaders. Portland Chapel was the exception; it reached its highest membership towards the end of the century, under the ministry of M.G. *Pearse. In the twentieth century, decline set in and the 'Chapel on the Hill' closed in 1970.

As a result of the dispute between the *Conference and the New Room trustees in 1794, a new city centre chapel was built in Old King Street (1795; closed during redevelopment in 1954). It was modelled, not on the New Room, but on Oldham Street chapel in Manchester. Its day school in North Street ran from 1858 to 1928.

PM came to Bristol in 1823, but its first chapel, Ebenezer in Midland Road, was not built till 1849 (closed 1938). St George, Rose Green was opened in 1855. In 1854 the WR (later UMFC) built Hebron, Bedminster (closed 1967) and also Milk Street, which anticipated *Methodist Union by uniting in 1929 with Old King Street.

At the end of the twentieth century there were six Methodist circuits covering the city. Victoria, Clifton, is the base for the Methodist chaplaincy to the University. And *Wesley College, successor to *Didsbury and *Headingley Colleges, is at Westbury-on-Trym.

J.S. Pawlyn (1877); *MR(W)* 1901 pp. 48–57; Conference Handbooks 1923 (WM), 1935, 1959; WHS(B), various publications

EAC

Britton, George Bryant (1857–1929), UM industrialist, of *Kingswood, Bristol, established the boot- and shoe-making firm of Bryant and Britton and was an advocate of conciliation and arbitration in industrial disputes. He was Superintendent of a UM Sunday School numbering over 1,000, As a *Bristol City councillor he was responsible for initiating the tramway between the city and Kingswood and was Lord Mayor of *Bristol in 1920 and Coalition Liberal MP for East Bristol 1918–22.

Bristol Times and Mirror 9 Aug. 1921

CJS

Broadbelt, John Arthur (1878–1962; e.m. 1901), WM minister under whose preaching ministry the missions at *Hull (1908–14), Southall (1914–22) and *Bristol (1922–29) were established. After three years at the Tooting Mission, in 1932 he succeeded S. *Chadwick (an early influence) as Principal of *Cliff College and guided its post-war development. He was secretary and then President of the *Southport Convention. During his Bristol years he was closely involved in the purchase and restoration of the *New Room and CW's house. His keen advocacy of *overseas missions led in 1920–21 to a world tour of all the WM overseas districts.

M.L. Edwards (1949); *MR* 29 Nov. 1962

JAV

Broadhurst, Henry (1840–1911), *trade unionist, born at Littlemore, Oxon, the youngest of 12 children. He was early associated with WM and remained a committed member. His great aim in life was to work for the betterment of the common people. After serving as an apprentice stonemason he left *Oxford for *Norwich and in 1865 moved to *London. Following a dispute in the London building trade he organized the Stonemasons' Union, becoming its General Secretary in 1875, the year in which he also became General Secretary of the TUC. From 1873 he was also General Secretary of the Labour Representation League which sought to promote working men as Parliamentary candidates. In 1880 he was elected Liberal MP for *Stoke-on-Trent and in the 1885 election successfully contested Bordesley in *Birmingham. In 1886 Gladstone appointed him Under Secretary for the Home Office, the first working man ever to hold a ministerial post. After a period out of the House, he was returned for *Leicester in 1894 and sat as a Lib/Lab member until 1906.

T. Parr in *PMQR* vol. 44; *DLB* vol.1

NADS

Brockless, Dr George Frederick (1887–1957), organist, born at Fritwell, Oxon. Educated at New College and Queen's College, Oxford, he obtained his LRAM, ARCM and FRCO before the age of 21. He held two important posts at Grahamstown, South Africa 1908–28, returning to England to take his MusB and DMus at Durham. He held posts at Hornsey, Kensington and Battersea Polytechnic, lectured at *Westminster College and acted as conductor on many important occasions. In 1933 he became music adviser, with F. L. *Wiseman, to the Methodist Tune Book Committee and six of his tunes appeared in the 1933 *MHB*. He was organist at *Westminster Central Hall from 1944 until his death.

MR 5 Dec. 1957

PLC

Bromley, James (1785–1860; e.m. 1811), WM minister who was a friend and supporter of S. *Warren, opposed the suspension of J.R. *Stephens in 1834, and was censured for supporting the Warrenites the following year. At the time of the *Fly Sheet controversy he again supported the Reformers, being one of the few who voted against the expulsion of *Everett, *Dunn and *Griffith. He was himself expelled the following year. He wrote a number of polemical tracts at the time of the Fly Sheets, but did not ally himself with the Reformers after 1849.

B. Gregory (1898)

OAB

Bromley (Kent) A preaching house was built c.1770 in nearby Widmore and JW preached there in December 1772 and on two later occasions. Methodists from Widmore formed a society in a room in Bromley market place in 1816 and in 1826 Zion Chapel in the Upper High Street was opened. The population doubled in the decade after the coming of the railway in 1858 and Zion was replaced in 1876 by a large neo-Gothic chapel, itself replaced in 1965 by the present building. Bromley WM Circuit was formed from Deptford in 1866. The Rev. G.S. *Rowe became a well-loved member of the society in his retirement.

WHS(LHC) 1 (1965)

NM

Brontë Family Patrick Brontë or Brunty (1771–1861), perpetual curate of Haworth from 1820, was introduced to JW's teaching through the Rev. Thomas *Tighe. He was appointed examiner of *Woodhouse Grove School and married the niece of the headmaster, Maria Branwell, of Cornish Methodist stock. 'Aunt Branwell' cared for the Brontë children after their mother's death. The influence of W. *Grimshaw was still prevalent in Haworth and there were many similarities between the two men, including puritanical discipline, evangelical fervour and family misfortunes. Years before Patrick had found comfort and help in the home of J. *Fletcher. G.E. *Harrison traced the tragic trend in *Wuthering Heights* to the spiritual stories of conversion, of dramatic changes from darkness to light and of startling conflicts in the soul which Emily Brontë found in old *Methodist Magazines* belonging to her aunt. Anne and Charlotte went through phases of Calvinistic depression, but their treatment of Christian topics suggests that they tended towards *Arminianism. Anne's poems found a place in successive Methodist hymn-books, notably, 'Believe not those who say/The upward path is smooth' (*HP* 708).

G.E. Harrison (1937); G.E. Harrison (1948)

EWD

Brook, David, DCL (1854–1933; e.m. 1875), UMFC minister, was converted and entered the ministry through J. *Dodgson. As a circuit minister he took a leading part in the negotiations resulting in the Union of 1907 and became the chief UMC advocate of *Methodist Union in 1932, being Chairman of the Union committee of his own Church as well as of the interdenominational committee from 1922 to 1932. He was President of the UMFC Assembly and also of the FCFC in 1901.

MR 30 March 1933

OAB

Brown, Arthur Ernest, CIE (1882–1952; e.m. 1904), son of a WM missionary, **John Milton Brown, K-i-H, CIE** (1843–1934; e.m. 1865; in Ceylon and India 1866–1901), was educated at *Kingswood School and Cambridge, where he was a Wrangler in the Mathematics Tripos. He served in the Bengal District 1904–36 and was Principal of Bankura College 1917–18 and Chairman of the District 1924–29, before returning to circuit work in England.

MR 13 Nov. 1934, 24 July 1952

JAV

Brown-Westhead, Joshua Procter, MP (1807–77), the son of a *Manchester merchant who was a friend of J. *Bunting, was the partner of J. *Wood in a Manchester cotton firm and helped to set up the conservative *Watchman* in 1835. As Liberal MP for Knaresborough 1847–52 and *York 1857–65 and 1868–71, he supported Irish Disestablishment and voting by ballot. His career illustrates the way in which leading WM laymen moved left politically in the mid nineteenth century.

DEB

JHL

Brownsword, Thomas (1801–67; e.m. 1819), one of the earliest PM itinerants, known as 'the boy preacher'. He preached with great energy in the open air and was imprisoned in *Worcester gaol in 1820. He resigned in 1825 and settled as a *local preacher in Wednesbury. His sister **Ann Brownsword** (fl.1819–22) was also engaged in early missionary work and was arrested at Stourbridge and gaoled for persisting in open-air preaching. She reverted to local-preacher status on marrying Charles John Abraham, a Burslem druggist.

PMM, 1868, 1872; H.B. Kendall (1906); Petty (1880); WHS(WM) vol.1

EDG

Bryan, John (1776–1856), Welsh-speaking itinerant. Born in Llanfyllin, Montgomeryshire in 1776 (not 1770 as generally given), he was known as 'Bryan bach' because of his small stature. He was converted in *Chester in 1798 and after a period with the CMs began to preach with the WMs. Having been admitted on trial as an itinerant in 1801, he assisted O. *Davies and J. *Hughes in the Welsh Mission. He moved to English circuits in 1815, left the ministry in 1824 and set up as a grocer, first in *Leeds and, from 1831, in Caernarfon. He was a popular, forceful and original preacher, a little impetuous but wholly straightforward in his dealings. He produced Welsh versions of several biographies (J. *Haime, J. *Nelson, Arminius) and of polemical works and contributed frequently to *EW*; but his lasting monument is some 55 translations of CW's hymns, many still in use.

DWB; W. Davies (1900)

GTH

Bryant, Thomas (c. 1740s–c. 1804; e.m. 1758), an active outdoor evangelist and popular Yorkshire preacher described by JW as 'rough as W

*Darney [but] much changed for the better.' Ordained by Bishop *Erasmus, he insisted on wearing a gown. After JW expelled him in January 1765, he led a secession in *Sheffield and became Independent minister of the Scotland Street chapel. He invited A. *Kilham there in 1796 and it became MNC after his death.

WJW 21 p. 448n; J. Everett (1823) pp. 185–9; W. Parkes (1965)

JHL

Buck, Mary Clarissa (1810–76), PM itinerant. Converted at the Annual *Lovefeast and Watch Meeting at Griffydam WM chapel, she joined the PMs, becoming a *hired local preacher in 1835 and itinerant in 1836. Despite being extremely popular and in great demand, she resigned in 1847 because of the strain of itinerancy and a 'call' to take special services and anniversaries throughout the Connexion. Although based in *Leicester, she travelled extensively for 25 years. The 1866 Conference granted her an annuity of £20.

PMM, 1842–3, 1852–4, 1877; Kendall (1906); E.D. Graham (1989) pp. 6–7

EDG

Buckenham, Henry (1844–96; e.m. 1869), the first PM missionary in *South Africa (1870–75), where he single-handedly pioneered work among separate black and white congregations at Aliwal North. After service at home and in Fernando Po (now *Equatorial Guinea), he agreed to establish a mission in Mashukulumbweland (*Zambia). His party crossed the Kalahari Desert and the Zambezi and reached their destination after a journey of nearly five years (1889–94), held up both by the Lozi king, who said his Ila vassals would butcher them, and by the repeated need to make replacement wheels for the ox-wagons. In spite of illness and injury he established two widely separated posts, but died returning south.

A. Baldwin (n.d.)

JRP

Budd, William Robert (1853–1943), General Secretary of the Irish HM Fund, 1908–30, was born in *Waterford, the son of a Methodist businessman. He used his financial and administrative skills to complete the transfer of responsibility for the Irish Missions from the British to the Irish Connexion. He was noted for his patience, kindness and courtesy. His most radical proposal, presented to the General Committee in 1915, was to appoint what amounted to a separated Chairman with stationing powers to the Clones District. This was considered uncharacteristically high-handed and was never implemented.

ICA, 1 Dec. 1933, 11 June 1943;

RPR

Budgett, Samuel (1794–1851), born at Wrington, Som, was the co-founder of a grocery firm at *Kingswood which prospered by initiating country rounds and by moving into wholesaling. He gained a reputation for uprightness in his business dealings and considerate treatment of his staff. The firm prospered and moved to *Bristol in 1841. His unostentatious giving to charity amounted to £2,000 a year and he was a generous contributor to WM funds. His son **James Smith Budgett** (1823–1906), son-in-law of T. *Farmer and a missionary supporter, moved to Guildford and opened a London branch of the firm in 1857. He served as lay treasurer of the WMMS 1874–83. A younger brother, **William Henry Budgett** (1827–1900) maintained the *Bristol business, was active in public affairs (including the building of the Colston Hall in 1861), in the Bristol *Stranger's Friend Society and in local Methodism.

W. Arthur (1852); *WMM* 1851 pp. 606–7; *DNB*; D.P. Lindegaard (1988)

CJS

Buller, James (1812–84; e.m. 1837) left Cornwall for *New Zealand in 1835 in the hope of taking up missionary work. He was appointed to the Kaipara, a new station which he occupied until 1854 and where his ministry was noted for his commitment to Maori education. In 1839 he made an overland journey largely on foot to Port Nicholson to secure the site for the new mission station. He was ordained in 1844. At Wellington 1855–60 and Christchurch 1860–65 he achieved a position of prominence among the settlers. He was President of the Conference in 1875. During retirement he spent four years in England and published *Forty Years in New Zealand* (1878) and *New Zealand Past and Present* (1880).

B. Gadd (1966)

DJP

Bulmer, Mary (Mrs Leuty) (?-post 1934) was born at Wylam-on-Tyne and became an accredited PM *local preacher in 1891, several years after she had begun working as a very successful evangelist. At times she acted as a *hired local preacher and virtual itinerant, especially in the Stanley and Chester-le-Street Circuits. She married John E. Leuty (1855–1945; e.m. 1889) in 1906 and continued active both in his circuit work and beyond, e.g. in *Christian Endeavour. She was the first *woman representative to the PM Conference.

W.M Patterson (1909); *Local Preachers' Who's Who* (1934)

EDG

Bultitude, Elizabeth (1809–90) PM itinerant, converted at a camp meeting on Mousehold Heath, *Norwich, 14 May 1826. She became an exhorter in March 1830, a *local preacher in June and an itinerant two years later, working chiefly in East Anglia. She was remembered as having a 'large round rubicund face in a poke bonnet', for using 'ejaculatory prayers with many fervent repetitions' and as a stickler for propriety. On superannuating in 1862 she received an annuity and settled in Norwich, where she continued to preach and attend her class. She itinerated longest and was the last of the PM female preachers, dying after a long, painful illness. As the only female itinerant to 'die in the work' she alone has an obituary in the PM *Minutes*.

PMM 1891 pp. 564–5; E.D. Graham (1989) pp. 7–8

EDG

Bumby, John Hewgill (1808–40; e.m. 1830), WM missionary, born at Thirsk. After nine years in circuit work, in 1839 he was sent to take charge of the *New Zealand mission, one of a group intended to counteract colonial exploitation of the Maori people at a time when the organized settlement of New Zealand was in prospect. Gifted as a leader and preacher, he immediately set about assessing the needs of the Mission. He undertook a voyage to the south, accompanied by a number of younger Maori, trained at the Mission, whom he left at strategic places as native teachers. The Treaty of Waitangi was signed in February 1840 while he was in Sydney seeking further support for the Mission. He was drowned on his way home when the canoe overturned in crossing the Hauraki Gulf. He was mourned as a man of energy and great promise.

A. Barrett (1864); I. Whyle (1990)

MJF/DJP

Bundy, James (1750–1818), WM *local preacher, born at Dymock, Glos. He began as a shepherd boy, but after learning to read and write became a foreman in a *Bristol brewery. His success as a preacher brought him increasing notice and a number of legacies, all of which he redistributed among the testators' lawful heirs. He started his own brewing business and for over 30 years was a dedicated prison visitor, first in Bristol and later in London, often passing the night in a criminal's cell. He was a member of Portland Street chapel and a founder member of the Bristol *Strangers' Friend Society.

———————

T. Wood (1820)

CJS

Bunting, Dr Jabez (1779–1858; e.m. 1799), the architect of the WM Church, described by W.R. Ward as 'undoubtedly one of the front rank churchmen of the nineteenth century', was a more representative figure than the crude dictator vilified by his opponents. Born in *Manchester, the son of a radical tailor, he studied medicine there under Dr Thomas Percival. His circuit ministry was spent mainly in the North. After 1832 he resided in London as the first Secretary and master mind of the WMMS and from 1835 President of the *Hoxton Theological Institution. He was *Connexional Editor, 1821–24. As early as 1806 he had been Assistant Secretary of the Conference, becoming Secretary in 1814–19 and 1824–27. He was four times President (1820, 1828, 1836 and 1844), a record only equalled by Dr R. *Newton.

J. *Pawson said in 1805 that Methodism was a body without a head. Bunting gave much-needed leadership, not only for ministers but for wealthy and articulate laymen. The *'Liverpool Minutes' of 1820, responding to a decline in membership, was his work, as were the *Regulations of 1835. He promoted the election of younger ministers (including himself) to the *Legal Hundred, the annual Pastoral Address, the right to memorialize Conference, the place of laymen on key committees, the proper training of ministers and their *ordination by laying-on of hands. He was the epitome of 'high Methodism', which stressed the *Connexion', the national, the international (including foreign missions). He saw Methodism as an independent body between Church and Dissent – not unlike Thomas Chalmers of the Scottish Free Kirk. Though often typecast as a Tory, he supported Catholic Emancipation in 1829 and in the 1840s opposed Peel on the Maynooth Grant, the Dissenters' Chapel Bill and Graham's Edu-

cation Bill. Later he championed Methodist *day schools.

When defending the supremacy of Conference, he declared that 'Methodism was as much opposed to democracy as to sin' (*Nottingham Review*, 14 Dec. 1827). His policies provoked opposition leading to the secession of *Protestant Methodists (1828) and the *Wesleyan Association (1835), and finally to the *Fly Sheets controversy. Clearly there was an air of clericalism about 'High Methodism', the marks of a Connexion becoming a Church, but having to attain too quickly the maturity of a national institution. Bunting showed an inflexibility and insensitivity and his opponents a cantankerousness which precluded any hope of genuine partnership between ministry and laity for a generation.

Bunting received an MA from Aberdeen and a DD from Connecticut Wesleyan University, USA. Before his death he declared that he had sought to be a true Methodist, an Evangelical Arminian, as in his classic sermon on *Justification by Faith (1812).

William Maclardie Bunting (1805–66; e.m. 1824), the eldest of his three sons by his first wife Sarah (*née* Maclardie), was educated at *Kingswood School, retired from circuit life in 1849. He was not afraid to oppose his father in Conference, and was a minor hymn writer (MHB 296, 571, 750). As Hon. Secretary of the Evangelical Alliance from 1858 he was perhaps the first non-Anglican to lead prayers in Lambeth Palace. His brother **Thomas Percival Bunting** (1811–86), his father's biographer, became a solicitor in Manchester. As a member of the *Committee of Privileges he strongly supported his father. T.P. Bunting's son **Sir Percy William Bunting** (1836–1911), an alumnus of Pembroke College, Cambridge, was called to the Bar in 1862, was a promoter of the *Forward Movement, The *Leys School and the FCFC. He edited the monthly *Contemporary Review* from 1882 to 1911, when Miss Evelyn Bunting and his nephew Dr J.S. *Lidgett became co-editors. He was associated with the ecumenical *Review of the Churches* (1891–96) and the Grindelwald Conferences of Church leaders.

———————

G.S. Rowe (1870); G.J. Stevenson (1884–6) 2 pp. 249–60; T.P. Bunting & G.S. Rowe (1887); J.H. Rigg (1905); J. Kent (1956); W.R. Ward (1972, 1976); A.J. Hayes & D.H. Gowland (1981); K.G. Greet (1995); D. Hempton (1996) pp. 91–108

JMT

Burdsall, Richard ('Dicky') (1735–1824), *local preacher and buckle-maker, born at Kirby Overblow, Yorks, nicknamed 'Old Chapter and Verse' because of his ability to quote scripture. Convinced of sin under the preaching of W. *Grimshaw in 1751, he found peace with God and cleansing from sin in 1762. He was a simple but effective preacher in the *Leeds Circuit and as far afield as N. Lincs, *Hull and the N. and E. Ridings, but declined to become an itinerant or an Independent pastorate. In *York from 1782, he became the leader of a large class. His son John Burdsall (*c.* 1776–1861; e.m. 1796) and grandson J. *Lyth both entered the ministry.

R. Burdsall (1797)

JAV

Burgess, William (1845–1930; e.m. 1866), missionary in the Madras District, *India 1866–96. He pioneered a mission among the outcastes at Ikkadu, but is chiefly remembered for the successful evangelical mission he launched in Hyderabad State in 1879, where he built up congregations and churches in the twin cities of Hyderabad and Secunderabad and initiated rural work which laid the foundations of the future Mass Movement. His wife was closely involved in the establishment of girls' schools and the Wesley Boarding and Normal Training School, but died in a shipwreck. Under his superintendency of the Mission in *Italy 1902–18 a union with the Evangelical Free Church was effected.

MR 11 Sept. 1930

EMJ

Burgin, Dr Edward Leslie, MP (1887–1945), WM solicitor who obtained a First in both university and professional final examinations and an LLD in 1913. He became Principal and Director of Studies at the Law Society in 1925. From 1929 to his retirement in 1945 he was Liberal (from 1931 Liberal Nationalist) MP for Luton. He was Parliamentary Secretary to the Board of Trade 1932–37, Minister of Transport 1937–39 and Minister of Supply 1939–40. His special interest was international relations and he was a British Delegate to the League of Nations in 1935.

Times 17 Aug. 1945; M. Stenton & S. Lees vol. 3 (1979)

CJS

Burials The rights of Nonconformists to be buried in parish churchyards and of Nonconformist clergy to conduct the burial service were issues, linked to the question of the validity of Nonconformist *baptism, which flared into controversy, chiefly in rural areas, at several points in the nineteenth century. As WM became a body recognizably distinct from the CofE, it was drawn into the controversy. In 1808 the refusal of the vicar of Belton (Rutland) to bury a child because it had not received Anglican baptism led to a test case and the vicar's suspension for three months. A similar case arose at Gedney (Lincs) in 1842 and was taken by the *Committee of Privileges to the Court of Arches, which ruled in favour of WM, a verdict later confirmed on appeal to the Privy Council. The issue was finally resolved by the Burial Laws Amendment Act of 1880, supported by H.H. *Fowler and opposed by Bishop Wordsworth of Lincoln. Reinforced by the Burials Act of 1900, this permitted burials in churchyards without the use of the *BCP* or the attendance of a clergyman.

O. Chadwick vol. 2 (1970) pp. 202–7; J.M. Turner (1985) pp. 132–3

JAV

Burma *see* **Myanmar**

Burnet, Amos (1857–1926; e.m. 1880), WM missionary in *India, who ministered to the English congregation in Bangalore, 1881–93 and was superintendent of the work in the Transvaal, 1902–19, in the wake of the Boer War. In 1919 he became one of the Secretaries at the *Mission House and was President of the 1924 Conference.

MR 5 Aug. 1926

JAV

Burnett, Richard George (1898–1960), journalist, author and *local preacher who, after working on papers in *Plymouth and *Sheffield, became assistant editor of the *Methodist Times* in 1932 and managing editor of the *Methodist Recorder* in 1952. He actively supported the *LPMAA, was co-author of its centenary history, *A Goodly Fellowship* (1949) and became its president in 1953. A class leader in the Finsbury Park circuit, he had close links with the *East End Mission, writing about its work in *These My Brethren* (1946) and serving as its circuit steward. He was a founder member and director of Religious Films Ltd and wrote a biography of J. *Rank, *Through the Mill* (1945).

WDH

Burslem *see* **Stoke-on-Trent**

Burt, Thomas (1837–1922), northern miners' leader, was born at Murton Row, Northumberland. He began work in 1847 as a trapper boy in Haswell pit and later at Choppington. In 1865 he was elected secretary and agent of the Northumberland Miners' Association, which quadrupled under his leadership. Despite his parliamentary work he remained as its secretary until 1905. In 1874 he was elected MP for Morpeth, holding the seat until 1918. He was Parliamentary Secretary to the Board of Trade in the Liberal Government of 1892–95, was a member of three Royal Commissions and was made a Privy Councillor in 1906. His parents were PM and as a boy he attended Sunday School 'with the utmost regularity' and chapel services. Although never a member, he later testified to the stimulus he had received from PM preachers and wrote an article on 'Methodism and the Northern Miners' for the *PMQR* (1882, pp. 385–97).

See also **Trade Unionism**

T. Burt (1924)

NADS

Burton, Dr Henry (1840–1930; e.m. 1865), WM minister, born in Swannington, Leics, in the house where his grandmother had begun the first *JMA in 1818. He moved with his parents to *America and graduated from Beloit College, which later granted him a DD for his contributions to theological literature. After a brief period of pastoral oversight in Wisconsin, he entered the WM ministry in England and married a sister of M.G. *Pearse. Three of his hymns appeared in *MHB* (1933). He is remembered chiefly for the hymn 'There's a light upon the mountain' (*HP* 246) and the song 'Pass it on'.

MR 1 May 1930

PLC

Bury St Edmunds JW's 17 visits between 1755 and 1790 were made often on his way to *Norwich. Anglican dominance in rural Suffolk, coupled with a strong Dissenting presence in the town, meant that the society remained small, though JW spoke more of their spiritual strengths than of their weaknesses. The first chapel was not built until 1812 and was replaced by the present one, Trinity, nearer the town centre, in 1878. A second church was opened in 1957 to serve the needs of post-war housing developments. The first PM chapel was built in 1830, a year after their arrival. The early success of their mission necessitated larger premises in 1851 and again in 1902. In 1934 they united with the WM in the latter's premises. What is now *Culford School was founded in the town in 1881, followed on the site by the East Anglian School for Girls until the amalgamation in 1972. The Martins *MHA opened in the town in 1962.

WHS(EA) 3 (1960) pp. 3–4, 6 (1961) pp. 6–7, 10 (1964) p. 4, 13 (1965) pp. 5–7

WDH

Buss, Frederick Harold (1876–1964), civil servant and an accredited *local preacher from 1898, who was active in the *LPMAA, joining its general committee in 1912 and serving as honorary secretary 1926–56. He was its President in 1932 (when he worked to incorporate PM and UM preachers into what had been a WM movement) and again in 1949, its centenary year. The founding of Mutual Aid Homes owed much to him. A frequent contributor to Methodist periodicals, he was the co-author of *A Goodly Fellowship* (1949), a centenary history of the Association.

WDH

Butler, Dr John Francis (1909–82; e.m. 1933), missionary in *India, born at Ashby-de-la-Zouch. Educated at Magdalen College, Oxford, he gained his MA at Harvard (where he had a Henry Travelling Fellowship) and a PhD at Manchester for a thesis on the Epistemology of Theism. After two years as Assistant Tutor at *Didsbury College, he was Professor of Philosophy at Madras Christian College 1937–41, then served in the Army as Captain and later chaplain. From 1947 to 1951 he worked for the Christian Literature Society in Madras and was examiner at Serampore and Madras Universities, before returning to English circuits. His research into inter-relationships between religions, art, architecture and culture world-wide led to two books, *The Holiness of Beauty* and *Christian Art in India* (1986) as well as contributions to other publications. His extensive library is housed in the Centre for the Study of Christianity in the Non-Western World at Edinburgh University.

MR 22 July 1982

JAV

Butler, Dr Joseph (1692–1752), Bishop of *Bristol 1738 and of *Durham 1750, was brought up as a Presbyterian and educated at a dissenting academy; then conformed and studied at Oriel

College, Oxford 1715–18. JW spoke approvingly of his answer to Deism, *The Analogy of Religion* (1736). In the summer of 1739, as Methodism was developing rapidly in Bristol, JW had three interviews with the bishop in which he defended his irregular preaching activities, claiming that as Fellow of Lincoln College he had a roving commission. He distanced himself from any claim to 'extraordinary revelations and gifts of the Holy Ghost', which the bishop characterized as 'a very horrid thing'. Butler's proposal in 1750 for establishing colonial bishops might have radically changed the development of Methodism in America after the Revolutionary War.

W.A. Spooner (1901); E.C. Mossner (1936); *PWHS* 42 pp. 93–100

JAV

Butler, William (1818–99) was born in *Dublin and entered the WM ministry in Ireland in 1844. He emigrated to *America in 1850 and pioneered MEC missions in *India (1856–64) and in Mexico (1873–78). He had a broad vision of mission. In India, for example, he advocated the use of printing presses, schools, orphanages and agricultural projects as well as preaching. He saw the education of women as a priority. In Mexico he advocated the promotion of evangelical concerns among Roman Catholics in a 'Christian and unsectarian manner'.

C. Butler (1902); N.W. Taggart (1986) pp. 168–80

NWT

Butterfield, Sir Herbert (1900–79), historian and *local preacher, born at Oxenhope, Yorks. He was educated at Cambridge, where he became Fellow (1923–55) and Master (1955–68) of Peterhouse. He was Professor of Modern History (1944–63) and Regius Professor (1963–68), and from 1959 to 1961 was Vice-Chancellor of the University. He brought his Christian faith and his historical scholarship into fruitful interplay in his *Christianity and History* (1949), *Christianity in European History* (1951) and *Christianity, Diplomacy and War* (1953). His special period was the reign of George III, but he ranged widely from *The Whig Interpretation of History* (1931) to *The Origins of Modern Science 1300–1800* (1949). He was knighted in 1965 and had 14 honorary doctorates.

Telegraph, 23 July 1979; *MR* 2 Aug. 1979; *PWHS* 46 pp. 1–12

JAN

Butterworth, James ('Jimmy') (1897–1977; e.m. 1922) was born near Oswaldtwistle, Lancs. His World War I experience fired him with a passion for providing a better world for the next generation. While at *Didsbury College he started a youth club in *Manchester which shaped the pattern of his whole ministry. In 1922 he was sent to Walworth, South London, and remained there for 54 years. He organized the replacement of the old Walworth chapel by the first Clubland, opened in 1929 as a lively centre for youth activities in an area of great deprivation. He had a great gift for enlisting the support of celebrities such as Bob Hope. Though 20 years' work was destroyed by bombing in 1941, he arranged the building of even better premises after the war.

J. Butterworth (1970); *MR* 14 April 1977

JDB

Butterworth, Joseph, MP (1770–1826), son of a Baptist minister in *Coventry, became a very successful law bookseller in Fleet Street, London. A. *Clarke, his wife's brother-in-law, influenced him to become a Methodist and he undertook the publication of Clarke's *Commentary*. He was the second Methodist MP, representing Coventry as an Independent (1812–18) and Dover (1820–26). He was a founding member of the *Committee of Privileges. He was well known for his philanthropy and as an anti-slavery campaigner. As treasurer of the WMMS 1819–26 he was able to use his gifts and influence to promote religious and social rights in many parts of the world. The initial meeting of the Bible Society was held at his home. Neither high office nor success affected his concern for the poor and he valued highly his service as *class leader. He regretted the tendency towards a high doctrine of the *Pastoral Office.

DNB; G.J. Stevenson (1872) pp. 353–5; G.J. Stevenson (1884–6) 4 pp. 561–4

EWD

Button, Robert Arthur (1872–1937) trained as a teacher at *Westminster College and became a *local preacher and ardent Sunday School worker. He showed his organizational skills as secretary of the First London District Sunday School Council and in 1923 was appointed connexional WM Local Preachers Secretary – the first and only lay secretary after the 1932 Union. A great encourager, he travelled the Connexion, pioneering *local preachers' studies and conferences.

Described as 'always gentle, ever sincere, scrupulously painstaking and with quiet passion,' he received a standing ovation from Conference on his retirement in 1937, only a short while before his death.

MR 2 & 9 Sept. 1937; J.C. Bowmer in *Preacher's Handbook* no.9 pp. 1–13; G. Milburn & M. Batty (1995) pp. 84–93

PB

Cadman, Samuel Parkes (1864–1936), an eminent American preacher, born in Shropshire and nurtured in British PM, was accepted for the WM ministry in 1886. After training at *Richmond College he left for New York, which enabled him to marry immediately in defiance of WM regulations. He had a highly successful career as a Methodist and then Congregational minister, as the first 'radio pastor', and as a prolific journalist and author. He travelled regularly to Geneva as an envoy to the League of Nations and maintained his links with the Lawley Bank WM chapel, Shropshire, returning to the county regularly to preach.

MR 16 July 1936; F. Hamlyn (1930); F. M. Ridge (1936)

JHL

Callard, Mary Pauline (1917–), Principal of *Southlands College 1965–77, was born in Torquay. She was educated at Lauriston Hall and *Queenswood School and graduated in both Commerce and Social Studies. She served with UNRRA in its Mission to Austria immediately after World War II, then became a lecturer in Statistics and then in Sociology at Exeter University, before being appointed to Southlands College. She became an Honorary Fellow of the Roehampton Institute and in retirement served as Honorary Treasurer of MCOD and on the Connexional Boards of Education, of Ministries and the Candidates' Committee.

PMW

Calvert, James (1813–92; e.m. 1838), pioneer missionary to *Fiji. Born in Pickering, he was apprenticed to a printer. While training for the ministry at *Hoxton, he responded to an urgent call to join J. *Hunt and others in a mission to Fiji. He and his wife landed at Lakemba in 1838 and remained in Fiji for the next 17 years. They were instrumental in the conversion of Thakombau [Cakobau], the most powerful chief in the island. James used his printing skills in revising and publishing a translation of the Bible. After five years' further work on the translation in Britain, he returned to Fiji as Chairman of the District, followed by eight years (1872–80) in the Diamond Fields of South Africa. His wife **Mary Calvert** (*née* Fowler) (1814–82) was born at Aston Clinton, Bucks and was well known there as a nurse who cared for the sick during a cholera epidemic. She married after a whirlwind courtship and within a few days was on her way to Fiji. Her nursing skills saved the lives of many women and even brought her into the chief's court, where Thakombau was greatly influenced by her care. Convinced of the need for more women missionaries, she persuaded the newly formed Ladies' Committee to send a Miss Tookey to Fiji in 1861.

G.J. Stevenson (1884–86) 3 pp. 409–20; C. Hall (1918); P.M. Webb (1958) pp. 13–23

PMW

Calvinism The key elements in the theological system associated with the Swiss reformer John Calvin (1509–64) were an emphasis on the absolute sovereignty of God, the predestination of certain 'elect' people to *salvation, the *perseverance of the saints and an insistence on ecclesiastical discipline. Whether Calvin actually taught the 'horrible decree', i.e. of predestination to *damnation*, in the manner often ascribed to him has been questioned, but it was certainly propagated by his spiritual heirs. A distinction is sometimes made between the 'High' Calvinism which insisted on this extreme form of predestinarian teaching and the 'low' Calvinism which did not concern itself with such issues as whether the 'decrees' predated the Fall.

Calvinism was widespread in *Puritanism, and hence among both Anglican and dissenting evangelicals, in the eighteenth and early nineteenth centuries. JW strongly opposed it over predestination, final perseverance and its attack on his doctrine of *Christian perfection, believing that it denied the universal availability of *grace and the power of the Spirit to 'save to the uttermost'. Many of CW's hymns (e.g. HP 520, 'Father of everlasting grace') were written to refute the limited availability of salvation. In turn, JW was bitterly attacked, especially during the controversy of the 1770s, his teaching on perfection being perceived as 'popery'. The intermittent dispute impaired the co-operation between Wesleyan and other evangelicals, notably G. *Whitefield and Lady *Huntingdon. The issue, with the related one of *antinomianism, was discussed at the Conferences of 1744 and 1745 and, above all, 1770.

See also **Welsh Calvinistic Methodism**

A.C. Outler (1964) pp. 425–91; H.D. Rack (1989) pp. 198–202, 450–61; A. Brown-Lawson (1994) pp. 301–54

DJC

Camborne *see* **Redruth and Camborne**

Cambridge Methodism came to Cambridge despite JW's neglect: he never preached there and visited only briefly, in 1731. At the end of that decade a *religious society similar to the *Holy Club had a brief existence, with W. *Delamotte among its members, but this had dispersed by 1740. In the 1760s a group of undergraduates met for study, preached and visited the sick and needy for a time, after the manner of the Oxford 'Holy Club'. They were led by the *Calvinist Rowland *Hill. After his graduation in 1769 the movement was suppressed by the University authorities. It was left to C. *Simeon, minister of Holy Trinity 1782–1836, to represent the Evangelical Revival in Cambridge. Despite some earlier preaching in nearby villages, the Cambridge WM society had only a room in the yard of the 'Brazen George' inn until Barnwell Chapel, Fitzroy Street (later the scene of Gipsy *Smith's conversion) was opened *c*.1818. Despite this, Cambridge WM Circuit was formed from Bury St Edmunds in 1816. Later chapels included Hills Road (1866–1972). In 1901 the WM Conference appointed a special committee on Methodism in Cambridge, which led to the building of Wesley (1913) at the corner of Christ's Pieces, which became the home of the Cambridge MethSoc. Modernization and reordering were completed in 1990. PM chapels were built in St Peter Street (forerunner of Castle Street Church), opened by W. *Clowes (1823), Panton St (1860s) and Sturton St (1875). Restrictions on Nonconformists at Oxford and Cambridge were lifted in 1871. This led to the opening of The *Leys School (1875). *Wesley House was opened in 1921 for ministerial training.

F. Tice (1966); John D. Walsh in Peter Brooks (1975), pp. 249–83

SJH

Cambridge, Alice (1762–1829), pioneer Irish *woman preacher, was born in Bandon, where she joined the Methodists in 1780. Her spiritual experience compelled her into an increasingly public ministry, Wherever she went she drew large crowds and many responded to her appeals. Reacting to criticism, she sought JW's advice, which was, 'Obey . . . in all things, as far as your conscience permits. But it will not permit you to be silent when God commands you to speak.' In 1802 the Irish Conference withdrew membership from women who persisted in preaching, but she did persist, drawing such large outdoor congregations that by special resolution in 1811 the Conference readmitted her, though without rescinding the ban on women preachers.

C.H. Crookshank (1882) pp. 191–203; P.W. Chilcote (1991) pp. 203–4, 232–3, 254–5

RPR

Cambridge Group, the origin of the later MethSocs, began informally in 1929 when 18 friends among the students at *Cambridge met, in an 'atmosphere of freedom and comradeship' and against the background of declining Christian allegiance among young people, to prepare for Methodist Union. They were encouraged by W.H. *Beales, minister of Wesley Church and were also much influenced by W.R. *Maltby. Their manifesto *A Group Speaks* was published in 1931, followed by a series of 'Cambridge Group Manuals'. There was a similar group at *Oxford called the John Wesley Society. A number of lay and ministerial figures prominent in Methodism since 1932 were influenced by the groups and 'MethSoc' groups were formed at other universities.

See also **Coulson, C.A.**

J.M. Turner (1998) pp. 76–8

JAV

Camp Meetings were American in origin. The American evangelist Lorenzo Dow wrote a pamphlet, *An Account of the Origin and Progress of Camp Meetings and the Method of conducting them*. Dow visited England 1805–7, and both H. *Bourne and *Clowes heard him preach at Congleton in November 1806. The pamphlet and Dow's personal advocacy of camp meetings suggested the idea of holding them in England. Camp meetings involved short and varied preaching or exhorting by a number of speakers, in the context of fervent prayer. The first, held on Mow Cop on 31 May 1807, was mainly a meeting for prayer. Thousands came from the towns in Cheshire. Further meetings (which included preaching) were held at Mow Cop on 19 July, at Langtoft-on-the-Wolds near Driffield and at Brown Edge on 16 August, and at Norton-in-the-Moors on 23 August. The WM Conference's judgment on them was: 'They are highly improper . . . we disclaim all connexion with them,' and Bourne was expelled from the society. The birth of the *PM Connexion was a result. Camp meetings became a feature of the movement and many were held in different parts of the country, especially at the time of District Meetings and when the Conference assembled. They were characterized by processions, singing and preaching.

W. Garner (1857); A. Wilkes & J. Lovett (1942); W.E. Farndale (1950)

WL

Canada Information on the origins of Methodism in Canada is fragmentary and confusing. It was introduced into the maritime provinces of Newfoundland in 1765 by L. *Coughlan and of Nova Scotia in 1781 by W. *Black. Both of these featured in T. *Coke's 1786 missionary appeal, though the missionaries designated by that year's Conference were in the event all stationed by Coke in the *West Indies. John McGeary was sent to Newfoundland the following year. In Nova Scotia Black's labours were first reinforced by American preachers appointed in 1784 by the Christmas Conference in Baltimore and then, in 1789, by the English preacher James Wray.

Palatine emigrants from New York brought their Methodist faith with them to Montreal in 1778. The first Methodist sermon in Quebec is said to have been preached in 1780 by a soldier and *local preacher named Tuffey while stationed there. A cavalry major named George Neal, who was an Irish local preacher, settled near Niagara and began preaching in Upper Canada around 1787. Methodist developments in Ontario are bound up with the settlement of the Ryerson family in Victoria County in 1799.

The later development of Methodism in British North America was complicated (and sometimes hampered) by a number of factors: the vastness of the sparsely populated territory, its heterogeneous population (Upper Canada being predominantly English, Lower Canada French), and a series of tensions: between American and British influences, between urban and rural cultures, and especially between Canadian Methodism and the WMMS (e.g. in their attitude towards the Anglican establishment).

The MEC at first supported the work in Nova Scotia, but severed the link in 1800. *Asbury paid a belated visit in 1811, but the MEC's work in Upper and Lower Canada was hampered by anti-American feelings, aggravated by the War of

1812–14. Conflict between American and WM missions led to an agreement in 1820 whereby the MEC withdrew from Lower Canada and the WMMS from Upper Canada. The 1824 General Conference of the MEC created a Canadian Conference which became the autonomous 'MEC of Canada' in 1828. For some years relations between Canadian Methodists and the WMMS were also marked by tension and conflict, but these were largely resolved in 1847. Finally, in 1855 WM throughout eastern Canada was united under a single autonomous Conference.

PM was introduced by a local preacher, William Lawson, who had migrated from Cumberland. In 1831 the PM Conference sent its first itinerants, Nathaniel Watkins and William Summersides; the work remained largely urban and centred on Toronto, and was placed under the *Hull Circuit. H. *Bourne visited the mission in 1844–45. The BC Conference of 1831 sent its first two missionaries: Francis Metherall to Prince Edward Island and John Hicks Eynon to Upper Canada. In 1837 the MNC Conference responded to appeals from Upper Canada by sending J. *Addyman and a link was established with a breakaway group, the 'Canadian WM Church'. Union between the various Methodist bodies in Canada was effected in 1874. In 1925 Methodists joined with Congregationalists and Presbyterians to form the United Church of Canada. This is the largest Protestant denomination in Canada and is affiliated to the World Methodist Council.

W. Moister (1871) pp. 69–108; T.W. Smith (1877); A. Sutherland (1903); F&H 1 pp. 256–510

JAV

Candidates JW accepted men as *itinerants on the recommendation of the circuit *Assistant (or *Superintendent) and after interview in the Conference. There was usually a one-year period of *probation, extended in 1784 to four. Over the years WM evolved a more elaborate system, substantially parallelled in other branches of Methodism, which has survived, with modifications, to the present. Its main features are: nomination in the Circuit Meeting and approval by the Ministerial Synod, written examinations and trial sermons, personal interview and psychological assessment, examination by District and connexional committees, and recommendation by the Ministerial to the Representative Session of Conference, where the final decision rests. Candidates must be local preachers, possess basic educational qualifications and give an account of their

Christian experience and sense of call. Special procedures exist for those who apply to transfer from the ministry of other Churches.

Until 1956 it was rare for candidates to be married or above 25 years of age. By 1996 the average age had risen to 41. *Women were not accepted until 1973. From 1956 until 1988 a special category of Senior Candidate was open to those aged 55 or over (50 for women) who were available for stationing without training and who would not require pension provision.

The 1998 Conference adopted a radical change, dividing candidature into two stages, the first (determined by a District committee) for initial training for authorized ministry (whether ministerial, diaconal or lay), the second (determined by Conference as above) specifically for training as minister or deacon.

HMGB 1 pp. 248–9; G.T. Brake (1984) ch. 6
BEB

Cann, William Henry (1857–1942; e.m. 1879), BC preacher, born in Huckworthy, Devon, the son of a miner. He went down the mine at 10, was converted at 16, became a local preacher and trained for the ministry at *Shebbear College. He was sent to Adelaide, South *Australia in 1884, where his most important ministry was the establishment of the Adelaide Central Mission, with its vigorous social and evangelistic work. He established the Mission's Children's Homes. The Sunday evening service, with his evangelical preaching and powerful congregational singing, attracted 1,000 worshippers weekly. He preached in the open air, broadcast regularly and contributed to the *Australian Christian Commonwealth*. He was President of the South Australian Conference in 1912.

DG

Canterbury JW paid the first of 39 visits in 1750. The 'Round-house' or 'Pepper-box' chapel, King Street was opened in 1764 and replaced by St Peter's Street (designed by W. *Jenkins) in 1812. Canterbury belonged to the widespread London Circuit until 1765. A *Day School opened in premises behind the chapel in 1871 and *Kent College for Boys in 1885. A PM chapel in St. John's Place, Northgate was registered in 1839 as part of a mission under the *Hull Circuit; it became a separate Circuit in 1859. A new chapel opened in the Borough in 1876.

J.A. Vickers (1961)

JAV

Capey, Ernest F. H. (1865–1924; e.m. 1888), MNC minister, trained at *Ranmoor College. He edited the monthly magazine *Young People*. In 1916 he published an influential book of responsive services *Sanctuary Worship*, followed by the less successful *Young People's Worship* (1920). He was President of the UM Conference in 1922.

EAR

Capper, Joseph (1788–1860), *Chartist and PM local preacher. Born near Nantwich, Cheshire, he later moved to Tunstall and was converted at the first Mow Cop *Camp Meeting. Unusually, neither his *Chartism nor his Primitive Methodism arose from poverty. Described as 'a sort of saintly John Bull', he was a powerful preacher and popular radical orator. Following the Plug Plot disturbances in 1842 he was charged with sedition and conspiracy and sentenced to two years' imprisonment at Stafford, where he testified that his only consolation was that 'no one could deprive him of communion with his Saviour'. He later became a prominent agitator against the 'papal aggression' of 1850.

C. Shaw (1903) pp. 141–54; 172–81; D. Thompson (1984) p. 197

JAH

Cardiff Both JW and CW preached in the city and ministered to prisoners in the County Gaol in St Mary Street. JW first preached, in the Castle precincts (as on later occasions) on 18 Oct. 1739. On his visit in 1843 a 'room' had just been built. This was replaced later in the century by a chapel in Church Street (rebuilt on the same site, 1829). Cardiff became a separate circuit (from Swansea) in 1796. Wesley Chapel, Charles Street, opened in 1850, was rebuilt after a fire in 1895, became the Central Hall, but was damaged in World War II. As the city expanded, Methodism followed the population into the suburbs. Roath Road was opened in 1871; Roath Park replaced an iron chapel in 1898. The first Cathays church (1862) was replaced by larger premises and a new church in the 1880s, following the ministry of Dr J.S. *Lidgett. WM Conferences met in Cardiff in 1893 and 1911 and the Methodist Conference met there in 1990.

A PM mission was launched in 1857 from the Pontypool Circuit and came under the care of the General Missionary Committee before becoming a circuit in 1879. Later there were two circuits, based on the Mount Tabor and Canton churches built in the 1860s. Llandaff North in Coplestone Road was built in 1897. PM's most eminent local layman, Alderman Joseph Ramsdale JP, came to

Cardiff in 1870. UM had a number of chapels, most of which were damaged in World War II. All but Penarth Road (1893) had disappeared by 1970.

WM Conference Handbook 1911

MRH

Cargill, David (1809–43; e.m. 1832) and **Margaret Cargill** (*née* Smith, 1809–40), missionaries in *Tonga and *Fiji. Their arrival in Tonga after a 16-month journey coincided with a charismatic awakening. A graduate of Aberdeen (the WMMS's first graduate missionary), he took up the translations work begun by other missionaries. In 1835 they and W. *Cross launched a mission in Fiji, where Christians from Tahiti and Tonga had begun preaching. After four years on the island of Lakemba they moved in 1839 to Rewa on Vita Levu. Supply schooners were unreliable and mail often took two years. Repeatedly, both on moving and after hurricanes, they built a home from scratch. In spite of invariable seasickness, six pregnancies and physical weakness, 'Maggie' learned Tongan and Fijian and shared her husband's ministry amid local intrigue, warfare and cannibalism. After her death he went through much mental suffering, but remarried while on furlough in England. He died by his own hand in Vava'u, Fiji, soon after his return to the Pacific.

M. Dickson (1976); J. Telford (1895) pp. 91–104

JRP

Caribbean and the Americas *see* **West Indies**

Carlisle   JW paid 12 visits between 1764 and 1790. It became the head of a circuit in 1801 and was the head of a District from 1805. There has been Methodist worship in Fisher Street since 1785. The first chapel was replaced on a new site in 1817; this in turn was rebuilt as the Central Hall in 1923, its first minister being G.B. *Evens. PM began in a hat warehouse in 1822; a circuit was formed the following year. Willowholme chapel (1826) proved unsuitable and was superseded by Cecil Street chapel in 1852 (closed 1966). Early WMA enthusiasm led to the building of Lowther Street Tabernacle (1836; closed 1933), a cause later boosted by an influx of WR. The post-Union Carlisle District was renamed Cumbria in 1978.

EL

Carr, Ann (1783–1841) joined the WMs at 18 and with her friend Sarah Eland led revivals. In 1818 she began preaching for the PMs in *Hull and with Sarah Eland and Martha Williams was sent to *Leeds, probably as revivalists. But unwilling to accept circuit discipline they seceded and started the Female Revivalist Society. 'Ann Carr's Chapel' in Leyland, opened in 1825, was noted for its social work. On her death she bequeathed the property to Martha Williams on condition she continued the work.

M. Williams (1841); D.C. Dews (1982)

EDG

Carter, Henry, CBE (1874–1951; e.m. 1901) was born in *Plymouth and worked for ten years for a firm of ironmongers in *Cardiff before training at *Handsworth College. As a Secretary of the *Temperance Committee, 1911–19 and the Temperance and Social Welfare Department, 1919–42 he was a keen advocate of total abstinence and created an ecumenical Temperance Council. He was made CBE for his work on the legislative control of the drink trade. He expanded the agendas of his Department to cover many related social concerns. A pacifist, he founded the *Methodist Peace Fellowship in 1933 and was much involved in refugee relief work after World War II.

MR 28 June 1951

KGG

Carvosso, William (1750–1834), saintly Cornish revivalist, began to associate with the Methodists through his sister's influence and in revulsion against the cock-fighting and Sabbath-breaking prevalent in his day. He was soundly converted in 1771. He gave up farming to move around the Cornish countryside visiting classes, sometimes as many as eleven in a week. He compensated for his lack of formal education by his evangelical fervour. His memoirs (edited by his son, 1860), a classic WM biography, give one of the most vivid accounts of an early Methodist class leader. His son **Benjamin Carvosso** (1789–1854; e.m. 1814) was a pioneer WM missionary in *Australia and served in New South Wales and Tasmania from 1820 to 1830, opening the new chapel in Hobart in 1825. He was the main instigator of the *Australian Magazine*, the earliest Methodist periodical and literary journal on that continent. Its suppression by the Missionary Committee in London was resented by the Australians. Ill-health compelled his return to England in 1830.

WMM 1835 p. 156; L.F. Church (1948) pp. 104–6, 133–5, 165–6; T. Shaw (1967) pp. 50–1; F&H 3

EWD

Castillo, John (1792–1845), WM local preacher and author, brought from Ireland to Lealholm Bridge (Yorks) at the age of 3. He became a stonemason and was converted from Roman Catholicism in 1818. Impressed by the spoken dialect of his evangelical seniors under whose influence he became a preacher, he began to use it in his writing. The standard edition of his work was *Poems in the North Yorkshire Dialect* (1878). Stanzas of his most memorable poem, *Awd Isaac*, could still be repeated by local countrymen a century after its first appearance in 1832.

––––––––

MR(W) 1896, pp. 31–3; WHS(Y) no. 9 (1966) pp. 4–8

CJS

Castlebar (Co. Mayo), a county town in the West of Ireland, was visited by JW 14 times between 1756 and 1789. In 1763 it was one of the first seven circuits into which the Irish societies were divided. It covered the whole province of Connacht and neighbouring counties and took the itinerant six weeks to visit all the societies and keep his appointments, with only three days in the circuit town. It has the only chapel in Ireland of which JW laid the foundation stone (in 1785). Work there ceased in 1959; the chapel was leased, and sold in 1992.

JWJ
DALC

Caughey, James (1810–91), an Irish Presbyterian who renounced *Calvinism after emigrating to the USA. He became an MEC preacher, widely known on both sides of the Atlantic as a travelling evangelist and revivalist. English Methodists differed sharply in their views on him, partly because he was independent of connexional discipline. His extravagant oratory contrasted with the more formal style of other preachers of the time. Conflict reached a peak in 1847 when he was denied the use of WM pulpits and premises.

––––––––

R. Carwardine (1978); J. Kent (1978)

NWT

Cennick, John (1718–55) was born in *Reading, where JW first met him in March 1739. He became one of W's first lay preachers in the *Bristol area and was the cause of a 'great awakening' in north Wiltshire. The evidence for his involvement in the colliers' school in *Kingswood is more problematical. By the end of 1740 he had become more closely associated with the *Calvinists and G. *Whitefield. After a visit to the *Moravians in Germany, he was ordained as a Moravian deacon in London in 1749 and served as a minuister in *Dublin His reference in a sermon to 'the Babe that lay in swaddling clouts' is said to have led to the Irish Methodists being dubbed 'Swaddlers'. He published sermons and three collections of hymns, but of his three hymns in *MHB* (1933) only the evening hymn 'Ere I sleep' has survived into *HP*.

––––––––

F. Baker in *PWHS* 28 pp. 149–50; A.G. Ives (1970) pp. 231–2

JAV

Centenary Fund, established by the WM Conference to mark the centenary of the first Methodist societies in 1739. (Noticeably, there was no celebration of the centenary of JW's Aldersgate Street 'conversion'.) £222,589 (approximately £10m today) was raised. The major allocations included Foreign Missions and Centenary Hall as the London headquarters of the WMMS, the Theological Institution and the Chapel Fund. Another Centenary Fund, created by the MNC in 1897, raised some £100,000 (approximately £6m today) and was used mainly for work in circuits, but also for connexional projects.

DRF

Centenary Hall *see* **Mission House**

Central Finance Board was set up under the Methodist Church Funds Act of 1960 and was given much greater freedom to invest in equities than had previously been allowed. Charitable funds were greatly restricted at that time, with a high emphasis on fixed-interest funds. Local Churches were encouraged to invest their various funds with the Board, with a choice of different types of investment, all managed by experts. Within a year or two the funds had risen to several million pounds and by 1997 £660m was managed on behalf of local churches and connexional funds. The Board was also charged with managing a Covenant scheme which took advantage of the provisions of successive Chancellors of the Exchequer to recover tax paid on gifts and donations received under deed of covenant or the Gift Aid arrangements.

DRF

Central Halls *see* **Architecture; Forward Movement**

Ceramics The closing decades of JW's life coincided with the development of the Staffordshire pottery industry. On one of his visits to the area, probably in 1781, he gave five sittings to the young and gifted Burslem potter E. *Wood. Many factories from the early nineteenth century to the present day have copied the resulting bust. One of the earliest potters to represent JW was Josiah Wedgwood with basalt intaglios and jasper portrait medallions produced around 1775. Around 1840 Minton produced both bisque, parian and earthenware figures of JW. From the time of the WM Centenary in 1839 potters in Staffordshire, North East England, Yorkshire and South Wales produced not only busts but representations of JW on plaques, crockery and figures, e.g. in a pulpit. (There were also ceramic money boxes in the shape of a WM chapel, medals, Stephengraph silk bookmarks, silk pictures, love-feast cups, chapel crockery with transfers of JW, ceramic and metal silhouette figures of DRV standing by his mother's grave, a large parian representation of the same subject, iron door stops, ceramic window stops, scent bottles, profile pictures in wax, ivory or metal, letter seals, prints, etc.)

In the National Portrait Gallery is a marble bust of JW attributed to Roubillac (d.1762) which was reproduced in parian a century later. Wesley items are still being made, some from early moulds, copies of early figures and busts, and others newly modelled.

Other Methodist figures commemorated in ceramic include CW, G. *Whitefield, A. *Clarke, J. *Fletcher, H. *Bourne, W. *Clowes and J. *Bryan. The only other Methodist denomination to produce a significant number of ceramic busts, crockery and commemorative ware was the PM Church. Plates were produced only 20 years after the denomination was founded, with special commemorative plates and other crockery for the centenaries of the first *camp meeting (1907) and of the PM Connexion (1910), along with busts of H. *Bourne and W. *Clowes.

Important displays can be seen at the Museum of Methodism, *Wesley's Chapel, London, and at *Epworth Old Rectory (both of which include items from the Botteley collection); also the *New Room, Bristol, Mount Zion, Ogden, *Halifax (the Horace Hird Collection), and Parc Howard, Llanelli.

R. Lee (1988)

DHR

Ceylon see Sri Lanka

Chadwick, Samuel (1860–1932; e.m. 1886), WM minister, was the leading Methodist evangelical preacher of his time, linking with the *holi-

ness tradition on which he had a profound influence, not least in his concern for social action. He came of humble origins in Burnley. His time as a lay agent at Stacksteads in *Rossendale before being accepted, at the second attempt, for the WM ministry in 1883, was normative for his later tactics. At *Didsbury College the influence of Dr W.B. *Pope was great and he learned his technique of expository preaching while in *Glasgow. He had a notable ministry at Oxford Place in the *Leeds Mission (1894–1907), where he combined a fervent evangelistic and teaching ministry with Bible study a deep concern for poverty and deprivation. He also developed Lenten devotions, being expert in Catholic spirituality. Membership rose from 294 in 1894 to 957 in 1907.

From 1907 to 1932 he was Tutor, then Principal of *Cliff College. His regime was firmly Methodist with a happy, almost Franciscan style of spirituality. The 'Cliff Trekkers' of the 1920s were very much in the Chadwick style. The *Southport Convention was a significant part of his influence. As Chairman of the Sheffield District, 1911–26, he pioneered the South Yorkshire Coalfields Mission (1912). He was President of the Conference in 1918 and later President of the National Council of Evangelical Free Churches. He was editor of *Joyful News, where much of his writing is to be found. While never obscurantist – a 'high church evangelical Methodist' – he roundly criticized the Churches for missing the opportunity to evangelize the nation after World War I and for forgetting that learning without fervour and spirituality is deadening.

MR(W) 1897 pp. 43–7; MR 20 Oct. 1932; Dunning (1933); K.E. Bowden (1982); D.H. Howarth (1983)

JMT

Chairman see District Synod; Districts

Champness, Thomas (1832–1905; e.m. 1857), WM minister and evangelist, was born in Stratford, East London and brought up in *Manchester. Converted in *Stockport, he was called to preach in 1856. Accepted for the ministry the following year, he was sent without college training to *Sierra Leone, where he served as a missionary until ill health forced him home in 1863. After serving as assistant to G. *Osborn at the WMMS, he embarked on a circuit ministry in 1865. In 1878 he was appointed Newcastle District Missionary, moving to *Bolton in 1882. While there he embarked on evangelistic publication as editor of *Joyful News. Moving to *Rochdale, he opened

his home as a Centre for training evangelists. In 1889 he was released from circuit work and made Castleton Hall the centre for his publishing and evangelistic activity, the 'Joyful News Mission'. He published *The Mission Minstrel or Songs of Saving Grace* (1895) and many homely works for spiritual revival. He preached widely and campaigned for temperance throughout the Connexion until his retirement in 1903. A Chapel was built in his memory in Rochdale.

MR 2 & 9 Nov. 1905; J. Mee (1906); E.M. Champness (1907); J.I. Brice (1934); T.D. Meadley (1983)

TSAM

Channel Islands   Two Jerseymen involved in the fishery trade with Newfoundland were influenced by L. *Coughlan's ministry and on their return home formed the first Methodist society in 1774. In 1783 R C. *Brackenbury responded to an appeal for a bilingual preacher and spent the next seven years in the islands, supported by the native preacher J. *de Quetteville. T. *Coke visited him at the beginning of 1786 and the Channel Islands were one of the areas included in his missionary *Address* of that year. A. *Clarke was sent out as a second preacher and JW himself paid a visit in 1787. In the early days the movement spread despite great opposition. Military service was compulsory during the Napoleonic wars and Methodists were fined or imprisoned for conscientious objection to Sunday exercises, until Coke successfully intervened on their behalf with the Government.

In Jersey the medieval 'Chapelle de Notre Dame des Pas' was purchased in 1782 and the first chapel built in 1809. Separate English and French circuits existed until 1947. A BC mission was launched in 1823 and PM work began in 1832. A single Methodist circuit was formed in 1960. In 1976 a joint Anglican/Methodist 'Communicare Centre' was opened.

Jerseyman Pierre Arrivé, then living in Guernsey, heard of the movement and while visiting Jersey was taken to a class meeting. Converted, he invited Brackenbury to visit Guerney. The first chapel was opened in 1789. There were separate French and English circuits. The BCs opened a chapel in 1826; PM work began in 1832 and amalgamated with the WM English Circuit in 1933. A single island circuit was not established until 1976. The first chapel in Alderney was opened in 1790 and in Sark in 1797. Both are within the oversight of the Bailiwick of Guernsey Circuit, but in 1991 they became the responsibility of the Channel Islands District.

MR 1903 pp. 61–2; F. Guiton (1846); M. Lelièvre (1885); R D. Moore (1952)

FLeB

Channon, Thomas, a Methodist soldier who, while quartered in *Dunbar in 1759, was asked to teach the inhabitants 'church-musick' and when in *Aberdeen taught the congregation of Monymusk Kirk the novel style of four-part singing by 1761. This took on and he was invited to introduce it in other kirks, providing perhaps the most fruitful effect of Methodism on the Scottish Church in that century.

A.F. Walls (1973) p. 6

MB

Chapel Affairs   JW's injunction was: 'Let all preaching places be built plain and decent, but no more expensive than is absolutely unavoidable.' But by the early nineteenth century WM chapel debts were becoming burdensome. As early as 1817 a Fund for Distressed Chapels was instituted, followed in 1827 by a Chapel Loans Fund, to which some of the better-placed Trusts contributed. But the first Chapel Committee was not appointed until 1854, when William Kelk (1795–1866; e.m. 1820) submitted a paper on 'Our Chapel Debts' and was appointed the first full-time Chapel Committee Secretary. The first PM Chapel Committee and General Chapel Fund had been set up as early as 1831. (H. *Bourne wanted simple buildings that could easily be converted to cottages should the need arise.) The BCs, MNC and UMFC all made similar provision. Following the 1932 *Union a Chapel Affairs Department was established in *Manchester, where the WM committee had been based since 1855. In 1973 this became the Property Division and from 1996 the Property Committee. This not only scrutinizes and advises on local schemes, but includes experts on legal and financial matters and is concerned with the link between architecture and theology.

See also **Architecture**; **Trustees**

JAV/PAK

Chapel Aid Association (Methodist) was launched within PM in 1890 to assist debt-ridden chapels by offering them long-term loans at 3.75% interest. A group of forward-looking ministers and laymen conceived the scheme, but its implementation and success were largely due to the business acumen, integrity and generosity of W.P.

*Hartley, its first chairman (1890–1922). The Association raised its funds from personal deposits, so that it became in effect the PM savings bank, offering an attractive 3.5% Despite the tiny margin of profit, it enjoyed considerable success and did much to ease the burden of debt which had plagued PM in the later nineteenth century. No comparable organization existed in the other Methodist bodies and in 1932 the Association enlarged its scope by offering its services to Methodism as a whole, as it has continued to do. From the outset its offices have been in *York, shared originally with the PM Insurance Company which predated it by 24 years and in some important respects provided a model for it.

———

G.E. Milburn (1990)

GEM

Chapel Stewards   In order to carry out their responsibilities, the *trustees appointed their own stewards who received and disbursed seat rents and organized collections for the reduction of debt. The resulting division of authority and responsibilities between the Leaders and the Trustees was sometimes unfortunate. Since autonomous local trusts were abolished by the *Methodist Church Act of 1976, these stewards have become Property Stewards responsible to the *Church Council.

———

Minutes, 1794; *CPD* vol. 2 bk III, SO 941

MB

Chaplaincies *see* **Armed Forces**; **Higher education**; **Industrial chaplaincy**; **Residential schools**

Chapple, Frederick (1845–1924), WM teacher, born in London. Although his parents were Presbyterians, he was sent to a WM day school and was converted during a mission led by the Rev John Smith. He became a pupil-teacher at the school at 14, attained degrees in both Arts and Science at London University and trained at *Westminster College. From 1876 to 1914 he was headmaster of Prince Alfred College, Adelaide and developed the school on English Public School principles, with strong emphases on both academic and sporting success, so that it became one of the leading schools in South Australia. He believed in a 'muscular Christianity', the authority of Scripture and the potential of past and present PAC scholars. In 1894 he experienced a spiritual uplift during a mission led by T. *Cook. He was a member of the Council of the University of Adelaide, edited the *Methodist Journal* and was active in the development of the Adelaide YMCA and Our Boys Institute.

DGH

Charles, Rev. Thomas (1755–1814), Anglican clergyman and *Welsh Calvinistic Methodist leader. He was converted through hearing D. *Rowland preach in 1773. Ordained deacon in 1778, and priested in 1780, he served in various curacies in Somerset until he migrated to Bala in 1783. He was appointed curate of nearby Llanymawddwy in 1784, but owing to his support for the Methodists was soon dismissed. Having thrown in his lot with the Methodists, he made Bala the centre of their activities in North Wales. He established schools and produced literature which included a catechism, a Bible dictionary and a periodical called *Y Drysorfa Ysbrydol* (The Spiritual Treasury). Due to the demand for Welsh Bibles, he worked, with others, towards the establishment of the British and Foreign Bible Society in 1804. In 1811 he took a leading role in the ordinations which marked the secession of Welsh Methodism from the Church of England.

———

D.E. Jenkins (1908); R.T. Jones (1979); *DWB*; *DEB*; *DNB*

GT

'Charlestown Hymn-book'   JW's first *hymn-book, prepared during his ministry in Georgia, was published at Charleston SC in 1737 as *A Collection of Psalms and Hymns*. (He published another with the same title on his return to London the following year, and a third in 1741. The latter, enlarged in 1743, was frequently reprinted, while the Charleston book was forgotten for many years. Only two copies are known to have survived.) The 1737 book was probably the first hymn-book ever published in America and reflected the *Moravian influence JW had encountered on the way to Georgia and also the effect of Isaac Watts on English hymnody. It included 37 hymns by Watts, 6 by George Herbert, 3 by Joseph Addison and one by Thomas Ken; also 9 by JW's father and 5 by his brother Samuel. CW's contribution was still in the future. In August 1737 one of the charges brought against W in Savannah was that he had introduced 'compositions of Psalms and hymns not respected or authorised by any proper judicature.'

———

PWHS 3 pp. 57–63, 14 pp. 3–5, 31 pp. 186–93

JAV

Chartism, a predominantly working-class movement, unsuccessfully petitioned Parliament in 1839, 1842 and 1848 for the People's Charter with its celebrated six points: universal manhood suffrage, equal electoral districts, annual Parliaments, payment of MPs, secret ballots and no property qualifications for MPs. All the Methodist connexional authorities dissociated themselves from the movement and a member of the WM Conference of 1839 was enthusiastically applauded when he proclaimed that he 'should be sorry if we fraternize with Chartists'. For their part, Chartist leaders viewed Methodism with disdain. Feargus O'Connor dismissed it as 'the religion of retail and shop', while R G. Gammage, the Chartist historian, declared that 'if there is a body of men in England who . . . uphold principles of despotism, that body is the Wesleyan Conference.' Some Methodist historians, however, notably R F. *Wearmouth, have emphasized the influence of Methodism upon Chartist leadership and organization and identified ex-Methodists among its grass-roots supporters. Others, such as M.S. Edwards, have argued that Methodist involvement was untypical and that Chartism was largely secular in 'inspiration and outlook'.

Only rarely are the religious affiliations of Chartists revealed in contemporary evidence. Of 73 Chartist prisoners questioned in 1840–41, 15 were Methodists, the largest group apart from Anglicans (which may have included a number of sceptics). The involvement of a minority of former ministers and local preachers is more fully documented. The former included J.R *Stephens, J. *Barker and J. *Skevington; and the latter T. *Cooper (WM) and John Markham (PM) of *Leicester, J. *Capper (PM), B. *Rushton (MNC) and William Thornton (WM) of *Halifax, and W. *Lovett.

R F. Wearmouth (1948); M.S. Edwards in *LQHR*, 1966 pp. 301–10; N.A.D. Scotland in WHS(B) Bulletin 77 (1997)

JAH

Checkland, Sir Michael (1936–), Vice-President of the Conference, 1997, took a degree in history at Oxford and became an accountant. He joined the BBC in 1964 and was its Director-General 1987–92, a period of radical change. Among various other offices, he is Chairman of *NCH.

MR 19 June 1997

JAV

Cheltenham G. *Whitefield preached in 1739 in what he described as 'a poor struggling hamlet, with a few thatched cottages'. The town did not grow in style and prominence till the end of the century, and in population between 1801 and 1831. Ebenezer, the first purpose-built chapel, dates from 1813; Wesley Chapel (1839) was one of a hundred built to mark the centenary of Methodism. Both still stand, converted to residential use. Cheltenham became head of a WM circuit in 1813 and united with Tewkesbury Circuit in 1991.

The PM presence, from about 1840, was slight. They took over Ebenezer chapel in 1859 and used it until 1934. There is some evidence of WMA activity in the town about 1840, with an imposing chapel in the town centre from 1865 to 1936.

DFM

Cheshunt College *see* **Trevecka**

Chester Methodism was introduced by J. *Bennet in 1747. JW's visits, from 1752 on, were generally made *en route* to Ireland, sailing from Parkgate on the Wirral. By 1765 the society was confident and wealthy enough to erect an octagon chapel seating 600 and a preacher's house. Services were not held in church hours until 1806. Chester became the head of a circuit, covering the western half of the county, in 1764. J. *Crawfoot recollected JW's use of the term 'primitive Methodists' on his last visit in 1790. St John Street WM church was opened in 1812. The MNC maintained a precarious existence throughout the nineteenth century and its Conference met in the city five times between 1811 and 1856. PM established a strong presence from 1819 onwards. A chapel was opened in Steam-Mill Street in 1823 and several new ones in the late nineteenth century: Tarvin Road (1884), George Street (1888) and Hunter Street (1899)), each of which became head of a circuit. The PM Conference met there in 1894. At the time of *Methodist Union there were one WM and three PM circuits. The former WM church in City Road was converted into a Central Hall in 1933.

F.F. Bretherton (1903); *Chester PM Centenary 1819–1919* (Chester, 1919); Conference Handbook 1939, 1949

EAR

Chester, Harold Guylee, OBE (1887–1973), a grandson of a UMFC minister, Samuel Chester (1824–97; e.m. 1860) was a member of Lloyd's for 70 years. He was a generous benefactor to Methodism and other causes and Vice-President of the Conference in 1954. After his wife's death he gave their intended residence at Muswell Hill to the local church for community use. Deeply committed to young people, he was Treasurer of the Youth Department throughout its existence. When its lease in Ludgate Circus ended, he established Chester House, a young people's hostel and departmental offices next door to his home, Hazlehyrst. The bequest of the latter completed North Bank Estate as Methodist property. Extensive grounds, long-time home of a tennis club, now also include *MHA residential and sheltered accommodation and the rebuilt local church.

See also **Youth Work**

MR 8 July 1954, 25 Oct. & 15 Nov. 1973

CHS

Chew, Richard (1827–1905; e.m. 1847), WMA minister who spent most of his ministry in the north of England and was chiefly known as an administrator. He was a member of the Connexional Committee for 35 consecutive years and was twice elected President of the Assembly (1867 and 1881). He wrote the standard biographies of J. *Everett (1875) and W. *Griffith (1885).

G.J. Stevenson (1884–86) pp. 1008–14; E. Boaden (1896)

OAB

Chichester A Countess of Huntingdon chapel was built in 1774, but WM did not reach the city until 1790, when R.C. *Brackenbury, after an overnight stay, preached from his carriage drawn up by the Market Cross. There is no evidence of a society being formed until 1804 when a local schoolmaster, William Woodroffe Phillips, registered a room in his house in North Pallant. Chichester became part of the Lewes and Brighton Mission and in 1810, with 12 members, was given its own missioner, though it did not become fully independent until 1815. The first chapel was built in East Walls in 1818 and rebuilt as Centenary Chapel in 1840. Stalwart leadership through the middle years of the century was given by William Ballard, landlord of the Dolphin Hotel, and his wife Maria, sister of Dr G. *Osborn. In 1877 the society moved to a new chapel in Southgate, designed by A. *Lauder.

The first BC preacher, M. *Toms, came over from the Isle of Wight in 1833, and a missionary was appointed in 1834. Bethel chapel in Orchard Street opened in 1836. The Leng family provided

leadership for many years and in 1865 a new Jubilee chapel was built in The Hornet (closed 1968). PM preachers came from Buriton in the 1860s and opened a chapel at Fishbourne in 1872 (closed 1971). Chichester was made a separate station in 1874 and its Broyle Road chapel (in the working-class Summerstown area) opened the following year, but only after the wife of the missioner, Sarah Clarke, had been killed by a bottle thrown during disturbances. For some years before *Methodist Union Chichester was part of the Portsmouth PM Circuit. The Broyle Road chapel closed in 1956. In 1982 the Methodist/URC Christ Church premises were opened on the site of the former Southgate chapel.

J. & H. Vickers (1977)

JAV

Childe, Donald Braithwaite (1901–93; e.m. 1929), WM missionary, designated to South *China in 1930. He served as District Chairman and was interned by the Japanese, 1942–45. He went back to China in 1947, then returned to England to serve as MMS Secretary for China and Burma, 1949–65, and also for India and Ceylon from 1959. With China closed to missionaries, he initiated new work among the Chinese of South East Asia.

MR 5 Aug. 1993; G.R. Senior (1995)

GRS

Children Eighteenth-century children were seen and treated as small adults and in evangelical and Methodist circles this was intensified by an almost obsessive concern for their salvation. The Wesley children learned the Lord's Prayer from their mother as soon as they could talk. As they grew up, she taught them in turn, insisting that the girls learnt to read before they began needlework, and held regular conversations with them. In a letter of 24 July 1732 she gave JW a detailed account of her methods. His awareness of children's needs, particularly in the new urban environments, led to the establishment of day schools for poor children at *Kingswood, the *New Room and the *Foundery and, in 1748, the first residential school at *Kingswood. JW urged his preachers to relate to children, to encourage their parents and to preach about education. CW's hymns provided prayers for parents ('for grace to guide what grace has given') and for children ('to train and bring them up for heaven').

Between 1800 and 1950 millions of children passed through Methodist *Sunday Schools. *Day schools flourished from 1837 until 1902 and further *residential schools, beginning with *Woodhouse Grove School in 1811, were established. T.B. *Stephenson founded the *NCHO in 1869. The Methodist Church is involved in ecumenical and voluntary organizations for the well-being of children: toddlers' clubs, playgroups and Shell Groups (for mixed 7 to 11s) exist in many churches. After the Children's Act (1989) child protection guidelines were applied to Church life. Most recently, parenthood training and the result of a study project on Afro-Caribbean spirituality in this country are contributing to the direction and quality of future work with children.

The section 'For little Children' in *MHB* (1933) acknowledged their place in *public worship. In new areas, churches have often developed from work with children. Infant *baptism, the sacrament of belonging to the Church, is the basis of all-age worship and of sensitivity to children's spirituality. Children 'received into the congregation of Christ's flock', and thus accepted for themselves, are regarded as capable of worship and of contributing to it. The *Big Blue Planet* song-book (1995) offers contemporary material for this purpose.

See also **Education**; **Sunday Schools**; **Youth Work**

L.F. Church (1948) pp. 236–46; P. Sangster (1963); J.A. Newton (1968); D.S. Hubery (1977)
CHS

China When British Methodism withdrew from China in the early 1950s, its work was spread over seven Districts. Three were started by the WMMS (South China, Hubei and Hunan); and four by the three bodies which became the *United Methodist Church in 1907: the MNC (North China), the UMFC (Ningbo and Wenzhou) and the BC (South West China). The first British Methodist missionary to China was G. *Piercy of the WMMS, who arrived in *Hong Kong in January 1851. He was followed by many distinguished workers, including D. *Hill of Hubei and S. *Pollard of South West China. Medical work began with the arrival in Hankou of Dr F.P. *Smith in 1864. The Sino-Japanese war (1937–45) brought disruption to the Church and 70 missionary workers were interned by the Japanese. With the capitulation of Japan, civil war broke out between Chinese Nationalists (Kuomintang) and Communists and the resulting Communist victory led to the severing of ties with foreign mission boards. By the end of 1951, a century after Piercy's arrival, all British missionary workers had withdrawn from China. A survey in 1950 indicated that there were 21,000 full members and a Christian community of 57,000 in the Chinese Methodist Church. Under Communist rule Chinese Christianity became self-governing, self-supporting and self-propagating and contact with the outside world was lost until 1978.

F&H 5 pp. 421–562; Mrs T. Butler (1924); Smith, Swallow & Treffry (1932); G.R. Senior (1994)
GRS

Choirs The hearty congregational singing of the Methodist Revival inevitably led to the formation of choirs (referred to in the early days as 'the singers'), which in some cases became quite large by the late nineteenth century. JW approved of anthems, provided they were not of a fugueing type, and included simple ones in some of his hymn-books (e.g. in *Sacred Harmony*, 1780). But he and his preachers sometimes had problems with their choirs (e.g. at *Warrington in 1781), rather like those experienced in the Anglican Church. This became more pronounced after his death and the *Large Minutes of 1797 forbade both anthems and organs without Conference permission. But anthems were popular with congregations and that same year a collection of 'Hymns, Odes and Anthems as sung at the Methodist Chapels in the *Sheffield, Rotherham, *Doncaster and *Nottingham Circuits' was published. This issue was debated again by Conference in 1805 and 1815. Some writers consider that congregational singing deteriorated with greater dependence on organs and choirs towards the end of the nineteenth century; but the more recent steady decline in choirs and four-part singing did not mean a resurgence in congregational song; rather, the emergence of music groups which often sang in unison.

Methodism and Music' in P.A. Scholes (1938); Miriam Tuckwell in *MCMS Bulletin*, July 1978
PLC

'Christ and the Cosmos' *see* **Gowland, W.**; **Science**

Christian Advocate (1830–39), the first British Methodist newspaper, angered the WM leadership by attacking *Bunting's alleged vote for a pro-slavery candidate in the 1832 election. Its editor John Stephens (brother of J.R. *Stephens) became a Wesleyan Reformer and the paper openly sided with S. *Warren (1834–36). It also suffered through its more discreet support of the editor's brother, since WR was not over-sympathetic to factory reform. Two changes of editor made it less Methodist-centred, but did not improve its fortunes, and it merged with the *Patriot* in 1839.

MSE

Christian Brethren In 1841 the MNC Conference expelled two preachers, J. *Barker and William Trotter, for doctrinal reasons. Barker's followers formed themselves into churches, taking the name 'Christian Brethren'. They opposed a 'hired ministry' and believed in the complete equality of all members. Other characteristics were pacifism, refusal to take oaths, the rejection of force as means of government and, in some cases, refusal to accept laws and government. At its height the movement had about 200 churches, but its later history is lost in obscurity. Some churches became Unitarian and others UMFC or BC.

The name 'Christian Brethren' was also used by some churches in Yorkshire which seceded from local WM, MNC or PM churches and adopted free gospel principles. It is doubtful whether they had any connection with Barker's movement. They eventually became IM and a few still continue.

H. McLachlan (1923)

JAD

Christian Citizenship *see* **Social Responsibility**

Christian Commando Campaigns C.A. *Roberts, Secretary of the HM Department in 1939, was concerned about the shape post-war society would assume. In 1940 Conference adopted a Forward Movement Report recommending plans for evangelistic work over a period, in co-operation with other Free Churches and the CofE where possible. Out of this grew the Commando Campaigns, which adopted the military idea of trained people making forays into places where the gospel was not normally heard – works canteens, cinemas, clubs, pubs, schools, colleges etc. Their theme was 'New Men for a New World'. Roberts provided the Team Leaders and Team Members, but arrangements for campaigns in the larger urban areas were made locally. They reached a climax in Greater London in 1947. Those who participated in the Campaigns found that it profoundly changed the nature of their ministry. W. *Gowland was an outstanding example of this.

C.A. Roberts (1945)

JWH

Christian Community, a philanthropic and worshipping society originally founded by *Huguenots in East London in 1685 and re-organized in 1772 under the patronage of JW. Though independently administered and with their own preaching plan, its members were nevertheless treated as part of the membership of *Wesley's Chapel. Because of their sympathy with the Reformers of 1849, many were expelled in 1850 and the work became totally independent, though there was some link-up with W. *Booth's 'Christian Mission'.

PWHS 20 pp. 98–100

WP

Christian Endeavour, a non-denominational movement inaugurated in *America by the Rev. Francis E. Clarke, a Congregational minister, in 1881. It provided fellowship and training for young people and flourished in England in nonconformist churches, including PM, where it was a parallel movement to the *Wesley Guild. For some years there was a PM *CE Year Book*.

JAV

Christian Lay Churches A body which originated in 1877 as the result of a rift in the *Sunderland PM Circuit. The immediate cause was a proposal to divide the circuit, despite opposition by a substantial number of members. This was finally enforced by the Connexional General Committee. A group of local preachers seceded in protest and established a Church which had no paid ministry. About 200 members followed. By 1882 there were 21 churches in five circuits and the Northern Counties Confederation of Christian Lay Churches was formed. In 1895 the Confederation merged with the IM Connexion and remains a constituent part of it.

G.E. Milburn (1977)

JAD

Christian Library, published by JW in 50 volumes, 1749–55, included extracts from the Early Fathers such as Ignatius and Polycarp, Anglican writers ranging from J. *Taylor to Archbishop Tillotson, Catholic *mystics like Fénelon and Molinos, and Cambridge Platonists such as Cudworth, More and Patrick. Yet he drew most fully on the English Puritans: Robert Bolton, John Preston, John Bunyan, Richard Baxter and many others. He abbreviated and revised his authors, to remove controversial statements and provide consistent Christian instruction. He selected 'the Choicest Pieces of Practical Divinity . . . in the English Tongue', and took advice from the leading Dissenter, P. *Doddridge. In October 1764 he urged: 'in every Society where you have not an experienced preacher, let one of the leaders read the *Notes* [*on the NT*] or the *Christian Library*. The price of the volumes may have limited sales and in 1783, urged to reprint them, W replied, 'I have lost above a hundred pounds by it before: and I cannot well afford to lose another hundred.' A later edition in 30 volumes, edited by T. *Jackson, (1819–27) apparently sold better. The *Library* is a monument to W's keenness to educate his preachers and people, and to his catholicity in drawing so widely on the resources of the Christian tradition.

R.C. Monk (1966); J.C. English in *PWHS* 36 pp. 161–8

JAN

Christian Methodist Church was the name adopted by a small transient group of dissidents in Cheshire who left the Brown Knowl PM society c.1880 over the continuing practice of 'lining out' the hymns. They issued *class tickets and a *preaching plan and held an annual 'tea meeting' similar to the PM *camp meetings. They flourished in the Bickerton area under the leadership of a local preacher, Robert Thomas, but did not survive his death in 1902.

PWHS 37 p. 131

JAV

Christian Mission *see* **Salvation Army**

Christian Perfection was for JW the central emphasis of the Methodist movement; indeed, he believed that it was to spread 'scriptural holiness' that God had providentially raised it up. His doctrine, however, was controversial in his lifetime and has remained so. He argued that it was God's purpose to bring all believers to a state where they no longer sinned, but were 'made perfect in love'. At first he seems to have regarded this as a 'second blessing', given instantaneously. Later he understood that it could be gradually bestowed. He believed, moreover, that the blessing could be lost, so that the believer is as dependent on *grace to retain it as to gain it.

W set out his teaching in his *Plain Account of Christian Perfection* (1766). Recognizing that the notion of 'perfection' is open to misunderstanding, he argued that Christian perfection is compatible with 'sinful' tempers not yet recognized, and with sinning through ignorance, and that it does not involve perfect knowledge. His teaching was vilified by Calvinists who held that a saved person remained always and necessarily a sinner – *simul justus et peccator*. The adequacy of his doctrine of *sin as primarily conscious has also been challenged. It is notable that although JW encouraged his followers to testify when they had experienced Christian perfection, he never claimed it for himself.

See also **Holiness**; **Sanctification**

R.N. Flew (1934); W.E. Sangster (1943); H. Lindstrom (1946)

DJC

Christian Social Union, an unofficial PM organization, originally called the Social Services Union and similar to those in the UM and WM, originated at the Conference of 1906, with the aim of increasing the sense of social responsibility and the social implications of the gospel. S. *Horton was General Secretary and W.E. Curry Organizing Secretary.

See also **Union for Social Service**

DCD

Chubb Family   The house of **Charles Chubb** (d.1804), blacksmith at Breamore, Hants, was licensed for Methodist meetings in 1768. His son **Charles Chubb junr** (1772–1846) started a hardware business in *Winchester, moved to Portsea in 1804 and to London in 1824. He and his brother **Jeremiah Chubb** (b. 1790) patented the detector lock which was virtually unpickable. With his son **John Chubb** (1815–72) he developed a successful lock and safe business, with factories in *London and *Wolverhampton. In 1851 Chubbs made the cage in which the Koh-i-noor diamond was displayed at the Great Exhibition and John Chubb was awarded the Telford Silver Medal for his paper on locks presented to the Institute of Civil Engineers. He served on the WM Education and Missionary Committees, the management committee for *Richmond College and the *Committee of Privileges. He had three sons, who became managing directors of the family firm when it became a private limited company in 1882: **John Charles Chubb** (1846–99), **George Hayter Chubb** (1848–1946) and **Henry Withers Chubb** (1857–1905). George Hayter Chubb married Sarah Vanner *Early in 1870. He was created a knight in 1885, a baronet in 1890 and first Baron Hayter of Chiselhurst in 1927. He served on several connexional committees and was a governor, chairman of governors and treasurer of The *Leys School. It was largely through him that during World War I the WM Soldiers Homes were established. His son **Charles Archibald Chubb**, 2nd Baron Hayter (1871–1967) and his grandson **George Charles Hayter Chubb**, 3rd Baron (b.1911) were both educated at The Leys.

KEC

Chudleigh, Frederick W. (1878–1932; e.m. 1902) was born in *Bristol where he came under the influence of S.E. *Keeble. After training at *Didsbury College, he spent most of his ministry in the East London Mission. From 1906 to 1911 he worked with P. *Thompson at St. George's, Stepney. After five years in the South London Mission, he returned to the East End as minister of *Lycett Memorial Church, Stepney, then as Superintendent of Stepney Central Hall from 1919 until 1932. He had considerable musical gifts and showed much practical concern for the slum children of the neighbourhood. His pioneering Sunday evening film services drew crowds to the Central Hall. Fifteen thousand poor people lined the streets for his funeral and a street was named after him.

MR 25 Feb. 1932; R.G. Burnet (1932); R.G. Burnett (1946) pp. 94–110

JDB

Church, Dr Leslie Frederic (1886–1961; e.m. 1908), WM minister and historian, born at Chester-le-Street. He trained for the ministry at *Headingley College. He taught Church History at *Richmond College 1929–35 and was *Connexional Editor 1935–53. He was a gifted preacher, broadcaster and writer. His *Fernley-Hartley Lecture, published as *The Early Methodist People* (1948) and *More about the Early Methodist People* (1949), were pioneering studies of the Methodist *laity. During his presidential year (1943–4) his house was destroyed in an air-raid, but he continued to serve both the home Church and those serving in the *Armed Forces, for whom he provided books and devotional material.

MR 26 Jan.1961

JAN

Church, Rev. Thomas (1707–56), vicar of Battersea 1740–56 and prebendary of St Paul's from 1744, wrote polemical works against Deism and Methodism. These included a defence of the Anglican doctrine of *regeneration in 1739 and an attack on *Whitefield in 1744. In 1745 he published *Remarks* on the 4th Extract from JW's *Journal* 'shewing ... the many errors relating both to faith and practice which have already arisen among these deluded people'. JW in his *Answer* distanced himself from the *Moravians and dealt with misrepresentations of his teaching on *justification and with charges of *enthusiasm. The following year Church returned to the fray with *Some farther remarks ... together with a few considerations on his 'Farther Appeal'*, to which JW responded in turn with his *Principles of a Methodist Farther Explained*. W deemed him 'a gentleman, a scholar, and a Christian'.

DNB

JAV

Church Council is the body which, since *restructuring in 1974, combines functions previously exercised by the *leaders' meeting and the *trustees and exercises authority and leadership over the whole area of the local church's life. Its functions include the managing trusteeship of local property, the appointment of officers and committees, pastoral oversight (in conjunction with the Pastoral Committee) and the approval of persons to be admitted to *membership.

CPD vol. 2 bk III section 61

SRH

Church of England JW and CW remained *Anglican clergymen to the end, though the former's vision of Methodism as an order within the established Church became less realizable as time went on. JW's own actions, not least his *ordinations, hastened separation. Many of the Methodist people, converts from the new industrial populations or, later, from depressed rural society, had no allegiance to the state Church; it had not provided for them and some of its ministers repelled them from the altar. It has always been a problem for Methodism that there were those who retained Anglican loyalties, emphasized that they were not Nonconformists, cherished Prayer Book worship and turned to the parish church for rites of passage and sometimes for the Sacrament, and others, particularly among the non-

Wesleyans, who owed little to the Establishment except in many cases its contempt.

As early as the 1750s separation from the Church was a living issue, discussed in the Conferences. JW held the line, but at the cost of concessions and irregularities deplored by CW. Proposals put forward by J. *Fletcher and J. *Benson in 1775 with a view to keeping the Methodists within the Established Church proved stillborn. In the decade after JW's death the gulf between 'Church Methodists' and 'new planners' widened and the nineteenth century aggravated the differences. Methodist enthusiasm and noise offended staid and sober Anglicans and seemed to vulgarize the Christian solemnities.

As late as 1868 the Tractarian E.B. *Pusey made fruitless overtures, but as the Oxford Movement developed into Anglo-Catholicism and the Roman hierarchy was restored, Methodists had become fearful of a Roman take-over and increasingly associated with the Nonconformists. As a counterblast to Anglican superiority, they insisted that world-wide Methodism had become far larger than Anglicanism, due to the great numbers of American Methodists and the movement's missionary successes.

Estrangement eventually gave way to *rapprochement*. Parish church worship became more popular in form with the wider use of hymns. Christian Socialism brought Anglicans and Methodists together and those who worked in the cities and the slums were united in social concern. Whereas J.H. *Rigg deplored F. D. Maurice as much as he did J.H. Newman, J.S. *Lidgett was a disciple of the former and Methodists came to admire Anglicans such as Dean Church, 'the Anglican reply to Newman' with his unerring moral judgments. His lecture on Bishop *Butler asserted that, in spite of his horror at claims to special inspiration, Butler had anticipated 'all that was deepest and truest in the Methodist appeal to the heart'. The opening of the ancient universities to non-Anglicans was a decisive step. Shared scholarship meant shared understanding. The revision of the AV in the 1880s brought together Anglican biblical scholars and the Methodist W.F. *Moulton.

In the long term, the *Anglican-Methodist Conversations, following Archbishop Fisher's Cambridge University sermon in 1946, were almost inevitable. Since the failure of the Scheme and the subsequent proposal of 'Covenanting for Unity' (though not necessarily in consequence) both Churches have declined. Due to the divisions in, and decline of, Anglo-Catholicism and the predominance of Anglican evangelicalism, the agenda is now less dominated by questions of ministry. If ecclesiology fails, economics may force the Churches together.

R.W. Church (1895); A.W. Harrison (1945); F. Baker (1970)

GSW

Church of the Nazarene (UK), one of the churches that grew out of the nineteenth-century *Holiness Movement. Now an international denomination affiliated to the World Methodist Council, its British beginnings were simultaneously in *Glasgow and *London in 1906. Dr George Sharpe, a Congregationalist minister strongly committed to the Wesleyan emphasis on Christian holiness, founded the Pentecostal Church of Scotland. Mr David Thomas, a Welsh draper with business at Clapham Junction, organized the International Holiness Mission in Battersea. Both Sharpe and Thomas ardently believed that the new movements were called, in JW's words, to 'spread Scriptural holiness across the land'. In 1915 the Pentecostal Church of Scotland united with the Church of the Nazarene and the International Holiness Mission joined in 1952. The Calvary Holiness Church, formed in 1934, joined in 1955. Wesleyan in its doctrinal convictions, the denomination is congregationalist in church government and holds representative District Assemblies annually. Missionary enterprise is central to the denomination's ethos and ethically it stands in the evangelical Pietist tradition. Its theological college, founded near *Paisley in Scotland in 1944, is now Nazarene Theological College, *Manchester, offering both graduate and post-graduate courses in affiliation with Manchester University.

J. Ford (1968)

HMG

Church Stewards *see* **Society Stewards**

Churchey, Walter (1747–1805), attorney and versifier, and one of the early supporters of English WM in Brecon. A friend of T. *Coke from his schooldays, he began corresponding with JW in 1771 and later claimed to have suggested to him the publication of the *Arminian Magazine* which appeared in 1778. Wesley's letter of 18 October 1777 confirms that they were exchanging views on the subject. A writer of indifferent religious verse, he had an inflated view of his own poetic gift and published several volumes despite the discouraging advice of both JW and William Cowper.

W.I. Morgan in *Brycheiniog* 16 (1972) pp. 79–102; *DNB*; *DWB*; SL, vols 5–8 passim

GT

Circuit By 1746 JW had divided his growing *societies into seven circuits or regional preaching 'rounds', each with an itinerant preacher or '*Assistant' to look after it in his absence. The circuits grew in number and decreased in size year by year. Most had two or more itinerants stationed in them. *Membership figures for each society were reported each year. The itinerants travelled a monthly or six-weekly circuit round all the societies, with only an occasional return to the circuit town. By about 1753 *Quarterly Meetings, consisting of all the circuit and society stewards and preachers, local and itinerant, were being held. The *Circuit Stewards kept the accounts and paid the preachers. At the 1791 Conference circuits were grouped in *Districts under a Chairman to provide the oversight JW had given. The circuit system enabled strong societies to support the weak and preachers to mission new areas as opportunities or invitations occurred. The *Superintendent minister in each circuit was responsible for making the *preaching plan, for chairing circuit committees, including the Quarterly Meeting, and for the exercise of pastoral discipline. Ministers were appointed to (and later invited by) and paid by the circuit, not by individual societies or churches.

All the Methodist denominations adopted the circuit system. PM circuits often had 'Branches' and 'Missions' as part of their growth during the period of rapid proliferation. By the end of the nineteenth century many of them were single-man stations. In the twentieth century circuits have been divided for administrative purposes into sections, each group of churches being in the pastoral care of one minister. Outside the Central Missions pastorates, such as have become commonplace in American Methodism, are almost unknown. Circuit funds are raised mainly by an assessment on local churches, which pays ministerial stipends, travel costs and the provision of manses. A circuit may also have reserve funds to finance future building or other projects.

See also **Itinerancy**

HMGB 1 pp. 231–242; G.T. Brake (1984) pp. 306–7

JHL

Circuit Meeting *see* **Quarterly Meeting**; **Restructuring**

Circuit Stewards In early Methodism the *Assistant appointed from among the *society stewards of the Circuit a 'General Steward' who had responsibility at the *Quarterly Meeting for receiving the quarterly class money from each society and the ticket money collected by the Assistant and for disbursing it, mainly in paying the itinerants' allowances. As their obituaries show, those chosen for this office were usually in easy circumstances, ready to give financial support to struggling societies and itinerants, and experienced office-bearers in the local societies. Today they are called Circuit Stewards and are appointed by the Circuit Meeting, and with the ministers are responsible, like their predecessors, for the spiritual and material well-being of the Circuit.

Minutes, 1797; *WMM* 1813 pp. 306–7; *CPD* vol. 2 bk III section 53

MB

Clapham Family of *Yarm on Tees. **Robert Clapham** (d.1901) was briefly a PM itinerant (1839–46) before establishing a grocery and a rope works in Yarm and Stockton. He was Vice-President of the PM Conference in 1891. His son **John Robert Clapham** (1847–1923) prospered greatly in business and was active in local government, philanthropy and PM. He donated £10,000 to the Itinerant Preachers' Friendly Society in 1919.

G.E. Milburn in *PWHS* 44 pp. 72–3

GEM

Clark, Thomas (1775–1859), musician, was born and spent most of his life in *Canterbury, where he worked as a boot and shoemaker, but spent every spare moment with music and became choirmaster at St. Peter's WM chapel. At the age of 27 he published the first of several sets of 'psalm and hymn tunes', adopting in 1830 the new title *Sacred Gleaner*. In 1837 he was co-editor of the popular *Union Tune-Book* for the Sunday School Union and his *David's Harp* (1843) contained settings of the whole Book of Psalms. His tune 'Cranbrook', set to Doddridge's hymn 'Grace, 'tis a charming sound', has survived as the music of 'Ilkley Moor baht 'at'. His nationwide reputation was clearly seen in the preface written by contemporaries for his *Lyra Sacra* (1840).

H. Wallace (1983)

PLC

Clarke, Dr Adam (*c.* 1760–1832; e.m. 1782), WM minister and polymath. He was born in Co. Londonderry, the son of a schoolmaster. He travelled to England in 1782, met JW in *Bristol and was sent into circuit. Unusually, he was received into full connexion after only one year in the itinerancy. He became a leading figure and a moderating influence in British Methodism after W's death. Three times President of the British Conference (1806, 1814 and 1822), he also presided over the Irish Conference on four occasions.

His scholarship was outstanding and wideranging. His chief reputation was as a linguist, particularly in Middle Eastern and Oriental languages; this enabled him to play an important part in the work of the Bible Society. In 1808 he received an honorary doctorate from Aberdeen and was elected a member of the Geological Society in 1823. He was also a foundation member of the Royal Asiatic Society and was elected to the Royal Irish Academy. In 1808 he was engaged to edit a new and more complete edition of Thomas Rymer's *Foedera*, a collection of State Papers from the time of the Norman Conquest to the accession of George III, a task to which he gave much time during the next decade. His major publication was his eight-volume *Commentary on the Bible* (1810–26), which was enriched by his extensive linguistic studies and was widely used for many years. There was controversy over his unorthodox views on the Eternal Sonship of Christ.

He was a keen advocate of missions at home and overseas, of which he claimed first-hand experience through his service in the *Channel Islands, 1786–89. He supported the moves in 1813–14 to create District missionary societies. In 1818 he undertook the Christian instruction of two Buddhist priests from Ceylon. They were baptized in 1820, but problems arose in Ceylon after their return. In the 1820s he had oversight of the *Shetlands Mission and in 1831 established six mission schools in counties Londonderry and Antrim. He died of cholera and is buried close to JW at *Wesley's Chapel.

Life by 'members of his family' (1833); J.W. Etheridge (1858); S. Dunn (1863); J. Everett (1866); G.J. Stevenson (1884–6) 2 pp. 222–37; M.L. Edwards (1942); R.H. Gallagher (n.d.); N.W. Taggart (1986) pp. 87–103

NWT

Class Leaders *see* **Class Meetings; Leaders' Meeting**

Class Meeting In JW's growing societies, the solution of the problem of exercising adequate pastoral oversight of the members was a byproduct of a financial expedient used to pay off the debt on the *New Room. On the suggestion of a Captain Foy, in 1742 the *Bristol society was divided into 'little companies or classes', each numbering about twelve and having one person responsible for receiving one penny per week from the members and handing it to the stewards. 'Class' implied no teaching element or, at first, any pastoral function, but was simply the English form of the Latin *classis* (division). But almost immediately JW saw its potential, and within a few months other societies were similarly divided and a system established whereby the class was to meet weekly for this pastoral purpose under the leadership of class *leaders. These class meetings gradually increased in significance compared with the *band meetings and attendance at class was a condition of *membership of the society. The class's members were listed on a class paper, later in a class book, with quarterly *class tickets being issued.

The same discipline of meeting in class, and the issue of class tickets, was followed in e.g. MNC and PM from their inception, and the centrality of group fellowship and pastoral care was integral to all branches of Methodism. In the nineteenth century, the class meeting continued as the basic unit for Methodist fellowship and pastoral care. But the system came under considerable pressure, particularly in WM, for two reasons. First, class meetings were criticised in terms of their purpose, content and leadership. Secondly, the rule that church membership was based exclusively upon class membership (and, officially, attendance) excluded many from both membership and office. The system was eventually modified in the 1880s and 1890s. A committee appointed in 1887 reported to the WM Conference of 1889, asserting the essential link between membership and attendance at class. Nevertheless, the traditional basis of class membership was being eroded and was greatly reduced in significance by meeting in class ceasing to be a condition of membership. In 1890 the class-book was replaced by a roll-book of members of the society. Similarly in the MNC the formal conditions of membership in 1889 were relaxed to include attendance at a class, fellowship or church meeting.

The 1932 *Deed of Union emphasized the duty of members to seek to cultivate fellowship, and affirmed the weekly class meeting as having proved to be 'the most effective means of maintaining among Methodists true fellowship in Christian experience'. It provided that all Methodist members should have their names entered on a class book and be placed under the pastoral care of a class leader (the phrase 'or pastoral visitor' being added in 1974). Meetings for fellowship of various kinds have developed (e.g. *Wesley Guilds). The traditional class meeting has continued to decline, although in some churches there are still classes meeting regularly (but not usually weekly). But the continued importance of every member being placed in local pastoral care was recognised by the 1974 addition to the Deed of Union quoted above.

—————

WM *Minutes*, 1890, Report on 'Church Membership and the Class-Meeting'; B.E. Jones in *PWHS* 36 pp. 135–7; *HMGB* 1 pp. 222–3; 3 pp. 158–62; L.F. Church (1948) ch. 4; H.D. Rack in *PWHS* 39 pp. 12–21; D.L. Watson (1985)

SRH

Class Tickets Tickets of membership, first issued in *Bristol in 1741 as 'society tickets', were later known as class tickets and were quarterly until the introduction of an annual ticket in the 1980s. In earlier years, some carried emblems or other decoration and a verse of Scripture. Because they were used to restrict admission to *society meetings, *love-feasts and the *Covenant Service, a large capital letter indicated the quarter of issue. Separate *band tickets were also issued, later superseded by a letter 'b' printed on the class ticket and discontinued in 1880. Some members made a lifelong collection of their tickets and even had them placed in their coffin. In December 1893 the heading 'Wesleyan Methodist Society' was replaced by 'Wesleyan Methodist Church'. (A similar change was made on PM tickets in 1902.) Junior membership tickets, introduced in the late nineteenth century, were discontinued in 1961. Other branches of Methodism issued similar tickets.
See also **Class meeting**; **Membership**

—————

PWHS 1 pp. 129–37; 5 pp. 33–44; 29 pp. 43–5; 31 pp. 2–9, 34–8, 70–3

JAV

Claxton, Marshall, RA (1813–81) was born in *Bolton, the son of a WM minister of the same name, and became a pupil of J. *Jackson. He studied at the Royal Academy from 1831 and first exhibited in 1832. He painted a number of historical and biblical scenes; also scenes from

JW's life, such as the *'Holy Club', the *Wednesbury riots and the deathbed scene ('Holy Triumph', exhibited at the RA in 1842). In 1850 he went to Australia to institute a school of art and stimulate interest in painting, but was unsuccessful and then went to India and Egypt before returning home in 1858. Though an ambitious and industrious painter, he failed to reach the first rank of artists of the period.

—————

DNB; J. Telford (1927)

PSF

Clayton, Albert (1841–1907; e.m. 1862), WM minister who served on many connexional committees and was WM President in 1906. As Secretary of the *Twentieth Century Fund he was largely responsible for its success. Two sons served as missionaries. **Albert C. Clayton** OBE (*c.* 1869–1956; e.m. 1892) served in *India. **George Alfred Clayton** (1870–1947; e.m. 1895) went to Hupeh, China in 1895, serving the Central *China Religious Tract Society 1916–30. He wrote *Methodism in Central China* (1903).

—————

WMM, 1907, pp. 12–13, 778–80; *MR* 19 Sept. 1907, 23 Aug. 1956; 9 Jan.1947

JAV

Clayton, Rev. John (1709–73), son of a *Manchester bookseller, went to Brasenose College, Oxford in 1726, met JW in 1732 and became associated with the *'Holy Club'. At his suggestion they began observing the stationary *fasts on Wednesdays and Fridays. Returning to Manchester in 1733, he was appointed chaplain at the Collegiate Church. A close friend of the non-jurors John Byrom and Dr T. *Deacon, his Jacobite sympathies led to his suspension by the bishop of Chester in 1745 and he opened a school. JW visited him both before and after his Georgia venture, but Clayton distanced himself from the Wesleys after their evangelical conversion. JW heard him read prayers in 1752 and CW heard him preach in 1756, but without any renewal of their friendship.

—————

L. Tyerman (1873) pp. 24–56; *DNB*

JAV

Clegg, George (1839–95), WM industrialist and pioneer of women's ministry. The son of a *Halifax grocer and stone merchant, he assisted his father as a quarry worker. He became bookkeeper for a local textile firm and later formed a highly successful worsted spinning partnership with Abraham Hollingrake. An influential member and Sunday School Superintendent of Rhodes Street WM chapel, *Halifax, he became chapel secretary for the Halifax and Bradford District and a member of the connexional HM Committee. A fervent supporter of the *Holiness Movement, he assured the Conference in 1886 that it was the teaching of holiness that brought conversions every Sunday at his mission room in Halifax. In 1887, after hearing a *Salvation Army girl's testimony, he established a female evangelists' home in Halifax as a branch of the *Joyful News Mission.

JAH

Clegg, William Ernest (1871-post 1947), a PM local preacher in *Leeds, served on the *Methodist Union Committee and was Vice-President of the PM Conference in 1928 and of the Methodist Conference in 1940. A director of an insurance business, he was a Liberal who, after establishing a short-lived party, became a Conservative.

DCD

Cliff College, a small Georgian country house at Calver, near Sheffield, was leased in 1875 by Henry Grattan Guinness for training evangelists for work in the East End of London. In 1903, the property, then called 'Hulmecliffe College' (after its Congregationalist founder James Hulme) was bought by the WM *Home Mission Committee to locate the Joyful News Training Home and Mission, building on the earlier work of T. *Champness in *Rochdale. Its first Principal, T. *Cook, united *holiness teaching with evangelistic zeal. He was succeeded in 1912 by his assistant, S. *Chadwick, the editor of *Joyful News*. Chadwick established the mission teams and developed the summer schools begun by Cook. In the 1920s he began the Whitsuntide meetings, first in *Sheffield and then at Cliff. The summer evangelistic campaigns by 'trekkers' toured the country for two or three months. The first women students were admitted in 1965. More recently, as well as lay training for evangelism and preaching schools, further ministerial education has been provided through an MA in Evangelism. The College is a designated college of the University of Sheffield, offering a range of courses in Evangelism, Missiology and Apologetics. Chadwick's successors as Principal were J.A. *Broadbent (1932–48), J.E. *Eagles (1948–57), T. *Meadley (1957–65), H. *Belben (1965–77), A.S. *Wood (1977–83), William R. Davies (1983–94) and Howard Mellor.

W.F. Moulton (1928); J.I. Brice (1934); D.W. Lambert (1954); A.S. Cresswell (1983)

TSAM

Clogg, Dr Frank Bertram (1884–1955; e.m. 1908) was educated at Emmanuel College, Cambridge and *Richmond College. After three years as Assistant Tutor at the latter, he was in circuit until returning to Richmond College in 1920 as Tutor in NT Language and Literature. He remained there until his retirement, becoming Principal in 1951. He was also a Professor at London University from 1937. Best known for his textbook, *An Introduction to the NT* (1937), a mark of his primary interest in teaching, he also wrote *The Christian Character in the Early Church* (1944).

MR 16 June 1955

CSR

Clough, Benjamin (1791–1853; e.m. 1813), the youngest of the missionaries who accompanied T. *Coke to Ceylon (now *Sti Lanka) in 1814. He was stationed in Galle and Colombo and was Chairman of the South Ceylon District, 1825–37, a time of critical importance for the consolidation of the Methodist presence there, through the building of churches and the founding of schools. He engaged actively with Buddhism, both in dialogue and confrontation, and became a scholar of Sinhala and Pali, stressing the necessity for missionaries to learn about Buddhism through the original languages. He published Sinhalese dictionaries and a Pali grammar.

W.J.T. Small (1964)

EJH

Clough, Dorothea (1889–1971), WM missionary in *India, served in the Hyderabad District 1920–52. As Principal of the Wesley Girls' Middle and Normal Training School, Secunderabad, she gave outstanding service to women's education in the town and District, preparing able girls for higher education. Her crowning achievements were the school's promotion to full High School status and her handing over to the first Indian Principal in 1946. Her last six years were spent in rural schools where many of the staff were her own former pupils.

EMJ

Clowes, William (1780–1851), son of a Tunstall potter, was converted in 1805, spent some time distributing Bibles and tracts and became a WM class leader. He attended the *camp meeting on Mow Cop on May 31, 1807. He preached during the second camp meeting and was placed on the Burslem WM plan as a preacher on trial. Although he was expelled from WM membership in 1810 he continued to preach. He and his followers joined forces with those of H. *Bourne and J. *Steele, and his name appeared as preacher no. 5 on the hand-written preaching plan for Tunstall in 1811. J. *Nixon and Thomas Woodnorth gave him financial support, enabling him to extend his travels into nearby counties, where he established many societies. In 1819 he reached *Hull, and this became the centre from which he extended his travels as far afield as London and Cornwall, until his retirement in 1844. His name is linked with that of H. *Bourne as a founder of the PM Connexion and he was President of the Conference for three successive years, 1844–46. Part of the tension between him and Bourne was due to the fact that, unlike Bourne, he was a powerful and persuasive preacher. He had lived a wild and dissipated life before his conversion, but thereafter revealed a gentle and generous character. A more traditional Methodist than Bourne, he contributed significantly to the rapid growth of the PM movement by his success as an evangelist.

W. Garner (1868); F.H. Hurd (1872) pp. 37–57; G.J. Stevenson (1884–6) 5 pp. 669–84; J.T. Wilkinson (1951)

WL

Clulow, William (d.1811), JW's London solicitor, was the son of John and Elizabeth Clulow of *Macclesfield, where his father was a masterbaker and his mother one of the earliest Methodist converts. He practised as a solicitor from 1783. In 1784 he drafted the *Deed of Declaration in conjunction with T. *Coke. In November 1787 JW had a long conversation with him about the 'execrable' Conventicle Act. Clulow convinced him that it was best to license both chapels and itinerants under the *Toleration Act, describing them simply as 'preachers of the gospel'. He and his mother were witnesses to JW's will.

JAV

Cobban, George Mackenzie (1846–1905; e.m. 1872) was born of Presbyterian stock at Fyvie, Aberdeenshire. He came under Methodist influence in *Manchester, was trained at *Headingley College and in 1876 sailed for *India,

where he made a study of Hindu religious and philosophical literature. Working among Tamils in the Madras area (from 1886 at the Hindu stronghold of Tiruvallur), with his colleague W. *Goudie he pioneered work in the villages. His open-air preaching was particularly effective and he won the confidence of many Hindus, being elected as one of their representatives to the Indian National Congress. Failing health forced him to return home in 1892.

MR 27 April 1905

JAV

Codling, Arthur Dean (1876–1950), son of William E. Codling (1844–1903; e.m. 1865), was born in Lancashire. Educated at *Rydal School and London University, he joined the Civil Service and in 1900 was posted to the Local Government Department in *Dublin. In 1923 he elected to remain there and was transferred to the Department of Finance in the Irish Free State. He was very influential in establishing its standards. He served on the Irish Connexional Committees on Public Questions and Overseas Missions and represented Irish Methodism on the Committee of the MMS. He was secretary of the *Strangers' Friend Society, *Dublin.

D.A.L. Cooney in *DHR*, Spring 1994

DALC

Coke, Dr Thomas (1747–1814), 'father of overseas missions' and bishop of the MEC, was born in Brecon, educated at Jesus College, Oxford, and ordained priest in 1772. He obtained his DCL in 1775, but at Easter 1777 was forced out of his curacy at South Petherton, Som., because of his Methodistical leanings. Having met JW at Kingston St Mary the previous August, he joined the Methodists and became W's right-hand man during his remaining years.

Wesley used him as a trouble-shooter, especially in the disputes over the *chapel deeds at *Birstall, Dewsbury and North Shields, and he helped to draft the *Deed of Declaration. Despite his championing the aspirations of the itinerants, his social and educational superiority made him suspect to many of them. CW deeply resented his enjoyment of his brother's confidence and accused him of self-seeking ambition, especially when he learned of Coke's *'ordination' as 'Superintendent' for *America.

In 1784 Wesley set Coke apart by imposition of hands and sent him out to *America to establish what became the autonomous Methodist Episcopal Church. At the 'Christmas Conference' in Baltimore, F. *Asbury was ordained as fellow-Superintendent (soon changed to 'Bishop' despite Wesley's disapproval). Coke paid eight further visits to America, but was marginalized by his lengthy absences and British citizenship. He did not return after his marriage in 1805. During this period, support for the growing missions, through both personal giving and begging, made enormous demands on his time and energies. His first missionary proposal in 1783/4 foundered for lack of support from JW, but in 1786 his 'Address to the Pious and Benevolent' led to the first Methodist *overseas missions in the *West Indies, as well as in British North America, the *Channel Islands and northern *Scotland.

Although Coke may have seen himself as Wesley's natural successor, he was not elected President until 1797 (and again in 1805), though for some years he alternated with Wesley in presiding over the Irish Conference. Among his publications were a six-volume *Commentary* (1801–7), a *History of the West Indies* (1808–11) and (with H. *Moore) a life of Wesley (1792). He died at sea on his way to fulfil a long-cherished dream of an *Indian mission.

J. Crowther (1815); T. Coke (1816); S. Drew (1817); J.W. Etheridge (1860); J.A. Vickers (1969)

JAV

Colbeck, Thomas (1723–79) of Keighley, Yorks. A grocer and mercer converted by John Wilkinson *c*. 1743. He and Wilkinson established the first Methodist society at *Haworth in 1744–45. JW accepted him as an itinerant in 1748. In that year, with W and *Grimshaw, he faced the fury of the mob at Roughlee and Barrowford. He was in charge of two Classes from 1764 and became Steward of the Haworth Circuit in 1765. 'The refined and gentle Colbeck,' as Grimshaw described him, died of a fever caught while undertaking visitation work.

J.W. Laycock (1909); F. Baker (1963)

SRV

Colchester JW visited the town 20 times, usually en route to *Norwich. There was a Methodist meeting a year prior to his first visit in 1758 and he encouraged them to build the twelve-sided 'great round meeting house' in Maidenburgh Street (1759, rebuilt 1800). When its successor Culver Street chapel (1835) was refronted in 1900 the Trustees resolved that the wording on the

façade be changed from Chapel to Church 'in order to conform with modern usage'. It in turn was replaced by the Castle (1970). In 1768–69 F. *Asbury was in charge of the Colchester Circuit, which had been formed in 1765. The former PM chapel in Artillery Street is now Spurgeon Memorial Evangelical Church, named to commemorate the conversion of Charles Haddon Spurgeon there in 1850.

WHS(LSE) 3 (1966), 50 (1994)

NM

Cole Family Three brothers from Pickering, set up a shop in *Sheffield in 1847. It grew into a large department store, Cole Bros of Fargate, was taken over by Selfridges in 1919 and joined the John Lewis Partnership in 1940. The oldest brother was **John Cole** (1814-after 1896). **Thomas Cole** (1824–1902), a prominent WM, was a *temperance advocate and philanthropist. His son, another **Thomas Cole,** (b.1854) served on six connexional committees and was involved in the building of the Victoria Hall, Sheffield, which he opened in 1908; and his daughter **Annie Littlewood Cole** (1856 1939) married J.V. *Early in 1880. The third brother **Skelton Cole** JP (1827–96) was one of the first laymen elected to the WM Conference (in 1878); he served on the connexional *Education Committee and the *Headingley College committee. His son **Thomas Skelton Cole** (b.1853) was organist at Norfolk Street WM chapel, and his grandson **Maurice Cole** (1890–1980) was treasurer at Victoria Hall and involved with Boys' Brigade and Sunday School.

KEC

Cole, Richard Lee (1878–1963; e.m. 1900), Irish Methodist minister, educated at *Methodist College, Belfast. His circuit ministry was mainly in *Dublin. He became widely known as a preacher and administrator and was involved in educational affairs. He was Secretary of the Irish Conference 1926–32 and President of the Irish Church in 1933. A keen student of history, he gave the WHS Lecture in 1938 on *John Wesley's Journal*. He was made a Fellow of Methodist History by the *WMC in 1956 and was President of the Irish Branch of the *WHS. He supplemented C.H. *Crookshank's history of Irish Methodism with a fourth volume covering the century from 1860 and wrote histories of Dublin Methodism (1932) and of *Wesley College, Dublin (1963).

NWT

Collection of Hymns for the use of the People called Methodists (1780), the most important of the many *hymn-books published by JW, was extolled by B.L. Manning as comparable with the Book of Psalms, the *BCP* and the Canon of the Mass. JW began work on it in September 1773, when he was confined to the *New Room, Bristol by a heavy cold, and took it up again at Tullamore during his Irish tour in 1778. His Preface explains that it was published because of the number of earlier books in use; the most important of these, *Hymns and Spiritual Songs* (1753) being too small (only 84 hymns). All but a few of the hymns are by CW (with some editing by JW). They are 'carefully arranged under proper heads, according to the experience of real Christians' and so amount, in JW's words to 'a little body of experimental [i.e. experiential] and practical divinity'. The central part of the book is a kind of Methodist 'pilgrim's progress', from spiritual awakening through to full salvation. One result of this is the absence of any hymns for use on the great festivals; CW had already written his masterpieces for these, but they were not included until a supplement was added in 1831. A new supplement appeared in 1876 and the *Collection* was not replaced in WM until the entirely new book of 1904. Meanwhile the MNC, WMA and UMFC had all adopted the 1780 book with variations.

B.L. Manning (1942) pp. 7–31; F. Hildebrandt & O.A. Beckerlegge (1983); J.R. Watson (1997) pp. 217–21

JAV

Collection of Psalms and Hymns *see* **'Charlestown Hymn-book'**

Collier, Samuel Francis (1855–1921; e.m. 1879), WM minister, born in Runcorn, the son of a grocer and trained at *Didsbury College. In 1886 he founded the *Manchester and Salford Mission, the earliest and one of the largest of the enterprises of the *Forward Movement. The Mission had 93 members in 1887; by 1902 it had 3,521, with a number of ordained staff and 'Sisters of the People' similar to those in London. He lost no time in combining evangelism with social action, funding and organizing homes, hospitals and other institutions. He became a leading member of the WM *Union for Social Service and featured social concern in his Presidential address in 1913. He was the longest serving in Missions of the 'great three', F.L. *Wiseman and S. *Chadwick being lifelong friends. In 1912 he made a successful visitation of *American Methodism. He died in harness, while still Superintendent of the Manchester Mission.

MR 9 & 16 June 1921; G. Jackson (1923); J. Banks (1996)

JMT

Collins, Rev. Brian Bury (1754–c.1807), evangelical clergyman, born in Stamford. After his father's death, he was brought up by his maternal uncle, Thomas Bury of Linwood Grange, Lincs, went to St. John's College, Cambridge in 1771 and was ordained deacon in 1776. He was dismissed from a curacy at Rauceby and Cranwell, Lincs for *field preaching. In 1778 he was an assistant curate in *Hull and in 1779 was assisting the Rev. J. *Berridge at Everton. About this time he met JW, preaching occasionally for him and the Countess of *Huntingdon, and sought to reconcile the *Arminian and *Calvinistic Methodists. He also assisted the Rev. D. *Simpson at *Macclesfield. In 1781, after refusing the previous year, Bishop Porteus of Chester ordained him priest. His peripatetic ministry took him as far afield as *Bath and *Newcastle and JW found him too independent for comfort. By 1787 their friendship had cooled and he was preaching in the Surrey Chapel, London. He inherited Linwood Grange on his uncle's death in 1799 and took the name Bury. He retired to Westminster and his only son was buried at *Wesley's Chapel in 1807.

G.J. Stevenson (1872) pp. 450–51; *PWHS* 9 pp. 25–35, 49–58, 73–85, 24 pp. 95–8

WL

Collins, Thomas (1810–64; e.m. 1832), WM revivalist and powerful exponent of the doctrine of *holiness, was the last major figure in the strongly revivalistic and mission school associated with W. *Bramwell and J. *Smith. He was widely revered as one who adorned the doctrine he preached. Although he was in difficulty from time to time with the Conference leadership, large increases attended his circuit ministry. Though remaining faithful to WM, he forged friendships with revivalists in other branches of Methodism.

S. Coley (1868)

WP

Colton, Sir John (1823–1902), WM legislator and merchant, born at Habertonford, Devon, the son of a farmer. After working as a harness maker, he emigrated to *Australia and in 1842 began his own saddlery business. In 1859 he was elected to Adelaide City Council and was Mayor in 1874–75. Elected to the House of Assembly in 1862, he introduced a Stamp Duties Bill (the second in Australia) and in 1876 became Premier. He was a trustee of more than 100 WM churches, a Sunday School teacher and local preacher and promoted Methodist policies on social issues. He supported the building of Pirie Street WM Church with the gift of £100 towards the £600 required. The Colton Wing at Prince Alfred College is a memorial to his generosity and the leading part he played in its establishment.

                                                                 DGH

Committee of Privileges The Conference of 1803, faced by the issue of Sunday drilling of militia, answered the question 'How may we guard our religious privileges in these critical times?' by appointing a committee of ten which became known as the Committee of Privileges, annually elected by the Conference. It was also to be consulted prior to the commencement of any law suit in which the connexion was involved. The initial members were two preachers, T. *Coke and J. *Benson, and leading laymen, with T. *Allan appointed as the Conference's 'general solicitor'. It was thus the first 'mixed' (ministerial and lay) committee.

Through Allan it played a very active part in the opposition to the *Sidmouth Bill and in the enactment of the new *Toleration Act (1812). It later acted for the WM Church on various occasions e.g. in opposing the 1839–40 proposals for a State teacher training college and in prosecuting the 1842 Gedney case on burial. It had full power to take action on all national occasions and in all cases affecting the interests, duties, rights or privileges of the Church, subject to Conference resolutions. An acting sub-committee (later 'the Committee of Exigency') was appointed from 1843. Provision was made in 1882 for an extraordinary committee to be convened when deemed expedient, eventually to include lay and ministerial representation from each district.

By 1932 the Committee comprised 20 connexional officers, 15 ministers, 12 laymen from the London area and 10 from the country. Its functions were then assumed by the *General Purposes Committee.

                                                                 SRH

Common Cash With a branch of the Midland Bank conveniently on its site at *Westminster Central Hall, and most of its connexional accounts at that branch, the Church has continued an arrangement dating from 1886 for most of its accounts nominally to be held together, so that overdrawing on one account could be offset by credits in others. Eventually, most connexional money throughout the country joined this scheme and the Church avoided considerable bank charges while earning interest on the overall credit balance.

                                                                 DRF

Communion Stewards *see* **Poor Stewards**

Community House Fellowship *see* **Barker, R.J.**

Community Roll *see* **Membership**

Conference The annual Methodist Conference is the church's supreme legislative body, and is responsible for the oversight of the church's life and for the definition and interpretation of its doctrine.

JW held the first such conference in 1744 with CW, four other Anglican clergymen, and four of his lay preachers who were invited to join them. It lasted for six days, and the business was conducted (as continued for many years in the official courts of Methodism) in question and answer form. It deliberated about 'what to teach, how to teach and what to do i.e. how to regulate our doctrine, discipline and practice'.

Thereafter the Conference was called together annually and increased in size, being composed of certain preachers who were selected and summoned by JW (who normally presided), to 'advise, not govern' him. Other preachers were permitted to attend. It originally met in *London, *Bristol or *Leeds (and *Manchester from 1765). Its business was wide, one main concern being the choice, training, *stationing and *discipline of the preachers in connexion with JW. Discussion of 'temporal affairs' was open to other interested lay people. In 1784, by the *Deed of Declaration, the Conference was legally defined (as the *Legal Hundred) and provision made for the election of the *President and *Secretary, and for the formal Conference resolutions and other acts to be recorded in the 'Journal' (see below).

Following JW's death, the 1791 Conference agreed that all preachers in full connexion should have every privilege possessed by legal members of the Conference, so far as the 1784 Deed allowed (and the more senior preachers acquired the further right to vote for President and Secretary from 1814). It was therefore customary for preachers other than the Legal Hundred to meet and share in the discussions, including those elected by *District Meetings and any *Superintendent who wished to attend. It was not until 1878 that WM lay members were admitted, although there had been 'mixed committees' (beginning with the *Committee of Privileges) previously. Thereafter, a Representative Session met, having equal numbers of ministerial and lay representatives. The ministerial Pastoral Session met separately. Each session dealt with its own exclusive business, but all was subject to ratification by the Legal Hundred.

The other Methodist connexions followed the pattern of annual Conferences (as did the emerging American church). A. *Kilham first advocated lay representation to the Conference, and this became the rule for the *MNC in its conferences from 1797, with *Guardian Representatives providing continuity. The *BCs held their first Conference in 1819 and from 1824 lay representatives from District Meetings attended with the preachers. By their 1831 Deed every fifth conference was to have exact parity of lay and ministerial numbers. The first PM annual Conference was held in 1820, composed of two laymen to each travelling preacher (as later provided in the PM Deed Poll). The Conference came to consist of about 80 members, including 12 permanent ones. Election as representative depended upon seniority, and the Conference came to be seen as lacking in vigour and significance compared with the *District Meetings, at which *ordinations and stationing took place.

The secessions of 1827, 1835 and 1849 all related to the authority to be exercised by the WM Conference and its composition (e.g. the *Warrenite controversy and Lord Lyndhurst's judgment in favour of the Conference's authority). The resulting Methodist groups all formed annual Assemblies or Conferences of mixed representation, but not necessarily with the equivalent authority over the membership. Similarly, from 1806 the Annual Meeting of IM was not a legislative but a deliberative body.

*Methodist Union in 1932 brought together the traditions of WM and PM and that of the UMC (which had adopted a conference of one session, with lay and ministerial parity). The Legal Hundred was dissolved, in favour of a number of Conference-elected representatives to provide continuity. A separate Ministerial Session continued to deal with its exclusive business e.g. as to ministerial candidates, training and discipline, with a Representative Session of equal lay and ministerial numbers having exclusive jurisdiction over many other matters. The post-1932 Conference which numbered 900 people has progress-

ively reduced in size to 384 in 1998. The parity requirement was replaced, with effect from 1998, by a minimum of one-third lay and one-third ministerial representation.

The reduction of the scope of exclusively ministerial business and the introduction of a category of 'shared business', requiring the concurrence of both sessions, was adopted in 1989. In 1998, consequent upon the decisions about the *diaconate, Conference resolved to create a Diaconal Session, with equivalent status and authority to that of the Ministerial Session.

The Journal of the Conference, duly signed and attested, continues to be the official legal record of its acts and proceedings. It is compiled by the Journal Secretary from the Daily Record of the Conference's decisions upon the matters which come to the Conference either through the Agenda (published in advance) or by Notices of Motion brought by members of the Conference. The Daily Record (which dates from 1838 in the WM Conference) is printed daily and circulated to Conference members for approval, with confidential matters dealt with in closed session being recorded only in manuscript form. The *Minutes of Conference, published later, also serves as an Annual Directory. Legislative changes are published in *CPD.

See also **Memorials**

HMGB 1 pp. 242–51; 4 pp. 67–70; W.L. Doughty (1944); B.L. Semmens (1971); Conference Agenda, 1987, pp. 718–41

SRH

Conference Executive Committee see **General Purposes Committee**

Conference Office see **Secretary of the Conference**

Conference Rules of 1835 were a constitutional consequence of the *Leeds Organ Case and the *Warrenite controversy over the Theological Institution. The new rules were set out in a Special Address to the WM societies and covered four basic areas: (1) Financial affairs (2) the expulsion of members (3) meetings for communication with the Conference or on general matters concerning the Connexion and (4) the proposed revision and clarification of the Rules in general. In the case of expulsion from *membership, individuals were provided with more safeguards, including an appeal to the District Meeting which had not been allowed for in 1827. A final appeal to Conference was also possible. The third area was the beginning of *Memorials to Conference from the circuits, though the memorials were to bear the signatures of those who voted for them. (This sowed seeds which came to fruition in the anonymous *Fly Sheets of the 1840s.) It can be argued that the *Pastoral Office was strengthened, though fairly, by these regulations, which did not appease the more liberal element in WM. The historian G. *Smith declared them 'too late and too limited'.

————

G. Smith (1858–61) 3 pp. 344–50 and Appendix P; J.C. Bowmer (1975) pp. 137–44

JMT

Confirmation *see* Membership

Connect see Missionary Magazines

Connexional Editor   JW was his own editor until T. *Olivers was appointed in 1776 as 'Corrector of the Press'. Outstanding among his successors were J. *Benson, J. *Bunting, T. *Jackson, B. *Gregory, J. *Telford and L.F. *Church. The office ceased to be full-time in 1971. For some years his principal task was to edit the (*Wesleyan*) *Methodist Magazine*, but as *publishing expanded so did his duties, until he was an incessant reader of manuscripts, recommender to the Book Committee, corrector of work submitted and writer of editorials. He was in charge of the various connexional periodicals, including magazines for children. His duties were defined in WM in 1904 and again after *Methodist Union in 1932. He was responsible for all the publications of the Publishing House, which involved the selection of readers. He was to seek out competent authors, to aim at 'producing books that will appeal to all sections of Methodists and to the public generally'. He must write good English himself.

His task was a difficult one, with the chance of errors of judgement, sometimes due to the reports of expert readers. Nineteenth-century editors often feared criticism in Conference. There was often a conflict of interest between works of substance and creativity which might be unprofitable and lightweight material, deplored by some, but which sold well.

————

F. Cumbers (1956)

GSW

Connexional Team *see* Restructuring

Connexionalism   In the eighteenth century 'connexion' was a term used generally, in e.g. political, commercial and religious contexts, to refer to the circle of those connected to some person or group, and to the relationship thus created. But it was the particular character of the connexion JW maintained with his *members, his *societies and his *preachers that gave the term its technical significance in Methodism. All were in connexion primarily with him and thence with each other. The 'connexion' came to be in some senses equivalent to 'denomination' and, later, to 'Church', and 'connexionalism' was descriptive of a particular principle and pattern of church life which emphasized the interdependence of the constituent parts (over against independency). The WM Conference of 1891 endorsed the use of the word 'Church' rather than 'Connexion' and it replaced *'Society' on *class tickets in December 1893.

Whilst the various non-WM branches differed in the balance of authority accorded to the various levels of church government, all accepted some form of connexionalism. This was manifested in, for example, a common bond of *discipline and usage for the societies with transferable membership, and the *itinerant ministry of those 'in full connexion' with the Conference and stationed by the Conference.

This connexional principle continues to be intrinsic to Methodism, as a structural expression at all levels of church life of essential interdependence, through fellowship, consultation, government and oversight The Methodist understanding of the nature of the Church is set out in two official statements, *The Nature of the Christian Church* (1937) and *Called to Love and Praise* (1999).

————

B.E. Beck in *ER* 18 (1991) no. 2 pp. 48–59, no. 3 pp. 43–50; Conference Agenda 1995 pp. 195–8

SRH

Conservative Evangelicals in Methodism (CEIM)   was the more scholarly, doctrinally and ethically aware wing of the *Methodist Revival Fellowship, but always shared with the Fellowship in concern for prayer and revival. It provided an annual platform for discussion at its residential conferences and through a widely circulated periodical and occasional papers. Aware of the need for evangelical influence in the wider Church, it fostered opportunities for the evangelical position to be represented in the courts of the Church, especially at the *Conference. In 1987 it joined with the Revival Fellowship to form Headway.

————

A.S. Wood (1987)

WP

Constitutional Practice and Discipline (CPD) This volume was first published in 1951, the outcome of a resolution passed by the Conference in 1946 directing the preparation of a volume summarising the constitution and *discipline of the Methodist Church. The editors were H. *Spencer and E. *Finch and the work was frequently referred to, until 1974, by their names. It included the Standing Orders of the Conference, the framework of which had been adopted by the Uniting Conference in 1932, and which had subsequently been increased and modified and were now re-ordered, together with the historic foundation documents of the church and Declarations of the Conference. Four further editions were published between then and 1974, the intervening amendments to Standing Orders being printed in the *Minutes of Conference for relevant years. The 6th edition in 1974, being part of the *restructuring process, was the work of John C. Hicks and was in a completely changed arrangement and format (allowing for subsequent updating via loose-leaf replacements). Since 1988 Volume 2 (containing all but the Acts of Parliament and historical documents) has been re-issued annually.

There were various earlier codifications of WM laws and usage. Of these, J.S. *Simon's *Summary of Methodist Law and Discipline* (1896, with several revisions before the 1932 Union) was prepared by order of the Conference as a new edition of the *'Large Minutes' and was accorded official status. Other digests did not have such official status, although 'Williams', first published in 1880, was prepared at the request of the Book Committee. Equivalent non-WM volumes included the *General Rules* of the MNC (1800 etc.), *A Digest of the Rules, Regulations and Usages of the Bible Christians* (1838 etc.), *A Handbook of PM Church Principles, History and Polity* (1898 etc.) by H.B. Kendall, and *The Free Methodist Manual* (1899) by E. Askew,

See also **'Large Minutes'**

SRH

Contingency Fund *see* **Finance, Ministerial**

Conventicle Act *see* **Toleration Act**

Cook, Dr Charles (d. 1858; e.m. 1816), WM minister, was stationed in *France in 1818 and spent the rest of his 40-year ministry in the French-speaking work, in a working pattern closely modelled on JW's own itinerant ministry. His obituary judged that 'to trace his labours in France would be to write a history of Methodism in that empire.' He was sent to Palestine in 1824 to examine the feasibility of establishing work there, but this opening was not developed. Returning to France, in 1841 he oversaw progress in the south and an extension of the work to Lausanne, J. *Fletcher's birthplace. Until his death he presided over the affiliated French Conference set up in 1852.

F&H 4 pp. 446–54; *Missionary Notices* April 1858 pp. 62–3; *EWM*

MJF

Cook, Raymond (1899–1972), Methodist local preacher and travel agent, grew up in *Portsmouth and Dover, where he lived for much of his life. Between the wars he was a horticulturalist and in World War II lectured first for the 'Dig for Victory' campaign and then to the Forces on a variety of subjects. He led his first party to Palestine in 1935, followed by tours in Norway. After the War he built up a very successful Christian travel service, which was sold in 1962, though he did not retire until 1967. He wrote an autobiography, *Life in Many Parts* (1972).

MR 12 & 26 Oct. 1972

JAV

Cook, Thomas (1859–1912; e.m. 1882), WM evangelist, born in Middlesborough. At 16 he was converted and became a local preacher in 1878, after a call received during a sermon by W.M. *Punshon. Turned down for the ministry, he became a lay evangelist in the Halifax and Bradford District. His outstanding success in preaching for conversions led to his acceptance for the ministry in 1882 and his appointment as Connexional Evangelist as part of the *Forward Movement. He took part in many *Southport Conventions, toured extensively in the British Isles and visited Norway, Africa and Asia. He succeeded T. *Champness as leader of the *Joyful News Mission and was appointed first Principal of *Cliff College in 1903.

MR 26 Sept. 1912; H.T. Smart (1913); V.C. Cook (1914); A.S. Wood (1983)

TSAM

Cooke, Joseph (1775–1811), founder of the *Methodist Unitarian Movement, was born near Dudley, became a local preacher and was accepted on trial for the ministry in 1795 and into *full connexion in 1799. Appointed to *Rochdale in 1803, he proved a popular preacher. But his intellectual independence, together with his study of the Bible, led him in 1805 to preach sermons on *justification by faith and the *witness of the Spirit which were criticized as heretical. He was examined in Conference and appointed to *Sunderland on conditions which he was deemed to have broken by both preaching on the same subjects and publishing the offending sermons (though he denied this). Expelled in 1806, he returned to Rochdale, where his followers built Providence Chapel. A pamphlet war between him and Edward Hare, his successor at Rochdale, led to *Bunting's sermon on *justification by faith, preached and published in 1812 at the Conference's request. Cooke's thinking moved from Socinianism towards Unitarianism, a direction in which the Movement continued after his early death. His publications included *A Sunday Evening's Companion for Parents and Children* (1810) and a hymn book published posthumously.

H. McLachlan (1919) pp. 1–30

JAV

Cooke, William (1806–84; e.m. 1826), MNC minister and theologian. Largely self-taught, he established his reputation by the effective reorganization of the MNC Irish Mission, 1836–41, and by his defence of orthodoxy in a ten-day debate with J. *Barker in 1845. He wrote over 60 theological works, notably his *Christian Theology* (1846), which went into five editions. From 1849 he lived in London, where selected ministerial students lodged with him for theological training. One of these was W. *Booth. He was Editor and *Book Steward 1849–70 and President of the Conference in 1843, 1859 and 1869.

G.J. Stevenson (1884–6) 4 pp. 608–15; S. Hulme (1886)

EAR

Cooling, James (1841–1915; e.m. 1871), missionary in *India, was born in *Newark. He was Assistant Tutor at *Richmond College before being stationed in the Madras District in 1876, where he was a Fellow of Madras University and influential in educational matters. Wesley College, Royapettah was his lasting achievement. Vernacular work increased during his period as Chairman of the District from 1885 and he was widely known and respected by Indian Christians. After his sudden death while still engaged in this important work, it was officially recorded that 'no

man ever served the Society [i.e. the WMMS] more faithfully and few more ably'.

F&H 5 pp. 243–4

MJF

Cooper, Thomas (1805–92), *Chartist leader, born in *Leicester. In his early years he worked as a shoemaker, reading and learning at the same time; then began work as a journalist, first as correspondent on the *Lincolnshire, Rutland and Stamford Mercury* and later as editor of the *Kentish Mercury* and then of the *Midland Counties Illuminator*. In the early 1840s he became the leader of the Leicester Chartists. His commitment to Chartism was costly. He had heated arguments with O'Connor and was sentenced to two years in prison in 1843. His literary output continued. His *Plain Pulpit Talk* (1872) and *Cooper's Journal* (1849–50) both sold well. In his teens he was a PM, but later became a WM local preacher. However, after an argument with the *Lincoln Circuit leaders, he left the Connexion, having denounced his superintendent minister and J. *Bunting. In 1856, following a period of doubt, he became a highly popular Christian lecturer, with as many as 2,000 gathering to hear him speak on the inerrancy of the Bible. His autobiography was published in 1872.

MR 16 March 1905; G.D.H. Cole (1941)

NADS

Cork, the chief port and city in the South of Ireland, was visited by CW in 1748 and by JW 17 times between 1749 and 1789. In 1749 and 1750 for a period of 14 months the Butler riots subjected Irish Methodists to their severest and longest persecution. Members and their property were attacked by mobs incited by a ballad-seller named Nicholas Butler. The civil authorities refused to defend the Methodists and the Grand Jury blamed CW and the Methodist preachers for being the cause of the disturbance, praying that they might be transported. The Assize judge was more wisely persuaded. It was, however, the support of the Army for the Methodist preachers that eventually discouraged the rioters. The Methodist Conference which meets in Cork about once in ten years is the only governing body of an Irish Church to meet so far south.

JWJ; C.H. Crookshank (1885) vol. 1

DALC

Corrin, James Robertson (1878–1972), *IOM local preacher and founder member of the

Manx Labour Party (1902), was elected to the House of Keys in 1919 and served in the Manx Government for 36 years. From 1927 he was a member of the Electricity Board, responsible for bringing power to all parts of the Island.

FC

Cory Family of Morwenstow **Andrew Cory** (1794–1833), a BC itinerant who held various district and connexional offices and was President of the 1829 Conference, was drowned at St. Germans. Two of his sisters entered the itinerancy. **Ann Cory** (fl.1819–30) was sent with Catherine *Reed to the Kent Mission, where they aroused much curiosity. In 1822 she went to London,and formed a number of societies there. Of her sister **Sarah Cory** (fl.1819–21) little is known. Two other members of the family later entered the BC ministry.

F.W. Bourne (1905); T. Shaw (1965)

EDG

Côte d'Ivoire (Ivory Coast) William Wadé Harris, a Liberian evangelist (known as 'Prophet Harris') preached on the coast for some fifteen months around 1914 before being expelled by the French authorities. In 1923 a British missionary, W.J. *Platt, found groups of his converts still worshipping together. Missionaries from Britain, France and *Dahomey were sent to consolidate the work, which was at first concentrated in the South-East of the country. Initially part of the French West Africa District, a separate Ivory Coast District was formed in 1957 and became an autonomous Conference in 1984. Its circuits now cover almost all the country and it is the largest Protestant Church in Côte d'Ivoire. There is extensive educational work and a Methodist Hospital opened in Dabou in 1968, thanks to fund-raising efforts fronted by MAYC.

G. Haliburton (1971)

JRP

Coughlan, Rev. Laurence (d. *c.* 1784), an Irish RC who became a Methodist preacher. On JW's recommendation he was ordained by the Bishop of London and was sent by the SPCK as a missionary to Conception Bay, Newfoundland, 1767–73. He continued to follow Methodist practices, forming converts into classes and corresponding with JW, and is therefore regarded as the founder of Methodism in Newfoundland. A colourful and controversial figure, he aroused both support and criticism. His *Account of the Work of*

God in Newfoundland was published in 1776.

C. Atmore (1801) pp. 80–3; T.W. Smith (1877)
NWT

Coulson, Charles A., FRS (1910–74), Vice-President 1959, was educated at Clifton College and Trinity, Cambridge, where he achieved 1st class honours in both Maths and Natural Science and became a Fellow. His special field was molecular physics. In 1947 he was appointed Professor in Physics at King's College, London; in 1952, Rouse Ball Professor of Applied Mathematics, Oxford; and in 1972 the first Professor of Theoretical Chemistry there. He received many academic honours, became an FRS in 1950 and was frequently in demand abroad as visiting lecturer. Besides over 300 scientific papers, his 1954 Rede Lectures on *Science and Religion* and his *Beckly Lecture on *Science, Technology and the Christian* (1960) were influential contributions to the ongoing debate. At a more popular level, *Science and Christian Belief* (1955) was an important work of Christian apologetics in which he was concerned to show the inadequacy of a 'God of the gaps'. From 1965 to 1971 he was Chairman of OXFAM.

Times, 8 January 1974; *MR* 9 July 1959, 17 January 1974

JAV

Countess of *Huntingdon's Connexion In 1779 the Consistory Court in London disallowed the Countess's claim that as a peeress she had the right to appoint as many chaplains as she chose and to employ them in public ministry. She responded by registering the 67 proprietary chapels she had built as dissenting places of worship under the *Toleration Act and they became part of her 'Connexion' in 1781. A 'General Association', similar to that of the *Welsh Calvinistic Methodists, formed in 1790 and divided into 23 Districts with an annual Conference, met with little approval, resulting in the bequest of her chapels to four trustees, including T. *Haweis and his wife. The Anglican liturgy was used in services, and from 1849 fraternal links were established with the newly formed Free Church of England, whose Constitution framed in 1863 was based on the abortive Huntingdon one of 1790, although no formal union took place. In the *Religious Census of 1851 the Connexion was reported as having 98 chapels and 11 other places of worship; but an increasing tendency to Congregationalism over the years and the inevitable closures had reduced the number of churches by 1999 to 23, with 20 ministers and a reported membership of *c.* 1,000. The Connexion has recently developed closer ties with the IM and WRU Churches. It has an overseas branch in *Sierra Leone, where freed slaves from Nova Scotia were evangelized by John Marrant, one of G. *Whitefield's converts.

G.W. Kirby (1972)

PWG

Court, Lewis Henry (1871–1960; e.m. 1892), BC minister, born at Kingsbrompton, Som. He served mainly in the South West. His important collection of BC books and manuscripts are now in the Methodist *Archives at *Manchester. His publications include *The Romance of a Country Circuit* (1921) and *Some Dartmoor Saints and Shrines* (1927)

MR 4 Feb. 1960

TS

Courtice, William (1794–1865; e.m. 1820), BC itinerant, born at Twitching, Dorset. He helped to deal with the financial problems in the Connexion in the years following the departure of W. *O'Bryan. He was Connexional and Missionary Society Treasurer in 1827 and 1844–65. Under his guidance the debt of more than £1,400 on the Book Room was dealt with and the Missionary Society's income rose from just over £1,000 to more than £5,000.

TS

Coussins, Jonathan (1757–1805; e.m. 1780), early itinerant, born in *Reading. Brought up a strict Anglican, he was awakened by a sermon in the Countess of *Huntingdon's *Bristol chapel and converted in 1776 through P. *Newman of *Cheltenham. Finding him perplexed over the controversy between election and general redemption, she lent him JW's *Predestination Calmly Considered*. They were married in 1782. J. *Valton encouraged him to enter the *itinerancy. Despite his self-deprecation, JW had a high opinion of his abilities and included him as one of the youngest members of the *Legal Hundred. Both he and his wife suffered from periodic ill health and in April 1804 he had a stroke. In 1962 his remains were discovered under the floor of the chapel at Diss and reinterred at North Lopham.

PWHS 34 pp. 58–60; *WMM* 1806 pp. 286–96, 337–44, 385–9

JAV

Covenant Service   JW derived from *Puritanism the custom of making an explicit covenant with God. He published and used forms composed by the Puritans Richard and Joseph Alleine. The service came to be held on the first Sunday of the year as a corporate renewal of individual discipleship. It first appeared in a full service book in the WM book of 1882. It there consisted of a long exhortation followed by a covenant prayer, but usually included a hymn (now *HP* 649) written by CW for the purpose, and was followed by a Communion Service. In subsequent service books it has been extensively revised, but still includes a sentence or so from the original prayer.

D.H. Tripp (1969)

ARG

Coventry   JW first visited Coventry and Foleshill in July 1779 and returned in 1782 and 1786. The society had various meeting places, including an auction room in the Women's Market and a former Baptist chapel in Jordan Well, before occupying its first chapel in Gosford Street in 1808. After a period of rivalry between Wesleyan and Calvinistic parties, it became an established WM chapel until a new chapel was opened in Warwick Lane in 1836. This in turn was replaced by the Central Hall in 1932. In the Foleshill area a group met in a weaver's cottage from 1809 until Lockhurst Lane chapel was built in 1825 (rebuilt 1875 and 1928; closed 1974). Other chapels were built as the suburbs expanded. Coventry was at first in the Northampton Circuit, was transferred to the Birmingham Circuit in 1791, then to the Leicester Circuit in 1792 and to the Hinckley Circuit in 1800, becoming a separate circuit in 1811.

Following a visit by J. *Garner, a PM group began to meet in 1819 in a room in Muston's Court off Gosford Street. Grove Street chapel was opened in 1836 (replaced by Ford Street, 1895). In 1823 another society began to meet at Paradise, Stoney Stanton Road, Foleshill and built a chapel, known as Bethesda or Paradise Chapel, in 1828 (rebuilt 1856). The three circuits in existence following *Methodist Union in 1932 were reorganized into two in 1946, one of them, the Coventry Mission Circuit, based on the Central Hall. These became a single circuit in 1993. There were several Free Methodist causes which were unaffected by Methodist Union: Station Street West, Durbar Avenue and Alderman's Green.

A.E. Peck (1979)

AEP

Cownley, Joseph (1723–92; e.m. 1746), from Leominster, was converted through the preaching of JW. Called into the itinerant ministry, he became one of W's longest-serving and most trusted preachers, serving circuits in England and Ireland. He was also a close friend of G. *Whitefield. Illness led to his semi-retirement for twenty years. He was appointed to *Edinburgh in 1788 but after one year his failing health forced him to retire in *Newcastle. He was known as a diligent pastor and a very accomplished preacher. His biographer recounts JW saying of him that he was 'one of the best preachers in England'.

C. Atmore (1801) pp. 90–4; *EMP* 2 pp. 1–47

HMG

Cox, Josiah (1829–1906; e.m. 1852), WM missionary appointed to serve with G. *Piercy in Canton (Guangzhou), *China in 1852. He was responsible for opening new work in Wuchang, which became a separate District in 1865. After 24 years he returned home because of ill-health and served for six years before retiring to Jersey.

MR 18 Oct. 1906

GRS

Coy, Sister Dorothy (d.1902), Wesley *Deaconess (formerly Mary Foster Coy) was from a religious middle-class family and trained as a nurse. Entering the Wesley Deaconess Order in 1892, she became sister-in-charge for ten years of the second Branch House, Calvert House in *Leicester, opened in November that year. She trained deaconesses there and had a great influence in the area as a Guardian of the People. The House was furnished initially by her father, **John Coy** (1829–1905), a shrewd businessman, who became treasurer in 1896.

Flying Leaves 1905 p. 202

EDG

Cozens (later Cozens-Hardy), William Hardy (1806–95), born at Sprowston, Norfolk of Methodist parentage, was articled at 17 to a solicitor in *Norwich. In 1842 he inherited Letheringsett Hall from a uncle on condition that he added 'Hardy' to his surname. He was prominent in local government and for many years was the only nonconformist JP in Norfolk. A staunch supporter of the Reform movement, he argued the case of the three ministers expelled in 1849 and was himself expelled by a District Meeting in 1850. Controversy between the Conference and the Reform party in Holt over responsibility for chapel debts led to a court case won by the latter. In 1863 he built an impressive Gothic chapel for the UMFC on Obelisk Plain, which survives as the present Methodist church. Of his nine children one daughter married Jeremiah J. Colman MP of Norwich and one son, **Herbert Hardy Cozens-Hardy** (1838–1920), 1st Baron Cozens-Hardy of Letheringsett, became Lord Justice of Appeal and Master of the Rolls.

W.H. Cozens-Hardy (1852); G.J. Stevenson (1884–6) 6 pp. 1023–7; B. Cozens-Hardy (1957)

OAB/JAV

Cracknell, Kenneth Robert (1935– ; e.m. 1958) was educated at Oxford and *Richmond College, taught theology in East Nigeria, 1962–67 and at Loughborough 1969–78. He was Secretary of the BCC's Committee for Relations with People of Other Faiths 1978–88 and has been involved in numerous inter-faith bodies. Since 1995 he has been Director of Global Studies and Research Professor of Theology and Mission at Brite Divinity School, Fort Worth, Texas. He has written many books and articles on inter-faith dialogue, including *Towards a New Relationship: Christians and People of Other Faith* (1986).

PB

Crane, Roger (1758–1836) joined the WM society in *Preston after a controversy in the Presbyterian church in which he grew up. He became a close friend of W. *Bramwell and both became local preachers and, together with M. *Emmett, were known as 'the Apostles of the Fylde'. He was revered as a fine Christian gentleman, known for his eloquent and powerful expository preaching. He entertained JW in 1781 and 1784. With financial means, a keen mind and deep piety, he contributed generously to the first WM chapel in Back Lane.

J. Taylor (1885); W. Pilkington (1890)

EWD

Crawfoot, James (1758–1839), known as 'the Old Man of the Forest' or 'the Forest Mystic', was hired by H. *Bourne as the first itinerant in what became Primitive Methodism. A former WM local preacher and admirer of JW, he formed small bands of highly charismatic followers, known as *Forest (or Magic) Methodists, most (though not all) of whom became part of the PM movement. He placed great emphasis on the interpretation of dreams, trances and prophecy. His gifts were best suited to small groups and he led many into a deeper prayer life. He separated from PM in 1813, possibly over personal difficulties with Bourne.

Kendall (1906) 2, pp. 147–54; *PWHS*, 30 pp. 12–15

WP

Creighton, Rev. James (1739–1819), a native of Cavan, Ireland, educated at Trinity College, Dublin and ordained by the Bishop of Kilmore. While curate at Swanlinbar, he read the **Appeals* which sent him in response to an enquiry and met W himself in 1773. His Methodist irregularities and his preaching of *salvation by *faith antagonized both his parishioners and local Catholics. In 1783 he became one of JW's assistants at *Wesley's Chapel, reading prayers and administering the sacrament there and elsewhere in the London Circuit and helping to edit the **Arminian Magazine*. In 1784 he was named in the *Deed of Declaration as one of the *Legal Hundred and assisted at the *ordination of T. *Coke and preachers for America. His numerous writings include *Elegiac Stanzas* marking CW's death (1788) and *A Dictionary of Scripture Proper Names* (1808) with a preface by A. *Clarke. He retired in poor health in 1810.

AM 1785 pp. 241–4, 297–302, 354–9, 398–403; A. Stevens (1864) pp. 599–601

JAV

Crookshank, Charles Henry (1836–1915; e.m. 1859), Canadian-born Methodist minister and historian. He came to Ireland as a boy. He was treasurer of the Supernumerary Fund for more than 20 years and edited the *Irish Christian Advocate* 1888–93. His three-volume *History of Methodism in Ireland* (1885–88) tells the story of the Church up to 1859. He was Vice-President of the Irish Conference in 1899, an office later held also by his son, **C. Henry Crookshank** (d.1955; e.m. 1899).

NWT

Crosby, Mrs Sarah (*c.* 1729–1804) was attracted by G. * Whitefield's preaching, but influenced by JW's sermon on *Christian Perfection joined the *Foundery society and became a class-leader in 1752. Having been deserted by her husband in 1757, she travelled to *Derby in 1761 to support the work of her friends the Dobinsons, and faced with a dramatically enlarged class was

moved to begin exhorting. She wrote to JW about female preaching and received qualified encouragement. In response to many invitations, she made extensive preaching tours during the next 40 years and was closely associated with M. *Bosanquet and S. *Ryan in their work at Leytonstone and Cross Hall. Many of JW's letters to her survive.

Z. Taft, 2 (1828) pp. 23–115; L.F. Church (1949); J. Burge (1996)

EDG

Cross, William (1797–1842; e.m. 1827), WM missionary in *Tonga and *Fiji, born in Cirencester. His appointment to New Zealand as a colleague to N. *Turner was overruled by the Sydney Synod, which sent both men to the failing Friendly Isles mission, where they soon achieved both baptisms and Bible translations. Cross's just and straightforward attitude was universally appreciated. In 1835 he and D. *Cargill volunteered for the Tongan-pioneered Fiji work. Though lacking Cargill's brilliance, he was quietly effective despite considerable privation and personal loss. Dying in Fiji from exhaustion and dysentery, he was mourned as 'one of the excellent of the earth'.

J. Hunt (1846); A.H. Wood (1975, 1978)

MIF

Crothers, Thomas Dickson (1831–1902; e.m. 1850), MNC minister, born in *Ireland, served in 15 circuits before becoming third Principal of *Ranmoor College in 1886. A shy, austere man, he was criticized for an excessive emphasis on *Butler's *Analogy of Religion* in the college curriculum. He was son-in-law of the first Principal, J. *Stacey and retired in 1898, by which time there was strong pressure to modernize the course of study. He was President of the 1884 Conference.

EAR

Crowther, Jonathan, senr (1759–1824; e.m. 1784), WM itinerant who wrote several books on Methodism, including *The Methodist Manual* (1810) and *Portraiture of Methodism* (1811); also a life of T. *Coke (1815). His concern for Methodism's growing burden of debt, which he attributed to chapel building and the proliferation of *Home Mission stations, was voiced in his *Thoughts upon the Finances of the Methodist Connexion* (1817). He was President of the Conference in 1819. His nephew, **Jonathan**

Crowther junr (1794–1856; e.m. 1823) was educated at *Kingswood School and became a good classical scholar. At the age of 19 he became Classics Master and, briefly, acting Headmaster, at *Woodhouse Grove School, proving himself a stern disciplinarian. From 1823 to 1826 he taught at Kingswood, and in 1837 was sent out to superintend the missions in *India. In 1849 he became Classics Tutor at *Didsbury College, having published a *Defence* of the Theological Institution against S. *Warren's criticisms in 1834.

F&H 5 pp. 193–7

JAV

Cudworth, William (1717–63) was the leading spirit of an off-shoot from *Calvinistic Methodism. For a period he associated with G. *Whitefield, but launched his own movement and ministered to a small congregation in Spitalfields, London. In 1751 he was in *Norwich, preaching at the Tabernacle before erecting his own chapel in St Margaret Street. He edited *Holy Meditations and Contemplations of Jesus Christ*, the work of an unknown author, and published his own pamphlets, mostly in the nature of theological controversy. JW met him, weighed his opinions and wholly distrusted him, partly because of his *antinomian tendencies and partly because he soured Wesley's relationship with J. *Hervey. His connexion had dissolved before the end of the century.

PWHS 12 pp. 34–6

WL

Culford School, near Bury St Edmunds, was founded in 1881 by local Methodists as the East Anglian Propietary School for Boys. In 1904 it became one of the original *Board of Management Schools and changed its name in 1935 when it moved to Cadogan Hall, Culford. Its former buildings housed the new East Anglian School for Girls until 1972, when the two schools merged on the Culford site to form the first Methodist co-educational boarding school. It reverted to full independence in 1976, following the withdrawal of the government's Direct Grant regulations. In 1997 it had 650 boarding and day pupils from nursery age to 18.

F.E. Watson (1980); S. & J. Roebuck (1995)

DBT

Culshaw, Wesley James (1904–75; e.m. 1926), missionary in *India, was born in Bengal and educated at University College, London and *Richmond College. He served in Bengal from 1927, becoming Chairman of the District in 1943. His wife **Freda** (*née* **Cox** had been a Women's Work missionary in Bengal from 1925. He was fluent in Bengali, Hindi and Santali and from 1957 to 1967 was Translations Secretary for the BFBS, first in Bangalore and then in Canberra. As Translations Co-ordinator to the United Bible Societies 1966–67 he was in close contact with RC scholars. He wrote an anthropological study of the Santal tribe, *Tribal Heritage* (1949) and a textbook *A Missionary Looks at his Job* (1937), widely used in missionary training. His sister **Kathleen Culshaw** (1906–86), born in India, graduated from Manchester University and was an accomplished linguist. She spent most of her 30 years of missionary service as a *deaconess in Hyderabad City, where she ministered pastorally to Muslim women in their homes, showing a sensitivity to their traditional religious faith and customs and exercising a wide influence.

MR 10 April 1975

JAV

Cumbers, Frank Henry (1905–91; e.m. 1929), a Methodist through and through, graduated from *Richmond College and was always *au fait* with the latest scholarship, though himself a traditionalist and strongly opposed to the *Anglican-Methodist unity Scheme. After 18 years in circuit he became *Book Steward, serving during difficult years (1948–69) in which, as he put it, Methodist *publishing 'lost money to the glory of God'. He published some 90 titles a year, some of them influential in theology. His *WHS Lecture (1956) was a history of the Book Room. A lively personality, his wider interests included the *Fellowship of the Kingdom, music, drama and football. He loved preaching above all. A difficult colleague, ill-at-ease with other connexional officers, he was at the same time generous and kind, not least to those with whom he disagreed, who were never out of his prayers.

MR 15 Nov. 1979, 12 Sept. 1991

GSW

Curnock, Nehemiah (1840–1915; e.m. 1860), WM minister, son of a minister of the same name (1810–69; e.m. 1834), was born at Great Bridge, Tipton. From 1886 to 1906 he edited the *Methodist Recorder*. He helped to prepare the *MHB* (1904 and the *Methodist School Hymnal* (1911). He actively supported both Army chaplaincy and the work of *NCH, of which he wrote a popular history. In retirement he made a major contribution to Methodist historiography by editing the 'Standard Edition' of JW's *Journal* (1909–16), though he did not live to see the last two volumes off the press.

MR 4 & 11 Nov. 1915; SJ (Bicentenary reprint, 1938) 8 pp. 349–50

JAN

Cutler, Ann (1759–94), early WM female travelling evangelist, born at Thornley, near Preston. W. *Bramwell, under whom she was converted, was impressed by her piety and prayer life. There was something medieval about the stringency of her spiritual exercises and she became known as 'Praying Nanny'. In the Fylde she was mocked and persecuted for her oddity. Rising at four, she led a simple life, surviving on a diet of milk and herb tea. Her prayers were pithy and pointed, but awakened faith. She travelled in many circuits, including *Preston, *Bradford, *Manchester and *Derby. Her grave in *Macclesfield has an inscription describing her simple manners, solid piety and extraordinary power in prayer.

W. Bramwell (1796)

EWD

Dahomey *see* **Benin**

Daily Record *see* **Conference**

Dale, Alan Taylor (1902–79; e.m. 1926) entered the UM ministry from teaching in 1923. From 1929 to 1935 he served in the North *China District, but returned to English circuits on health grounds. From 1953 to his retirement in 1967 he lectured in Religious Studies at Dudley Training College. His *New World* (1967) and *Winding Quest* (1972) were an imaginative re-presentation of the heart of the NT and OT.

MR 15 Feb. 1979

JAV

Dales Circuit The Pennine Dales, most of them busy with lead mining, became an important centre of Methodist activity from the mid-eighteenth century on. JW's visits were few and brief. He first came to Weardale and Barnard Castle in 1752 and to Swaledale in 1761, but does not mention Richmond until 1768. (A house there in which he preached in 1774 is marked with a plaque.) Bishop Auckland does not feature in his

Journal; his main interest was in the upper parts of the Dales.

Many Methodist societies, especially in the remoter parts of the dales, resulted from local initiatives. In 1747 Joseph Cheesewright, a shoemaker who had heard Methodist preachers in Leeds, returned to Barnard Castle and witnessed to his new-found faith. The first local preachers were Catherine Graves, Joseph Garnett and John Loadman. C. *Hopper came from *Newcastle in 1748 and J. *Rowell in 1749. As a result of 12 years' preaching in Upper Teesdale by Hopper, Rowell and M. *Lowes, in 1759 a preaching house was built at Newbiggin-in-Teesdale, believed to be the oldest Methodist chapel in the world in continuous use. (When JW writes of coming to Teesdale, he is referring to Newbiggin, as his main centre of operations.) Others which survive (though not all in current use for worship) are High House Chapel at Ireshopeburn (1760), Wolsingham (1776), Westgate (1791) and Stanhope (1800) in Weardale, and Reeth in Swaledale (1796). In Richmond, Centenary Chapel was built in Ryder's Wynd in 1839.

The importance of the dales to Methodism was clearly indicated by the formation of the Dales Circuit in 1757, with Barnard Castle as its head. It was one of the 13 on the first printed list of circuits in 1765 and originally included not only the dales of the northern Pennines, but also much of Westmorland. In 1757 it had about 400 members; by 1772 they had increased to 1,000 in 21 societies (which increased to 40 by 1791). JW declared in 1791 that the circuit was too extensive and that 'five or six others might be taken out of it'. The process of division had already begun with the formation of the *Yarm Circuit in 1764 and continued with the formation of the Richmond Circuit in 1807 and the Bishop Auckland Circuit in 1838. Reeth Circuit was separated from Richmond in 1846; in 1997 these were reunited as the Swaledale Circuit. Since 1978 Barnard Castle and Teesdale have been united in one circuit.

PM was introduced by preachers from the *Hull Circuit. The first society was formed at Wolsingham in Weardale in 1821, after a visit by Samuel Laister. Although he was not the first PM preacher, T. *Batty has been called the 'Apostle of Weardale' and played a prominent part in the great revival which swept through the dale between 1823 and 1826. Thousands attended a *camp meeting at Westgate on 1 June 1823 and in 1824 Westgate was made a separate Branch of the Hull Circuit, with J. *Oxtoby ('Praying Johnny') at its head. W. *Clowes visited in 1828 and opened a chapel at Frosterley. In Teesdale chapels were opened at Holwick (1837) and Bowlees (1845). At Countersett, a remote hamlet in upper Wensleydale, a PM society formed in 1872 shared a Quaker meeting house. PM chapels from the 1820s survive at Wearhead, Brotherlee, Frosterley and Barnard Castle, though not all in Methodist use.

See also **Race, George**

MR(W) 1898 pp. 23–7, 31–5, 1900 pp. 25–8, 61–7, 1904 pp. 38–9; A. Steele (1857); J. Ward (1865); H.L. Beadle (1980); H.L. Beadle (1984); M. Batty (1985); M. Batty (1993b)

APC/BB/ML/GEM

Dall, Robert (1745–1828) noted for his courage and simplicity, was born in *Dundee, began to preach in 1768 and was admitted on trial in 1772. From *Aberdeen and on foot he pioneered Methodist work along the Moray coast and to *Inverness, Dingwall and Tain; after which he spent three years in *Ireland. In 1778 he was sent to the *Isle of Man, where he married and disappeared from the *Minutes* until 1787. He then re-emerged, again on trial, at *Dumfries. There he built a splendid chapel and was admitted into full connexion in 1788. From 1796 he served in England.

G.W. Davis (1995)

MB

Dallinger, William Henry (1842–1909; e.m. 1861), WM minister, born in Devonport, the son of an artist and engraver, was trained at *Richmond College. As Principal of *Wesley College, Sheffield 1880–88 he modernized the curriculum. On his resignation, in recognition of his scientific work he was, exceptionally, allowed to retain ministerial status without pastoral office. His primary interest as a microscopist was in monads or flagellates (simple organisms developed in organic infusions) and abiogenesis (the spontaneous generation of living matter). Elected FRS in 1880 he was President of the Royal Microscopical Society 1884–87. After 1888 he devoted himself to public lecturing and literary work, which included editing the *Wesley Naturalist*, popular articles for the *WMM* and the 1896 *Fernley Lecture on *The Creator and what we may know of creation*.

G.J. Stevenson (1884–6) 4 pp. 530–8; *MR* 11 Nov. 1909; *WMM* 1910 pp. 46–50; *Journal of* the Royal Microscopical Society 1909 pp. 699–702; *Proceedings* of the Royal Society, Series B, 1910 pp. iv-vi

CJS

Dalton, Dr Edwin (1845–1925; e.m. 1867), PM minister who travelled in the Leeds and York District before becoming *Book Steward, 1905–10. He was President of the Conference in 1911 and a Director of PM *Chapel Aid 1914–25. He collapsed and died during the *Scarborough Conference of 1925.

DCD

Darlington (Co. Durham) The old market town (with an influential Quaker element) was greatly enlarged by the development of railways and engineering in the nineteenth century. The seeds of Methodism were sown through the witness of J. *Nelson on his way north as an army conscript in 1744. In 1753 local preachers and a former *Moravian lady helped to establish a society, which met in hired premises until the building of the first chapel on Bondgate in 1778. Originally part of the *Dales Circuit and then transferred to *Yarm, it became the head of a separate circuit in 1805. JW made ten visits between 1761 and 1788, preaching on the first occasion at the home of the Allan family, Blackwell Grange, just south of the town. The handsome new Bondgate chapel (1813), followed by purpose-built Sunday and day schools, signalled the growing strength of WM. Industrial expansion led to further chapels (e.g. North Road, 1872) later in the century.

W. *Clowes introduced PM in 1820. F.N. *Jersey and Samuel Laister were other PM pioneers in the town, the latter soon to die from his labours. In 1822 the first PM chapel in Co. Durham was opened on Queen Street, from where missions went out to many surrounding villages. The zenith of PM's progress was the opening of the Greenbank chapel in 1879 under the ministry of H. *Gilmore. At that same time the *Christian Lay Churches were establishing a cause in Darlington and took over the Queen Street PM chapel. The WMA built Coniscliffe Road chapel, which was later strengthened by WR seceders. The MNC was represented by Victoria Road chapel, a late development built in 1884 with the help of a gift of £1,000 by the widow of J. *Love. Chapel building continued in the late nineteenth and early twentieth centuries as the town grew. One striking development was the bold conversion in 1932 of Elmridge, a former Quaker mansion, into a splendidly appointed chapel through the generosity of Mr G.M. Harroway.

R. Wilson (1890); R. Trotter (1913); G.W. Weatherill (1953); H. Burgin (1988)

GEM

Darney, William (1709–74) was converted in the Scottish awakening of 1733–40. Of sturdy build and 'terrible to behold', he earned his living as a clogger and pedlar and became an itinerant evangelist in October 1741. From 1742 he was active on both sides of the Lancashire and Yorkshire Pennines, founding a number of societies which were brought under Methodist discipline in 1747, when Darney was recognized as a Methodist preacher on W. *Grimshaw's recommendation. Grimshaw shielded him from the Wesleys' intermittent criticism of his *Calvinistic tendencies, his doggerel verse and general uncouthness. When the 1768 Conference prohibited preachers from following a trade, Darney left the itinerancy and returned to the *Rossendale area as a local preacher.

C. Atmore (1801) pp. 100–1; F. Baker (1963)

JAH

Dart, Elizabeth (1792–1857), one of the earliest BC female itinerants (1816–33), was from an Anglican background, becoming WM in 1811. She retired in 1833 on marrying John Hicks Eynon, a convert under her preaching. They were the first ministerial couple to go to Canada, where Elizabeth continued as itinerant and class leader. They revisited England in 1848, preaching extensively in Devon and Cornwall.

Z. Taft, vol. 2 (1828) pp. 210–9; F.W. Bourne (1905); E.G. Muir (1991)

EDG

Dartmouth, William Legge, 2nd Earl (1731–1801), described by William Cowper as 'one who wears a coronet and prays', was educated at Westminster School and Trinity College, Oxford. He succeeded his grandfather in 1750 and had a distinguished public career, being made a Privy Councillor in 1765 and serving as President of the Board of Trade (1765–66), Colonial Secretary (1772–75) and Lord Privy Seal (1775–82). Dartmouth College in New England (incorporated 1769) was named in his honour. He embraced Methodism through the preaching of G. *Whitefield and opened his home for preaching when his private chaplain was excluded from the parish church. JW also knew him and sought his support in an attempt to unite the evangelical clergy in 1764. On the eve of the Revolutionary War JW wrote to him and to the Prime Minister Lord North, urging against the use of force against the colonists on both moral and prudential grounds. Sandwell Park, his home in West Bromwich, was close to F. *Asbury's boyhood home; they both attended All Saints Church and the Methodist society in Wednesbury.

B.D. Barger (1965)

WL

Davey, Cyril James (1911–98; e.m. 1933), minister and prolific author, was born in *Liverpool and was trained at *Handsworth College. He was Garrison Chaplain in North India, 1939–46. From 1965 he was Home Secretary and Area Secretary for Europe at the Mission House and edited *Now* magazine, being known as 'Father of the House' before retiring in 1976. Among the causes with which he was involved were *MHA and Casa Materna, Naples. His numerous publications include plays, biographies, travel books and two popular missionary histories, *The March of Methodism* (1951) and *Changing Places* for the 1986 Bicentennial celebrations. He was also a gifted speaker.

MR 5 Nov. 1998

PB

Davey, Dr Thomas Frank, CBE (1908–83; e.m. 1932) studied medicine and trained for the ministry simultaneously in Manchester. He was appointed in 1936 to the Uzuakoli Leprosy Hospital, *Nigeria, where he served as both doctor and minister. He pioneered a new treatment of leprosy with the drug Dapsone. In 1951 he became Leprosy Adviser to the Nigerian Government and was awarded the OBE and later the CBE in recognition of his work. From 1959 to 1968 he served with distinction as Medical Secretary of the MMS; then went out to take charge of the Leprosy Settlement at Dichpalli, *India. In retirement from 1973 he continued to contribute to leprosy work, becoming editor of the *Leprosy Review* and co-editor of the 2nd edition of *Leprosy in Theory and Practice*. Together with his wife **Kathleen Davey** (*née* Barnes, 1904–96) he wrote *The Compassionate Years – a Medical Te Deum* (1964).

See also **Medical missions**

MR 7 April 1983; G.R. Senior (1996)

GRS

Davies, Edward Tegla (1880–1967; e.m. 1904), Welsh WM minister born at Llandegla, Denbighshire, adopted the middle name Tegla and was widely known by it. After a period as a pupil teacher, he trained at *Didsbury College. His service in North Wales provided the background to some of his prose works. He was President of the Welsh Assembly in 1937 and was in much demand as a preacher throughout Wales. He regarded himself as primarily a minister of the Gospel, but he was also a leading figure in twentieth century Welsh literature. Much of his earlier work appeared in the denominational journals *Y Winlan* and *Yr Eurgrawn Wesleyaidd*, both of which he later edited. His 25 or so published volumes include the most widely read children's books of their day, novels, allegorical fantasies, translations, short stories, essays and radio talks, sermons and an autobiography, *Gŵr Pen y Bryn* (1922), translated as *The Master of Pen y Bryn* (1975) and into Catalan (1985), has been called the greatest Welsh novel. He was awarded a DLitt in 1958.

MR 19 Oct. 1967; H. Ethall (1980); I.F. Elis (1956); P. Davies (1983); *OCLW*

GTH

Davies, John (1784–1845; e.m. 1806) became a WM under the influence of the preachers of the English-speaking *Chester Circuit. After two North Wales circuits, he spent the rest of his ministry in South Wales. Though a staunch *Arminian he took no part in the doctrinal controversies of his time, but was highly regarded as a wise leader and competent administrator. He was Chairman of the Welsh District 1827–28 and, after its division, of the South Wales District 1828–29. He was Secretary of the South Wales Synod 1833–43 and Chairman of the District for a second time from 1843.

W. Rowlands (1847); *DWB*

IGPL

Davies, John Cadvan (1846–1923; e.m. 1871), Welsh WM minister, from Llangadfan, known by his bardic name 'Cadfan', had a distinguished 40-year ministry in North and Central Wales, becoming President of the Welsh Assembly in 1910. He excelled as a poet, winning the crown at the National Eisteddfod more than once and being elected Archdruid of Wales in 1923. He published four selections of his poetry and contributed many hymns to Welsh WM hymnals, the best of which survived into the 1927 book still in use.

DWB; *EW*, 102 p. 309, 103 p. 1–7

EHG

Davies, Owen (1752–1830; e.m. 1789), born in Wrexham, went to work in London as a youth and eventually joined the WM there. JW observed his gifts as a preacher and brought him into the ministry. He became Chairman of the Redruth District, but when the Welsh Mission was formed in 1800 he agreed to become its superintendent and set out for Ruthin with J. *Hughes of Brecon as his colleague. He served the mission for 16 years, becoming Chairman of the Welsh District formed in 1804. In the financial crisis of 1816, he was transferred back with others in the Welsh work to an English circuit. Ill-health soon caused him to retire from the active work. Though limited in his ability to preach and write in Welsh, his strong personality and gifts of leadership and administration were largely responsible for the success of the early Welsh WM. He wrote much in defence of *Arminianism against Calvinist attacks, notably his *Defence of Wesleyan Methodism* (1806) and *The Dialogues* (1807).

A.H. Williams (1935) pp. 85–146; *DWB*; *WMM* 1832 p. 389

IGPL

Davies, Dr Rupert Eric (1909–94; e.m. 1933), scholar and author, educated at St Paul's School, London, Balliol College, Oxford and *Wesley House, Cambridge. As a Finch Scholar he spent the year 1934–35 studying the Reformers at Tübingen. He was chaplain of *Kingswood School 1935–47, Tutor in Church History at *Didsbury College, Bristol 1952–67 and Principal of the united *Wesley College 1967–73. He was President of the Conference in 1970 and Warden of the *New Room 1976–82.

He was convener of the *Faith and Order Committee. A convinced ecumenist, he worked closely with Oliver Tomkins, Bishop of Bristol, and was a member of the *Anglican-Methodist Union Commission, also serving on the WMC, the WCC (on both its Assembly and its Faith and Order Commission) and the BCC. He was a fine teacher, handling a range of subjects with the versatility of a Balliol man. He and his wife Margaret worked tirelessly for the *ordination of *women and the full participation of women in the life of the Church. A skilful popularizer and communicator, his Penguin original on *Methodism* (1963) is still a standard introduction. His numerous other titles include *The Problem of Authority in the Continental Reformers* (1947) and the 1968 *Fernley-Hartley Lecture *Religious Authority in an Age of Doubt*. The University of Bristol, in which he was for many years a Recognized Teacher, awarded him an honorary DLitt in 1992.

J.M. Turner in R.E. Davies (1993); *MR* 25 June 1970 & 14 July 1994; *PWHS* 50 pp. 21–2
DJC/JAN

Davies, Samuel (1818–91; e.m. 1843), 'the Second', joined the WM in Abergele. His outstanding preaching, literary and administrative gifts, his wide educational and cultural interests, and his wise judgment and leadership made him one of the most trusted and respected Welsh Christian leaders of his day. He edited *Y Winllan* 1854–55 and *Yr Eurgrawn* 1859–65 and 1875–86 and was for some years in charge of the connexional Book Room in Bangor. He was Secretary (1858–65) and Chairman (1866–86) of the North Wales District and was elected to the *Legal Hundred in 1875. He was a founder member of the Council of the University College at Bangor in 1884. Among his many publications were biographies of T. *Aubrey (1877) and of Samuel Davies 'the first' (1866).

H. Jones (1904); *DWB*; *EW* 83 pp. 305–8
IGPL

Davies, William (1784–1851; e.m. 1807), WM missionary to *Sierra Leone, known as 'Davies Affrica', was born in the Vale of Clwyd. In partnership with E. *Jones he established Welsh-speaking Aberystwyth and Llandeilo Circuits in 1807 and 1808. Responding to an appeal for overseas service, in 1815 he and his wife arrived in Sierra Leone, where he worked in close co-operation with the CMS missionaries, despite repeated bouts of malarial fever. His wife died after only ten months and he was forced to return home after three years. He became Chairman of the Welsh District (1821–26) and Secretary of the South Wales Welsh-language District on its formation in 1829. But subject to repeated bouts of malaria, he eventually succumbed to mental illness which after his retirement in 1841 led to his exclusion from *full connexion and to his death in tragic circumstances. Among his published work was a diary of his ministry in Africa. His pioneering work in Wales and Sierra Leone

were given belated recognition by the Conference of 1999.

DWB; *EW* 1909 pp. 210–15; H.Jones (1911–13) 2 pp. 712–16
SRH

Davies, Dr William (1820–75; e.m. 1843), Welsh WM minister, received a good education, enhanced by a fondness for reading to the detriment of his progress as an apprentice shoemaker. Soon after becoming a WM member in 1840 he was accepted for the ministry and quickly became popular as a preacher. His ministry was enriched by his administrative ability, skill as a debater and wide literary and musical interests. He was *Book Steward at Bangor 1867–75 and in 1870 received an honorary American doctorate. He edited *Y Winllan* 1857–60 and *Yr Eurgrawn* 1866–75, contributing countless articles. Among his books in Welsh were a Bible Dictionary (1857), an Introduction to the Scriptures (1866), a work on the Atonement (1873) and a study of J. *Bryan (1867).

DWB; T.R. Roberts (1908); *EW* 67 pp. 386–87; *Y Geninen* 1886 pp. 145–52
IGPL

Davies, Sir William Howell (1851–1932), WM layman, born in Narberth, Pembs. He became a tanner and leather merchant in *Bristol, where he was on the City Council from 1885, Mayor in 1896 and alderman from 1897. He was Chairman of the Finance Committee 1902–29 and of the Docks Committee 1899–1908, where he introduced the motion for the construction of the Avonmouth Dock. He was knighted in 1908. He was Liberal MP for South Bristol 1906–22.

Bristol Times and Mirror 8 Aug. 1921
CJS

Davison Family   **James Davison** (1810–80), born near Wooler, Northumberland, was converted by the PMs in his mid-twenties and gave them loyal service, particularly in the Hexham area, during more than 40 years as headmaster of Dean Raw School in lower Allendale. He served as a local preacher in the huge Hexham Circuit and was a frequent representative at District Meetings and Conference. He was keen *temperance advocate. Tradition affirms that five of his pupils became Presidents of the PM Conference. One of these was his son **Matthew P. Davison** (1853–

1922; e.m. 1875) who trained at the *Sunderland PM Institute 1870–71 and was President in 1919. His son **Hugh Allan Davison** (1892–1973; e.m. 1917) and grandson **Richard M. Davison** (1924– ; e.m. 1948) followed him into the ministry.

MR 20 Dec. 1973; WHS(NE) no. 21 March 1974

GEM

Davison, Leslie (1906–72) was born in Penshaw, Co. Durham and entered the UM ministry in 1924. During his years in the London Mission, he became an alderman in the Borough of Bermondsey. After serving as Chairman of the Wolverhampton and Shrewsbury District, he was appointed to the *HM Department in 1957 and in 1962 was President of the Conference, making history by being the first President to be granted a papal audience. In 1965 he became General Secretary of the HM Department. He wrote extensively on mission and evangelism, notably in *Sender and Sent* (1969). He was active in promoting closer relations between Methodist and Anglicans and also in seeking to understand the charismatic movement.

MR 5 July 1962, 20 Jan. 1972

KGG

Davison, W. Theophilus (1846–1935; e.m. 1868), WM scholar and author, son of **William Davison** (1818–93; e.m. 1840). He became head boy at *Kingswood School, but did not take up an Oxford scholarship because of his father's dread of the influence of Tractarianism and of *Essays and Reviews*. He served as Classics Tutor at *Richmond College from 1881, then as Theological Tutor at *Handsworth College, 1891–1904. As one who helped WM to come to terms with modern biblical scholarship, he had to face a heresy charge during his early career. Leaving the Book Room with some relief after one year as *Connexional Editor, he returned to Richmond as Theological Tutor and was Principal from 1909 to 1920, serving also as Dean of the Theology Faculty of London University. He was editor of the *Methodist Recorder* 1883–86. An ecumenist with wide-ranging interests, including poetry and music, he contributed to the *ERE* and the Hastings Bible Dictionaries and gave the 1888 *Fernley Lecture on *The Christian Conscience* (1888). Though small of stature, he was recognized as an outstanding preacher. He was President of the 1901 Conference. His wife was a grand-daughter of J. *Stanley.

MR 25 July 1901, 14 Nov. 1935

JAV

Dawson, William (1773–1841), WM farmer and colliery agent at Garforth, Yorks, and a local preacher from 1801. Though never ordained, he was in popular demand nationally as a preacher known for his godliness and homespun style. He was involved in the launching of the Leeds District *Missionary Society in 1813 and from 1837 the Conference gave him an allowance to travel, preach and promote the missionary movement. He was also a staunch *temperance advocate.

J. Everett (1842); G.J. Stevenson (1884–6) 4 pp. 565–8

PSF

Day Schools (Methodist), attached to chapels and under the supervision of the *Education Committee, represented WM's contribution to the *education of the poor. By 1873 there were 912 schools, with limited state aid, offering elementary education with Bible-based religious teaching and a conscience clause. Further growth was halted by increasing Methodist support for the new publicly funded Board Schools and the Conference of 1891 resolved to support the establishment of a single national system of education. Most of the Methodist day schools were eventually handed over to local authorities. In 1997 there remained 56 'voluntary schools', publicly funded, of which 28 were joint Anglican-Methodist foundations, the result of a policy of co-operation which developed during the 1950s.

Methodist Education Reports, 1839 onwards; J.T. Smith (1998)

DBT

de Quetteville, Jean (1761–1843; e.m. 1786), pioneer of WM in the *Channel Islands, was born at St Martin, Jersey and educated at Winchester, where he was confirmed. He returned home in 1777, came under Methodist influence and was converted in 1783. He felt a call to preach and did so in Jersey until 1786, when the Conference accepted him as an itinerant on the recommendation of R C. *Brackenbury, sending him as a bilingual preacher to Guernsey. As a colleague of Brackenbury, and later of A. *Clarke, he also worked in Alderney and Sark and faced bitter hostility. His offer to serve in Nova Scotia was not taken up. Instead, he was ordained by T. *Coke, who took him on an abortive mission to Paris. In 1804 his health began to deteriorate and he became a *Supernumerary in 1816, though continuing to preach and visit the sick. In retirement he edited a new edition of the 1795 hymnbook (1818) and a Sunday School hymnal (1835), founded and edited *Le Magasin Méthodiste* from 1817 to 1841, and translated a number of religious books into French.

R D. Moore (1952); G.R. Balleine (1948)

FLeB

Deacon, Dr Thomas (1697–1753), *Manchester non-juror and author of *A Complete Collection of Devotions* (1734) which JW read on the voyage to Georgia, having been introduced to him by J. *Clayton just before he embarked. The *Collection* was based on the 'Apostolic Constitutions' and other early liturgies and on the first Prayer Book of Edward VI. Deacon advocated prayers for the dead and the signation in *baptism and held a view of the eucharistic sacrifice similar to that taken by the Wesleys from Daniel Brevint. His influence can be clearly traced in JW's practices during his Georgia ministry. The *Collection* also included hymns which, though of indifferent literary quality, may have given JW the idea of publishing the *'Charlestown Hymn-Book'.

DNB; *PWHS* 13 pp. 26–9

JAV

Deacon in the NT means 'servant' or 'minister' and in Phil.1:1 and 1 Tim. 3:8 clearly refers to a church officer, though the duties are not specified. As forms of ministry developed it came to refer to the third order of ministry, after bishop and presbyter (priest), concerned with care of the poor, administration, teaching and assistance in worship. But in time the office became chiefly a step on the way to the priesthood and was restricted to men. This has remained so in the Orthodox, RC and Anglican Churches until very recently, when a permanent diaconate has been reintroduced. Among Churches of the Reformation and in English Dissent deacons were introduced in various ways, but as lay officers concerned with administration and charity. In the nineteenth century orders of deacons and deaconesses for the relief of poverty and need proliferated, exemplified in Methodism by the *NCH Sisters, the West London Mission Sisters and the *Deaconess Orders.

JW ordained some of his preachers deacons prior to their *ordination as elder. This practice

was retained in *American Methodism until 1996, but was soon abandoned in Britain. Official British statements have tended, as late as 1960, to regard *stewards in their administrative and financial roles as the equivalent of NT deacons. But during the twentieth century the office of deacon has undergone widespread reappraisal in most Churches and this has influenced more recent Methodist thinking, resulting in a new *Diaconal Order. The Methodist Church therefore now recognizes two orders of ministry, the presbyteral and the diaconal. Deacons, both men and women, are ordained for life and on reception into *full connexion are admitted to membership of the Order. They are itinerant and their calling is to represent and make visible the servant ministry of Christ and the Church's calling to servant ministry in the world. In 1996 a similar position, without itinerancy, was adopted by the UMC.

See also **Diaconate**

Conference Agenda, 1993, pp. 223–44

BEB

Deaconess Orders   The Wesley Deaconess Institute was founded in 1890 by T.B. *Stephenson, who recognized that an Order of dedicated women had a valuable part to play in the life of the Church. Initially the Institute was closely connected with the Children's Home (later the *NCII), but in time the two organizations became separate entities. Its first residential House was in London, and others were opened in *Norwich, *Leicester and Salford. Stephenson was Warden of the Order as well as Principal of the NCH until 1900, when he moved to the Ilkley Circuit. The headquarters of the Order was transferred there when a former boys' school was purchased in 1902 and remained there until transferred to *Birmingham in 1967. Until 1901 deaconesses were 'recognized'; between 1902 and 1936 they were 'consecrated'; and from 1937 on they were 'ordained', following an order of service included in the new *Book of Offices. *Ordination was to lifelong service, but until 1965 they were required to resign on marriage. They met together in an annual Convocation. The Sisters engaged in pastoral, mission, evangelistic, social and prison work, and in nursing, teaching and work overseas. The Order was closed to recruitment from 1978 to 1987 and renamed the Methodist Diaconal Order when it was opened to both women and men in 1988.

In 1891 the UMFC started a Deaconess Institute organized along very similar lines, but with more emphasis on evangelistic and mission work. At the Union of 1907 the Deaconess Institute became part of the *United Methodist Church. PM did not have an organized 'order', but there were deaconesses who 'learned on the job', though they attended some lectures at the UM Institute. With Methodist Union in 1932 the WM Order and UM Institute were united, with the 22 PM Sisters joining in 1934.

See also **Diaconate**

MR 6 July 1939; *Highways and Hedges: The Children's Advocate*, passim; *Flying Leaves, the Organ of the WDO* (1907–15), passim; H. Smith (1913)

EDG

Deed of Declaration   JW executed a Deed Poll, enrolled in Chancery on 9 March 1784, to deal with his societies and the future of the connexion after his death by clearly defining the identity, constitution and powers of 'the *Conference of the People called Methodists'.

By this Deed of Declaration he gave authority for the *Legal Hundred to be the supreme legislative body, and laid down rules for the annual meetings, procedure, records and officers (i.e. *President and *Secretary) of the Conference. The Conference thus constituted had the right to admit preachers on trial, to receive them into full connexion and expel them where necessary. For those preaching houses and other property settled upon JW or JW and CW, the Conference was to be the body referred to in the trust deeds as having after their death the power to appoint preachers to the chapels. In the *Warrenite controversy the Deed was the basis of the litigation which resulted in the decision of Lord Chancellor Lyndhurst upholding the authority of the Conference.

A similar Deed Poll declaring the names, objects, rules and fundamental regulations of the PM connexion was executed in 1831. Other branches of Methodism used the same method (MNC, 1846; UMFC in 1857, adopting the 1840 Foundation Deed of the WMA; BC, 1831) culminating in the Deed of Foundation of the UMC in 1907.

Under the authority of the Methodist Church Union Act 1929 the Uniting Conference of 1932 adopted the *Deed of Union which superseded the previous Deeds.

J.S. Simon in *PWHS* vol. 12 (1919–20) pp. 81–93; text of Deed: *NHM* vol. 2, App. B.

SRH

Deed of Union   Under the power given by the Methodist Church Union Act 1929, the Uniting Conference of 1932 adopted the Deed of Union setting out the basis of the union, including the constitution and doctrinal standards of the united Church. The *Deed of Declaration (1784) and its equivalents were therefore superseded. The Act gave the Conference the power, provided specific procedure was followed, to amend the Deed, apart from the *doctrinal standards clause. The Deed has been amended in many respects since 1932, and was extensively rearranged and revised in form in 1990.

Under section 5 of the *Methodist Church Act 1976 (a provision which provoked controversy at the Bill stage) the Conference's power was extended to amending the clause (now clause 4) defining the doctrinal standards. This power has been exercised once, to enable the recognition of the *diaconate as an order of ministry, in 1995.

CPD vol. 2 bk II part 1

SRH

Deed Poll *see* **Deed of Declaration**

Delamotte Family   **Thomas Delamotte** was a London sugar merchant and magistrate, of Huguenot descent. His eldest son **Charles Delamotte** (*c.* 1714–86), much to his father's disapproval, accompanied JW to Georgia in 1735, desiring to 'give himself up entirely to God'. He was W's closest companion and confidant, though not afraid to question his attitude in the Sophy Hopkey affair. He devoted himself to teaching the young and his musical ability helped JW to introduce German hymns into worship. On W's departure he kept the mission going in the face of hardship and ridicule. Back home in 1738 he found that the family home, Blendon Hall, near Bexley, had become a haven for the Methodist preachers. He joined the *Fetter Lane society and later the *Moravians. On the premature death of his brother he joined the family business, settled in Barton on Humber and supported B. *Ingham's work in Yorkshire. He and JW met again in 1782. His younger brother **William Delamotte** (1718–43) was a sizar at St Catherine's College, *Cambridge was a member of a small group of Methodists which existed briefly in the 1730s. Increasingly drawn to the Moravians, his preaching won many converts. He maintained an intimate friendship with CW. Ill-health compelled him to leave Cambridge in 1740 without a degree. He joined the Moravians in Yorkshire, settling briefly at Smith House, Lightcliffe.

SJ 1 & 2; J. Nayler (1938); John D. Walsh in P. Brooks (1975) pp. 249–83

EWD

Denovan, Alexander (1794–1878) was born and lived in *Glasgow, where with others he established an IM Church in 1820. He founded the *IM Magazine* in 1823 and was its editor 1823–29, 1847–9 and 1865–68. He was President of the denomination for thirty years and architect of the connexional constitution (1852) which made what had been a loosely related group of churches into a recognizable denomination. He put in writing the principles which held the churches together and gave the unpaid ministry an ideological basis which remained unchallenged until the late twentieth century. He was the author of *Election according to Holy Scripture* (1832) and *Appeal to the Christian World* (1866).

IM Magazine Feb. 1879

JAD

Derby On his first visit in 1762, JW preached at the home of a Mr Dobinson. He returned in 1764, when he was granted permission by the mayor to preach in the market place, but was hindered by a noisy mob. The old malthouse behind St Michael's Church was opened that year as a preaching house. JW, CW and J *Fletcher all preached in the first chapel (1764), which stood on St Michael's Lane, and Derby's first Sunday School was started there in 1785, only five years after Raikes' began his in Gloucester. A more spacious church was built in King Street in 1805, replaced in turn in 1841 by an impressive building frequently referred to as 'the mother church of Derby Methodism', complete with mahogany pulpit and one of the finest organs in British Methodism.

PM began when R. *Winfield, farmer and pioneer evangelist of Ambaston, invited S. *Kirkland to conduct a lovefeast at Ambaston in 1815. Three who were present from Derby invited her to preach in Derby the next day, a class was formed and Derby became the second circuit in PM. Its first church was built in Albion Street c.1817–18; replaced by one in Traffic Street. An old barn at Normanton, often called 'the Cathedral', was the predecessor of the St Thomas' Road Church. When W. *Griffth, Superintendent of the Ripley Circuit, was expelled by the WM Conference of 1849, he settled in Derby and ministered for 22

years at the Becket Street UMFC church, built in 1857. The MNC's Temple Church was replaced in 1900 by a new church in Dairyhouse Road. At the time of *Methodist Union in 1932 there were 29 WM, 18 PM and 5 UM churches in and around Derby.

See also **Arminian Methodists; Original Methodists**

MR(W) 1896 pp. 35–8; J. Jones (1883)

DMG

Derby Faith Folk *see* **Arminian Methodists**

Devotion and Piety 'Spiritual respiration' is the key metaphor in Wesleyan piety. The Holy Spirit breathes 'life' into the soul of the faithful person, who responds by ministering to others and using all the means of grace.

The four elements of prayer, according to JW are 'deprecation, petition, intercession and thanksgiving'. He took seriously St Paul's admonition, 'Pray without ceasing.' Wesley encouraged the 'practice of the presence of God' which Brother Lawrence exemplified and private prayer at regular times, morning and evening. These prayers might follow a set form or they could begin with meditative reading. The Bible, the hymn-book and Kempis's *Imitation of Christ* were appropriate texts, among others, for this purpose. As aids to devotion W published forms of prayer and extracts from ancient (e.g. 'Macarius the Egyptian') and modern authors (including Henry Scougal, A.H. Francke and Blaise Pascal).

Beginning in 1736, JW rejected *'mysticism' as he understood it. The term represented the 'dark' contemplative piety of Johann Tauler and the *Theologica Germanica*. Contemplation is prayer which does not employ ideas, words or images. W believed that the 'mystics' tended towards pantheism and antinomianism. For him, 'resemblance' between God and the faithful person, not the 'union' of the finite and the Infinite, is the fulfilment of the Christian life. W rejected concepts such as 'absorption', 'deification' and 'equality' between God and perfected individuals and hesitated to use symbolism based on marriage. In later years he spoke appreciatively of W. *Law and other spiritual writers whom he had earlier upbraided, although he began to criticize Boehme and Swedenborg.

JCE

Diaconate Although recruitment to the Wesley *Deaconess Order ceased in 1978, there were still those who believed themselves called to a diaconal ministry and in 1986 the Conference re-opened that possibility. In 1988 it resolved that the re-opened order should be called the Methodist Diaconal Order and be open to both women and men (called 'deaconesses' or 'deacons' according to sex). The members of the Methodist Diaconal Order received into full membership of the Order were to be 'ordained to the diaconate in the Church of God'.

In 1993 the Conference adopted a report upon the theological and constitutional issues raised by these 1988 decisions, which concluded that 'the Methodist Church recognises and has received from God two orders of *ministry, the presbyteral and the diaconal'; thus the members of the Order should no longer be regarded as 'lay'. The 1995 Conference confirmed the amendment of the *doctrinal standards clause of the *Deed of Union (for the first time) by removing any wording that might appear to exclude the diaconate as a form of ordained ministry. Further reports were adopted in subsequent years which re-affirmed the diaconate as a separate order of ministry, as well as being a religious order, and reflecting this in various changes. These included the creation of a separate diaconal session of Conference (from 1999), and provisions for reception into full connexion upon ordination and for stationing by the Conference. In 1998 the Conference received all existing members of the Methodist Diaconal Order into full connexion and resolved that 'deacon' should be the official usage for all members of the Order.

See also **Deacon**

―――――

Conference Agendas: 1993, pp. 223–44; 1995, pp. 713–20; 1997, pp. 165–91; 1998, pp. 503–77

SRH

Diaries of JW   Influenced by the advice of J. *Taylor's *Holy Living*, which he read when preparing for ordination, in Lent 1725 JW began to keep a diary. Unlike his later *Journals, this was a private record, though he later drew on it in preparing his Journal extracts for publication. His method changed over the years. In January 1734 he adopted a tabular format, which he referred to as his 'exacter method' and which made possible a concise and detailed record of his spiritual state hour by hour. After the Methodist movement got under way, the diaries became less introspective and more a record of his travels and other activities. He maintained the practice throughout his life, though none of the diaries

have survived for the period 1742–1783 and some early ones are also missing.

The diaries were written in a combination of shorthand, abbreviations, symbols and cipher. They were partially decoded by N. *Curnock, who used them in his Standard Edition of JW's Journal; but his work has now been superseded by that of R.P. Heitzenrater in the Bicentennial Edition of JW's *Works*.

―――――

SJ 1 pp. 3–5, 36–77; R.P. Heitzenrater in *MH* 12 (July 1974) pp. 110–35; W.R. Ward & R.P. Heitzenrater (1988) pp. 299–307

JAV

Dickinson, Rev. Peard (1758–1802), born at Topsham, was influenced by reading the *Puritan divines and especially Richard Baxter's *Saints' Everlasting Rest*. Apprenticed to a *Bristol jeweller whose wife was a Methodist, he was converted and joined the local society, finding peace with God after a lengthy period of spiritual anguish. Helped by a widowed relative, in 1779 he went to St Edmund Hall and then to Hertford College, Oxford. During vacations in London, JW took him sick-visiting. He was ordained deacon in 1783 and was curate to V. *Perronet, whose granddaughter Elizabeth Briggs he married. After other curacies in Notts and Lincs, in 1786 he was summoned to London by JW (who called him 'a very pious and sensible young man') to assist him at *Wesley's Chapel.

―――――

J. Benson in *WMM* 1802 pp. 537–55

JAV

Didsbury College was established in *Manchester in 1842 as the Northern Branch of the WM Theological Institution. Its first theological tutor, Dr J. *Hannah, was succeeded in 1867 by W.B. *Pope and in 1886 by M. *Randles, representing between them the weight of WM theological reflection in the nineteenth century. Early in the twentieth century J.H. *Moulton made the College's chief contribution to biblical, religious and theological studies. On re-opening after World War I, it worked more closely with other Methodist colleges and with the university in Manchester. Following closure during World War II, the property was sold and the proceeds put to the purchase of property in *Bristol, where a new college was opened in 1951 to serve the West and Southwest, known since 1967 (when it amalgamated with *Headingley College) as *Wesley College. It established strong links with the University of Bristol through the contribution of K. *Grayston and others.

MR(W) 1902 pp. 70–5, 1903 pp. 39–42, 1906 pp. 92–100; W.B. Brash (1935) pp. 55–68; W.B. Brash & C.J. Wright (1942)

TSAM

Dimond, Dr Sydney George (1881–1968; e.m. 1904), son of UMFC minister **Richard Dimond** (1845–1925; e.m. 1873), trained for the ministry at *Victoria Park College and was appointed to some of the Connexion's leading circuits. He wrote books on psychology, including *The Psychology of the Methodist Revival* (1926). He was Resident Tutor and lecturer in Church History at *Richmond College, 1935–41 (and also in retirement after the War) and Secretary of the *Ministerial Training Committee, 1943–48.

MR 18 July 1968

OAB

Dingle, Lilian Mary (*né* Grandin) (d.1924), medical missionary, daughter of a leading BC Jerseyman. She qualified in medicine specifically for service in Yunnan, *China, where she served with distinction from 1906 to 1913. Following an unhappy marriage, she retrained and returned to her missionary appointment in 1923, but died of typhus in Chaotung within 16 months.

RKP

Dinnick, William (1840–1901; e.m. 1860), one of five brothers who entered the PM ministry, was born at Stoke Damerel, Devon), of BC parents. He combined considerable organizing and administrative ability with great energy and physical strength. During his ministry in Ramsgate (1868–76) despite setbacks, he also missioned Margate. In 1878 he began a 23-year ministry in *Brighton, during which he raised funds for and built eight chapels, and also re-established PM in mid-Sussex, around Horsham and Haywards Heath. He was taken ill during a service and died the next day.

J.A. Funnell (n.d.)

JAV

Discipline Methodist 'discipline' encompassed for JW the ordering of the life of the *societies and their members, both in personal and ecclesiastical terms. Personal discipline was strongly enforced by e.g. the General Rules of the United Societies, first published in 1743 and regularly handed out and explained to new *members (with stricter rules for the *bands). JW himself frequently examined the societies and purged the membership lists during his tours. Between his visits, discipline was exercised by the *Assistants and other itinerants, whose own itinerancy and stationing were under the authority of JW and later of the Conference. The *Large Minutes periodically summarised the Conference decisions on such matters. The use of the term 'discipline' to refer to the ordering of church life in its various aspects has continued, from the *Form of Discipline* of 1797 to the modern *Constitutional Practice and Discipline*.

Within this broader sense, jurisdiction in 'disciplinary' matters has always been exercised where, upon a charge being brought, misconduct is found to justify the removal of a person from ministerial or lay office or membership. Originally, the *Deed of Declaration vested in the Conference the general power to exclude from the ministry, but rules were adopted e.g. in the *Plan of Pacification for the procedure to be followed in the trial of such preachers through District Committees. Charges against lay members came to be dealt with by the *Leaders' Meeting, with the Local Preachers' Meeting having jurisdiction over *local preachers with respect to their exercise of that office. Provisions for appeal were made, including a final appeal to the Conference.

The rules relating to the exercise of disciplinary jurisdiction evolved, with variations, in the different branches of Methodism, and have been revised several times since 1932. Ministerial and diaconal discipline is now dealt with by a connexional discipline committee, with appeal to a connexional appeal committee. Lay matters continue to be dealt with initially below connexional level, but with an appeal to a connexional committee. The final appeal in all cases continues to be to the Conference (nowadays, in the Ministerial, Diaconal or Representative Session, according to the status of the person charged). From 1998, this Conference jurisdiction is exercised, other than in doctrinal cases, by a committee of thirty members of the previous Conference acting in its name.

HMGB 1 pp. 183–209; *CPD* vol. 2 bk III section 02

SRH

District Synod When the WM Connexion was divided up in 1791 into geographical *Districts, the *Assistant of any Circuit was given authority to summon the preachers of the District in full connexion where a 'critical case' occurred, in order to deal with the business, subject to any Conference resolution. They were to choose a chairman for the occasion, who was to lay the minutes of this District Committee before the next *Conference. At the Conference of 1792 this *ad hoc* arrangement was replaced by provisions for the appointment of a Chairman for the District.

The District Committee, or District Meeting, became an important part of the connexional economy, meeting annually in May, still technically as a committee of the Conference and with regulations for its business laid down in 1812. The preachers and those on trial for the ministry were obliged to attend. By 1817 laymen (generally *Circuit Stewards) obtained the right of attendance when financial matters were discussed. In 1819 a financial District Committee was created, i.e. the September District Meeting. In WM two sessions developed, the ministerial and the joint ministerial and lay session. The authority of the Conference to overrule the District Meeting was at stake in the *Leeds Organ Case.

Cases of *discipline were dealt with by a 'Minor District Meeting', usually comprising four itinerant ministers and the Chairman. Lord Lyndhurst's judgment in the *Warrenite controversy confirmed that the meeting's jurisdiction generally extended to suspending or removing a preacher, subject to the decision of Conference.

The MNC created District Meetings in 1844, with equal ministerial and lay representation, and the UMC constitution provided similarly in 1907. District Meetings were of particular importance in the PM connexion, especially in the mid-nineteenth century, because of the restrictive rules about membership of the *Conference; hence the culture of this period is described as 'Districtism'. Stationing of ministers took place there until 1879 and ordinations until 1932. The District Meeting in WM was officially renamed the 'District Synod' in 1892, a term already in common usage, and a similar process took place elsewhere.

Since *Methodist Union in 1932, District Synods have been held in the Spring and Autumn, comprising all those stationed in the District, lay representatives of each Circuit (including Circuit Stewards), and various District officers. Attendance is compulsory for ministers, deacons and probationers. A separate Ministerial Session continues, but the jurisdiction of the Minor Synod was replaced by that of a connexional Pastoral (later Discipline) Committee in 1985. From 1999 the Synod is only required to meet once a year.

SRH

Districts Following the suggestions made in the *Halifax Circular, the WM Connexion was first divided into Districts in 1791 as a basis for administration between the annual *Conferences: initially, 19 in England, 2 in Scotland and 7 in Ireland. Each District appointed one preacher to represent it and its circuits when preachers were stationed by the next Conference.

Districts, with their boundaries defined by Conference, remained an essential part of the Methodist structure, though there has been little attempt to relate their boundaries to those of secular or other ecclesiastical bodies. During the nineteenth century they proliferated and by 1932 there were 35 British Districts in WM (increased to 46 as a result of *Methodist Union), with 7 in Ireland.

The first District Chairmen were chosen for a limited period and with circumscribed powers. They continued to be ministers with pastoral charge. For both historical and ecclesiological reasons, the appointment of 'separated' Chairmen (i.e. without pastoral charge) was a much debated issue, not finally resolved until 1957. The Chairman's threefold role was defined in 1955 as that of *Pastor pastorum*, evangelical leader and District administrator. Until 1957 (except in Scotland) most Chairmen were either circuit ministers or District Missioners. In that year the number of Districts was reduced from 45 to 31 and separated Chairmen became the norm. Pastoral oversight and the exercise of Methodist discipline continue to be their primary responsibilities and they are ex-officio members of Conference, the Stationing Committee, and the Methodist Council (formerly the Connexional HM Committee and General Purposes Committee). From the time of the *Anglican-Methodist Conversations, there has been continued consideration of the roles of the Chairman and of the Circuit *Superintendent in relation to that of a Diocesan Bishop.

Similar patterns developed in the other branches of Methodism. In early PM, despite the predominance of circuit initiatives, circuits were grouped into four Districts as early as the 1820s and Conference representation was transferred to them from the circuits. BC Districts were first organized in 1824, each under a Superintendent who had the right to preside at the Circuit *quarterly meetings if he so chose. The *UMFC had District Meetings from the outset, but their powers and functions were limited.

As the Church's missionary work developed, overseas Districts were formed and continued until each in turn became an autonomous Conference (or part of one). By 1999 only the *Togo and *Gambia Districts remained as part of the British Methodist Church.

The purpose of the District has been set out in *CPD* as (1) to advance the mission of the Church by enabling circuits to work together and support each other, and together to engage in mission to the wider society of the region in which they are set and (2) to link the Connexion and circuits, especially in training, and also by approving applications for grant aid to circuits.

NHM 1 pp. 587–93; G.T. Brake (1984) pp. 70–78; *CPD* vol. 2 bk III part 4

JWH/PWS

Divisions *see* **Restructuring**

Divorce *see* **Sexual Ethics**

Dixon, Dr James (1788–1871; e.m. 1812), WM itinerant born in Castle Donington, began his long ministry in *Hereford which he called 'the poorest Circuit in all the Kingdom'. He quickly gained a reputation as a preacher, with a special concern for *slavery, missions and the Bible Society. A notable pastor, he had a fear of bureaucracy and centralization. Though high Wesleyan and Tory, he had an affinity with Liberals like J. *Beaumont and T. *Galland. Blind in later years, Dixon was one of the notable characters of early Victorian WM. He was President of the Conference in 1841 and received a DD from Philadelphia University. He presided over the *Canadian Conference in 1848 and wrote a book on *Methodism in America* (1849). In 1870 he asserted: 'Methodism was the most glorious development of the grace and power of God ever known in the world, but the horrors of that darkest hour [1849] shook my confidence.' His third wife, Mary, was the daughter of R. *Watson and one of his sons was R.W. Dixon, Anglican priest, poet and historian.

R.W. Dixon (1874); G.J. Stevenson (1884–86) 2 pp. 307–19

JMT

Docton, William (1810–79), born in Padstow, became a tailor. Converted in 1830, he joined the Padstow WM and became a local preacher. He moved to *St Ives in 1835 and following a visit from the *temperance lecturer James Teare became a prominent advocate of total abstinence in 1838. As secretary of the influential St Ives teetotal society he led a secession of some 400 WM teetotalers in the area and they formed the *Teetotal WM Connexion in 1841. Docton was Liberal Mayor of St Ives in 1876.

MNCM 1879 pp. 305–7

EAR

Doctrinal Standards Definitions of official Methodist doctrine go back to the 1763 *Model Deed. The 1932 Deed of Union contains clauses defining Methodism's doctrinal standards, carefully phrased to avoid their becoming a theological strait-jacket. Hence they refer to the doctrines 'contained' in the historic creeds, without fixing their formulation for all time. In particular, they stress that JW's '44 sermons' and *Explanatory Notes upon the NT* are not intended rigidly to prescribe thought. The 1976 *Methodist Church Act permits the Conference to alter the doctrinal clauses.

From JW's time Methodism has distinguished between fundamental doctrines (e.g. the atonement and the Trinity), which all Methodists should accept, and what W called 'opinions', over which Christians might reasonably differ. At the same time, ministers and local preachers have always been expected to 'believe and preach our doctrines', including such emphases as *assurance and *Christian perfection. The range of permitted diversity now permitted has become much wider in the twentieth century.

See also **Beet, J.A.**; **Hell**

'Doctrinal Minutes' (1749); A.R. George in C.S. Rodd (1987); G. Wainwright (1995) pp. 189–206, 231–36, 261–76

DJC

Dodd, John (1916–87), RAF prisoner-of-war who returned home physically and mentally scarred by his harsh treatment in Japanese hands. He was converted through the influence of his future wife. Visiting inmates in Parkhurst on the Isle of Wight made him aware of the problem of recidivism among discharged prisoners. In 1958 he helped to found the Langley House Trust to provide Christian care and rehabilitation for ex-offenders and was its first General Secretary. Launched with Methodist support, it gained official approval in 1966. Elderfield at Otterbourne, Hants, opened in 1959 as a 'half-way house' and there are now residential homes and 'move on' projects throughout the country.

Times, 4 Feb. 1987; D. Norman (1970)

JAV

Doddridge, Philip (1702–51), Independent minister, author and hymnwriter, the grandson of one of the ejected clergy of 1662. Ordained as minister of the Castle Hill church, *Northampton in 1730, he remained there for the rest of his life. Fame and influence came from his preaching and tutorship at his Dissenting Academy. JW, G. *Whitefield and the Countess of *Huntingdon were in his circle of acquaintances. JW spoke to his students and consulted him on the reading list for his itinerants. Opposing high *Calvinism, he sought to unite Dissenters, though he was disenchanted with the *Moravians. Wilberforce was converted through reading his *Rise and Progress of Religion in the Soul* (1745). Aberdeen University awarded him a DD. A number of his hymns have remained in general use, including 'Hark the glad sound! The Saviour comes' (*HP* 82) and (in altered form) 'O God of Bethel' (*HP* 442). CW described him as a 'loving, mild and judicious Christian'.

DNB; *ODCC*; W.S. Kelynack in *LQHR* Oct. 1951 pp. 327–33; G.F. Nuttall (1951); M. Deacon (1980)

EWD

Dodds, Frederick W. (1884–1966; e.m. 1908), PM missionary in Eastern *Nigeria 1909–39. He was a pioneer evangelist among the Ibo people during a period of rapid growth, making long journeys along forest paths on foot or bicycle. He was District Chairman at the time when *Methodist Union brought rapprochement with WM work in Western Nigeria. As Africa Secretary of the MMS 1939–50, he was a prolific letter-writer, especially when travel was restricted by the War.

MR 21 July 1966

JRP

Dodgson Family   **Joshua Dodgson** (1795–1870), local preacher of Elland, Yorks, set up a successful dyeing business and joined the WR at its outset, providing them with a local meeting place in his warehouse. Among his sons: **Jonathan Dodgson** (1820–1909) was an outstanding WR local preacher and evangelist. He had an experience of the 'new birth' at the 1832 WM Conference and became a local preacher in 1841. Returning from Sowerby Bridge to his native Elland, he formed a class from which came a number of local preachers, some of whom entered the ministry in America and others (including Dr D. *Brook) the WR ministry. Of his brothers,

James Davy Dodgson (1824–92; e.m. 1849) was a WM minister who trained at *Richmond College and emigrated to *Australia on health grounds, where he became President of the Victoria Conference in 1880; and **Aquila Dodgson** (1829– ?) was active in the Reform movement, served for a time as a WR minister in *Hull and Lancashire and was later curator of the *Leeds Philosophical Society's museum.

O.A. Beckerlegge, in D.C. Dews (1987) pp. 33–46

JAH

Doncaster   Although JW visited the town as early as 1743, the first society was not established until 1762. Its rented room was replaced in 1770 by a chapel in Skinners's Yard, known as the 'Rookery' but described by JW as 'one of the neatest in England'. In 1797 Doncaster Circuit was formed (from Sheffield) and by 1828 had 30 preaching places and 1,000 members. Priory Place chapel, seating 1,300 and with its sanctuary modelled on *Wesley's Chapel, opened in 1832. In the 1851 *Religious Census a morning congregation of 800 and an evening one of 1,200 were recorded. In 1872 a second large town-centre chapel was built at Oxford Place, which became head of a second circuit in 1884.

PM was introduced in 1820 with the first of many *camp meetings. Duke Street chapel was bought in 1843 from the MNC, which had only a struggling existence. By 1853 the PM Circuit had 29 preaching places and the following year a large new town chapel was opened in Spring Gardens. A second PM circuit was formed in 1870.

In the early twentieth century the South Yorkshire coalfield extended to the Doncaster area and WM responded in 1912 by establishing the South Yorkshire Coalfields Mission under S. *Chadwick. A UMC South Yorkshire Mission was formed the same year and in 1920 PM followed suit. This work continued for many years, with strong links between chapel, pit and union. Between 1944 and 1974 six separate Doncaster circuits became one. Large and once flourishing urban churches closed, notably Spring Gardens (1955), Oxford Place (1968) and Nether Hall Road (1971). Priory Place remained, with a much reduced membership. About a score of village chapels have closed since 1966, but two suburban churches have prospered.

T.S.A Macquiban (1978); G.M. Morris (1988)

GMM

Doncaster, Martha (*c.* 1806–75) converted in Derbyshire at the age of 9, began to preach at 17 and became a PM itinerant in 1822. In 1824 she became the second wife of John Ride (1790–1862) who in 1821–22 had been one of the early PM pioneers in the USA. The Rides seem to have been equal partners in the work and endured the many hardships of early PM mission stations, notably as pioneers in the Brinkworth District. In 1849 they sailed as missionaries to Victoria, *Australia. John superannuated in 1852 and they settled at Benalla. Widowed in 1862, Martha died at her son-in-law's home.

_____

PMM, 1862 pp. 5–6, 1875 p. 553; E.D. Graham (1989) p. 10

                                                    EDG

Downes, John (1722–74) was one of JW's first lay preachers and one of those invited to attend the fourth *Conference in 1747. He had been pressed as a soldier and imprisoned. Tyerman describes him as 'one of Wesley's untaught itinerants' and his mathematical and mechanical gifts caused JW to declare him to be 'as great a genius as Sir Isaac Newton'. He was also artistically gifted and engraved a portrait of JW as the frontispiece to his *Explanatory Notes. He married Dorothy Furly, sister of the Rev. Samuel Furly and one of JW's frequent correspondents. When he ceased to travel because of failing health, he became JW's printer.

_____

C. Atmore (1801) p. 109–10

                                                    WL

Draper, Daniel James (1810–66; e.m. 1834), born at Wickham, Hants to Anglican parents and apprenticed to his father, who was a carpenter. He became a Methodist, was ordained in 1835 and sent to *Australia, where he exercised an impressive 30-year ministry in the colonies of New South Wales(1836–46), South Australia (1846–54) and Victoria (1854–66) as Chairman of the District. In Adelaide he built the Pirie Street church, known as 'the Cathedral of South Australia Methodism' His election to Conference offices, including the Australasian Presidency, was a recognition of his genial leadership, enthusiasm for church building and financial ability. He was a founder of Wesley College, Melbourne and a pioneer of inter-church co-operation. His first wife died in childbirth and his second wife was drowned with him when the ship on which they were returning from an official visit to the British and Irish Conferences sank in the Bay of Biscay. Survivors testified to his courageous exhortations and prayers as the ship was sinking.

_____

J.C. Symons (1870)

                                              DGH/TMO

Dredge, James (1796–1846), son of a cabinet maker in *Salisbury, became a local preacher in 1807 and started a school in the city in 1821. He was appointed one of four Assistant Protectors of the Aborigines by the Secretary of State for the Colonies (another being his fellow Methodist E.S. Parker of London) and sailed to New South Wales in 1838. Due to the antagonism of settlers and colonial administrators in and around Melbourne, he relinquished the post in 1840 and opened a china and glass business in Melbourne, which failed the following year. He was engaged as a paid local preacher in the Methodist Church and stationed at Geelong, but his offer for the ministry was declined. With continuing ill-health he was advised to take a voyage back to England, but died at sea one day from home. His daughter, Mary Ann Truckle, married Edward John *Ensor of Milborne Port.

_____

C.A. McCallum (n.d.)

                                                    DE

Drew, Samuel Thomas (1765–1833) Cornish shoemaker and local preacher, born in St Austell. He was deeply influenced by Dr A. *Clarke, for whom he later acted as secretary. The first Methodist layman to make a name in philosophy, he had the confidence to reply to Thomas Paine's *Age of Reason* and Polwhele's *Anecdotes of Methodism*. There followed *Essays on the Immateriality and Immortality of the Human Soul* (1802), the *Identity and Resurrection of the Human Body* (1809) and the *Being and Attributes of Deity* (1811). He also wrote a history of Cornwall and an indifferent life of T. *Coke, another mentor. He edited the *Imperial Magazine* and was superintendent of the Caxton Press, first in *Liverpool, then in *London. Dubbed the 'English Plato', he was granted an MA at Aberdeen and offered the Chair of Moral Philosophy at London.

_____

J.H. Drew (1834); G.J. Stevenson (1884–6) 4 pp. 557–60; J.T.Wilkinson (1963)

                                                   JMT

Dublin JW paid his first visit to *Ireland in 1747, a Methodist society having been formed by an officer of the British garrison. Their first meeting place was later attacked and the furnishings burnt. CW visited the city in 1747 to restore calm and extend the work. In all JW's 21 visits to Ireland, Dublin was his principal base. There was a dispute with J. *Cennick and the *Moravians over the use of a chapel in Skinners Alley.

In 1752 the Methodists built a chapel in Whitefriar Street and later enlarged the site to include a Boys' Free School, a Book Room, a Widows' Almshouse, a Female Orphan School and houses for two ministers. When the lease expired, these moved to various sites, the headquarters of the Church being located in St Stephen's Green. The Widows' Almshouse continues today.

In 1818 the *Primitive Wesleyan Methodists built a headquarters in South Great George Street. In the 1890s this was adapted for the Dublin Central Mission, serving the local poor. In the twentieth century it pioneered housing projects for the elderly and the rehabilitation of offenders.

Dublin Methodists managed several primary schools (of which one continues), established *Wesley College for secondary education, and for some years ran a teacher training college in Hardwick Street.

MR(W) 1904 pp. 78–81; R.L. Cole (1932)
DALC

Duckworth, Francis (1862–1941), organist, born at Rimington in Ribblesdale, Yorks on Christmas Day, 1862. At 5 he moved with his family to the nearby village of Stopper Lane, where he received his only music lessons. At 12 he became organist of Stopper Lane WM Chapel, moving to Colne in 1882 to work for his brother, a printer. Seven years later, following in his father's footsteps, he founded a successful grocery business. He was organist at Albert Road WM Chapel, Colne, 1894–1929. The hymn tune 'Rimington', printed in 1904 though written long before, has proved internationally popular, often set to Watts's words 'Jesus shall reign where'er the sun' (*HP* 239).

PLC

Duckworth, Sir James (1849–1915), UMFC layman, born in *Rochdale, where he founded a substantial firm of provision merchants bearing his name and took a prominent part in local affairs. He was mayor in 1891–93 and again in 1910–11, and was twice Liberal MP (1897–1900 and 1906–10) and was one of only two laymen elected President of the UMFC (1894). He was knighted in 1908.

Who Was Who 1897–1916   OAB

Dudley, Hannah *see* **Fiji**

Dugdale, Bennett (*c*. 1756–1826), the leading printer and bookseller in *Dublin at the beginning of the nineteenth century. He became a Methodist in his teens, a local preacher and a visitor in the *Strangers' Friend Society. He married a sister of H. *Moore. In 1817 he joined the *PWM and laid the foundation stone of their headquarters chapel in Dublin. He was also the principal supporter, and for some time proprietor, of Wesley Chapel, Dublin.

D.A.L. Cooney in *DHR* Autumn 1993
DALC

Dumfries   Although JW visited the town several times after 1753, he preached there only in 188 and 1790. The society was founded by R. *Dall, who walked the 60 miles from Ayr in 1787. He built a preaching house in Queen Street in 1788, which the society left in 1868 after buying St Mary's Episcopal Church in Buccleuch Street. A Dumfries Circuit was formed in 1790, but debts caused it to be put under the control of the Carlisle District Chairman in 1885 and made part of the Carlisle circuit in 1899. It revived between 1905 and the Depression years and the chapel was completely refurbished in 1966; but, being found in a dangerous condition, it closed in 1981.

J. Burgess in WHS(S) 1980 part 2 pp. 5–8; H. Phillips & G.W. Davis in WHS(S) 1999 pp. 5–10
MB

Dunamis Revival Fellowship was the final name of a loosely-knit movement (eschewing organization) which sought to bring together those involved in the charismatic renewal movement within Methodism. A publication *Quest* existed between 1961 and 1965 and from 1968 a *Newsletter* circulated among those interested in Holy Spirit renewal. *Dunamis*, which had a much wider influence, first appeared in 1972. Both the magazine and the 'organism' which centred on its readership ceased in the mid '90s because of the conviction that the charismatic witness had been established. Dunamis had some shared activities with the *Methodist Revival Fellowship and Headway.

See also **Conservative Evangelicals**

WP

Dunbar Dragoons quartered in the town after the Disarming Act of 1746 began daily prayer meetings; the first society was formed and in 1752 Andrew Affleck, a baker, became its leader for over 50 years. His property in the Sea Port (now Victoria Street), rebuilt in 1761, was given over to the use of the society, probably in 1764. On this site and adjoining land given by Affleck a new chapel was built, spoken of by JW in 1770 as 'the cheerfullest in the kingdom' and now the oldest church building still in use in the town. T. *Rankin and Dr J. *Hamilton were among its trustees. It was extended in 1857 and renovated in 1890, when an oak pulpit and stained glass window from the High Kirk of St Giles, Edinburgh, were installed.

_MR(W)_ 1894 pp. 39–42, 1907, pp. 48–50; A.T. Pepper in WHS(S) 1984 pp. 3–9

MB

Dundee C. *Hopper preached there in 1759, returning in 1761 with JW, who made a further 13 visits. By 1763 Methodism had been established through T. *Hanby. Like other Scottish societies it was almost destroyed by the publication of J. *Hervey's 'eleven letters' in 1764. Dundee became a circuit in 1766. The society met in a former convent, then moved in 1773 to a former Episcopalian chapel in Tally Street. During the anti-Conference agitation of 1836 D. *Shoebotham and more than half the members left, becoming first IM and then Congregationalists. PM arrived in 1835, led by John Johnson. After his death in 1864 the strong PM society in Peter Street joined with the WM in a new church at Ward Road; but by 1869 a social divide led to a separation of the two societies. Ward Road is the only surviving Methodist Church in Dundee.

A.N. Cass in WHS(S) 1973 pp. 3–7

MB

Dunn, Samuel (1797–1882; e.m. 1819), WR minister, the son of a Megavissey sea-captain and erstwhile smuggler who later became a Methodist. He entered the WM ministry under the influence of Dr A. *Clarke and in 1822 responded to Clarke's appeal for missionaries to the *Shetlands. There his work was crowned with amazing success, so that when he left in 1825 there were over 600 members.

Back in England he was quickly involved in controversy. In *Rochdale he warmly supported a circuit memorial criticizing the handling of the

*Leeds Organ Case and joined in disputes relating to Church-state relations. This, and the suggestion that his theology was unsound, caused his reception into full connexion to be delayed until 1836, despite his success as an evangelist. (After six months in Camborne, he reported an increase of 300 members, with over 1,000 on trial.) When the *Fly Sheets appeared in the 1840s, although he had nothing to do with them, he published the _Wesley Banner and Revival Record_ partly in their defence, was asked to cease publication and was expelled. After travelling in support of reform he finally became minister of a chapel in Camborne and, after a visit to the USA, preached wherever he was invited. His voluminous writings included a life of A. *Clarke and selections from the theological works of the *Puritan divines.

J.D. Dinnick (1890); T.R. Harris (1963); O.A. Beckerlegge (1996)

OAB

Dunnell, Mary (fl.1805–12), female preacher, loosely associated with WM and the early PMs. One of the 'Christian Revivalists' of *Macclesfield early in the century, she was present at the first *camp meeting on Mow Cop and was on her way to take part in the camp meeting at Norton in August 1807 when the Circuit WM Superintendent dissuaded her by offering her the Tunstall pulpit. On a later visit she was refused the same pulpit and so began her official association with the earliest PM leaders. A woman of independent spirit and given to over-frequent visions, H. *Bourne recognised her gifts and the success of her preaching in the *Derby area, but found her a somewhat unstable character; and following a break with the Derbyshire Methodists she disappeared from the records in 1812, under suspicion of marital irregularities.
See also **Women**

J.T. Wilkinson (1952) pp. 56–7, 73–9; _North Staffordshire Journal of Field Studies_ 9 (1969) pp. 69–73; _MR_ 11 March 1999

PB

Dunstone (or Dunstan), Edward (_c._ 1724–49; e.m. 1744), little known early itinerant who was preaching in the *Newcastle area in 1744 and 1746/47 and went to the Cheshire Circuit in 1748. J. *Bennet informs us that he was 'a young man from Cornwall' who became an itinerant at an early age, and that 'in Derbyshire, Cheshire and Lancashire he was very usefull drawing great multitudes after him wherever he went.' Due to constant ill health and over-exertion, he died at J. *Nelson's house, Birstall, on 6 January 1749.

J. Bennet, *Journal* and *Letter Book*, Methodist Archives, Manchester

JHL/SRV

Dunwell, Joseph Rhodes (1806–35; e.m. 1834), WM missionary hastily despatched to the Gold Coast (now *Ghana) in response to a request for Bibles from a group of Christians meeting in Cape Coast. The swift decision to send not only books but a missionary enabled him to join the ship on its return voyage. Landing on New Year's Day 1835, he survived the climate for only six months, but encouraged the African 'Bible band' and laid foundations on which T.B. *Freeman and others were to build from 1838.

F.L. Bartels (1965) pp. 1–19

JRP

Durbin, Henry (1719–99), WM layman, a chemist of Redcliffe Street, *Bristol who often entertained JW and CW. Though retaining his association with St Thomas's Church, where he was Senior Warden in 1760, he was a member at the *New Room and a trustee. He belonged to the party of 'Old Planners' or 'Church Methodists', who held that preachers should be appointed by the Trustees and the sacraments administered only by ordained clergymen, and so was involved in the sacramental controversy of 1794.
See also **Horton, J.**

PWHS 2 pp. 40–1, 6 p. 101n, 19 pp. 138–9

CJS

Durham City, though physically dominated by signs of Anglican strength (its cathedral and epis-copal castle) nevertheless became a lively Methodist centre. Contributory factors were that it was a market town on the old North Road (JW's route), had a lively professional and business class and was at the heart of a great coal-mining region. A society was formed in 1743, a year before the first of JW's 22 visits. CW came also and on one occasion 'communicated at the Abbey'. From the first there was patronage by the wealthy, such as Miss Mary Lewen, and the support of prosperous lawyers, including Thomas Parker (d.1829), John Bramwell (1794–1882), son of the itinerant W. *Bramwell and John Ward (1771–1857), though the latter transferred his allegiance to the MNC.

The first chapel was in Rotten Row (1770), replaced by one off Old Elvet, opened by J. *Bunt-ing in 1808. This was succeeded in turn in 1903 by a Gothic building also in Old Elvet. James Willans, a local businessman, gave £1,000 towards the £11,000 cost and raised £1,450 more. The MNC presence was supported by Joseph *Love (1796–1875), a self-made millionaire who started life as a pit-boy. Bethel Chapel (1854) with its attractive Renaissance front, was largely promoted by him.

PM missionaries arrived in 1824 and the first chapel dates from 1825. In 1860 John Bramwell and Sir W. *Atherton (both sons of WM ministers who had served in Durham) took part in the stone-laying of the PM Jubilee Chapel (1861). Two of its leading members were J. *Wilson and John Johnson, both leaders of the Durham Miners Association and MPs. The long-standing links between Methodism and the Durham miners were celebrated in the launching of the *Durham Methodist Big Meeting in 1947.

W. Thwaites (1909); W.M. Patterson (1909); G.E. Milburn in *PWHS* 44 pp. 45–92

GEM

Durham Methodist Big Meeting, an annual event from 1947 to 1997 on a June Saturday, modelled on the long-established Durham Miners' Gala, popularly known as the 'Big Meeting'. The initiative came from the HM and Chapel Commit-tee of the Sunderland and Durham WM District, on the suggestion of an Easington local preacher, George Walker. Principal elements in the early meetings were processions with bands and banners, a service in Durham Cathedral, an open-air gathering with distinguished speakers (includ-ing most Presidents and Vice-Presidents of the Conference) and evening rallies. The programme was streamlined over the years in accordance with changing tastes, to include music, drama and dance and an evening rock concert. Industrial, social and religious changes led to the decision in 1997 to abandon the Meeting in favour of a biennial ecumenical act of witness, beginning at Pentecost in 2000.

MR 3 July 1997

GEM

Dymond Family **John Dymond** (1835–1910; e.m. 1857), BC minister, was born at Bea-ford, Devon and served first as a *hired local preacher. He was President of the 1879 Confer-ence and addressed the 1881 Ecumenical

Methodist Conference on 'Training Young Men for the Ministry'. He advocated the opening of mission stations in the populous northern towns and was judged one of the saints of the Connexion whose face 'shone with the radiance of the divine light within'. His son, **George Pearse Dymond**, UM layman and educationalist, was born in *Barnstaple. From 1888 to 1937 he was headmaster of Hoe Grammar School, *Plymouth, which he built up from 50 to 400 boys (including I. *Foot). His educational ideals and practice set standards for Plymouth. He twice visited the USA on educational missions, including the Morley Commission of Teachers, 1906–7. He was a JP, a Liberal Councillor from 1917 on and mayor of Plymouth in 1931. One of the UM *Guardian Representatives 1910–32, he was secretary of the UM Conference in 1913 and, as a representative ex-UM layman, was Vice-President of the 1934 Methodist Conference. He wrote a life of his fellow educationalist T. *Ruddle. Another son, the Rev. **Francis John Dymond** (1865–1932; e.m. 1886) served his whole ministry in the Yunnan Mission in *China. When revival among the tribes people imposed acute strains on the unity of the Mission, his steady, balanced leadership was of paramount importance. He married a colleague, **Maud Cannon** from New Zealand and their son and three daughters also became missionaries in China.

MR 19 July 1934, 14 Jan. 1937, 5 Oct. 1939; *UMM* 1908 pp. 296–8; *Transactions* of Devonshire Association, 1940 p. 16

RFST/RKP

Dyson, John B. (1815–1904; e.m. 1839), a much respected WM minister who was the author of substantial histories of Methodism in the Leek and Congleton Circuits (1853, 1856) and the Isle of Wight (1865). His son **George Dyson** (1858–1928) was accepted for the ministry in 1880, but left under a cloud after being implicated in the Adelaide Bartlett murder case (1886). He emigrated to America under the name of John Bernard Walker, where he gained a wide reputation as a journalist in scientific and engineering topics and became the editor of *Scientific American*.

J. Hall (1927); Y. Bridges (1962)

JAV

Eagar, Edward (1787–1866), pioneer Methodist layman in New South Wales A solicitor in Ireland, he was sentenced to death in 1809 for uttering a forged document. In the death cell he experienced conversion and his sentence was commuted to transportation for life. Arriving in Sydney in 1811, he was assigned to the Rev. R. Cartwright to teach his children. He formed a Methodist *class meeting in Windsor and was associated with T. *Bowden in appealing for a preacher to be sent to the colony. On the arrival of S. *Leigh in 1815 he provided him with accommodation and introduced him to Governor Macquarie. He was pardoned in 1818. In Sydney he was active in the emancipists' cause and in 1821 was chosen to take their petition to London. There he was successful in obtaining some redress of their grievances. He also worked strenuously for the appointment of liberals to the Legislative Council. He never returned to Australia.

ADB

EGC

Eagles, James Edward, MC (1891–1980; e.m. 1916) was born in Peterborough and became a teacher in Melton Mowbray. Soon after training for the ministry at *Handsworth College he joined the RAMC, serving in Egypt and Palestine. He was ordained in Cairo and became a chaplain. He was stationed at the *Manchester and Salford Mission (1931–36) and at Champness Hall, *Rochdale (1936–46), leaving to become Principal of *Cliff College (1946–57). In retirement he continued for many years to edit *Joyful News* and to preach every Sunday.

MR 18 Dec. 1980

WL

Early Family of Witney has been involved with blanket making since 1669 and with Methodism since JW preached in the streets of Witney in the 1770s. **John Early** (1783–1862) did much to build up the local WM society and was the prime mover in the building of High Street WM church (1849–50). His son **Charles Early** (1824–1912) was a local preacher and largely responsible for moving the local blanket-making from a cottage industry to a factory process. He married Sarah *Vanner of the prominent WM Huguenot family, and his sister Maria married J.E. Vanner. Charles' daughter **Sarah Vanner Early** (1849–1941) married Sir G.H. *Chubb. His sons, **Charles William Early** (1850–1943) and **James Vanner Early** (1853–1920) ran the family business while being much involved in WM connexionally – The former in *Home Missions and social issues, the latter in *overseas missions.

J.V. Early married into the Cole family of

*Sheffield. Two of his sons became missionaries. Dr **Philip Vanner Early** (1886–1939) was a medical missionary at Fatshan, China 1913–37 and **Charles Gordon Early** (1889–1975; e.m. 1914) went to Burma (*Myanmar) in 1914, then joined C.W. *Posnett in Medak 1916–54. His retirement was devoted to animal welfare in *India. Their two brothers continued in the family business, displaying a progressive approach to the welfare of their employees. **James Harold Early** (1881–1958) was on the MMS Committee and President of the Methodist Laymen's Missionary Movement in 1939 and was much involved with the Boys' Brigade. **Edward Cole Early** (1883–1940) was a local preacher who served on the editorial committee for the *MHB* (1934). He married Margaret Lyth Foster (1889–1964), daughter of Henry Joseph Foster (1845–1910; e.m. 1871), the granddaughter of R.B. *Lyth and sister-in-law of W.F. *Lofthouse. She was a treasurer of the MMS.

A. Plummer & R.E. Early (1969); K.E. Crawford (1996); *MR* 22 May 1975

KEC

Easter Offering originated in the Manchester District with a suggestion that at Christmas ladies should give a penny for women's missionary work and that this might be adopted throughout the Connexion as 'Christmas Pennies for Missionary Funds'. The Auxiliary Committee (i.e. *Women's Work) of the WMMS considered Easter a more appropriate time and asked women to raise 'a penny a head' in their Easter Offering. The practice dates from 1883 and later on circuits arranged a circuit service in which the Easter Offerings were dedicated. The practice has survived the merger of the General and Women's Work Funds.

C. Davey & H. Thomas (1984)

JWH

Easter People A celebration event which began in 1988, involving training, education, music, drama and evangelism. It is held annually during Easter week and is arranged by the Rob Frost Organization. It first met at Camber Sands and has since been held at Blackpool, Torquay, Llandudno, *Scarborough and Bournemouth. By 1999 it had grown from 800 to 12,000 participants and planned in future years to divide between several regional venues.

PWS

Easterbrook, Rev. Joseph (*c.* 1752–1791), evangelical clergyman, the son of a *Bristol bell-man, was educated at *Kingswood School. In 1768 he was appointed the first 'head master' of Lady *Huntingdon's college at *Trevecka, but stayed only a short while. He was ordained in 1779 and presented to the living of the Temple Church, Bristol. JW spoke of his 'incessant labours' in the parish and he was remembered for the frugal life-style which enabled him to set an example of relieving the poor. He sent his converts to the Methodist societies, which he regarded as the Church's spiritual and pastoral agents. H. *Moore preached his memorial sermon from the *New Room pulpit.

Atmore (1801) pp. 110–16

JAV

Eastern Counties (Norfolk, Suffolk, Essex) Rural East Anglia held little attraction for JW. *Norwich, which he first visited in 1754, was his main destination on his forays from London into the region. He also made frequent visits to *Bury St Edmunds (from 1755), Lakenheath (1757), *Colchester (1758), *Great Yarmouth (1761) and Lowestoft (1764), because these places were on his routes to Norwich. His role was that of consolidator: societies were mostly established by his preachers or local lay people gathering groups in homes or farm buildings for worship. They faced an uphill task: opposition from the clergy and squirearchy was compounded by opposition from Old Dissent, which was strong in these counties. Despite this, until the secessions of the 1830s and 40s, the number of societies and members grew slowly. Although neighbouring villages were evangelized from the towns and chapels were built, WM was never strong.

PM had greater success, particularly in Norfolk, spreading south from *Nottingham and *Lincoln in 1821. At a time when WM was becoming increasingly 'respectable', PM was regarded as the 'people's' Church. It gave agricultural workers a sense of community at a time of social upheaval and fostered the skills of future *trade union leaders. It also recognized the ministry of *women: E. *Bultitude served most of her 29 years as a travelling preacher in the Norwich District. The *WMA (in the *Ipswich area), the *WR (mainly in north Norfolk) and the *UMFC flourished only briefly in the eastern counties.

The 1851 *Religious Census recorded 740 Methodist places of worship in the Eastern Counties Division, divided almost entirely between WM (346) and PM (338). By 1989 there were only 438 churches, over half of them in Norfolk.

Total attendances recorded in 1851 were 136,407 (12.2% of the population) with evening services (usually the best attended) totalling 48,652 (4.4%). In Norfolk, where the Reform movement had greater influence, WM was outnumbered by PM in both chapels and attendances. In 1989 both membership and adult worshippers represented 0.8% of the population, the highest figures (1.1% and 1.2%) being in Norfolk.

C. Jolly (n.d); N. Scotland (1981); N. Virgoe & T. Williamson (1993); T.C.B. Timmins (1997); J. Ede & N. Virgoe (1998)

WDH

Eastern Orthodoxy   JW, like his father, was devoted to the early theologians of the East and prescribed the reading of them for his preachers. Though he thought them non-intellectual, they were closest to the purity of Christian origins, as he idealized it, and held authentic Christian faith. He derived his account of the character of a Methodist from Clement of Alexandria's Christian Gnostic, and Albert Outler has claimed that his dynamic doctrine of *Christian perfection or perfect love was influenced by the 4th-century Cappadocian Father, Gregory of Nyssa, through the so-called Macarius the Egyptian. Ephrem Syrus (c. 306–373), 'the man of a broken heart', he found 'the most awakening of all the ancients', protagonist as he was of Nicene orthodoxy who made hymns the vehicle of his theology. The example of his nonjuring mother Susanna was another factor, since those who could not accept Hanoverian allegiance, having sworn the oath of loyalty to the Stuarts, were drawn towards Eastern liturgy. The doctrine of theosis (deification), though Protestants of the Barthian school have deemed it dangerous, is found in the Wesley hymns. However, the centrality of Liturgy is not found in Methodism, nor the tradition of Prayer as taught by Metropolitan Anthony Bloom.

Methodism as a branch of Western Christianity largely in the theological tradition of St Augustine of Hippo, has had little association with the East, except on the part of individuals such as P. *Ineson. But a little symposium in 1965 *We Belong to One Another*, edited by A.M. Allchin, showed among other things a common belief in God's Spirit inflaming the lives of ordinary people and a note of joy in worship – a perpetual alleluia in spite of the trembling awesomeness of much in Orthodoxy.

Dialogue between Orthodoxy and the WMC began in 1992. The Orthodox have participated in the WCC and shared in the Lima document on *Baptism, Eucharist and Ministry*. They have shown alarm since the Canberra Assembly that syncretism is increasing and that there has been departure from the Trinitarian basis of the WCC. In parts of Orthodoxy there are disturbing tendencies: a repudiation of the accord between Pope Paul VI and Metropolitan Athenagoras, even a belief that ecumenism is anti-Christian, together with new religious discrimination in Russia. But Orthodox spirituality remains a treasure store for Western Christianity, e.g. the Jesus Prayer; and Methodists could well follow their founder's patristic precepts.

See also **Erasmus**; **Ineson, P.**

T.A. Campbell (1991); G. Wainwright (1995) pp. 161–85

GSW

Eayrs, Dr George (1864–1926; e.m. 1887), UM minister, born in *Leicester, entered the MNC ministry from a solicitor's office. Despite having no college training he had a passion for Methodist history and published several important studies, including an edition of JW's letters (1915). He suggested, planned and largely edited the *New History of Methodism* (2 vols, 1909). In 1924 he was awarded the Durham PhD for work on JW as 'Christian Philosopher' (published 1926). In his will he endowed the Eayrs Essay, an annual prize for an historical essay by a junior Methodist minister. It was first awarded in 1935/6, but has been in abeyance since 1988.

UMM 1927 pp. 13–14

EAR

Eckett, Robert (1797–1862; e.m. 1838), WMA minister, was born in *Scarborough, but early moved to London, where he became a successful builder. He was expelled from the WM Church for writing a pamphlet on the *Leeds Organ Case and joining in the agitation over the Theological Institution. He became the chief architect of the *WMA, planning the Foundation Deed (1840) which embodied its fundamental principles. He was President of the Association three times, Connexional Secretary several times and thirteen years its editor. A clear thinker and powerful debater, he was viewed with some suspicion by the Reformers of 1849 as a 'Warrenite Bunting'. But despite his personal antipathy to *Everett, he shared with him the creation of the *UMFC in 1857 and was elected its second President in 1858. In addition to many polemical writings, he drew up a *Covenant Service for the UMFC and 'Directions to Penitents and Believers'. He died suddenly on his way to the 1862 Annual Assembly.

M. Baxter (1865); G.J. Stevenson (1884–6) 6 pp. 922–28; O.A. Beckerlegge (1957)

OAB

Ecumenism JW's sermon on the 'Catholic Spirit' might be regarded as a proof text for Methodism's commitment to ecumenism. It is not surprising that Methodists have played active and often leading roles in the ecumenical movement. The first Ecumenical Methodist Conference in 1881 brought delegates from 30 Methodist bodies to London. This helped to heal the divisions at national level. Through developing international relationships within *World Methodism, British Methodists shared the vision of such ecumenical pioneers as the American Methodist layman, John R. Mott, who chaired the International Missionary Conference at *Edinburgh in 1910. Methodists from the British missionary movement partici- pated fully in plans for future co-operation and comity in the work overseas. Methodism was similarly represented in the Life and Work move- ment, which held its first World Conference in 1920, and in the Faith and Order Conference in 1927.

In 1939 Conference welcomed the plans, springing from these two movements, to form a World Council of Churches and appointed an Ecumenical Committee to consider questions affecting such matters as the representation and financial contribution of Methodism to the ecu- menical movement. In 1940 Methodism joined the newly constituted FCFC. In 1942 it became a founder member of the BCC and continued as a full member of the wider ecumenical body, the Council of Churches in Britain and Ireland (CCBI), which succeeded it in 1990. British Methodism has sent delegates to every Assembly of the WCC and been represented on its Central and Executive Committees. Two of the four Gen- eral Secretaries of the WCC have been Methodists: Dr P.A. *Potter and Dr Emilio Castro.

The Ecumenical Committee, now under the office of the Secretary of the Conference, is responsible for relations with all ecumenical bodies at both international and national levels, including the WCC, the Conference of European Churches and the FCFC. It also monitors the relations and bilateral conversations between the different Christian traditions in Britain. Ecumeni-

cal Officers with similar responsibilities are appointed in each District.

See also **Davies, R.E.**; **Lunn, Sir H.S.**; **Roberts, H.**; **Wainwright, G.**; **Webb, P.M.**

PMW

Edgehill College, Belfast is the Irish Methodist theological College. Prior to 1868 Irish ministers were trained in England. In that year *Methodist College opened in Belfast and included a ministerial training department. This was moved in 1918 to a house called Edgehill and in 1928 Edgehill College was separately con- stituted. During the 1950s co-operation was developed with the Presbyterian Assembly's (now Union) College, training ministers for both Churches. In 1984 a lay training department, Edgehill Christian Education Centre, was opened, offering day, evening and correspondence courses.

W.L. Northridge (1952)

DALC

Edgehill College, Bideford opened in 1884 to provide an education for girls of BC families equal to that for boys at *Shebbear. The school was strong enough to survive a devastating fire in 1920 and to be regarded as the girls' grammar school of North Devon. In 1951 it was taken over by the *Board of Management. Following the withdrawal of the government's Direct Grant regulations it reverted to full independence in 1976. The only Methodist girls' school to admit senior boys, in 1997 it had 448 boarding and day pupils aged 3–18.

R. Pyke (1934); A.M. Shaw (1984)

DBT

Edinburgh JW made the first of 21 visits in 1753. From 1761 to 1765 the society, led by Robert Miller, ironmonger and local preacher, met in Baillie Ffyfe's Close and then in their own Octagon Chapel until 1814, when it was sold to enable Waterloo Bridge to be built and Nicolson Square was built (opened 1816). To the anger of connexional leaders like A. *Clarke, who thought they were letting in *Calvinism, the trust, deep in debt, let the chapel from 1829 to 1833 to a Kirk congregation while repairs to St Giles were taking place, leaving it to the Methodists on Sunday evenings. In mid-century the Reform movement gravely weakened the Edinburgh Circuit, which fell from 570 members in 1850 to 375 in 1860; but after that it strengthened each decade, reaching 724 in 1910. In 1916, to celebrate the centenary, the adjoining Epworth Halls were built to house the Sunday School.

As Edinburgh expanded, new chapels were required and from 1888 G. *Jackson led a powerful mission which resulted in the erection of the Central Hall in 1901. Abbeyhill WM was built in 1896. JW preached in Leith in 1765 and in a 'new room' there in 1772. A chapel was built in 1818. The society moved to Great Junction Street in 1868, where the present building dates from 1932.

From 1826 a PM mission from *Sunderland Circuit to Edinburgh met successively in James Court, Melbourne Place and the Magdalene Chapel of 1541, before building Ebenezer chapel in Victoria Terrace in 1861. At the turn of the century, led by S. *Horton, it moved to Livingstone Hall (now demolished) in South Clerk Street. Pioneering work was carried out through the Home for Friendless Girls (1903) and there were satellite missions in Leith and Niddrie. PM churches at Tranent (1870) and Cockenzie (1878) are still in use.

H.B. Kendall (1906) 2 pp. 516–18; A.J. Hayes (1976)

MB

Edmondson, Jonathan (1766–1842; e.m. 1786), WM itinerant who graduated MA with a view to taking Anglican orders, but became a Methodist. He was secretary of the Missionary Committee 1814–15, immediately after *Coke's death, and President of the Conference in 1818. He published a number of sermons, *An Essay on the Christian Ministry* 'for the use of young preachers' (1828) and *Scripture Views of the Heavenly World* (1835) which went into numerous American editions.

JAV

Education Methodism has been involved in education since JW and other members of the *Holy Club taught *children of the poor in *Oxford. He realised the importance of education, read widely on the subject and visited schools at home and abroad, but was influenced especially by his mother's example. A surprising amount of what he published was educational in purpose, but he is not renowned as an educationalist because his evangelical concern to save children from hell restricted his view of the scope of education. In the 1740s he founded two single-sex charity day schools and two single-sex fee-paying schools for boarders (including the forerunner of the present *Kingswood School) at *Kingswood, a charity

school in the *New Room, Bristol and another at the *Foundery in London. He actively supported the girls' schools founded by M. *Bosanquet at Leytonstone and Morley, H. *Owen at Publow and M. *Bishop at Keynsham. In contrast to his efforts, and those of the Irish Mission, the WM Conference took few educational initiatives until the 1830s, when an *Education Committee was appointed. The WM Church then rapidly became a powerful force in education and its spokesmen (e.g. J. *Scott and J.H. *Rigg) were national figures. Methodism pioneered the idea of open elementary schools with Bible-based religious teaching, extended its *Sunday Schools, founded *Westminster and *Southlands Colleges, ran the *NCH and established local education committees. The opening of the Universities of Oxford and Cambridge to nonconformist students in 1871 encouraged the growth of Methodist *Residential Schools, although some middle-class Methodists had moral reservations about sending their sons to university. In the twentieth century, with the growth of state education, the emphasis slowly changed. Many *day schools were closed or handed over to local authorities and few new ones were opened. Co-operation with other denominations increased; and from the 1970s Westminster and Southlands Colleges were encouraged to diversify, the purpose and practice of the Residential Schools were subjected to Conference-directed reviews, and children's homes closed as NCH was refocussed on 'Action for Children'.

See also **Higher Education**

MR 22 June 1939; A.H. Body (1936); H.F. Mathews (1949); D.F. Hubery (1977); F. C. Pritchard in *HMGB* 3 (1982), pp. 279–308; D.B. Tranter in T.S.A. Macquiban (1996)

DBT

Education Committee (Methodist), permanently established in 1839 by the WM Conference, had responsibility for the promotion and oversight of the *Sunday Schools and *day schools which represented the Church's contribution to the religious and elementary education of the *poor. Its work expanded in the second half of the century with the foundation of *Westminster and *Southlands Colleges and the Methodist *Residential Schools. In the twentieth century, as the number of day schools dwindled, the Committee increasingly co-operated with other denominations whilst retaining its freedom to comment on government policies. In 1973 its main responsibilities were assumed by the new

Division of Education and Youth. In 1985 a non-executive Education Committee was created to promote connexional interest in education and advise on policy matters.

Methodist Education Reports (1839 onwards)

DBT

Edwards, Sir George (1850–1933), *trade unionist, born at Marsham, Norfolk. Beginning as a crow-scarer at the age of 6, he worked as an agricultural labourer for most of his life. He was converted in a PM chapel in 1869 and subsequently became a local preacher. He was active in Norfolk agricultural trade unionism, including J. *Arch's National Union, until the 1890s. In 1906 he founded the National Allied and Agricultural Workers' Union and the same year was elected for the Liberals to the Norfolk County Council. After World War I he changed his allegiance to the Labour Party and was elected MP for South Norfolk in 1920. His autobiography *From Crow-scaring to Westminster* was published in 1922.

R.F. Wearmouth in *LQHR* Jan.1952 pp. 40–43; N. Edwards (1998)

NADS

Edwards, John (1714–85), converted under G. *Whitefield in *Ireland, became a lay preacher and then an itinerant in Ireland in 1747. Despite civil unrest, he had a successful ministry in *Dublin and *Limerick and later in England, but in the mid-1750s, with four others, became dissatisfied with the itinerancy and with being 'mere evangelists' and withdrew. He ministered at the 'White Chapel' in *Leeds until his death. He had strong *Calvinist leanings.

Ev. Mag. 1793 pp. 221–30; C. Atmore (1801) pp. 117–18; C.H. Crookshank (1885–88) 1 pp. 93, 97–8, 107–8

NWT

Edwards, Dr Maldwyn Lloyd (1903–74; e.m. 1926), church historian, was born at *Liverpool. After service in central missions, he became Secretary of the *Temperance and Social Welfare Department 1945–48, Superintendent of the *Birmingham Central Mission 1948–56 and Chairman of the Cardiff and Swansea District 1957–71. He was President of the Conference in 1961. His preaching combined scholarship with passionate Welsh eloquence. His extensive writings on Methodist history and biography include a notable

trilogy on Methodism's social and political influence: *John Wesley and the eighteenth Century* (1933), *After Wesley (1791–1849)* (1935) and *Methodism and England (1850–1932)* (1943). His *WHS Lecture (1942) was on Dr A. *Clarke and he was President of the Society 1963–74 and of the International Methodist Historical Society 1966–71. In retirement he was Warden of the *New Room, Bristol 1971–74.

MR 6 July 1961, 17, 24 & 31 Oct. 1974; *PWHS* 39 pp. 166–7, 50 pp. 54–8

JAN

Ellis, James John, K-i-H (1883–1962; e.m. 1907), WM missionary to *India, born at Wacton, Norfolk, a son of the manse. After taking his MSc, he began training at Didsbury to become a missionary doctor. He spent 31 years in the Trichinopoly District. He taught science at the Findlay High School, Mannargudi, later returning as Vice-Principal. As an evangelist in Dharapuram he baptized the first converts in the mass movement.

MR 19 July 1962

JAV

Ellor, James (1819–99), self-taught musician, born in Droylsden, Lancs. He became choirmaster of Droylsden WM Chapel and worked in a local hat factory until 1843, when he emigrated to *America, resuming his hat-making until he became blind. He is chiefly remembered for the popular hymn tune 'Diadem', usually set to 'All hail the power of Jesu's name' (*HP* 252).

PLC

Elmfield College ('The Jubilee School'), a PM boys' school in *York, opened in January 1864. A good all-round education within the context of sound religious teaching was its basis. Ministerial training was also given there for about two years. The school survived various problems, but in 1904 financial difficulties forced its closure. However, some old boys put together a rescue package and the college was able to continue until in 1932 the development of state education and the imminence of *Methodist Union led to its joining with *Ashville College, Harrogate.

E.D. Graham (1998) pp. 6–23

EDG

Ely On his only visit, in 1774, JW preached in a private house and admired the cathedral as 'one of the most beautiful' he had seen. The earliest reference to local Methodists is in 1807. A barn was registered for worship in 1808, followed by several other buildings. The Littleport Circuit, formed in 1808 from Thetford Circuit, became the Ely Circuit in 1812 and by 1814 extended as far as *Cambridge and March. The first chapel was opened in Chapel Street in 1818 by Dr J. *Bunting and was replaced by the present larger building on the same site in 1858. A PM chapel (no longer in existence) was erected in Victoria Street in 1847. The Countess of Huntingdon's Connexion's chapel of 1879, also in Chapel Street, replaced a smaller building of 1785 on the same site.

E. Jakes (1988)

EJ

Englesea Brook, Cheshire, was an early PM preaching place, appearing on the September-December 1811 preaching plan. A local resident, Sarah Smith, who ran a dame school, extended an invitation through those associated with W. *Clowes. A small chapel was built in 1828, enlarged in 1832 when Clowes returned to preach at the re-opening. H. *Bourne often preached there, staying with his niece at a nearby farmhouse, and in 1852 was buried in the graveyard. In 1860 his brother James was buried in the same grave, and in 1889 T. *Russell, who died at Dover, was brought to be buried as near to Bourne as possible. In 1983 the chapel was saved from closure and more recently a Museum of Primitive Methodism has been established there.

SGH

English, Dr Donald, CBE (1930–98; e.m. 1958), an evangelical, conservative in his Inter-Varsity Fellowship days, his great achievement has been, through an eirenical and mediating realism, to restore evangelicalism to Methodist leadership. He was Theology tutor at *Hartley Victoria College and *Wesley College, Bristol 1972–82 and General Secretary of the *HM Division 1982–95. He is the only minister since the Union of 1932 to be elected twice as President of the Conference (1978 and 1990). He was Moderator of the FCFC in 1986 and Chair of the WMC Executive 1991–96. The author of many books seeking to relate Christianity to modern society, he was a noted biblical expositor at conferences.

B. Hoare in *ER*, April 1998 pp. 26–35; *Guardian* 29 Aug. 1998; *Times* 1 Sept. 1998; *MR* 3 Sept. 1998

GSW

Enlightenment The Enlightenment in England was both 'conservative' and 'liberal' in character. This helps to explain JW's attitude towards it. He accepted, with reservations, Locke's theory of knowledge, Newtonian natural philosophy and Hartley's psychology, partly because they seemed to support, or at least be congruent with, traditional Christian doctrines. He welcomed the practical application of the new science, e.g. in the medical use of electricity. Certain idea which he had inherited, such as the 'reasonableness' of Christianity (however that concept is interpreted) fitted the newer ways of thinking.

W did not sympathize with calls for change in the established political order, although he criticized specific policies and abuses. He believed that Great Britain and her colonies enjoyed as much civil and religious liberty as they could legitimately desire. 'Civil liberty' refers particularly to the rule of law; 'religious liberty' to freedom of worship. He opposed American independence and rejected Price's political theory. Perhaps inconsistently, he condemned the institution of *slavery.

W vigorously criticized representative figures of the French and Scottish Enlightenments, including Voltaire, Montesquieu, Raynal and (especially) Rousseau on the one hand, and Hume, Lord Kames and Robertson on the other.

JCE

Enniskillen Although JW recorded only four visits, he must have passed through on other occasions. The 'Protestant mob' mentioned by him in a letter to CW in 1773 stoned his chaise from one end of the town to the other. The first class was formed in the early 1760s by John Smith. Successful WM Camp Meetings were held on an island in Lough Erne between 1861 and 1863, reflecting the more evangelical ethos of Protestant church life in Ireland.

A.G. Hanna (1967)

DALC

Ensor Family The Ensors trace their family back to one of the early Methodist itinerants Thomas Rought (d. 1845) and to the *Salisbury local preacher J. *Dredge. **William Walters Ensor** (1890–1967; e.m. 1914), WM minister, was the son of **Charles Ensor**, a doctor and local preacher at Stalbridge, Dorset and grandson of W.D. *Walters. He was known and respected for his outspokenness on matters of principle. His son **David Ensor** OBE (b.1924) was educated at

*Kingswood School and the London College of Printing. Following wartime service in the Royal Signals, he had a career in printing and publishing and was President of the London Printing Industry Association in 1976–7, the quartercentenary of Caxton's first printing press, Vice-Chairman of the Press Council 1982–90 and Chairman of the Methodist Newspaper Company 1981–96. He was Vice-President of the Conference in 1981. His son Dr **Peter W. Ensor** (b.1951; e.m. 1975) became a tutor at St Paul's United Theological College, *Kenya in 1984 and Principal in 1995. The family also includes three Anglican priests and the historian Sir R.C.K. Ensor (1877–1958).

MR 8 June 1967, 2 July 1981

PB

Enthusiasm was a term of abuse in the eighteenth century, implying the rapturous self-delusion of people that they were under the immediate inspiration of the Holy Spirit. Convinced that they had received a direct revelation from God, contrary arguments from reason or even morality were rejected. In its early years, allegations that Methodism's 'wild and pernicious enthusiasm' undermined 'the bases of true religion' seemed to be substantiated by cases of uncontrollable weeping or fainting. Extempore prayer and the preaching of *Christian perfection and *assurance were all dismissed as 'enthusiasm'. JW replied that the test of these and other purported gifts of the Spirit was in their fruits, such as love, joy and peace. When J. *Butler, Bishop of Bristol, told him in 1739, 'Sir, the pretending to extraordinary revelations and gifts of the Holy Ghost is a horrid thing, a very horrid thing,' W replied, 'I pretend to no extraordinary revelations or gifts of the Holy Ghost: none but what every Christian may receive and ought to expect and pray for.'
See also **French Prophets**

L. Tyerman (1878) 1 p. 246; R.A. Knox (1950); B. Semmell (1974) pp. 13–17; H.D. Rack (1989) pp. 275–8

MB

Entwisle, Joseph (1767–1841; e.m. 1787), born in *Manchester and converted at 14, began to preach two years later. Having been one of JW's travelling companions, he took a leadership role in the connexion after 1791, being twice elected President of the Conference (1812, 1825). In 1834, when a senior minister was needed to help shape the new Theological Institution at *Hoxton, he was appointed 'House Governor', a post he held until retirement in 1838. Responsible for domestic matters and the pastoral care of students, he met them weekly in class and was held in respect by them.

J. Entwisle (1848)

WDH

Episcopé Methodism has always insisted on the importance of *episcopé* or 'oversight' in the life of the Church and has argued that, though it does not have the 'historic episcopate', it nevertheless provides for the proper oversight of God's people through both the pastoral ministry and the courts of the Church.

During his lifetime JW exercised oversight over the *Connexion both directly and through the *itinerants, and always presided over the *Conference. After his death, the final *episcopé* passed to the Conference corporately ('The Conference is the living Wesley'). WM regarded *episcopé* as residing primarily in the pastorate, though consultation with the *Leaders' Meeting was always part of any disciplinary machinery involving lay members. The ministers exercised *episcopé* over each other. In the non-Wesleyan traditions, *episcopé* was shared with lay leaders. At and after the 1932 Union it was made clear that *episcopé* is always shared between ministers and lay leaders. In *American Methodism *episcopé* is exercised jointly by the bishops and the Annual and General Conferences. British Methodism has discussed (in connection with the Covenanting Proposals) how personalized episcopacy might fit in with the corporate *episcopé* of the Conference.
See also **Discipline; Pastoral Office**

DJC

Epworth was the home of the *Wesley family from 1697 to 1735. Both JW and CW were born there. The Old Rectory, rebuilt by Samuel Wesley after the fire of 1709, was purchased by the World Methodist Council in 1956 and is a major centre of Methodist pilgrimage from March to October. JW returned in 1742 to find a society already established there and came every other year until 1790. He preached often in the old market place and on one memorable occasion, in 1742, when refused the pulpit in the parish church, on his father's tomb in the churchyard. Epworth was never a Methodist stronghold. The first chapel (1758) was replaced by a larger in 1821. An Epworth Circuit existed briefly 1765–66 and more permanently from 1776. Wesley Memorial (1889) is still the head of a small circuit reaching Crowle in the north and Wroote (where JW was his father's curate 1727–29) in the south.

PM arrived in 1821, with a small chapel replaced by more extensive premises in 1883. Its circuit was coterminous with the WM one. Epworth was also the birthplace of A. *Kilham and a MNC cause was established in 1797, with a circuit extending into Yorkshire. In 1860 Kilham Memorial Church replaced an 1803 chapel.

MR(W) 1907 pp. 61–4; P. Marshall (1988)
                                                                            WL

'Epworth Quadrilateral' *see* 'Four Alls'

Equatorial Guinea   PM missionaries began work on the island of Fernando Po (known as Bioko after independence from Spain) in 1870. It was the springboard for the mission in eastern *Nigeria and later on Methodism on the island ministered extensively to migrant Nigerian plantation workers. Links with Nigeria were severed when the colony became part of independent Equatorial Guinea, the plantation workers were expelled in 1973 and a period of persecution ensued, after which Methodism was compelled into a loose union with other Protestant groups.

N. Boocock (1912)
                                                                            JRP

Erasmus (*fl.* 1760s), Orthodox Bishop of Arkadia in Crete, arrived in England in 1763 and was befriended by JW as 'a stranger perishing from want'. They conversed in Latin and Greek. With only limited support from Anglican clergy and a growing need to supply his followers with the *sacraments, W was tempted to see Erasmus as a providential means of obtaining *ordination for some of his preachers. He carefully examined his credentials and got J. *Jones to write to the Patriarch of Smyrna, who confirmed them. J. *Newton and the Countess of *Huntingdon both saw the Bishop as a means of establishing 'a new ministry'. Against CW's advice, Jones was ordained by Erasmus at some date before March 1764. But JW soon had cause for misgivings about the legality and advisability of the step; and he was quick to repudiate some of his preachers (including L. *Coughlan) who, without his knowledge or consent, persuaded Erasmus to ordain them. In 1775 the incident provided A. *Toplady with the opportunity to accuse him of bribing Erasmus to consecrate him a bishop, so that he might ordain his 'ragged regiment of lay-preachers'. Both Jones and Coughlin later

obtained Anglican orders and JW waited another 20 years before taking matters into his own hands by ordaining preachers for *America. The bishop's authenticity, long a matter of controversy, seems now to have been established.

See also **Ordination**

F. Baker (1970) pp. 200–1; A.B. Sackett in *PWHS* 38 pp. 81–7, 97–102
                                                                            JAV

Errington, Matthew (1711–88), a tailor, born at Houghton-le-Spring, Co. Durham, who was converted in London in 1741 and joined the *Foundery society, where, at JW's request, he undertook domestic duties. In 1742 he accompanied CW on his first visit to *Newcastle upon Tyne. A journey on foot with T. *Meyrick to Cornwall exposed him to physical danger, weakened his health and left him penniless. In 1749 he returned to Newcastle, where he became keeper of JW's books at the *Orphan House for the rest of his life.

AM 1789 pp. 22–5
                                                                            CJS

Essame, Enid M., headmistress of *Queenswood School 1944–71, where she had taught since 1929. During a year in the USA on a travelling scholarship from Newnham College, Cambridge, she travelled extensively and wrote an MA thesis comparing British and American independent schools. Following the long reign of Miss *Trew, she was a forward-looking and liberalizing headmistress under whom academic standards rose, and outside contacts were fostered. She expressed her ideal as 'socialized individualism' and was a champion of equality of the sexes. She also served abroad under the British Council.

N. Watson (1994)
                                                                            JAV

Etheridge, Dr John Wesley (1804–66; e.m. 1827), WM minister, born near Newport, IOW. Ill-health entailed a period as supernumerary in 1838 and from 1843 to 1845 he lived in Paris, then Boulogne, where he became pastor of the English Methodist Church. Returning to English circuit work in 1846, he served mainly in Cornwall, to whose people he was devoted. A lifelong student, he had a flair for languages, especially Hebrew and Syriac, and Heidelberg awarded him a doctorate in 1847 for his work in Semitic Studies.

His writings include lives of A. *Clarke (1858) and T. *Coke (1860).

J. Harris (1871); T. Smith (1871)

J A N

European Methodism Methodism in continental Europe has both British and Irish, and also American, origins. In *Spain and *Italy missions were launched by the British Conference. Elsewhere, the first steps were taken by laymen and later followed up by the Conference: in *Gibraltar (1769 and then 1792), *France (1791), *Sweden (1804), *Germany (1813), and *Portugal (1853 and 1868). In France, Italy and Spain Methodism has more recently entered into union with other evangelical minority Churches, though still affiliated to the World Methodist Council. The work in Germany and Sweden was eventually taken up by the MEC and present-day Methodism in Central and Northern Europe is affiliated to American Methodism from which it stems.

F&H Vol. 4, Part IV; W.P. Stephens (1998); *WMC Handbook 1997–2001*

S J P

Euthanasia *see* **Medical Ethics**

Evangelists Home, *Birmingham was established in September 1888 by J. *Odell, assisted by his wife, who attended to the domestic arrangements. The staffing increased from two to twenty in the first six months. Its purpose was to train PM evangelists for special work. In 1889 30 young men were sent out to give assistance in circuits needing additional help. Later 13 men were sent out to *America. Among those who trained at the Home were John B. Bayliffe (1868–1950), shown in the Stations prior to 1917 as 'Connexional Evangelist', Bert Coulbeck (1876–1949), Connexional Evangelist 1916–31, and Tom Holland, a layman who was a travelling evangelist for most of his active life. The Home survived until 1904.

W L

Evans, Dr David Tecwyn (1876–1957; e.m. 1902) entered University College, Bangor in 1895 as one of the first Welsh WM ministers to receive a university education and attained great popularity as a preacher in both English and Welsh and for his scholarly but popular lectures and numerous articles. An acknowledged authority on the Welsh language and a great linguistic purist, he translated many classics of English prose, poetry and hymns. As editor of *Yr Eurgrawn*, 1931–51, he made that denominational journal an organ of national significance. But he remained first and foremost a preacher of the gospel, and is chiefly remembered as one of the last of the princes of the Welsh pulpit. He was President of the Welsh Assembly in 1929 and Chairman of the Second North Wales District 1936–41 and received an honorary DD from the University of Wales in 1951.

MR 31 Oct. 1957; D.T. Evans (1950); *EW* 150, pp 1–2; 168, pp. 145–208; *YBC3* (1997) pp. 49–50

O E E

Evans, Elizabeth Ann (*née* Tomlinson) (1776–1848), featured as 'Dinah Morris' in her niece George Eliot's *Adam Bede*, was a staunch defender of revivalism and female ministry. With M. *Taft, she was the focus of contention in WM over *women preachers. She gained wide attention through her ministry to the condemned child killer Mary Voce in *Nottingham. Living by lace repairing, she preached widely in the Midlands, where she and her husband **Samuel Evans** (1777–1858) established several societies. She also worked in *camp meetings with H. *Bourne and for a time joined with the *Arminian Methodists. She was close to Elizabeth Fry and leading evangelical and Quaker women.

Z. Taft vol.å 1 (1825) pp. 145–58; W. Parkes in P. Taylor (1996) pp. 9–15

W P

Evans, James (1801–46; e.m. 1827), born in *Hull, emigrated to *Canada in 1822 and entered the ministry there. In 1840 the WMMS appointed him General Superintendent of the new mission in the Northwestern Territories, where he worked among the Indians, invented a syllabic script for the Cree language and went to some effort in order to print and distribute hymns for them. Though at first supported by the Hudson Bay Company, differences arose between them, e.g. over Sunday trading. This and the blame for the death of an Indian brought his Canadian ministry to an end in 1846 and he died suddenly after his return to England. In due course his name was cleared of any blame. His younger brother **Dr Ephraim Evans** (1803–92) also served in Canada and was the leader of the pioneer mission to British Columbia in 1858.

F&H 1

J A V

Evans, John (1723–1817), CM preacher, born near Wrexham. He moved to Bala in 1742 and joined the CM society there in 1745. Though soon an exhorter, he was not recognised as a preacher until 1765. Later he was to work closely with T. *Charles and took a leading part in the first Methodist ordination service in 1811. He translated three of JW's publications into Welsh: *Primitive Physick* in 1759, and the *Rules of the United Societies* and the *Short Account . . . of Nathaniel Othen* in 1761.

A.H. Williams (1935); G.P. Owen (1997); *DWB*
GT

Evans, John (1840–97; e.m. 1861), Welsh WM minister, invariably referred to as John Evans, Eglwysbach, or even 'Yr Eglwysbach' after his birthplace, and sometimes called 'the Welsh Spurgeon', began to preach at 17 and to draw great crowds while still working on his father's farm. He went to minister in Anglesey in 1860, though not stationed there by Conference until 1861. Ordained in 1865, he served in nine Welsh circuits (including *Liverpool and *London) and made American preaching tours in 1873 and 1887. After three years in the English work in London, he returned to Pontypridd in 1893 to found a Glamorgan Mission and became Chairman of the South Wales District in 1895. He edited *Win* 1878–79 and published his own monthly *Y Fwyell* 1894–97. Strikingly handsome and with a voice of great purity and charm, he appealed not only through his dramatic powers, but also through his profound sincerity. He published three volumes of sermons and a biography of JW in Welsh.

DNB; *DWB*; J.P. Roberts & T. Hughes (1903), including an unfinished autobiography; *EW* 1897
GTH

Evans, John Hugh (1833–86; e.m. 1860), Welsh WM minister, from Ysceifiog, Flints, known by his bardic name 'Cynfaen', was the younger brother of W.H. *Evans. Having inherited a rich family tradition of Welsh literary culture, radical Liberal politics and WM piety, he played a notable part in Welsh WM in the latter half of the nineteenth century. Having been a miner and teacher and experienced a dramatic conversion, he entered the ministry and while in Welsh circuits in *London, *Liverpool and *Manchester developed his gifts of intellect and poetic imagination. He excelled as preacher, lecturer, teacher, writer, poet and literary adjudicator. Besides his many published articles, essays and poems, he did much to preserve the memory and works of his ministerial forebears; e.g. by composing a poetic elegy on T. *Aubrey, editing S. *Davies's sermons and the sermons and lectures of R. *Hughes.

W.H. Evans (1888); *DWB*
EHG

Evans, William Hugh (1831–1909; e.m. 1856), Welsh WM minister, older brother of J.H. *Evans, was known by his bardic name 'Gwyllt-y-mynydd'. Beginning life as a miner, he began to preach at 18 and spent a year as a lay agent before entering the ministry. He was a powerful preacher and a man of deep spirituality, firm convictions and fervent concern for *Sunday Schools, Board Schools, *Temperance, peace and Disestablishment. His literary output was remarkable for one whose educational opportunities had been sparse and whose life was so busy. He edited *Y Winllan* 1864–67 and also the denominational weekly paper *Y Gwyliedydd* he helped to found in 1877. He contributed regularly to *Yr Eurgrawn*, excelling as biographer, e.g. in his memorial volume for his brother. He in turn was fittingly commemorated by his son, W.O. *Evans.

EHG

Evans, William Owen (1863–1936; e.m. 1887), son of W.H. *Evans, was educated at *Woodhouse Grove School and Llanrwst Grammar School. After a brief apprenticeship to a shopkeeper, he began to preach at 18, became a lay agent and was an outstanding ministerial student at *Didsbury College. In him the natural gifts of his father and uncle were enhanced by greater educational opportunities and wider experience of ministry. After two years in the English work, he chose to minister in his own native land and language. President of the Welsh Assembly in 1914 and Chairman of the Second North Wales District 1924–33, he was elected to the *Legal Hundred in 1933. His literary achievements included commentaries on Romans and Mark and a biography of T. *Coke. His hymns included translations of CW and Watts, and he played a prominent part in preparing the joint CM/WM hymn-book of 1927. A wise and generous counsellor and encourager of younger ministers, he claimed to be the first to recognize the literary genius of E.T. *Davies.

DWB; *Bathafarn* 1 (1946) pp. 54–6, 3 (1948) pp. 18–25; 19 (1964) pp. 5–26, 20 (1965) pp. 3–28; *EW* 102 passim, 133 passim
EHG

Evens, George Bramwell ('Romany') (1890–1943; e.m. 1907), WM minister, naturalist, author and broadcaster, was born in *Hull, the son of two WM evangelists (who had worked for the *Salvation Army) and nephew of 'Gipsy' *Smith. Educated at *Queen's College, Taunton and *Handsworth College, he was an attractive personality who began to write while stationed in the *Carlisle Circuit, where he also organized activities for munitions workers. His 'Out with Romany' series was broadcast on BBC 'Children's Hour' from 1933 to an audience that reached 13 millions. In addition to two series of nature books featuring his spaniel Raq, he wrote a regular article in the *Methodist Recorder* over his pseudonym 'The Tramp'. His gipsy caravan, the 'Vardo', is preserved at Wilmslow and a 'Romany Society' preserves his memory.

———

MR 25 Nov. 1943; E. Evens (1946); H.L. Gee (1949); G. Loveridge (1995)

JHL

Everett, James (1784–1872; e.m. 1807), WM and UMFC minister, author and leading Reformer, was born at Alnwick of Methodist parents. He met JW a year before his death and developed a lifelong veneration for him. Apprenticed to a grocer, he was converted in 1803 and became a local preacher in 1804. The brothers Thomas and Jacob Stanley encouraged him to enter the ministry, though as a result of his own hesitation he was not received into full connexion until 1811. In Barnsley he became firm friends with the poet-printer J. *Montgomery, who published many of his works. He had already written a reply to an attack on Methodism, which he submitted to J. *Bunting for criticism. The two struck up a measure of friendship which may explain his appointment to London to assist at the Book Room. Though he stayed less than a year, it gave him the chance to meet CW's widow just before her death.

He had already superannuated because of persistent bronchitis. He now set about writing in earnest, producing histories of Methodism in *Sheffield and *Manchester and biographies of A. *Clarke and D. *Isaac. At the Conference of 1841 he was accused of being the author of *Wesleyan Takings* (1840), and later of the *Fly Sheets, which began to appear in 1844; and because he refused to answer the charge unless evidence was produced, he was expelled in 1849 for contumacy. The next few years were devoted to Reform meetings up and down the country. In addition he edited a Reform hymn-book and one for the UMFC (1860). He chaired the meetings to prepare for that union and, almost inevitably, was elected the first UMFC President.

———

R. Chew (1875); G.J. Stevenson (1884–86) 6 pp. 913–21; B. Gregory (1898); O.A. Beckerlegge (1957); O.A. Beckerlegge (1996); PWHS, 44 pp. 135–44

OAB

Everson, Frederick Howell (1898–1961; e.m. 1920), WM minister, born in Guildford. He used his training as a journalist in contributing a children's feature in the *Daily Mail* and, as 'FHE', in the *Methodist Recorder* under the title 'Thursday Teatime'. Under the pseudonym 'Epsilon' he also contributed impressions of the annual *Conferences. He wrote books and plays and in 1945 was Director of the connexional 'How Great a Flame' exhibition.

———

MR 30 Nov. & 7 Dec. 1961

WL

Exchange of Pastorates, a programme of the *WMC initiated in 1947 to encourage greater understanding between member Churches. Initially, and still mainly, between Britain and the USA, the programme involves ministers from two countries exchanging residences and duties for five or six weeks during the summer. The annual number of exchanges averages about 40. In recent years the programme has been extended in small numbers to other parts of the world and for longer periods, and to include retired ministers and lay people.

BEB

Exeter   Although JW visited the county town with CW in 1739 and preached in St Mary Arches church, his visits were infrequent until 1773, when the influence of *Calvinistic Methodism had waned. G. *Whitefield visited in 1743 and a Calvinistic congregation under Henry Tanner met in Rock Lane (and later, from 1769, in their Coombe Street Tabernacle). They suffered rioting in 1745. Bishop *Lavington's notorious attack on Methodist *enthusiasm was published in 1751. On JW's recommendation, the old Musgrave's Alley chapel became the home of the WM society in 1778 and he preached there in 1779. In 1813, encouraged by Dr *Coke, they bought the old Arian Meeting House and built the new Mint

Chapel, later enlarged and rebuilt in 1970. A chapel was opened in 1905 in Sidwell Street, a unique baroque domed edifice of reinforced brickwork and concrete.

In the nineteenth century WM, BC and Free Methodism all had chapels there and there was a short-lived PM presence. Seven BC Conferences were held in the town between 1853 and 1905, and one UM Conference in 1915. Samuel Sebastian Wesley, grandson of CW, was cathedral organist 1835–41 and is buried in the Bartholomew Street cemetery.

'Impartial Hand' (1746); E. Chick (1907); B. Le Messurier (1962)

RFST

Exhorters played an important part in early Methodism by encouraging their hearers in word and by prayer. Preachers began as exhorters, speaking in a class meeting and then to the society, usually warning against sin and urging repentance. Some exhorters began to read a Bible passage and comment on it. The crucial transition from exhorting to preaching came when an exhorter, whether male or female, 'took a text' and expounded it. Although in WM *women were not officially allowed to preach, exhorting was permitted, as it took place mainly within the family or in the classes. By 1770 exhorters were recognized as an important element in Methodism. M. *Bosanquet (Fletcher), probably the best known example of a WM exhorter, went on to preach, but refused to go into the pulpit, always speaking from the steps.

Minutes 1770; G. Milburn & M. Batty (1995) pp. 15–18

EDG

Exley, Thomas (1774–1855), scientist and schoolmaster, born at Gowdall, Yorks. He married A. *Clarke's sister Hannah and came to *Bristol, where he was a member at Old King Street and ran a school in Kingsdown. After his wife's death in 1810 he remarried, started a new school in Kingsdown and joined Portland Street chapel. He lectured at the Baptist College 1809–25 and was a popular tutor at *Kingswood School 1816–49. He produced around 40 papers on chemical and physical subjects and four textbooks; also *A Short Treatise on the Deluge* (1844) and a collaborative *Imperial Encyclopedia*, both obsolescent on publication. Though he was an early member of the British Association for the Advancement of Sci-

ence, his spiritual qualities served his reputation better than his science.

Transactions of Bristol and Gloucestershire Archaeological Society, 1993 pp. 201–8

CJS

'Experimental Religion' was a phrase used by JW to describe the vital, inward religion of faith and love which was a feature of his own 'conversion' and which he always longed for others to share. He asserted that 'This experimental knowledge [of God], and this alone, is true Christianity,' and in his preface to the 1780 *Collection of Hymns* described the book as 'a little body of experimental and practical divinity'. In the eighteenth century 'experimental' carried the meaning 'experiential', but in a scientific context was beginning to be used in the sense of actual experiment, putting a conviction to a practical test. W certainly wished to convey both meanings. The words from Luther's 'Preface to the Epistle to the Romans' which he heard read at the Aldersgate meeting on 24 May 1738 offer a good insight into W's understanding of the term: 'Faith is a living, daring confidence in God's grace, . . . a living, busy, active, mighty thing, . . . so it is impossible for it not to do good works incessantly.' In his sermon on 'The Witness of the Spirit' JW asserted that experience was not sufficient to *prov* a doctrine unsupported by Scripture, but *was* sufficient to *confirm* a doctrine grounded in Scripture. It has become part of twentieth century Methodist orthodoxy to see experience as one side of the *'Wesleyan quadrilateral'.

See also **Assurance**

H.M. Hughes (1915); H. Bett (1937) pp. 93–104; T.A. Langford (1998) pp. 57–9

GEM

Explanatory Notes upon the NT JW began compiling these *Notes* on 6 January 1754, at a time when he was not well enough to preach or ride, and finished them in September 1755. They were published the same year and were reprinted four times in his lifetime. Intended for use by the Methodist preachers, they have since gone through many editions, partly because of their place in the *Model Deed* as part of the *doctrinal standards of Methodism. In his Preface JW acknowledges his debt to Bengel's *Gnomon* (1742), to Dr John Heylyn's *Theological Lectures* (1749), to Dr John Guyse and to *Doddridge's *Family Expositor*. He was also indebted to Dr Robert Gell. In 1765 he also published similar

Notes on the OT and at the end of his life produced a new translation of the NT with 'an analysis of the several books and chapters'.

See also **Scripture**

WL

Extension Fund was established in 1874 to increase the funds of the *HM, Chapel and Theological Institution committees, but ultimately was confined to the support of new church building. The 1897 Centenary Fund made a substantial grant to it, and this was considerably augmented by a bequest of £45,000 (approximately £2.7m today) from John Henry Wadhurst. It was charged with the task of establishing new societies.

DRF

Faith for JW was an absolute pre-condition for the total work of *salvation: 'In asserting salvation by faith we mean this: 1. That pardon (salvation begun) is received by faith producing works; 2. That holiness (salvation continued) is faith working by love; 3. That heaven (salvation finished) is the reward of this faith.' JW conceived of faith primarily as trust, not belief, a gift received through God's gracious offer in Christ which must be initially grasped through repentance. 'It is a sure confidence that a man has in God.' 'Faith is then not only an assent to the whole gospel of Christ, but a full reliance on the blood of Christ . . . as given for us and living in us.' *Grace always precedes faith. The Methodist doctrine is thus entrenched in the classical Reformation teaching on *justification, to which is added the distinctive element of 'from faith to faith', bearing fruit in *holiness and perfect love. Such faith is available to all, it is available now, it is based on the atonement, and its application may be inwardly resisted.

JW, sermons on 'The Scripture Way of Salvation', 'Salvation by Faith', 'Justification by Faith'; *Minutes*, 1744; C.N. Williams (1960) pp. 61–6; R.L. Maddox (1994) pp. 172–6

WP

Faith and Order Committee The various Methodist connexions appointed representatives to the World Conference on Faith and Order from about 1913, and a WM committee for this purpose was first appointed in 1921. The Committee continued after *Methodist Union, and from 1951 became known as the Committee on Faith and Order, to be appointed annually by the Conference.

Whilst its responsibilities in relation to ecumenical matters and bodies (e.g. WCC) continue, as well as its function of reporting on all matters touching the faith and order of the Church, others have been added over the years and they now include the encouragement of theological reflection and study throughout the church. Major theological reports over a wide range of the church's life (e.g. *baptism, *ordination) have been produced.

The committee is also responsible for the preparation and revision, for the Conference's approval, of forms of service authorised for Methodist use, and under its aegis the *Methodist Service Book* of 1975 and its successor the *Methodist Worship Book* of 1999 were prepared, as well as *Hymns and Psalms* in 1983.

Statements . . . 1933–1983 (1984)

SRH

Fargher, Robert (1803–63), Manx LP who established a radical newspaper, *Mona's Herald*, in 1833 to promote universal suffrage on the *IOM and to encourage nonconformity and temperance. He was one of the four representatives of the Island in negotiations with Westminster to advance political reform. He spent three spells of imprisonment in Castle Douglas for publishing material on the self-elected members of the House of Keys, but died three years before his vision of a freely-elected House was realised. He was also an active promoter of teetotalism and founded the *Isle of Man Temperance Guardian and Rechabite Journal*. His son followed in his political footsteps and came near to imprisonment.

W.T. Kneale in *Journal of Manx Museum*, vol. 6 no. 76 (1959–60)

FC

Farmer, Thomas (1790–1861), WM industrialist, the philanthropist son of a chemical manufacturer. He was converted in 1809 and attended *Wesley's Chapel, London, serving as a Sunday School teacher and superintendent and as a class leader. Friendship with A. *Clarke brought him into prominence. As treasurer of the WMMS 1836–60, he offered £1,000 towards extending the work in *Hong Kong. He was treasurer of the Theological Institution and had a decisive influence on the choice of site for *Richmond College. He also contributed generously to the Bible Society (of which he was Vice-President), the *Strangers' Friend Society and the Evangelical Alliance. He declined invitations to stand for Parliament. His wife **Sarah Farmer** (*c*.1794–1868) was the first President and Treasurer of the

Women's Auxiliary, and one of his five daughters, **Sarah S. Farmer** (d.1867), was its first Home Secretary, edited the *Quarterly Paper* and wrote one of the earliest accounts of *Tonga and the Friendly Islands* (1855).

G.J. Stevenson (1885) 4 pp. 569–71

EWD

Farndale, Dr William E. (1881–1966; e.m. 1904), PM minister, born in *York, trained at *Hartley College. After Methodist Union he became Chairman of the Lincoln and Grimsby District (1933–52). He was President of the Conference in 1947 and Moderator of the FCFC 1950–51, and in 1952 became a tutor at *Cliff College. He received an honorary DD from Victoria University, Toronto. He wrote several books on PM history, including *The Secret of Mow Cop* (WHS Lecture, 1950).

MR 17 July 1947, 10 Feb. 1966

WL

Farrar, Dr Dorothy Hincksman (1899–1987), came from a family of wealthy *Halifax WM industrialists and was named after a maternal great-grandparent who had been a missionary in the West Indies. She was educated at London University, developing a specialist interest in psychology, one of the subjects she taught at the Wesley *Deaconess College, Ilkley from 1936. Having been persuaded by her mentor W.R *Maltby to become a local preacher in 1927, she encountered prejudice against *women preachers during her early years in the *Halifax Circuit. She remained an active and inspiring preacher on that plan for 53 years and contributed articles on the use of the imagination and on prayer to the *Preachers' Handbooks* published in 1949 and 1953. She was ordained a deaconess in 1936 and was vice-president of the Order in 1941 and 1958 and vice-principal of the college from 1942 to 1962. In 1952 she became the second woman to be elected Vice-President of the Conference and was the sole woman Methodist representative in the *Anglican-Methodist Conversations, 1955–63, and at the Second Assembly of the WCC at Evanston in 1954. She was deeply disappointed by the failure of the Conversations and by the cessation of recruitment to the Wesley Deaconess Order in 1978.

JAH

Farrar, John (1802–84; e.m. 1822), son of a WM minister of the same name, was one of the first pupils at *Woodhouse Grove School. He was Governor and Tutor at Abney House, the Preparatory Branch of the Theological Institution, until the opening of *Richmond College in 1843, where he became classical tutor. In 1858 he became Governor of Woodhouse Grove and in 1868 the first Governor at *Headingley. He was also Chairman of the Leeds District, 1858–77 and secretary of the Book Committee etc. He was Secretary of the Conference 1851–64 and President in 1854 and 1870. Among his biblical works was a *Biblical and Theological Dictionary* (1851) which went through several editions.

G.J. Stevenson (1884–86) 3 pp. 340–49; *WMM* 1885, 14–28

JAV

Farringtons and Stratford House School, Chislehurst, was formed in 1994 by the merger of two girls' schools on the Farringtons' site. Farringtons was founded by local Methodists in 1911 to provide an education equalling that for boys at The *Leys. By the 1920s increasing numbers led to the first of several extensive building programmes. After a short evacuation to Babbacombe in 1939, the school closed until 1946. It was taken over by the *Board of Management in 1949. It attracted national media attention in 1964 by selling 45,000 copies of the first charity celebrity cook book. In 1997 it had 420 boarding and day girls aged 3–18.

J. Waymark (1986)

DBT

Fasting   JW and members of the *'Holy Club', influenced by the writings of the non-juror, Robert Nelson, followed the practice of the early church in fasting on Wednesdays and Fridays. W continued the practice in Georgia. From 1744 he encouraged the itinerants, as a spiritual discipline, to fast on Fridays. This largely meant abstention from meat. From then on days of fasting and prayer were enjoined on the societies, for example, at times of perceived connexional failure or national crises. By 1790 W lamented that fasting was 'almost universally neglected by the Methodists'. After his death the WM Conference ordered quarterly fast days, sometimes for specific causes and through much of the nineteenth century fast days were noted on circuit plans.

Minutes 1812; J. Pawson (1994–5) 3 p. 2

MB

Federer, Charles Antoine (1837–1908), bibliophile and historian, was born in Switzerland and came to England in 1857, working as a teacher at Bakewell, Gildersome and Wetherby before settling in *Bradford. He published various books on dialects including his *Materials for French Translation* (1891). Some time after 1864 he renounced Roman Catholicism and became a Methodist, attending the White Abbey WM chapel. His collection of books and memorabilia (including many Methodist items) is in the Bradford Central Library.

S.R. Valentine in WHS(Y) April 1998 pp. 18–22

SRV

Fellowship of the Kingdom (FK) brings together Methodist ministers in local areas on a regular basis for discussion and fellowship. Originating in World War I, it was formally launched in 1919. It 'aims to enable them to engage in deep thought on biblical, theological, ethical and pastoral issues' in order to foster 'a deepening spirituality . . . without being confined to any one theological perspective'. In recent years its annual conference has been opened to spouses and other lay people.
    See also **Ministry**

GRS

Fenton (Staffs) *see* **Stoke-on-Trent**

Fenwick, John James (1846–1905) began work as a draper's apprentice, was appointed manager of a silk mercer's in *Newcastle upon Tyne and in 1882 launched his own high-class fashion store on Northumberland Street, where the business still operates under his family name. A WM with Swaledale roots, he was an active supporter of WM in the Newcastle (Brunswick) Circuit, serving as *Sunday School superintendent and *Circuit Steward.

DBB; R. Pound (1972)

GEM

Ferens, Robinson (d.1892), MNC layman, son of a *Durham draper. He carried on the family business until 1857, when he married the widow of J. *Love's son. As Love's associate, he managed his collieries near Willington and was his partner in opening new pits. A member of the *MNC from the time of his marriage, in 1875 he replaced Love as a MNC *Guardian Representa-

tive, but did not finance church projects on the scale of his former partner.

PWHS 44 pp. 73–4

EAR

Ferens, Rt Hon Thomas Robinson (1847–1930), WM businessman and benefactor, whose career was largely spent in the service of the Quaker firm of Reckitt & Sons Ltd of *Hull. Born the son of a miller at Shildon, Co. Durham, he became confidential clerk to James Reckitt in 1868 and enjoyed rapid promotion within the company, becoming its Chairman in 1927. He was a generous donor, particularly to the WM Church and its boarding schools and to Hull University College, whose launch was largely facilitated by his gift of £250,000. The College (now the University) chose as its motto 'Lampada Ferens' ('bearing the torch'). Hull Art Gallery was also established by his generosity. He attended Brunswick Chapel, Hull and served as superintendent of its Sunday School for over 40 years. He endowed a Chair of Philosophy at Hull and a Chair of NT Language and Literature at *Headingley College in the 1920s (later transferred to *Wesley College, Bristol). He was Liberal MP for East Hull 1906–18 and was appointed a Privy Councillor in 1912.

Ours (the Reckitts' magazine), 11 (June 1930) pp. 612–32; *MR* 8 May 1997; *DBB*

GEM

Ferguson, Dr Joseph (1838–1904; e.m. 1861), PM minister and Fellow of the Royal Astronomical Society, was the first editor of the *PM World*. In 1897 he delivered the first *Hartley Lecture, on the Holy Spirit. He was President of the 1891 Conference and a delegate to three Ecumenical Methodist Conferences. His son **Robert William Ferguson** (1874–1922) entered the ministry in 1900.

WL

Fernando Po *see* **Equatorial Guinea**

Fernley, John (1796–1874), WM layman from *Stockport. A highly successful cotton manufacturer, he abandoned his early attachment to the Established Church. J. *Bunting, whom he supported during periods of agitation, recommended him as treasurer of the Chapel Fund. He was a founder manager of *The *Watchman* and a strong supporter of the theological college at *Didsbury. He introduced times of prayer in his factory and was eager to give a good account of the stewardship of his wealth. His philanthropy was catholic, supporting hospitals, mental institutions and dispensaries in *Manchester, Stockport and Lancaster. During retirement in *Southport, he financed the building of *Trinity Hall School and Trinity Duke Street chapel. He instigated the *Fernley Lecture in 1869.

WMM 1874 pp. 193–204, 289–300; G.J. Stevenson (1884–6) 4 pp. 576–9; WHS (NL) Bulletin no. 20

EWD

Fernley-Hartley Lecture An amalgamation of two lectureships, one WM, the other PM. In 1869 J. *Fernley founded a lectureship to be given at the WM Conference, particularly for the benefit of those to be ordained, but also to give opportunity for publication to young and scholarly, but hitherto unknown ministers (though the first, Dr G. *Osborn in 1870, was already a connexional figure). It resulted in some important theological works by men destined for eminence, such as J.S. *Lidgett's *The Spiritual Principles of the Atonement* (1897). The Hartley Lecture was endowed by Sir W.P. *Hartley in 1897, the first being delivered by Dr J. *Ferguson. John *Watson's on *The Fatherhood of God* (1898) was the first to be published. Among later lecturers were J. *Odell on *Evangelism* (1903) and John Ritson on *The Romance of Primitive Methodism* (1909). A.S. *Peake was the only one to give two Lectures (1904 and 1919); he and Atkinson *Lee were the only laymen to lecture. The last was given by H.G. *Meecham in 1932, on *The Oldest Versions of the Bible*.

The two lectureships were amalgamated after the 1932 Union and some subsequent lectures, such as R.N. *Flew's *Jesus and His Church* (1938) have made an original contribution to theology and have been widely studied. A fuller version of the lectures as delivered was published in book form by the Epworth Press, but with increasing losses later lecturers were left to make their own arrangements for publication. More recently the lecture has appeared, if at all, as a pamphlet or, since 1998 as an article in the *ER. For a list of titles, see B. A. Barber (1932); K.B. Garlick (1983)

GSW/WL

Fetter Lane Society During a visit to England in the spring of 1738, P. *Böhler formed a group of eight young men belonging to *religious societies in the City of London into a Moravian-style *band. By October this had grown into a society of 56, divided into separate bands for youths and married men. The W brothers, G. *Whitefield and B. *Ingham were all associated with it; and J. *Hutton was a key figure. They met weekly in a room off Fetter Lane for prayer and mutual confession of their faults. The members were Anglicans, but many features (e.g. the *Lovefeast) were derived from *Moravianism and reappeared in the shape and ethos of Methodism.

Differences arose after a visit from the Moravian P.H. Molther. Disgusted by the groans and bodily contortions he witnessed, he advocated abstention from the *means of grace until the believer knew he was fully sanctified, lest he should think he had earned his salvation. Failing to convince the society that this *stillness was misguided teaching, JW left the society in July 1740 and established his own society at the *Foundery.

Under the influence of A.G. Spangenberg, the society was formally settled as a Moravian congregation in 1742 and continued to meet off Fetter Lane until its 'Great Meeting House' (originally built by Elizabethan Puritans) was destroyed by bombing in 1941. In 1959 the congregation moved to Moravian Close, Chelsea.

C. Podmore in *PWHS* 46 pp. 125–53, 47 pp. 156–86; C. Podmore (1992)

MB

'Field Bible', known as such because printed by John Field in 1653 in pearl 24mo. In the copy JW obtained in 1766 from Thomas Short, he listed a few misprints on the last flyleaf, adding the note: 'By these three marks know a genuine Field Bible.' In 1788 he gave it to H. *Moore, whose executors handed it to the WM Conference in 1844. This is the Bible which is handed down from President to President at the opening of each *Conference.

PWHS 13 pp. 121–3; 24 pp. 126–9

WL

Field Preaching was resorted to by G. *Whitefield in 1739 as a means of reaching the *Kingswood miners and other unchurched people in the *Bristol area. The W brothers had serious reservations because of its past association with Dissent and political disaffection. But on April 2, 1739, JW 'submitted to be more vile' and, encouraged by the precedent of the Sermon on the Mount, took over Whitefield's open-air witness in Bristol. He later gave as his main reason his exclusion from the parish churches. By the end of May CW too had overcome his misgivings and field preaching became a major element in the Methodist revival, provoking charges of breaking the Conventicle Act. JW developed techniques for making himself audible to great numbers. At the 1747 Conference, he declared that it enabled the Methodist preachers to reach many who would never enter a church, but admitted that, while it aroused popular curiosity, it 'rarely made any impression at all till the novelty of it was over'. He had already found, especially in *Wales and Cornwall, that preaching not followed up by forming *societies was ineffective.

W confessed in 1759 that he persisted in open-air preaching in spite of his preference for the ease and comfort of an indoor pulpit. He himself preached his last open-air sermon in Winchelsea at the age of 87, on October 7, 1790. With W no longer present to spur them on, the WM itinerants soon abandoned the open air, leaving it to the early PM and BC preachers. The nearest twentieth century equivalent is the 'ministry of controversy' exemplified by the open-air witness of Lord *Soper.

W.L. Doughty (1955); Horton Davies (1961) pp. 146–50

JAV

Fielden, John, MP (1784–1849), *Methodist Unitarian of *Todmorden, the son of a Quaker, Joshua Fielden of Haslingden. He became actively involved in factory reform and a champion of the cause of women and children factory workers. In 1832 he was elected, with William Cobbett, as MP for Oldham and though not an eloquent speaker became recognized as sincere and down-to-earth. He was re-elected in 1835, 1837 and 1841, but not in 1847. He opposed the New Poor Law of 1834, which replaced outdoor relief by the workhouse system, and in 1847 succeeded in carrying the Ten Hours Bill through Parliament. He was an active Chartist, but against resort to violence. Following his sudden death the Fielden Society was formed to further his aims by constitutional means.

H. McLachlan (1921); *PWHS* 12 pp. 178–80

JAV

Fiji In 1835 two missionaries, W. *Cross and D. *Cargill sailed to Fiji to begin a mission there and were joined in 1838 by J. *Hunt. The paramount chief Ratu Seru Cakobau (Thakombau) became a convert in 1854 and many others followed. Christianity has had a profound effect on the social life and culture of Fiji, which came under British rule in 1874. Until 1946 most of the educational work was in the hands of the Church, which still runs the Navuso Agricultural college, medical work and the Davuilevu Theological Institution for ministerial training. From 1879 on there was an influx of indentured labourers from India. The Indian Mission launched in 1892 was given new impetus by the arrival of Hannah Dudley in 1897. Dudley Church and Dudley High School are named in her honour. An independent Fijian Conference was inaugurated in 1964.

F&H 3 pp. 363–469; A.H. Wood, vol. 2 (1978)

JAV

Finance, Local Raising the money to pay the preachers was far from methodical in early Methodism. Preachers were sometimes supported only by personal gifts of money or in kind. Collections taken at *Love Feasts were often divided between the circuit preachers. From 1742 a weekly penny (plus, from 1788, one shilling a quarter) was collected from those who belonged to a *class meeting. The taking of a collection at services was a later development: at first occasional and for specific causes, but gradually becoming the chief means of providing for the circuit preachers, though at first without any calculation of what was needed. The upkeep of church premises, formerly the responsibility of local Trustees, was paid for (particularly in WM) mainly by *pew or seat rents, supplemented by giving at Anniversaries. Trust funds were kept separate from Society funds, which mainly paid for the circuit assessment. The 'envelope scheme' (which had come into general use by the time of Methodist Union) and, more recently, giving by bank Standing Order were introduced to take account of absence from worship from time to time. At present each Circuit makes an assessment on all its churches, in order that the cost of the ministry and other expenditure should be shared out fairly. One among the attempts to work out a fair system, and approved by a number of Conferences since 1932, takes into account not only membership figures, but also how a minister's time is apportioned and the ability of each church to pay. The last two are sometimes difficult to measure and many circuits take the easy option of assessing only on membership, despite the risk of its being a disincentive to enrol new members.

W.A. Sturdy (1932)

DRF

Finance, Ministerial   JW was at first against any formal provision for his itinerant preachers; indeed, he enjoined them to accept only food and shelter. As Methodism developed, however, this proved impractical and a system of carefully calculated allowances was instituted, covering only basic necessities (e.g. £12 p.a. in 1752). In 1769 an allowance of £10 p.a. was added for a preacher's wife. The **Ministers' Children's Fund** was not established until 1819, although as early as 1748 there was a yearly public collection for *Kingswood School. Direct contributions gave way to support from the **General Assessment** and later by the **Mission and Service Fund**. The fund made small grants in respect of each minister's child and contributed to various Methodist schools, including Kingswood, so that ministers could send their children to a denominational boarding school. Eventually the grants to each child were phased out, with a compensating increase in stipend. Under the latest restructuring, support of Methodist schools has been drastically curtailed; educational grants now fall directly on the *Methodist Church Fund and the Ministers' Children's Fund has been abolished.

The term 'stipend', in place of 'allowance', is quite recent, many ministers objecting to the term because it suggested payment for the Lord's work; but the word has now become fashionable and officially recognized: ministers are no longer paid solely on the basis of the cost of necessities, but with careful regard to what is paid by other denominations and comparable professions. Note is taken annually of movements in the Index of Retail Prices and various earnings indices. The minimum stipend is mandatory on all circuits and is now paid centrally. In the past each Methodist denomination had a **Sustentation Fund** which enabled poorer circuits to be supported by those able to raise more money, in order than a minimum stipend could be paid to the ministers. In the 1970s this function was taken over by the Home Mission Fund, to enable grant-making to circuits to be streamlined.

Almost from the outset there have been arrangements for financing ministerial travelling. In earlier days many circuits had a Horse Hire Fund or owned a preachers' horse. Soon after World War II, a **Rural Travel Fund** was set up to contribute to the cost of car travel in rural areas. As motor transport advanced, an **Urban Travel Fund** was also established. The two funds were eventually merged and concentrated on making provision for car depreciation. This was assessed as a cost to the circuits and was invested, to be repaid with interest when a minister was obliged to change his car. As tax regulations relating to benefits in kind became more stringent, ministerial stipends were increased and the fund abolished. Mileage allowances were a circuit responsibility.

From early in the twentieth century the **Invalid Ministers' Rest Fund**, supported by benefactions and legacies, provided properties, with funds for their maintenance, to be used by sick ministers for recuperation. In the 1980s the properties were sold and the proceeds added to invested capital, so that enhanced grants could be paid to sick ministers. The **Contingency Fund** was started after Divisional restructuring in 1973 to make grants to Circuits when a minister was sick for more than six months and when other difficult ministerial situations arose. Such grants are now made direct from the Methodist Church Fund.

Provision for *Supernumeraries was, for many years, on an ad hoc basis, often relying on local generosity. Ministers were often obliged to continue in the active work well into their 70s. A **Preachers' Fund** was established in 1763, but without JW's initial approval, as such funding for old age seemed at odds with an entire reliance on God and was considered too worldly. Two years later somewhat reluctant provision was made, with benefits quoted at £10 p.a. In 1805 it was renamed the **Preachers' Merciful Fund** and later became the **Worn Out Ministers' Fund**. Each of the uniting Churches in 1932 had its own **Annuitant Society**, but the provision made by these bodies was comparatively small. The 1946 Conference set up the **Ministers' Retirement Fund** to provide a more reasonable, but still small, pension for all retired and active ministers. Circuits bore contribution rates much greater than normal liabilities to ensure that the Fund eventually reached an actuarially sound position. Pensions are still based on cash stipends and do not include the value of the manse provided, although this is offset by the properties available through the Housing Society. An **Auxiliary Fund**, successor to the Preachers' Fund and at one time an adjunct to the Ministers' Retirement Fund, is used to make grants to impecunious Supernumeraries, their spouses, widows or widowers to supplement pensions. After World War II rented accommodation was scarce and social changes meant that ministers no longer wished to retire to their children's homes. The **Ministers' Housing Association** (now Society) was formed to acquire property to rent to Supernumeraries, beginning with flats built in Barrow on Trent and financed mainly by the local authority and the Ministers' Retirement Fund. Through generous donations from local churches, the Joseph *Rank Benevolent Fund and many bequests, the number of properties rapidly increased. The Society provides not only for retired ministers and their widows, but also for deacons and deaconesses and a few lay missionaries. In 1998 it owned over 900 homes entirely free of debt.

See also **Manses**

W.A. Sturdy (1932)

DRF

Finch, Edwin (1876–1965; e.m. 1908), born at Stockton-on-Tees, was trained for the WM ministry at *Handsworth College. In 1920 he became assistant to H. *Carter in the *Temperance and Social Welfare Department. From 1937 to 1950 he was Secretary of the Conference, and as such was responsible for *The *Constitutional Practice and Discipline of the Methodist Church*, first published in 1951.

MR 7 & 14 Oct. 1965

WL

Findlay, Dr George G. (1849–1919; e.m. 1870), the son of a WM minister, was born at Welshpool and educated at *Woodhouse Grove School. He took a BA in Classics at London University and spent all his working life in ministerial training: first as Assistant Tutor at *Headingley and *Richmond Colleges, then as Classical Tutor at Richmond (1874–81) and Tutor in Biblical Languages and Exegesis at Headingley (1881). He excelled as a teacher, but also wrote extensively on the OT prophets, the Pauline and Johannine epistles, and on Methodist doctrine in the *ERE*. At the time of his death was working on the Centenary *History of the WMMS* (1921). His son **James Alexander Findlay** (1880–1962; e.m. 1903) was born at *Richmond, Surrey. After graduating at Cambridge, he was appointed Assistant Tutor at *Handsworth College (1904) and in 1919 became Tutor in NT Language and Literature at *Didsbury College both in Manchester and later in Bristol. He was awarded an honorary DD by St Andrews University. His supreme aim was to interpret Jesus, which he did both in his teaching, preaching and writing, and through his own attractive character.

MR 6 & 13 Nov. 1919

CSR

Findlay, William Hare (1857–1919; e.m. 1880), WM missionary to *India, born at Malton, Yorks, the younger brother of G.G. *Findlay.

He was educated at *Woodhouse Grove School, London University and Merton College, Oxford and served in the Madras District 1881–1900, where he was Principal of the Negapatam High School and founded Findlay College at Mannargudi. He made an effective defence of India missionaries in the *Missionary Controversy of 1890 and as a Missionary Secretary from 1900 to 1910 made a vital force of the new Home Organization Department. He spent a year publicizing the Edinburgh World Missionary Conference of 1910 and, returning to India to carry out a missionary survey, died in Madras.

MR 11 Dec. 1919

JAV

Finney, John W. (1913–97), IM minister and missionary to *India, 1945–79, was born in Prescot, Merseyside. From 1949 he worked with the American Methodist missions, developing Christian-based technical education, establishing a Technical School at the Ingraham Institute, Ghaziabad and a Methodist Technical School at Baroda. From 1972 to 1979 he was Executive Secretary for all Methodist Technical Education in India.

John Finney, Pioneer of Technical Education in India (Wigan, 1972); *The Connexion* July and Aug. 1997

JAD

Firth, Mark (1819–80), MNC industrialist, the son of a *Sheffield steel smelter. In 1842, with his father and brother, he founded a steel works, Thomas Firth & Sons, which grew into a large and profitable concern. From 1850 he was head of the firm, which for many years forged all the 80-ton guns for the Royal Navy. Active in Sheffield life and mayor in 1865, his benefactions included almshouses (1869), a public park (1875) and Firth College (1880), which became Sheffield University. Though prominent in the MNC as Mission Treasurer and then College Treasurer, towards the end he came to prefer Anglican worship. His brother **Thomas Firth junr** (1821–60) was a member of the MNC and had a long-standing concern for ministerial education, by enabling students to lodge with leading ministers for theological and practical training. His bequest of £5,000 made possible the opening of *Ranmoor College in 1864.

See also **Ranmoor College**

DNB; G.J. Stevenson (1884–6) 4 pp. 653–5; *MNCM* 1860 p. 409

EAR

Fish, William (1764–1843; e.m. 1785), one of the early missionaries to the *West Indies, appointed in 1792 to Jamaica, where he served for 13 years, four of them alone. He sought to make the Montego Bay mission a centre for the evangelizing of West Jamaica, but had to leave because of adversity caused by the Maroon rebellion in 1797. He returned to England in 1805 in failing health.

GRS

Fisher, Philip John (1883–1961; e.m. 1905), PM minister, born in Maidenhead. He trained at *Hartley College and was a chaplain in France and Flanders throughout World War I. His advocacy of overseas missions led him to serve as chairman of the 'Western Committee' and he was also a member of the *Faith and Order Committee. He was editor of the *Methodist Leader* 1930–33 and co-editor of the *Methodist Times and Leader* 1933–37. His books included plays, devotional works and poetry.

MR 13 July 1961

JAV

Fitchett, Dr William Henry (1841–1928; e.m. 1865), Australian minister, born in *Grantham. When he was 7 his family emigrated to *Australia, where his father, who was consumptive, died within a year. Working from an early age as a quarryman near Geelong and a jackaroo in Queensland, he was self-educated, proving a voracious reader. Converted at 16, he was called to fill a ministerial vacancy caused by illness and graduated at Victoria University, which later granted him an honorary LLD. He was the founder and, for 46 years, the Principal of the Methodist Ladies' College at Hawthorne, Melbourne, was twice President of the Victoria WM Conference and once of the Australasian Conference. He was an indefatigable and influential journalist, edited the interdenominational *Southern Cross* and the monthly magazine *Life* (which he had founded) and was engaged by Lord Northcliffe to report the coronation of George V. His many books included imperialistic works such as the popular *How England Saved Europe* (in Napoleonic times) (4 vols, 1899–1900), the *Fernley Lecture of 1905 on *The Unrealized Logic of Religion*, which deeply influenced L.D. *Weatherhead, and a major study of *Wesley and his Century* (1906). His implacable opposition to modern biblical scholarship (especially the work of E.H. *Sugden and A.S. *Peake) was expressed

in *Where the Higher Criticism Fails* (1922).

C. Irving Benson in *Heritage* October 1960

JAV

Fitzgerald, Lady Mary (1725–1815), born Lady Mary Hervey, was successively daughter, sister and aunt to Earls of Bristol, and also aunt to the 2nd Earl of Liverpool (prime minister 1812–27). Her marriage to George Fitzgerald was an unhappy one, ending in a separation. About 1765 she rejected the life of high society, devoting herself to the spiritual life and her wealth to charitable work. She was a close friend of JW and one of J. *Fletcher's correspondents. She is buried at *Wesley's Chapel, London.

WMM 1815 pp. 522–32

PSF

Fitzgerald, William Blackburn (1856–1931; e.m. 1877), WM minister, a son of the manse, born at Barnard Castle and educated at *Kingswood School and *Headingley College. In 1890 he formulated the idea of the *Wesley Guild to bridge the gap between Sunday School and Church. The method worked at Roscoe Place, *Leeds and was adopted by the 1896 Conference. In 1906 Fitzgerald was set apart to be secretary of the Guild at Oxford Place Chambers, *Leeds. He edited the *Guild Magazine*, pioneered the Guild Holiday Homes and its support for medical missions. The *'Four Alls of Methodism' originated with him in 1903.

L.E. Ingram (1945)

JMT

Flanagan, James (1851–1918; e.m. 1891), a *Mansfield coal miner, born to a drunken Irish RC father, was converted at Bath Street PM chapel in 1872 and became a local preacher in 1874. Gaining a reputation for evangelism, he was appointed *Nottingham City Missioner in 1885 and in 1887 Superintendent of the Albert Hall. Entering the PM ministry in 1891, he served in the Southwark Circuit, which became the London South East Mission following the opening of St George's Hall in 1905. His autobiography, *Scenes from my Life* was published in 1907.

MR(W) 1907 pp. 51–3; D. Crane (1906); R.W. Russell (1920)

DCD

Flesher, John (1801–74; e.m. 1822), PM minister, son of a Silsden schoolmaster, began preaching at 20 from the doorstep of his father's house. He had exceptional gifts as both preacher and administrator. He was sent to *Edinburgh to sort out problems in that city and to *London when difficulties arose there. As Connexional Editor 1842–52, he gave a new lease of life to the connexional magazines and organized the removal of the Book Room from *Bemersley to the Sutton Street premises which he had built in London. He established the General Missionary Committee, published the Consolidated Minutes (1850) and a new PM Hymn-book (1853).

F.H. Hurd (1872) pp. 216–35

WL

Fletcher Family of Silsden. **Joshua Fletcher** (1802–75), a wool-comber, was converted under John *Flesher and became a PM local preacher in 1822. He was elected a member of the PM Deed Poll in 1873 and gave financial support to a number of chapels. His son **William Fletcher** (1828–86), a successful manufacturer and chairman of the Silsden Liberal Association, was treasurer of the General Chapel Fund. He attended eight PM Conferences. William's son **Richard Fletcher** (b.1851) was a manufacturer of fancy goods, a JP, a member of the Urban District Council and County Councillor. He was Vice-President of the Conference in 1907. Another son, **Tom Fletcher** (b.1854), a coal merchant, was Vice-President of the Conference in 1911. He was Vice-President of the Liberal Association for the Skipton Division and Chairman of the District Council. All were local preachers and held many offices in the local PM church and Sunday School.

W.J. Robson (1910)

WL

Fletcher, Rev. John William (1729–85), born Jean Guillaume de la Fléchère, of an aristocratic family in Nyon, Switzerland. He attended Geneva University (1746), but rejected the ministry to pursue a military career. Thwarted in this, he came to England in 1750 and became tutor to the sons of Thomas Hill, a Shropshire MP. He experienced an evangelical conversion in January 1755, was ordained in 1757 and became involved with JW, CW and Lady *Huntingdon in London Methodism.

Nominally curate of *Madeley, Salop on ordination, he was drawn to that parish, which included Coalbrookdale, the 'cradle of the Industrial Revolution', and was notorious for 'the ignorance and profanity of its inhabitants'. Inducted as vicar in 1760, his ministry was outstanding for its preaching and pastoral qualities, especially in the new industrial areas. He also developed a wider ministry, but firmly resisted JW's attempts to persuade him to itinerate and to be nominated as his successor. In 1775 he and J. *Benson proposed a plan to keep Methodism within the CofE.

In 1768 he was appointed President of Lady *Huntingdon's College at Trevecka, but the reaction against JW's 1770 *Minutes* led to his resignation, and the damaging *Calvinistic controversy, in which he was the main exponent of the *Arminian position. His *Checks to Antinomianism* (1771–75) were long regarded as the model of Arminian doctrine, arguing chiefly for the moral necessity of good works accompanying faith. His main adversaries were A.M. *Toplady, Sir R. *Hill and the Rev. R. *Hill. His final contributions to the controversy suggest that Calvinism and Arminianism should co-exist. His collected *Works*, edited by Benson, were published in 9 volumes, 1806–1808.

By 1775 the strain of his writing commitment, alongside an assiduous parish ministry and an ascetic lifestyle, led to a breakdown in health and he spent periods convalescing in London and *Bristol, then in Switzerland (1778–81), which he had also revisited in 1770. He travelled also in France and Italy with his friend and patron, James Ireland, a Bristol sugar merchant. In Nyon his ministry was initially welcomed, but later rejected. On 12 November 1781, after many years' acquaintance, he married M. *Bosanquet. They ministered together in Madeley and visited *Dublin in 1783. Fletcher died of typhoid during an epidemic in Madeley. Recognized increasingly as a saint during his lifetime, his reputation grew posthumously and in many ways he exemplified JW's teaching on *Christian Perfection.

J. Wesley (1786); C. Atmore (1801) pp. 125–42; J. Benson (1804); L. Tyerman (1882); G.J. Stevenson (1884–6) 1 pp. 128–41; F.W. Macdonald (1885); G. Lawton (1960); F. Baker in *LQHR* Oct. 1960 pp. 291–8; B. Trinder (1973) pp. 267–81; P.S. Forsaith (1994)

PSF

Flew, Dr Robert Newton (1886–1962; e.m. 1913), a leading NT scholar and ecumenist, taught NT at *Wesley House, Cambridge, 1927–55 (Principal from 1937). He was President of the Conference in 1946. A magisterial theologian and a leader of the inter-war Faith and Order Movement, his *Idea of Perfection in Christian Theology* (1934) was a comprehensive survey of the history of the doctrine, with a valuable restatement of the WM tradition in modern terms. His *Fernley-Hartley Lecture, *Jesus and his Church* (1938) dealt with NT ecclesiology in the light of modern scholarship, and the Conference statement on 'The Nature of the Christian Church' (1937), the first comprehensive ecclesiological statement formally approved by British Methodism, bears the marks of his influence. He was co-editor with R.E. *Davies of *The Catholicity of Protestantism* (1950) and in 1953 gave the WHS Lecture on *The Hymns of Charles Wesley*.

MR 18 July 1946, 13 & 20 Sept. 1962; F. Tice (1966) pp. 124–30; G.S. Wakefield (1971)

DJC

Fly Sheets, a series of anonymous papers, circulated to WM ministers between 1844 and 1849. For some years there had been growing resentment at the power of J. *Bunting and what was regarded as a small clique of ministers in London. In 1846 WM ministers received an anonymous pamphlet, *Fly Sheets from the Private Correspondent*; a second was issued later in the year, a third in 1847, a fourth in 1848, and a fifth after the expulsions. They were critical of what they called 'centralization', of Mission House extravagance, of the Connexional Committee and of the *Stationing Committee. On almost every page Bunting's name appeared in a bad light. They were answered in 1849 in five 'Papers on Wesleyan Matters', published by the Book Room. These were also anonymous and even more scurrilous than the Fly Sheets, which were reprinted as a result. Instead of investigating and answering the complaints, Bunting's friends set about trying to discover the author(s) of the Fly Sheets. G. *Osborn was authorized to distribute a declaration for signature by the ministers, stating that they abhorred the attacks and had nothing to do with their production. But by the Conference of 1849 36 signatures were still lacking. Osborn tried to examine them one by one in the Conference. Everett was sent for from *York, but asked why he should be singled out. Told that he was the main suspect, he replied that in that case they must have evidence and demanded that it be produced. When he refused to answer in the absence of evidence, he was expelled, as were two others, S. *Dunn and W. *Griffith. This led to the eventual formation of the *UMFC.

B. Gregory (1898); E.C. Urwin (1949); O.A. Beckerlegge (1957)

OAB

Foot Family   **Isaac Foot senr** (1843–1927), a WM *local preacher of evangelical bent, was born in Horrabridge, Devon. He worked as a carpenter and undertaker and as a young man moved to *Plymouth, where he established a large building business. He built the independent Mission Hall in Notte Street, Plymouth. His son **Isaac Foot junr** (1880–1960) was born in Plymouth and educated at Hoe Grammar School under G.P. *Dymond. After a spell in the Civil Service he trained as a lawyer and set up practice in Plymouth as Foot and Bowden. He was Liberal MP for Bodmin, 1922–24 and 1929–35 and Minister for Mines, 1931–32. He last contested an election in 1945, when three of his sons also stood. He was Lord Mayor of Plymouth in 1945–46 and Vice-President of the Conference in 1937. Like his father, he was a *temperance advocate. A compulsive bibliophile with a remarkable memory, he lived in later years at Pencreber, Callington, which housed his vast library, sold on his death to the University of California. He habitually annotated his books heavily, but was the author only of a few booklets. His children included: **Sir Dingle Mackintosh Foot QC** (1905–78), barrister, Liberal MP for *Dundee 1931–45 and later Labour MP for *Ipswich and Solicitor General in the Labour Government of 1964–67; **Hugh Mackintosh Foot**, later Lord Caradon (1907–90), Governor of Cyprus in the 1950s and Permanent Representative to the UN 1964–70, maintaining his Methodist connection; **John Mackintosh Foot**, later Lord Foot (1909–), Plymouth solicitor; and **Michael Mackintosh Foot** (1913–), journalist, author, keen pacifist, Labour MP and leader of his party in opposition, 1980–83.

Times 20 June 1978, 6 Sept. 1990; *MR* 15 & 22 Dec. 1960, 20 Sept. 1990; H. Foot (1964); S. Foot (1980)

RFST

Forest Methodists (otherwise known as 'Magic Methodists') were a group in Delamere Forest, Cheshire, under the leadership of J. *Crawfoot, a *local preacher and mystic. At service held in his home people fell into trances and claimed to experience visions in which preachers admired in their circle were shown in a certain hierarchy. They believed that spiritual power could be called down by prayer and conveyed by the laying on of hands. Crawfoot exercised a strong influence on H. *Bourne and W. *Clowes, who regarded him for a time as a spiritual mentor. However, the visions of the Forest Methodists were short-lived and little was heard of them after 1811. They represented a phase in PM development which passed as Bourne started to teach that *grace and power could be present without spectacular gifts.

G. Herod (1855); H.B. Kendall (1906) 1 pp. 147–54; H.D. Rack (1996)

JAD

Forsyth, Samuel (1881–1960; e.m. 1908), Irish evangelist, born in Co Tyrone to farming parents. He emigrated to *Australia in 1901 and in 1929 was appointed Superintendent of the Adelaide central Mission. He was an excellent fundraiser and organizer, with a very real concern for those in need. During the 1930s Depression he established Kuitpo Colony as a self-supporting community for unemployed men. In 1940 it became a home for the rehabilitation of alcoholics. He was responsible for the purchasing of radio station 5KA in 1944 and the establishment of Aldersgate Village to provide homes for the elderly.

DGH

Forward Movement began in the 1880s, partly in response to *The Bitter Cry of Outcast London* (1883), which focussed attention on the desperate plight of the urban poor in the late Victorian age. Under the leadership of men like H.J. *Pope in *Manchester and H.P. *Hughes in London, a determined effort was made to bridge the widening gap between WM and the working classes. One feature was the building of 'Central Halls', beginning with *Manchester Central Hall in 1886 and ending with Archway, London in 1934. These were secular in their architecture and furnishings and in the activities they provided as an alternative attraction to the music hall and public house. Much effective social work was done before the advent of the Welfare State, but the impact began to wane as their novelty wore off in the twentieth century; and they were palliative rather than remedial in their treatment of political and social evils.

C. Oldstone-Moore (1999)

JAV

Foster, David Blyth (1858–1945), born at Holme-upon-Spalding Moor, became a WM *local preacher at 17. Entering the drapery trade in Pudsey, he became a manager in Morley, he launched his own successful business in *Leeds in 1887. Because of his Tolstoyan Christian Socialist beliefs, he gave up his business in 1897 to become an electrician on a worker's wage. He set up the

Tolstoyan Brotherhood movement in Holbeck, Leeds in 1892, joined the Labour Church in 1895 and then formed his own Christian Socialist Church. Though he appears to have ceased to be a local preacher, he continued to preach. After many attempts, in 1911 he was elected as a Labour Councillor in Leeds and was Lord Mayor in 1928.

DCD

Foster, John (1897–1973; e.m. 1922) WM missionary in *China, studied at *Handsworth College and served in the South China District 1922–37. He lived simply, learned Chinese and was known to his Chinese colleagues as 'the gentle scholar'. He lectured in Cantonese on doctrine and church history in the Union Theological College. From 1937 he was Professor of Church History at Selly Oak, Birmingham, then became the first professor (and later Dean) in the Faculty of Divinity at Glasgow who was not a minister of the Kirk. He had a gift of combining scholarship with popular and lucid presentation and was a successful broadcaster. In retirement he published two volumes of a projected history of the Church: *The First Advance* (1972) and *Setback and Recovery* (19).

MR 22 Nov. & 13 Dec. 1973

JAV

Foulger, Thomas Robert (1896–1998; e.m. 1921), WM missionary in *India, born in Hastings. After war service he trained at *Richmond College and soon after arriving in Madras in 1923 became headmaster of Wesley College High School, Royapettah and in 1937 founder and first Principal of Meston Training College for postgraduate men teachers. The title of his MA thesis, obtained while on furlough in 1930, was 'The Psychological Approach to Religious Education'. He was at various times President of the Faculty of Teaching and chairman of the Board of Studies in the University of Madras, and held the chairs of Educational Psychology and of Comparative Education. In addition he served as Secretary and Chairman of the Madras District. From 1939 on he was involved in the discussions leading to the formation of the CSI and was credited by Bishop Stephen Neil with having broken the log-jam at a crucial point in the negotiations.

MR 21 Jan.1999

JAV

Foundery, London For over 45 years JW's headquarters in London was the former royal arsenal on Windmill Hill to the north of Moorfields, which had stood empty since an explosion seriously damaged it in 1716. In 1739 JW acquired the lease for £115, spent £700 repairing and equipping it and held the first service there on 11 November. When he withdrew from the *Fetter Lane society in July 1740, the Foundery became the home of the first Methodist society in London. It was a multi-purpose building, with two entrances, one into the preaching house and the other into the living quarters and band-room, which also served as schoolroom and book room (where Methodist publications were stored and sold). There was also stabling for the preachers' horses. The preaching house, complete with galleries, held 1,500, with men and women segregated Moravian-style. The living quarters included rooms for JW himself, his mother during her closing years, some of his preachers and a number of poor widows. He insisted on a common table for the whole 'family'. The school for poor children had two teachers and 60 pupils and for many years was in the charge of S. *Told. One of the earliest ventures was the first free dispensary in London, for which JW later engaged an apothecary and a surgeon. By 1776 the lease was running out and JW made plans for a move to his 'new chapel in the City Road'. But the Foundery was not finally given up until November 1785.

G.J. Stevenson (1872) pp. 13–60; J.H. Martin (1946) pp. 20–9; M.W. Woodward (1966) pp. 17–33

JAV

'Four Alls'   A convenient summary of the 'Methodist gospel', sometimes called the 'Epworth Quadrilateral'. It was formulated by W.B. *Fitzgerald in 1903: 'All need to be saved; all can be saved; all can know themselves to be saved; and all can be saved to the uttermost.' This pinpoints four characteristic emphases that derive from the *Arminianism of JW's own teaching and preaching; i.e. the cardinal doctrines of *original sin, *salvation by *grace through *faith, *assurance and *sanctification. In 1909 Dr G. *Eayrs added a fifth clause: 'All should declare their salvation,'(echoed at the Ecumenical Methodist Conference in 1951 by W.E. *Sangster as 'All must witness to their salvation').

JAV

Fowler, Joseph (1791–1851; e.m. 1811), WM minister, born at Horton near *Bradford. Despite being an upholder of Methodist discipline, he became a leading opponent of J. *Bunting in the *Conference and B. *Gregory's *Sidelights* was based on the record he kept of the Conference debates between 1827 and 1849. He was appointed Secretary of the Conference in 1848, but his health failed shortly afterwards. His younger son **Henry Hartley Fowler** (1830–1911), born in *Sunderland and educated at *Woodhouse Grove School, became a solicitor and moved to *Wolverhampton in 1855, becoming mayor in 1863 and chairman of the first School Board in 1870. He was elected MP for the town in 1880–1908 and joined the Cabinet in 1892 as President of the Local Government Board. He married Ellen Thorneycroft, the daughter of a local ironmaster. He was Secretary of State for India 1894–95, was considered a possible successor to Gladstone as leader of the Liberal Party, and was Chancellor of the Duchy of Lancaster 1905–8 and Lord President of the Council 1905–10. From 1876 he was a partner of R. *Perks and as Viscount Wolverhampton (1908) was the first Methodist to sit in the Lords. His daughters, **Ellen Thorneycroft Fowler** (Mrs A.L. Felkin, 1860–1929) and **Edith Henrietta Fowler** (Mrs W.R. Hamilton, b. 1865) were both novelists. *Concerning Isabel Carnaby* (1898) by the former was partly autobiographical.

Times 27 Feb. 1911, 24 June 1929; E.H. Fowler (1912)

JAV

Foy, Captain, of Bristol *see* **Class Meetings; New Room**

France   Methodism was first taken into France from the *Channel Islands at the instigation of a Guernsey businessman, Jean Angel. He encouraged T. *Coke to visit Paris in 1791 and two of his friends, W. *Mahy and J. *de Quetteville, began a mission with Coke's support. After the Napoleonic Wars it was taken under the wing of the WMMS and from 1819 was consolidated under the leadership of C. *Cook. A semi-autonomous French Conference was formed in 1852. But financial dependence on British Methodism continued and in the wake of the Franco-Prussian War the 1871 Conference was persuaded by Cook's son Emile to launch a special Relief Fund. Methodism was found mainly in the Paris area, Normandy, parts of central and eastern France, the Midi and French-speaking Switzerland. In 1939 all but a minority of churches and members united with the French Reformed Church to become the Evangelical Methodist Church. Those which stayed out were in the Midi, where relations with the state-supported Reformed churches had been unhappy. An English-speaking church was located in the Rue Roquépine, Paris from 1862 until 1977, its first pastor being W. *Gibson. The Evangelical Methodist Church is affiliated to the *WMC and in 1997 reported 950 members and a total community of 1,550.

See also **Cook, Charles**; **Cornforth, William**; **Gallienne, Matthieu**; **Hocart, James**; **Lelièvre, Matthieu**; **Toase, William**

F&H 4 pp. 444–59; Th. Roux (1941); C.J. Davey (n.d.); W.P. Stephens (n.d.); J. Waller in *PWHS* 45 pp. 97–115

SJP

Francis, David Noel (1904–92; e.m. 1930), born in London, was educated, after a brief spell in banking, at Peterhouse and *Wesley House, Cambridge. After service in the Home Organization Department of the *MMS, in 1933 he went for eight years to Hyderabad; then in 1958 became secretary of the Local Preachers' Department. He was a founder member of the Young Laymen's League and for some years its general secretary. For eight years he edited the *Bulletin of the *Fellowship of the Kingdom*. He wrote several books, the last entitled *Jesus – Our Way to God*.

MR 11 June 1992

KGG

Free Gospel Churches, a term used to describe churches which operated on an unpaid local ministry. Some IM churches went under this name. The *Original Methodists and the *Protestant Methodists also worked on this basis, but had a much shorter history.

JAD

***Free Methodist** see* **United Methodist**

Free Methodist Church, a conservative *holiness body which separated from the MEC in 1860 in an agitation over perfection, 'episcopal despotism' and free pews. The Canadian Holiness Movement Church, which began work in Ulster in the 1890s, united with the Free Methodists in 1957 and the new larger body extended the work in *Ireland with some success. However, a division in the 1970s led to half the churches forming the Fellowship of Independent Methodist Churches (not connected with *IM). The Free Methodist Church in England (not to be confused with the former *UMFC or with the *WRU churches that use that title) originated with a loss of members and ministers in the North Lancashire District during the earlier *Anglican-Methodist

Conversations. Currently there are both Irish and British Conferences.

L.W. Northrup (1988)

WP

Freeman, John (1880–1929), poet and critic, was born into a Methodist family at Dalston, Middx. His health was permanently impaired by scarlet fever in early childhood. At 13 he joined the Liverpool Victoria Friendly Society as a junior clerk and rose to become Secretary and Director in 1927 and a leading figure in the insurance world. He was a *local preacher. But he was more widely known in the literary world, where he enjoyed the friendship of such figures as Alice Meynell and Walter de la Mare. His first book of poems, published in 1909, was followed by many others, marked by his 'grave and quiet rhythms' and including *Collected Poems* (1928). *Poems Old and New* (1920) won him the Hawthornden Prize for imaginative literature. He wrote on literary matters for the *New Statesman* and the *London Mercury* and his prose works included a *Portrait of George Moore* (1922), *English Portraits* (1924), *Herman Melville* (1926) and a play *Prince Absalom* (1925). A field adjoining the churchyard at Thursley, Surrey, was given to the National Trust in his memory.

DNB; *Times*, 25 Sept. 1929; *MR* 3 Oct. 1929; J.C. Squire in J. Freeman (1930)

JAV

Freeman, Thomas Birch (1809–90; e.m. 1837), WM missionary, the son of an English mother and African father (a freed slave?). He became a Methodist while working as a gardener near *Ipswich. In 1837 he was sent to the Gold Coast (now *Ghana), where he found that all five of his predecessors had died within thirteen months. Freeman, with his African blood, survived. He not only planted churches in the coastal area, but made several difficult expeditions inland and along the coast. In the Ashanti capital, Kumasi, where human sacrifices were being offered, he was viewed with suspicion. But his 1842 journey is regarded as the beginning of Methodism in *Nigeria, *Benin and *Togo. He was at the heart of the anti-slavery struggle. In 1857 he resigned from the ministry after overspending his budget and became the civil commandant of the Accra District; but he still preached and was reinstated in 1873. Although he never learned an African language, he was an effective pastor and in 1877 alone baptized over 1,500 people.

F.D. Walker (1929); N.A. Birtwhistle (1950); P. Ellingworth (1995)

JRP

French, E. Aldom (1868–1962; e.m. 1893), WM minister, born in *Taunton and educated at *Queen's College. In 1928 he became secretary of the *Methodist Union Committee and travelled the country advocating union and supporting it in Conference. When this was achieved in 1932, he became secretary of the Commemoration Fund established by the Uniting Conference. A committed evangelist, he never saw union as a substitute for evangelism and much of his ministry was in mission appointments and in the *HM Department (1936–38). In *Brighton he initiated the Dome Mission. He edited *Evangelism: a Reinterpretation* (1921).

MR 2 Aug. 1962

WDH

French Prophets or 'Camisards', a Huguenot sect who came into the Wesleys' orbit in 1739. While claiming to be under the influence of the Holy Spirit, they prophesied the imminent visible rule of Christ on earth, spoke in tongues and claimed the gifts of healing and perfection. Some of the more 'enthusiastic' Methodists were attracted to them, partly because of their eschatological, supernatural and perfectionist emphases, but mainly because they too believed God to be directly in control and to make himself known through supernatural intervention. J&CW were not convinced of their authenticity, but suspended judgment until CW's investigation of one of them concluded that she was a fraud.
See also **Enthusiasm**

R.A. Knox, (1950) ch. 15; H. Swartz (1980)

MB

Froggatt, George (1839–1912), a prominent PM layman, born in Shropshire. Arriving in *New Zealand in 1864, he worked as a roading contractor, then set up a butchery in Invercargill which developed into a stock and station agency. He served as a town councillor for 30 years and was twice mayor (1885 and 1903). In 1872 he established the first PM society in the town and was active as a *local preacher. He was involved in connexional affairs for 50 years, notably as treasurer of the Supernumerary Fund, and gener-

ously supported the establishment of stations throughout the country. In 1888 he became only the second layman to be elected President of the PM Conference in New Zealand.

DJP

Frost, Sir David Paradine, OBE (1939–), TV producer and presenter on both sides of the Atlantic. The son of **W.J. Paradine Frost** (1900–67; e.m. 1928), he was active in the youth club and drama group in his formative years and Billy Graham has remained a significant influence since the 1954 Harringay campaign. He became a *local preacher in 1958, the year he went to Caius College, Cambridge, and became a household name in the satirical 'TW3' programme of the 1960s. In his *Autobiography* (1993) he pays a warm tribute to his father and acknowledges the influence of Methodism, especially on his work ethic. Religion has continued to play a part in his life. He was knighted in 1993.

MR 20 June 1963, 30 Nov. & 28 Dec. 1967; W. Frischauer (1971)

JAV

Full Connexion was a status granted in the eighteenth century to the *itinerant preachers associated with JW after a period on trial. He regarded them as a supplementary lay ministry, but with no right to administer the *Lord's Supper In 1795 the *Plan of Pacification allowed a circuit to ask *Conference to grant this right to its preachers in full connexion, and this led to the belief that such preachers were virtually ordained. The 1836 Conference adopted the procedure of reception into full connexion a few hours before *ordination by the laying on of hands. Exceptional arrangements were made for those going overseas or serving as chaplains to the Forces. Since 1932 ministers who complete their probationary period are received by a standing vote of Conference into full connexion with the Conference earlier on the day of their ordination.

A.R. George in *HMGB* 2 p. 143

JWH

Fullerton, Alexander (1839–1922), Irish Methodist preacher, took a leading part in the great 1859 Irish Revival. His autobiography was entitled *Fifty Years an Itinerant Preacher* (1912). Five gifted sons survived childhood. **Alexander Moffit Fullerton** OBE, KStJohn (1865–1947), was a civil servant in *Dublin and Secretary of the MCI Twentieth Century Fund. **William Moore**

Fullerton (1870–1954), Chairman and Director of the Ulster Bank, 1931–42 and Governor of *Methodist College, Belfast where Fullerton House was named after him. **Thomas William Archer Fullerton** (1867–1907), surgeon in the Indian Medical Service, was awarded the Kaiser-I-Hind medal for his role in the eradication of plague. **Andrew Fullerton** (1868–1934), the first *Belfast surgeon to become president of the Royal College of Surgeons in Ireland, became an Anglican. **Moore Beattie Fullerton** (b.1872) was a Westminster Bank manager.

RPR

Furz, John (1717–1800; e.m. 1758), early itinerant, born in Wilton. After a lengthy period of searching, he was converted. Finding no spiritual help from the local dissenting meeting he began to preach and gained the support and encouragement of the Earl of Pembroke. Through an acquaintance with J. *Haime he travelled as far afield as Shaftesbury and Wincanton. About 1758 JW encouraged him to become an itinerant, despite family commitments, and sent him into West Cornwall. He served in many circuits, especially in Lancashire and Cheshire, before retiring to the *Salisbury Circuit in 1782. His closing years were marked by mental decay.

C. Atmore (1801) pp. 148–54; *EMP* 5 pp. 108–34

JAV

Gainsborough JW first preached in Sir Neville Hickman's Baronial Hall in 1759 and paid a further nine visits. The first chapel was built in 1785, replaced by a large galleried one in Spittal Terrace in 1804. Later chapels were built in Bridge Road (1883) to the south and Ropery Road (1899) to the north. The WM Circuit was formed from Lincolnshire West in 1776. PM was introduced in 1818 by William Braithwaite and T. *Cooper was converted there. The first chapel was in Spring Gardens (1837). The largest, Trinity Street, opened in 1878. A short-lived MNC society, formed in 1825, sold its Hickman Street chapel (1832) to WM in 1841. The UMFC cause, established in 1856, also had a chapel in Hickman Street (1868; closed 1948).

A new society formed at Whiteswood in 1955 built a chapel in 1959. St Stephen's (1968) is on the site of the 1804 Spittal Terrace chapel. Gainsborough is the head of a country circuit east and west of the Trent.

WL

Gallagher, Ernest William (1918–84; e.m. 1943), missionary to *India. After training at *Edgehill College, Belfast, he was appointed to the Hyderabad District in 1943 and then served in the Medak Diocese of CSI until 1966. His fluent Telugu enabled close relationships with local colleagues and the effective training of ordained and lay workers. On returning to *Ireland in 1966 he served as General Secretary of MMS Ireland, as well as in other areas of the Church's life. His ministry was shared and enhanced by the educational work of his wife **Muriel Gallagher** (*née* Hyman), a *Women's Work missionary. He was President of the Irish Conference in 1981 and became Principal of Edgehill College in 1982.

MR 1 March 1984

MJF

Gallagher, Robert Henry (1881–1965; e.m. 1908), Irish Methodist minister and historian, exercised most of his ministry in the north of Ireland. An able administrator, he served as secretary and, from 1941, Chairman of the District and as secretary of the Orphan Fund 1931–46. His influence encouraged a number of people to enter the ordained ministry. He published several historical works, including a study of Dr A. *Clarke (1963), *Pioneer Preachers of Irish Methodism* (1965) and an autobiography *My Web of Time* (1959). He helped to organize the Church's records and was President of the Irish Branch of the *WHS. He was elected President of the Irish Methodist Church in 1946. His son **R.D. Eric Gallagher** (1913–99; e.m. 1938) was Superintendent of the *Belfast Central Mission 1957–79 and Secretary of the Irish Conference 1958–67. He was elected President in 1967. A committed ecumenist, he was Chairman of the Irish Council of Churches 1967–69 and Vice-President of the BCC 1979–80. From the 1960s he played a leading role in encouraging consultation and co-operation between the Protestant and Roman Catholic Churches in Ireland. He was awarded the CBE in 1987 for distinguished service to community relations.

MR 11 Feb. 1965; Dennis Cooke in *ER*, Oct. 1998 pp. 38–46; *MR* 13 Jan. 2000

NWT

Gallatin, Lt-Col Bartholomew (d.1778) A career Army officer of Swiss origin, he and his wife were in the *Whitefield-Lady *Huntingdon circle and through it came to know CW, his family and JW. From *Manchester in 1749, Mrs Gallatin sent gifts to W. *Grimshaw for his work, and in 1751 Gallatin invited JW to Musselburgh. J&CW both stayed with them at Lakenham in 1756, while transcribing the *Explanatory Notes upon the NT and heard from them of J. *Wheatley's conduct. They retired to Ham (Kent) and on Gallatin's death CW called this 'bosom friend' 'gentle, generous and sincere'.

————————

CWJ; WMM 1900, 198–204
                                                    MB

Gallienne, Matthew (1812–1900; e.m. 1835), WM minister born near St Peter Port, Guernsey, the son of a *local preacher and lawyer of the same name. Converted in 1831, he became a Sunday School teacher and local preacher and in 1835 responded to a challenge by James Hocart to join him in the work in the south of *France, where he was stationed until 1859, except for five years in Switzerland. He was elected President of the French Conference in 1859, then returned to the *Channel Islands as Chairman of the District 1859–71. He edited the Magazin Méthodiste until his eyesight failed in 1897 and two sons, Matthew and Edward, joined him in the ministry. After seven years in the *Bath, Liskeard and Bridport Circuits, he retired to Guernsey in 1878.

————————

J. Walle (1989)
                                                    JAV

Galpin, Frederick (1842–1932; e.m. 1866), UMFC missionary, appointed to Ningpo (Ningbo), *China in 1866. He was Superintendent of the Mission for 27 years and after 30 years service returned to circuit work in England. He was elected President of the UMFC Assembly in 1900.

                                                    GRS

Gambia, The From the outset in 1821 Methodist preaching bore fruit among the Aku people – freed slaves and their descendants – in Bathurst (now Banjul) but there were fewer converts upriver and among the largely Muslim indigenous Gambians. The Methodist community never numbered more than two thousand but ran significant educational, medical and agricultural work. At the end of the twentieth century Gambian Methodism remained an overseas District of the British Conference.

————————

B. Prickett (1960)
                                                    JRP

Gambling is defined by the Conference as those practices whose characteristic features are a determination of the possession of money or value by the appeal to chance; the gains of the winners being made at the expense of the losers; and the gain secured without the return of an equivalent of the gain obtained. The Conference condemns gambling on account of its anti-social effects and addictive qualities, and because it debases sport. It is judged to be alien to the Christian understanding of divine Providence. The Church has often addressed the Government on its responsibilities for controlling a dangerous practice and was opposed to the National Lottery, declining to apply for grants from its proceeds. This stance was modified in 1999 to allow applications for Lottery funding through Good Causes.

————————

E. B. Perkins (1958)
                                                    KGG

Gambold, Rev. John (1711–71), Anglican priest and Moravian bishop, was the son of a Pembrokeshire vicar. While a student at Christ Church, Oxford, he became associated with the *'Holy Club' in 1730. He was ordained in 1733 and became vicar of Stanton Harcourt, where he indulged in philosophical and mystical studies. The attraction of *stillness led to an estrangement from the Wesleys and in 1742, influenced by P. Böhler, he gave up his living and joined the *Moravians. He became the minister of their London congregation and was consecrated Bishop in 1754. He compiled the first English Moravian hymn-book in 1754, played a prominent part in the Synod of Marienborn (1764) and founded the Moravian settlement at Cootehill, Co. Cavan, in 1765. His poems and a tragedy on The Martyrdom of Ignatius were published posthumously.

————————

D. Benham (1865); L. Tyerman (1873) pp. 155–200; DNB
                                                    JAV

Gammon, John (1815–98; e.m. 1837), BC minister, born at Folkestone. He was Treasurer of the BC Preachers' Annuitant Society, President of the Conference in 1859 and 1876, and Governor of *Shebbear College 1873–85.

————————

G.J. Stevenson (1884–86) 6 pp. 896–902
                                                    TS

Garland, Charles Hughlings (1848–1917; e.m. 1876), born in London, where his father worked in the WM Seamen's Mission. He was trained at *Headingley and *Handsworth Colleges and went to *New Zealand in 1881 as a circuit minister. He was Secretary of the Century Commemoration Fund, 1899–1900. Though lacking university training, he was well read and intelligent, an original thinker and preacher. His Conference lecture on *The Bearing of Higher Criticism on Leading Evangelical Doctrines* (1893) was significant in the liberalization of Methodist theology in New Zealand. He was President of the Conference in 1901 and in 1912 became Principal of the Theological Institution. His relatively early death deprived the Church of a theologian and leader of outstanding ability.

DJP

Garner Brothers **John Garner** (1800–56; e.m. 1819), PM minister, born at Kegworth, was the first Secretary of the General Committee and one of the preachers named in the original Deed Poll. He was six times President of the Conference. His brother **William Garner** (1802–81; e.m. 1822) was twice President. Among his several books were biographies of W. *Clowes (1868) and of his brother (1856). Another brother, **James Garner** (1809–95; e.m. 1830) served for five years as Secretary of the General Missionary Committee and was twice President. He wrote several books on biblical history and theology.

F.H. Hurd (1872) pp. 119–30, 159–79; G.J. Stevenson (1884–6) 5 pp. 685–95

WL

Garrett, Charles (1823–1900; e.m. 1846), WM missioner and temperance advocate, was born in Shaftesbury. As a young man he worked for the Anti-Corn Law League and during his ministry in *Preston (1860–63) was active in relief work among the victims of the Cotton Famine. He was involved in the founding of the *Manchester and Salford Mission and later of the *Liverpool Mission. He campaigned tirelessly against the drink trade and other social evils. He was one of the founders of the *Methodist Recorder*. In wide demand as a preacher, he was President of the 1882 Conference.

MR 25 Oct. 1900

JAV

Gateshead JW first passed through the town on his way to Newcastle in 1742. In March 1743 he preached to the colliers of Chowden(e), 'the very Kingswood of the North'. Caught in a snowstorm on Gateshead Fell in February 1745, he

vowed 'never again', and there is no further record of him visiting the North East during winter months. He preached for the first time in Gateshead town in September 1745, and in 1753 in a house in Gateshead Fell belonging to William Bell, a baker. A meeting room added to it the following year was possibly the first Methodist chapel in the (then) county of Durham. A Sunday School was opened there in 1789. JW also visited several villages and townships now within the Gateshead boundary, including Ryton, Whickham, Swalwell and Lamesley.

Gateshead WM Circuit was formed in 1812 and divided in 1875. Prominent WM ministers stationed there included H. *Casson (1827–30) and P. *Mackenzie (1865–68). M.L. *Edwards was the first minister at the Central Hall when it opened in 1933 at the height of the Depression.

The MNC was introduced by **Joseph Forsyth**, expelled from the WM ministry in 1833, taking with him a large following. In 1835 he allied himself with the MNC. Bethesda Chapel, opened in April 1736, was a notable MNC edifice, where W. *Booth was minister 1858–61, just before he left the connexion. Another name notoriously linking Gateshead and the MNC was J. *Barker, expelled in 1841 on doctrinal grounds.

PM arrived in 1821 with the preaching of J. *Branfoot. A Gateshead Circuit was formed in 1837, although because of financial irregularities it was included in the Newcastle Circuit from 1841 to 1862. The PM author J.G. *Bowran ('Ramsey Guthrie') was born there in 1869. The UMFC was represented locally from 1852 by WR, a separate Gateshead Circuit being formed in 1858. There was a small IM group there from 1819, with a chapel opened in 1823.

W.M. Patterson (1909); F.W.D. Manders (1973) pp. 148–56

NFM

Geden, John Drury (1822–86; e.m. 1846), WM minister and Hebraist, educated at *Kingswood School and *Richmond College. He was Hebrew and Classics Tutor at *Didsbury College 1856–82 and contributed to the Revised Version of the OT (1885). In 1853 he became joint editor of the *London Quarterly Review* and his *Fernley Lecture in 1874 was on *The future Life as contained in the OT Scriptures*. St Andrews gave him an honorary DD in 1885. His son Dr **Alfred Shenington Geden** (1857–1936; e.m. 1881) was Assistant Tutor at Didsbury 1883–84 and from 1886 to 1889 was Principal of Royapettah College,

Madras. From 1891 to 1915 he was Tutor in OT Languages and Literature at *Richmond College. His scholarship, especially in Semitic languages, led to his collaboration with W.F. *Moulton on his NT *Concordance*. He also contributed to Hastings' *ERE*. In addition to biblical studies, he wrote books on comparative religion. In retirement at Harpenden he worked for the *NCHO and also for the BFBS, being at one time its Vice-President.

MR 13 Aug. 1936

EWD/WL

Gedye, Alfred John (1898–1969; e.m. 1922), born in *China, the son of **Ernest F. Gedye** (1869–1922; e.m. 1893, Principal of Wesley College, Wuchang). After training for the ministry, he returned to China in 1922, serving there for 28 years. He was interned by the Japanese and on returning to England served in English circuits.

GRS

Gee, Herbert Leslie (1901–77), a native of Bridlington, trained at *Leeds as a teacher and taught for ten years before becoming a journalist and prolific writer whose books were widely read and treasured. In 1932 he became one of Arthur Mee's collaborators on the 'King's England' series and was a regular contributor to the *Children's Newspaper*. From 1939 to 1973 he compiled the annual 'Friendship Books' under the pen-name of Francis Gay and he wrote as the 'Friendly Man' in the *Methodist Recorder*. Bestsellers like *Nodding Wold* (1940), in which his wife Mary featured as 'Judith', were characterized by his humour, gaiety and a buoyant optimism. His latest title was the highlight in the Epworth Press's year and his appearance with L.F. *Church at 'Book-Lovers' Meetings' during Conference drew record crowds. Royalties from his *Easter at Epworth* (1944) went to *Wesley Memorial Church's endowment fund.

MR 31 Mar. & 7 April 1977

JAV

Gelder, Sir W. Alfred (1855–1941), architect and civic leader in *Hull. The son of a WM farmer, he built up an extensive architectural practice, including mills and warehouses for his friend J. *Rank. His WM chapels and Central Halls used new structural methods to achieve wide roof spans. and several display art nouveau features. He was active in Hull's social and political life and during five successive terms as mayor of Hull (1899–1904) inspired and directed the extensive

rebuilding of the city centre. He was knighted in 1903 and made a Freeman of Hull in 1930. He was Liberal MP for Brigg, 1910–18. A lifelong Methodist, he served both as Sunday School teacher and *local preacher and designed many WM churches in Hull (e.g. Brunswick (1877), Princes Avenue (1905), Queen's Hall Mission (1905), Anlaby Road (1910) and Newland (1928)) and elsewhere.

G.E. Milburn in *PWHS* 44 pp. 51, 75

GEM

General Assessment *see* **Finance, local**

General Church Meeting *see* **Society Meeting**

General Purposes Committee was constituted at *Methodist Union, the membership consisting of certain ex-officio members, a Treasurer, ministerial and lay representation from each District and members elected by the Conference. It took over the functions of the WM *Committee of Privileges, and the relevant functions of the PM General Connexional Committee and the UMC Connexional Committee. It was authorised to act as the Conference between Conferences and to deal with matters not referred to other committees, with power to delegate to an executive and other sub-committees. It administered the General Purposes Fund, to meet connexional expenses not chargeable elsewhere.

The war-time Conferences of 1942–44 appointed it, with certain additional members, as the Conference Executive Committee, to exercise all powers vested in the Conference which could lawfully be delegated.

In 1964 it became the 'General Purposes and Policy Committee', with additional responsibilities to keep in review the life of the church and its work and witness, to indicate ways to increase its effectiveness and to give spiritual leadership. With the creation of the *President's Council in 1971, it reverted to its former name and functions. In 1994, it was abolished, its functions being once again amalgamated with the policy functions of the President's Council in the Methodist Council, a body containing nearly 70 members, including connexional officers and ordained and lay District representatives on a rota basis.

SRH

Genetic Engineering *see* **Medical Ethics**

George, A. Raymond (1912–98; e.m. 1936), outstanding liturgical scholar and ecumenist, born in *Gloucester. He taught at *Headingley (1946–67; Principal, 1961–67), *Richmond (Principal, 1968–72) and *Wesley College, Bristol (1972–81), earning a reputation as a great encourager of students. The reputation he earned by his *Fernley-Hartley Lecture *Communion with God in the NT* (1953) was consolidated by many scholarly articles. He served on key ecumenical liturgical bodies and had a major influence on the 1975 *Methodist Service Book*. He served on the WMC executive 1956–81, on the WCC Faith and Order Committee 1961–75, on the International RC-Methodist Committee 1971–86, and as co-chair of the British RC-Methodist Committee 1971–93. He was President of the 1975 Conference and Moderator of the FCFC 1979–80. In retirement he served as Warden of the *New Room, Bristol.

J.A. Newton in ER, Jan. 1997; *MR* 26 June 1975, 9 July 1998

DJC

Germany A German layman, C. Gottlieb Müller, came to England in 1806 to escape conscription into the Napoleonic army, came under Methodist influence in London and, returning in 1813, began an evangelical ministry in the Stuttgart area. A plea from a group of Moravians meeting in his father's house met with no immediate response from the WMMS; but in 1831 they appointed Müller himself as a lay missionary. Despite his intention of working within *Lutheranism, he met with opposition from the Church leaders. The year after his death in 1858, J. *Lyth was sent to supervise. The work in Germany was eventually taken over by the MEC, so that present-day German Methodism is affiliated to the United Methodist Church.

F&H 4 pp. 460–74; W.P. Stephens (n.d.)

SJP

Ghana Methodism came to the Gold Coast (as the British colony was known until independence in 1957) in 1835. The first missionary, J. *Dunwell, and five others died before T.B. *Freeman, who arrived in 1838, established the work along the coast and made pioneering journeys inland. Alongside the growth of the Church went the development of education, including the prestigious Mfantsipim (boys) and Wesley Girls' Schools in Cape Coast. There is a fine musical tradition, in which lyrics in traditional style have a proud place. The Ghana District became an autonomous Conference in 1961 and continued to grow rapidly.

F.L. Bartels (1965)

JRP

Gibbs, Dr John Morel, OBE (1912–96) came from a family of shipping magnates. From The *Leys School he went to St John's College, Cambridge to read law and later studied psychology, which he taught at University College, Cardiff and during periods as a Visiting Lecturer in Louisiana and Kentucky. In 1939 he registered as a conscientious objector. A generous philanthropist, his services to Methodism included work with the *NCH, *MAYC and Clubland. He was chairman of Aldersgate Productions and was the inspiration behind the *Methodist Collection of Twentieth Century Christian Art. He was a Sunday School teacher for 37 years and a *local preacher for 49 years and was Vice-President of the Conference in 1958.

MR 10 July 1958, 4 July 1996; J.M. Gibbs (1982)

KGG

Gibraltar A society was begun on the Rock in 1769 by Sgt. Henry Ince, who had heard JW preach in Ireland. In 1792 a group of soldiers began meeting under the leadership of another soldier, A. *Armour. Long-standing opposition from the military authorities came to a head in 1803, but ended the following year with the appointment of a new Commander. In 1804 the first preacher, J. *M'Mullen, and his wife both died of yellow fever within a month of arrival (leaving a young daughter who became the mother of J.H. *Rigg). The second preacher, William *Griffith senior, arrived in 1808 and built the first church in 1809. In the 1830s W.H. *Rule championed religious toleration and successfully appealed against the punishment of soldiers for being Methodists. The Welcome Home and Institute, opened in 1898, served generations of servicemen and after World War II a 'Gibraltar Club' back home perpetuated the fellowship experienced on the Rock. The present Church is part of British Methodism.

O.S. Watkins (1906); W.H. Rule (1844); W.H. Rule (1886)

SJP

Gibson, Edmund (1669–1748), Bishop of London 1720–48, the author of the authoritative *Codex Juris Ecclesiastici Anglicani* (1713) and other scholarly works. He ordained CW to the priesthood in 1735 and in 1738 questioned both brothers about their teaching on *justification, *assurance and the rebaptism of dissenters. He agreed that *religious societies were 'not conventicles', but in 1739, in a pastoral letter, criticized both JW and G. *Whitefield. He supported the *Islington parishioners in their dispute with G. *Stonehouse. In 1740 he questioned JW on his understanding of *Christian perfection and professed himself satisfied. But the anonymous *Observations upon the Conduct of a Certain Sect* (1740) was widely attributed to him. A further attack in 1747, in a Visitation Charge dealing with Methodist doctrines, provoked JW's *Letter to Dr Gibson*, deemed to be 'direct but courteous' and exemplifying 'his controversial style at its best'. The two men had a common concern about the prevailing moral laxity and a strong pastoral concern.

DNB; N.H. Sykes (1926); G.R. Cragg (1975) pp. 327–51

JAV

Gibson, William (1832–94; e.m. 1952), son of a WM minister, was appointed to the new Ruc Roquépine church, Paris, in 1862, remaining until the 1870 seige. From 1878 on he concentrated his intellectual gifts and prodigious capacity for hard work on developing the 'Mission populaire', which extended from Paris to the Channel coast. He introduced working people to his own evangelical hymn-book and such hitherto unfamiliar activities as Bible classes and *youth and *temperance societies. He travelled widely in Europe and crossed the Atlantic frequently, raising funds and promoting the Mission, despite opposition from the Missionary Committee in London, and died in harness in 1894.

See also **France**

MJF

Gilbert Family of Antigua. **Nathaniel Gilbert** (*c*. 1721–74), son of a prosperous planter, was articled at Gray's Inn, London in 1741 and called to the Bar in 1747. Returning home, he succeeded his father as a representative in the island's Assembly. In England 1757–59 he met JW, who preached in his Wandsworth home and baptized two of the family slaves. Back in Antigua, he began preaching to his slaves (in effect, the start of Methodist overseas work) and formed a society which was led after his death by two local women. Re-elected to the Assembly, he was Speaker from 1763 until retiring from public life in 1769.

His younger brother, **Francis Gilbert**, at first a profligate, was converted and became an itinerant in England in 1758. He tried to take up his brother's work in Antigua, but had to return to England in poor health and died in 1779. His widow **Mary Gilbert** returned to Antigua in 1781 and helped to build up the St. John's society. One of the sisters, Grace, married Thomas *Webb; another, Mary, was the mother of the Rev. M. *Horne.

F. Baker in *LQHR*, Jan. 1960, pp. 9–17; E.W. Thompson (1960)

JAV

Gill, Frederick Cyril (1898–1974; e.m. 1921), born at Clapham. After military service in France, where he was both wounded and gassed, he entered *Didsbury College. His literary and cultural interests are reflected in his Liverpool MA thesis, published as *The Romantic Movement and Methodism* (1937), and he wrote popular studies of JW and CW, as well as scripts for radio and TV. After retirement in 1974 he became North West area Secretary for the United Society for Christian Literature.

MR 4 July 1974

WL

Gill, Rt Rev. Kenneth E. (1932– ; e.m. 1957), born in Nidderdale, Yorks, the son of a *local preacher in the Pateley Bridge Circuit. He was accepted for the ministry at 22 and trained at *Hartley Victoria College. He was designated to the Church of South *India, where he was ordained. He was the first elected bishop of the Karnataka Central Diocese in 1972 and the only non-Indian bishop of any Church in India when he left in 1980. From 1980 he served as Assistant Bishop of Newcastle (twice acting as Diocesan Bishop) until his retirement in 1998. Throughout his active ministry in both India and England he retained his status of Full Connexion with the Methodist Conference.

GEM

Gill, Silas (1805–75), pioneer *local preacher in New South Wales. He was converted in Beckley, Sussex, under the ministry of Thomas Collins, who said as Gill responded to his invitation, 'Here comes a giant for Jesus.' Arriving in NSW in 1837, he worked on farms and as a farmer in the Camden district, the Hunter, Hastings and Macleay Rivers. His preaching to convicts and settlers resulted in many hundreds of conversions and the establishment of Methodism in several country places. He is representative of – and pre-eminent among – a galaxy of local preachers who pioneered the work in many places in *Australia, resulting in its phenomenal growth in the latter half of the nineteenth century. Five hundred attended his funeral and attested to his gracious influence in their lives.

E.G. Clancy (1972); *ADEB*

EGC

Gill, Walter (1914–95; e.m. 1940), Methodist minister, trained at *Didsbury College, Manchester. In 1964, at the Ministerial Synod, he gave a qualified reply to the question, 'Do you believe and preach our doctrines?': 'Yes, with the exception of the doctrine of the deity of Christ, my interpretation of which Conference refuses to accept.' Heresy charges ensued and he left the ministry. In 1986 he applied for reinstatement and was able to convince the Conference that his views were compatible with Methodist doctrine. He was reinstated as a supernumerary minister.

PWS

Gilliver, Alfred J. (1920–), civil servant, educated at St Dunstan's College, Catford. His career began in 1938, but was interrupted by wartime service in the Royal Signals, spent mainly in India. He became a *local preacher in 1947. His experience in the Registry of Friendly Societies and later as Principal in the Department of Employment enabled him to give invaluable service to the *LPMAA and took him so often to Brussells that he was dubbed LPMA's 'Mr Europe'. He served on the *LPMAA Committee from 1960 and was Hon. Secretary 1967–87 and President 1976–77. He wrote a history of the Association's residential homes, *More Precious than Rubies* (1989). He was Chairman of Lay Training in the Division of Ministries, 1974–76 and in 1975 was one of the first Open University students to graduate BA with Honours.

PB

Gilmore, Hugh (1842–91; e.m. 1865) was an orphaned street-urchin reared in a *Glasgow slum, where he first came into contact with PM. Leaving Scotland with the intention of emigrating to America, he found employment in *Newcastle upon Tyne, where he was converted and became a PM *local preacher at *Gateshead. After two years as a *hired local preacher, he began itinerating in 1865, travelling in the north-east until 1883.

His experiences in the Blyth Circuit led him to write *The Black Diamond: a tale of life in a colliery village*. Appointed to Adelaide, South *Australia, in 1889 he had a brief but influential ministry at Wellington Square chapel, where he built up a large congregation. Politically an active, radical Liberal with Christian Socialist leanings, he supported the strike of the predominantly Irish RC dockworkers, advocated tax reform, and showed a willingness to consider RC views, e.g. on baptism. J. *Ritson's novel *Hugh Morrigill, Street Arab* is based on his early life.

PM Mag, 1900, pp. 27–32 etc.; A.D. Hunt (1977)

DCD

Girls' League, founded in 1908, enabled girls (who were not expected to accompany their mothers to missionary meetings) to support the Jubilee Effort of the WM Women's Auxiliary. The committee that was set up in 1909 suggested a more permanent project supporting medical work in North *India. An Annual Report and eventually a periodical *The Lamp* were published. The PM and UMC established their own 'Girls' Branches' of the Women's Missionary Association' and 'Girls' Missionary Auxiliary' respectively. They united to become part of the Methodist Girls' League in 1932, with a membership of *c*. 9,000. This League strengthened the whole Church through its commitment to prayer, study and stewardship, with young women offering service both at home and overseas. A Young Laymen's League (later known as the Young Men's League) was formed in 1925 with a similar purpose and was influential in prompting many to offer for missionary service. The two Leagues were integrated into the *Youth Missionary Association in 1953.

MJF

Glasgow   JW made the first of 15 visits in 1753 at the invitation of Dr John Gillies of the College Kirk, who held class meetings and provided a canvas pulpit for JW's outdoor preaching. T. *Taylor formed a society and rented a room in 1765 in the Barber's Hall in Stockwell Street. The first chapel was opened in John Street in 1787 by J. *Pawson, who angered JW by appointing seven 'elders' to lead the society, a move swiftly countermanded. WM immigrants from England and Ireland divided the society in the 1830s, with the Scots forming the John Street and Calton societies and the immigrants chiefly at Bridge Street and Anderston. In 1840 the circuit membership totalled 1,224, with congregations developing in the Clyde shipbuilding towns to the west and in mining towns inland. John Street, compulsorily sold in 1881, is now the site of the City Chambers. The new chapel in Sauchiehall Street (1882) was replaced by Woodlands in 1974. Methodism expanded in the mid- and late-Victorian period of Glasgow's economic optimism, with WM chapels opening in the suburbs.

In 1825 the Carlisle PM Circuit sent J. *Johnson to mission Glasgow. By 1827 it had become a circuit, missioning Paisley in its turn. English PMs came from the *Black Country to establish and work in the iron foundries and blast furnaces around Wishaw, where they built a chapel in Young Street (1858). Pollokshaws, missioned from Paisley, was built in 1883. The great success of PM, however, was in open-air work and gatherings in rented premises. The MNC had a chapel in East Clyde Street from 1814 to 1828. The WMA. WR and IM also had societies and buildings c.1830–90.

MR 28 Mar 1912; J. Ritson (1926); O.A. Beckerlegge in *PWHS* 29 pp. 161–2, 30 pp. 7–11

MB

Glasson, Dr Thomas Francis (1906–1998; e.m. 1933)

was born in *Derby and trained for the ministry at *Richmond College. He was appointed NT Lecturer at New College, London in 1960, where he remained until the college closed and he retired in 1972. His main interest was in eschatology, as seen in his two major works, *The Second Advent* (1945) and *Greek Influence in Jewish Eschatology* (1961). He contributed a commentary on Revelation to the Cambridge Bible series and also wrote a study of Moses in the Fourth Gospel (1963).

MR 27 Aug. 1998

CSR

Glenorchy, Willielma, Viscountess (1741–1786)

an evangelical *Calvinist who, with Lady *Maxwell, rented St Mary's Chapel in Niddry Wynd, *Edinburgh in 1770, with the ecumenical intention that services be held outside church hours by Episcopalian and Presbyterian ministers and Methodist itinerants in turn. The scheme predictably foundered on doctrinal grounds.

T. Snell-Jones (1822); E.D. Graham, in WHS(S), 3 pp. 15–20; 4, pp. 13–17

MB

Gloucester

G. *Whitefield, a native of the city, belonged to the dissenting congregation which met at the Cobblers Hall in Kimbrose under the evangelical preacher Thomas Cale. In 1735, after coming within the orbit of the Holy Club, he spent nine months in the city and gathered together a small group. He was ordained in the Cathedral in 1736 and in 1739 preached there several times, in the Booth Hall, Westgate Street and in the open air. JW first visited the city on Sunday, 15 July 1739, preaching to some 4,000. On his many later visits he preached in the open air or at the Tolbooth (later known as the Tolsey). The small society met in one another's houses until the Cobblers Hall was taken in 1770 and a Gloucestershire Circuit was formed, with John Glassbrook as its first Superintendent. When JW met the society in 1787 it was decided to build a chapel in Lower Northgate (opened July 1787; extended 1824 and 1831). The present chapel with frontage to Northgate Street was opened in 1878. There was a WM meeting in Yew Tree Cottage, Hucclecote from 1843 to 1848, when a chapel was opened (rebuilt 1929). Other WM chapels were at Hartpury (1828, rebuilt 1846 and 1887), Tibberton (1839) and Churchdown (1849, rebuilt 1902). The Countess of Huntingdon's Connexion opened a chapel at Birdwood in 1814, taken over by WM in 1848.

PM began open-air preaching in 1837 and built the first chapel in Barton Street in 1856 (enlarged 1882), followed by Stroud Road in 1897. The UMFC also built in Stroud Road in 1903. The two Stroud Road congregations were later united at St Luke's (rebuilt 1967). St John's, Northgate, is now a Local Ecumenical Project and large housing developments are served at Quedgeley by a chapel first built in 1885 and at Abbeydale by another Local Ecumenical Project in the newly built Christchurch complex.

SMEC

Gogerly, Daniel John (1792–1862; e.m. 1823),

a London *local preacher, trained as a printer, who arrived in Colombo to superintend the Mission Press in 1818, entered the ministry and devoted the rest of his life to Ceylon (*Sri Lanka). As Chairman of the South Ceylon District from 1838, he gave a new impetus to an ailing mission. Despite his lack of formal education, he mastered Pali (the language in which the texts of Theravada Buddhism are written) and became an acknowledged expert on Buddhism and its literature, exposing what he perceived as its weaknesses and publishing many papers on the subject, including some of the first English translations from the Pali texts (collected edition, Colombo, 1907). Although his Sinhala work *Kristiyani Prajñapti* ('The Evidences and Doctrines of the Christian Religion') (1849) ushered in a new, more polemical stage of the nineteenth-century Buddhist-Christian controversy in Sri Lanka, that did not prevent T.W. Rhys Davids, founder of the Pali Text Society in Britain, declaring him to be 'the greatest Pali scholar of his age'.

F&H, 5 pp. 80–1; W.J.T. Small (1964) pp. 116–23

EJH

Gold Coast, *see* **Ghana**

Goodrich, William *see* **Primitive Methodist Magazine**

Gospel Pilgrims, a group which came into existence *c*. 1830 and by 1834 had several chapels and over 20 societies in West Yorkshire and also a widespread rural circuit in Norfolk. Linked with IM (whose 1838 Annual Meeting was held at their Little Horton chapel), but retaining their own identity, the origin of the Gospel Pilgrims remains a mystery. But their regular *camp meetings suggest that it may have resulted from a PM disruption. Some of their societies were highly radical politically and there were *Chartists among their unremunerated preachers. They survived as a body into the 1850s. Dewsbury IM church remains as the sole survivor of the tradition.

WP

Goudie, William (1857–1922; e.m. 1881), WM missionary in *India. A Shetlander, he was trained at *Richmond College and served in Madras 1882–1906, becoming fluent in Tamil. He was a champion of the outcastes, noted for his nursing of cholera victims. Catholic in his sympathies, he fostered understanding between the denominational missions in India and became recognized as a missionary statesman and advocate. He attended the World Missionary Conference in *Edinburgh (1910) and was secretary of the committee that organized the Centenary celebration of the WMMS in 1913. He was designated President of the 1922 Conference, but died following surgery.

MR 13 April 1922

JAV

Gowland, William (1911–91; e.m. 1935) was born near Darlington, the youngest son of a farm-labourer. After training at *Victoria Park, Manchester, he began a ministry characterized by strong evangelical convictions and concern to bridge the gap between Church and society. His ministry at Tilehurst, near Reading, and elsewhere saw rejuvenated churches and new ventures in outreach. He served as a part-time chaplain during World War II and played a leading part in the *Christian Commando Campaigns. A pioneer of *industrial chaplaincy, he founded and became Principal of the *Luton Industrial College. He visited many countries and wrote *Militant and Triumphant* (1954). He was President of the Conference in 1979. In retirement, influenced by C.A. *Coulson, he launched the Christ and the Cosmos initiative to promote the study of the interrelationship of science and religion.

D. Gowland & S. Roebuck (1990); *MR* 21 June 1979, 30 May & 6 June 1991

KGG

Grace is the term used in classical Christian theology for the outworking of God's loving regard towards humankind. In the West, both in medieval times and later, it was often regarded as referring more to a 'substance' than, as in the Bible, to a living relationship. JW laid particular emphasis on prevenient (or 'preventing') grace, active even before a person could apprehend his need of it. This grace – and here JW was in strong disagreement with *Calvinism – was at work in everyone, awakening them to their sinful condition and need of salvation, and then enabling them to respond in faith to the Gospel. JW also emphasized the importance of the *means of grace in the lives of justified believers 'pressing on to full salvation'. Recent Wesleyan theology has emphasized 'responsible grace', i.e. the extent to which the grace of God necessarily evokes and requires a human response.

E.A. Nilson in *LQHR* Oct. 1959 pp. 188–94; P.S. Watson (1959); R.L. Maddox (1994)

DJC

Graham, Charles (1750–1824; e.m. 1790), a native of Sligo who, as a fluent Irish speaker, was called into the itinerant ministry in 1790 and sent to Kerry, where there was no Methodist witness. In 1799 with two others (J. *McQuigg and G. *Ouseley) he was appointed as a General Missionary to take the gospel throughout the country. Their business was 'to preach, exhort, advise and pray' with people who were not already involved with Methodism. He and Ouseley worked as a team from 1799 to 1804, which were particularly fruitful years.

C.H. Crookshank (1885–8) esp. vol. 2; R.H. Gallagher (1965) pp. 86–7

NWT

Grantham A meeting was registered in Great Gonerby in 1774 and a year later a society was formed in the town in the house of Robert Derry, a shoemaker in Swinegate. From 1781 to 1787 it met in Derry's new home in the main street. JW passed through the town four times and in 1781 preached in the open air and in the parish churches at Rauceby and Welby, where the incumbents John Pugh and William Dodwell were Methodist sympathizers. (Both were present at the Conference that year.) A room above a smithy in Back Lane served the Grantham society until Finkin Street chapel was opened in 1803 (replaced by a larger chapel in the same street, 1841). Later WM chapels were Ebenezer, Wharf Road (1835) and Wesley, Spitalgate (1876); Signal Road and its successor Harrowby Lane 1951, rebuilt 1963) were post-Union. The Grantham Circuit was formed from Newark in 1803.

A PM mission was established in 1817 by J. *Wedgwood, who was imprisoned for preaching (the first PM to be so treated). Progress was slow until revival in the 1830s, which led to the building of chapels in Commercial Road (1837) and later Broad Street (1886). In 1850–51 a majority of the Finkin Street congregation left to form a WR society, meeting in a theatre, then in the Westgate Corn Exchange, and finally in a former Congregationalist chapel in 1869. All three Grantham circuits extended into Leicestershire. Alfred Roberts, grocer, mayor and WM *local preacher, was the father of Baroness *Thatcher, who grew up in the town.

T. Cocking (1836)

WL/BJB

Gratton, Enoch (1837–1931; e.m. 1861), MNC and BC minister, born in Hanley. Brought up in the MNC, he went to work in a pottery at 7, was converted at an early age and began to testify and work for God. In 1861 he was sent to *Newcastle on Tyne to fill the vacancy caused by the resignation of W. *Booth and exercised a successful ministry there. He devoted himself to literary activity and gained access to the public press, was a helpful counsellor to the young and

kept abreast of the latest theological learning. In *Birmingham (1865–67) he was closely associated with the Gladstone-Bright school of political thought which held that 'that can never be politically right which is morally wrong'. In 1883 he was appointed to Maughan MNC Church, Adelaide before transferring to the BC Church in 1888. He served as a tutor for ministerial candidates at Way College, Brighton, SA and was President of the BC Conference in 1894.

DGH

Grayston, Dr Kenneth (1914– ; e.m. 1938) was born in *Sheffield and obtained a major scholarship to St John's College, Oxford, where he read Chemistry. Trained at *Wesley House, Cambridge, he worked as Assistant Head of Religious Broadcasting at the BBC, before being appointed NT Tutor at *Didsbury College in 1949. He became the first Professor of Theology at Bristol University in 1965 and built up a lively department. From 1976 until retirement in 1979 he was Pro-Vice-Chancellor of the University. As well as his major study of the meaning of the death of Christ in the NT, *Dying, We Live* (1990), he wrote commentaries on Galatians and Philippians (1957), Philippians and Thessalonians (1967), the Johannine Epistles (1984), John's Gospel (1990) and Romans (1996).

CSR

Great Yarmouth In 1754 T. *Olivers, came to preach, but encountered noisy and violent hostility and was driven back to *Norwich. A further effort was made in 1760 by H. *Harris, whose regiment, the Welsh Fencibles, was stationed in the town. By a clever ruse he gained a peaceable hearing, guarded by his fellow-soldiers. JW paid ten visits, describing the town as 'eminent for wickedness and ignorance'. A chapel built in 1793 was sold and converted to houses and shops when a large church, seating 1,400, was built in Southdown in 1837. A large WM Mission Hall and Sunday School opened in Tower Street in 1904.

Two PM preachers from Norwich, J. Brame and J. Turnpenny, missioned the town in 1821. A house in Row 60 was licensed for worship in 1823, the year Yarmouth joined the Norwich Circuit. Meetings were also held in a hayloft above a stable until the Tabernacle was built in 1829 (enlarged 1850). The 1851 PM Conference was held there. Queen's Road chapel dates from 1867 and the huge Italianate Temple on Priory Plain, 'a gross design' (Pevsner) built at the enormous cost of £7,000, from 1875 (demolished 1972).

Strong WR sympathies were given great

impetus when Thomas Rowland (1792–1858; e.m. 1813) was disciplined by the WM Conference for refusing to condemn two men for discussing Reform issues. As a result, large numbers were attracted to the Reformers, there were expulsions of WM members in December 1850 and a WR society was formed, with a permanent chapel in Regent Road in 1856. It became part of the UMFC, together with the MNC chapel of 1835. The Newtown UM Church was built in 1907.

A. Watmough (1828); A.H. Patterson (1903)

NV

Green, Frederick Pratt (1903– ; e.m. 1927), described by Erik Routley as the first and most obvious successor to CW, was educated at *Rydal School and trained for the ministry at *Didsbury College. He was Chairman of the York and Hull District 1957–64. The kindling of his latent skills as an author in the 1940s led to three volumes of poetry, and also plays, including *Farley Goes Out* (1928). Towards the end of his active ministry his talent as a hymn writer led him to serve on the working party set up to produce *Hymns and Songs* (1969), a supplement to the 1933 *MHB*. His prolific retirement bore fruit in two collections of *Hymns and Ballads* (1982 and 1989). He was co-editor of the 1979 *Partners in Praise* and a number of his hymns are included in *Hymns and Psalms*, the 1989 United Methodist *Hymnal*, etc. He has been honoured by the Hymn Societies of Great Britain and Ireland and of America and was awarded an honorary doctorate by Emory University, Atlanta. The Pratt Green Trust gives assistance to projects in church music and hymnody.

MR 17 Oct. 1963, 20 Sept. 1979

PLC

Green, Richard (1829–1907; e.m. 1853), WM minister and historian, born in *Birmingham. He laid the foundations of Methodist work in *Italy 1860–62 and was Governor of *Didsbury College, Manchester 1888–1900. As one of a small group of historians who strove to put Methodist historical studies on a more scholarly footing, he was the founder and first President of the *WHS. He gave the *Fernley Lecture on *The Mission of Methodism* in 1890. His bibliographies of *The Works of John and Charles Wesley* (1896; enlarged edn, 1906) and of *Anti-Methodist Publications* (1902; revised edn by C.D. Field, 1991) provided valuable research tools. His advocacy

led to the 'Standard Edition' of JW's *Journal* edited by N. *Curnock.

MR 26 Sept. 1907; *PWHS* 6 pp. 61–3

JAN

Greenfield, Thomas (1813–94; e.m. 1836), PM minister and theological college tutor. Born of humble parentage in *Newcastle on Tyne, he served his entire ministry in the North. Though largely self-educated, he became a very competent biblical scholar, linguist and theologian in the *Puritan mould and a frequent contributor to the PM connexional magazines. He published *Expository Discourses* on Romans 5–7 (1875). He was a tutor at the *Sunderland PM Theological Institute 1877–81 and principal until its closure in 1883, admired and loved by his students for his learning, kindliness and humour.

PMM 1894 pp. 786–92 ; G.E. Milburn (1982)

GEM

Greenhalgh, William *see* **Southport**

Greenwood, Paul (d.1767), early itinerant, probably from Ponden near Haworth. Converted *c*. 1741 by reading a religious tract, he began to itinerate in 1747 and was stationed in *Dublin at the outset of Methodism's work in *Ireland. As one of 'Mr *Grimshaw's men' he preached throughout *Rossendale, Lancs and Yorks and was also associated with J. *Bennet. On Whit-Sunday 1752 he faced the fury of a mob at Middleton in Teesdale. In 1758 he was one of those appointed as trustees of Grimshaw's chapel at *Haworth. He was stationed in the *Manchester Circuit in 1766, but died of a fever at *Warrington. J. *Pawson described him as 'a truly apostolical man, and exceedingly loved by the people'.

J. Pawson in *AM* 1795 pp. 148–9; C. Atmore (1801) pp. 164–5; J.W. Laycock (1909) pp. 85–92

SRV

Greet, Dr Kenneth Gerald (1918– ; e.m. 1943) gained a reputation in his circuit ministry as a fine preacher. He was a secretary in the Christian Citizenship Department 1954–71. As Secretary of the Conference 1971–84 he was highly regarded as an ecumenical statesman, faithful to Methodist principles, yet a trusted and knowledgeable partner in reconciliation. He was President of the 1980 Conference and Moderator of the FCFC in 1982. He also held office in both the WMC and the WCC. A moral theologian whose most considerable published work is *The Art of Moral Judgement* (1970), he is a lifelong pacifist dedicated to world disarmament.

_____

K.G. Gree (1997)

GSW

Greeves Family, a WM ministerial dynasty, beginning with **John Greeves** (1791–1846; e.m. 1815), born at King's Lynn and trained for the ministry at *Hoxton. All three of his sons entered the WM ministry: **John W. Greeves**(1823–94; e.m. 1846), Financial Secretary to the *HM Committee 1876–94; **Francis Wakefield Greeves** (1825–94; e.m. 1849), secretary of the Conference Memorials Committee for 22 years; and **Frederic Greeves** (1833–95; e.m. 1855). Frederic, born in *Bedford and educated at *Kingswood, obtained a doctorate and became well known in the Connexion. He was Chairman of the Oxford District, was appointed to the Legal Hundred in 1875 and was President of the 1884 Conference. He was Principal of *Southlands College, 1886–95. His sons **John Henry Greeves** (1863–1924; e.m. 1886) and **Edward Greeves** (1871–1942; e.m. 1894) continued the succession. Edward in turn had three ministerial sons. **Frederic Greeves** (1903–85; e.m. 1925) graduated at Manchester and was Assistant Tutor at *Didsbury College. At Oxford he was a founding member of OXFAM. He was a broadcaster and chaired the West of England Religious Broadcasting Advisory Committee. He returned to Didsbury in 1946, becoming Principal in 1949. He delivered the Fernley Hartley Lecture in 1956 on *The Meaning of Sin* and the Cato Lectures in 1960 on *Theology and the Cure of Souls*. He was President of the 1963 Conference. His brother **Hubert Trevor Greeves** (1905–70; e.m. 1928) was a gifted pianist and poet. A younger brother, **Derrick Amphlet Greeves** (1913–91; e.m. 1935) was an RAF chaplain during World War II and minister of *Westminster Central Hall, 1955–64. A gifted preacher and broadcaster, he served on the Central Religious Advisory Council and wrote many sermons for the *Methodist Recorder*.

_____

MR 14 & 21 March 1895, 23 Oct. 1924, 16 July 1942, 9 April 1970, 4 July 1963, 7 March 1985, 28 March 1991

WL

Gregory, Arthur S. (1895–1989; e.m. 1922), WM minister, read Classics at Trinity College, Oxford and was Assistant Tutor at *Handsworth College before entering circuit work in 1926. An acknowledged expert on CW's hymns, he was a founder member of the *MCMS and of the *Methodist Sacramental Fellowship, and a member of the editorial committee of the 1933 *MHB*. He wrote *Praises with Understanding* (1935; revised and enlarged 1949), a notable landmark in Methodist hymnology.

_____

MR 15 June 1989

PLC

Gregory, Benjamin (1820–1900; e.m. 1840) belonged to a distinguished family that produced several generation of WM ministers. From 1868 to 1893 he was *Connexional Editor and played a leading part in the 1882 revision of the 'Book of Offices', being keen to eliminate anything 'unscriptural' or 'sacerdotalist' from the services derived from the BCP. He was an able historian and ecclesiologist. His *Sidelights on the Conflicts in Methodism, 1827–52* (1897) is a key source for that troubled period. His *Fernley Lecture *The Holy Catholic Church* (1873) is still the only systematic exposition of the doctrine of the Church by a British Methodist. In other works he gave detailed and careful expositions of the polity of WM.

_____

MR 30 Aug. 1900; B. Gregory (1903)

DJC

Gregory, Theophilus Stephen (1897–1975; e.m. 1922), WM minister, from a long line of Methodist preachers, was born in Benares of missionary parents. He graduated at New College, Oxford and won the MC in World War I. He was a charismatic figure, much loved and long remembered, as a circuit minister. Always a high churchman, he was prominent in the Swanwick *Schools of Fellowship. He had drawn up the constitution of the *Methodist Sacramental Fellowship in 1935 when, in the course of writing his book *The Unfinished Universe*, he converted to Rome, feeling that Methodism was insufficiently God-centred and, strangely, that Roman Catholicism made possible a more open and adventurous attitude to the scheme of things. He became editor of the *Dublin Review* and Religious Controller of the BBC Third Programme. He took his devotion to CW with him and wrote an exposition of his hymns, *According to Your Faith*, as the Methodist Lent Book of 1966.

_____

G.S. Wakefield (2000)

GSW

Griffith, Sidney (d.1752), known as 'Madam Griffith', daughter of Cadwaladr Wynne of Plas y Foelas, Denbighshire, married William Griffith of Cefnamwlch, Caernarfonshire early in the 1740s. Converted in 1747, the couple showed an interest in Methodism and in October 1748 she met H. *Harris in North Wales. In 1749, claiming to have separated from her husband, she appeared at *Trevecka and began a close friendship with Harris which soon led him to regard her as a prophetess with God-given powers of discernment. Though an uneasy relationship, their friendship caused widespread rumours in Wales and heightened the tension between Harris and D. *Rowland, which led to the separation within Welsh CM in 1750. In Harris's plans for a Christian community at Trevecka early in the 1750s, Griffith was included (rather than Harris's wife) as the 'Mother', while he was to be the 'Father'. Towards the end of 1751 her health deteriorated and following her death from TB in London Harris retired from public life.

G.T. Roberts (1951) pp. 58–60; E. Evans (1985) pp. 277–8

GT

Griffith, William (1806–83; e.m. 1828), Wesleyan Reformer and UMFC minister, son of **William Griffith** senr (1777–1860; e.m. 1808). He followed his father into the WM ministry, after initial misgivings. An invitation to him in 1838 to go to Australia was vetoed by *Bunting. The *Fly Sheets appeared while he was in the *Ripley Circuit. He declined to sign the 'Declaration of Abhorrence' issued 'for the voluntary signatures of those who may approve of it' and he was consequently expelled. He spent the next few years in Reform activities and eventually became minister of the WR chapel in *Derby, where he remained for the rest of his life. He was thrice elected President of the *UMFC, but declined to serve. He was a radical in politics as well as in the Church and a republican who had his effigy burned in *Derby market place; but his ministry was truly Methodist and evangelical.

MR(W) 1899 pp. 21–2; R. Chew (1885); B. Gregory (1898); O.A. Beckerlegge (1957); O.A. Beckerlegge (1996)

OAB

Griffiths, Douglas Allen, MBE (1898–1982; e.m. 1922), WM minister, trained at *Didsbury College. In 1943 he became Secretary of the Methodist Youth Department and as such initiated MAYC. He founded 'Friendship House', Wandsworth Road and another at Rotherham, and initiated luncheon clubs for the elderly, advice centres, clinics and youth clubs. He wrote on *youth work and published some of his broadcast talks.

MR 7 Oct. 1982

WL

Grimsby J. *Nelson, the first to preach there, met with much opposition, but formed a society of 15. JW paid six visits and in 1757 opened the first preaching house, in William Blow's yard. With the opening of the new haven in 1800 the population grew rapidly and several substantial WM chapels were built during the nineteenth century, including New Street (1808), George Street (1847) and Victoria, following the opening of the Royal Dock by the Queen in 1852. Further large chapels and small mission halls were scattered east and west across the town. Grimsby became the head of a WM Circuit in 1776.

PM was introduced in 1819 by Thomas King (1788–1874; e.m. 1819), who preached from a wheelbarrow in Victoria Street. By 1880 a number of large chapels, including Garibaldi Street (1863), Hainton Street (1869), Ebenezer (1871) and Flottergate (1880), housed large congregations. Four PM Conferences were held there. and by 1900 there were three PM circuits. The fishing industry produced leading figures in both civic and religious life, some becoming mayors of the borough. C.K. *Watkinson and Sir Thomas *Robinson were Vice-Presidents of the PM Conference. Sir James *Blindell was an MP in the post-Union era. G. *Jackson and G. *Stampe were among the notable ministers and laymen born in the town.

The Grimsby circuits included Cleethorpes and many close-knit villages, with congregations drawn from the agricultural community. A post-Union Central Hall (1936) replaced three large chapels in the dockland area, but its influence declined in recent days.

G. Lester (1890); W. Leary (1996)

WL

Grimshaw, Rev. William (1708–63), evangelical incumbent of Haworth, Yorks, described by Frank Baker as 'the first beneficed clergyman in northern England to exercise an unrestrainedly evangelical ministry' and 'the commander-in-chief of revival in the north'. Born at Brindle, near Preston, he graduated from Christ's College,

Cambridge in 1730. After curacies at Little-borough and *Todmorden, he moved to Haworth in 1742. He was hostile to Methodist preaching until he came under the influence of W. *Darney, provoking the gibe, 'Mad Grimshaw is turned Scotch Will's clerk.' He received first CW and then JW at Haworth, forging a firm friendship with them. They entrusted him with the superin-tendency of an extensive preaching circuit known as the Great *Haworth Round, encompassing parts of North and West Yorks, Lancs and Cumbria. He was the only Anglican incumbent to act as secretary of a Methodist *quarterly meeting, held near Todmorden in 1748.

Grimshaw reported to the Archbishop of York in 1749 that during his incumbency summer com-municants at Haworth had increased from a mere dozen to some 1,200. By then JW was ready to name him as successor to himself and his brother, but in the event Grimshaw died in 1763 from a fever caught while visiting a sick parishioner. His genuine pastoral concern and deep spirituality have often been obscured by the caricature of the over-zealous cleric, horsewhipping backsliders into worship, most grotesquely by Glyn Hughes in his novel *Where I used to play on the Green* (1982). His behaviour and 'language of the market place' were certainly robust, but as JW wrote: 'a few such as him would make a nation tremble . . . he carries fire wherever he goes.' His favourite text, 'To us to live is Christ, to die is gain' was inscribed on the chapel he built for the Haworth Methodists in 1758.

C. Atmore (1801) pp. 165–9; G.C. Cragg (1947); F. Baker (1963); A. Longworth (1996)

                                                              JAH

Grindrod, Edmund (1786–1842; e.m. 1806), a gifted teacher, noted for his piety, integrity and uprightness. His rigid adherence to the consti-tution of Methodism and his view of the *pastoral office made him refuse to compromise in the *Leeds Organ Case and his health was impaired. He became Secretary of the WM Conference in 1833 and was President in 1837. The most lasting benefit he conferred on the Connexion was his *Compendium of the Laws . . . of WM* (1842)

B. Gregory (1898); *PWHS* 29, 146

                                                              MB

Grist, William Alexander (1869–1942; e.m. 1889), BC missionary to *China, born in Ryde, IOW. He read Chinese at Oxford before serving in South West China from 1896 to 1902. With his

wife and C.E. *Hicks he took the risk of remaining in Tung Chuan throughout the Boxer troubles. Author of the definitive biography of S. *Pollard, he was President of the UM Conference in 1926. He became Foreign Missions Secretary in 1928 and in preparation for *Methodist Union was appointed China Secretary of the WMMS in 1930, an office he held until 1936.

MR 7 Jan.1943

                                                              RKP

Groves, Charles Pelham (1887–1973; e.m. 1910), PM scholar, born in Wisconsin. His family settled in England in 1897, then in *Sierra Leone, where his father became superintendent of the *Countess of Huntingdon's Connexion mission. He himself was Principal of the PM Training Institute for teacher-evangelists at Oron, Eastern *Nigeria, 1911–23. From 1926 to 1954, apart from two years as a visiting Professor in the USA, he taught at *Kingsmead College, Selly Oak, becoming Professor of Missions in 1945 and influencing many generations of missionaries. His *magnum opus*, *The Planting of Christianity in Africa* (1948) earned him the nickname 'the Euse-bius of Africa'.

MR 5 April 1973

                                                              JRP

Grundell, John (1761–1815; e.m. 1780), WM and later MNC itinerant, born in *Sunderland. Though blind from his early childhood, he became a *local preacher in his teens and entered the ministry. While stationed at *Newcastle upon Tyne in the early 1790s he became minister of a private chapel at Byker where the sacrament was celebrated by himself and other preachers against the wishes of the more conservative WM circuit leaders. He threw in his lot with the MNC from the outset, was its first Conference secretary and President in 1799.

W. Salt (1827) pp. 55–70

                                                              GEM

Guardian Representatives were created by the MNC Deed Poll (1846). Twelve ministers and twelve laymen, representative of all parts of the Connexion, were appointed for life by Confer-ence, to have permanent seats in Conference and vacancies were filled by Conference. A minimum of six Representatives had to attend Conference to give it a legal existence, but they had no power to obstruct business. The UM Constitution also included Guardian Representatives, but they were elected for six years only.

EAR

Guest Family, iron masters at Dowlais, Glam. **John Guest** (1721?-87), a Wesleyan, migrated from Broseley, Shropshire, to Dowlais in 1759 and was appointed manager of the iron works there in 1767. In 1782 he secured for himself a share in the company, and when he was succeeded as manager in 1785 by his son, **Thomas Guest** (1749?-1807), a period of expansion began. Thomas's son, **Josiah John Guest** (1785–1852), through further expansion, succeeded in making Dowlais the biggest producer of iron in South Wales. By 1840 there were 18 furnaces under his control, and by 1851 he was the sole owner of the company. Elected MP for Honiton in 1825, and Merthyr in 1832, he was knighted in 1838. His second wife, **Lady Charlotte Elizabeth Bertie** (1812–95), translated and edited the Mabinogion. Though brought up a Wesleyan, and despite his father's having preached from time to time in local WM chapels, J.J. Guest returned to the Anglican fold. His religious convictions were expressed through his keen interest in the welfare of his workers and their families. He helped to establish schools, made donations to the local churches and chapels, supported Sunday schools, and set up friendly societies and a savings bank. During his final years he lived at Canford Manor, Dorset.

G. A.Williams (1988); J.A. Owen (1972); L. Ince (1993); C.M. Vaughan (1975); *DWB*; *DNB*

GT

Guier, Philip (d. 1778), master of the German-speaking *Palatine school at Ballingrane, was one of six preachers received by JW at the first Irish Conference in *Limerick (1752). He never itinerated, but as class leader and *local preacher became spiritual father to the infant society at Limerick and neighbouring Palatine settlements, among whom he is credited with upholding high moral standards when they had no other pastoral care. His most notable pupils were Philip Embury (1728–73), a pioneer of New York Methodism, and Thomas *Walsh. It was said that, even a century after his death, locals would say of the Methodist itinerants, 'There goes Philip Guier who drove the Devil out of Ballingrane.'

WMM 1828 pp. 214–15

RPR

Guild of Methodist Braillists was formed in 1952 by Geoffrey Treglown MBE (1919–91; e.m. 1941) who had been seriously wounded and blinded as an army chaplain. (In retirement he became an Anglican priest in 1960.) The RNIB supported the Guild by providing the first braille transcribers. The Guild's aims are 'to proclaim the gospel to blind people by transcribing agreed literature into braille and by helping to increase the number of Methodist books in particular in the National Library for the Blind and RNIB Library' and 'to promote the interests of blind Methodists at home and abroad'. Volunteer transcribers qualify by taking the RNIB Proficiency Test and work from home, transcribing books from the Book Selection Committee's list. More than 1,000 books have been produced. Special requests that have been met include the Four Year Lectionary, chorus books and training material for blind *local preachers.

JAV

Guppy, Henry (1861–1948), WM Librarian of the John Rylands Library, Manchester for 49 years, so that it was said, 'Mrs Rylands founded the John Rylands Library, Henry Guppy made it.' Born in London, he went from Sion College Library to Manchester in 1899 and became Librarian there in 1900. Gifts from the Rylands family (whose primary intention had been to assist further study for Nonconformist ministers) enabled him to embark on prodigious collection-building. He edited the Library's *Bulletin* from 1908 until his death and did extensive editorial work over the Library's imprint. He was made Honorary Fellow (1902) and President (1926) of the Library Association, and after World War I reconstituted Louvain University Library.

WM Conference Handbook 1932; *Bulletin of the John Rylands Library* 31 (1948) pp. 173–9; *Library Association Record* 1948 pp. 255–6

JAV

Gurteen Agricultural College in North Tipperary was opened in 1947. The Irish Methodist Council on Social Welfare feared that post-war emigration from rural Ireland would denude the countryside of its Protestant population. Gurteen House and a farm of *c.* 300 acres were bought and the buildings adapted to accommodate 44 students. The College soon won a high reputation. It now holds *c.* 700 acres and welcomes up to 95 students of all denominations. Its board is appointed by the Irish Conference, to which it reports annually.

J.W. Mckinney & W.S. Sterling (1972); H. Perdue (1997)

DALC

Gutteridge, Michael (1842–1935), business-man and philanthropist whose working life was spent in Naples, where he was widely respected for his Christian principles and integrity. After retirement he attended the WM Conference of 1911. Lacking university education himself, he sought the highest standards for ministers and the 1912 Conference accepted his proposal that *ministerial training be started in *Cambridge, towards which he initially contributed £5,000. War delayed the implementation of his plan, but it led to the opening of *Wesley House, where a college Chair in systematic theology bears his name.

WDH

Guttery, Thomas (1837–1895; e.m. 1857), PM minister, born at Brierley Hill, served for eight years (1871–79) in Toronto. He wrote a life of W. *Clowes and died in the active work at Newcastle. His son **Arthur Thomas Guttery** (1862–1920; e.m. 1883) followed his father into the ministry, was President of the Conference and of the FCFC in 1916, and General Missionary Secretary, 1908–13. He was a leader of the Passive Resistance Movement in opposition to the Education Act of 1902.

J.G. Bowran (1922)

WL

Guttridge, John (1819–86; e.m. 1838), UMFC minister. Born in *Birmingham of Methodist parents, he was converted when 12 and became a *local preacher four years later. He entered the *WMA ministry and became one of the most popular preachers of his generation. He was equally at home in the pulpit, lecture hall (he was a keen temperance advocate) or open air. He spent most of his ministry in Lancashire, from which he drew material for his *Life among the Masses* (1884). He held many connexional posts and was elected UMFC President in 1863.

OAB

Gwennap Pit, Carharrack, Cornwall, is thought to be the result of subsidence in an old mine working. JW used it as a preaching place on 18 occasions between 1762 and 1789 and drew large crowds from miles around. In 1806 it was remodelled, terraced and reduced in size as a memorial to W's visits. The annual Whit Monday service (held on the Spring Bank Holiday since 1976) began in 1807. A visitors' centre, with an exhibition on World Methodism, was added to the adjoining chapel and opened in 1991.

T. Shaw (1992)

TS

Gwynne Family of Garth, Breconshire. The family's first contact with Methodism was through **Marmaduke Gwynne** (1692–1769) who entered Jesus College, Oxford, on 5 May 1710 and Lincoln's Inn in 1711, but then abandoned his education and married Sarah Evans, Fynnon Bedr, Cardiganshire, on 27 July 1716. Converted through hearing H. *Harris preach in 1737, he became involved in the revival by giving his support to the leaders and also by intervening on behalf of Methodists when they were threatened with prosecution. He helped H. Harris in the matter of his marriage to Anne Williams of Skreen in 1744, was present in *Bristol in 1745 at JW's second Conference, and on 8 April 1749 his daughter, **Sarah Gwynne** (1726–1822), became the wife of CW. After the wedding Gwynne removed to Ludlow; two years later he returned to Wales and resided at Brecon until his death in 1769. **Howell Gwynne**, his eldest son, was MP for Radnorshire, 1755–1761, and for Old Sarum, Wiltshire, 1761–1768. By the beginning of the nineteenth century, the family was no longer living at Garth but at Glanbrân near Llandovery, and Llanelwedd near Builth Wells.

DWB; A.H. Williams, in *Brycheiniog*, XIV (1970) and XVII (1976–77); A.H. Williams in *Journal of the Historical Society of the Presbyterian Church of Wales*, 55 (1970)

GT

Hackworth, Timothy (1786–1850), railway engineer who built up his career from relatively humble origins as a colliery blacksmith at Wylam on Tyne. In 1825 he became resident engineer and manager at Shildon (Co. Durham) for the Stockton and Darlington Railway and began to win a reputation as a leading locomotive designer. He established his own company at Shildon in 1840. He was cheerful in manner and popular as an employer. He served as a WM *local preacher. By his own hard work and financial generosity he did much to strengthen WM in the Bishop

Auckland Circuit and was a generous supporter of connexional causes.

MR(W) 1907 pp. 36–8; R. Young (1923); G.E. Milburn, in WHS(NE), Aug. 1975 pp. 4–33

GEM

Haigh, Dr Henry (1853–1917; e.m. 1874) missionary in *India, served in Mysore 1874–1903. An accomplished Kanarese scholar, he founded and edited a Kanarese newspaper and was reviser-in-chief of the Kanarese Bible. From 1903 to 1912 he was Chairman of the Newcastle District and was President of the Conference in 1911. A General Secretary of the Missionary Society from 1912, he died in Hankow during a visit to *China.

MR 19 July 1917

JAV

Haime, John (1710–84), early itinerant, born in Shaftesbury, Dorset. He enlisted in the army and came to faith, greatly helped by his contacts with J. *Cennick and CW. Serving with his regiment in France, his zeal led him to form a religious society and he became known as the 'soldier-preacher'. He narrowly escaped death at the battle of Fontenoy in 1745. On returning from the continent he introduced Methodism into his native town. Despite his falling later into depression and doubts that lasted twenty years, JW made him a travelling preacher in 1747 and personally befriended him. He continued active in the Methodist ranks until his death. A later member of the family, **Charles Haime** (1775–1854; e.m. 1804) was also in the WM ministry.

C. Atmore (1801) pp. 172–76; *EMP* 1 pp. 269–311; J.W. Haime (1970) pp. 45–65

HMG

Hale, William John (1862–1929), *Sheffield architect, was educated at *Wesley College, Sheffield and articled to the Congregationalist C.J. Innocent, who specialized in school buildings. He had his own practice from 1892. In his most active periods, 1896–1909 and 1924–29 he designed a number of WM churches, notably the Victoria Hall (1908) taken over from W.A. Waddington, the octagonal Wesley Hall, Crookes (1908), Attercliffe Mission Hall (1926) and Banner Cross UM Church (1929). His work was influenced by the Arts and Crafts movement and Art Nouveau. He was related to the Fordham family, which included a cousin, William Henry Fordham (1860–1918),

a Sheffield GP and Tory city Councillor, and WM missionaries in *Fiji and *China, and he and his daughter married into two other influential WM families, the Toothills and the *Coles.

N.D. Wilson in *Miscellany 1* (The Chapels Society, 1998) pp. 51–73

JAV

Halévy Thesis Elie Halévy, the eminent French historian and political scientist, in the early twentieth century developed a thesis on popular evangelicalism and the absence of revolution in early industrial England which has exercised a remarkable influence on the historiography of Methodism. His formidable intellect was engaged by what he regarded as a profound paradox at the centre of English history in the age of European revolutions. By comparison with some other European states England had the weakest executive, the smallest army, the most dynamic economy and the highest degree of individual freedom; yet it was also characterized by an unusual amount of social and political stability. According to Halévy, England did not experience revolutionary change because of the 'powerful moral authority' exercised by freely organized evangelical sects in general, and Methodism in particular, over their middle and upper working-class members. Halévy's views have been challenged by historians who have suggested that he exaggerated both the fragility of early industrial English society and the power of evangelical Protestants to make such a decisive difference. The Halévy thesis is both unproven and probably untestable, but over the years it has excited much debate and controversy. In 1963 it was given a notorious psycho-sexual and Marxist twist by E.P. *Thompson in his infamous chapter on the 'transforming power of the cross' in *The Making of the English Working Class*.

E. Halévy (1961); B. Semmel (1971); G.W. Olsen (1990)

DNH

Halifax JW made the first of 25 visits in 1742, but Methodism first became established in the parochial out-townships of Lightcliffe (where there was an early *Moravian settlement) and Skircoat Green (where J. *Nelson preached in 1741). A society was formed in Halifax itself following JW's open-air preaching in 1748. The first purpose built preaching house, in Church Lane (1752), was replaced by South Parade Chapel, opened by JW in 1777. A second chapel was opened in Broad Street in 1829. Halifax became the head of a circuit in 1785 and of one of the first *Districts in 1791.

Superintendents of the Circuit included W. *Thompson, the first WM President after JW, W. *Thom, the first President of the MNC, and J. *Bunting, who faced the challenge of the *Luddite disturbances during his Halifax ministry. In the *Religious Census (1851) it was the only large town in the West Riding where WM, reduced by 45% during the WR controversy, was outnumbered by the other branches of Methodism. During the second half of the century, the MNC exerted considerable influence on municipal politics, the first nonconformist civic service being held at Salem Chapel (1799) in 1877, which also hosted six MNC Conferences between 1817 and 1895. The imposing Ebenezer PM Chapel, rebuilt in 1922 to commemorate the centenary of the first PM society in Halifax, was the last to be built there before *Methodist Union.

After 1932 circuit amalgamations and chapel closures reduced the number of circuits from eight to one by 1971, but new churches were opened at St Andrew's (1965), Salem (1970) and Highgate (1978). The oldest surviving chapel in the circuit, at Mount Zion (1773), seized from WM by the MNC in 1796, is now a centre for Methodist heritage, with a display of *ceramics from the Hird Collection.

Conference Handbook 1937, 1950

JAH

'Halifax Circular'   A letter addressed to 'The Preachers in general and the *Assistants in particular' was signed by nine senior itinerants who met in Halifax on 30 March 1791, four weeks after the death of JW. The nine were W *Thompson, J. *Pawson, R. *Roberts, J. *Allen, R. *Rodda, S. *Bradburn, T. *Tennant, T. *Hanby and C. *Hopper. The purpose of the Circular was to advocate a corporate form of connexional government, rather than 'another king in Israel' as Wesley's successor. The 1791 Conference chose its prime mover, Thompson, as the first President and adopted many of its proposals, including an annual presidency and the formation of *Districts with Chairmen authorized to exercise disciplinary powers between Conferences. The more controversial sacramental issues were left unresolved.

G. Smith, (1858–61) 2, pp. 85–7; *PWHS* 30, pp. 165–6

WL

Hall, Robert (1754–1827), MNC layman, who went into business as a bleacher and cotton spinner at Basford, Notts. He joined the Methodists in 1771, occasionally entertained JW and solicited his help in the building of Hockley Chapel, *Nottingham. In 1797, like many other Nottingham Methodists, he joined the MNC, where his wealth gave him a leading position. He was Secretary of the MNC Conference in 1799 and 1800 and was the principal editor of the first *Life* of A. *Kilham (1799).

MNCM 1828 pp. 1–7, 45–50

EAR

Hall, Rev. Westley (1711–76), a member of the *'Holy Club' and an early associate of JW and CW, who deceitfully proposed to their sister Keziah while already secretly engaged to her sister Martha. He married Martha in spite of her parents' disapproval and to her lifelong regret and 'Kezzy' never recovered from the experience. Despite this, he remained close to the W brothers and JW spoke of his piety; but he proved to be a man of great charm who pursued his own interests ruthlessly, ignoring the consequences of his debauchery. After a curacy at Wootton Rivers, Wilts, he moved to *Salisbury, where he established one of the first Methodist societies. He became increasingly idiosyncratic and morally irresponsible, defending polygamy and deserting his wife, and eventually left with his mistress for the West Indies. JW conducted his funeral in *Bristol in 1776 and wrote of his 'deep repentance'.

See also **Antinomianism**

Tyerman (1873) pp. 386–411; F.E. Maser (1988) pp. 86–97

EWD

Hall, William Nelthorp (1829–78; e.m. 1848), MNC minister. In 1859 he was appointed, along with J. *Innocent, to begin new work in North *China. Under his leadership a Training Institute for native preachers was opened in Tientsin (Tianjin) in 1871. He died in China of typhus.

GRS

Hall's Circuits and Ministers   In 1873 Joseph Hall (1835–1902; e.m. 1862) published *The Wesleyan Methodist Itinerancy*. A second edition appeared in 1885 under the title *Hall's Circuits and Ministers*. The third edition appeared in 1897. Circuits were arranged alphabetically, with ministerial appointments to each listed in chronological order. Departmental appointments and other offices were also included. In 1912 T. Galland Hartley (1847–1931; e.m. 1868) revised and enlarged Hall's work and in 1925 produced a supplementary volume, bringing it up to 1923.

'Hall's' (as it came to be known) was updated in manuscript from 1924 until 1932 and after Union was enlarged to include the whole Connexion, down to 1980. Copies of this manuscript list are in the Methodist *Archives Centre, Manchester and in the WHS Library.

PWHS 17 pp. 96–8

WL

Hamilton, James, MD, FRCPEd (1740–1827) born at *Dunbar, from 1759 to 1763 was a Surgeon's Mate in the Navy. Returning home to medical practice, he joined the fledgling Methodist society and became a *local preacher. His house was home for the itinerants and he helped JW organize Methodism in *Scotland. As a leading Town Councillor he organized the defence of Dunbar against French attacks. In 1790 he moved to *Leeds, married into a wealthy family and in 1794 became Physician to the London Dispensary and an influential member at *Wesley's Chapel.

M. Batty (1998)

MB

Hammet(t), William (*c.* 1756–1803), an Irish preacher who sailed with T. *Coke and two other missionaries in September 1786, bound for Nova Scotia. Violent storms drove them south to the *West Indies, where they landed in Antigua on 25 December. Hammet pioneered WM missions in St Kitts (1787), Tortola and Santa Cruz (1788) and Jamaica (1789), where the first society of eight people was formed in August at his lodgings in Kingston. Bitter persecution by influential leaders of the white community followed his success and led to his physical breakdown. In 1791 Coke took him to Charleston SC to recover his health in the hope that he might return to the work. Hammet, however, settled in Charleston, gathered his own following and initiated the first schism (the 'Primitive Methodist Church') in *American Methodism. This brand of Methodism did not survive in America, but was introduced into the Bahamas, where traces remained at least into the 1820s.

E.S. Bucke (1964) 1 pp. 617–22; N.W. Taggart (1986)

NWT

Hampson, John, senr (*c.* 1732–95), born at Chowbent, of Unitarian stock, became an itinerant in 1752, but resigned in 1765, referring slightingly to the Church as 'Old Peg'. He settled at Little Leigh and became the leader of the Methodist society there; then returned to the itinerancy in 1776, but finally withdrew in 1784 because JW did not include him in the *Legal Hundred. He became an Independent minister at Southborough, Kent. When he became ill, he received help from the Preachers' Fund and JW found him a teaching post. His son **John Hampson junr** (1753–1819; e.m. 1777) was educated at *Kingswood School and St Edmund Hall, Oxford. He was stationed in Ireland and northern England, but left the itinerancy with his father in 1784, partly because of a disagreement with S. *Bradburn and partly because of an offer by some *Sunderland laymen to fund him through Oxford. He was ordained and became a curate, and later rector, in Sunderland, 1795–1819. His three-volume biography of JW (1791) was the first to appear after JW's death; it was too candid to be acceptable by contemporary Methodists, but its value has become increasingly recognized.

C. Atmore (1801) pp. 176–8; *WMM* 1845 p. 15, 1880 p. 932; *PWHS* 20 pp. 131–5; R.P. Heitzenrater (1984) 2 pp. 168–70; *DEB*

JHL

Hanby, Thomas (1733–1796; e.m. 1754), early itinerant. A native of *Carlisle, he moved with his parents to Barnard Castle and joined the local Methodist society. At the 1755 Conference he was made a travelling preacher and dedicated himself to forty-three years of tireless and fruitful ministry. Appointed to *Dundee in 1763 he witnessed the bitter anti-Wesleyan controversy sparked off in *Scotland by the publication of J. *Hervey's *Letters*. He was ordained by JW for Scotland in 1785 and on his return to English circuits in 1787, persisted in the practice of baptizing children and administering the Lord's Supper in spite of JW's disapproval. Although JW feared that he would leave Methodism for an independent ministry, Hanby outlived him, was elected President of the Conference in 1794 and lived to be the oldest minister in the Connexion.

C. Atmore (1801) pp. 179–81 *EMP* 2 pp. 131–57

HMG

Handsworth College, Birmingham, was opened in 1881 as a result of a decision of the

WM Conference in 1868 to establish a theological college in the Midlands out of moneys from the *Thanksgiving Fund. It opened with 40 students. Its first theological tutor was F.W. *Macdonald. Other outstanding staff members included W.T. *Davison and J.G. *Tasker. Extensions to the building in 1931 included lecture rooms and a chapel. Links with the University of Birmingham were forged by the strong teaching team of W.F. *Lofthouse, C.R. *North, H. *Bett and W.F. *Howard, specializing in biblical studies and Pastoral Theology. During World War II the College was taken over by the Public Health Department. After the War, G.W. *Anderson and P.S. *Watson continued its strong contribution to biblical and historical theology. In 1967 the training centre of the Wesley *Deaconess Order transferred to Handsworth from Ilkley. After closure in 1970 the name was transferred to a new residential building for married students in the ecumenical *Queen's College, Edgbaston.

W.B. Brash (1935) pp. 92–102

TSAM

Hanham Mount see **Kingswood**

Hanley see **Stoke-on-Trent**

Hannah, Dr John (1792–1867; e.m. 1814) Born in *Lincoln, on entering the WM ministry he was offered a place in T. *Coke's party of missionaries bound for India, but stayed in the home work. His intellectual ability was shown by his graduating as MA and DD. The Conference recognized his talents and eloquence and appointed him Tutor in Theology at the newly established Theological Institution in *Hoxton, and he spent the rest of his ministry in theological training. He was several times Conference Secretary and was twice President (1842 and 1851). He was a first-rate biblical expositor and a gifted public speaker, enthralling congregations by his command of language, his animating voice and his noble oratory. He was commemorated in Lincoln in the 'Hannah Memorial' chapel built in 1875.

WL

Hardy, Robert Spence (1803–68; e.m. 1825), born in *Preston and educated in Yorkshire. He was a missionary in Ceylon (now *Sri Lanka), 1825–48 and again 1862–65, as Chairman of the South Ceylon District after the death of D. *Gogerly. He became a scholar of both Buddhism and Sinhala language, literature and culture and published four major books on Buddhism, including *A Manual of Buddhism in its Modern Development* (1853), which contained pioneering translations of Sinhala texts. His attitude to Buddhism became increasingly condemnatory, e.g. in *The Legends and Theories of the Buddhists compared with history and science* (1866). His tract *The British Government and the Idolatry of Ceylon* (Colombo, 1839) spearheaded missionary criticism of perceived government leniency towards Buddhism.

EJH

Hargreaves, Peter (1833–1917; e.m. 1857), WM missionary, spent his entire ministry in *South Africa, with only two appointments in 44 years. He arrived in Clarkebury (Transkei) in 1857. By 1880 membership had increased ninefold and a number of outstations and a Training Institution had been opened. From 1882 to 1901 he was stationed at Emfundisweni in Pondoland, then an independent territory troubled by tribal warfare. He argued for its annexation by the Cape Colony to discourage random European speculators, and when it was peacefully ceded in 1894 a period of stability allowed the Church to grow. He was Chairman of the Clarkebury District from 1885 and President of the South African Conference in 1891.

JRP

Harris, Howel(l) (1714–1773), founder of *Welsh Calvinistic Methodism, born at *Trevecka. Initially intended for holy orders, his father's death in 1731 interrupted his education and he began his career as a schoolmaster. Converted in 1735, he was soon involved in an itinerant ministry and in setting up societies. He made several applications for ordination, but was turned down, and therefore remained an Anglican layman throughout his life.

He met *Whitefield and the Wesleys in 1739; a long period of co-operation followed despite doctrinal differences with JW. He often travelled to London to assist at Whitefield's Tabernacle, but during the latter half of the 1740s he was suspected of heresy. This, coupled with his autocratic manner and the presence of 'Madam' S. *Griffith as his travelling companion, led to tension which resulted in his separation from D. *Rowland and the majority of Welsh Methodists in June 1750. Following the death of 'Madam' Griffith in 1752, he retired to Trevecka and established a Christian community that became known as the 'Trevecka Family'. Fearful of a Catholic invasion in the late 1750s, he joined the militia, and when the regiment was disbanded in 1762, he was reconciled with his former co-revivalists and resumed itinerating. By then, a new revival had broken out in Wales which centred on Llangeitho, and Harris was marginalised by a new generation of Methodists. Following the death of his wife in 1770, Harris' own health began to deteriorate. He is buried at Talgarth.

H. Harris (1791); H.J. Hughes (1892); G.T. Roberts (1951); G.F. Nuttall (1965)

GT

Harris, Dr William (1813–1900), born in *Barnstaple, the son of a German Jew, was a *local preacher on the Dunster WM Circuit plan until he moved to London in 1843. He was a founder member and first President of the *LPMAA and, despite becoming an IM minister in South London in 1854 (serving in England and the *Channel Islands for 40 years), continued his interest in the LPMAA. He was the first editor of the *Local Preachers' Magazine* (1851–57) and a trustee of the local preachers' retirement home at Fillongley. He lived to attend the Association's Jubilee meeting in London in 1899, but the next year was taken ill and died following the World Temperance Congress.

MR 5 July 1900; F.H. Buss & R.G. Burnett (1949), pp. 81–2, 145–50

PB

Harris, Dr William Butcher (1913–92; e.m. 1937), missionary to *India, was educated at Wadham College, Oxford and *Wesley House, Cambridge. He served in the Madras District 1941–47 and then in CSI. He was involved in education and village evangelism. He taught first in the Tirumaraiyur Theological Seminary and then with his second wife Margaret (*née* *Valentine) in the joint Tamil Nadu Theological Seminary in Madurai, where he also became involved in prison chaplaincy. He wrote several NT commentaries and received an honorary DD from Serampore University.

MR 30 April 1992

JAV

Harris, William Wadé *see* **Platt, W.J.**

Harrison, Dr Archibald Walter, MC (1882–1946; e.m. 1905), WM minister and historian, graduated at University College, Nottingham and trained for the ministry at *Didsbury College. He served in World War I, first as a combatant, then as chaplain. In 1921 he became Vice-Principal of

*Westminster College, succeeding H.B. *Workman as Principal in 1930. He was President of the Conference in 1945, but the strain of the war years contributed to his sudden death while in office. He was a devoted student of Bunyan and the *Puritans, cherished the evangelical *Arminianism of the Wesleys and was a leading member of the *WHS. He was a champion of *Methodist Union in 1932 and his publications include two books on Arminianism and *The Evangelical Revival and Christian Reunion* (*Fernley-Hartley Lecture, 1942). His wife, **Grace Elizabeth (Elsie) Harrison** (1886–1964), the daughter of Dr J.S. *Simon, was trained in the Manchester History School under T.F. Tout and made her own distinctive contribution to Methodist biography and history. Her *Son to Susanna: the private life of John Wesley* (1937) provoked widespread debate. Her other writings include *Methodist Good Companions* (1935) and the 1937 WHS Lecture *Haworth Parsonage*.

F.B. Harvey (1946); *MR* 10 & 17 Jan. 1946, 7 Jan. 1965; *PWHS* 25 pp. 65–7

JAN

Harrison, Richard (1743–1830), a native of Halkyn, Flintshire, was converted in 1766, joined the WM society in *Chester and later the society at Bryngwyn. Eventually he formed a society that met in his home at Northop and became a *local preacher in the *Chester Circuit. After attending a preaching and Communion service conducted by JW in the Chester Octagon in 1774, he devoted his time and energy to preaching *Arminianism in Wales. A weaver by trade, his dedication to preaching and visiting the societies left him poor for life. He unflinchingly faced vicious opposition and when the first WM missionaries to *Welsh-speaking Wales, E. *Jones and E. *Roberts, arrived they found that he had long been preparing the way for them and benefited greatly from his help and advice.

D. Young (1893) pp. 381–2, 390; A.H. Williams (1935) pp. 45–100; *DWB*

IGPL

Hart, Sir Robert (1835–1911), Irish layman, born near Portadown, the son of a WM mill-owner. He entered Queen's College (now University) at 15 and went to *China as a student interpreter with the British Consular Service. At 28 he became inspector-general of the imperial maritime customs, a post he held with outstanding ability and great distinction until his retirement in 1906, revisiting Europe only twice. The *Irish Christian Advocate* occasionally referred to his achievements and to the many Chinese and European honours bestowed on him.

DNB; *Times* 10 Jan. 1899; J. Bredon (1909); S.F. Wright (1950)

NWT

Hartlepool JW's seven visits were to old Hartlepool, formerly a busy port which by the eighteenth century was in decline. His purpose was evangelical, but may also have been related to the presence there of the family of W. *Romaine. Typically, he recruited the services of a substantial man of business to oversee the budding society, John Middleton (1724–95) a corn miller who was instrumental in establishing Methodist meetings and building preaching houses. Originally part of the great Yarm Circuit, Hartlepool was later transferred to Darlington. Methodism profited from its industrial and commercial progress, in the course of which both urban and social development, including church life, moved towards West Hartlepool. A clear sign of its strength was the building in West Hartlepool of the 'Wesley' chapel of 1873, whose imposing classical portico survives. PM arrived on the headland of old Hartlepool in 1822, where a fishermen's chapel was soon built; but the PMs soon migrated towards the new town, WR/UMFC was also active and all three Methodist denominations built chapels in outlying colliery villages.

C. Sharp (1851); W.R. Owen (1909); WHS(NE) Bulletins nos. 9–10, 27–9, 30, 47–8

WB

Hartley, Marshall (1846–1928; e.m. 1868), the son and grandson of WM ministers, was educated at *Woodhouse Grove School. As a Secretary of the Missionary Society, 1888–1929, he visited *South Africa, *China and *India. He was Secretary of the Conference from 1895 to 1902 and President in 1903.

MR 28 Dec. 1928

JAV

Hartley, Sir William Pickles (1846–1922), jam-maker and devout PM layman who used his considerable wealth and influence to promote the advancement of the PM Connexion. Born in Colne, Lancs, he worked for a short while in the little family shop, before commencing business on his own in 1862. His home-made jams were

so successful as to encourage him to open a small factory in Bootle (1874) before transferring to extensive premises at Aintree (1886), with an additional factory in London from 1901. A conscientious and paternalist employer, he built a model village for his employees at Aintree and in 1889 introduced a profit-sharing scheme. A private vow on New Year's Day 1877 to devote 1/10th of his gross annual income to religious and charitable purposes proved a landmark in his career and in his later years he was giving away up to 1/3rd of his entire income, while also encouraging the recipients of his generosity (especially the PM Church) to give more willingly themselves. The major beneficiary was the Theological Institute in Manchester, known from 1906 as *Hartley College and he was largely responsible for the recruitment of A.S. *Peake to its staff in 1892.

His influence on PM was evidenced in many other ways, including the establishment in 1890 of the *Chapel Aid Association, of which he served as Chairman and Treasurer until his death. He was also a generous benefactor to Colne, providing almshouses (1911) and a hospital, opened by his daughter in 1924. He was knighted in 1908 for his commercial and philanthropic work and was Vice-President of the 1892 Conference and President in 1909. Among his sons-in-law were the PM minister J.T. *Barkby and J.S. Higham MP.

G.J. Stevenson (1884–6) 5 pp. 852–8; A.S. Peake (1926); A.S. Peake in *Holborn Review*, 1923 pp. 1–7, 101–6; G.E. Milburn in *ER* Sept. 1983 pp. 33–41; *DBB*

GEM

Hartley College, Manchester, the main PM theological college, opened in 1881. PM ministerial training was provided from 1865 by *Elmfield College, York, as a one-year preparation for circuit work. This was superseded by the *Sunderland Theological Institute in 1868. A second college opened thirteen years later in Manchester. Through the generosity of Sir W. *Hartley, the PM Church was enabled to support a two-year training programme in an extended building housing over 60 students and erected between 1897 and 1906. The College's most notable tutor was A.S. *Peake. It amalgamated with *Victoria Park College in 1934 to form the *Hartley Victoria College.

A.L. Humphries & W. Barker (1931); W.B. Brash (1935) pp. 123–47

TSAM

Hartley Lecture was endowed by W.P. *Hartley in 1897 and was given annually except for a break in World War I until it became part of the *Fernley-Hartley Lecture after *Methodist Union.

JAV

Hartley Victoria College, Manchester, was formed as a union of the *Hartley (PM) and *Victoria Park (UM) Colleges after *Methodist Union. The Duckworth, Lewins and Ranmoor chairs perpetuated links with the UM tradition on the Hartley site. During World War II the college was taken over by the YMCA, but reopened in 1945. After three years of indecision about rede-veloping and upgrading the premises to provide a major theological college accommodating 80 stu-dents, the Conference of 1972 decided to close the Manchester college, rather than the Bristol one, on financial grounds. Its students were transferred to the Northern Baptist College, where they con-tinued to take courses in the University. The Col-lege premises were sold and now house the Royal Northern College of Music; but the staff remained to form part of a federation providing theological education. The title 'Hartley Victoria' is retained within the Manchester Christian Institute, situated at Luther King House, Brighton Grove.

Hartley Victoria Methodist College, 1881–1981: The First Hundred Years (1981)

TSAM

Harvard, William M. (1790–1857; e.m. 1810), one of the young missionaries who accompanied T. *Coke to Ceylon in 1814, became their leader after Coke's death. After four years in Colombo, he returned home in poor health, and wrote a detailed *Narrative of the . . . Mission to Ceylon and India* (1823). He later served in the Isle of France and Madagascar and was sent to *Canada in 1836, a time of political unrest. His insensitive handling, as President of the Canadian Conference, of the situation at the time of the 1837 rebellion created problems for the Church there. From 1855 to 1857 he was Governor of *Richmond College.

JAV

Harwood, Margaret (1887–1979), the pen-name of Mrs Sybil Fern Haddock, wife of a village schoolmaster on the Isle of Wight, where she lived for nearly 70 years, though born in Yorkshire. A contributor to the *Methodist Times* and *PM Leader*, she was best known for her column 'Ask Margaret Harwood' which ran in the *Methodist Recorder* from 1937 until 1975. Harwood House, Cram-lingham, commemorates her support of *MHA, for which she made a special Christmas Appeal in the *Recorder*. She opened 'Green Meadows', their home in Freshwater, IOW, in 1963.

MR 31 May & 14 June 1979

JAV

Haslingden *see* **Rossendale**

Haslope, Lancelot, JP (1766–1838), born in Pembrokeshire, served in the Army, mainly in the West Indies, before becoming a prosperous London merchant noted for his military bearing. He was a member of the *Committee of Privileges. He was associated with the WMMS from its inception and succeeded J. *Butterworth as its lay treasurer in 1828. He also served on the committee of the Bible Society. He had initial misgivings about the wisdom of setting up a theological insti-tution, but was won over. In 1836 he left Highbury on health grounds for Selly Hall near *Birming-ham. He was buried at *Wesley's Chapel, his funeral service being conducted by J. *Bunting.

Gentleman's Magazine 1838 p. 670; G.J. Stevenson (1872) pp. 363–4

JAV

Hastings, John Patrick, MBE (1927–98; e.m. 1948), missionary to North *India. After training at *Hartley Victoria College he was appointed to the Bengal District, where his prime concern was the development of literacy materials in Santali and Bengali. He founded the Bengal Christian Literature Centre which trained writers and editors. Challenged by desperate poverty in the slums, he developed inter-faith joint action for slum improvement. Returning to England in 1971 he was called to serve in the Division of *Social Responsibility as secretary for Relief, Development and Community and Race Relations (1975–81). In 1982 he accepted an invitation to work for the Christian Commission for Develop-ment in Bangladesh, where he set up adult literacy schemes and the Bangladesh Inter-Religious Council for Peace and Justice. In 1991 he returned to Dakha and with colleagues founded the 'Nijera Shikhi' ('Let's Teach Ourselves'), a non-profit company that developed a people's movement to combat the literacy problem. He was awarded the MBE in 1995 and returned to England in 1997 due to illness.

MR 26 March 1998

GRS

Haweis, Rev. Thomas (1734–1820), evangelical clergyman, converted under the Rev. S. *Walker. He was educated at Christ Church and Magdalen Hall, Oxford and in 1757 became the leader of a group of students described by Tyerman as a 'second Holy Club'. He became assistant to Martin Madan at the Lock Hospital Chapel, London; then rector of Aldwinkle, Northants from 1764. He was manager of the Countess of *Huntingdon's College at *Trevecka and one of her trustees and executors. He edited J. *Newton's *Authentic Narrative* (1764) and wrote a life of W. *Romaine (1797) and a *History of the Rise, Declension and Revival of the Church* (1800), in which he spoke highly of JW's character and ministry despite their disagreement over the doctrine of election.

DNB; A.S. Wood (1957)

                                                    J A V

Haworth Round, the name given to the circuit established by W. *Grimshaw and his assistants in Lancs, Yorks and Cumbria. As elsewhere, this circuit, although regularly visited by both JW and CW, was founded by others prior to, and without the assistance of, the Methodist leaders. Societies were formed in Yorkshire by B. *Ingham as early as 1738, and by J. *Nelson in the following year. John Wilkinson, a journeyman shoemaker and pioneer *local preacher, invited Nelson to preach in Keighley and formed the first society there in 1742. At the same time T. *Colbeck, J. *Maskew, Paul *Greenwood and others were active as preachers in Keighley and the Wharfe valley. W. *Darney's societies, mainly in Lancashire and *Rossendale, were incorporated into this Round in 1747, as were other groups formed by J. *Bennet. Despite fierce opposition, such as the mob riots organized by the Rev. Wickham of Guiseley and the Rev. George White of Colne, such preachers as these (known aptly as 'Mr Grimshaw's men') extended the Circuit from Birstall and Otley in the south to *Whitehaven, Workington and Cockermouth in the north, and from Bacup and *Preston in the west to Pateley Bridge in the east. It was the Haworth Round that held the first Methodist *Quarterly Meeting at Todmorden Edge on 18 Oct. 1748. In 1763 (the year of Grimshaw's death) Keighley became the head of the Circuit.

J.W. Laycock (1909); Conference Handbook 1961; S.R. Valentine (1997)

                                                    S R V

Hayes, Ernest Henry (1881–1969), pioneer in *Sunday School teaching methods. His *The Child in the Midst* (1916) was frequently reprinted and had considerable influence. As secretary of the British Lessons Council for 35 years, he was responsible for the *Concise Guides*, predecessor of *Partners in Learning*. He later worked for the Religious Education Press and produced material for day-school use.

MR 25 Sept. 1969

                                                    J A V

Hayes, Helen Elizabeth Thompson (Mrs L.J. Williams) (1873–1950), *New Zealand *deaconess, born on the *Isle of Man. She went to New Zealand in 1892, became the first President of the Young Women's Bible Class Union in Wellington and its first national President in 1906 (and again 1918–20). She trained as a nurse and was the first deaconess appointed to work with Maori at Okaiawa in South Taranaki. During 12 years in this appointment she trained younger Maori women for work among their own people and successfully advocated the compulsory registration of births, marriages and deaths among the Maori. During the influenza epidemic of 1918 she organized an emergency hospital at Hawera. The 1912 Conference confirmed her as a deaconess and she became known as Sister Nellie. Retiring shortly afterwards and marrying in 1921, she remained actively involved in Maori welfare in Hawera.

W.A. Chambers (1987)

                                                    D J P

Headingley College, Leeds, was opened in 1868 to provide for the training of more ministerial students when *Richmond College was sold to the WMMS. There were places for 40 students, with two residential tutors, J. *Lomas and Benjamin Hellier, transferred from Richmond. Its first Governor, J. *Farrar, was a great supporter of the new college. One of its most distinguished students was D.T. *Young. Two others became Anglican bishops: Watts-Ditchfield (Chelmsford) and J.W. *Hunkin (Truro). Between 1914 and 1930 the College was taken over by Leeds Education Committee. On re-opening it developed important links with the Theology Department of Leeds University. Its strengths were in Church History and Biblical Studies, ably served by V. *Taylor and N. *Snaith. During World War II it was taken over by the WRNS. A.R. *George, appointed in 1946, became its last Principal. In

1967 it amalgamated with *Didsbury College, Bristol, to form *Wesley College, its name being perpetuated in a new worship and teaching block on the Bristol site.

MR(W) 1904 pp. 72–4; W.B. Brash (1935) pp. 79–91

TSAM

Headway *see* **Conservative Evangelicals**; **Dunamis Revival Fellowship**; **Methodist Revival Fellowship**

Heald, James (1796–1873), a successful banker whose wealth gave him much influence in WM. Born in *Stockport, the son of a calico printer, he moved to Parrs Wood, south of *Manchester, in 1825. He was responsible for the Northern branch of the Theological Institution being established at nearby *Didsbury in 1842. He was circuit steward, *local preacher and class leader in the Stockport North circuit and Tory MP for Stockport 1847–52. A generous benefactor to many WM funds, he served as treasurer of the WMMS and was one of the original guarantors of the *Leys estate in Cambridge. St Paul's WM church, Didsbury (1877), which also served as the College chapel, was built by his sisters in his memory.

W.B. Pope (1876); G.J. Stevenson (1884–6) 4 pp. 572–5

EAR

Heaps Family of *Leeds. **Christopher Heaps** was a plumber and former Presbyterian who retained 'staunchly dissenting' opinions when he became a Methodist in the 1790s. He was an early supporter of A. *Kilham and a trustee of Ebenezer Chapel, Leeds, opened in May 1797 and the scene of the first MNC *Conference. His son **John Heaps** (1799–1856) was a MNC *local preacher who itinerated for one year (1800–1801) and was instrumental in replacing Ebenezer by Woodhouse Lane Chapel in 1858. John's son **Joshua Garred Heaps** (?1811–88) continued the family business and was a Liberal councillor and alderman. He was MNC Chapel Fund Treasurer 1864–80 and became a *Guardian Representative in 1874.

MNCM 1904 pp. 48–9

EAR

Heaven The teaching of J&CW on the final state of bliss of those with true faith in Christ had several aspects. First, they stressed the close fellowship of believers in the Church below with 'our friends above' (*HP* 812). Second, Christian

fellowship and love were affirmed as a foretaste (or 'antepast') of heaven, experienced especially in worship: 'the heaven of heavens is love' (*MHB* (1904), 687). JW believed strongly in the eschatological transformation of all nature in 'the new heaven and new earth' promised in the Apocalypse: 'To crown all, there will be . . . a constant communion with the Father and His Son, Jesus Christ, through the Spirit; a continual enjoyment of the Three-One God, and of all creatures in Him.'

R.L. Maddox (1994) ch. 9

DJC

Heginbottom, Samuel (1756–1829), a prominent MNC layman, born in *Ashton-under-Lyne and brought up an Anglican. He came under Methodist influence at 28 and identified with the MNC on its establishment. He became its financial adviser and the architect of its funds for the care of disabled ministers and their widows and for the education and support of ministers' children. He suffered disablement through a riding accident, but throughout his life proved a wise counsellor and a good friend to the Connexion.

G. Packer (1897) pp. 97–8

EWD

Hell In classical Christian theology the eternal state after death of the finally impenitent and unbelieving. The traditional teaching was strongly upheld by J&CW and most of the early Methodists. It is arguable, however, that JW stressed it less than many contemporary evangelicals. In the 1870s the doctrine, though never discarded, gradually dropped out of normal Methodist preaching. Conservative WMs in particular continued to insist on it, their depth of feeling being shown in the works of M. *Randles and in attacks on J.A. *Beet's *The Last Things* (1897), which suggested that the punishment of the damned would not last for ever. In modern Methodism the subject is not often raised, but, when it is, hell is most often interpreted in terms of alienation from God.

C. Williams (1960) p. 199; *PWHS* 34, pp.12–16

DJC

Helper *see* **Assistant**

Henderson, Arthur (1863–1935), Labour MP, was born in *Glasgow, where as a young man he attended the Elswick Road WM Mission church. In later years he became a regular reader of H.P. *Hughes' *Methodist Times*. In 1883 he joined the Friendly Society of Iron-Founders and became secretary of his local branch. In 1892 he also served his union as a district delegate. Sponsored by the Labour Representation League, he was elected to Parliament in 1903 and from 1908 to 1911 was Keir Hardie's successor as leader of the Parliamentary Labour Party. In the post-war years he played a major role in building up the party organization. He served briefly as Home Secretary in 1924 and as Foreign Secretary in the Government of 1929.

MR 24 March 1966; M.A. Hamilton (1938); A. Wilkinson (1998) pp. 210–11

NADS

Henderson, John (1757–88), son of the itinerant **Richard Henderson** (*fl.* 1760s) The father, described as 'of a timid, diffident, reasoning spirit', was born in *Ireland and came to England in 1762. After leaving the itinerancy he set up a school and later kept a private asylum at Hanham, near Bristol. His son was a child prodigy who was sent to *Kingswood School at an early age, was teaching Latin at 8 and at 12 went to teach Classics at *Trevecka College. A protégé of Hannah More and Dean Tucker of *Gloucester, he went to Pembroke College, Oxford, where he attracted the attention of Samuel Johnson as 'a student . . . celebrate for his wonderful acquirements in alchemy, judicial astrology and other abstruse and curious learning'. JW recognized his genius, but was concerned about his lack of occupation. He died young without any lasting achievement.

AM 1793 pp. 140–44; C. Atmore (1801) pp. 183–5;

JAV

Hepburn, Thomas (1795–1864), *trade unionist, was the second son of a colliery worker at Pelton, Co. Durham. Converted at 26, he became a PM class leader and later a *local preacher on the *Gateshead Circuit. While working at Hetton colliery he took a leading part in the great strike of 1831 and initiated the first Northumberland and Durham Miners' Union. He was a skilful negotiator, but the Union was short-lived. For a while he parted company with PM, but returned in later life and was active as a local preacher and in their Sunday Schools.

H. Phillips in *PMM* 1865 pp. 546–7; T. Burt in *PMQR* 24 (1882) pp. 385–97; *Durham Advertiser*, 16 Dec. 1864

NADS

Heptonstall (Yorks) JW made 20 visits to this hill-top industrial village near Halifax between 1747 and 1786, but the Methodist society originated in the evangelical activities of W. *Darney. The society met in a cottage at Northgate End until an octagonal chapel was built in 1764 (extended in 1802). By 1818 there were no fewer than 1,002 children enrolled in the Sunday School. Membership, which reached 446 in 1821, had fallen by 1939 to 50; but the church, in the Upper Calder Circuit, remains as one of the oldest surviving Methodist chapels in continuous use.

C.H. Gee (1939); E.V. Chapman & G.A. Turner (1964)

JAH

Hepworth, Joseph (1834–1911), MNC layman, born near *Huddersfield. From the age of 10 he worked in the mill as a half-timer, but ultimately established a very successful firm of multiple tailors, based in *Leeds. He was Mayor of Leeds in 1906 and Treasurer of the MNC *Centenary Fund 1894–8. He was elected a MNC *Guardian Representative in 1892. He retired to Torquay and established there the only MNC cause in Devon.

MNCM 1894 p. 239–44; *DBB*

EAR

Heraldry Methodism's attitude to coats of arms over the years can only be described as misinformed and cavalier. The fact that the *Wesley family's genealogy cannot be traced with any certainty further back than JW's great-grandfather Bartholomew Westley vitiates any claim to the use of any arms belonging to earlier generations, even if genuine. Furthermore, even if JW's right to bear arms could be established, this would not carry with it the right to their use by the Methodist Church or any other Methodist organization.

The Board of *Trustees for Methodist Church Purposes applied for and received a Grant of Arms by the College of Arms, as have *Westminster College and some Methodist theological colleges and *residential Schools. Other institutions have adopted coats of arms of their own devising (sometimes variations of what they believed to be the Wesley family arms); but in the absence of a grant by the College of Arms these remain spurious. At least some of the coats of arms with which F.O. *Salisbury embellished his Methodist portraits appear to be figments of his own imagination.

A.W. Saunders in *PWHS* 35 pp. 110–14

JAV

Hereford JW passed through the city only once and without staying to preach. In 1770 Richard *Rodda visited from Brecon and was roughly treated as he attempted to preach near St Nicholas Church. A cottage meeting eventually led to a *society which in 1804 rented the Assembly Room in East Street. Hereford was one of the Home Mission stations formed in 1807 at T. *Coke's instigation. It became the Hereford and Ledbury Circuit in 1812. Bridge Street church (1829, extended 1866) was the centre of the Herefordshire Mission 1907–21. A second chapel, Holmer Road, was opened in 1879.

A small PM society was formed in 1826, but made little headway in the face of opposition. The arrest of John Morton (1809–52; e.m. 1829) for preaching in the open air evoked considerable local support and brought official (but not popular) hostility to an end. About 1830 a hayloft in Union Street was rented as a meeting place. The chapel in St Owen Street which replaced it in 1838 was rebuilt in 1880. Originally in the Pillowell Circuit, Hereford became a separate circuit in 1840. A second chapel in Chandos Street (replacing one in Clifford Street) was opened in 1909. Following *Methodist Union in 1932, the amalgamation of the two circuits was completed in 1942. The WM and PM societies in the city centre, together with Holmes Road, united in 1967 in the St Owen Street premises, renamed St John's and with rebuilt ancillary premises.

A Brief Sketch of the Rise of Methodism in the County and City of Hereford (Hereford, 1929); *St John's Methodist Church, Hereford 1880–1980* (Hereford 1980)

JAV

Hervey, Rev. James (1714–58), student at Lincoln College, Oxford under JW and a member of the *'Holy Club'. He served as C. *Kinchin's curate at Dummer, but because of poor health retired to Stoke Abbey, Devon at the invitation of Paul Orchard. In 1752 he obtained a Cambridge MA and succeeded his father as incumbent of Weston Favell, Northants. As early as March 1739 JW was defending himself against Hervey's criticisms of his 'irregularities'. He published several books of meditations and reflections; the last, *Theron and Aspasio or a Series of Dialogues and Letters on the most Important Subjects* (1755), was intended to commend *Calvinism to 'people of elegant manners and polite accomplishments'. In *A Preservative against Unsettled Notions in Religion* (1756) JW criticized its doctrine of the 'imputed righteousness of Christ' as leading to *antinomianism. This caused a rift between them which continued after Hervey's death. A reprint in *Edinburgh of Hervey's posthumous *Eleven Letters* defending his views antagonized Presbyterians and hindered Scottish Methodism for many years.

DNB; C. Atmore (1801) pp. 185–90; L. Tyerman (1873) pp. 201–333; J.S. Simon (1927) pp. 164–7; A. Brown-Lawson (1994) pp. 70–75, 227–69

JAV

Hewitt, John Harold ((1907–87)), poet and art critic, son of a Methodist Primary School principal in *Belfast and educated at *Methodist College and Queen's University. He was Keeper of Art at the Ulster Museum, Belfast 1930–57 and for a time writer-in-residence at Queen's University. He was a member of the Irish Academy of Letters. His many volumes of poetry gave voice to the Ulster Protestant identity and attempted to define the relation of the planter stock to Ireland's past and present. His sonnet sequence *Kites in Spring – a Belfast Boyhood* captures a Belfast Methodism of the early twentieth century, although he himself became agnostic.

F. Ormsby in J.H. Hewitt (1991)

RPR

Hick, Sammy (1758–1829), village blacksmith at Micklefield, Yorks. Born into a poor family at nearby Aberford, he received little education and was apprenticed at 14. He heard J. *Nelson preach in Aberford and JW in *Leeds, but came to a conversion experience following the later death of his mother-in-law. Becoming a *local preacher, he built up the societies around Aberford, Garforth and Barwick, where his simple enthusiasm led to a notable ministry. As his popularity spread he was in demand farther afield and in his closing years spent much time in *London in support of the missionary movement. His chief appeal lay in the transparent simplicity and cheerfulness of his faith.

J. Everett (1830)

PSF

Hicks, Charles Edwin (1871–1932; e.m. 1892), BC missionary to *China, born in *Portsmouth. He went to Yunnan in 1895 and with W.A. *Grist, at considerable risk, chose to remain in Tung Chuan throughout the Boxer troubles. He excelled as a teacher and did much to develop both the school and the training institute in Chaotung. He also worked among the Nosu people to whom his forceful personality greatly appealed. In 1901 he married **Maria Bush**, a fellow BC missionary from Victoria, Australia. Their daughter, **Irene**, also became a missionary in Yunnan.

RKP

Higher Education   What JW called 'the first rise of Methodism' occurred in a university setting, but, especially after he had resigned his Lincoln fellowship in 1751, the link between Methodism and Oxford University was severed and the expulsion of six (Calvinistic) Methodist students from St Edmund Hall in 1768 formalized the divorce. For several generations, Methodists, treated as Nonconformists, were effectively debarred from Oxford and Cambridge, and in the mid-nineteenth century parental fear of 'Tractarian perverting influence' deprived men like R.N. *Young and H.H. *Fowler of a university education. When the restrictions were lifted in the 1870s, a case still had to be made for exposing young Methodists to the cultural and spiritual influence of university life and a Conference committee was appointed to consider what provision should be made for them. Methodist participation both at Oxford and Cambridge and in the new generation of universities and colleges increased steadily from then on.

A modern form of class meeting was discovered when W.H. *Beales invited Cambridge students, including C.A. *Coulson, to meet in preparation for *Methodist Union in 1932. Groups flourished after the 1944 Education Act gave many more Methodists access to higher education. Student numbers, including ex-service people, increased in congregations near universities and student Methodist Societies were formed, often in comfortably furnished rooms in a local church. MethSoc groups, with duly appointed leaders, studied and prayed together, gave mutual support and affirmation, undertook preaching and social work and often held Easter missions. Many vocations to ordained ministry and lifelong Christian commitment occurred. In 1963 Conference decided to explore the possibility of a student chaplaincy service. As universities expanded following the Robbins Report (1963), **Douglas A. Brown** (1922– ; e.m. 1948), under the aegis of the HM Department, established chaplaincies throughout the country. Ministers were appointed to pastoral care of Methodist students, some as part of full-time campus-based teams. From 1988

more new universities, and their variety, created a situation beyond the capacity of denominations to provide individual chaplains. Some universities appointed ecumenical or Free Church chaplains. In the Further Education sector, an Advisor appointed jointly with the Church of England in 1990 produced material to help the newly incorporated colleges consider values, religious and moral education and pastoral care.

See also **Cambridge Group**; **Education**; **Residential Schools**

Report of the Student Work Committee (1968); 'Methodist Chaplaincy in Higher Education Today' (Report to Conference, 1993); *HMGB* 4 pp. 536–40

CHS

Hildebrandt, Franz (1909–85), German theologian, entered the *Lutheran ministry in 1932, served as assistant to Martin Niemöller and was a close friend of Dietrich Bonhoeffer. He joined the 'Confessing Church' which led the opposition to Hitler within the German Evangelical Church. After leaving Germany he became pastor of the refugee German Lutheran congregation in *Cambridge and was transferred to the Methodist ministry in 1946. In 1953 he went to Drew University, where he established himself as an authority on Wesleyan hymnology and the relationship between the Wesleyan and Lutheran traditions. His major works were *From Luther to Wesley* (1951), *Christianity according to the Wesleys* (1956) and *I Offered Christ: a Protestant study of the Mass* (1967); and he was an editor of the 1780 *Collection of Hymns* for the new edition of JW's *Works*. He was a Methodist observer at Vatican II. Back in Britain, he opposed the Majority Report in the *Anglican-Methodist Conversations and resigned from the ministry when he felt Methodism was abandoning its principles.

MR 19 Dec. 1985, 18 Feb. 1999; F. Baker in *MH* July 1986

DJC

Hill, David (1840–96; e.m. 1863), outstanding WM missionary appointed to Central *China in 1864. He gave unstinting devotion to the Chinese people, influencing great numbers by his self-giving love. His prayerful personality and dedicated life were also an inspiration to many in Britain who felt the call to follow him to China. He became General Superintendent of the Wuchang District in 1885 and was elected to the *Legal Hundred in 1888. He died of fever in Hankow

(Hankou). His nephew, Joseph Kimber Hill (1867–1952; e.m. 1890), was born in *York and educated at The *Leys School. In 1890 he went to the Wuchang District in China, serving there until 1921 without any cost to the WMMS and becoming District Chairman in 1916. A Home for Destitute Boys was founded in memory of his son. J.K. Hill's niece **Dorothy Hill** also served in the District as a teacher in Hankow from 1927 until her marriage to the Rev. James Clegg in 1933. Another scion of the Hill family, Dr **Philip Keith Hill** (1883–1948) was appointed as a lay missionary to the Tayeh Hospital, Wuchang District in 1914. In 1921 he succeeded Dr Arthur Morley at the Hill Memorial Hospital, Teian. Serious civil upset precluded his return after furlough in 1927 and he took up work in *Nottingham. The historian **Christopher Hill** (b.1912) belongs to the same family.

W.T.A. Barber (1898); H.B. Rattenbury (1949)
GRS/MJF

Hill, Sir Richard Bt, MP (1732–1808), and the **Rev. Rowland Hill** (1744–1833), prominent evangelicals, were the sons of Sir Rowland Hill of a leading Shropshire family. Richard, a controversialist educated at Westminster School and Magdalen College, Oxford, travelled in Europe 1755–57. His *Pietas Oxoniensis* (1768) criticized the university authorities following the expulsion of Methodist students from St Edmund Hall. Though influenced by J. *Fletcher, he supported G. *Whitefield, defending *Calvinistic Methodism in the controversy of the 1770s and continuing to write polemically in its support. As MP for Shropshire 1780–1806 he championed the evangelical cause. His brother Rowland was educated at Shrewsbury, Eton and St John's College, Cambridge. Holding religious convictions from his youth, he preached and visited the sick and prisoners while at Cambridge. After some difficulties, he was ordained in 1773 and as curate at Kingston, Devon developed an itinerant evangelistic ministry. At the Surrey Chapel, London from 1783, his preaching continued to attract large numbers. He supported the Religious Tract Society and Bible Society, was an early advocate of vaccination and published *Village Dialogues* (1810).

E. Sidney (1834); E. Sidney (1839); *DNB*
PSF

Hill, William (1828–89) commenced his architectural practice in *Leeds in 1851 after being articled to Perkin & Backhouse. He designed public buildings, notably *Bolton Town Hall (1865), many Nonconformist chapels, and *Ranmoor College, Sheffield. Many of the main MNC chapels were by him, including Woodhouse Lane, Leeds (1853–8), where he attended, and Manville, *Bradford (1875).

DCD

'Hill's Arrangement' The earliest chronological list of WM ministers was published in 1795 by J. *Pawson under the title *A Chronological Catalogue*. C. *Atmore's *Methodist Memorial* (1801) included a similar list in an appendix, as did the 1813 edition of William Myles' *Chronological History*. Another appeared in J. *Crowther's *Portraiture of Methodism* (1815). William Hill (*c.* 1771–1827; e.m. 1804) first published his *Alphabetical Arrangement* in 1819, listing WM ministers and the circuits in which they were stationed. (Preachers who had 'died in the work' before 1819 were not included, but these were eventually listed by Kenneth B. Garlick in his *Mr Wesley's Preachers* (1977).) It was followed by a second, updated edition in 1824, including a list of ministers who had 'died in the work'. Three editions between 1827 and 1841, together with a supplement dated 1833 continued to carry Hill's name, though he had died in 1827. John P. Haswell was responsible for five editions between 1847 and 1866. He was succeeded by Marmaduke C. Osborn (four editions, to 1881) and David J. Waller (seven editions) and Arthur Twigg, who produced the 1912 and 1926 editions. After *Methodist Union J. Henry Martin produced three editions, as did J. Bernard Sheldon, the last being in 1968. No further editions have appeared since that date, but a ms edition has been updated annually since 1968, a copy of which is in the Methodist *Archives Centre, Manchester. All editions since 1932 include all former PM and UM ministers, with lists of the Presidents of Conference in the pre-Union connexions, PM Vice-Presidents, Presidents of the Methodist Church in *Ireland (from 1868) and of the Welsh Assembly (from 1899).

PWHS 30 pp. 134–5; 40 pp. 2–5, 45–7
WL

Hincksman, Dorothy (née Hobson, 1802–59) Born into an Anglican family at Cobridge, Staffs, she found comfort and help among the Methodists when her mother died. Her father opposed the association and compelled her to leave home, though later receiving her back when she was desperately ill. She married a young missionary, Thomas Jones (c. 1802–26) and in 1825 they arrived in Antigua, where she established a school. In February 1826, returning with her husband from a District Meeting on St Kitts, she was the sole survivor of five missionaries and their families when the mail-boat sank in a storm. Returning to England, in 1832 she married **Thomas Crouch Hincksman** (1799–1883) of *Preston. They were responsible for much mission work there and later at Lytham. Always frail in health after her ordeal, she died in 1859.

See also **Farrar, D.H.**

J. Taylor (1885)

EWD

Hindmarsh, Dr W. Russell (1929–73), atomic physicist and *local preacher. Graduating from Wadham College, Oxford, he gained his PhD for research on atomic spectra and was appointed to a Chair at Newcastle in 1961. He wrote *Science and Faith (1968)*, was Vice-President of the Conference in 1970 and gave a memorable address to the 1971 World Methodist Conference in Denver.

MR 25 June 1970; 10 & 17 Jan. 1974

JAV

Hired Local Preachers were sometimes employed by PM circuits as ancilliary to the *itinerant ministry, often to meet an opportunity for mission or extension. They were employed for a limited period only and were not subject to being stationed by the Conference. Their nearest equivalent in more recent Methodism is the 'minister in local appointment'.

G.E. Milburn & M. Batty (1995) pp. 182–4

JAV

Hirst, Dr Edward Wales (1870–1952; e.m. 1893), MNC and UM minister, trained at *Ranmoor College, where he returned as tutor in 1903. He resigned in 1913 to become minister of Broom Hill Congregational Church, *Glasgow. In 1920 he was readmitted to the UM ministry and appointed a tutor at *Victoria Park College. Among his books on ethics was *Studies in Christian Love* (1941).

MR 8 May 1952

OAB

Hobbs, John (1800–83; e.m. 1824), Kentish blacksmith and lay WM missionary, who made his own way to Tasmania in 1822 and accompanied N. *Turner to the newly founded *New Zealand mission in 1823. In full connexion from 1828, he became fluent in the Maori language, which was significant in the establishing of New Zealand Methodism. All his ministry was in the North Island, where he became the senior missionary. He survived the sacking of the first station at Kaeo and was in charge at Mangungu on the Hokianga, where a fresh start was made in 1827. His building skills and medical knowledge were enhanced by resourcefulness. Difficulties with William *White led to his moving to *Tonga in 1833, where he acted as the Mission's printer. Returning to New Zealand in 1838, he accompanied J. *Bumby on a journey round the North Island coast in search of new openings, especially around Port Nicholson. He was active in promoting the Treaty of Waitangi (1840) among the chiefs of the Hokianga. In 1855 he became Governor of the Three Kings native training institution in Auckland. Despite difficult relations with some colleagues, he was respected and loved by both Europeans and Maoris.

DNZB; T.M.I. Williment (1985)

MJF/DJP

Hobill Library was a large collection of Methodist material formed by George Alexander Kilham Hobill (1842/3–1912), a schoolmaster at Pensnett, who later retired to London. A lifelong member of the MNC, in 1894 he presented the collection to the MNC and it was housed until 1917 at *Ranmoor College and then at the nearby Nether Green UM Church. The books later went to *Hartley Victoria College, but the associated mss remained forgotten at Nether Green for over 30 years. When Hartley Victoria closed in 1973 the books went to the John Rylands Library, Manchester, where they were later reunited with the mss recovered from *Sheffield. The collection's special value lies in its rare and sometimes unique MNC pamphlets and tracts. In 1921 it was said to include JW's Greek NT and A *Kilham's ordination certificate (now at *Wesley's Chapel).

PWHS 20 pp. 40–2

EAR/WL

Hocken, Edward (1788–1875; e.m. 1825), BC itinerant, born at Treveighan, Michaelstow, Cornwall. He helped to establish the BC Preachers' Annuitant Society and the monthly *Arminian* (later *Bible Christian Magazine*. He was Secretary to the Conference in 1836, but then resigned. He was among those who resisted *O'Bryan's suspected take-over of the chapel properties and it may be significant that the chapel he built at Treveighan in 1828 survives, with his initials still on the datestone over the door.

TS

Hocking Family   James and Elizabeth Hocking of St Stephen in Brannel, Cornwall had two sons who entered the UMFC ministry . **Silas Kitto Hocking** (1850–1935; e.m. 1869) had a popular ministry in *Southport, 1883–96 before devoting himself to writing and Liberal politics, resigning from the ministry in 1906. He wrote nearly 100 novels and his second book *Her Benny* (1879) sold well over one million copies. He wrote an autobiography, *My Book of Memory* (1923). His brother **Joseph Hocking** (1860–1937; e.m. 1884) also wrote nearly 100 novels, in which Cornwall, an idealized Methodism, war, jingoism and papistical infiltration of England (e.g. in *The Scarlet Woman*) were prominent themes. In 1909 the Catholic Truth Society published a collection of pamphlets entitled *A Brace of Bigots (Dr Horton & Mr Hocking)*. Hocking and R.F. Horton replied the next year with *Shall Rome Reconquer England?* His daughter **Anne Hocking** was also a prolific novelist. **Salome Hocking** (d. 1927), sister to Silas and Joseph and married to the London publisher A.C. Fifield, was the author of about ten novels similar to those of her brothers, some of them published by the UMFC and WM Book Rooms.

A.C. Fifield (1927); R.F.S. Thorne (1978)

RFST

Hodges, Rev. John (*c.* 1700–77), rector of Wenvoe, near Cardiff 1725–77. He graduated from Jesus College, Oxford and was associated with the evangelical revival from the early days through an association with H. *Harris. He held both English and Welsh services, with a weekly communion and a society meeting on Sunday evenings. He first met CW in November 1740 and probably introduced him and JW to R. *Jones of Fonmon. Both CW and JW preached in his church. He attended the first three Conferences in London and Bristol, but later became disillusioned, perhaps because of the shortcomings of the *Cardiff society, perhaps through his growing interest in *mysticism. In 1758 he wrote a frank letter reproving JW for the 'tartness' of his controversial writings. Wesley in turn disapproved of the 'cold, dry, careless manner' in which Hodges read the church service in August 1763.

WMM 1902 pp. 425–31; A.S. Wood (1992) pp. 3–7

JAV

Holborn Review   In 1854 the Sunderland PM District Ministerial Association began to publish lectures given at its meetings in a periodical at first named *The Christian Ambassador*. In 1878 its scope was enlarged and its title changed to the *PM Quarterly Review*. This was in turn changed to the *Holborn Review* in 1910, an allusion to Holborn Hall which,through the initiative and generosity of Sir W. *Hartley,had just been acquired to serve the PM London headquarters. From the outset it was remarkably modern in spirit and influential in fostering liberal opinion in PM and in highlighting educational and cultural issues. Among its editors were C.C. *M'Kechnie, J. *Watson, H.B. *Kendall and A.S. *Peake. At *Methodist Union in 1932 it was amalgamated with the WM *London Quarterly Review.*

GEM

Holden, Sir Isaac (1807–97), son of a Cumbrian WM *local preacher, lead miner and tenant farmer who moved to *Paisley to find work as a coal miner, decided in 1824 to candidate for the WM ministry. Finding the physical demands too great, he became a teacher at *Sigston's Academy in Leeds, but lost his post in refusing to join the *Protestant Methodists. By 1839 he was in the employment of Townends at Cullingworth, where, during his 16 years, he perfected woolcombing machinery. He went into business by himself in 1846 and built up a *Bradford textile empire with business interests in France, aided by his marriage into the Sugden WM family which had a worsted manufacturing business in the Worth Valley. A *local preacher and member of Eastbrook Chapel, Bradford, his wealth was used in WM causes, including the *Metropolitan Chapel Building Fund and the building of chapels at Knaresborough (1865) and Manningham St John's, Bradford (1879). He was Liberal MP for Knaresborough in 1885 and for Keighley, 1885–95. His grandson, **Sir Isaac Holden Holden** was Vice-President of the Conference in 1939.

MR 20 July 1939; K. Honeyman & J. Goodman (1986); C. Giles & I.H. Goodall (1992); E. Jennings in *PWHS* 43 pp. 117–26, 150–58

DCD

Holden, William Clifford (1813–97; e.m. 1836), WM missionary, regarded as the pioneer of Methodism in Natal, where he was sent on J *Archbell's resignation in 1847. In fact, he spent most of his ministry (1839–47 and 1851–81) in the Eastern Cape, but wrote a *History of the Colony of Natal* (1855), as well as *The Past and Future of the Kaffir Races* (1866) and *A Brief History of Methodism and of Methodist Missions in South Africa* (1877)

JRP

Holiness is used in Scripture to express the absolute perfection of the Divine nature. God alone has underived holiness, so that when the term is used in connection with persons, places or things it is because of their relationship to God. Both the OT *qodesh* and the NT *hagiosuné* mean 'separation', 'set apart'. Holiness therefore the quality of being like God and in Christian theology is the goal of *sanctification. For JW this is realizable in this life and from as early as 1725 he records that he was praying for and aiming at 'inward holiness' (JWJ, 24 May 1738) Throughout his writings he used the term as synonymous with 'entire sanctification' or 'perfect love'. In the 1763 *Minutes* he declared that Methodism originated in 1729 when he and CW 'saw they could not be saved without holiness' and that God's purpose in raising up the Methodist preachers was 'to spread scriptural holiness over the land'. He spoke frequently of 'holiness of heart and life', 'inward and outward holiness' and 'holiness or true religion', most often citing Heb. 12:14: 'Holiness without which no man shall see the Lord'.

In re-emphasizing this aspect of JW's teaching, the nineteenth century *Holiness Movement urged 'second-blessing holiness' as the eradication of inbred sin, as against W's more usual emphasis on holiness as love perfected. It was proclaimed as an instantaneous blessing, whereas JW's most mature judgment, made in 1784, was that the dispute about an instantaneous as against a progressive experience was 'not determined – at least, not in express terms – in any part of the oracles of God'. The Movement also saw holiness or entire sanctification as being accomplished by the Baptism of the Spirit, which JW had not endorsed, telling J. *Benson that the phrase 'receiving the Holy Ghost' was 'not Scriptural and not quite proper' as a synonym for holiness or perfect Love (SL 4 p. 215).

See also **Christian Perfection**

H. Lindstrom (1946); M. Dieter (1980)

HMG

Holiness Movement This movement arose in mid-nineteenth century *America and was a blend of historic *Pietism, American *revivalism and Wesleyan perfectionism. It was widely disseminated by the growth and popularity of the *Camp Meetings and characterised by revival preaching and encouragement to every Christian to seek the 'second blessing' and bear witness to it. All over America groups of Christians came together to further a Wesleyan understanding of the doctrine of *Christian perfection. Eventually denominations emerged, the largest being the *Church of the Nazarene. Leading figures in this Movement in America were Timothy Merritt, founder editor of the influential periodical, *Guide to Christian Perfection,* Mrs Phoebe Palmer, who organised the Tuesday Meeting for the Promotion of Holiness and Dr Asa Mahan of Oberlin College. The Movement was promoted in Britain in the 1860s and 70s through the preaching of Mrs Palmer, the Rev. William Boardman and Mr and Mrs Robert Pearsall and Hannah Whitall Smith. Conventions were held at Broadlands, Romsey (Hants), *Brighton and *Oxford and these prepared the way for the first Keswick Convention in 1875. In England the holiness theme was much less definitely Wesleyan and it took the generic title of the 'Higher Life Movement'.

J. Kent (1978); M. Dieter (1980)

HMG

Holy, Thomas (1752–1830), an early member of the *Sheffield WM society, which he joined in 1766, was educated at a Dissenting Academy in Northampton. He developed the family button-making business into an international concern, later diversifying into mining and other mineral activities. He entertained JW on his final visits to Sheffield and later his home was the venue for some of T. *Coke's missionary *ordinations. Despite holding no local society or circuit office, he was later described as the town's 'business man *par excellence* and the financier of Sheffield Methodism'. He was closely involved in the building of Carver Street WM Chapel in 1805. His only connexional service was on the Committee of the WMMS, to which he was a generous subscriber. A visit to the newly formed United States inspired a revulsion against the institution of *slavery and misgivings about their abandonment of the security of the monarchy and the Common Law in favour of the hazards of democracy. His son **Thomas Beard Holy** (d. 1867) was one of the original trustees of what became Wesley College, Sheffield.

T.A. Seed (1907)

ANC

'Holy Club' was a nickname, rather than an actual organization. JW returned to *Oxford in 1729 to find that CW had begun to meet with other religiously inclined students for prayer, reading the Bible and other literature, religious conversation and weekly church-going. Though these activities later became more regular, there was no formal organization or membership; rather, several loosely connected groups with a fluid composition. JW's seniority and natural flair for leadership gave him an informal influence, but no official status. Their activities attracted little attention in the University as a whole until, at the suggestion of William Morgan, they began in August 1730 to visit the debtors and condemned prisoners in the Castle and later in Bocardo, the city gaol. This drew them to the public attention and they were variously dubbed 'Sacramentarians', 'Bible Moths', 'Supererogation Men', the 'Godly Club' or 'Holy Club'.

Biographers and historians have fostered a popular version of the 'Holy Club' reinforced by M. *Claxton's romanticized painting, which embodies and perpetuates several widespread misconceptions: (1) At no time were all those depicted in the painting at Oxford together; (2) they rarely met in groups of more than six and there was no single meeting-place; (3) they engaged in discussion rather than listening to JW or any other individual; (4) they spent more time in acts of benevolence than in either devotions or discussion. JW himself inadvertently contributed to the myth by describing these activities, retrospectively, as 'the first rise of Methodism'.

PWHS 42 pp. 90–1; R.P. Heitzenrater (1995) pp. 33–58

JAV

Home Missions The earliest Home Mission ventures can be credited to T. *Coke, who included the Highlands and islands of *Scotland among the areas singled out in his missionary appeal of 1786. Largely at his instigation, vernacular missions were launched in *Ireland in 1799 and in North *Wales in 1800, and in 1806 the WM Conference appointed its first 'home missionaries' to areas in England where Methodism had not yet taken firm root. These mission circuits were not conspicuously successful and proved a drain on resources.

The first Home Missions committee was set up in 1856 in response to evidence that Methodism remained weak in some urban and rural areas. Ministers were designated for special work there and this was picked up in the 1880s by the *Forward Movement through its Central Missions.

The HM Division which was set up in 1973 and became part of the Connexional Team in 1996 comprised the former HM Department and London Mission. It was charged with the task of promoting evangelization and fostering the spiritual life and growth of churches in Britain. It had responsibility for urban and rural mission and for specialist ministries in the services, in prisons and in business, industry and commerce. Other aspects of the work include *Mission alongside the Poor, *Cliff College, the work of the Rob Frost team and of the London Committee. The Division was a resource for the work of local churches and circuits through the preparation of study programmes, apologetics material and a grant aid programme. Approximately 20% of circuits applied for HM grants, predominantly those in the inner cities and urban areas. In its final year, these grants accounted for £1.5 million, approximately half its annual expenditure, and this aspect of its work is continued through the Resourcing Mission group of the Connexional Team. *Easter People, one of the activities of the Rob Frost Team, is one of the latest Home Mission ventures.

MR 15 June 1939

PWS

Honey, John Cleverdon (1834–1912; e.m. 1856), BC minister, born at Bridgerule, Devon and educated at *Shebbear College. During his ministry at Waterloo Road Chapel, London he began extensive open-air work. He was President of the Conference in 1878 and in 1881 became Secretary of the BC Fire Insurance Association. At Barry he took a leading part in an anti-liquor and anti-licence campaign.

TS

Hong Kong Methodism was introduced in 1843 by British Methodist soldiers. In 1851 a WMMS missionary, G. *Piercy, arrived with the purpose of preaching the gospel in *China, but it was not until 1884 that a catechist sent by the Guangzou Methodist Church established a Chinese Cantonese-speaking congregation in the colony, followed in 1893 by an English-speaking congregation. In the early 1950s, after the withdrawal of missionaries from China, the American Methodist Board of Missions also began work in

Hong Kong among the many Mandarin-speaking refugees. In 1975 the British and American strands united to become the autonomous Methodist Church, Hong Kong, joined in 1988 by the English-speaking congregation. In 1997 the Church had some 12,000 baptized members and claimed a total community of 160,000, including 17,000 students studying in its schools and 142,000 through a number of social service centres, providing a variety of services for people of all ages and back-grounds.

J. Roser (1951); B. Ream (1988)

GRS

Hooker-Stacey,   Professor   Morna (1931–) graduated at Bristol and was awarded a Research Scholarship at Manchester. She trans-ferred to the University of Durham in 1959 and became a lecturer at King's College, London in 1961. She was subsequently a university lecturer in NT at Oxford and Lady Margaret Professor at Cambridge. She was elected President of the Society for NT Studies in 1988. Her major works are *Jesus and the Servant* (1959), *The Son of Man in Mark* (1967), *Mark* (Black Commentaries, 1991), *Not Ashamed of the Gospel* (1994) and the Shaffer Lectures, *The Signs of a Prophet* (1997). Her textbook *Studying the NT* reflects her concern for instructing lay preachers and her expository interests. She married D.W. *Stacey in 1978.

ER May 1996

CSR

Hoole, Dr Elijah (1798–1872; e.m. 1819), WM minister and missionary in *India (1818–28). His expertise in oriental studies was used to good effect on the committee for revising the Tamil versions of the Bible. He published a 'personal account' of his years in India (1829). As a devoted Secretary of the WMMS from 1834 to 1872, he was gracious in personal relations, but firm over matters of dispute, and was not afraid to make hard decisions, especially about the financing of the mission stations. In 1835 he married Elizabeth *Chubb (d.1880) of Portsea. Their hospitality was proverbial. At a time when the Mission House served as a hostel for newly appointed mission-aries, she excelled in their care and established communication with every part of the mission field. She was involved in the founding of the Ladies' Committee, forerunner of *Women's Work and was its 'Foreign Correspondent'. Her letters, needlework and other gifts were more than welcome to missionary families. Their son **Elijah**

Hoole jun. RIBA (d.1912) was a successful archi-tect who designed many London churches, Toynbee Hall and the *Bermondsey Settlement and supervised the 1891 restoration of *Wesley's Chapel.

EWD

Hooper, Dr John Stirling Morley, K-i-H (1882–1974; e.m. 1905), missionary to *India, son of **John H. Hooper** (1844–1917; e.m. 1871) was educated at *Kingswood School and Corpus Christi, Oxford. He was in educational work in the Madras District 1905–32, becoming Principal of Wesley College, Madras in 1926. A Tamil scholar, from 1932 to 1947 he served as the first Secretary of the Bible Society of India, Burma and Ceylon and wrote *The Bible in India* (1938). He was secretary of the Joint Committee for Church Union 1935–47 and preached at the inaug-ural service of CSI in Madras Cathedral in Sep-tember 1947. In 1957 he received an honorary DD from Serampore University.

MR 23 May 1974

JAV

Hooson, Thomas James Stewart (1862–1931), son of a PM itinerant, **Stewart Hooson** (1832–1903; e.m. 1856), was educated at *Elm-field College, York and *Bourne College, Bir-mingham, where he quickly joined the staff. On its move to Quinton in 1882 he was appointed headmaster, serving throughout its existence. He took his London BA in 1884 and then a BSc at Mason College (later Birmingham University) and believed in a broadly based education catering for the whole person. He was the first layman to be listed on the PM stations.

E.D. Graham (1998)

EDG

Hopkins, Joseph H. (1848–1934; e.m. 1871) was born in Montgomeryshire and went to *Dids-bury College in 1868. After a remarkable two-year ministry at the fashionable Barry Road WM Church, East Dulwich, he became the first Super-intendent of the South London Mission (1889–1906). He toured the country raising funds to build London's first Central Hall in Bermondsey. After seventeen exhausting years he returned to less exacting circuit work, before retiring to New Barnet in 1915.

MR 19 July 1934; J.D. Beasley (1989)

JDB

Hopper, Christopher (1722–1802; e.m. 1749) from *Durham, was a schoolmaster before becoming an itinerant. He was JW's travelling companion in England, Wales and Scotland (the first Methodist itinerant to venture north of the border). He travelled for a total of forty-seven years and was one of JW's most regular correspondents. Recognising his gifts of preaching and leadership, JW appointed him 'Lord President of the North' in 1768. This gave him jurisdiction over the Methodist Societies from Cumberland to Lincolnshire. He was one of the veteran preachers named in the *Deed of Declaration.

EMP 1 pp. 179–239

HMG

Hornabrook, John (1848–1937; e.m. 1871) was born in Kingston, Jamaica, the son of a WM missionary, **Richard Hornabrook** (1802–88; e.m. 1827) and educated at *Woodhouse Grove School. He served as Secretary of the *Chapel Committee, 1897–1932, and as Secretary of the Conference, 1903–10, being elected President in 1910. His outstanding powers of leadership earned him the reputation of being the 'elder statesman' of the Church. He married a daughter of Luke H. *Wiseman.

MR 14 July 1910, 6 May 1937

JAV

Hornby, George Goodall (1876–1964; e.m. 1899) followed his father **George S. Hornby** (1841–1911; e.m. 1866) into the MNC ministry after a year at *Ranmoor College. In 1922 he became a tutor at *Victoria Park College, whose history he wrote (1934), and continued as Church History tutor at *Hartley Victoria College until 1940.

EAR

Horne, George (1730–92), bishop of *Norwich 1790–92. A Hutchinsonian, he championed revealed as against natural religion. Like JW he admired and followed W. *Law's devotional rules, but rejected his *mysticism. In 1762 JW wrote a letter protesting at Horne's misrepresentation of his teaching in a University Sermon on 'Works wrought through Faith', but later commended his commentary on the Psalms (1776) as 'the best that ever was wrote'. Horne was of a magnanimous nature. He deplored the expulsion of the six Methodist students from St Edmund Hall, Oxford in 1768, forgave JW's plagiarism of his work and as bishop refused to hinder him

from preaching in the parish church at Diss in 1790.

W. Jones in Horne (1799); *DNB*; W.K.L. Clarke (1944) pp. 102–6; G.R. Cragg (1975) pp. 437–58

JAV

Horne, James (1788–1856; e.m. 1814), a Scotsman who was converted in 1811 under G. *Ouseley while serving in the army in Ireland. He went as a missionary to Jamaica in 1817 and served in the *West Indies for 35 years. He was believed to have been the secretary of a group of missionaries which in 1824 drafted compromising resolutions on *slavery in response to charges and threats by white settlers. In Britain the resolutions were repudiated by the WMMS as contrary to the 'no politics' rule. Horne protested that he had not been present at the meeting and resisted his transfer to Bermuda.

F&H 2, pp. 84, 86–8; N.W. Taggart (1986) pp. 158–60

NWT

Horne, Rev. Melville (1762–1841), born in Antigua, son of a barrister and nephew to N. *Gilbert, joined the Methodists at 15. In 1783 he offered for the itinerancy and served in *Liverpool, *Chester and *Wolverhampton Circuits before following J. *Fletcher at *Madeley in 1785. There was a degree of estrangement between him and the Methodists from 1791, when he ceased to appear on the stations. He served in *Sierra Leone 1792–94, under the auspices of the London Missionary Society; then in the parishes of Olney 1796–99, Christ Church, *Macclesfield 1799–1811, West Thurrock 1811–14, Marazion 1814–16 and Salford 1817–23, when his health deteriorated.

DEB

PSF

Horton, John (*c.* 1739–*c.* 1802), London merchant and Member of the Common Council. A member at the *Foundery and At *Wesley's Chapel, he was a close friend of JW and one of his executors. In his will JW entrusted to him and others 'his books, now on sale and copies of them, in trust for the General Fund of the Methodist Conference'. W often used his home, Highbury House, as a retreat. His wife was Mary *Durbin of *Bristol. They had the sorrow of losing two small children and she died in 1786 at the age of

34. Unhappy differences after W's death induced him to leave Methodism, though he never lost his affection for it and began attending services again before he died in Bristol.

SJ 6–8 passim; G.J. Stevenson (1872) pp. 569–70; L. Tyerman (1878) 3 p. 17

EWD

Horton, Samuel (1857–1949; e.m. 1881), PM minister and novelist, born at Prees, trained for the ministry at the *Sunderland Theological Institution. After 30 years, mostly in northern circuits, he became General Missionary Secretary (1913–18) and while in his last circuit, Kennington Park, London, was elected President of the 1921 Conference. He wrote 40 novels and his series of 'Wentworth' stories gave him a wide readership.

MR 28 April 1949

WL

Hosie, Lady Dorothea (1885–1959), UM laywoman. Born in Ningpo, the daughter of W.E. *Soothill, she married Sir Alexander Hosie, Consul-General. A prominent UM, she served on many educational and charitable bodies, particularly relating to *China, and was President of the FCFC's Women's Council, 1932–33. In addition to assisting her father with some of his works, she was a considerable author in her own right, especially on China. Her *Jesus and Woman* (1946) was revised and republished in 1956.

Times 16 Feb. 1959

OAB

Howard, Dr Wilbert Francis, FBA (1880–1952; e.m. 1904) was born at *Gloucester. After taking a degree at Manchester University, he trained for the WM ministry at *Didsbury College. He became NT Tutor at *Handsworth College in 1919, where he remained until his retirement in 1951, becoming Principal when the College reopened after World War II. He was President of the Conference in 1944 and was Joint Chairman of the World Methodist Conferences of 1947 and 1951. An internationally renowned scholar, he was awarded honorary degrees at St Andrews and Manchester. His main scholarly work was in NT Greek and St John's Gospel. He was editor and joint author of Vol. II of J.H. *Moulton's *Grammar of NT Greek* and was working on Vol. III at the time of his death. As well as *The Fourth Gospel in Recent Criticism and Interpretation* (1931) and *Christianity according*

to *St John* (1943), he wrote the more popular *The Romance of NT Scholarship* (1949), based on his Drew Lectures of 1947, and also contributed 1 & 2 Corinthians to the *Abingdon Commentary*.

Times 12 July 1952; *MR* 20 July 1944, 17 July 1952; W.F. Lofthouse in *LQHR* Dec. 1952 pp. 246–51; W.F. Lofthouse (1954)

CSR

Howdill, Thomas (1840–1918), PM *local preacher and connexional officer, was born in Tadcaster and moved to *Leeds in 1863, where he began business as a joiner. In 1873 he set up an architectural practice. His son **Charles Barker Howdill** (1863–1941) became a partner in 1893. They designed many chapels, mainly PM and predominantly in the West Riding, Lancashire and London, and a *Leeds tannery (1892) for W. *Beckworth.

DCD

Howell, George (1833–1910), *Chartist and *trade unionist, was born at Wrington, Som, the eldest of eight children. He attended village schools and later studied at evening classes. In his early years he became a self-employed builder like his father, but in 1843 lost everything in a lawsuit in which he failed to recover a large debt from a contractor. In 1848 he became an active Chartist and in the same year underwent a conversion experience in the WM church. He became a Sunday School teacher and an advocate of teetotalism. In 1855, working in London as a bricklayer, he joined the Operative Bricklayers' Society and represented them at their national conference in Derby in 1861. He became secretary of the London Trades' Council that year and in 1867 appeared before the Royal Commission on Trades Unions and testified to their success and value. From 1885 to 1895 he was Liberal MP for Bethnal Green and devoted the rest of his life to writing on labour issues.

NADS

Hoxton Theological Institution, a former dissenting academy, was rented in September 1834 to house the first WM *ministerial training. J. *Entwisle senr. was appointed its first Governor and, more controversially and in the face of opposition (notably from S. *Warren), J. *Bunting its President. J. *Hannah was its theological tutor and Samuel Jones the classical and mathematical tutor to the junior preachers in training. Despite initial opposition to ministerial training, it proved itself in the formation of students, who spent two years studying the liberal arts, Bible and theology and sermon preparation. Its earliest students included two missionaries to Fiji, J. *Hunt and J. *Calvert, W. *Arthur and W.B. *Pope. In 1839, when the Hoxton accommodation became inadequate, Abney House, Stoke Newington was acquired as a 'Preparatory or Auxiliary Branch' with J. *Farrar as Governor. By 1840 it had 25 students, sleeping three to a room. Expanding numbers led to the replacement of both Hoxton and Abney Park by *Didsbury and *Richmond Colleges in 1842–43.

W.B. Brash (1935) pp. 34–41; *PWHS* 39 pp. 104–12

TSAM

Hubbold, Lucy (1809–1860), PM itinerant, converted when she went out of curiosity to hear PM preaching. At first very reluctant to preach, in 1835 she became an itinerant. While in the Longton Circuit she broke a bone in her foot, which forced her to give up itinerating, but she continued as a *hired local preacher until her voice failed. She located at Longton, as a *local preacher and class leader. In 1847 William Belcher left her a house there as a token of respect.

PMM 1861 pp. 200–4; E.D. Graham (1989) pp. 13–14

EDG

Hubery, Douglas Stanley (1916–88; e.m. 1940), born at Hednesford, was trained at *Handsworth College. In 1953 he became a tutor at Westhill College, Birmingham. His original contribution was to apply principles of experiential learning to both informal and formal Christian education. Appointed successively Secretary (1960) and General Secretary (1961) of the Youth Department, Secretary of the *Education Committee (1970) and the first General Secretary of the Division of Education and Youth (1973), he contributed by speech and writing to the Youth Service and to educational thinking, partly through the FCFC Education Committee. He travelled in Europe, Africa and the USA, advising on Youth programmes.
See also **Youth Work**

CHS

Huddersfield was a strong but turbulent centre of early Methodism. Though itinerants were active in the vicinity in the 1750s and 1760s and JW paid his first visit in May 1757, the first chapel did not open until 1776, following the departure of the popular evangelical vicar H. *Venn in 1771. This Old Bank society was almost wiped out when the MNC took possession of the chapel in 1797. A new WM start was made in Queen Street (1800). Both connexions thrived; the MNC opened a new chapel in High Street (1815) after losing a legal battle to retain Old Bank, and WM built a new Queen Street chapel, seating 2,000, in 1819. This was soon filled and Old Bank was redeveloped as Buxton Road chapel in 1837, becoming head of its own circuit in 1844. PM was weak in the area, with its first chapel being built only in 1847. But WM was again torn apart by the *Fly Sheets controversy of 1849. After contesting possession of Queen Street chapel, in 1757 the Reformers moved out and opened Brunswick in 1859, but did not join the UMFC until 1866. As the town grew in the later nineteenth century, the MNC opened a large gothic chapel in High Street in 1867 and formed a second circuit in 1876; the UMFC had three circuits by 1884 and WM, whose numbers equalled those of the other two combined, formed a third circuit based on a new suburban chapel at Gledholt in 1888. Queen Street eventually experienced a new lease of life as a Central Mission from 1906, with a range of activities and a membership far in excess of any since 1850. Following *Methodist Union in 1932 and circuit amalgamations the other central chapels had closed by 1960, the centre of gravity moved to the suburbs and then to the suburbanized villages. But the Queen Street Mission remained active, moving to King Street in 1970 and to Lord Street in 1998.

J. Mallinson (1898); Conference Handbook 1937, 1950; E. Royle in E.A.H. Haigh (1992); E. Royle (1994)

ER

Hudson, John Rathbone (1879–1932; e.m. 1906), WM missionary to *India, trained at *Didsbury College. He went to the Lucknow and Benares District in 1907 and, after a period with the YMCA in France, served in the Mission to the Doms in Benares, where he supervised the expansion of the Wesley Industrial School and its removal to Benares in 1920. In 1931 he agreed to serve for three years in British Guiana while a younger Hindi-speaking man trained for the East India Mission there, but died of malaria and enteric fever after only one year.

MR 15 Sept. 1932

JAV

Hudspeth, William Harrison (1887–1976; e.m. 1909), UM missionary in *China, born at Willington, Co. Durham. Joining the Yunnan mission in 1909, he was one of only four missionaries to master the Miao language. His charismatic personality endeared him to Chinese and Miao alike. After the death of S. *Pollard, he supervised the publication of the Miao NT and also undertook its revision in 1936, the year he was appointed China Secretary for the Bible Society in Shanghai. Interned during World War II, he suffered savage spells of torture and interrogation. Subsequently he served as General Secretary of the Bible Society in *Canada.

MR 20 May 1976; W.H. Hudspeth (1937)

RKP

Hughes, Donald Wynn (1911–67), schoolmaster, the son of H.M. *Hughes, was educated at The Perse School and Emmanuel College, Cambridge, where he read Classics and then English. He was Senior English Master at The *Leys 1934–46 and Headmaster of *Rydal School 1946–67, serving on the Committee of the Headmasters' Conference from 1960. At Colwyn Bay he was a JP and held various public offices. He wrote extensively on education; also plays, light verse and operettas (including *The Batsman's Bride*, which was broadcast). His books include *Reason and Imagination* (1948) and *The Apostles' Creed* (1960) and three of his hymns are in *HP*.

MR 17 Aug. 1967; P. Heywood in *Donald Hughes, Headmaster* (1970)

JAV

Hughes, Dr H. Maldwyn (1875–1940; e.m. 1898), Principal of *Wesley House, Cambridge, 1921–37. Educated at *Kingswood School and the University College of Wales, he was a sound scholar, respected by his students and the University, but an indifferent lecturer. He published *What is the Atonement?* (1924) and a much used textbook, *Christian Foundations: an Introduction to Christian Doctrine* (1927). An eloquent preacher with a social concern, he was elected President of the WM Conference in 1932, but served only during the brief interval before *Methodist Union. *See also* **Hughes, Dr John**

MR 22 Aug. 1940

WDH

Hughes, Hugh (1778–1855; e.m. 1807), Welsh WM minister, born in Caernarfonshire. He

worked as a gardener before moving to *Liverpool, where he joined the WM in 1805. He was Chairman of the South Wales District 1828–43 and in 1834 became the first Welsh member of the *Legal Hundred. He founded many new churches and revived others. He wrote extensively for *Yr Eurgrawn*, which he also edited 1819–21, and was joint translator of JW's *Explanatory Notes upon the NT* into Welsh. He wrote an autobiography, posthumously edited by his son-in-law I. *Jenkins (1857). He was the grandfather of H.P. *Hughes.

DWB; *Bathafarn* 28 (1974–6) pp. 42–70

IGPL

Hughes, Hugh (1842–1933; e.m. 1866), Welsh WM minister, known as 'Hugh Hughes Fawr' because of his height. He was born at Tregarth near Bangor and worked in slate quarries, beginning to preach at 19. Though lacking early educational opportunities, he worked hard to qualify himself for the ministry. His outstanding personality, melodious voice and skill in sermon construction and delivery made him one of the most popular Welsh preachers during his long life. He contributed frequently to *Yr Eurgrawn* and *Y Winllan* and published a volume of sermons.

EW 125 pp. 235–8, 241–5

IGPL

Hughes, Hugh Price (1847–1902; e.m. 1867), WM minister, born in Carmarthen. Following his grandfather, Hugh *Hughes, into the ministry, while training at *Richmond College he met his wife, the daughter of A. *Barrett, the College Governor. As Superintendent in *Oxford, he revitalized the circuit. Returning to London in 1884, he became the first Superintendent of the West London Mission, part of Methodism's response to *The Bitter Cry of Outcast London* through its social and evangelistic work among the urban poor. As preacher, pastor and organizer, he was leader of the *Forward Movement in the 1880s and 1890s, creating a high profile for reform and innovation. As editor of the *Methodist Times* from 1885 he raised social issues as part of the 'Nonconformist Conscience', particularly with regard to *temperance, *gambling and social morality. In opposition to Parnell's adultery which contributed to his downfall, Hughes asserted: 'What is morally wrong cannot be politically right.' He was a committed ecumenist and became the second President of the Free Church Congress. Despite his sturdy independence (as shown in his

support for H. *Lunn in the *missionary controversy of 1889–90), he was elected President of
the WM Conference in 1898. His volumes of
sermons on *Social Christianity* (1889), *The Philanthropy of God* (1890), *Ethical Christianity*
(1892) and *Essential Christianity* (1894) were
widely read as models of Methodism's marrying
of evangelism and social action, embodied in a
range of agencies in the Mission.

See also **Hughes, Katherine Price**

MR 20 & 27 Nov. 1902, 6 Feb. 1947; D.P. Hughes
(1904); A. Walters (1907); J.H.S. Kent in G.V.
Bennett & J.D. Walsh (1966) pp. 181–205; D.W.
Bebbington (1982); C. Oldstone-Moore (1999)

TSAM

Hughes, John (1776–1843; e.m. 1796) 'of
Brecon', received a good education, his father
being a well-to-do tradesman. He joined the English WM society and after hearing JW preach
decided to become a *local preacher; then entered
the ministry at the cost of his worldly prospects.
In 1800 he was sent by his fellow-Breconian T.
*Coke as colleague to O. *Davies in the new North
Wales mission. His sacrificial efforts resulted in
the formation of many Welsh-speaking societies
despite his limited fluency in Welsh, the difference
of background and education between him and
his colleagues (whose preaching often seemed to
him like the 'outpourings of ranters'), and the
difficulty of accepting the authority of O. *Davies.
Seeing the danger of division, Coke removed him
to the English work for most of his remaining
ministry. His interest in the Welsh mission, however, continued and he strove hard to provide it
with religious literature. He produced a Welsh
hymn-book which included a number of his own
compositions.

W. Rowlands in *EW* 1848–9 A.H. Williams
(1935) pp. 69–146; *Bathafarn* 5 (1950) pp. 6–
22, 11 (1956) pp. 5–53, 12 (1957) pp. 5–22;
DWB; *WMM* 1847 pp. 209–21

IGPL

Hughes, Dr John (1842–1902; e.m. 1868),
Welsh WM minister, born near Aberysywyth,
known by his bardic name 'Glanystwyth', worked
on farms and in lead and slate mines from the age
of 12. Beginning to preach in his early twenties,
he became renowned in both South and North
Wales as a gifted preacher, author and poet. He
edited *Y Winllan* 1874–76 and *Yr Eurgrawn*
1897–1902, and was chiefly responsible for establishing *Y Gwyliedydd* in 1877–78. He was Book

Steward for the last five years of his ministry.
Belonging to the radical Welsh Liberal tradition,
he was an outspoken and eloquent advocate of
Nonconformity, Disestablishment, Board Schools
and Land Law Reform and an opponent of the
Boer War and the amalgamation of English and
Welsh WM in Wales. He was instrumental in
establishing the Welsh Assembly in 1899 and in
the creation of two Districts in North Wales in
1903. His voluminous publications include works
on the life of Christ (1891) and on the early
ages of the world (1892), both attempts to help
Christians come to terms with Darwinism and
Biblical Criticism, a biography of the Rev. Isaac
Jones and a commentary on Colossians (1900).
An acknowledged national poet and literary
adjudicator, he was the chief editor of the 1900
Welsh WM hymn-book and some of his hymns
are still in common use. He was the father of Dr
H.M. *Hughes.

D.G. Jones (1904); *EW* 94 pp. 161–94; *EE*; *DWB*;
H.T. Hughes (1979) pp. 42–56

EHG

Hughes, Katherine Price (*née* Mary Katherine Howard Barrett) (1853–1948), daughter of A.
*Barrett, Governor of *Richmond College 1858–
68, and wife of H.P. *Hughes, whom she first met
as a student at the college. She was a pupil at
Laleham and acknowledged the influence of the
headmistress, H.E. *Pipe. Her husband always
stressed the importance of her partnership and
support in his ministry, not least in conceiving
and bringing into existence a Sisterhood within
the West London Mission, offering opportunities
for women in the Church to serve the needs of the
disadvantaged and ostracized sections of society.
J.S. *Lidgett's verdict was that, while being a
moderating influence on her excitable husband,
she gave practical support to his platform oratory
which perpetuated his influence. Following his
early death, she continued to be actively involved
in the work of the Mission, especially through her
leadership of the 'Sisters of the People'. Despite
distancing herself from the more extreme aspects
of the suffragette movement, she played an active
part in advancing the status of *women in society
and Church, was one of the first women elected
to the WM Conference in 1911 and was the first
woman to address that bastion of male supremacy.

MR 22 Jan. 1948; D.P. Hughes (1907); K.P.
Hughes (1945)

JAV

Hughes, Lot (1787–1873; e.m. 1808), Welsh WM minister, from Abergele, converted through the preaching of E. *Jones (Bathafarn), began to preach in 1806. Personal contact with such pioneers as O. *Davies and J. *Hughes, a quite exceptional memory, assiduous diary-keeping and letter-writing, all combined to make him a mine of information about early Welsh WM. Not himself a professional historian or a polished writer, he collected the raw material that was published in *Yr Eurgrawn* and elsewhere as 'Tremau' (historical sketches), putting all subsequent historians in his debt. As a preacher and pastor he was much respected for his honesty, sensitivity, outspokenness and mild eccentricity. In later life he took pride in belonging to the *Legal Hundred.

E.H. Griffiths in *Bathafarn* 29 pp. 3–147; *DWB*
EHG

Hughes, Rowland (1811–61; e.m. 1832), Welsh WM minister, brought up in Dolgellau and apprenticed to a tailor. Converted under WM preaching in 1827, he served as a *local preacher and lay agent before being accepted for the ministry. He gained a wide reputation as a preacher and popular lecturer on religious subjects. A volume of his sermons was published in 1877. He published a *Defence of Wesleyanism* against the *Fly Sheets (which had troubled circuits in Wales) and a revised translation of JW's *Explanatory Notes upon the NT*, and was one of the editors of the Welsh hymn-book of 1845.

EW 55 pp. 133ff. etc.; *DWB*
IGPL

Hughes, Thomas (1854–1928; e.m. 1879), Welsh WM minister, born at Rhuddlan, trained at *Headingley College, was President of the Welsh Assembly in 1907, Chairman of the Second North Wales District, 1911–24, and a member of the *Legal Hundred from 1910. A great encourager of scholarly activities, he published a commentary on Acts (1906) and was joint author of the biography of J. *Evans (Eglwysbach) (1903) and editor of *Yr Eurgrawn*, 1912–28 and *Y Winllan*, 1894–97. While serving on the Council of University College, Bangor, he established a fund to enable ministerial candidates from the Welsh Districts to study for University of Wales degrees. A keen advocate of Church unity, he was one of the initiators of the joint CM/WM *Hymn-book (1929).

YBC p. 370; *DWB*, 391–2; *EW*, 121 pp. 41–69
OEE

Hughes, Thomas Isfryn (1865–1942; e.m. 1890), born near Ruthin, trained for the ministry at *Handsworth College and became one of the most venerated and theologically learned of Welsh ministers. His scholarly calibre was demonstrated in his frequent doctrinal articles in *EW* and other Welsh journals, his contributions to the standard Welsh Dictionary of the Bible, *Geiriadur Beiblaidd* (1926) and his commentary on Philippians and Philemon (1916). He was President of the Welsh Assembly in 1918.

USMR 7 Jan. 1943; USYBC2 p. 22; *EW* 135 pp. 101–7
OEE

Huguenots Huguenot refugees and their descendants, both in Britain and North America, were caught up in the Methodist movement from its beginnings. The best known (e.g. the *Delamotte, *Riggall and *Bosanquet families) were only the tip of an iceberg. One tenth of the 740 members at the *Foundery in London in the early 1740s bore French names and the *Bristol society reveals similar evidence, though on a smaller scale. Both the housekeeper (Sarah Clavel) and steward (Melchior Teulon) at the Foundery were Huguenots, as were the *Vanners; and JW was later to marry a Huguenot widow, Mary Vazeille. Redundant Huguenot chapels proved to be invaluable to him, especially those at *West Street and Spitalfields, London, which he acquired in the early 1740s. West Street, being episcopally consecrated, was of particular importance in Methodism's sacramental life.
  See also **Vanner Family**

G.E. Milburn in *PWHS* 45 pp. 70–9
GEM

Hulbert, Charles (1878–1957; e.m. 1903) WM minister, was influenced in his youth by Gipsy *Smith, Campbell Morgan and T. *Champness and on leaving *Didsbury served under S. *Collier in the *Manchester Mission. His ministry was spent in various city missions, including Blackburn (where he built the Queen's Hall), Southall and Archway, London. From 1937 he served as Home Missions Evangelist.

MR 9 Jan. 1958
JAV

Hull, a mediaeval port which grew rapidly with the new docks after 1774, became both a PM and a WM *Conference town. Elizabeth Blow from

Grimsby established a society there about 1746. JW's first visited in 1752 and on a return visit in 1759 met his old friend C. *Delamotte. The Manor House tower, used for meetings from 1757, was replaced by George Yard Chapel in 1787. This became the centre for the new Hull WM Mission, but was replaced in 1905 by the Queen's Hall. Other Central Halls were the King's Hall and Thornton Hall. One prominent early Methodist was T. *Thompson MP, who in 1791 drafted the 'Hull Circular', a pleas for Methodists to remain luyal to the CofE. The early twentieth century was notable for T.R. *Ferens, A. *Gelder and J. *Rank.

A business trip to Nottingham in 1817 brought Richard Woolhouse into contact with PM and the activities of female revivalists, including A. *Carr; and this marked the origins of Hull PM. W. *Clowes came to the town in January 1819 and Mill Street chapel opened that September. Hull became his base and he is interred in Spring Bank Cemetery. Clowes Memorial, Jarratt Street, was opened in 1851. Hull was the centre of rapid PM expansion, especially in the north; in 1825, for example, the circuit included East Yorkshire, the North East, part of Cumbria, London and Sheerness. In the 1830s also it had missions as far afield as the Hampshire coast and Isle of Wight. But it was adversely affected by the secession of John Stamp in 1841.

The MNC opened Bethel in 1799. One prominent MNC family was the Needlers, confectionery manufacturers. W. *Booth had a successful ministry in the town before leaving the MNC to launch his own movement. There was also a small UMFC presence.

W.H. Thompson (1895); J. Hogg (1987); D. Neave (1991); *Conference Handbooks* 1920 (WM), 1938

DCD

Hulme, Samuel (1806–1901; e.m. 1828), leading MNC minister, despite a timid personality and delicate health. From an Anglican background, he spent a year preparing for the ministry with T *Allin, married Allin's daughter and was his ally against J. *Barker and in moves to raise the status of the MNC ministry. He was Secretary of Missions 1863–79, having persuaded the Conference in 1858/59 to embark on a mission to *China, and tutor at *Ranmoor College 1864–66. He was President of the Conference in 1842, 1855 and 1866.

G.J. Stevenson (1884–6) 4 pp. 616–22

EAR

Hulme, Thomas Ferrier (1856–1942; e.m. 1878), WM minister who served for many years in the Bristol District. As a Separated Chairman, he took the lead in the restoration and endowment of the *New Room. He was President of the 1923 Conference.

MR 19 July 1923, 5 Nov. 1942

JAV

Humphreys, Joseph (b.1720–1722), a *Moravian described by JW many years later as 'the first lay preacher that assisted me in England in the year 1738'. Converted by G. *Whitefield, he led a society for converts at Deptford and in 1740 began preaching and acting as W's assistant at the *Foundery. Eventually he reverted to his hereditary *Calvinism, joined Whitefield and wrote critically of the Wesleys. Falling out with Whitefield, he obtained Presbyterian and then episcopalian ordination. In spite of his earlier evangelical enthusiasm, he eventually abandoned his belief in inward *holiness and personal religion.

JWJ 9 Sept. 1790; C. Atmore (1801) pp. 202–3; R.P. Heitzenrater (1995) pp. 114–15, 122–3

EWD

Humphreys, Thomas Jones (1841–1934; e.m. 1865), born at Darowen, Mont., Welsh WM minister, was educated at the Normal College, Swansea and served as a lay agent before beginning a long and distinguished ministry. He was President of the Welsh Assembly in 1906 and served as President of the *Manchester FCFC while stationed there, being prominent in the causes of education and temperance. A prolific writer, he published several biblical commentaries and works on doctrinal, ecclesiastical and philosophical subjects, as well as many articles for *Yr Eurgrawn*. He is specially remembered for his hymns and works on Welsh WM history and hymnody, and was honoured by election to the Bardic Circle of Wales.

DWB; *EW* 104 pp. 321–4; 126 pp. 127–32

IGPL

Humphries, Albert Lewis (1865–1950; e.m. 1887), Cambridge-educated son-in-law of S. *Antliff. As a tutor at *Hartley College, 1902–35, his contributions to theology and biblical criticism included his *Hartley Lecture, *The Holy Spirit in Faith and Experience* (1911) and (with William Barker) a Jubilee History of the College (1931).

He was President of the PM Conference in 1926.

MR 6 April 1950; A. Wilkes & J. Lovett (1942) p. 114

DCD

Hunkin, Joseph William (1887–1950), Bishop of Truro 1935–50. Brought up a strict WM in Truro, he became, like his father, a *local preacher in the Truro Circuit. He was educated at *Truro School, The *Leys and Caius College, Cambridge. Accepted for the ministry in 1910, he spent one year at *Headingley College and another in circuit before withdrawing in favour of the Anglican priesthood, for which he trained at Ridley Hall. After distinguished wartime service as an army chaplain, he returned to Cambridge. In 1935 he was consecrated Bishop of Truro, proving a controversial, but largely popular leader. He remained friendly towards Methodism and on Whit Monday 1936 was the first non-Methodist to preach at *Gwennap Pit. His Penguin Special *The Gospel for Tomorrow* (1941) anticipated some features of the *Anglican-Methodist unity proposals of the 1960s, but (perhaps predictably) provoked an adverse response from Cornish Methodists.

Times 31 Oct, 10 Nov. 1950; A. Dunstan & J.S. Peart-Binns (1977)

JAV

Hunmanby Hall School, Filey, opened in 1928 primarily as a girls' boarding school and was the only school founded by the *Board of Management. It grew quickly and developed a reputation for a good all-round education with a strong emphasis on pastoral care. However, its rural and coastal location limited its ability to recruit day pupils as national boarding numbers plummeted in the 1980s. In July 1991 it closed because its September role of 170, from nursery age to 18, was neither educationally nor financially viable.

Hunmanby Hall School Jubilee (1978)

DBT

Hunt, John (1812–48; e.m. 1838), WM missionary to *Fiji, born near Lincoln in humble circumstances and self-educated, he attended the *Hoxton Theological Institution 1835–38. He was recommended as 'of scarcely any literary attainments, but with a clear, sound understanding, a right judgement in the things of God, and a just conception of the way of salvation'.

Enhanced by study, his outstanding ministry was in the pioneer Fiji Mission from 1838. Facing isolation, privation and danger on the various islands and with the unfailing support of his wife Hannah, he evangelized by teaching, preaching and translation, all unmistakably grounded in his love for the Fijians and lit by his personal grace and goodness. His colleagues, like his converts, were unstinting in their love and respect, despite the challenge of his example. As Chairman of the District from 1842 and only 'happy when on full stretch', he overworked relentlessly, until his strength broke down and he died at 36. *Letters on Entire Sanctification*, an exposition of the doctrine enriched with his own insights, was published posthumously and became a required text for ministerial students.

A. Birtwhistle (1954); A.H. Wood vol. 2 (1978)

MJF

Hunter, William (1728–1797; e.m. 1767), a Northumbrian who was converted through hearing Methodist preaching. As an itinerant he continued to serve faithfully until his death. Of quiet disposition and genial temper, he was one of JW's lesser-known preachers, being little involved in either the business of the Conferences or the theological arguments of the day. A devoted pastor throughout his circuit ministry, JW described him as 'not the best, though not the worst, of our preachers'. In life and testimony and preaching he was a strong advocate of *Christian perfection.

EMP 2 pp. 240–261; C. Atmore (1801) pp. 203–14

HMG

Huntingdon, Selina Hastings, Countess of (1707–91), born Selina Shirley, daughter of Earl Ferrers. She married Theophilus, Earl of Huntingdon in 1728. They came under *Moravian influence through B. *Ingham, were converted in 1739 and associated with the Wesleys, though the Earl's religious convictions were less deeply rooted than his wife's. After his early death in 1746, she successfully managed the extensive family estates (including Donington Park, Leics) and dedicated much of her life to supporting the evangelical cause, initially from her Leicestershire base and among her aristocratic acquaintances. Becoming associated with G. *Whitefield and the *Calvinistic Methodists, she opened chapels in many places, including such fashionable resorts as *Bath and *Brighton. Failing to get the support she needed from the Anglican hierarchy, she sponsored a number of Evangelicals seeking ordination, appointing some of them as her 'chaplains', and in 1768 founded a college at *Trevecka to train young men for the ministry. Whitefield bequeathed her the 'Orphan House' at Bethesda, Georgia, which she ran after his death. Her proprietorial attitude to the college at Trevecka annoyed JW and though she did not actively participate in the Calvinistic controversy of the 1770s, she used her influence to oppose the *Arminians. Legal action over her chapel at Spa Fields, London led to the formation of the Connexion which bears her name.

See also **Countess of Huntingdon's Connexion**

S. Tytler (1907); G.W. Kirby (1990); P.W. Gentry (1994); E. Welch (1995); B.S. Schlenther (1997)
PSF

Hurd, F.H. *see* **Primitive Methodist Leader**

Hurrell, Elizabeth (1740–98) was converted under the ministry of the Rev. J. *Berridge of Everton. JW approved of her preaching and she travelled extensively in Yorks, Lancs and Derbyshire. She corresponded with JW and with other women preachers. W. *Warrener is said to have been one of her converts. In 1775 there seems to have been a confrontation between her and J. *Benson, one of the leading opponents of *women's preaching. Around 1780 she decided to give up her preaching and moved to London. She was buried in the crypt of *Wesley's Chapel.

Z. Taft vol. 1 (1825) pp. 175–81; SL vol. 6; P.W. Chilcote (1991) pp. 156–9, 270–1
EDG

Hutchinson, John *see* **Thomas, John**

Hutton, James (1715–95), Moravian bookseller at the 'Bible and Sun' in London. The son of a non-juring clergyman, John Hutton, he was educated at Westminster School. He formed a friendship with the Wesleys and he and his sister were among JW's converts. He published many of JW's early works and later G. *Whitefield's Journals. Under the influence of the Moravians, he was a founder member of the *Fetter Lane society and became one of the leading figures in the *Moravian Church in England, while remaining on good terms with the Wesleys and Whitefield. In 1741 he was instrumental in the formation of the Society for the Furtherance of the Gospel. Over-borrowing led to financial problems and he worked strenuously to avert bankruptcy. Marriage

to a Swiss wife helped him to consolidate Moravian work in Switzerland.

R.P. Heitzenrater (1989) pp. 75–90
EWD

Hymn-books The early Methodists were taught to sing their faith and their theology. JW's first hymn-book, *A Collection of Psalms and Hymns* (the *'Charlestown Hymn-book') was published as early as 1737, while he was in Georgia. After May 1738, hymns flowed from CW's pen, while his brother published many collections, beginning with *Hymns and Sacred Poems* (1739). Some had a specific theme (e.g. *Hymns on the Lord's Supper* (1745) and *Hymns on the Great Festivals* (1746); others were of a more general nature, including a 1743 *Collection* later known as the 'Morning Hymn-book', *Hymns and Spiritual Songs* (1753) and, most importantly, the *Collection of Hymns for the use of the People called Methodists* (1780), intended to supersede all earlier books. W's first tune book was published in 1742, followed in 1761 by *Hymns with Tunes Annext* (also known as *Sacred Melody*), which he prefaced with advice on hymn-singing. His finest tune book was *Sacred Harmony* (1789; edited and revised by CW junior in 1821).

The 1780 hymn-book was reissued with additions or supplements in 1831 and 1876, but was not replaced in WM until the *MHB* of 1904. The MNC used it with supplements until a new book was produced in 1834, followed by *Hymns for Divine Worship* in 1864. For the PMs H. *Bourne produced a 'Large Hymn-book' in 1825; J. *Flesher's revised and enlarged edition of 1853 aroused considerable controversy and was in turn replaced in 1886 (with a supplement in 1912). There were BC enlargements of JW's 1780 book in 1838 and 1862; they eventually produced a new hymn-book in 1889. The UMFC made changes in editions of 1860 and 1889.

The WM book of 1904 was the first to change from the experiential arrangement of the 1780 *Collection* in favour of a thematic one, which subsisted in its successor, the *MHB* of 1933, an early fruit of *Methodist Union in 1932. A supplement *Hymns and Songs* was issued in 1969. The present book, *Hymns and Psalms* came out in 1983, fifty years after the 1933 *MHB*.

Each denomination also produced Sunday School hymn-books; the *School Hymn-book* published in 1950 by *MYD has been supplemented by the all-age *Partners in Praise* (1979), *Story Song* (1993) and *Big Blue Planet* (1995).

The first Welsh WM hymn-book, *Diferion y Cyssegr* was published by J *Hughes, (Brecon, 1802). Much altered and enlarged editions appeared in 1804, 1807, 1809 and 1812. Like all subsequent hymnals, these depended heavily on the Calvinist W. *Williams, Pantycelyn. The connexion itself published books in 1817, 1845 and 1900, and in 1927 joined with CM in what has been the most highly regarded Welsh collection, with a supplement in 1985.

————

R. Watson & K. Trickett (1988) pp. 18–33
PLC/GTH

Hymn-singing   In the words of the Preface to MHB (1933), 'Methodism was born in song,' fuelled by CW's unparalleled output of hymns. The rise of Methodism followed closely on the transition at the turn of the seventeenth century from metrical psalms to hymns, of which Isaac Watts was the chief catalyst, CW the chief heir and the Methodist people the first beneficiaries. JW had learned from his *Moravian companions on the way to Georgia the value of hymn-singing as a corporate expression of faith. He translated hymns from the German and published the first of many collections, the *'Charlestown Hymnbook', while still in America. CW's outburst of poetic fervour began at the time of his conversion and was sustained over half a century. Hymns were an essential ingredient of the preaching service, which was intended to supplement, not replace, the worship of the parish church. In the open air they were used to attract a congregation (a technique also used by PM preachers in the next century). There is much testimony to the effectiveness of hymn-singing in both arousing and giving expression to faith as people responded to the preaching of the 'Methodist gospel'. At the same time they were experiencing what JW saw as the essentially social nature of religion and, however unconsciously, were learning what he called 'all the important truths of our most holy religion, whether speculative or practical' – a safeguard, still necessary, against empty emotionalism.

In an age when literacy was limited, the practice of 'lining out' prevailed, the words being given out, usually two lines at a time, before being sung. This rather tedious practice died hard: as late as the WM Conference of 1844 there were complaints that whole verses were being given out at a time. Conference expressed its disapproval of this innovation and made further attempts in 1860 and 1877 to maintain the earlier custom, which nevertheless succumbed to the rising tide of popular education and survives only in the custom (rare in Anglican circles) of announcing a hymn by reading out at least the opening line.

————

S.G. Dimond (1926) pp. 101–3, 119–24; L.F. Church (1949) pp. 228–36; J. Bishop (1950); J.R. Watson (1997)
PLC/JAV

Hymns on the Great Festivals and Other Occasions (1746) contained 23 hymns by CW and one by his brother Samuel, with musical settings by J.F. *Lampe, the first original tunes written for Methodist hymns. It included three hymns on death, characteristic of the early Methodists' claim to 'die well'.

————

Introduction to facsimile reprint (1996)
JAV

Hymns on the Lord's Supper (1745) went through nine editions in the Wesleys' lifetime. It was based on *The Christian Sacrament and Sacrifice* (1673) by Dr Daniel Brevint, a Caroline divine who became Dean of Lincoln after the Restoration, and is a reminder of the sacramentalism which was complementary to, and integrated with, early Methodist evangelicalism. The book was in two parts: a lengthy extract prepared by JW from Brevint's treatise was followed by a series of 166 hymns, mostly by CW, which formed a series of versified meditations on Brevint's words. The hymns celebrate the sacrament as not only a memorial but a *means of grace and a 'pledge of heaven'. They do not hesitate to speak of Christ's 'real presence' and express a 'high' doctrine of the sacrament which anticipated the Anglo-Catholic revival by a hundred years, but was lost to nineteenth-century Methodism in its reaction against high Anglicanism. A number of the hymns remain in use; e.g. 'God of unexampled grace' (*HP* 166), 'Jesus, we thus obey' (*HP* 614) and 'Let him to whom we now belong' (*HP* 698). (Cf. *HP* 298, 596, 602,629.

————

J.E. Rattenbury (1948); J.C. Bowmer (1951) pp. 166–86
JAV

Ibberson, Herbert (1880–1959), MNC and UM layman, born at Mapplewell, near Barnsley. He was educated at Leeds University and became a solicitor. He served as a Liberal Councillor and later Chairman of Darton UDC. An outstanding *local preacher, he was treasurer (1923–27) and then secretary (1927–32) of the UM Local Preachers' Committee, organizing preachers' schools for many years. He was also Co-Secretary of the *LPMAA. As a member of the Methodist Union Committee he argued for an equal number of lay and ministerial *ex officio* members at Conference.He was Vice-President of the 1942 Conference.

MR 24 July 1941, 16 July 1942, 6 Aug. 1959
JHL

Independent Methodism, a small denomination originating from Methodism's age of disunity, exists mainly in the north of England. Its distinctive features are its unpaid ministry and independent system of church government.

An attempt was made in 1803 by W. *Bramwell to bring together various groups of *Methodist Revivalists, but this came to nothing. In 1806 they held a general meeting and formed a union, known as Independent Methodists, though each group retained its local name: *Quaker Methodists (Warrington), *Band Room Methodists (Manchester), Independent Methodists (Oldham), Christian Revivalists (Macclesfield/Stockport) and in various places *Free Gospel Churches. Most had broken away from *WM or the *MNC. Further growth followed the Peterloo massacre (1819) when churches were formed in *Bolton and the North East by groups which included many Radical Reformers.

Other groups were added at various times during the nineteenth century: *Gospel Pilgrims (Yorkshire and Norfolk), Independent Primitive Methodists (Nottinghamshire), Church Presbyterians (Glasgow), *Christian Brethren (Yorkshire), *Christian Lay Churches (North East) and, briefly, *Wesle Bach (Minor Wesleyans) in North Wales. The Connexion itself has changed its title – Churches of Christ, United Free Gospel Churches and (since 1898) the Independent Methodist Connexion of Churches.

The rejection of a paid ministry was usually a reaction against what was perceived as the abuse of authority by itinerant preachers, but as the years passed non-payment was given a strong ideological basis. Preachers were appointed by local churches and circuits. The concept of a connexional ministry with legal recognition dates only from the present century.

Today the Connexion's Resource Centre in Wigan serves as headquarters and a facility for the churches. A Connexional Committee manages the work of the Connexion, but final authority rests with its Annual Meeting, at which each church may be represented. The Connexion is a member body of Churches Together in England, CCBI, the Free Churches' Council and the Evangelical Alliance.

A.Mounfield (1905); J. Vickers (1920); J. Murray (1955); D. Valenze (1985); J. Dolan (1996

JAD

India   Until the renewal of its charter in 1813, Christian missions in India were severely hampered by the policy of the East India Company. Despite this, T. *Coke had envisaged a mission to Asia as early as 1784, when he corresponded with Charles Grant, a merchant in the East India Company, about the Indian situation. Though other commitments delayed this project for many years, in 1800 he persuaded the Conference to authorize the sending of a missionary to Madras and in 1805–6 was in contact with the East India Company through Col. William Sandys. Nothing, however, materialized until the end of Coke's life. James *Lynch, one of the six young missionaries who accompanied him to Asia in 1814, was designated for India, but remained with the others in Ceylon and did not reach Madras until 1817. From this small beginning the India mission grew very slowly in the face of an ancient and complex culture and of the prevalent Hinduism. Educational work came to be seen as a way forward, but the work did not gather pace or extend far beyond the Madras area until the second half of the century, when interest and concern were stimulated in the Church at home by the Indian Mutiny of 1857. Then there was a period of expansion: south-west to Negapatam and Trichinopoly, inland to Bangalore in Mysore State and northwest into Hyderabad State. In Hyderabad and also in Bombay, military personnel played a part in establishing the first missions. Calcutta and Bengal at first proved barren soil, but a fresh initiative in the 1880s was more successful. Work was developed among the primitive Santal tribesmen of Bengal, and to the north-west the Lucknow and Benares District was the scene of a mass movement among the Gonds and Chamars and the Doms of Benares. Missionaries also moved into Burma (now *Myanmar) to the north-east.

The *'Missionary Controversy' of 1889 seriously weakened confidence in the work of the Indian mission, but resulted for a time in greater awareness of the need for the missionary to live and work alongside his flock, rather than apart from it. A recurring issue was the relative value and success of educational work among the higher castes and village evangelism among the lower castes and outcastes. The first *medical mission began in Madras in 1884 and in Calcutta in 1887. Medical work, in which the contribution of women missionaries and wives was particularly valuable and effective, expressed the love of God at such centres as the Holdsworth Memorial Hospital at Mysore (1906), the leprosy settlements at Bankura and Dichpali and many village clinics and dispensaries. The long ministry of C.W. *Posnett at Medak saw a mass movement in the villages of Hyderabad in the early twentieth century. A considerable network of institutions for ministerial and lay training laid foundations for a well qualified and skilled indigenous ministry at a time when schemes for wider union and for autonomy were being considered. While American Methodism held aloof, the South India Province of the British Methodist Church joined with Anglicans and former Presbyterians and Congregationalists in the Church of South India (1947), the most important ecumenical break-through of the twentieth century. An even wider range of denominations came together in the Church of North India (1970).

W. Moister (1871) pp. 459–510; F&H 5 pp. 119–418; *HMGB* 3 pp. 96–102; B. Sundkler (1954)

JAV

Industrial Chaplaincy The 1934 Conference adopted a Report on 'A Christian View of Industry in relation to the Social Order' (revised, 1960), a response to the concern shown by writers like R.H. Tawney and William Temple over the separation of industrial society and the Churches. In the 1950s the HM and Christian Citizenship Committees, in the context of discussions at the BCC, began to consider industrial chaplaincy as a means of evangelism amongst those working in industry. It was envisaged that chaplains would see this as part of their circuit work and recognized that the responsibility of representing the Churches in industry belonged primarily to the lay people employed there. A Church in Industry Committee was established in the Home Mission Department. The reports *Work and Witness* (1975) and *Shaping Tomorrow* (1981) and the 'Luton Papers' set out to educate Methodists about industrial matters and to encourage lay witness to the faith. A few full-time and many more part-time industrial chaplains were appointed to work ecumenically. They were paid by the Church and

their appointment was approved by management and employees in the factories they visited.
See also **Luton Industrial College**

JWH

Ineson, Percy (1883–1953; e.m. 1909), WM minister, born at Cramlington and trained at *Handsworth College. From 1922 to 1944 he served in the *London Mission, where his social work at St John's Square, Clerkenwell and during the war years at Stepney Central Hall was notable, especially through his chairmanship of the LCC Care Committee. He exercised a reconciling ministry among exiled Orthodox priests in England, had a special interest in prison reform and was an active member of the *Methodist Peace Fellowship. The closing years of his ministry were spent with the BCC's Refugee and Inter-Church Aid Commission.

MR 11 June 1953; R.G. Burnett (1946) pp. 134–51
WL

Ingham, Benjamin (1712–72), born at Ossett (Yorks), was a member of the *'Holy Club'. He accompanied J&CW to Georgia and, with them, came under the influence of the *Moravians. He began to preach in his native Yorkshire and in 1738 travelled with JW to Herrnhut. The *Fetter Lane disputes of 1740 led to a rift between JW and Ingham, who remained under Moravian influence until 1751. In 1741, in spite of opposition from her family, he married Lady Margaret Hastings (1700–68), sister-in-law to the Countess of *Huntingdon. They lived at Aberford, Yorks and she encouraged his ministry in the North of England. His preaching resulted in over 40 societies by 1741. He received Moravian support in this ministry and, lacking JW's ability and zeal for administration, placed his societies under their care in 1742, in order to concentrate on preaching. But by 1750 he was seeking independence from them and by 1756 was ordaining his own preachers. In 1760 he was attracted to the Glasites or Sandemanians, a Scottish sect, and adopted their heretical teaching and practices. In spite of the Countess of Huntingdon's intervention, this resulted in a schism which decimated the Inghamite societies and destroyed much of his life's work.

DEB; L. Tyerman (1873) pp. 57–154; C.W. Towlson (1957)

WDH

Innocent, John (1829–1904; e.m. 1852), MNC missionary appointed to North *China along with W.N. *Hall in 1859. On his return to England in 1897 he was elected President of the Conference. When ill health prevented his return to China, he was made a permanent member of the Missionary Committee and was appointed a *Guardian Representative in 1900.

GRS

Invalid Ministers' Rest Fund see **Finance, Ministerial**

Inverness In 1746 a Jacobite Methodist, Ninian Dunbar, was accompanied to the gallows by Methodist soldiers on the government side who sang and prayed with him. C. *Hopper came in 1759, 1860 and 1761 and JW first visited in 1764. In 1770 he found that Benjamin and William Chappel, wheelwrights waiting three months for a ship to return them to London, had employed the time in meeting people every night to sing and pray. The society rented a disused malt kiln off Academy Street, then moved to New Street until in 1798 Inglis Street chapel was opened (rebuilt on the same site in 1868). With an increase in numbers, the society moved to the Music Hall in Union Street in 1922, leaving Inglis Street for use as Sunday School and institute. The Union Street premises were burned down in 1961 and were replaced in 1965 by a church in Huntley Street.

T.P. Addison (1964)

MB

Inwood, Dr Charles (1851–1928; e.m. 1872), born at Woburn Sands, Bucks, became a Methodist *local preacher in *Ireland in 1869. Ordained in 1876, he continued in circuit work in Ireland until 1897 when the Irish Conference, recognising his evangelistic and convention ministry, released him for wider work. His emphasis on JW's doctrine of Christian *holiness, which he interpreted as full consecration, led to his being invited to preach at the Keswick Convention in 1892. From then until his death he was the most regular WM preacher at the Convention. His growing reputation as a convention preacher and his life-long interest in missionary work resulted in thirty years of itinerant ministry that took him to all five continents.

A.M. Hay (n.d.)

HMG

Ipswich JW's only recorded visit was in 1790, to change horses. No society is mentioned until 1805. In 1808 Thomas Morgan was appointed to the 'Ipswich Mission', initially under the *Colchester Circuit. It became a circuit in its own right in 1811, the year in which the first small chapel was opened in Long Lane, soon replaced by one seating 800 in Market Lane (1816) and later by Museum Street (1861). PM beginnings in the town are not documented; but the first QM minutes date from 1836 and a chapel was opened in Rope Walk in 1839. This was the head of a PM Circuit until it united with the Museum Street (formerly WM) Circuit in 1953. Norwood in Park Road, the residence of the Anglican bishop from 1914, became an MHA home in 1979. By arrangement with the Church Commissioners, the house was exchanged for the nearby home of Arthur Hill, a prominent Methodist surgeon and his wife Elsie. *Conference is to meet in the town for the first time in 2001.

T.N. Ritson (1908)

EW

Ireland G. *Whitefield visited Ireland as early as 1738. It was, however, JW's 21 visits between 1747 and 1789 that played a vital part in the development of Irish Methodism. He presided over the Conference as often as possible, alternating with T. *Coke in later years. His Irish tours were generally based on *Dublin, where he established the Irish Methodist headquarters at Whitefriar Street. His commitment to Ireland reflected a conviction that her problems – including poverty, moral depravity, political instability and violence – required spiritual solutions. Preachers and people alike experienced considerable hardship from the harsh conditions and fierce opposition. As an early preacher observed, 'No one is fit to be a preacher here who is not ready to die any moment.'

By 1789 Methodist membership exceeded 14,000, representing a 500% increase in 20 years. This total had doubled by 1814, partly as an indirect result of the insurrection of the United Irishmen in 1798. Its leaders included Catholics, Anglicans and Presbyterians. Methodists generally supported the Government and in Wexford one preacher, Andrew Taylor, narrowly escaped being piked to death by the insurgents. T. *Coke, believing that evangelical conversion was the only preventative, urged the Irish Conference to act and in 1799 it established the General Mission under three Irish-speaking preachers, C. *Graham, J. *McQuigg and G. *Ouseley. (Irish speakers and bilinguals were in a majority at that time.) The Mission's aim was 'the subjugation of

Irish popery to the faith of Christ'. By 1839, more than 100 missionaries had been appointed and it played a major part in the nineteenth-century growth of Irish Methodism.

The main division within Irish Methodism – between Wesleyans and *Primitive Wesleyans – took place in 1816, when limited authority was given to the Irish preachers to administer the sacraments. Those opposed to this development established a separate Primitive Wesleyan Conference in 1818, with A. *Averell as President. The two bodies were reunited in 1878, to form the Methodist Church in Ireland, which remains united despite the political division of the country in 1922. Three of its eight Districts straddle the border. One unique feature is the tradition whereby the British President presides over the Irish Conference, while the President of the Methodist Church in Ireland, sits on his right, as Vice-President of the Conference (and may be invited to preside over some sessions).

Through city missions in *Belfast, *Dublin, Newtownabbey and *Londonderry, and by other means, the gospel is related in practical ways to the whole of life. The Church's contribution in the vital area of education is highlighted by *Wesley College, Dublin and *Methodist College, Belfast, together with *Gurteen Agricultural College.

The failure of the potato crop in 1846/47 caused major famine and out of a population of 8 millions about one million died and another million emigrated. Methodist membership, fell from a peak of 44,000 in 1844 to 26,000 in 1855. Five ministers and an unknown number of lay people died of fevers. More than 15,000 members emigrated between 1840 and 1859. In 1997 membership stood at under 18,000, with a total Methodist community of over 57,000. From the start, Irish Methodism had most influence among people from the Established Church and migrant European minorities (e.g. *Moravians, *Palatines and *Huguenots). It also had a strong base within the army. Less impact was made on Roman Catholics and Presbyterians. These factors help to account for its uneven distribution.

Emigrants helped to build the Church in the lands of their adoption. Foremost among Irishmen whose ministry was located largely in Britain were A. *Clarke and *W. Arthur. Both Robert Strawbridge in Maryland and Barbara Heck and Philip Embury in New York had come from Ireland. More than 200 Irish-born ministers served in *Canadian Methodism before 1900. Through involvement in the mission agencies of Methodism in Britain and elsewhere, the Irish also played an important role in the World Church.

C.H. Crookshank (1885–88); J.C. Bowmer in *LQHR* Oct. 1953 pp. 252–62, Jan. 1954 pp. 38–45; R.L. Cole (1960); F. Jeffery (1964); N.W. Taggart (1986); D. Hempton & M. Hill (1992); D. Hempton (1996) pp. 29–48; D.A.L. Cooney in WHS(I) Autumn 1996

NWT/DALC

Ironside, Samuel (1814–97; e.m. 1837), WM missionary, born in *Sheffield and trained at the *Hoxton Theological Institution. Arriving in *New Zealand with J.H. *Bumby in 1839, he was appointed first to Hokianga Station, where he quickly became fluent in Maori. In 1840 he travelled overland to select sites for new missions on the west coast of North Island; then moved to South Island, where he pioneered work in Nelson and Marlborough from the Port Underwood Mission station. The mission had to be abandoned after the Wairau Affray in 1843 and he spent the next six years in Wellington, where he was a trusted negotiator between Maori and settler, particularly in 1845 when relations were strained. At Nelson 1849–55 he was involved in moves to organize freehold settlement by working men and in New Plymouth 1855–58 fostered education among both Maori and settler. He needed all his accumulated knowledge and understanding of Maori thought in those years when the country was being opened up to colonial influences; as did his wife Sarah who was often left alone and in charge of the mission during his travels. He left for *Australia in 1858, where he served in Sydney, Adelaide, Melbourne and Hobart.

W.A. Chambers (1982); *DNZB*

MJF/DJP

Isaac, Daniel (1788–1834; e.m. 1800), WM minister, born at Caythorpe, Lincs, became an outstanding theologian and preacher. His sermons were controversial rather than oratorical, full of humour, often satirical, but combined with deep and touching emotion. Though he retained the Lincolnshire dialect, he so distinguished himself as a thinker as to earn the title given him by J. *Everett, 'the Polemic Divine'. When his friends wished him to occupy the Presidential chair, he absented himself from the Conference. His extensive writings were republished in a collected edition (3 volumes, 1840–41) by J. *Burdsall.

MR(W) 1905 pp. 36–8; J. Everett (1839)

WL

Isaac, Evan (1865–1938; e.m. 1891), Welsh WM minister. A native of Tre'rddôl, he grew up under the influence of the 1859 Revival. Having worked in local mines from the age of 10, he moved to the South Wales coalfields and began to preach. After training at *Handsworth College, he spent the whole of his ministry in the South Wales District, of which he was Chairman from 1917 (when he was elected President of the Welsh Assembly and a member of the *Legal Hundred) to 1932. A bachelor of warm friendliness and shrewd judgment, he was held in respect and affection by all. A man of varied interests and rich literary gifts, his widely read volumes on Welsh hymn writers (1927), on H.R. *Jones and the 1859 Revival (1930) and on Welsh folklore (1938) are of abiding value.

EW 131 pp. 43–50; *DWB*

EHG

Isbell, Digory (*c.* 1718–95) and his wife Elizabeth (*c.* 1718–1804), Cornish hosts to JW and the early itinerants in their home at Trewint, Altarnun. J. *Nelson and J. *Downes discovered their house on Bodmin Moor in 1743 and JW was welcomed there in 1744. Isbell was a stonemason and built a two-room extension to his cottage for the preachers' use. Their tombstone at Altarnun describes them as 'the first who entertained the Methodist preachers in this County, and lived and died in that Connection, but strictly adhered to the Duties of the Established Church'.

WMM 1809 p. 165

TS

Isle of Man The first Methodist to visit the Island was J. *Murlin in 1758, but J. *Crook in 1775 made greater impact, instituting the Manx Conference and personally examining all candidates for *local preaching. JW visited in 1777 and when refused the church at Peel preached on the beach. In 1781 he was very impressed by the 22 preachers he met and by the Manx singing, but not by the Manx language. A Manx hymnbook was not published until 1799. George Holder (1788–90, 1792–97 and 1806) contributed much to Manx Methodism. Despite initial opposition membership grew rapidly; by the turn of the century there were more members in the Island than in London, rising to 3,500 by 1834.

John Butcher introduced PM in 1822, establishing 18 preaching places in two years. Both branches of Methodism became firmly rooted in Manx society. An MNC Home Mission station was formed in 1886. The work prospered mainly in Douglas and Ramsey and survived until about the early 1920s.

At the time of the 1851 *Religious Census there were 59 WM and 26 PM chapels, with one WR meeting house. The total attendances during Census Sunday were 14,376.

Methodism strongly influenced Manx social and political life. In the early twentieth century 14 out of 24 members of the House of Keys were Methodist, 12 of them *local preachers.

MR(W) 1895 pp. 17–23; 1896 pp. 24–8, 1901 pp. 33–6, 1905 pp. 75–7

FC

Islington JW and CW preached in the old St Mary's parish church 1738–42, during the incumbency of the Rev. G. *Stonehouse. It was the scene of one of the most concentrated evangelical efforts of early Methodism, until protests by the Vestry brought it to an end. JW continued to minister in Islington and Finsbury from the *Foundery and *Wesley's Chapel. The New Wells, near to Sadler's Wells, was a Methodist 'Tabernacle' from 1752 to 1756 and JW preached there in 1754. He frequently retreated to 25 Highbury Place, home of J. *Horton, a drysalter and member of the Common Council of London, dining there for the last time on 22 February 1791, a few days before he died. In 1821 Wesley's Chapel hired a butcher's shop in White Lion Street and established a Sunday School which evolved into the Liverpool Road WM Chapel (1826). Sir F. *Lycett and S.D. ('Judge') *Waddy were members there and notable ministers included J.H. *Rigg, W.M. *Punshon and L.H. *Wiseman. The church closed in 1930 and the society joined with Drayton Park to become Islington Central Hall under the ministry of D.O. *Soper, who held open-air meetings in Highbury Fields. The congregation moved to St Albans Place in 1953 and then in 1963 to Palmers Place as Islington Central Methodist Church.

There were *Calvinistic Methodist chapels in Providence Place and Gaskin Street. The first two ministers of Union Chapel in Compton Terrace (1806) were former Methodists who became Congregationalists. In Cross Street from 1860 to 1866 a WM Missionary College founded by Dr Andrew Kessen taught Tamil and other languages to a dozen students from *Richmond College preparing for work in India and Ceylon. The headquarters of *NCH Action for Children is at 85 Highbury Park.

WHS(LHC) 26 (1982) and 36 (1987)

NM

Italy   In 1861 W. *Arthur persuaded the WM Conference to send two missionaries to Italy to support work begun in Florence by a convert from Roman Catholicism, Bartholomeo Gualtieri. H.J. *Piggott spent 40 years there. A former priest, Benedetto Lissolo, was accepted for the ministry. The work was centred on Milan, Padua and Florence, and following the siege of Rome the first Methodist service in Rome was held on Easter Day, 1871. The degree of religious freedom enjoyed under Pope Pius IX diminished under his successor Leo XIII (1878–1903) and still further under Fascist rule, following the Concordat of 1929. The Mission launched by American Methodism in 1873, with its emphasis on educational institutions, suffered more than the British-based work. British and American work was united in 1946 to form the Chiesa Evangelica Metodista d'Italia, which remained a District within British Methodism until becoming an autonomous Conference in 1962. Ministers were trained at the Waldensian Seminary and in 1979 Italian Methodism entered into a covenant union with the Waldensian Church. The Casa Materna chidren's home in Naples has received much support from British Methodism. In 1997 the Chiesa Evangelica Metodista reported 3,700 members and a total community of 6,500.

W.P. Stephens (n.d.); R. Kissack (1960)

SJP

Itinerancy   The earliest Methodist preachers employed by JW were itinerant in a double sense: (a) because he moved them from one area to another at frequent intervals (in the early days at least annually) and (b) because he insisted that they travel round their *circuit on a regular basis, spending only a limited time in the 'circuit town'. The itinerant system made for flexible deployment at the expense of continuity of ministry and strengthened the *'connexional' element. It survived, both in Wesleyanism and in other branches, though in increasingly modified form and with exceptions such as appointments to connexional office or to the urban missions of the *Forward Movement. Preachers are still stationed by the *Conference through the *Stationing Committee and the circuit *preaching plan reflects the fact that, at least in theory, they are appointed to a

circuit rather than to an individual pastorate.

NH, 1,294–8; *HMGB* (1965) 1, 232–4; H. Rack (1989) pp. 243–5

JAV

Ivory Coast *see* **Côte d'Ivoire**

Jackson, George (1864–1945; e.m. 1887), born in Grimsby, was sent to *Edinburgh in 1888 to evangelize new suburbs. His modern outlook coupled with loyalty to the gospel drew widespread support for building the Central Hall. In 1906 he went to a Toronto circuit, where he encountered fundamentalist hostility for accepting scientific evidence of the creation of the universe and man. He later taught at Toronto University. His Fernley Lecture, *The Preacher and the Modern Mind* (1912), aroused opposition in the Conference to his appointment to *Didsbury College, where he was as Tutor in Pastoral Theology, 1913–16 and in English Literature, 1919–28. He was Free Church correspondent of the *Manchester Guardian* and regularly contributed 'A Parson's Log' to the *Methodist Recorder*.

MR 19 April 1945, 27 June 1963; A. Jackson (1949); D.W. Bebbington in W.J. Shiels (1984) pp. 421–33

MB

Jackson, George Basil (1898–1973; e.m. 1922), son of G. Jackson, was a missionary in Ceylon (now *Sri Lanka) 1926–66. He was Principal of the training college for Sinhala-speaking teachers at Peradeniya, 1928–41, and Chairman of the S. Ceylon District, 1942–43 and 1945–50. As founder and first Director of the National Christian Council's Study Centre in Colombo (renamed The Ecumenical Institute for Study and Dialogue in 1977) he published a monthly commentary on social and political affairs. In 1963 he became first Principal of the Theological College of Lanka, the first Protestant institute to provide training in Sinhala and Tamil.

MR 3 May 1973, 27 May 1999

EJH

Jackson, John, RA (1778–1831), Methodist artist, born at Lastingham, N. Yorks. He was early influenced by Joshua Reynolds' painting and worked as a miniaturist in *York. He was painting in London by 1804, when he first exhibited at the RA. He became a prolific and successful society portraitist and produced likenesses of leading Methodists from 1813 for the

WM *Magazine*. His well-known but unsatisfactory synthesized image of JW was painted in 1827 and was followed by portraits of J. *Fletcher and others. John Constable paid tribute to his Christian qualities.

―――――

H. Honour in *Connoisseurs' Year Book* 1957 pp. 91–5; *PWHS* 3 pp. 190–1; 47 pp. 191–2

PSF

Jackson, Samuel (1786–1861; e.m. 1806), younger brother of the WM minister T. *Jackson, became a leading advocate of popular *education. The WM Conference of 1833 considered proposals for week-day schools in association with local churches, and in 1836 Jackson with two others was asked to report on both Sunday and day school work. Their findings led to the formation of the WM *Education Committee in 1839. He was President of the 1847 Conference and house governor of *Richmond College, 1848–55. In the Church controversies of his day he was an anti-reformist.

WDH

Jackson, Thomas (1783–1873; e.m. 1804), WM minister and historian, son of a farm labourer at Sancton, Yorks. With little formal education he became a distinguished scholar, serving as *Connexional Editor (1824–37 and 1839–41) and tutor at *Richmond College (1842–61). He was President of the Conference in 1838 and 1849. He was an able apologist for Methodism against the High Anglican attacks of E.B. *Pusey and others. His most significant publications were *The Centenary of Wesleyan Methodism* (1839), a life of CW (1841) and editions of JW's *Works* (1829–31), CW's *Journal* (1849) and the *Lives of the Early Methodist Preachers* (1837–8; 3rd edition, enlarged, 1865–6). He also wrote lives of R. *Watson and R. *Newton. His *Recollections of My Own Life and Times* (1873) is a rich quarry for students of nineteenth-century Methodism.

―――――

G.J. Stevenson (1884–6) 2 pp. 272–85; E.G. Rupp (1954)

JAN

Jackson, Thomas (1850–1932; e.m. 1876), PM minister, was born in Belper. He was sent to Bethnal Green in 1876 and served in London's East End for the next 56 years. In 1896 he bought the Home for Working Boys next to Whitechapel station and began the Whitechapel Mission in Brunswick Hall opposite. He offered a home and educational help to many boys, especially first offenders. He founded the Garment Workers' Union to combat sweated labour in Whitechapel and was President of the PM Conference in 1912.

W. Potter (1929); R.C. Gibbins (1995)

JDB

Jackson, William Christopher (1874–1944; e.m. 1898), UMFC minister, quickly established himself not only as an outstanding preacher, but as a church statesman. He was Chapel Secretary from 1919 to 1932. His gentlemanly courtesy as an administrator served the Church in good stead during the Union negotiations. He was the last UM President and President of the Methodist Conference in 1935.

OAB

Jaco, Peter (1729–1781; e.m. 1754), a Cornishman who made his first acquaintance with JW when he helped to protest him from a mob near *Penzance. Some months later, under Methodist influence, he found pardon at a communion service. JW encouraged him to preach in 1751 and the 1754 Conference made him a full-time itinerant. He continued to travel until 1779. He experienced considerable mob violence in various circuits and was forcibly taken for a soldier near *Truro but later released by the magistrate.

―――――

C. Atmore (1801) pp. 215–17; *EMP* 1 pp. 260–8

HMG

James, Francis Bertram (1882–1968; e.m. 1906), WM minister, whose older brother **Walter James** (1878–1908; e.m. 1904) was also in the ministry. (His book of prayers, *The Unveiled Heart* (1909), was published just after his early death). Francis was trained at *Handsworth College. Recognized as an expert on worship and spirituality, he contributed to the volume of broadcast talks on *How Christians Worship* (1942) and wrote *The Way of Prayer* (1952). The devotional series 'For the Quiet Hour' in the *Methodist Recorder* was begun in 1933 by W.R. *Maltby, but soon taken over by James, who sustained it at a high level for over 30 years. Both his son **David W. James** (1913–97; e.m. 1935) and his daughter **Margaret James** (1920–), headmistress of Kent College, Pembury (1966–83), served as missionaries in *India.

―――――

MR 8 Oct. 1908, 19 Sept. 1968, 7 Aug. 1997; D.W. James (1982); F.B. James (1991)

JAV

Jeffery, Frederick, OBE (1914–1997) was born in *Sunderland and trained as a teacher at *Westminster College. Appointed to *Methodist College, Belfast in 1937, he became Vice-Principal in 1966. An effective *local preacher, communicator and administrator, he was for many years Lay Secretary of the Church's Council on Social Welfare. He did much to promote emergency relief and world development. He was President of the *WHS (Irish Branch) 1974–93 and wrote much on historical topics. He was awarded the OBE in 1964 for services to education and youth welfare.

NWT

Jenkins, Dr Ebenezer E. (1820–1905; e.m. 1845), WM missionary in *India, born in South Wales of Methodist parents. He showed early intellectual promise. He served in India 1845–63, mainly in the Madras District, where he did educational and evangelistic work among the lower castes and established Royapettah College. Back home he spent 40 years advocating the missions and from 1877 was a General Secretary of the WMMS. He was President of the 1880 Conference and lived to be the oldest member of the *Legal Hundred.

G.J. Stevenson (1884–6) 4 pp. 497–507; *MR(W)* 1892 pp. 89–94; *MR* 20 July 1905

JAV

Jenkins, Isaac (1812–77; e.m. 1835), Welsh WM minister of Ystumtuen, born into one of the pioneer WM families of Cardiganshire, received a better education than most of his contemporaries and was trained at *Hoxton Theological Institution. He was appointed Assistant Secretary of the South Wales District Synod while still a probationer and throughout his ministry he held office continuously in that District, as Assistant Secretary, Secretary and Chairman. He was equally a fine preacher, scholar and writer, contributed erudite articles on biblical, historical and biographical subjects to *Yr Eurgrawn* (which he edited 1839–41 and 1857–59) and other journals, wrote elegies in Welsh on J. *Bunting and H. *Hughes (his father-in-law) and edited a memorial volume to the latter. He composed a hymn, still in use, on the *Witness of the Spirit and was chief editor of the 1845 Hymn-book.

W.I. Morgan (1976); *EW* 101 pp. 401–6; *DWB*

EHG

Jenkins, William (1763–1844; e.m. 1789) trained as an architect before entering the WM ministry. After ill health forced him to retire in 1810, he practised from Red Lion Square, London in partnership with a cousin and was involved in building a number of chapels in *London (including Kings Cross, Great Queen Street and Lambeth) and in the provinces (e.g. the Mint, *Exeter, Walcot, *Bath, Waltham Street, *Hull, St Peter's, *Canterbury and Carver Street, *Sheffield). His designs are carefully proportioned and often feature delicately detailed Classical porticos placed centrally on otherwise flat façades. His son and namesake was also an architect.

WMM 1844 p. 775; G.W. Dolbey (1964) pp. 177–8

BWB

Jessop, Dr Thomas Edmund, OBE, MC (1896–1980), UM and Methodist layman and *local preacher, Professor of Philosophy at Hull University. In addition to philosophical writings, he was an active apologist for the Christian faith, especially in booklets for the Forces during World War II. He was one of the Methodist representatives in the *Anglican-Methodist Conversations and was one of the signatories to the Minority Report. His acute critical and philosophical mind produced two trenchant analyses of the Scheme. He was Vice-President of the Conference in 1955. His books include *Law and Love: a study of the Christian ethic* (1940) and the A.S. Peake Lecture *On Reading the English Bible* (1958).

MR 7 July 1955, 2 Oct. 1980

OAB

JMA originally stood for 'Juvenile (from 1974 'Junior') Missionary Association', becoming 'Junior Mission for All' in 1991. Its purpose was to raise funds, stimulate interest and 'prepare children for future usefulness'. Local Juvenile Societies predated the formal constitution of the WMMS in 1818 and for 50 years Joseph Blake of Harrow promoted a scheme encouraging *Sunday School children to collect weekly contributions. Opposed by J. *Bunting, who feared lay control of Sunday Schools, the scheme was officially sanctioned in 1865. In 1903 medals embossed with the motto 'For Zeal for Christ' were first awarded to those collecting £5. A new medal was struck in 1976; the qualifying amount was increased to £10 in 1981 and abolished in 1991. From 1932 four-fifths of the income went overseas and one-fifth to home mission. Blake's monthly paper *Juvenile Offerings*, free to collectors, was superseded in 1879 by *At Home and Abroad* and in 1974 by the quarterly *Windows*, which eventually became *Rainbow*. The annual total raised through JMA reached almost £1 million in the 1980s, but declined with the number of Sunday School scholars.

See also **Sowton, Stanley**

JRP

Jobson, Frederick James, DD (1812–81; e.m. 1834), WM minister. Having served an architectural apprenticeship with Edward Willson of *Lincoln, his advocacy of Gothic, especially in his *Chapel and School Architecture* (1850) was a major influence on Methodist and Nonconformist building styles. He was also a persuasive missionary advocate and represented British Methodism at the MEC General Conference of 1856 (reported in his *America and American Methodism*, 1857) and at the Australian Conference in 1860. Succeeding J. *Mason as *Book Steward in 1864, he expanded Methodism's literary horizons and strengthened the Book Room's finances. He improved both the format and the circulation of the **WM Magazine* and was responsible in 1876 for the new Supplement to the *Hymn Book. He was elected President of the Conference in 1869.

MR 7 Jan. 1881; G.J.Stevenson (1884–6) 3 pp. 369–81; F.H. Cumbers (1956) pp. 98–9

JAV

John Finch Travelling Bursary Under the will of John Finch, a grocer from North Esher, Surrey, a bequest of £5,000 was left to charitable trustees, to be invested in order to fund foreign travel for Methodist ministers. Under its terms ministerial candidates, probationers and ministers were to be given grants to enable them to make educational visits abroad in order to enlarge their vision, amplify their knowledge and extend their experience, the purpose being that 'they may become better fitted to discharge their duties or future duties as Methodist Ministers'. The Fund is administered by three lay and two ordained trustees. Since the first meeting of the trust in 1945 some 192 ministers have received grants.

DARB

Johnson, Elizabeth (1808–60) PM itinerant. Though from a WM background, she was converted by PM preaching in *Shrewsbury, and quickly began to exhort, becoming an itinerant in 1824. Her first preaching appointment, at 16, was in a large foundry in South Wales. During her ministry she faced opposition from noisy musicians, 'drunks' and clergy. After marrying **W. Brownhill** of Darlaston in 1828, she became a *local preacher and class leader. Three of her seven sons became Mayors of Walsall.

PMM, 1861 pp. 206–8; Kendall (1906) vol. 2; E.D. Graham (1989) p. 15

EDG

Johnson, George Edward Hickman (1883–1966; e.m. 1906), WM missionary in *India, born in *Birmingham and trained at *Handsworth College. During his ministry in the Hyderabad District 1906–19, he laid particular emphasis on lay evangelists as key figures in the Mass Movements. Espousing Indian independence, he urged equal status for women and Christian emancipation of the lower castes. As Home Organization Secretary of the MMS from 1927 to 1948 he worked with his colleagues to transform the old *Mission House regime into a united family team.

MR 24 March 1966

JAV

Johnson, James (d.1864) a hatmaker, was sent by *Carlisle PM circuit in 1826 to evangelize *Glasgow. He soon enlisted volunteers to mission *Paisley, then moved to *Dundee in 1835 and remained there as pastor of the Peter Street congregation, labouring daily among the poor and outcast.

WHS(S), 2 pp. 4–6

MB

Johnson, John (1725–1803; e.m. 1755), a shoemaker, born in Somerset of RC parents, was converted in London through the preaching of G. *Whitefield. Received as an itinerant in 1758, he was appointed to *Ireland where he spent the remainder of his life. Highly regarded by JW, he had an uneven career. At one time General Superintendent of the Irish work, he became for a period the centre of some dissent and was disloyal to W. He retired early due to ill health and settled in Lisburn, where he continued as a *local preacher.

R.H. Gallagher (1965)

RPR

Johnson, Dr Robert Crawford (1841– 1914; e.m. 1865), Irish minister, born in Antrim and educated at *Wesley College, Dublin and

*Didsbury College. He was a key figure in initiating the *Belfast Central Mission, becoming its first Superintendent (1889–1905) and establishing its headquarters at the first Grosvenor Hall. He laid the foundation for the Mission's high-profile ministry, through open-air preaching, work with the needy and civic contacts. He became Secretary of the Irish Conference in 1893 and was Vice-President in 1898.

MR 9 April 1914; R.D.E. Gallagher (1989)

NWT

Johnson, Simpson (1852–1920; e.m. 1873), WM minister, was stationed for many years in the industrial areas of *Hull, *Manchester, *Liverpool and *Leeds, before joining the *HM Department in 1902. As *Secretary of the Conference and of the newly formed *London Committee from 1910, he initiated the *New London Movement. He was President of the 1917 Conference.

MR 26 Aug. 1920

JAV

Johnston, Edward (d.1858; e.m. 1809), Irish minister, born in Co. Tyrone. He responded to an appeal for preachers for *Canada and travelled out via New York in 1817. In *America he enjoyed friendly contacts with MEC preachers and this led him to question Canadian WM criticism of the American Methodists. Refusing to become embroiled in what he called 'a religious war', he returned to Ireland without Conference authority. Though severely censured by the WMMS, he was treated more leniently by the Irish Conference. His ministry highlights contemporary tensions on both sides of the Atlantic. His later offer to return to Canada was not accepted.

N.W. Taggart (1986) pp. 81–5

NWT

Jones, David Gwynfryn (1867–1954; e.m. 1894) was brought up in Cwm Rhondda and worked for years in coal mines. He began to preach at 17, but his entry into the WM ministry was repeatedly barred by ill-health. His ministry lasted 60 years, though for the sake of his health he was once sent to Cape Town and later left circuit work to edit various Welsh denominational publications. With little formal education, he demonstrated outstanding ability, culture and breadth of interests. He was Chairman of the First North Wales District, 1934–38, and President of the

Welsh Assembly in 1924. An orator of powerful intellect and fiery passion, he was equally at home in the pulpit and on the political platform. He began as a Liberal and an ardent friend and supporter of Lloyd George; but his pacifist stand during Word War I led him to the Labour Party. He helped to establish it in Flintshire and became President of the North Wales Labour Federation. He twice stood unsuccessfully for Parliament.

EW 147 pp. 31–3; 150 passim; *YBC3* (1997) p. 93

OEE

Jones, David Llewelyn (1898–1973; e.m. 1923), Welsh WM minister, born at Borth, Cardiganshire, was educated at University College, Aberystwyth and *Wesley House, Cambridge. He spent the whole of his ministry in the South Wales District and was its Chairman 1954–63. The outstanding quality of his preaching and his literary and linguistic criticism in both denominational and national periodicals, earned him both scholarly and popular acclaim throughout Wales. He was recognized as one of the most judicious book reviewers writing in Welsh and for many years worked as a reader for the ongoing *University Dictionary of the Welsh Language*. He edited *Yr Eurgrawn*, 1954–66, maintaining its high-standing reputation, and was President of the Welsh Assembly in 1952.

MR 13 Dec. 1973; *EW* 166, pp. 1,4–9

OEE

Jones, Edward (1778–1837; e.m. 1802), known as 'Edward Jones, Bathafarn', after the farmhouse in Ruthin in which he grew up. He had a good education at Ruthin Grammar School. Soon after entering the *Manchester cotton industry *c.* 1796, he underwent conversion and became a zealous WM. On his way home in 1799 for health and family reasons, he called on the *Chester circuit to send preachers to Ruthin. He hired a room there in 1800, conducting prayer meetings to supplement the preachers' visits. When a society was formed, he himself began to preach in both languages. As a minister he furthered the Welsh mission in various parts of Wales. The curtailment of Conference funding of the Welsh work in 1816 led to his transfer to the English work for the rest of his ministry. He became a member of the *Legal Hundred in 1834. He has generally been regarded as the 'father of Welsh WM' and the integrity of his character left an indelible impression on Welsh Methodism. His gravestone was brought from

Leek in 1869 to the new Bathafarn Memorial Chapel in Ruthin.

D. Young (1893) pp. 388–412; A.H. Williams (1935) pp. 45–150, 283–6; *DWB*

IGPL

Jones, Rev. Griffith (1683–1761), sometimes called 'the morning star of the Methodist revival in *Wales', was born in Carmarthenshire of Nonconformist stock, but ordained into the Anglican priesthood in 1708. His brother-in-law Sir John Phillips presented him to the living of Llandowror in 1716. His preaching tours throughout South Wales, especially at the time of the Easter and Whitsuntide Wakes, made him the outstanding preacher of his day. One of his converts was D. *Rowland and H. *Harris held him in high regard. With the support of the SPCK he threw himself into organizing charity schools for both adults and children and raised funds to provide teachers of 'circulating schools', thus contributing both to increased literacy and to the spread of Methodism in Wales.

DNB; *DEB*; D. Jones (1902)

JAV

Jones, Sir Harold Spencer, FRS(1890–1960), Astronomer Royal. After a distinguished career at Cambridge, he was appointed to Greenwich in 1913 and to the Royal Observatory, Cape of Good Hope in 1923. He returned to Greenwich as Astronomer Royal in 1933 and initiated the move to Herstmonceux. His research on irregularities in the earth's rotation and the system of astronomical constants won him international recognition, including ten honorary doctorates and an honorary fellowship at Jesus College, Cambridge. In World War II he worked on ways of combatting magnetic mines. He was President of the International Astronomical Union, 1945–48. His other interests included horology and geomagnetism.

Biographical Memoirs of FRS, 7 (1961); DNB; *MR* 17 Nov. 1960

JAV

Jones, Dr Hugh (1837–1919; e.m. 1859), a leading figure in Welsh WM, was nurtured in the Caernarfon society. Beginning his probation as Chairman's Assistant under T. *Aubrey, his exceptional preaching, writing and organizing gifts soon marked him out as the latter's natural heir. He became Chairman of the North Wales

District in 1893 and, after its division, of the Second N. Wales District 1903–11. He was President of the Welsh Assembly in 1901 and a member of the *Legal Hundred from 1893. A staunch Free Churchman and an outspoken Liberal in politics, he was active in many moral, social, educational, legal and political issues. Despite this, his literary output was phenomenal, including the four volumes of *Hanes Wesleyaeth Gymreig* (1911–13), a comprehensive history of Welsh WM, a biography of S. *Davies the Second (1904) and a lecture on Welsh Nonconformity (1898). He edited the 1904 collection of Welsh WM hymns and tunes and was editor of *Yr Eurgrawn* 1902–11. He received an honorary DD from Kansas City University (1902) and at the Golden Jubilee of his ministry in 1909 was honoured by the Welsh Assembly.

O.M. Roberts (1934); *EW* 111 pp. 241–57, 126 pp. 125–27; *DWB*

EHG

Jones, Humphrey Rowland (1832–95), Welsh revivalist, known as 'Humphrey Jones Tre'rddol' after the village in whose WM chapel he was nurtured. He became a *local preacher while working as a farm labourer and witnessed many conversions. In 1854, when Welsh WM was not accepting candidates for the ministry for financial reasons, he joined his family in Wisconsin and preached to scattered Welsh congregations there. Accepted for the MEC ministry in 1855, he resigned in 1856, feeling too restricted, and became a peripatetic preacher among his fellow expatriates. He 'caught fire' in a New York revival and became 'Humphrey Jones, Y Diwygiwr' ('The Revivalist') in the Welsh-speaking churches. In 1858 he returned to Tre'rddol, convinced that he was called to bring the Revival to Wales by following the example of the revivalists Charles G. Finney and Jeremiah C. Lanphier. Some 100,000 converts were added to the churches at Tre'rddol and other places. But he had to withdraw at Aberystwyth under the mental strain and eventually entered a mental hospital. He was later taken back to Wisconsin, where he recovered only to relapse from time to time.

E. Isaac (1930); E. Evans (1980); R.G. Gruffydd (1959); *DWB*

EHG

Jones, James (d. 1783), a native of Tipton, Staffs, who was one of JW's earliest converts in the West Midlands. Though he became an itinerant for a time in the Staffordshire Circuit and endured fierce persecution at Wednesbury, his talents as a preacher were limited. He married and settled near *Birmingham, continuing to preach occasionally. A man of considerable property, he built the first chapel at Tipton Green at his own expense.

See also **Black Country**

C. Atmore (1801) p. 225; W.C. Sheldon (1903) p. 8

JAV

Jones, Rev. John (*c.* 1711–1785), one of JW's most able and loyal early associates, graduated from Trinity College, Oxford 1739 and obtained a medical degree in 1745. While teaching in *Wales he made the acquaintance of H. *Harris and was caught up in the Welsh revival. Failing to get himself ordained, in 1746 he offered his services to JW, who used him intensively in *London 1746–48, then as 'first master' at *Kingswood School when it opened in 1848. Having served there through its difficult opening years, in 1752 he became W's *Assistant in the *Bristol and Cornwall Circuits, then in the London Circuit as a curb to T. *Maxfield 1758–67. The Countess of *Huntingdon failed to obtain a living and Anglican orders for him, but in 1764 he was ordained by Bishop *Erasmus. For health reasons he left Methodism at the end of 1769, was ordained by the Bishop of London and became curate and, by 1780, vicar of Harwich. He remained on terms of warm friendship with both CW and JW, though the latter clearly regretted his 'defection'.

C. Atmore (1801) p. 224; A.B. Sackett (1972)

JAV

Jones, John Roger (1879–1974; e.m. 1906), outstanding Welsh WM minister from Conwy, was the first to graduate at University College Bangor with Class I honours in Philosophy before training at *Didsbury College. Most of his long ministry was spent in the First North Wales District, but his reputation as a preacher of phenomenal physical, intellectual and oratorical power spread throughout Wales and also into England and *Ireland. A voracious student with an incisive analytical intellect and encyclopaedic memory, able to communicate lucidly, convincingly and inspiringly, he could have filled a university chair in philosophy or theology, but chose to remain a circuit preacher, combined with lecturing to extra-mural and WEA classes and broadcasting. His preferred medium of communication was the

spoken rather than the written word, though he did publish occasional articles, a volume of sermons (1963) and a commentary on Matthew (1937–38). He was President of the Welsh Assembly in 1948, remained in the active ministry until his 80th year and preached regularly to within a week of his death at 94.

EW 166 passim

EHG

Jones, Robert (1706–42), a fellow student of CW's at Christ Church, Oxford, was born at Fonmon Castle, Glam., the family home. He became a local magistrate. Greatly impressed by the preaching of H. *Harris, he set up the dining-room at the Castle as a chapel with a pulpit for use by Methodist preachers, including the Wesleys. He and his wife Mary (*née* Forrest, of Minehead, d.1788) became Methodists in 1741 and after his sudden death his widow continued to entertain the preachers at Ffontygari Farm and gave herself to various charitable works.

DWB; E.A.Morgan in *Bathafarn* 9 (1954) pp. 38–41

WL

Jones, Thomas (1785–1864), early IM leader in *Liverpool, was expelled from the *Welsh WM society in 1818 for his objections to the use of the Poor Fund and the payment of ministers. He founded an IM church on the basis of the equality of all members and an unpaid ministry and was President of the IM Connexion 1834–35. At his own expense he sent missionaries into Wales to establish churches and as a result the Minor Wesleyans (*Wesle Bach) movement joined the IM for a time. The Liverpool church seceded in 1838 and joined the *WMA and Jones served for a time on the WMA Connexional Committee.

UMFC Magazine 1866 p. 634

JAD

Jones, Dr Thomas (1802–91; e.m. 1828), born at Mydreilun, Cardiganshire, a preacher of great power and eloquence. He became the acknowledged leader of Welsh WM in South Wales in the mid-nineteenth century, being Chairman of that District 1846–66. He initiated and was first editor (1848–49) of *Y Winllan* and edited *Yr Eurgrawn*, 1836–39 and 1857–59. In 1839 he published a volume in Welsh to celebrate the centenary of WM and in 1866 received an honorary DD from the University of Lawrence, Wisconsin.

EW 83 pp. 347–9; 101 pp. 12–91

OEE

Jordan, Sir William Joseph, PC, KCMG (1879–1959), born in Ramsgate, the son of a lifeboatman, was apprenticed as a coach painter, but then joined the Metropolitan Police Force. He became a PM *local preacher at an early age and remained an active churchman. Emigrating to *New Zealand in 1904, he became a trader in Waihi and Secretary of the New Zealand Labour Party when it was formed in 1907. He was wounded during service in France in World War I, entered the New Zealand Parliament in 1922 and became President of the Labour Party. From 1936 to 1951 he was High Commissioner in London, representing New Zealand at many international conferences and at the 1946 Paris Peace Conference. He was President of the League of Nations Council in 1938. On retirement he was knighted and returned to live in Auckland.

B.J. Foster in *An Encyclopedia of New Zealand* (Wellington 1966)

DJP

***Journal* of John Wesley** Unlike his *diaries, JW's Journal was deliberately written for publication. During his time in Georgia, he had sent back a number of reports in the form of 'Journal-letters', but the first of the 21 printed 'Extracts' from his Journal, covering that period, was not published until the early summer of 1740 and was a response to charges brought against him by Capt Robert Williams. The second Extract, covering the period of his Aldersgate Street experience and visit to the *Moravian settlement at Herrnhut, appeared later in 1740. In the fourth (published in 1744) he distanced himself from the Moravians and recorded his breach with the *Calvinists. In each case the polemical motivation was close to the surface. Further instalments were published on average every three years during the rest of his lifetime, the 21st being brought out by his executors very soon after his death. The Journal offers a picture of eighteenth century England that reflects JW's extensive travels throughout the British Isles and reveals such diverse aspects of his character as the extent to which he was influenced by the Enlightenment and his residual superstition (e.g. his belief in special providence). More importantly, it chronicles the development of that segment of the evangelical revival associated with him, but viewed through the eyes of one man and with the advantage of hindsight, and was one means by which he maintained remote control over the growing Connexion. Because of the time-lag between events and the compilation of the Journal, W's memory sometimes failed him or was coloured by hindsight. The record was understandably selective; damaging or sensitive topics (e.g. the Grace *Murray affair, his subsequent marriage, and the 1784 *ordinations) were omitted or played down. Versions of the Journal appeared in W's collected *Works*, including Jackson's edition. The latter presented a better text than *Curnock's 'Standard Edition', though lacking Curnock's editorial apparatus. The latest edition is that of W.R. *Ward in the Bicentenary Edition of Wesley's *Works* (1988–99).

R. Lee Cole (1938); W.R. Ward, WJW 18 (1988) pp. 37–104

JAV

Joyce, Matthias (1754–1814; e.m. 1783), Irish itinerant, brought up a Roman Catholic in *Dublin, was apprenticed to a printer and bookseller. His career in the printing business was troubled by a fiery temper and frequent changes of employment in both Dublin and England. Impressed by JW on his 1773 visit to Dublin, he began an erratic spiritual journey marked by a self-doubt which continued beyond his conversion to Methodism and first appointment as an itinerant in 1783. But he became an effective preacher and from 1795 to 1806 was the first *Book Steward of the Irish Conference.

R.H. Gallagher (1965)

RPR

Joyful News , a newspaper begun in 1883 by T. *Champness to encourage revivalism: 'a Sunday paper for Smockfrock and Co.' The profits were used to train evangelists for the 'Joyful News Mission', especially for the villages. Mrs Champness did the editorial work and on his retirement it was taken over by S. *Chadwick and W. Hammond Heap, his successors at *Cliff College. Originally full of reports from missions all over the country, by 1910 it had become more theological. It was taken over by the *Methodist Recorder* in 1955.

MR(W) 1894 pp. 49–56; J. Brice (1934)

JHL

Jukes, Richard (1804–67; e.m. 1825), PM itinerant and hymn writer. Born in the Clun valley, the son of a stonemason, he worked in that craft when young. When PM came into the valley in 1825, he became a *local preacher and was soon enlisted as an itinerant, serving in Midland and southern circuits until 1859. His native love of poetry and music was applied fully in his ministry and he published many hymns and songs of his own composition, becoming known as 'the bard of the poor'. These sold in large numbers, but very few were used in connexional hymn-books. One of his hymns is *MHB* 403, 'My heart is fixed, eternal God'. He helped in the production of the *PM Revival Hymn-book*.

A. Wilkes & J. Lovatt (1942) pp. 87–94
                                                                                          GEM

July Committee, the connexional committee for examining *candidates for the ministry, originally held in July and for long called by that name, even when meeting earlier. The committee now meets in April.
                                                                                          BEB

Justification, defined by JW simply as 'forgiveness', together with *sanctification links Methodism with classical Reformation doctrine. 'Justification is what God does for us through his son,' whilst sanctification is what 'God works in us by his Spirit'. It is 'to be pardoned and received into God's favour; into such a state that, if we continue therein, we shall be finally saved.' *Faith is the sole necessary condition of this justification: it does not depend on any human merit. God has responded through the sacrifice of his Son to our creaturely alienation, offering the pardon which reconciles us to him and restoring us in *holiness. This is realisable through penitence and faith in the universal atonement of Christ. Former sins are pardoned, *regeneration is begun and the sinner is freed from condemnation 'because the Son of his love hath suffered for him'. Perhaps not surprisingly, given his stress upon holiness, JW seems to have toyed with the idea of 'double justification', i.e. a present acceptance and forgiveness and a 'final justification' which includes being 'perfected in love'.
See also **Christian Perfection**

J. Wesley, sermon on 'Justification by Faith'; *Minutes* 1744; W.R. Cannon (1946); J.W. Deschner (1960) pp. 181–96; R.L. Maddox (1994), pp. 166–72
                                                                                          WP

Kay, Dr James Alan (1904–62; e.m. 1930), born in *Southport, read English at Downing College, Cambridge, where he was one of the founder members of the *'Cambridge Group'. He trained at *Wesley House and was chaplain at *Westminster College 1931–34. After five years in the *HM Department and fourteen years in Circuit work, he became *Connexional Editor in 1953, serving with distinction. As an accomplished musician with a fine singing voice, he played a leading part in the *MCMS. His PhD thesis (Edinburgh) was on the arts and Christian worship. He wrote *The Nature of Christian Worship* (1953) and edited an anthology of CW's 'prayers and praises' (1958).

MR 30 Aug. & 6 Sept. 1962
                                                                                          JAV

Kay, William Whittle, MD (1896–1980) was born in *Bolton, but spent most of his life in the south of England. A consultant pathologist by profession, he became an *IM minister who represented the denomination nationally and promoted its involvement in the wider Church. He was Moderator of the FCFC 1960–61, President of the National Sunday School Union 1961–62 and of the IM Connexion 1962–63 and 1965–66, and Vice-Chairman of the British Lessons Council. He was joint editor of the *IM Magazine* 1963–70 and one of the compilers of the new IM Hymnal (1974).

IM Magazine April 1980
                                                                                          JAD

Kedward, Roderick Morris (1881–1937; e.m. 1903) was born at Westwell, Kent. He was sent to Worcester Gaol for causing an obstruction during street services. After training at *Richmond College he became a Home Mission Connexional Evangelist. He had a successful ministry at King's Hall, *Hull, before going to the South London Mission in 1916 and becoming Superintendent two years later. He was elected MP for Bermondsey West (1923) and for Ashford, Kent (1929–31).

MR 11 March 1937; J.D. Beasley (1989)
                                                                                          JDB

Keeble, Samuel Edward (1853–1946; e.m. 1878) WM minister, born in London and converted at *Wesley's Chapel, was also author, Christian Socialist and pacifist. As early as 1889 he mastered Marx's *Das Kapital*, appreciating both its strengths and weaknesses. His first book *Industrial Daydreams* (1896) controversially proclaimed that 'a purified Socialism is simply an industrially applied Christianity'. During the Anglo-Boer War he successfully opposed a dinner invitation to Joseph Chamberlain at *Wesley's Chapel. He founded the *Methodist Weekly*, the WM *Union for Social Service (1905) and the WM Peace Fellowship (1916). His books influenced P. *Snowden towards Socialism. He gave the *Fernley Lecture on *Christian Responsibility for the Social Order* (1922) and the first *Beckly Lecture in 1926. He chaired the International and Industrial sub-committee of the WM Temperance and Social Welfare Committee, 1922–32, attended COPEC in 1924 and served on the resulting Christian Social Council. His Conference obituary proclaimed him 'a major prophet within our church'.

MR 12 Sept. 1946; M.L. Edwards (1949); M.S. Edwards (1977)

MSE

Keen, Samuel (1818–71; e.m. 1848), BC missionary, born in South Molton. Coming under BC influence when about 20, he became a *local preacher in the villages around Bideford. After some months at *Shebbear College, he was ordained in 1852 and offered to go to Australia. He and his wife Sarah (née Ingerson) arrived in Port Adelaide in March 1853 and were sent to Gawler. During two terms on Gawler Plain, riding from farm to farm seeking a verdict for Christ, he started 15 congregations and built more than a dozen chapels. It became known as the most Methodist area in the colony.

DGH

Keene Family **Arthur Keene** (d.1818) and two bothers came to *Dublin from England as working goldsmiths. His marriage to Isabella Martin at St. Bride's Church, Dublin in April 1775 is the only wedding JW is known to have conducted in Ireland. He was a steward of the Dublin society and W's letters to him reveal warm friendship. They indicate his importance in connection with the Whitefriar Street School and the Widows' Almshouse. He quarrelled with W over the times of Methodist services and the administration of the Sacrament and declined to meet him on his last visit to Ireland. His sons **Martin Keene** (d.1846) and **James Keene** (d.1872) were members of the committee which drafted the *PWM Constitution in 1818. Martin was King's Printer in Ireland and a founding member of the

Hibernian Sunday School Society (1809) and his grandsons, **Charles H. Keene** (d.1915) and **James B. Keene** (d.1919) were respectively the first Professor of Greek in University College, Cork and Bishop of Meath.

SL vols 6–8 passim; D.A.L. Cooney in *DHR* Spring 1995

DALC

Keig, Thomas (1829–96), PM *local preacher who became the first Mayor of Douglas, *IOM and died during his year of office. Becoming involved in Town affairs in 1874, he was chairman of the Town Commissioners on five occasions. His considerable engineering skills were used for both Town and Church and he designed and supervised the building of Lock Parade PM Church. He founded a photographic business still in existence in 1997.

FC

Keighley *see* **Haworth Round**

Kellett, Ernest Edward (1864–1950), WM schoolmaster and author, educated at *Kingswood School and Wadham College, Oxford, where he graduated in both Maths and Classics, 1st Class. He brought his deep and wide scholarship to his teaching at The *Leys School, 1889–1924, where he was also a housemaster. His *Musa Leysiana* (two volumes, 1901 and 1904) reflects his affection for the school. He was a prolific author on a wide range of topics, mainly literary and historical, such as *Religion and Life in the Early Victorian Age* (1938). His light verse appeared in *Punch* and other periodicals and his linguistic skills were evidenced by several works of translation. His *As I Remember* (1936) draws on personal reminiscences of his early years.

GEM

Kelly, Charles Henry (1833–1911; e.m. 1857), WM *Book Steward from 1899 to 1907. During this time the name of the Book Steward was introduced as an imprint, a practice discontinued in 1948. He was President of the Conference in 1889 and again in 1905. His *Memories* (1910) throw interesting light on the introduction of lay representation in the WM Conference. As Secretary of the WM *Sunday School Union he co-operated with W.B. *Fitzgerald in forming the *Wesley Guild. In retirement he was a regular visitor at Wandsworth Prison.

MR 13 April 1911; F.H. Cumbers (1956) p. 99

EWD

Kendall, Holliday Bickerstaffe (1844–1919; e.m. 1868), PM minister and connexional historian, one of five sons of **Charles Kendall** (1818–82; e.m. 1839; President of the Conference, 1881) who all served in the PM ministry. He began to preach when a boy and entered the ministry at 19, serving in north-eastern circuits. He obtained an external degree at Durham and, following a breakdown in the mid-1880s, taught at a private theological college near *Leeds. As *Connexional Editor from 1892 to 1901 he renamed the PM monthly and quarterly periodicals *The Aldersgate* and the *Holborn Review* respectively. His *History of the PM Connexion* (1889) was revised and enlarged in 1902 and substantially rewritten in 1919 as the *History of the PM Church*. His *magnum opus*, the two-volume illustrated *Origin and History of the PM Church* (1906) appeared first in monthly parts. The largest work ever produced by the PM Book Room, it immediately became the authoritative account of PM history, especially for the earlier decades of the movement.

PMM 1900 pp. 723–4; G.E. Milburn in *PWHS* 50 pp. 108–12

GEM

Kendall, Richard Elliott (1915–92; e.m. 1939), missionary in *China and Africa. After training at *Handsworth College, he began his ministry among the Miao people in South West China in 1939, during the Sino-Japanese War. He was eventually deported by the Communist regime in 1951, but only after gaining the release of a colleague charged with espionage. From 1957 to 1967 he served in post-Mau Mau *Kenya, was the last Chairman of the Kenya District and played a key role in the preparations for autonomy. Back in England he worked for the Conference of British Missionary Societies and as Director of the BCC Community and Race Relations Unit. He advocated the WCC's controversial Programme to Combat Racism and in retirement worked for the abolition of Apartheid in *South Africa. He sought to persuade the British Churches to take ethical investment seriously. He wrote several books on China, Africa and race relations and his *End of an Era* (1978) was a prophetic work on mission in Africa.

MR 15 & 22 Nov. 1992

JRP/GRS

Kendrick, John (1779–1813), a Sergeant in the Light Dragoons, born in Wokingham (Berks),

was converted by G. *Morley. While stationed in Cape Town in 1806 he helped establish a society on the strict Methodist pattern, which flourished despite official disapproval and the regimental officers' fear of 'enthusiasm' in the ranks. Letters requesting a missionary were sent to England. Although J. *McKenny was appointed in 1814, the mission was not effectively founded until the arrival of B. *Shaw in 1816. Meanwhile Kendrick had died in November 1813.

MJF

Kent, Dr John Henry Somerset (1923– ; e.m. 1950), Methodist historian, son of the PM minister **Walter Harold Kent** (1889–1951; e.m. 1916), was educated at Emmanuel College, where he gained a 1st Class in the Historical Tripos, and *Wesley House, Cambridge. In 1950 he was awarded a PhD for his thesis on 'The clash between radicalism and conservatism in Methodism, 1815–1848'. During his first year as assistant tutor at *Headingley College (1951–53), he was President's Assistant to Dr H. *Watkin-Jones. He taught History at Emmanuel College, Cambridge 1955–59 and Church History and English at *Hartley Victoria College 1959–65; and from 1965 to 1988 he was successively Lecturer, Reader and Professor of Ecclesiastical History and Doctrine in the University of Bristol. He was British Editor of the *Encyclopedia of World Methodism* (1974). His published works, which include *Jabez Bunting, the Last Wesleyan* (WHS Lecture 1955), *The Age of Disunity* (1966) and *Holding the Fort: Studies in Victorian Revivalism* (1978), are consistently marked by a keen and incisive intelligence, an impatience with shibboleths, and a readiness to question received wisdom.

JAN

Kent College, *Canterbury, was founded in 1885 by the Kent Methodist Schools Association as a 'middle class school' for boys and was taken over by the *Board of Management in 1920. It gradually built up a strong academic and sporting reputation, enabling it to compete with Kent's grammar schools. C.W. *Posnett was a pupil teacher 1888–92 under the headmastership of his elder brother Leonard W. Posnett. The England wicket keeper Godfrey Evans was a pupil there and the musicologist Dr Percy A. Scholes was on the staff 1900–1903. An extensive building programme in the 1980s was facilitated by the sale of property bought privately by the former headmaster J. *Prickett. Girls were first admitted in 1973. The school reverted to full independence in 1976 following the withdrawal of the government's Direct Grant regulations. In 1997 there were 709 boarding and day boys and girls from nursery age to 18.

C. Wright (1985)

DBT

Kent College, Pembury, was founded in Folkestone in 1886 by the Kent WM Schools Association for training girls 'for home and business life, and for further study at university based on broad religious principles'. A government inspection in 1933 resulted in the school's staying open in the afternoons. It moved to its present site in 1939 and was taken over by the *Board of Management in 1942. A sustained building programme beginning in the 1950s led to increased numbers and improved academic standards. In 1997 there were 417 boarding and day girls from nursery age to 18.

M. James (1986)

DBT

Kenya   The UMFC mission, inspired by the travels of a German missionary, J.L. Krapf, began with the arrival of T. *Wakefield in 1862 and was concentrated for fifty years around Mombasa and its hinterland. Then J.B. Griffiths and R.T. *Worthington, together with Kenyan Christians from the coast, pioneered work in the foothills of Mount Kenya with increasing results among the Meru people. A hospital was opened at Maua in 1930. Since autonomy in 1966, there has been new evangelistic enterprise in the fast growing capital Nairobi, among the Maasai people and also in Tanzania and Uganda. Church Union negotiations in the 1960s foundered but ecumenical ministerial training was instituted at St Paul's Theological College, Limuru. The Kenya Methodist University near Meru, fruit of a long educational tradition, also provides training through its theological institution.

Z.J. Nthamburi (1982)

JRP

Kerr, George McGlasham, K-i-H (1874–1950; e.m. 1899), served in *Rhodesia 1901–1904. In 1907 he and his wife Dr **Isabel Kerr, K-i-H** (*née* Gunn (1875–1932)) went to Nizamabad in the Hyderabad District, *India, where she realised the need for long-term care and treatment of leprosy patients. This led to the founding of the Victoria Leprosy Hospital at Dichpalli, where she served in an honorary

capacity until her death. She was held in high honour for her vision, medical skill and the great advancement in treatment as more effective drugs were introduced. Her husband proved adept at dealing with government bureaucracy.

MR 29 Dec. 1932, 11 May 1950

EMJ

Kerridge, Jessie, MBE (1902–), co-founder of the *Deaconess Order in the *West Indies. Born in *Cambridge, she trained first as a teacher and then as a deaconess. In 1927 she and Muriel Ellis (who had grown up in Trinidad) answered a call for two deaconesses to work in Jamaica. They established Deaconess House and through both the *Girls' League and the Guide Movement began training women for leadership. In 1938 she recommended the establishment of Deaconess Houses in all the Caribbean islands. She became a member of staff at Caenwood Theological College, where West Indian deaconesses were trained alongside ministerial candidates.

B. Baynes (1995)

PMW

Kershaw, James (1730-1797), one of JW's first itinerants, converted by H. *Venn. He accompanied JW on some of his journeys, then withdrew for some years. After finally retiring, he lived at *Gainsborough and became a vendor of medicines, described as riding through the countryside 'in his own vehicle, preaching in the villages and giving medical advice to the labouring classes, thus manifesting a laudable concern both for the bodies and souls of the people'. He was gifted as a preacher and writer, but Atmore's judgment was that his unstable character limited his usefulness. He published a reply to the preface written by Dr John Erskine for the republication of J. *Hervey's *Eleven Letters* to JW. His poem *The Methodist; attempted in Plain Metre* (1780), a sort of Wesleyan epic, caused some concern as bringing reproach on the Methodists and prompted JW to impose a censorship over the preachers' publications.

C. Atmore (1801) p. 237; L. Tyerman (1878) 2 p. 531, 3 p. 362

EWD

Kershaw, Jonathan (1772–1846) known as the apostle of the Dales due to the pioneering work he undertook in establishing Wesleyan Methodism in Garsdale, Dentdale and other areas of *Yorkshire and Cumbria. Working as an itinerant tea merchant during the day and preaching at night he founded several Methodist societies including that at Sedbergh and 'Low Smithy,' Garsdale. He and his wife lived in the cottage adjoining the Garsdale Chapel and are buried in the graveyard.

SRV

Key, Robert (1805–76; e.m. 1828), PM itinerant, born at All Saints South Elmham, Suffolk and converted at *Great Yarmouth in 1823. He pioneered the work in East Anglia, where he spent all his ministry. A powerful open-air preacher, especially at camp meetings, it has been suggested that he was the preacher at the camp meeting described in Borrow's *Lavengro*. He wrote *The Gospel among the Masses* (1866).

T. Lowe (1881); G.J. Stevenson (1884–6) 5. pp. 708–23

DCD

Kilham, Alexander (1762–98; e.m. 1785), radical WM itinerant and founder of the MNC, was the third son of *Epworth Methodists. Converted at 18 in a local revival, he became a *local preacher in 1782 and as assistant to R.C. *Brackenbury accompanied him to the *Channel Islands. During a further year in Lincolnshire he professed himself a Dissenter to obtain a preaching licence and became an itinerant in 1785. He played a leading part in the constitutional debates following JW's death. His first pamphlet defended J. *Cownley for having celebrated the *Lord's Supper. For this he was censured by the Conference in 1792 and 'banished' to *Aberdeen, where his encounter with Presbyterianism confirmed his hostility to episcopacy and the Church of England. He went on to produce a stream of tracts expounding the case for Methodist reform and for lay representation in Conference, and thus became the spokesman for those who wished to separate totally from the Establishment. His doctrinaire approach, coupled with his exposure of petty abuses among the itinerants, earned the hostility of his colleagues. They closed ranks following his most strident pamphlet *The Progress of Liberty* (1795) and expelled him the following year.

Kilham spent the next year soliciting support through a periodical, *The Methodist Monitor*, and by preaching in northern towns. When Conference again rejected lay representation, three preachers withdrew, met with Kilham and a few laymen and inaugurated the *MNC. Kilham went to *Sheffield, the largest MNC circuit, where, his

first wife having died some months earlier, he married a former Quaker, Hannah Spurr (1774–1832). The 1798 Conference moved him to *Nottingham, where he died in December, following a visit to Wales. He had combined evangelical passion with a zeal for constitutional reform, but lacked the discrimination needed to change WM from within. His widow returned to the Society of Friends and became an early missionary to *Sierra Leone.

DNB; *WMM* 1887 pp. 689–96, 773–82, 1888 pp. 375–81; C. Atmore (1801) pp. 237–9; J. Blackwell (1838); G.J. Stevenson (1884–6) 4 pp. 595–9; W.J. Townsend (1890); *HMGB* 2 pp. 281–90; M. Dickson (1980)

EAR

Kilner, John (1824–89; e.m. 1847), WM missionary to Ceylon (now *Sri Lanka) during nearly 30 years (1847–75) with one short interval (1849–52) in southern *India. Despite his lack of college training, he became familiar with the Tamil language and identified himself closely with Tamil life and culture. He devoted himself to the task of training a native ministry and promoting a self-supporting Church. Back in England, as one of the Missionary Secretaries from 1875, he had particular responsibility for the finances. In 1879 he was sent on a visit to the *South Africa Missions and presided over the meetings which brought into being an autonomous South African Conference.

JAV

Kilner, William (1826–93), WM layman, born at Hunslet, *Leeds. Starting work at eight in his father's glass bottle-making business in Castleford, he built up a company which gave its name to the Kilner preserving jars. Converted at 15, he was a class leader for 35 years and a *local preacher for 45 years. Moving to London in 1864, he belonged to Finsbury Park and was involved in mission work at Essex Hall, supporting the building of five chapels. He was one of the first lay representatives to the WM *Conference, attending 12 between 1878 and 1893, and was President of the *LPMAA in 1888.

MR 14 June 1888, 24 Aug. 1893; G.E. Milburn & M. Batty (1995) p. 209

PB

Kinchin, Rev. Charles (d.1742), a member of the *'Holy Club' and fellow of Corpus Christi, Oxford, who became rector of Dummer, Hants in

1736, where, according to G. *Whitefield, the inhabitants were 'poor and illiterate'. He visited from house to house, catechized the children, held public prayers twice a day and endeared himself to his parishioners. When he was elected Dean of Corpus Christi at the end of that year, he appointed J. *Hervey as his curate. He accompanied JW on his visits to *Manchester both before and after the Georgia mission, and in March 1739 invited him to preach at Dummer at a time when many pulpits were denied him. Under *Moravian influence he resigned his living and his Oxford posts, intending to becoming an itinerant preacher, but died in January 1742. His widow Esther, a sister of J. *Hutton, became a Moravian.

L. Tyerman (1878) pp. 363–70

JAV

King, Horace Maybray, Baron Maybray-King (1901–86), son of a Teesside steel worker and educated at Stockton-on-Tees Secondary School and King's College, London. His key interests were education and politics. He taught English at Taunton School 1922–46 and was Headmaster of Regents Park School 1946–50. MP for *Southampton from 1950 to 1971, he was Speaker of the House of Commons from 1965 and was created a life peer in 1971. He was National President of the Brotherhood Movement in 1963.

MR 11 Sept. 1986

JWH

King's Lynn Methodism owed its origin to two of JW's converts, a Mr and Mrs Crawford, who moved there from Newcastle upon Tyne. JW himself visited the town a dozen times and the Lynn Circuit was formed in 1776. The first chapel, built in Clough Lane (now Blackfriars Street) in 1786, was replaced by Tower Street, opened in 1813 by R. *Newton, which, with enlargements, survived until 1943. One stalwart was Sir Alfred Jermyn, founder of a local department store, whose grand-daughter Enid became a missionary in India. North End (1862), the chapel of the old fishing community, closed in 1963 and the proceeds of sale were used to build on the new North Lynn estate. A WM chapel in London Road South (1888) closed in 1964.

John Oscroft and Thomas Charlton and other preachers from the Nottingham PM Circuit missioned the town in 1821, 'carrying all before them'. But there was a setback when one of their colleagues, William Wildbur, divided the infant society. Despite this, Lynn became a separate circuit in 1824 and the work was consolidated in 1825–27 by G.W. Bellham (1797–1854; e.m. 1821), a native of the town. The circuit spawned a number of new circuits, such as Swaffham, Downham, Thetford, Docking and Peterborough. The first meeting place, in St Nicholas Street, was soon replaced by a chapel in London Road (1826) where the PM Conference met in 1836 and 1844. At the former the first Consolidated Minutes were drafted, and at the latter H. *Bourne, then aged 72, volunteered to go as a missionary to *Canada. London Road, a new chapel built in 1859 and also known as St James, was opened by R. *Key and has recently been modernized. One indication of the spate of chapel building is the fact that the long-serving Circuit Steward, William Lift, is named on no fewer than 22 foundation stones.

The MNC, WMA and UMFC were all active in the area, but their local history is sketchy.

W. Sampson (1998)

JG

Kingsmead College, Selly Oak, Birmingham was from 1906 a Quaker missionary college which also trained UM women from 1915 and WM women from 1917. Methodists were soon the largest group in the student body and the college came under Methodist control in 1946. Prior to 1932 both men and women from all three branches of Methodism had been trained there, but from Methodist Union until 1966 it was the *Women's Work college, while men were prepared at St Andrew's College nearby. From 1967 it was again a joint college, still serving Scandinavian missionary societies too and increasingly welcoming students from Africa, Asia and the Caribbean. New buildings were added from time to time. In 1993 Kingsmead closed and its work was carried on jointly with the USPG in what became the United College of the Ascension.

JRP

Kingston Eighteenth-century Surrey was sparsely populated and there are no references to JW's visiting Kingston. But in March 1760 *Lloyd's Evening Post* reported that a 'terrible riot' precipitated by a Methodist preacher had to be controlled by Iniskilling Dragoons. The Kingston society was at first attached to the Hammersmith Circuit and the first chapel was built in 1836 on an isolated part of Canbury Fields. Baroness Burdett-Coutts attended worship there and was a generous patron to the society. It was replaced in 1862 by a larger chapel on the Kingston Hall Estate, succeeded by the Eden Street Church and

then the Fairfield Methodist Church. Vigorous mission work undertaken by society members and *Richmond College students resulted in new WM chapels in New Malden (1868, replaced 1933), Kingston Hill (initially in the temporary 'Iron Church' taken over from the Anglicans; then in a new London Road church, 1886) and Surbiton (1876).

A PM society took over the former WM Canbury Fields chapel, then erected a chapel in Richmond Road, Kingston (1872 and 1914). Open air services were led by PM missioners J. *Smith, T. *Batty and R. *Key. The work of mission bands from Croydon resulted in chapels at Norbiton (1871) and Surbiton (1879).

WHS(LHC) 2–7 (1966–8) and 23

NM

Kingswood, Bristol was a former Royal Forest which in the eighteenth and nineteenth centuries saw the development of coal mining and the dependent brass- and copper-smelting industries and of a distinct forest settlement of outcast squatter communities. On his first visit to Bristol, in 1739, JW accompanied G. *Whitefield and heard him preach in the open air at Hanham Mount. That spring Whitefield took the first steps to established a colliers' school and preaching house, leaving JW to carry the project into effect. J. *Cennick was appointed the first schoolmaster. The school continued until 1803, but in 1741, as doctrinal differences widened, Whitefield and Cennick founded another school at what became known as Whitefield's Tabernacle. In 1748 JW, in his turn, founded the present *Kingswood School, now at Bath. He was frequently at Kingswood during his many visits to Bristol.

In the main, the work throughout Kingswood began and continued in humble homes and makeshift rooms; but A. *Clarke recorded in 1799 that 'the work goes on gloriously'. The first recorded WM chapels were built in Warmley Tower in 1800, Downend (1804), Kingswood Hill (1809) and Bridgeyate (1810). A further nine chapels followed. The first PM chapel was built on Kingswood Hill in 1833, followed by Mangotsfield (1857) and Bourne, Staple Hill (1869). Between 1850 and 1870 the UMFC built rival chapels in almost every Kingswood settlement where WM had built in 1830–50.

The bicentenary of JW's birth in 1903 saw the building of Wesley Memorial Church (opened 1907) in Hanham, with the good wishes and support of other branches of Methodism. To com-memorate the Festival of Britain in 1951, the Hanham Mount site, also used by persecuted Bristol Baptists in the seventeenth century, was laid out as a public open space, with a replica of the pulpit from Kingswood School chapel and dedicated to 'the Field Preachers 1658–1739'.

A.G. Ives (1970) pp. 227–33

EAC

Kingswood School was founded by JW in 1748 to educate the sons of Methodist families 'in every branch of useful learning'. The regime was rigorous, with long hours of study, hard beds, no play and no holidays. From just after W's death until 1932 the school, supported by the Connexion, was set aside for preachers' sons. There were riots against excessive beatings in 1820, but gradually the regime was relaxed and the curriculum broadened. In 1851 the school moved from its site east of Bristol to new premises overlooking *Bath, designed by J. *Wilson. To promote interest in higher education, it was reorganized in 1873 as an upper school, with *Woodhouse Grove School as its junior department for eight years. It began to establish and sustain an academic reputation and by the turn of the century 111 of its old boys had won awards at Oxford and Cambridge. It achieved public school status in 1922 and during the headmastership of A.B. *Sackett entered a new, more liberal phase. Priors Court, near Newbury, became its preparatory school during World War II and closed in 1998. Girls were first admitted in 1972. In 1997 there were 817 day and boarding pupils aged 3–18 in the upper school and the two preparatory schools, Priors Court and the Day Preparatory School (opened in 1991). The School reports annually to *Conference, which appoints its Governors.

J. Wesley (1749); A.G. Ives (1969); G. Best (1998)

DBT

Kinsman, Richard (1803–81; e.m. 1829), BC itinerant, born at Stratton, Cornwall. He served as Secretary of the Chapel Committee 1837–39, of the General Committee 1841–42 and of the Foreign Missions Committee 1855–56. He was Secretary of the Conference in 1837 and 1854 and President in 1840 and 1851.

TS

Kipling, John Lockwood (1837–1911), son of Joseph Kipling (1805–1862; e.m. 1831), was educated at *Woodhouse Grove School and in

1865 joined the newly formed Bombay School of Art as 'Architectural Sculptor'. From 1875 to 1893 he served as the first Principal of the Mayo School of Art and curator of the Central Museum, Lahore. Himself a skilful artist in various media, he had an exceptional knowledge of oriental art, shown in *Beast and Man in India* (1891). Against the imperialistic, westernizing trend of his time, he fostered traditional Indian art and architecture and was commissioned by Queen Victoria to design the Durbar Room at Osborne House. In 1865 he married Alice *Macdonald and their son was Rudyard Kipling, some of whose books he illustrated.

Times 30 Jan. 1911; *MR* 2 Feb. 1911; Mahrukh Tarapor in *Victorian Studies* Autumn 1980 pp. 53–81; A.R. Ankers (1988)

JAV

Kirkgate Screamers *see* **Sigston, J.**

Kirkham Family One of the four earliest members of the *'Holy Club' was **Robert Kirkham** of Merton College, son of the Rev. Lionel Kirkham of Stanton, Glos. He became his uncle's curate and disappears from the records. He introduced JW and CW into the family circle, including his oldest sister **'Sally' Kirkham**, nicknamed 'Varanese' and she may have been the 'religious friend' whose influence caused JW to become more serious in 1725. Through them he also came to know the neighbouring Granville family, including the future Mrs Mary Pendarves ('Aspasia'). The circle of friends indulged in cultural dalliance. If, as seems likely, JW was in love with 'Varanese', then her marriage to the schoolteacher Jack Chapone was the first of his disappointments in love.

L. Tyerman (1878) pp. 1–4; G.E. Harrison (1937) pp. 55–84; V.H.H. Green (1961)

JAV

Kirkland, Sarah (1794–1880) of Mercaston, commonly regarded as the first female PM itinerant, started to preach in 1813/14. As a PM itinerant from 1814 she undertook many missions in which the novelty of a young female preacher drew great crowds and she received many preaching invitations. In 1818 she married her fellow itinerant John Harrison (1795–1821), a pioneer in the east Midlands, where he launched the Leicestershire Mission in 1818. They worked together until his health forced their retirement. She was never stationed by the Connexion, having retired before the first PM Conference. In 1825 she married a fellow *local preacher, William Bembridge, and continued as local preacher and class leader until her death.

PMM 1881 passim; G. Herod (1855); J. Walford (1855–7); Kendall (1906) vol. 1

EDG

Kirsop, Joseph (1825–1911; e.m. 1851), WR and UMFC minister. A Scotsman who entered the ministry in *Glasgow, from 1853 he was in English circuits and from the 1860s held a number of District and Connexional offices, being elected President in 1875. A keen supporter of overseas work, he published several missionary biographies and in 1894 became editor of the newly founded *Missionary Echo*. Among many other works he wrote the valuable *Historic Sketches of Free Methodism* (1885).

G.J. Stevenson (1884–6) 6 pp. 984–91

OAB

Kissack, Reginald (Rex) (1910–98; e.m. 1934) was born in *Liverpool. During his ministry in *Oxford he played a part in the reorganization of the WMC and initiated the *Oxford Institute of Methodist Theological Studies. While serving in Rome, 1955–63, he promoted the independence of *Italian Methodism (1962), made the first official Methodist contact with the Vatican and was Observer at the first session of Vatican II (1962–63). This helped him, as Chairman of Liverpool District (1965–75), to foster ecumenical relations in that city. His *Church or No Church* (1964) was an important contribution to Methodist ecclesiology. Retiring to the IOM, he served as Chaplain to the House of Keys, 1991–96. His wife **Elizabeth Kissack** (*née* Hutchinson) (b.1916) founded the Sunday School of Ponte S. Angelo in Rome and taught at the Overseas School. On returning to the UK she served at District and Connexional levels with the *Women's Fellowship and the MMS and was one of the first three women on the *President's Council. She was area President for UK and Ireland of the World Federation of Methodist Women 1971–76, and as World President 1976–81 steered the Federation to seek Nongovernmental Status at the UN.

MR 28 May 1998

FC

Knight, Titus (1719–93) was a collier converted 1746–7 under J. *Nelson in *Halifax. His name heads the list of trustees of the first WM preaching house (1752), next to the cottage in which he had opened a small academy. In 1762 he adopted Independency, taking with him 15 of the 31 members of the WM society. With the help of W. *Grimshaw and the Countess of *Huntingdon, he converted cottages into a meeting house. This was replaced in 1772 by the Square Chapel described by JW as 'superb' and 'finished with the utmost elegance'. Besides maintaining 'a respectable congregation in Halifax', he also preached regularly in London and two of his sons entered the Anglican ministry.

Ev. Mag. 1793 pp. 89–97; J. Sutcliffe (1996)

JAH

Knox, Alexander (1757–1831), born in *Londonderry in a Methodist home where JW and other preachers were entertained, he broke with Methodism at the age of 20 and became an Anglican. Despite poor health in early life, he became private secretary to Lord Castlereagh. But soon tiring of politics, he sought the advice of a Methodist preacher and spent the rest of his life in seclusion and a quest for *holiness. He corresponded with Hannah More, visiting her at Barleywood, and corresponded frequently with JW, whose teaching on holiness influenced him deeply. He anticipated some of the principles of the Oxford Movement. Towards the end of his life he wrote some useful 'Remarks' on JW's life and character. His *Remains* were published in 4 volumes in 1834–37

PWHS 22 pp. 67–71

WL

Koynonya, founded in 1975, is a Methodist-based ecumenical organization with the purpose of promoting and widening contacts between Christians in all parts of the world. It encourages and facilitates exchange visits by both individuals and groups.

JAV

Lackington, James (1746–1815), born at Wellington, Som, began life as a shoemaker. He joined the Methodist society in Cullompton in 1770 and went to *London almost penniless in 1773. With a £5 loan from the *Foundery *Lending Stock he became a highly successful London bookseller on the principle of 'small profits and quick returns', calling his premises the 'Temple of the Muses'. But in prosperity he turned his back on Methodism, which he dismissed con-

temptuously in his *Memoirs* (1791). Following a further change of heart, his *Confessions* (1804) repudiated his infidelity. He built three Methodist churches, each named 'The Temple': at Thornbury, Glos (1803), *Taunton (1808) and Budleigh Salterton (1813).

PWHS 18 pp. 85–92; J.G. Hayman (1871) pp. 51–3; M. Hewlett (1921) pp. 128–37

JAV

Ladies College, Clapham was a short-lived PM venture that opened in 1876 with William Rowe (1826–1914; e.m. 1844) as Governor. It provided a broad-based education for the daughters of itinerants and members. Though academic standards were good and success was achieved, the small numbers of pupils resulted in financial problems and the school was forced to close by 1887.

E.D. Graham (1998) pp. 24–30

EDG

Ladies' Committee/Auxiliary *see* **Women's Work**

Laity JW believed that Methodism was raised up to renew the community by giving it a new understanding of God's nature, new life through faith in Christ and new power from the Holy Spirit to live without voluntary sin. Those wanting to be involved in this put themselves under obedience to JW who, as a minister of the gospel, saw his role and that of the *itinerants as 'to feed and guide, teach and govern' them. In this system the members of society had no status, apart from the only one that mattered to them, that of knowing themselves to be loved and accepted by God in Christ.

The rapid proliferation of societies needed more supervision than JW's clerical associates or his itinerant preachers could provide and he (sometimes hesitantly) accepted the development of lay leadership: *class leaders, *local preachers, *exhorters, *prayer leaders, *Sunday School teachers (all including some *women), *society stewards, *poor stewards and *trustees. These appointments were made by the Circuit *Superintendent. They provided opportunities for the exercise of responsibility and gifts of leadership otherwise denied to the lower classes at that time.

After 1791 the itinerants became ministers in all the usually accepted senses of the word. Organized by means of their annual *Conference into a collective pastorate, they gradually increased their authority by methods which weakened that of the laity, apart from the trustees, with whom they arrived at a system of mutual support. By 1878, when laymen were finally admitted to the WM Conference, much of the vitality and responsible involvement of local laity, characteristic of JW's day, had been lost or transferred to the other branches of Methodism.

In the mid-nineteenth century laymen were appointed as 'Home Missionaries' to take the gospel to new places or to revive the work where it had declined. In 1871 they became 'Lay Agents' to 'save unsaved souls', forerunners of the later *Lay Pastors. More recently, during a shortage of ministers in 1979, the employment of paid lay workers at Circuit and District levels was revived. In 1980 they became 'Lay Pastoral Assistants' to support the pastoral work of the ministry and in 1985 'Lay Workers' providing 'a distinctive and complementary ministry' that was neither a substitute for nor subordinate to the presbyteral ministry. A Board of Lay Training was set up in 1966; its outstanding contribution was to ensure that ministers recognize lay training as part of their normal work. *Cliff College continues to train lay people in evangelism, the majority returning to their secular work.

It is arguable that every secession from WM arose from dissatisfaction with the Conference's authority, particularly the veto over local affairs exercised through Superintendents. Again, since ministers were paid by the circuit, WM was publicly perceived as a system of 'taxation without representation'. Down to the middle of the nineteenth century the growing national demand for representative government added to the pressure for laymen to have a greater involvement in connexional affairs. In all the branches of reformed Methodism, laymen had a place in decision-making at both connexional and local levels.

Methodism's popular reputation as a denomination whose organization is sustained by the laity is only partially justified. Although in 1932 the *Deed of Union asserted that ministers had no priesthood differing in kind from that which is common to all the Lord's people, lay administration of the *sacraments, held by PM and UM to be part of the doctrine of the priesthood of all believers, was thereafter regarded as acceptable only as an exception, i.e. when no minister was available. Many non-WMs were unhappy that an important principle had been sacrificed.

Since 1932 a careful balance has been developed so that the Representative Session of the Conference has a minimum of one third lay and one third ministerial members and the *Vice-President is always either a lay person or a deacon. At the local level, general oversight and approval (or otherwise) of proposed new members is by the *Church Council. Both the Church Council and the General Church Meeting are chaired by a minister, but in the 1970s' *restructuring provision was made for subsidiary committees to be under a lay chairman.

By 1998 the nature of ministry, both lay and ordained, paid and unpaid, was being entirely rethought and a course of integrated development for lay people, ministers and deacons devised. The heart-searching about the training and use of lay people that seems to have recurred once a generation, both before 1932 in the various branches of Methodism and after it in the united Church, is perhaps a sign of healthy self-criticism.

See also **Deacon**; **Lay Pastor**; **Pastoral Office**

SL 2, 292–311; *LQHR* January 1962; M. Batty (1993a); C. Warren (1995)

MB

Lake, Octavius (1841–1922; e.m. 1863) was born in Monmouthshire, where his BC parents moulded his religious character from birth. He was educated at *Shebbear College, later serving as Assistant Master. In 1869 he emigrated to South *Australia, where he was appointed to Auburn. He was an effective speaker with strong convictions and a champion of many social reforms. He was President of the BC Conference in 1886 and of the Methodist Conference in 1915. He edited the *Australian Commonwealth* and wrote many devotional meditations and hymns. His wife **Serena Lake** (née Thorne, 1842–1902), the daughter of S. and M. *Thorne, was born at Shebbear. Educated at home and filled with evangelistic fervour, she became a *local preacher and was known as 'the girl preacher' of North Devon. In 1865 she was sent to Brisbane to establish BC work in Queensland. Moving to South Australia in 1870, she preached each Sunday to crowded congregations in the Adelaide Town Hall. She and Octavius renewed acquaintance and were married in 1871. She remained a leading woman preacher and organized the BC Women's Missionary Board. She was a lifelong total abstainer and opponent of the liquor trade.

DGH

Laleham School *see* **Pipe, H.E.**

Lamb, George (1809–86; e.m. 1829), PM itinerant, born in *Preston of Quaker origins and converted at a *Camp Meeting in 1826. In 1829 H. *Bourne persuaded him to become an itinerant. His circuit ministry (1829–85) was spent largely around *Hull and in London. He was a keen advocate of temperance and social reform. He was *Book Steward 1870–75 and twice President of the Conference (1866 and 1884), and was appointed by Conference to visit the PM churches in N. America in 1876. Throughout his ministry he gave a rising proportion of his income to charities and a scholarship fund was founded in his name to assist candidates for the PM ministry.

F.H. Hurd (1872) pp. 107–18; G.J. Stevenson (1884–6) 5 pp. 736–47; *PMM* 1887 pp. 242–5; 1879 p. 181; *DEB*

GEM

Lampe, John Frederick (1703–51), musician, born in Saxony, who came to England *c.* 1725 as a bassoon-player at Covent Garden Theatre and in Handel's band. He was one of the finest bassoonists of his time, published books on music and composed several burlesque operas and many songs. He met CW at the home of J. *Rich and towards the end of 1745 became interested in Methodism and spent some time with JW. He wrote 24 hymn tunes, of which two are in *HP* and collaborated with CW on *Hymns on the Great Festivals* (1746; 1996 reprint, Madison NJ), and published *A Collection of Hymns and Sacred Poems* (Dublin, 1749). Many of his tunes are in the florid style of the day, but were popular with the Methodists. CW wrote a lyric ode in his memory.

PWHS 3 pp. 237–9; 8 pp. 155–6

PLC

Lamplough, Williamson (1854–1925) and his brother **Edmund Sykes Lamplough** (1860–1940) were descended from Dr J. *Hamilton. Williamson was an enthusiastic supporter of *overseas missions and of the Bible Society. His office was close to the Bishopsgate *Mission House and he served as WMMS Treasurer for 27 years. Edmund, an underwriter and deputy-chairman at Lloyd's, was Vice-President of the Conference in 1935. An avid collector of Wesleyana and President of the WHS from 1926, he was a generous benefactor of the *New Room and *Wesley's Chapel. The brothers built Sunfields Chapel, Blackheath, as a memorial to their parents and held office there for many years, Williamson

as Sunday School Superintendent and Edmund as organist.

PWHS 22, pp. 169–72; *Times*, 28 & 29 Oct. 1940; *MR* 15 Oct. 1925, 20 Oct. 1940

JAV/PLC

'Large Minutes' In 1753 JW published a compendium of the published and unpublished *Minutes of the Conferences from 1744. Five further revisions were made in his lifetime, the last in 1789. It became the custom to give an inscribed copy of these 'Large Minutes' to a preacher when he was received 'on trial' and another when he was received into *full connexion. The 1789 edition continued in use until Lord Chancellor Lyndhurst's judgment in Dr *Warren's case in 1835 described it as 'a mere guide and assistant to the preacher', treating as legally authoritative instead the 'Collection of Rules, or Code of Laws' adopted by the Conference in 1797. The latter Code was therefore substituted as the Large Minutes, and continued substantially unaltered until it was superseded in 1896 by J.S. Simon's *Summary of Methodist Law and Discipline*. The PM equivalent was known as the 'Consolidated Minutes', first published in 1828.

See also **Constitutional Practice and Discipline**

W.F. Swift in *PWHS* vol. 31 (1957–8) pp. 158–9

SRH

Lark, William Blake (1838–1913; e.m. 1859), BC minister, born at Fowey, began to preach at 16. During an extensive circuit ministry, he became known at *Exeter for a popular series of lectures on the Bible and drew great crowds at *Portsmouth by his discourses on Christianity and Free Thought. In 1900 he was appointed Governor of *Shebbear College. He contributed articles to the *BC Magazine* over the signature 'B.W. Kral'. He was President of the Conference in 1882, 1898 and 1907 and represented the Connexion at the Ecumenical Methodist Conferences between 1881 and 1901. Believing that 'the kingdoms of this world are also the Kingdom of God', he used wit, humour, repartee, scorn, denunciation and ridicule in dealing with political and social wrongs.

TS

Lauder, Alexander (1836–1921), Methodist architect, born in *Barnstaple. He studied art and architecture in Edinburgh and practised as an architect in Barnstaple. He also ran an art pottery. He married Eliza M. Widlake, a WM, and became a leading layman. Among the WM chapels he designed were a dozen locally, including South Molton (1882), Boutport Street (1869) and Newport Road (1911), both in Barnstaple, five in London and Southgate, *Chichester (1877). W.R. Lethaby (1857–1931), brought up in a BC home in Barnstaple, was his pupil and assistant from 1871 to 1878 and went on to become an eminent Arts and Crafts architect and Surveyor of Westminster Abbey.

RFST

Lavington, George (1684–1762), Bishop of Exeter 1747–62, author of *The Enthusiasm of the Methodists and Papists Compared* (1749 and 1751; new edition edited by R. Polwhele, 1820), provoked by a false charge of immorality brought against JW at the height of anti-Jacobite feelings. In addition to recording scurrilous charges, it denied the operation of the Holy Spirit in Methodist conversions, attributing them to physical and psychological factors. It produced replies by G. *Whitefield (1749), V. *Perronet (1749) and JW himself (1750, 1751, 1752). A reconciliation took place in 1762, when JW dined with the bishop after receiving the Sacrament with him in *Exeter cathedral, within weeks of his death.

DNB; F. Baker in *PWHS* 34 pp. 37–42; G.R. Cragg (1975) pp. 353–436; O.A. Beckerlegge (1980)

JAV

Law, William (1686–1761), scholar, writer, ascetic and mystic who was an early influence on JW. In 1714 he forfeited his fellowship at Emmanuel College, Cambridge by refusing to take the oath of allegiance to George I. Founding a girls' school in 1727, he then became tutor, chaplain and spiritual adviser to the family of Edward Gibbon (father of the historian). In 1740 he retired to Northants, where he lived a secluded life, offering spiritual direction and practising the strict spiritual disciplines advocated in his *Treatise on Christian Perfection* (1726) and *A Serious Call to a Devout and Holy Life* (1728). In his *Oxford years JW was much influenced by these treatises and by the *Theologica Germanica* to which Law introduced him. He visited Law in 1732, became a disciple and was encouraged by him to go to Georgia. But after meeting P. *Böhler he became disenchanted with Law's asceticism and openly reproached him for not having taught

him true faith. The rift between them widened in Law's later years to the point where his increasingly *mystical stance led JW to publish a letter in 1756 attacking his position.

See also **Devotion**; **Mysticism**

J.B. Green (1945); E.W. Baker (1948); A.K. Walker (1973)

WDH

Law and Polity Committee In 1897 the Pastoral Session of the WM Conference appointed an advisory Committee on the Law of Appeal. In 1902 the Session appointed a standing committee (comprising 23 ministers) replacing this, to consider Pastoral questions and other matters relating to Methodist legislation and administration. It became known as the Committee on Methodist Law. After *Methodist Union (1932) it operated as a Sub-committee (of the *General Purposes Committee) on Methodist Law and Polity, and included both ministerial and lay members. Since 1945 it has been a standing connexional committee responsible *inter alia*, for considering questions concerning Methodist legislation and administration, advising the Conference upon interpretation, examining and correlating the elements of the constitution and scrutinizing new legislative proposals. It appoints a Conference Sub-committee to discharge these functions during the Conference.

SRH

Lawrence, Sarah ('Sally') (1759–1800), orphaned niece of S. *Ryan. She was taken into M. *Bosanquet's school at Leytonstone at the age of 4 and moved with the school to Cross Hall in 1768. When her aunt died in 1768 Miss Bosanquet became her adoptive mother and on her marriage to J. *Fletcher Sarah went with her to *Madeley, where she worked with children and visited the sick. She began to take meetings and even ventured into the local public houses. She started to preach and pioneered the work in the hamlet of Coalport.

Z. Taft vol. 1 (1825) pp. 41–8; M. Fletcher (1820); P.W. Chilcote (1991) pp. 199–200, 272–3

EDG

Lawry, Walter (1793–1859; e.m. 1817), WM missionary, born near Bodmin. Appointed to New South Wales in 1817 as colleague to S. *Leigh, he sailed on a convict ship, preaching to the prisoners. Relations with Leigh became strained and he moved to *Tonga in 1822, largely financing his own transfer, together with that of two artisan helpers and a translator, to establish the first WM work in the Pacific. In 1823, with no successor appointed and no measurable progress made, he was ordered to Van Dieman's Land (Tasmania), but chose to return home. After an interval in English circuits, in 1843 he was appointed 'General Superintendent for *New Zealand and Visitor of the Missions in the Friendly Islands and Fiji' in succession to J. *Waterhouse. Based in Auckland, he travelled throughout New Zealand and revisited in Tonga a work that had been successfully established despite his own apparent failure. In 1844, with a government land grant, he established an institution in Auckland to train young Maoris as potential missionary 'assistants'; and in 1850 he had a major hand in establishing the Wesleyan College and Seminary in Auckland to provide education for missionary children and others. Relationships with his colleagues gradually worsened, due partly to his undefined powers, and he had to defend himself against complaints to the Missionary Committee in London. A deputation sent to New Zealand eventually exonerated him, but he retired in 1854 to Sydney. As an evangelist rather than a missionary, he lacked the ability to relate to indigenous people, and he was primarily an administrator.

F&H 3 passim; E.W. Hames (1967); A.H. Wood 1 (1975) pp. 19–25; EWM

MJF/DJP

Lawson, John ('Jack'), Lord Lawson (1881–1965), mineworker and MP, was born at *Whitehaven. When he was 9 the family moved to Boldon, Co. Durham, where he began work at the local colliery. He was an active WM *local preacher for 60 years. In 1906 he attended Ruskin College, but did not graduate. In 1913 he was elected to Durham County Council and from 1919 until his retirement in 1949 was MP for Chester-le-Street. In the 1924 Labour administration he was financial secretary to the War Office and in the Attlee government of 1945 was Secretary of State for War with the task of managing demobilization as efficiently as possible. In 1945 he was made a Privy Councillor, was Lord Lieutenant of Durham 1949–58, the first working man to hold the office, and was created 1st Baron Lawson of Beamish in 1950. He wrote an autobiography, *A Man's Life* (1932) and lives of Peter Lee (1936) and Herbert Smith (*The Man in the Cap*) (1941).

Times 4 & 7 Aug. 1965; MR 12 Aug. 1965; DLB
NADS

Lawson, John James (1909– ; e.m. 1932) was trained in agricultural science before entering the WM ministry and studying at *Wesley House, Cambridge. From 1955 to 1976 he was a lecturer in the Candler School of Theology, Emory University, Atlanta GA. He is an authority on Irenaeus and the theology of J&CW, and has written a number of books, including *Notes on Wesley's 44 Sermons* (1946), and the chapter on 'Our Discipline' in Volume 1 of *HMGB*. He is a member of the Editorial Board of the Bicentennial Edition of JW's *Works* and editor of the unit on the *Explanatory Notes upon the NT*.

RFST

Lawton, Rev. Dr George (1910–93; e.m. 1934) was trained at *Richmond College, but after eleven years in circuit went to *Queen's College, Birmingham and was ordained priest in 1950. As vicar of *Madeley he followed an illustrious predecessor, J. *Fletcher, on whom he gave the WHS Lecture, *Shropshire Saint*, in 1960. From 1959 to 1977 he was rector of Checkley, Staffs. An assiduous scholar, he spent many years on a meticulous study of JW's English, resulting in articles in the WHS *Proceedings* on his use of slang, proverbial expressions etc. and in a book *John Wesley's English* (1962). He also wrote a life of A.M. *Toplady, *Within the Rock of Ages* (1983).

JAV

Lax, William H. (1868–1937; e.m. 1895), commonly known as 'Lax of Poplar', was born in *Manchester and trained for the WM ministry at *Didsbury College. From the West London Mission he was moved to the Poplar Mission in 1902, becoming Superintendent in 1907. His 35 years in the Mission are described in his five books, particularly his autobiographical *Lax of Poplar* (1927) and *Lax: His Book* (1937). A colourful and popular figure, he became Mayor of Poplar in 1918 and was featured in the Religious Film Society's first talking picture, *Mastership* (1934).

MR 11 Feb. 1937

JDB

Lay Pastor From the late nineteenth century on, some *local preachers were engaged as assistants to circuit ministers and came to be known as lay pastors. After the 1932 *Methodist Union most full-time paid lay ministry was through the Lay Pastorate. The *HM Department/Division maintained an official list of approved Pastors, who worked under its authority and oversight in the circuits to which they were appointed. Many had trained at *Cliff College. They appeared on the Circuit *Preaching Plan alongside the ministerial staff and often had a dispensation to administer the Sacrament. In 1947 and again in 1963 Conference expressed misgivings about this form of ministry. Lay Pastors were not paid the full ministerial stipend, yet were often appointed to undertake full presbyteral ministry. A District Chairman commented that the system was either an injustice to the man in that he was not accorded ministerial status and emoluments or an injustice to the Church in that it was using as ministers those who had not been fully trained for the role. In 1948 the Church made it possible for Lay Pastors to offer for the presbyteral ministry on the evidence of acceptable service in the circuits. Many of the 95 who offered were accepted and became ministers.

See also **Diaconate**

G.T. Brake (1984) pp. 651–3

PWS

Lay Witness Movement originated in the Institute of Church Renewal, Atlanta, USA and extended to British Methodism following an exploratory visit in 1975 by officers of the Institute. The first mission was in Bolsover in 1976. Developing largely under lay leadership, it is now a registered charity. Weekend missions offer three different programmes, with an emphasis on deeper commitment within the local church. Missions are not restricted to Methodism and the Movement, whilst officially recognized, is not directed by the Church.

WP

Laycock, John William (1836–1923) an iron merchant of Keighley, W. Yorks. He served as a WM *local preacher for 68 years, being appointed President of the *LPMAA in 1872. He is better known as a writer of early Methodist history, especially *Methodist Heroes of the Great *Haworth Round* (1909).

SRV

Leaders' Meeting The first 'Leaders' Meeting' seems to have been held in *Bristol on June 6 1739, followed by one in London on September 5. With the inauguration of *class meeting the function of the leaders of the classes in exercising pastoral care became crucial. These leaders (men and women) were appointed on the basis of their perceived spiritual gifts.

The duties of a leader were laid down in the 'General Rules of the United *Societies' (1743) as being, first, to see each person in the class at least weekly to exercise spiritual oversight and to receive their financial contributions, and secondly to meet the itinerant and stewards once a week so as to inform them of any that 'are sick or walk disorderly', and to account for money received. The regulation that the preachers should meet the leaders weekly remained in the *Large Minutes until shortly after JW's death.

The Leaders' Meeting originally possessed only advisory powers, but in 1797 was given the right of veto in the admission or expulsion of members. The appointment and removal of leaders and stewards (by the minister) was to be 'in conjunction with the meeting'.

Leaders' meetings were part of the polity of many other branches of Methodism, although having a different relationship to the exercise of ministerial authority. For instance the MNC provided from the outset for leaders in new places to be appointed by the mutual concurrence of the travelling preachers and the people, with replacements being subject to the veto of the class involved. In the Digest of Rules of the BC Conference (1838) the term 'Leaders' Meeting' was altered to 'Elders' Meeting'.

In WM its membership was formally defined in 1874, as consisting of the circuit ministers and probationers, the leaders, society and poor stewards, and any circuit stewards who were members of that society. Representatives of the local society, directly elected, were added in 1908.

The leaders' meeting was always a central part of local church organization, exercising pastoral oversight and being the first court of *discipline over members. But its place at the spiritual centre of the society was increasingly called into question, particularly in WM. After *Methodist Union, it continued in existence and acquired an increasing number of functions. It met at least quarterly and included (other than for disciplinary cases) other local officers and leaders of fellowship groups.

In the 1974 *restructuring, the 'dual control' exercised over the local church by leaders' and *trustees' meetings was replaced by the *Church Council, having oversight of the whole of the church's life. The council is now required to appoint a Pastoral Committee to exercise functions in relation to *membership, *discipline, fellowship and other pastoral matters.

See also **Class Meetings**

L.F. Church (1948); *HMGB* 4 pp. 59–61; 573–5.

SRH

Leamington In 1817 William Scott, a London barber, and his wife began holding services in a loft in Barnacle's Yard, Satchwell Street, then in a larger room in Brunswick Street. The first chapel was in Portland Street, then known as Quarryfield (1825; extended 1835 and 1846). A day school was built at the rear in 1839. In 1870 the congregation moved to Dale Street, a large Victorian chapel, which was rebuilt on the same site in 1972, incorporating the former PM congregation from Warwick Street. The Young Men's Mutual Improvement Class sent several men into the ministry. In the southern part of the town Trinity was opened in 1877. It developed a strong musical tradition and is now Radford Road Methodist/URC Church. Originally in the widespread Coventry Circuit, Leamington became head of a separate circuit in 1837.

———

P. Bolitho (1987)

PBo

Lee, Atkinson (1880–1955), born in Driffield, the son of a PM minister, **George Lee** (1851–1919; e.m. 1872). He was educated at Peterhouse, Cambridge, then became lecturer in Education at University College, Aberystwyth (1903–8). On the recommendation of A.S. *Peake, he was appointed tutor at *Hartley College, Manchester (1908–47), also lecturing in the Philosophy and Psychology of Religion at Manchester University. He was a man of wide-ranging knowledge and penetrating thought, coupled with a sensitivity which won the affection of his students. He gave the Hartley Lecture in 1927 on *Sociality: the Art of Living Together*, contributed a chapter on religious experience to *Methodism in the Modern World* (1929) and also published *Groundwork of the Philosophy of Religion* (1946).

———

MR 20 Jan. 1955

EDG

Lee, Peter (1864–1935), *trade unionist, born at Trindon Grange, Co. Durham of gypsy ancestry. His working life began at the age of 9 in a cotton mill. He went down a coal mine for the first time in 1874 and for many years lived a roving life, working as a miner in various parts of England, *South Africa and the USA. He was virtually illiterate until early manhood. Converted in 1888, he became a PM *local preacher, consistently proclaiming that the Christian faith could not be divorced from social concern and urging the need for service in the community. Education, chapel membership and a settled life style became the

basis of his later achievements. He rose through the ranks to become General Secretary of the Durham Miners Association in 1930 and President of the Mineworkers Federation in 1932. He became Chairman of the Durham County Council in 1919. and his selfless work on behalf of the people of Co. Durham was celebrated in the 1950s by the naming of Peterlee new town after him.

———

J. Lawson (1936)

GEM/NADS

Leeds emerged in the early eighteenth century as the leading West Riding market town and grew to be a major industrial centre. B. *Ingham and the *Moravians were active in the parish, but the father of Methodism was J. *Nelson from nearby *Birstall. The first society was established in Armley in 1742. Soon afterwards a society of ten was formed in Leeds itself under the leadership of W. *Shent in his Briggate barber's shop. After various other meeting places, the 'Boggart House' was opened in 1751. Several *Conferences met there, including the one in 1769 which sent R. *Boardman and J. *Pilmore to America.

The Leeds society experienced difficulties, including the expulsion of Shent. In 1753 the itinerant **John Edward** seceded over *Calvinism and the Independent White Chapel was opened for him. **William Hey** (1736–1819), senior surgeon at Leeds Infirmary, who had been *circuit steward since 1764, presented a paper on the widening gap between WM and the CofE at the Leeds Conference of 1781 and left the Connexion in 1784.

In the 1790s, with a sympathetic printer and bookseller, Leeds was for a time A. *Kilham's base and a Kilhamite stronghold. One of his leading supporters was Richard *Oastler's father Robert. Having failed to obtain their demands at the Leeds Conference of 1797, Kilham's followers withdrew to Ebenezer Chapel (obtained from the Baptists) and held the first MNC Conference. In 1858 Ebenezer was replaced by Woodhouse Lane chapel, where, on 18 October 1859 W.N. *Hall and J. *Innocent were commissioned for China.

The great West Riding revival of 1794, inspired by W. *Bramwell, led to a rapid increase in WM membership and new chapels. The secession in 1803 led by J. *Sigston (the 'Kirkgate Screamers') was short-lived. In 1819 an expelled class at Wesley, Meadow Lane, joined the *Hull PM Circuit and in 1821 Leeds became a PM Circuit and a Conference town. There was already an established tradition of women preachers in Leeds, with S. *Crosby, M. *Bosanquet and A. *Tripp, and this continued under the PMs with A. *Carr, who seceded to form the Leeds Female Revivalists.

The installing of an organ in 1826 at Brunswick (opened 1825) brought to a head existing discontent over the division of the circuit and in the Sunday Schools. As a result, Sigston and M. *Johnson led the *Protestant Methodist secession of 1827, which later joined the WMA. Their Lady Lane Chapel (1840) housed the Annual Assembly when it met in Leeds nine times between 1839 and 1890. Although the WR agitation from 1849 onwards affected the Leeds circuits, its greatest impact was in the Bramley Circuit. The influence of Bramley-born J. *Barker was locally responsible for membership losses in both the MNC and PM in the 1840s.

By the 1830s Leeds was a strong Methodist centre, but the revival of Anglicanism under Dr W.F. Hook was at Methodism's expense. Faced with declining inner-city congregations, in 1889 WM responded by making Wesley a mission centre, resulting in 1899 in the Leeds Mission based on Oxford Place, with the influential ministry of S. *Chadwick at Wesley and Oxford Place. Later, Lady Lane (UMFC), Rehoboth (PM), Park Lane and Dewsbury Road (MNC), West Hunslet also became central missions. There were notable ministries at Brunswick under A.E. *Whitham (1918–25) L.D. *Weatherhead (1925–36) and W.E. *Sangster (1936–39).

Leeds is associated with WM *overseas missions, particularly the establishment of the first District Missionary Society in 1813 and the fundraising Missionary Breakfasts from 1849 under the influence of the wealthy merchant W. *Smith of Gledhow. *Headingley College was opened in 1868 and the first *Wesley Guild was formed at Roscoe Place Chapel in 1894.

MR(W) 1894 pp. 62–7; Conference Handbooks, 1914 (WM), 1930 (WM), 1938, 1956; T. Hardcastle (1871); W. Beckworth (1910); D.C. Dews in *PWHS* 51 pp. 96–103, 117–25

DCD

Leeds Organ Case *see* **Protestant Methodists**

Legal Hundred By the *Deed of Declaration (1784) JW defined the *Conference for legal purposes as consisting after his death of one hundred preachers (including eleven Irish-based) listed by him, with provision for their succession in perpetuity. This numerical limit and his choice of names created some dissension and resignations.

The 1791 Conference, in response to JW's letter, read after his death, unanimously resolved 'that all the preachers in full connexion with them shall enjoy every privilege that the members of Conference enjoy', and it became customary for these other preachers to meet and share in discussions. Their rights were extended to some extent with regard to elections in 1814; but ratification by the Legal Hundred of all elections and decisions continued to be necessary in the WM Church, even after the introduction of the Representative Session in 1878, until the Legal Hundred was abolished at *Methodist Union in 1932.

J.S. Simon (5th edn., 1923), pp. 382–6; J.S. Simon in *PWHS* Vol 12 (1919–20) pp. 81–93

SRH

Legion of Service and the associated Fellowship of Service were launched by the 1922 UM Annual Assembly. The Legion claimed to be different from either the *Christian Endeavour or the *Wesley Guild in that 'its spiritual aims and devotional plans' were 'based on modern educational principles'. The Fellowship's aim was to help leaders in every type of young people's work. Its outlook was wider than the circuit and it aimed to make leaders aware of their connexional responsibility. Both movements grew steadily and brought into the Union of 1932 a form of youth service especially valuable in towns where the UMC was strong.

H. Smith, J.E. Swallow & W. Treffry (1932) pp. 181–2

WL

Leicester Markfield to the north-west was an early centre of Methodism. From there in 1753 JW responded to an invitation to visit Leicester and preached in the Butt Close on Whit Sunday. Most of over a dozen later visits were brief. A society was formed by John Brandon, a dragoon who later became an itinerant. They met first in the house of William Lewis, a Presbyterian hosier in High Street, who then provided them with a thatched barn, known as the Tabernacle, in Millstone Lane. A chapel built on the same site was opened by Dr *Coke in 1787. It was in the Derbyshire Circuit until a separate circuit was formed in 1776. In 1816, at a time of economic depression, the opening of Bishop Street (formerly Bishopsgate Street) chapel, designed by W. *Jenkins, in 1816 (extended and remodelled several times later in the century) heralded a new era, with the population doubling by 1840. The Sunday School continued at Millstone Lane and in new premises in Metcalf Street. Membership decline after 1881 was due partly to its position as a downtown church and partly to the opening of new causes, including mission halls, elsewhere in the town. A 10-year Circuit Extension Scheme was launched in 1893. In 1944 this became part of the new Central Mission. Meanwhile Humberstone Road (1863) and King Richard's Road (1874) became the head of new circuits in 1873 and 1906. Between 1788 and 1917 the WM Benevolent Society provided a response to local poverty and sickness.

The MNC formed a rival cause in 1797, but seems to have disappeared by 1815. Between 1859 and 1890 a new MNC congregation, perhaps the result of unrest at Bishop Street, worshipped in St Paul's chapel at the junction of Station Street and London Road. PM swept through the Leicestershire villages in the second decade of the nineteenth century. W. *Clowes preached in Belgrave Gate in 1818. The PM chapels opened in George Street (1819) and York Street (1839) were united in 1873 in new premises at St Nicholas Street. During the twentieth century Methodism has continued to adapt to changing circumstances and opportunities.

Conference Handbook 1934; B.J. Biggs (1965); J. & R. Stevenson (1988)

BJB

Leigh, Samuel (1782–1852; e.m. 1812), first WM missionary to *Australia and *New Zealand, was trained at the Gosport Congregational seminary. He went to New South Wales in 1815 to an itinerant ministry based in Sydney, but extending over 150 miles. He found it difficult to work with his colleague W. *Lawry, but established a close relationship with the Anglican chaplain Samuel Marsden, who enabled him in 1819 to recuperate his health by a voyage to New Zealand. Back in England in 1820, recovering from his exhausting labours, he successfully advocated a mission to New Zealand and was appointed to return there. By 1823 he had established the ill-fated 'Wesleydale' mission at Kaeo on Whangaroa Bay. He maintained good relations with the CMS staff at the Bay of Islands. Of undoubted abilities, but unable to husband his energies, he was obliged to return to Sydney in 1825 and to English circuit work in 1831.

DNZB; A.E. Keeling (1896); D. Wright & E. Clancy (1993) pp. 4–17

MJF/DJP

Lending Stock   One of JW's responses to the poverty he encountered in *London was to set up a fund at the *Foundery in 1746 from which interest-free loans of up to £1 (later raised to £5) could be made as an alternative to resorting to a pawnbroker. To launch it he begged £30 from London friends. Two stewards were appointed to administer the fund at the *Foundery every Tuesday morning. Loans were to be repaid weekly within three months. In its first 18 months over 250 loans were made. In January 1748 a public collection increased the lending stock to £50 and in 1767 it rose to £120. Its most famous beneficiary was the bookseller J. *Lackington in 1774.

PWHS 3 pp. 197–8, 5 p. 192

JAV

Lenton, Mary (*née* Foster) (1913–98), born in *Whitby into a staunchly Methodist home, read English at St Hugh's College, Oxford, where she was a founder member of the John Wesley Society and came under the influence of H. *Roberts. She married **Arthur Lenton** in 1940 and from 1946 they were tutors in child care at the Princess Alice College, *Birmingham. She fully supported him in his role as Governor of the Birmingham Branch of *NCH from 1948 and was elected to Conference. In London from 1968 to 1980, where Arthur was at NCH headquarters, she taught in a secondary school for 5 years, became chairman of *Women's Fellowship, a governor of *Southlands College and treasurer of the *General Purposes Fund and served on the *President's Council. She was Vice-President of the 1978 Conference. The welfare of children, spiritual growth, worship and Christian reunion were foremost among her concerns.

MR 22 June 1978, 30 July 1998

JAV

Lessey, Theophilus (1757–1821; e.m. 1786), WM minister who 'united ardent zeal with scriptural knowledge'. His son **Theophilus Lessey Junr** (1787–1841; e.m. 1808), was baptized by JW and educated at *Kingswood School. A powerful preacher, he was much in demand on special occasions such as the opening of Brunswick Chapel (1825) and Oxford Place Chapel (1835), *Leeds. He was President of the Conference in 1839, the WM Centenary year, the first minister's son to be elected to that office.

WL

Lewis, Greville Priestley (1891–1976; e.m. 1915), descendant of Joseph Priestley, became a *local preacher while in the VI Form at *Kingswood School and trained for the ministry at *Handsworth College. As secretary of the *Local Preachers' Department (1946–58) he was concerned that preachers should be fully trained ánd resourced. He initiated residential conferences and summer schools, published five biennial vol- umes of the *Preachers' Handbook*, edited the *Epworth Preacher's Commentaries* and distributed a report on *The Local Preacher and Evangelism* (1949). He wrote *An Approach to the New Testament* (1954) and edited *An Approach to Christian Doctrine* (1954). He served on the board of the *Methodist Recorder* and on the book committee of the Publishing House.

MR 18 March 1976

WDH

Lewis, Hywel Meilir Pennant (1919–97; e.m. 1940), elder of two brothers who followed their father into the Welsh WM ministry. Graduating in Arts and Divinity at Manchester University, he was a man of wide reading and culture and deep spirituality, one of the most influential ministers of his generation. As a scholar he specialized in the lives and works of Christian saints and the history of Welsh WM. He was secretary of the Historical Society of the Methodist Church in Wales from its foundation in 1946, becoming its Chairman in 1980 and later an Honorary President. He made valuable contributions to its journal *Bathafarn*, as well as to *Yr Eurgrawn* and other Welsh periodicals.

USMR 30 Jan. 1998; *Y Gwyliedydd*, Feb.-March 1998

OEE

Lewis, Mrs Mildred Clarissa (1886–1982), daughter of Henry Babb (1852–1933; e.m. 1878), was educated at *Trinity Hall, Southport and married **David Lewis** of Bilston, an iron-founder who was active in public affairs, especially education. Following his sudden death in 1942 she took over much of his public work, served on many connexional committees, including *Women in the Ministry, *Ministerial Training, Church *Membership and the *'July Committee'. She had a special interest in mental health. A gracious and friendly personality, in 1948 she became the first woman to be elected *Vice-President of the Conference and in that office attended the first WCC meeting in Amsterdam.

MR 15 July 1948, 25 Feb. 1982   JAV

Leyland, Arthur Stanley (1901–92), born in Shropshire, was baptized after his uncle **Albert Stanley**, a *local preacher and trade union leader, and inherited musical skills from his father. He stood unsuccessfully for Parliament, entered the PM ministry in 1922 and trained at *Hartley College. He was first Record Secretary, then Assistant Secretary of the Conference and was convener of the committee which arranged for ministers to own their own furniture. He developed the *WMC ministerial exchange programme and himself led many groups on overseas visits. He wrote hymns, poetry and plays and for many years contributed a children's page to the *Methodist Recorder*.

MR 1 Oct. 1992

KGG

Leys School, The, opened in *Cambridge in 1875 as a Connexional School to meet demands for higher education and to enable the sons of Methodists to enter Oxford or Cambridge. The traditions established by its first headmaster, Dr W.F. *Moulton – high academic standards, broad curriculum, pastoral care, sporting prowess and impressive building programmes – have always characterized the school. W.H. Balgarnie, a master for 37 years, was immortalized by ex-pupil James Hilton in his novel *Goodbye Mr Chips*. In 1997, with its preparatory school St Faith's, The Leys had 880 boarding and day pupils of both sexes, aged 4–18.

F. Tice (1966) pp. 79–90; D. Baker (1975)

DBT

Leysian Mission, London was founded in 1886 and from then until the present former pupils of The *Leys School have engaged in every aspect of its work. Its first premises were in Whitecross Street. The first resident lay worker was appointed in 1887, visiting the homes of the sick and poor and conducting a Mothers' Meeting with some 200 members. Activities included medical work, a working men's club, educational classes for boys, a large Sunday School and weeknight entertainments. The Mission moved to larger premises in Erroll Street in 1890, and again in 1904 to extensive premises at the junction of Old Street and City Road. A Commission appointed by the London Committee met in 1988 to consider its future and an amalgamation with *Wesley's Chapel, City Road took place in 1989, bringing together two complementary traditions. Sale of the Leysian Mission premises enabled alterations to be made at Wesley's Chapel to accommodate the local and wider ministry. It also supports ministry among those experiencing deprivation in inner London and elsewhere, in keeping with the Mission's original purpose.

The Leysian Mission 1886–1986: A Century of Caring (1986)

PWS

Licensing of Preachers The *Toleration Act of 1689 gave a measure of protection to Dissenting preachers by providing for them to register as such either at the episcopal or archdiaconal courts or at the Quarter Sessions, on condition that they demonstrated their loyalty by taking oaths and making declarations. This presented a dilemma to JW, once he had begun to rely on lay preachers (whether local or itinerant) and he hesitated for a long time, insisting that the Methodists were not Dissenters but Anglicans. In a letter of 19 July 1768 he admitted that, for their own protection, some of the preachers had applied to be licensed and some had been refused on the grounds that they were not 'Protestant Dissenters'. The right of the magistrate or court to refuse a licence was successfully contested by T. *Brisco, but W was still hesitating in 1787. After consulting his solicitor, W. *Clulow, he then reluctantly agreed to the licensing of preachers, but as 'preachers of the gospel', not as Dissenters. Several test cases brought before the courts between 1793 and 1812 were settled in favour of the Methodists. But abuse of the Toleration Act during the Napoleonic Wars to avoid military service was condemned by the Conference, eager for Methodism to be seen as patriotic. Following the defeat of the *Sidmouth Bill in 1811 the Conventicle and other Acts were repealed by 52 Geo.III c.155, a new Toleration Act which provided for preachers to take the oaths and make declarations before a JP.

John S. Simon in *PWHS* 11 pp. 103–11,130–7

JAV

'Lichfield Plan' An unofficial meeting of senior itinerants, convened by T. *Coke, was held on 1–2 April 1794 at Lichfield, where there was as yet no Methodist society and secrecy might therefore be preserved. Its purpose was to consider the future government of the Connexion. Those attending were A. *Mather, T. *Taylor, J. *Pawson, S. *Bradburn, J. *Rogers, H. *Moore and A. *Clarke. Coke's offer to ordain those present who were not already ordained and so enable them

to administer the Sacrament, met with general approval, but Moore and Mather persuaded them to take no action without consulting the Conference. It was agreed to propose (a) that preachers be 'received into *full connexion' by ordination as deacons, (b) that those approved by Conference be ordained elders, and (c) that the Connexion be organized into eight 'divisions', each under an annually appointed *'Superintendent'. Although this was in line with the organization of *American Methodism, the plan was rejected by Conference as 'tending to create invidious and unhallowed distinctions among brethren', partly because its proposers had nominated all but one of themselves as 'Superintendents'.

G. Smith (1858–61) 2 pp. 99–104, 691; *HMGB* 3 pp. 257–60

JAV

Lidgett, Dr John Scott, CH (1854–1953; e.m. 1876) WM minister, born in Lewisham. While serving in the *Cambridge Circuit he became acutely aware of the gulf between rich and poor and the evils of poverty, bad housing and unemployment. Encouraged and supported by W.F. *Moulton, he established the *Bermondsey Settlement, where he was Warden from 1892 to 1949. His numerous church and civic offices included being President of the WM Conference 1908, Superintendent of the South London Mission 1909–18 and 1942–43, first President of the Methodist Conference after the 1932 Union, leader of the Progressive Party on the London County Council, Vice-Chancellor of London University and chairman of the executive committee of the Central Council for Nursing. Sometimes described as 'the greatest Methodist since Wesley', he was made a Companion of Honour in recognition of his work in Bermondsey and towards *Methodist Union. He was editor of the *Methodist Times* 1907–18. Notable among his theological works were his *Fernley Lecture on the Atonement (1898) and *The Fatherhood of God* (1902). His two autobiographical works were *Reminiscences* (1928) and *My Guided Life* (1936).

MR 25 June 1953; J.D. Beasley (1989); R.E. Davie (1957)

JDB

Lightley, John William (1867–1948; e.m. 1892) was WM minister of the Methodist Church in Paris 1901–7, OT Tutor at *Headingley College 1910–16 and Chairman of the Leeds District 1915–30. He was President of the 1928 Conference. Returning to Headingley as Principal and Resident Tutor from 1930 to 1936, he fostered closer relations with the University of Leeds. His publications included the 1919 *Fernley Lecture on *Jewish Sects and Parties in the Time of Christ*.

MR 17 June 1948

JAV

Lightwood, James Thomas (1856–1944), musicologist, born in *Leeds, the youngest son of the Rev. Edward Lightwood (d. 1892; e.m. 1841). After leaving *Kingswood School he worked as a draper in *Lincoln before embarking on a scholastic career. In 1879 he joined his brother E.R. Lightwood in opening Pembroke House, a boarding school in Lytham, Lancs. In 1910 he became the founding editor of *The Choir* magazine and from then on became the connexional adviser on musical matters (including finding the unique 1761 Snetzler organ for the *New Room). His books include *Hymn Tunes and their Story* (1905), *Methodist Music of the eighteenth Century* (1927), USThe Music of the Methodist Hymn-book (1935) and *Samuel Wesley, Musician* (1937). But none of his five tunes in *MHB* has survived into *HP*.

PLC

Limerick   JW visited the city on 17 occasions between 1749 and 1789. The first Irish Conference met there in 1752 and the third in 1758. P. *Embury and B. *Heck, pioneers of Methodism in New York, sailed from there in 1760, and it was the home of JW's correspondent Mrs E. *Bennis.

JWJ; JWL

DALC

Lincoln   JW did not preach in the city until 1787. A society of four members was formed that year in the home of Dorothy Fisher, who paid for the first chapel at Gowt's Bridge. Wesley Chapel (where the WM Conference met in 1909 and 1925) was opened in 1836; Hannah Memorial (commemorating J. *Hannah) in 1864. A WM day school, opened in 1845 in the Wesley Rooms, moved to premises in Rosemary Lane in 1859 and closed in 1932. The Lincoln WM Circuit was formed from Gainsborough in 1801.

PM was introduced in 1818 by W. *Clowes, who preached in Castle Square and was mobbed. Their first chapel in Mint Lane (1819) was replaced by Portland Place (1839) and then by High Street (1905). Six smaller chapels were opened in work-ing-class areas. The Reform movement led to the secession of 500 members from WM in 1851, resulting in the Silver Street UMFC chapel (1857) with three offshoots, including Portland Street, a cause started by the parents of W.C. *Jackson.

Methodist businessmen who were also office-holders in the Church became Mayors or Sheriffs. Miss Lena J. Wallis JP (1868–1962) was the first woman to represent the Lincoln District in the WM Conference (1911).

A. Watmough (1829); George Barratt (1866); W. Leary (1969)

WL

Lister, William (1804–80; e.m. 1827) was born into an Anglican family at Old Washington, Co. Durham, but became a WM in his youth. On moving to Tyneside, the family joined Wallsend PM society in 1822. After working as a coal miner, he entered the PM ministry and travelled mainly in the North East. He served as *Book Steward 1865–70, was President of the Conference in 1868 and a Deed Poll member from 1871, as well as being Conference Secretary and Treasurer of the Superannuated Ministers' Fund.

F.H. Hurd (1872) pp. 188–203; G.J. Stevenson (1884–86) 5 pp. 696–707

DCD

Literature   Methodism (or the Evangelical Revival as a whole) has been seen (e.g. by F.C. *Gill and T.B. Shepherd) as a precursor of the Romantic Movement. Both were a reaction against the more formal Augustan age that preceded them. Of the considerable volume of literature produced by eighteenth century Methodism, little would be generally acclaimed as of lasting literary value. Nevertheless, JW was a master of unadorned prose (not least in his voluminous correspondence), which contrasts sharply with the ponderous Johnsonese style of his day. He contributed to popular literacy through a pocket dictionary and a simple English grammar and was a pioneer anthologist, e.g. in his *Collection of Moral and Sacred Poems* (1744). Both he and his brother Charles were well read in the English poets, notably Milton, Herbert, Prior and Edward Young. But for appreciation of the literary qualities of his own verse CW had to wait two centuries for a George Sampson and a Donald Davie. Robert Southey wrote one of the earliest lives of JW (1820) and in 1928 Evelyn Waugh was working on another, but this came to nothing apart from satirical references in *Vile Bodies* (1930).

Despite a lack of major literary figures in its own ranks, Methodism was a significant element in the family background of the *Brontës, George Eliot, Arnold Bennett and Rudyard *Kipling. It produced several minor novelists (such as 'John Ackworth' (F.R. *Smith), the *Fowler sisters, M.G. *Pearse, the *Hocking brothers, 'Ramsay Guthrie' (J.G. *Bowran), J. *Riley and writers popular at least with Methodist readers, such as H.L. *Gee, W.J. *May and W. *Storey. James Hilton went to The *Leys School and Emlyn Williams attended a Methodist Sunday School. Howard Spring was a *local preacher for a short period in his youth. Methodism was more prolific of writers of dialect verse (e.g. T. *Wilson, J. *Castillo, O. *Ormerod and E. *Waugh), popular in the nineteenth century, especially in the north. More serious poets have included J.W. *Thomas and E. *Tatham in the nineteenth century, and in the twentieth, J. *Freeman and F.P. *Green. G.H. *Vallins was a skilful parodist. Country writers and broadcasters include R. *Whitlock, C. *Porteus and G.B. *Evens ('Romany'). The twentieth century also produced E.J. *Thompson, a literary scholar of the calibre of Professor B. *Willey, a literary journalist like G.O. *Thomas and the children's writer Lucy M. Boston. Irish and, even more, Welsh Methodists have made a notable contribution to their national literature both in the vernacular and in English.

————

F.C. Gill (1937); T.B. Shepherd (1940); D. Davie (1978)

JAV

Litten, John Howard, CBE (1878–1954; e.m. 1903), Principal of *NCH. He trained as a teacher and taught at *Westminster College before entering the ministry. In 1917, when he joined the NCH, his distinctive life's work began. As Principal, 1933–50, he founded the Sisters' Training School at Highbury and Princess Alice College, *Birmingham to provide training in Child Care; established small mixed family groups throughout the NCH; instituted the Convocation lecture; built children's flats and accepted many refugee children; and founded the National Council of Associated Children's Homes. He served on the Curtis Committee, whose report led to the Children's Act of 1948. Restless and energetic, he was a shrewd selector of colleagues, who returned his loyalty. He retired in 1950 to Australia.

————

MR 30 Sept. 1954

WDH/JHL

Liverpool Methodist beginnings are obscure, but a chapel (the first in the north-west) was opened in Pitt Street in 1750, despite being far to the west of the main centres of Methodist activity in Lancashire. On his first visit, in April 1755, JW was impressed by both the people and the elegant streets. Liverpool became head of a circuit in 1766 and the growing population led to a second chapel in 1790. The WM Conference met in Liverpool for the first time in 1807 and again in 1820, when the *'Liverpool Minutes' were passed. In 1876 the first Central Mission in Methodism was established by C. *Garrett at the old Pitt Street chapel, but a purpose-built Central Hall had to wait until 1903.

A WM minority seceded to the MNC in 1797, but remained small in numbers relative to the WM. Despite this the MNC Conference met there in 1824, 1836, 1848 and 1861.

PM evangelists from Cheshire missioned the town in 1821, opening a chapel in Maguire Street, but they too were unable to emulate WM success. In the 1890s Liverpool was widely regarded as PM's 'problem city', but expansion followed in Edwardian times. The PM Conference met there in 1888 and 1923.

Anti-Conference sentiment grew in WM in the 1830s, finding expression in the local publication of a *Circular to Wesleyan Methodists* (1830–33). A damaging secession occurred in 1834, although Free Methodism was never as strong as in *Rochdale or *Manchester. IM established a cause in 1826 and the IM Conference met there seven times up to 1932.

————

Conference Handbook 1939, 1949, 1960; F.M. Parkinson in *PWHS* 1 pp. 104–8; 2 pp. 65–8; I. Sellers (1971); C. Gwyther (*c.*1975); D.A. Gowland (1979)

EAR

'Liverpool Minutes' The Conference of 1820 was held in *Liverpool, with J. *Bunting in the Presidential chair. A decrease of 4,688 members was reported, the first ever recorded in the British circuits. (*Ireland, in contrast, reported an increase of 1,220.) This led to some soul-searching and renewed attention to JW's 'Rules of a Helper' and other parts of the *Large Minutes. The outcome was a series of resolutions in which the preachers rededicated themselves to their duties as pastors and preachers. Among the measures they pledged themselves to were: a renewal of *field preaching and *Home Mission activities, public prayer meetings; attention to children, young people and 'backsliders'; pastoral visiting and meetings with *class leaders; encouragement of Sabbath observance and attendance at the *Lord's Supper; the preparation of catechisms and resumption of quarterly schedules; discouragement of 'the spirit of strife and debate' in *Leaders' and *Quarterly Meetings, and a day of special *fasting and prayer. How much of this was put into effect is difficult to determine, but it became a standard practice for these 'Liverpool Minutes' to be read annually at Circuit and District meetings, until they were replaced in 1885 by fresh 'Resolutions on Pastoral Work'.

Minutes 1820, 1885; *HMGB* 4 pp. 367–72
JAV

Lives of the Early Methodist Preachers

were autobiographical records collected by T. *Jackson chiefly from the *Arminian Magazine* and from personal accounts sent to JW. The first edition in three volumes was published in 1837–8; followed by a second edition in five volumes (1846), a third in six volumes (1865) and a fourth, also in six volumes and 'with additional lives' (totalling 41) in 1871. The lives vary widely in length and reflect the very varied backgrounds and education of the early itinerants. They are written with artless simplicity and sincere conviction, each detailing his own conversion and experience in the itinerancy. In 1912–14 J. *Telford re-edited them under the title *Wesley's Veterans*; he omitted five, but added in most cases an obituary taken from the *Minutes of Conference*.

PWHS 22 pp. 102–5
WL

Lloyd, Henry (d.1799), one of the earliest Methodist preachers, was born in Rhydri (Glam). From 1747 he itinerated widely, but because he could speak Welsh spent most of his time in South Wales and interpreted for JW on at least one occasion. He co-operated with the Welsh CM and wrote admiring elegies on both H. *Harris and G. *Whitefield. He also translated works by J&CW. He visited *Trevecka frequently and like J. *Evans of Bala and T. *Ffoulkes was regarded as the very embodiment of a spirit of co-operation and goodwill among Methodists of all shades.

C. Atmore (1801) pp. 243–44; A.H. Williams (1935) pp. 31–6; *HMGB* 3 p. 257
OEE

Lloyd Webber, Dr William Southcombe, CBE, FRCM, FRCO (1914–82), organist and composer, was Professor of Theory and Composition at the London College of Music from 1946 and its Director from 1964. He was music director at All Saints, Margaret Street and from 1958 music director and organist at *Westminster Central Hall. He was the father of the highly successful composer **Andrew Lloyd Webber** (b.1948; knighted 1992) and the cellist **Julian Lloyd Webber** (b.1951).

MR 11 Sept. 1997
JAV

Loane, Dr Edith M. (*née* McKinney) (1926–) was born in Co. Armagh and educated at *Methodist College and Queen's University, Belfast. She qualified in medicine, specializing in psychiatry. Among her many national and international roles, she has been treasurer and President of the World Federation of Methodist and Uniting Church Women and chairperson and treasurer of the National Women's Council of Ireland. In 1999 the WMC made her a member of its new Honorable Order of Jerusalem. Her father, the Rev. J.W. McKinney (1895–1974; e.m. 1921), was founding Principal of *Gurteen Agricultural College, of which her husband Dr Oscar Loane also became Principal.

NWT

Local Preachers are lay persons, voluntary and part-time, who have served Methodism from the earliest days as evangelists and in conducting services, largely within the circuits in which they reside and alongside the full-time paid itinerants ('ministers'). T. *Westell and T. *Maxfield were two of the earliest Methodist lay preachers, though working in circumstances very different from the settled patterns of later years. About the time of JW's death there were an estimated 2,000 local and 300 itinerant preachers. Virtually all local preachers at that time were male, though JW did admit a few *women preachers who had an 'extraordinary call'. With no formal training demanded, the only requirement was that they should exhibit the necessary 'gifts, grace and fruits'. Their appointments came to be arranged by the *Superintendent minister and set out on a quarterly *preaching plan.

Matters relating to the status and discipline of local preachers came to a head after 1791, as many became restive under the controls increasingly imposed by their circuit ministers and the all-ministerial *Conference. Predictably, they were active in the secessions from WM from 1797 on and many found greater scope and freedom in the new non-Wesleyan connexions. This included the use of women as local preachers. WM did not give women preachers equal status with men until 1918.

By 1900 there were some 40,000 local preachers, compared with 5,000 ministers, in the Methodist denominations as a whole. Yet, while being essential to the continued existence of Methodism, little was done formally to equip them for their work. Voluntary training programmes began to be offered towards the end of the nineteenth century, but it was not until 1937 that a compulsory written examination was introduced for all new preachers. The current training scheme, based on units integrating biblical study, theology and liturgical practice and supervised by local tutors, was introduced in 1990. More recently, a programme for the 'continuing development' of all local preachers has been introduced.

There has been little formal organization of local preachers. Quarterly preachers' meetings in each circuit began in 1796 and continue today, together with committees at District level. A connexional Local Preachers Department (now Office) was established in 1932. All but the first of its full-time secretaries have been ministers. The *LPMAA, began to care for local preachers in need in 1849.

Local preachers have always been drawn from all walks of life and are accorded much freedom with regard to dress in the pulpit and their mode of leading worship. Some non-Wesleyan connexions allowed them to celebrate the *Lord's Supper, but since the 1932 *Methodist Union this has been permitted only in exceptional cases. There are at present c. 12,500 local preachers in British Methodism, some 10,000 of them active.

G.E. Milburn & M. Batty (1995) and sources listed therein, pp. 339–44

GEM

Local Preachers Mutual Aid Association

Several local initiatives in the years before 1849 (e.g in *Bolton, *Bristol and *Cambridge) foreshadowed the formation of the LPMAA. The society formed in Bristol expressed its purposes as 'promoting brotherly love, relieving the distressed, administering to the wants and necessities of the afflicted, and smoothing the pillow of death'. In June 1849 Francis Pearson, a *local preacher in the Cromford Circuit, initiated a correspondence in the *Wesleyan Times which led to an Aggregate Meeting of over 600 WM local preachers in London on 3–4th October. This formally established the WM LPMAA, adopted resolutions for the preparation of rules, appointed officers and elected a General Committee. W. *Harris, who had chaired the meetings, was elected the first President. Each circuit was invited to send a representative to the annual Aggregate Meeting.

From 1851 the Association retained in membership any local preachers who were expelled from or left the WM as a result of the Reform movement. In consequence of this it was eschewed by the WM establishment for nearly a quarter of a century. Local preachers of the UMFC (1857), WRU (1859), MNC (1896), BC (1907) and PM (1932) became eligible for membership as circumstances made this necessary or appropriate. Notable laymen who have served as President of the Association include 'Judge' S.D. *Waddy (1870), Sir W.H. *Stephenson (1883, 1895), Sir John Barnsley, a *Birmingham builder (1899), Sir Thomas Rowbotham, magistrate and Mayor of Stockport (1909) and R.J. *Soper MP (1939).

Following World War II the LPMAA diversified its provision to include residential care homes and now maintains five, at Westcliff-on-Sea, Grange-over Sands, Woodhall Spa, Minehead and Rickmansworth. It shared with *MHA in creating a sheltered housing development in *Sheffield (1989) and continues to provide financial and personal help for local preachers and their dependants in their own homes. The Association formally became part of the connexional structures in 1996. Its periodical *The Local Preachers Magazine* has been published without a break since 1851 and now appears quarterly.

F.H. Buss & R G. Burnett (1949); C.A. Parker in G. Milburn & M. Batty (1995); C.A. Parker (1998)

WL

Lockhart, James (1861–1943; e.m. 1884), PM minister, born at Stewartstown, Co. Tyrone. He was Principal of *Hartley Victoria College 1918–23, President of the Conference in 1925 and President of the FCFC in 1932.

MR 18 March 1943

JAV

Lockhart, Richard A., OBE (1893–1963; e.m. 1918), Irish minister and missionary, born in *Belfast and educated at *Methodist College. In 1922 he went out to the Gold Coast (now *Ghana), where he became Principal of Mfantsipim School. Under his leadership the school played an important part in the life of the community. After seven years (1936–43) in Irish circuits, he was invited by the government of *Kenya to become Principal of Kagumo teacher training college. His twelve years there overlapped with the emergence of the Mau Mau movement.

A.A. Boahen (1996) pp. 241–330

NWT

Lofthouse, William Francis (1871–1965; e.m. 1896), generally considered the widest-ranging Methodist scholar of his time, was tutor at *Handsworth from 1904 to 1965 and Principal 1925–40. He was President of the WM Conference in 1929. Early influenced by J.S. *Lidgett, he saw, ahead of many, the need to study social conditions in the light of the Gospel and was a founder member of the *Union for Social Service. His consistent concern with ethics as a key branch of theology was expressed most clearly in his *Ethics and Atonement* (1906). He was also a philosopher and OT scholar (writing a commentary on Ezekiel) and active in both the 'Life and Work' and 'Faith and Order' sections of the inter-war ecumenical movement. He had a profound influence on generations of Handsworth students.

Times 6 July 1965; *MR* 8 & 15 July 1965

DJC

London JW was familiar with the city from his schooldays and it became his main base after his return from Georgia in 1738. Between preaching tours his winters were spent in and around London. His headquarters for nearly 40 years was the *Foundery in Moorfields, replaced by *City Road Chapel in 1778. In addition he had *West Street Chapel in the West End, Snowsfields Chapel, Southwark and others in Spitalfields etc.

Compared with Cornwall or the industrial North, London Methodism grew slowly. The London Circuit was divided into East and West in 1807 and further sub-division did not take place until the 1820s. A major boost to chapel-building was provided in the rapidly expanding outer suburbs by the *Metropolitan Chapel Building Fund in the 1860s. In the inner suburbs the East End Mission was launched by the Conference of 1861 under the leadership of A. M'Aulay at Bow and from the 1880s on was part of the *Forward Movement. At the time of the 1851 *Religious Census the London Registration Division extended from Kensington to Poplar, and south of the river from Greenwich and Lewisham westwards to Lambeth and Camberwell, taking in parts of Middlesex, Surrey and Kent. The Census

recorded 154 Methodist places of worship, of which 98 were WM and 21 PM. Otherwise, only the WMA and WR had any significant presence in the capital. Total attendances on Census Sunday were 62,442 (80% of them WM). This represents 2.6% of the population and 7% of attendances across all denominations.

By 1902–3 the number of chapels had risen to 383 (231 in the County of London, plus 152 in Greater London) and 254 of these were WM. Adult attendances totalled 21,169 in the morning and 39,531 in the evening; 85% of them WM. The overall Methodist total of 60,700 represented 9% of all recorded attendances. By the 1980s the 33 boroughs and the City of London had a population of *c*. 9 million; in 1997, *c*. 7 million. By 1989 there were only 252 Methodist Churches in the London area (90 in Inner London, 162 in Outer London, reflecting the outward shift of population). Two thirds of these were in the north, but the largest congregations were in the southwest. Total adult attendances were 20,600 (7,900 in Inner and 12,700 in Outer London). Membership stood at 24,000 (5,800 in Inner and 19,100 in Outer London).

The 1990s have seen a reversal of the post-war migration to the suburbs and new towns, with new growth in the inner city, largely as a result of the rise of multi-racial congregations. Methodist worship now occurs in several languages: Cantonese and Mandarin at Kings Cross; Urdu and Punjabi at Southall; Tamil at Hammersmith; and Korean in several places. Church plants from these congregations are to be found throughout the region. Methodism ministers to the needy and is a participant in the London Churches Group and the London Church Leaders Group. Most inner-city Missions have day centres and other social work programmes caring for the homeless and the poorest. Until 1957 there were six Methodist Districts covering London and most of the South-East, but with the appointment of separated Chairmen these were reduced to four. A proposal to create a new Greater London District in the 1980s was rejected in favour of retaining the four Districts, with a co-ordinating task given to the London Committee. The Committee administers the London Mission Fund, which supports work in the region in regard to both ministry and property.

See also **New London Initiative**

MR 29 June 1939; *WMM* 1865 pp. 438–48; R. Mudie-Smith (1904); Hugh McLeod (1974); London Mission (1961)

PWS

London Quarterly Review , first advocated by J.H. *Rigg, began publication in September 1853, with the backing of Rigg, W. *Arthur, G. *Osborn, W.B. *Pope and F.J. *Jobson and the financial support of two laymen, John Robinson Kay and J.S. *Budgett. Recurrent commercial difficulties made it dependent on the help of the WM Book Room until it became connexional property in 1897. Under the long editorship of Pope (1862–86) and Rigg (1883–98) its scope was wide-ranging and its tone broadly conservative. The third series, launched in January 1899, carried signed articles for the first time. J. *Telford, editor 1905–34, saw the post-Union merger with the PM *Holborn Review, which was in financial trouble despite the herculean efforts of A.S. *Peake (editor 1919–29). A further amalgamation with the Church Quarterly Review (1968) produced the short-lived Church Quarterly, which ceased publication in 1971. After an interval, in 1974 its place was taken by the Epworth Review.

William Strawson in The Church Quarterly, July 1968 pp. 41–52

MW

Londonderry A small society was formed in 1753. JW visited the town on ten occasions between 1765 and 1789 and on his first visit was treated with unaccustomed deference by the Mayor. His hosts were the parents of A. *Knox, who became secretary to Lord Castlereagh.

JWJ; C.H. Crookshan (1886) vol. 2

DALC

Long, G. Ernest (1910–93; e.m. 1932), missionary in *India, was born in *Southport and gained 1st class honours in Classics at Liverpool University. After training at *Wesley House, Cambridge, he served 1934–51 in the Hyderabad District and then in the Medak and Dornakal Dioceses of CSI. As well as being a circuit minister, he was Vice-Principal of the Medak Evangelists' Training School and Principal of Andhra United Theological College, Dornakal. From 1953 to 1970 he taught Church History at *Handsworth College, but valued above all being a preacher of the gospel.

MR 23 Sept. 1993

JAV

Longbottom, William (1799–1849; e.m. 1827), WM missionary to *India and *Australia, born in Bingley, Yorks. After seven years in

Madras, he went to Cape Town to recover his health and was then appointed to the Swan River Mission in Perth, WA. Arriving in Hobart early in 1835, he sailed for Fremantle in a small brig which was wrecked off the South Australia coast, After various vicissitudes the party reached Adelaide in August 1838, where a WM society had been formed the previous year. He organized the church there by introducing 'the whole system of our admirable discipline'.

ADEB; J. Haslam (1886)

DGH

Longridge, Michael (1757–1815), prosperous WM draper and mercer of *Sunderland. As a *local preacher he pioneered Methodist expansion in the vast Sunderland Circuit and was largely responsible for the establishment of Sunday Schools in Sunderland in 1786. In the troubled years after JW's death he steered a middle course and worked hard for reconciliation, befriending A *Kilham but retaining his own loyalty to WM. He was actively involved in drafting the *Plan of Pacification A man of culture, steeped in *Puritan theology, he owned a large library and promoted libraries in Sunderland. He was a 'father and friend' to the young local preacher J. *Everett and encouraged the education of local preachers in general.

WMM 1815 pp. 481–6, 561–8; G.E. Milburn, in WHS(NE) 23 (Feb. 1975) pp. 22–8

GEM

Longton see **Stoke-on-Trent**

Lonsdale, Mrs Marjorie Walton (1915–), educationalist and Vice-President of the Conference in 1961. Born into a Methodist family in the mining village of Coundon, Co. Durham, she became a *local preacher and national Vice-President of the *Order of Christian Witness. On her marriage in 1939 she moved to Sussex. Her husband was killed in action in the RAF. In 1952 she joined the staff of *Trinity Hall, Southport, where she served as Headmistress from 1957 until the school closed in 1970. She then became Deputy Head at *Hunmanby Hall until her retirement.

MR 6 July 1961, 16 July 1970

PMW

Lord's Supper Through the influence of his parents and then for a while the Non-Jurors, JW held a high view of the Lord's Supper or Holy

Communion at a time when it was widely neglected in the Church of England. The Oxford Methodists (or *'Holy Club') were nicknamed 'Methodists' or 'Sacramentarians' largely because they communicated regularly. JW's heart-warming experience in Aldersgate Street in 1738 did not diminish this, though it added new elements to his experience. He advocated 'constant Communion' and continued to receive it on an average once every four or five days. In due course he began to celebrate it not only in Anglican but also in Methodist buildings such as *West Street Chapel, London. He believed it to be a 'converting' and not merely a 'confirming' ordinance; but it called for sincere penitence and before long he required the production of a class ticket or a special communion note for admission to it in Methodist buildings. Society members were expected to communicate regularly. In 1745 he and CW published *Hymns on the Lord's Supper, expressing 'higher' sacramental doctrines than are now common in Methodism. In the *Sunday Service (1784) JW slightly revised the Anglican service.

After JW's death the administration of the Sacrament by the unordained itinerants was one of the most divisive issues that had to be faced. This was largely resolved by the *Plan of Pacification in 1795. There were various further revisions and some branches of Methodism before 1932 permitted lay administration and followed a more informal pattern, as in other Free Churches. The service was extensively revised in the 1975 *Methodist Service Book and further revised in the 1999 *Methodist Worship Book. Most town churches have had Communion about monthly; village churches quarterly. There was a widespread custom in the past that between the preaching service and a much abbreviated Communion there was a break during which many worshippers departed. This has now largely died out; Communion services are slightly more frequent and the full service is often used.

See also **Means of Grace**; **Sacraments**

J.C. Bowmer (1951); J.C. Bowmer (1961); J.E. Rattenbury (1948)

ARG

Lot, Use of Decision by lot, following Acts 1:26, was a *Moravian practice stemming, like 'opening the Bible' at random, from belief in divine providence. Both were adopted by JW when in spiritual distress or perplexity. The Conference of 1792, quoting Prov. 18:18, decided by lot that the Sacrament would not be administered in the ensuing year, but the usage gradually faded out and in 1804 was rejected as a method of settling a dispute. Many Methodists continued to look for guidance by opening the Bible at random or used 'promise boxes' (which are still being produced).

Minutes 1 (1812) p. 263; SJ 2 pp. 56, 158

MB

Lott, Dr Eric J. (1934– ;e.m. 1958), missionary in *India, was trained at *Richmond College and received his M.Litt and Ph.D. from Lancaster University for studies in Hinduism. He served in Andhra Pradesh 1959–77, where he became proficient in Telugu and Sanskrit, later also learning Kannada. From 1962 he taught at the Andhra Union Theological College and from 1977 to 1988 at the United Theological College, Bangalore, where he was Professor of Religion and Culture, editor of the *Bangalore Theological Forum* and Dean of Doctoral Research, specializing in eco-theology. Among numerous other publications, his pioneering writings on the Indian religious traditions (e.g. *Vedantic Approaches to God* (1980) and *Vision, Tradition, Interpretation* (1988)) address the issue of theological inculturation. On returning to Britain he had an inner-city ministry in *Leicester 1988–94.

D.C. Scott in *Re-Visioning India's Religious Traditions* (Bangalore 1996)

JAV

Louth was visited by JW four times between 1766 and 1788. The first extant class book lists four members in 1769, when a chapel was built in Eastgate (replaced 1808, enlarged 1835; interior modernized 1972). The Louth Circuit was formed from Grimsby in 1799.

The town was missioned for PM in 1820 by Thomas King; a chapel was built in 1836, replaced by a larger one in 1850. The WMA had a small cause for a few years before 1862. The Reform movement was introduced in 1849. J.B. Sharpley, corn merchant, alderman, magistrate and three times mayor was its chief spokesman. A chapel with eight Corinthian pillars was built in 1854. During the later nineteenth century and until *Methodist Union the three circuits spread across the marshes and wolds.

W. Leary & D.N. Robinson (1981)

WL

Love, Joseph (1796–1875), MNC layman, born near North Shields. He followed his father down the mine, working as a trapper-boy until 1821. He then became a hawker of drapery and groceries. After other commercial ventures, the turning point came in 1840 when he and a partner purchased the Brancepeth coal royalties and sank a mine. Other collieries followed until he became one of *Durham's leading proprietors. A MNC *local preacher from 1819, he gave generously to the Church, chiefly to finance chapel-building and so facilitated the great MNC expansion in the Durham coalfield, 1850–75. He was elected a MNC *Guardian Representative in 1857 and died virtually a millionaire.

PWHS 44 pp. 79–80

EAR

Love-feast, a communal meal, usually traced to the *Agape* of the Early Church which, in turn, may have had its roots in Jewish feasts and had close similarities with the daily common meal of the Essenes. NT passages linked with the Agape include Acts 2:42, 46, 1 Cor. 11:18–34 and Jude 12. The *Moravian Brethren in Germany, in the 1720s, revived this practice in the form of a common meal of worship and celebration. Almost certainly JW was introduced to it through his contact with the Moravians. He recounts a moving Love-feast held at *Fetter Lane on 1 January 1739. Early Methodists celebrated a quarterly Love-feast with 'a little plain cake and water', together with singing and testimony. JW explained the origin and purpose of the Love-feast in Methodism in a letter to V. *Perronet in December 1748. The Love Feast continued in all the various branches of nineteenth-century Methodism, but began to wane toward the close of that century. This was because Eucharistic practices became more fixed in Methodist worship, revivalist services were on the decline and there seemed to be less need for it as more set worship patterns were established.

F. Baker (1957)

HMG

Loveless, George (1796–1874), Dorset farm labourer and WM *local preacher. In 1833 he formed 'the Friendly Society of Agricultural Labours' at Tolpuddle. In an excessively repressive reaction to the social unrest represented by the 'Captain Swing' riots and rick-burning, he and his five fellow members (the 'Tolpuddle Martyrs'), all but one of whom were Methodists, were convicted of taking an unlawful oath and sentenced to seven years' transportation to Van Diemen's Land. Public outcry followed (in which the WM leadership remained conspicuously silent) and a full pardon was eventually granted. Returning home in 1837, Loveless wrote *The Victims of Whiggery*. After living briefly in Essex, where he was active in the *Chartist agitation, he emigrated with his wife and family to Ontario. They farmed at Siloam, where they were instrumental in building the first Methodist church.

See also **Trade Unionism**

MR(W) 1907 pp. 41–4; O.Rattenbury (1931); G.E. Fussell (1948); J. Marlowe (1974); *HMGB* 4 pp. 432–4

NADS

Lovett, William (1800–77), *Chartist, born in Newlyn, near Penzance and brought up by his mother as a strict Methodist. He was for a time a BC *local preacher, but later became a free thinker. In 1821 he moved to London to find work and there became active in the Owenite co-operative movement. In 1836 he became secretary of the London Working Men's Association, which aimed to achieve equal political and social rights. Helped by Daniel O'Connell and a few radical MPs, the Association drew up the 'People's Charter', which was published in 1838, and Lovett became secretary. After opposing a police attack on a peaceful crowd in *Birmingham in 1840, he was committed to prison, where he wrote *Chartism or a New Organisation of the People* (1841). He was active in the Anti-Slavery League and ended his days as a teacher of anatomy.

NADS

Luddism was the name given by contemporaries to the activities of machine-breakers in the Midlands and North during the period 1811–16. Historians have long debated the causes and character of the movement, focusing particularly on whether it was primarily a form of industrial protest motivated by economic hardship or part of a wider insurrectionary political movement. Historians of Methodism have sought to establish the character and extent of Methodist involvement in the disturbances, which occurred in some of the areas of most rapid Methodist expansion in that decade. Connexional leaders were anxious to demonstrate their loyalty in order to remove any justification for restrictions on itinerant preaching threatened by the *Sidmouth Bill of 1811; hence the exhortations of WM preachers to 'fear the Lord and the King, and meddle not with them that are given to change'. But D. Hempton has questioned the effectiveness of such injunctions and W.R. *Ward has suggested that Methodists 'stood on both sides of the conflict'. Some Methodist employers, for example **Daniel Burton** of Middleton, Lancs and **Francis Vickerman** of *Huddersfield, were certainly targeted by the Luddites. But evidence for Methodist participation in the riots has proved more elusive. For J. *Bunting, who had sanctioned the burial of a Luddite son of Methodist parents in the graveyard of his *Halifax chapel, the 'awful fact' that of 17 Luddites hanged at *York in January 1813 no fewer than six were 'sons of Methodists' demonstrated the failure of Methodist parents and suggested that Methodist progress in the West Riding had been 'more swift than solid; more extensive than deep'.

W.R Ward (1972); D. Hempton (1984); J.A. Hargreaves in *Northern History* 26 (1990) pp. 160–85
JAH

Luke, John (1849–1916; e.m. 1871), BC minister, born in Cornwall and apprenticed to an iron founder before becoming a teacher in South Wales and a *hired local preacher in 1870. He was very much a social reformer and loved debate on any public platform. He was Connexional Secretary 1896–99 and Secretary of the Chapel Committee for nine years, and was President of the BC Conference two years running, 1900 and 1901, and of the UM Conference in 1912. He was a BC representative at the Ecumenical Methodist Conference in 1901.

WL

Lumb, Matthew (1761–1847; e.m. 1783), one of the early missionaries appointed by T. *Coke to the *West Indies. In 1788 he was stationed in Antigua, and then in St Vincent, where he was imprisoned for preaching to Negro slaves. On his release he served in Barbados, but returned to England in 1793 due to ill health and worked in home circuits until his retirement in 1826.

GRS

Lunn Family Sir Henry Simpson Lunn (1859–1939; e.m. 1882), WM minister, medical missionary and Liberal politician, came from an old Lincolnshire Methodist family. He was educated at *Headingley College and Trinity College, Dublin. His missionary service in *India (1887–88) was curtailed by illness and on returning to England he published articles severely critical of WMMS policy. The ensuing *missionary controversy led him to resign from the ministry (1893)

and redirect his energies into journalism and action for Christian unity. He edited the strongly ecumenical *Review of the Churches* (1891–96) and organized a series of high-level conferences on unity at Grindelwald, Switzerland. Following the 1920 Lambeth Conference he initiated another series of Anglican-Free Church unity talks at Mürren. (Though he originally had no commercial motive, his organization of overseas travel and accommodation developed into the Lunn Travel Company.) In 1910 he was confirmed as an Anglican, though continuing to see himself, like JW, as 'a Methodist member of the Church of England'. In 1920 he published *Reunion and Lambeth*. As well as being a pioneer ecumenist, he was a 'Catholic' Methodist, publishing a series of books in the spirit of JW's *Christian Library, designed to open up to Methodists the classic treasures of Christian devotion: *The Love of Jesus* (1911), *Retreats for the Soul* (1918) and *The Secret of the Saints* (1933). He wrote two volumes of autobiography, *Chapters from my Life* (1918) and *Nearing the Harbour* (1934). Politically he was a staunch Liberal, endorsing Irish Home Rule and taking a pro-Boer stance in the war of 1899–1902. He was knighted in 1910. The best known of his three sons, **Sir Arnold Lunn** (1888–1974), author and pioneer of the sport of ski-ing, wrote a life of JW (1929). After engaging in public controversy with Mgr Ronald Knox, he became a Roman Catholic. His grandson, David, became a Benedictine monk at Downside, eventually left the Order (though remaining a Roman Catholic) and married the daughter of a Methodist family. He taught history at Bristol Grammar School until his death in 1996. Another of Sir Henry Lunn's sons, **Hugh Kingsmill Lunn** (1889–1949), was a versatile, prolific and iconoclastic author.

MR 23 March 1939; *DNB*; M. Holroyd (1964)
JAN

Lutheranism Although JW had learned German on his way to Georgia, there is no evidence that he read Luther except in translation. Luther's commentary on *Galatians* and his Preface to *Romans* played a key part in the conversion experiences of CW and JW respectively in May 1738. But it is interesting that there are none of Luther's hymns among JW's translations from the German and nothing from Luther's writings was included in the *Christian Library*. W's knowledge of Lutheranism was mediated through *Moravian pietism; as he himself put it in a letter of 22 Aug. 1744: 'I love Calvin a little; Luther more; the

Moravians, Mr. Law, and Mr. Whitefield far more than either.' This involved some degree of distortion, e.g. in his charging Luther with two of his chief bugbears, *antinomianism and *mysticism. H. Lindström identified a difference of emphasis between them, Luther focusing on *justification, JW on *sanctification. However, Archbishop N. Söderblom provocatively suggested that JW might be seen as 'the Anglican version of Luther' and Methodism as the English equivalent of the Protestant Reformation. Not until the twentieth century was Methodism's understanding of Luther deepened by the studies of F. *Hildebrandt, P.S. *Watson and E.G. *Rupp.

F. Hildebrandt (1951)

JAV

Luton Industrial College, the brainchild of W. *Gowland, opened in April 1957, with the active encouragement of W.E. *Sangster. Beginning in the run-down premises of Chapel Street Methodist Church, it expanded into two tower-blocks, initially with the supprt of of Lord *Rank. Its threefold purpose was set out in its Charter. At the centre was Gowland's concern to make the Christian faith relevant to industrial society. Its courses were designed for non-Christians as well as Christians and for both trade unionists and management. Before long the *HM Department placed all the training of industrial chaplains in the hands of the College, but Gowland continued to stress that industrial mission was the task of the local church as well as of individual ministers. A number of lectures given by experts in various fields were published. Methodism's support was often equivocal. In 1985 Harold S. Clark (1940– ; e.m. 1967) became Principal. The College closed in 1996.

G.T. Brake (1984) pp. 668–9; D. Gowland & S. Roebuck (1990) pp. 115–81

JAV

Lycett, Sir Francis (1803–80), businessman and philanthropist. The glove-making firm of Dent & Allcroft prospered under his direction and he retired, a wealthy man, in 1867. A sheriff of London (1866), he was knighted in 1867. He stood unsuccessfully for Parliament as a Liberal candidate on three occasions. A member at *Islington, he gave large sums to WM causes, particularly through the *Metropolitan Chapel Building Fund. In 1870 he offered £50,000 for fifty new chapels. He was a founder of The *Leys School, Cambridge and a trustee of *Wesley's Chapel. Lycett Memorial Church, Stepney (1883) was built in his memory.

G.J. Stevenson (1884–86) 4 pp. 580–3

WDH

Lynch, James (1775–1858; e.m. 1808) was born in Co. Donegal and converted from Roman Catholicism in youth. He was one of the missionaries led by Dr T. *Coke in 1813 on a mission to Asia. After Coke's death at sea, he became the leader of the team. He served in Jaffna, Ceylon (now *Sri Lanka) until 1817, then moved to Madras to extend the mission to *India. He recognized the importance of education and of a trained local ministry and was open to the possibility that Hindus were not idol-worshippers in the biblical sense. His relations with the WMMS became strained owing to poor communication and he returned to Irish circuits in 1824, retiring to *Leeds in 1842.

N.W. Taggart (1986) pp. 104–28

NWT

Lyon, Alexander Ward, MP (1931–93), barrister and *Leeds *local preacher, represented *York 1966–83 and, it has been claimed, was one of the most able government ministers of his generation. He was Vice-Chairman of the BCC Board for Social Responsibility 1970–74.

DCD

Lyth Family of *York, associated with Centenary WM Chapel from its opening in 1840. **John Lyth** (1777–1853), a seed merchant and Freeman of the city, married Mary Burdsall (1782–1860), daughter of the early WM preacher R. *Burdsall. Among their sons were **R.B. *Lyth** (1810–87; e.m. 1836), Fiji missionary and Dr J. *Lyth. A grandson, D. *Hill and great-grandson, J.K. Hill (1867–1952; e.m. 1890) were both China missionaries.

H. Lee (1987)

DCD

Lyth, Dr John (1821–86; e.m. 1843) was apprenticed to a bookseller in *Hull, where he became a close friend of W.M. *Punshon, with whom he later collaborated on a book of poems. In 1859 he was sent to Würtemberg, Germany, where he introduced Methodist organization and discipline and campaigned for religious freedom against Lutheran restrictions. Returning to England, he was successively Chairman of the Sheffield, Hull, Nottingham and Newcastle Districts, retiring in 1883. His wide-ranging scholarly interests included philosophy, science and poetry. He contributed to the Sunday School hymnal and wrote a history of *York Methodism (1885).

WMM 1887 pp. 326–33

JAV

Lyth, Richard Burdsall, FRCS (1810–87; e.m. 1836), WM missionary to *Tonga (1838–39) and *Fiji (1839–55). Born in *York, he was the first medically qualified ministerial missionary. After 18 months in the Friendly Islands he joined J. *Hunt in extending the Fiji Mission to the stony field of Somosomo. The two men shared the same quiet, deep, spiritual faith which sustained them (and their wives) through years of barren struggle. Though an effective physician to both colleagues and flock, he was primarily a pastor and teacher, developing a system for the local training of catechists and teachers and making a major contribution to the extensive Bible-translation programme. Following Hunt's death in 1848 he became Chairman until his own health broke down and he left for *New Zealand in 1855. He was chaplain to the Forces in *Gibraltar 1869–73.

F&H 3; A.H. Wood vol. 2 (1978)

MJF

MacAfee, Daniel (1790–1873) was born in Bushmills, Co. Antrim. Received as a preacher in the Irish PWM Connexion in 1822, he quickly demonstrated a talent for controversial and anti-Catholic pamphleteering. In 1825 he was one of two preachers sent to England by the PWM Conference to assist M. *Robinson and other leaders at Beverley in establishing an English 'Church Methodist' Connexion on similar lines to their own economy. The experiment was short-lived and ended in mutual recrimination. In 1827 MacAfee was received into the Irish WM itinerancy and subsequently gained some celebrity by his *Letters to Daniel O'Connell* (1840). He died in London.

Irish Evangelist 1 Feb. 1873

RPR

McAllum, Duncan (?1755–1834; e.m. 1775), a Highlander with little formal education but enormous learning and wisdom, taught himself Latin, Greek, Hebrew, Syriac, civil and religious history. He was an itinerant for 50 years. On Sundays he often preached twice in English and twice in

Gaelic. JW called him 'the North Star', named him in the *Deed of Declaration and in 1787 ordained him for Scotland.

WMM 1834 p. 717; W.F. Swift (1947) p. 38

MB

M'Arthur, Sir William (1809–87) was born at Malin, Co. Donegal, the son of an Irish preacher. Apprenticed in *Enniskillen at 12, he built up his own woollen drapery business in *Londonderry. With his brother Alexander he extended the business to *Australia. In 1857 he moved to *London, where he became sheriff (1867), then alderman (1872) and Lord Mayor (1880). The following year he entertained the first Ecumenical Methodist Conference at a reception in the Mansion House. He was knighted in 1882. He was Liberal MP for Lambeth 1868–85 and was noted for supporting many philanthropic projects, including church extension and *overseas missions. He never lost his connection with Irish Methodism. After the introduction of lay representation he was a member of both the British and the Irish Conferences and was a key figure in establishing *Methodist College, Belfast.

See also **Watering Places Fund**

G.J. Stevenson (1884–86) 4 pp. 584–87; T. M'Cullagh (1891); N.W. Taggart (1986) pp. 59–63, 188–9

NWT

M'Aulay, Alexander (1818–90; e.m. 1840) was born in *Glasgow, where his father had been baptized by JW. After working in the Glasgow Infirmary, in 1838 he moved to London's East End and became a *local preacher in the WM chapel in Brick Lane, Spitalfields. He returned to Spitalfields as a minister in 1858 and after addressing the Conference of 1861 on the need for new initiatives in East London was appointed to Bow, to launch the East End Mission. He was responsible for the building of new churches and the creation of five new circuits in the East End. He was President of the Conference in 1876 and was appointed General Secretary of the *HM Committee. In retirement he travelled widely and died in Cape Town.

G.J. Stevenson (1884–6) 3 pp. 421–33; *MR* 11 Dec. 1890; W. Sampson (1896); R.C. Gibbins (1995)

JDB

Macclesfield was in J. *Bennet's Round as early as 1745. A chapel was built in 1764, which had to be enlarged in 1779 and again in 1799. During the Rev. D. *Simpson's evangelical ministry at Christ Church, 1775–99, there was close Anglican-Methodist co-operation and his was the only Anglican pulpit in Cheshire in which JW preached regularly. The town supplied JW with his solicitor (W. *Clulow) and J. *Bunting with his wife (Sarah Maclardie) and was the home of H.A. *Rogers (née Roe). Head of a circuit from 1770, WM membership was 5.1% of the population in 1794. PM arrived in 1819 and ultimately built three chapels. Both the MNC and the UMFC established very large chapels. The IM Conference met in the town in 1811. The undenominational Sunday School was founded by Methodists.

B. Smith (1875); G. Malmgreen (1985)

EAR

McClure, John (1778–1817), first Irish MNC preacher, was born at Malone, *Belfast. He was called out in 1799 by the thirty-four leaders at Lisburn who had withdrawn from WM. The following year he responded to a request to establish a MNC cause in *Dublin. The struggling societies were unable to support a married preacher and, although he made various attempts to supplement his income, he was gaoled for five months in 1814 for several small debts. His son **William McClure** (1803–71) also became an Irish MNC preacher, but during a period of retraction in the Irish Mission transferred to *Canada and became theological tutor and Assistant Superintendent of the Canadian work.

W. McClure (1872)

RPR

McConnell, H. Ormonde, MBE (1904–98; e.m. 1930), Irish missionary in Haiti, son of **Henry McConnell** (1866–1953; e.m. 1893), was educated at Methodist College and Queen's University, Belfast. He served in Haiti from 1933 until his retirement in 1970. A man of faith, prayer and vision, he played a central part with the government in developing an extensive literacy programme in which Haitian Creole was written phonetically and the Laubach teaching method was adapted to local conditions. He helped to establish Nouveau College Bird, enabled the world Church to respond to natural disasters in Haiti and encouraged rural rehabilitation projects.

His son **Patrick M. McConnell** (1935– ; e.m. 1958) also served in Haiti.

H.O. McConnell (1976)

NWT

M'Cullagh, Thomas (1822–1908), born of Anglican parents in Athlone, was converted through Methodism at Kilkenny while employed with the Ordnance Survey of Ireland. Transferred to Skipton, he was nominated for the itinerancy in 1844. In his early circuits he was, like his friend W.M. *Punshon, a preacher of extraordinary power and popularity. Over the years he modified his pulpit style. Though he wrote several biographies and many articles, preaching remained his chief delight. He was President of the British Conference in 1883.

G.J. Stevenson (1884–6) 4 pp. 508–18; *MR(W)* 1892 pp. 58–63; *MR* 19 Nov. 1908; H.H. M'Cullagh (1909)

RPR

Macdonald Family, a remarkable WM dynasty with connections in the world of politics art and literature. **James Macdonald** (1761–1835) was one of JW's itinerants from 1784. He wrote the life of J. *Benson (1822). His son was **George Browne Macdonald** (1805–1868; e.m. 1825), among whose pastorates were Hinde Street, London and Trinity, *Wolverhampton (the home church of H.H. *Fowler). He and his wife Hannah had a remarkable brood of daughters. Alice (1837–1910) married J.L. *Kipling and their son was the writer and poet Rudyard Kipling (1865–1936). Georgiana (1840–1920) married (Sir) Edward Burne-Jones (1833–98), the pre-Raphaelite painter. Agnes (1846–1906) married the painter Sir Edward J. Poynton (1836–1919). Louisa (1845–1925) was the wife of Alfred Baldwin (1840–1908), the Bewdley iron-master. Their son, Stanley Baldwin (1867–1947) was later Prime Minister and became the first Earl Baldwin of Bewdley. The youngest sister Edith (1848–1947) remained single and wrote the family *Annals* (1927). Their brother, **Frederic William Macdonald** (1842–1928; e.m. 1862) was a third-generation WM minister, who had a distinguished circuit ministry, following student days at Owens College, Manchester. He was a tutor at *Handsworth College from 1881 to 1891 and then Secretary of the WMMS. He was President of the Conference in 1899. He was a littérateur at a time when Handsworth was a centre of West Midlands Methodism and wrote two autobiographical volumes (1913 and 1919), lives of J. *Fletcher (1885) and W.M. *Punshon (1887) and *Recreations of a Book-lover* (1911).

MR(W) 1904 p. 74; A.W. Baldwin (1960); I. Taylor (1987)

JMT

Macdonald, Dr Roderick J.J. (1859–1906; e.m. 1884), WM medical missionary, born in *Doncaster. He went to the hospital at Fatshan (Fushan), *China in 1884 and in 1897 began medical work in Wuchow on the West River, founding a church, hospital, boarding school for boys and girls and a leprosy colony. His ministry ended tragically when he was murdered by pirates while tending the captain of the boat on which he was returning from Synod.

Mrs R. Macdonald (1908)

GRS

Mace, Dr David Robert (1907–90; e.m. 1929) was actively involved in the early days of the Young Laymen's League. During World War II he became increasingly concerned about marriage failure and in 1942 founded Marriage Guidance (now 'Relate'). In 1949 he was appointed to a teaching post at Drew University. He went on many lecture tours and spoke at conferences throughout the world, wrote over thirty books and many articles. In later years his interest focused on 'marriage enrichment'. He held degrees from London, Cambridge and Manchester and honorary degrees from several American universities.

MR 10 Jan. 1991

JAV

McElwain, Archibald (1792–1874), a prominent businessman in Coleraine, was associated with the commercial, educational and religious prosperity of his adopted town. He contributed of his time and considerable wealth to his local Methodist society, as prayer leader, class leader and circuit steward and to the wider Connexion as a member of Conference committees. He was prominent, along with his brother-in-law Thomas A. *Shillington and his son-in-law Sir W. *McArthur, in the promotion and realization of *Methodist College, Belfast with its provision for ministers' children and ministerial training.

Irish Evangelist 1 Feb. 1875

RPR

M'Kechnie, Colin Campbell (1821–96; e.m. 1838), PM itinerant, born into a *Paisley Presbyterian family. Converted as a boy, he became a PM *local preacher at 15 and began a lifelong process of self-education. In his first circuit appointment, still in his teens, he was influenced by J. *Spoor, an unlettered preacher of great spiritual power. He served for nearly 50 years in the Sunderland PM District and was the agent of remarkable revivals in several circuits. A keen advocate of improved educational provision for *local preachers and ministers, he was active in launching the Sunderland District Ministerial Association in 1850 and its journal *The *Christian Ambassador* (1854, renamed the *PM Quarterly Review* in 1879), which he edited until 1887. He took a leading role in establishing the *Sunderland Theological Institute in 1868. The five-year rule was suspended to allow him to serve as *Connexional Editor 1876–87. In that role he produced the new *PM Hymnal* (1887) and launched the magazine *Springtime* in 1886. An advocate of a better informed laity and of ministerial training, he combined scholarship with evangelicalism. He was President of the 1880 Conference.

F.H. Hurd (1872) pp. 131–41; G.J. Stevenson (1884–86) 5 pp. 783–90; J. Atkinson (1898)

DCD/GEM

McKenny, John (*c.* 1788–1847; e.m. 1813), Irish missionary, born in Coleraine. In 1814 he went to Cape Colony, *South Africa as the first WM missionary, served in Ceylon (now *Sri Lanka) 1816–1835, and from 1836 as chairman of the New South Wales Mission. He was wise, far-seeing and industrious, his sharp eye for opportunities led to the strategically important Kollupitiya site in Colombo being acquired. He stressed the importance of a native ministry in Ceylon, yet pressed the claims of 'white' colonial missions at a formative stage in their development. At the New South Wales Mission he strengthened its discipline and persuaded the government to give it legal status. He led several remarkable campaigns, resulting in WM advances in many places in the colony.

ADB; N.W. Taggart (1986) pp. 128–45

NWT/EGC

Mackenzie, Peter (1824–95; e.m. 1859), WM minister, Scottish by birth. He moved to Co. Durham in 1844, finding employment as a miner. Converted in 1849, he became a *local preacher the following year and his exceptional pulpit gifts led to his being accepted for the ministry. He trained at *Didsbury College. Although all but two of his ten circuits were in the North, he attracted large congregations throughout the country, bringing many people to faith. His lectures, delivered with humour and dramatic effect, raised considerable sums for chapel building and missionary projects. Generous of his time, energy and money, he maintained a heavy schedule of engagements to the end.

————

MR 28 Nov. 1895; J.Dawson (1896)

WDH

Mackintosh, John P. (1868–1920), MNC businessman,moved to *Halifax in infancy and followed his father into the mill there. He was actively involved in the Sunday School, choir and Band of Hope at Queens Road MNC chapel, which his family attended, and met his future wife there. In 1890 he and his wife launched a pastry shop, specializing in home-made toffee. From this small beginning grew the internationally famous Mackintosh's Toffee, produced from a Halifax factory which ultimately employed over 1,000. He became a MNC *Guardian Representative in 1896 and was a frequent delegate to the MNC and UM Conference. His eldest son **Harold Vincent Mackintosh** (1891–1964), first Viscount, became head of the firm in 1920. Knighted in 1922, he received further honours for his leadership of the National Savings Movement and other charitable work and was made Viscount in 1957. In later life he lived in *Norwich and played a large part in establishing the University of East Anglia. His wife **Constance Mackintosh** (1891–1976) shared in his public work, was a JP and a governor of *Hunmanby Hall school and served on the Methodist Education and *MHA Committees

————

MR 31 Dec. 1964, 8 Jan. 1976; G.W. Crutchley (1921); H.V. Mackintosh (1966); *DBB*

EAR

McLellan, Edward (1870–1967; e.m. 1893), one of the last great PM orators, was born at Woodley and trained at *Hartley College. He became Connexional Editor (1921–26) and wrote extensively. In 1929 he delivered the *Hartley Lecture on *Jesus the Reformer*. He was President of the Conference in 1931.

————

MR 26 Jan. & 2 Feb. 1967

WL

McMullen (or M'Mullen), James (d.1804; e.m. 1788), Irish preacher, appointed to *Gibraltar in 1804 as pastor of the small congregation. It was hoped that his appointment would facilitate the attendance of Methodist soldiers, following an earlier court-martial and other prejudicial treatment by the army authorities. Arriving in September, he reported an outbreak of yellow fever, to which his daughter (later the mother of J.H. *Rigg) succumbed but eventually recovered. He himself fell ill on 10 October and died on the 18th, survived by only a few days by his wife. He was not replaced until 1808.

MJF

McMullen, Dr Wallace (1819–99; e.m. 1841) had a unique authority and influence in the Irish Conference for much of the later nineteenth century. He was a leader in every movement of importance, notably the introduction of lay representation in the Conference and union with the *Primitive Wesleyans. For 24 years he was associated with what became the Home Mission Fund, and as General Secretary of the united Church after 1878 he guided the redistribution of ministerial staff, the amalgamation of circuits and the disposal of redundant property. He had the unique honour of being elected to the Irish vice-presidency on four occasions.

————

ICA 22 Oct. 1926

RPR

M'Nab, Alexander (1745–97; e.m. 1766), early itinerant, born at Killin, Perthshire. He went to sea at 14 despite parental opposition. Returning to *Edinburgh in 1763 he joined the society, began to preach in 1766, was accepted as an itinerant and appointed to *Newcastle. Returning after three years in *Ireland he found the Edinburgh preaching house in urgent need of repair. Though recognising his ability and integrity, JW judged him 'too warm and impatient of contradiction' and disapproved of his alienating Scottish Presbyterians by preaching against 'final perseverance'. In 1779, as *Assistant in the *Bristol Circuit, he fell foul of JW by challenging his invitation to the Rev. E. *Smyth to preach in the *Bath chapel, but (in spite of CW's implacable hostility) he had the support of most of his fellow itinerants and was reinstated at the 1780 Conference. T. *Taylor commended his 'integrity and uprightness' and Thomas Rutherford spoke of his 'natural, simple oratory'. He left the itinerancy in 1783 and became pastor of a small Independent chapel in *Sheffield.

AM 1779 pp. 240–9; C. Atmore (1801) pp. 291–4; Tyerman (1878) 3 pp. 303–13; *PWHS* 29 pp. 21–2

JAV

McNeal, George Henry (1874–1934; e.m. 1896), pastor, evangelist and one of the leading Central Mission ministers, was converted by Gipsy *Smith and trained by S. *Collier. Sent in 1905 to develop a new mission in *Sheffield, he filled a theatre, built the Victoria Hall, raising the £46,000 needed in three years. He built up the congregation and pioneered its social witness (e.g. the Labour Yard). At *Wesley's Chapel 1924–35 he restored the building and rescued the graveyard from near-terminal neglect.

MR 20 &27 Dec. 1934; H. Murray (1935) pp. 81–4; N. Farr (1991) pp. 10–34

JHL

Macpherson, James (1814–1901; e.m. 1833), PM itinerant and scholar. Born in *Edinburgh, he entered the ministry at 19. He made up for educational deficiencies by a gruelling course of self-education, mastering Hebrew, Greek, Latin, German and French and becoming a formidable expositor of Scripture. Having worked with J. *Petty in *Sunderland and the *Channel Islands, he later edited Petty's *Memoirs* (1870) and the revised edition of his PM *History* (1880). His ministry was largely spent in the Manchester District, where he acted as theological tutor to probationers. As Principal-elect of the Manchester theological college he had helped to promote he was responsible for fund-raising and his full duties did not begin until 1881 in difficult circumstances. It was he who sought the support of W.P. *Hartley, but his approach did not have full effect until after his retirement in 1889. He was awarded, but never publicly acknowledged, an American DD.

F.H. Hurd (1872) pp. 142–8; G.J. Stevenson (1884–6) 5 pp. 759–71; G.E. Milburn (1981)

GEM

McQuigg, James (fl. 1799–1815), an Irish preacher with an exceptional knowledge of the Irish language. In 1799 he was appointed a General Missionary with C. *Graham and G. *Ouseley. The rigours of work in the Mission compelled him to return to the circuit ministry for the sake of his health. After 26 years as an itinerant, he

was expelled by the Irish Conference in 1815 for adultery, though he denied the charge. After his death his name was cleared.

C.H. Crookshank (1885–88) vol. 2

NWT

Maddern, John and Molly (fl.1745–82) John Maddern was born in Cornwall (where JW sheltered in his home in 1745) and had become an itinerant by 1746. In 1751 he married Molly Francis, the mistress of the girls' school at *Kingswood and he himself was the English master at Kingswood, 1756–57. They left after the fire in 1757, Mrs Maddern being succeeded by Grace *Murray. Maddern was dead by 1770, but W thought highly of his wife's service at Kingswood and from 1770 to 1782 she was housekeeper at the *New Room.

A.G.Ives (1970) pp. 40,50

JHL

Madeley was an area of major industrial development 1760–1815, symbolized by the first cast-iron bridge erected in 1779 by Abraham Darby III of Coalbrookdale, where coke had been first used to smelt iron. Through the patronage of Sir Thomas Hill of Tern Hall J. *Fletcher became first curate (in the late 1750s), then vicar of Madeley in 1760. His congregations grew. He founded religious societies in 1762 in the parish and beyond (e.g. Broseley, Trench and Coalpit Bank by 1765). In 1777 he built a large preaching house at Madeley Wood and before his death in 1785 another was built at Coalbrookdale. In 1781 he married M. *Bosanquet. His widow, aided by his non-resident successor and by curates (including M. *Horne) whom she helped to choose, remained in control until her own death in 1815, living in the vicarage and using the nearby barn for religious meetings. The Methodists continued to attend the parish church. With Coalport and Coalford these Madeley societies formed a kind of sub-circuit in which the vicarage ladies led classes and preached. Through Mrs Fletcher and her adopted daughter M. *Tooth, Madeley remained a centre of Evangelical pilgrimage as late as the 1840s. They encouraged other women preachers such as M. *Taft and D. *Thomas. After 1815, the Anglican/Methodist co-operation gradually broke down. Miss Tooth moved from the vicarage, but was allowed to continue meeting in the barn until its demolition in 1831, as a result of which a Methodist chapel was built near the parish church in 1833 (replaced by Fletcher Memorial, larger and further away, in 1841).

Because of the Fletchers' ministry, Methodism became the 'established church' of the Shropshire coalfield, with 3,500 members and over half the church attendances in the 1851 *Religious Census. Revivals were common in the nineteenth century and every mining community had one or more chapels. A MNC chapel (1860) stood in Park Street, Madeley until 1901 and a PM chapel (1881) in High Street until 1977. Among notable Methodists who came from the area were V. *Ward, G.T. *Perks, S.P. *Cadman and A.S. *Leyland.

B.S. Trinder (1973) pp. 267–310; B.S. Trinder (1991)

JHL

'Magic Methodists' *see* **Forest Methodists**

Mahy, William (1764–1813) was a native of Guernsey, employed by 1790 as a preacher in Jersey and Guernsey. Sent in 1791 to launch a mission in Normandy, he had about 800 people around Caen, including a number of Roman Catholics, under instruction. In the face of formidable difficulties, he persevered throughout the years of the Revolution, forming a number of small Methodist societies. He remained in Normandy until 1808, then returned to England, suffering from deep depression, and died in a mental home near *Manchester.

R D. Moore (1952) pp. 69–72; Th. Roux (1941) pp. 6–18

WL

Major, Harry (1795–1839; e.m. 1817), BC itinerant, born at Northlew, Devon. He was Secretary of the General Committee 1823–25, *Book Steward 1825–26 and President of the Conference in 1830. *O'Bryan and J *Thorne consulted him about sacramental theology.

TS

Mallett, Sarah (Mrs Boyce) (1768-*c*. 1845), a native of Loddon, Norfolk who in her teens began to preach during epileptic fits. JW met her at Long Stratton in 1786, was convinced of her call to preach and gave her encouragement and support. They corresponded frequently in his closing years. With the approval of the 1787 Conference she worked mainly in East Anglia, but received invitations from elsewhere. She later gave up her preaching, perhaps after her marriage or because of the 1803 Conference's prohibition of female preaching.

Z. Taft, vol. 1 (1825); SL, Vol. 8; *Eastern Daily Press* 21 Aug. 1961

EDG

Mallinson, Sir William (1854–1936), UMFC layman and philanthropist. A Londoner by birth, he was a prosperous timber merchant who pioneered the manufacture of plywood. In 1893 he became treasurer of the connexion's London Church and Extension Committee, a post he held for 40 years. Under his leadership 30 chapels were built in London and he endowed a trust for their benefit and carried through a scheme for the extinction of all debt in London. He also founded the Shern Hall Building Society in 1922 to help his fellow Methodists. Gipsy *Smith was once in his Sunday School class. He was created a baronet in 1935.

W. Mallinson (1936); *MR* 7 May 1936

OAB

Maltby, Dr W. Russell (1866–1951; e.m. 1893), WM minister, trained at *Headingley College. From 1920 to 1940 he was Warden of the Wesley *Deaconess Order. President of the WM Conference in 1926, he was an advocate of *Methodist Union. He exercised a powerful ministry among students through university missions and conferences. The Methodist *School of Fellowship and *Fellowship of the Kingdom owed much to his spiritual guidance. The theme of his preaching and of his books *The Significance of Jesus* (1929) and *Christ and his Cross* (1935) was the centrality of a personal relationship with Jesus.

MR 18 Jan. 1951, 15 Dec. 1966

WDH

Manchester JW visited his friend, the Rev. J. *Clayton, in Manchester three times before his 'conversion'. G. *Whitefield paid the first of seven visits in December 1738 and was followed by B. *Ingham in 1742. J. *Nelson preached at Manchester Cross in either 1742 or 1743, but no society was formed until CW's visit in January 1747. J. *Bennet added it to his Round in March 1747 and JW came in May, preaching at Salford Cross. A chapel in Birchin Lane was completed in 1751 and in 1752 Manchester became head of a circuit covering much of Lancashire and Cheshire. In 1753 the town society had 250 members. JW visited the town 49 times, recording 1,600 communicants in 1790. In 1765 the Conference met in Manchester for the first time. Membership grew rapidly with the increasing population and the shortcomings of Anglican provision. Birchin Lane was replaced in 1781 by Oldham Street chapel, which rivalled *Wesley's Chapel in size. By 1799 there were 2,225 members in Manchester and Salford. Expansion continued until 1834, despite a secession to the MNC in 1797. A second circuit was created in 1824, with Grosvenor Street at its head: for many years it was the wealthiest in the British connexion. In 1886 the first WM Central Hall was opened on the site of Oldham Street chapel. Under the leadership of S. *Collier it developed into the Manchester and Salford Mission. The largest and most successful of all the WM provincial Missions, with an impressive array of social agencies, for 20 years it claimed the 'largest Methodist congregation in the world' at the Free Trade Hall.

PM activity began in 1819. Jersey Street chapel, Ancoats was opened in 1823, but progress was slow. The PMs compensated for their failure to establish a successful central chapel by building a 'cathedral' at High Ardwick in 1878. Seven PM Conferences met there between 1827 and 1926. The *Warrenite secession in 1834 cost the four WM circuits 1,000 members and many more Sunday School scholars. The resulting WMA had 11 chapels in the city by 1851.

The WM Department for *Chapel Affairs was established in Manchester in 1855 and its present equivalent remains there, as does the *Methodist Insurance Company. Manchester was a centre for ministerial training, with *Didsbury College (WM, opened 1842), the UMFC *Victoria Park College (1876) and the PM *Hartley College (1881), the latter two amalgamating after *Methodist Union. The Methodist *Archives and Research Centre was transferred from London to the John Rylands University Library in 1977.

_____

MR(W) 1894 pp. 43–9, 1897 pp. 39–43; J. Everett (1827); Conference Handbook 1932(WM) 1955, 1970; F.H. Everson (1947); J. Banks (1977); W. Barker (1928); D.A. Gowland (1979)

EAR

Manning, Rev. Charles (1715–99), vicar of Hayes, Middx 1739–57. He was an active supporter of Methodism from 1742 and he attended the Conferences of 1747 and 1748. His evangelical preaching drove many of his parishioners to Hillingdon church. JW preached for him on various occasions, e.g. when he was seriously ill in 1749, and in 1750 noted a marked improvement in the deportment of his congregation. He is said to have officiated at W's marriage in 1751. He resigned in 1757, after which nothing is known of him.

_____

PWHS 4 pp. 34–5; A.S. Wood (1992) pp. 23–5

JAV

Manses By the beginning of the nineteenth century some circuits owned houses for their preachers, but the majority were still housed in lodgings. Those in Methodist property were greatly inconvenienced by being expected to provide lodgings to any travelling Methodist. By the beginning of the twentieth century, most ministers (except probationers) were housed in fully furnished manses. After World War II provision of soft furnishings was abolished; the existing linen, crockery and cutlery was given to the ministers then in residence and they were required to provide their own in future. Eventually all manse furniture was sold at generous prices to the ministers and circuits provided only carpets, cookers and curtains from then on. Minimum standards of size and condition of a manse are required by the Conference.

DRF

Mansfield, Ralph (1799–1880; e.m. 1819), WM missionary to *Australia, born in Toxteth Park, *Liverpool. Arriving in Sydney in 1820, he became the leader of all Methodist activities, as secretary of the Auxiliary WMMS, editor of the _Australian Magazine_ etc. In Hobart (Tasmania) 1823–26 he built the first chapel. Back in Sydney he became involved in the growing tension between the colonial missionaries and the Home Committee in London and resigned from the ministry in 1828, though continuing to serve as a *local preacher. Thereafter, with Robert Howe, he was joint editor of the _Sydney Gazette_ and also contributed to the _Colonist_. He had a broad range of interests and occupied a number of secular positions. In 1841 he became editor of the _Sydney Morning Herald_.

_____

ADB

EGC

Mansfield WM was introduced in 1788 by John Adams, a Nottingham *local preacher who conducted an open-air service in the market place. The society that was formed met for a time in temporary premises, but opened its own chapel in 1791. Six years later a majority of its members seceded to the MNC and appropriated the chapel. After a time of struggle, the WM society acquired Stanhope House, Bridge Street, a one-time home of the Earls of Chesterfield, converting it into a chapel and rebuilding on the site in 1864, despite losing half its membership in the Reform agitation of 1849–50. That secession led to the formation of a WR/UMFC (later UM) church. Meanwhile PM had arrived in 1816. By 1900 the MNC church had closed, but WM, PM and UMFC were all strongly supported, were each the head of a circuit and boasted fine chapels. In the rationalization that followed *Methodist Union in 1932 the PM church closed. The other two, Bridge Street WM and Nottingham Road (UM) survived and are still the head of their respective circuits.

J.R. Raynes (1907)

MJJ

Manton, John Allen (1807–64; e.m. 1830), WM missionary in *Australia. Arriving in Sydney in 1831, he was appointed to Parramatta. In 1833 he became the first chaplain to the new penal settlement at Port Arthur, Tasmania, where he organized schools for adult convicts and instructed 70 convict boys. At Campbelltown (Tasmania) he helped establish Horton College, a WM school for boys, and became its first principal. He suggested that the WM Church establish a second college in Sydney, and when Newington College opened in 1863 he became its first principal. He became Secretary of the Australian Conference when it was formed in 1855 and in 1857 was elected President.

ADB

EGC

Mantripp, Joseph C. (1867–1943; e.m. 1892), PM minister, born in Lowestoft. He was *Connexional Editor, 1926–31 and in the latter year delivered the *Hartley Lecture on *The Faith of a Christian*. He also wrote on *The Devotional Use of the MHB* and contributed to several periodicals, including the theological journals of other Churches.

MR 11 Feb. 1943

WL

Markfield *see* **Leicester**

Marriage *see* **Sexual Ethics**; **Trustees**

Marriott Family   Thomas Marriott (d. 1775), a London baker, was a member at the *Foundery,

London and a steward of the Spitalfields society. His wife, **Webster Marriott**, was one of the first members of the Foundery society in 1739. Their son **William Marriott** (1753–1815) was educated at *Madeley under the eye of J. *Fletcher and became a London stockbroker. In 1788 he was appointed society steward and a class leader at *Wesley's Chapel. By this time he was wealthy and wrote to A. *Mather (who had worked for his father before entering the ministry), asking advice on disposing of part of his property for charitable purposes. Mather later wrote to tell him how many people had been helped. For more than 20 years he supported two schools for 100 poor children. He kept a modest journal in which he recorded business and private activities. He was an executor of JW's will. He had two sons. **William Marriott** (1777–1834) was one of the founders of the *Sunday School Union, compiled text books and in 1805 launched *The Youth's Magazine*. He was treasurer of the *Strangers' Friend Society 1815–24, in succession to his father. **Thomas Marriott** (1786–1852) was one of the first collectors of Wesley manuscripts. He bequeathed his library and manuscripts to G. *Osborn and his considerable fortune to the WMMS and the Worn-out Preachers' Fund.

WMM 1815 pp. 801–10, 881–9

WL

Marsden, George (1773–1858; e.m. 1793), WM minister. In his youth he became a sick visitor under the newly formed *Strangers' Friend Society in his native *Manchester. He was 49 years in the active work. As Superintendent of the *Leeds Circuit in 1813, he took the initiative in calling the inaugural meeting of the first District *Missionary Society and was General Secretary of the WMMS 1824–30. He was twice President of the Conference (1821 and 1833) and in 1833 represented British Methodism at the *Canadian Conference.

WL

Marshall, Dr I. Howard (1934– ; e.m. 1958), NT scholar, born in *Carlisle. He read classics and Divinity at Aberdeen, trained at *Wesley House, Cambridge and studied at Göttingen University. Since 1964 he has been lecturer and then Professor of NT Exegesis at King's College, Aberdeen University. A leading British evangelical scholar, he has written important commentaries on *Luke* (1978), *The Epistles of John* (1978), *Acts* (1980), *1 & 2 Thessalonians* (1983), *1 Peter* (1991) and *Philippians* (1992), as well as *Luke:*

Theologian and Historian (1970), *I Believe in the Historical Jesus* (1977), *The Origins of New Testament Christology* (1977), *Last Supper and Lord's Supper* (1980) and *The Acts of the Apostles* in the 'New Testament Guides' series (1992). He has also edited important collections of articles, including *New Testament Interpretation* (1977) and since 1981 has been the editor of *The Evangelical Quarterly*. His writing is noted for its clarity, fluency, lucid ordering of material, extensive knowledge and extremely fair treatment of views with which he does not agree.

CSR

Martin, Sir George William, KBE (1884–1976), the principal director of Wilkinson & Warburton, *Leeds wholesalers, was the son of a WM minister, **Edward Martin** (1849–1916; e.m. 1873), who married a daughter of Dr G. *Osborn, and brother of **E. Osborn Martin** MC (1877–1937; e.m. 1899). The family, active in Leeds Methodism from the eighteenth century, helped to form the Leeds District *Missionary Society in 1813 and inter-married with the *Chubb and *Marshall families. Sir George was Conservative Lord Mayor of Leeds in 1946, President of the Chamber of Commerce 1948–52 and High Sheriff of Yorkshire 1954. He was made a Freeman of the city in 1966. He served on numerous local and national bodies, was Chairman of *MHA and established the George Martin Charitable Trust.

Times 20 Oct. 1976; *MR* 28 Oct. 1976; I. & W. Martin (1969)

DCD

Maskew, Jonathan (1718–93) born at Otley, Yorks. Following his conversion he lived with W. *Grimshaw, accompanying him on preaching excursions into Lancashire and Yorkshire. In 1752 he was at *Newcastle upon Tyne, while the following year he assisted J. *Haughton in the *Manchester Circuit. On being appointed to the *Haworth Circuit he settled at Dean Head, a farm near *Rochdale. Apparently adopting *Calvinistic views, he acted as an Independent pastor for several years, before returning to Methodism. W remarked of him: 'Ten such preachers would carry the world before them.'

AM, 1798, pp. 21, 473–78; *EMP* 2, 241–74; C. Atmore (1801) pp. 253–6

SRV

Mason, William (1790–1873; e.m. 1817), BC itinerant and President of the 1828 Conference.

A farmer's son, by the time he met W. *O'Bryan in 1815 he was the champion wrestler of Devon. Converted under O'Bryan, he became a class leader and *local preacher, and then an itinerant. His wife **Mary Mason**, *née* Hewett (1803–53), was a Quakeress, born at Wellington, Som. She joined the BC in 1825 and became a female itinerant. When she was appointed to Devonport in 1827 she lodged with the O'Bryans at Mill Pleasant and was married from there. The Masons travelled in many circuits and brought up eight children.

L. Deacon (1951)

TS

Mather, Alexander (1733–1800; e.m. 1757), an early itinerant. A Scotsman working in a London bakery, he was converted by JW in 1754. He was the first married married man accepted for the *itinerancy and proved himself an effective evangelist and writer. As one of JW's close advisers he played an important part in connexional administration. W named him in the *Deed of Declaration and in his will as permitted to preach in the new chapels in London and *Bath. In 1788 W ordained him as a *'Superintendent'. Though his fellow preachers ignored this after W's death, being unwilling to have another 'King in Israel', he became the second President of the Conference in 1792. In 1791 he approved of the *'Hull Circular' urging the preachers in Conference to retain Methodism's links with the Church. At the *Lichfield meeting in 1794 he, with H. *Moore opposed any immediate step to ordain without first consulting the Conference and in the *Bristol dispute that year took a conciliatory position. He was one of the preachers who drew up the *Plan of Pacification the following year.

C. Atmore (1801) pp. 256–66; *EMP* 2, pp. 158–239; G.J. Stevenson (1884–6) 1 pp. 156–64

WDH

Mathews, Dr Horace Frederick (1914–74), educationalist, trained for the ministry at *Didsbury College and was chaplain at *Rydal School, 1938–44 and 1946–50 before leaving the ministry for education. He taught RE at the Cheshire Training College, Alsager 1951–59 and was Deputy Principal of Shenstone Training College, Kidderminster 1959–63, Principal of Summerfield College 1963–71 and of Scawsby College, Doncaster 1971–74. His MA thesis was published as *Methodism and the Education of the People 1791–*

1851 (1949) and his (unpublished) doctoral thesis (1954) was a sequel to that. He wrote extensively on education and the study of the Bible, and for many years contributed children's addresses to the *Expository Times*.

MR 12 Dec. 1974 & 16 Jan. 1975; *Expository Times*, Jan. 1975 p. 100

EDG

Maughan, James (1826–71; e.m. 1848), MNC minister, born at Hepburn, Nothumberland into a poor family. After only a few years' schooling he went down the mine. He was converted, became a MNC *local preacher and in 1848 was appointed to the *Bradford Circuit. After 14 years in English circuits he was sent to Australia and held his first service in Adelaide on 21 December 1862. Franklin Street church, built in 1864, became the first Central Methodist Mission in Adelaide in 1900. Conservative in his theology and earnestly evangelical in his preaching, he was a good preacher and organizer. He had a lively interest in science (especially chemistry) and philosophy and won a prize for an essay on diseases in wheat. Debilitated by a chest disease, he died at 44 and is commemorated in the name of the church which replaced the earlier Franklin Street church in 1965.

ADEB

DGH

Maurice, Michael *see* **Skinner, Conrad**

Maxfield, Thomas (d. 1784) experienced a dramatic conversion while JW was preaching in *Bristol in 1739 and soon became Wesley's lay assistant. Learning that Maxfield had begun to preach, W was about to intervene, but after hearing him acknowledged his call from God and appointed him one of the first of his lay preachers, referring to him as his first 'son in the gospel'. He was later ordained by the Bishop of Derry to give W support; but in the 1760s, supported by the visionary G. *Bell, he ran to fanatical extremes over *Christian perfection and apocalyptic predictions. Both JW and CW tried, unsuccessfully, to reason with him, but he left Methodism in the early 1760s and became the leader of a breakaway group. He later opened a large chapel in Moorfields, London. In 1767 he published a *Vindication* very critical of both the Wesleys, but JW did not reply until Maxfield had returned to the attack in 1778. Before he died there was some healing of the rift and JW preached in his chapel twice in 1783 and visited him in his final illness.

JWJ, 28 April 1763; C. Atmore (1801) pp. 266–9; *PWHS* 10 p. 116; R.A. Knox (1950) pp. 543–7; *HMGB* 1 pp. 78–9

HMG

Maxwell, Lady Darcy (1742–1810), widowed at 19, became a lifelong member of the society at *Edinburgh. JW was often her guest and she was most generous to the itinerants stationed in Edinburgh, where she founded a free day school in 1770 and a Sunday School in 1787. Lady *Glenorchy, a long-standing friend despite their doctrinal disagreements, made Lady Maxwell her executrix in establishing a *Calvinistic chapel in *Bristol in spite of W's grieved opposition. She is buried in Greyfriars Kirkyard, Edinburgh.

WMM 1816 pp. 721–31, 801–14, 881–92; J. Lancaster (1821)

MB

May, William John (1882–1959; e.m. 1908) was born in Falmouth and trained at *Handsworth College. The interest in and concern for individuals which marked his ministry were reflected in his many books and articles in the *Methodist Recorder*. He began writing for children, then for SS teachers, and his sketches and talks for women's meetings made him a popular author (especially in his 'Mary-Martha' series) as far afield as America and Australia.

MR 3 & 10 Sept. 1959

JAV

Mayer, Matthew (1740–1814), WM preacher, born at Portwood Hall, *Stockport, son of a farmer. About 1760, with John Morris, he began house prayer meetings around *Ashton-under-Lyne and Dukinfield. In 1763 JW encouraged him to begin preaching in *Birmingham, from where he extended his work throughout Staffordshire and northwards as far as south Lancashire, notably in Oldham. He declined ordination, seeing his special mission as that of preaching to the poor. But his growing reputation brought him prominent ministerial friends and JW consulted him on local problems. After two decades of travelling, he confined his work to the Stockport area, especially encouraging the growth of Sunday Schools.

WMM 1816 pp. 3–11, 161–70, 241–51

CJS

Meadley, Donald Thomas (1909–89; e.m. 1933), son of a PM minister, entered *Hartley Victoria College in 1930. P.T. Forsyth was an important early influence. In 1957, at the instigation of W.E. *Sangster, he was appointed Principal of *Cliff College, where he initiated a period of change before returning to circuit work in 1965. His convictions led him to register a dissentient vote on the Report to Conference on the *Anglican-Methodist Conversations in 1963. He contributed to the revision of the *Book of Offices. The best known of his books was *Top Level Talks ... studies in scriptural holiness* (1969).

MR 8 June 1989

WL

Meakin, Henry T. (1855–1913; e.m. 1892) was born in Chellaston, near Derby, and worked for the Midland Railway before joining the newly formed South London Mission as organizing secretary in 1889. His success in filling Locksfields Chapel led to his entering the WM ministry in 1896. His vision inspired the opening of London's first Central Hall, at Bermondsey, in 1900. He was Superintendent of the South London Mission from 1906 until his health broke down two years later.

MR 29 May 1913; J.D. Beasley (1989); F. and L.F. Church (1914)

JDB

Means of Grace according to JW's sermon of that title are 'outward signs, words, or actions, ordained of God, and appointed for this end, to be the ordinary channels whereby He might convey to men, preventing, justifying or sanctifying grace'. The chief means are prayer, whether in private or with the congregation, searching the *Scriptures, and receiving the *Lord's Supper. According to the *Minutes of Conference* in 1744, in addition to such instituted means there are also prudential means of grace, such as the meetings of *Society, *Class and *Band. JW advocated their use in opposition to the doctrine of *'stillness'.

ARG

Medical Ethics JW was a keen amateur physician in an age when medical help was rudimentary and beyond the reach of the poor. He was ahead of his time in stressing the importance of hygiene and diet, and in experimenting with electrotherapy. His followers in the twentieth century, how-ever, because of spectacular advances in medical science, face profoundly complex issues with which he was unfamiliar. In addition to Conference statements on contraception and abortion (*see* Sexual ethics) Methodism has encouraged informed debate on human genetics, the status of the unborn human, the ethics of gene therapy, the issues involved in sex selection, the use of donated ovarian tissue and other matters which are emerging from the rapidly developing science of genetic engineering. In 1977 Conference adopted a Declaration on *The Church and the Ministry of Healing*, and in 1995 came a statement on the ethics of health care delivery, *Limited Resources, Unlimited Demand*. A 1974 Conference statement on euthanasia reached the conclusion that the need is not so much to change the law as to alter the attitude of society towards death. The Methodist Church has participated in ecumenical discussion of many issues in the field of medical ethics and played a leading part in the production of the British Council of Churches Report *Human Reproduction* (1962).

See also **Primitive Physick**

J. Atkinson (1976)

KGG

Medical Missions As in the ministry of Jesus, healing the sick has long been seen as part of missionary outreach, but the early missionaries and their wives found themselves responding to local needs with little medical knowledge and no formal qualifications. In 1839, the first medically qualified WM missionary, R.B. *Lyth, was called to treat Fijian chiefs and gained a wide reputation as a healer. In the wake of the Taiping Rebellion, J. *Cox planned a mission to Hankow in Central *China that was to be medical as well as evangelistic and educational; and in 1864 Dr F.P. *Smith found patients waiting even before news of his arrival was announced. In 1886 Dr Arthur Morley established work in Teian and more centres were set up in Anlu, where Dr Ethel Rowley (*née* Gough), the first fully qualified woman doctor (Hankow, 1896) served after her marriage. 1871 saw C. *Wenyon founding Fatshan Hospital in S. China and successfully training medical students. R. *Macdonald joined him in 1884, extending the work to Wuchow in 1897. Other distinguished colleagues followed in all the China Districts, but Dr George Pearson, who built a hospital at Shaoyang, Hunan in the 1920s, was one of the last before enforced withdrawal followed the 1950 Communist take-over.

In 1884 the *Women's Auxiliary sent Agnes Palmer, a Eurasian, to *India as their first Zenana medical worker in Madras. Facing smallpox and cholera epidemics, she opened a dispensary, enrolled for full medical training and became the first WMMS woman doctor in 1889. Similar appointments were made in Calcutta and in 1887 the brief service of H. *Lunn, the first medically qualified missionary in India, saw an extension into Tiruvalur. Emilie Posnett (C.W. *Posnett's sister) and Sarah Harris began their unique ministry in 1896, setting up village dispensaries in Hyderabad. Hospitals followed: the Holdsworth Memorial Hospital, one of South India's great institutions, opened in Mysore in 1906 and smaller institutions flourished elsewhere.

John Bond, a *'Joyful News' lay missionary, opened a dispensary at Igbo-Ora, *Nigeria in 1904. In 1912 Dr J.R.C. Stephens, first medically qualified missionary in West Africa, extended this work and established the *Wesley Guild hospital at Ilesha. Dispensary and hospital work was also developed elsewhere in this region by the different Methodist missionary societies. In 1968 the Dabou Hospital, *Côte d'Ivoire, built by volunteer labour and funds from young Methodists, was opened. Qualified practice in the Rhodesias (now *Zambia and *Zimbabwe) began in 1914 when Dr Sydney Osborn was appointed, at government invitation, to a hospital at Kwenda; in 1915 Dr H.S. Gerrard went to the PM work at Kasenga, and in *Kenya the UMs founded Maua Hospital in 1928. The first work in South Africa came with the appointment of a doctor to the hospital at Mahamba, Swaziland (1926).

Pioneer work in the cure and rehabilitation of leprosy patients was done in Burma (*Myanmar), Nigeria and India at such places as the Home for Lepers in Mandalay (1892), the settlements in India at Bankura (1902) and Dichpalli (formally opened, 1915). One of the most significant achievements was the work of leprologist T.F. *Davey in Eastern Nigeria. More recently, smaller institutions such as Ngao Hospital, Kenya, have been handed over to government care. Scarce personnel have been effectively used in establishing primary care in the community and specialist care for such groups as those suffering from mental illness and AIDS.

There is much to be proud of and enormous benefits to all parts of missionary work have resulted from over 150 years of service, despite constant curtailment through underfunding and lack of personnel, the nightmare companions of all such activity.

F. & K. Davey (n.d.); C.J. Davey (1951) pp. 140–51; C.J. Davey (1988) pp. 109–18

MJF

Meecham, Henry George (1886–1955; e.m. 1911), PM minister and scholar, was born in *Manchester and trained at *Hartley College. In 1929 he succeeded A.S. *Peake as lecturer in NT studies at Hartley College and became Principal in 1948, after a period in circuit in *Sheffield during the War. His main publications were: *Light from Ancient Letters* (1923), *The Oldest Version of the Bible* (Hartley Lecture, 1932), *The Letter of Aristeas* (1935) and *The Epistle of Diognetus* (1949) (for the last of which he was awarded the Manchester DD). He was one of the translators on the Apocrypha panel for the NEB and in retirement revised J.H. *Moulton's *Introduction to the Study of NT Greek*.

MR 1 Sept. 1955

CSR

Mellor, Eleanor G. (1887–1957), missionary to *India, educated at Manchester University. Appointed to the Trichinopoly District in 1910, she served the MMS for over 40 years. In Trichinopoly City she took the lead in establishing a Girls' High School; in Dharapuram she pioneered a boarding school for village Christian girls. Returning home in 1935, she was a tutor at *Kingsmead College preparing women missionary candidates for overseas service.

RA

Melson, Dr John Barritt (1811–98), physician, scientist and magistrate, the son of a radical WM minister, **Robert Melson** (e.m. 1803) who left the ministry in 1852 after protesting against Conference policies, and his wife Elizabeth (*née* Barritt, niece of M. *Barritt). He studied medicine at Trinity College, Cambridge, became a successful doctor in *Birmingham and one of the founders and first physicians of the Queen's Hospital. He was a noted science lecturer and corresponded with Michael Faraday and Isambard Brunel, contributing significantly to railway technology. He introduced electroplating, telegraphy and photography to Birmingham. A lifelong member of the Cherry Street WM chapel, he was an active *local preacher, a founding member of the *LPMAA and of the Evangelical Alliance.

W.C. Sheldon (1903) pp. 53–4   EDG

Membership The first members of Methodist societies were admitted on acceptance of the 'Rules of the United *Societies' and entry on a 'class book'. The requirement was not a statement of faith, but the evincing of a desire 'to flee from the wrath to come, to be saved from their sins'. Membership continued to depend on the earnest desire to grow in *holiness through meeting in class, evidenced in the continued quarterly issue of the *class ticket. Other branches of Methodism followed an essentially similar pattern of membership.

The evolution from class-based to church-based membership, and the exploration of its relationship to membership of the church universal, was a gradual process. In WM the issue of the relationship between mandatory attendance at *class meetings and membership, and the consequent barring from membership of many regular worshippers, was repeatedly raised. The resolutions of the 1889 Conference led to increasing stress being laid on the reception of people into church membership, with greater attention being given to the nurture of baptized children of members and to the appropriate rite to mark the solemnity of the occasion.

The existing practice between and within the various branches of Methodism on this last point varied. New members were approved by the *Leaders' Meeting; in some cases an official reception or recognition took place in a society meeting or a service of worship. No liturgical forms were produced until in 1894 an order of service for the 'Recognition of New Members' was added to the WM *Book of Offices; around the same period the UMFC and BC also produced recognition services, as did the UMC in 1913. The 1936 *Book of Offices contained an order of service for the 'Public Reception of New Members'. From 1962, consequent upon a report by the *Faith and Order Committee on the Methodist understanding of church membership (and its relationship to baptism), the title was amended to 'Public Reception into Full Membership, or Confirmation'. As a result of a further Faith and Order Committee report in 1992, the *Deed of Union was amended to provide that, as the name of the service implied, persons were admitted to membership in the liturgical act. This reflected a departure from the long tradition that it was the act of the Leaders' Meeting (later, *Church Council) which admitted into membership. The Church Council's function now is to approve the names of those to be received in the service. It may also approve the admission into

membership of persons received from other Christian communions.

The present basis for membership in the *Deed of Union is that: 'All who confess Jesus Christ as Lord and Saviour and accept the obligation to serve him in the life of the Church and the world are welcome as members of the Methodist Church.'

A person received into membership always holds a membership based in a local church, and will come under the care of a class leader or pastoral visitor. This membership also has a connexional dimension, however, being transferable to any other local church. Membership may cease through lapse, resignation or expulsion. Certain offices and functions in the church continue to be limited to members. Besides the membership roll, each local church has a more broadly based community roll, recording the names of all those linked with the life of the local church and within its pastoral care. There are continuing discussions about the appropriateness of the concept of membership in contemporary Methodist and ecumenical church life and society.

See also **Society Meeting**

Statements . . . 1933–83 (1984), pp. 75–89; Conference Agenda 1992, pp. 107–12; S.A. Bell in *PWHS* Vol 48 (1991–2) pp. 1–10; 25–40

SRH

Membership Statistics From the outset the Methodist community has been divided into an inner core of members of *society and an outer fringe of adherents and 'hearers', the latter typically outnumbering the former by more than two to one. As the *class meeting declined in the nineteenth century, the distinction between members and adherents tended to blur, but is still manifest in the generally deeper spiritual experience and more regular attendance at worship and church activities of the former.

The first full set of membership statistics for Great Britain and Ireland was published in 1767, when 26,000 members were reported. From the 1780s to the 1840s membership increased rapidly, both absolutely and relative to population, so that by 1850, on the eve of major losses sustained through the *WR agitation, there were 379,000 WM members (including 21,000 in Ireland) and a Methodist total of 534,000, or 3% of the adult population. Any reported decline (as in 1820, the year of the *Liverpool Minutes) was viewed with concern.

During the later nineteenth century, Methodism

continued to grow absolutely, but contracted relatively, membership of all branches reaching a total of 881,000 by 1907, the year in which the *UMC was formed. This represented the effective pinnacle of Methodism's statistical success, after which decline set in, modestly at first, to reach a membership of 869,000 by the time of the 1932 *Union. In common with most other Christian Churches a more dramatic decrease ensued, with 784,000 members by the end of World War II (1945), 614,000 when the *Anglican-Methodist Conversations failed (1972) and a mere 402,000 in 1995.

These totals can be disaggregated in various ways. Denominationally, WMs were always at least twice as numerous as PMs who, in turn, comfortably outstripped the branches of UM put together. Nationally, England accounted for the lion's share of membership, Wales (excluding Calvinistic Methodism), Scotland and Ireland never exceeding 54,000, 14,000 and 33,000 members respectively. In gender terms, *women have constituted an increasing majority, two thirds or more today. During the twentieth century there has been a progressive ageing of members, with Methodist death rates well above the civil average. With marital status, contrary to folklore, Methodism does not seem to have appealed disproportionately to single persons, but to have had a mostly above average marriage rate. In occupational terms, there has been evidence from the earliest days of a growing bias towards skilled manual workers and the lower middle class and, since 1945, of an almost exclusively non-manual following.

R Currie, A.D. Gilbert & L. Horsley (1977); various editions of *UK Christian Handbook* and *Irish Christian Handbook*.

CDF

Memorials Subordinate bodies have traditionally addressed the *Conference directly by means of a written 'Memorial'. In WM the question of which individuals or bodies had the right to do so was the subject of periodic debate and direction, until the process became more formalized in 1852, when the Conference confirmed the authority of Circuit *Quarterly Meetings to send such memorials on any connexional subject. All memorials this received were referred to a committee of Conference members, to be reported on at the relevant session of the Conference. That procedure still continues; the Memorials Committee, comprising connexional officers and District

representatives, proposing to the Conference the reply to be sent to the Circuit.

The parallel procedure for *District Synods to address the Conference was by means of a 'Suggestion', dealt with in a similar way. In 1992 the usage was finally standardized to 'Memorial' for those coming from both sources.

SRH

Mercer, John, FRS (1791–1866), WM calico printer and chemist, of Harwood near Blackburn, who invented the process of mercerizing cotton fabrics. He displayed great fertility of innovation in chemistry (especially in the discovery of dyes) and at the British Association in 1842 propounded the theory of catalytic action. A brief acquaintance with Richard Cobden influenced his liberal and reforming views. He joined the WM in 1813 and applied his faith to his business and research activities. Though he returned to the Established Church in 1849, he and his family were great benefactors to their local WM church and to the townships of Great Harwood and Clayton-le-Moors. The Mercer Memorial Chapel at Clayton-le-Moors was built in 1914.

DNB

EWD

Meriton, Rev. John (*c.* 1698–1753), evangelical clergyman, who resigned his Norfolk living and was converted during a period in the *IoM. He met JW in 1741 and soon afterwards became his travelling companion and secretary. Though also associated with G. *Whitefield, he inclined towards the *Arminianism of the Wesleys. In 1744 he went with CW on his tour of Cornwall, attended the Conference in London and accompanied JW to *Oxford when he preached his last University sermon at St Mary's. In 1747 he and CW were mobbed in Devizes. After 1748 he and JW were estranged, JW describing him as 'one that has the fear of God, but with small measure of understanding'. CW in an elegy says he was 'born to a double share of woe' and 'long tossed on life's tempestuous sea'.

WMM 1900 pp. 495–501; *PWHS* 4 pp. 65–7

JAV

Merryweather, George (fl. 1750s–early 1800s), a merchant of *Yarm on Tees who, from the late 1740s was an active promoter and generous patron of Methodism, especially within the extensive Yarm Circuit. He provided the first meeting place in Yarm, before supporting the building of the Yarm *Octagon in 1763. He was a good friend to JW and the itinerants, while retaining independence of mind on connexional policies. Many letters to him from JW and leading itinerants were preserved by his daughter, Mrs Naylor.

G.E.Milburn, in *PWHS* 44 pp. 47, 80–1; SL 4–7

GEM

Methodism   The term has a lengthy pedigree. JW himself traced it back to a first century school of medicine, though the link is tenuous. More plausibly, he saw it as referring to the 'regular method of study and behaviour' adopted under his leadership by the Holy Club. He himself had begun to be methodical during his student days, monitored in the *diary he began to keep. Samuel Johnson picked this up in his *Dictionary* (1755) when he defined a Methodist as 'one of a new kind of puritan lately arisen, so called from their profession to live by rules and in constant method'. R.P. Heitzenrater has identified a significant theological root in the late seventeenth century use of the term 'new Methodists' by orthodox *Calvinists to denote those who deviated from predestinarianism by finding a place for free will and human initiative in the process of salvation. They thereby foreshadowed JW's Arminianism.

The earliest application of the word in print to JW and his circle was in *Fog's Weekly Journal* on 9 December 1732, in a scathing attack on the 'Oxford Methodists'. JW treated it as a nickname applied by others 'by way of reproach'. He habitually spoke of 'the people commonly [or 'vulgarly'] called Methodists', though it gradually became a less opprobrious label.

The first Methodist *societies were in direct line with the *religious societies of the late seventeenth century and, like them and the *Moravian societies, were intended to be *ecclesiolae in ecclesia*, a spiritual leaven within the Church and a means of spreading 'scriptural holiness throughout the land'. JW often spoke of a threefold 'rise of Methodism', first at *Oxford, then in Georgia and finally in the movement of which he became the leading figure. In his accounts of its development (e.g. in his *Plain Account of the People Called Methodists*, written for V. *Perronet in 1748) he confined himself to that part of the evangelical movement of which he was leader and found no place for the role of G. *Whitefield or of H. *Harris and other Calvinistic Methodists in Wales. Later WM historians developed a tunnel vision

which similarly equated 'Methodist' with *'Wesleyan'. But throughout the eighteenth century 'Methodist' had a wider connotation, virtually synonymous with 'evangelical' and applicable to any manifestation of *'enthusiasm'. *Calvinistic Methodism, in particular, was very much a part of the Methodist movement, especially but not exclusively in Wales. It was often more in the public eye than the Wesleyans, with Whitefield seen as the quintessential Methodist, if only because he was easier to lampoon or caricature. Apart from the *Countess of Huntingdon's Connexion, it was much more loosely organized than the WM connexion.

WM increasingly became the dominant strand in the Evangelical Movement through JW's flair for organization, his instinct for leadership and the incessant travelling by means of which he nurtured and controlled the societies 'in connexion with' him. The more localized work of other evangelists such as W. *Grimshaw and W. *Darney was assimilated into WM and swelled its numbers.

Seeing Methodism as a movement primarily (though not exclusively) within the CofE, JW consistently defined the word in terms of the *BCP* and defended its message by reference to the Homilies as well as to *Scripture. He insisted that a Methodist was no more (and no less) than 'one who has the love of God shed abroad in his heart by the Holy Ghost given unto him' and so disclaimed any desire to be the head of a sect or party. In line with this, the only 'thing needful' for admission to *membership of a Methodist society (despite W's proclivity for drawing up rules) was 'a desire to flee from the wrath to come'. The reality, inevitably, deviated further and further from the ideal until separation from the Church became little more than a matter of time and JW could be compared (by J. *Beaumont) to a rower looking in the opposite direction from the one in which he was travelling.

The characteristic features of Methodist organization (e.g the *class, *society and *circuit, the *quarterly meeting, *field preaching, the *itinerancy, *local preaching and the annual *Conference), the preaching service, *Covenant Service and other forms of *public worship, were adopted pragmatically from various sources in response to changing circumstances and developments. JW's zeal to recover the pattern of the 'Primitive Church' led him to encourage *fasting, *watchnights, vigils, *lovefeasts etc. Though he remained the focal point and chief unifying factor in the growing *'connexion', towards the end he began to exercise his authority through such individuals as T. *Coke, and to share it with an inner 'Cabinet' of preachers. In 1784 he provided for its continuance by legally defining the *Conference in the *Deed of Declaration. Despite this, after 1791 the ambiguities and unresolved tensions inevitably surfaced and led to controversy and dissention, out of which *Wesleyanism was born.

J. Wesley (1742); R.P. Heitzenrater (1989) pp. 13–32

JAV

Methodist Archives Centre *see* **Archives**

Methodist Association of Youth Clubs (MAYC) *see* **Youth Work**

Methodist Church Acts The authority of the Uniting Conference in 1932 to promulgate the *Deed of Union was conferred by the Methodist Church Union Act 1929. (The 1907 Union had similarly been enabled by the United Methodist Church Act 1907.)

The Methodist Church Act 1939 constituted and incorporated the *Trustees for Methodist Church Purposes. The Methodist Church Funds Act 1960 constituted and incorporated the *Central Finance Board and widened the investment powers.

In 1976 the 1929 Act was repealed and replaced (not without controversy at the Committee stage) by the Methodist Church Act 1976 which is now the principal legislation upon which the constitutional structure of the Methodist Church is built. The 1976 Act, *inter alia*, provided for the definition of the purposes of the Methodist Church and extended the Conference's power to amend the Deed of Union to include the *doctrinal standards clause. It altered the position of *trustees by replacing the *Model Deed by Model Trusts (Schedule 2 to the Act), with power for Conference to amend them. It vested Model Trust property in custodian trustees and defined the managing trustees.

See also **Finance, Connexional**; **Trustees for Methodist Church Purposes**

CPD vol. 1 (1988); G.W. Dolby in *PWHS*, 41 (1977–8), pp. 97–103; G.T. Brake (1984) ch. 5

SRH

Methodist Church Collection of Modern Christian Art In the early 1960s Douglas A. Wollen (1909–98; e.m. 1939), who wrote regularly on art for the *Times*, the *Methodist Recorder* etc., collaborated with Dr J. *Gibbs in forming a collection of modern Christian art. Under the title 'The Church and the Artist' the collection was taken on a tour throughout England and Wales which included major art galleries. Exhibits included photographs, drawings and actual examples of church design and furnishings, in the hope of raising the quality of design within church life. The collection was then housed at *Kingswood School, with individual items being lent to other Methodist schools and colleges. It is one of the finest denominational collections of twentieth century art, offering an exploration of Christian themes to a wide audience, and includes works by Burra, Frink, Rouault and Sutherland. Since 1998 it has been based at *Westminster College, Oxford.

R.A. Wollen (1993); *MR* 5 Nov. 1998

PSF

Methodist Church Fund (previously called PSF the Mission and Service Fund and before that the General Assessment) is raised by a levy on the Districts, which in turn assess their Circuits. The fund defrays such central costs as the running of the Conference Office, District Chairmen's stipends and much of the other expense at connexional level. The present fund has wide powers of recommending how money should be distributed, as most needed, among Methodist funds, subject to any limitation of previous legal constraints on money given for specific purposes.

DRF

Methodist Church Music Society (MCMS) Shortly after publication of the 1933 *MHB*, Dr W.R. *Maltby arranged a retreat for organists and choir masters, from which emerged the MCMS 'to cultivate and co-ordinate all the musical resources of Methodism in public worship'. Its first secretary was the Rev. E.C. *Barton and its committee was chaired by Dr F.L. *Wiseman. The Methodist Conference of 1948 gave it official status. One of the first developments, the annual conference, has continued, apart from the war years, until the present. Choirs and organists, very much in evidence in the 1930s, were at the centre of the Society's work; and the annual conference always included the rehearsal and singing of a major choral work. Some conferences have been shared with the Local Preachers' Department, partners in 'Creative Arts' and the official music bodies of other denominations. The annual summer school, 'Youth Makes Music', was initiated in 1964 in partnership with MAYC and has expanded to include dance and drama. More recent initiatives include the British Methodist Youth Choir (1982) and the National Organ Advisory Service, joined in 1993 by an Organ Training Scheme and more recently by a training scheme for 'Leaders of Music in Worship'.

PLC

Methodist College, Belfast was opened in 1868, partly in response to the growth of the city. Secondary education under WM auspices had been available in *Dublin since the 1840s. Sir W. *McArthur was prominent among the early benefactors. Composed of both a 'college' and a 'school', it aimed from the outset at providing education for boys from the earliest stages of schooling to the completion of a degree or entry into business life. Within months of opening it was agreed that 'young ladies' be admitted on equal terms. The school had places for day pupils and boarders and for the children of Methodist ministers. The college was for candidates for the ministry (transferred in 1919 to *Edgehill College) and for lay undergraduates at the nearby Queen's College (later Queen's University). W. *Arthur was appointed its first Principal. In 1999 Methodist College had almost 1,900 pupils, including nearly 200 boarders and 500 in the preparatory departments.

R. Marshall (1968)

NWT

Methodist Congress The first Congress, held in *Bristol in October 1929, was the idea of Dr T.F. *Hulme, Chairman of the Bristol and Bath District and anticipated the Union of 1932. It brought together 1,000 delegates from Districts in the West of England and Wales. The addresses presented were published under the title *Methodism: its Present Responsibilities*. A second Congress, held in *Sheffield in February, 1931 addressed the subject of Methodism's *Message for To-day*.

JAV

Methodist Council *see* **General Purposes Committee**; **President's Council**; **Restructuring**

Methodist Diaconal Order *see* **Deaconess Orders**; **Diaconate**

Methodist Homes for the Aged The 1943 Methodist Conference gave official approval to the proposal of the Rev. Walter Hall (1876–1966;

e.m. 1906) to establish residential homes for older people, provision at that time for poorer people being mainly in the workhouse. In 1944 the name of Methodist Homes for the Aged (MHA) was approved and a Conference Committee appointed. The first home to be opened was Ryelands at Wallington, Surrey in 1945.

From 1975 until *re-structuring in 1996 MHA operated in relationship with the Division of *Social Responsibility, but always as a separate charity with a separate Board of Trustees, the headquarters being based in London until moving to Derby in 1990. The Charity expanded into sheltered housing as well as residential care, and a sister Housing Association was set up in 1977. It has more recently extended into other forms of care, including specialized dementia care and community-based 'Live at Home' schemes. Its facilities are open to all, irrespective of religious belief. In 1998 the annual turnover was over £24 million and its operation included 41 residential care homes.

C.J. Davey (1976); C.J. Davey (1983); D.L. Wigley (1997)

SRH

Methodist Insurance Company Ltd was formed on 7 April 1933 by the amalgamation of the three groups undertaking insurance on behalf of the three branches of Methodism united in 1932 (the WM Trust Assurance Company, set up in 1870, the PM Insurance Company (1866) and the UM Church Guarantee Fund). It specializes in the insurance of properties belonging to the Methodist Church and its associated organizations, but in recent years has broadened it scope to serve a wide public. As part of its Christian witness its investment portfolio is constructed on a basis consistent with the moral stance and teachings of the Methodist Church. In 1999 the company merged with Ecclesiastical Insurance.

Methodist Insurance Company (1970)

GRS

Methodist International Houses The first House, a former hotel acquired through the exertions of H. *Porter, was opened in Bayswater, London in 1950 to provide a home for overseas students. Others followed in a dozen other university cities. Some later closed as new higher education policies led to changed needs. Bayswater MIH was replaced in 1998 by a modern building near Euston, with residential and non-residential facilities. The Lambeth MIH was a separate venture, initiated by the Lambeth Mission with support from the British Council and the London Mission Committee. It opened in 1968 and closed c.1987.

JRP

Methodist Magazine see *Arminian Magazine*

Methodist New Connexion was inaugurated on 9 August 1797 at Ebenezer Chapel, *Leeds, by A. *Kilham, W. *Thom, two other former WM itinerants and 13 laymen. This followed Kilham's expulsion in 1796 and the refusal of the WM conference in 1797 to allow lay representation. The 5,000 or so WM members (c. 5%) who joined the new body were those who felt that the *Plan of Pacification and the further slight concessions of 1797 did not go far enough. They came chiefly from the industrializing towns of the North and formed about 66 societies, all north of a line from Stoke to Nottingham. A minority held radical political views. The MNC Conference of 1798 adopted the constitution proposed by Kilham and Thom, in which Preachers and people had separate 'rights'. Each circuit elected one Preacher and one layman to *Conference, in contrast to the all-ministerial WM Conference. The Connexion was given a legal basis by the Deed Poll of 1846 (the MNC equivalent of the *Deed of Declaration), which appointed twelve Preachers and twelve laymen as *Guardian Representatives.

Kilham's early death in 1798 left Thom as the leading figure. His cultured and orderly approach left a permanent mark. The Connexion grew very slowly, taking 25 years to reach 10,000 members. It benefited from troubles within WM in 1834 and 1849–53, but lost 21% of its own members when J. *Barker was expelled in 1841. Ministerial status rose in the 1840s and *ordination was by imposition of hands at least by 1855. *Ranmoor College opened in 1864. The MNC was the most urban of all Methodist bodies, but was weak in the large cities. Its natural habitat was the medium-sized Northern manufacturing town. From 1798 there was an Irish mission (see below). Membership reached 40,000 by the time of the 1907 Union with *BC and the *UMFC to form the *UM Church.

See also **Overseas Missions**

<hr>

J.S. Simon in *LQR* Oct. 1885 pp. 136–58; *PWHS* 47 pp. 241–53; *NHM* 1 pp. 488–502, 524–7, 540–3; *HMGB* 2 pp. 290–4, 3 pp. 167–9; G. Packer (1897)

EAR

Methodist New Connexion in Ireland The tensions which led to the formation of the MNC had parallels in Ireland in areas as far apart as Lisburn, *Dublin and *Cork. In 1795 a petition to the Irish Conference from the stewards and leaders at Lisburn (then the largest Irish circuit) to allow the administration of the Lord's Supper by their own preachers was rejected. In 1798 32 of the Lisburn leaders petitioned Conference for lay representation at the District meetings and Conference. Against a background of widespread rebellion and civic unrest the petition was dismissed as 'Jacobinism'. The Irish dissidents were recognized by the 1798 MNC Conference, which planned to send missionaries to Cork and Lisburn. For the next 25 years the few Irish societies remained isolated, but in 1824 the MNC decided to make Ireland its first mission field. The plan was to strengthen and extend the existing societies in the north east and later expand into the south. But there was no serious missionary thrust among the RC population until 1836. Under the leadership first of W. *Cooke the work began to expand rapidly. At this stage they had their own Conference and under his leadership started their own monthly journal and established causes in Dublin, Cork, *Waterford, Rathkeale (Co. Limerick), Galway and the Aran Islands, employing Irish-speaking missionaries and teachers.

The Irish Mission suffered from lack of resources and adequately trained and equipped indigenous personnel. The crisis over J. *Barker, coinciding with a period of general economic hardship, resulted in a cut in the annual subvention of £1,000 to the Mission. The first to suffer were the southern stations: missionaries were withdrawn and stations closed. The Irish MNC contracted again to a few causes in the linen triangle of Ulster. An initiative of the Irish Conference's Bangor society to purchase the MNC premises there led to the transfer in 1905 of the other nine remaining MNC causes in Ireland for the sum of £4,000. By that time the looked-for rights which had led to the original split in Ireland had long been granted.

RPR

Methodist Peace Fellowship, an association of pacifists founded in 1933 by H. *Carter, following an earlier WM initiative by S.E. *Keeble, to inform and unite Methodists who covenanted together 'to renounce war and all its works and ways'. It has for many years been incorporated in the inter-denominational Fellowship of Reconciliation. It holds a public meeting during Conference and provides speakers for student and other societies. It administers a fund in memory of R.J. *Barker, which provides bursaries enabling young people to attend peace conferences or participate in development projects.

KGG

Methodist Philatelic Society was formed in 1970 for the study and encouragement of philately associated with Methodism and those united churches and ecumenical activities with which it is associated. Churches, individuals and anniversaries featured on postage stamps, postmarks, philatelic covers and meter frankings have been reported from over sixty countries in the Society's newsletter, which includes articles on stamps featuring biblical illustrations and hymns, Methodist postcards and the postal history of missionary correspondence. Many churches have marked an anniversary or other special event by issuing a souvenir cover, and since 1970 there have been annual covers in connection with the British *Conference.

JAV

Methodist Recorder was launched in 1861 as a more liberal alternative to *The *Watchman* by six WM ministers, including C. *Garrett, G.T. *Perks, W.M. *Punshon, G. *Smith and F.L. *Wiseman. The first issue, on 4 April 1861 under the title of *The Methodist Recorder and General Christian Chronicle*, bore the motto 'The truth in Love'. A layman, John Willey, was named as one of the editors, but Punshon was in effective control. At the end of 1862 the *Recorder* and the *Watchman* were brought under the same management. The first illustrations in the news pages appeared in 1865, the first photographs in 1896. Between 1892 and 1907 an annual 'Winter Number' was published, containing substantial articles and some fiction. The first lay managing editor, J.B. Watson, served from 1906 to 1934. Following *Methodist Union the *Recorder* absorbed the *United Methodist* in 1932 and the *Methodist Times and Leader* in 1937, taking over from the latter R.G. *Burnett, M. *Harwood and E.W. *Tattersall. In 1983, after 122 years in Fleet Street, the offices moved to Golden Lane and the following year the first 'District Supplement' was published. In March 1997 **Moira Sleight** became the first woman and the youngest editor in the paper's history.

MR 6 Apr 1961, 27 March 1986

JAV

Methodist Relief and Development Fund, formerly the Methodist Relief Fund, was started under the aegis of the Christian Citizenship Department and its Secretary H. *Carter in response to the desperate needs of World War II refugees. By the time of its first detailed report to Conference in 1955 its annual income had passed £4,000 and by 1999 grants amounted to over £900,000 annually. It relies entirely on voluntary giving and responds to human need 'irrespective of race, religion, gender or age'. Working through local Methodist Churches and in conjunction with other agencies, it has three main purposes: (a) humanitarian assistance in disasters and emergencies, (b) support for long-term programmes that offer hope to the poor, particularly through the promotion of sustainable agroforestry, improved water supply and literacy and (c) raising awareness of the factors in Britain, such as international debt and fair trade issues, which inhibit human development in the poor world.

G.T. Brake (1984) pp. 529–30

DRF

Methodist Revival Fellowship originated in 1952 and was recognized by Conference in 1955 as an evangelical grouping emphasizing prayer for revival, loyalty to the Scriptures and the *'Four Alls' of Methodism. Its organ was *Sound of Revival*. In January 1987 it linked with the *Conservative Evangelicals (which had concentrated on doctrinal and ethical issues) to form Headway.

A.S. Wood (1987)

WP

Methodist Revivalists, a term used loosely at the beginning of the nineteenth century to describe groups of a revivalist character which operated on the fringes of Methodism. They included the 'Kirkgate Screamers' of *Leeds, the *Bandroom Methodists of *Manchester and the Christian Revivalists of *Macclesfield, all of which W. *Bramwell tried unsuccessfully to bring together in 1803.

JAD

Methodist Sacramental Fellowship held its inaugural conference in 1935. It seeks 'to reaffirm the Catholic faith', based on Holy *Scripture and the Nicene Creed; 'to restore to Methodism the sacramental worship of the Universal Church and in particular the centrality of the Eucharist'; and 'to work and pray for the restoration of Catholic unity in Christ's Church'.

It also embraces the sacrament of *baptism, believing it to be 'a sign and mark of entry into the Church and of regeneration by the Holy Spirit'. It supports Methodism's view of infant baptism as the norm, rejecting any usage purporting to be baptism of anyone known to be already baptized.

GRS

Methodist School of Fellowship was started in 1916 by W.R. *Maltby and his educationalist brother Mr. T. Maltby, originally to train *class leaders. Several series of study booklets ('Manuals of Fellowship') were published. Held biennially at the Hayes Conference Centre, Swanwick, Derbys, the School now welcomes people of all ages, including families, and offers the opportunity to discover spiritual insights and learn leadership skills in the setting of a holiday of physical and spiritual refreshment. Speakers and audience have never been exclusively Methodist, but come from many denominations and walks of life. Many return from year to year.

JAV

Methodist Service Book (1975) was the result of work begun in 1963 to revise the *Book of Offices* of 1936. It retained the 1936 Communion Service (essentially the Anglican rite of 1662, with some light revisions by JW) but preceded it with a new order called, after JW's abridgement for the American Methodists, 'The *Sunday Service'. This was much influenced by the Liturgical Movement which, beginning in Rome, has controlled revisions in all the mainstream Churches, so that the shape of the liturgy is now virtually the same in them all. Its main principles are (a) that the Eucharist (the preferred ecumenical name, though not yet widely used in Methodism) is the central and normative act of Christian worship, (b) that it is a union of word and sacrament and must include the Bible lections and preaching as well as the *Lord's Supper, (c) that it is the congregation and not the presiding minister who 'celebrate' and therefore there must be as much participation of the people as possible and (d) that the Supper has a fourfold shape, following Jesus's actions in the Upper Room – he took (offertory); he gave thanks (the long central prayer rehearsing God's mighty act and the Lord's institution); he broke the bread to share it, and he distributed the bread and wine to the disciples (communion). This seeks to go back beyond Cranmer and the medieval rites to the earliest known orders. Where there is no Lord's Supper, the service has a eucharistic shape. The *Covenant Service, Marriage and *Ordination similarly, and Confirmation (the

alternative name for public reception into *membership). Infant *baptism is still presupposed as the usual custom, with the emphasis on what God in Christ has done for the child. The optional giving of a candle is included. The book was compiled independently of the CofE and for the first time Methodist liturgy is free of direct Anglican influence; but the Joint Liturgical Group was consulted throughout. The position of the Lord's Prayer to conclude the intercessions and the Ministry of the Word is a departure from tradition on URC advice. The *Service Book* was used beyond all expectations, but was superseded in 1999 by the *Methodist Worship Book*.

See also **Public Worship**

K.B. Westerfield Tucker (1996); G.S. Wakefield (1998).

GSW

Methodist Times, an anti-Conference weekly newspaper, published by John Kaye and Co. at 80 Fleet Street, which ran from January 1849 until 1869. Until August 1867 it was entitled the *Wesleyan Times*.

PWHS 28 p. 37

JAV

Methodist Union In 1907, the *MNC, the *BC Church and the *UMFC united as the *United Methodist Church. The Conferences of each were formally adjourned to a Uniting Conference at *Wesley's Chapel on 17 September 1907, when the motion to unite was carried unanimously. This followed votes of about 90% in favour by *Quarterly Meetings in 1904–5. The Union took place under the United Methodist Church Act 1907; the Foundation Deed was duly adopted under that Act and a new *Model Deed executed in 1908.

Negotiations were first opened for further union in 1913, the first tentative scheme being reported to the WM, PM and UM Conferences in 1920. WM opposition, known as 'the Other Side', was led by J.E. *Rattenbury and H. *Lunn. The leading UM opponent was J.N. *Higman. Among PMs there were strong misgivings about sacerdotalism and bureaucracy, but the influence of A.S. *Peake in favour of union carried the day. After many revisions, the proposals were approved in 1925 by the PM and UM Conferences but the required majority of 75% was not achieved in the WM Pastoral Session until 1928.

The Methodist Church Union Act 1929 was enacted (after strong arguments before the Parliamentary Select Committees) thus enabling the union to take place. In 1932 the three Conferences formally adjourned to a Uniting Conference on 20 September 1932 in the Royal Albert Hall, London. This Uniting Conference adopted the *Deed of Union as setting forth the basis of union and declaring and defining the constitution and *doctrinal standards of the Methodist Church, and a new *Model Deed was executed. A lengthy period of adjustment followed, before the effects of the Union were widely felt at the local level.

H. Smit, J.E. Swallow & W. Treffry (1932); R.N. Wycherley (1936); J. Kent (1966) pp. 1–43; R.Currie (1968) pp. 217–89; A.J. Bolton (1994)
SRH

Methodist Unitarian Movement began in *Rochdale in 1806, following the expulsion of J. *Cooke from the WM ministry for heresy. (Its members were sometimes called 'Cookites'.) Cooke was joined early on by three Rochdale *local preachers: John *Ashworth, a self-educated woollen weaver, James Taylor, fuller and cloth-dresser and James Wilkinson, shoemaker. Their first chapels were 'Providence' at Rochdale (1806) and 'Bethlehem Chapel' at Newchurch-in-*Rossendale (1809) and they had a number of other preaching places on either side of the Lanca-shire/Yorkshire border, including Oldham, Bury and *Todmorden. The first annual meeting of their Association was held in Rochdale in 1818. They adopted a Methodist style of organization, includ-ing circuit *preaching plans. With a largely artisan membership, they were actively involved in the Reform and Co-operative movements, in *Chart-ism and in *Sunday School work, especially at Todmorden, where the Superintendent was the radical J *Fielden. Contact with the preacher Richard Wright and other local Unitarians, together with their study of the Bible, led them to reject Trinitarian orthodoxy and after the 1850s, as their leading figures died, their congregations became independent and Unitarian.

H. McLachlan (1919); G. Smith (1858–61) 2 pp. 431–4; *PWHS* 12 pp. 178–8
JAV

Methodist Weekly (1900–1903) a *Man-chester-based newspaper founded and (from 1902) edited by S.E. *Keeble. Unlike the existing WM press, it resisted the spirit of the age, opposed the Boer wars and imperialism, supported the new Labour Representation Committee and cham-pioned social Christianity inside and outside the Church. The financial crisis resulting from its principles being too politically advanced and uncompromising for Wesleyan taste proved its undoing.
MSE

Methodist Worship Book (1999) A revision of the 1975 *Methodist Service Book* was necessary due to the need for inclusive language and for a wider range of material, including versions of the Eucharistic Thanksgiving suitable for different seasons of the Christian Year. The resulting book is more extensive than any of its predecessors. It is a Methodist Prayer Book, with orders for morning and evening worship, as well as for the Sacraments and the occasional offices. There are a whole series of services for Holy Week and an Easter Vigil and, in all, nine orders of Holy Communion, as well as orders for its use in home and hospital and for extended communion, when the elements consecrated at the service in church may be taken to those unable to attend. Though it is very 'catholic', 'us' is an alternative to 'you' in blessings and absolutions, and in one thanksgiving God is controversially addressed as 'Father and Mother'. The book should assist, rather than inhibit, a proper use of extempore prayer.
GSW

Methodist Youth Department *see* **Youth Work**

Methodists for World Mission, founded in 1912 as the Wesleyan (later, Methodist) Laymen's Missionary Movement, became renowned for its annual conference at Swanwick, Derbyshire, with outstanding speakers and international flavour. The change of name and full involvement of women came in 1986. Between 1961 and 1975 the MLMM raised £256,000 as a working capital fund for the MMS to obviate bank charges, but the movement's primary aim has been to raise awareness rather than funds.
JRP

MethSoc *see* **Cambridge Group**; **Higher Edu-cation**

Metropolitan Wesleyan Chapel Building Fund, the brainchild of W. *Arthur, was launched in 1861 as a WM response to the rapid growth of *London and the situation revealed by the *Religious Census of 1851, in which London recorded the lowest overall rate of attendance anywhere in the country. Arthur and F. *Lycett were appointed treasurers; W.M. *Punshon and Edward Corderoy secretaries. Its threefold purpose was 'to promote the erection of commodious chapels in suitable situations in and around the metropolis, to assist in the enlargement of existing chapels . . . and to secure eligible sites, especially in the new localities'. This was seen as 'indispensably necessary to the stability and permanence of the work of God'. The Fund played a major part in almost doubling the number of WM chapels in London by the end of the century. Lycett himself gave £1,000 towards each of 50 chapels. By 1914 grants totalling £301,241 had been made towards 190 new chapels, including £117,000 towards the new *Leysian Mission premises. But the percentage of the population (3.3%) which London Methodism could accommodate still fell far short of the 11.9% average in England and Wales as a whole.

London Mission Report (1985)

JAV

Mewburn, William (1817–1900), successful WM businessman, born of humble parentage at Stokesley, N. Yorks. Beginning in a solicitor's office, he set up as a stockbroker in *Halifax and then in *Manchester, specializing in railway shares. He became Chairman of Star Life Assurance and of the South Eastern Railway and a director of other companies. On a visit to *Banbury for a stonelaying, he found the Wykham Park estate on the market and set himself up there in 1865, becoming High Sheriff and then Deputy Lieutenant of Oxfordshire. He tithed his income and was a generous benefactor of the Banbury WM Circuit and of the *NCHO. His fourth daughter married Sir Robert *Perks. His son, also **William Mewburn** (1852-post-1933), born in Halifax, studied at University College, London and lived at Hawkwell Place, Pembury. He continued his father's business and philanthropic activities, including the lay treasurership of the Ministers' Children's Fund. When he retired in 1926, father and son had completed 61 years of continuous service in that office.

B. Trinder (1965) pp. 20–2

JAV

Meyrick, Rev. Thomas (d. 1770), born in Cornwall, was educated for the law before becoming an itinerant. In March 1745 he wrote at length to JW about his spiritual state and was present at the Conference that year. He later obtained episcopal ordination and became a curate near *Halifax (also keeping a school there). He fell from grace, but just before his death was appointed afternoon lecturer at Halifax parish church.

C. Atmore (1801) pp. 270–2

JAV

Middlebrook, Sir William, Bart (1851–1936), a native of Birstall, Yorks, he became a solicitor, but interested himself in politics and became secretary of the Spen Valley Liberal Association, 1885–95. Created an Alderman in 1894, he was Lord Mayor of *Leeds in 1901 and 1911. From 1908 to 1922 he was MP for Leeds South. He was a member of the *Wesley Guild General Council and treasurer of the WM Chapel Committee.

MR 2 July 1936

WL

Middleton, George, FGS (1830–1907; e.m. 1854), PM itinerant, the son of a Derbyshire mine-owner. He was a Sunday School teacher, prayer leader, *exhorter and *local preacher before entering the itinerancy. Most of his ministry was spent in the Midlands. While in *Birmingham he built five chapels and was the prime-mover in the establishment of *Bourne College, of which he was Governor for 31 years, also serving as secretary, chaplain and caretaker-in-chief. He was also active in the local PM church and circuit.

E.D. Graham (1998)

EDG

Miller, Dr Harold, OBE (1909–1995), physicist, *local preacher and staunch pacifist, came from Derbyshire PM stock. Graduating from St. John's College, Cambridge, he became a research student in the Cavendish Laboratory in the pioneering era of atomic physics under Rutherford and Chadwick, before working in the Research Department of EMI, where he was involved in the development of the first successful domestic TV system. From 1942 as Medical Physicist to the *Sheffield National Centre for Radiography he was involved in cancer research. He was President of the Hospital Physicists Association and of the British Institute of Radiology, and consultant to the International Atomic Energy Agency. He gave the Chapel Aid lecture on *Growing Up with PM* in 1995.

MR 16 Nov. 1995

EDG

Million Guinea Fund *see* **Twentieth Century Fund**

Mills, Edward D., CBE, FRIBA (1915–98), architect involved in innovative work in many parts of the world. He was involved in the Festival of Britain (1951) and the Brussels Expo (1958) and designed the National Exhibition Centre, *Birmingham (1976). His book on *The Modern Church* (1956) highlighted trends in the use of contemporary materials and open planning pioneered by Walter Gropius (with whom he had been associated) and had a widespread effect on post-war church design. Much of his Methodist work is in the *London area (e.g. Colliers Wood, Mitcham, Woking and Upper Norwood). He also refurbished a number of W.A. *Gelder's Central Halls and designed buildings for *Kent College, Canterbury and *Queen's College, Taunton. His *Methodist International House at Penarth won a Civic Trust award. He received an honorary DLitt from the University of Greenwich in 1993.

BWB

Milner, Rev. John (*c.* 1710–77), vicar of Chipping, Lancs, who met JW *c.* 1741 and attended a gathering of Methodist preachers in *Leeds convened by CW. He welcomed JW to his church, despite local objections. Summoned before the bishop in 1752 'for the high offence of letting Mr. Wesley preach in my pulpit', his defence was heard with 'much mildness and candour'. In March 1754 W found him suffering from acute depression. He worked closely with W. *Grimshaw and attempted to reconcile JW and B. *Ingham.

J.W. Laycock (1909) pp. 77–83

JAV

Milson, Dr Frederick William (1913–83; e.m. 1935) was brought up in *Sheffield and trained for the ministry at *Headingley College. He served for 20 years in Central Missions. At *Leeds, 1955–60, he was Methodist university chaplain. Succeeding D.S. *Hubery at *Westhill College in 1960, he developed the Community and Youth Department and shared in the development of MAYC. He advised successive British and *Hong Kong governments on Youth Service, helped to establish Youth Service in Israel and led *youth work trainees on visits to Berlin during the partition of Germany. He chaired the Local Radio Advisory Committee, the National Council for Voluntary Youth Service and the Bessey Committee. The Milson sub-committee of the Youth Service Development Council made a major contribution to the seminal report *Youth and Community Work in the 70s* (1969). He wrote prolifically on sociology and youth work and sustained a syndicated weekly newspaper column.

See also **Youth Work**

MR 22 Sept. 1983

CHS

Ministerial Training was considered as early at 1744, when the first Conference considered the question 'Can we have a seminary for labourers?' JW's answer was, 'Not yet'. During his lifetime he directed the preachers' studies, drew up reading lists and provided them with the *Christian Library*. But there was a preference for practical piety over lettered learning and resistance to proposals by J. *Fletcher, A. *Clarke and others to establish a college. At the turn of the century, Methodist itinerants were looked down on by the better-educated Nonconformist ministers. In the 1830s the growing WM denomination determined, though with considerable dissension, to provide residential training for its ministers. A Literary and Theological Institution was set up at *Hoxton, with a preparatory branch at Abney House. Despite initial opposition the principle was accepted and in 1842 two Branches, North and South, were established at *Didsbury and *Richmond. During the rest of the century provision for theological education increased dramatically, until most ministers received three or four years of residential training. New colleges were opened at *Headingley (1868) and *Handsworth (1881); and in 1921 what became *Wesley House, Cambridge received its first students.

From the outset, while encouraging their itinerants to be studious as well as committed, the PMs were strongly suspicious of theological colleges, fearing that they might encourage 'soft and sedentary habits' and foster clerical ambition to the detriment of the essentially lay character of the Connexion. So their theological education was for many years dependent on individual and local initiatives. Ministerial associations sprang up in some Districts in the 1850s and led to the appointment of District theological tutors on the recommendation of the 1860 Conference. Two Scottish itinerants, C.C. *M'Kechnie and J. *Macpherson, supported by the new journal, the *Christian Ambassador*, were leading advocates of a theological institution. From 1865 provision for ministerial training at *Elmfield School, York and then at *Sunderland predated the establishment of *Hartley College, Manchester in 1881. Among the other branches of Methodism, the MNC and UMFC had *Ranmoor College, Sheffield (1864) and *Victoria Park College, Manchester (1876) respectively.

In the twentieth century many of these colleges were attached to university departments of Theology in London, Leeds, Birmingham, Manchester and Bristol. More recently, new centres linked to Church colleges developed at *Durham, *York, *Sheffield and *Oxford and there was a growing emphasis on ecumenical provision. The closure of the *deaconess college at Ilkley and the development of the Methodist *Diaconal Order have brought together the training of deacons and presbyters. The fierce controversy of the late 1960s and early 70s over the closure of colleges because of fewer ministerial candidates persisted. Non-residential courses and in-service training brought ministerial training and lay theological education into closer relationship. Throughout the second half of the twentieth century there have been moves to integrate the traditional academic subjects (OT, NT, Church History and Systematic Theology) with preparation for the practice of ministry, to relate initial training more closely to on-going education and, most recently, to develop modular forms in which an initial stage would be equally suitable for presbyteral, diaconal and lay training, with subsequent specialization In 1999 an initial stage of 'foundation training' for those judged to have a vocation to some form of either ordained or authorized lay ministry was introduced.

See also **Probation**; **Warrenite Controversy**

MR 11 May 1939; W.B. Brash (1935); *PWHS* 44 pp. 93–102, 47 pp. 113–24; K.D. Brown (1988); G.E. Milburn (1981); R.E. Davies (1993) pp. 6–18

TSAM/GEM/BEB

Ministry in current usage may refer to (a) Christ's service for the world in its redemption, (b) any service done in his name by the Church corporately or by a church member, (c) a particular form of such service ('the ministry of *local preachers', 'healing ministry'), (d) the specific service rendered by those ordained as presbyters or deacons and (e) most often, in its narrowest sense, the service of those ordained as presbyters. What follows deals with that last sense. 'Minister' usually refers to such persons. 'The ministry' means life devoted to such service or the ministers considered as a body (as in 'entering the ministry').

Apart from a small number of *Anglican clergy, those who assisted JW were laymen and their primary task was to preach and oversee the societies on W's behalf. The chief distinction was between those who were locally based and those who were subject to *itinerancy. The latter were officially described as 'travelling preachers' well into the twentieth century, although 'pastor' soon came into use. 'Ministry' and 'minister' began to be used in WM as early as 1810, as understanding of the nature of the role broadened, partly as a result of the *Plan of Pacification (1795) and the regular use of *ordination from 1836. There were similar developments in the other Methodist bodies (although some like IM had no paid ministry). In the late twentieth century, influenced by ecumenical discussion and the inauguration of the *diaconate, the ancient term 'presbyter' began to come back into use.

Whereas American Methodism retained JW's threefold ordination of deacon, elder and superintendent (bishop), in Britain, until the recognition of the diaconate as an order of ministry, there was only one order. British Methodism's current understanding is set out in a number of official documents: clause 4 of the *Deed of Union, *Ordination* (1960 and 1974) and *The Ministry of the People of God* (1988). Methodist ministers are presbyters in God's Church, ordained for life to the ministry of word and sacraments, with a 'principal and directing', but not exclusive, part in preaching and pastoral care. They 'hold no priesthood differing in kind from that which is common to all the Lord's people'.

Ministry was originally seen as full-time commitment to circuit work. Those who were unable to give full-time service were expected to resign or become *supernumerary. Eventually, the concept of 'without pastoral charge' was developed, later to become 'without appointment', a category introduced with the admission of *women in 1973, extended to include men in 1984 and replacing the *President's List in 1993. Towards the end of the nineteenth century ministers were permitted to serve with other Christian organizations, later in other types of appointment, from which *sector ministry developed. In 1989, after decades of debate, Ministers in Local Appointment were introduced; these were ordained and stationed, but not subject to itinerancy. All alike are subject to common procedures of *candidature, *probation, *discipline and becoming supernumeraries, and all are shown on the *stations.

See also **Finance**, **Ministerial**

J.C. Bowmer (1975); J. Kent (1966) pp. 44–85; G.T. Brake (1984) pp. 289–339; *HMGB* 1 pp. 198–203, 225–38, 2 pp. 143–60

BEB

Ministry, Men who Left 54% of JW's preachers left the itinerancy, for a variety of reasons. Many (e.g. William Orpe (1743–1810; e.m. 1764/65) and Francis Woolf (1740–1807; e.m. 1768) married and settled down, usually as *local preachers. Some like J. *Pilmore took Anglican orders; others went into business or 'located' for health reasons. Some quarrelled with JW, e.g. because they were left out of the *Deed of Declaration (the *Hampsons) or would not accept their stationing. Doctrine was sometimes a reason (e.g. Samuel Edwards who travelled 1783–89). This might lead to joining another Church or even founding a new one (J. *Blades, and later A. *Kilham, W. *Booth). JW and CW periodically examined the itinerants and purged their ranks, not only on moral grounds (e.g. J. *Wheatley), but for involvement in trade (e.g. W. *Darney) or lacking the necessary gifts (e.g. Thomas Readshaw, travelled 1779–83; died 1788). Most of these reasons still operated after JW's death. R. *Newton's brother Jacob Newton left on health grounds in 1812. Jonas Jagger (e.m. 1800) was expelled in 1824 for drunkenness; Edwin Tindall (e.m. 1858) in 1883 for embezzlement, and one probationer, G *Dyson, was even implicated in a murder case. The rate of loss dropped in every decade until the 1960s, as the length of service in a circuit grew longer and circuits decreased in size. Since 1850 doctrinal issues have become more important (e.g. the case of W. *Gill); marriage regulations continued a factor (e.g. S.P. *Cadman) and in the late twentieth century some have left because of a marriage break-up. Some left because they were not permitted to work in the 'sectors' – a result of a more highly qualified ministry at a time when the State had taken over aspects of the Church's role. Others continued to be attracted into the Anglican ministry (e.g. Bishop J. *Hunkin) or that of other denominations. The period 1957–73 saw a rise in the number of transfers to the Church of England and of resignations (e.g. F. *Hildebrandt) in protest against the *Anglican-Methodist proposals. At the same time there was a rise in the numbers of those returning, following a pattern exemplified earlier by R. *Dall.

R.P. Heitzenrater (1995) pp. 182–6; K.D. Brown (1988)

JHL

Minutes of Conference The first published minutes of Conference proceedings were two pamphlets produced by JW in 1749, entitled 'Minutes of some late conversations between the Revd Mr Wesleys and others'. These summarized the decisions of the Conferences held from 1744, and were popularly known as the 'Doctrinal Minutes' and the 'Disciplinary Minutes'. The latter was revised and enlarged in 1753 to become the *Large Minutes.

There are relatively few other records of Conference proceedings before 1764. The first annual *Minutes of Conference* was published in 1765, and the series has continued on an annual basis to the present. Two collected editions were published, in 1812 (8vo) and 1862 (12mo). A useful *Handbook and Index*, edited by Charles E. Wansborough, was published in 1890.

The Annual Minutes from 1765 contained the list of itinerant *preachers and their stations, connexional *membership returns, some account of connexional *finance, and new legislation. Later the ministerial obituaries and Address to the Societies were included. The published Minutes for the annual Conferences of the other Methodist connexions are generally in similar form. From 1965 the volume was entitled 'Minutes and Yearbook' and from 1988, 'Minutes and Directory', indicating its breadth, although the core content remains essentially similar. It is, however, the Conference 'Journal', not the *Minutes*, which is the authoritative record of its proceedings.

W.F. Swift in *PWHS* vol. 31 (1957–8) pp. 155–60

SRH

Mission Alongside the *Poor, a fund dedicated not so much to the relief of poverty as to the support of Methodist work of all kinds in impoverished areas. It highlights the Church's commitment to the poor and disadvantaged by making grants for personnel and property schemes which further this aim. It was a prominent part of Methodist outreach in poor areas in the period 1985–95, after which it became largely subsumed within wider funding. It is financed largely by voluntary contributions and grants. The fund assisted the growth of small churches, often moving into alternative premises such as houses, shops, public houses and community centres. The concept of 'Mission Alongside' rather than 'to' the Poor emphasizes an incarnational and co-redemptive thrust, whereby Methodism seeks to continue and expand its street-level commitment in deprived neighbourhoods. From this vantage point 'Mission' takes place where the total human experience and environment are seen as part of God's redemptive purposes. Out of this presence, 'local churches should reflect theologically upon, and publicize the realities of life in cities, the problems, struggles and achievements, to policy makers and the wider public'.

See also **Poor**

David Calvert (1992); NCH (1997)

DRF/JJV

Mission House   The first headquarters of the WMMS was at 77 Hatton Garden and included accommodation for a residential Secretary and for missionaries and candidates while in London. In 1840 the London Tavern in Bishopsgate was bought from the proceeds of the *Centenary Fund and adapted to become the Mission House, becoming known as 'Centenary Hall'. It was rebuilt in 1902–3. Work on a new Mission House at 25 Marylebone Road began in 1939, but the premises were occupied by the BBC until 1946. Since 1996, with the move of connexional offices from *Westminster Central Hall, the building has been known as Methodist Church House. The cost of upkeep at both the Bishopsgate and the Marylebone Road premises has come from lettings.

F&H 1 pp. 98–109

JAV

Missionary Controversy   (1889–90) This began with four articles in the *Methodist Times* by H. *Lunn, who had recently returned from *India. The WMMS had sent him to establish a hospital, but illness forced him to return within a year and he was then stationed in the West London Mission with H.P. *Hughes, editor of the *Methodist Times*. Lunn and Hughes criticized the supposedly elitist English-medium education policy and the allegedly lavish lifestyle of the WM enterprise in India, both entailing preoccupation with the higher castes and aloofness from the masses. They were supported in the *Joyful News* by T *Champness, who had recently sent evangelists to India under an independent low-budget arrangement. The WMMS resisted the charges and conciliatory resolutions were passed by the 1889 Conference; but support for foreign missions, which had been waning, was further undermined. Protests from India led to a commission of enquiry chaired by the President, which found the allegations unsustained. The 1890 Conference endorsed its findings and Lunn soon resigned from the ministry.

The Missionary Controversy (1890); F&H vol.1 pp. 137–60; N.C. Sargant in *LQHR* vol.190, 1965, pp. 304–10; *HMGB* 4 pp. 575–84

JRP

Missionary Magazines   *Missionary Notices* 'relating principally to the Foreign Missions first established by the Rev. John Wesley, MA, the Rev. Dr Coke and others . . .', first published in 1816, was intended to furnish 'regular and early communications of Missionary intelligence' without supplanting the fuller versions found in the *Methodist Magazine*. It included verbatim extracts from missionaries' correspondence and journals, and extensive reporting of WMMS Annual Meetings and committees. Other features included missionaries' travel, auxiliary branches, subscriptions and, from 1820, limited numbers of illustrations. It was succeeded by *The Foreign Field* in 1904. Meanwhile, *Work and Workers in the Mission Field*, edited by F.W. *Macdonald and intended for a wider readership, was published from 1892 to 1904. The UM counterpart was the *Missionary Echo* (from 1894) and there were *Monthly Notices* (later, *Records*) of the PM Missionary Societ, continued as *The Record*, then *The Herald* and finally *Advance* (from 1923). After Methodist Union all four were merged into *The Kingdom Overseas* as the magazine of the *MMS. Under the editorship of F.D. *Walker, the number and quality of the illustrations and the special contributions from missionaries made a wide appeal. Wartime paper restrictions changed the format, but the magazine survived until 1970, when *NOW* magazine appeared. Under the editorship of C.J. *Davey *NOW* was to be even more topical and universal in its treatment of the whole mission of the Church. After 1992 *Connect* magazine, edited until 1999 by Jan. Sutch Pickard, assumed these and other responsibilities.

MJF

Missionary Ships   The scarcity and unreliability of shipping in the Pacific prompted the WMMS to acquire its own vessel, the *Triton*, bought with a grant from the 1839 *Centenary Fund. In 1846 it was sold and a larger and swifter vessel, the *John Wesley*, was built. Management of the ship passed to the Australasian Conference when it became autonomous in 1855. In 1858 it was almost wrecked and in 1865 it foundered on a Tongan reef. A replacement, the *John Wesley II*, was built in *Aberdeen and sailed in 1867. Management reverted to the WMMS in 1873 and it was sold in 1881, made redundant by a more regular shipping service.

JRP

Missionary Societies   The MMS was formed in 1932 to administer the *overseas missions of the three uniting Churches. The WMMS had been formally constituted at connexional level by the Conference of 1818, but District Societies, the first in *Leeds, the result of local (and strongly lay) initiatives, had existed since 1813, so that the WMMS celebrated its jubilee in 1863 and its centenary in 1913. The PM and UM Churches did not formally constitute missionary societies, though PM reports used the term from 1844; their overseas work was under the direct authority of the respective Conferences. A *CM Missionary Society was formed in 1840 with *India as its mission field.

The WMMS had overseas Districts in the Caribbean, much of W. Africa, the Rhodesias (now *Zambia and *Zimbabwe), *India, Ceylon (now *Sri Lanka), Burma (now *Myanmar) and *China, as well as in *France, *Italy, *Spain and *Portugal. UM activity was in China (MNC, BC and UMFC) and in Jamaica, *Kenya and *Sierra Leone (UMFC). The PMs had work in Fernando Po (now *Bioko, Equatorial Guinea), *Nigeria and Northern Rhodesia. Earlier work done by the various branches of British Methodism in the USA and the dominions was all by 1932 autonomous.

A revision of the MMS constitution in 1942 stated explicitly that 'every member of the Methodist Church as such is a member of the Methodist Missionary Society', and from 1973 to 1996 the MMS was coterminous with the Overseas Division. Unlike the other Divisions, it officially served both the British and Irish Conferences.

Bicentenary celebrations were held in 1986, 200 years after the first missionaries were appointed by the Conference to overseas stations. By then, sending and supporting missionaries and the provision of grants and scholarships were part of a strategy of partnership in mission with *autonomous Churches. Old relationships in the Pacific had been revitalized and new ones in Latin America were being forged.

By 1996, when the Divisions were merged in the connexional Team, the number of mission partners (as they were now called) serving abroad was much reduced, while ministers from overseas were regularly stationed in Britain under the World Church in Britain/Ireland Partnerships.

___

MR 27 April 1939; E.W. Thompson (1955); C.J. Davey (1988)

JRP

Mitchell, George (1827–1901), UMFC *trade unionist, born at Montacute, Som. He began work at the age of 5 as a crow-scarer for 6d a week, but escaped from this harsh life by taking up his father's trade as a stone-mason, subsequently becoming a successful marble merchant in London. Although prospering, he remained deeply aware of the plight of the farm labourer and played a major part in organizing meetings of J. *Arch's National Union of Agricultural Labourers in 1872, especially in Somerset and the South West. He was a trustee of the Union *c*. 1880–1886, when he fell out with Arch over the use of money from the Sick Benefit Fund to defray general expenses. He nearly ruined himself by investing some £20,000 in the farm labourers' cause. His *The Skeleton at the Plough: or the Poor Farm Labourers of the West* (1874) included his own autobiography.

___

R. Groves (1949); *Winchester Gazette*, 1 Feb. 1901

NADS

Mitchell, Thomas (1726–1785), early itinerant from Bingley (Yorks). Having served in the army, he joined the Methodists and was helped to faith by the preaching of J. *Nelson. After *exhorting for some time in various parts of Yorkshire, he was made a travelling preacher in 1751. Serving in Wiltshire he 'discovered' the young T. *Olivers and recommended him to JW. He experienced his share of mob violence, including being half-drowned when thrown into a pond at Wrangle (Lincs). A man of modest abilities, he was nevertheless an effective preacher and the 1785 Conference saluted him as 'an old soldier of Jesus Christ'.

___

C. Atmore (1801) pp. 274–6; *EMP* 1 pp. 240–59

HMG

Mitton, Dr Charles Leslie (1907–98; e.m. 1929) was born in *Liverpool, the son of **Charles William Mitton** (1873–1959; e.m. 1897). Educated at Manchester University, he was appointed Assistant Tutor at *Headingley College in 1930 and after some years in circuit became NT Tutor at *Handsworth College in 1951, becoming Principal in 1956. He was largely responsible for the successful outcome of the negotiations with the *Queen's College in 1970, when he retired. His main publications are: *The Epistle to the Ephesians, Origin and Purpose* (1951), *The Formation of the Pauline Corpus* (1954), and commentaries on Mark (1956), James (1973) and Ephesians (1978). He was editor of *The Expository Times* from 1965 to 1976 and was awarded an honorary DD by the University of Aberdeen in 1964.

MR 27 Sept. 1979, 2 Apr 1998; *Expository Times*, June 1998

CSR

Model Deed   In settling the preaching-houses upon *trustees, JW had to ensure their continued use for the Methodist societies and by authorized Methodist preachers. Various forms of deed were tried, and the *Large Minutes from 1763 pre-scribed a model, or pattern, deed which was a revised form of the 1751 settlement for Birchin Lane, *Manchester. This limited the use to persons appointed by the annual *Conference (later defined by the *Deed of Declaration) and defined the approved doctrine to be preached. Successive Conferences encouraged the use of such forms, rather than local variants, and subsequent forms appeared in the Large Minutes and Code of Rules of 1797. In 1832 a Model Deed was executed, which was legally able to be incorporated by reference into individual settlements, rather than requiring a full recital in each case.

The other branches of Methodism used similar legal forms (e.g. PM, 1864; BC, 1863; MNC, 1846; UMFC, 1865; UMC, 1908). All of these were superseded in 1932 by the Model Deed, still similar in form, which was authorised by the Methodist Church Union Act 1929. Existing church property could be transferred onto it by the trustees' deed of declaration and the vast majority was so transferred. Under the *Methodist Church Act 1976, Model Deed property became subject instead to the *Model Trusts.

See also **Birstall Chapel Case**; **Doctrinal Standards**

E.B. Perkins (1952)

SRH

Model Trusts   Under the *Methodist Church Act 1976, all existing property held on either the 1932 *Model Deed or those which it replaced was vested in custodian trustees (i.e. generally the *Trustees for Methodist Church Purposes), with groups of managing trustees defined for each type of property e.g. local or circuit. The property was to be held, not on the trusts laid down in a specific document executed as a model or pattern deed, but instead on the 'model trusts' which were enacted as Schedule 2 to the Act itself. Trustees of other church property and future settlors of property could also adopt the Model Trusts. The provisions of the Schedule are in most cases amendable by the Conference, using a specified procedure, and have been amended from time to time.

CPD vol.2 bk II part 2

SRH

Modern Media   Methodism's reliance from the outset on the printed as well as the spoken word was exemplified in JW's extensive *publishing activity (including the *Arminian Magazine*) and, as literacy became more widespread, in its nine-teenth century newspapers. During the twentieth century Methodists were closely involved with the new communications media as they developed. F.W. *Chudleigh and T. *Tiplady were pioneers in the use of films to attract an audience. Lord *Rank recognized film as an important medium for evangelism and the *HM Department, for which he was a treasurer, became a distributor for religious films. In addition he encouraged local ministers to visit his Odeon Cinemas on Good Friday to deliver an appropriate message in the interval between films.

In the case of radio and television the policy has been to contribute to broadcasting in general, rather than seeking to own a separate channel. Josie Smith became Methodism's first Local Broadcasting Officer in 1982. The Churches Tele-vision Centre at Bushey, supported by the Arthur Rank Foundation and with a succession of Methodist directors, was established to train the clergy to present epilogues that were broadcast by both BBC and ITV companies. Now reconsti-tuted as the Foundation for Christian Communi-cation with a wider brief, it has become a major independent supplier of programmes to broadcast-ing networks. Among Methodists who have played an important part in broadcasting are P.M. *Webb and C.M. *Morris. There is a connexional web site and many Methodist churches and organ-izations now have web sites on the Internet.

See also **Cadman, S.P.**; **Evens, G.B.**

JDBr

Moister, William (1808–91; e.m. 1830), WM missionary, appointed to the *Gambia in 1831. He left in 1833 due to ill health and was then appointed to the *West Indies, where he served in Demerara, Barbados, Grenada, Tobago, St Vincent and Trinidad (1834–46). Suffering from exhaustion, he returned to England, but again offered for overseas and was General Superintend-ent of the Cape of Good Hope District, *South Africa 1850–60. In later years he wrote several books, including a *History of Wesleyan Missions*

(1871), *Missionary Pioneers* (1871) and *Missionary Worthies* (1885); also *The Story of my Life and Missionary Labours* (1886).

M(W) 1907 pp. 71–3

GRS

Monahan, Charles Henry, K-i-H (1869–1951; e.m. 1893), missionary in *India, educated at Trinity College, Dublin and *Richmond College. He served in the Madras District 1893–1940, in village evangelism, and the training of evangelists and in higher education. He was Chairman of the Madras District for over 20 years and twice Chair of the South India Provincial Synod. An early member of the Joint Committee, he was an influential proponent of the Scheme which led to the inauguration of CSI seven years after his retirement. He devoted seven years of retirement to completing the revision of the Tamil Bible.

RA

Montgomery, James (1771–1854), hymnwriter, the son of a *Moravian minister at Irvine, Ayrshire. He trained for the *Moravian ministry, but abandoned this to become an apprentice baker and then a shop assistant. Moving to *Sheffield in 1792, he maintained a close association with Methodism. In 1794 he took over a radical newspaper, the *Sheffield Register*, renamed it the *Sheffield Times* and edited it for the next 31 years. Imprisoned twice for publishing radical material, he became a well-known critic of the slave trade, the employment of child chimney sweeps and lotteries, and as a supporter of the Bible Society, foreign missions and WM *Sunday Schools. He wrote over 400 hymns and published *Songs of Zion* (1822), *The Christian Psalmist* (1825) and *Hymns for Public, Private and Social Devotion* (1853). A memorial statue stands in the grounds of Sheffield cathedral and a city hall is named after him. Erik Routley judged him to be 'the greatest English lay hymnwriter'.

A.S. Holbrook & J.A. Kaye in *LQHR* April 1954 pp. 134–45

PLC

Moon, James Sladin (1904–82; e.m. 1930), missionary in *India, born in Wigan. He read History at Sheffield, trained at *Wesley House and spent one year in Germany as a Finch scholar. A year in Egypt gave him a lifelong interest in Islam. He served in the Lucknow and Bombay Districts 1933–70, effectively combining teaching and management, mostly at Cutting Memorial

Boys High School. He was also District Treasurer and an influential senior missionary at a time of great change. He contributed to the dialogue with Islam at the Henry Martyn School of Islamic Studies, and in retirement was involved with Amnesty and the Ecumenical Society of the BVM.

MR 15 July 1982

JAV

Moore, Henry (1751–1844; e.m. 1779), WM itinerant, born near *Dublin. Despite showing academic promise, he was deprived of a university education by his father's death and became a wood engraver. While in London he heard JW preach, but was unimpressed. Back in Dublin, he was converted in 1777, became a *local preacher and opened a school. JW met him in *Liverpool in 1779 and sent him into the Coleraine Circuit, where he became friends with A. *Knox. For two years, 1784–86, he was stationed in London as JW's travelling companion and amanuensis, declining to go out to America in 1785 because of his mother's health. He was one of the three preachers ordained by JW in 1789 for the English work. As one of W's literary executors he was involved in the dispute with Dr J. *Whitehead over W's papers and hastily prepared an official biography, published in 1792 over his and *Coke's names. (It was rewritten and enlarged in 1824–25.) He later wrote a life of Mary *Bosanquet Fletcher (1817).

Moore attended the unofficial meeting at *Lichfield in 1794, but opposed any moves lacking the prior approval of the Conference. Later that year his involvement in a celebration of Holy Communion in *Bristol led to his being barred from the *New Room pulpit by the trustees and a bitter dispute between them and the Conference. A somewhat similar dispute occurred in 1812 while he was stationed at *Wesley's Chapel, London; it was not until 1826 that he became one of the first itinerants to administer the Sacrament there. He was twice elected President of the Conference, in 1804 and 1823. By 1836 he was the only surviving itinerant to have been ordained by JW himself, but was not invited to participate when *ordination by laying on of hands was reintroduced by Conference.

Mrs. R. Smith (1844); G. Smith (1858–61) 2 pp. 25–9, 107–19; G.J. Stevenson (1884–6) 2 pp. 201–11; R.P. Heitzenrater (1984) 2 pp. 177–9

JAV

Moravian Church or Unitas Fratrum (Unity of the Brethren) had its roots in the 15th-century Hussite reformation and eighteenth-century German *Pietism. Fleeing from persecution in Bohemia, a number of the Brethren were given refuge at Herrnhut by Count *Zinzendorf. The new society there was marked by a belief in salvation by faith, personal conversion and a personal devotion to Jesus. Their emphasis was on spiritual nurture rather than evangelism and settlements for communal living were planted in England, the Netherlands and America. JW first encountered them on the voyage to Georgia and was deeply impressed by their simple faith and their serenity when threatened by shipwreck. Their central teachings and 'heart theology' deeply influenced his spiritual development during this period of searching. On his return to England he met P. *Böhler, who advised him to 'preach faith *until* you have it, and then, *because* you have it, you will preach faith.' He also became convinced that instantaneous conversion was both biblical and also presently possible. After his visit to their main settlement at Herrnhut, JW became more critical of the Moravians, and especially of Zinzendorf's style of leadership, and challenged their *'stillness' and what he saw as their *antinomianism. They in turn described him as still 'homo perturbatus' and excluded him from the Sacrament. Although from then on he distanced himself from them, the *Love-feast and the *Watchnight service were Moravian features incorporated into Methodism. The Moravian Church in England was established in the 1740s, retaining a threefold order of ministry. Later attempts to unite the two movements came to nothing.
See also **Fetter Lane Society**

C.W. Towlson (1957); E.G. Rupp (1986) pp. 330–8; H. McGonigle (1993); C. Podmore (1998)

EWD

Morgan, Dr Irvonwy (1907–82; e.m. 1932) was born at Trefeglwys, Montgomeryshire and was the first non-graduate to be admitted to *Wesley House, Cambridge. In 1932 he joined W. *Lax in the Poplar and Bow Circuit. In 1951 he became Secretary of the London Mission and its Extension Fund and was responsible for planning the rebuilding of the capital's Methodist churches destroyed in the Blitz. He was President of the Conference in 1967, Moderator of the FCFC in 1972 and chairman of the Bible Lands Society.

He received his London Ph.D. for a thesis on *The Nonconformity o Richard Baxter* (1946).

MR 7 Oct. 1982

JDB

Morgan, John (1792–1872; e.m. 1820) was the first missionary sent to the *Gambia in response to a request from the Governor, Sir Charles Macarthy. His instructions were to establish work up the river Gambia (but he was defeated by the climate) and to learn Mandinka (but he decided Wolof would be more useful). He had more success in ministering to liberated slaves in St Mary's (now Banjul) and as a result Gambian Methodism has always flourished mainly in the Aku community. After four years he was forced to return to Britain for health reasons in 1825.

JRP

Morgan, William (1712–32) of *Dublin, one of the original members of the *Holy Club at Oxford, gave shape to the social activity of the group in visiting prisons and serving the poor. Shortly after leaving Oxford he died and it was rumoured that this was the result of his ascetic lifestyle. JW sought to rebut this charge in a letter to Morgan's father **Richard Morgan Senr** (1679–1752), explaining the rise and design of 'Oxford Methodism'. Their correspondence was sufficient to persuade him to entrust his second son, also **Richard** (1714–85) to the Wesleys' care. He in turn joined the Methodists and retained at least some contact with JW on his return to Dublin.

PWHS 3 pp. 47–50

RPR

Morisonians, a name given to supporters and active followers of the Rev. Dr **James Morison** (1816–93), leader of the Evangelical Union which grew out of his expulsion in 1841 from the United Secession Church of Scotland for abandoning *Calvinistic doctrine in favour of universal atonement and resistible grace. The evangelical conversion he experienced in the course of his religious quest attracted ministerial and lay support. Revivals resulted as Morisonian 'missionaries' travelled through Scotland and into parts of northern England, especially Tynedale and other Pennine valleys, notably the Haltwhistle area. Converts attached themselves to nonconformist bodies, including Methodism. Conversely, the Morisonians learned from Methodist example.

The Evangelical Union united with the Congregational Union in 1897.

F. Ferguson (1876); *PMM* 1894 pp. 144–6, 1898 pp. 430–4; W.M. Patterson (1909) pp. 198–200
GEM

Morley, George (1772–1843; e.m. 1792), WM minister, born at Calverton, Notts, was a friend of T. *Coke and took a particular interest in *overseas missions. He organized the first 'Auxiliary *Missionary Society' in *Leeds (1813) to raise funds for the missions and in 1821 was appointed General Treasurer of the WMMS, becoming resident Secretary at Hatton Gardens three years later and corresponding with missionaries on foreign stations. He was President of the Conference in 1830 and in 1831 was appointed Governor of *Woodhouse Grove School.
WL

Morley, Robert (1863–1931), *trade unionist, born at Knaresborough, was in his early days a member of Skircoat WM chapel and served as a *local preacher. His work took him to *Halifax where, in 1839, he began to organize the gas workers and soon established the largest branch of the Workers' Union. His success as an organizer was recognized in 1900, when he was elected the Union's President.

DLB
NADS

Morley, Dr William (1842–1926; e.m. 1862), son of WM parents in Nottinghamshire, he worked as a student teacher before being accepted for the ministry in 1862. His family emigrated to *New Zealand the following year and he began a 36-year ministry there. He was twice President of the Conference, in 1879 and 1884, attended the second Oecumenical Methodist Conference in 1891 and became Connexional Secretary in 1893 and President of the Australasian General Conference in 1894. The administrative structure of New Zealand Methodism owes more to him than to any other person. He received a DD from Emory and Henry College, Virginia in 1898. His *History of Methodism in New Zealand* was published in 1900. Problems in Australian Methodism led to his transfer in 1902 to the Victoria Conference, where he managed the Supernumerary Fund until his retirement in 1914.

DNZB; B. Gadd (1964)
DJP

Morris, Dr Colin Manley (1929– ; e.m. 1952), renowned preacher, author and broadcaster. Born in *Bolton and educated at Oxford and Manchester Universities, he served as a missionary in *Zambia 1956–69 and was elected first President of the United Church of Zambia. He was a close friend of President Kenneth Kaunda, with whom he worked in the negotiations for Zambia's independence. He became minister of *Wesley's Chapel, London in 1970 and General Secretary of the Overseas Division in 1975. He was President of the Conference in 1976. In 1978 he joined the BBC and became Head of Religious Broadcasting. From 1987 to 1991 he was Controller of BBC Northern Ireland. A prolific writer on preaching, on popular theology and on the media, his books include *Include Me Out* (1968) and *Raising the Dead* (1996).

MR 24 June 1976
PMW

Mortimer, Mrs Elizabeth *see* **Ritchie**

Moss, R. Waddy *see* **Waddy Family**

Moulton Family Beginning with William Moulton (1769–1835; e.m. 1794), there have been eight members of the family in the WM ministry. In the third generation there were two ministerial brothers. **James Egan Moulton** (1841–1909; e.m. 1863) was a missionary in Tonga and translated the Bible into Tongan. His older brother **William Fiddian Moulton** (1835–98; e.m. 1858) was born at Leek and educated at *Woodhouse Grove School, *Wesley College, Sheffield and London University, where he had a brilliant career, winning the gold medal in mathematics and natural philosophy. He was appointed Assistant Tutor at *Richmond College in 1858 and became Classics Tutor there in 1868. In 1875 he moved to *Cambridge to found The *Leys School, remaining there as Headmaster until his death. The Leysian Mission in London was established on his initiative. He also assisted in the 1876 revision of the WM Hymn-book and was elected President of the Conference in 1890. His main scholarly work was his translation of Winer's *Grammar of NT Greek* (1870). With A.S. *Geden he compiled *A Concordance to the Greek Testament* (1897). He was a member of the committee which produced the NT section of the Revised Version of the Bible and worked on the RV Apocrypha with Westcott and Hort. He was awarded an honorary DD by Edinburgh University and an honorary MA by Cambridge University. His son

James Hope Moulton (1863–1917; e.m. 1886) was born at *Richmond, Surrey and educated at The Leys School. With a First in Classics at Cambridge and the Chancellor's Medal, he was the first nonconformist minister to be elected Fellow of a Cambridge college (King's). He taught at The Leys from 1886 to 1902, when he was appointed Tutor in NT Language and Literature at *Didsbury College and also became Greenwood Professor of Hellenistic Greek at Manchester University. He was among the first to recognize the importance of the Greek papyri discovered in Egypt for NT studies, which he popularized in *From Egyptian Rubbish Heaps* (1916). His outstanding achievements were his *Grammar of NT Greek* (1906) and *The Vocabulary of the Greek Testament Illustrated from the Papyri* (completed by G. Milligan, 1930). He was also a pre-eminent expert on Zoroastrianism, knowing Zend and Sanskrit, and his lectures in India on the subject were posthumously published as *The Treasure of the Magi* (1917). He was honoured by doctorates from the Universities of Edinburgh, Grønigen, Durham and Berlin. While returning from India, his ship was torpedoed in the Mediterranean and he died from exposure after three days in an open boat. His son **Harold Keeling Moulton** (1903–82; e.m. 1926) was the last of the ministerial line. Educated at The Leys, King's College, Cambridge and *Didsbury College, he was appointed to Findlay College, Mannargudi, S. India in 1929 and in 1932 moved to the United Theological College at Bangalore as Professor of NT Studies. He worked on the revision of the Tamil NT and contributed to the important CSI Liturgy. In 1957 he became translations secretary at the BFBS. In retirement he revised the Moulton and Geden Concordance of the NT and was awarded an honorary DD by Serampore University.

MR 10 Feb. 1898, 12 & 19 April 1917, 23 May 1935, 17 June 1982; W.F. Moulton (1899); G.G. Findlay (1910); W.F. Moulton (1919); J.E. Moulton (1921); W.F. Moulton (1926); F. Tice (1966) pp. 99–115; H.K. Moulton in *PWHS* 43 pp. 49–58

CSR

Mounfield, Arthur, FRHistS (1870–1941), writer, historian and antiquarian, was born and lived in *Warrington. He edited the *IM Magazine* from 1901 to 1941 and was compiling editor of *A Short History of Independent Methodism* (1905) to mark the denomination's centenary. He wrote *The Quaker Methodists* (1924), *The Beginnings of Total Abstinence* (1903) and other books on IM history and polity and was awarded a Fellowship by the Royal Historical Society for his published thesis *Early Warrington Nonconformity* (1923). He had strong Quaker sympathies and was a staunch pacifist. As theological examiner for students for the IM ministry, his liberal views strongly influenced the theological trend of the denomination in the first half of the twentieth century.

IM Magazine Dec. 1941

JAD

Mountstephen, Sir William Henry, Bart (1869–1946), WM layman, a leather merchant and JP, who was chairman of the Home for the Blind and of the Mercantile Association in his native Devonport. He was a member of the *Wesley Guild General Council and its Vice-President for a time and represented the District at seven Conferences.

WL

Mow Cop *see* **Camp Meetings**

Murlin, John (1722–1799; e.m. 1754), early itinerant from Cornwall, sometimes called 'the weeping prophet'. A convert of Methodist preaching, he served as a *local preacher until in 1754 JW invited him to become a full-time travelling preacher. He gave 45 years to a ministry that took him to circuits in Ireland and England and was marked by much fruitfulness. JW described him as 'a wise and zealous man . . . and wherever he goes the work of God prospers in his hand.' A Christian poet, he published *Sacred Hymns on Various Subjects* (1781) and an elegy on J. *Fletcher (1788). At his request he was buried in JW's vault in the graveyard at *Wesley's Chapel.

C. Atmore (1801) pp. 288–91; *EMP* 3 pp. 293–306

HMG

Murray, A. Victor (1890–1967), leading PM layman and educationalist, born at Choppington, Northumberland. A *local preacher from his teens, he studied at Magdalen and Mansfield Colleges, Oxford, intending to become a PM minister, but abandoned this in favour of service with the SCM as a travelling secretary (1914–22). He was a conscientious objector in World War I. From 1922 to 1933 he taught at Selly Oak Colleges. His book *The Schoool in the Bush* (1928) was the fruit of a travelling scholarship to Africa. In 1932 he was Vice-President of the last PM Conference.

From 1931 to 1945 he was Professor of Education at Hull. His Hartley Lecture *Personal Experience and the Historic Faith* (1939) won him a Cambridge BD. He was President of Cheshunt College, Cambridge, 1945–59 – a surprising appointment for this dissenting theological college. He was Vice-President of the Methodist Conference in 1947. His later published works were largely based on lecture series in Britain and America on educational, religious and philosophical themes.

MR 17 July 1947, 15 June 1967; A.V. Murray (1992)

GEM

Murray, Grace (Mrs John Bennet) (1716–1803) Born in *Newcastle upon Tyne, in 1736 she married Alexander Murray, a seaman who died at sea six years later. She became housekeeper at the *Orphan House, where she met both JW and J. *Bennet, one of his preachers. She accompanied W on one of his preaching tours in Ireland, where they contracted a marriage *de praesenti*, a form of betrothal. Bennet also proposed marriage to her. After a long period of hesitation on W's part and increasing bewilderment on hers, she was finally persuaded by CW to marry Bennet. After his death she continued to lead meetings for prayer and fellowship. She settled in Derbyshire, where she was renowned for her saintliness.

MR(W) 1902 pp. 21–32; A.Leger (1910); G.E. Harrison (1935) pp. 13–32; F. Baker in *LQHR*, Oct. 1967 pp. 305–15; M.L. Edwards (n.d.) pp. 33–8; S.R. Valentine (1997)

PMW

Murray, Lionel (Len), Baron Murray of Epping Forest (1922–), *trade unionist, born at Hadley, Shropshire, was educated at Wellington Grammar School and Queen Mary College, London. After army service he studied Politics, Philosophy and Economics at Oxford, then joined the staff of the Trades Union Congress and was its General Secretary from 1973 to 1984. He was made a Life Peer in 1985 in recognition of his distinguished public service. In retirement he has served as Vice-Chairman and Treasurer of *NCH.

MR 1 Nov. 1973

PMW

Music *see* **Choirs**; **Methodist Church Music Society**; **Organs**

Myanmar (formerly Burma) Upper Burma was missioned by British Methodism and Lower Burma by American Methodists. Upper Burma was annexed by the British in 1886 and the following year the first two MMS missionaries, J. Milton Brown (d. 1934; e.m.1865) and W.R. *Winston, arrived in Mandalay from Ceylon, with two Sinhalese colleagues. Progress in the face of the prevailing Buddhism was slow until 1952, but accelerated when evangelism was begun among ethnic groups in the Chin Hills and the Kale Valley. The Church became autonomous in 1965, a year before all expatriate missionaries were expelled, Christian hospitals and schools being taken over by the state. In 1997 the Methodist Church of Upper Myanmar reported a membership of 18,766 and a total community of 37,769.

F&H 5 pp. 381–91; *HMGB* 3 pp. 102–3

JAV

Myles, William (1756–1828; e.m. 1777) was born in *Limerick, where he joined the Methodist society following JW's visit in 1773. After travelling for five years in Irish circuits at his own expense, he was accepted for the English work and in 1782 was the first Irish preacher to be received into *full connexion. Just two years later he was one of those named in the *Deed of Declaration. He retired to Liverpool in 1824. He is mainly remembered for his *Chronological History of the Methodists* (1798; 4th enlarged edition 1813), which usefully included in its list of the itinerant preachers those who had left or been expelled from the ministry. He also wrote a life of W. *Grimshaw (1806).

WMM 1797 pp. 209–12, 261–65, 313–17, 1831 pp. 289–307; C.H. Crookshank (1885–88) 2 passim; R.H. Gallagher (1965) pp. 156–8

JAV

Mysticism In the 1720s W. *Law convinced JW that his search for genuine Christianity would be furthered by the writings of such mystics as Mme Guyon, Fénelon and de Renty. W made a thorough study of these and other mystics and was fascinated by their presentation of religion as a quest for perfect love and a personal encounter with the Divine. He later admitted that he had felt their alluring 'enchantment' and had almost been trapped by them. Nevertheless, by 1736 he believed that he had saved his faith from being 'wrecked on the rock' of mysticism. He rejected the mystics' 'refined' form of Christianity, branding them as unhealthily introvertive, self-obsessed and prone to devise 'religions of their own'. He condemned the 'quietism' of much RC mysticism and the obscurity of Protestant mystics such as J. Boehme. Convinced that mysticism 'stabbed Christianity in the vitals', he exposed it wherever he found it, even detecting its 'tincture' in *Luther.

However, while rejecting certain of its forms, the Wesleys may still have preserved the essence of mysticism. If Christian mysticism signifies a direct and loving union with God in Christ, it is arguable that the *experiential element in their theology promulgated a popularly comprehensible form of 'biblical' mysticism and celebrated it magnificently in their hymns. Moreover, JW continued to commend the lives of de Renty and Mme Guion as edifying reading.

See also **Devotion and Piety**

D. Dunn-Wilson in *PWHS* 35 pp. 65–7, 181–4; W.R. Cannon (1946); M. Schmidt (1962, 1973); R.G. Tuttle (1978)

DDW

Nash, David Foot (1902–72), *Plymouth solicitor, son of James L. Nash and Janie Foot, eldest daughter of I. *Foot Senr. In 1921, at the age of 18, he became a WM *local preacher of evangelical bent, associated with Plymouth Central Hall. During the *Anglican-Methodist Conversations of the 1960s, he was at first strongly opposed to the proposals, but later wrote *Their Finest Hour* (1964) in support of them. He was Vice-President of the Conference in 1963.

MR 4 July 1963, 23 March 1972

RFST

National Children's Home and Orphanage (now NCH Action for Children) was founded in 1869 by T.B. *Stephenson along with two Methodist friends, Alfred Mager and Francis Horner. Moved by the plight of children in Lambeth, they conceived the idea of a home for young boys in an environment free from poverty, crime and godlessness. Their first house was in Exton Street, Waterloo. Girls were admitted when new premises were opened in Bethnal Green in 1871. In 1872 the gift of a farm at Edgworth, Lancs, where Mager was the pioneer, brought further expansion. Property at Hamilton, *Canada (1873) facilitated emigration and an 'Industrial School' at Gravesend (1875) tackled juvenile delinquency. Princess Alice Orphanage in *Birmingham (1882) was for children of Christian families. The number of children increased rapidly, but Stephenson knew that, because they needed love as well as

food and shelter, care must be offered in family units with not more than 12–15 children in the care of mature staff. The NCH Sisterhood, founded in 1878 for women dedicated to the care of children, was a forerunner of the Wesley *Deaconess Order.

Children were placed in foster homes as early as 1905 and adoptions were arranged, a few before and many after the Adoption Act (1926). The two PM children's homes at Alresford, Hants and Harrogate became part of the NCH following *Methodist Union in 1932. The recommendations of the Curtis Committee on Child Care (of which J.H. *Litten was a member) were put into effect by the Children's Act (1948). The NCH had set up its own training college in 1935 – Stephenson Hall, London, the country's first college for training residential care workers – and already had a high percentage of fully trained staff. As the training of local authority staff rapidly improved, NCH, led by Gordon E. Barritt (e.m. 1943; Principal 1969–84), was more able to co-operate with them. In the 1950s NCH expanded residential special education and community-based work in family centres, where the emphasis is on preventive action. Residential care became limited to small units for children with severe disabilities or emotional and learning difficulties. A home-finding service continues and aims to match children with special needs with adoptive or foster parents. Counselling is provided for victims of sexual abuse and for divided families. The proportion of children referred and paid for by public authorities has steadily increased until two-thirds of annual income comes from that source.

Work in *Scotland began in 1954. In the Third World a Sister was working in *Nigeria in the 1960s. To mark the centenary in 1969, a home and training centre were opened in Jamaica and social workers and training staff were sent to the Eastern Caribbean, Belize and *Zimbabwe. From 1990 the ministerial Principal has been replaced by a lay professional, but the NCH still reports annually to Conference.

C.F. Walpole (1941); C.F. Walpole (1947); A.A. Jacka (1969); G.E. Barritt (1972); T. Philpot (1994)

JHL/GRS

Natural Philosophy, a forerunner of 'modern' science, illustrates from the order of nature the attributes of God and explains the secondary causes of natural phenomena. JW's major statement on this subject is his *Survey of the Wisdom of God in the Creation* (2 vols, 1763; 3rd edition,

5 vols, 1777). He was comfortable with a natural philosophy based upon description and classification. Parts of the *Survey* are reminiscent of Aristotle's *History of Animals*. His attitude towards Sir Isaac Newton was ambiguous. W praised him, but was worried about a natural philosophy stated in mathematical terms, perhaps because he associated mathematics with the rejection of particular Providence. At times, therefore, he was attracted to the 'Mosaic physics' of the anti-Newtonian John Hutchinson. While Hutchinson based his natural philosophy upon the unpointed Hebrew text of Genesis 1.1–18, he was heavily indebted to Descartes.

See also **Science**

JCE

Nelson, John (1707–74), a travelling stonemason, was 'like a wandering bird, cast out of the nest' until he heard JW preach at Moorfields, London, in 1739. Returning to his native Birstall, he founded the first Methodist society there in 1741. JW travelled to West Yorkshire in 1742 to encourage him in the work and found that 'the whole town wore a new face . . . and [God's] word sounded forth to . . . all the West Riding of Yorkshire'. Episcopal visitation returns for 1743 confirm the profusion of Methodist activity around Birstall unparalleled elsewhere in the diocese. Nelson preached initially from the doorway of his cottage, often still wearing his leather apron. His opponents had him impressed for military service in 1744, but his discharge was secured by the Countess of *Huntingdon and he became a frequent companion of JW in his travels. In 1751 Wesley found 'the societies of Yorkshire, chiefly under the care of John Nelson . . . all alive, strong and vigorous of soul . . . and increased in number from 1,800 to upwards of 3,000'.

C. Atmore (1801) pp. 295–8; *EMP* 1 pp. 2–178; *MR(W)* 1898 pp. 77–81

JAH

Nettleship, Sister Gertrude (d.1933) entered the Wesley *Deaconess Order in 1896 and was 'recognized' in April 1897 before sailing for Puttur, Jaffna. She was the first Wesley Deaconess in Ceylon (now *Sri Lanka) and spent the rest of her 35-year service there.

EDG

New, Charles (1840–75; e.m. 1860), early UMFC missionary to *Kenya and campaigner against slavery in East Africa. Trained as a bootmaker, he equipped himself for his ministry by reading widely. His travels were distinguished by careful observation and diligent recording. The first person known to have reached the snowline on Kilimanjaro (in 1871), he died returning from a fruitless attempt to establish a mission post near the mountain. He wrote *Life, Wanderings and Labours in Eastern Africa* (1874).

MR 24 May 1951; R.E. Kendall (1978)

JRP

New birth *see* **Regeneration**

New London Initiative   In 1910 the *Metropolitan Chapel Fund was merged with the London Mission Fund in order to 'carry the gospel to such regions of London as are the most spiritually destitute and degraded'. S. *Johnson was appointed Secretary of the new London Mission and Extension Fund, bringing together the interests of mission and property. An appeal was launched to raise £150,000. In the following years a new generation of Central Halls were built in strategic locations, such as Dagenham, Southall, Tooting, Uxbridge and Archway. J. *Rank, converted under Johnson's ministry, was a very generous, though anonymous, benefactor, giving over half a million pounds to found these Central Halls. In 1939 there were over 100 Mission Centres served by 80 ministers plus lay workers, deaconesses, sisters and doctors. In that year over 113,000 Londoners attended clinics at these centres to consult a doctor.

London Mission Report (1985)

JWH

New Mills   A creation of the water-powered textile industry and close to J. *Bennet's base at Chinley, this small industrial town early became a Methodist stronghold. A chapel was opened in 1766 which, as JW noted in 1776, was the only place of worship in the town. (Its pulpit is now at Abbot Hall Guest House, Cumbria.) JW paid eight visits between 1768 and 1788. It became a separate circuit (from Stockport) in 1808 and a larger chapel was opened in 1810. The PMs built a chapel in 1828 and the WMA built nearby in 1838, each becoming the head of a circuit in due course.

S. Evans (1912)

EAR

New Room, Bristol was the first preaching house built by JW. In 1739, soon after he had begun preaching in the open air in *Bristol, he found himself ministering to religious societies which met in private houses in Baldwin Street and Nicholas Street. Their numbers soon outgrew their domestic settings and on 9 May 1739 he bought land in the Horsefair to provide them with a home. They thereby became the first of the 'united societies' in association with JW. The New Room was opened on 3 June. It was intended for preaching and expounding the Scriptures, but also housed a school for poor children and a dispensary with free medicines for the poor. It was enlarged in 1748 and thereafter has been little altered. Above the preaching room were living quarters – a common room, library, studies and bedrooms for the itinerants stationed in the Bristol circuit and sometimes for visiting preachers. JW had his own rooms here, where he spent nearly 1,500 nights in the course of his ministry. CW also lived here for a time, before his marriage in 1749. In 1742, in response to the need to pay off the debt on the building, Captain Foy's suggestion of 'a penny per member' each week eventually led to the introduction of the *class meeting. The second *Conference met at the New Room in 1745, the first of 18 to meet there in JW's lifetime, including 1790, the last before his death.

After JW's death, divisions within Bristol Methodism came to a head in 1794–95 and led to a rift in the New Room society. The building was sold in 1808 to the *Welsh Calvinistic Methodists, who owned it until 1929. It was bought back for WM that year through the generosity of E.S. *Lamplough and was restored by Sir George Oatley. As the oldest Methodist building in the world it has become a centre of international pilgrimage. Two associations in particular link it with *American Methodism. At the Conference of 1771, F. *Asbury offered for the work in America, where he was to become the leading Methodist figure. In 1972 the remains of Capt. T. *Webb, known as 'American Methodism's no. 1 Layman' were reinterred in the Broadmead forecourt. Wardens in recent years have included M.L. *Edwards (1972–74), R.E. *Davies (1976–82) and A.R. *George (1982–95). In its worship and witness it is linked to both the Bristol (Centre) Circuit and to the Charles Wesley Heritage Centre, based on the family home of Charles and Sarah Wesley at 4 Charles Street.

C.F. Stell (1986) pp. 68–9; K. Morgan (1990); M.L. Edwards (1995);

JAN

New Zealand Encouraged by Samuel Marsden, the evangelical chaplain in Sydney, S.

*Leigh began a mission at Kaeo, North Island, in 1822. This settlement, 'Wesleydale', was destroyed by a Maori attack in 1827, but a new mission on the Hokianga Harbour the following year had greater success among the Maoris. In 1840 both Anglican and Methodist missionaries had a hand in the Treaty of Waitangi, which helped to protect Maori rights; but the Maori Wars of 1845–69 hampered the mission and there was a gradual shift of emphasis towards the European settlers, whose numbers were increased in the 1870s by rural immigrants from the English shires. In 1855 New Zealand was included in the Australasian Conference. It became a separate Conference in the Australasian Church in 1873 and an autonomous Conference in 1913. Meanwhile, smaller Methodist bodies had begun work there. PM work was begun in New Plymouth in 1844 by R. *Ward and spread to other towns and cities. In 1841 a BC *local preacher Henry Gilbert began a society at New Plymouth which later joined the PM cause. In 1873 a fresh start was made in Christchurch by the BC *local preacher Edward Reed and among the missionaries sent out were John Orchard and W. *Ready. In 1868 M. *Baxter gained a foothold for the UMFC in Christchurch, but the work there and in other towns was always overshadowed by the WM presence. Both BCs and the UMFC united with the WM in 1896 and in 1913 PM joined the newly autonomous Methodist Church of New Zealand ('Te Haahi Weteriana O Aotearoa'). In 1997 this reported a membership of 12,238 and a total community of 45,980.

—————

F&H 3 pp. 165–253

DJP/JAV

Newark A society was established in Millgate in 1776 and a chapel built in Guildhall Street, opened by JW in 1787. It became a school when Barnbygate Chapel was opened in 1846. Another WM chapel was opened at North End in 1868 and the Charles Street Sunday School mission room for the poor of the area in 1886, with a church there in 1905–6. The Newark Circuit was formed in 1793. The MNC had a chapel in Barnbygate. PM established itself in the face of opposition. Following a visit from W. *Clowes and J. *Wedgwood, another preacher William Lockwood was drenched by a fire hose while attempting to preach in the market place in 1817. Nevertheless, Newark eventually became the head of a separate circuit in 1862.

In 1935 a church was established in Hawtonville to meet the needs of a housing estate. A church hall was opened in 1955 and a new church built in 1968.

S V

Newbiggin-in-Teesdale *see* **Dales Circuit**

Newcastle-under-Lyme JW regularly passed through the town which was, as now, on a major north-south route. A chapel was registered by 1777. A MNC society was formed in September 1797 with a chapel, Ebenezer (1799) which is now part of the Sunday School building. J. *Barker, was stationed in the Newcastle MNC Circuit in 1831–32 and appears to have mediated in settling the potteries strike of 1836–37. In the 1840s the Unitarian Meeting House was linked with Barker's *Christian Brethren. A secession from the WM society to WR some time between 1849 and 1851 led to a UMFC circuit based on the Lower Street chapel (1799; purchased in 1863 after the WM had moved to a new chapel, Brunswick, in 1861). A cotton mill at Cross Heath appears on the first PM printed plan in 1812 and a PM chapel was built at Higherland in 1823. From time to time in the nineteenth century the southern Potteries were in the Newcastle WM and PM circuits.

———

VCH: Staffordshire 8 (Oxford, 1963); *150th Anniversary, Ebenezer Methodist Church, Newcastle, 1800–1950* (Newcastle 1950)

JHA

Newcastle upon Tyne On his first visit in May 1742, JW preached on the Quayside. CW formed a Methodist society during his eventful visit in September that year and for some years shared with his brother in the oversight of Methodism on Tyneside. But it was JW who was the dominant influence, with some 50 visits over half a century. Here he wrote and printed the *Rules of the United Societies* in 1743 in response to the need he found for greater discipline among his followers. The Keelmen's Hospital (1701) which still overlooks the Quayside was the site of early Methodist activity. With the *Orphan House as his base, Newcastle quickly became the heart of JW's northern work and the centre of a circuit which initially stretched from *Berwick-upon-Tweed to *Osmotherley. Since 1791 it has been the centre of a District.

Newcastle itself and the coal mining and fishing communities in its hinterland proved fruitful soil for the growth of Methodism. Important factors were effective lay leadership and the patronage of wealthy businessmen, such as W. *Smith in the early years and later on the *Bainbridges, *Fenwicks, *Stephensons and *Lunns. The New Road (1813) and Brunswick (1820) chapels were early fruits of the solid respectability they represented. The Duke of Northumberland contributed to the building of Brunswick, being reassured as to Wesleyan loyalty to king and country. Bainbridge Memorial chapel (1885) was demolished and replaced (1991) by a worship area in the ancillary premises. The Westgate Hall (1902), a fine survival of the *central hall movement, is now the base of the former Prudhoe Street Mission, another fruit of patronage by Methodist businessmen, as was the first of the Moody and Sankey campaigns in the north east in 1873.

Except for the BC all the major non-WM movements took root in Newcastle, including the early IM evicted from WM for alleged radicalism at the time of Peterloo and later reinforced by several *Christian Lay Churches in the 1870s. The MNC opened its first chapel, Bethel, in 1799 and that movement's story was enlivened by the controversy surrounding J. *Barker and the Barkerite secession c.1840. *J. Branfoot was the pioneer PM evangelist here in 1821 and within two decades a handsome chapel was erected on Nelson Street at the heart of the new town being built by Dobson and Grainger (the latter a product of the Brunswick Sunday School). Central, Northumberland Road (1899) was built under the ministry of A.T. *Guttery. The UMFC also flourished there, as evidenced by such chapels as New Bridge Street (1852), Prudhoe Street (1862) and Gosforth (1877, still in use). Both WM and other Methodist Conferences have met a number of times in the city.

Despite its important influence on the religious and social life of Tyneside, Methodism was not dominant in statistical terms. The 1851 *Religious Census shows total Methodist attendances as one thirteenth of the population, compared with one sixth for the CofE and one tenth for non-Methodist Nonconformity. Newcastle today has three Methodist circuits, serving the eastern, western and central areas of the city.

———

PWHS 47 pp. 202–20; W.R. Surman (1902); W.M. Patterson (1907); Conference Handbook 1936, 1958; G.E. Milburn (1987);

GEM

Newchurch-in-Rossendale *see* **Rossendale**

Newman, Penelope (Mrs Coussins) (fl.1775–1805), a bookseller in *Cheltenham, was converted on one of JW's visits some time after 1766 and banished plays and novels from her shelves. Soon after becoming a Methodist she started to take part in prayer meetings, travelling to *Tewkesbury and elsewhere to publish 'the glad tidings of saving grace'. Occasionally she exhorted and preached. She became one of W's correspondents and he encouraged her efforts. She was instrumental in the conversion of J. *Coussins; they were married in 1782 and had a daughter Philadelphia.

PWHS 25 86ff; SL, vols 5–7; Z. Taft, vol. 1 (1825) pp. 290–5

EDG

Newton, Rev. John (1725–1807), evangelical clergyman, who spent his early years at sea, in the navy and then in the slave trade. He was converted in 1748. His religious convictions were strengthened through the influence of G. *Whitefield and of JW, who met him in *Liverpool in 1758 and in 1760 deplored the fact that he had been refused ordination because he lacked a university education. Despite this he was ordained in 1764 by the bishop of Lincoln and became curate at Olney. His autobiographical *An Authentic Narrative* was published in 1764. He collaborated with William Cowper in producing the *Olney Hymns* (1779). Eight of his hymns are in *HP*. In 1780 he moved to St. Mary Woolnoth, London, where he exercised a strong evangelical influence and lent support to Wilberforce's anti-slavery campaign.

DNB; *ODCC*; B. Martin (1950); J.C. Pollock (1981); D.B. Hindmarsh (1996)

JAV

Newton, Dr John Anthony (1930– ; e.m. 1956) A church historian and ecumenist, his varied ministry included teaching at *Wesley College, Bristol (1965–72; Principal, 1973–78) and at Limuru Theological College, *Kenya (1972–73). In 1978 he became Superintendent of the West London Mission in succession to D.O. *Soper. As Chairman of the Liverpool District (1986–95) and local Free Church moderator, he became a third member of the partnership established by Bishop David Sheppard and Archbishop Derek Worlock. He was President of the Conference in 1981 and Moderator of the FCFC 1989–90 and 1992–9, and served on the English RC-Methodist Committee and on the 7th international RC-Methodist Dialogue Commission (1996). His books include studies of Susanna Wesley (1969) and Bishop Edward King of Lincoln (1977); and

he is an honorary canon of Lincoln. He gave the 1985 WHS Lecture on Samuel *Annesley.

MR 2 July 1981

DJC

Newton, Dr Robert (1780–1854; e.m. 1799) WM minister. Born near *Whitby, the son of a farmer, he followed his brother **Booth Newton** (1768–1811; e.m. 1790) into the ministry and served almost entirely in northern circuits. As an advocate of *overseas missions he raised enormous sums. At home equally on platform or in the pulpit, he preached sometimes twelve times a week. Opening innumerable chapels, he was well known on the coach and railway circuits. He was frequently Secretary of the Conference from 1821 on and, like *Bunting was President four times (in 1824, 1832, 1840 and 1848), on the last occasion after being criticized in the *Fly Sheets. In 1834 as Chairman of the Manchester District he had taken action against J.R. *Stephens for advocating separation of Church and state and had suspended Dr S. *Warren at a District Meeting. He made a very popular visit to the USA in 1840 and the Wesleyan University of Middletown, Conn, granted him a DD. In his later years he was given an assistant, so that he could be freed from pastoral work during the week.

Newton was the classic WM popular preacher, offering the heart of the gospel and often using the same basic sermon. Two volumes of his sermons were published in 1856. He was loyal upholder of the 'high Wesleyan' position in connexional affairs and a Protestant stress in political matters.

MR(W) 1905 pp. 67–8; T. Jackson (1854); G.J. Stevenson (1884–86) 2 pp. 261–71; D.T. Young (1907)

JMT

Nicholas, Dr William (1838–1912; e.m. 1861), theological professor and sixth President (1889–1908) of *Methodist College, Belfast. Born of English parents at Wexford, he was a theological Prizeman at Trinity College, Dublin. An outstanding speaker, he attracted large crowds wherever he preached. He was also a writer of considerable ability and was chosen by the Evangelical Alliance to deliver papers at three international conferences. He was a traditionalist in his attitude to social issues and his theological outlook. He campaigned vigorously against Home Rule during the campaigns of 1886 and 1892 and became increasingly identified with the Ulster Loyalist cause. The *Methodist Times* saw in him all that was anathema to radical thinkers, dismissing the rhetoric of his *Fernley Lecture on *Christianity and Socialism* (1893) and branding him an extreme individualist. He was a member of the Senate of the Royal University of Ireland and on its dissolution received an honorary LLD. He was elected Vice-President of MCI in 1894 and 1904.

———

ICA 27 Sept. 1912

RPR

Nigeria James Ferguson and other former slaves who, after some time in *Sierra Leone, moved on to settle at Abeokuta in western Nigeria, appealed for Christian teachers. In 1842 T.B. *Freeman, at the request of the Missionary Committee in London, went from the Gold Coast and established work which after many trials gained a foothold among the Yoruba peoples. In the 1870s a PM mission was launched in eastern Nigeria. The two Districts remained separate until an autonomous Nigerian Conference was inaugurated in 1962. Shortly afterwards Church Union negotiations foundered and the adoption of a very hierarchical form of church order in 1976 led to a schism in Methodism which was not healed until the new constitution was modified in 1989. A strong commitment to *medical work, embodied in such places as the *Wesley Guild hospital in Ilesha and the renowned leprosy settlement at Uzuakoli, was not diminished by government take-overs and new developments in the 1990s included pioneering work among mentally ill destitutes at Amaudo in the east.

———

F.D. Walker (1942)

JRP

Nightingale, Charles Thomas (1876–1961), son of a WM minister, was a prominent *Edinburgh solicitor and circuit steward. A *local preacher, he helped G. *Jackson establish the Albert Hall Mission in the west of Edinburgh. An Asquithian Liberal JP, he was concerned about juvenile delinquency and led a Sunday School in one of the mining villages. As Vice-President in 1943, he gave a memorable address on 'Discipleship' and was the first Vice-President to preach during Conference.

———

MR 15 July 1943

JHL

Nightingale, Joseph (1775–1824), critic of WM. Influenced in his youth by the writings of Joseph Priestley and Tom Paine he became a Deist, but was converted and joined the Methodists in 1796, but left them in 1804. After teaching in *Macclesfield, he became a Unitarian minister (though without pastoral charge) in London in 1805. His many publications included history, topography and natural history and he contributed frequently to the *Monthly Repository*. His highly critical *Portraiture of Methodism* (1807) did some damage to the movement, but at the end of his life he expressed regret for 'that foolish book' and was reconciled with WM.

———

WMM 1823 pp. 750–1; G. Smith (1858–61) 2 pp. 283–4, 440–2

JAV

Niles, Daniel Thambyrajah (1908–70; e.m. 1932), *Sri Lankan minister and internationally renowned Church leader, began training for the law. Before World War II he was World Secretary of the YMCA at Geneva. He was a speaker at the World Conference of Christian Youth in Oslo, 1947 and was appointed co-chairman of the WCC Youth Department. He also served as chairman of the World Student Christian Federation. From 1957 to 1968 he was secretary of the newly formed East Asia Christian Conference, of which he was elected President in 1968. He was a delegate to the WCC and one of its Presidents at the fourth Assembly (Uppsala, 1968). He was a Vice-President of the World Methodist Council. His book *Upon the Earth* (1962) was an important contribution to the theology of mission. Three of his hymns are in *HP*.

———

MR 23 July 1970

JAV

Nixon, James (1785–1857), converted at Burslem, became an associate of W. *Clowes in the early days of the PM revival in Cheshire. He and Thomas Woodnorth each gave five shillings to Clowes to enable him to be free of employment in order to preach. His name appears on the first Tunstall PM plan for 1811, but with only three appointments.

WL

Noble, Dr Walter James (1879–1962; e.m. 1900) missionary in Ceylon (*Sri Lanka), was born at Darlington and employed by the North Eastern Railway before offering for the ministry. After training at *Didsbury College, he went out to southern Ceylon, where he served for 22 years (1900–22) before becoming one of the MMS Secretaries (1922–47), proving himself a skilful chairman of committees and a lucid and compelling missionary advocate. He was President of the 1942 Conference and in retirement was active in the WMC. A keen cricketer, he once took the wicket of George Hirst with one of his leg breaks and was also remembered for his BBC Epilogue on the evening of the death of George VI.

W.J. Noble (1957); *MR* 16 July 1942, 1 March 1962

JAV

North, Dr Christopher Richard (1888–1975; e.m. 1912) was born in Dulwich and educated at a school for orphans. He worked in a London office before being accepted for the WM ministry and was trained at *Didsbury College. He obtained his MA at the School of Oriental and African Studies while a minister at Chertsey and Walton-on-Thames, and after two years in N. *India was appointed OT tutor at *Handsworth College in 1925. After World War II he was appointed to the Chair of Hebrew at the University College of North Wales, Bangor. His main publications were *The Suffering Servant in Deutero-Isaiah* (1948) and a commentary on Isaiah 40–55 (1952). He received an honorary DD from Aberdeen University. He was active in the Society for OT Study and was elected its President in 1949.

Times 4 Aug. 1975; *MR* 7 Aug. 1975

CSR

North Midland Counties (Leics, Rutland, Lincs, Notts, Derbys) Between 1742 and 1790 JW visited his birthplace, *Epworth, every other year on his northern journeys. Otherwise, except for *Grimsby which he visited 19 times, he gave very little attention to Lincolnshire. It was left largely to local initiative and the itinerants to establish societies there. Methodism was strongest in Lindsey, where there was a larger concentration of population, compared with Holland and Kesteven, where it also encountered Baptist and Catholic influence respectively. Elsewhere in the North Midland Region JW was similarly selective. In the early years of his itinerant ministry he paid several visits to Lady *Huntingdon's home at Donington Park, Leics, but later concentrated on the county towns: *Nottingham (30 visits), *Leicester (18 visits) and *Derby (16 visits).

In the nineteenth century PM became by far the largest of the non-WM bodies, especially in Lincs, where *Lincoln, *Gainsborough and *Grantham were early centres and it had a follow-

ing among the agricultural labourers. *Scotter (where the PM Conference met in 1829) became a circuit town and the centre of widespread missionary activity, extending as far as the *Channel Islands. In mid-century *Louth, *Lincoln, *Grantham, *Derby and *Nottingham became strongholds of WR.

In 1851 the *Religious Census recorded a total of 1,554 Methodist places of worship in the North Midland Division (including WM:963; PM: 470). Total adult attendances on Census Sunday were 279,237 (23% of the population) with evening services (usually the best attended) totalling 136,753 (11.3%). As a percentage of the population, attendances at both WM and PM services were higher in Lincs than elsewhere in the Division. With approximately 50% of the WM figures (despite a much lower morning attendance), the PM presence was a significant one across the Division. Though WR attendances morning and evening were only 10% of the WM totals, this represented substantial inroads into the WM membership, despite the small number (66) of WR chapels at that date. WM faced less rivalry in Notts from either PM or WR than elsewhere in the Division.

By 1989 the number of Methodist churches was down to 798, with the largest concentration in Lincs and Derbys. Attendances totalled 32,500 (1.2% of the population) and membership 25,500 (0.9%)

W. Leary (1988); J. & R. Stevenson (1988)

JAV/WL

North West England (Lancashire and Cheshire) South East Lancashire and East Cheshire, with their large parishes, dispersed settlements and residual Puritanism, were fertile fields for the early Methodist preachers, notably J *Bennet who was active here in the 1740s. Following his break with JW in 1751, a WM circuit based on *Manchester was created. This embraced the two counties and beyond and was progressively subdivided. The industrial revolution gave Methodism great opportunities as the population grew. Chapels were opened in Manchester and *Liverpool in 1751, but West Lancashire, with its ancestral Catholicism, poor communications and lack of industry, remained something of a Methodist backwater for many years.

From the 1750s JW paid annual visits, usually travelling north from the Potteries. Oldham Street Chapel, Manchester, opened in 1781, rivalled

*Wesley's Chapel in size and opulence; but Methodism was also successful in rural Cheshire and the growing mill towns. In the nineteenth century all branches of Methodism were active there, but WM was dominant except in *Rochdale, a stronghold of the WMA, and *Ashton-under-Lyne, where the MNC was largest. PM was strong in rural Cheshire and mining areas. Manchester was the centre of the WMA agitation in 1834 and the scene of the expulsion of W. *Griffith, J. *Everett and S. *Dunn in 1849. *Warrington was the cradle of IM in 1796 and industrial Lancashire has remained an IM heartland.

*Didsbury College was established in Manchester in 1842, followed by *Victoria Park UMFC College in 1872 and the PM (later *Hartley) College in 1881. In 1883–86 Oldham Street chapel was replaced by Methodism's first purpose-built Central Hall. This was the nucleus of the Manchester and Salford Mission which flourished under S. *Collier and claimed the largest regular Methodist congregation in the world at the Free Trade Hall. Prior to this the first Central Mission had been established in *Liverpool, but not in special premises. After 1850 Blackpool and *Southport became strong centres.

In 1851 the *Religious Census recorded 932 Methodist places of worship in the two counties (including WM 496, PM 238 and WMA 133). By 1989 there were 807 churches serving a much larger population. Total attendances recorded in 1851 were 266,628 (10.7% of the population; significantly higher in Cheshire than in Lancashire). In 1989 adult worshippers averaged 1.3% of the population, again higher in Cheshire than in the conurbations.

EAR

Northampton by the eighteenth century was a stronghold of 'respectable' Dissent, notably during the ministry of P. *Doddridge. From 1752 the neighbouring Weston Favell was the scene of the Rev. J. *Hervey's evangelical ministry. G. *Whitefield made frequent visits; the first in 1739, when he preached on the racecourse. JW visited the town 24 times between 1741 and 1790 and on his second visit lectured to Doddridge's students. But the first society was not formed until around 1767, by a Captain Scott of the Royal Horse Guards. It met in the Regimental Riding School; then, after his departure, in other places including premises on the Green previously used by Presbyterians and Strict Baptists. By 1793, when the first chapel was built in King's Head Lane, there were 55 members, which grew to 200 by 1813 and to

353 by 1821. It became the Sunday School when a larger chapel, designed by W. *Jenkins, was built in Gold Street in 1815. A second chapel, opened in Todd's Lane in the 1830s, was replaced by Regent Square in 1876, when a third chapel was built in Queen's Road.

PM was introduced from the Burland Circuit by James Hurd in 1834, but made slow progress until 1840, when the Horsemarket Chapel was built (rebuilt 1872; closed 1942). J. *Petty had a difficult ministry there 1842–44, but there was new growth later in the century and a second chapel was opened in 1880 at Kettering Road (later Queensgrove) with the support of Joseph Gibbs, a leading boot and shoe manufacturer. The circuit was divided into two in 1886 and two PM Conferences met there, in 1891 and 1918. After lengthy delay caused by the war years Park Avenue church opened in 1925. The WMA had a chapel, the Tabernacle, in King Street. In 1857 it did not join the UMFC, but formed a short-lived WR circuit. At the time of Methodist Union there were one WM and three PM circuits; after 1932 both circuits and churches were progressively amalgamated.

In 1929 two local PM businessmen, J.W. Arnold and C.J. Pearce, saw a local need for accommodation for elderly Methodists and founded the Methodist Homestead, anticipating the work of *MHA. It has developed into a complex of 24 individual Homes, operating as a private trust.

G. Lawton in *PWHS* 25 pp. 88–94, 104–7; H.B. Kendall (1906) 1 pp. 416–9

JAV

Northern Counties The four northern counties of Durham, Northumberland, Cumberland and Westmorland contained some of Methodism's strongest concentrations, largely owing (in socio-economic terms) to the region's industrial and commercial activity. *Newcastle upon Tyne, a historic town increasingly surrounded by collieries and a flourishing trade centre, became the Wesleys' northern base as early as 1742. JW visited Tyneside 50 times in almost as many years, often staying for extended periods (especially in the early years) and using Newcastle as a base from which to make great forays into the surrounding region. The *Orphan House (1743), Methodism's first building in the north, provided him and his preachers with living quarters.

The coal-mining areas of south-east Northumberland, north-east Durham and West Cumbria commanded most of JW's attention. Large areas of central and northern Northumberland and the agricultural area of south eastern Durham were ignored completely. He made a series of brief but important forays into the northern dales to evangelize lead-mining communities, and also worked the coastal ports and the towns which lay along his routes; e.g *Berwick, Alnwick, Hexham, *Durham, *Darlington and *Yarm. Cumbria was visited either via Weardale, Nenthead and Alston to *Whitehaven, or along the Tyne valley to *Carlisle. Methodism was slow to establish itself in Cumbria, until many former members of *Inghamite societies founded some 20 years earlier transferred their loyalties in the 1760s.

By 1791 the distribution of Methodist chapels in the north reflected the geographical strategy outlined above. But new industrial developments, population growth and rapid urbanization in the nineteenth century stimulated a massive growth and expansion of its presence in the region. This was due partly to vigorous new WM initiatives, but also to the appearance of all the non-Wesleyan branches, some in a relatively modest way (MNC, BC, IM), but others (PM, WMA, WR, UMFC) in very considerable numbers. Of all these, PM made the biggest overall impact, filling the gaps in the rural areas and being especially active in pit villages, and towns such as *Whitehaven and *Sunderland, the latter (according to the 1851 *Religious Census) having more PM worshippers than WM by the mid-nineteenth century.

The massive impact of Methodism on religious life in the north is demonstrated by the Census figures for County Durham, where its attendances equalled those of the Church of England and Dissent put together. According to the Census figures, Methodism in the four northern counties had 767 places of worship (WM 441, PM 214, WMA, 52; MNC 32, WR 28). Total attendances on March 31st were 138,339 or 14.3% of the population (morning, 37,648; afternoon, 32,382; evening, 68,309). In 1989 the figures for the equivalent geographical area were: 568 places of worship; total attendances throughout the day, 44,200 or 1.6% of the population.

R. Moore (1974); J. Burgess (1980); G.E. Milburn (1987); C.C. Short (1995)

GEM

Northridge, Dr William L. (1886–1966; e.m. 1910), distinguished Irish preacher, scholar and writer, educated at *Methodist College, Belfast. In 1922 he obtained his PhD at Queen's University,

which conferred an honorary DD on him in 1957. As tutor at *Edgehill College in 1926 and Principal from 1943, he exerted great influence on the training of both ministers and lay people. He played an important part in the development of educational policy in Northern Ireland and was President of the Irish Methodist Church in 1944. He was much in demand as a speaker on both sides of the Atlantic. His books include *Psychology and Pastoral Practice* (1947) and *Disorders of the Emotional and Spiritual Life* (1961).

MR 22 Dec. 1966

NWT

Norwich   A form of Methodism first arrived with J. *Wheatley, a preacher expelled by JW. He attracted huge crowds and a meeting place named The Tabernacle was provided in Timberhill, but public hostility led to its destruction. A more permanent building, designed by Thomas Ivory and also named the Tabernacle, was erected in Bishopgate. The local 'Hell Fire Club' violently persecuted the Methodists, often with the tacit support of the magistrates. JW and CW both came in 1754. As John was gravely ill, Charles hired an old foundry in Orford Hill in response to the support his preaching attracted. S. *Larwood was left in charge. In 1759, after the disgrace of Wheatley, JW took over the lease of his Tabernacle for seven years. He had great difficulty with the Calvinist congregation, which was eventually taken over by Lady *Huntingdon.

JW opened Cherry Lane chapel in 1769, financed largely by his own gift of £270. The congregation transferred in 1811 to a new and larger chapel in Calvert Street. St Peter's, Lady Lane, was opened in 1824 – at this time it was noted that more than 2,000 people were worshipping in Methodist churches in the city – and New City Chapel in 1839.

W. *Clowes declared that Norwich, 'notwithstanding its thirty-six parish churches and numerous clergy is *fearfully wicked*'. It was missioned in 1820 by the Nottingham PM Circuit. Open-air meetings were held on Mousehold Heath. The first chapel was a hayloft in Rose Yard. Lakenham Old Chapel was built in 1823 and replaced by a much larger one on Queen's Road in 1872; the PM Conference met there in 1892 and 1912. Cowgate chapel converted from a brewery, opened in 1842; Dereham Road replaced an earlier chapel in 1864; Shipfield Chapel opened in 1875 (rebuilt on Wroxham Road, 1958) and Nelson Street chapel in 1879. Scott Memorial in Thorpe

Road (1902) was designed by the architect A.F. Scott in memory of his father, Jonathan Scott (1823–1900; e.m. 1846). Plumstead Road chapel (1910), destroyed by bombs in 1942, was replaced by Heartsease Lane (1946). Dereham Road (1850; rebuilt 1864), also bombed, was eventually succeeded by Bowthorpe Road, with a permanent building in 1974. The number of PM chapels in Norwich mirrors its great success in Norfolk as a whole.

The WR agitations convulsed Norfolk more than any other county and WM membership in Norwich dropped by 4/5ths. The Reformers took over Calvert Street, New City (from the Baptists, replaced by Chapelfield Road, 1881) and Sun Lane (rebuilt in 1908 as Rosebery Road). Only at the end of the century had WM membership recovered sufficiently to warrant the building of St Peter's, Park Lane (1895) and Sprowston Road (1909). When the City Council determined on the compulsory purchase of the Lady Lane chapel's Sunday School premises in the late 1930s, the congregation united with that of Park Lane and a new St Peter's church was built (1939). Mile Cross church, a splendid example of art deco by Cecil Yelf, opened in 1934, the result of co-operation between the three strands of Norwich Methodism.

W. Larkin (1825); J. Ede, N. Virgoe & T. Williamson (1996)

NV

Nottingham Methodism is said to have begun through the preaching of a merchant hosier, John Howe, who had met the Wesleys during business visits to London. Preaching was at first in the market place and in private homes. To accommodate more hearers, Matthew Bagshaw of Crossland Place made a hole in his living room ceiling; men sat upstairs and women downstairs, with the preacher standing on a chair on the table. The first purpose-built chapel was the Octagon in Boot Lane. JW made the first of 28 visits in June 1741 on the invitation of Lady *Huntingdon. In 1783 he opened the new chapel in Hockley, which was taken over by the MNC when the majority of members sided with A. *Kilham in 1797. Another MNC chapel, Parliament Street, opened in 1817 (rebuilt 1875).

PM arrived when S. *Kirkland was invited to preach in a disused factory in Broad Marsh on Christmas Day, 1815 to a congregation of 1,000. A small group of *Protestant Methodists was formed in 1827. In March 1833 the *Arminian Methodist connexion was formed at Salem Chapel, Barker Gate. There were *Original Methodists in Radford for a few years around 1849; and the 'Wesleyan Congregational Free Church' existed for two years from 1855, under the patronage of Richard Mercer. WR and WMA leaders conferred in Nottingham on 27 February 1855, with the result that the UMFC was formed in 1857.

In 1902 the WM bought the impressive Albert Hall and made it their centre for preaching and mission. It was destroyed by fire in 1906 and rebuilt and reopened in 1909, remaining the centre of their Mission until 1985, when the congregation moved to the Parliament Street church.

See also **Boot, Jesse**; **Booth, William**

G.H. Harwood (1872); Conference Handbook (1924); R.C. Swift (1982)

JC

NOW *see* **Missionary Magazines**

Oastler, Richard (1789–1861), son of Robert Oastler (*Leeds cloth merchant and *local preacher, a founder member of the MNC, although he later rejoined the WM; d.1820, aet.71). Educated at the Fulneck Moravian school and trained as an architect, he became a commission agent in 1810, began preaching, but became bankrupt in 1819. In 1820 he became the steward of the Fixby Estate, left Leeds in 1821 and emerged as a Tory-Anglican factory reformer. His letter on 'Yorkshire Slavery', written to the *Leeds Mercury* 29 September 1830, is seen as marking the start of the campaign for factory reform. His opposition to the new poor law led to his eventual imprisonment for debt 1840–44. He was a close friend of J.R. *Stephens and M.T. *Sadler.

J.R. Stephens (1838); C. Driver (1946)

DCD

Oats, Sister Evelyn (d.1937) entered the Wesley *Deaconess Order in 1892 and sailed in 1894 for Durban, *South Africa, the first WM Deaconess to become a foreign missionary. From Durban she moved to Johannesburg, where she established 'Stephenson's Cottage' as her base and opened a convalescent home in 1897. She continued her ministry through the Boer War and in 1907 became Principal of Kilmerton Native Women's Industrial College, Pretoria. Failing health forced her to retire from active work in 1909.

EDG

O'Bryan, William (1778–1868), founder of the *Bible Christians, was born at Luxulyan, Cornwall, the son of William O'Bryan, farmer and tinner, and his wife Thomasine. They were a 'Church Methodist' family and both father and son served as churchwardens. William junior received JW's blessing as a child: 'May he be a blessing to hundreds and thousands.' A studious and deeply religious boy, it seemed likely that he would 'take the gown' and receive Anglican ordination; but under the influence of A. *Clarke and other visiting Methodist preachers he became a *local preacher in 1800 and developed into an itinerant free-lance evangelist, operating on the fringes of the WM circuits. Rejected for the ministry because of his family responsibilities, he engaged in independent evangelizing in parts of Cornwall and Devon largely uninfluenced by WM. His relationship with the circuit superintendents became more and more strained on account of his disregard of Methodist rules and his apparent self-sufficiency, and he was twice expelled from membership. At Stratton near the Devon border, although no longer a Wesleyan, he, with the circuit steward, made a proposal to the circuit which would have given him some recognition within the circuit and at the same time allowed him to pursue his independent mission work. This was not acceptable and on October 1st 1815 O'Bryan wrote: 'I entered on my circuit at Mary-Week and Hex.' He had become a church founder. Within a week 22 members had been enrolled at Lake Farm, *Shebbear, among them the teenager J. *Thorne. The following decade saw the rapid spread of BC, but also witnessed the deteriorating relationship between O'Bryan and his followers, which led to a final break in 1829. Following this he emigrated to North *America, living there in self-imposed exile, the denomination continuing without him.

His wife **Catherine O'Bryan**, (*née* Cowlin, 1781–1860) helped to manage her father's draper's shop in Roche, near St Austell. They were married in 1803. She became a preacher and helped her husband in many ways, emigrating with him to America. She wrote poetry and, it is thought, a few hymns.

All his life O'Bryan was a tireless, indeed a compulsive, traveller. His evangelistic tours in Devon, Cornwall, London and Kent were succeeded by long journeys from New York to Ohio and across the Canadian border, and he published a journal of his American travels. He preached wherever he went, but never saw the results that he had seen back home. He died in New York in 1868 and was buried in the Greenwood cemetery, Brooklyn, where he is named 'Bryant', having dropped his preference for what he had supposed to be the correct form.

See also **Thorne Family**

G.J. Stevenson (1884–86) 6 pp. 861–67; S.L. Thorne (1878)

TS

Octagons *see* **Architecture**

Oddie, James (1730–90), born near Gisburn in the W. Riding, itinerated mainly in the North. A gifted and penetrating preacher, he was the instrument of J. *Pawson's conversion in 1758. He defied JW by persisting in trade (for which he was removed from the itinerancy), by petitioning on behalf of the itinerants not included in the *Deed of Declaration, and by pressing for the administration of the sacraments by the itinerants. He became a class leader, but was removed in 1787 when his unhappy second marriage ended in bankruptcy, and left the society.

C. Atmore (1801) pp. 298–300; J.W. Laycock (1909), pp. 172–4

MB

Odell, Joseph (1846–1923; e.m. 1866), PM minister. From 1876 to 1880 he was stationed in Brooklyn, New York, where he established the 'Odell Temperance League' and seems to have come into contact with ideas that shaped his future ministry. In 1885 he began a 20-year ministry in *Birmingham, which resulted in considerable PM progress in the city, notably in the opening of the Conference Hall, 1895. Inspired by a *Holiness Convention in *Grimsby, he founded the *Evangelists' Home. He was President of the Conference in 1900 and gave the *Hartley Lecture in 1903 on *Evangelism*.

J. Pearce (1935), pp. 87–96

DCD

Olivers, Thomas (1725–1799), early itinerant from Wales, a convert of G. *Whitefield. He became one of JW's preachers in 1753 and spent 46 years in the itinerant ministry in England, Ireland and Scotland. Of a literary and theological bent of mind, he actively supported JW in the disputes with *Calvinism. He was less successful when in charge of JW's printing projects, including the *AM*, and was removed by JW for his lack of editorial skills. A considerable poet and polemicist, he is best remembered for his hymn,

'The God of Abraham praise'. Among his other poems was an *Elegy on the Death of John Wesley*. The ascription of the tune 'Helmsley' to him is debatable.

———

EMP 2 pp. 48–106; C. Atmore (1801) pp. 302–6; G.T. Hughes (1979)

HMG

Olver, George William (1829–1905; e.m. 1851), WM minister, son of Henry Vyvyan Olver (1790–1872; e.m. 1812). He was educated at *Kingswood School and taught at *Queen's College, Taunton before training at *Didsbury College, where he was also Assistant Tutor 1851–53. He served in turn as Secretary of the *Education Committee (1866–71), as Principal of *Southlands College (1871–81) and as a Secretary of the WMMS (1881–1900).

———

MR 2 March 1905

JAV

Order of Christian Citizenship During the 1930s the *Temperance and Social Welfare Department inaugurated the Youth and Christian Citizenship Movement. Out of this grew the OCC, dedicated to instruction and guidance in social witness and service. Meetings and conferences were held throughout the country and thousands were enrolled. A quarterly magazine, *The Christian Citizen*, was published, incorporating an earlier publication, *On Active Service*, aimed at keeping members in touch with the Department's work.

KGG

Ordination On 1 September 1784, JW, long persuaded by his reading of Bishop Stillingfleet and Lord Peter King that 'Bishops and presbyters are essentially of one order', responded to the post-War situation in *America. Assisted by T. *Coke and J. *Creighton, both Anglican priests, he ordained two of his preachers as deacons and the next day as elders. He also ordained Coke as 'Superintendent'. With them he sent to America *The *Sunday Service of the Methodists* which included services for the ordination of deacons, elders and superintendents. At the 'Christmas Conference' in Baltimore Coke, assisted by others, ordained F. *Asbury successively as *deacon, elder and *Superintendent and the Methodist Episcopal Church began its separate existence. In 1785 JW ordained preachers as elders for *Scotland. He continued to ordain men going overseas and in 1788 ordained A. *Mather

for England, probably as Superintendent. In 1789 the word 'presbyter' replaced 'elder' on the ordination certificates.

After JW's death there were a few ordinations at District Meetings, but the 1792 Conference put a stop to these and in 1793 abandoned the distinction between ordained and unordained. The *Plan of Pacification (1795) permitted any itinerant 'authorised by the Conference' to administer the *Lord's Supper in certain circumstances and this soon became a universal practice. Coke, however, continued to ordain with the imposition of hands men going overseas, regardless of whether they were actually in *full connexion, and this custom continued in the WM Church. The idea gradually arose that the preachers in full connexion were 'virtually' or 'in essence' ordained. The 1836 Conference resolved to introduce the imposition of hands as a general practice. In 1846 the three forms of ordination in the *Sunday Service* were replaced by a single service, based loosely on that for elders, but including elements from those for deacons and superintendents. The present custom is for the President or an ex-President to preside at each ordination service, with other ministers taking part in the imposition of hands.

Members of the *Deaconess Order were first ordained in 1937, and the *Diaconate was seen as an ordained order of ministry from its inception in 1988.

The other Methodist bodies differed from WM both in their understanding and in their practice. In BC there was no ordination by imposition of hands, despite the fact that reception into full connexion was described as 'ordination' from 1892 on. PM practice is difficult to establish, but probably varied locally, especially in the early years. The UMFC was strongly opposed to the imposition of hands as reflecting high church superstition. Candidates were received into full connexion at the annual Assembly, following a vote by all present on each individual.

A.R. George in *HMGB* 2 (1978) pp. 143–60; *PWHS* 39 pp. 121–7, 153–7

ARG

Organs date from 200–300 BC and are by far the oldest keyboard instrument. Their use at Roman pagan events ensured that they were not used by the Church until the 10th century; but by the sixteenth century they were to be found throughout western Europe. JW objected strongly to the long voluntary (and probably to the poor quality of the music chosen and the playing!) in the middle of Anglican services as 'an unreasonable and unmeaning impertinence'. But on occasions he was most appreciative of the organ playing in worship. A bass viol was at first the only instrument permitted in Methodist chapels. Although a few Methodist organs appeared at the turn of the century, they were not officially sanctioned until 1820 and then, as at *Leeds, could prove a cause of contention. However, by the end of the nineteenth century pipe organs adorned many chapels, often being seen as a status symbol. By the end of the twentieth century many churches were smaller, with more flexible worship areas, electronic organs had become highly sophisticated and a number of churches supplemented their organs with instrumental groups. Fortunately, some good pipe organs survived and continue to give good service. A 1996 survey showed that over 90% of British Methodist churches have an organ (46% pipe organs, 44% electronic and 5% reed organs).

See also **Bath**

PLC

Original Methodists   There were no fewer than three serious divisions within Nottinghamshire PM between 1829 and 1839, centred on the *Nottingham, Bingham, Belper and *Mansfield areas. The division arose during the Superintendency in the Belper Circuit of William Carthy, ostensibly over ministerial payment. They were joined by a second stream from the *Mansfield Circuit. The Original Methodists in the Belper and Mansfield circuits were the largest and longest surviving group, extending at one stage into Derbyshire and strong enough to have their own monthly publication, *The Original Methodist Record, A Free Gospel Magazine*. All three groups held *'Free Gospel' convictions similar to those of IM, the Nottingham and Bingham groups ultimately uniting with that body. The 'Originals' (also known as the 'Selstonites' from the village where the schism first occurred) remained independent until the 1870s, when some of the surviving societies returned to PM whilst most linked with the UMFC. The link with churches having a paid and separated ministry appears odd for a group which had resisted union with IM because of the IM's occasional practice of supporting evangelists financially.

D.M. Grundy in *PWHS* 25 & 26 (1966–8)

WP

Original Sin   To speak of 'original sin' is both to affirm that sin is universal and to suggest an explanation of how this comes to be the case, viz that every human being is contaminated by the sin of Adam. JW's one essay in truly systematic theology was on this subject. He considered the Arianism of Dr John Taylor's *Scripture Doctrine of Original Sin. Proposed to Free and Candid Examination* (1740) the greatest threat in Britain to the historic faith. His reply, *The Doctrine of Original Sin according to Scripture, Reason and Experience* (1756–57), draws heavily on Watts, Jennings, Hervey and others in defence of traditional teaching. JW believed that any attack on the doctrine, if successful, rendered incarnation and redemption unnecessary. But while, for JW himself, all are under Adam's fall, none need carry Adam's guilt. Prevenient *grace stimulates our response to the call to repent and believe, and saving grace is the great nullifier of sin's disease. Subsequent biblical, patristic and scientific scholarship has placed serious question marks beside the doctrine as JW and others formulated it. It is, after all, sin, not original sin, that necessitates redemption; and original sin is not found in the Greek Fathers, but becomes central only with Augustine, who based it upon six or seven texts whose interpretation is now seriously disputed.

See also **Sin**

C.W. Williams (1960), pp. 47–56; R.L. Maddox (1994), pp. 73–82; G.T. Eddy in *ER* April 1999 pp 88–98

GS

Orkney *see* **Shetland and Orkney**

Ormerod, Oliver (1811–79), son of a WM tanner in *Rochdale, whose occupation he followed. A trustee of Baillie Street UMFC chapel, in 1844 he became editor of the radical *Rochdale Spectator* and also contributed to *The Vicar's Lantern*, a paper arguing for greater freedom of religious opinion. In 1851 he produced *Ful, tru, un pertikler Okeawnt*, a humorous account of a visit by a Lancashire lad to the Great Exhibition. In a sequel (1862) one encounters, for the first time in dialect writing, alert, lively-minded urban artisans in place of the usual rural clodpoles. An unpublished account of a visit with ten companions in 1868 to the Holy Land was summarized in the Memoir by H.C. March published with his *Writings* in 1901.

CJS

Orphan House, Newcastle, the earliest Methodist building in the north of England and JW's principal base there. It stood outside the

Town Walls on the west side of what is now Northumberland Street. (The site is now marked by a plaque.) Building began in late December 1742 and full occupation began probably when G. *Murray took up her duties as housekeeper in the summer of 1743. The total cost was about £700, of which £100 was donated by a sympathetic Quaker as the result of a dream.

Like the *Foundery and the *New Room, it was a multi-purpose building, consisting of a chapel (with later galleries) on the ground floor, rooms for the *Bands and *classes on the first floor, and domestic rooms on the second floor. Despite the name, it does not appear that orphans were ever housed there, though the care and education of needy children were no doubt important parts of the work. The Wesleys spent much time there, including long spells in the 1740s, and JW continued to lodge here up to his last visit to Tyneside in 1790. A study, reached by stairs from the 2nd floor, was built for him under the roof. In addition to accommodating the travelling preachers, the Orphan House gradually acquired a longer-term residential community, including women and retired preachers. It also became the regular home of the Newcastle preachers who (following reductions in the size of the circuit) lived here with their families for lengthening periods in some of the upper-floor rooms.

Controversies between the conservative high-church trustees and the more radical members and itinerants broke out after JW's death. Secessions led to the building of new chapels, including Brunswick (1821) nearby. Partly as a result of this, the old building lost its *raison d'être* and was demolished in 1857. It was replaced by WM *day schools, opened in January 1858, but no longer in existence.

W.W. Stamp (1863); WHS(NE) Sept. 1986, March 1993

GEM

Orton, Joseph (1795–1842; e.m. 1826), WM missionary, born in *Hull. He embarked for Jamaica in 1826 and was stationed at Montego Bay. He visited the Maroons of Accompong, but encountered hostility towards the WM preachers and was imprisoned. Though he left by 1829 in poor health, he had made sufficient impression to be appointed to *Australia as Chairman of the New South Wales District in 1831, where he gave much-needed leadership. As Chairman of the Tasmania District he pioneered Methodist work in the newly-colonized mainland state of Victoria,

where he helped establish the Buntingdale Wesleyan Mission among the aborigines. He published *Aborigines of Australia* (1836) and pleaded with new settlers to protect the native population. His judgment that a General Superintendent was necessary to oversee the Australasian and Pacific work led to the appointment of J. *Waterhouse. His health suffered under the pressures of this work and he died at sea while returning home.

F&H 2 and 3; *ADB*

MJF/EGC

Osborn, Dr George (1808–91; e.m. 1828), WM minister who served as a secretary of the WMMS 1851–68 and as theological tutor at *Richmond College, 1868–85. An able scholar, he wrote a preface to JW's *Collection of Psalms and Hymns*, edited the *Poetical Works of J&CW* in 13 volumes (1868–72) and compiled a *Wesleyan Bibliography* (1869). He gave the first *Fernley Lecture in 1870 on *The Mission and Work of the Holy Spirit*. Twice President of the Conference (1863 and 1881) he was a powerful Conference speaker. Steeped in and jealous of the traditions of WM, his ministry was in the mould of J. *Bunting, conservative and authoritarian. He had an acute legal mind and took a leading role in cases involving Methodism. He espoused the cause of popular education and supported WM *day schools. He was a founder of the Evangelical Alliance (1845). His nephew **Thomas George Osborn** (1843–1910), a Fellow of Trinity Hall, Cambridge and one of the first lay representatives to the WM Conference, was headmaster of *Kingswood School 1866–85. Described as 'Kingswood's Dr Arnold', he raised the school's academic level and introduced the prefectorial system before resigning to found *Rydal School (where he was succeeded by his son G.F.A. Osborn). He was the father-in-law of F.F. *Bretherton.

G.J. Stevenson (1884–6) 3 pp. 360–8; *MR* 23 April 1891; *PWHS* 46 pp. 93–6, 47 pp. 13–19

WDH

Osborn, George Robson (1905–79; e.m. 1928) served in *China from 1930 to 1951. He worked with the YMCA, as a teacher and as superintendent of a refugee camp which became a prison camp after the Japanese invasion. After Pearl Harbour he was interned at Langwha. Under his headship the Camp School achieved high academic standards. Latterly he served under a Chinese head and subject to communist surveillance. From 1951–1970 he was Secretary of the Education Department. He renewed collaboration with the Government, developed teacher education, supervised *Westminster College's move to Oxford and nurtured the early MethSocs. As Chairman of Governors at *Westhill College, Birmingham, he encouraged the development of Religious Education and the training of teachers of pupils with learning difficulties.

See also **Education**

CHS

Osmotherley, a Cleveland village which in the eighteenth century housed a mixed community of farmers, craftsmen and linen spinners and weavers. In addition to the parish church there were Quakers and RCs (served by Franciscan friars) in the village. On the urgent invitation of one of the Catholic clergy, JW visited the village in April 1745 and preached in the middle of the night and early next morning to what was probably a mixed RC, Anglican and Quaker congregation. Within a short while a Methodist society became yet another element in the village's religious life and JW returned 15 times. It was one of the ten preaching places in the Newcastle upon Tyne Circuit when it was formed in 1748. A chapel built in 1754 (replaced in 1864) was restored in 1935 and rededicated as a Methodist chapel in 1977. There was also a PM chapel.

PWHS 3 pp. 89–95, 7 pp. 28–31

GEM

O'Sullivan, Seumas (James Sullivan Starkey) (1879–1958), Irish nationalist poet and essayist, the grandson of two Irish Methodist preachers, William Starkey (*c.* 1802–47; e.m. 1830) and James Sullivan (*c.* 1798–1851; e.m. 1824). The latter preached in Irish and wrote small books in Gaelic under the name Seumas O'Sullivan, later chosen by his grandson as a pseudonym. As editor of *The Dublin Magazine* 1923–58, he encouraged young Irish writers such as Samuel Beckett, Patrick Kavanagh and Mary Lavin, who started their literary career in its pages. He retained an affection for his Methodist upbringing, but saw himself as a Wesleyan in his regard for the Church of Ireland.

J. Russell (1987)

RPR

Ouseley, Gideon (1762–1839; e.m. 1799), born in Co. Galway, was appointed a General Missionary in 1799 with C. *Graham and J.

*McQuigg. A fluent Irish speaker and colourful personality, he was the longest-serving and most effective Irish evangelist of his day. With ready wit, homely illustrations and everyday turns of phrase, he established a close rapport with his hearers. He presented *Roman Catholicism as an oppressive system, exposing what he saw as its errors and longing for the conversion of Roman Catholics. Many of his converts emigrated to *America.

W. Arthur (1876); T. MacCullagh (1906); D. Hempton (1996) pp. 130–9

NWT

Ovenden, Grace (1915–55), missionary in *Kenya. Born in *Brighton, she grew up wanting to be a missionary in Africa and, after training at *Kingsmead College, was sent to Kenya, where her job was to encourage parents to send their daughters to a newly opened girls' school in Meru. Once this was flourishing she was sent to build up another in Ribe on the coast. Her main attention there was given to teacher training. She became caught up in the Revival Movement in Kenya, along with many of her African friends who became victims of the Mau Mau movement. She herself was killed in a road accident in Meru.

P.M. Webb (1958) pp. 115–31

PMW

Overseas Mission Methodism began to spread outside the British Isles in the 1760s with the preaching of N. *Gilbert in Antigua and of Irish emigrants in *America. Appeals for preachers for West Africa in the 1770s had no immediate result and T. *Coke's first 'Plan' for missionary work misfired in 1784. But his *Appeal* of 1786, backed by JW, led to the first stationing of missionaries in the *West Indies. Asia, however, had to wait until missionaries reached Ceylon (now *Sri Lanka) in 1814 and *India in 1817.

Initial steps to make the missions a responsibility of the *Conference included a Committee of Finance in 1798 and a Missionary Committee in 1804, but with Coke still named as Conference's agent for the overseas work the shift from personal to corporate responsibility was only gradual, culminating in the creation of a connexional *missionary society in 1818. Meanwhile, following earlier abortive ventures, the first mission to West Africa began in *Sierra Leone in 1811.

The nineteenth century saw the worldwide proliferation of missions and all the main Methodist bodies eventually established work overseas, ranging from the Caribbean to China. The heroic exploits of missionaries and their wives in hazardous and exotic (and hitherto unfamiliar) parts of the world making a stirring appeal for support back in the home Church. In 1859 the Ladies' Committee (later *'Women's Work') sent out its first woman missionary, to Belize. The steady, and sometimes dramatic, growth of the Church in many lands owed much to the ability, energy and faith of indigenous converts whio became partners in the enterprise.

Education was a recognized part of mission from the early days and *medical missions grew in importance, as in the twentieth century did agricultural and other specialist ministries. In 1932 all this overseas work was effectively integrated under the MMS, set up at the time of *Methodist Union. Since World War II there has been a fundamental shift of outlook and policy. The Overseas Consultation held in Skegness in 1961 on the initiative of D.W. *Thompson, then General Secretary of the MMS, was a landmark in the shift from 'overseas missions' to 'World Church Partnerships' between *autonomous Churches.

See also **Missionary Magazines**; **Missionary Societies**

F&H; W. Moister (1871); H.B. Kendall (1906) 2 pp. 481–506; G.G. & M.C. Findlay (1913); C.J. Davey (1951); O.A. Beckerlegge (1957) pp. 79–94; D.W. Thompson (1962); T. Shaw (1965) pp. 65–7; A. Birtwhistle in *HMGB* 3 pp. 1–116; C.J. Davey (1988); R. Pyke (n.d.) pp. 163–74; J. Telford, *Short History* (n.d.);

JAV

Owen, Samuel (1774–1854), WM layman and mechanical engineer from *Norwich, went to *Sweden in 1804 to develop and build steam engines. Seeing an opening, he wrote to the Missionary Committee in 1825, requesting a 'young man of good abilities' to preach to his family, workmen and any others willing to attend. Underwriting the costs of the appointment, he overcame Swedish legal restrictions on missionary activity. Esteemed by government and decorated by the king, he made possible the development of a chapel and regular, well-attended Methodist worship under J.R. *Stephens.
MJF

Owen Family of Publow. In the 1770s, with JW's encouragement and advice, Mrs **Hannah Owen** (c.1725–85) and her three daughters ran a girls' school for up to 20 boarders, including some

of the itinerants' daughters. W paid a number of visits to what he called 'the lovely family' and spoke highly of the school, likening it to M. *Bosanquet's community at Leytonstone, though he later expressed some reservations. The oldest of the sisters Elizabeth married William Pine, JW's Bristol printer and when her mother and sisters left Publow she started a school for poor children in nearby Pensford, before settling in Bristol. The youngest sister Mary (c. 1750–1809) married Joseph Beardmore (c. 1746–1829) of London, a friend of JW and a trustee and Trust Treasurer at *Wesley's Chapel.

JWJ; G.J. Stevenson (1872) pp. 384–5

JAV

Owens, Thomas (d.1808; e.m. 1785), after some years in Irish circuits, spent 12 years in the *West Indies and was well thought of by T. *Coke. He saw much success during his ministry on Nevis and established a small society on Grenada. By good management he brought persecution to an end on Tortola and he also worked on St Kitts, In 1794 he was sent to reopen the Mission on St Vincent, which had closed when M. *Lumb had been imprisoned, and the following year was able to report a membership of 454.

GRS

Oxford can claim to be the birthplace of Methodism, since it saw what JW called 'the first rise of Methodism' in the informal meetings of students associated with the W brothers and nicknamed 'the *Holy Club'. Both brothers were students at Christ Church (as had been their brother Samuel) and JW was elected fellow of Lincoln College in 1726, resigning only in 1755, four years after his marriage. He regularly preached in churches in the city, including University Sermons from the pulpit of St Mary the Virgin, until his outspoken sermon on 'Scriptural Christianity' led to his exclusion in 1744. In 1757 a group of religiously-minded students, under the leadership of T. *Haweis, began to meet in what L. *Tyerman described as 'a society . . . analogous to the Holy Club of the Wesleys'. It survived Haweis' departure in 1762, but in March 1768 six Calvinistic Methodist students were expelled from St Edmund Hall, despite the support of their Principal, Dr Dixon. The earliest evidence of a WM society in the city is the opening of a chapel in New Inn Hall Street in 1783, replaced in 1818 by a larger one by W. *Jenkins in the same street. Following the opening of the University to non-Anglicans in 1871, the Victorian Gothic Wesley

Memorial Church, by Henry Firth, was opened in 1878. The short ministry (1881–84) of H.P. *Hughes marked the beginning of a notable period in the church's history. It was later the home of the Oxford MethSoc, the 'John Wesley Society'. The older building became a Sunday School, was sold to St Peter's in 1932 and demolished in 1968. There were PM chapels in New Street and Pembroke Street. The UM work was at Rose Hill and in the villages. The World Methodist Conference of 1951 met in the Sheldonian Theatre. *Westminster College moved from London to its present site at North Hinksey in 1959.

MR(W) 1898 pp. 17–21; *PWHS* 29 pp. 73–5
TSAM

Oxford Institute of Methodist Theological Studies

was formed in 1958 as part of the programme of theological reflection promoted by the WMC, to which it is affiliated. Held originally in Lincoln College, Oxford, it has continued to meet every four or five years, bringing together scholars and pastors from around the world to reflect on aspects of Methodist theology, history, identity and practice. At the Tenth Institute, held in August 1997, the 200 invited participants were drawn from over 30 countries including many younger scholars and women from Third World countries, groups under-represented in earlier years.

TSAM

Oxtoby, John (1767–1830; e.m. 1821) was born at Givendale on the Yorkshire Wolds. On his conversion in 1804, he joined the WM and by his praying converted others, becoming known as 'Praying Johnny'. He joined the PM in 1819 and itinerated from 1821, mainly in the Yorkshire Wolds. He was instrumental in the 1823 revival at Filey, which resulted in a strong society among the fishermen, and later gave fresh impetus to the revival in Weardale.

H. Leigh (1855); G. Shaw (1894)
DCD

Pacifism *see* **Methodist Peace Fellowship**; **War**

Packer, George (1843–1920; e.m. 1865), MNC minister whose administrative gifts brought him connexional prominence. He was College Secretary for eight years, Secretary of the 1888 Conference, secretary of the Centenary Fund 1894–98, Missionary Secretary 1897–1900 and

President in 1895. He played a key role in the negotiations which led to the 1907 Union and was Connexional Secretary of the UM Church 1907–20. He was elected UM President in 1911.

EAR

Paisley Methodism may have been introduced by English workmen building the canal in 1807. A large chapel was erected in George Street in 1810, but in the Warrenite agitations of 1834 half the members seceded, eventually calling themselves the Congregational Methodists. They returned to George Street when the resulting financial problems forced the WM congregation to move to a smaller property in New Sneddon Street, but in 1851 George Street was bought by the Swedenborgians. The WM society died out by 1862, but the PMs had been active since 1828 under the inspiration of J. *Johnson of Carlisle. After renting various premises including the Philosophical Hall in Abbey Close, in 1874 they bought a property in Canal Street, replaced in 1884 by one in St James Street, where they remained until amalgamating with the Central Mission in 1960. The WMA also had a cause until the late 1850s.

WM was reactivated in 1896, but made little progress until 1904, when the Rev. W.H. Rolls and the evangelist Josiah Nix made a strong impact, notably on John Slack, a notorious gambler and drunkard. After his conversion he worked with Rolls to establish the Paisley Central Mission (1908), which from the first has accommodated community groups, including the Suffragettes, whose local leaders were members of the church.

A. Leitch (1983)
MB

Palatines, Irish immigrants to Ireland from the Lower Rhenish Palatinate, the chief Calvinist centre in seventeenth/eighteenth century Germany. In 1709 the periodic invasions by Louis XIV and a disastrous winter led to the emigration of over 13,000 Palatine people. Queen Anne sent ships to bring them to England and some continued to America. The largest settlement in Ireland was at Courtmatrix, Killeheen and Ballingrane in Co. Limerick. In the 1750s T. *Walsh introduced them to JW and many became Methodists.

By 1760 the eight or twelve acres originally granted to each family were overcrowded and Philip Embury led a party to New York. This included his cousin Barbara Heck (*née* Ruttle) who in 1766 encouraged Embury to begin Methodist work in New York. This was one of the roots of *American Methodism. In 1770 Embury and Heck moved to Camden Valley, NY, where Embury died in 1783. Following American Independence, in 1784 the Hecks moved to *Canada and introduced Methodism there. Barbara died in 1804 at Prescott, Ontario. Descendants of those who remained in Ireland preserve their Palatine and Methodist heritage in Co. Limerick.

E.C. Lapp (1977); C.A. Heald (1994); P.J. O'Connor (1989)

DALC

Parker, Henry Perlee (1793–1873), prolific artist, born in Devonport. He spent most of his career in the north-east, painting street life, historical and marine subjects, which earned him the nickname 'Smuggler Parker'. He exhibited at the Royal Academy and elsewhere and from 1840 was Drawing Master at *Wesley College, Sheffield. He was also associated with J. *Everett and the UMFC. He is best known in Methodist circles for his 1840 painting of the fire at *Epworth rectory, 'A Brand Plucked from the Burning'.

DNB; Exhibition Catalogue, Laing Art Gallery, Newcastle upon Tyne (1969)

PSF

Parker, James, MP (1863–1948), trade unionist and Labour politician, attended a WM school and Brunswick UMFC after he came to *Halifax in 1883. Finding employment first as a navvy and then as an engineering warehouseman, he became an active trade unionist and a leading figure in the ILP. He was elected MP for Halifax in 1906 and subsequently lost the chairmanship of the Parliamentary Labour Party to Keir Hardy by only one vote. He was appointed secretary of the party in 1909 and junior Lord of the Treasury in 1917. On retiring as MP in 1918 he received the honorary freedom of the borough.

J.A. Hargreaves (1999)

JAH

Parkin, George (1846–1933; e.m. 1869), PM minister, born at Eston near Middlesborough. He was one of the first intake of students at the *Sunderland Theological Institute. Beginning in *Glasgow in 1869, his first ten years were spent in the Scottish PM missions. He gained MA and BD degrees from Glasgow University, one of the first PM ministers to graduate. After a successful urban ministry in the North and Midlands of England, from 1898 to 1903 he was Principal and also tutor in Hebrew at the PM Theological Institute in *Manchester. He was President of the Conference in 1906 and gave the *Hartley Lecture in 1908 on *The New Testament Portrait of Jesus*.

PMM 1907 pp. 3–4

GEM

Parrinder, Dr Edward Geoffrey (1910 ; e.m. 1932), deemed by Prof. Ursula King 'the doyen of Methodist scholars in the field of interfaith studies'. Born at New Barnet, he trained at *Richmond College. He became a missionary in French West Africa in 1933 and from 1949 in *Nigeria, carrying out extensive field research in both places. In 1966–69 he gave the Wilde Lectures in Natural and Comparative Religion at Oxford. He aimed to strike a balance between relativizing differences between religions and stressing the unique claims of the Christian faith. A prolific author, he was a pioneer in popularizing the study of world religions and helped to introduce the teaching of other faiths into schools.

G. Ainger in *ER* Jan. 1995; M. Forward (1998)

DJC

Parsons, Charles Richard (1842–?1918), WM layman, born at Merriott, Som. He became a shopkeeper in Glastonbury and started a Bible class there in 1866. Moving to *Bristol, in 1880 he established the Old Market Street Bible Class, with Savings Bank, Mutual Aid, Medical and Burial Societies incorporated. His evangelization through mass meetings, street canvassing, band processions and Saturday evening temperance assemblies, laid the foundation of later work by the Bristol Mission and Central Hall and is described in several autobiographical accounts (1883, *c.* 1900, 1914). Among his socio-religious tracts and novels, the title of *The Man in the White Hat* (1885) provided the sobriquet by which he became well-known.

MR(W) 1892 pp. 64–6

CJS

Parsons, Harry (1878–1952; e.m. 1899), BC missionary in *China, born in *Barnstaple. He went out to the Mission in Yunnan in 1901 and shared in the first Miao baptisms in 1905. Fluent in their language, he and his wife **Annie Parsons** (*née* Bryant, 1875–1965), called by W. *Hudspeth the 'Apostle to the Miao', served the Miao people until invalided home in 1926. He was responsible for many building schemes and famine relief projects. By introducing improved varieties of produce and through a mutual aid insurance scheme, he sought to improve living standards. He concentrated on leadership training, supervised the publication of the Gospels in River Miao and strongly advocated self-support. Their twin sons, **R. Keith Parsons** (1916– ; e.m. 1938) and **P. Kenneth Parsons** (1916– ; e.m. 1940) also served in Yunnan.

RKP

Pastoral Committee *see* **Church Council**; **Leaders' Meeting**

Pastoral Office   WM held a high doctrine of the 'Pastoral Office', believing that the *ministry was of divine institution and, according to the NT, had final responsibility before God for the souls committed to it. Though it did not believe, with RCs and Anglo-Catholics, that this ministry had to be transmitted in unbroken tactile succession from the Apostles, it stressed the obligation of Christians to submit to the pastors of the Church they had chosen to enter (cf. Heb. 13:17) and the responsibility of the ministry to appoint and train its successors. These convictions underpinned the refusal in the earlier nineteenth century to admit laymen to the *Conference. Non-Wesleyans, and other Free Churchmen, accused WM of denying the proper rights of the *laity in Church government. At the end of the century, with the admission of laymen to the Conference and closer relations with the Free Churches, the doctrine became attenuated, though it did not entirely disappear. The *Deed of Union stresses that ministers have 'no exclusive cure of souls' (thus rejecting traditional high Wesleyan claims), but also emphasizes that they are 'Stewards in the household of God and shepherds of his flock'. The 1937 statement on the *Nature of the Christian Church according to the Teaching of the Methodists* describes ministry as a gift of the Spirit to the Church.

A.Barrett (1854); J.C. Bowmer (1975)

DJC

Patterson, Saidie (1906–85), trade union activist and peace worker, was born and lived off *Belfast's Shankill Road. When she was 12 her mother died in childbirth and she went to work in the Belfast Linen Mills. She became a leading fighter for women's rights in the linen industry.

The advent of Northern Ireland's conflict led her back into public life as a founder member of the 'Women Together' peace movement. She was a person of strong faith who drew inspiration from Methodism and was for a time in Moral Rearmament. She was the recipient of the first World Methodist Peace Prize.

D. Bleakley (1980)

RPR

Pawson, H. Cecil, MBE (1897–1978), son of a WM minister, was lecturer (1917–48) and Professor of Agriculture (1948–57) at Hull University. As a *local preacher (from 1917) he always 'preached for a verdict' and 3,000 responded to his call. He was Vice-President of the 1951 Conference. He wrote many articles for the religious press. Among his books were *Cockle Park Farm* (1960), *Agriculture of Northumberland* (1961), *Personal Evangelism* (1968) and an autobiography, *Hand to the Plough* (1973).

MR 12 July 1951, 28 Dec. 1978, 4 Jan. 1979; D. English, in WHS(NE) no. 31, Feb.1979; E. Thompson (1990)

JHL

Pawson, John (1737–1806), early itinerant, of Thorner, near Leeds, first encountered Methodism in *Hull, where he was learning the building trade. He became an itinerant in the *York Circuit in 1762. In 1785 he was ordained for the work in *Scotland; but when brought back to England in 1787, he was forbidden to continue administering the Sacrament. Bewildered and frustrated, he became closely involved in the debates and events which shaped the Connexion after W's death. He was President of the Conference in 1793 and 1801. He was deeply concerned by the threat to the internal unity of Methodism and by its lack of effective central government between Conferences. He attended the *Lichfield meeting in 1794 and published his *Affectionate Address to the Methodist Societies* the following year. He was in favour of allowing the Methodists to receive the Sacrament in their own chapels and from their own ministers.

A man of deep but simple piety, he is remembered for having burnt JW's annotated copy of Shakespeare, which he considered 'unedifying'. His misgivings at the loss of Methodism's 'primitive' simplicity were expressed in a *Serious and Affectionate Address to the Junior Preachers* in 1798. His extensive correspondence, especially with C. *Atmore and J. *Benson, gives an intimate and detailed insight into the state of the Connexion.

EMP 4 1–108; G.J. Stevenson (1884–6) 2 pp. 165–74; J. Pawson (1994–5)

JAV

Payne, Frederick (1814–95; e.m. 1838), WM minister who spent 41 of his 57 years in the ministry in the Liverpool District. He pioneered English-speaking Methodism on the North Wales coast, opening chapels in Llandudno, Rhyl, Colwyn Bay, Prestatyn, Conway and Penmaenmawr.

MR(W) 1897 pp. 85–9

JAV

Peace *see* **Methodist Peace Fellowship**; **War**

Peake, Dr Arthur Samuel (1865–1929) the son and nephew of PM ministers, was born in Leek and went to St John's College, Oxford in 1883. In 1890 he accepted a lectureship at Mansfield College, Oxford and was elected to a Theological Fellowship at Merton College. In 1892 he was recruited by W. *Hartley to the staff of *Hartley College, Manchester, where he remained for the rest of his life, accepting concurrent lectureships at Lancashire Independent College in 1895 and the UM College in 1904 (resigning from both in 1912 because of his University commitments). In 1904 he was appointed Professor of Biblical Exegesis at the University and Dean of the Faculty of Theology, and in 1925 became Pro-Vice-Chancellor. He was elected President of the Society for OT Study in 1924 and edited the Society's first volume of essays, *The People and the Book* (1925). He received honorary degrees from Manchester (1906), Aberdeen (1907) and Oxford (1920) Universities. Best known for the one-volume *Commentary* which he edited (1919), his most important biblical studies are *The Problem of Suffering in the OT* (1904), *A Critical Introduction to the NT* (1909), *The Bible: Its Origin, its Significance and its Abiding Worth* (1913) and commentaries on Hebrews (1902), Colossians (1903), Job (1905), Jeremiah and Lamentations (1910, 1912) and Revelation (1919). He remained a layman, but played a vital part in enabling PM ministers and others to accept critical biblical scholarship without losing their faith. He was also prominent in the endeavour for church unity, being one of the PM representatives on the *Methodist Union Committee from 1918, one of six representatives of the Free Churches at meetings with the Anglicans at Lambeth Palace

from 1922 to 1925, and attending the Lausanne meeting of Faith and Order in 1927.

L.S. Peake (1930); W.F. Howard (1938); J.T. Wilkinson (1971); E.R. Burnett in *LQHR* July 1954 pp. 213–16; *MR* 16 Aug, 1979

CSR

Pearse, Mark Guy (1842–1930; e.m. 1865), WM preacher and prolific author. Born in Camborne, his writings reflect his lifelong devotion to his native Cornwall. He was briefly a medical student at Bart's before entering the ministry. From 1887 to 1904 he was a colleague of H.P. *Hughes in the West London Mission, working especially to build up the Mission's Sisterhood. He undertook world-wide preaching tours on its behalf. His popularity as a preacher and speaker owed much to his vivid imagination, sense of humour and mellifluous delivery. Volumes of his Sunday morning sermons were published, but he was best known for his fiction, notably *Daniel Quorm* (1879).

G.J. Stevenson (1884–86) pp. 548–56; *MR* 9 Jan. 1930; Mrs G. Unwin & J. Telford (1930)

JAV

Pearson, Francis *see* **Local Preachers' Mutual Aid Association**

Penrhos School *see* **Rydal Penrhos School**

Penzance Despite a slow beginning, a Methodist society of 34 members was formed in the town by 1767 and in 1789 JW described the preaching house as 'considerably the largest and, in many respects, far the best, in Cornwall'. Chapel Street church (1814) was extended in 1864 and has a profusion of stained glass windows, notably by H.J. *Salisbury of London and St Albans (1914) and memorials to R. *Treffry jun, the banker W. *Carne, Maria Elizabeth Branwell, mother and aunt of the *Brontë sisters. Richmond WM Church was built in 1907 in the 'arts and crafts Gothic' style. Other denominations were represented by High Street (BC, 1879), Alexandra Road (MNC, 1903) and Parade Street (UMFC, 1890). The pulpit at Wesley Rock chapel, Heamoor, stands on a granite block from which JW and others preached between 1743 and 1760.

TS

Percival, Peter (d. 1873; e.m. 1825), a convert from Anglicanism, served as a WM missionary in North Ceylon (*Sri Lanka) without a break, 1826–1851 (from 1838 as District Chairman), apart from a brief period spent in an abortive mission to Calcutta (1830). In the face of native prejudice and the rival policy of his colleague, Ralph Stott, who favoured more direct evangelism, he and his wife developed educational work, especially for girls, opening schools in Jaffna (including the forerunner of Jaffna Central College) and in a number of villages. An outstanding Tamil scholar, he produced translations of the Bible, hymns, etc. His revision of the Protestant Tamil Bible, the fruit of 15 years' work, was never given the recognition it deserved. On his return to England in 1851, he resigned over differences with the Missionary Committee, on property issues, reconverted to Anglicanism and returned to *India as a Professor at Presidency College, Madras. He was in Jaffna at the time of the Hindu Revival and had close contact with one of its leaders, Arumuka Navalar.

F&H 5 pp. 33–7, 348–50; W.J.T. Small (1964) pp. 196–8, 215, 217; R.F. Young & S. Jebanesan (1995)

EJH

Perkins, Dr Ernest Benson (1881–1974; e.m. 1903) was born in *Leicester. He trained at *Handsworth College and served as a Chaplain to the Forces in World War I. In 1920 he was appointed to the *Temperance and Social Welfare Department, developing a special interest in gambling and its social effects; then, after ten years in the *Birmingham Mission (1925–35), he became Secretary of the Chapel Committee. He was President of the Conference in 1948, Vice-President of the BCC 1952–54, and Moderator of the FCFC in 1954. He wrote *Gambling in English Life* (1958) and an autobiography, *So Appointed* (1964); and gave the 1952 WHS Lecture on *Methodist Preaching Houses and the Law*. In retirement he devoted much time to the *WMC.

MR 15 July 1948, 3 Oct. 1974

KGG

Perks Family George Thomas Perks (1819–77; e.m. 1840) was born in *Madeley of an old Methodist family (his great-uncle was J. *Fletcher's churchwarden), entered the WM ministry and became a notable preacher. He was Secretary of the Conference in 1872 and President in 1873. He was one of the founders of the *Methodist Recorder* as a more Liberal rival to the *Watchman*. His son **Sir Robert William Perks** (1849–1934), solicitor, civil engineer and politician, was educated at *Kingswood School

and London University. He became a partner of Sir Henry *Fowler and was Chairman of the Metropolitan District Railway. Among his major contracts were the Manchester Ship Canal, the London Underground Circle Line, the Buenos Aires Port Works and the Transandine Tunnel. Having long advocated lay representation, he attended Conference from 1878 and proposed a motion that year on *Methodist Union. As Secretary of the *Committee of Privileges he helped bring about the Burials Acts of 1880 and 1900, enabling Nonconformists to be buried in churchyards. He was treasurer of the London Mission Fund and the *Twentieth Century Fund and was instrumental in purchasing the prestigious site of *Westminster Central Hall, whose triumphalism reflects his ideas. As Liberal MP for *Louth, 1892–1910, he saw himself as 'MP for Nonconformity' and in close collaboration with H.P. *Hughes and the leader of the pro-Rosebery Imperialist faction created a Nonconformist parliamentary committee (1898). As Treasurer of the National Council of Evangelical Free Churches he unsuccessfully opposed the 1902 Education Act, though his efforts helped the Liberal triumph of 1906. He became a baronet in 1908. and at the age of 83 was elected Vice-President of the Uniting Conference in 1932 as the man most responsible for Methodist Union. He was chairman of the *Methodist Recorder*'s Board of Governors. His son, **Sir Robert Malcolm Mewbury Perks** (1892–1979), a civil engineer, was involved in the building of Broadcasting House, London, the Singapore Naval Base and the Nag Hammadi Dam on the Nile. He continued his father's involvement with the London Mission, Westminster Central Hall and the *Methodist Recorder*.

MR 1 June 1877; 4 Oct.1979; 6 & 13 Dec. 1934; D. Crane (1909); R.W. Perks (1936); S.E. Koss (1975)

JHL

Perronet, Rev. Vincent (1693–1785), son of a Swiss father from Chateau d'Oex who came to England *c*. 1680. A scholarly child, he was educated at a school in the north of England and at Queen's College, Oxford. He was curate of Sundridge and from 1728 Vicar of Shoreham (Kent), where he encountered opposition for much of his incumbency. In 1746 he invited JW and CW into his parish. CW on his first visit described the riotous reaction as that of 'wild beasts'. Resistance to the Methodists continued, but grew less extreme. Both brothers relied heavily on Perronet's advice and support. He attended the 1747 *Conference and JW addressed his *Plain Account of the People Called Methodists* to him. He became known as the 'Archbishop of the Methodists' and on at least one occasion mediated between the brothers. Only after the death of his wife Charity (*née* Goodhew) in 1763 was a Methodist society in Shoreham formally established. Previously meetings had been held in the vicarage. Known both for great holiness of life and for his scholarship, he published pamphlets defending Locke's *Essay on the Human Understanding*.

His later years were saddened by the death of his children, including his favourite daughter Damaris and his son William, who died while returning from a visit to Switzerland and was buried at Douai. **Edward Perronet** (1721–92) and **Charles Perronet** (1723–76) were both Methodist preachers for a time. Edward, remembered as the author of the hymn 'All hail the power of Jesu's name' (*HP* 252), published a poem *The Mitre* (1757) critical of the Church of England and became pastor of the Countess of *Huntingdon's chapel and then of an Independent congregation in *Canterbury. Charles helped to form a Methodist society in *Dublin. They were estranged from the Wesleys through their advocacy of separation from the Church. Their sister **Damaris Perronet** (*c*. 1727–82) was a leading member of the Methodist society in Shoreham and anticipated the work of Elizabeth Fry by her prison visiting in Maidstone gaol.

C. Atmore (1801) pp. 317–36; *WMM* 1799 pp. 1–8, 53–8, 105–10, 157–62; *WMM* 1902 pp. 52–6, 215–20, 373–9, 660–64; WHS(LSE) 30 pp., 32 pp. ?

PSF

Persecution   The eighteenth century was a violent age in which the means of law enforcement were rudimentary. Methodism was perceived by the authorities as a proletarian movement, nationally organized, a new generation of 'Levellers' which disrupted the social fabric, threatened law and order in both Church and State, and was a challenge to the prevailing moralism of the parish *clergy. (*Justification by faith was seen as leading to *antinomianism.) It did not help that the *Toleration Act was of dubious relevance to Methodists so long as they claimed to be Anglicans, not Dissenters. Physical persecution, often at the instigation of clergy and gentry and carried

out by the local mob, occurred where civil authority was weak (as at *Wednesbury in 1743 and Colne in 1748), or where Methodism had clashed with vested interests such as the theatre, or as a result of general outrage at the incursion of strangers threatening the accepted patterns of behaviour. A mob incited to violence by their 'betters' and plied with drink was unlikely to be deterred merely by reading the Riot Act. Nor did Magistrates always act against rioters, though the government was in principle opposed to persecution for religious opinion; but JW knew the law and was prepared to demand its application to those who violated it. The persistent courage of preachers and members did much to transform hostility into admiration. By 1791, Methodism had a footing in national life and persecution had largely ceased. It resurfaced against the BC and PM preaching, especially in southern counties, and later against the *Salvation Army. *local preachers were evicted from their farms, cottagers risked loss of employment for allowing a room to be used for a religious meeting, and the law was sometimes used as a pretext for persecution.

D.D. Wilso (1969); J. Walsh in G.J. Cuming & D. Baker (1972) pp. 213–27; J.L. Waddy (1976)
MB

Perseverance   Wesleyan teaching on this is summed up in W.B. *Pope's *Compendium* (1880): 'Provision is made in the Christian covenant for the maintenance of religion in the soul to the end. The source of this grace is the effectual intercession of Christ. The manifestation of it is the power of the Holy Spirit; in its nature and operation it is superabundant and persistent; not indefectible however, but conditional on perseverance in fidelity.' The last clause indicates rejection (following JW) of the *Calvinist doctrine of the 'final perseverance of the saints', according to which the elect cannot fall irrevocably from *grace and *salvation. Pope discusses the texts usually cited in the controversy.

DJC

Perth   In 1768 JW found 'not above two believers, and scarce five awakened persons' there, but in 1772 he was presented with the Freedom of the City. Nevertheless, in 1774 he wrote that the 'generality of the people' were 'so wise that they need no more knowledge, and so good that they need no more religion'; so he gave them three rousing sermons, two on *hell and one on the day of judgment. The early society met in a room in the Meal Vennel; a property in South

Street was bought in 1836 and finally in 1880 the present church in newly laid-out Scott Street was built.

————

S. Davis, in WHS(S), 1981 pp. 10–14

MB

Petty, John (1807–68; e.m. 1826), PM minister. From 1822 visiting PM preachers stayed at his boyhood home at Salterforth in Craven. When stationed at Haverfordwest in 1826 he became the first missionary to be accredited by the General Missionary Committee. He served as Assistant *Connexional Editor in 1851 and Editor 1852–57, and was President of the Conference in 1860. In 1864 he became first Governor of *Elmfield College and was the first Theological Tutor of candidates for the PM ministry. Among his many publications were a *History of the PM Connexion* (1st edition 1859), *Systematic Theology* (1873) and *The PM Catechisms*. Petty Memorial (later Trinity), Monkgate, *York, was opened in his memory in 1903.

————

J. Macpherson (1870); F.H. Hurd (1872), pp. 58–73; G.J. Stevenson (1884–6) 5 pp. 724–35

DCD

Pew Rents   In early Methodism there were no regular weekly collections at Sunday services. To meet the cost of chapels the custom arose of regular worshippers, whether members of society or not, paying a 'rent' for their seats. This was paid annually, sometimes quarterly, and was always a modest amount, according to the position of the seat, varying from 1/- to half a crown a quarter. Sometimes a ticket was issued as a receipt, often bearing a print of the chapel. In older chapels small brass frames may sometimes be seen at the end of seats, on the hymn-book ledge, to hold the cards giving the pewholder's name. The *Religious Census showed the widespread use of this source of income in 1851 by differentiating between 'appropriated' and 'free' sittings. It was gradually superseded by the weekly offertory, though it was still in use in some chapels as late as the 1960s.

OAB

Phillips, Peter (1778–1853) was born and lived in *Warrington, a chairmaker by trade who at an early age became a preacher and leader in the local IM church. Part of his childhood was spent in a *Quaker home and he encouraged several Quaker practices, such as silent times of worship and the use of plain dress, so that his church was in its early days termed *'Quaker Methodist'. His views on unpaid ministry came from the same source. He visited and drew together other churches of similar character to form the IM Connexion, of which he was regarded as founder. He was a close friend of H. *Bourne and spoke at the first Mow Cop *Camp Meeting. He pioneered Sunday School work, promoted the *temperance movement and opposed violent means of social reform. His wife **Hannah** (*née* Peacock) (1780–1858) supported him and had a practical philanthropic ministry of her own.

————

Zion's Trumpet 1855 p. 175; *Free Gospel Advocate* Sept. 1859

JAD

Pickard, Benjamin (1842–1904), *trade unionist, born at Kippax, near Pontefract and described by R.F. *Wearmouth as 'the most prominent trade union leader to emanate from WM'. He grew up in WM, emerging as a strict Protestant and staunch supporter of the Lord's Day Rest Association. In 1881 he was appointed secretary of the West and South Yorkshire Miners' Association. He was President of the Miners' Federation of Great Britain from 1899 to 1904. 'A canny Yorkshireman' and 'every inch a fighter', he was the dominant personality in the organization for more than a decade.

————

R.F. Wearmouth (1954) pp. 173–4

NADS

Piercy, George (1829–1913; e.m. 1851), first WM missionary in *China, travelled to *Hong Kong at his own expense in 1851 because the WMMS felt unable to undertake work in China. After some months in Canton (Guangzhou), he again offered his service and the Society responded by ordaining William Beach and J. *Cox for China, sending a letter of ordination for Piercy and naming him as Superintendent of the Mission. His fiancée Joan Wannop sailed with them. A boys' school was opened in Canton in 1853 and some months later Mrs Piercy opened what became the first boarding school for girls in China, with accommodation in their own home. Piercy chaired the first WM Synod in China in December 1853 and during his 31 years' ministry the WM mission was firmly established under his leadership. Mrs Piercy died in 1878 and, after being invalided home in 1882, he spent his closing years working among the Chinese in the Port of London.

GRS

Piers, Rev. Henry (1694–1770), vicar of Bexley, Kent, 1737–70. Of aristocratic Irish descent, he graduated from Trinity College, Dublin. Meeting CW and John Bray at Blendon Hall in 1738 he was introduced to the evangelical understanding of *justification and in 1739 was arraigned by Archbishop Potter for his Methodistical sympathies. The Visitation sermon on 1 Cor. 4:1–2 which he prepared with JW's help for a deanery meeting in 1742 gave great offence to his fellow clergy by its pointed reference to their shortcomings. In 1744 he introduced JW to V. *Perronet. He attended the 1747 Conference, but seems to have withdrawn gradually from contact with Methodism, concerned at what he saw as its *antinomian tendencies. JW could not persuade him to itinerate beyond his own parish. His closing years were shadowed by financial worries arising out of the mismanagement of a family estate in Montserrat.

WMMag 1902 pp. 133–40; *PWHS* 5 pp. 225–7; A.S. Wood (1992) pp. 8–14

JAV

Pietism, a spiritual movement which arose in Germany in the latter half of the seventeenth century as a protest against what was perceived to be the growing arid intellectualism of *Lutheranism. Its main proponent was Philip Jakob Spener (1635–1705), whose tract *Pia Desideria* prescribed the way to spiritual renewal, including personal conversion, systematic Bible study, and good works as expressive of true faith. Pietism was further promoted by the life and work of A. H. Francke (1663–1727) whose *Pietas Hallensis* was an account of the movement's activities at Halle University. Pietism deeply influenced Count von *Zinzendorf (1700–60) and the *Moravians, some of whom, in turn, strongly influenced the W brothers.

P.J. Spener (1964)

HMG

Piggott, Henry James (1831–1917; e.m. 1852), pioneer of Methodism in *Italy, was the son of **William Piggott** (1798–1886; e.m. 1822, a missionary in *Sierra Leone 1824–28). He was educated at *Kingswood School and London University and in 1861 went with R. *Green to open the Italian mission. He became General Superintendent in 1870 and from 1873 was stationed in Rome, where he trained two generations of Italian ministers before retiring in 1903. He sought to promote Protestant unity in Italy and was involved in the revision of the Italian Bible.

MR 6 Dec. 1917; T.C. Piggott & T. Durley (1921)

JAV

Pilgrim Wesleyan Holiness Church consists largely of people of Caribbean origin associated with the Pilgrimage Holiness Church, which originated in the USA in 1897. In 1977 it had 13 churches and about 500 members in Britain, with headquarters in Handsworth, *Birmingham. Its parent body united with the Wesleyan Methodist Church of America (not connected with British WM) in 1968,, adopting the name 'Wesleyan Church'. The British denomination retains the words 'Pilgrim' and 'Holiness'.

C.E. Jones (1987); P.W. Thomas & P.Wm Thomas (1992)

WP

Pilmore, Rev. Joseph (1743–1825; e.m. 1765), pioneer itinerant in *American Methodism, 1769–74, was born at Fadmoor, N Yorks, the illegitimate son of Sarah Pillmoor and Joseph Foord, a Quaker (later a successful watercourse engineer) who denied the paternity, though it was accepted in court. Converted by JW, probably *c.* 1759, he went briefly to *Kingswood School, then entered the itinerancy. With R. *Boardman he volunteered to go as the first itinerant to America in 1769. A popular preacher, he tended to stay in Philadelphia, which led to friction with F. *Asbury and to his recall by JW in 1774. He withdrew briefly from the ministry, but returned in 1776 and served until 1785, when he finally withdrew, possibly because he was not included in the *Legal Hundred, partly because he wished to return to America and settle there, and partly because he saw Methodism as a society within the CofE. Returning to the USA, he was ordained in 1785 and became rector of St Paul's, Philadelphia, an evangelical on good terms with Asbury.

F.E. Maser & H.T. Magg (1969); J.P. Lockwood (1881); W.C. Barclay (1949) pp. 22–3; E.S. Bucke (1964) 1, pp. 80–9; I. McLean (forthcoming)

JHL

Pipe, Hannah Elizabeth (1831–1906), granddaughter of John S. Pipe (1768–1835; e.m. 1790) and niece of John Willson Pipe (*c.* 1799–1836; e.m. 1818), was educated at Chorley High School. She opened her first school for girls in *Manchester in 1848, taking in boarders four years later. Moving to London in 1856 she founded the Laleham Boarding School for Girls, which provided an enlightened education in arts and science with a strong emphasis on religious and moral education. In 1875 she attached an orphanage to the school, to enable her pupils to have contact with the poor. Although a convinced Wesleyan, she was free from denominationalism and not all her pupils were Methodist. Retiring to Limpsfield in 1890 she was instrumental in building a convalescent home for women in neighbouring Oxted.

A.M. Stoddart (1908); K.P. Hughes (1945) pp. 31–9

GRS

Plan of Pacification Immediately after JW's death, the diverging views about the relationship of the connexion with the Established Church, and in particular about the administration of the sacraments by the itinerant preachers and the times of preaching services, came to the fore. The 1791 Conference resolved simply 'to follow strictly the plan which Mr Wesley left us'. This was open to conflicting interpretations and much disturbance followed, with successive Conferences reflecting the tension between the 'Church Party' and their opponents, and also the issue of local as against connexional control of chapels.

The 1795 Conference therefore chose a committee of nine preachers to draw up a plan to bring peace. Their Plan was passed unanimously, and approved also by the assembled trustees. It marked a crucial stage in the separation of Methodism from the CofE. It laid down that the Sacrament of the *Lord's Supper should not be administered in any chapel except where both a majority of trustees and a majority of stewards and leaders allowed it and the Conference sanctioned it. The same rules applied to *baptism, burial and services in church hours. Holy Communion was to be administered only by those authorised by the Conference (i.e. itinerant preachers in *full connexion). Rules as to the time and order of services were laid down. Not all societies availed themselves of these provisions immediately, but eventually the Lord's Supper became an integral part of Methodist worship.

With regard to the powers of trustees, it was provided that *stationing of preachers was solely by the Conference, but moral or doctrinal charges or disputes about a preacher's abilities could be heard by a District court. The failure of the Plan to give greater authority to the *laity led to the secession of A *Kilham and, despite the 'Leeds

Concessions' of 1797, the beginning of the MNC.

J.S. Simon in *LQR* Oct. 1884 pp. 1–24; J.C. Bowmer (1975); J.M. Turner (1985) pp. 75–7; *HMGB* 4 pp. 264–9

SRH

Platt, Dr Frederic (1859–1955; e.m. 1882), WM minister, was born at *Bolton, Lancs and educated at Liverpool College and Durham University, followed by a brief period in banking. He taught at *Didsbury College (1905–10) and *Handsworth College (1910–16 and 1919–25), where he became Principal in 1923. During retirement at Clevedon he co-operated with T.F. *Hulme in restoring the *New Room as a Methodist shrine and served as its first Warden 1930–45. He gave the *Fernley Lecture in 1915 on *Immanence and Christian Thought*, and also published *Miracles, an Outline of the Christian View* (1913) and *Certainty and the Christian Faith* (1926).

Times 25 Jan. 1955; *MR* 27 Jan. & 3 Feb. 1955

CJS

Platt, Dr William James (1893–1993; e.m. 1916), WM missionary. On leaving *Didsbury College at 23, he was appointed to the Lagos District, which then covered a vast area of *Nigeria, Dahomey (now *Benin) and *Togo. As a fluent French speaker he was stationed in Dahomey In 1923 he visited the Ivory Coast (now *Côte d'Azure) to intercede with the French authorities for the small Methodist community there. He was alerted to the mass movement initiated in 1913–15 by the Liberian 'prophet' William Wadé Harris, a movement hitherto unknown outside the Ivory Coast. He persuaded the WMMS to take responsibility for following it up and in 1924 became Chairman of the new French West Africa District. He was an effective organizer in Africa and a powerful advocate in Britain. In 1930, frustrated by policy differences, he left the Missionary Society and served for over 30 years with the Bible Society, eventually becoming its General Secretary.

MR 19 Aug.1993; G.M. Haliburton (1971) pp. 173–206

JRP

Plymouth The modern city combines the former 'Three Towns' of Devonport, Stonehouse and Plymouth. Andrew Kinsman (1724–93), born in Tavistock, heard G. *Whitefield preach in 1744, moved to Plymouth in 1745 and joined the *Calvinistic Methodist society there. Its Tabernacle chapel was built on his wife's land, which gave him a controlling position in Plymouth Methodism. In 1753 he opened a chapel called the 'Upper Room' in Devonport. He was ordained at Broadmead Baptist Church, Bristol in 1763 and for 30 years was the leading figure in Plymouth Methodism. After his death both his congregations became Independent. The Moravians also had congregations in both Plymouth and Devonport, the latter's James Street church surviving until 1916.

JW preached in Plymouth in 1746, but because of the prevailing Calvinistic influence he concentrated on Devonport until 1766 and it was there that WM spread most rapidly, though not without problems. The first WM preaching house was built in Lower Street, Plymouth in 1779 and JW preached there in August 1780. In February 1785 he went down to Devonport to deal with a secession and preached in the shell of Ker Street chapel. Plymouth Central Hall, converted in 1940 from the Ebenezer WM chapel of 1815 in Eastlake Street, was the last such to be opened. There have been close links with the armed services. In Devonport the WM built the 'Welcome' sailors' hostel in 1908, enlarged into the Central Hall in 1926, rebuilt after the War, but closed in 1986. Other chapels such as the Stonehouse Mission in Union Street (1813, rebuilt 1857, now closed) were parade chapels.

Being the largest conurbation in the South West, Plymouth became BC's connexional stronghold, centred on its Greenbank Chapel (1886, closed 1976). Administratively, Methodist history has been complex: by 1900 there were nine overlapping circuits – four WM, two UMFC, two BC and one PM. The city has hosted 15 BC, 3 WM and 2 UM Conferences and two since *Methodist Union. World War II brought devastation to buildings (seven in Devonport alone), resulting in a short-lived city-wide circuit. The great WM King Street Conference chapel was destroyed. Post-war rebuilding with war damage compensation in the outlying estates was only partially successful. In 1999 there were two circuits.

See also **Dymond, G.P.**; **Foot Family**

Conference Handbook 1913 (WM), 1929 (WM), 1965

RFST

Pocock Family William Pocock (1750–1835), a carpenter employed by Samuel Tooth,

builder of *Wesley's Chapel, met his wife Hannah Fuller at the *Foundery and both were present at the laying of the foundation stone of the Chapel. Pocock went into business on his own account and in 1782 obtained the freedom of the Carpenters' Company. He became a cabinet maker in Leyton and is said to have made the first extending dining table. His eldest son **William Fuller Pocock** (1779–1849) was apprenticed to his father and in 1840 was elected Master of the Carpenters' Company. He became an architect (described as 'competent but unremarkable') and was an early member of the Institute of British Architects, entering unsuccessfully the competition for the design of the new Palace of Westminster in 1835. He and his wife Fanny (née Wilmer) were members of Sloane Terrace chapel, Chelsea (which he had designed) near their Knightsbridge home. His designs included the headquarters of the London Militia, Bunhill Row, Finsbury (1828), Kensington WM chapel (1836), Christchurch parish church, Virginia Water (1837) and the Centenary Hall (WM *Mission House), Bishopsgate, London (1840). The eldest of their four sons, **William Wilmer Pocock** (1813–99), entered his father's practice in 1837 and became FRIBA in 1843. He was one of the first students at King's College, London and graduated at London University. In 1861 he designed Spurgeon's Metropolitan Tabernacle in Newington Butts; in 1875, the Central WM chapel at Hastings and in 1878 the chapel, school and Soldiers' Home at Aldershot. He was a trustee of Wesley's Chapel for 49 years and closely associated with the renovation of 1891. A 'sensible, sound' *local preacher, but 'never very effective or popular', he became President of the *LPMAA in 1875 and is commemorated in a stained glass window at Wesley's Chapel. His brother **Thomas Wilmer Pocock** (1817–89) became a doctor at Brompton and retired early to' Glenridge', a cottage his father had built at Virginia Water. He served on the connexional Home and Overseas Mission Committees and served as a *local preacher over a wide area. With his older brother he planted Methodism in the area between Guildford and Portsmouth (sometimes described as 'the Methodist wilderness'), fostering *HM efforts there. His eldest son, also **Thomas Wilmer Pocock** (1846–1929; e.m. 1876), was a missionary in South Africa 1876–1929 and his youngest son, **Percy Wilmer Pocock** (d.1941), was a solicitor, local preacher and Sunday School Superintendent at Egham. One of Percy's sons, also **Percy Wilmer Pocock** (1885–1986), followed the profession of his great grandfather and became an architect, dying in 1986 at the age of 100.

C. Binfield in J. Garnett & C. Matthews (1993) pp. 153–82; WHS(LHC) 38 pp. 12–14, 39, 41, 43

NM

Pocock, George (1774–1843) was born in Hungerford, the son of the Rev. John Pocock, and joined the WM in Frome in 1796 or 1797. In 1800 he became the proprietor of Prospect Place Academy in *Bristol, joined Portland Chapel and soon afterwards became a *local preacher and trustee. Described as 'impulsive and at times capricious', he both owned and played the Portland Chapel organ. Using his practical skills, in 1814 he constructed a tent capable of holding 500 people, which he and others used in and around Bristol to supplement existing WM resources. He and two others were expelled in 1820 because he would not accept WM control of the tents and chapels he had financed. He became the leader of the *Tent Methodists, but in 1835 gave up his independent preaching and regained his status as a WM *local preacher. His inventive skill was demonstrated in the 'char-volant', a kite-impelled road vehicle which he exhibited around the country. He expounded his aeronautical theories in *The Aeropleustic Art* (Bristol, 1817). One of his grandsons was the famous cricketer, W.G. Grace.

J.L. Hodgson (1924) pp. 370–1; A.J. Lambert (1930) pp. 50–55

JL/CJS

Politics   It was never JW's intention for his followers to become a political people, but it proved impossible to draw a clear line between religion and politics in the prevailing conditions of eighteenth- and nineteenth-century Britain. W himself flirted with High Tory causes in the 1730s and 40s, spoke out against political corruption, castigated the revolutionary actions of the American colonists, disavowed slavery and railed against riches and conspicuous consumption. He bequeathed to his followers a strong ethos of loyalty to the established order, an enthusiasm for civil and religious liberty, a deep suspicion of *Roman Catholicism and an ecclesiastical system that mobilized and trained the *laity. It proved an unstable legacy for his followers who had to cope with spectacular Methodist growth in a period of rapid social, economic and political change. In the early nineteenth-century Methodists were rela-

tively united in their determination to resist state interference in the form of the *Sidmouth Bill against itinerant preaching and in their resistance to the political demands of Irish Roman Catholics; but they found it more difficult to absorb the class tensions of early industrial England. Some Methodists flirted with radical causes; others rose to leadership in mining and agricultural *trade unions; still others signed their names to anti-slavery petitions. But most were relatively uninvolved in politics and simply obeyed the injunctions of their leaders not to meddle with those given to change.

But Methodism could not avoid the political context of its own growth. Class tensions mingled with ecclesiastical conflicts and produced manifold secessions from WM. Most new Methodist denominations, such as the PMs, were on the whole less deferential to Anglican and Tory causes than the original Connexion. As the nineteenth century unfolded Methodists, in common with the rest of Nonconformity, found it easier to unite on religious and moral crusades such as *temperance and *sabbatarianism than on such great political issues of the day as Home Rule for Ireland and the running of the Empire. Over the past two centuries Methodist engagement with the world of politics has been engagingly eclectic. Kilhamite radicals, trade unionists and early socialists are as much a part of the Methodist canon as Buntingite tories and Welsh liberals. In fact, MPs from Methodist backgrounds have shown up in all the major political parties and in recent times have supplied three successive Speakers of the House of Commons. As JW himself understood, religion and politics are hard to separate and even harder to unite.

See also **Chartism**; **Committee of Privileges**

E.R. Taylor (1935); D. Hempton (1984); M. Watt (1995); D. Hempton (1996)

DNH

Pollard, Samuel (1864–1915; e.m. 1886), BC missionary in *China, was a son of the manse. He was appointed to the newly opened Yunnan Mission in 1886. A superb linguist with great personal charm, he was an ardent evangelist and fearless in his denunciation of social evil. In 1891 he married Emmie Hainge, a missionary with the China Inland Mission. He received the first Miao enquirers in 1904 and guided the development of the great movement that followed. Mastering their language, he devised an ingenious script for it, undertook the translation of the NT and published a hymn-book. Constantly travelling and preaching, he never spared himself. He died of typhoid and was buried on the hillside behind Shimenkan (Stonegateway), the mission station he had founded. His grave was destroyed by the Red Guards, but rebuilt by the Government in 1995 as a lasting tribute to the work of the missionaries. His three books on China were republished in 1995 as *The Sam Pollard Omnibus*.

———————
W.A. Grist (1920); R.E. Kendall (1954); G.R. Senior (1999)

RKP

Poor, The JW's preference for the life and company of the poor has continued as an irritant within Methodism. In the twentieth century, the rise of Central Halls in the cities and the persistence of street-corner chapels in poor areas continued until World War II. Since then most Central Halls have closed and most street-corner chapels have succumbed to outward and upward mobility. In 1973 the Conference appointed an Inner City Committee, which led to the *Mission Alongside the Poor. Methodism, largely now a middle-class phenomenon, still manifests itself in small, often innovative congregations in inner cities and deprived housing estates, and some middle-class Methodists see in the 'preferential option for the poor' of Liberation Theology a return to at least some of JW's 'preference'.

———————
J. Vincent (1984); M. Marquardt (1992)

JJV

Poor Stewards In JW's time the poor were dealt with on behalf of the society by 'visitors of the sick' and the *society stewards, who disbursed financial help. After his death it became customary for a collection for the poor to be taken during the *Lord's Supper by the Poor's Stewards (now called Communion Stewards), who prepare the elements and direct the communicants to the Lord's table. The office was often seen as the lowest rung on the ladder of lay office. The offering, now called the Benevolence Fund, is used primarily to relieve local poverty and distress.

———————
J.C. Bowmer (1961) pp. 32–3; *CPD* vol. 2 bk III, SO6372 section 65

MB

Pope, Dr Henry J. (1836–1912; e.m. 1858), WM minister, born in March, Cambs, entered the ministry from *Hull. During eight years in Scottish circuits he sought to promote evangelistic missions through the Relief and Extension Fund. He was Secretary of the Chapel Committee 1876–97; then moved to the *HM office. He was closely involved in initiating the *Manchester Central Mission and the *Forward Movement which it inaugurated. He was President of the 1893 Conference. In retirement his literary interest focused especially on the mystics.

———————
MR 18 July 1912

WL

Pope, William Burt (1822–1903; e.m. 1841), the outstanding WM theologian of the nineteenth century, whose 3-volume *Compendium of Christian Theology* (1880) remained a standard text for over a generation. (In his own view, however, the shorter *Higher Catechism of Theology* (1883) was a more balanced and felicitous statement of his position.) He taught at *Didsbury College 1867–86, was President of the Conference in 1877 and served as Chairman of the Manchester District, 1877–85. He gave the *Fernley Lecture in 1871 on *The Person of Christ*. Stressing the Methodist contribution to theology, he wrote an important essay (1873) on its particular ethos and contributed a classic chapter to the *Wesley Memorial Volume* (1881). In his own theological work, however, he also drew widely from patristic, reformed and eastern traditions. He laid particular emphasis on the inner trinitarian dynamics of salvation, on the eternal sonship and what he called 'the great obedience' of the incarnate Son; and he stressed the inner witness of the Spirit and the doctrine of perfect love. A meticulous textual scholar, he was, like many of his generation in the WM ministry, suspicious of the 'higher criticism' and of the notion of 'evolution'. His work thus marks the end of an era, though his encouragement of J.S. *Lidgett undoubtedly contributed to new and important developments in Methodist theology.

———————
G.J. Stevenson (1884–6) 3 pp. 434–7; *MR* 9 July 1903; R.W. Moss (1909); G. Slater in *ER*, May 1988

DJC

Porteous, Crichton (1901–1991), Derbyshire farmer and author, who contributed frequently to the *Methodist Recorder*. His many books on farming and country life included *Farmer's Creed* (1938, *Teamsman* (1939) and (with S.J. Looker) *Richard Jefferies, Man of the Fields* (1965).

———————
MR 25 Jan. 1940

JAV

Porteous, Mary (née Thompson) (*c.* 1783–1861), PM itinerant. Brought up in a strict Presbyterian family, she married in 1803 and became a WM in 1807, becoming a prayer leader, class leader (1814), sick visitor and Sunday School teacher (1816). After hearing PM preachers, she felt a call to preach. Despite reservations about female preaching, in January 1824 she became a PM *local preacher and a year later an itinerant. Delayed by family commitments, she went to the *Whitby Circuit in January 1826. She worked chiefly in the North, but ill health forced her retirement in 1840, though she continued as a *local preacher for another 21 years.

J. Lightfoot (1862); E.D.Graham (1989) pp. 18–19

EDG

Porter, Hilda, MBE (1892–1976), founder of *Methodist International Houses. She began her working career with her father's engineering firm in *Barnsley. In 1920 she offered to the WMMS for work in *China and after elementary medical training served in Suichow, Central China for five years. In 1934 she was appointed Secretary for *Women's Work (China) and Home Organization. She became particularly concerned for overseas students seeking accommodation in post-war Britain. A Committee for the Care of Overseas Students was formed and eventually she became warden of the first International House, in Inverness Terrace, London.

P.M. Webb (1963) pp. 71–6; *MR* 9 Dec. 1976

PMW

Portsmouth JW did not visit the town until 1753, on his way to the Isle of Wight. He preached on the Common.He did not return until 1758 and 1767. A society had been formed in 1746 by J. *Cennick and a Whitefieldite Tabernacle opened in 1758. That year Wesley found the society torn by disputes. The infrequency of his visits may have been connected with the strength of local Dissent and the prevalent *Calvinism among the Methodists. From 1767 on, when his followers began meeting in a room in Warblington Street and then built a chapel in Bishop Street, Portsea, he was there almost annually. In Portsmouth, Oyster Street chapel (c.1786) was replaced by Green Row (later Pembroke Road) in 1811, but was hampered by debts. Meanwhile, in Portsea, St. Peter's Chapel was bought from an Anglican group in 1800 (enlarged 1810). Until 1790 Portsmouth was part of the far-flung Salisbury Circuit.

Mary Billing launched a BC mission from the Isle of Wight in 1825. Their earliest chapels were Emmanuel in York Place, Landport (replaced by Stamford Street, 1861) and Bethesda, Little Southsea Street (replaced by Grosvenor Street and taken over by WM in 1847). The first BC Conference outside Devon was held at Grosvenor Street in 1852. Following a visit to the area by W. *Clowes, the Hull PM Circuit set up missions in Portsmouth, Southampton and the Isle of Wight in 1833. They had a Green Row chapel in Landport (unconnected with the WM chapel), but in 1851 were the weakest of the three Methodist denominations locally. In the *Religious Census that year, despite its chapel building efforts (most recently, Wesley Chapel, Arundel Street (1845)), Portsmouth Methodism could accommodate only 5 % of the rapidly growing population, the lowest percentage anywhere in southern England outside London. New churches continued to be built as Portsea Island became steadily more urban, notably Victoria Road (1878) and Trinity, Albert Road (1901), both in Southsea; while the WM Central Hall, Fratton (1889; with new buildings in 1900, 1928 and 1992), the PM Central Hall in Albert Road, Southsea (1901) and Eastney Central Hall (WM 1928, on the site of the Victoria Soldiers' and Sailors' Home and successor to an 1867 chapel in Highland Street) belonged to the era of the *Forward Movement.

H. Smith (1894); W.D. Cooper (1973); J.A. Vickers in *Portsmouth Archives Review* 4 (1979–80) pp. 25–43

JAV

Portugal A Cornish mining engineer, Thomas Chegwin, began the first *class-meeting at the Palhal Mines in northern Portugal in 1853. Another layman, James Cassels, introduced Methodism into Oporto and in 1868 built the first Methodist chapel, in Vila Nova de Gaia. In the early years the work was supervised from *Gibraltar. The first missionary, Robert K. Moreton, was sent to Oporto in 1871 and was Superintendent for 43 years. He was supported by two converts from the RC priesthood and later by Alfredo da Silva, who succeeded him as Superintendent. Early in the twentieth century a flourishing work began in Lisbon, which was later handed over to another evangelical body. The work in the north, centred on Oporto and Aviero, continued as an Overseas District of the British Conference until it gained autonomy in 1996. In 1997 it reported a membership of 1,500 and a total community of 3,500.

See also **Aspey, A.**

F&H 4 pp. 437–43; W.P. Stephens (n.d.)

SJP

Posnett, Charles Walker, K-i-H (1870–1950; e.m. 1895), WM missionary to *India, was the son of **Robert Posnett** (1831–1908; e.m. 1855) and was educated at *Kingswood School and *Richmond College. He served from 1896 to 1940 among the 'untouchables' of Hyderabad, showing deep compassion for the victims of famine and disease. His outstanding powers of leadership made the village of Medak the centre of a Mass Movement among Malas and Madigas. The mission included hospitals, schools and the great central church which he built in Medak itself and which became the CSI's largest cathedral. A gifted teacher, he established a training centre for student-evangelists, for whom he wrote 'Outlines of Biblical Characters'. Many outcastes were converted, but also a number of caste Hindus. He served as Chairman of the Provincial Synod in South India. His sister **Emilie Posnett** K-i-H (1866–1966) trained at the London Hospital. With her close friend Sarah Harris (d.1955) she served as a medical missionary in Medak 1896–1939, becoming known to her Indian friends as Pedda Dorasani ('the great lady'). They campaigned vigorously against both social prejudice and appalling sanitary conditions. At the time of the mass movement in Hyderabad, working in close co-operation with Posnett, they organized the training of young Indian wives as Bible Women. Emilie died two days before her 100th birthday.

MR 5 & 12 Oct. 1950, 8 & 15 Dec. 1966; F.C. Sackett (1951)

EMJ

Potter, Dr Philip A. (1921– ; e.m. 1947), a leading figure and renowned preacher in the international ecumenical movement. Born in Dominica, he trained for the Methodist ministry at Caenwood, Jamaica and *Richmond College. As Secretary of the British *SCM he led the youth delegation to the first WCC Assembly in 1948. After service in Haiti he was appointed to the Youth Department of the WCC in 1954. In 1960 he was elected President of the World Student Christian Federation and in 1961 became the first overseas minister to be a Secretary of the MMS. He was appointed Director of World Mission and Evangelism in the WCC in 1967 and was elected General Secretary of the WCC, 1972–84. In that office he promoted programmes to combat racism and injustice.

ER July 1999 pp. 45–53

PMW

Preachers *see* **Itinerancy**; **Local Preachers**; **Ministry**; **Ordination**

Preachers' Fund *see* **Finance, Ministerial**

Preaching Methodism was born as much in sermons as in song. JW and CW were both preachers, nervously at first, in the open air, but soon with dramatic effect. And also in their own places of worship. JW believed that should the 5 a.m. preaching cease it would be the end of Methodism. He recruited preachers from among his converts, only a few of whom were clergymen. The dependence of Methodist worship on lay people began almost at once.

The call to the *itinerant ministry was until recently primarily a call to preach, with experience as a *local preacher a prior requirement. There was an inescapable sense that preaching must be for a verdict. JW, however, deplored so-called 'gospel preachers' who provided 'cordials' rather than the pure milk of the Word. He insisted that preaching must be of both law and gospel.

Methodist piety was based on preaching, which for both preachers and congregations often meant an exercise in the classic technique of meditation. To go to worship often meant 'to hear so-and-so'. Until the mid-twentieth century there were popular preachers who could draw large congregations. Methodist preaching was less intellectual than that of the Reformed tradition, less restrained than the Anglican. Illustrations from many aspects of life were what held people and often contributed to their education, for sermons were a method of teaching which in the utterances of a master could be very effective.

Modern educational methods have disparaged preaching. The monologue has been thought to fall on deaf ears, the attention span said, wrongly, to be limited, and the visual has replaced the verbal through television. The decline of Sunday evening services has seriously diminished preaching opportunities at an hour when working people could attend and there was undistracted openness to the gospel. Methodist preaching has become shorter and increasingly related to the lectionary; less a virtuoso performance than part of the ministry of worship.

See also **Field Preaching**; **Local preachers**
                                                         GSW

Preaching Plans The circuit preaching plan has been a feature of Methodism from very early days, and was common to all branches of British Methodism. It originated as a hand-written list of preaching appointments. Compiled by the circuit *Superintendent, in its simplest form it is a grid showing the times and frequency of services in all the places of worship throughout the circuit, and the ministers and *local preachers responsible for each service. Each plan usually covers a three-month period. In the eighteenth century there were separate plans for *itinerants and local preachers. The modern 'combined' plan became standard early in the nineteenth century. Victorian plans usually consisted of a single sheet printed (sometimes on silk) on one side only, with numbers used to indicate the preachers. Over the years plans have become more elaborate and informative, but their essential purpose has remained unchanged. They are the only convenient source of information on the local preachers in each circuit. The Methodist *Archives Centre has a large though random collection of plans from the past 200 years and the Marriott Collection (now at Drew University, but available on microfilm) is a complete collection of WM plans dating from 1825. The Society of Cirplanologists and its journal *Cirplan* exists to preserve and study preaching plans.

PWHS 37 pp. 50–4

                                                         EAR

Presbyterian Church of Wales *see* **Welsh Calvinistic Methodism**

Prescott, Charles John (1857–1946), WM minister and noted educationalist in New South Wales, was educated at *Kingswood School, Worcester College, Oxford and *Handsworth College. Arriving in Sydney in 1882, in 1886 he became the first Headmaster of the Methodist Ladies College, Burwood NSW and also established a co-educational kindergarten, probably the first in the colony. In 1900 he moved to Newington College, Stanmore as President and Headmaster, the first to hold that dual office. He became spokesman for other headmasters in negotiations with government, university and Department of Education. He was founder and several times chairman of the Teachers Association of NSW, the Headmasters' Association (foundation chairman, 1923) and the Teachers Central Registry. He was elected President of the Australian Conference in 1910.

P.L. Swain (1978); *ADB*

                                                         EGC

President of the Conference JW called together the first *Conference as a consultation with friends and supporters. During his lifetime he always presided, except in 1780, when C. *Hopper was elected in his absence. The *Deed of Declaration established its legality. In the event of W's death a President was to be elected by the *Legal Hundred. In March 1791 the *Halifax Circular proposed that there should be 'no more kings in Israel', which led to W. *Thompson being elected the first President after W's death. The Conference of 1792 laid down that the same person was not to be elected President more than once in eight years. J. *Bunting and R. *Newton each held the office four times. In the MNC, where this rule was not adopted, W. *Thom was President six times. Several of the post-1932 Presidents (J. *Scott Lidgett, F.L. *Wiseman, W. *Younger, W.C. *Jackson and R. *Pyke) had been Presidents of pre-Union Conferences, but since then only Dr D. *English has been elected twice. The first woman President was Dr K.M. *Richardson in 1992.

The other Methodist bodies all adopted the Presidency. The UMFC elected two laymen to the office – Henry T. Mawson (1883) and Sir James *Duckworth (1894). PM had one lay President – Sir W.P. *Hartley (1909). It also instituted the office of *Vice-President.

The office owes not a little historically to the Church of Scotland; Bunting, indeed, preferred the title of Moderator. The President has disciplinary powers between Conferences; he has normally presided at the reception of preachers into full connexion and, after 1836, at *ordinations, and also at Departmental (and Divisional) Boards. But the custom of the President touring the Districts (and World Methodism) began with the railway age and is not of the essence of the office. If a President should die in office (e.g. Dr A.W. *Harrison in 1946) his predecessor resumes office.

The annual election by ballot has opened the office to people of distinctive gifts and emphases. Many now advocate a longer period of office (if only for the media's sake!). This would mean the Presidency becoming a more executive office. more akin to that of the *Secretary of Conference.

CPD various editions; *HMGB* 1 pp. 246, 280
                                                         JMT

President's Council The 1969 Report on Departmental Structure and Function recommended that policy matters should become the responsibility of a President's Council, with the *General Purposes and Policy Committee reverting to its former functions.

The Council was appointed from 1971, with responsibility, *inter alia*, to keep in constant review the life of the Methodist Church; to give spiritual leadership; to supervise and promote liaison in the work of the connexion; to formulate policy development.

Its functions in advising the Conference on connexional budgeting matters were subsequently given to the Mission and Service Fund Budget Committee in 1979.

It consisted of 33 members, including ministerial and lay district representation on a rota basis, 4 Conference-elected members (to include two women) and Divisional General Secretaries.

In 1994, following its 1992 Report on Divisional Structure and Function, the Council was abolished, its functions being amalgamated with those of the General Purposes and Budget Committees and (in 1996) those of the Divisional Boards in the Methodist Council.

SRH

President's List or List of Reserve. A list of accepted candidates not immediately wanted for stationing was first printed in the WM Minutes of 1791. These were available to supply emergency vacancies during the year. In 1807 authority was given to the President to appoint such 'supplies'. Similar arrangements obtained in the other Methodist denominations. In time the list included ministers who on compassionate or other grounds needed temporary respite from stationing, and in practice the list came to be confined to these. It was abolished in 1993, such cases thereafter being listed as 'without appointment'.

BEB

Preston, Raymond (1861–1950; e.m. 1914) was a successful evangelist in Britain for many years. In 1913 W.G. *Taylor invited him to conduct a mission at the Central Methodist Mission in Sydney, NSW. Received into the *Australian ministry in 1914, he conducted successful missions in many places. Many of his converts entered the ministry. He had a fine tenor voice and was a forceful temperance advocate.

ADEB; W. Kingscote-Greenhead (1930)

EGC

Preston The first Methodist in the town is deemed to have been Martha *Thompson, rescued by JW from a lunatic asylum in London. On her return home she joined a society in a nearby village and was instrumental in forming the first Preston society in 1774. The society grew under the preaching of M. *Crane, M. *Emmett and W. *Bramwell. JW paid his first visit in 1780 and in 1790 preached in the first chapel, erected in Back Lane in 1787. Preston became a separate circuit in 1799. A secession in 1802 resulted in the loss of one third of the members and the formation of a MNC society. But by 1817 there were 300 members and a larger chapel was opened in Lune Street. In 1825 the Countess of *Huntingdon's Connexion had a chapel in Pole Street. The WMA chapel at Orchard joined the UMFC in 1857 and there was also a group of Quaker Methodists. The 'Seven Men of Preston', led by Joseph Livesley, promoting total abstinence and the signing of the pledge, found encouragement among local non-WMs. Meetings were held on their premises and the first children's *Temperance Society was formed at Lawson Street PM chapel. At Lune Street a Missionary Society and Samaritans' Society were well-known for fund-raising and promoting practical social awareness; e.g. giving much help at the time of the 'cotton famine' during the American Civil War. Work continues from that centre among the homeless and destitute. A WM Day School opened at Moor Park in 1864; in the 1930s it had nearly 500 pupils. At the time of *Methodist Union in 1932 there were two WM, two PM and two UMC circuits. The Methodist Conference met in Preston in 1952, 1963 and 1976.

R. Allen (1866); W. Pilkington (1890); Conference Handbook 1952; W.F. Richardson (1976)

EWD

Prickett, John (1907–96), headmaster of *Kent College for Boys, Canterbury, 1933–60, including the problematic war years. On retirement he worked with maladjusted adolescents at Finchden Manor; then as educational secretary of the British Council of Churches from 1967. As secretary of the Standing Conference on Inter-Faith Dialogue in Education, 1973–83, he contributed to Lutterworth Press's 'Living Faith' series. His third wife was the daughter of Bishop J. *Hunkin.

MR 18 Jan. 1996

JAV

Priestley, Eber (1901–72; e.m. 1923) was born and spent his whole ministry in *India. After training at *Handsworth College, he worked in the Muslim stronghold of Hyderabad from 1923 and later in training village evangelists. Though staunchly opposing union with the Anglicans, he gave his wholehearted support to the CSI after 1947 and in 1960 became Bishop of Medak, a huge and diverse diocese experiencing divisive tensions.

MR 20 Jan. 1972

JAV

Primitive Methodism developed from early nineteenth-century revivalism, which was localized in a prayer meeting at Harriseahead, Staffs, in 1800. The American Lorenzo Dow, visiting the area, introduced the idea of *Camp Meetings. This fired the imagination of H. *Bourne and other revivalists, but the WM Conference judged them 'highly improper' and disclaimed all connection with them. Bourne's association with the revival led to his expulsion from WM in 1808. W. *Clowes was drawn into the movement and soon had a following (known as 'Clowesites'). After his expulsion in 1810, he and his followers joined with the Camp Meeting Methodists.

Two events in 1811 marked the birth of a new denomination: Bourne issued a ticket of membership and the first PM chapel was built at Tunstall. The following year the name 'Society of Primitive Methodists' was adopted. A preaching plan for the Tunstall Circuit, printed in 1812, virtually confirmed the (self-styled) 'Ranters' as a separate denomination. The Conference of 1829 approved a Deed Poll, giving the denomination legal status.

The movement was at first confined to the Burslem area, but after 1816 it grew more rapidly and under the guidance of Bourne and Clowes missionary activity escalated. Clowes missioned *Hull in 1819 and the first PM *Conference was held there in 1820. Outstanding missionaries to other parts of the country included Thomas *Batty in Weardale, Thomas *Russell in Berkshire, William *Braithwaite in Lincolnshire and Robert *Key in Norfolk. Outstanding among the *women preachers were the pioneer Sarah *Kirkland and the long-surviving Elizabeth *Bultitude.

A Book Room was established at *Bemersley in 1820, which eventually moved to Holborn Hall, London. A connexional Magazine and other monthly publications became part of its output. There was a series of hymn-books, the *Hartley Lecture, a weekly newspaper and books by promi-

nent writers in the connexion. A theological institute opened in *Sunderland in 1868, to be succeeded by *Hartley College in 1881. *Elmfield College, York and Bourne College, Quinton, Birmingham were educational establishments. Orphanages were opened at Harrogate and Alresford.

The period from 1829 to 1850 was one of rapid expansion. Circuits mushroomed throughout the country and it was the leading circuits, rather than the Conference, that took the initiative through their 'Branches' and 'Missions' for the new outreach. The strength of PM lay chiefly in the north – Yorkshire and Co. Durham; but it also flourished in the agricultural areas of East Anglia and the south, chiefly among the lower classes, but as time passed with a sprinkling of successful manufacturers and businessmen. As *Districts and *Circuits were defined, chapel building became a dominant activity. The towns built on a grand scale; the villages erected utilitarian, box-like chapels. PM moved from an aggressive type of evangelism to a distinctive ministry of preaching, buttressed by prayer meetings, open-air witness and later the *Christian Endeavour societies. Laymen were highly influential at connexional level and occasionally laymen (T. *Bateman and W.P. *Hartley) were elected President of the Conference. The Vice-Presidency (from 1872 on) was open to ministers or laymen, but after 1883 was almost always held by a layman.

At the time of Methodist Union in 1932 there were 222,000 members with over 1,000 ministers and nearly 13,000 *local preachers.

See also **Overseas Missions**

J. Petty (1880); H.B. Kendall (1906); J.S. Werner (1984)

WL

Primitive Methodist Leader, a PM newspaper, launched as the *Primitive Methodist* in 1868. It changed its name in 1905 to the *Primitive Methodist Leader*, incorporating the *Primitive Methodist World* from 1908. In 1926 it was again renamed the *Methodist Leader*. In 1932 it amalgamated with the *Methodist Times* to form the *Methodist Times and Leader*, which was incorporated in the *Methodist Recorder* in 1937 For many of its early years it was edited by a layman, F.H. Hurd. But the most notable of its numerous editors was George Bennett (1856–1930; e.m. 1875) whose 25 years of editorship wielded great influence and moulded connexional opinion.

WL

Primitive Methodist Magazine In April 1818 H. *Bourne printed a small magazine of 24 pages under the title *A Methodist Magazine ... conducted by the Society of people called Primitive Methodists*. A second number was printed in July. It was largely a failure, but a second attempt to introduce a magazine was made in 1819, with William Goodrich, a preacher in Loughborough, as editor. It was called *A Methodist Magazine ... conducted by the camp meeting Methodists*. There were eight monthly parts and then no more until June 1820. H. *Bourne was officially appointed editor from 1820 and it was renamed the *Primitive Methodist Magazine*. In 1831 it became octavo in size and continued as such until 1898 when the page size was enlarged and the title became *The Aldersgate Primitive Methodist Magazine*. As with other connexional magazines, it included portraits of the travelling preachers and their obituaries as well as of many prominent lay members. There were also reports from the circuits, news of chapel openings and anniversaries, extracts from preachers' journals and foreign mission reports. The final issue was in August 1932.

W L

Primitive Physick was an expression of JW's concern for the health of the poor at a time when professional medical help was both expensive and rudimentary. First published in 1747, it went through 23 editions in his lifetime. It contains remedies for a great variety of illnesses. The preface gives his reasons for compiling the book and stresses the importance of exercise, a balanced regimen, correct dress and adequate sleep. He acknowledges his debt to Dr George Cheyne's *Book of Health and Long Life*. In later prefaces he explains why he had left out some remedies and added new ones. Many of the recommended cures are marked as 'Tried' (i.e. either on himself or on a patient). Although many were merely folk remedies, he was ahead of his time in recommending Electricity as coming 'the nearest to a universal medicine of any yet known in the world' and as a cure for baldness, deafness and many other ailments. He was also a firm believer in hygiene and in such natural resources as herbs, along with hot or cold baths.

PWHS 18 pp. 149–53; 21 pp. 60–7; A.W. Hil (1958)

W L

Primitive Wesleyan Methodists The early Irish Methodists had more support from landed and entrepreneurial classes than the English and this prolonged their link with the Established Church. It was not until 1814 that the Irish Conference was strongly urged to allow the administration of the *sacraments. After two years' considerable agitation, in 1816 the Conference gave conditional approval.

Opponents convened a conference at Clones in October and stationed 19 *local preachers as itinerants. In January 1818 a committee formulated their Constitution, which was adopted in July, with the name Primitive Wesleyan Methodist Society. They took approximately one third of the WM membership. PWM members continued to receive the sacraments in the Church of Ireland. A. *Averell was elected President for life. In time the Society's ministers adopted clerical style and dress. It did not extend its work beyond Ireland. The Disestablishment of the Irish Church in 1870 raised the question of the PWM future. Several of its preachers were ordained to fill vacant Church of Ireland parishes, leaving Methodist interests to prevail. The WM and PWM Conferences reunited in 1878 as the Methodist Church in Ireland.

C.H. Crookshank (1885–8) 2 pp. 402–66, 3 passim; R.L. Cole (1960) pp. 20–32

D A L C

Pritchard, Edward Cook (1833–1918; e.m. 1856), PM missionary in *Australia. After brief service in England, he arrived in Hobart, Tasmania in 1860 and exercised ministries there and in NSW until 1875 and 1882–88. A noted evangelist, many experienced conversion under his ministry and church membership grew considerably. He spoke at many *camp meetings where attendance were as high as 800. In 1886 he was elected President of the PM Assembly of NSW.

E.C. Pritchard (n.d.)

E G C

Pritchard, Dr Frank Cyril (1911–79), schoolmaster, the son of Frank Hubert Pritchard (1883–1947; e.m. 1906), was born at Grassington. He was a London graduate in English and obtained his doctorate with a thesis on *Methodist Secondary Education* (published in 1949). After war service in the Middle East he was headmaster of *Woodhouse Grove School 1950–72, where he oversaw an extension and modernization of the school buildings. He wrote the school's history (1978) and a history of *Westminster College (1951).

J A V

Probation Initially, accepted candidates for the *ministry were trained by a system of apprenticeship, under which they were placed in the care of their *Superintendent for a period. From 1784 the period was four years, to which was added after 1834 two (later three) years spent in the Theological Institution. Studies were prescribed and annual reports made to the probationer's *District Meeting (Synod). The other branches of Methodism developed similar systems and in outline this survives today. Two years in a carefully selected circuit or similar appointment is regarded as the minimum. The studies are designed as one element in a wider programme for the early years of ministry. During this period probationers preside at the *Lord's Supper only if authorized by the Conference. In 1956 a ban on the marriage of probationers was lifted. Probation is considered complete on reception into *full connexion.

HMGB 1 pp. 248–50

BEB

Property Stewards *see* **Chapel Stewards**

Protestant Methodists, a small secession from WM which eventually became part of the UMFC. In 1827 it was proposed to put an organ into the new Brunswick Chapel in *Leeds; but this was rejected unanimously by the *Leaders' Meeting. The trustees unwisely took the matter to the District Meeting, where permission was again refused. But the trustees then got the ear of influential men at Conference, including J. *Bunting, and despite its own resolutions of 1820 Conference acceded to the application. The upshot was the loss of 1,000 members in Leeds and the formation of the Protestant Methodist Connexion, which held its first Assembly in 1828. When it amalgamated with the *WMA in 1836, it had just under 4,000 members.

J.S. Simon in *LQR* July 1888 pp. 271–91; O.A. Beckerlegge (1957) pp. 16–19; *HMGB* 2 pp. 314–15

OAB

Public Worship JW declared that he believed there to be 'no liturgy in the World . . . which breathes more of a solid, scriptural, rational Piety, than the Common Prayer of the Church of England' and, though he early came to accept extempore prayer alongside it, he strove to make the Anglican liturgy the foundation of Methodist worship. He urged his followers to attend their parish church for both worship and the Sacrament and resisted grassroots pressure for Methodist services to be held in 'church hours'. In 1784 he revised and abridged the 1662 Book of Common Prayer for use as *The *Sunday Service of the Methodists in North America*. This was less widely used in England than the full order, though the latter was only in a minority of leading chapels. It often became reduced to Morning Prayer as the staple. Contrary to his wishes, JW's 5 a.m. preaching service became the distinctive Sunday order. In this the sermon was supplemented by elements of confession, praise and intercession, which could be sparse fare unless enlivened by *hymn-singing and by preaching for conversions, particularly on Sunday evenings. Though hymn-singing brought inspiration, warmth and a sense of unity, JW himself realised that it had its dangers, could be half-hearted or unthinking and he prescribed rules for it. The Methodist tradition of combining liturgical and free prayer is recognized in the Preface to the 1936 *Book of Offices*.

Methodism's contributions to worship, apart from 'our hymns', were the *Covenant Service, the *Watchnight and the *Love-feast, all borrowed by JW from elsewhere, but given new significance. The non-Wesleyan branches of Methodism eschewed set forms, until they came to realise that there were certain solemn occasions which should not be left entirely to the discretion of the worship leader. In the 1950s there was a feeling that Methodist worship had become 'slovenly'. A Conference commission was appointed and resulted in a revision of the *Book of Offices* and the authorization of the *Methodist Service Book* (1975), replaced in 1999 by the *Methodist Worship Book*. In recent years all-age worship has been introduced in many places. Some are unhappy with this as replacing liturgy by gimmicks, Wesley hymns by choruses, and as lacking a sense of the numinous. Methodism has never provided for Children's Eucharists as in Roman Catholicism and the Church of Scotland.

J. Bishop (1950); H. Davies (1961) pp. 184–209; T. Dearing (1966); R.J. Billington (1969); G.S. Wakefield (1998)

GSW

Publishing JW wanted the Methodists to be a reading people. It has been estimated that he and his brother published during their lifetime about 500 separate titles that contained their own writings or edited works, some of them running into several editions. These included sermons, hymns, tracts, abridgements of classic works, a pocket dictionary, *Primitive Physick* and the wide-ranging extracts collected in the fifty volumes of the *Christian Library*. This last, JW's most ambitious venture, was a publishing disaster in his lifetime.

W did much to remove literature from the confines of scholarship and make it available in cheap and popular form for the common people. He made precise arrangements for distribution: the itinerant preachers were to take books with them and sell them to reinforce the sermon, though not on Sundays. The MNC and PM were as keen as the WM to encourage reading and by the end of the nineteenth century no ministry was better read than that of PM.

JW established a 'book room' at the *Foundery in 1739. It was transferred to the 'new Chapel' in City Road in 1778 and in course of time it moved a little to the south along City Road. After the Union of 1932 Epworth House, a seven-storey building, housed Methodist publishing until 1969, being still known affectionately as 'the Book Room'. It then moved first to Wimbledon and in 1988 to Peterborough.

In 1918 the Epworth Press imprint was adopted, partly to distinguish official publications such as the Agenda and *Minutes* of Conference, hymnbooks and Service Books from more general titles. These included literature, theology, devotional works and biography and helped to subsidize less profitable works. There were also periodicals such as the *Methodist Magazine* and the *London Quarterly Review*.

The first PM book room was housed besides H. *Bourne's home at *Bemersley, Staffs, though PM and the MNC eventually had book rooms in London.

Welsh Methodism, in spite of its small numbers, had a publishing programme which produced over 400 books and pamphlets during the nineteenth century. Its Book Room (Y Llyfrfa) was first at Dolgellau, then in Llanfair Caereinion and Llanidloes, and from 1859 in Bangor. *Yr Eurgrawn* (from 1809 until merged into the interdenominational *Cristion* in 1983) became the oldest continuously published periodical in Welsh. *Y Trysor i Blentyn* (1825–42) and *Y Winllan* (1848–1963) were children's monthlies. *Y Gwyliedydd* (from 1877; since 1910, *Y Gwyliedydd Newydd*), is the connexional newspaper.

See also **Book Steward; Connexional Editor**

F. Baker (1984); D. Young (1893) pp. 717–24; T. Jones-Humphreys (1900); F.H. Cumbers (1956)
GSW/GTH

Pugh, Philip (1817–71; e.m. 1837), PM itinerant, born in *Shrewsbury. Until 1839 he served on the Irish Mission. He was *Connexional Editor from 1867 until his death and President of the Conference in 1869. He was a polemicist whose major disputations were with the Mormons and the hyper-Calvinist Samuel Cozens, a Willenhall Baptist minister, producing a series of pamphlets beginning in 1852.

J. Pritchard (1871)

DCD

Punshon, William Morley (1824–81; e.m. 1845), WM minister, born in *Doncaster to a Methodist family with trading connections in *Hull and *Sunderland, where he became a *local preacher. His uncle B. *Clough encouraged him to enter the ministry and he trained at *Richmond College. He was appointed to Hinde Street, London in 1858 on the strength of his growing reputation as a preacher and public lecturer. His lectures on Bunyan, Wilberforce and the Huguenots were highly popular and raised much money for the *Watering Places Fund and the *Metropolitan Chapel Building Fund. His wife's death and overwork ruined his health, which he tried to restore by a grand tour of Europe. He went to *Canada as British representative to its Conference and served as its President 1868–73. It was this period which made it possible for him to marry his sister-in-law. Returning to Britain he was elected President in 1874 and was Secretary of the WMMS from 1875 until his early death. Proceeds from his published lectures went to the *Thanksgiving Fund and his *Sabbath Chimes* was a well loved devotional on the Christian year. He was a founder and director of the *Methodist Recorder* and its first editor.

MR(W) 1905 pp. 67–8, 1907 pp. 47–8; F.W. Macdonald (1887); W. MacCullagh (1881); G.J. Stevenson (1884–6) 3 pp. 464–79; J. Dawson (1906)

TSAM

Purdy, Victory (1747–1822), WM *local preacher, born in *Bristol, son of **John Purdy** (d.1759), a member of the *Fetter Lane society and one of JW's earliest associates in Bristol. Victory became a counting-house clerk in a colliery office, but declined promotion, either through lack of confidence or from unwillingness to work on Sundays. A meticulous recorder of his activities, he calculated that in 41 years he had preached 2,882 sermons, travelling 22,896 miles, mostly on foot, and had read the Bible through 40 times, becoming known as 'the Walking Bible' and being allegedly capable of quoting over 100 texts in the course of one sermon. The anonymous contribution on 'Gospel Preachers Described and Directed' in the *Magazine* for 1819 was from his pen. He was a prolific hymnwriter and his *Poetical Miscellanies* (1826) included a memoir.

_____

PWHS 22 pp. 31–8; G. Pocock (1822); J. Edwards (1984)

CJS

Puritanism Dr Johnson's definition of 'Methodist' as 'a new kind of Puritan' contains a vital truth. Both Samuel and Susanna Wesley came from Puritan, Dissenting stock, whose influence was not obliterated by their conversion to High Church Anglicanism. Susanna ordered her *Epworth family life according to a careful 'method', with set times for teaching her children, prayer and meditation, and keeping a spiritual journal. She read Puritan authors, notably Richard Baxter, and drew up 'Rules' for family governance.

After 1738, JW rediscovered this Puritan tradition and injected it into his Methodism. It is the English Puritans who are most fully represented in his *Christian Library*. Like the mainstream Puritans, he sought to reform the CofE from within, and therefore empathized strongly with the Dissenting clergy forced out of the Church in 1660–62. He relished the 'Practical Divinity' of the great Puritans and used part of Baxter's *Reformed Pastor* as a manual of pastoral practice for his preachers. His *Covenant Service was derived from the Puritans Joseph and Richard Alleine, but transformed from an individual act of devotion into a corporate act of the worshipping community.

_____

F. Baker in *LQHR* July 1962 pp. 180–6; J.A. Newton (1964); R.C. Monk (1966)

JAN

Pusey, Rev. Dr Edward Bouverie (1800–82), Regius Professor of Hebrew at Oxford from 1828, contributed to the *Tracts for the Times* and was a leading Tractarian, especially after Newman's withdrawal in 1845. His *Letter to the Archbishop of Canterbury* (1842) condemned the Methodist doctrine of *assurance as the heresy of 'justification by feeling', leading to *antinomianism, in place of repentance, good works and the Sacraments. T. *Jackson's *Letter to the Rev. E.B. Pusey* (1842) was a vigorous and

detailed refutation of this. In 1868 Pusey's attempt to enlist Methodist and Nonconformist support for the Anglican monopoly of University education was rebuffed by the WM Conference.

_____

H.P. Liddon (1893–7); P. Butler (1983); *HMGB* 4 pp. 457–60, 532–3

JAV

Pyer, John *see* **Tent Methodism**

Pyke, Richard (1873–1965; e.m. 1894), BC minister and historian, born at Sampford Courtenay, Devon, the son of an agricultural labourer. Leaving school at 11, he worked for eight years on a farm but continued to educate himself. After a year's training at *Shebbear College under T. *Ruddle, he had a long and distinguished ministry which included appointments at Shebbear College as Governor (1915–22) and Bursar (1942) and culminated in his election as President of the UM Conference in 1927 and of the Methodist Conference in 1939. He wrote histories of the BCs (*The Golden Chain* (1915) and the WHS Lecture of 1941), of *Edgehill College, Bideford (1934 and 1957) and of Shebbear College (1953), and an autobiography, *Men and Memories* (1948).

_____

MR 30 Sept. 1965

TS

Quaker Methodists, one of the groups which came together to form the IM Connexion in the early nineteenth century. It was based in *Warrington. Initially its members were WM dissidents who were later joined by former Quakers. The group adopted a number of Quaker characteristics, including times of silent waiting upon God, plain dress and speech, non-sacramentalism and the rejection of paid ministry. However, it also retained Methodist elements such as *classmeetings, *band meetings, a *circuit and a *preaching plan. By the middle of the century the name was dropped and the group became known as 'Independent Methodist', having lost most of its Quaker characteristics.

See also **Phillips, P.**

_____

A. Mounfield (1924)

JAD

Quakerism JW's churchmanship inevitably led him to repudiate many aspects of Quaker belief and practice, especially its use of *Scripture, its theology of *salvation, its abandonment of the sacraments of *baptism and the *Lord's Supper, its silent worship and, not least, its willing acceptance of *women preachers. In his 'Letter to a Quaker' he writes: 'Friend, you have an honest heart but a weak head – come back, come back to the weightier matters of the law, to spiritual, rational scriptural religion.' So, at a formal level the relationship between Methodism and the Society of Friends was cool; but the larger picture is more complex and more positive. J W himself rejoiced at receiving a substantial contribution from a rich Quaker towards the cost of building the Newcastle *Orphan House and one of his earliest evangelical bases in the north was a Quaker farmhouse at Hindley Hill in Allendale. In day-to-day contacts there was a good deal of mutual interest and attraction between Quaker and Methodist layfolk. Some Methodists turned Quaker, but in general the trend was in the opposite direction, largely owing to the attractions of the vigorous young Methodist movement to Quakers aware of the decline in zeal of Quakerism. In this process Methodism began to learn from the Quakers. The first Methodist *quarterly meeting (a Quaker practice) was held in a Quaker farmhouse near *Todmorden. Quaker influence was stronger on the more radical non-Wesleyan Connexions, especially *IM and *PM. H. *Bourne, though never persuaded to throw in his lot with them, adopted some Quaker practices. The first PM Conference (1820) was described as an 'Annual Meeting' and was preceded in 1819 by a 'Preparatory Meeting' – both terms being in Quaker use. The PMs also adopted a Quaker simplicity and plainness in dress and a 'natural' hair style for men. Both Bourne and W. *Clowes were described as like Quakers in appearance. But perhaps the most radical Quaker influence on the PMs was the example they offered of the potential of women preachers and the divine legitimacy of their call.

Telford (1931) pp. 116–28; F. Baker in *LQHR* 1948 pp. 312–23, 1949 pp. 239–48; J.C. Bowmer in *Religion and Life* 23 (1954); G. Nuttall (1967) pp. 204–13; G.E. Milburn in WHS(NE) Feb. 1981 pp. 13–17

GEM

Quarterly Meeting This part of Methodism's organization, derived from the Quakers, was introduced by J. *Bennet and evolved with the *Circuit system. The 1748 Conference had stated that the societies should be more firmly and closely united together, and the first circuit Quarterly Meeting was presided over by W. *Grimshaw at *Todmorden Edge on

October 18 1748. Others soon followed, the development being particularly encouraged by Bennet, and in 1749 the Conference laid down that an *Assistant responsible for a Circuit had a duty 'to hold Quarterly Meetings, and therein diligently to enquire both into the spiritual and temporal state of each Society'. By 1753 they were established in all 12 existing Circuits. They were gatherings of the preachers, the *circuit stewards and the *society stewards and *leaders from the various societies, meeting to deal with financial matters and other activities and to exercise spiritual oversight, and including a time of worship and fellowship (and often dinner).

In 1852, following the recent agitations and secessions, the WM Conference made the Quarterly Meeting more representative, clearly defining its constitution for the first time. It was to include ministers and probationers stationed there, circuit stewards, and all society and poor stewards, class leaders, *local preachers of three years standing and trustees in the Circuit. (Other responsible officers were later added.) It also gave the meeting the right to hear appeals in certain *discipline cases and to approach Conference directly and freely via a *Memorial, whilst reserving 'the integrity of the pastoral office, the inviolability of the connexional principle and the authority of District Committees'.

Other Methodist connexions followed a similar pattern of quarterly meetings (sometimes under other names e.g. 'Quarter Day Board'), and the meeting's constitution continued essentially unaltered in 1932. In the 1974 *Restructuring it was eventually replaced, in a reduced form, by the Circuit Meeting which was to meet at least twice annually.

PWHS 7 pp. 78–81, 26 pp. 105–9; *LQHR* 1949 pp. 28–37; *HMGB* 1 pp. 239–42; H.W. Williams (1881) pp. 87–98

SRH

Queen's College, Taunton, founded in 1843 by local Methodists as the West of England Proprietary Grammar School, became a Collegiate Institute of London University in 1846 and a centre for ministerial training, attracting scholarship boys from *Kingswood and *Woodhouse Grove schools. Its buildings were designed by J. *Wilson. There was a change in status from the 1870s, following freer access to the old universities and the growth of civic universities. Queen's became a *Board of Management school in 1930 and has maintained its high academic standards and its reputation for games, music and drama. In 1997 it had 700 boarding and day boys and girls aged 4–18.

H.J. Channon (1957)

DBT

Queen's College, The, Edgbaston, *Birmingham, was formed as the first ecumenical theological college in Britain by the transfer of the proceeds from the sale of *Handsworth College to the Anglican Queen's College, originally a medical college founded in 1828. This had been recognized since 1934 for the training of ordinands. On its opening in 1970, there were 87 students from six denominations, men training for the ordained ministry and women for the Wesley *Deaconess Order. Close links were developed with Oscott (RC) and the Selly Oak Colleges. Since 1972 it has been the home of the West Midlands Ministerial Training Course for non-residential students. In 1996 the College was reformulated as the Queen's Foundation, of which the College, the Training Course and a Theological Research Centre are constituent parts.

TSAM

Queenswood, founded in 1869 in Clapton, East London, as a school for ministers' daughters, acquired its present name when it moved to Clapham. Soon after its closure by Conference in 1893 it reopened as a limited company. It moved to its present site near Hatfield in 1925. From its early years it offered a sound liberal education and had its first success in Cambridge Entrance in 1913. It established a national reputation for music under the directorship of Professor Ernest Read (1920–65). In the 1980s it launched an extensive building programme and achieved a strong sporting and academic reputation, with emphasis on science and technology. In 1997 it had 378 boarding and day girls aged 11–18.

N. Watson (1994)

DBT

Quetteville *see* **de Quetteville**

Race Family (WM and PM) of Weardale. **Anthony Race** was one of the most active WM *local preachers in the dale in the later eighteenth and early nineteenth centuries. His son, also **Anthony Race**, joined the PMs on their arrival in Weardale and served for several years in the 1820s as an itinerant. **George Race** (1810–86), son of Anthony junr, a grocer and draper in the dale, was a leading PM layman in the North for

half a century, and one of its most learned and scholarly preachers. His son, also **George Race** (d.1911), an architect and builder, designed a number of attractive PM chapels in the north-east, including that at Westgate where the Races themselves worshipped.

PMM 1883 pp. 155–60; 1892 pp. 20–4

GEM

Race, Philip (1916–), older son of an old Wesleyan family from Weardale. Both his grandfather **Joseph Race** (1848–1880; e.m. 1872), a missionary in China with D. *Hill, and his father died young. Following in his father's footsteps he became a *Lincoln solicitor. He spent 15 years writing scripts for and producing drama at MAYC London Weekends and became its Vice-President in 1950. He helped to form the Westminster Laymen's Movement in 1954 and was Vice-President of the Conference in 1957. He was the youngest and only lay member of both the *Anglican-Methodist Conversations, 1955–63 and the Anglican-Methodist Unity Commission, 1965–8. His younger brother **Steve Race** (1921–) made his name as a musician and broadcaster.

MR 11 July 1957; S. Race (1979); S. Race (1988)

JHL

Ramsden, Alfred (1827–92), the son of John Ramsden, a schoolmaster who moved to *Halifax in 1832, where he joined his brother's corn-marketing business and became one of the original trustees of New Hanover Street MNC chapel. Alfred, after 16 years as a druggist, joined the *Halifax Courier* as a reporter in 1857, subsequently becoming editor and joint-proprietor. Prominent in local Liberal politics, he became a town councillor in 1876, alderman in 1880, mayor in 1883–4 and in 1886 became the first provincial newspaper editor to be appointed a magistrate. He taught a large adult class at the Hanover Street Sunday School for nearly 20 years and for 15 years was *local preacher's secretary. He was secretary of four MNC Conferences between 1869 and 1889.

J.A. Hargreaves in WHS(Y) 49 (Sept. 1986)

JAH

Randles, Marshall, DD (1826–1904; e.m. 1852) was Tutor in Systematic Theology at *Didsbury College, 1886–1902. His *Fernley Lecture on *The Design and Use of Holy Scripture* (1892) including a chapter predictably defending the

Bible against the 'Higher Criticism'. He was President of the Conference in 1896.

MR 7 & 14 July 1904

JAV

Rank, Joseph (1854–1943) was born in *Hull and converted in Kingston Chapel. From humble beginnings he became a highly successful flour miller, noted for his great benevolence especially to Methodist causes such as the *Twentieth Century Fund. He supported the building of central halls as part of the *Forward Movement, especially at Tooting (opened 1910) where he lived in later years. His son **J(oseph) Arthur Rank** (1888–1972; knighted 1957) took over and diversified the family business in 1952. The Lord Rank Research Centre at High Wycombe was set up to promote food technology. To improve the effectiveness of Christian witness, he promoted the Religious Film Society in 1933 and later the Churches Television Centre. He set up Pinewood Studios in 1936 and gained control of most of the British film industry. Despite differing from the Methodist line on *gambling, he served for many years as treasurer of the *Home Missions Department and of *Westminster Central Hall. Many causes have benefited from the Joseph Rank Benevolent Trust and from the Rank Foundation which Arthur Rank set up to safeguard his assets from an American take-over. Its aims include the promotion of education, of 'the Christian religion by any lawful means' and of 'the study of the history of the Christian faith'.

See also **Arthur Rank Centre**

MR 18 Nov. 1943, 6 & 13 April 1972; *Times*, 5 April 1972; R.G. Burnett (1945); G. MacNab (1993); M. Wakelin (1996)

JAV

Rankin, Thomas (1738–1810; e.m. 1761), early itinerant from *Dunbar, East Lothian. Religiously awakened by the preaching of G. *Whitefield, he was later attracted to WM. JW appointed him to his first circuit in 1761 and he was destined to have one of the longest and most influential ministries of all W's preachers. In 1773 JW sent him as Superintendent of the work in *America where he gave five years of strenuous labour in building up the Methodist societies. In June 1773 he had the distinction of presiding at the first American Methodist Conference. He returned to England in 1778, and from 1783 until a few months before his death was a very active supernumerary in London. Noted as a man of unbending principle and a rigid disciplinarian, his relations with colleagues were not always easy. JW, however, thought highly of him, named him as one of the *Legal Hundred in 1784 and ordained him for the work in England in 1789. In the last decade of JW's life Rankin was one of a small number of the senior preachers who constituted a kind of 'inner cabinet' which advised him on many matters, though he was never elected President of the Conference after W's death.

EMP 5 pp. 135–217

HMG

Ranmoor College was opened in Sheffield in 1864 as a base for training for the MNC ministry, with a £5,000 bequest from T. *Firth Junr. This was the culmination of a 30-year effort which had begun in 1835 with the personal tuition offered by T. *Allin. The college accommodated 16 students, who normally followed a two-year course, but it was rarely, if ever, full. The funds were sufficient only for the Principal, supported by part-time staff. The Union of 1907 meant that the UMC had two colleges, neither of which was large enough. In 1910 the normal course was extended to three years and from 1913 Ranmoor provided for first-year students only, who then transferred to *Victoria Park College for two years. After requisition in World War I Ranmoor was sold to Sheffield City Council in 1919, the proceeds endowing the Ranmoor Chair at *Hartley Victoria College. The building was demolished in the 1960s.

See also **Hobill Collection**

W.B. Brash (1934) pp. 152–6; D.C. Dews (1987) pp. 11–22

EAR/TSAM

Ranson, Dr Charles Wesley (1903–88; e.m. 1927), Irish missionary to *India. Born in Ballyclare, Co. Antrim, he was educated at *Methodist College, Belfast and Oriel College, Oxford and went to India in 1929. He was secretary of the National Christian Council of India, Burma and Ceylon, 1943–45, and of the International Missionary Council, 1946–58, Director of the IMC's Theological Education Fund, 1958–62, and professor, then Dean, at Drew University, NJ, 1962–68. He was President of the Methodist Church in Ireland, 1961–62. He wrote *A City in Transit: Studies in the Social Life of Madras* (1938) and *The Christian Minister in India* (1945).

MR 11 Feb. 1988; C.W. Ranson (1988)

NWT

Ranston, Dr Harry (1878–1971; e.m. 1901), biblical scholar, born Harry Ramsbottom at Keighley, Yorks. He started work at 10, but through night school obtained scholarships to higher education and joined the local PM society. At *Hartley College he came under the influence of A.S. *Peake. He arrived in *New Zealand in 1902, changing his name c. 1904, when he transferred to the WM Conference. While serving in South Island circuits he completed his MA in Greek and Semitic languages. Moving to Auckland in 1916 he taught part-time at the Theological College. In 1923 he gained a DLitt for a thesis published as *Ecclesiastes and the Early Greek Wisdom Literature* (1925). *The Old Testament Wisdom Books and their Teaching* (1930) established him as a scholar of some international repute. He is credited with having secured for Trinity College, Auckland its reputation as a teaching institution, giving it its strong biblical basis. He served on the Auckland University Council and was examiner in Hebrew for the University of New Zealand. His unsophisticated character endeared him to his students.

DJP

Rattenbury Family **John Rattenbury**, WM minister (1806–79; e.m. 1828) was born in Tavistock, grew up in *Manchester and was converted by R. *Newton. He was an almost hypnotic preacher and revivalist, who attracted many hearers, had many conversions and adopted the penitent form and the prayer meeting following the service. He launched the *Metropolitan Chapels Building Fund and was elected President of the 1861 Conference. His son **H. Owen Rattenbury** (1843–1904; e.m. 1863) had two sons who also became ministers. **J. Ernest Rattenbury** (1870–1963; e.m. 1893) was closely associated with Central Halls. He was responsible for setting up the Albert Hall, *Nottingham (1902–7) and was sent to revive the West London Mission after the death of H.P. *Hughes. He built the Kingsway Hall and filled it with 'fiery sermons rebuking eminent sceptics'. In 1903 he helped to found the WM *Union for Social Service. He led the WM opposition to *Methodist Union in 1932. He founded the Methodist *Sacramental Fellowship. Notable among his writings are *The Conversion of the Wesleys* (1938), his Fernley-Hartley Lecture *The Evangelical Doctrines of Charles Wesley's Hymns* (1941) and a pioneering study of *The Eucharistic Hymns of John and Charles Wesley* (1948). His brother **Harold Burgoyne Rattenbury** (1878–1961; e.m. 1902) was a missionary in Hupeh, *China, 1902–35, arranging for the first Chinese national to become Chairman of the District. As Missionary Secretary in London he advocated decentralization of the Chinese Church, facilitating its survival under Communist rule after 1949. He wrote a number of popular books about China and was President of the 1949 Conference.

———

MR 7 July 1949, 4 Jan. 1962, 24 & 31 Jan. 1963; H.O. Rattenbury (1884); H.M. Rattenbury (1994); P.W. Chilcote on J.E. Rattenbury in *MH* 21 (1982–3) pp. 207–24

JHL

Reading JW's early visits were at the invitation of J. *Cennick, but on later occasions he found the local population unresponsive. The society had ceased to exist by 1804 and a new start had to be made in 1811 when Reading was made one of the early *Home Mission stations. The ministry of J. *Waterhouse in 1816–19 gave new impetus to the cause and the first purpose-built chapel was opened in Church Street in 1817; but the debt on the property was not finally cleared until 1867. It was then replaced by 'Wesley'(1873), a much larger gothic chapel in Queen's Road. Later chapels included Oxford Road (1893) and Whitley Hall (1906). The PM Shefford Circuit missioned Reading in 1835 and a circuit was formed in 1837. Their London Street chapel, built as a Mechanics' Institute in 1843, was taken over in 1866, and they opened chapels in Cumberland Road (1871) and West Reading (1906). Wartime conditions hastened the union of the Queen's Road and London Street congregations in 1940.

———

M.F. Jordan (1973)

JAV

Ready, William (1860–1927; e.m. 1885), BC minister in *New Zealand, was born in a London workhouse to Irish RC parents. Orphaned at 5, he lived by his wits on the streets, but at 12 was sent to George Müller's orphanage in *Bristol, where he received his education. Converted at 17, in 1884 he was he went for training to *Shebbear College. He arrived in New Zealand in 1887 in answer to a call for help. The highlight of his ministry was the nine years in which he established the Dunedin Central Mission, where he is said to have preached to the largest congregations in New Zealand. His open-air work brought him into contact with pressing social needs and in response he initiated the Sisters of the Poor. Undoubtedly his childhood experiences gave him both sympathy for the plight of the poor and a passion for social justice. Coupled with his exceptional gifts as both street and pulpit orator, these made him an influential figure in the Church of his time. He was an active temperance advocate, particularly through the work of the Good Templars. Visiting England in 1897, he toured the BC circuits raising funds for overseas missions. He was President of the New Zealand BC Conference in 1912.

L.H. Court (1935)

DJP

Redruth and Camborne and the adjoining area (including *Gwennap) were a flourishing centre of tin-mining when the Wesleys first visited West Cornwall in 1743. Between 1743 and 1789 JW paid 29 visits to Redruth and 10 to Camborne. At Redruth his hosts included Andrew and Elizabeth Harper and he later published 'Extracts' from Elizabeth's Journal to exemplify *Christian perfection. Soon after his death in 1791, a meeting of 51 representative Methodist laymen was convened at Redruth and adopted a series of resolutions aimed at democratizing Methodism. These anticipated the future reformed branches of WM and the UMFC. In Redruth the *Lombardo-Venetian style WMA chapel (1865) reached its centenary before being destroyed by fire in 1973. The successive PM chapels (1827 and 1884) and the BC chapel (1864) are still standing, but Wesley Chapel (1826) is now the only Methodist Church in the town.

At Camborne JW formed a friendship with Richard Trevithic. Wesley Chapel (1828, modelled on *Wesley's Chapel, London) hosted four WM Conferences between 1862 and 1903. Prominent figures associated with the chapel include Charles Thomas of Killivose (1798–1868), founder of the fortunes of the important Dolcoath mine, and the historians G. *Smith, and J.W. *Etheridge. Centenary Chapel was built in 1839. Trelowarren Street chapel was one of the very few MNC causes in Cornwall.

TS

Reed Family, of Holwell, *Shebbear, Devon, was one of the oldest BC families. **William Reed**, farmer, and his wife **Catherine**, opened their home to W. *O'Bryan and his preachers from c. 1816. From them descended three generations of BC leaders and their daughter **Catherine Reed** married J. *Thorne. **William Reed** (1800–58; e.m. 1820) was President of the Conference in 1832, 1837, 1845 and 1855. His son **William Bryan Reed** (1836–1936; e.m. 1860) was one of

the first pupils at Prospect School, *Shebbear. Before entering the ministry he worked as a chemist in London. His annual introduction to the Home Mission report revealed his width of outlook, evangelical spirit, mental grasp and literary style. He was Secretary of the Conference 1879–80 and President in 1881, and was the first Governor of *Edgehill College, Bideford, 1883–1909. In the next generation, his son **John Ford Reed** (1869–1962; e.m. 1887) was resident governor of Shebbear College 1922–36 and President of the Conference in 1931.

J. Thorn (1869); G.J. Stevenson (1884–6) 6 pp. 881–7

TS

Reed, Bryan Holwell (1905–91; e.m. 1926), fourth-generation minister of the BC tradition. By directing the Church's attention to alienated young people, he enabled a response to the changing society of the 1960s. He early took initiatives in youth ministry, establishing a 'Clubland' at Walthamstow. In 1946 he became lecturer in Youth Work at Westhill College, *Birmingham, training youth leaders for the post-war world. His survey *Eighty Thousand Adolescents* (1950) became a basic document. As General Secretary of the Youth Department from 1953, he nurtured the growth of MAYC. He personally conducted the 'Million Half-Crowns' appeal which, with the generosity of H.G. *Chester, made possible MYD's move from Ludgate Circus to Chester House, Muswell Hill.

See also **Youth Work**

MR 9 Jan. 1992

CHS

Reed, William (1820–85; e.m. 1838), WMA and UMFC minister. Becoming a *local preacher when only 15, his early ministry was spent largely in the north before being appointed to a succession of connexional offices. Though he himself wrote very little, he served as *Book Steward 1860–65 and *Connexional Editor 1860–70. In his public speeches and in debate he was one of the most vociferous defenders of the UMFC principles of free representation and circuit independence. He was President of the 1862 Conference.

G.J. Stevenson (1884–6) 6 pp. 960–8

OAB

Rees, Ronald David (1888–1975; e.m. 1913), WM missionary. After two years as Assistant

Tutor at *Handsworth College, he worked for the Student Christian Movement. In 1922 he went to the South *China District and in 1930 was seconded to the National Christian Council of China for 17 years. Returning home in 1947 he served as International Secretary of the BCC.

————

MR 15 Jan. 1976

GRS

Reeth *see* **Dales Circuit**

Reeves, Rev. Jonathan (d. 1787) one of W's earliest *'Assistants,' active in Cornwall, Ireland and northern England. J. *Nelson, stated in 1744: 'On my return to *Leeds, I found that the Lord had greatly blessed the labours of Jonathan Reeves and John Bennet: several being converted by their preaching both there and at Birstal.' Reeves attended the Conferences of 1746, 1747 and 1748. In 1746 he was appointed a trustee of the *Orphan House, Newcastle. In 1758 he left Methodism and became the first Chaplain of the Magdalen Hospital, London. He later became a curate in Whitechapel and lecturer at West Ham.

C. Atmore (1801) pp. 345–6

SRV

Regeneration (or 'new birth') is the entry into salvation by the pardoned sinner, the full realisation of becoming a child of God. Fear and sin are replaced by adoption through *faith in Christ into the family of the redeemed. This inward change in the believer, enables growth into the image of God. *Baptism may be the sign of the reality of the new birth or a sealing in anticipation of its fulfilment. Regeneration must lead to increasing *holiness, or it may be made void by falling away from proffered *grace. For JW it was imperative for the life of faith. It is not a static condition or relationship, but must demonstrate the marks of the new birth, such as ever-developing transformation and anticipation of the full potential of grace.

————

JW, sermons on 'The New Birth' and 'The Great Privilege of those that are Born of God'; K. Collins (1989); R.L. Maddox (1994) pp. 77–9

WP

Regnal League A WM minister Donald Standfast (1884–1951; e.m. 1908) with a particular concern for the welfare of young people and involved in the early Scout movement, served in World War I, first as a private and then as a chaplain during the Battle of the Somme. In 1918

he formed the 'League of Friendship' at Bethune, with branches throughout the British Army. After the war this developed into the Regnal League with the ideal of wholeness of life and the aims of developing body, mind and spirit through Christian fellowship and service. Local groups, known as 'Circles' were attached mainly, but not exclusively, to Methodist churches. Women's Circles were also formed and at its height the League had nearly 400 Circles. These were reduced to fewer than 50 by the end of World War II. After 'Padre' Standfast's death leadership passed to David ('Dai') Samuel, MBE (1907–93), a layman and *local preacher from Rhondda.

————

MR 15 Nov. 1951; D. Samuel (1993)

JAV

Reid, Alexander (1821–91; e.m. 1848), WM missionary to *New Zealand, was born a Scottish Presbyterian and taught in both Scotland and England before entering the ministry. In New Zealand he took charge of the Native Training Institution in Auckland and was its Principal for ten years, earning for high esteem with the government. His success with the Maori students led to his appointment to Waipa in Northland 1858–63, followed by 21 years in major circuits. He was President of the Conference in 1876, having been its Secretary for two years and a District Chairman for six. He attended the first Oecumenical Methodist Conference in 1882. He ended his ministry at the Three Kings College (1885–91), which had reopened for the training of both European and Maori students for the ministry.

DJP

Religious Census of 1851 A census of places of worship and attendances was held as part of the decennial population census in March 1851, despite objections and some boycotting, chiefly Anglican. The main questions related to the number of sittings and the actual or average attendances. A *Report* was published in 1854, containing many statistical tables at national, county and registration district levels. There was considerable disquiet that only around 50% of the population attended at least one service on Census day and, among Anglicans, that Protestant and Catholic nonconformists made up half of those attending. Methodism was found to be the largest Nonconformist body, with Wesleyanism recording 6,579 places of worship, providing 1,361,443 sittings and an overall total of 1,513,304 worshippers at all services.

Interpretation of the original returns (now at

the Public Record Office in Kew) is problematical, but considerable scholarly attention has been given to them in recent years and the returns for a number of counties have been published.

HMGB 4 (1988), 499–505; J.A. Vickers (1996)

JAV

Religious Societies In or about 1678 a group of young men began to meet under the leadership of Dr Anthony Horneck, Prebendary of Westminster, to promote their own spiritual and moral life and to support charitable causes. They were the first of a number of such 'religious societies', both in and around London and further afield. Samuel Wesley senior formed one at *Epworth in 1701. Before and after his Georgia ministry, JW was in touch with a several of these societies, including one meeting at the home of the *Huttons in London, and another at *Oxford. In some respects, e.g. in the Rules they adopted and the appointment of 'Stewards' whose function resembled that of Methodist class leaders, they anticipated the later *societies under JW's leadership. But they were not evangelistic and the original rule that they should place themselves under a clerical director, was gradually abandoned. The support they received from the SPCK, including the gift of books, ceased soon after the rise of the Methodist movement.

See also **Fetter Lane Society**

D. Pike in *PWHS* 35 pp. 15–20, 32–38; R.P. Heitzenrater (1989) pp. 33–45

JAV

Residential Schools (Methodist) There are thirteen independent schools which report annually to *Conference through the Methodist Council. Apart from The *Leys, *Kingswood and *Woodhouse Grove, they are the survivors of a number of boarding schools founded by local initiatives to enable children from middle-class Methodist homes to progress beyond elementary education: *Shebbear College (BC, 1834), *Queen's College, Taunton (1843), *Ashville College, Harrogate (1877), *Truro School (1880), *Rydal Penrhos School, *Colwyn Bay (comprising the former Penrhos (1880) and Rydal (1885) schools), *Culford School, Bury St Edmunds (1881), *Edgehill College, Bideford (1884), *Kent College, Canterbury (1885), *Kent College, Pembury (1886) and *Farringtons, Chiselhurst (1911). Their development was quickened by the success of the Irish schools – the Wesley Connexional School (1845) and its successor,

*Wesley College, Dublin (1879) and *Methodist College, Belfast (1868) – and by the opening of the Universities of Oxford and Cambridge to Nonconformists in 1871.

As qualified lay headmasters and mistresses replaced ministerial 'Governors', school chaplains were appointed, usually separated from circuit responsibilities. They were responsible for arranging school worship, taught (but not necessarily RE), exercised pastoral care of staff and pupils, and offered training for church membership or confirmation.

In 1997 there were some 8,700 day and boarding pupils in these schools, from a variety of religious and social backgrounds.

See also **Education**

J.M. Gibbs (1989)

DBT

Restructuring Since *Methodist Union, there have been two major periods of organizational change, in the early 1970s and the early 1990s.

With regard to **local and circuit structure**, a committee reported to the 1970 Conference with proposals for replacing the 'dual control' of the local church through the *trustees and *leaders' meetings with a single *Church Council having oversight over the church's life and working usually through various defined committees. Provision was made for lay persons to chair such committees. The replacement, in official usage, of the term 'society' by 'local church' was also a significant change. The committee further recommended a considerable reduction in the size and minimum number of meetings of the Circuit *Quarterly Meeting, re-naming it Circuit Meeting, again with specified circuit committees to be appointed.

These changes came into effect in 1974, except that it was not until the 'appointed day' under the *Methodist Church Act 1976, i.e. April 16 1977, that *model trust property became vested in custodian trustees and the Church Council and Circuit Meeting assumed responsibility as managing trustees. Since then, particularly in 1992–3, the Conference has approved considerable 'de-regulation' with regard to local and circuit structures and constitution of meetings.

Connexional re-organization resulted from the Report on Departmental Structure and Function to the Conference of 1969. From 1973, various connexional bodies, committees and boards were formed into new groupings, comprising (in addition to the *General Purposes Committee and *President's Council) seven **Divisions**, responsible respectively for: Education and Youth, Finance, Home Mission, Ministries, Overseas Mission, Property and Social Responsibility. Each was headed by a General Secretary and oversight exercised by an elected Divisional Board.

The *President's Council's Report on Divisional Structure and Function in 1992 recommended that to achieve more effective and flexible use of resources a more unified structure was required. From 1996 the work carried out in the Divisions became the responsibility of a single Connexional Team, led by four Co-ordinating Secretaries (in collaboration with the *Secretary of Conference) having general responsibility respectively for the areas of church life, church and society, inter-church and other relationships, and central services. The Methodist Council assumed responsibility for the oversight of the work formerly under the Divisional Boards, and also took over the functions of the *General Purposes Committee and *President's Council, all these bodies being abolished.

Conference Agendas: 1969, pp. 538–58; 1970, pp. 39–88; 1992, pp. 605–30; 1993, pp. 650–96; 1995, pp. 766–827; T. Shaw in *PWHS* vol. 41 pp. 129–32; G.T. Brake (1984) pp. 77–87

SRH

Retford (formerly East Retford) JW must have passed through frequently after the Great North Road was diverted through the town in 1766. According to local tradition he addressed a rowdy crowd in the market square in 1779 and another visit is recorded in his *Journal* in 1786. A Scottish cattle drover had formed a society about 1776 and the first chapel, in Spa Lane, was registered in 1781. Originally in the Epworth Circuit, Retford became the head of its own circuit in 1802. In 1822 a larger chapel, flanked by preachers' houses, was erected in Grove Street for a membership of 250 in a circuit of 820. This was replaced on the same site by the present chapel in 1880. Other chapels were opened in Albert Road (1898) and Ordsall.

PM missionaries from Nottingham arrived in 1819 and within two years Retford was the centre of a new circuit. Temporary premises were replaced in 1841 by the purchase of a Georgian theatre in Carolgate, dubbed, following alterations, the 'Swingboat' Chapel. With an average congregation of 270 this was replaced on the same site in 1870.

A *Countess of Huntingdon chapel was built

privately in Chapel Gate in 1795, but soon foundered. Following Congregationalist use, in 1851 a newly-formed WR society (head of yet another Retford Circuit) moved in. It became UMFC and was rebuilt in 1879.

B.J. Biggs (1970)

BJB

'Reverend'   Wesley drew a clear distinction (e.g. in his 'Korah' sermon of 1789) between his lay itinerants ('prophets') and the ordained clergy ('priests'). He allowed the itinerants he ordained for *Scotland in 1785 to use the title 'Reverend', but not when they returned to England. After his death some advocates of separation from the CofE, such as S. *Bradburn, began using the title. But the 1792 Conference ruled against its use in the interests of 'simplicity and plainness'. This was modified the following year to a ban on its being used 'by us toward each other', along with the distinction between those ordained and the rest of the preachers. Unofficially its use continued to grow and was reinstated in 1818 (in place of 'Preacher of the Gospel'). Dissidents included Dr A. *Clarke who in 1821 disclaimed any right to its use because he was not episcopally ordained. Anglican disapproval of the extension of the title to Nonconformist ministers was highlighted in 1874 when the WM Conference went to law over a refusal by the incumbent at Owston Ferry, Lincs, to allow it on a tombstone. Outside WM, the title was generally adopted, though J. *Thorne was long opposed to its use in BC, condemning it as 'unscriptural and a badge of popery'. The WMA abandoned it between 1836 and 1845 and as late as 1876 there was an attempt by W. *Griffith to persuade the UMFC Conference to discontinue its use.

See also **Burials**; **Ordination**

PWHS 33 pp. 134–6; J.M. Turner (1985) p. 133; *MR* 6 Nov. 1975

JMT

Revivalism denotes the deliberate organizing or planning for a revival of religion. Success was not assured, but during the century after JW's death such efforts, predominantly but not exclusively Methodist and often under American influences, did lead to large periodic increases of membership in Cornwall and many parts of the North and Midlands. Associated with such WM figures as W. *Bramwell, J. *Smith, H. *Casson and T. *Collins, and W. *Booth in the MNC, revivalism penetrated all branches of Methodism.

The WM, PM and MNC sought to diminish the influence of revivalists, and the WM interdict on J. *Caughey was a secondary factor in the WR agitation.

J. Kent (1978); C.H. Goodwin (1994)

WP

Revivalist Methodists *see* **Winfield, R.**

Rhodes, Benjamin (1743–1815; e.m. 1766), an early itinerant, born at Mexborough, Yorks was apprenticed in his youth in the wool and worsted business. For a time he came under the influence of CM, but at 21 heard P. *Jaco and joined the WMs, first as a class leader and then itinerant preacher. When stationed in Cornwall, he was advised by JW not to give class tickets to those 'who deal in stolen goods' (i.e. smugglers). He wrote several hymns, some for children, the best-known being 'My heart and voice I raise' (HP 268).

EMP 6 pp. 223–34

WL

Rhodesia *see* **Zambia**; **Zimbabwe**

Rich, John (*c.* 1682–1761), born in London, the son of Christopher Rich, patentee of Drury Lane theatre, which he was forced to leave. John and his brother took over the new theatre his father had built in Lincoln's Inn Fields as a rival to Drury Lane, and then built the first Covent Garden theatre. His third wife, a waitress before going on the stage, was one of the first worshippers at *West Street Chapel. A notable convert of the Wesleys, she threatened to make a public testimony if her husband forced her to return to the stage. Despite considerable opposition and derision from friends and colleagues, Rich eventually became a close friend of the Methodists, especially CW and his family, and it was at his home that CW met J.F. *Lampe.

PLC

Richards, Rev. Thomas (1717–98), early Methodist itinerant and Anglican clergyman, educated at Trinity College, Oxford (but without graduating). Influenced by the Rev. John Thorold, JW's predecessor as Fellow of Lincoln College, and by the Rev. G. *Jones of Llanddowror, he associated himself with the Wesleys and JW later referred to him, along with T. *Maxfield and T. *Westell, as one of his first lay assistants. In 1744 he was an itinerant in Yorkshire and Derbyshire and was present at the first two *Conferences in 1744 and 1745. In 1746 JW made him a trustee of his properties in *Bristol and *Newcastle. He became language master at *Kingswood School in 1748, but was not a success in the classroom and returned to the itinerancy in 1751. He left in 1759 and with the Countess of *Huntingdon's support was ordained, serving for over 30 years as curate of St Sepulchre's, London.

DEB

JAV

Richardson, Amy (1872–1953), missionary in Eastern *Nigeria, the first single woman to become a PM missionary. With 15 years' teaching experience in *Leeds, she was appointed to the new Girls' Institute at Jamestown, Eastern Nigeria, in 1909. During her 44 years in West ASfrica she helped to build up the Institute, which included a girls' boarding school and a teacher training centre. After its removal to Oron, under the name of the Mary Hanney Memorial School, it became renowned throughout Nigeria. Her appointment was hailed as the beginning of a new epoch in PM Missions and led to the formation of a Women's Missionary Federation, which gave particular support to the first women missionaries. She was the main speaker at its first public meeting and aroused such enthusiasm that there was a steady stream of missionary candidates. By *Methodist Union in 1932, there were 18 PM women missionaries and over 30,000 members of the Federation.

See also **Women's Work**

PM Missionary Society's *The Herald*, 1905–31 passim

JRP/PMW

Richardson, Charles (1791–1864), born at Fullerby, Lincs, had no schooling, but early in life developed a thirst for books and was self-taught. He became a farm-labourer and was known as 'the Lincolnshire Thrasher'. As a preacher and class leader he was in popular demand. In 12 years he opened no fewer than 38 chapels and soon was travelling into neighbouring counties and as far away as Cornwall and Wales. In 1844 he preached at *Wesley's Chapel, London. He kept a diary and wrote many letters to his wife.

J.E. Coulson (1865)

WL

Richardson, Rev. John (1733–92), son of an alehouse keeper of Kirkleatham, Yorks. While curate at Ewhurst, Sussex (1759–62), his prejudices were dispelled by contacts with local Methodists and he was converted by T. *Rankin in 1762. His evangelical preaching drew large congregations, but also complaints to the rector. Dismissed from his post in November 1762, he joined JW in London and later was one of the Readers at *Wesley's Chapel, where he conducted JW's funeral service in 1791.

C. Atmore (1801) pp. 356–65; *PWHS* 15 pp. 3–4, 21 pp. 97–101

JAV

Richardson, Dr Kathleen Margaret, OBE, Baroness Richardson of Calow (*née* Fountain, 1938–), trained in religious education at Stockwell College. She entered the Wesley *Deaconess Order in 1961 and, resigning on marriage in 1964, worked as pastoral assistant in a Methodist/Anglican Church in Stevenage. Accepted for the ministry in 1976, she trained at *Wesley House and was ordained in 1980. In 1987 she became the first woman appointed to a *District Chair (West Yorkshire) and in 1992 the first woman President of the Conference. In 1995 she became Co-ordinating Secretary for Inter-church and Other Relationships and in 1998 was the first ordained woman to enter the Lords as a life peer.

MR 7 Feb. 1991

PMW

Richmond (Surrey) Methodism probably began in a small room in Water Lane in the early nineteenth century. The society belonged successively to the London, West London and Brentford (later Hammersmith) Circuits before becoming a separate circuit in 1861. Kew Road chapel (1871) served the dual purpose of school during the week and place of worship on Sundays. V. *van Gogh was associated with it and the Petersham chapel during his time at Isleworth. *Richmond College opened in 1843. There were PM chapels at Cambridge Road, Kew and at Barnes, the latter on the site of an earlier WM chapel which the society left for larger premises in 1907.

WHS(LHC) 8 (1969) and 24 (1981)

NM

Richmond (Yorks) *see* **Dales Circuit**

Richmond College, London, opened as the Southern Branch of the Theological Institution in 1843 and was built with some of the proceeds of the *Centenary Fund. The architect was J. *Wilson of Bath. It was later sold to the WMMS and used from 1869 to 1885 to train missionaries for work overseas. Its first Theological Tutor (from 1843 to 1861) was T. *Jackson and among his successors were J.A. *Beet (1885–1905), W.T. *Davison (1905–15) and C.R. *Smith (1920–32). W.F. *Moulton and A. S. *Geden made notable contributions to biblical studies. Other members of staff included W.T.A. *Barber, G. *Osborn, F.B. *Clogg, L.F. *Church and E.S. *Waterhouse. Its students included many future Presidents, such as W.M. *Punshon and H.P. *Hughes. During World War I it housed *Westminster Training College and in World War II became the administrative headquarters of the University of London, with which it had developed important links through theological education. The college was a victim of the 1960 cuts and closed in 1972, its last Principal being A.R. *George. It was sold and is now an American university campus.

MR(W) 1903 pp. 42–4; W.B. Brash (1935) pp. 69–78; F.H. Cumbers (1944)

TSAM

Ride, John *see* **Doncaster, M.**

Ridgway, Job (1759–1814), MNC industrialist, born in the Potteries, though his formative years were spent elsewhere. He returned to Hanley in 1781 as a trained potter and an enthusiastic Methodist. He opened his own factory in 1792. He played a leading part in the events which led all but eight of the Hanley Methodists to join the newly formed MNC and founded Bethesda Chapel, which became the largest and most important in the connexion. As Connexional Treasurer he was a 'nursing father' to the infant connexion. In 1802 he built a model manufactory at Cauldon Place, Hanley. His eldest son **John Ridgway** (1786–1860) followed him into the pottery business and the MNC. With his brother he became joint owner of the Cauldon Place works, which had a high reputation for hygiene and efficiency. He was Potter to the Queen and won a Prize Medal at the 1851 Exhibition. A leading Liberal, he dominated Hanley political life for nearly 40 years, being the first Mayor in 1856. His industrial and political experience helped to shape the MNC administration and put it on a sound business basis. His biographer stated that 'To no other single individual . . . does the Connexion owe so much.'

J. Stacey (1862); G.J. Stevenson (1884–6) 4 pp. 650–2; D.J. Jeremy (1988) pp. 47–71

EAR

Rigg, Dr James Harrison (1821–1909; e.m. 1845), a leading WM educationalist, theologian, ecclesiologist and ecclesiastical statesman, was Principal of *Westminster College from 1868 until his retirement in 1903. He vigorously defended WM against both Anglican and Congregationalist detractors. Deeply loyal to the Conference during the 1849–51 disruption, he nevertheless advocated reform and a greater participation of the laity in church government. He was President of the Conference in 1878 and 1892.

He published a volume of substantial *Essays for the Times* (1866) and wrote major studies of European elementary education (1873) and of comparative ecclesiology, *Principles of Church Organization* (1887). He strongly defended the retention of WM elementary schools against those who wanted them placed under the new School Boards. In this and other matters he was increasingly seen as out of date in the more liberal atmosphere at the turn of the century.

G.J. Stevenson (1884–6) 3 pp. 480–96; *MR* 22 April 1909; J. Telford (1912); D. Carter (1994); J.T. Smith (1998)

DJC

Riggall Family Of Huguenot origins, they settled in Lincolnshire. By the eighteenth century some of them were Methodists. **Paul Riggall** (1749–1836) and **William Riggall** (1752–1821) farmed on the edge of the Wolds near Horncastle. William's son **Robert Riggall** (1787–1865) and Paul's son **William Riggall** (1784–1875) married sisters, Rebecca and Elizabeth Kirkby and were the grandparents of **Marmaduke Riggall** (1851–1927; e.m. 1872), an enthusiastic founder member of the *WHS. Other branches of the family were also Methodists and farmers. William's son **Francis Riggall** (1806–93) took a farm at Dexthorpe in 1836 and with his wife **Elizabeth** (*née* Mawer) opened his farm kitchen for Methodist services. Servants and labourers were among the 40 or so members on their class books. Paul's son **Francis Riggall** (1788–1857)became a draper in Alford, but became a *local preacher and soon gave up his business to become a travelling Tract Distributor and founder of Tract Societies. He retired to *Louth and left legacies to the Theological Institution and the two Methodist schools.

PWHS 16, pp. 71–2; Lincs FHS 1 June 1990

WL

Riley, William (1866–1961), son of **Joseph Riley** (1838–1926), a *Bradford stuff merchant until bankrupted in 1902. Both were WM *local preachers in the Bradford Circuit. Joseph Riley supported the *NCH by giving magic lantern slide lectures and this led to the founding of Riley Bros Ltd, a major provider of lantern slides for illustrated lectures, especially to Sunday Schools. With the outbreak of World War I and the rise of the cinema, this business also went into bankruptcy. William Riley turned to writing. In six years the royalties from his first and probably most popular novel *Windyridge* (1912), based on the village of Hawksworth and the first to be published by Herbert Jenkins, covered his business losses. He wrote 36 books, mainly in the inter-war years, including an autobiography, *Sunset Reflections* (1957). He later went to live at Silverdale.

MR 21 Nov. 1957; C. Gordon (1980)

DCD

Ripley, Dorothy (1767–1831), daughter of **William Ripley** (1739–84), a *Whitby builder and pioneer *local preacher in the North East whose *Memoirs* she later published. Her home was open to the Methodist preachers, and she met JW there. Under *Quaker influence, in 1801 she crossed the Atlantic to work among negro slaves. She had no money, but lived and travelled by faith. She secured the support of Thomas Jefferson and moved from city to city, pleading the cause of the slaves, especially in Charleston. She visited prisons, preached to the Indians and in 1806 preached before Congress in Washington DC. She crossed the Atlantic eight or nine times, kept a journal for 30 years, and published an autobiographical *Account* of her *Extraordinary Conversion and Religious Experience* (1817).

PWHS 7 pp. 31–3; *MR(W)* 1907 pp. 74–6

WL

Ritchie, Elizabeth (Mrs Mortimer) (1754–1835), the daughter of an Otley surgeon, John Ritchie, came under the influence of JW as a girl and was soon accompanying him on some of his journeys. They corresponded frequently. She was living in his London house during the last months of his life and became close friends with Hester Ann *Rogers. She was present at his death in 1791 and wrote an account of his last days. In 1801 she married Harvey Walklake Mortimer, a widower with six children. In spite of poor health when in her twenties, she lived to a good age. She is buried in the crypt at *Wesley's Chapel.

MR(W) 1904 pp. 21–4; A. Bulmer (1836); E.K. Brown (1983)

WL

Ritson, Dr John Holland (1868–1953; e.m. 1891), WM minister. As a general secretary of the *BFBS from 1899, he travelled widely and was involved in reorganizing the work in *Canada and *Australia. He played a part in the first International Missionary Council in Edinburgh, 1910 and, as a member of the *Ministerial Training Committee, was closely involved in the opening of *Wesley House, Cambridge. He was President of the 1925 Conference and received honorary doctorates at Oxford and Montreal.

J.H. Ritson (1939); *MR* 16 July 1925, 3 Sept. 1953

JAV

Ritson, Joseph (1852–1932; e.m. 1874), outstanding PM preacher, much loved in the Scottish circuits which he brought into order. He wrote for the *PM Magazine* over a long period and was Connexional Editor 1906–11. He wrote an influential bestseller on *The Romance of Primitive Methodism* (*Hartley Lecture, 1909) and was President of the PM Conference in 1913.

MR 18 Aug. 1932

JHL

Roberts, Colin Augustus (1886–1975) was born in Dawley, Shropshire and trained at *Cliff College and *Didsbury College. Forced by ill-health to withdraw from the ministry in 1909, he served Wellington Congregational Church. Returning to Methodism in 1912, he became an army chaplain in 1915. He was ministerial secretary to the Wesley *Deaconess Order, 1922–26, then Chairman of the London NE District, before being appointed Secretary of the *HM Department in 1939. He helped raise the War Emergency Fund to assist Methodist congregations in stricken areas and launched the *Christian Commando Campaigns. He became President of the Conference in 1952.

MR 10 July 1952; 18 Dec. 1975

KGG

Roberts, Evan (1756?-1833), a Welshman born at Oswestry, became a WM *c.* 1777 when he heard JW and T. *Coke preach in *Liverpool.

Moving to *Manchester he was present at the opening of Oldham Street chapel by JW. Returning to Liverpool he helped to form the first Welsh CM society there, joining it for linguistic and patriotic rather than theological reasons, but later rejecting *Calvinism for WM. In 1784 he settled in Denbigh, where he preached in Welsh and formed the first WM society in North Wales that was more Welsh than English in character. His success there determined the *Chester preachers to bring the cause of Wales to the notice of the 1798 Conference, so that he deserves at least as much credit as E. *Jones of Ruthin for the founding of *Welsh WM.

A.H. Williams (1935) pp. 54–9; *HMGB* 3 p. 257

OEE

Roberts, Griffith Thomas (1912–91; e.m. 1936) studied Welsh and Welsh history at University College, Bangor and trained for the ministry at *Headingley College. He quickly attained a position of leadership and influence in *Welsh Methodism and recognition as an outstandingly versatile scholar and writer in several fields, including biblical studies and theology and the history of Methodism (both CM and WM) in Wales. He assisted A.H. *Williams in founding and editing *Bathafarn*, succeeding him as editor (1970–90). In English he wrote on *Howell Harris* (WHS Lecture, 1951) and the chapter on Welsh Methodism in *HMGB*. In Welsh he produced a standard work on the controversies of early Methodism, many booklets and countless articles. No less prominent as an ecclesiastical statesman, he was Chairman of the Second North Wales District 1962–74 and President of the Welsh Assembly in 1968. He played a leading role in the unity conversations between the four nonconformist denominations (1957–73), in the *Anglican-Methodist Conversations and in the Covenanting in Wales conversations and subsequent Commission of Covenanted Churches (1964–84), drafting and/or editing most of their bilingual reports. From 1961 to 1989 he was also secretary of the inter-Church Committee responsible for the new Welsh translation of the Bible (1988).

O.E. Evans (1993); *EW* 160, pp. 117–19

OEE

Roberts, Dr Harold (1896–1982; e.m. 1919), Methodist statesman, born at Ashley, Cheshire and brought up in Welsh Methodism in *Manchester. He was educated at University College of North Wales, Bangor and *Wesley House, Cambridge. A friend of D.O. *Soper, L.D. *Weatherhead and W.E. *Sangster, all of whom consulted him, he was considered a better preacher than any of them, but a less effective writer. As minister at Wesley Memorial Church, *Oxford 1929–34, the 'LD' (Learned Doctor) had an immense influence over a mixed group of undergraduates, including Harold Loukes, A.R. *George, R.E. and M. *Davies. He became tutor in theology, first at *Headingley College (1934–40), then at *Richmond College (1940–68, with a wartime interlude in the *Ipswich Circuit) where he was Principal from 1955. Through his report on *The Mission and Message of Methodism* (1946) he had much influence on the post-war Church. As Methodist Chairman of the *Anglican-Methodist Conversations he was responsible both for the scheme devised and for defending and commending it to his fellow Methodists. He was President of the 1957 Conference and President of the WMC 1951–56, helping to set up a new mechanism for linking *World Methodism more closely, moderating some of the American ideas and ensuring a place for Third World participation. He was Chairman of the Governors of both *Westminster and *Southlands Colleges during the post-war period of growth and change. He encouraged *women and the younger generation (e.g. P.M. *Webb) to speak in Conference.

Times 7 Oct. 1982; MR 11 July 1957, 21 Oct. 1982; *The Old Chariot*, 1968; J.H. Lenton (1995)

JHL

Roberts, Joseph (c. 1794–1849; e.m. 1818), early WM missionary in Ceylon (*Sri Lanka) and *India. After serving in Tamil areas in Ceylon 1819–31 and an interval in English circuits, he became General Superintendent of the Madras District in 1843. He produced translations from Tamil and was on the Translation Committee of the Madras Auxiliary Bible Society. He published *Oriental Illustrations of the Sacred Scriptures* (1833) and a treatise on 'Caste and its bearing on Christianity and Missions'.

JAV

Roberts, Richard (1823–1909; e.m. 1845) was brought up by Welsh relatives in *Manchester. Having begun to preach in Welsh, he returned to Wales in 1841 and quickly gained popularity as a preacher. He trained at *Didsbury College, intending to serve in the Welsh work, but was appointed to an English circuit and the whole of

his subsequent ministry was spent in England, though he remained loyal to his first love. He became a prince of the English pulpit. A member of the *Legal Hundred, in 1885 he was the first Welsh-speaking minister to become President of the WM Conference.

MR 2 Dec. 1909; *EW*, 101, pp. 281–8; 102, pp. 36, 62–5

OEE

Robin Hood's Bay Methodism may have begun in this seafaring village as early as 1747, but JW's first visit was not until May 1753, seven years before he went to *Whitby. He preached twice near the quay and found them 'all attention', perhaps because of his hostility to the prevalent smuggling. On his 10 later visits he sometimes preached in the Square. Once, told that the mob would pull down the house where he was staying, he went up the hill to sleep at Normanby. A preaching house was built by 1764 and in 1779 JW opened a new chapel (enlarged 1841). Another chapel at Fylingthorpe, one mile away (1818, replaced by a larger one in 1891), was built on land given by Francis Newton, brother of Dr R. *Newton. By 1825 there was also a PM chapel at Bay, though that did not last. In the 1851 *Religious Census the total WM attendances at the two services was 480, plus 90 in the afternoon at Fylingthorpe. A WM day school (by 1861; closed 1923) proved popular. But the opening of a Congregational chapel (1840) and the movement of the parish church closer to the village in 1870 provided more competition. Population in the village declined, though Fylingthorpe expanded as a retreat for the wealthy. Faced by the threat of cliff erosion, Methodism bought the Manor House overlooking the village and in 1937 transformed it into a new church with seating for 200 and ample parking. Part is now let as flats. The older chapel in Bay Town was restored and is used as a crafts centre and concert hall.

E.W. Dickinson (1925); J. Marsland (1978); E. Wyman (1997)

JHL

Robins, Paul (1804–90; e.m. 1823), BC itinerant, travelled in home circuits until emigrating to *Canada in 1846. He was Secretary of the Conference and Financial Secretary several times and President in 1836 and 1843; Secretary of the Chapel Committee 1842–46, of the Missionary Committee 1844–46 and of the Home Missions

Committee 1847–51. He continued his ministry in Canada and died at Bowmanville.

See also **Taylor, M.A.**

TS

Robinson, Sir Thomas (1855–1927) Born in Cleethorpes, at 14 he was cabin boy on a fishing smack and within 14 years had become a master smack owner. By 1883 he had given up going to sea and had his own fleet of fishing vessels. In World War I he handed over 14 of his ships to the government, went to the Canadian Pacific to acquaint himself with local conditions and then built three trawlers designed for work in that area. He was knighted for his work with Cecil Harmsworth's Food Control. He supported the PM orphanages at Alresford and Harrogate and was Vice-President of the PM Conference in 1923. He was a JP and member of the Lindsey County Council. He died soon after embarking on a Mediterranean cruise.

WL

Rochdale Methodism dates from 1747 and became established quickly, despite the hostility recorded by JW on his first visit in October 1749. A chapel was built in Toad Lane in 1770 and the size of its 5 a.m. congregation greatly impressed JW in 1787. The first resident minister was appointed in 1791; Union Street chapel was opened in 1793, complete with burial ground and manse, and in 1795 Rochdale became head of a circuit. Its 380 town members were 2.6% of the population. Its Sunday School, opened in 1782, was one of the earliest. In the 1830s, along with Liverpool and Manchester, Rochdale was a storm-centre of the anti-Conference agitation which led to the formation of the WMA in 1834. WMA's principal chapel, Baillie Street, was opened in 1837. At the time of the *Religious Census in 1851 WMA attendances exceeded WM ones. The WMA Annual Assembly and UMFC Conference met 11 times in the town before 1907, and the UM Conference met there in 1916 and 1927. Prominent local Methodists included Sir J. *Duckworth and the asbestos manufacturer Robert Turner. T. *Champness brought his infant *Joyful News Mission there in 1886 and in 1889 bought Castleton Hall to train lay evangelists; in 1903 the institution moved to Calver and became *Cliff College.

Conference Handbook 1952; D.A. Gowland (1979)

EAR

Rodd, Dr Cyril Stanley (1928– ; e.m. 1951), a wide-ranging scholar and OT specialist, who was tutor at *Handsworth College 1956–67 and at *Southlands College and the Roehampton Institute 1969–91. He gained his MSocSc at Birmingham on 'The social teaching of the Churches' and a London PhD on 'the teaching of Jesus in Mark'. He has been the editor of the *Expository Times* since 1975 and was Editorial Secretary of the Epworth Press 1991–6. He has written Epworth Commentaries on the Psalms (1963, 1964) and Job (1990) and volumes for the 'Thinking Things Through' series on the Bible, Evil and Suffering and Life after Death.

GSW

Rogers, David (1783–1824; e.m. 1805), *Welsh WM minister, born in Denbighshire and converted by E. *Jones, Bathafarn in 1800. He became a *local preacher in 1803 and served in *Liverpool before entering the ministry. Thereafter he served with O. *Davies and J. *Bryan in the Welsh mission and in 1816 succeeded Davies as Chairman of the Welsh District, until transferred to the English work in 1819. An eminent preacher and a man of acute intellect with widely varied literary and theological interests, he wrote much to enrich the early Welsh WMs. He edited *Yr Eurgrawn* 1812–14, contributing much himself, and was editor of the 1812 hymn-book and jointly responsible for that of 1817.

H. Jones (1911–13) 1 pp. 370–80; *DWB*

IGPL

Rogers, Edward (1909–97; e.m. 1932) was born in Fleetwood and educated at Manchester University and *Hartley Victoria College. In 1950 he became a secretary and, in 1953, General Secretary of the Christian Citizenship Department. He wrote *A Commentary on Communism* (1951) and many other books, but his most sustained literary output was his weekly column in the *Methodist Recorder*, a masterpiece of compression and informed comment on contemporary affairs. For many years both before and after retirement he contributed a Conference diary to that paper, full of humour and incisive comments. He was President of the Conference in 1960 and Moderator of the FCFC 1961–62.

MR 7 July 1960, 6 Nov. 1997

KGG

Rogers, James (1749–1807; e.m. 1774) and **Hester Ann Rogers** (*née* Roe, 1756–94). Born at Marske, Yorks, his first appointment as an itinerant was to *York. In 1778 he married Martha Knowlden and they had two children. After her death, in 1784 he married the daughter of the Rev. James Roe of *Macclesfield. She was well-read, especially in Roman and English history. She had been converted under the preaching of S. *Bardsley. During her husband's three years in *Dublin, she led a class and wrote her *Spiritual Letters* (1796) which, together with extracts from her diary, became for many a book of devotions. She also contributed to the *AM* and wrote some verse. In 1790 they moved to *Wesley's Chapel and were present at JW's death. James found himself involved in the disputes between trustees and preachers over J. *Whitehead's appropriation of W's papers. Hester died in *Birmingham after the birth of her seventh child. James retired in 1805.

EMP, 4 pp. 274–329; H.A. Rogers (1796)

WL

Romaine, Rev. William (1714–95), Anglican priest, a student at Christ Church, Oxford and ordained in 1738. He was attracted to JW, but parted company with him over *Christian perfection and became a leading exponent of *Calvinism and one of the Countess of *Huntingdon's chaplains. His support for G. *Whitefield in 1755 cost him his lectureship at St George's, Botolph Lane, London. From 1765 he was rector of St Anne's, Blackfriars and of St Andrew by the Wardrobe. He edited a Hebrew concordance (1748) and published a *Treatise upon the Life of Faith* (1763).

DNB; A. Brown-Lawson (1994)

JAV

Roman Catholicism   JW, in many ways a Hanoverian Protestant high churchman, shared the prevalent fear of Rome and late in his life showed sympathy for Lord George Gordon, leader of anti-Catholic riots. Yet he was drawn to Catholic *holiness, encouraging his followers to read two minor Catholic Reformation saints, Gregory Lopez and M. de Renty. In 1749 he wrote a letter to a Roman Catholic in *Dublin which is one of the most remarkable documents of *ecumenism, pleading for emphasis on what is held in common. To the outrage of the Roman Bishop Richard Challoner, some charged Methodism with being covert Catholicism, seeing the *class meeting as the confessional.

There has always been a certain kinship in the pursuit of holiness, and Romans have found the W hymns spoke to them, not least in devotion to Christ's passion and the doctrines of the Real Presence and Sacrifice in the Eucharist. Methodist suspicion of Rome continued until World War II and afterwards. But theologians such as R.N. *Flew emphasized affinities and Vatican II, together with the Liturgical Movement, made dialogue possible. Since 1967 Joint RC and WMC Commissions have issued regular reports. The Mass is no longer the Methodists' *bête noir*, and some hardline RC ethical attitudes (such as those of the Pro-life movement) have Methodist supporters, such as the distinguished American Stanley Hauerwas. The dialogue is not likely to be broken off and there are Methodists, influenced by the best RC theologians such as Hans Urs von Balthasar, who will not rest satisfied with any union which does not include Rome.

D. Butler (1995); G. Wainwright (1995) pp. 37–106

GSW

Rose, Professor Geoffrey, CBE (1926–1993), a leading specialist in the epidemiology and treatment of heart disease, was the son of **Arthur N. Rose** (1892–1979; e.m. 1914; *Ministerial Training Secretary from 1948). Educated at Oxford and St. Mary's Hospital, London, from 1959 he lectured at the London School of Hygiene and Tropical Medicine, then as Professor of Epidemiology from 1970 gained an international reputation, especially though his involvement in INTERSALT, an international study of blood-pressure patterns which emphasized prevention by linking individual health and that of whole communities.

Times, 29 Nov. 1993

JAV

Rose, Dr John Richard (1910–98), *medical missionary, studied medicine at Queen's College, Cambridge and sailed for *China in 1932. He served in the hospital at Fatshan and was interned by the Japanese. Returning home after release, he went back to China in 1946 and served there until 1951. He was then appointed to Africa, where he helped build up the Nixon Memorial Hospital in *Sierra Leone. In 1958 he returned to Britain and became a GP. He wrote *A Church Born to Suffer* (1951), *Kwashiorkor in SE Sierra Leone* (1956) and an autobiography *Traveller's Joy* (1991).

MR 27 Dec. 1998

GRS

Rosevear, Thomas Pope (1781–1853), WM and WMA layman, of Boscastle, Cornwall; merchant, slate quarry owner, Lloyds agent, boat owner and diarist. He was a circuit steward and *local preacher and trustee in the Camelford WM Circuit. He had a great interest in political reform and became the local champion of Methodist Reform, leading some 90% of the Camelford Circuit members and local preachers into the WMA.

––––––––

T. Shaw in CMHA 7 (1986) pp. 71–6

                                                        TS

Rossendale, adjoining the Lancashire Pennines between *Rochdale and Burnley, was visited several times by JW, though only once by CW (in January 1757). JW reputedly preached at Goodshaw in 1745, but the first visit recorded in his *Journal* was on 7 May 1747, when he 'came down to the fruitful Valley of Rossendale', preaching in the vicinity of W. *Darney's cottage at Miller Barn. He made at least nine other visits to different areas of Rossendale, including riding to Broad-Clough with W. *Grimshaw in July 1759 and preaching in the 'new preaching-house at Bacup' (Mount Pleasant, the mother of Methodist churches in Rossendale) in July 1761 and at Newchurch-in-Rossendale in July 1766. On his last visit, in April 1788, he preached from the steps in Town Gate, Haslingden and complained about the state of the roads, 'sufficient to lame any horses and shake any carriage to pieces'. After being in the *Haworth Round, then in the Colne (1776), Blackburn (1787) and Rochdale (1795) Circuits, in 1811 Rossendale became a circuit in its own right.

PM arrived in 1824, aided by a visit from H. *Bourne and established North Street, Bacup (1854–1941) as their principal circuit church. The *Unitarian Methodists came into the area from Rochdale. Beula, Britannia (1852) and Eden, Lumb (1874) are ex-UM churches still in existence.

––––––––

W. Jessop (1880)

                                                        KFB

Round *see* **Circuit**

Rouquet, Rev. James (1730–76), Anglican clergyman of *Huguenot ancestry. JW appointed him as a master at *Kingswood School, 1751–55(?). Despite W's hopes of his becoming an itinerant, he chose parish work, but retained his love for the spirituality of Methodism and introduced Captain *Webb to the *Bristol Methodists. He devoted much of his time to improving prison conditions in Bristol. Theologically he occupied the middle ground between *Arminianism and *Calvinism. The Countess of *Huntingdon counted him an intimate friend, but he also remained a close confidant of JW who, when he thought he was dying in 1768, bequeathed all his manuscripts to him. His death was mourned by clergy both regular and irregular, Lady Huntingdon's followers, Baptist Dissenters, Huguenots and Methodists, together with the sick and poor of Bristol.

––––––––

A.B. Sackett (1972)

                                                        EWD

Rowe, Dr George Edwards (1858–1926; e.m. 1880), WM minister, trained at *Richmond College. He served in South *Australia; then in Western Australia, where, at the time of the gold rush, he organized spiritual provision for the mining camps. When they were swept by epidemics, he organized the 'Sisters of the People' to minister to the sick. In 1896 he established a mission to the Chinese in Perth. He was elected President of the Western Australia Conference when it was set up in 1900. In 1905 he became Superintendent of the Central Mission in Brisbane (Queensland) and under his ministry there the Church became a greater moral and spiritual force than ever before. He was a strong personality, a forceful and eloquent speaker and a great organizer.

                                                        EGC

Rowe, George Stringer (1830–1913; e.m. 1853), WM minister, born in Margate, educated at *Wesley College, Sheffield and at *Didsbury College. He was President's Assistant in 1857. In his circuit ministry he found the training of young people particularly congenial and the hymn for which he is chiefly remembered, 'Cradled in a manger meanly' (*HP* 98), first appeared in the Christmas number of *At Home and Abroad* and in the *Sunday School Hymn-Book* of 1879. He was Governor and tutor in Pastoral Theology at *Headingley College 1888–1904, wrote biographies of the missionaries J. *Hunt and J. *Calvert and *The Psalms in Private Devotion* (1884), and completed the *Life* of J. *Bunting by his son (1887).

––––––––

MR 21 Aug. 1913

                                                        JAV

Rowland, Daniel (1711–1790), Anglican clergyman and pioneer of *Welsh Calvinistic Methodism. Born at Nantcwnlle, Cardiganshire, he was ordained deacon in 1734, and priest in 1735. He then served as a curate in the parishes of Llangeitho and Nantcwnlle, but having met H. *Harris during 1737, he enlarged the sphere of his activity in order to promote the revival in Wales. Following the 1750 separation, he continued with the revival work, and when a new revival occurred at Llangeitho in 1762, he was deprived of his curacy. Some of his hymns, sermons and translations into Welsh have appeared in print, but it was for his powerful preaching that Rowland was renowned.

E. Evans (1985)

GT

Rowlands, William (1802–65; e.m. 1829), the leading Welsh bibliographer of the century, known as 'Gwilym Lleyn'. He followed his father's trade as a weaver, but began preaching at 19. His itinerancy enabled him to search for books in many parts of Wales and he began to publish his *Cambrian Bibliography* in the CM monthly *Y Traethodydd* in 1852. After his death the work was edited by Daniel Silvan Evans and published in 1869 as a volume of over 750 pages, an astonishing achievement at a time when no major libraries existed in Wales. He edited *EW* 1842–45 and 1852–56.

EW, 1868; *DNB*; *DWB*; *OCLW*; *Bathafarn* 1953 pp. 5–23; B. Thomas in *Caernarvonshire Historical Transactions*, vol. 45 (1984) pp. 79–92

GTH

Ruddle, Thomas (1839–1909), born at Trowbridge, the son of a woollen yarn spinner, became a student teacher and, after studying at Borough Road Training College, London, taught at Lewisham and *Weymouth. A natural student and omnivorous reader, particularly in English literature, his interests also included music and chemistry. In 1864, at the age of 23, he became the headmaster of the small BC grammar school at *Shebbear and held the post for 45 years. Under him it developed into an outstanding school of its kind and he heard himself described as the Thomas Arnold of North Devon.

G.P. Dymond (1913)

TS

Rule, Dr William Harris (1802–90; e.m. 1825), WM minister, born in Cornwall. Intellectually gifted, he mastered ten languages. After trying to make a living as a portrait painter and school-

master, he was ordained in 1826 and served as a missionary in Malta and St Vincent, where he was outspoken against slavery. During nine years in *Gibraltar (1832–41) he worked unsparingly among the garrison, providing the first chapel and the first charity school. He won from the War Office the right for Methodist and nonconformist soldiers to attend their own religious services. The appointment of a colleague enabled him to devote time and energy to the circulation of the Scriptures in *Spain, where he travelled extensively and attempted to establish Methodist classes, confronting RC opposition with courage and determination. After returning to the English work, he became joint editor at the Book Room (1851–7). His *History of the Inquisition* was published in 1874.

W.H. Rule (1886); *MR* 2 Oct. 1890; F&H 2 p. 182, 4 pp. 419–20

EWD

Runciman, Walter (Lord Runciman) (1847–1937), WM shipowner and generous benefactor, was born at Cresswell, Northumberland, where both Methodism and the sea were profound influences on his life. He ran away from home at 12 and for 25 years sailed the seas, captaining his ships from 1873. In 1885 he established himself as a shipowner at South Shields, and later at *Newcastle upon Tyne. He built up the Moor Line and later acquired a controlling interest in the Anchor Line, building up a considerable fortune. He was active in civic and political life and was Liberal MP for *Hartlepool 1914–18. He was knighted in 1906 and raised to the peerage in 1933. He remained a dedicated Methodist and served as a *local preacher. His son, also **Walter**, was raised to the peerage as Viscount Runciman of Doxford shortly before his father's death.

Times 14 Aug. 1937; *MR* 19 Aug. 1937; G.E. Milburn in *PWHS* 44 pp. 83–4; *DNB*; *DBB*

GEM

Rundle, Robert Terrill (1811–96; e.m. 1840), pioneer WM missionary in the Hudson Bay Territory, *Canada, was born at Mylor, Cornwall, the grandson of W. *Carvosso. He was one of four missionaries sent out in 1840 following an agreement between the WMMS and the Hudson Bay Company. During a successful ministry among the Cree Indians he introduced the Cree script invented by J. *Evans and founded an agricultural settlement to combat the recurring starvation among the Indians. In the course of extensive journeying he gained the confidence of the Black-foot and other Indian tribes, but his Canadian ministry was ended by an accident in 1848. His work anticipated (but was eclipsed by) the RC missions which began in 1842, but it prepared the ground for later missionaries to the area.

JAV

Rupp, Professor Ernest Gordon, FBA (1910–86; e.m. 1934), born in London and worked in commerce and a bank before reading History at King's College, London under Norman Sykes. Having trained for the ministry at *Wesley House, he studied at Strasbourg and Basle. He taught Church History at *Richmond College 1947–52 and in the Cambridge Divinity Faculty 1952–56. He was awarded the DD (Cantab) in 1955 and in 1956 became the first Professor of Ecclesiastical History at Manchester University, where as Public Orator his proverbial wit and eloquence found full scope. He returned to Cambridge in 1967 as Principal of Wesley House and played an active part in forming the Cambridge Federation of Theological Colleges. The University appointed him Dixie Professor of Ecclesiastical History and Emmanuel College made him a Fellow. He was President of the Conference in 1968. A distin-guished Luther scholar, he published his researches in *Luther's Progress to the Diet of Worms* (1951) and *The Righteousness of God* (1953). His last book was *Religion in England 1688–1791* (1986). A committed ecumenist, he served on the Central Committee of the WCC and was an official observer at the Second Vatican Council.

MR 13 June 1968, 1 & 8 Jan. 1987; E.G. Rupp (1994)

JAN

Rural Travel Fund *see* **Finance, Ministerial**

Rushbrooke, Frederick William, JP (1861–1953), was the son of Joseph Rushbrooke, baker, confectioner and grocer of Willenhall, Staffs, a staunch Methodist and *local preacher. Educated at *Queen's College, Taunton, he saw the opportunity offered by the rapidly growing cycle industry and in 1892 started his own business in *Birmingham. His rigid principles, honesty and determination made Rushbrooke and Co. a commercial success and in 1907 the business became a limited company as the Halford Cycle Co., of which he was joint managing director. He retired in 1947, but continued as Chairman. He served as treasurer of the Hospital for Wounded Soldiers at Sutton Coldfield 1915–18, and from 1931 as senior treasurer of the Princess Alice Orphanage, Sutton Coldfield.

B.A. Jones (1981)

EDG

Rushton, Benjamin (1785–1853), handloom weaver, *Chartist and itinerant preacher, was born at Dewsbury. He joined Salem MNC chapel, *Halifax in 1815 and later served as Sunday School teacher and popular *local preacher at Ovenden, appearing at chapel anniversary ser-vices in a clean brat, patched knee breeches, highly polished clogs and a tall hat. He appears to have withdrawn from the MNC *c.* 1821, but continued to preach in Methodist pulpits, despite official disquiet, until about 1830. Thereafter he preached for radical and secessionist congregations across the West Riding. He requested that no paid minis-ter should speak at his funeral, which was organ-ized by the Chartists and drew great crowds.

J.A. Hargreaves in K. Dockray * K. Laybourn (1999) pp. 72–7, 80

JAH

Russell, John, RA (1745–1806), evangelical artist, son of the mayor of Guildford, was con-verted in 1764 under Martin Madan's preaching. He was well known for his fervent evangelism and the Countess of *Huntingdon tried to persuade him to become a minster. A talented and pro-ductive portrait artist (often working in chalks), he depicted evangelical leaders (G. *Whitefield, Lady *Huntingdon, the *Wesleys, William Wil-berforce and others) as well as aristocracy and gentry. He was a particular friend of the Wesleys and painted a number of portraits of CW's family. He became 'painter to the King and Prince of Wales' in 1790. He was also an amateur astron-omer who invented an apparatus for lunar observa-tion and made a lunar map.

G.C. Williamson (1894); I.C. Rhodes (1986); *PWHS* 25 pp. 52–6; 47 pp. 190–1

PSF

Russell, Thomas (1806–89; e.m. 1829), PM itinerant, born at Kinderton, Cheshire, began to preach at 19. By the time he was 23 he became known, along with J. *Ride, as the apostle of Berkshire, where they led a remarkable mission in the face of much persecution. He was imprisoned for a time in Abingdon. From 1855–62 he served in Irish circuits. He was three times married, his first wife being his fellow itinerant, E. *Smith. Although he died at Dover, he was buried at his own request at *Englesea Brook, close to his father-in-God H. *Bourne.

T. Russell (1869); W.M. Kilby (1986)

WL

Russell, Wilfrid H. (1898–1981; e.m. 1926), missionary in *India, born at Sawley, Derbys and trained at *Handsworth College. In the Lucknow and Benares District 1927–52 he mastered Urdu and was involved in training primary teachers and missionary candidates. From 1952 to 1965 he served with the Mission to Lepers and as its secretary from 1960 travelled world-wide.

MR 30 April 1981 JAV

Rutledge, John (d.1826), Irish missionary to New Providence in the Bahamas from 1804 to 1814, when he was forced to resign after marrying a white woman who had inherited slaves. Their proposal to free them gradually, as legal restrictions permitted, was unacceptable to the WMMS. Despite this, he maintained his contacts with the Missionary Committee and continued to serve unofficially, being more experienced than other missionaries in the area. He strongly supported the interests of the slaves and in 1817, despite his mild disposition and conservative outlook, vigorously opposed legislation prohibiting worship during the hours of darkness when slaves were free to attend.

F&H 2 pp. 228–33; N.W. Taggart (1986) pp. 161–2

NWT

Ryan, Mrs Sarah (1724–68) was of humble origins and began her working life in domestic service. At the age of 20 she married a sailor who proved to be a bigamist. After further misfortunes she found a spiritual home at the *Foundery in London and a spiritual friend in S. *Crosby. She became a confidant and correspondent of JW's, and the object of his wife's jealous suspicion. He appointed her housekeeper (1757–61) at the *New Room, Bristol. Back in London because of ill-health, in 1763 she joined M. *Bosanquet at her school for orphans at Leytonstone. This moved to Cross Hall, Morley, near *Leeds in 1768 in the hope that country air would improve her health, but she died shortly afterwards.

S. Ryan (1763); *AM* 1779, 1781, 1782; J. Burge (1996); JWL, vols 3–5

EDG

Rydal Penrhos School, Colwyn Bay, was formed in 1995 by the merger of Rydal School with the nearby Penrhos School for Girls, founded in 1880 by local Methodists. Penrhos was not a connexional school and its Methodist links were gradually severed. Rydal Mount School for Boys was founded in 1885 by T.G. *Osborn, formerly headmaster of *Kingswood School. It became a connexional school in 1905 and built up a strong academic and sporting reputation. Famous old boys include the Tudor historian, Sir Geoffrey Elton and Wilfred Wooller, excused lessons to play Rugby for Wales and later captain of Glamorgan County Cricket Club. The school had strong links with the *Bermondsey Settlement and the Old Rydalians support a boys' club in *Liverpool. In 1997 there were 767 boarding and day boys and girls aged 4–18.

E.B., *Rydal School 1885–1985 Centenary Booklet* (1985)

DBT

Sackett, Alfred Barrett, OBE (1862–1951; e.m. 1889), WM minister, who trained at *Richmond College and spent much of his ministry as a Forces chaplain, including 15 years (1903–19) in Gibraltar. He superintended the Soldiers' Homes in *Gibraltar and Shorncliffe. His son, also **Alfred Barrett Sackett** (1895–1977) was educated at *Kingswood School and Oxford and saw war service at Gallipoli and Ypres, winning the MC. After six years as a housemaster at Christ's Hospital, he began a distinguished career as headmaster at *Kingswood School (1928–59), a period of liberalization and development despite wartime evacuation to Uppingham. He was a member of the World Methodist Council 1950–66.

MR 8 Feb. 1951, 6 Oct. 1977; A.G.Ives (1970) pp. 207–21; J. Walsh (1979)

WL

Sackett, F. Colyer (1876–1953; e.m. 1901), WM missionary in *India and brother of A.B. *Sackett, trained for the ministry at *Headingley College and from 1901 to 1945 served in the Hyderabad District, succeeding C.W. *Posnett as Chairman in 1939. In a largely urban ministry, he built up a strong Christian witness in the twin cities of Hyderabad and Secunderabad. He wrote two books on the Hyderabad Mission and a life of Posnett (1951)

MR 14 May 1953 JAV

Sacraments JW held, as Methodism still does, the normal Protestant view that there are two sacraments ordained by Christ in the Gospel, namely *Baptism and the *Lord's Supper. They are *means of grace by which God works invisibly in us and not only quickens but strengthens and confirms our faith in him. The administration of the sacraments by the *itinerant preachers was one of the most contentious issues facing Methodism after JW's death.

_____

O.E. Borgen (1972)

ARG

Sadler, Michael Thomas (178–1835), born at Snelston, Derbys, into a family who were the first Methodists in the district. In 1817 he wrote a stinging pamphlet, *An Apology for the Methodists*, and soon afterwards began preaching. He moved to *Leeds *c*. 1800 to go into business with his brother Benjamin, a linen merchant. On his marriage he became an Anglican and was elected to the corporation. An enthusiastic Tory, he was elected MP for *Newark in 1829 and for Aldborough 1830–32. With his friend R. *Oastler he advocated and campaigned for factory reform, moving the reading of the Ten Hour Bill in 1831.

_____

R.B. Seeley (1842); J.T. Ward in *University of Leeds Review* Vol. 6 (1960) pp. 152–60

DCD

St Ives (Cornwall), then becoming established as a mining centre, was the prime destination of the Wesleys and their companions when they set out from Bristol in 1743. They were further attracted by the news of a religious society being formed there. Under JW's influence, it became one of his Methodist societies and when the Cornwall Circuit was divided in 1764 became the head of the Cornwall West Circuit.

PM arrived in 1829 and Fore Street Chapel (1831) was for many years regarded as the fisherman's chapel. It contains three charcoal drawings by the artist W.H.Y. *Titcombe: 'Primitive Methodists at Prayer', 'A Mariners' Sunday School' and 'Piloting her Home'. The *Teetotal Methodist denomination was formed in St Ives in 1841, but after a brief history the St Ives society united with the MNC. One of the members at Bedford Road (MNC, 1900) was the shipping magnate Edward Hain MP, mayor of St Ives and Sheriff of Cornwall, for whom Treloyhan Manor was built in 1892. The house became a *Wesley Guild Holiday Home in 1948.

TS

Salisbury was the focal point of Methodism in southern England throughout the eighteenth century. JW's earliest visits were because of family connections and his brother-in-law W. *Hall formed the first society at Fisherton in the early 1740s. But Hall's leadership proved a mixed blessing; his immoral behaviour brought the society into disrepute and in 1748 JW had to salvage what he could, putting it under the pastoral charge of J. *Furz. Despite this, Salisbury was the first society established in central southern England. The first chapel was opened in St Edmund Church Street in 1758 (rebuilt in 1810 and remodelled in 1992). When the Wiltshire Circuit was divided in 1868 into Wiltshire North and South Circuits, Salisbury became the head of the latter, embracing Hampshire, Dorset and the Isle of Wight; and, despite rivalry (and some animosity) between Salisbury and Portsmouth, there was no further division until 1790. Asbury was acting Superintendent of the Circuit before offering for *America in 1771.

PM preachers came from Motcombe in 1827. The society met first in the former WM chapel in Fisherton Street and there was a proliferation of small village causes, mostly without a home, but sometimes in former WM chapels. A Salisbury circuit was formed as early as 1831. In 1869 a new chapel was built on the opposite side of Fisherton Street (replaced by Dews Road, 1917). Salisbury was one of the few places in the south seriously affected by the *Fly Sheets controversy. Expulsions from the Church Street society in 1850 led to a revolt of Sunday School teachers and scholars who, in April 1851, took possession of the Salt Lane school premises and held rival services there. The protest spread to the village causes and by June 1853 they claimed 270 members, including 164 in the city. When they eventually affiliated to the UMFC in 1861, some village causes (notably Downton and Wilton) remained aloof. The first Milford Street chapel was rebuilt in 1879.

Methodist Union was not effected until 1949, when the three Salisbury circuits, together with Woodfalls PM Circuit, came together. In 1984 the four city congregations became one in the Church Street premises.

_____

Methodist Church, Church Street, Salisbury: Bi-Centenary [1959]; *Primitive Methodist Church, Salisbury Circuit: Centenary Celebrations 1827–1927, Souvenir Handbook* [1927]

JAV

Salisbury, Frank Owen, CVO (1874–1962), born in Harpenden, served an apprenticeship at his brother's *stained glass works in St. Albans and continued to work in that media (e.g. in Medak Cathedral and at *Wesley's Chapel, London), though celebrated mainly for his portraits and paintings of historic occasions. While studying at the Royal Academy he won the Landseer Scholarship, which made possible a formative visit to Italy. A skilful and productive artist in the tradition of the English School, his autobiography, *Portrait and Pageant* (1944) is a roll-call of the great and illustrious who sat for him. His posthumous portraits of early Methodists, include three of JW (now at JW's house, *Westminster Central Hall and the WMC headquarters, Lake Junaluska). He wrote and illustrated a book on the Lord's Prayer and also illustrated *The Prophets of Israel* by S.P. *Cadman. After his wife's death he became a member of The City Temple under L.D. *Weatherhead. His home, 'Sarum Chase', Hampstead, was left to the BCC.

B.A. Barber (1936); *Times* 1 Sept. 1962; *MR* 6 Sept. 1962

JAV

Salvation The Wesleyan tradition has a carefully nuanced understanding of the 'order of salvation', which JW distinguished from both the *Calvinist and Tridentine Catholic positions, e.g. in his sermon on *Justification and in his contributions to the *Calvinist controversy of 1770. He sets out the stages by which an individual comes to saving faith in his sermon on 'The Spirit of Bondage and Adoption'. First, the 'natural man' is content with his situation in blissful ignorance of the demands of God; then, 'under the law' he has the 'faith of a servant'; next, moved by prevenient *grace and recognizing his sinfulness and the impending judgment of God, he repents and begins to produce 'fruits meet for repentance', but still lives in fear of judgment and in awareness of his inability to save himself; and, finally, receiving 'justifying *faith' in Christ and the full sufficiency of his atonement, he is a 'son' with 'the spirit of adoption'. The process is not complete, however, until he has 'pressed on to entire *sanctification' or 'perfect love'. In his open letter to T. *Church (1746) W wrote of repentance as the 'porch' of religion, faith as its 'door' and holiness as 'religion itself'.

C.W. Williams (1960); R.L. Maddox (1994)

DJC

Salvation Army, an organization founded in London's East End by W. *Booth, a former MNC minister, in 1865. It was known at first as 'the Christian Mission' (also the Christian Revival Association) and retained such Methodist features as *circuits, *itinerancy, *local preachers, *class leaders, *class tickets, *love-feasts, *camp meetings and *watchnights. Its government was a modified form of the MNC system. The name was changed to 'the Salvation Army' in 1878, reflecting its military organization and requirement of unquestioning obedience. In doctrinal matters it is evangelical, but without either of the sacraments. Its most conspicuous features are its open-air witness and wide-ranging social activities. Brass bands were first introduced in *Salisbury, by the Methodist Fry family, to counteract violent hostility. It is now an international organization, operating in over a hundred countries. Queen Elizabeth II attended the International Centenary celebrations in 1965.

R. Sandall, A. Wiggins & F. Coutts (1947–86)

JDB

Samoa In 1828, under the influence of a Samoan chief who had visited *Tonga, Christianity of a WM persuasion was introduced. After a visit to request a missionary and in the wake of the Tongan 'revival', in 1835 P. *Turner arrived with Tongan missionaries and found 2,000 converts. Meanwhile work had also begun under the London Missionary Society and the early years were marred by misunderstanding and rivalry, despite attempts at comity. The Methodists withdrew until 1857, when the newly autonomous Australian Conference, encouraged by the veteran J. *Thomas, decided to resume the mission despite continuing difficulties. The Samoan Methodist Church remained small, but became autonomous in 1964. In 1997 it reported a membership of 31,979 and a community of 35,625.

F&H 3 pp. 338–62; A.H. Wood 1 (1975) pp. 251–335

JAV

Sanctification is the process, in classical Christian theology, by which the Holy Spirit transforms believers and renews them in the image of Christ. *'Holiness' is the state of believers thus transformed. JW, while not regarding sanctification as necessary for 'present' salvation, held that the true believer would persevere in faith and go on to seek perfection. *'Christian perfection', or 'perfect love', would be granted to some in this life, to others only at the moment of death – since 'without holiness, no man shall see the Lord' (Heb. 12:14). According to W, faith 'active in love' was essential to growth in holiness and though he emphasized sanctification as the gift of God, he also stressed the necessity of human co-operation. People were to await the gift in 'universal obedience and attendance upon the *means of grace'. However, he repudiated any idea that sanctification was achieved by 'merit'; rather, the Christian should be confident in the great promises of God, who commands nothing that he does not give power to achieve. In this way, the quest for holiness need not become burdensome.

W's apparent underplaying of the role of the Spirit in sanctification probably reflects the practical emphasis in his teaching, which stressed what a person had to do to co-operate with divine grace. By contrast CW stressed the role of the Spirit (e.g. in HP 300), offers a more lyrical treatment of the 'glorious hope of perfect love' and shares some of the insights of the *Eastern Orthodox tradition of 'theosis' and participation in the divine energies (e.g. MHB (1933) 568).

J. *Fletcher, in his *Last Check to Antinomianism* (1775) emphasized the Trinitarian dynamics of sanctification. In the next century W.B. *Pope gave a clear analysis of the role of the Spirit in his *Compendium* (1875–6) and J.A. *Beet, in his *Holiness* (1880) and *The New Life in Christ* (1895) presented holiness as the divine claim on creation and the human response to the outflow of the divine love which is its enabling source.

———

H. Lindstrom (1946); R.L. Maddox (1994)

DJC

Sanderson, William (1811–99), a *Liverpool man, began as a WM but joined the *Warrenite secession in 1835 and briefly served the WMA as a paid evangelist. Returning to his trade as a tailor, he left the WMA in 1840 and started a *Free Gospel Church which joined the IM Connexion in 1841. He was connexional President on four occasions, secretary for eleven years and editor of the *Free Gospel Advocate* (1849–52, 1859–62). He travelled widely, was a strong advocate of unpaid ministry and was instrumental in adding churches to the Connexion during the middle years of the century. In 1853 he published the first IM hymnal.

———

W. Sanderson (1899); *IM Magazine*, Feb.1899

JAD

Sandwith, Humphry (1792–1874), prominent WM layman, a surgeon at Bridlington and from 1842 lecturer on the theory and practice of medicine at the *Hull School of Medicine. He made a name for himself by his opposition to the attempts of Mark Robinson of Beverley in 1825 to bring Methodism back into the Anglican fold. As a *Bunting supporter in 1835 he was appointed the first editor of the *Watchman*. His son, also **Humphry Sandwith** (1822–81), born at Bridlington, had a varied and colourful career as army surgeon, rising to be head of the medical staff in Armenia and distinguishing himself during the siege of Kars in the Crimean War. He then abandoned medicine for the diplomatic service, serving as colonial secretary in Mauritius and Serbia. His novel *Minsterborough* (1876) was based on memories of his own youth.

———

DNB; T.H. Ward (1884)

JAV

Sangster, Dr William Edwin (1900–60; e.m. 1922) was born in London. He had no family connection with Methodism, but attended Radnor Street Sunday School and mainly through its influence offered for the WM ministry. He trained at *Handsworth and *Richmond Colleges. His outstanding gifts as a preacher drew large congregations, especially at *Scarborough (1932–36) and Brunswick, *Leeds (1936–39). His appointment to *Westminster Central Hall coincided with the opening of World War II and for 16 years he exercised a powerful ministry there. During the war he lived in a small flat on the premises, so that contact could be maintained with people who sheltered each night in the crypt. His post-war Sunday evening congregations were the largest in London. He was alive to contemporary thought and his sermons were relevant to the human situation. He was elected President of the Conference in 1950 and five years later became General Secretary of the *HM Department. He was a prolific author. Among his most widely influential titles were *Methodism Can Be Born Again* (1938; revised edn, 1941) and *Methodism's Unfinished Task* (1947), together with his books on preaching, reprinted as *The Art of the Sermon* (1954). His doctoral thesis was published as *The Path to Perfection* (1943). He gave the Sam P. Jones Lectures at Emory University (*Let Me Commend*, 1948) and the Cato Lecture (*The Pure in Heart*, 1954) in Australia. He was forced to retire in 1959 through muscular dystrophy, but during two years of illness continued to write and to promote prayer cells.

Times 25 May 1960; *MR* 13 July 1950, 26 May & 2 June 1960; P. Sangster (1962)

JDB

Sargant, Norman Carr (1909–82; e.m. 1931), missionary in *India, born into a well-known London Methodist family. He was educated at The *Leys School and *Handsworth College. He served in several circuits of the Kanarese-speaking Mysore District from 1931 to 1947, and then in the Mysore Diocese, CSI until 1972. Becoming Bishop in 1951, he not only travelled even more widely, but poured his great energy and administrative ability into meeting diocesan needs. He was a noted supporter of Indian nationalism. In retirement he became an honorary canon of *Bristol Cathedral and was working on a history of the Church in Mysore when he died.

MR 7 Oct. 1982

JAV

Sargant, Dr William Walters (1907–88), controversial pioneer in chemotherapy and other physical forms of treatment for mental disorders, had a Methodist background and was educated at The *Leys School and St John's College, Cambridge. He was visiting professor of Neuropsychiatry at Duke University Medical School, Durham NC, 1947–48 and physician in charge of the Department of Psychological Medicine at St Thomas's Hospital, London, 1948–72. He received the Starkey Memorial Prize of the Royal Society of Health in 1973. In *Battle for the Mind* (1957) he strongly criticized JW's evangelistic methods as a form of brainwashing and indoctrination. He was answered at a theological level by M. Lloyd-Jones in *Conversions Psychological and Spiritual* (1959) and by I. Ramage in *Battle for the Free Mind* (1967), a trenchant critique of both his philosophical assumptions and his treatment of historical data.

Times 31 Aug. 1988

JAV

Saville, Jonathan (1759–1842), *local preacher, born at Great Horton, *Bradford. As an orphan he grew up in the workhouse and was lamed before seeking employment in *Halifax in 1782. Convinced of 'the necessity of a change of heart' at a *Covenant Service in 1784, he emerged as a powerful prayer leader during a period of

revival in the 1790s, became an *exhorter in 1803 and subsequently a *local preacher, gaining inspiration for his sermons while working at his spinning jenny. A popular preacher at missionary and Sunday School Anniversary services, he was invited by J. *Bunting to preach at a memorial service in South Parade Chapel for a *Luddite killed in the attack on a mill in 1812. He was subsequently stoned when attending his class meeting, but escaped unhurt.

F.A. West (1843)

JAH

Savin, Lewis (1864–1918; e.m. 1887), BC missionary in *China, born in Faversham. After teaching and circuit work in England he undertook medical training at the request of the Missionary Committee and joined the BC mission in Yunnan in 1896 as both minister and doctor. He married a missionary colleague, Kate Howe, in 1898. Retiring and reserved, he disliked publicity, but was meticulous and exact in all his work. After the Boxer troubles in 1900 he set up the Mission Hospital in Chaotung, where his medical skills and caring concern won him universal respect and trust.

RKP

Sawday, George William (1854–1944; e.m. 1875), WM missionary in *India, was born in Sidmouth and trained at *Headingley College. Except for six years (1894–99) his whole ministry was spent in the Mysore District, as Superintendent of the Tumkur Circuit (18 years) and of the Mysore District (32 years). He founded the Holdsworth Memorial Hospital in Mysore City and built chapels and schools in many towns and villages. Retiring in 1932, he died in Mysore City.

MR 28 Sept. 1944

JAV

Sayers, Jack (1911–69), legendary liberalizing editor of the *Belfast Telegraph*, Ulster's largest-selling newspaper, and one of its most remarkable journalists, succeeded his father John Sayers (1879–1939) and uncle Robert Sayers (1898–1970) in an editorial dynasty lasting over forty years. He gathered round him journalists of calibre and established a paper which straddled the sectarian divide. Under his leadership it helped to sustain and mould a popular moderate consensus unique in twentieth-century Ulster. The Sayers family owed much and contributed much to the

Methodist Church of which they were active members.

A. Gailey (1995)

RPR

Scarborough, a mediaeval port that later became a spa and holiday resort, saw the first of many visits by JW in 1759. George Cusson, founder of the Naval and Military Bible Society and later a member at Hinde Street, London, played a leading role in the early society. JW preached in the shell of the first chapel in 1772. Queen Street Central Hall was built in 1922, with W.E. *Sangster its minister from 1932 to 1936. A PM society was formed in 1821 following W. *Clowes' preaching and a chapel was built the same year. Expansion came with the opening of Jubilee (1861) and the second St Sepulchre Street chapel (1866). The Independent Primitive Methodists, led by M. *Baxter, seceded in 1831, but had joined the WMA by 1836. Scarborough seems to have replaced York as the PM Conference town; it hosted the Conferences of 1877, 1887, 1905 and 1925. The Methodist Conference met there for the first time in 1998.

DCD

Scarborough, William (1841–94; e.m. 1863), WM minister, appointed along with D. *Hill to Hankow (Hankou), *China in 1864. He returned to England in 1885 because of his health and was appointed Chairman of the Whitby and Darlington District in 1891. His mastery of Chinese language and literature found expression in his *Collection of Chinese Proverbs* (1875; revised and enlarged by C.W. *Allan, Shanghai, 1926).

GRS

Scarth, William Gilyard (1780–1853), master dyer and *local preacher in *Leeds. As a close friend of J. *Bunting and treasurer of the Leeds trustees, he was an opponent of democracy, sided with the Conference party in the dispute over the Brunswick organ in 1827 and opposed the *Warrenites in 1834. He was a member of the committee appointed in 1838 to organize the celebration of the centenary of Methodism.

JAV

School Chaplains *see* **Residential Schools**

Science JW's interest in *natural philosophy derived largely from its theological and apologetic value, just as his interest in electricity was as much pragmatic as theoretical. In the early decades of the nineteenth century Methodists like the railway engineer T. *Hackworth and manufacturers like J. *Mercer contributed to applied science in engineering and industry, rather than to scientific knowledge for its own sake; while the transition to pure science was exemplified in the career of Dr J.B. *Melson, who also did much to popularize scientific discoveries. The response of Methodists, as of other Christians, to the challenge of Darwinism was more positive than is credited in popular mythology, though WM tended to be more negative and conservative than the others. The need to bridge the widening gap between the latest science and traditional religion was nevertheless a real one and was met by men like the WM microscopist W.H. *Dallinger and the PM J.P. *Bellingham in their books and magazine articles. The *Wesley Naturalist*, published between 1887 and 1889, was the journal of the Wesley Scientific Society. In the later part of the century J.C. *Adams was a distinguished astronomer. Contributors to the continuing debate between religion and science in the twentieth century included the mathematical physicist C.A. *Coulson and the atomic physicist W.R. *Hindmarsh, both Vice-Presidents of the Methodist Conference. Professor H. *Butterfield made a historical contribution in his *Origins of Modern Science 1300–1800*. More recently, the interaction between science and religion has continued to be explored through the 'Christ and the Cosmos Initiative', initiated by W. *Gowland.

JAV

Scotland Methodism was probably first brought to Scotland by government troops sent after the 1745 rebellion. JW paid the first of 22 visits in 1751 at the invitation of Capt. *Gallatin, commander of dragoons at Musselburgh. His second visit was to *Glasgow in 1753, at the invitation of John Gillies, minister of the College Kirk. In the next 20 years evangelists like C *Hopper, T. *Taylor, Thomas Cherry, T. *Hanby, D. *Wright, D. *McAllum, A. *McNab and R. *Dall spread Methodism from *Dunbar through *Edinburgh and Leith to *Perth, *Arbroath, *Dundee, *Aberdeen, the Moray coast and *Inverness, and out from Glasgow to Greenock, Port Glasgow and Ayr.

By then the welcome given to the message of Christ as universal saviour had alarmed the Scots Kirk and Methodism was severely set back when the revered and influential minister John Erskine published his opposition to its Arminian doctrine. The consequent refusal by many ministers to administer the Communion to Methodists or to baptize their children persuaded W in 1785 to ordain preachers for Scotland and to allow the *Lord's Supper to be administered in the Presbyterian manner, preceded by the production of metal tokens by communicants. Many believed that his intention, only prevented by death, was to form a separate Scottish connexion, as in *America and *Ireland. This failure was later seen as the reason for Methodism's lack of success in Scotland.

Despite this, membership crept upwards, the message of a universal salvation was eagerly heard and, in the early nineteenth century, the number of hearers persuaded V. *Ward, then District Chairman, to build many chapels from a conviction that preaching in private homes inhibited the progress of Methodism. However, the debts incurred soon crippled the societies. It seemed to some that the WM Conference, which had enthusiastically supported the development of the Free Church of Scotland, was ready for it to take over Scottish Methodism.

By 1851 the *Religious Census showed WM as having only 0.12% of total attendances. The reason for its slow development, apart from continuing debt, was perceived to be the refusal of the Connexion to separate the message from its forms of expression, by insisting on the regular transfer of the itinerants, on the exclusion of leaders from decisions affecting members, and on attendance at class meetings as a condition of *membership. In spite of allowing non-members to communicate on presenting a 'token' and later an 'admission ticket' (a practice which survived, e.g. in *Arbroath, into the twentieth century), many, notably the potential leaders, were lost to the Congregational and Free Churches, a move made easier by the decline in both Churches of anti-Arminian doctrines such as predestination. However, after the creation of the Relief and Extension Fund for Scotland in 1866 and lay representation in Conference from 1878, District membership rose from 2,594 in 1860 to 6,674 in 1900. WM's strength lay in the central and east-coast towns as far north as the Moray coast.

The MNC, which had germinated in the mind of A. *Kilham in Aberdeen in 1792 and whose first President was the Aberdonian W. *Thom, had little impact except around Glasgow between 1810 and 1830. But sympathy for its aims produced IM churches which gravitated towards Congregationalism, which, in contrast to Methodism, was strikingly successful in Scotland.

PM launched missions in Edinburgh and Glasgow in 1826, where their open-air preaching and emphasis on the social gospel found ready hearers among the poor. They avoided ruinous property debts, but for many years failed to turn hearers into members, because, it was said, they had too few chapels. They had only 0.008% of total attendances in 1851, but from the 1880s they developed strong bases in Glasgow, *Paisley and Edinburgh, among miners and factory workers and in the fishing villages on the Berwickshire coast. Membership rose from 1.046 in 1884 to 1,574 in 1889.

Despite the hard soil both WM and PM, led by outstanding preachers, became tough if tiny plants. By 1900 WM had 6,674 and PM 1,574 members and at the 1932 Union totalled 11,997 (9,713 of them WM). Attendances in the 1994 Church Census were 6,000 and in 1995 there were 5,883 members. A proposed union with the Church of Scotland was rejected by the Scotland Synod in 1979, but in 1998 Methodism was actively engaged in the current Scottish Churches' Initiative for Church Unity.

See also **Shetland and Orkney**

D. Wilson (1850); T.L. Parker (1867); W.M. Patterson (1909); W.F. Swift (1947); *HMGB* 3 pp. 265–78

MB

Scott, Abraham (1777–1850; e.m. 1801), MNC minister, who wrote at least 44 theological tracts, many of a polemical nature. Some were in reply to J. *Barker. He also crossed swords with *Calvinists, Socinians and *Roman Catholics and challenged A. *Clarke's views on the eternal sonship of Christ. He was President of the MNC Conference in 1817 and 1837.

EAR

Scott, Dr George (1804–74; e.m. 1830), WM minister, sent to *Sweden in 1830 to take over the work begun by J.R. *Stephens. He helped to found the Swedish Tract Society, the Swedish Missionary Society and the Swedish *Temperance Society. But his adverse comments on the *Lutheran state church during a visit to America aroused hostility in Sweden. He opened an English Church in Stockholm in 1840, but was forced to abandon the mission in 1842. On a return visit in 1859 he was well received. In 1866 he was appointed President of the *Canadian Conference. His son **James Scott** (1835–1911; e.m. 1859) was born in Stockholm and became a missionary in *South Africa, first among the Botswana in Thaba 'Nchu 1861–71 and then mainly in Bloemfontein. He was secretary of the South African Conference 1889–91, President in 1892 and 1897 and acting President in 1898. The pall-bearers at his funeral included a RC priest and a rabbi.

F&H 4 pp. 424–6

JRP/JAV

Scott, John (1792–1868; e.m. 1811), WM minister, born at Copmanthorpe, *York. His early interest in overseas missions persisted and he was Treasurer of the WMMS 1852–68. He was twice President of the Conference, in 1843 and 1852. His passionate concern for education led to his appointment as chairman of the General *Education Committee in 1843. Under his dynamic leadership there was a rapid increase in WM *day schools, but he supported state involvement in education. In 1851 he became the first Principal of *Westminster College. His annual lectures on education were well received. He combined gifts of financial administration with theological insight and love of the trained mind with evangelical zeal. As administrator of the *Auxiliary Fund he showed himself a wise, faithful and sympathetic friend of retired ministers and their widows.

G.J. Stevenson (1884–6) 2 pp. 286–94; F.C. Pritchard (1951); *HMGB* 2 pp. 242–5

EWD

Scott, Dr Percy (1910–91, e.m. 1933) trained for the ministry at *Richmond College and Marburg University. In 1947 he became Tutor in Theology at *Hartley Victoria College, and as Principal (1960–73) unsuccessfully opposed the closure of the college. He was a member of the Faculty of Theology of Manchester University. His wide-ranging interests included industrial mission, youth camps, Rotary, Probus and soccer, and he conducted the memorial service at Old Trafford after the Manchester United air disaster in 1958.

MR 7 Feb. 1991

WL

Scotter, a village north of Gainsborough, is notable for having been the head of a PM *District 1821–23. The first chapel (1819) was sold to the MNC in 1849, when a new one was built. The PM Conference of 1829, meeting there, saw the signing of the Deed Poll and sent four missionaries (including one woman, Ruth Watkins) to *America.

JW visited the village in 1764 and 1766; a WM

society was formed and a chapel built in 1774 (replaced in 1815 and 1900). The MNC (in the Gainsborough Circuit) continued to use the former PM chapel until 1948.

WL

Scripture   One nickname for members of the *Holy Club was 'Bible Moths'. JW called himself *homo unius libri*, a man of one book, i.e. the Bible, but was so widely read that he clearly meant that Scripture was the primary, rather than the exclusive authority for him. In Outler's *'Wesleyan Quadrilateral' it takes precedence over, but is associated with, reason, experience and tradition. In their early years both JW and CW were given to seeking guidance by opening on a text at random. Both were steeped in the Greek NT. But JW was far from uncritical in his acceptance of the Bible as authoritative, rejecting parts of the Psalms as being 'highly improper for the mouths of a Christian Congregation'. In compiling his *Explanatory Notes on the NT*, he drew on Bengel's revised Greek text in making his own revised English version and on the commentary of J.A. Bengel (1687–1752) for his exegesis. His translation, which he also published separately in 1790, anticipated the Revised Version of 1881 at many points.

Other commentaries were produced by T. *Coke, A. *Clarke and J. *Benson. During most of the nineteenth century Methodist scholars remained conservative in their biblical exegesis. The *Wesleyan Bible Union was founded in 1913 to oppose G. *Jackson's qualified advocacy of modern biblical scholarship. A.S. *Peake was largely instrumental in making critical biblical scholarship acceptable within PM and beyond. Other Methodist scholars who have made major contributions to biblical studies in the twentieth century include G.W. *Anderson, C.K. *Barrett, W.F. *Howard, W.F. *Moulton, C.R. *North, N.H. *Snaith, V. *Taylor and M. *Hooker-Stacey.

C.W. Williams (1960) pp. 23–8; R.L. Maddox (1994) pp. 36–40; S.J. Jones (1995)

JAV

Scripture Playing Cards   A misnomer, since they were never used for playing card games. They seem to have originated with the *Moravians, who since 1731 have published an annual *Losungsbuch*, a book of texts and verses from a hymn. The cards were about the size of *class tickets, had Scripture on one side and hymn verses (usually by CW) on the other, and were in sets of 30–100 and usually numbered. They were passed round in *class meetings and similar groups and each text became the subject for conversation.

PWHS 1, pp. 15–25; 4, pp. 6–8, 40–3; 29, pp. 136–8

OAB

Scriven, Sister Miriam (d.1924) was a Sister in the *NCH before entering the Wesley *Deaconess Order in 1893. After four months in Pontefract she went out to Johannesburg, *South Africa, in 1896. She remained there until 1907, doing splendid work during the Boer War. In 1908 she took up an appointment at Otley, but retired in 1915.

Agenda: The Organ of the WDO (1924)

EDG

Secker, Dr Thomas (1693–1768), Bishop of *Bristol 1734 and of *Oxford 1737; Dean of St Paul's, 1750 and Archbishop of Canterbury from 1758. Brought up as a Dissenter, he obtained Anglican orders in 1722. He 'deprecated the progress of Methodism, but did not persecute its adherents'. His identification with JW's anonymous correspondent 'John Smith' in 1745–8 is now generally discounted.

DNB; T. Secker (1988)

JAV

Secretary of the Conference   The *Deed of Declaration 1784 required the annual election of a Secretary of the Conference. The Secretaries, including the first, T. *Coke, and J. *Bunting, often served for a number of years, and in WM the office was combined with a circuit or another connexional appointment. The Secretary was always a minister and a member of the *Legal Hundred.

In PM the Secretary was a circuit minister appointed annually simply to minute the Conference proceedings. There was also a 'General Secretary of the Church and Secretary of the General Committee' separated from circuit work and in office for five years. The UMC appointed annually from 1911 a layman as their Conference secretary, the constituent groups having previously had differing practices.

After Methodist Union E. *Finch was, in 1937, the first to be elected to the office of Secretary without other circuit or connexional appointment. The Conference Office was located in *Westminster Central Hall from then until it moved to 25 Marylebone Road in 1995. The designation

'Conference Office' first appeared on the stations in 1943.

K.B. Garlick (1983), Appendices; *PWHS* vol. 38 pp. 94, 118–120

SRH

Sector Ministry has more recently come to be called 'Ministry in other appointments', that is, outside the circuit, District and connexional ministry. For many years a few ministers were given permission to serve in senior appointments, usually in universities. From the 1960s the concept has been widened by a Conference decision that the Church should be represented by ministers serving in social work, hospital chaplaincies, the Health Service, industry, the media, education, counselling and even bus driving. The Conference Advisory Committee on Ministerial Appointments considers all applications to serve in 'the Sectors' and reports on them to the *Stationing Committee.

PWS

Sellon, Rev. Walter (1715–92), Anglican clergyman, of Huguenot descent. Before his ordination he was a baker and a *local preacher, having met JW in 1745 and shed his prejudice against Methodism. He taught at *Kingswood School 1748–50. Under the patronage of the Countess of *Huntingdon he held several livings, including from 1770 that of Ledsham, Yorks, but in 1770 supported JW in the *Calvinistic controversy. He made a study of John Goodwin's *Arminian writings in order to answer A. *Toplady's Calvinistic polemics. His *Answer to Aspasio Vindicated* (1767) was a contribution to the controversy that surrounding J. *Hervey's *Theron and Aspasio*. At JW's suggestion, he wrote *A Defence of God's Sovereignty* (1770) as a reply to a book by Elisha Cole first published in 1673.

C. Atmore (1801) pp. 381–84; A.G. Ives (1970); A. Brown-Lawson (1994)

JAV

Selston, the largest parish in Nottinghamshire. WM made no headway there, but PM spread among the framework knitters and other working-class inhabitants. The village was missioned from the Belper Circuit in 1823–24 and Portland Row chapel was built in 1824 (replaced in 1882), with six more in other parts of the parish between 1827 and 1904. A schism in 1839 led to the formation of the *Original Methodists, whose first chapel (known from its location as the 'Middle Chapel') was built in Selston and became the head of one of the four circuits and branches of this new body. At Pye Hill the UMFC chapel (1874) and the PM chapel (1882) were within a few yards of each other.

DMG

Selstonites *see* Original Methodists

Sermons on Several Occasions In the summer of 1746 JW interrupted his itinerant schedule for several weeks to prepare a volume of sermons for publication. It was designed to 'exhibit the substance of what I have been preaching for between eight and nine years last past' and he hoped it would reveal in the clearest manner 'what those doctrines are which I embrace and teach as the essentials of true religion'. A second set followed in 1748 and a third in 1750, making 36 sermons in all. A fourth volume was added in 1760, bringing the total to 43 and a 44th sermon was inserted in the 2nd edition of volume 3 (1762): hence 'Wesley's Forty-four Sermons'. In the *'Large Minutes' of 1763 these four volumes were cited in the *model deed as defining the content of Methodist preaching. (*See* Doctrinal standards.)

In 1770 JW began to publish a collected edition of his *Works*. Volumes 1–4 were the 44 sermons plus a further nine, totalling 53. In 1785 he published a new and final collection in 8 volumes, totalling a hundred sermons. In this edition he discarded 8 of the 9 additional sermons from the 1770 edition. He himself understood this corpus of sermons as definitive of his role as preacher, teacher, evangelist and pastor. The successive volumes reflect his thoughts as they unfolded over the years.

J. Lawson (1946) pp.xix–xxi; A.C. Outler (1984–7) 1 pp. 29–55

JWH

Seward Family of Badsey, near Evesham, were early supporters of both *Calvinistic and *Arminian Methodism and of JW's *New Room, Bristol. Both JW and CW declined offers from them to cover the cost of their preaching tours. **William Seward** (*c.* 1702–40) was an Anglican layman and a financial expert employed in the South Sea Office of the Treasury. Coming under the influence of CW in 1738, he was converted and associated with G. *Whitefield, whom he accompanied to Georgia. While accompanying H. *Harris on a preaching tour in South Wales in September 1740, he was mobbed and struck in the eye by a stone. He died the following month, though the later accounts of his 'martyrdom' at Hay on Wye have been questioned and lack contemporary evidence. His brother **Benjamin Seward**, educated at Cambridge, was converted in 1739 and was a close friend of the Wesleys despite the opposition of his Baptist brother **Henry Seward**. He accompanied JW on his secession from the *Fetter Lane society in 1740. Another brother, **Thomas Seward**, was an Anglican clergyman.

PWHS 17 pp. 187–91, 39 pp. 2–5

EWD

Sexual Ethics The Conference Declaration on *The Christian View of Marriage and the Family* (1939) states that from the time of Jesus the life-long union of one man with one woman has been the norm and standard of Christian marriage, which is intended to serve the dual purpose of fellowship and parenthood. Methodism stresses the importance of sex education, preparation for marriage and chastity before marriage. The principle of family planning is commended and the use of contraception approved. Abortion as a means of family limitation is condemned, but the Methodist Church has assented to the provisions of the law which allows abortion in carefully defined situations, especially where the life of the mother is in jeopardy. The Church recognizes the fact of marriage breakdown and judges that divorce should be granted only when the breakdown is irretrievable. The remarriage of divorced people in church is permitted in certain cases. The Conference has declared that no person should be debarred from the Church on grounds of sexual orientation in itself, but has directed that the traditional teaching of the Church should be made clear to all candidates for the ministry, office or membership.

G.T. Brake (1984) pp. 456–76

KGG

Shadford, George (1739–1816; e.m. 1768), born at *Scotter, Lincs, was a keen wrestler in his youth and loved football and dancing. In 1758 he joined the militia and while stationed at *Gainsborough heard a Methodist preacher at the Old Hall. This led to his conversion and he became an itinerant. At the Conference of 1772 in *Leeds he responded to Capt. *Webb's plea for preachers to go to *America. As he embarked the following spring, JW wrote to him: 'I let you loose, George, on the great continent of America . . . Do all the good you can.' Returning to England in 1780, he gave a further eleven years to the itinerancy and died at Frome after 25 years in retirement. He was one of those named by JW in the *Deed of Declaration.

EMP 6 pp. 137–81

WL

Shafto, Robert Ingram (1770–1848), country squire and committed PM, was converted when working as a solicitor in *Sunderland. On inheriting Bavington Hall in the Tyne Valley in 1828, he threw in his lot with the PMs and became not only a sincere and generous patron, but also a preacher within the enormous Hexham Circuit and a warm advocate of *temperance and *Sunday Schools. He is said to have enjoyed a *Camp Meeting with as much zest as his shepherd or ploughman. His son showed no inclination to continue supporting the PMs, but Shafto's patronage was of much importance in their pioneering days in Tynedale.

PMM 1848 pp. 513–16

GEM

Sharp, Dr John Alfred (1856–1932; e.m. 1881), WM minister, born at Shaftesbury, Dorset and apprenticed to a carpenter. He was converted under A. *M'Aulay, who also kindled his interest in Methodist history and literature. He was trained at *Didsbury and *Handsworth Colleges. In *Northampton (1888–91) his encounter with Charles Bradlaugh kindled an interest in social issues and in *Birmingham (1894–97) he took a prominent part in educational affairs. In 1906 he became Connexional *Temperance Secretary. As *Book Steward from 1911 to 1932 he strengthened the Book Room's links with the book trade and with overseas Churches. He saw through the press the final volumes of N. *Curnock's edition of JW's *Journal*, J. *Telford's edition of JW's *Letters*, E.H. Sugden's edition of the 'Standard Sermons' and Findlay and Holdsworth's history of the WMMS. He himself wrote books on Abraham Lincoln and David Livingstone and produced a catalogue of the library and Wesleyana at the Book Room. He was elected President of the Conference in 1921 and in 1930 was President of the FCFC. At the age of 55 he became a Mason and was Assistant Grand Chaplain of the Grand Lodge. His native town made him a Freeman in 1921, the first to be so honoured.

MR 10 March 1932; W.H. Armstrong (1932); F.H. Cumbers (1956) pp. 99–100

WL

Sharpe, John (1820–95; e.m. 1848), PM minister appointed to Sydney NSW in 1854, where he revived a feeble PM cause founded in the colony in 1845. For 20 years he provided effective leadership, encouraging the growth of churches in Sydney, Parramatta, Newcastle etc., as well as in Melbourne (Victoria) and Launceston (Tasmania). A man of deep piety, he was an excellent and indefatigable administrator. He helped establish temperance societies, criticized the treatment of aborigines, opposed capital punishment and founded and edited the *New South Wales PM Messenger*.

ADEB

EGC

Sharpley, John Booth (1800–72), corn merchant and Methodist reformer, born at *Louth. He became a *local preacher in 1822. In the *Warrenite dispute of 1835 he was an energetic reconciler of the rival factions. But in 1849, when the Reform agitation was felt in the *Louth Circuit, he was its leading spokesman, was expelled from WM membership and gave himself to the establishment of the UMFC chapel at Eastgate. He was three times mayor of Louth (1839, 1841 and 1854), a Justice of the Peace and an alderman.

WL

Shaw, Barnabas (1788–1857; e.m. 1810), WM missionary, who spent most of his ministry in *South Africa, where his was effectively the first missionary appointment. Within months of arrival in 1816 he had seized an opportunity to begin work in Namaqualand and established a base at Leliefontein, 300 miles north of Cape Town. From there or the Cape he oversaw the steady expansion of Methodist witness and his advice guided WMMS policy. He was strict about discipline, critical of the London Missionary Society for its laxity, and himself sometimes criticized as dictatorial.

JRP

Shaw, Charles (1832–1906; e.m. 1853), MNC minister, born in Tunstall. He spent part of his childhood in the workhouse and part working on the pot-banks, recounting his experiences in his autobiography *When I was a Child* (1903; reprint, 1977) and they form the (unacknowledged) basis of chapter 5 of Arnold Bennett's *Clayhanger* (1910). He joined the local MNC Sunday School and was in the ministry from 1853 to 1861. Between 1861 and 1897 he managed a cotton mill in Oldham, expressing his ardent Liberalism in the leaders he wrote for the Radical *Oldham Express*. He re-entered the ministry in 1897.

PWHS 40 pp. 51–3

EAR

Shaw, William (1798–1872; e.m. 1820), WM missionary in *South Africa 1820–33 and 1837–56, initially as chaplain to the British settlers. In 1824 he began to open a string of mission stations among the Xhosas. His wife's words as they set out were the theme of South African Methodism's 150th anniversary in 1956: 'Let us go in the name of the Lord.' In his second tour, as General Superintendent for South East Africa, he extended the chain to Natal and Methodism came to have more black members than any other mainline denomination in the country. Back in England he drew up a scheme for a South African Conference which was not realised for 20 years. He wrote *The Story of My Mission* (1860) and was President of the 1865 Conference.

G.J. Stevenson (1884–6) 3 pp. 329–39; W.B. Boyce (1874); H. Davies (1951) pp. 30–9; C. Sadler (1967)

JRP

Shaw, Dr William (1854–1937; e.m. 1878), born at Newport, Salop, entered the MNC ministry in 1882. After several English circuits he was sent to Melbourne, Victoria to superintend the Richmond MNC Circuit. In 1888 the MNC withdrew from Australia and Shaw negotiated a merger with WM. He served, as a WM minister, 11 years in Victoria and 6 in Tasmania, before transferring to South Australia and ministering at Archer Street, North Adelaide until his retirement. Interested in young people, he became State and National President of the *Christian Endeavour movement. He was President of the South Australia Conference in 1918. After retirement he led an evangelical programme called the Spiritual Advance Crusade. A powerful expository preacher, he was a careful, conservative scholar prepared to accept much of the new biblical scholarship. His textbook *Christian Theology* (1928), written at the request of the General Conference, gained him a DD from McGill University, Montreal.

DGH

Shebbear, a remote and rural parish in north-west Devon which in BC tradition became their equivalent of Epworth. Lake Farm near Shebbear village was the home of the *Thorne family. The support they gave to W. *O'Bryan and his newly formed denomination ensured its survival and growth. James Thorne succeeded O'Bryan as its leader and his brother Samuel became the denomination's printer. A chapel was built on the farm in 1818 (rebuilt 1841 and enlarged more recently). Its burial ground is the denomination's Valhalla. Samuel built Prospect House on the farm as a home and printing works; contemporary plans and pamphlets bear the Shebbear imprint. In the 1830s he and his wife Mary O'Bryan began a school for local children there, which is now *Shebbear College. Eight BC Conferences were held at Shebbear between 1821 and 1868, by which time the movement had developed from a folk religion to a denomination.

RFST

Shebbear College, Devon, a BC Conference proprietary grammar school for boys from 1842, began as a private school founded in 1834 by S. *Thorne. It was taken over by the *Board of Management in 1951. Many of its early pupils went as missionaries to *Australia and *Canada. Its roots are firmly in the North Devon countryside and for over 50 years until 1975 it accepted pupils funded by the local authority. Local support in 1993 led to the withdrawal of proposals to merge it with *Edgehill College on the Bideford site. In 1997 there were 297 boarding and day boys and girls aged 3–18.

R. Pyke (1953); A. Fairchild (1987)

DBT

Sheffield In 1780, on one of his several visits, JW preached at the opening of Norfolk Street Chapel (transformed in 1905 into the Victoria Hall, one of the Central Missions inspired by the *Forward Movement) and was the guest of T. *Holy. Carver Street Chapel hosted no fewer than 13 WM Conferences between its opening in 1805 and 1922. The *Cole family was influential in establishing Board schools and also Wesley College (1838), which was transferred to the local education authority in 1906 as King Edward VII Grammar School. One of its governors, W.H. *Dallinger, also preached in local PM chapels.

In 1797, following his expulsion from WM, A. *Kilham took with him part of the Norfolk Street congregation, taking over the Scotland Street Chapel built in 1764 for an earlier dissident, T. *Bryant. This closed in 1963. Notable among MNC laymen were the *Firth family and J. *Ward. No fewer than 24 Conferences of the MNC, the UMFC and the UMC were held in

Sheffield, plus 6 PM Conferences. In 1932 there were 6 WM, 7 PM and 5 UMC circuits in the city, the non-Wesleyans equalling the WM in ministers and members. They were reorganized into 8 new geographically-based circuits, in response to the rapidly expanding and diversifying conurbation. By 1997 Carver Street Chapel was no longer a place of worship and Methodism was involved in the Inner City Ecumenical Mission, in the *Urban Theology Unit and in theological education in co-operation with *Cliff College, the Church Army and the University of Sheffield.

See also **Ranmoor College**

J. Everett (1823); T.A. Seed (1907); Conference Handbooks 1922 (WM), 1940

ANC

Shent, William (1715–87), a *Leeds barber and peruke maker, was converted by three Marys – Mary Maude, his wife (*née* Musgrave) and Mary Whedale – all three being converts of John *Nelson. His Briggate shop became the first home of the Leeds society. Nelson first preached there just after Christmas 1742 and CW the following May. As leader of the Leeds society and *local preacher, he is recorded in 1755 as being a half-itinerant in the Yorkshire Circuit. He subsequently 'fell into sin and was publicly expelled from the society', the cause being business failure and drink. Following a moving letter from JW in 1779, recalling how Shent had stood by him when stones were flying on every side, he was restored to membership.

SL 6 pp. 333–4

DCD

Shern Hall Building Society *see* **Mallinson, W.**

Shetland and Orkney The Scottish islands were among the proposed mission fields mentioned in *Coke's missionary *Address* in 1786. But an appeal to Coke in 1808 for the launching of a mission to Shetland came to nothing. In 1819 John Nicolson, converted by Methodists while in the Army, returned to his native Shetland and in two years had formed a 'circuit'. He asked for Conference's help and, with A. *Clarke's support, John Raby (1790–1858; e.m. 1811) and S. *Dunn were sent in 1822. Despite opposition from the Kirk, by the time of Nicolson's death in 1828 there were four circuits and 1,000 members. From then on, in spite of heavy emigration, Methodism remained comparatively strong and at the 1932

Union there were 1,398 members. By 1995 there were only 379.

Methodist work was initiated in Orkney by A. *Clarke in 1825. S. *Dunn made a preaching tour and a few societies were established, of which Stronsay was the strongest under the leadership of John Knowles. But they gradually declined and those who remained joined the Free Church after its formation in 1843. In the 1980s, however, a Methodist 'house congregation' was formed in South Ronaldsay.

H. R. Bowes in *PWHS* 38 pp. 136–46; *WMM* 1835; WHS(S) 4 pp. 17–20; 6 pp. 9–20

MB

Shillington, Thomas (1767–1830), founder of a wealthy family business in *Ireland and generation of public-minded Shillingtons who contributed to Methodism's growth in Portadown and the wider Connexion. At the time of the *PWM division he chaired the 'Dungannon Committee' which ensured for the WMs legal control of Trust property. His son **Thomas Averell Shillington** (1800–74) followed the tradition of connexional and public service. He was treasurer of the Chapel Fund and played a leading role in the founding of *Wesley College, Dublin and *Methodist College, Belfast. He served on the Senate of Queen's University, Belfast.

J. Dwyer (1875)

RPR

Shirley, Rev. Walter (1725–86), Anglican clergyman related to the Countess of *Huntingdon and the Earl of Ferrers. 'A typical hunting parson', he was converted under H. *Venn. His evangelical preaching as rector of Loughrea, Co. Galway from 1758 was condemned by the Bishop of Clonfert. As one of the Countess's chaplains, he rallied the Calvinistic opposition to the Wesleyan *Minutes* of 1770, led the deputation of protesters at the Conference of 1771 and composed the circular letter for the Countess in 1772, accusing the *Arminians of heresy. He wrote a number of hymns.

DNB; A. Brown-Lawson (1994)

JAV

Shoebotham, Daniel K. (fl.1827–44), entered the WM ministry in 1827 and served in several English circuits before spending one year in *Shetland (1832–33). During his ministry in *Perth (1833–35) and *Dundee (1835–36) the *Warrenite controversy erupted. He sided with S.

*Warren against the Conference and in March 1836 divided the *Dundee society over the issue, taking with him two thirds of the membership and most of the leaders. He and his following (known locally as 'Shoebothamites' or 'Shuffelbottamites') joined the WMA, but his name disappears from their *Minutes* in 1838. In that year he opened a chapel seating 1,000, and both he and his Dundee congregation had become Independent by 1840. He was opposed to the Factory Acts of 1833 and 1844 on the grounds that they violated parental rights.

A.N. Cass in WHS(S) Sept. 1973 pp. 3–4
                                                         MB

Shrewsbury   The first society was formed in 1744 by a 'poor woman' who made her living mending stockings. JW did not visit it until 1761, when he preached in a cottage at 1 Fish Street belonging to a tin man called Perks. His frequent visits from then on were because of J. *Fletcher's ministry at *Madeley. He also preached in the private chapel at Berwick. The society at Shearman's Hall (from 1761) owed much to John Appleton, a currier who preached four times a week and built the first chapel in Hill's Lane (1781). He was followed by Thomas Brocas, a gardener turned Staffordshire pottery seller and a very acceptable *local preacher whom JW described as the 'father of Methodism in Shrewsbury', The Shrewsbury Circuit was formed (from Wolverhampton) in 1792. Membership grew from 302 in 1793 to 850 in 1802. Brocas encouraged the building of a chapel at St John's Hill in 1805 (rebuilt 1879).

PM arrived with Sarah Spittle and James Bonser (who was imprisoned for a day) in 1822. They built a chapel at Castle Court (1826), missioned Bishops Castle and, further afield, Brinkworth (Wilts) and *Belfast, the last causing major financial problems. Preachers sent out from the circuit included E. *Johnson, Richard Davies (Book Steward 1859–65) and P. *Pugh. In 1926 the PM chapel was used for prayer meetings by striking railwaymen. The defection of a son of Thomas Brocas led in 1834 to the opening of the first MNC chapel, an Italianate building on Town Walls, now part of the Girls High School. The UMFC built a chapel in Albert Street in 1857.

W. Phillips (1896); W.E. Morris (1961)
                                                         JHL

Shrewsbury, William James (1795–1866; e.m. 1815), WM missionary appointed to the *West Indies in 1815, where he served for nine years on Tortola, Grenada and Barbados. On Barbados he suffered severe persecution from those interested in upholding *slavery and had to flee for his life. In 1826 he was appointed to *South Africa and pioneered the work of the Butterworth Station in Kaffirland, returning to the home work in 1836.

J.V.B. Shrewsbury (1856)
                                                         GRS

Shum (or Schumm) Family, five brothers who emigrated from Niederstettin, Germany in the 1770s, settling in *London and *Bath, where they became associated with the Methodists. In Bath, **John Jacob Shum** prospered as a baker and became an enthusiastic and generous Methodist, affectionately known as 'Daddy Shum'. He was a *class leader and chapel steward and an assiduous visitor of the poor and sick. He outlived his younger brothers, dying in 1822. Of his brothers, **George Shum** also settled in Bath and was attracted to the *Moravians; **Frederick Shum**, a pork butcher, became a class leader and *local preacher; and **John Michael Shum** (d. 1831) was a *society steward. His son, also **John Michael**, was musically gifted and became the organist at New King Street at the age of 12 and held the post for 64 years. Another of the second generation, **John Caspar Shum** (1760–1836), came to England in his youth and eventually settled in London, becoming *class leader, steward and *trustee at Great Queen Street. He and other members of his family were buried at *Wesley's Chapel.

WMM 1824–1836 passim; *MR(W)* 1893 pp. 76–81; G.J. Stevenson (1872) p. 468
                                                         JAV

Sidmouth Bill (1811) was introduced in Parliament by Lord Sidmouth at a time of political nervousness in government circles, to deal with the perceived threat of a growing number of preachers licensed under the *Toleration Act. It would have effectively put in jeopardy Methodism's use of *local preachers and even threatened the *itinerancy. As a threat to religious liberties it was opposed by the *Committee of Privileges, led by T. *Allan and J. *Butterworth, and by the Protestant Dissenting Deputies. A public petition was organized and in the face of growing opposition the Bill was dropped after its second reading. The incident marked a significant point in Methodism's self-awareness and a mutual hardening of attitudes on both sides of the Anglican/Nonconformist divide.

W.R. Ward (1972) pp. 54–62; J.M. Turner (1985) pp. 120–6; D. Hempton (1984) pp. 98–104; D. Hempton (1996) pp. 110–13

JAV

Sierra Leone There were Methodists in the first party of freed slaves from Nova Scotia which landed in Freetown in 1792, but their pleas for missionaries were at first unavailing. In 1796 T. *Coke organized a mission to the Fula people of the interior which proved abortive. It was not until 1811, after Sierra Leone became a Crown Colony in 1808, that a fresh start was made; G. *Warren died within months, but the work survived. Disputes between the Freetown congregations and with missionaries led to a period of fragmentation from 1821, as a result of which several different kinds of Methodist Church were still in being in the Freetown area at the end of the twentieth century. In 1896 the hinterland was proclaimed a Protectorate and Methodist work among the Mende and Kissi people gradually developed. Colony and Protectorate became an independent nation in 1957 and in 1967 the Sierra Leone District became an autonomous Conference, with extensive educational, medical and agricultural work. In the civil strife and turmoil of the 1990s many congregations were dispersed and the Church struggled to care for refugees in Guinea and displaced people in Freetown and Segbwema, where the Nixon Memorial Hospital continued its ministry in spite of repeated looting.

C. Fyfe (1962)

JRP

Sigston, James (1776–1865), Protestant Methodist leader who ran a school, Sigston's Academy, in *Leeds and was locally active in radical politics. Originally a WM *local preacher, he was greatly influenced by W. *Bramwell, whose *Life* he wrote. He led a small revivalist secession, the 'Kirkgate Screamers', in Leeds in 1805, returned to WM in 1807, but with M. *Johnson was a leader of the opposition in the *Leeds Organ Case in 1827. He drew up a constitution for the *Protestant Methodists, was their first President in 1829 (and again in 1833), and opened the first Protestant Methodist chapel. He was President of the *WMA in 1839.

OAB

Simeon, Rev. Charles (1759–1836), Anglican evangelical, Fellow of King's College and incumbent of Holy Trinity, *Cambridge 1782–1836. A friend of H. *Venn and his son John, he was also acquainted with J. *Fletcher and JW. He began small group meetings for his parishioners comparable to Methodist *class meetings. He held conversation parties and sermon classes in his rooms at King's for aspiring ordinands and in this way helped to revitalize much of the CofE. In the preface to his sermon outlines (*Horae Homileticae*) he recorded a conversation with JW on 20 Dec. 1784 on the common ground between *Calvinists and *Arminians. Reviled and criticized at first, he was later widely respected and influential. He was one of the founders of the CMS and of the Simeon Trust for the appointment of suitable clergy to benefices purchased from his funds.

DNB; *ODCC*; H.C.G. Moule (1892); H.E. Hopkins (1977)

SJH

Simon, Dr John Smith (1843–1933; e.m. 1863), WM minister and historian, born in *Glasgow, of Scottish and Welsh ancestry. His father was the Rev. John Simon (1802–61; e.m. 1831) and he traced his Methodist ancestry back to 1748 in Birstall. He was Governor of *Didsbury College, Manchester 1901–13 and President of the Conference in 1907. His DD was conferred by Victoria University, Toronto. He wrote a history of Methodism in Dorset (1870) and the article on the history and polity of Methodism in the *ERE*, and made substantial contributions to the *LQR*. His early experience in a solicitor's office enabled him to write on the constitution and discipline of WM. He gave the 1907 *Fernley Lecture on the eighteenth century revival of religion in England. He devoted his retirement in *Southport to a scholarly, comprehensive, five-volume history of eighteenth-century Methodism, beginning with *John Wesley and the Religious Societies* (1921), the final volume being completed by his son-in-law Dr A.W. *Harrison. He was President of the *WHS 1907–33. His wife was the sister of J.C. and W.G. *Adams and his three daughters all married into the WM ministry. His son **Alfred Gordon Simon** (1884–1962; e.m. 1910) was a missionary in Wuchang, *China 1910–27 and was Principal of Wesley College, Kumasi, Gold Coast 1930–34.

MR 6 July 1933, 13 Sept. 1962; *PWHS* 19 pp. 49–51, 50 pp. 15–18; G.E. Harrison (1935) pp. 139–54; R.P. Heitzenrater (1984) 2 pp. 193–4

JAN

Simpson, Rev. David (1745–99), Anglican clergyman, born near Northallerton and educated at St John's College, Cambridge, where he became acquainted with R. *Hill. He was converted in 1767 under the preaching of the Unitarian Theophilus Lindsey and in 1772 was offered the curacy at *Macclesfield in succession to H.A. *Rogers' father. When he had been twice suspended and eventually prevented from taking the living because of his Methodistical preaching, Mrs Rogers' uncle Charles Roe built Christ Church for him and installed him as incumbent in 1779. He is said to have started a Sunday School there as early as 1778. B.B. *Collins was one of his curates and JW preached and helped to administer the Sacrament there on several occasions. He fostered the local Methodist society and was present at the 1784 Conference. Among his many publications, some of them in defence of Methodism, *A Plea for Religion and the Sacred Writings* (1797) was frequently reprinted.

C. Atmore (1801) pp. 388–97; B. Smith (1875)
JAV

Sin as the act of sinning has its roots in *original sin. For JW, sin cannot reign in the regenerated, but does remain, even though past sin is pardoned and the stain of guilt removed. While it is too simplistic to limit his understanding of sin to 'a voluntary transgression of a known law' (which is certainly scriptural, even if not the full biblical understanding of the nature of sin), this definition is vitally important for his teaching on the state of a justified Christian who does not knowingly sin, and those who have gone on to *Christian perfection or 'perfect love'. For those who have advanced in the Christian life, the principle of sin has itself been destroyed and the carnal mind remaining in the believer utterly cleansed. But JW recognized the continuance of 'ignorance, mistake, temptation, and a thousand infirmities' in those who had experienced a second distinctive work of *grace. He often spoke of sin in terms of a disease from which we need to be healed – a therapeutic concept he shared with *Eastern Orthodox theologians. (Cf CW's 'The seed of sin's disease/Spirit of health remove' etc.) The line he drew between actual sins and human weaknesses has been considered by critics as dealing too loosely with the reality of inward, unrecognized, involuntary sin.

JW, sermons 'On Sin in Believers' and 'Repentance of Believers'; R.L. Maddox (1994) pp. 73–83, 163–5
WP

Singapore *see* **South East Asia**

Skevington, John (1801–50), *Chartist leader, born in Loughborough, where his father Joseph Skevington was one of the founders of the PM society. At 14 he acquired fame as the 'boy preacher' in the local circuit. He was an itinerant in *Halifax, Barnsley and Bradwell from 1822 to 1824, then returned to Loughborough. He severed his links with the PMs following a dispute over the Dead Lane chapel, of which he was treasurer. Shortly after this he became the organizer of the Loughborough Chartist district and represented them at the National Convention in 1839. Although he became a national Chartist leader, it is unlikely that he countenanced the use of physical force advocated by some of his fellows.

DLB; S.Y. Richardson in D.C. Dews (1982)
NADS

Skevington, John (1814–45; e.m. 1839), WM missionary. A *Nottingham lacemaker, he sailed to *New Zealand in 1839 on the *missionary ship Triton's maiden voyage. Learning his job from colleagues in Tasmania and New Zealand, he was appointed in 1842 to the new station at Taranaki. Escorted there by a group of enthusiastic Maoris, he and his wife pioneered the work. After a brief but effective ministry, he collapsed and died in Auckland, aged only 31, the victim of unrealistic expectations of human strength.
MJF

Skinner, Conrad Arthur (1889–1975; e.m. 1912), WM minister and author. In 1910, 1911 and 1912 he coxed for Cambridge in the university boat race and later was coach of the Jesus College boat and rowing correspondent of the *News Chronicle* and its predecessor for nearly 40 years. He was Assistant Tutor at *Richmond College 1912–15 and teacher and (from 1918) chaplain at The *Leys School 1917–49. Unable for health reasons to preach, he published devotional and popular theological works, including *Concerning the Bible* (1928), *The Gospel of the Lord Jesus* (1937) and *An Approach to Church Membership* (1946); also ten novels and plays under the pseudonym 'Michael Maurice'. In retirement he discovered that he possessed the gift of radiesthesia ('Odic force') and exercised it in a healing ministry. His son **Michael J. Skinner** (1919– ; e.m. 1943) was tutor at *Wesley House, Cambridge 1959–74 and Principal 1974–80. Two grandsons entered the Methodist and one the Baptist ministry.

MR 4 Dec. 1975

BEB

Slack, Agnes Elizabeth (*c.* 1859-post 1941), born at Ripley, Derbys, the sister of Sir J.B. *Slack, in 1895 became secretary of the British Women's Temperance Union and the World Women's Christian Temperance Union founded by her close friend Frances Willard. She travelled through the British Isles and the world, speaking and preaching in churches of many denominations, but especially WM, and was the first woman allowed to speak at *Wesley's Chapel, London. She wrote *People I Have Met and Places I have Been* (1941)

A. Tillyard (1926)

JHL

Slavery In the eighteenth century England wrung from Spain and France a virtual monopoly of the slave trade and contracted to supply the Spanish West Indies 144,000 negroes within 30 years. But it was from England that the movement for emancipation sprang. Inspired by the Quaker Anthony Benezet, JW attacked what he called 'this execrable villainy' in his *Thoughts upon Slavery* (1774) and other writings. He urged William Wilberforce to continue his battle against the trade. Visiting the newly independent American States in 1784–85, T. *Coke found slavery to be too controversial an issue for open denunciation without damaging Methodism's appeal to the *American people; and in the nineteenth century it was one which split the MEC as well as the nation. Early missionaries in the *West Indies suffered through their opposition to slave-owning. The Emancipation Act which came into force on 1 August 1834 owed much to the zeal and conviction of the evangelical leaders of the day.

R.T. Anstey (1975)

KGG

Smales, Gideon (1817–94; e.m. 1837), WM missionary from *Whitby. He sailed to *New Zealand in 1839 on the *missionary ship Triton's maiden voyage. Although devoted to his work, he had a turbulent ministry, causing difficulties with both colleagues and flock. He married J.H. *Bumby's sister, Mary Anna, and served in several stations on North Island, including 'Beecham-

dale'. He left the mission voluntarily in 1856 in order to provide for his family.

MJF

Smetham, James (1821–1889), artist and writer, son a WM minister of the same name (1792–1847; e.m. 1812). He was educated at *Woodhouse Grove School and became a painter, known for his prodigious output, his 'squarings' (miniature visual jottings) and also his 'ventilations' (penning of passing thoughts). He was the first drawing master at *Westminster College. An associate of D.G. Rossetti and the Pre-Raphaelites, his adherence to Methodism distanced him from the mainstream of artists and he never achieved the success he might have done. During his closing years he suffered from severe mental illness, exacerbated by the inner conflict between his art and his Methodist allegiance.

J. Smetham (1892); S. Casteras (1995)

PSF

Smethurst, Henry (1819–92), son of a PM itinerant **Samuel Smethurst** (1781–1863; e.m. 1821) who left the *itinerancy in 1824 for financial reasons and sought work in *Grimsby. Henry built up a thriving business in the fish trade. After his conversion, he began to preach and as a staunch *temperance advocate was instrumental in building the Grimsby Temperance Hall. He also gave sites for two large chapels. He became a member of the town Council and an Alderman and was twice Mayor. He served as a JP and as Chairman of the School Board. His success was based on hard work and inflexible integrity, but misfortune befell him in later years. He went blind, but remained generous to the town and to Methodism. A marble monument in his memory was placed in the People's Park in 1894.

WL

Smith Family of *Leeds **George Smith** (d.1846 aet. 82), was a *local preacher who began as a clothier but became a thread manufacturer and partner in the bank of Perfect, Smith & Co. His son **William Smith** (1785–1868), a wealthy Tory woollen merchant, was a trustee of Brunswick chapel who supported the installing of an organ and paid for its extension in 1846. A keen supporter of *overseas missions, he was on the first committee of the pioneering Leeds District WM Missionary Society and is credited with having founded the annual missionary breakfast, first held at his warehouse in 1839. With his father and his brother **George Smith** he became a director of the family's Leeds & West Riding Joint Stock Banking Co. (1835), but never fully recovered from its collapse in 1846. In 1865 a grateful Methodism presented him with a portrait by Samuel Sidley, formerly in the Mission House, London, and on his death a memorial, now destroyed, was placed in Brunswick chapel. His brother **Samuel Smith** (1790–1867) was a surgeon at Leeds Infirmary from 1819 and founder of the Leeds School of Medicine.

DCD

Smith, Dr Charles Ryder (1875–1956; e.m. 1895) was born at *Mansfield and educated at *Kingswood School. After a period as Assistant Tutor at *Headingley College and twenty years in English Circuits and Bombay, he was appointed Tutor in Systematic Theology at *Richmond College in 1920, where he remained until retirement in 1940, becoming Principal in 1929. He was also a Professor in the University of London and Dean of the Faculty of Theology. His series of Studies entitled *The Bible Doctrine of* . . . are marked by a careful survey of the evidence and include one on *Womanhood* (1923). He was a member of the *Methodist Sacramental Fellowship, his 1927 Fernley Lecture being on *The Sacramental Society*. In 1931 he was elected President of the WM Conference and played an important part in the movement towards *Methodist Union.

MR 16 July 1931, 29 March 1956

CSR

Smith, David Howard (1900–87; e.m. 1923), UMC missionary appointed to North *China in 1925. He taught at the Wuchang Theological Seminary, Hupeh, 1932–33 and was Chairman of the North China District from 1933 until his internment by the Japanese in 1943. From 1953 he taught at Manchester University. A student of Chinese philosophy and religion, he contributed to various publications and wrote several books, including *The Wisdom of the Taoist Mystics* (1980).

GRS

Smith, Edward (1849–1902; e.m. 1871), WM minister, born in *Bolton into a working-class family and trained at *Didsbury College. A powerful and persuasive preacher, he proved himself a conspicuously successful evangelist, especially through his rapport with the working class. The highlight of his strongly pastoral ministry was his three years (1886–89) at St John's Square, Clerkenwell, London, where he made many con-

verts and reinvigorated a failing mission. He suffered for many years from a weak heart and died soon after moving to the *Scarborough Circuit.

MR 12 June 1902; E. Smith (1889)

JAV

Smith, Dr Edwin William (1876–1957; e.m. 1897), born at Aliwal, *South Africa, the son of **John Smith** (1840–1915; e.m. 1859), was a PM missionary there (1898–1902) and in Central Africa (1902–15). In *Zambia he researched Ila linguistics and culture and made translations into Ila. Serving with the Bible Society 1916–39, he encouraged accessible Bible translations in *The Shrine of a People's Soul* (1929). He taught missionaries and African Americans in the USA, 1939–44 and his influential publications promoted respect for Africans. *The Golden Stool* (1926) showed his comprehensive understanding of African issues and *Aggrey of Africa* (1929) expressed enthusiasm for multiracial cooperation. *The Ila-Speaking Peoples of Northern Rhodesia* (1920), with A.M. Dale, was an anthropological classic. He was President of the Royal Anthropological Institute, 1933–35. He advocated adaptation to African culture in *The Christian Mission in Africa* (1926) and pioneered African Christian theology in *African Beliefs and Christian Faith* (1936). His writing on African religion culminated in *African Ideas of God* (1950).

MR 2 Jan. 1958; M. McVeigh (1974); *DNB, Missing Persons* (1993)

JRP

Smith, Elizabeth (Mrs Russell) (1805–36) early PM itinerant, brought up by her grandmother and apprenticed to a dressmaker, went to work at 16 in London. Her conversion at Christmas 1825 cost her her job. She became a *local preacher the following year and an itinerant in 1828. Particularly successful at 'opening' new areas, she faced much hostility from clergy, rowdy youths and musicians, especially in the Brinkworth District, where female preaching was a great novelty. She worked in Darlaston and Bilston during the cholera epidemic of 1832 and married fellow-itinerant Thomas *Russell on Easter Monday 1833.

PMM 1830–33 passim, 1837 p. 25; E.D. Graham (1989) p. 21

EDG

Smith, F.W. Ambery, K-i-H (1861–1929; e.m. 1886), WM missionary, born in *Manchester. In his early years he was influenced by W.B. *Pope. After training at *Richmond College, he served in the Bengal District from 1886 to 1911. He established leper asylums at Raniganj and Bankura and his own home was open to those in need as orphans, sick, refugees and disowned converts.

MR 14 March 1929

JAV

Smith, Dr Frederick Porter (d.1888), the first British lay *medical missionary, was educated at Wesley College (now *Queen's College), Taunton and King's College, London and appointed to *China. He arrived in Hankow (Hankou) in May 1864 and began medical work with J. *Cox as interpreter. In 1866 he built the first hospital in Central China and also opened a dispensary in Wuchang. He returned home in December 1870, weakened in health and was unable to offer for a second term of service. He died on 29 March 1888 from taking poison during a bout of depression due to overwork.

GRS

Smith, Frederick R. (1845–1917; e.m. 1878), WM minister who wrote under the pen-name 'John Ackworth'. After training at *Headingley College he served mostly in northern circuits. In 1896 he published *Clogshop Chronicles*, a collection of Methodist tales set in a Lancashire mill village and featuring dialect humour. Its immediate success led to nine other novels in the next 11 years, including *The Minder* (1900), which probably contains autobiographical material, and *The Coming of the Preachers* (1901). A popular preacher, he also published a volume of sermons and *The Making of the Million* (1899), tales of the *Twentieth Century Fund.

J. Sutherland (1988)

EAR

Smith, Dr George (1800–68), Cornish businessman and historian, born at Camborne. The son of a carpenter, he left school at 11, but embarked on a course of self-improvement while working at a mine and then as a gentleman's servant boy. He joined the WM society in 1821 and became a *local preacher in 1823. He set up in business as a builder in 1824 and in 1826 married Elizabeth Burall Bickford, daughter of the inventor of the miner's safety fuse. On William

Bickford's death in 1832 he took over the management of the Fuse Factory at Tuckingmill and developed it into a profitable business. He left an estate of *c*. £35,000 in 1868.

His social work, literary interests and work for Methodism developed alongside his business career. He became Chief County Magistrate, was a pioneer in developing the railway system in Cornwall, was a Fellow of the Society of Arts, a member of the Royal Asiatic Society and the Royal Society of Literature and received a DL from the University of New York. His first book was *An Attempt to Ascertain the true Chronology of the Book of Genesis* (1842). Firmly loyal to WM in the period of the WR movement, he published *The Wesleyan Ministers and their Slanderers* (1849) and *The Doctrine of the Pastorate* (1851). His three-volume *History of Wesleyan Methodism* (1857–61) remains a standard work.

T.R. Harris (1968)

TS

Smith, Dr Gervase (1821–82; e.m. 1844), WM minister, born in Derbyshire and was a pupil at the WM grammar school in *Sheffield. After a distinguished circuit ministry, which included *Wesley's Chapel, London (1865–68), he was elected President of the Conference in 1875. An accomplished author and administrator, he worked closely with Sir Francis *Lycett in support of the *Metropolitan Chapel Building Fund. He toured *Canada, the South Pacific islands and *Australia as a representative of British Methodism.

G.J. Stevenson (1884–6), 3 pp. 448–63

EWD

Smith, John (1794–1831; e.m. 1816), WM evangelist, was born at Cudworth and apprenticed at 14 to a *Sheffield grocer, but was sent home because of his conduct. Converted in 1812, the following year he went to *Sigston's Academy, Leeds. Here he came under the influence of **David Stoner** and became a *local preacher. He gained a reputation as a revivalist, going in 1816 to the *York Circuit as an evangelist and itinerating from 1817. Ill health forced him to superannuate in 1828–29. The 1831 Conference appointed him to Sheffield, but his health deteriorated rapidly and he died there. The John Smith Memorial WM Chapel at Cudworth was opened in 1892.

R. Treffry (1832)

DCD

Smith, Rodney ('Gipsy') (1860–1947), colourful evangelist, born in a gipsy tent near Epping Forest, son of Cornelius and Polly Smith. His mother died early; his father was converted and became an evangelist. Rodney, who never went to school, was converted in a PM chapel in 1876 and became an evangelist, first for W. *Booth (1877–82), then independently when Booth tried to move him from Hanley. He then became 'evangelist to the world', visiting *America, *Australia and *South Africa. He spent 1889–91 working for S.F. *Collier at the *Manchester Mission, where he converted G. *McNeal. From 1897 he was employed by the FCFC as 'Travelling Evangelist'. His singing and emotional appeals had much success, though some saw him as an anachronism. He was a frequent visitor to *Cliff College. His autobiography was published in 1906.

See also **Evens, G.Bramwell**

————

MR 7 Aug. 1947; H. Murray (1937); D. Lazell (1997)

JHL

Smith, Sarah ('Hesba Stretton') (1832–1911), daughter of a bookseller and *local preacher in Wellington (Shropshire). 'Hesba' was an acronym formed from her own and her four siblings' initials. She became a leading evangelical author of 'waif' children's books, her best-selling *Jessica's First Prayer*, first serialized in 1866, topping 2 million copies by 1911. Her older sister sent her first story to Dickens without her knowledge, giving rise to the legend that she was his friend. She helped to found the London Society for the Prevention of Cruelty to Children, forerunner of the NSPCC. She wrote 56 books, mostly as Sunday School prizes for the Religious Tract Society, helping to form the social conscience of the late nineteenth century. Her attempts at novels about the upper classes were unsuccessful.

————

M. Cutt (1979)

JHL

Smith, William (1736–1824), an influential layman who, as JW's step-son-in-law, enjoyed a unique influence in north-eastern Methodism. A native of Corbridge on Tyne, he settled in *Newcastle as a young man, establishing business interests which ensured his prosperity. He joined the society meeting at the *Orphan House and was appointed a class leader by JW at the age of about 20. He married Jane Vazeille in 1769. (Their daughters were regarded by JW as his grand-

children. Mary married John Stamp (d. 1831; e.m. 1787); Jane married Christopher *Sundius.) He became an invaluable aide to JW through his faithful service to Methodism and in preventing a serious accident when Wesley's carriage horses bolted in 1774. Anxious to preserve peace within Methodism after 1791 and despite his liberal inclinations and friendship with A. *Kilham, he remained loyal to WM. In 1820 he was a founder member of Brunswick Chapel, which replaced the Orphan House.

See also **Wesley, Mrs Mary**

————

W.W.Stamp (1863) pp. 121–2; *PWHS* 16 pp. 125–7; 44 pp. 64–5, 85

GEM

Smith, William Henry, MP (1825–91), son of Methodist parents of Duke Street, Grosvenor Square, London. Baulked by parental opposition to his preparing for the Church at Oxford, he joined the family business in the Strand, became a junior partner in 1846 and developed it into the leading firm of newsagents in the country, by exploiting the growing demand for station bookstalls and recognizing the potential for public advertising. His other innovations included cheap reprints and circulating libraries. His policy of boycotting 'pernicious literature' earned him the sobriquet of 'the North-Western Missionary'. He entered Parliament in 1868 as MP for Westminster and became a member of the first London school board in 1871. His career was marked by integrity rather than brilliance. He served as First Lord of the Admiralty (1877) under Disraeli and as First Lord of the Treasury and Leader of the Commons (1886) in the Salisbury administration. *Punch* dubbed him 'Old Morality'. In 1890 he was appointed Lord Warden of the Cinque Ports. Among his philanthropic activities he was treasurer of the SPCK.

————

DNB; G.R. Pocklington (1949)

JAV

Smith, William Hodson (1856–1943; e.m. 1880) served as a missioner under C. *Garrett in the *Liverpool Mission, where he was also actively involved in public affairs. From 1912 to 1933 he was Principal of the *NCH in a period of expansion. He was President of the 1927 Conference.

————

MR 14 July 1927, 20 May 1943

JAV

Smithies, John (1802–72; e.m. 1828), WM missionary, born in *Sheffield. After serving in Newfoundland 1828–37, he was sent to Western *Australia, where it was expected that his earlier experience would help in establishing a mission amongst both settlers and Aborigines in the new Swan River Colony. With inadequate funding he laboured alone in a million square miles, trying unsuccessfully to reconcile western expectations with traditional Aboriginal culture. When a colleague was appointed in 1852, he removed the Aboriginal work to the easier ground of York, but after his transfer to Tasmania the work soon lapsed and was not taken up again until 1951.

F&H 3

MJF

Smithies, Thomas Bywater (1817–83), WM layman, publisher and *temperance advocate. He began the first temperance society in *York and pioneered missionary meetings for children. Aware of the power of the written word, he devoted the rest of his life to cheap and beautifully illustrated publications bearing his initials 'T.B.S.'. His monthly periodicals included *The Band of Hope Review*, *The British Workman* and *The Weekly Welcome*. These were attractively produced, with engravings and articles from the most popular moral authors of the day. He gave full support to the evangelist J. *Caughey and was agent for his publications.

G.J. Stevenson (1884–6) 4 pp. 588–91

EWD

Smyth, Rev. Edward (fl.1770–90), curate of Ballyculter (Co. Down), was ejected from the parish in 1776 for Methodist tendencies and for rebuking his patron for adultery. For several years he assisted JW at City Road, London and as a 'general missionary' in Ireland. He proved problematical and W wrote of him, 'I doubt Edward needs a bridle.' More than once he urged W to leave the Church (e.g. at the Irish Conference in 1778). He was the focal point of dissension in *Bath in 1779, when A *McNab protested at his authority as Superintendent being abrogated. Despite her poor health, his wife Agnes (*née* Higginson, d. 1783) provided strong spiritual support to his ministry. He left the itinerancy in 1784 and in 1786 his brother William built Bethesda Chapel to give him a settled base in *Dublin. JW preached at Bethesda in 1787 and 1789 in spite of ill-natured attacks by Smyth in the Dublin press. Smyth's *Bethesda Hymn Book*

(showing the influence of JW's 1780 *Collection of Hymns*) is evidence of the penetration of Methodist influence on wider evangelical circles. His last years were spent in a *Manchester parish.

SJ vols 6–7; SL vols 6–8; C.H. Crookshank (1885–88) 1 passim

DALC/RPR

Smyth, William Henry (1864–1949; e.m. 1886), Irish minister, born in Co. Down. A skilled debater and able administrator, he served with particular distinction in educational affairs. When the Northern Ireland Parliament was established in 1921, he was appointed a chaplain. He became Vice-President of the Methodist Conference in Ireland in 1921, the first to be known as President of the Methodist Church in Ireland, and was again President in 1927.

MR 21 July 1949; A. McCrea (1931); R.L. Cole (1960)

NWT

Snaith, Dr Norman Henry (1898–1982; e.m. 1921), the son and grandson of PM ministers, read mathematics at Corpus Christi and trained for the PM ministry at Mansfield College, Oxford. He was appointed OT Tutor at *Headingley College in 1936, becoming Principal in 1954. He was President of the Conference in 1958 and retired in 1961. Proud of his PM heritage, he opposed the proposals for *Anglican-Methodist union in 1963, rejecting the historic episcopate. An internationally renowned OT scholar, President of the Society for OT Study in 1957, he received honorary doctorates from the universities of Glasgow and Leeds. His most famous book was *The Distinctive Ideas of the OT* (1944), but he also wrote *The Jewish New Year Festival* (1947) and *The Inspiration and Authority of the Bible* (1956), as well as more popular works. His Hebrew scholarship is seen both in his little books on the Hebrew text intended for students and in his editing of the BFBS Hebrew Old Testament (1958). His son **John Graham Snaith** (1934– ;e.m. 1958) is a lecturer in the Cambridge Faculty of Oriental Studies.

Times 6 March 1982; MR 10 July 1958, 18 March 1982

CSR

Snowden, Philip, 1st Viscount (1864–1937), a leading figure in Socialist circles for nearly 30 years, was born at Cowling, Yorks, deriving strong religious and ethical principles from his Methodist upbringing, though in later years he had no denominational affiliation. He was in the Excise service until crippled in a cycling accident. Having moved from Liberalism into Socialism, in 1895 he unsuccessfully contested the Keighley division against Sir I. *Holden, but in 1906 was elected at Blackburn and later represented Colne Valley. He was one of the architects of the Labour Party, serving as Chancellor of the Exchequer in 1924 and again in 1929. He received the freedom of the City of London for his part in the Hague Conference of 1929. Having served briefly in the National Government of 1931, he did not stand at the 1931 election, but was created Viscount in the Dissolution Honours and was Lord Privy Seal until his resignation in 1932. 'Most autocratic of democrats', his public truculence covered a personal charm. His numerous books included two volumes of autobiography. His wife, **Ethel Snowden** (*née* Annakin) shared his political and religious convictions and was known in her own right as a writer and speaker on social and moral issues. She was a Governor of the BBC, 1927–33.

Times 17 May 1937; *VMR* 27 May 1937
JAV

Social Responsibility, Division of Formed in 1919 as the *Temperance (and from 1942 the Temperance and Social Welfare) Department, and renamed 'Christian Citizenship' in 1950, in 1973 this became the Division of Social Responsibility. Its task was to assist the Methodist Church in the effective presentation of Christian social witness. The changes of name reflect an ever-expanding agenda and the range and depth of Methodism's concern to stimulate thought and action on the social, political and international issues which confront the Church and its members. The Division's history also demonstrates the interrelatedness of those issues. Beginning with a concern about alcohol abuse, it went on to study other addictions such as compulsive *gambling. This in turn led to an interest in marriage and mental breakdown and crime. The Division has produced definitive Methodist statements on divorce (1946), peace and *war (1957), industry (1960), the treatment of animals (1961), race (1961) and a number of other subjects of fundamental importance. It administers the *Methodist Relief Fund and has assisted, both in Britain and in overseas Methodist Churches, the application

of JW's insistence that 'there is no holiness but social holiness.'
See also **Medical Ethics**; **Sexual Ethics**; **Temperance**

MR 1 June 1939; G.T. Brake (1984) pp. 433–580
KGG

Society JW frequented several of the *religious societies in London, including that at *Fetter Lane and had had the experience of leading the *Holy Club and a group which met in the Savannah parsonage. The *New Room was built to house two such societies in *Bristol in 1739 and a London society was formed at the *Foundery when JW left Fetter Lane in July 1740 with 18 or 19 members and 48 women adherents. As *field preaching brought in numbers of 'seekers', W realized that the 'society' provided a framework for the support, discipline and nurture which they needed and a network of 'United Societies' developed. Being 'in connexion' with him, an Anglican clergyman, their meetings were protected, he hoped, from prosecution as illegal conventicles. Each society was in the care of one of the itinerants, who received into membership those who had satisfactorily completed a period on trial and each was divided into *Classes under a *Class Leader. Societies were soon grouped into *Circuits, each in the charge of an *Assistant. This pattern was to be repeated in all the branches of Methodism.

R.E. Davies WJW 9 (1989)
MB

Society Meeting In addition to the *class meeting, the Society Meeting was from the early days an integral party of Methodist organization, admission being by means of the *class ticket. Regular meetings of the Society (consisting of all the members in the local place) were seen as important in fostering Christian fellowship and the consideration of the work of God in the congregation and neighbourhood, including the reading of the Pastoral Address of the Conference to the Methodist societies. The meeting gradually came to have other functions, such as the election of representatives to the *Leaders' Meeting, but met less regularly, though required to do so once a year.

In the restructuring of the 1970s, the Society Meeting was replaced by the General Church Meeting, again comprising as voting members the lay members of the local church and those ordained persons active in its life and work, but being open also to all other persons on the community roll. It is required to meet at least annually and is for fellowship, consideration of the life of the local church (including financial matters) and election of Church Stewards and representatives to the *Church Council and various other bodies.

See also **Membership**

SRH

Society Stewards were appointed by JW (and later by the *Superintendents) to manage the temporal affairs of each *Society, though after his death the societies were consulted about the choice. Most societies had two stewards and JW insisted that one should be changed each year. They received the weekly 'class pennies' from the *class leaders, dealt with the running expenses of the society and were its representatives at the *Quarterly Meeting. If they noted anything amiss in the itinerants' doctrine or life, it was their responsibility to say so. A. *Kilham argued that every society should choose its own leaders and stewards, and this became the practice in the non-Wesleyan branches of Methodism.

Now called 'Church Stewards', their duty is to exercise corporate leadership and responsibility with the minister for the life and activities of the local church. They have specific duties in connection with the weekly services and the offertory.

SL 2 p. 305; *Minutes* 1766; *CPD* vol. 2 bk III SO 632–34

MB

Soldiers' Homes *see* **Armed Forces**; **Chubb Family**

Soothill, William E. (1861–1935; e.m. 1882), distinguished UMFC missionary appointed to Wenchow (Wenzhou), *China in 1882, where he served for 25 years until his appointment as Principal of the Imperial University of Shansi. In 1911 he was appointed President-elect of the proposed Central China University. In that year he became secretary of the Chinese YMCA. He retired in 1919 due to ill health and in 1920 accepted the Chair of Chinese at Oxford. An outstanding Chinese scholar, his many books included *A Pocket Dictionary of Four Thousand Characters* (1899), *The Analects of Confucius* (1937) and a lecture on *The Three Religions of China* (1913). His younger brother **Alfred Soothill** (1863–1926; e.m. 1885) was Headmaster of *Ashville College, Harrogate.

GRS

Soper, Donald Oliver, Baron Soper of Kingsway (1903–98; e.m. 1925) was born in London and educated at St Catherine's College and *Wesley House, Cambridge. He became Superintendent of the West London Mission in 1936, supervising its extensive social work and serving as chaplain at Holloway and Pentonville prisons. At Kingsway Hall he preached to large crowds and became famous as an open-air orator on Tower Hill and in Hyde Park, a ministry he sustained for over 60 years. He early established a reputation as a superb broadcaster. He was President of the Conference in 1950 and was President of the *Methodist Sacramental Fellowship, of the *Methodist Peace Fellowship and of the Fellowship of Reconciliation. His pacifism and support of the Labour Party sprang directly from his understanding of the gospel. In 1965 he entered the House of Lords. He travelled throughout the world to preach and speak and in retirement maintained a heavy programme of work, battling courageously into his nineties against loss of mobility. He was the author of many books, especially on Christian apologetics and social concerns.

MR 9 July 1953, 29 Jan. & 31 Dec. 1998; D. Thompson (1971); W. Purcell (1983); B. Frost (1996); A. Wilkinson (1998) pp. 183–7

KGG

South Midland Counties (Middlesex, Herts, Bucks, Oxon, Northants, Hunts, Beds, Cambs) This Registration Division, fanning out northwestwards from the London area, with the two university cities at its extremities, was predominantly rural. In Methodist terms it had neither cohesion nor recognizable characteristics apart from the absence of any Methodist strongholds. JW passed through the area on many of his journeys to or from the north, and had friends and supporters here and there (e.g. Miss Elizabeth Harvey of Hinxworth, J. *Berridge, vicar of Everton, and P. *Doddridge at *Northampton), but remained a bird of passage. Except in the vicinity of London, his societies were widely scattered.

In 1851 WM predominated, but with a significant PM minority in Cambs and Bucks. The *Religious Census recorded 702 Methodist places of worship in the Division (including WM: 493; PM: 188; WR 18). By 1989, with the disappearance of Middlesex, there were only 450 churches. Total attendances reported in 1851 were 187,688 (15.2% of the population), with evening services (usually the best attended) totalling 77,978 (6.3%). In 1989 adult worshippers and members totalled between 0.6% and 1% of the population, with no very marked difference between the counties.

E.R. Bates (1972); B.P. Sutcliffe & D.C. Church (1988)

JAV

Southampton Beginning in 1765, several houses were registered for Methodist meetings, but with little lasting effect. JW passed through in 1753, but did not preach until 1767 and then did not return for another 20 years. By 1787 a small society had been formed with the encouragement of the Fay family of Above Bar Independent Chapel, until they began to meet at the same time as services at the chapel. The first members were mostly poor and the town was in economic decline. Their various meeting places included a disused auction room and then a scaffold loft in Hanover Buildings. A turning point was reached in 1791 when they won the support of the Independent minister, William Kingsbury. Southampton became a separate circuit in 1798, although the first chapel, in Canal Walk, was not opened until 1799. It was enlarged in 1823 and replaced by the larger gothic East Street chapel in 1850. In 1925 a Central Hall was opened in St Mary Street (sold 1965). Meanwhile, suburban chapels opened as the town expanded and its fortunes revived later in the nineteenth century. In 1928 the St James Road Church replaced the chapels at Church Street, Shirley (1843) and Howard Road, Freemantle (1907).

A BC attempt to mission the town from the Isle of Wight in 1825 was unsuccessful, but in 1851 a new start had been made in St Mary's parish. The Traveller's Lodging House in Simnel Street was taken in 1852 and Jubilee Chapel, Princess Street, Northam opened in 1863, replaced in 1874 by St Mary's Road (formerly Baptist? closed 1934).

Following a visit by W. *Clowes, in 1833 a PM mission was launched by the Hull Circuit, supported by James Crabbe. This became an independent circuit in 1852. Their first chapel, St Mary Street (1837), was in the working class area, replaced by one in South Front by 1887.

J.W.M. Brown (1986)

JAV

Southcott, Joanna (1750–1814), daughter of William Southcott, farmer, of Gittisham, East Devon, worked in a shop and in domestic service in Honiton and then in *Exeter, where she wor-

shipped both in the cathedral and in Methodist services. In 1792 or 1793 she formally joined WM 'by divine command'. At Easter 1792 she made a confused statement in a class meeting about providential guidance. This was not well received. At her sister's home in Plymtree she wrote rambling prophecies and returning to Exeter broke with the Methodists. But she continued to regard herself as loyal to the Church and continually sought the clergy's approval of her claims. In her role of prophetess she gathered supporters, some of whom formed congregations, with chapels and preachers. In 1801 she began printing her works and wrote at least 65 books. Moving to London in 1802, she claimed to be the mother of the Divine Child 'Shiloh', but died at the time of the expected birth.

See also **Enthusiasm**

E.P. Wright (1968); J.K. Hopkins (1982)

RFST

South East Asia In 1957 British Methodism launched a new initiative to serve the Chinese dispersion, in co-operation with the American Methodist Board of Missions and its work in South East Asia. The plan was to supply and support British Missionary personnel to serve the Chinese under American direction and the authority of the local church. The Asia Secretary of the MMS, D.B. *Childe, hoped that this would help train a new generation of China missionaries in case the door into *China, which had closed in 1951, should reopen. The initiative started with the appointment of a former China missionary, J.N. Foster, and three probationer ministers, J.L. Hodgkinson, D.H. MacDonald and G.R. Senior, to the Church in Sarawak. Earlier, in 1954, a former China missionary, C.H. Smith, had been appointed to the Chinese faculty of Trinity Theological College, Singapore, and in 1958 another, C.G. Baker, was appointed to the Chinese Methodist Bible School, Medan, North Sumatra.

G.R. Senior (1989)

GRS

South-Eastern England (Surrey, Kent, Sussex, Hants, Berks) was an area in which Methodism was, and remained, relatively weak. Predominantly rural, with compact Anglican parishes, it remained largely unaffected by the Industrial Revolution.

JW spent little time here, apart from winter forays into east Kent (*Canterbury, Dover) and along the Kent-Sussex border (Tunbridge Wells,

Rye), where societies had been formed. Until 1790 Hampshire was part of a widespread *Salisbury Circuit, which included the Isle of Wight and Dorset. The Hampshire/Sussex borders in particular, became known as the 'Methodist desert'. Population growth was slow, except in *Portsmouth and *Southampton, where the older Dissent was already established. The later nineteenth century saw the growth of suburban congregations in the metropolitan parts of Surrey and Kent.

The BCs came along the south coast in the 1820s, gained a firm foothold on the Isle of Wight and from there missioned Portsmouth and Southampton, but failed to penetrate the hinterland, apart from the Farnham area. A Portsmouth District was formed as early as 1826. Other missions were launched further along the coast and in Kent, beginning in the Medway area, from where both *London and *Brighton were missioned.

As a result of northern initiatives, PM came into Hampshire in the 1830s from a base at Shefford, Berks and was centred on Micheldever and Andover. Their main success was among the impoverished agricultural labourers in the era of the 'Swing' riots. At the same period the *Hull Circuit initiated missions in the coastal towns and on the Isle of Wight.

Neither the MNC nor the later Reform movements made any significant impact on the South-East. In 1851 the *Religious Census recorded 685 Methodist places of worship in the SE Division (including WM: 432; PM: 156, mainly in Berks and Hants; BC: 81). By 1989 there were only 380 churches. Total attendances reported in 1851 were 131,947 (8.1% of the population), with evening services (usually the best attended) totalling 58,872 (3.6%). In 1989 adult worshippers ranged from 0.63% of the population in Berks to 0.51% in Surrey. Membership was highest in Berks (0.82% of the population) and lowest in Sussex (0.67%).

W.W. Pocock (1885); R.C. Swift (1987)

JAV

Southern Africa   A Methodist society was formed among soldiers in Cape Town in 1806 and W. *Shaw accompanied the 1820 settlers from Britain to the Eastern Cape, while from 1816 work among Africans was initiated by B. *Shaw. W. Shaw opened a chain of mission stations among the Xhosa people, and missionaries accompanied the Barolong on their migrations. By the time a Southern African Conference was created in 1883 there were Methodist churches throughout the country, though work in Transvaal and Swaziland remained under the British Conference until 1931. In the face of apartheid the Conference in 1958 declared the Methodist Church of Southern Africa to be 'one and undivided', but Church leadership remained a white prerogative until, and even after, the first black President, S. Mokitimi in 1963. Only with the appointment in the 1980s of M.S. Mogoba first as Secretary and then as President of the Conference did the MCSA become a recognisably non-racial body. The President became the Presiding Bishop with the introduction of a functional episcopate in 1990. The Methodist Church of Southern Africa comprises six countries: Botswana, Lesotho, Mozambique, Namibia, South Africa and Swaziland. A Methodist, Nelson Mandela, became the first democratically-elected President of South Africa.

JRP

Southlands College opened in Battersea in 1872 as a teacher training college for women, drawing some of its first students from *Westminster College. With the development of infant work it quickly gained a reputation for the teaching of reading. From 1903 onwards a few students followed degree courses, but in 1930, coinciding with the move to Wimbledon Parkside, only a two-year certificate course was permitted by the Board of Education. In the 1960s, as extended certificate and degree courses were introduced, the college broke new ground by admitting men, offering diversified academic courses, and, in keeping with its foundation, introducing professional training courses concerned with inner-city schools and ethnic minorities. Southlands survived the college closures of the 1970s by joining with Digby Stuart (RC), Whitelands (CofE) and Froebel Colleges to form the Roehampton Institute of Higher Education in 1975. Each college retained its Principal and governing body and the Institute acknowledged their traditions and purposes. In 1997, when Southlands moved to Roehampton Lane, close to Digby Stuart and Froebel Colleges, the Institute had 6,557 full and part-time students following undergraduate and postgraduate degree programmes and professional course validated by the University of Surrey. Of these, 1,294 were members of Southlands College.

E. Williams (1972); D. Milbank (1972)

DBT

Southport   Methodism has been present since the beginning of the town's development. Beginning as a cottage meeting in 1806, WM built a succession of chapels culminating in Mornington Road (1861), said to have been the first WM chapel with a spire. Methodism benefited from the generosity of several notable figures who retired to the town. J. *Fernley moved there from Manchester in 1857 and financed Trinity, Duke Street in 1864 and *Trinity Hall girls' school in 1872. William Greenhalgh and M. *Gutteridge provided much of the capital for the establishment of *Wesley House, Cambridge. Dr Peter *Wood was the town's first mayor. WR had a cause by 1855 and opened Duke Street UMFC in 1879. S. *Hocking was pastor there 1883–96. PM arrived in 1833 and was strengthened when Sir W.P. *Hartley moved there in 1904. In 1907 he was largely responsible for building Church Street (1907) PM chapel (now St Mark's) with its fine memorial windows to Mr and Mrs Hartley and A.S. *Peake. His daughter Christiana was Mayor in 1921–22. The PM Conference met there in 1909 and 1928. IM work dates from 1860 and the MNC from 1864. Since 1885 the town has been the venue for the annual *Southport Holiness Convention. The Methodist Conference of 1999 met in the town.

F.P. Argall in *UM Magazine*, 1910 pp. 247–53; E. Bland (1911); Conference Handbook 1939, 1949, 1960

EWD/EAR

Southport Holiness Convention began in 1885 as a WM expression of the renewed stimulus to the *Holiness and Higher Christian Life movement which emerged in Britain in the last quarter of the nineteenth century. With the exception of some wartime years it has continued as an annual gathering. The trustees own the land and property in Mornington Road given by the *Wood family. Many leading figures have been associated with it over the years, not all of whom have been exponents of the distinctively WM position. There have always been strong links with *Cliff College.

J.B. Atkinson (1945); A.S. Wood (1985)

WP

South-Western Counties (Cornwall, Devon, Somerset, Dorset, Wilts) JW was summoned to *Bristol by G. *Whitefield in the spring of 1739, and it quickly became a focal point of his itinerant ministry, second only to *London. During his visits he frequently visited *Bath (where the Countess of *Huntingdon also built a chapel) and the woollen towns of west Wiltshire. So Methodism took root there early.

Family connections brought JW to *Salisbury early on, but the society formed at Fisherton faltered through the notoriety of Westley *Hall. A Wiltshire Circuit, formed in 1758, was divided into North and South in 1768. Salisbury became the base from which Methodism spread slowly through Hampshire and Dorset, the Circuit remaining undivided until 1790. Shaftesbury, the birthplace of J. *Haime and C. *Garrett, became head of a circuit in 1809.

Cornwall was a potent mixture of remoteness, a Celtic population and industrialization against a harsh but picturesque landscape. The diocesan bishop was far away in *Exeter and the Church was failing to provide for the new mining settlements, especially in the far west. JW arrived in the county in 1743, preceded by a few weeks by CW. Both travelled the length of the county as far as *St Ives. In 1756 JW recorded 'about 34' societies in the county. By 1767 the membership had risen to 2,160. Aided by periodic revivals between 1782 and 1821 and by the rapid population increase, it reached 9,405 in 1813, 12,891 in 1821, and a peak of 26,227 in 1840. The 'Great Revival' of 1814 added 5,000 members, many of whom became the next generation of Methodist leaders.

JW travelled through Devon many times on his way to and from Cornwall. He preached in *Tiverton (where his brother Samuel had been headmaster of Blundell's School from 1730 to 1739) from 1750 on and it became the centre of a widespread Devonshire circuit which included part of Somerset. *Plymouth contained supporters of Whitefield (who first visited the town in 1744) under the leadership of Andrew Kinsman. So until 1766 JW concentrated on the neighbouring Devonport, which became the strongest cause in the county. His visits to *Exeter were infrequent until 1773, when Calvinistic influence had waned.

At the beginning of the nineteenth century WM was concentrated in the more prosperous southern half of Devon, leaving the deeply rural north-west to be evangelized by the *Bible Christians from their stronghold at *Shebbear, though Plymouth eventually became the effective centre of the denomination, with Cornwall as its heartland. BC membership in Cornwall grew to 2,605 by 1826, with many country chapels. Rural West Somerset was the eastern limit of the BC heartland. East of a line from Bridgwater to Yeovil, PM took over as the liberal alternative to WM, and there were only isolated BC circuits, e.g. on the Isle of Portland.

In both Devon and Cornwall the BC presence

hindered the spread of PM as a rival to WM, but after the mid-century it did establish itself in the ports and watering places of South Devon, probably through members retiring from the Midlands. To the east, a Wiltshire Mission launched by the *Shrewsbury PM Circuit led to the formation of Brinkworth Circuit (1826) and Motcombe Circuit (1828). From there the work spread through rural Dorset, where it was particularly strong in the Shaftesbury area. The other branches of Methodism made little impact on Somerset and Wiltshire. In Devon, the UMFC was confined to the urban centres of Plymouth, Tavistock, Exeter and Newton Abbot. Only one chapel, Silverton, is known to have been taken over by the Reformers.

In 1851 the *Religious Census recorded 1,757 Methodist places of worship in the South West Division, two thirds of them (1,029) being WM. Total Methodist attendances were 348,044 (19.3% of the population); evening services (usually the best attended) totalled 175,044 (9.7%). In Somerset the BCs and WR had overtaken PM as the main rival to WM, but in Wilts and Dorset PM was still its only serious rival. There was a marked contrast between the strength of Methodism in the two adjacent counties of Devon and Cornwall. WM attendances in Cornwall were three times the level of those in Devon, where the parish system was operating much more effectively. In Cornwall, Methodist places of worship outnumbered parish churches by 3 to 1; total Methodist attendances (WM 28% of the population; BC, 8.4%) far outstripped the Anglican ones, most notably in the evening.

By 1989, even with Bristol included, the number of Methodist churches had dropped to 1,071, nearly one third of them in Cornwall. Attendances were recorded at 1.6% of the adult population in the south-west as a whole (4.5% in Cornwall). Membership stood at 52,000 (1.5%), the highest being in Cornwall (3.8%).

J. Pearce (1964); T. Shaw (1967); A.G. Pointon, 1982; M. Wickes (1985); B.J. Biggs (1987)
TS/RFST/JAV

Sowerby Bridge (Yorks) A Methodist society existed in this expanding riverside settlement near Halifax by 1782. Successive chapels were built in 1787, 1806 and 1832. The deed drawn up for the conveyance of the site of the imposing Bolton Brow chapel became the *model deed for all future transactions of this kind throughout the WM Connexion. In 1979 the former Bolton Brow

WM society amalgamated with the former Tuel Lane UMFC/UM society, and after the latter's premises were burned down in 1988 impressive new premises were opened in 1991 by K.M. *Richardson. In 1997 the Sowerby Bridge Circuit, now reduced to two churches, became part of the new Elland and Ryburn Circuit.

J.A. Hargreaves (1994)

JAH

Sowton, Stanley (1875–1958), a conspicuously successful Circuit Missionary Secretary who gave up a career in banking to join the Mission House staff in 1906 and worked in its finance department until his retirement in 1942. A prolific writer, he was a tireless missionary advocate. As 'Uncle Ned' he reorganized *JMA and introduced its DSO award. He instigated the purchase and preservation of the *Isbell cottage at Trewint. For many years Sunday School Superintendent at Muswell Hill, he held many other offices, except that of Local Preacher, but declined to stand as *Vice-President.

MR 19 Feb. 1953, 28 Aug. 1958

JAV

Spain In 1832 W.H. *Rule launched a mission from *Gibraltar, mainly through distribution of the Scriptures. A *class meeting was formed in Cadiz, but the venture came to an end in the face of fierce opposition, in which his young son was murdered. Following the 'September Revolution' in 1868, a new opportunity was seized in Catalonia and the Balearics. Colporteurs were sent from Gibraltar and a lay missionary from England, W.T. Brown, opened a school and preaching places in Barcelona. After his ordination in 1879 he moved to the Balearic Islands. The work was taken up by Franklyn G. Smith, who spent 32 years (1884–1916) in the mission. Evangelical work elsewhere in Spain came under the MEC, but was seriously affected by the Civil War of 1936–39. In 1955 Methodists became part of the Spanish Evangelical Church which in 1997 reported a membership of 3,000 and a total community of 6,000.

F&H 4 pp. 427–37; W.P. Stephens (n.d.)

SJP

Spencer, Arthur Marshman (1886–1943; e.m. 1911), WM missionary in *India, the son of **William Marshman Spencer** (1856–1935; e.m. 1879, missionary in the Bengal District 1880–92). He was educated at *Kingswood School and

*Headingley College and shone as an athlete. His ministry at Sarenga 1911–32 and then in Calcutta was marked by his special concern for the poor and for Indian national aspirations. His strong leadership was in evidence in the crisis summer of 1942, especially in the support he gave to Burma and China missionaries at that time.

MR 22 April 1943

JAV

Spencer, Harold (1876–1966; e.m. 1900), WM minister and missionary, born at Bethnal Green. He began his career as a teacher and after training at *Richmond College spent 21 years in Mysore, *India, where he became Principal of Hardwick College and edited the local newspaper. He compiled a grammar of the Karanese language and designed a hospital. Returning to England in 1923, he was for some years secretary of the Ministers' Missionary Union and was Conference Memorials Secretary for ten years, noted for his 'unfailing memory for precedent'. He collaborated with E. *Finch on the *Constitutional Practice and Discipline of the Methodist Church.*

MR 21 April 1966

WL

Spiritual Quixote, The, a 'comic romance' by Richard Graves (1715–1804), rector of Claverton near Bath from 1749, which is a genial satire on itinerant preachers and preaching. Begun about 1757 and eventually published in 1773, the butt of its ridicule is ill-timed effusions of *enthusiasm and their ludicrous effect upon the gentlemanly Geoffrey Wildgoose, a convert to Methodism, and his cobbler companion Jerry Tugwell, while travelling in the West Country and Derbyshire, meeting with JW himself on the way.

C. Tracy (1967); C. Tracy (1987)

CJS

Spoor, Joseph (1813–69; e.m. 1835), PM itinerant and revivalist, born at Whickham, near Gateshead. He began life as a keelman on the Tyne, was converted under H. *Casson, becoming first a WM, then a PM. He was taken on in 1831 as a *hired local preacher to work in the Hexham Circuit between Morpeth and Rothbury at the expense of Squire *Shafto and later did similar work in and around Northallerton, showing the charismatic power and revivalist fervour which were strong features of his ministry. He entered

the full itinerary in 1835 and served several circuits within the Sunderland PM District.

E. Hall (1870)

GEM

Sport The early Methodists distanced themselves from the popular 'sports' of their day such as bear- and bull-baiting, cock-fighting and bare-fisted prize-fighting, with the drunkenness and gambling that accompanied them. In the course of the nineteenth century these were displaced by sports with which Methodism could much more readily identify itself and church-based football, cricket and tennis clubs became common. Aston Villa is an example of a professional club that had Methodist origins. Before World War II there was a Methodist Sports Association, with sections for different sports. We read of a Durham County Methodist Cup Tie and football teams around the country competed for the *Methodist Recorder*'s 'All Britain Challenge Trophy'. There was a Wesleyan Cricket Association in London and tennis clubs associated with local churches were common. The extent to which sport had become acceptable in evangelical and liberal circles in the late Victorian Church found a Methodist example in the figurative use of it made by Thomas Waugh (1853–1932; e.m. 1882) in his book *The Cricket Field of the Christian Life.*

Individual Methodists were actively involved at a professional level. William McGregor was one of the founders of the Football League in 1888. Charles and Arthur Sutcliffe, members at Langholme, Rawtenstall and strong *temperance supporters, served on the Football Association committee 1898–1927, and Charles's son Harold Sutcliffe was involved with the Football League until 1967. Wilf Harrop was Vice-President of the League 1950–56. Fred Howarth was FA Secretary 1935–56 and was succeeded by Alan Hardacre 1957–79. Walter Tull, grandson of a Barbadian slave and brought up by the *NCH at Bethnal Green, played for Preston North End. Among ministers who were former professional footballers, Norman H. Hallam (1920–97; e.m. 1949) and Philip J. Lockett (e.m. 1969) both played for Port Vale. Garry Shelton played for Walsall. Alan Merritt (Manchester United) is a *local preacher in the Stretford and Urmston Circuit and Howard Kendall (Preston, Birmingham City and Everton) is a church organist. John Motson, football commentator with the BBC since 1968, is a son of the manse.

W.G. Grace, one of the monumental figures in

the history of cricket, was of Methodist stock. In first-class cricket, Jack Bond captained Lancashire for many years. Wilfred Wooller, captain of Glamorgan, was an old boy of *Rydal School. Godfrey Evans, the England wicket-keeper, was an old boy of *Kent College, Canterbury. Harold Dennis ('Dickie') Bird was an internationally acclaimed umpire. Methodists are actively involved in the organization 'Christians in Sport'.

D. Brailsford (1997)

BW

Squire, Ethel Maud and **Letitia ('Lettie') Olivia** ('Othen'), BC missionaries in *China, were the daughters of **Richard Squire** (1850–1931; e.m. 1873) and sisters of **Ernest Richard Squire** (1883–1960; e.m. 1903). Both graduated at London University, became teachers and volunteered for work in the Yunnan mission in South West China. Maud was appointed in 1903 to Chaotung and was associated with the Girls School until 1919. Lettie (b. 1879) followed in 1908 in response to an appeal from Mrs Sam *Pollard. She taught with her sister and took her place when Maud was invalided from the work in 1919. They were pioneers in the emancipation of women, China's greatest change for centuries, establishing their school at a time when girls' education was unheard of and foot-binding was universal. Lettie retired in 1939, but stayed on in China until forced out in 1951 by the coming of Communism. Both sisters retired to East Anglia and were still alive in 1965.

MJF/RKP

Sri Lanka (formerly Ceylon) A mission to Asia was the long-cherished vision of T. *Coke, who was consulting with Charles Grant about it as early as 1784. The renewal of the East India Company's charter in 1813 provided the eventual opportunity. Coke sailed with six young missionaries at the beginning of 1814 and the first missionaries landed at Galle on 29 June, following Coke's death at sea. Welcomed and aided in government circles, three of them began work among the Tamils – J. *Lynch and T. Squance in Jaffna and W. Ault in Batticaloa, where he died within months. Meanwhile B. *Clough at Galle and G. Erskine at Matara began a Sinhalese mission in the south. W.M. *Harvard's arrival in Colombo in 1815 marked the beginning of the work there and the Dam Street Church in the Pettah survives as the first Methodist church built in Asia. A mission in Kandy led by R.M. *Hardy in 1836 came to nothing. But a fresh start was made there

in 1867 and an Extension Fund, set up in 1874, supported pioneer work in the central highlands and the remoter parts of the east and south. From as early as 1817 the opening of village schools was a vital part of the missionary strategy, despite financial constraints imposed by the WMMS. The missionaries were champions of vernacular education, which brought them at times into conflict with the colonial authorities. The earlier high schools set up in Colombo and Galle were handed over to the government. Later in the century several secondary schools were opened, including two in Colombo: what became Methodist College (1866) for girls and Wesley College (1874) for boys.

The first Sinhalese minister was appointed in 1819 and the first Tamil in 1825. Among the missionaries were notable Tamil scholars (e.g. P. *Percival and J. *Kilner) and students of Pali and Buddhism (D.J. *Gogerly; R.S. *Hardy and later Charles Haddon Spurgeon Ward (1876–1957; e.m. 1902; in Ceylon 1902–35). Missionaries were involved in the debates with Buddhism at the time of the Buddhist Revival in the latter part of the 19th century. The main Christian protagonist in the famous Panadura Debate in 1873 was the Sri Lankan WM minister David de Silva (1817–74; e.m. 1841), a pupil of Gogerley. More recently, dialogue has replaced confrontation. With this in view, the Study Centre (now the Ecumenical Study Institute for Study and Dialogue) in Colombo was established by Methodists in 1951. The Rev G.B. *Jackson was its first secretary and its most outstanding Director (from 1962 until his death in 1982) was the Sri Lankan Methodist minister, Lynn A. de Silva (1919–82; e.m. 1947), a remarkable scholar of Buddhism. Ministers are trained at the ecumenical Theological College at Pilimatalawa near Kandy. With other Churches Methodism has been actively involved in reconciliation of the Sinhalese and Tamil communities and in caring for the victims of violence.

The Methodist Church in Sri Lanka became autonomous in 1964 and in 1997 reported a membership of 28,000 and a total community of 50,000.

See also **Niles, D.T.**

F&H 5 pp. 15–115; W.J.T. Small (1964)

JAV

Stacey, Dr James (1818–91; e.m. 1839), MNC minister, appointed first Principal of *Ranmoor College after some years of training ministerial students at his home. He was sole tutor 1865–76, then classical tutor 1876–79. His sensitive and cultured piety had a lasting influence on those who went through his hands. He was Missions Secretary 1859–63 and 1879–86 and was elected President of the 1860 and 1881 Conferences. His books included *The Christian Sacraments Explained* (1856) and a life of J *Ridgway (1862).

G.J. Stevenson (1884–6) 4 pp. 628–34; W.J. Townsend (1891)

EAR

Stacey, Dr Walter David (1923–93; e.m. 1947) was born in *Bristol and educated at *Handsworth College, where he remained as Assistant Tutor (1951–53) before becoming chaplain at *Queen's College, Taunton, then Lecturer in Biblical Languages and Literature at *Wesley College, Bristol, 1967–71. After a period as lecturer in Religious Studies at Homerton College, Cambridge, and Chaplain to Robinson College, he returned to Wesley College as Principal in 1977, married M. *Hooker in 1978 and retired in 1987. He was Book Editor of *The Epworth Review* from 1974. His works include *The Pauline View of Man* (1956), *Prophetic Drama in the OT* (1990) and a commentary on Isaiah 1–39 (1993).

MR 9 Dec. 1993

CSR

Stained Glass JW's *Puritan roots were reflected in the austerity of the architecture he approved and his immediate successors remained suspicious of ornamentation in chapels. Stained glass was not reintroduced into Britain until the Anglo-Catholic Revival of the mid-nineteenth century; but its high-church connotations delayed its acceptance in Methodist circles until the 1880s. Methodist windows are dominated by orthodox scriptural themes and the heroes of Protestantism. Haloes, the commonest features of high-church saints, rarely feature. The non-WM denominations seldom succumbed to portraiture; more often their chapel windows were filled with geometrical, multi-coloured patterns.

The most celebrated Methodist glazier was Clement Heaton (1824–82) of Heaton, Butler & Bayne, one of the largest firms of the Victorian period which survived into the 1950s. His experiments with pigments produced a wide range of gentle colours, until then unknown in stained glass. His technical experiments resulted in his 'indestructible colours' for the English climate

which were adopted by all the leading firms. In 1880 he rediscovered the flux used by medieval glassmakers. Though the son of a WM minister, James Heaton (1782–1862; e.m. 1806), it is unlikely that any of his work appeared in Methodist chapels. Two quality Methodist firms among the hundreds active between 1850 amd 1900, the heyday of stained glass, were Hawes and Harris of Harpenden (who produced two windows for Westminster Abbey) and H.J. Salisbury of St Albans (who produced windows for St Albans Abbey, The *Leys School chapel, *Wesley's Chapel and Muswell Hill Methodist church, North London). In 1933 his brother F.O. *Salisbury became the only Methodist to be elected Master of the Worshipful Company of Glaziers and Painters on Glass. An outstanding series of windows was commissioned by H.G. *Chester for Muswell Hill as a memorial to his wife who died in 1927.

Beauty in the Sanctuary: the Methodist Church, Muswell Hill (*c.* 1937); N. McMurray (1999)

NM

Stamp, Sir Josiah Charles, CBE, FBA, DSc, LLD, Baron Stamp of Shortlands (1880–1941), WM layman, born at Kilburn. He studied economics and political science at London University before entering the Civil Service in 1896. He held various positions in the business world, including Secretary and Director of Noble Industries and of ICI. In 1928 he became a Director of the Bank of England and served on Royal Commissions in England and Canada. He was raised to the peerage in 1935. A member of the Beckenham Church, he was a lay member of the Conference, a Governor of The *Leys School and Treasurer of the *NCHO. He delivered the first *Beckly Lecture on Social Service (1926). He and his wife and son were killed by a bomb in April 1941.

Times, 18 April 1941; *MR* 24 April 1941

WL

Stamp, William Wood (1801–77; e.m. 1823) of *Bradford, Yorks. Originally apprenticed to a surgeon, but having been converted in 1822 and showing ability as a preacher, he became an itinerant. He was elected President of Conference in 1860. For many years he was editor of the Wesleyan Year Book. His publications include *Wesleyan Methodism in Bradford* (1841) and *The Orphan House of Wesley* (1863).

WMM 1885 pp. 86–94; 169–77

SRV

Stampe, George (1836–1918), WM layman, born at Tetney, Lincs. He became a timber merchant in *Grimsby and was in business there for 60 years. His chief interest was in collecting books, letters, pamphlets, portraits etc. relating to JW and early Methodism. He was a founder member of the *WHS and its treasurer for many years. He gave considerable help to N. *Curnock in preparing his Standard Edition of JW's *Journal*.

PWHS 12 pp. 1–2

WL

Standing Orders, a term adopted in 1844 in place of the Conference resolutions previously listed in the WM *Minutes* under the heading 'Miscellaneous Orders and Resolutions'. These were mainly temporary, but included some intended to have more permanent effect, e.g. as to annual returns of *membership. In the 1844 *Minutes* this latter group, nine in all, was entitled 'Standing Orders' (following Parliamentary usage), with a separate group of 'Miscellaneous Resolutions' preceding it. The number of Standing Orders increased substantially over the years. Other branches of Methodism similarly adopted General Rules under various names. At *Methodist Union in 1932 the new Church adopted a body of some 222 Standing Orders. For later developments see *Constitutional Practice and Discipline*.

SRH

Staniforth, Sampson (1720–99) Born in *Sheffield, he enlisted and served in Flanders and was helped to faith by a fellow soldier, one of *J. Haime's converts. Leaving the army in 1748, he built a preaching house at Deptford in 1757, preached there and in adjacent areas and later gave the lease of the building to JW. Ordained by the Greek Bishop *Erasmus in 1764, he declined to use his credentials, knowing it would 'offend' his brethren. JW encouraged him in the work and he later opened another preaching house in Rotherhithe in 1771. A devoted Wesleyan, he was a Methodist preacher, though never strictly an 'itinerant', for almost fifty years.

C. Atmore (1801) pp. 400–7; EMP 4 pp. 109–51

HMG

Stationing Committee At first the appointment of itinerant preachers to their circuits was made by JW himself, and from 1765 the list was published annually in the *Minutes of Conference.

After his death the Conference appointed a Stationing Committee, with a representative from each *District, to prepare a draft for the Conference to adopt. In 1818 the Missionary Committee was given responsibility for preparing the overseas stations. As early as 1803, however, the practice had arisen of petitioning the Conference for particular appointments and this led to direct invitations from circuits to ministers. The same dual system developed in the other Methodist denominations (although in the early decades most PM stationing was done at District level) and has persisted to the present. The final decision remains with the Conference, although the President has power under the *Deed of Union to alter the stations in emergencies between Conferences.

Stationing is annual, although circuits may invite and the Conference designate for longer periods. JW's *Deed of Declaration imposed a legal limit of three years on appointments, although various devices were developed in time to evade its rigour, especially with respect to the central missions created from the 1880s on under the *Forward Movement. During World War I the rule was suspended under the Wesleyan Methodists (Appointments during the War) Act 1917. The other Methodist denominations similarly limited the length of appointments. The rule was abolished by the *Methodist Church Union Act (1929) and five years is now the circuit minimum. Extensions to seven or nine years or more are not uncommon.

The Stationing Committee now comprises the Chairman and a lay representative of each District, together with some connexional officers, and works largely through sub-committees, of which the most important is the Policy Sub-Committee, introduced in 1984 to advise on priorities in an attempt to balance the needs of individual circuits with an overall connexional strategy in the deployment of ministers.

The stationing of *deaconesses was from the beginning the responsibility of the Warden of the Order, their stations being printed in the Minutes from 1946. In 1998 the stationing of ministers and deacons was combined and the Stationing Committee given responsibility for both.

HMGB 1 pp. 230–4, 251

BEB

Stedeford, Charles (1864–1953; e.m. 1883), BC minister, born in *Bristol. He was Foreign Missions Secretary from 1904 and UM Missionary Secretary from 1909 to 1933. During those years he was deeply involved in Methodist work overseas, visited Africa and *China and was a member of the Council of the Selly Oak Colleges, *Birmingham. After his retirement he was made an honorary MMS secretary.

MR 16 April 1953

TS

Stedeford, John Britton (1857–1929; e.m. 1878), BC minister, born in *Bristol. He was General *Sunday School Secretary 1899–1904 and was President of the BC Conference in 1906 and of the UM Conference in 1915. He wrote a *Guide to Church Membership* (1917) for the UM.

TS

Steele, James (1767–1827), PM *local preacher, who had been *local preacher, *class leader, *Sunday School superintendent, *trustee and *Chapel Steward in the Burslem WM Circuit. He was expelled, with members of his class, for his association with W. *Clowes and his name appears as No.2 on the first Tunstall PM plan in 1811. He became the first PM steward in 1812, when it was decided to provide financial support for the promoters of the newly formed 'Society of the Primitive Methodists'. H. *Bourne conducted his memorial service at Tunstall.

WL

Stephens, Joseph Rayner (1805–79; e.m. 1825) the first WM missionary to Stockholm (1826–29), resigned in 1834 after a Conference trial for advocating disestablishment and became the minister of a 'Stephenite' circuit in the *Ashton-under-Lyne area. A man of independent judgment and combative spirit, his pastoral ministry in a major cotton centre convinced him of the need for Christian activism and with his friend Richard *Oastler he campaigned for the abolition of child and female factory labour, a ten (later eight) hours working day for men and the repeal of the hated Poor Law Amendment Act of 1834. He held sway over thousands through his fervent, earthy but biblical oratory. In 1838 he was briefly associated with the *Chartists. His violent language led to arrest and imprisonment (1839–41), but on release he continued to reject party politics and to demand justice for the poor. In the cotton famine (1862–65) he championed the local operatives and was accused, unjustly, of instigating the Stalybridge riot. Ministerial duties were combined with new factory campaigns, education, *trade unionism, politics and journalism. The

Stephenites disbanded in 1875. For Methodists he represents a lost ideal of social holiness.

M.S. Edwards (1994)

MSE

Stephenson, John (*c.* 1749–1819; e.m. 1788), Irish itinerant, sent as the first WM missionary to Bermuda in 1799. His reception by the governor and other leading citizens was cool because of his Irish background and his association with JW's opposition to *slavery. Despite treading warily, his faithfulness and humanitarian concern for the blacks drove him to defy new legislation passed early in 1800 to prohibit non-conformist preaching. He was convicted and served a six-month sentence, during which he is said to have preached to his black supporters through his prison window. He returned to Ireland on his release, but his health precluded his returning to circuit work.

F&H 2 pp. 240–45

NWT

Stephenson, Dr Thomas Bowman (1839–1912; e.m. 1860), WM minister and architect of a more socially-minded Methodism, through the establishment of two major institutions. The son of **John Stephenson** (1799–1861; e.m. 1822), he was born at *Newcastle upon Tyne and baptized by R. *Newton. A Liberal in politics and musically gifted, his ministry was untypical. He sang in the streets and was the first to hire a theatre for use in his mission. In 1869, with the help of two laymen, he founded the *NCH and in 1873 was set apart as its Principal. Always eager to use everyone's talents (including the laity and *women), he had employed a deaconess at *Bolton in 1868. A visit to Kaiserwerth deaconess centre in Germany in 1871 encouraged him to develop opportunities for women to serve in the Church, through the 'Sisters of the Children' in the NCH and later through the Wesley *Deaconess Order, following the publication of his book *Concerning Sisterhoods* (1890). He was the chief mover behind the admission of laymen to the WM *Conference, first speaking for it in 1873 and becoming secretary of the *Thanksgiving Fund in 1878. An expert money-raiser and publicist, he began magazines such as *Highways and Hedges*, wrote many hymns, especially for children, and composed a service book for them. He was President of the Conference in 1891. Excessive work and money-raising tours affected his health and forced him to relinquish his responsibility for the

NCH in 1900 and for the Deaconess Order in 1907. His daughter **Dora Stephenson** (b.1867), a Sister in the Home and the first Wesley Deaconess, was an important spokeswoman for both organizations, e.g. at the Chicago Deaconess Conference in 1893. She emigrated to *Canada after marrying in 1910.

MR 18 July 1912; G.J. Stevenson (1884–6) 4 pp. 519–29; W.Bradfield (1913); C.J. Davey (1968); G.E. Barritt (1996)

JHL

Stephenson, William H., a WM *local preacher who, in 1819, following the Peterloo massacre, addressed a huge Radical Reform meeting on *Newcastle Town Moor and was disciplined by the local circuit. His case was finally resolved by the *Committee of Privileges in London, whose decision was not only to suspend him as a local preacher but to expel him from membership unless he promised to refrain from Radical Reform activities in future. Stephenson and others left their societies and within a year had formed fourteen IM churches in the North-East.

H. Kelly (1824); W.R. Ward (1972) pp. 21–4

JAD

Stephenson, Sir William Haswell (1836–1918), WM layman and Tyneside industrialist, a descendant of John Stephenson (d. 1761) who sold JW the site of the Newcastle *Orphan House. Educated at *Wesley College, Sheffield, he was soon involved in a variety of industrial undertakings, some of them building on initiatives taken by his father. He quickly became prominent in the commercial and civic life of *Newcastle, serving as a Tyne Improvement Commissioner, School Board member, and conservative City Councillor. He was elected mayor several times between 1875 and 1911 and Sheriff in 1886. He provided several branch libraries and the statue of Queen Victoria near Newcastle cathedral. He was knighted in 1900. A dedicated WM, a local preacher from 1859 and a staunch supporter of *LPMAA, he was a generous patron of WM causes and donor of the Elswick Road chapel where he worshipped. He served as chairman of *Woodhouse Grove School and was a founder and governor of The *Leys School.

MR 2 Dec. 1909; A.D. Walton in WHS(NE) no.32 pp. 8–13 & no. 33 pp. 13–20

GEM

Stevenson, George John (1818–88), born in Chesterfield. On leaving school he worked in a bookselling business. He then trained at St John's College, Battersea and became in succession head of a reformatory school (1846–48) and of an endowed parochial school (1848–55), before returning to bookselling and publishing. Though vacillating between Anglican and Methodist leanings, he showed by his published works which was his paramount interest. From 1861 to 1867 he owned and edited the *Methodist Times* and edited the *Union Review*. Among his voluminous writings were *The WM Hymn-book and its Associations* (1870), *City Road Chapel* (1872), *Memorials of the Wesley Family* (1876) (written after he had classified papers bequeathed by JW to Henry Moore) and six volumes of *Methodist Worthies* (1884–86), containing sketches of ministers and laymen of all the main branches of Methodism, complete with excellent portraits.

DNB; *PWHS* 28 pp. 33–4

EWD

Stewards *see* **Chapel Stewards**; **Circuit Stewards**; **Poor Stewards**; **Society Stewards**

Stewardship   The basic tenet of stewardship is that we are accountable to God for the ways we treat his creation. Therefore our time, talents and treasure (or money) belong to God and a proper proportion of them should be given to him. Stewardship campaigns were introduced into Britain by the Wells organization in the late 1950s. The Methodist Stewardship Organization was set up in 1960–61 under **J. Morrison Neilson** MBE (1906–74; e.m. 1927) and Mr **John Longworth** in *Manchester. It became part of the Connexional Funds Department in 1970 and from 1972 of the HM Department, being seen as one way of renewing the life of local churches. Stewardship was encouraged within each District by a District Secretary.

G.T. Brake (1984) pp. 161–5

JWH

Stewart, Robert Michael Maitland, MP, Baron Stewart of Fulham (1906–90) was educated at Christ's Hospital and St John's, Oxford, where he took 1st Class Honours and was President of the Union. He was a *local preacher and during the War served in the Intelligence Corps and Education Corps. In 1945 he was elected MP for Fulham and held ministerial office in the Attlee administration. As Foreign Secretary in the Wilson government he supported America in the Vietnam War. In opposition, he was a spokesman for housing and local government. In 1975 he headed the British delegation to the European Parliament. He became a Life Peer in 1979.

R.M.M. Stewart (1980)

JAV

Stillness In 1739–40 there were controversies in the *Fetter Lane Society, London, over the issue of 'stillness'. The visiting *Moravian P.H. Molther reacted against the extravagant behaviour and disorder he witnessed and encouraged the members to wait passively for the gift of faith and abstain from the *means of grace until they had received it. Such views were deeply influenced by Lutheran fears of 'works righteousness' and 'Quietist' notions. JW repudiated this teaching and separated from the Society over it. He believed that the *Lord's Supper and other 'means' were 'converting ordinances', that there were degrees of faith and that experience showed the importance of using the means of grace at all stages of Christian growth. There was, nevertheless, a role for 'stillness' in waiting on God, as expressed in CW's lines: 'For this, to Jesus I look up,/I calmly wait for this' and in the hymn 'Open, Lord, my inward ear' (HP 540).

H. Rack (1989) pp. 202–5

DJC

Stinson, Dr Joseph (1801–62; e.m. 1823), WM minister, born at Castle Donington, was appointed to the *Canada District in 1823, where he formed valuable contacts with both American and other colleagues. From 1828 to 1833 he served in *Gibraltar. When the church in Upper Canada reunited with the British Conference in 1833 he was appointed Superintendent of the Indian Missions. Through his extensive travels he gave them a new impetus and proved an effective champion of native interests. He became President in 1839. An eloquent and charming man with a gift for friendship, he worked for the unity of Canadian Methodism. He withdrew from the Canadian complexities in 1842, but in 1857 was welcomed back as President of the newly amalgamated Conference.

F&H 1

MJF

Stockport A society was formed by J. *Bennet in 1748 and survived his departure from

Methodism in 1752. The first Methodist chapel in Cheshire was opened there in 1759 (rebuilt 1784). A minority seceded in 1797 to join the MNC. Both PM and WMA subsequently gained a foothold, but WM was always dominant. Stockport Circuit was formed in 1786 from Manchester. Tiviot Dale was opened in 1826 as the second WM chapel. The undenominational Sunday School, which became the largest in the world, was founded by Methodists. Prominent local Methodists included M. *Mayer, JW's host on his visits after 1760 and J. *Heald MP, who was instrumental in locating the northern Theological Institution at *Didsbury. The IM Conference met in the town in 1817 and 1844 and the MNC Conference in 1887 and 1902.

H. Jutsum (1876); W.H. Lockley (1909)

EAR

Stoke-on-Trent, ('the Potteries') was created in 1910 from six North Staffordshire pottery towns, Tunstall, Burslem, Hanley, Stoke-upon-Trent, Fenton and Longton, each of which retained its own town centre and identity. JW first visited Burslem in 1760; his last visit to the area was in March 1790. In 1933 there were 87 Methodist chapels within the city in 12 circuits. In 1999 there were 39 chapels in 7 circuits.

In **Tunstall**, a chapel built in 1788 for a society dating from 1783 was replaced by Wesley Place (1835). PM, which originated at nearby Mow Cop, built its first chapel in Tunstall in 1811 and the name 'Society of Primitive Methodists' was adopted at a meeting there on 12 February 1812. A new chapel (1821, extended 1834) was rebuilt as Jubilee Chapel for the Jubilee Conference of 1860 and became revered as the 'mother church' of the connexion. Eight PM Conferences met there. A MNC society existed by 1821 and opened Mount Tabor chapel (1823; replaced 1857) on a site secured by J. *Ridgway at the top of the new Market Square. The society was seriously disrupted by J. *Barker and his supporters in the 1840s. A UMFC chapel was opened in Bank Street in the 1860s. Following post-war closures and amalgamations, Queens Avenue church opened in 1975.

Burslem was in J. *Bennet's round in 1744. JW's first visit was in 1760. The first chapel (1765) was replaced in 1801 by one on Swan Bank (called 'Duck Bank' by Arnold Bennett, who was baptized there in 1867); this became the Burslem Mission (rebuilt 1971). Five WM and Methodist Conferences have met in Burslem. In

1798 J. Ridgway built Zoar Chapel for the MNC society (one of eight formed in the Potteries within six weeks of the first MNC Conference in 1797). It was replaced by Bethel, Waterloo Road (1824), with the Dr Cooke Memorial School (1877), commemorating Dr W. *Cooke, at the rear. W. *Clowes was born in Burslem in 1780. A PM society was formed in 1819, with a chapel built in 1822. Their acquisition of the former MNC Zoar chapel in 1842 left the trust with a grave financial burden. Clowes Memorial (1878) fell victim to mining subsidence and was replaced by Clowes Church, Hamil Road (1959). The Burslem Sunday School, founded in 1787, broke with WM in 1836, built a large chapel at Hilltop (1837) and joined the WMA in 1848.

Hanley's first chapel was opened in 1783 and JW preached there in 1784. In 1797 J. *Ridgway and others led a revolt against a trust dominated by 'high church' Burslem potters and the society was almost extinguished by defection to the MNC. Bethesda MNC chapel, Albion Street (1798; enlarged 1812) was rebuilt in 1819 to seat 2,500. Its members dominated the commercial and political as well as the religious life of the town as it developed into the commercial heart of the Potteries. By 1840 one tenth of the MNC's membership was in the Hanley and Longton Circuits. The MNC Book Room was in Hanley from 1808 to 1832. Bethesda hosted nine MNC and two UM Conferences. WM recovered sufficiently to build a large chapel in Old Hall Street (1819). PM, established in Hanley by 1819, proved comparatively weak. Their first chapels (1824 and 1835) both failed; a third, in Marsh Street (1857) was the first of the town centre churches to close (c.1940). The only remaining Methodist presence in the town centre is the Methodist Book Centre on the site of the PM Sunday School.

Stoke-upon-Trent society, with 13 members, was in the new Burslem Circuit formed from Macclesfield in 1783. Lewis Bostock, an ironfounder, acquired sites for a chapel (1799) and a Sunday School (1805), Wesley Chapel (1816) seated 900. Mount Zion MNC chapel (1816) opened nearby, on the site of an earlier one registered in 1806. Houses were registered for PM worship at Penkhull (1819) and Stoke Lane (1820). The PM chapel in Penkhull (registered in 1830) was replaced in 1836. The second PM chapel in Stoke in John (now Leese) Street (1834) was succeeded by chapels in Queen Street and Londsdale Street (1878). Stoke and Penkhull Methodists now worship in part of the Epworth Street Youth Centre, built in 1957.

A MNC society was formed in **Fenton** in 1798 and Mount Tabor chapel built in Park Street. When a larger chapel opened in Market Street in 1811, the old chapel was kept for the Sunday School. The whole was rebuilt in 1870. A WM chapel in Temple Street (1812) was rebuilt in 1873. China Street PM chapel, taken over by Congregational Methodists (a secession from the MNC) in 1843 was bought by the CofE in 1849. Further PM chapels were built in Whieldon Road (1860), Bourne Street (1878) and Victoria Road (1884, rebuilt 1904).

JW made the first of several visits to **Longton** in 1783 and a chapel was registered that year. A new chapel was built in 1804, replaced in 1842 by a large chapel in Stafford Street, which in 1933 became the Longton Central Mission. Following a secession in 1797, Union Street MNC chapel opened in 1798. Zion MNC chapel in Commerce Street (1803) was enlarged in 1812 and 1822 and rebuilt in 1841. The town was missioned for the PMs by John Walford, who registered Vauxhall schoolroom in 1834. In 1843, on the foreclosure of the mortgage on their Victoria Place chapel (1836), the PM society rented Ebenezer chapel in High Street (now Uttoxeter Road), built in 1841 for an IM society. They moved to a new chapel in Sutherland Road in 1858 and finally to Bourne Chapel, Stone Road in 1901, on a site given by the Duke of Sutherland. By 1851 a second WM chapel (1812) in High Street had seceded to WR, which also took over the former PM Victoria Place chapel by 1860. By 1876 the latter had seceded from the UMFC to the WRU.

John H. Beech (1883); H. Smith & A.H. Beard (1899); J.W. Chappell (1901); J. Ward (1902); J. Young (1903); J.P. Langham (1911); H.J. Watts (1937); J.H. Anderson (1975); H.E. Beech (1999); Conference Handbook 1962

JHA

Stonehouse, Rev. George (1714–93), Anglican clergyman, born at Hungerford, Berks. He graduated from Pembroke College, Cambridge and became vicar of *Islington in 1738, but resigned and sold the living in 1740. Under *Moravian influence he became very critical of the Church. JW and CW were often in his parish church in 1738, though there is no supporting evidence for the assertion that CW was ever his curate. In conversation with JW in May 1740 he rejected any 'degrees of faith'. He appears to have married into money and in January 1745 JW found him 'gay and worldly'. The influence of

Moravianism had waned. He spent his later years at East Brent and he may have been the 'G.S.' whom JW met in *Bristol in August 1781.

JAV

Storey, Dr Christopher (1908–94), born in *Newcastle upon Tyne, obtained 1st class honours in French at Durham and a PhD from the University of Strasbourg for a thesis on St Alexis, on whom he published a life (1946; revised edn, 1968) and other works in French. As senior French master at the City of London School 1936–42, he became a freeman of the City. While Head of the Johnston Boys' Grammar School, Durham, 1942–51, he was appointed Officier d'Academie for his services to the French language. His 20 years as Head of *Culford School, 1951–71, saw improvements to the school premises and the amalgamation with the East Anglian School for Girls.

MR 26 Jan. 1995

JAV

Storey, Samuel (1841–1925) Trained as a teacher, he abandoned education in favour of business in his home town of *Sunderland. Publishing and politics soon became his dominant concerns and he was one of the group of radical businessmen who launched the *Sunderland Echo* in 1873. He later worked with Andrew Carnegie on a national newspaper syndicate. An advanced Liberal, he was MP for Sunderland 1881–95 and served on the Durham County Council 1892–1913 (for nine years as Chairman). Brought up in Free Methodism, he attended Dock Street UMFC/UM chapel, Sunderland and was an active supporter of the Brotherhood Movement.

GEM

Storey, Winship (1891–1950), a Tyneside *local preacher, was prevented by poor health from entering the ministry and became a partner in the family estate agency. His frequent contributions to the *Methodist Recorder* were characterized by whimsical humour, 'charity in judgment, but scorn for all that is petty and sordid'. He contributed to *The Message and Mission of Methodism* (1946) and towards the end of his life wrote *And Hearts are Brave Again* (1949) and *Give God Something to Build On* (1951).

JAV

Story, George (1738–1818), Yorkshire-born itinerant. He was awakened in London by the preaching of G. *Whitefield and came to full faith by hearing the Methodist preachers in his native Harthill. A printer by trade, the 1762 *Leeds Conference accepted him as an itinerant and he spent 29 years in circuits in England, Scotland and Ireland. In 1792 he was editor of the *Arminian Magazine* and from 1793 to 1804 manager of the WM printing office and *Connexional Editor. His obituary spoke of him as 'an old disciple and faithful labourer in the Lord's vineyard'.

EMP 5 pp. 218–41

HMG

Stovin, Cornelius (1830–1921), born at Binbrook Hall, Lincs, the son of a farmer. He had little education, but took to reading, especially science and natural history. He too became a farmer at Binbrook. He travelled widely and his thirst for learning took him to the Bodleian Library, Oxford. He became a *local preacher and was known as a keen evangelical and a zealous Bible expositor. He was a leading advocate of Methodist reform. He married into the *Riggall family. Under the Education Act of 1870 he founded a free Methodist School. He served as an overseer of the poor and a member of the Board of Guardians. He gave up farming in 1892 and retired to Hogsthorpe.

J. Stovin (1982)

WL

Stow, David (1793–1864), a pioneer of teacher training. In 1827, with the support of the Glasgow Education Society, he founded the first 'Normal School' in the UK, in which religious and moral concern undergirded the curriculum. In 1841 it came under the control of the Church of Scotland, but after the Disruption of 1843 he re-established it as the Free Church Normal College, which he directed until his death. Students were encouraged to follow his novel method of 'picturing out', i.e. encouraging pupils' interest through vivid oral lessons. His teachers proved successful and the WM Education Committee, with money from the *Centenary Fund, sent students to Glasgow for training until *Westminster College was founded in 1851, largely on Stow's principles.

W. Fraser (1868); *DNB*

MB

Strangers' Friend Societies were an important aspect of the voluntary social welfare work of Methodism in urban areas. JW encouraged a number of such projects to help the poor, particularly in times of distress. In 1785 John Gardner, a member at *Wesley's Chapel, London started a scheme to collect weekly contributions from members and distribute them among the deserving poor. JW gave this his support with an initial donation of a guinea and the promise of 3d a week. A similar society was started in *Bristol the following year. It was stipulated that the recipients of the charity were not to be Methodists, but 'poor, sick, friendless strangers', irrespective of religious and ethnic background. After W's death, A. *Clarke supported societies in Bristol, *Dublin, *Liverpool and *Manchester.

L. Tyerman (1878) 3 pp. 252–4; *PWHS* 29 pp. 32–4

TSAM

Stroud (Glos) In 1739 G. *Whitefield, CW and JW each made visits to the area and JW's Journal records at least 50 visits before his last in 1790. By 1756 there was what CW described as a 'little steady society' of 43, based on Wallbridge. In 1763 an octagonal preaching house was erected in Acre Street. On the last of his numerous visits JW noted that it was 'far too small'. It was enlarged c.1797 and about the same time a Stroud Circuit was formed. A more spacious chapel was built in Castle Street in 1876 and in 1879 the original 'Round House' became (and remains) the Salvation Army Citadel.

The PM society was the result of mission outreach from the Midlands c.1823, at first in the form of the Stroudwater Branch of Brinkworth Circuit. A PM Circuit was formed in 1830 with fewer than 200 members. They met at first in the local theatre, until a chapel was built in Parliament Street in 1835. Following *Methodist Union, in 1933 the WM and PM Circuits became one. By 1947 the Parliament Street chapel had been sold and became the Cotswold Playhouse. The Castle Street premises were sold in 1980, and the local Methodists found a 'home' with the Anglicans in St Alban's Church, Parliament Street.

WJC

Sugden, Dr Edward Holdsworth (1854–1935; e.m. 1874), WM minister, born at Ecclesfield, *Sheffield, the son and grandson of WM ministers. He was educated at *Woodhouse Grove School, Owen's College, Manchester (taking a London BA with prizes in classics and Greek Testament) and *Headingley College. While Assistant Tutor at Headingley 1874–80, he took a London BSc. As Master of Queen's College in the University of Melbourne 1887–1928, he

tackled the problems of uncompleted buildings and substantial debts, while exercising a formative influence on generations of students. For the first 12 years his wife served as college matron. His encouragement of drama and music and his liberal biblical scholarship, though combined with JW's evangelical zeal, drew criticism in the Victorian Conference. He was a member of the University Council and a trustee of the Public Library and the National Gallery of Victoria. He was elected President of the Victoria-Tasmania Conference in 1906 and of the Australasian Conference 1923–26. He gained a DLit in 1918 for a thesis on Shakespeare and gave the *Fernley Lecture in 1928 on *Israel's Debt to Egypt*. Sugden Tower was built in his memory, but his chief memorial is the two-volumes edition of JW's *Standard Sermons* (1921) which he edited. He also wrote a little book on JW's London (1932).

ADB; M.F. Sugden (1941); D. Eakins (1959)

TMO/JAV

Suggestions *see* **Memorials**

Sunday Schools H. *Ball started her Sunday School in High Wycombe in 1769 and there were numerous similar local initiatives. From 1780 onwards, through publicity about Robert Raikes' work in *Gloucester, Sunday Schools were founded in the major towns of England. Often motivated by the gospel, their founders also desired to reform behaviour by engaging children's minds. Children were in a 'lawless state' and 'allowed to run wild that day' (Raikes). Reading and writing were taught and teachers worked with small classes, nurturing literacy, social skills and Christian values, often with the Bible as the main resource. J. *Bunting opposed the teaching of writing on Sunday and at his insistence in 1827 the WM Conference adopted rules for the management of its schools. With the opening of Methodist *day schools, the religious character of Sunday Schools (which eventually included adults) became dominant.

By 1900 the Sunday School movement was an international lay-led movement among English-speaking Protestants, often in purpose-built premises and with a vision of the global use of the Bible. From 1916 the British Lessons Council provided thematic material, graded by age, of which *Partners in Learning* is the successor. 'Anniversaries', often with processions ('walks') included reunions of scholars and the presentation of songs and recitations in church. 'Outings' and 'Treats' provided rare pleasure for children from poor families. Between 1900 and 1932 the number of children in Methodist Sunday Schools in Britain dropped by half to just under one million. World War II brought further decline. During the 1960s changed use of Sunday, increased mobility and fewer children per family affected numbers. Sunday School sessions were moved to the morning, leading to the concepts of 'Junior Church' and 'Family Church', which integrated Sunday Schools into church life. Links between learning and worship led to all-age worship. In many places all that remains of the traditional Sunday School is the name and the use of curriculum material in classes led by lay teachers. Nevertheless, this method of Christian education is of immense importance throughout the world.

See also **Education**

MR 8 June 1939; W.R. Ward (1972); P.B. Cliff (1986); *HMGB* 4 pp. 373–5, 399–404

CHS

Sunday Service of the Methodists in North America With other Occasional Services

Prayer Book revision was commonplace in the eighteenth century. *The Sunday Service* was compiled by JW in 1784 and sent over with T. *Coke for the use of *American Methodists. It was an abridgment of the 1662 *BCP*, but on the whole was a conservative revision. It omitted Confirmation, the saints' days, some passages in *Baptism and a number of the Psalms, and shortened some services, but included a 'Form of Ordaining of a Superintendant', used in the case of F. *Asbury. There are two versions of the first edition, one containing the manual acts in the Communion and the signation in Infant Baptism. One possibility is that JW intended the inclusion of both, but Coke, supervising the printing, omitted them. When JW discovered this, he had corrected sheets printed, to be inserted when the copies were bound in America. This was accordingly done, but not in every case. Another edition in 1786 had various alterations, especially in infant baptism, possibly made by Coke. In this and numerous subsequent editions 'North America' in the title is omitted or replaced by other topographical references. Morning Prayer never gained widespread acceptance in America and in the 1792 *Discipline* was replaced by a simple rubric enjoining singing, prayer and scripture readings. In England the *Sunday Service* was not replaced in WM till 1882 and even then, though not widely used, continued in print for a while. Shorter versions, such as *Order of Administration*

of the Sacraments and other Services, contained only some of the services.

See also **Ordination**

W.F. Swift in *PWHS* 29 pp. 12–20, 31 pp. 112–18,133–43; Nolan B. Harmon in *PWHS* 39 pp. 137–44; F. Baker (1970), ch.14; J.F. White (1995); J.C. English in *MH* July 1997 pp. 222–32

ARG

Sunderland, a good example of an industrial and trading community whose socio-economic character proved favourable to all branches of Methodism. CW and then JW first came and preached at mid-summer 1743. C. *Hopper and J. *Nelson were among the early pioneers. Within a few years there were societies and chapels on both banks of the Wear. St Peter's, Monkwearmouth had evangelical ministers who invited JW to preach there. He visited Sunderland about 30 times between 1743 and 1790 and (despite his strictures against smuggling!) was a dominant influence on Wearside. The WM Circuit was formed in 1782 and until 1812 covered a wide area of north-east Durham, including many colliery communities. J. *Everett offers lively descriptions of lay folk and preachers in the circuit in books based on memories of his years as a youthful *local preacher.

Sunderland proved fertile ground for most non-WM connexions, notably PM, UMFC and WR. The 1851 *Religious Census recorded 12,881 Methodist attendances out of a total of 32,920: WM 3,960, PM 4,012 and others (MNC, UMFC and WR) 4,909, indicating PM's strength on Wearside after only 30 years. Sunderland was the heart of a huge PM District, stretching south to *Whitby, north to *Berwick and west to *Carlisle. The promotion of progressive causes, including ministerial education, resulted in the establishment of a PM Theological Institution in 1868. Resistance to the modernizing party in local PM in the mid-1870s resulted in the *Christian Lay Church secession in 1877. The seceders soon joined the IM and are still active as such. The PM Conference met there five times between 1825 and 1889 and the UMFC Conference four times between 1869 and 1903.

Sunderland's older surviving chapels reflect the strength of Methodism's appeal to both artisans and the middle class in the nineteenth and early twentieth centuries. St John's (WM, 1888) in the suburb of Ashbrooke, the finest of the city's Gothic chapels, replaced the central Georgian chapel on Sans Street (1793, now demolished), which was adapted as a mission hall serving the declining east end of the town.

See also **Hampson, John**

Conference Handbook 1936, 1958; G.E. Milburn (1987); G.E. Milburn (1988)

GEM

Sunderland PM Theological Institute
The Sunderland PM District was in the forefront of the mid-nineteenth century campaign for ministerial training, led by ministers such as C.C. *M'Kechnie and Thomas Southron. The training of men at *Elmfield College, York from 1865 was only a halfway house and the campaigners' demands finally bore fruit in 1868 with the conversion of Sunderland's former infirmary into a college, with an intake of about 20 students on a one-year course. The staff were Dr W. *Antliff (Principal 1868–81) and T. *Greenfield (Tutor, 1877–81; Principal, 1881–3). Between 1868 and 1883 some 300 students passed through the Institute, before it was replaced by the new purpose-built college in *Manchester. One of its first intake was George *Parkin who was himself to become Principal at Manchester 30 years later.

G.E. Milburn (1981)

GEM

Sundius, Christian (1754–1835) was a Swedish Army officer who served in the British Navy till 1780, when ordered from Sweden to enter the French service. This he refused to do, was converted the same year and joined the City Road society in London. His second wife (1798) was Jane Vazeille Smith, daughter of William *Smith and JW's step-granddaughter. He became a translator to the Admiralty, was a member of the *Committee of Privileges and in 1804 one of the founders of the BFBS. He was a director of the London Missionary Society and a trustee of the Swedish Protestant Church in London. The family grave was at *Wesley's Chapel.

WMM 1833 p. 464; G.J. Stevenson (1872) pp. 472–5; M.W. Woodward (1966) pp. 76–8

MB

Superintendent In JW's lifetime the word used for the preacher in charge of a *circuit was '*Assistant', (i.e. to Mr Wesley). The term 'Superintendent' was first applied to T. *Coke and F. *Asbury in 1784, in connection with the work in *America, where it was soon replaced by the title

'Bishop', evoking JW's strong displeasure. Later the term 'District Superintendent' replaced 'Presiding Elder' in American usage. In England 'Superintendent' replaced the term *'Assistant' in the 1796 Minutes. While the title can be seen as the Latin translation of the Greek episcopos, i.e. 'bishop', there was no suggestion in English Methodism that circuit Superintendents should be regarded as belonging to a different order and ordained or consecrated to their office. The Superintendent's name stands first (or alone) in the stations of a circuit. With their colleagues Superintendents determine the *preaching plan for their circuit and are responsible for Methodist *discipline in all its local churches (formerly *'societies'), subject always to the laws and regulations of the Conference. In conjunction with the *Circuit Meeting they are responsible for the effective use of the resources for ministry and mission within the circuit.

JWH

Supernumerary, 'a minister permitted or directed under the provisions of the Deed of Union or Standing Orders to retire from the active work of the ministry' and known in earlier days as a 'worn-out minister'. Ministers are permitted by *Conference to retire after travelling 40 years or reaching retirement age as defined by the Ministers' Pension Scheme, or on compassionate grounds such as ill-health. Supernumeraries are stationed in a circuit and are members of the *Circuit Meeting and Circuit Local Preachers Meeting. Unless they are active Supernumeraries (i.e. in pastoral charge of local churches), they are not members of *Church Councils or committees, unless elected to serve. They are members of the *District Synod, but are required to attend only the ministerial session of the Synod (unless granted a dispensation).

JWH

Sustentation Fund see **Finance, Ministerial**

Sutcliffe, Joseph (1762–1856; e.m. 1786), WM itinerant. While stationed in Cornwall, 1786–89, he introduced Methodism to the Scilly Isles. Later on, in *Bristol and with his interest probably aroused while in Cornwall, he published The Geology of the Avon (1822), a pioneer work on local economic geology. Among some twenty other works he wrote English grammars and a two-volume Bible commentary (1834). His four-volume manuscript 'History of Methodism' remained unpublished and is in the Methodist *Archives Centre. His last 18 years were spent in

London. Though in the ministry for 70 years, he was never President of the Conference.

PWHS 17 pp. 123–4

CJS

Sutton, Charles (*c.* 1765–1829), newspaper proprietor, was a founder member of the MNC in *Nottingham. He printed many of the connexion's early publications and was Secretary of the MNC Conference in 1804. In 1808 he founded the *Nottingham Review*, a Whig paper which supported the *Luddites in 1815. This earned him 18 months in prison. His only son **Richard Sutton** (1789–1856) took over the editorship in 1829. More radical than his father, he used the *Review* to advocate annual Parliaments and manhood suffrage, while remaining active in MNC affairs.

M.I. Thomis (1969)

EAR

Swaledale *see* **Dales Circuit**

Sweden   JW had contacts with Swedish visitors to England, including Karl Magnus Wrangel, chaplain to the Swedish King, who preached at the *New Room, Bristol in 1768, and Professor Johan Henrik Lidén of Linköping. But Methodism was introduced into Sweden by an engineer S. *Owen of *Norwich. J.R. *Stephens was sent over in 1826, followed in 1830 by G. *Scott. The 'English Church' was opened in Stockholm in 1840, but Scott's public criticism of the state of religion in Sweden provoked hostility and the mission was abandoned in 1842. Later Methodism in Sweden derives from the work of the Bethel Ship *John Wesley* among Swedish seamen in New York harbour.

See also **Sundius, C.**

F&H 4 pp. 460–74; W.P. Stephens (n.d.)

SJP

Sweetman, Dr James Windrow (1891–1966; e.m. 1916), missionary in *India, was born in *Liverpool and trained at *Didsbury College. He served in the Lucknow and Banares District 1919–22 and from 1934 to 1946 taught at the Henry Martyn School of Islamic studies, also serving as secretary and Chairman of the North India Provincial Synod. He received his DD from Serampore College in 1948. As Professor of Islamic Studies at the Selly Oak Colleges 1947–62, his expertise, demonstrated in his *Islam and Christian Theology* (1946–51), was widely

acknowledged, as was his charming, wise and stimulating personality.

MR 2 June 1966

JAV

Swift, Wesley F. (1900–61; e.m. 1924), Methodist historian, was trained at *Richmond College. He was a frequent contributor to the WHS *Proceedings*, which he edited from 1946 and was British Secretary of the International Methodist Historical Society. He gave the WHS Lecture in 1947 on *Methodism in Scotland* and compiled an invaluable guide to historical sources, *How to Write an Local History of Methodism* (1954). His *Ministers' and Laymen's Handbook* (1946) was for many years the circuit minister's *vade mecum*. After 36 years in circuit work, in 1961 he was appointed the first full-time Connexional Archivist and also the British editor of the *Encyclopedia of World Methodism*, but died shortly afterwards. His brother **Rowland Cook Swift** (d. 1984) had a successful career in commerce, was Registrar of the WHS for many years and wrote histories of Methodism in Nottingham and Sussex.

MR 4 Jan. 1962; *PWHS* 33 pp. 90–3, 44 p. 184

JAV

Swindells, Robert (d.1782), one of the English preachers who laid the foundations of Methodism in *Ireland. He joined the itinerancy in 1741 and accompanied JW on his 1748 Irish tour. Later that year he journeyed with CW when Methodism was introduced into important towns in the south of Ireland. He remained behind and was instrumental in converting several key figures, including T. *Walsh and E. *Bennis, as well as ministering to the *Palatine community. Another of his converts, Col. Pigot, provided him in gratitude with an annuity of £40. He died in England.

C. Atmore (1801) pp. 409–10; *Methodist Family* 1 Jan. 1870 pp. 30–1

RPR

Swindon   J. *Cennick visited the town in 1741, but met with a hostile reception said to have been encouraged by the Lord of the Manor, Pleydell Goddard. Methodism was eventually established there in 1814 by the Bristolian G. *Pocock and the *Tent Methodists. He preached in the Market Square and was entertained by one of his hearers, William Noad, parish clerk and well known businessman, who had registered his kitchen for worship. In 1824 a small chapel, holding 120, was opened at the back of the Square, thanks to the generosity of Thomas Bush of Lambourne. In 1837 the Great Western Railway chose Swindon as its base. The population exploded and the prosperity of the Methodist cause rendered the chapel too small. It was replaced by the 'Octagon Chapel' on the same site in 1862 and then by Bath Road church in 1880. Other chapels eventually proliferated throughout the town. A large building in Faringdon Road, erected in 1843 as a hostel for GWR workers, was converted in 1869 and became Wesley Chapel. It closed in 1959 and became the Railway Museum. The Central Hall, Clarence Street, opened in 1907, grew out of a WM mission in Princes Street. A new hall was added in 1957 and it became part of the ecumenical Central Church in the 1970s. The Swindon Circuit was formed from Hungerford in 1814. Between 1892 and 1911 there were two circuits, based on the Bath Road and Wesley churches.

PM was introduced in the late 1820s by preachers from the Brinkworth Circuit. Following a visit by H. *Bourne in 1840, a chapel was opened in Regent Street in 1849 (closed 1956). PM was particularly active in the last 20 years of the nineteenth century, when five new chapels were built. The Swindon Circuit, formed in 1877, divided into Prospect and Regent Street Circuits in 1890. After *Methodist Union, the three circuits (Bath Road, Prospect Place and Regent Street) eventually became a single circuit in 1959. In 1969 the Circuit church in Bath Road (1880) joined with Christ Church (Anglican) and Immanuel (Congregational, now URC) Church to form the Old Town Ecumenical Parish. Although there have been recent closures, mainly in the inner areas, the ecumenical movement continues to grow throughout the borough.

———

MR(W) 1898 pp. 45–8; E.R. Carter (1980); *Footprints of Faith: a History of Central Church, Swindon* (Swindon, 1988) pp. 69–92

BJC

Synod *see* **District Synod**

Tackaberry, Fossey (1796–1847), born in a staunchly Protestant home on Co. Wexford, was converted through the preaching of Andrew Taylor (d.1841; e.m. 1796), one of Ireland's General Missionaries who became his early mentor. For some time he worked on the family farm while travelling extensively as a *local preacher. Called into the itinerancy in 1823, his ministry

was characterized by revivalist and holiness preaching. He had a distrust of Roman Catholicism and opposed Catholic Relief. His final appointment was to Sligo where, after ministering to many victims of the Irish famine he himself succumbed to typhus.

———

R. Huston (1853)

RPR

Taft, Zechariah *see* **Barritt, Mary**

Tasker, Dr John Greenwood (1853–1936; e.m. 1875), WM minister, born at Skipton-in-Craven. After training at *Richmond College, he became Assistant Tutor, and later Classical Tutor, there. Four years at Cannstatt in Germany laid the foundations of an interest in German theology. In 1892 he moved to *Handsworth College as Tutor in Biblical and Classical Studies, later becoming Principal (1910–23). He delivered the *Fernley Lecture in 1910 on 'Spiritual Religion', was President of the 1916 Conference and in 1918 was a delegate to the Conference of the MEC South in the USA.

WL

Tatchell, Dr W. Arthur (1869–1937; e.m. 1905), WM medical missionary who went to *China in 1900 and served in hospitals at Tayeh and Hankow (Hankou) before going into private practice at Hankow. Returning to England in 1918, he resumed ministerial work in 1923, serving in English circuits until his retirement in 1929.

GRS

Tatham, Emma (*fl.* 1850–90), Methodist poet whose work won the approval of Matthew Arnold. She published *The Dream of Pythagoras and other Poems* (1854) and *On the Ocean of Time* (1890).

———

B. Gregory (1903) p. 409

JAV

Tattersall, Edward William (*c.* 1894–1987), a gifted photographer, born in Scotland, who specialized in landscape photography and whose work was featured in many calendars, books and magazines. His photographs, including those of *Conference and connexional events appeared in the *Methodist Times and Leader* and then in the *Methodist Recorder* from 1943 for over 30 years.

———

MR 28 May 1987

JWH

Taunton Methodism reached Taunton early, as it was usually JW's first stop on his way from Bristol to Cornwall. On his first visit, in August 1743, accompanied by J. *Nelson and J. *Downes, he preached at Taunton Cross. As a result a society began to meet at the Three Cups Inn (later the County Hotel and now the site of Marks and Spencer). Meetings were in members' homes until in 1776 JW opened a preaching house in Middle Street, the last of his 14 octagons. When they outgrew it in 1809, it was taken over by the Plymouth Brethren. From 1964 it was a night club, but in 1988 became the focal point of a preservation scheme. Its successor was built in Upper High Street by J. *Lackington and named The Temple after his business enterprise. In dispute with its owner, who stipulated that the preachers should be gowned, they soon moved back to the Octagon; it was then rented to the MNC, with whom Lackington also fell out. The WMs then bought it for £1,050 – half of what it had cost to build. Schoolrooms were added in 1866 and the interior redesigned on a new axis in 1869. It remains the circuit church, with Victoria Street chapel (1843), Rowbarton (1892) and Liseaux Way (1995) as part of its outreach. *Queen's College was founded in 1843.

The BCs reached Taunton when W. *Mason preached at the Cross in 1823 and a society belonging to the Kingsbrompton Circuit was started. It met in William Natcott's house in Canon Street, which was eventually bought and converted into a chapel. A purpose-built church, Ebenezer, replaced it on the same site in 1864. A single circuit was formed after *Methodist Union in 1932. But Ebenezer, hampered by debt, was sold in 1935 to the local council and was used as a fire station before being demolished in 1979 for residential development.

H.W. White (1988); H.W. White in WHS(B) Bulletin 79 (1999)

HWW

Taylor, David (d. 1780), the Countess of *Huntingdon's butler, who, after a conversion experience, preached in the villages near Donington Park and *Sheffield. From c. 1739 he travelled with B. *Ingham. At the invitation of J. *Bennet he visited the Derbyshire Peak District. On joining the Methodists, he accompanied J. *Nelson and, in May 1743, was with CW during the riots at Sheffield and Thorpe. Despite being influenced by *Moravian *stillness he was with JW at *Bolton in 1749. However, unsettled in his doctrinal views, he met with the *Quakers, but later returned to Methodism.

C. Atmore (1801), 412–13; J. Everett (1823)

SRV

Taylor, Henry James (1860–1945; e.m. 1881), PM minister, born in *Ireland and educated at *Sunderland College, *Hartley College and New College, London. He was an outstanding speaker, preacher and administrator, with a particular interest in *temperance and social topics. He served as Secretary of the PM Missionary Society and as President of the *Christian Endeavour Union and the National Sunday School Union. He delivered the 1921 *Hartley Lecture on *The Challenge of Freedom*. He was President of the PM Conference in 1922 and was a tireless worker for *Methodist Union.

CJS

Taylor, Jeremy (1613–67), Royalist and chaplain to Archbishop Laud and Charles I. Having survived the Civil War and Commonwealth, he was made Bishop of Down and Connor in 1661. During a period of retirement to Carmarthenshire, he wrote his best known works, *The Rule and Exercises of Holy Living* (1650) and *The Rule and Exercises of Holy Dying* (1651). JW was greatly influenced by these in 1725 and they were the basis on which he remodelled his own spiritual life, including the keeping of *diaries to monitor his spiritual progress. Taylor's continuing influence is seen in W's rejection of the more extreme versions of *salvation by *faith alone and his insistence on the pursuit of *holiness as part of Christian discipleship.

DNB; E. Gosse (1903); H.T. Hughes (1960)

JAV

Taylor, Joseph (1752–1830; e.m. 1777), itinerant preacher, born at Duffield, near Derby. He travelled 44 years, though often in poor health, owing to youthful over-exertion during a Cornish revival. He was included by JW in the *Legal Hundred and was one of the three preachers whom W ordained for *Scotland in 1785. A further deed in 1790 appointed him one of W's seven literary executors and he was President of the 1802 Conference. He was noted for his disciplined lifestyle and a frugality which enabled him to give generously to the poor.

JAN

Taylor, Joseph (1779–1845; e.m. 1803), WM missionary in the *West Indies 1803–11, serving on the islands of Tortola and St Bartholomew, where he restored the mission which had declined because of poor leadership. Returning to England, he became the first returned missionary to be appointed Resident Secretary of the WMMS, 1818–24. He was elected President of the Conference in 1834.

GRS

Taylor, Mary Ann (Mrs Robins) (d.1892) was a BC itinerant for about twenty years. Some of her converts became itinerants. In 1854 she married fellow-itinerant P. *Robins as his second wife and they went to *Canada, where he died in 1890. There is no record of her activity there.

F.W.Bourne (1905); E.G.Muir (1991)

EDG

Taylor, Thomas (1738–1816; e.m. 1761), born at Rothwell, near Leeds and in early life came under *Calvinistic influence. He met JW in 1761, who invited him to become a preacher and sent him into *Wales. He was a pioneer of numerous societies before being sent to *Ireland and then to *Scotland, where he established a society in *Glasgow. In early life he had shown a thirst for learning, and he taught himself Latin, Greek and Hebrew. He published a reply to Paine's *Age of Reason* (1796), a *History of the Waldenses and Albigenses* (1793) and an autobiography, *Redeeming Grace displayed to the Chief of Sinners* (1785). He was one of JW's close associates and after 1791 was an advocate of Methodist administration of the Sacrament. He was twice President of the Conference (1796 and 1809). J. *Montgomery wrote a poem, 'The Christian Soldier's Death', in his memory.

EMP 5 pp. 1–107

WL

Taylor, Dr Vincent, FBA (1887–1968; e.m. 1909) was born at Accrington and trained for the ministry at *Richmond College. He was appointed NT Tutor at *Headingley College in 1930, becoming Principal in 1936. Despite having had no university training (his first degree was the external London BD) he pursued his studies during his years in circuit and later published a series of NT studies, including trilogies on the atonement (*Jesus and his Sacrifice* (1937), *The Atonement in NT Teaching* (1940) and *Forgiveness and Reconciliation* (1948)) and on Christology (*The Names of Jesus* (1953), *The Life and Ministry of Jesus* (1955) and *The Person of Christ in NT Teaching* (1958)), as well as a major commentary on Mark's Gospel (1952). His account of form criticism in *The Formation of the Gospel Tradition* (1945) introduced it to many students in a readily understandable way. He was also noted for his championship of Streeter's Proto-Luke hypothesis (e.g. in *Behind the Third Gospel* (1926). He was elected President of the Society for NT Study and his scholarship was recognized by honorary degrees from the universities of Leeds, Dublin and Glasgow and the Burkitt Medal.

O.E. Evans in A.W.& E. Hastings (1966); *Times* 3 Dec. 1968; *MR* 5 & 19 Dec. 1968

CSR

Taylor, William George (1845–1934; e.m. 1870), WM minister who, in 1871 answered a call for preachers in *Australia. In 1884 he was appointed to the failing York Street Church in Sydney. By using such unorthodox methods as street preaching and brass bands he revived the church and in 1886 established in it the Sydney Central Mission (the first in Australia), gradually introducing a variety of service organizations, including a mission to seamen, the Sisters of the People (forerunners of the *deaconess order), Dalmar Children's Home and a shelter for 'fallen women'. He continued as Superintendent until his retirement in 1913. He was elected President of the NSW Conference in 1896. He placed great emphasis on prayer and on one occasion held a ten-day prayer meeting. Essentially an evangelist, revivals followed him wherever he went and ailing Methodist causes were renewed.

W.G. Taylor (1920); *ADB*; D. Wright & E. Clancy (1993) pp. 111–14

EGC

Teesdale *see* **Dales Circuit**

Teetotal Methodists, sometimes called the Temperance Methodists, existed chiefly in Cornwall. In September 1837 a young woman from Shropshire brought the teetotal message from *Preston and held meetings in *St Ives, with widespread success. But the *Superintendent minister frowned on them and the 1841 Conference passed motions condemning teetotalism. This led eventually to a separation from the parent body. Chapels were built in St Ives and elsewhere, and by 1845 the movement spread beyond Cornwall, particularly into South Wales. The desire for a regular ministry led to the break-up of the denomination, some chapels joining the *WMA and others the *MNC in 1860. The last known *class ticket is dated 1852.

See also **Docton, W.; Temperance**

M.S. Edwards in *PWHS*, 33 pp. 63–70; O.A. Beckerlegge (1957) pp. 56–7

OAB

Telford, John (1851–1936; e.m. 1873), WM minister, trained at *Didsbury College. His wife was the daughter of Dr J.H. *Rigg, whose life he wrote. As Connexional Editor 1905–34 he edited and published the 'Standard Edition' of JW's letters and a new edition of the **Lives of the Early Methodist Preachers* (under the title *Wesley's Veterans*). Among his other publications were popular lives of JW (1886) and CW (revised edition, 1900) and he gave the *Fernley Lecture in 1908 on *Man's Partnership with Divine Providence*. He succeeded J.S. *Simon as President of the *WHS in 1933. In his will £30,000 was left to the Methodist Church for ministerial training. After a legal dispute the High Court laid down the specific purposes of the 'Telford Bequest', with an emphasis on assistance to students and a bias towards study in Oxford or Cambridge. The bequest is now administered as part of the wider provision by the Methodist Church for such purposes.

MR 30 July & 6 Aug. 1936; *PWHS* 20 pp. 145–7, 191–3

BEB/JAV

Temperance In Methodist usage the word has come to be associated almost exclusively with the use of alcohol. Total abstinence has never been imposed as a condition of membership, but the Division of *Social Responsibility was charged with encouraging abstinence and warning about the dangers of alcohol abuse. Methodism played a prominent part in the Temperance Movement which developed in the nineteenth century (though, especially in the case of WM, only after many years of misgiving and actual opposition to the movement) and in such organizations as the Independent Order of Rechabites, the United Kingdom Alliance and the Band of Hope Union. The practice of total abstinence is no longer as widespread among Methodists as it was and few churches now maintain an 'abstainer's roll'. The once lively debate between 'prohibitionists' and 'moral suasionists' no longer excites much interest. But there is concern about the wider issue of drug addiction and a recognition that the abuse of alcohol is part of that larger problem. Alcoholism is seen as an illness and the Church is associated with centres for treatment and rehabilitation. The acknowledged dangers of 'drink driving' have added weight to Methodism's insistence on responsible attitudes and the legislative control of the drink trade. A further review of the Church's policy on the use of alcohol on Methodist premises was intitated by the 1999 Conference.

See also **Social Responsibility; Teetotal Methodists**

E.C Urwin (1943); K.G.Greet (1960); G.T. Brake (1984) pp. 433–43

KGG

Tent Methodism began among *local preachers in the *Bristol area, led by G. *Pocock and John Pyer, who were dissatisfied at the lack of evangelical outreach in WM. In April 1814 they pitched a tent and preached on waste ground at Whitchurch and that summer extended their activity to parts of North Somerset and South Gloucestershire, without formal authority from the *Superintendents of the circuits concerned. Despite initial approval from the WM Conference, like H. *Bourne and W. *O'Bryan they ran into increasing opposition and censure, which came to a head in 1820 with the expulsion of both Pocock and Pyer by the Bristol Superintendent. Their independence from WM was marked by issuing *class tickets, accepting the offer of a chapel, publishing a set of Rules and forming a *society of 35 members. In 1823 and, it is thought, 1824 a monthly Magazine was published. The movement spread to Wiltshire, *London, *Manchester and *Liverpool, but remained small in scale and eventually petered out. Pyer became a Congregational minister and Pocock eventually rejoined the Bristol WMs.

Tent Methodist Magazine 1823; K.P.Russell (1865)

JAV

Tewkesbury G. *Whitefield preached to large crowds in 1739, followed in 1744 by JW, who became a regular visitor, describing it as 'the liveliest place in the [Gloucester] Circuit'. He opened the first preaching house in 1777 (enlarged 1813). The present church in the town centre was built in 1878 by Thomas Collins, senior Circuit Steward and builder of many churches for all denominations. The Tewkesbury Circuit was formed from Gloucester in 1838, comprising at its zenith 12 chapels. It became part of the new Tewkesbury and Cheltenham Circuit in 1991. For a short time in the 1870s there was also a PM chapel.

DW

Thanksgiving Funds The MNC set up a Thanksgiving Fund in 1846 to mark its Jubilee and raised £7,700 in support of connexional projects. In 1877 a WM Thanksgiving Fund was established to celebrate the peaceful introduction of lay representatives in the Conference. It raised £297,518 (approximately £15m today) and was used to extinguish debts and to support extension work.

DRF

Thatcher, Margaret Hilda, Baroness Thatcher of Kesteven (1925–), right-wing Conservative politician, was born in *Grantham into a Methodist family and as a student at Somerville College, Oxford, was active in MethSoc. Through her family background she inherited JW's independence, industriousness, thrift and concern for public service, though not his distrust of surplus wealth or bias in favour of the poor. She was married in 1951 in *Wesley's Chapel, London and was called to the Bar in 1954. Becoming an MP in 1959, she was Secretary of State for Education and Science 1970–4 and Prime Minister 1979–90, the first woman to hold that office. She was made a life peer in 1992. She has published two volumes of autobiography (1993 and 1995).

H. Young (1989); J.A. Newton in *The Tablet*, 1 Dec. 1990

JAV

Theological Institution *see* **Ministerial Training**

Thom, William (1751–1811; e.m. 1774), cofounder of the MNC, was born in *Aberdeen and grew up in the Church of Scotland. He joined the Methodists and became an itinerant in 1774. JW included him in the *Legal Hundred in 1784. Although he played no part in the disputes of the 1790s, he withdrew from WM in 1797 to join A *Kilham and played a large part in drafting the MNC Constitution, which bore traces of Presbyterian polity. After Kilham's death Thom became the leading figure in the new denomination. He was a careful administrator rather than a charismatic leader, but ensured the MNC's survival.

He was six times President of the Conference and *Book Steward 1803–11.

W. Salt (1822) pp. 42–54; H. Smith (1893) pp. 15–28

EAR

Thomas, Diana (1759–1821), born at Brook Farm, Lyonshall near Kington, Herefords, joined the Methodists *c.* 1799 and began to preach under the influence of M. (*Bosanquet) Fletcher, whom she visited and with whom she corresponded. She had begun preaching by 1809 and encouraged M. *Tooth to continue preaching after Mrs. Fletcher's death. Invited to open both English and Welsh chapels, she travelled on her white pony over a wide area, preaching from Ledbury to Aberystwyth and Machynlleth and from Brecon to Bishops Castle. She was a formidable personality and persuasive speaker.

W. Parlby in *PWHS* 14 pp. 110–11; B.C. Redwood in *PWHS* 51 pp. 125–9; *WMM* 1821 p. 859

JHL

Thomas, George, Lord Tonypandy (1909–97), Labour MP and Speaker of the House, was born into a humble home in the Rhondda Valley. From early days he was associated with the Tonypandy Central Hall and learned some of his parliamentary skills in the Men's Parliament there. After training at University College, Southampton he became a teacher and a *local preacher. He was elected as Labour MP for *Cardiff West in 1945 and was Under-Secretary of State at the Home Office and then Minister of State at the Welsh Office. In that capacity he was deeply involved with the Aberfan disaster in 1966. In 1967 he became Minister of State at the Commonwealth Office and in 1968 Secretary of State for Wales, in which office he was responsible for arranging the investiture of the Prince of Wales and also read the lesson at the Prince's wedding. In 1976 he was elected Speaker of the House. On retirement in 1983 he entered the House of Lords. In the service of Methodism he has been Vice-President of the Conference (1960), Treasurer of the Department of Christian Citizenship and President of *NCH. He published his memoirs in 1985.

MR 7 July 1960, 25 Sept. 1997; R. Hunston (1981); E.H. Robertson (1992)

KGG

Thomas, Gilbert Oliver (1891–1978), after two unhappy years at The *Leys School, joined the editorial staff of Chapman and Hall in 1910 and went on to become a prolific literary journalist. Besides many essays, he wrote books on John Masefield (1932) and William Cowper (1935; revised edition, 1949) and an autobiography in 1946. *Paddington to Seagood* (1947) celebrates his enthusiasm for model railways. His son David founded the publishing firm of David & Charles.

MR 26 Jan. 1978

JAV

Thomas, John (1797–1881; e.m. 1824), WM missionary to *Tonga, born in Clent to a blacksmith family. He was converted by class leaders and became a *local preacher. With no formal training he was appointed to the Friendly Islands and sailed via Australia in 1825. The NSW ministers, without authority from London, had ordained John Hutchinson, expecting him to be Superintendent of the mission. Thomas's appointment caused such animosity on Hutchinson's part that the mission made little headway until Hutchinson left in 1829. Thomas remained the unsophisticated evangelical whose simplicity had so impressed the WMMS secretaries, an avowed Sabbatarian and devout literalist. He gave the Tongans the new faith and social structure they needed as Western 'civilization' spread. After two fruitful years, when hundreds were converted, baptized and put in classes, and made literate, in 1832 he was, to his dismay, made Chairman of the South Seas District (later including *Fiji and *Samoa), remaining so until 1848.

From the outset Thomas interested himself in Tongan history and culture and his unrivalled knowledge of the language at first made up for his ignorance of Hebrew and Greek, though it later exposed him to painful criticism from his college-trained colleagues. In England slanderous lies were told by a Captain Dillon, bent on increasing French influence in the Pacific and indignant at Thomas's efforts to protect Tongan women from his crew. His deep inferiority complex made him seem dictatorial in his later days, but he was trusted by many of the chiefs and brought to an end internal wars. Not having visited England or NSW for 24 years left him out of touch with changes in Church and society and he returned home in 1850 a disillusioned man. But Tonga was his true home and to the Free

Wesleyan Church he is still 'Father Thomas'.

J.L. Luckcock (1992); J.L. Luckcock (1998)

JLL/AY

Thomas, John Wesley (1798–1872; e.m. 1822), WM minister and scholar, remembered especially for his annotated translations in *terza rima* of Dante's *Divine Comedy* (*Inferno*, 1859; *Purgatorio*, 1862; *Paradiso*, 1866). Among his other poetry is a critical review of Byron's poem in *An Apology for Don Juan* (1824, enlarged 1855), *The Lord's Day, or the Christian Sabbath* (1865) and *Poems on Sacred, Classical, Medieval and Modern Subjects* (1867). He also wrote on *Exeter Methodism (1870). At the Conference of 1849 he made an impressive speech in support of the motion to expel J. *Everett, taking his stand not on Methodist law but on the 'universal law, those of Rome, Moses and King Alfred'. He was also a rabid anti-papist, and his opposition to teetotalism is forcefully expressed in a letter to J. *Bunting in 1839.

DNB; G.F. Cunningham (1965) pp. 102–8; W.R. Ward (1976) pp. 217–19

EWD

Thompson, Douglas Weddell (1903–81; e.m. 1925), WM missionary, appointed to Hunan, *China in 1925, where he worked, apart from a brief period in Calcutta, until 1939. During World War II he served as Chaplain to the Forces, was wounded and taken prisoner (as described in *Captives to Freedom* (1955)). After 13 years in English circuit work, he was appointed General Secretary of the MMS, 1958–68. He was President of the Conference in 1966. His autobiography, *A Mountain Road*, was published posthumously in 1983.

MR 19 March 1981

GRS

Thompson, Edward John (1886–1946), WM minister, son of **John M. Thompson** (1854–94; e.m. 1876), a WM missionary in India. He left *Kingswood School for a London bank. As a missionary candidate at *Richmond College, he took his London BA in 1909. While teaching at the Wesleyan College, Bankura, Bengal, he studied Bengali poetry and became friendly with Rabindranath Tagore, whose life he later wrote. After service as an army chaplain in the Middle East (for which he received the M.C.) he returned to Bankura in 1920 as Acting Principal. His interest in Indian politics led to a passionate advocacy of independence. Returning home in 1923, he left the ministry, though continuing to worship at Islip chapel. He became a prolific novelist, poet and historian and lectured in Bengali at Oxford, where he was Leverhulme research fellow, 1934–36, and Oriel research fellow in Indian history, 1936–46. He revisited India several times and counted Nehru and Gandhi among his friends. His novels, especially *Concerning the Arnisons* (1935) and *John Arnison* (1939), contain much autobiographical material. His younger son **Edward P. Thompson** (1924–93) went to Cambridge and became a social historian. His influential *The Making of the English Working Class* (1963) turns the *Halevy thesis into a charge against Methodism as a stabilizing political influence.

Times, 4 May, 1946; *MR* 2 May 1946, 9 Sept. 1993

JAV

Thom(p)son, Rev. George (1698–1782), vicar of St Gennys, Cornwall from 1732, welcomed JW and accompanied him on his tour of Cornwall in June 1745. Their relationship was strained by the strict *Calvinism, expressed in his *Original Hymns* (1776), but in August 1782 JW visited him on his deathbed and gave him the Sacrament. He has been wrongly identified as the 'Mr Thompson' whom JW met in Georgia in 1737.

G.C.B. Davies (1951) pp. 30–51

JAV

Thompson, John Day (1849–1919; e.m. 1871), son of Alexander Thompson, a prominent South Shields PM official and manager of a Jarrow chemical works. He trained for the PM ministry at the *Sunderland Institute. Following the death of H. *Gilmore, he was sent to Adelaide in 1892, where he supported the federation movement and the campaign for women's suffrage in South *Australia. A bold thinker and sworn foe of traditionalists, the liberal views expressed in his address 'The Simple Gospel' (1894) brought a reaction from the connexional conservatives, notably J. *Macpherson who attacked him for deviating from Methodist doctrine. At the 1896 Conference, in his absence, he was the first in the Connexion to be charged with heresy. Supported by W. *Beckwith and Dr J. *Watson, he was cleared of the charge. He returned to England in 1898 and was elected Conference Secretary in 1903, General Committee Secretary in 1909 and President of the Conference in 1915, when he tried to prevent

liberal theology being equated with German thought. His writings included his *Hartley Lecture, *The Doctrine of Immortality* (1908) and *The Church that Found Herself* (1912).

F. Tice (1966) pp. 116–18; S. Mews in S. Mews (1993) pp. 206–25

DCD

Thompson, Martha (Mrs Whitehead) (*c.* 1731–1820), a young *Preston girl who in 1750 went into domestic service in London. She came under the spell of JW's preaching at Moorfields and found new life in Christ. Her constant singing of Isaac Watts's words, 'And will this sovereign King/Of Glory condescend?' caused her master and doctors to believe she was suffering from religious mania. She was committed to Bedlam, where she wrote to JW. He sent doctors to investigate; she was discharged and cared for at the *Foundery. Later she accompanied JW on his journey north. She was counted as Preston's 'first Methodist' and was instrumental in forming the first class meeting there. Her story was dramatized in the musical *Ride! Ride!*

J. Taylor (1885) pp. 8–17; M.L. Edwards in WHS(N. Lancs) Bulletin 1 pp. 4–7

EWD

Thompson, Peter (1847–1909; e.m. 1871) was born at Esprick, Lancs and trained for the WM ministry at *Didsbury College. In 1885 he was appointed to St George's church, Cable Street, Stepney, to launch the first WM urban mission. He bought The Old Mahogany Bar, a notorious gin palace, and Wilton's Music Hall and converted them into mission premises. He was also responsible for building Stepney Central Hall in 1907.

MR 21 & 28 Oct. 1909; G.A. Leask (1909); R.B. Thompson (1910); R.G. Burnett (1946) pp. 46–60; R.C. Gibbins (1995)

JDB

Thompson, Thomas, MP (1754–1828), merchant and banker of *Hull, a partner in Smiths and Thompson's Bank and chairman of the Hull Docks Company 1810–18. As a young man he was influenced by the evangelical Joseph Milner, headmaster of Hull Grammar School. He was a *local preacher and married Philothea Briggs, a granddaughter of V. *Perronet. He was a stabilizing influence in the period that followed the death of JW and as a Church Methodist drafted the Hull

Circular of 1791 urging the Methodists to stay within the Church. He had an active concern both for the poor of Hull and for the conversion of the heathen and chaired the first District Missionary Meetings in both *Leeds and Hull in 1813. He was the first lay treasurer of the WMMS when it was formed in 1818. As MP for Midhurst 1807–18, the first Methodist to sit in the House of Commons, he supported the Corn Laws out of concern for the effect of cheap imports on agricultural labourers. He lived at Cottingham Castle and published a history of Holderness in 1821. He died in Paris on his first visit abroad and was buried there.

WM *Minutes* 1829; A.R.B. Robinson (1992)

JAV

Thompson, William (*c.* 1733–99), WM itinerant from Ulster, stationed for over 40 years throughout the British Isles. An articulate and inspiring evangelist and preacher, during the last decade of JW's life he became a trusted member of his entourage. In 1791 he moved quickly, calling a meeting of nine senior preachers to discuss the future governance of Methodism. The *Halifax Circular was adopted by the ensuing Conference, which also elected Thompson as President, preferring a relatively unknown and unordained moderate to more prominent connexional figures such as T. *Coke or A. *Mather. This self-styled 'man of peace' was criticized by radicals like A. *Kilham as a 'Church bigot' and a Pittite. He found himself increasingly isolated as the itinerants closed ranks on the centre ground in the face of the common threat posed by the Kilhamites.

C. Atmore (1801) pp. 416–23; *HMGB* 4 pp. 245–50, 259–60

JAH

Thomson, Rev. George *see* **Thom(p)son, Rev. George**

Thorne Family   John Thorne (1762–1842), of Lake Farm, *Shebbear, North Devon, had the reputation of being an honest and upright man and something of a 'Methodist', though no Methodist society had yet been formed locally. His family increasingly shared the evangelical fervour of the Shebbear curate, Daniel Evans. W *O'Bryan visited their home on 9th October 1815 and formed a society there of 22 members. This in effect completed the formation of the first BC circuit. One of the sons, **James Thorne** (1795–1872; e.m. 1816) became a member, a *local preacher,

an itinerant and assistant to O'Bryan in quick succession. Together they drew up the first Rules of Society in 1817, keeping, as Thorne wrote, 'as close as possible to Mr Wesley's Rules'. After O'Bryan's withdrawal from the connexion in 1829, Thorne became its virtual leader, being elected President of the Conference five times (in 1831, 1835, 1842, 1857 and 1865). From 1822 to 1868 he was closely involved with everything that happened in the life of the denomination. In his religious thinking he was a traditionalist, holding that Christian theology was a sacred deposit and that there could be no such thing as the development of doctrine. He supported the Evangelical Alliance and the Bible Society, but 'had no use for bigoted or narrow sectarianism'. He had some esteem for the Anglican liturgy, but was opposed to its establishment. He was a sturdy Protestant, but as a political Liberal supported RC emancipation. He was assistant editor of O'Bryan's *Arminian Magazine* from 1822 to 1829 and as editor of its successor, the *BC Magazine*, from 1829 to 1866 he guided the denomination in its religious, social and political thinking. Education was a particular interest and he took a leading part in the founding of the connexional school at Shebbear and its development into the college, of which he became the manager in 1844. His youngest son, **John Thorne** (1839–1914; e.m. 1873) was born at Langtree, Devon, worked in the connexional printing office and became a journalist in *Plymouth. In 1872 he offered for service in South *Australia. When farming settlements opened up in the north of the State in the 1870s he made several visits to the new towns and during the 11 years he superintended the BC work in the north he opened many preaching places, extended circuit boundaries and built churches. He was the main instigator of the Church's Bush Missions. He was President of the South Australia BC Conference in 1887 and 1899 (when he signed the Deed of Union on its behalf). While visiting England in 1895 he was President of the British BC Conference.

James's brother **Samuel Thorne** (1798–1873) was a BC itinerant from 1819 to 1822 and *Book Steward 1822–24 and 1827–36. In 1825 he married Mary O'Bryan (1807–83), daughter of the denomination's founder and a fellow itinerant. They settled for a time at Devonport, then at Shebbear, where Samuel was the denomination's printer and publisher. They both worked in the printing shop and at the same time opened a school at Prospect House, looked after the farm and brought up their ten children. Mary's journal reflects the ups and downs of their unequal, debt-ridden marriage. One of their grandsons was **Samuel Thomas Thorne** (1860–91), one of the first BC missionaries sent to *China in 1885. After twelve months in Yunnan Fu, he went alone to open a mission station in Chaotung, but the rigours of the climate, harsh living conditions and the magnitude of the task he had set himself undermined his health and he died in 1891 of typhus. After a furlough, his widow, Lois Anna Melpas of the CIM, returned to continue the work until her health also broke down and she died in 1904.

See also **Lake, Octavius**

J. Thorne (1873); S.L. Thorne (1874); G.J. Stevenson (1884–86) 6 pp. 868–80; F.W. Bourne (1895); S.L. Thorne (1889); T. Ruddle (1893); R.K. Parsons (1985)

TS/DGH

Thorp, Edgar Bentley (1905–91; e.m. 1928), son and grandson of WM missionaries in South *India, was one of three Methodists who became CSI bishops in 1947. He was born in Bangalore, where his father **William Hubert Thorp** (1870–1950; e.m. 1893) became Chairman of the Mysore District and was a member of the Joint Committee on church union. Educated at *Kingswood School and with degrees from Oxford and Cambridge, after a year studying Comparative Religion at Marburg, Edgar went to the Trichinopoly District in 1930. He was Principal of the Bible School at Dharapuram, training village evangelists. He was Chairman of the District 1945–47 and Bishop of the new Trichinopoly-Tanjore diocese 1947–64. His ministry among poverty-stricken village Christians in the Dharapuram mass movement area and on the tea plantations in Valparai, was underpinned by his simple lifestyle; and as Bishop, the impartiality of his leadership fostered unity between the Anglican minority and Methodist majority in his diocese.

JRP/RA

Threlfall, William (1799–1825; e.m. 1820), WM missionary, born in the Fylde. As a teenager, he believed himself called to work in Madagascar. He sailed for *South Africa in 1822 and after a year with W. *Shaw among the British settlers began work among Africans at Delagoa Bay. This isolated mission was aborted when malaria and dysentery caused his evacuation to Cape Town. After recuperating he was stationed at Liliefontein and in 1825 set out north with two African col-

leagues. They were murdered by robbers near Warmbad (Namibia).

S. Broadbent (1857); T.F. Cheeseman (1910); N.A. Birtwhistle (1966)

JRP

Tidmarsh, Henry Edward (1855–1939), artist, born into a WM home in London where craftsmanship and music were highly valued. He was offered a place in his father's carpentry firm, but studied to become an artist, becoming known as an illustrator (e.g. W.A. Shaw's *Manchester Old and New*, 1896) and as a prolific water-colourist. He painted a number of Methodist scenes and exhibited at the RA and elsewhere. A gentle man of strong principles, he was a Sunday School teacher, *local preacher, teetotaller, pacifist, vegetarian and Socialist whose views and faith were reflected in his art.

PWHS 49 pp. 208–21; R. Hyde (1993)

PSF

Tighe Family of Rosanna, Co. Wicklow. The **William Tighe** MP who built the family home had two children by his first wife Mary Bligh who were Methodist sympathizers. **William Tighe junr**, who also became MP for Rosanna, married in 1765 Sarah Fownes of Woodstock, Co. Kilkenny, who had come under Methodist influence in Dublin. She gave generous support to charitable causes and Methodist evangelistic activities. After her husband's death in 1782 she lived for a time in Harrow, where JW visited her, advising her on her charitable and educational work at Rosanna. In 1789, on his last visit to Ireland, he also visited Rosanna (the scene of a later painting by Maria Spilsbury, now at *Wesley's Chapel), and it remained an important staging post for T. *Coke and other Methodist preachers. Mary Tighe commissioned JW's portrait by Romney (1789/90) and her daughter Elizabeth, wife of the hymn-writer and Anglican evangelical Thomas Kelly, made one of several known copies.

Theodosia, daughter of William Tighe senr, and her daughter Mary, wife of **Henry Tighe** MP, lived for a time in London and were members at *Wesley's Chapel. She founded a House of Refuge in Dublin and corresponded with H. *Moore as her mentor.

One of William Tighe's sons by his second marriage (to Margaret Theaker) was **Thomas Tighe**. He became vicar of Drumgooland parish, Co. Down, and was a key figure in the emergence of evangelicalism in the Church of Ireland, though he welcomed Methodist preachers such as A. *Averell to the parish. He is also remembered for his influence on Patrick Brunty (later *Brontë).

Mrs R. Smith (1844) pp. 162–6; R.H. Ludlow in *WMM* 1910 pp. 527–33; *PWHS* 19 pp. 38–42

RPR/PSF

Tilsley, Gwilym Richard (1911–97; e.m. 1935), *Welsh WM minister, educated at University College, Aberystwyth and *Wesley House, Cambridge. He became well known throughout Wales and was President of the Welsh Assembly in 1969. One of the nation's leading poets, he was the chaired bard at the National Eisteddfod in both 1950 and 1957, and his two winning odes (the former in praise of the coal miner and the latter lamenting the decline of the slate quarrying communities) were included in a collection of his works, *Y Glowr a Cherddi Eraill* (1958). He was Archdruid of Wales, 1969–72 and wrote some notable hymns (both original and translated from English). His Pantyfedwen Lecture on the religious element in Welsh poetry, *Crefydd y Beirdd*, was published in 1977. He was the last editor of *Yr Eurgrawn*, 1966–83.

Cydymaith i Lenyddiaeth Cymru p. 577; *OCLW* p. 589; *MR* 9 Oct. 1997

OEE

Tiplady, Thomas (1882–1967; e.m. 1908) was born at Gayle, Wensleydale. During World War I he served as a chaplain on the Somme Front and wrote of his experiences in several books, including *The Soul of the Soldier* (1918). In 1922 he began a 32-year ministry in the Lambeth Mission. He was a pioneer in the evangelistic use of films and transformed the church into a cinema. He wrote of this in *Spiritual Adventure: the Story of the Ideal Film Service* (1935). Inspired in his youth by the poems of Robert Burns, he wrote over 250 hymns. *Methodist International House at Lambeth was the fulfilment of his dream.

MR 19 Jan. 1967

JDB

Titcombe, William Holt Yates (1858–1930), artist, son of the first Anglican Bishop of Rangoon. He lived for some years in *St Ives, Cornwall and later in *Bristol and exhibited a number of paintings on Methodist subjects at the Royal Academy, the best known being 'Primitive Methodists at Prayer' (at *St Ives, 1889; now in the Dudley Art Gallery). His 'John Wesley preaching before the Mayor and Corporation of Bristol, 1788' (1918, now in the Mansion House, Bristol) contrasts with his painting of JW preaching to the poor in the open air (said to be in Portland Square). Preliminary charcoal sketches for three of his paintings are in the St Ives Methodist Church.

Times 12 Sept. 1930; *MR* 4 July 1985; D. Tovey (1985)

JAV

Tiverton JW's first visit to this market and textile town was in November 1739, following the death of his brother Samuel, who had been headmaster of Blundell's School since 1732. Samuel's gravestone is fixed to the east wall of St George's parish church. Between 1750 and 1789 JW often preached there and founded a society which met in a room in St Peter's Street from 1752. Tiverton was the centre of the Devonshire Circuit formed in 1753. A surviving circuit book shows that in 1778 it still covered much of Devon and part of Somerset.

RFST

Toase, William (1782–1863; e.m. 1804), WM minister, born at Kilton, Yorks. Because of his knowledge of French he was appointed to the *Channel Islands in 1807. He became the first missionary to French prisoners of war on the Medway (1810–15) and then returned to the Channel Islands. The later years of his ministry were spent superintending the work in *France, notably in Boulogne (1836–7) and Paris (1837–48). He left retirement in Guernsey to take charge of the work in Boulogne.

Memorials by a Friend (1874)

WL

Todmorden was visited by JW 14 times between 1747 and 1790, but the early development of Methodism owed much to a former curate, W. *Grimshaw and the Scottish itinerant W. *Darney. Grimshaw's *Haworth Round held Methodism's first circuit *quarterly meeting on 18 October 1748 at Todmorden Edge Farm South, where one of Darney's societies had formerly met. Chaired by Grimshaw, it was attended by J. *Bennet, Darney and 31 class leaders, all but one of them men and including six from Todmorden. The first WM chapel was erected at Doghouse in 1783, and a second in York Street in 1827. Todmorden Circuit, formed in 1799, expanded rapidly in the following decade; but under the leadership of

John Fielden, cotton manufacturer and radical reformer, the town later became a leading centre of the *Methodist Unitarians. The *Religious Census showed that by 1851 Todmorden had a higher than average proportion of Nonconformist worshippers, nearly half of whom were Methodists. In 1942 York Street WM amalgamated with Bridge Street (founded during the WMA secession of 1835–37) and the united society later moved into the York Street Sunday School building, redesignated Todmorden Central Methodist Church.

M. & F. Heywood (1996)

JAH

Togo   T.B. *Freeman, returning from *Nigeria to the Gold Coast in 1843, persuaded local chiefs to allow both preaching and the establishment of schools. Under German and then French rule the Church remained small and confined largely to the coastal Minah people. The French West Africa District, of which Togo was a part, was reshaped as first *Côte d'Ivoire and then *Dahomey became separate Districts and eventually autonomous Conferences, leaving Togo planning its own autonomy for the year 2000. Like them the Togolese Church is a member of the Evangelical Community for Apostolic Action (CEVAA) which developed from the work of the Paris Missionary Society.

JRP

Told, Silas (1711–79), born in *Bristol, the son of a physician. In 1725 he enlisted in the navy and sailed to Jamaica. He spent eleven years at sea and saw not only war service but much cruelty associated with life at sea. He first came in touch with JW in 1740 and for a time taught at the *Foundery charity school in London. Moved by JW's sermon on 'I was sick and in prison and ye visited me not,' he began visiting the prisoners in Newgate, accompanying many of them to the gallows. The rest of his life was given to this ministry, through which he saw many prisoners reformed.

S. Told (1786)

WL

Toleration Act   The Conventicle Act 1670 had made it an offence for any group of people numbering more than five to meet for religious worship, except according to the liturgy and practice of the Church of England. The Act applied to meetings in houses, other buildings and the open air. The Toleration Act 1689 exempted 'Protestant Dissenters' if their buildings were registered and preachers licensed and the necessary oaths were taken. JW argued strongly that in neither their *field preaching nor preaching-houses were the Methodists within the penalties of the Conventicle Act; nor were they dissenters who should seek relief under the Toleration Act. Because of increasing difficulties with local magistrates he reluctantly agreed to registration being sought, finally concluding in 1787 that it was safer to register all chapels and travelling preachers, albeit not as dissenters but as 'preachers of the gospel', under 'that execrable Act'.

After his death there was growing political pressure to introduce more restrictive legislation, because of the perceived dangers of the large numbers of licensed preachers. Lord *Sidmouth's Bill of 1811 was dropped in the face of Nonconformist protests. In 1812 a new Toleration Act (drafted by T. *Allan) repealed the Conventicle Act and other penal legislation.

See also **Licensing of Preachers**

J.M. Turner (1985), pp. 15–18; 120–6; D. Hempton (1984) pp. 98–104; D. Hempton (1996) pp. 110–13

SRH

'Tolpuddle Martyrs' *see* **Loveless, G.; Trade Unionism**

Tomlinson, George (1890–1952) left Rishton WM Day School at 12 to become a cotton weaver and at 21 became President of the Weavers Union. From 1938 he was MP for Farnworth, Lancs, served under Ernest Bevin in the Ministry of Labour 1941–45 and became Minister of Works 1945–47. As Ellen *Wilkinson's successor at the Ministry of Education (1947–51), his experience on the Lancashire County Council and as President of the Association of Education Committees stood him in good stead in implementing the 1944 Education Act. As both *local preacher and politician he was dedicated to the gospel of 'evangelical socialism'.

Times, 23 Sept. 1952; *MR* 17 Feb. 1944, 25 Sept. 1952; F. Blackburn (1954)

JAV

Tomlinson, William Ernest (1877–1944; e.m. 1900), WM missionary in *India. Born in Hankow, the son of a missionary, he trained at *Didsbury College and served in the Mysore District except for two years in the Kanarese

Evangelical Mission in Bangalore. He had an un-rivalled knowledge of Kanarese and taught at the Union Seminary in Tumkur. He was also for many years the District Evangelist and strongly supported the scheme for union in South India.

MR 7 Sept. 1944; N.C. Sargant & A.M. Ward (1950)

JAV

Toms, Mary (1785–1871), a WM from Tintagel, joined the BCs in 1817 after hearing W. *O'Bryan preach and became an itinerant in 1820. Her services always attracted crowds and won many converts. In 1823 she became convinced of a call to become the first BC missionary to the Isle of Wight and raised the fare to get there. In 1824 she married William Warder and settled on the island. In 1833, though no longer an itinerant, she was the first BC to preach in *Chichester and form a society there.

BC Magazine, 1872; J. Woolcock (1897); F.W. Bourne (1905)

EDG

Tonga (the 'Friendly Islands') is made up of three main groups of islands extending over 500 miles in the South Pacific; from south to north: Tongatapu, Ha'apai and Vava'u. Following an abortive mission by the London Missionary Society in 1797, the first WM missionary, W. *Lawry, arrived in 1822, but was ordered to return to *Australia a year later because of local hostility and little encouragement or support from the WMMS. In 1826 J. *Thomas, accompanied by John Hutchinson, launched a more permanent mission. They were joined in 1827 by N. *Turner and W. *Cross, in 1831 by P. *Turner, J. *Watkin and W. *Woon and in 1834 by D. *Cargill. A break-through occurred in 1830 when King Taufa'ahau of Ha'apai, was converted and baptized . He became a *local preacher and, as King George Tupou I (from 1845) played a key part in the mission. The royal family remained Methodist after his death. Finau, king of Vava'u, was also converted, but more significant was the revival which spread through the islands in 1834, nourished especially by the ministry of P. *Turner. One significant result was the decision to extend the Tongan mission to *Fiji and *Samoa. J.E. *Moulton's service (from 1865 almost to his death in 1909) was marked by the founding in 1866 of Tupou College, intended for the provision of a superior education. Long-established dissension, centred on S.W. *Baker while Moulton was absent

in England 1878–80, resulted in the formation of the breakaway Free Wesleyan Church. Some of those loyal to Moulton and the WMMS faced persecution. Reconciliation (and then only partial) was not achieved until 1924, largely through the efforts of Queen Salote Tupou III, who reigned from 1918 to 1965 and whose visit to England at the time of the Coronation of Queen Elizabeth II was so memorable. Tongan Methodism maintained its Australian links until 1977, becoming fully autonomous at the time of the formation of the Uniting Church of Australia. In 1997 it reported a membership of 32,869 and a community roll of 70,000.

F&H 3 pp. 257–337; H. Luke (1954); A.H. Wood (1975) pp. 1–248

JAV

Tooth, Mary (1777–1843), companion and confidante of Mrs Mary Fletcher (*née* *Bosanquet) from *c.* 1804. She herself was active as a *class leader and preacher in the *Madeley/ Bridgnorth area both before and after Mrs Fletcher's death in 1815 and corresponded voluminously. As Mrs Fletcher's executrix, she preserved a wealth of letters etc, which were used by H. *Moore in writing his biography and now form part of the Fletcher-Tooth Papers at the Methodist *Archives Centre, Manchester.

PSF

Toplady, Rev. Augustus Montague (1740–78), hymnwriter, remembered especially for his 'Rock of Ages', was born at Farnham, Surrey. He obtained his BA at Trinity College, Dublin in 1760. Converted by a WM preacher in Ireland 1755/56, he turned to *Calvinism in 1758 and was ordained deacon in 1762 and priest in 1764. He was curate of Blagdon (Som) 1762–64 and vicar of Broad Hembury (Devon) from 1768. In controversy with JW and J. *Fletcher from 1769, his polemical writings (with such titles as *An Old Fox Tarr'd and Feather'd*, 1775) were characterized by both extensive doctrinal knowledge and vitriolic malice. Developing consumption in 1775, he died in London.

Gentleman's Magazine 1778 p. 335; A.M. Toplady (1778); W. Row (1794); G. Lawton (1983)

PSF

Torbay comprises the towns of Torquay, Paignton and Brixham. Torquay grew in the nineteenth century into an affluent watering place with a correspondingly varied and distinguished list of churches and chapels for residents and visitors. There were WM, BC and PM churches, as well as a single MNC mission chapel, the only one in Devon. The great Union Street WM chapel of 1879, seating 1,150, was replaced in 1976 by the distinctive modern Central Church (Methodist/ URC). The BC Conference met in their Torre Chapel in 1877. The WM chapel of 1816 in the ancient fishing port of Brixham was attended by Anne, the wife of the hymnwriter Henry Francis Lyte, which may have caused him some embarrassment as an Anglican priest.

RFST

Towlson, Dr Clifford W. (1889–1963) was born in *Norwich and brought up an Anglican. After graduating at Oxford he spent nearly 40 years teaching in Yorkshire, at Northallerton, Skipton and *Woodhouse Grove School, where he was headmaster 1922–40. He became a Methodist and a *local preacher, holding many other offices in the church, and was Vice-President of the Conference in 1950. He used his musical gifts as a member of the committees which produced the 1933 *Methodist Hymn Book* and the *School Hymnbook* of 1951 and was President of the *MCMS. His thesis for the London DPhil was published as *Moravian and Methodist* (1957).

MR 13 July 1950, 4 July 1963; F.C. Pritchard (1978)

JAV

Townley, Dr James (1774–1833; e.m. 1796), WM minister. An active supporter of J *Bunting, he was a Secretary of the WMMS 1827–32 and President of the Conference in 1829. Princeton awarded him a DD in 1822. He was a frequent contributor to the *WMM*. The most important among his religious works, *Illustrations of Biblical Literature* (1821) was judged well abreast of the scholarship of his time.

EWD

Townsend, William John (1835–1915; e.m. 1860), son of a MNC minister whose health forced him to retire, was born in *Newcastle upon Tyne. His studious inclinations were strengthened by attendance at Newcastle's leading school. His outstandingly successful ministry was acknowledged by his election as UM President in 1908. He was well-known beyond Methodism and was President of the National Free Church Council in 1902. He represented the MNC at Gladstone's funeral. He wrote ten books and was one of the editors of the *New History of Methodism* (1909).

G. Eayrs (1916)

EAR

Tract Societies The first Methodist tract was JW's *A Word in Season, or Advice to a Soldier*, published in 1743. This was followed by *A Word to a Smuggler, . . . to a Drunkard* etc. Initially, these four-page tracts were printed to make up a full sheet when printing long works, and it is only by their conjunction that they can be dated. They appeared without any indication of author, date or printer and went through numerous editions. In 1782 JW, with the help of T. *Coke, issued proposals for establishing a tract society. Subscribers received a number of tracts of their own choice for free distribution. Later tracts were more substantial and many of JW's sermons were published in tract form. Coke himself published a number of tracts in 1806–8.

The Tract Society was re-organized by the 1828 Conference. By 1871 there were 1,250 different titles and the number of copies issued ran into millions. In the second half of the nineteenth century local circuits and churches often had their own tract society. The tracts were slipped inside a stiff cover containing details of the local church's activities and these were distributed from house to house and exchanged for another a week or so later. Other branches of Methodism, notably the PMs, also published tracts and the Religious Tract Society, following the Methodist lead, was founded in 1799.

F.H. Cumbers (1956) pp. 7, 50

OAB

Trade Unionism An aspect of the British Labour Movement to which Methodism made a significant contribution was the origin and development of trade unions. These began to emerge following the repeal of the Combination Acts in 1825 and continued to do so throughout the nineteenth century.

Methodism contributed in several ways, most notably by providing a basic training in public speaking and business skills in a way that other denominations did not. In addition to the provision of *Sunday Schools, it gave men opportunities to stand in front of their fellows as *exhorters, *local preachers and *class leaders. Such offices as *chapel and *society steward provided the chance to learn simple business and administrative skills. In addition, Methodist conversion instilled in many ordinary men and women a sense of self-worth and dignity and gave them a desire to better their place in society. The result of all this was that many of the more articulate labourers were Methodists.

Methodist organization, with its three-tiered system of national *Conference, *circuit and local chapel provided a model which many trade unions either adapted or used wholesale. The National Agricultural Labourers' Union founded in 1837 by the PM J. *Arch had an annual conference, geographical districts somewhat akin to Methodist circuits, and local branches which often met in chapels. It is also possible that the union ticket and subscription derived from the Methodist *class ticket. Trade union meetings often had the air of Methodist chapel worship about them, as members sang hymns, uttered prayers, quoted scripture and concluded business with the grace or a benediction. A number of unions held *camp meetings which were clearly inspired by the Primitive Methodism of their leaders.

Many significant trade union leaders were active Methodists. Five of the six 'Tolpuddle Martyrs', including their leader G. *Loveless, in 1834 were WM. H. *Broadhurst, founder of the Stonemasons' Union, was WM, as was R. *Morley, President of the Workers' Union. T. *Hepburn (1795–1864), who formed the first mineworkers' union at *Durham in 1832, and G. *Edwards, founder of the Allied and Agricultural Workers' Union, were PM *local preachers. As the work of R.F. *Wearmouth demonstrates, this list could readily be extended and is indicative of the significant role Methodism played in providing trade union leadership.

R.F. Wearmouth (1959); R.F. Wearmouth (1972); N.A.D. Scotland (1981)

NADS

Trapp, Rev. Dr Joseph (1679–1747), Anglican priest, fellow of Wadham College and the first Professor of Poetry at Oxford. He held several London livings and lectureships and was President of Sion College. A poet and pamphleteer, he wrote against both Roman Catholicism and Dissent and was one of the earliest to attack Methodism in print. In 1739 he preached four sermons in London on 'The Nature, Folly, Sin and Danger of being Righteous Overmuch', in which he dismissed Methodists as a 'new set of *enthusiasts, or hypocrites or both', charging them with being a disruptive and corrupting influence in society. Their publication sparked off a considerable pamphlet

war in which G. *Whitefield was prominent and into which W. *Law was also drawn.

DNB; R. Green (1902)

JAV

Travis, James (1840–1919; e.m. 1859), PM itinerant. Born the son of a contractor on a remote Pennine farmstead, he was educated in village schools and the local Sunday School. He became a *local preacher in his mid-teens and an itinerant at 18, serving for 48 years in circuits in the *IOM and Lancashire. He took an active role in promoting ministerial education and served from 1875 as secretary of a committee whose work led to the establishment of the Manchester PM Theological Institute. Regarded as one of the ablest ministers in the PM connexion, he was secretary of the General Missionary Committee 1889–94, President of the 1892 Conference and of the National Council of Evangelical Free Churches 1903–4.

J. Travis (1914)

GEM

Treffry, Richard (1771–1842; e.m. 1792), WM minister, born at Cuby, Cornwall. In 1831 he became a Joint House Governor at *Woodhouse Grove School and in 1838 House Governor at *Hoxton Theological Institution. His unpublished journal is a mirror of the life and affairs of a WM preacher during the period 1802–9: his preaching, administration of Methodist discipline, his journeying to and from Conference and many aspects of daily life. His son **Richard Treffry junr** (1804–38; e.m. 1824) during his short ministry showed great promise as a historian, biographer and theologian. During his enforced retirement at *Penzance he wrote at his father's request a reasoned defence of 'Ministerial Power in the Excision of Unworthy Members of the Church' (1835) which, like his father's journal, reflects and supports the predominant WM view of the *pastoral office.

T. Shaw (1969)

TS

Tremberth, William (1867–1940; e.m. 1889), BC missionary in *China, born at St Austell. He joined the Mission in Yunnan in 1890. His companion, John Carter, died before they reached their station at Chaotung and within a year he was conducting S.T. *Thorne's funeral service. In 1894 he married a missionary colleague, Emily Bailey. In his devotion to the work he undertook much arduous travelling and constant preaching, often with scant response. He returned home in 1906, but an emergency in Ning-po, East China, called him back for four years in 1922.

RKP

Trevecka (or Trefeca) in the parish of Talgarth, Breconshire, was the birthplace of H. *Harris. In 1752 he partly demolished his home and began a building project with a view to establishing a Christian community there, modelled on those of the *Moravians. By 1755 the 'Trevecka Family' numbered over 100 and when JW visited in 1763 he described it as 'a little paradise'. After Harris's death it went into decline and from 1842 the buildings housed a theological college which moved to Aberystwyth in 1906. They were then used as a preparatory college for mature students but are now a centre for lay and youth activities. The Countess of *Huntingdon also established a college at what is now College Farm in 1768. J. *Fletcher was its President and J. *Benson its second Headmaster, until the dispute over *Calvinism resurfaced in 1770. Following the Countess's death the college was transferred to Cheshunt, Herts. In 1905 it moved to *Cambridge, where it was amalgamated with Westminster College in 1968 and survives as the 'Cheshunt Foundation'.

SJ 5 p. 25; G.T. Roberts (1951) pp. 63–71; E. Welch (1990)

GT

Trew, Ethel Mary (1869–1948), headmistress of *Queenswood School 1897–1943 (and 'Principal' for one year after that), was a native of South Petherton. The school was 'the consuming passion of her life', despite periods of ill health. She supervised its move from Clapham to Hatfield in 1927 and its growth from fewer than 20 to 330 pupils. Her imposing personality was combined with warm affection, though she became increasingly distant and authoritarian, being described by old girls as 'a benevolent despot' and 'like an ancient monument'.

MR 1 Nov. 1945, 16 Dec. 1948; N. Watson (1994)

JAV

Trewint (Cornwall), see **Isbell**

Trinity Hall, *Southport, opened in 1872 on a site donated by J. *Fernley as a boarding school for daughters of Methodist ministers. Its junior house began as a school opened by the mother of J.S. *Simon. The school was supported by connexional funds. Until 1906 girls left at the age of 16, but increasing opportunities in higher education led to the addition of an extra year. After a period of growth and academic success lasting into the 1960s, the Management Committee reported a financial deficit and the school was closed in 1970.

See also **Lonsdale, M.**

DBT

Tripp, Ann (1745–1823) was converted under T. *Maxfield. In 1763 she joined M. *Bosanquet's school at Leytonstone as a teacher and moved with them to Cross Hall. When Mary married J. *Fletcher and moved to *Madeley, Ann went to *Leeds with S. *Ryan. They became known as 'the Female Brethren' and wielded considerable influence in Leeds Methodism. Ann was a *class leader and probably preached. She lived to be one of the oldest members at the 'Old Boggart House'.

WMM 1823 p. 706

EDG

Truro   Because of the ministry of the Rev. S. *Walker at St Mary's, JW delayed establishing a society until 1760. Its first preaching house was off Boscawen Street. The Kenwyn Street chapel (1795, now a Salvation Army Citadel) was succeeded in 1830 by St Mary's, the present Methodist Church. Among Methodist associations in the Cathedral (completed 1903) are a Wesley window, and memorials to J.C. *Adams and Bishop *Hunkin. *Truro School opened in 1880. There are important Methodist collections in the Courtney Library at the Royal Cornwall Museum and in the Phillpotts Library at Diocesan House, Kenwyn.

TS

Truro School was founded by Cornish Methodists in 1880 as a 'middle class' boys' school and moved to its present site in 1882. In 1904 it became one of the original *Board of Management schools. In co-operation with the local authority it quickly established and maintained a fine academic reputation. It has two *Vice-Presidents of the Conference, A. Lowry Creed (1962) and Derek W. Burrell (1987), among its former headmasters. After a long period of debate it reverted to full independence in 1976, following the withdrawal of the government's Direct Grant regulations. Its records for 1980 contain a unique governors' resolution forbidding the construction of 'a second aircraft' – a cryptic tribute to an enthusiastic technology department.

In 1997 there were 981 boarding and day boys and girls from nursery age to 18.

N. Baker (1980)   DBT

Trustees As Methodist societies were established and preaching places built, it was necessary to safeguard their use for Methodist purposes. The appropriate legal mechanism adopted by JW was to settle them upon trust, and the *Model Deed and *Deed of Declaration were designed to define local trustees' powers and duties, after problems had arisen, e.g. at *Birstall. But the relationship between the rights of trustees (often quite powerful and wealthy men) and those of the Conference and its preachers, or in some cases of the local *leaders' meeting, continued to present problems after W's death (*see* **Plan of Pacification**). It was one of the causes of the secessions from WM, e.g. the *Protestant Methodists following the Leeds Organ case in 1827.

The provisions of the *Model Deed also regulated the procedure of trustees, requiring them to meet at least annually. The Trustees' Meeting made certain appointments, including the *chapel stewards and a treasurer. The ministers, other than the Superintendent who had the right to attend and vote, were not members of the Trustees' Meeting.

The Trustees Appointment Act 1890 (simplifying the appointment of trustees generally) was passed at the instigation of WM MPs, as was the Marriage Act 1898 permitting trustees to appoint an authorized person to solemnize marriages in registered places without the Registrar's presence.

The trust system was used by other branches of Methodism, and other non-conformist groups, and continued after *Methodist Union until it was modified under *restructuring in the 1970s. Under the *Methodist Church Act 1976, legal title was transferred to custodian trustees, with managing trusteeship remaining locally based. The trust system had been criticised for the 'dual control' of the local church by trustees and leaders and also for creating an autonomous, self-perpetuating body in office for life. The Act provided for the duties and powers of the managing trustees to be exercised instead by the *Church Council (or Circuit Meeting for circuit property).

E.B. Perkins (1952); *NHM* 1 pp. 514–516; *HMGB* 1 pp. 228–230, 282–284

SRH

Trustees for Methodist Church Purposes In 1863 the Conference resolved to create the Board of Trustees for WM Chapel Purposes, and a deed was duly enrolled in Chancery in 1866. It enabled property and funds given for various charitable purposes connected with the Church at all levels to be held by a group of trustees appointed by and reporting to the Conference, so providing the necessary continuity and skills to ensure that the purposes were properly and effectively carried out. In 1910, the Board was registered as a corporate body, enabling it to hold property in its own name and to act as a custodian trustee of property being directly managed by others.

In 1914 the UMC set up a similar Board for UM Church Purposes, but there was no equivalent PM body. The two boards were amalgamated by the *Methodist Church Act 1939 into the Board of Trustees for Methodist Church Purposes. The Board increased in significance with the provision in the 1932 *Model Deed for it to hold local and circuit proceeds of sale.

The 1976 *Methodist Church Act statutorily vested all existing and new *model trust property in the Board as custodian trustee (with separate provision for the Isle of Man and Channel Islands), so that it now holds the legal title to virtually all local, circuit and district property and much connexional property. The Board consists of 12 ministers and 12 lay people and continues to act as full trustee for certain individual trusts.

O.W. Phillipson (1966)

SRH

Trustees for Methodist Connexional Funds (Registered) is the custodial trustee body for the holding of Connexional Funds. It has no powers of its own, but is under the direction of the Managing Trustees of the connexional fund concerned. It can nevertheless be sued for negligence in a court of law if in some way it neglects its responsibility of caring for the assets entrusted to it.

DRF

Tunstall *see* **Stoke-on-Trent**

Turner, James (1818–63), WM class leader and *local preacher, born at Peterhead into a poor fishing family. He worked as a cooper, eventually establishing his own business, which included herring-curing. Setting aside early Presbyterian influences, he joined the Methodists. His preaching later developed into a campaign of personal evangelism, sometimes provocatively critical of ministers and office-holders whom he regarded as unconverted. His work fostered many societies in

*Aberdeen and along the Banffshire and Moray coast. In his own works he operated a profit-sharing scheme, never withdrawing wages from anyone who fell sick, and each day started with a scriptural reading and prayer.

E. MacHardie (1875); WHS(S) 1975 pp. 3–8

CJS

Turner, Nathaniel (1793–1846; e.m. 1821), WM missionary, born in Wybunbury, Ches. He was appointed to *New Zealand in 1822, serving there, latterly as *Superintendent in succession to W. *White, until forced to abandon the Wesleydale Mission in 1827. Proceeding to *Tonga, to aid the failing mission, he was censured by the London Committee for acting without authority, but his experience and resourcefulness probably saved the infant Church there. In failing health he went to Hobart in 1831, returning to New Zealand as District Chairman in 1835, following the departure of White, and had to deal with difficulties created by his predecessor. When J.H. *Bumby arrived as District Chairman, he returned to *Australia as senior minister in both Tasmania and Sydney. Although his health had never been robust, his obituary asserted that 'few ministers have preached the Gospel over a more extensive field.'

F&H 3 passim; J.G. Turner (1872); G.I. Laurenson (1972); J.M.R. Owens (1974) passim; A.H. Wood vol. 1 (1975); *EWM*

MJF/DJP

Turner, Peter (1802–73; e.m. 1829), WM missionary, stationed in *Tonga in 1834. A remarkable mass revival in 1834 encouraged the Synod in 1835 to extend the Mission to *Samoa and *Fiji in response to invitations and in spite of the legitimate LMS claim to that field. Turner was heartily welcomed as the first resident missionary, but was directed to leave the work and return to Tonga by 1839, when the LMS case could no longer be denied. In 1853 he retired to New South Wales.

A.H. Wood vol. 1 (1975) pp. 271–84 and passim; *EWM*

MJF

Turton, William (1761–1818; e.m. 1795), WM missionary in the *West Indies. The son of a respected planter in Barbados, he was converted by the preaching of missionaries. His obvious gifts and commitment brought him to the attention of J. *Baxter, who took him on as his assistant in the Mission. He pioneered work on Tobago and St. Bartholomew, and in particular in the Bahamas, where he was appointed as the first WM minister by the Conference of 1799. Arriving in Nassau the following year, he laid good foundations for the future despite discord caused by dissident Methodist preachers from America. He initiated new work throughout the islands and was appointed *Chairman and General Superintendent of the Mission. Though superannuating in 1816 due to ill health, he continued his active involvement in the work.

GRS

Twentieth Century Fund, commonly known as the Million Guinea Fund, was inaugurated by the WM Conference in 1898 under the skilful management of Sir R.W. *Perks. It aimed to raise one guinea from each of the 500,000 WM members, plus support from a substantial number of adherents and from other Methodist denominations. Rich and poor members were expected to contribute the same amount, but many wealthy members found as many as 500 poorer ones on whose behalf they could contribute. Some poor members saved their contribution by walking to work or forgoing modest luxuries. The Fund's aims included a new *membership drive, support for home and overseas missions and *NCH, and the building of what became *Westminster Central Hall, as a 'visible and monumental memorial'. The Fund was wound up in 1908, reaching a total of over £1m (approximately £60m today). An 'Historic Roll' containing the names of all who contributed is still housed at Westminster Central Hall.

See also **Smith, F.R.**

DRF

Twiddy, Mary *see* **Batchelor, Mary**

Tyerman, Luke (1820–89; e.m. 1844), WM minister, born at *Osmotherly and trained at *Didsbury College. His active ministry ended after 19 years because of ill health, but he devoted 25 years to Methodist history and wrote a number of standard works, including lives of Samuel Wesley senior (1866), John Wesley (1871), John Fletcher ('Wesley's designated successor') (1882) and George Whitefield (1876–7), and *The Oxford Methodists* (1873).

R.P. Heitzenrater (1984) 2 pp. 184–7   WL

Union for Social Service (WM) was founded in 1905 by S.E. *Keeble for the study of all social issues and the pursuit of social service on a non-party basis. The Union widened WM concentration on a few traditional social problems and attracted gifted young ministers, including J. Scott *Lidgett, J.E. *Rattenbury, W.F. *Lofthouse and H. *Carter. Through local branches, its magazine *See and Serve* and its tracts and publications, it influenced the thinking of younger church members and was one of the influences that led to the creation of the *Temperance and Social Welfare Department in 1918. Numbers declined after 1918 and when the *Beckly Lecture was established in 1926 the Union was dissolved.

See also **Christian Social Union**

M.L. Edwards (1949); M.S. Edwards (1977)

MSE

United Methodist, a 'weekly journal' which was a continuation of the *Free Methodist* (published from January 1886). It appeared throughout the lifetime of the *UM Church, 1907–32, then amalgamated with the *Methodist Recorder*.

JAV

United Methodist Church Formed in 1907, this was an amalgamation of the *UMFC, the *MNC and the *BC Church and had a life of 25 years before merging in the *Methodist Union of 1932. Though the UMFC membership outnumbered the other two, from the outset of negotiations committees were composed of equal numbers from each denomination. In spite of repeated earlier attempts to unite, it was not until the 1901 Ecumenical Methodist Conference that negotiations really began. These included the *WM, the *WR Union and the *PM; the last withdrew for financial reasons, the other two because the proposed terms of union were unacceptable. In 1905 the WM made an approach to the MNC, to the dismay of Dr J.S. *Simon and others, but the MNC gently but firmly rejected the overture and the three negotiating Churches accepted the scheme by overwhelming votes. Providentially, of the first nine Presidents of the UM Conference, there were three from each of the three Churches.

In the short period of its existence, no attempt was made to undermine local customs or force local amalgamations. Circuit boundaries were left largely unaltered, and there was in any case only limited geographical overlap between the BCs and the other two bodies. In the spring of 1908 the newly united Church held a nation-wide mission in which 5,000 decisions were registered.

H. Smith, J.E. Swallow & W. Treffry (1932); R.F.S. Thorne, in *PWHS* 51, pp. 73–95

OAB

United Methodist Free Churches, the largest of the three denominations which came together as the *UMC in 1907. As the name implies, they themselves were the product of a union of the *WMA and the *WR. Negotiations were opened between the two groups in 1851, and attempts were made in 1853 to broaden them to include others. Terms of a union were finally agreed in 1856 and a uniting Assembly met at Baillie Street chapel, *Rochdale, in 1857. Though the WMA had a slight majority, the Reformer J. *Everett was elected President. The UMFC was eager for union with other 'liberal' Methodists. Other Reform circuits joined individually over the next 10 or 15 years, so that the total membership grew between 1857 and 1867 from 39,968 to 67,488, with over 6,000 on trial.

The distinguishing features of the UMFC were circuit autonomy and freedom to be represented in the Assembly by whichever minister or layman they elected, with only four ex officio members. This represented an attempt to unite connexionalism and Congregationalism and worked in practice. In general, the UMFC had all the familiar features of Methodism, such as an annual *Conference (though called the Assembly), *circuits, *itinerancy and *class tickets. Everett produced a denominational *hymn-book, based on the WM one, with JW's portrait as its frontispiece. There was a *Magazine*, they published annual *Minutes of Conference*, and started *overseas missions.

See also **Overseas Mission**

M. Baxter (1856); J. Kirsop (1885); O.A. Beckerlegge (1957)

OAB

Urban Theology is an urban version of contextual theology and liberation theology. It was pioneered by Dr John J. Vincent (1929– ; e.m. 1953), whose Urban Theology Unit in *Sheffield has since 1970 been a centre for its development, alongside training in urban ministry and political action, as in the *Petition of Distress from the Cities* (1993), the Methodist Report on *The Cities* (NCH Action for Children, 1997) and *Gospel from the City* (1997) in the 'British Liberation Theology' series.

See also **Poor, The**

NCH Action for Children (1997) pp. 193–214; M. Northcott (1998)

JJV

Urban Travel Fund *see* **Finance, Ministerial**

Urwin, Evelyn Clifford (1884–1978; e.m. 1907), UM minister and son of Archelaus Urwin (until 1901, Uren; d.1933; e.m. 1876). After training at *Victoria Park College, a distinguished ministry led to his appointment as a secretary of the *Temperance and Social Welfare Department, 1933–53. He was a prolific author on temperance subjects and as a speaker had a remarkable command of facts and figures on that subject. He gave the 1949 WHS Lecture on *The Significance of 1849* and wrote *Religion and the Common Man* (1951) and a life of H. *Carter (1955). With Douglas Wollen he edited *John Wesley, Christian Citizen* (1937).

MR 19 & 26 Jan. 1978

OAB

Valentine, Olive Margaret (1913–89), (Mrs W.B. *Harris), missionary in *India. After studying at London University, she offered for the mission field and served in the Madras District and then in CSI. As Vice-Principal of Methodist Girls' High School, Royapettah, Madras, she pioneered training courses for recently baptized village women. Her pastoral and evangelistic work in Nagari (1946–51) and Madurantakam (1952–58) included training new converts. From 1958 to 1961 she was Director of Christa Seva Vidhayalaya, Madras, training women from throughout CSI for positions of responsibility in their dioceses. After their marriage in 1961,she shared her husband's work, training both theological students and their wives, in Tirumaraiyur and Madurai. Her visits to women in Madurai Central Jail led to the opening of Arulagam, a hostel and half-way house for women, including young prostitutes, on their release.

RA

Vallance, John (1794–1882), Lancashire-born *Chartist, who became active in the movement in 1839 in the Barnsley area. He served as chairman, speaker and delegate and after one meeting was arrested and imprisoned in *York Castle. He was a member and committed worshipper at Pitt Street WM chapel, Barnsley.

DLB   NADS

Vallins, George Henry (d. 1956) taught at Selhurst Grammar School, Croydon, where Malcolm Muggeridge was one of his pupils. After the War he was involved in teacher training in the Midlands and *Liverpool. He was an essayist and skilful parodist and, under various pen-names, contributed to *Punch, John o' London's Weekly*, the *Methodist Recorder* etc. Among his books on the English language were *Good English* (1951) and *Better English* (1953), and *The Wesleys and the English Language* (1957). He served on the Connexional Local Preachers Committee and Training Board.

MR 8 Nov. 1956

JAV

Valton, John (1740–1794; e.m. 1775), early itinerant. Born in London of French RC parents, he was drawn to Methodism by the preaching of JW and other London Methodists. Living in Purfleet, he worked in the Ordnance Office and began to preach in nearby societies. The 1775 *Leeds Conference made him a full-time preacher and he continued in that calling for 13 years. He suffered from a nervous complaint for most of his adult life and was given to bouts of depressive introspection. After becoming a *Supernumerary, he lived his final years with intense leg pain, but his Methodist labours continued until his death.

EMP 6 pp. 3–136; C. Atmore (1801) pp. 431–6

HMG

Van Gogh, Vincent Willem (1853–90), Dutch expressionist painter, came from a strong Lutheran family background and, like JW, was influenced by *The Imitation of Christ*. While in London in 1876 he was employed as a church worker and *Sunday School teacher by the Rev. Thomas S. Jones, Congregational minister at Isleworth and Turnham Green, and was also given preaching appointments at Kew Road and Petersham churches in the *Richmond (Surrey) WM Circuit. His sketch of Petersham chapel is now in the Courtauld Institute. Returning home in December 1876, he failed to become a minister in the Dutch Reformed Church and turned to painting. His compassion for the poor and his ideal of a community of artists may have owed something to the example of JW and the Methodist *class meeting.

JAV

Vanner Family The Vanners were Huguenots who were involved in silk weaving in Spitalfields, London from 1717. **Elizabeth Vanner** (1762–1841), the wife of John Vanner I, was buried at *Wesley's Chapel. Their son **John

Vanner II (1800–66) of Stamford Hill was a silk weaver and merchant and was circuit steward for 20 years. He was involved in the founding of the City Bank in 1856. He married Sarah Engelbert. Of their six children, one daughter, **Jane Vanner**, married G.S. *Rowe and three married into the *Early family. **John Vanner III** (1831–1906) married Elizabeth Early, lived at *Banbury and was HM treasurer. His sister **Sarah Vanner** married Charles Early. A brother **James Engelbert Vanner** (1831–1906) married Maria Early, lived at Stamford Hill and then at Campden Wood, Chiselhurst. As a Director of the City Bank he was largely responsible for its successful merger with the Midland Bank in 1898. He was HM treasurer, treasurer of the *NCHO, benefactor of the Wesley *Deaconess Institute and the *London Mission and author of the hymn 'Morning comes with light all-cheering' (MHB 928). Another brother **William Vanner** was treasurer of the Connexional *Sunday School Union and served on the Foreign Missions and *Auxiliary Fund Committees.

Stanley Chapman in *Textile History* 23(1) (1992) pp. 71–86

KEC

Vanstone, Isaac Balkwill (1827–1909; e.m. 1851), BC itinerant, born at *Shebbear, where he became a member of the parish choir. He joined the BCs in 1848 and worked for S. *Thorne in the BC Printing Office. He was Associate *Book Steward and Associate Editor, 1881–82, Foreign Secretary of the *Missionary Society 1885–1904 and Treasurer of the Preachers' Annuitant Society for 11 years. He was President of the Conference in 1873.

TS

Vanstone, Thomas Grills (1851–98; e.m. 1876) was a colleague of S.T. *Thorne in establishing the BC Mission in Yunnan, *China, in 1885. He worked chiefly in Yunnan Fu (Kunming), but also opened the station at Hweitseh (Tungchuan). He was invalided home in 1893 with persistent malaria, from which he never fully recovered.

W.B. R[eed] in *BC Magazine* 1898 pp. 422–30

RKP

Vasey, Thomas (1814–71; e.m. 1839), born at *Halifax and educated at *Woodhouse Grove School, worked as a commercial clerk and, following conversion in 1831, began to preach. Despite constant ill-health he served as a minister from 1839 to 1858, becoming Chairman of the Newcastle District. He was secretary of the WM *Education Committee, 1845–50. His evangelicalism and emphasis on holiness led J.H. *Rigg to describe him as 'one of the most powerful speakers in Conference' and to state: 'Perhaps Methodism never had a more original preacher'.

MR Oct.1871; M.J. Vasey (1874)

SRV

Vazeille, Mrs Mary *see* **Huguenots**; **Wesley, John**

Venn, Rev. Henry (1725–97), evangelical clergyman, influenced by W. *Law's *Serious Call*. After curacies in London and Clapham, he was vicar of *Huddersfield 1759–71, where his preaching drew large crowds. He visited many outlying settlements and preached in private houses. A discussion with JW in 1761 about Methodist preaching in the parish led to a compromise whereby the itinerants visited only once a month. A moderate *Calvinist and a sabbatarian, from 1771 he was vicar of Yelling, Hunts. His son **John Venn** (1759–1813), rector of Clapham 1792–1813, was a member of the 'Clapham Sect' and a founder of the CMS (of which *his* son **Henry Venn** (1796–1873) was secretary from 1841).

H. Venn (1834); A. Brown-Lawson (1994)

JAV

Vevers, William (1791–1850; e.m. 1813), WM minister who wrote two *Appeals to the Wesleyan Societies* (1834 and 1835) at the time of the *Warrenite controversy and various other works defending the WM ministry and discipline against its detractors, including *The National Importance of Methodism* (1831), *A Defence of the Discipline of Methodism* (1835), and *Wesleyan Methodism Vindicated* (1847). Just before his death he was appointed Governor of the WM Collegiate Institution at *Taunton.

JAV

Vice-Presidency There were Vice-Presidents of the PM Conference from 1872. After 1883 they were usually laymen, unless a layman was elected President. They were rarely active except during Conference, when they shared in presiding. WM had Vice-Presidents only in Ireland, where they were Irish ministers elected by the Irish Conference to take the chair at all committees during the year, while the British President presided over the Conference itself. The present office of Vice-President was created in 1932 at the suggestion of the non-Wesleyans. It was to be held by a lay person (or, after 1998, by a deacon) and was seen as a concession guaranteeing the rights of the laity. The earliest Vice-Presidents took little part during Conference and none preached at Conference until 1943. Until 1949 most were elderly and wealthy businessmen, honoured by the Church for their financial generosity. In 1951 H.C. *Pawson travelled 14,000 miles preaching, but there was little for him to do at Conference, except to preside for 20 minutes while the President met the ordinands. In the '50s D. *Blatherwick transformed the role and the following year P. *Race was told that the Vice-President, not the ex-President, automatically presided at all committees if the President was absent. The Vice-Presidents between 1950 and 1973 were younger, mostly professionals, often in law or education. The first woman elected was Mrs M. *Lewis in 1948, but there were only three others (including D. *Farrar and P.M. *Webb) before 1977. Between then and 1998 *women have provided 13 out of 22 Vice-Presidents.

Both the type of person elected and the role itself changed in the years 1973–83. Many lay servants of the Church (or their spouses) were chosen. There have been two black Vice-Presidents, the first Leon Murray (1938–) of Telford (1985). Vice-Presidents are no longer likely to be wealthy. The Vice-President takes the chair at Committees and at Conference if the President is absent; and in 1985 the *Deed of Union was amended to confirm the developing practice that the Vice-President was entitled to preside at the Representative Session on the President's invitation, even when the latter was present. By then the two were co-ordinating their programme of visits, sometimes going to a *District together. In 1982 the Vice-President was invited to assist at *ordination by laying on of hands and the matter became one of debate during the 1980s. The 1996 Conference by a very narrow majority reaffirmed the usage that only ordained ministers should lay on hands. Nevertheless the Vice-Presidency, though still less important than the Presidency, has become a more influential role, symbolic of increased theological emphasis on the co-operative ministry of the whole Church.

MR 8 July 1948, 22 June 1989

JHL

Vickers, James (1851–1923), IM minister in *Bolton and Secretary of the Connexion 1909–21. A journalist and editor by profession, he wrote many pamphlets on IM polity, notably his *History of IM* (1920), still a seminal work on its subject. During World War I, when IM ministers, being unpaid and non-clerical, received conscription papers, he arranged for a test case to establish that they fell within the legal definition of Ministers of Religion. This was successful and they were thereafter exempt from military service.

IM Magazine Jan. 1924

JAD

Vickery, Ann (1800–53), BC itinerant, converted at 19, was in the active ministry despite ill health from 1820 until she married her colleague, P. *Robins in 1831. They exercised a joint ministry, and she often fulfilled preaching appointments for other itinerants, sometimes taking her baby with her. She also visited the sick and led classes and prayer meetings. With their two small sons they went to *Canada in 1846 and despite her health she was virtually an itinerant until late 1847. Outspoken and strong-minded, she met with resistance and from 1850 is described only as a class leader.

BC Magazine, 1853 pp. 474–5; F.W. Bourne (1905); E.G.Muir (1991)

EDG

Victoria Park College, Manchester, began in 1871 as provision for the training of UMFC ministers. Thomas Hacking was appointed tutor and the library of J. *Everett was placed in a house in the city. Expanding numbers led to the acquisition of three houses in Victoria Park, which were subsequently enlarged and modified with a generous gift from J. *Duckworth to provide accommodation for 22 students. After the Union of 1907 the College provided for second- and third-year UM students after one year at *Ranmoor College. After it reopened in 1919 with 16 students, increasing co-operation with *Hartley College led to amalgamation soon after the Union of 1932 to form the new *Hartley Victoria College.

W.B. Brash (1935) pp. 148–51, 157–9

TSAM

Viney, Richard (fl. 1738–43), a London tailor and prominent member of the *Fetter Lane Society. In 1738 he accompanied JW to Herrnhut, where his knowledge of German was useful.

Admiring Count *Zinzendorf, he joined the *Moravians and became a minister at Oxford; but in 1743 he was expelled for criticizing them and the following year reinforced JW's growing prejudice against Zinzendorf. He rejoined the Methodists, but proved a disruptive influence at the *Orphan House, Newcastle and in Birstall.

————

JWJ 16 May 1744; *PWHS* 13–15 passim
JAV

Voice of Methodism, an association (VMA) formed in November 1963 in response to the organization of lay support for *Anglican-Methodist union through 'Towards Anglican-Methodist Union' (TAMU). An inaugural meeting was held at *Westminster Central Hall on 25 January 1964. Dr Leslie A. Newman (1904–87; e.m. 1927) was elected Chairman and A.E.D. Clipson (1902–64; e.m. 1927) secretary. The Association's stated purpose was to defend Methodism's *doctrinal standards, which were seen as under threat from the proposed union with the CofE, and to recall Methodism to its original evangelical mission. Some prominent critics of the Scheme of Union, such as Professor C.K. *Barrett, H.M. *Rattenbury, Professor T.E. *Jessop and Dr F. *Hildebrandt did not join. In September 1969 the VMA contested in the High Court the Conference's approval of Stage One of the Scheme, but its contention that this was *ultra vires* was rejected and judgment was given against them. Following the failure of the Scheme of Union the VMA continued to work for what it saw as Methodism's true calling, partly through a periodical *The Voice*.

————

A.E.C. Moore (n.d.); G.T. Brake (1984) pp. 106–8, 115–16, 139–42
JAV

Waddy Family Richard Waddy (1769–1853; e.m. 1793) was the first in a succession of six WM ministers. He married the sister of the Book Steward J. *Mason and wrote *A Vindication of the Methodists* (1804). Two of their sons entered the ministry: (1) Dr Samuel Dousland Waddy (1804–76; e.m. 1825) raised eyebrows early in his ministry by wearing a gown and bands in the pulpit at *Hull. He was instrumental in establishing *Wesley College, Sheffield, of which he was Governor and Chaplain 1844–62, and was a close friend of J. *Montgomery. He was President of the Conference in 1859. (2) Benjamin Bullock Waddy (1813–86; e.m. 1834). A daughter, Jane

Dousland Waddy (1817–94) was the mother of Dr R. Waddy Moss (1850–1935; e.m. 1869).

Samuel Dousland Waddy had a son John Turner Waddy (1836–98; e.m. 1859), a grandson, also John Turner Waddy (1865–1952; e.m. 1886) and a great-grandson John Leonard Waddy (1906–88; e.m. 1931), all in the ministry. His oldest son Samuel Danks Waddy QC (1830–1902), known as 'Judge Waddy', withdrew as a candidate for the ministry, but was in great demand as a *local preacher. He had a distinguished legal and political career. Between 1874 and 1894 he was a Liberal MP for *Barnstaple, *Sheffield, *Edinburgh and Brigg. Called to the Bar in 1858, he was Recorder of Sheffield from 1894 and a county court judge from 1896. He was counsel for the defence in the 'Maiden Tribute' trial of W.T. Stead in 1885.

————

A. Waddy (1878); G.J. Stevenson (1884–86) 3 pp. 349–59, 4 pp. 592–94; J.L. Waddy (1982)
JAV

Wainwright, Dr Geoffrey (1939– ; e.m. 1963), a liturgical scholar and World Methodism's leading ecumenist, taught at The *Queen's College 1973–79 before moving to America, first to Union Seminary, New York and then to Duke Divinity School. His *Doxology* (1980) was a pioneering attempt to write a systematic theology from a primarily liturgical perspective. He served on the Faith and Order Committee of the WCC from 1977 to 1991 and was co-ordinator of the 'Baptism, Eucharist, Ministry' Process that produced the 'Lima Report' of 1982. His involvement since 1986 in dialogues with Roman Catholics, Lutherans, Reformed and Anglicans is reflected in his *Methodists in Dialog* (Nashville, 1995) and he is currently involved in Orthodox-Methodist dialogue.

DJC

Wakefield, Dr Gordon Stevens (1921– ; e.m. 1943), a foremost liturgist and expert on the development of spirituality, was the youngest ever Fernley-Hartley lecturer with his *Puritan Devotion* (1957). His WHS Lecture, *Methodist Devotion: the Spiritual Life in the Methodist Tradition 1791–1945* (1966) filled a key gap. He later co-operated in many ecumenical studies of spirituality and edited *A Dictionary of Christian Spirituality* (1983). He was *Connexional Editor, 1963–72, Chairman of the Manchester and Stockport District, 1971–79 and Principal of The *Queen's College, 1979–87, being the first

Methodist minister to receive the Lambeth DD.

ER April 1997

DJC

Wakefield, Thomas (1836–1901; e.m. 1858), one of four UMFC missionaries who sailed for East Africa in 1861. The others were invalided home within months, but Wakefield settled at Ribe, inland from Mombasa, and began what eventually became the Methodist Church, *Kenya. He stayed for 25 years, often alone, often ill, and his first wife, infant son and three colleagues are buried at Ribe. He travelled throughout the coastal area and baptized the first 21 Kenyan converts in 1870. He made translations into Kiswahili and into the language of the Galla, who were believed to be far more numerous than proved to be the case. He was President of the UMFC Assembly in 1888.

E.S. Wakefield (1904)

JRP

Wakerley, John E. (1858–1923), WM minister, was noted for his evangelistic work, especially in the open air and as a Home Missionary at St John's Square, Clerkenwell (1890–1904) and East Ham (1904–11). He was the first minister appointed to *Westminster Central Hall (1911–14), but left in poor health, becoming Chairman of the East Anglia District in 1914, Secretary of the Conference, 1917–21 and President of the Conference, 1922.

MR 22 July 1922, 6 Sept. 1923

JAV

Wales: English-speaking WM   JW first preached in Wales at Devauden near Chepstow on 15 October 1739 and made frequent visits, often on the way to *Ireland. JW did not originally intend to form his own societies, as he worked closely with H. *Harris. But the first English-speaking society, formed in *Cardiff in April 1740, allied itself with JW rather than Harris the following year. Wales was in the first list of circuits in the 1747 *Minutes of Conference* and by 1770 there were three Welsh circuits: Pembroke, Glamorgan and Brecon. But progress was slow, especially in Mid and North Wales, and by 1791 there were only 600 members in the whole of South Wales.

Industrial development and an influx from England to work in mining and industry helped nineteenth century growth, especially in the south.

Leading industrialists such as Sir T. *Guest and Richard Crawshay had Methodist roots and gave practical support to WM. In North Wales incomers and the development of the holiday trade led to growth, particularly along the coast, supported by missionary outreach from the *Chester and *Shrewsbury areas. Until a separate North Wales District was formed in 1987, Methodist circuits there belonged to the Liverpool, Chester & Stoke and Wolverhampton & Shrewsbury Districts.

Many Cornish Wesleyans came to work in the Ceredigion mines and chapels were built as part of the missionary enterprise of Welsh-speaking Methodists among their English-speaking neighbours. BC migrants from Devon and Cornwall working South Wales industries established chapels which were often paired with chapels in the West Country. PM developed in Pembrokeshire and the Blaenavon/Pontypool area, in the first place as a mission from Oakengates, Shropshire. The Blaenavon (later Pontypool) Circuit missioned the Glamorgan and Monmouthshire valleys, and later Newport, *Cardiff and Swansea, reaching Cardiff in 1857.

There was an imaginative but unsuccessful WM experiment in bi-lingual work, based in the Brecon and Brynmawr areas, in 1814–17. A similar venture in Merthyr in 1912 survived much longer. The bi-lingual Ceredigion Circuit is a more recent move in the same direction. Welsh- and English-speaking Methodists tended in the main to go their own ways, apart from belonging to the same British Conference, meeting in the English Day in the Welsh Assembly, then in the Standing Committee (later the 'Consultative Council') for Methodism in Wales. Language and cultural barriers were transcended by friendships, fellowship and co-operation. In 1997 Y Gymanfa was formed for overall strategic planning and consultation, spear-headed by the All-Wales leadership team.

Welsh Methodism plays a full part, both nationally and locally, in Churches Together in Wales (CYTUN), and is committed to work towards visible unity in the Covenant which is the cutting edge of ecumenism in Wales. It is involved in many Local Ecumenical Partnerships.

D. Young (1893); H.B. Kendall (1906) 2 pp. 306–10; A.H. Williams (1971); G.T. Roberts in *HMGB* vol. 3 (1983) pp. 253–64

DGK

Wales: Welsh-speaking WM   Linguistic practicalities seem to have dictated a tacit agreement between JW and the eighteenth-century

Welsh evangelicals, by which he confined his activities almost exclusively to English-speaking societies. When he died there were some 600 members, mainly in South Wales, and, although the pace quickened markedly after 1790, Arminian Methodism was weak compared with old Dissent and the new Calvinistic Methodists. Ninety per cent of the population was still Welsh-speaking in the mid-eighteenth century, but Welsh-speaking WM was not established until 1800, when Conference, at the urging of T. *Coke, appointed O. *Davies and J. *Hughes as 'missionaries' to Wales. The work prospered in some parts only, and only in a few towns and villages – notably Coedpoeth, Llanrhaeadr-ym-Mochnant and Tregarth – did WM predominate. But by the beginning of the twentieth century the Welsh work had spread widely enough for there to be two Districts in the North and one in the South. Between 1899 and 1974 the Welsh Assembly, with considerable powers delegated to it by Conference, provided a unifying centre. In 1974 Welsh-speaking Methodism was restructured as one Cymru District. Little knowledge of, or co-operation with, English-speaking Methodism existed until the establishment of a Standing Committee for Methodism in Wales in 1957. This later became the Council for Methodism in Wales and was itself superseded in 1997 by a new, smaller Gymanfa or Welsh Assembly, representing all Districts in Wales.

Unlike CM, Welsh WM had no mission field of its own. Its first missionary, to *Sierra Leone in 1814, was W *Davies ('Davies Affrica'), followed by some 35 others, including H. Penri Davies (1889–1971), E. Armon Jones (1880–1950) and Edward John Jones (1898–1976). Welsh-speaking WM was, in the nineteenth century, often viewed as 'English' in its features (e.g. the position of the Conference, the training of ministers in England); but in its pattern of worship, its great preaching tradition (T. *Aubrey, J. *Evans, D. Tecwyn *Evans, E. Tegla *Davies, J. Roger *Jones), its *Sunday Schools, its eventual espousal of radical political issues (Disestablishment, Land Reform), it was by the turn of the century clearly in the mainstream of Nonconformity, even if a junior partner. In 1896 membership stood at just under 20,000 and in 1996 at just under 4,000.

See also **Welsh Calvinistic Methodism**

D. Young (1893); A.H. Williams (1935); H. Jones (1911–13); G.T. Roberts in *HMGB* 3 (1983) pp. 253–64; E. Edwards (1980)

GTH

Walker, Frank Deaville (1878–1945), journalist, editor and lecturer, born in *Manchester of Anglican parentage. He devoted his talents to furthering Methodist missionary history and home education, editing *Foreign Field* and *Kingdom Overseas* for 30 years and writing 38 annual Missionary Society reports. He was keenly interested in the missionary archives and important connexional and missionary artefacts held at the Bishopsgate Mission House and wrote lives of William Carey (1926) and T.B. *Freeman (1929) and books on Africa and India. In his youth he was challenged to dedicate his camera to the Lord's service and his work was frequently illustrated with the photographs he took on his travels.

MR 8 Nov. 1945

MJF

Walker, James Uriah (1812–64), letter-press printer and *local preacher of *Halifax. He wrote and published *A History of Wesleyan Methodism in Halifax* (1836) and from 1838 was proprietor and publisher of the *Halifax Guardian*. A *local preacher for 33 years, he was influential in the founding of the *LPMAA, recalling how as a Poor Law Guardian he had been moved when a venerable *local preacher had been obliged to seek poor relief in Halifax. A supporter of the Tory Radical factory reform movement, he was also a prominent campaigner for the release of R. *Oastler from prison.

A. Parker (1998)

JAH

Walker, Rev. Samuel (1714–61), evangelical clergyman, curate-in-charge at St Mary's, *Truro from 1746. He was converted under the preaching of George Conon, the Scottish headmaster of Truro Grammar School and became an influential local figure, described by JW as the only 'regular' minister who was successful in converting any of his own parishioners. He organized *religious societies in his parish and a 'Clerical Club' among his fellow evangelicals. He encountered some difficulty in dealing with the Methodist society in Truro and in 1755–56 did his best to dissuade JW from separating from the Church. After his death some of his congregation formed a church of their own and others joined the *Countess of Huntingdon's Connexion.

DNB; E. Sidney (1835); G.C.B. Davies (1951)

JAV

Wallbridge, Elizabeth (1770–1801) was born on the Isle of Wight, where her parents had a small dairy farm. She was converted in 1796 by a sermon preached by the WM itinerant James Crabb (1774–1851; e.m. 1794). At the funeral of her younger sister she met the Rev. Legh Richmond, the local Anglican priest. They exchanged letters and he often visited the family. Elizabeth was consumptive and on her death-bed urged Richmond to continue to visit her elderly parents and to conduct her burial service, the details of which she had arranged herself. He told her story in what became a popular classic, *The Dairyman's Daughter*.

J.B. Dyson (1865) chs 15–16

EDG

Waller, David J. (1835–1911; e.m. 1857) spent thirty of his 54-year ministry (1881–1911) as Secretary of the WM *Education Committee. He served on the Consultative Committee of the Board of Education and effectively represented Methodist views and interests in connection with the Voluntary Schools Act of 1897. He was closely associated with both *Westminster and *Southlands Colleges and played a major role in the re-organizing of *Queenswood School in 1894. He was President of the 1895 Conference. His daughter **Marion Waller** was appointed first headmistress of the new Queenswood, but resigned after three years to marry a Scottish Free Church minister, Alexander McGaskill, and die in childbirth.

MR 7 & 14 Sept. 1911

JAV

Wallis, James (1809–95; e.m. 1833), WM missionary from London, was appointed to *New Zealand in 1834. Although small in stature, he endured exhausting working and living conditions, constantly building and travelling to establish the work. Like his colleagues, he spoke the Maori language fluently. He encountered difficulties over land entitlement and hostility from Anglicans with patience and determination, entering into a more retired ministry after 1868. Other generations of his family also saw missionary service in the South Pacific.

MJF

Walsh, Dr John Dixon (1927–), Methodist historian, son of John S. Walsh (1895–1977; e.m. 1918). He was educated at *Kingswood School and Cambridge University, where his PhD was awarded for a thesis on 'The Yorkshire Evangelicals in the eighteenth century with especial reference to Methodism'. He is a Fellow of Jesus College, Oxford and has written extensively on the social, cultural and religious setting of eighteenth century Methodism. With G.V. Bennett he edited *Essays in modern English church history in memory of Norman Sykes* (1966) and with Colin Haydon and Stephen Taylor, *The Church of England c. 1689-c. 1833: from toleration to Tractarianism* (1993). His Friends of Dr Williams's Library Lecture on John Wesley (1995) was a magisterial study. By a combination of learning, insight and charity, he has effectively resisted the attempts of sociological reductionists to rewrite church history and has generously made available to others the ample resources of his own scholarship. *Revival and Religion since 1700: Essays for John Walsh* (ed Jane Garnett and Colin Matthew, 1993) paid a deserved tribute to his merits.

JAN

Walsh, Thomas (1730–1759), Irish RC from Co. Limerick who left the Catholic Church because of growing doubts about its doctrines and found the assurance of salvation among the Methodists. Very soon he began preaching in Irish with great effect and in the face of fierce hostility; then moved to circuit work in England in 1752. He returned to Ireland, dying of consumption, in 1758. His *Journal* reveals a man who knew the highest peaks, and the lowest troughs, in his fellowship with God. Intense, introspective and self-critical, his early rising, constant preaching out-of- doors in all weathers and with little regard for personal health precipitated his premature death. JW spoke of him as 'that man of God' and the best Hebraist he ever knew.

J. Morgan (1762); C. Atmore (1801) pp. 438–43

HMG

Walters Family **William Davis Walters** (1839–1913; e.m. 1865), WM minister, was born at Pontypool. After 24 years in circuit, he served as the first General Secretary of the London Mission 1889–1911, a crucial period in its history. He was a dedicated pastor and skilful fund-raiser. As a young minister in the Sherborne Circuit he became a close friend of two *local preachers, Charles and Edward John *Ensor and the two families became connected by marriage. One of his daughters married E.S. *Waterhouse and another was the mother of Bp N.C. *Sargant. Two of his sons became clergymen and three entered the WM ministry. **Charles Ensor Walters** (1872–1938;

e.m. 1895), after training at *Richmond College, became assistant to H.P. *Hughes in the West London Mission and at the age of 29 succeeded him in 1902 as Superintendent. He devoted 38 years of his ministry to London, becoming General Secretary of the London Mission and Extension Fund in 1921 and was specially loved by the poor. He was President of the Conference in 1936. He combined the gifts of pastor, preacher, administrator and advocate, and was one of the most popular platform speakers of his day. His brother Dr **Harold Crawford Walters** (1886–1958; e.m. 1909), the youngest of 15 children, was President of the Conference in 1956.

———

MR 19 June 1913, 22 Dec. 1938, 5 July 1956

KGG/JAV

Walton, Alice (1896–1980), Secretary of *Women's Work for over 25 years and elected Honorary Secretary on her retirement in 1958. Born in Elland, Yorks, she trained as a teacher and taught at the Girls' High School, Trichinopoly, 1924–29. When ill-health prevented her return to *India, she taught in *Colchester until joining the Mission House staff in 1933 as Women's Work Secretary, including responsibility for candidature. She travelled widely and took a particular interest in developing the leadership of women overseas. She was much in demand as a Women's Work speaker Her wide experience, shrewd judgment and sense of humour made her a most effective member of the Central Council in which she continued to play an active part in retirement.

PMW

Walton, Ernest Thomas Sinton (1903–95), son of **John A. Walton** (1874–1936; e.m. 1897) who was an amateur astronomer, inherited his father's natural curiosity, choosing the field of experimental physics at Trinity College, Dublin. From Dublin he went to the Cavendish Laboratory in *Cambridge, under Rutherford's supervision. In 1932 he and his colleague Cockcroft first 'split the atom', for which both were awarded the Nobel Prize in Physics in 1951. In 1934 he returned to Dublin to teach in the comparatively quiet backwaters of Trinity College. He remained a man of peace and deep religious faith throughout his life and was a governor of *Methodist College, Belfast and *Wesley College, Dublin. He died in Belfast.

———

B. Cathcart (1992) pp. 13–31

RPR

Walton, Sydney, CBE (1882–1964) began life as an office boy in Bishop Auckland and won an award to Durham University, where he took both an MA and a B.Litt with distinction and was President of the Union. After a brief spell of teaching, he became a prolific freelance journalist (e.g. as political commentator with the *Yorkshire Post*) and an accomplished publicist. His work for several government ministries earned him a CBE in 1918. He was a *local preacher for over 60 years, wrote several books and was closely associated with the *British Weekly*.

———

Times, 15 Dec. 1964; *MR* 24 Dec. 1964

JAV

War and Peace Several of the early Methodist itinerants (e.g. J. *Haime and S. *Staniforth) had served in the Army and Methodist soldiers were instrumental in establishing societies in many places, especially overseas. JW was ahead of his time in denouncing the evil of war ('that fell monster'), notably in his treatise on *Original Sin, where he dealt with its causes and condemned it as destructive of the 'work of God'. On the other hand, he responded to the threat of a French invasion in 1756 by offering to raise a 'company of volunteers' from among his followers. In the Napoleonic period Methodists were eager to demonstrate their loyalty, objecting only to drilling on Sunday.

The modern attitude of the Methodist Church to war is set out in the Conference Declarations of 1937 and 1957 and reflected in Conference resolutions on such specific issues as nuclear weapons, the arms trade and disarmament. Methodism acknowledges that war is contrary to the spirit, teaching and purpose of Christ, but recognizes that Christians are divided: some believing that loyalty to Jesus requires the total renunciation of the use of military force, others that there are situations in which resort to arms is the lesser of two evils. The Christian pacifist position is rooted in a theological interpretation of the Cross. The non-pacifist argues that sometimes the claims of peace and justice conflict and justice then has the prior claim. The Church is pledged to uphold the rights of conscience of both pacifist and non-pacifist. The development of weapons of mass destruction has led to a re-examination of the concept of a 'just war' and the conclusion that no war fought with such weapons can be just. The recognition that the search for military security is undermining the achievement of the environmental security on which the future of the planet

depends is leading to similar re-examination.
See also **Methodist Peace Fellowship**

G.T. Brake (1984) pp. 443–56

KGG

Warburton, William (1698–1779), Bishop of
*Gloucester 1759–79 and critic of Methodism.
Despite his slipshod scholarship he became a
prominent figure in the literary world and a friend
and executor of Alexander Pope. He directed his
violent and abusive invective at Hume, Gibbon
and JW. In Part II of *The Doctrine of Grace,
or the Office and Operations of the Holy Spirit
vindicated from ... the abuses of fanaticism*
(1762), he attacked Methodist teaching on *justification by faith as leading to *antinomianism and
JW as a hypocritical charlatan. JW's reply in a
open *Letter* (1763) protested against Warburton's
inaccurate quotation from his *Journal* and misrepresentation of Methodist doctrine.

DNB; A.W, Evans (1932); G.R. Cragg (1975)
pp. 459–63

JAV

Ward, Dr Arthur Marcus (1906–78; e.m.
1928), the son of a WM minister, was educated
at *Kingswood School, University College,
Southampton and *Wesley House, Cambridge,
where he won the Hulsean Prize. He spent most
of his career in ministerial training and theological
education, proving himself an outstanding teacher
at *Richmond College (1929–32 and 1955–72)
and at Bangalore (1936–54). He played a key
consultative role in the development of the Church
of South India and wrote the history of its first
five years, *The Pilgrim Church* (1952). He became
a member of the *Anglican-Methodist Conversations team in England and remained a deeply
committed ecumenist. He was the first ever Free
Church minister to teach at the RC Heythrop
College.

MR 8 June 1978; J.A. Newton (1984)

DJC

Ward, Joseph Neville (1915–92; e.m. 1938)
was born at Oxenhope, Yorks, son of John Ward
(1866–1949; e.m. 1892), and educated at *Kingswood School, Exeter College, Oxford and Manchester University. He trained for the ministry at
*Hartley Victoria College. His spirituality and
ability to appreciate many different traditions was
evident in his preaching and his books, particularly

The Use of Praying (1967) and *Five for Sorrow,
Ten for Joy* (1971).

MR 12 Nov. 1992

KGG

Ward, Robert (1816–76; e.m. 1835), PM
missionary in *New Zealand. Born in Norfolk, he
was converted at 15 and became a PM *local
preacher. After he had been in circuit for nine
years, he was chosen to be the missionary the
PM Connexion had decided to send to Australia,
though his destination was changed to New Zealand. He and his family sailed for New Plymouth
in 1844, but most of his ministry was spent in
Auckland and Wellington. A man of determination and common sense, he was remembered
for the intensity of his preaching. He had two
works published in England: *Lectures from New
Zealand addressed to Young Men* (1862) and *Life
among the Maoris of New Zealand* (1872). Two
of his sons, Charles and Josiah, served in the
Australian and New Zealand ministry.

J. Guy & W.S. Potter (1893)

DJP

Ward, Valentine (1781–1835; e.m. 1801)
spent half of his ministry in *Scotland, where
he was responsible for building or acquiring a
number of chapels on which crippling debts
remained for decades. A powerful, attractive
preacher, fiery controversialist, advocate of
denominational *Sunday Schools and opponent
of *slavery, he was sent in 1834 to superintend
the *West Indian missions, but died soon after his
arrival.

G.Smith (1861) vol. 3 passim; A.J. Hayes (1976)
pp. 96–105

MB

Ward, Prof. William Reginald (1925–),
emeritus professor of Modern History, University
of Durham, and a leading member of the Ecclesiastical History Society. He has been particularly
concerned with the interface between Church and
society, as in his *Religion and Society in England,
1790–1850* (1972). That work, with its emphasis
on the importance of the *Sunday School movement, exemplifies his concern with popular
religion as against over-concentration on church
hierarchies and establishments. His outstanding
contributions to Methodist historiography have
been his editing of the correspondence of J. *Bunting (2 vols, 1972 and 1976) and of the Bicentennial

Edition of JW's *Journals* (1988–99). His command of German and wide-ranging knowledge of German church history are manifest in his *Theology, sociology and politics: the German Protestant social conscience, 1890–1933* (1979). He has consistently sought to set English Methodism in a wider European context, e.g. of traditions like *Moravianism and the *Pietism of the Halle school. His astringent writing and breadth of intellectual concern have provided a bracing counterblast to any Methodist tendencies to parochialism.

JAN

Wardle, Dr William Lansdell (1877–1946; e.m. 1901), PM minister, son of **Arthur Temple Wardle** (1844–1914; e.m. 1867), was educated at Cambridge and *Hartley College. Apart from 1917 to 1919, when he was a forces chaplain, he was a tutor at Hartley (and Hartley-Victoria) College from 1903 to 1934, when he became Principal. An OT scholar, he gave the *Hartley Lecture in 1925 on *Israel and Babylon*. He was President of the Conference in 1938.

MR 5 Sept. 1946

DCD

Warren, George (d.1812; e.m. 1807), the first WM missionary to Africa. Born in Cornwall, he was recruited by T. *Coke and in 1812 sent to *Sierra Leone in response to an appeal from some of the liberated slaves who had settled there. After a 52-day voyage he was welcomed and helped by the Governor and the Anglican chaplain, and worked effectively for eight months before succumbing to the climate of what became known as the 'White Man's Grave'.

JRP

Warren, Gilbert George (1861–1927; e.m. 1886), WM missionary, sailed for Hupeh, *China in 1886, where he worked until 1907. As the first Chairman of the Hunan District, 1907–21, he encouraged Church growth under Chinese leadership. He and his wife, who predeceased him in 1918, are buried together in Changsha, Hunan.

MR 20 & 27 Jan. 1927; W.N. Warren (1929)

GRS

Warren, Dr Samuel (1781–1862; e.m. 1802), Methodist Reformer who entered the WM ministry after a career at sea. His scholarship and abilities soon earned him an influential position and he was stationed in some of the leading towns. In 1833 he was on a committee, along with J.

*Bunting, to formulate plans for the education of young ministers. Unfortunately the committee went beyond its brief and nominated Bunting, despite his existing offices, as 'President of the Theological Institution'. Warren consequently attacked the scheme in his *Remarks on the Theological Institution*, which went through several editions and led to an immense pamphlet warfare. He was suspended from his *superintendency, took the matter to court and lost, but in the course of this discovered that certain resolutions of Conference had not been entered in the official record. He was expelled and in 1835 formed the *WMA. He did not accept the constitution proposed at its first Conference in 1836 (over which he presided), left the WMA and became an Anglican.

S. Warren (1827); O.A. Beckerlegge (1957)

OAB

Warrener, William (1750–1825; e.m. 1779), WM missionary in the *West Indies, spent seven years in British circuits before offering for overseas. He was one of the three who accompanied T. *Coke across the Atlantic in 1786. Storms diverted their ship from Nova Scotia to Antigua, where Warrener began his service by taking over the Mission when J. *Baxter accompanied Coke on his tour of other islands. In 1789 he was appointed to St Christopher, where he gained hundreds of members during his ministry. After a further period in Antigua, ill health compelled him to return home in 1797. He continued to plead the cause of *overseas missions during his service in home circuits until 1818.

GRS

Warrenite Controversy ((1834)) was the result of a challenge from S. *Warren to the WM Conference, arising out of the proposal to set up a Theological Institution with J. *Bunting as its President. The agitation led to the formation of the *Wesleyan Methodist Association.

JAV

Warrington formed a staging post for JW between *Manchester or *Chester and *Liverpool; consequently he visited the town 21 times between 1755 and 1790. Bank Street chapel, opened 1778, was superseded by Bold Street (seating 1,300) in 1850. Isolation and the absence of a resident itinerant contributed to the secession of *Quaker Methodists in 1796, and Warrington remains an IM centre. A separate WM circuit was formed (from Northwich) in 1812. A small PM society, with a chapel in Legh Street, was established with difficulty. There was never any UM work.

A. Mounfield in *PWHS* 8 pp. 57–61, 81–85; Conference Handbook 1939, 1949, 1960; I. Sellers (1976)

EAR

Warwick   In 1801 Thomas Facer, a Yorkshire stonemason, began to preach in his own house and in the open air. The first Methodist building (1824) gave its name to Chapel Street (formerly Mellows Lane) and was opened by the President, Dr R. *Newton. The second chapel, in Stand Street (1839) was sold to the PMs in 1863 and replaced by Market Street. None of these buildings survives. Northgate Church (1893) underwent a complete renovation for its centenary. There was a daughter chapel in Avon Street (1838–1968)

PBo

Watchman, The , the first Methodist newspaper, launched to defend WM against its critics and would-be reformers at the time of the *Warrenite agitation. Its first editor was H. *Sandwith. It appeared weekly from 1835 to 1884, from 1849 under the title *The Watchman and Wesleyan Advertiser*. It continued to represent the conservative wing of the connexion, and was counterbalanced later by the more liberal *Methodist Recorder*.

PWHS 28 p. 37

JAV

Watchnight Service is a service held at night and continuing till after midnight. Such services had a precedent in the Vigils of the early Church. JW encountered them among the *Moravians, who held them on New Year's Eve. Hearing that they had started spontaneously at *Kingswood, he encouraged them monthly on the Friday night nearest the full moon, but this was gradually replaced by the Moravian practice. CW wrote hymns for them. The practice spread to other denominations, but in our own day has been largely replaced by the Christmas Eve Communion Service.

ARG

Watchorn, Robert (1858–1944) was born in Alfreton, Derbys and joined the PMs through the influence of friends. Their high moral standards had a lasting influence on his life. At 20 he emigrated to the USA, where he became secretary of the United Mine Workers and chief factory inspector in Pennsylvania. He led the fight against

sweat shops and child labour, was a member of the American Immigration service and later was highly successful in the oil business. He never forgot his humble beginnings and built the beautiful PM Watchorn Memorial Chapel (1928) in Alfreton, complete with playing fields and a library.

H.F. West (1958)

EWD

Waterford   A society was formed in 1749 by R. *Swindells. JW paid 13 visits between 1752 and 1789, having been prevented in 1750 by the presence in the city of Nicholas Butler from *Cork. Mrs. E. *Bennis wrote to JW about the work there and persuaded him to change his plans for the stationing of preachers there. The 'Catholic mob' which he mentions in a letter to CW in 1773 was in Waterford.

D.A.L. Cooney (1998)

DALC

Waterhouse, Dr Eric Strickland (1879–1964; e.m. 1901) trained at *Richmond College and in 1920 returned there as tutor. He was Principal from 1940 to 1951 and London University appointed him Professor of the Philosophy of Religion in 1931. As a railway enthusiast, he often travelled on the footplate. He was a writer and broadcaster, and a governor of Queenswood and Penrhos Schools.

MR 16 April 1964

KGG

Waterhouse, Esther (*née* Martin) (1908–95), Vice-President of the Conference, 1977. The daughter of Dr Frank Martin, a general practitioner in *Bradford, she herself became a doctor, graduating from the Royal Free Hospital in 1935. A year later she married **John Walters Waterhouse** OBE (1908–1971; e.m. 1930, the son of E.S. *Waterhouse) and shared wholeheartedly in his work for the *NCH, of which he was Principal 1950–69. She was medical adviser to *Good Housekeeping* and wrote the first of their books on baby care. After her husband's death she continued to work for NCH's Action for Children and with *MHA.

MR 10 June 1971, 11 May 1995

PMW

Waterhouse, John (1789–1842; e.m. 1809), WM minister, born near *Leeds. After 30 years in the home work he was appointed 'General Superintendent of the Wesleyan Missions in *Australia and Polynesia' in 1838. This involved oversight of nine Districts from New South Wales to *Fiji. From his base in Hobart, his extensive tours provided opportunity to advise and encourage, but proved too strenuous both physically and mentally for one man. His health gave way and he died in Hobart, having deeply influenced both colleagues and local people alike with his wise yet practical counsels. His son **Joseph Waterhouse** (1828–81; e.m. 1849) served in Fiji 1850–64 and again in 1874–78, when relations with his colleague Frederick Langham (d. 1903) were strained. He encountered cannibalism on the island of Bau off Viti Levu and faced a threat to his life at Davuilevu. His persistent attempts to convert chief Thakombau (Cakobau) were eventually successful. He wrote *The King and People of Fiji* (1866). He was drowned at sea while returning from New Zealand.

F&H 3 passim; A.H. Wood (1975, 1978)

MJF

Watering Places Fund In response to the growing popularity of annual holidays among middle-class Victorian families, the WM Conference of 1862 accepted an offer by W.M. *Punshon to raise £10,000 towards the building or improvement of chapels in seaside and inland resorts. To reach this formidable target, Punshon threw himself into a fresh round of preaching and lecturing and by 1867 it had been reached, though at some cost to his health. W. *M'Arthur served as the Fund's treasurer. It supported building ventures in some 37 places. Of the 24 new chapels built, Richmond Hill (1886) in the mushrooming resort of Bournemouth was predecessor of the present Punshon Memorial Church (though on a different site). Those at Folkestone (1866), *Weymouth (1867), Matlock Bath (1867), Malvern (1868), Lytham (1868), Rhyl (1868), Llandudno (1866) and Aberystwyth (1869) were still in use in 1998.

Report of the Committee for the Erection of Wesleyan Methodist Chapels in Watering Places (1867)

JAV

Watkin, James (1809–86; e.m. 1830), WM missionary, born in *Manchester. Appointed to *Tonga in 1831, he is remembered as the author of the famous 'Pity Poor Fiji' appeal, sent in 1838 on behalf of his colleagues, inspired by the recent revival in Tonga and finding in Britain a resurgence of missionary enthusiasm. Charged with a misdemeanour and confessing to it, he left, but after an interval in Australia, in 1840 he began an effective ministry as the first missionary of any denomination resident in South Island, *New Zealand. Settling in *Australia, he became President of the Conference in 1862 and undertook a deputation to Tonga in 1869. Three sons became WM ministers: (1) **William James Watkin** (1833–1909; e.m. 1857), who served in New Zealand and being bilingual helped to reconcile Maori and settlers. He was President of the New Zealand Conference in 1889. (2) **Jabez Bunting Watkin** (1837–1925; e.m. 1866), who served in Tonga, befriending and supporting the troublesome S.W. *Baker. Losing confidence in him, he applied to transfer to Australia in 1878. However, after resuming his involvement in Baker's activities and being Chairman of the Tonga District for one year (1880), he resigned to lead the breakaway Free Wesleyan Church of Tonga as its President from 1885 to 1924. He declined at the last moment to join the 1924 union with the WM remnant negotiated by Queen Salote. (3) **Edwin Iredale Watkin** (1839–1916; e.m. 1859) was awarded a DD by Victoria University, Canada and was President of the Victoria and Tasmania Conference in 1883.

F&H 3 passim; G.I. Laurenson (1972); A.H. Wood 1 (1975) *EWM*

MJF

Watkin-Jones, Dr Howard (1888–1953; e.m. 1912) was born at Ironbridge, Shropshire and educated at *Kingswood School, Gonville and Caius College, Cambridge (where he was organ scholar) and *Didsbury College. In 1930 he became a tutor at *Headingley College, specializing in church history and theology. He wrote two important books on the Holy Spirit, including *The Holy Spirit from Arminius to Wesley* (1929). He was Conference Precentor, 1918–29, Chairman of the Leeds District during the wartime closure of the College (1942–46), Moderator of the FCFC, 1934, and President of the Conference, 1951. He was much involved in the structures of the ecumenical movement.

MR 12 July 1951, 29 Oct. 1953

KGG

Watkins, Owen (1842–1915; e.m. 1864), WM minister, trained at *Richmond College, was prevented from missionary service for medical reasons. After a later illness doctors advised the South African climate and after four years in Pietermaritzburg he was designated Chairman of the Transvaal and Swaziland District in 1880. He purchased several mission farms, including Kilnerton where a major training institution was later established. He organized the African evangelists who had independently begun Methodist work in Transvaal, and pastoral care for the white communities drawn to the Witwatersrand by the discovery of gold. In 1891 he and Isaac Shimmin followed Cecil Rhodes' pioneer column to Mashonaland (the infant Rhodesia), where he obtained three mission farms and other property. He was invalided back to Britain after walking 200 miles to the coast at Beira. His son **Owen Spencer Watkins** CMG, CBE (1873–1957; e.m. 1896), educated at *Kingswood School and *Richmond College, followed in his father's footsteps in a distinguished career as an Army chaplain in Africa, took part in the memorial service to General Gordon at Khartoum and served in the Boer Wars and World War I. His books include *With Kitchener's Army* (1899), *Chaplains at the Front* (1901) and *Soldiers and Preachers Too* (1906), an account of Methodism in the army.

See also **Armed Forces**

MR 23 Dec. 1915, 9 Jan. 1957; F&H vol. 4
JRP

Watkinson, Charles K. (1858–1934), PM layman, born at Market Rasen, Lincs. At 17 he moved to *Grimsby, but soon left his apprenticeship to enter the fishing industry, where his business prospered. He was superintendent of the PM Sunday School for 40 years. A gifted singer, he was precentor at the PM Conference and later a member of the Methodist Hymnal Committee. He was Vice-President of the Conference in 1921. As a magistrate from 1914, he took a special interest in children's courts.

WL

Watkinson, Dr William L. (1838–1925; e.m. 1858), WM minister, born in *Hull, began his circuit ministry after only a few weeks in college and quickly rose to eminence. He was *Connexional Editor 1893–1904 and President of the Conference in 1897. A prolific writer, his books included several volumes of sermons and the *Fernley Lecture of 1886 on *The Influence of Scepticism on Character*.

MR 19 Feb. 1925
WL

Watson, Dr John (1832–1913; e.m. 1862), PM itinerant from Weardale. Converted at 14, having a widowed mother he served ten years as a *local preacher before entering the itinerancy. After 17 years in home circuits, he served in *South Africa (1879–83) and *Australia (1883–89). He was Principal of the Manchester Theological Institute 1893–98 and President of the 1895 Conference. He edited the *PM Quarterly Review* from 1906 and was actively involved in *Christian Endeavour and the FCFC. His *Hartley Lecture of 1898 on the Fatherhood of God was the first to be published. He received a DD from Victoria University, Toronto.

A. Wilkes & J. Lovatt (1942) pp. 110–11
GEM

Watson, Dr Philip Saville (1909–83; e.m. 1936), together with E.G. *Rupp, was a key figure in the renaissance of Luther studies in England. Educated at Durham and *Wesley House, Cambridge, he also did post-graduate work in Tubingen and Lund, where he profited from developments in Luther studies. From 1946 to 1955 he taught Theology at *Handsworth, where he was Principal from 1951, and after four years at *Wesley House, Cambridge became Professor of Systematic Theology at Garrett Theological Seminary, Evanston, 1959–73. His *Let God be God* (the Fernley-Hartley Lecture of 1947) offered a splendidly lucid introduction to Luther's teaching. He also published *The Concept of Grace* (1959). In America his academic focus switched to Methodist theology and the long introduction to his 'reader of instruction and devotion' *The Message of the Wesleys* (1964) was designed to present their teaching 'without myth'.

MR 30 June 1983
DJC

Watson, Richard (1781–1833; e.m. 1797) left the WM ministry for the *MNC in 1800 on doctrinal grounds, but returned in 1812. The first outstanding WM systematic theologian and a keen promoter of missions, he was President of the 1826 Conference. His greatest theological contribution was his *Theological Institutes* (1831), in which he was the first to bring JW's theology into a coherent system. He made no claim to originality, but, at a time when there was still no formal ministerial training, aimed to help ministers refute *Calvinist, Socinian and rationalist ideas when they threatened to disturb the Methodist people. While he undoubtedly shared the evangelical perspective of W's theology and reproduced its content, it is arguable that, because of his apologetic concerns, he failed to preserve its approach and style. Everything turns on whether for JW theology was immediately practical, informing and strengthening faith, whereas for Watson it served preaching indirectly, by supporting doctrine and clearing away intellectual encumbrances. Watson also wrote catechisms for young people and a life of JW (1831), compiled a *Biblical and Theological Dictionary* (1831) at the request of the WM Conference, and edited a revision of the WM *Hymn-book.

T. Jackson (1834); G.J. Stevenson (1884–6) 2 pp. 238–48; E.J. Brailsford (1906)

DJC

Waugh, Edwin (1817–90), born in *Rochdale, the son of a shoemaker. An outstanding product of WM *Sunday School education, he was apprenticed at 12 to a local printer. He was Assistant Secretary to the Lancashire Public School Association 1847–52, before turning to journalism and publishing his own verse. At 39 he found sudden fame with his broadsheet *Come Whoam to thi' Childer an' Me*, depicting the effects of drunkenness on family life. This sold 20,000 copies within days. His busy career of public readings ended when his health began to fail *c*. 1870 and poverty overtook him. He was granted a Civil List pension in 1883.

M. Vicinus (1984)

CJS

Waugh, Thomas (1785–1873; e.m. 1802), born of Presbyterian parents in Coleraine, was early attracted to Methodism and began to preach at 19. Called into the itinerancy in 1808, he became the most influential leader in his generation of Irish Methodism, shaping the deliberations and influencing the conclusions of the Conference and its committees. Often called 'the Irish Methodist Pope', he was autocratic and at times severe, but could also be a generous opponent. A friend and confidant of J. *Bunting, he was for over thirty years a representative at the British Conference. He exercised much of his ministry and influence from Bandon, where he was made a Freeman in 1823.

MR(W) 1898 pp. 52–5

RPR

Way, James (1804–84; e.m. 1826), BC minister, born at Morchard Bishop, Devon and con-

verted under the preaching of Ann Guest, a female BC preacher. Because of his poverty he had to walk the 75 miles to his first circuit, carrying his library of three books, a Bible, a hymn-book and a dictionary. His impressive circuit ministry was recognized when he was elected President of the Conference in 1847. In 1850 he went out to *Australia to form the first BC community in the Burra minefields north of Adelaide. Within months he had gathered a congregation and built a church at Bowden. In 1859 he conducted a revival among the Cornish miners at Burra. In 1892 a boys' school named Way College in his honour was opened. His son, **Sir Samuel J. Way** (1836–1916), born in *Portsmouth, was called to the Bar in 1861 and became a Q.C. in 1871. He was elected to Parliament in 1875 and became Attorney General. In 1876 he was appointed Chief Justice of the Supreme Court in South Australia, a position he held, along with that of Lieutenant Governor from 1890, until his death. The University of Adelaide (of which he was Chancellor from 1883), the Public Library, Museum, Art Gallery and Children's Hospital were among the institutions in his debt. He received doctorates from both Oxford and Cambridge. An old boy of *Shebbear College, he presented Lake Farm to his old school. He remained loyal to his BC roots, but strongly supported the move to unite Australian Methodists in 1902.

G.J. Stevenson (1884–86) 6 pp. 888–95; R. Pyke (n.d.)

EWD/DGH

Weardale *see* **Dales Circuit**

Wearmouth,   Robert   Featherstone (1882–1963; e.m. 1909), PM minister and historian, born into a mining family at Oxhill, Co. Durham. He went down the pit at 12, then into the Army, where he obtained a commission. Converted during a *Christian Endeavour mission, he was influenced and encouraged by John Clennell (1878–1962; e.m. 1905). After another period as a miner he trained at *Hartley College. As an army chaplain in World War I he went through the Battle of the Somme, writing of it later in *Pages from a Padre's Diary* (1958). During his circuit ministry he obtained a MA at Birmingham and a BSc and PhD at London. His series of pioneering studies of Methodism's social and political influence began with *Methodism and the Working Class Movements in England, 1800–1850* (1937), based on his doctoral thesis and was summed up in his WHS Lecture *Methodism and* *the Trade Unions* (1959). He meticulously documented the extent to which the working classes learned the arts of public speaking, organization and leadership through their involvement in local Methodism.

See also **Trade Unionism**

PWHS 43 pp. 111–16; R. Lowery (1982)

JAV

Weatherhead, Dr Leslie Dixon, CBE (1893–1976; e.m. 1915) was born in London and educated at Leicester University, *Richmond College and Manchester University. During World War I he became a chaplain to the Devonshire Regiment and from 1919 to 1922 served the English Methodist Church in Madras. After an outstanding ministry at Brunswick Chapel, *Leeds (1925–36) he became minister of the City Temple, London, where he drew great crowds. When the building was destroyed by enemy action, he held the congregation together in the Anglican Church of St Sepulchre's until the new City Temple was built. As a preacher he was known throughout the world, owing much to his impressive appearance and beautiful voice. He had a clarity of thought and expression which enabled him to convey truth in a way ordinary folk could understand. In addition to his London PhD, he received honorary doctorates from Edinburgh and two American universities. He was a prolific writer. His *Psychology, Religion and Healing* (1951) reflected his pioneer work in this field and he established clinics for the treatment of nervous disorders, developing helpful partnerships with distinguished medical men. In *The Christian Agnostic* (1965) he expounded aspects of the liberal theology which informed his preaching. He was President of the Conference in 1955. *The Transforming Friendship* (of Christ) – the title of one of his books (1928) – was at the heart of his ministry.

C. Maitland (1960); K. Weatherhead (1975); L. Price (1996); J.C. Travell (1999); *Sunday Times* 4 Jan. 1976; *MR* 7 July 1955, 8 & 15 Jan. 1976; M. Camroux in *ER* Jan. 1999 pp. 74–9

KGG

Weavind, George (1850–1916; e.m. 1871), WM missionary, appointed to *South Africa at 23. He learned Afrikaans, married into a Boer family, built the first church in Pretoria, succeeded O. *Watkins as Chairman of the Transvaal-Swaziland District (1892–1901) and was also Principal of the celebrated Kilnerton Training Institution.

JRP

Webb, Dr Pauline Mary (1927–), campaigner, broadcaster and missionary publicist. A daughter of Leonard F. Webb (1891–1973; e.m. 1915), she was educated at King's College, London and taught from 1949 to 1952 before joining the *MMS as Youth Education Secretary (1952–54), editor of *Kingdom Overseas* (1954–67) and area secretary for the Caribbean (1973–79). She reopened the issue of women's *ordination at the 1959 Conference and from 1965, the year in which she was Vice-President of the Conference, was a participant in the *Anglican-Methodist Conversations. The first woman to be elected an officer of the Central Committee of the WCC, she played a leading role, as Vice-Moderator 1968–75, in its Programme to Combat Racism. She was the first secretary of the Board of Lay Training, 1967–73 and organizer of Religious Broadcasting in the BBC World Service, 1979–87. She is co-editor of the *Dictionary of the Ecumenical Movement* (1991).

J.F. Bibb (1991)

JHL

Webb, 'Captain' Thomas (1725–96), lay pioneer of *American Methodism, born probably in *Bristol, but possibly in Ireland. He enlisted in the 48th Regiment of Foot *c.* 1745, was commissioned as Quartermaster in 1754, served in America under Wolfe and lost an eye at the battle of Montmorency in 1759. He was married in 1760 and chose to stay in America in 1764, as civilian Barrack Master at Albany, NY. During a visit to England after his wife's death, he was converted in Bristol, where J. *Rouquet introduced him to the Methodists and JW accepted him as a *local preacher. JW described him as 'a man of fire' and CW, more guardedly, as 'an inexperienced, honest, zealous, loving enthusiast'. He continued to preach back in Albany and as far south as Pennsylvania. He played a crucial role in the building of the first John Street Church in New York and in acquiring St George's Church, Philadelphia, and successfully appealed to the British Conference to send more preachers to America. In 1773 he married Grace *Gilbert, sister of Nathaniel. During the Revolutionary War he was arrested as a Loyalist and, though cleared of a charge of spying, his position became untenable. He finally returned to England in financial straits in 1778. Settling eventually in Bristol, he gave a lead in the building of Portland Chapel (1792), where he served as trustee, chapel keeper and class leader. His remains were reinterred at the *New Room in 1972.

C. Atmore (1801) pp. 444–48; E.R. Bates (1975); F. Baker (1976) pp. 51–69

JAV

Webber *see* **Lloyd Webber**

Wedgwood, John (1788–1869), PM preacher, a member of the famous family of potters. He inherited property near Tunstall from his father. Converted at 21, he associated with W. *Clowes and his name first appears on a Burslem plan in 1809. In 1819 he was imprisoned for preaching in *Grantham and he later took part in missions in *Leicester and in Cheshire. He became an itinerant in 1829, but does not appear on the stations after 1833. He was married in 1840 and appears to have settled in Crewe.

T. Bateman (1870)

WL

Wednesbury Riots (1743–44) The Wednesbury society, established in 1742, was known as 'the mother society of Staffordshire Methodism' and included members from Darlaston, Walsall and West Bromwich. CW preached there as early as the autumn of 1742 and JW followed in January 1743 – the first of 33 visits between then and 1789. The vicar, the Rev. Edward Egginton, was at first friendly and supportive, until injudicious criticisms by one of the itinerant preachers, Robert Williams, turned him into an implacable enemy. Mob violence, incited by local gentry and clergy, first broke out at Walsall, spreading to Darlaston and later West Bromwich. Homes were damaged and plundered, families victimized. JW arrived to give his support in the summer of 1743, but an appeal to the law proved fruitless. On 20 October, during a fresh outbreak, JW calmly faced the Wednesbury rioters, only to find himself in the hands of a rival mob from Walsall. He sought protection from the local magistrates in vain and barely escaped with his life. One notable result was the conversion of a ringleader, the local prize-fighter George Clifton ('Honest Munchin'). But violence continued until early 1744, reaching a climax of destruction and looting on 7 February. Belatedly the authorities were alerted and the storm of *persecution subsided. In answer to charges that the Methodists had instigated the violence, JW published a detailed account of events, *Modern Christianity exemplified at Wednesbury . . .* (1745)

See also **Black Country**

JWJ 15 Apr & 20 Oct. 1743; J.L. Waddy (1976); C.H. Goodwin (1994)

JAV

Welsh Calvinistic Methodism (or Presbyterian Church of Wales) was established as a result of the revival activities of H. *Harris, D. *Rowland and other Welsh revivalists who during the eighteenth century gave Welsh Methodism its distinctive *Calvinistic inclination. Contact was made with the English Methodists in 1739 and the first joint association meeting was held by the Calvinists at Watford near Caerphilly in 1743, the year before JW's first Conference. Despite pressure from many within the movement, the early leaders resisted calls for secession from the CofE, and this remained the general policy until the end of the eighteenth century. Uneasy relations between Harris and Rowland reached a climax in the disruption of 1750. Many of Harris's followers joined the Rowland camp, Harris withdrew to *Trevecka and the movement suffered a setback for some years.

Following the pioneering work of the early itinerant preachers in North Wales, further advances were made in the area through the labours of T. *Charles of Bala who joined the Methodists in 1784, but as persecution increased in the 1790s, preachers were forced to seek the protection of the *Toleration Act, thus becoming dissenters. Full secession followed in 1811 when *ordinations were held at Bala in the north and Llandeilo in the south. A Confession of Faith, based on the Westminster Confession was drawn up in 1823 and the Constitutional Deed was completed in 1826. In 1840 a missionary society was established to work in *India; missionaries were also sent to Brittany early in the twentieth century. Today, the Mission and Unity Board co-operates closely with the Council for World Mission.

Colleges for the training of ministers were established at Bala in 1837, Trevecka in 1842 and Aberystwyth in 1906. Theological training is currently conducted at Aberystwyth, while Bala and Trevecka are mainly used for youth and lay activities.

In 1919 a reconstruction Commission was inaugurated to streamline and modernize the constitution. A *Shorter Declaration of Faith* was published in 1921, but the 1823 Confession was retained as an historical document. The Calvinistic Methodist or Presbyterian Church of Wales Act (1933) created a legal identity for the church and gave equal standing to the two titles by which it is commonly known. By 1995 it consisted of 939 churches (of which 219 were English), employed 119 full time ministers, and had 51,720 members.

D.E. Jenkins (1911); G.M. Roberts (1973, 1978); *Agenda of the General Assembly of the Presbyterian Church of Wales*, 1996

GT

Wenyon, Dr Charles (1848–1924; e.m. 1871), WM missionary who sailed to *China in 1880. He founded the Fatshan (Fushan) hospital and its Medical Centre for the training of Chinese medical students. Ill health forced his return home in 1896. From 1901 to 1906 he was minister of *Wesley's Chapel, London.

GRS

Werrey, Mary Ann (fl. 1820–25), BC itinerant. After a successful ministry in the Isles of Scilly, in March 1823 she sailed to Guernsey, where she preached in a Baptist chapel and the open air. In Jersey she preached in a 'dancing room' before fitting up another room as a chapel. Responding to a dream which she interpreted as a call to *Scotland, she opened a Northumberland Mission at Blyth and reached *Edinburgh before her health failed.

F.W. Bourne (1905); C.C. Short (1995)

EDG

Wesle Bach ('Minor Wesleyans') was a protest movement within Welsh WM, primarily of *local preachers against ministerial authority. In August 1831 twelve local preachers met near Menai Bridge and proposed that there should be interchange of pulpits, lay and ministerial, between circuits and that local preachers should receive modest payment when travelling in circuits other than their own. These proposals received a hostile reception and the reformers seceded, throwing in their lot with IM (already home to a *Liverpool Welsh church that had seceded in 1818 under the leadership of T. *Jones) and hardening their attitude towards autocracy. They took control of Shiloh, Tregarth, one of the strongest churches (it returned to WM in 1837) and prospered for a few years, especially in Anglesey and Caernarfonshire. In 1838 they transferred their allegiance to the WMA, from which they expected more missionary help, but by the late 1850s only half a dozen societies remained.

The Reform movement of the 1850s met with little success in North Wales in the face of opposition from T. *Aubrey, but gained some 500 adherents in Liverpool and South Wales.

A.H. Williams (1935) pp. 221–52; G.T. Roberts in *Bathafarn* 3 (1948) pp. 42–52, 10 (1955) pp. 52–3

GTH

Wesley Family The Wesley brothers had *Puritan and Nonconformist ancestry on both sides of their family, but their parents both returned to the Cof E. JW's paternal great-grandfather **Bartholomew Westley** (an early form of the name) (*c.* 1596–1671) of Lyme Regis and grandfather, **John Westley** (*c.* 1636–70) of Winterborne Whitchurch, Dorset, and his maternal grandfather Samuel *Annesley (*c.* 1620–96) were all ejected from their livings after the Restoration.

Samuel Wesley senr (1662–1735) graduated from Exeter College, Oxford, was ordained priest in 1689 and after a brief interlude as a naval chaplain became rector of South Ormsby, Lincs, in 1691 and of Epworth in 1695, to which he added the nearby Wroote in 1722. Of considerable scholarly and literary ability, he produced a 'heroic poem' on *The Life of Christ* (1693) and a massive *Dissertations on the Book of Job* in Latin (1735). Despite this he failed to gain preferment, was unpopular with his rank-and-file parishioners and through poor financial management was imprisoned for debt at Lincoln.

His wife **Susanna Wesley** (*née* Annesley, 1669–1742) inherited her father's independence of character and intellectual ability. She educated each of her children from an early age and had a lasting influence on their lives, not least that of her middle son John; though it has been argued that what they gained intellectually they lost in warmth of affection.

Ten of their 19 children survived into adulthood. The oldest of the three sons, **Samuel Wesley junr** (1690–1739), was educated at Westminster School and Christ Church, Oxford, was employed as an Usher at Westminster 1713–33 (during which his brother Charles was a pupil there) and became headmaster of Blundell's School, Tiverton in 1733. Like his father and brothers he had some poetic ability.

All but one (the youngest, Kezzia, 1710–41) of the seven daughters married, mostly unhappily. Most disastrous were the marriages of the gifted Mehetabel ('Hetty', 1697–1750), forced by her father into marrying a plumber and glazier, William Wright, after an ignominious seduction by a young lawyer, and that of Martha ('Patty',

1706–91) to the flagrantly unfaithful Westley *Hall. She survived him, became a Methodist and a friend of Dr Johnson and remained close to her brother John, whom she is said to have resembled.

See also **Heraldry**; **Wesley, Charles**; **Wesley, John**

A. Clarke (1823); G.J. Stevenson (1876); M.L. Edwards (1949); M. Pinhorn in *Blackmansbury* Dec. 1964/Feb. 1965 pp. 36–51

J A V

Wesley, Rev. Charles (1707–88), preacher and hymnwriter, was the youngest of the three Wesley brothers and was still a baby at the time of the *Epworth fire in 1709. In 1716, at the age of 8, he entered Westminster School, where his brother Samuel was usher. He became a King's Scholar in 1721 and head boy in 1725–26 before going up to Christ Church, Oxford. By then JW had become a Fellow at Lincoln College, but was often away in Lincolnshire. Charles' pleasure-loving personality took a more serious turn and he found himself meeting with other students in what became known as the *'Holy Club'. Graduating in 1730, he became a Student (i.e. Fellow) at Christ Church. Preparing to accompany JW to Georgia as secretary to General Oglethorpe, in September 1735 he was ordained so that he might assist in his brother's parish duties. Failing to adjust to colonial life or to establish good relations with the settlers at Fort Frederica, he was back in England, a sick man, by the end of 1736.

The effect of his encounter with *Moravian settlers on the voyage to Georgia was reinforced by the influence of P. *Böhler and of John Bray with whom he lodged in London. On Whit Sunday 1738 he had a 'conversion' experience similar to that of JW in Aldersgate Street three days later. HP 706, 'Where shall my wondering soul begin?', is thought to be the hymn he wrote on this occasion, and from then on a spate of hymns and poems continued through the rest of his life. While JW was visiting Herrnhut, Charles had begun an evangelical ministry which included visiting Newgate and the Marshalsea prisons and accompanying condemned prisoners to Tyburn. To the end he was the more stalwart churchman of the two, resorting to *field preaching only after being refused the use of a parish church, harbouring reservations about the employment of lay preachers and recoiling at the news of JW's *ordinations in 1784 (which he blamed on the influence of T. *Coke).

For some years he shared in JW's peripatetic ministry and the leadership of the developing Methodist movement. He followed hard on the heels of his brother in visiting *Newcastle, where he formed the first society in September 1742, and faced mob violence at *Wednesbury and *Sheffield in 1743 and at Devizes in 1747. On his way to *Ireland in 1747 he met his future wife, Sarah *Gwynne, at Garth, Breconshire. They were married on April 8, 1749, after JW had guaranteed him an income of £100 a year from the sale of publications, and set up home in *Bristol (from 1766 at 4 Charles Street). From then on his ministry became more static and his last northern tour was in 1756. In 1771 the family moved to London, where the musical talents of his sons, **Charles Wesley** (1757–1834) and Samuel *Wesley (1766–1837, father of the composer and organist **Samuel Sebastian Wesley**), could be fostered and would be more appreciated. Recitals in their Marylebone home were attended by the upper classes.

Among the collections of CW's hymns published in his lifetime were *Hymns on God's Everlasting Love* (1741, 1742), *Hymns on the Lord's Supper* (1745), and *Short Hymns on Select Passages of the Holy Scriptures* (1762), together with others celebrating the major festivals of the Christian year. His hymns (variously computed as totalling 6,500 or as many as 10,000) are marked by their strong doctrinal content (notably the *Arminian insistence on the universality of God's love), a richness of scriptural and literary allusion, and the variety of his metrical and stanza forms. They have become part of the worship of Christians of many denominations throughout the world. His poetry included epistles, elegies and political and satirical verse.

See also **Collection of Hymns**; **Hymn-books**

T. Jackson (1841); J. Telford (1900); Frederick Luke Wiseman (1932); J.E. Rattenbury (1941); J.E. Rattenbury (1948); F. Baker (1948); F.C. Gill (1964); F. Baker (1988a); S.T. Kimbrough and O.A. Beckerlegge (1988–92); J.A. Vickers (1990); S.T. Kimbrough (1992)

J A V

Wesley, Rev. John (1703–91), born 17 June 1703 (OS), the second surviving son of the family at *Epworth rectory. His classical education as a 'gown-boy' at the Charterhouse, London (1713–20) built on foundations his mother had laid and prepared him for his years at Christ Church, Oxford (1720–24). The influence of a 'religious friend' (probably Sally *Kirkham at Stanton,

Glos) and his reading of Thomas à Kempis and J. *Taylor, together with the prospect of taking holy orders, cause him in 1725 to become more serious in his religious life and as part of his self-discipline he began to keep a *diary in which he plotted his spiritual health.

Ordained deacon in 1725 and priest in 1728, in 1726 he was elected Fellow of Lincoln College, but was soon absent helping his father in his two Lincolnshire parishes. He returned to Oxford in 1729 to find his brother Charles involved with other religiously inclined students in the activities of what became known as the *'Holy Club' and by seniority and natural ability became its leader. He was influenced at this time by the writings of W. *Law, especially his *Christian Perfection* (1726) and *Serious Call* (1729), distancing himself more and more from 'worldly' pursuits and pleasures and beginning to distinguish in his own mind and in his preaching between mere 'formal' religion and wholehearted devotion to God. But his own relation with God was, as he would later put it, still that of a servant rather than of a son.

Although he had found reasons for refusing a plea that he should leave Oxford in favour of the Lincolnshire livings, quite soon after his father's death in 1735 he agreed to go out to the newly established colony of Georgia as pastor to the first settlers in Savannah (and with some idea of evangelizing the local Indians). The venture was a humiliating disaster. His attempts to live by and to advocate strict rules of conduct, which he derived from primitive Christianity, were unacceptable to the majority of the settlers; and, inhibited by the ideal of clerical celibacy (and perhaps the still powerful influence of his mother), he seriously mishandled a love affair with Sophy Hopkey and was forced to leave in haste by a threat of legal action by her uncle, the storekeeper and chief magistrate. But he had learned some lessons in the process, if only negative ones, had translated hymns from the German and published his first *hymn-book (the *'Charlestown Hymn-book').

Above all, he had encountered the simple faith of the *Moravians and on his return to London early in 1738 was actively seeking it for himself. Influenced by P. *Böhler and others, on 24 May 1738, at a meeting of a *religious society in Nettleton Court, Aldersgate Street, and through hearing the words of Martin Luther, he felt his heart 'strangely warmed' by a realisation that the love of Christ, focused in the Cross, was for him personally. This did not bring an immediate end to his seeking, but did mark a significant turning point.

Whether 'Aldersgate Street' or his newly acquired seriousness in 1725 is to be accounted a 'conversion' experience has been debated at length and is largely a matter of definition.

The peripatetic ministry which occupied his remaining years did not begin immediately. He first visited the Moravian settlement at Herrnhut in Saxony, where he observed the community life and worship. *En route* he met its leader, Count *Zinzendorf. On his return he began to travel more widely, though at first only between London, *Oxford and *Bristol, with occasional visits to *Salisbury, where his widowed mother was now living with the Westley *Halls. In March 1739 he was persuaded by G. *Whitefield to 'become more vile' and begin *field preaching in Bristol, and soon afterwards undertook the building of the *'New Room' to house two religious societies which looked to him for leadership. In London his relations with the *Fetter Lane Society became strained as it increasingly embraced what he deemed to be the dangerous doctrine of *stillness and in July 1740 he led a number of the members in a secession, forming a new society in the *Foundery, which became his London headquarters for the next 40 years.

The Evangelical Movement had already begun, especially in *Wales, before JW's return from Georgia, and he and his brother Charles were now caught up in it. Societies looking to him for leadership began to be formed further and further afield and it was not only evangelical zeal, but the need for pastoral care of (and the exercise of discipline among) those who looked to him for spiritual guidance which led to his ever-increasing journeys throughout the British Isles. He defended his intrusion into other men's parishes by asserting that, as Fellow of an Oxford college, he looked upon the whole world as his parish. In 1742 he made his first visits to the north of England, where *Newcastle was to become his northern headquarters. In 1743 he first visited the *West Midlands, soon to be the cradle of the industrial revolution, and paid the first of many visits to Cornwall. In 1747 he crossed to *Ireland and in 1751 went north into *Scotland, despite the strong presence of a *Calvinistic Kirk. In many cases his first visit to a locality was in response to invitations from individuals or from groups which were already in existence and were happy to be linked with other societies 'in connexion with Mr Wesley'.

While he could not match the eloquent preaching of G. *Whitefield, JW was a born organizer and leader and so was able to consolidate the results of his own preaching and that of others, including the lay preachers on whom he increasingly relied to exercise spiritual oversight in his absence. His societies were provided with Rules and the members periodically examined to ensure that they were 'walking worthily' of the faith they professed. Because the danger of *antinomianism was a serious bugbear to anyone proclaiming *justification by *faith, W constantly reiterated the need to spread 'scriptural *holiness' and to pursue the easily misinterpreted '*Christian perfection'.

Relations with his brother Charles were intimate, but never easy, especially after CW's gradual withdrawal from their joint itinerant ministry following his marriage in 1749. CW was the stauncher Churchman and grew increasingly distressed and alarmed by the signs that his brother was drifting out of the Church.

From the outset JW had seen his mission in terms of the spiritual renewal of a lethargic *CofE and had no intention of creating a new denomination. He could, after all, claim merely to be extending to national level what other clergy had done locally in their oversight of religious societies. Nevertheless, the dynamics of the movement, reinforced by the limited response from within the Church, not least among his fellow clergy, meant that a gap steadily widened between them and was virtually, if still not formally, complete by the time of his death. The succession of irregularities (such as *field preaching coupled with his peripatetic ministry, the employment of lay preachers and, later, his *ordinations for *America and elsewhere) into which he was persuaded in response to changing circumstances and challenges made an eventual separation inevitable.

*Politically, JW was a Tory and a loyal Hanoverian; hence his support of the Government against the American colonists in 1775, despite his earlier counsels of moderation. In matters of doctrine he went to great lengths to insist that he taught nothing that was not part of Anglican teaching, citing the Articles and Homilies extensively to support that claim. It has been an academic commonplace that he was no theologian, i.e. that he produced no systematic theology to which his name could be attached. More recently A.C. Outler (1991) has promoted him as a 'folk-theologian' whose teaching, though designed to instruct the masses, had its own coherence. R.L. Maddox (1994) has shown the extent to which, despite his repeated claim to consistency over decades, W's teaching was modified in some key respects, in response to changing circumstances

and to incorporate new insights. Maddox and other American scholars have demonstrated that his theology, however pragmatic and pastorally motivated, warrants serious scholarly attention. Wesley was steering a middle course between the moralistic heresy of *salvation by works and the ultra-Protestant, potentially *antinomian heresy of salvation by *faith alone, to arrive at a doctrine of salvation by *grace which left room for both divine initiative and human response: from one point of view a characteristically Anglican *via media*. 'Faith working by love' (Gal. 5:6) was one of his favourite phrases. His preoccupation with the process of salvation justifies the view that his teaching was not so much a theology as a soteriology.

An aspect of both W brothers that was underplayed or conveniently overlooked by nineteenth century Wesleyanism is their sacramentalism. A century before the Oxford Movement, and in the face of a widespread neglect of the Eucharist in the eighteenth century Church, JW urged 'constant communion' on his followers. He himself both received and administered the *Lord's Supper as often as circumstances allowed, seeing it as a 'converting ordinance' and a vital *'means of grace'. He published his brother's sacramental hymns in *Hymns on the Lord's Supper* (1745), stressing the 'real [though spiritual] presence' of Christ, and the sacrament as a 'sacrifice' in a way uncharacteristic of eighteenth century Anglicanism as a whole.

His hesitant and ineffectual approaches to marriage culminated in the tangled affair with G. *Murray, which CW aborted in 1749 by marrying her off to J. *Bennet, to his brother's deep distress. Just over a year later, on the rebound, he precipitately married Mrs Mary Vazeille, the widow of a City banker. The marriage was probably doomed from the outset by his determination not to travel one mile or preach one sermon less than before and was embittered by his wife's understandable jealousy of his intimate (albeit innocent) correspondence with women friends. When she died in 1781 they had been separated for some years.

JW was a man of his age in at least two contrasted ways. His instinctive appeal to reason and experiential evidence was characteristic of the *Enlightenment, though in his public debates it often took the form of logic-chopping as much as reasoned argument. At the same time, he shared the popular belief in witchcraft and was given to finding the hand of providence in an escape from accidents or a timely change in the weather. Throughout his life he remained the Oxford tutor, e.g. in his concern for the education of the itinerant preachers and his society members as a whole, in his educational ventures and above all in his writing and *publishing (notably in the *Christian Library). Pamphlets and more substantial volumes on a wide variety of subjects and totalling around 500 titles poured from his pen, despite his extensive travels.

The object in earlier years of many and varied charges, ranging from 'hypocrite' and 'charlatan' to 'Jacobite' and 'Papist', and above all *'enthusiast', JW outlived most of his critics (except for the new generation of *Calvinists exemplified by R. *Hill) and came to be seen as a venerable institution of the national life, even by many who held aloof from Methodism itself. Seven years before he died he made provision for the continuance of the movement through the *Deed of Declaration; but his own stance remained sufficiently equivocal to provide his heirs and successors with a legacy of conflicting attitudes towards the Church from which he had never formally separated or been excluded, despite flouting its lax discipline whenever it hindered the progress of his mission.

The earliest biographies were by J. Hampson (3 vols, 1791), a hastily compiled official biography by T. Coke and H. Moore (1792) and its rival by J. Whitehead (2 vols, 1793, 1796). In the early nineteenth century there were lives by H. Moore (2 vols, 1824, 1825) and, from outside Methodism, by Robert Southey (2 vols, 1820). Later major works include L. Tyerman (3 vols, 1870–71; 4th edition 1878), J.S. Simon (5 vols, 1921–34) and M. Schmidt (3 vols, 1962, 1972, 1973). Single-volume lives, both popular and scholarly, have continued to appear, most recently those of H. Rack (1989; revised 1992) and R.P. Heitzenrater (1995). For the significance of his 'conversion', see J.E. Rattenbury (1938) and R.L. Maddox (1990).

Collected editions of Wesley's *Works* appeared in 1771–74, 1809–13 (edited by J. Benson) and 1829–31 (edited by T. Jackson). Editions of his *Journal* (edited by N. Curnock, 1909–16), his *Sermons* (edited by E.H. Sugden, 1921) and his *Letters* (edited by J. Telford, 1931) are in the process of being superseded by the on-going *Oxford* (now *Bicentennial*) *Edition*, begun in 1975.

Wesley as preacher is dealt with by W.L. Doughty (1955), A.C. Outler (1984) and R.P. Heitzenrater (in R. Sykes (1998) pp. 12–40). His theology is examined by Colin W. Williams (1960), A.C. Outler (1964 & 1991), W.S. Gunter (1989), J.A. Newton (1989) and R.L. Maddox

(1994); his social ethics in M. Marquardt (1992). For his relations with the Church of England, see F. Baker (1970).

J. Stacey (1988) approaches him from a variety of perspectives.

JAV

Wesley, Samuel (1766–1837), younger son of CW, born in Bristol. He showed musical talent at the age of 3 and at 8 presented a draft of his oratorio *Ruth* to William Boyce, who had described him as 'the English Mozart'. He entered enthusiastically into London's musical life, but found many church openings barred to a 'Wesley'. Disillusioned with the general quality of church music, he became for a time a Roman Catholic, attending the Chapel of the Portuguese Embassy where his friend Vincent Novello was music director. For many years he was chiefly remembered as the first English apostle of J.S. Bach and the father of the cathedral organist and composer **Samuel Sebastian Wesley** (1810–76). However, later research and reassessment has shown that he was one of the greatest English performers and composers, whose output, though varied, included organ voluntaries, harpsichord and piano pieces, anthems, symphonies, concertos and choral works. In later life he was music adviser to WM and published a book of *Original Hymn Tunes, adapted to every metre in the collection of the Rev. John Wesley AM*.

G.J. Stevenson (1876) pp. 490–538; J.T. Lightwood (1937); E. Routley (1968) chs.4–6; F. Routh (1973)

PLC

Wesley Banner and Revival Record , a monthly periodical edited by S. *Dunn, ran from 1849 to 1854, from 1852 under the title *Wesley Banner and Christian Family Visitor*. Contributors were named and included W. *Griffith and J. *Everett. The first issue contained little that was inflammatory, apart from 'Reasons for not signing Mr. Osborn's Declaration', protesting at a permitted declaration being turned into a compulsory test. It denied any support for such innovations as lay delegates to Conference and claimed merely to be the voice of the minority in Conference. The periodical was nevertheless condemned by the Nottingham and Derby District Meeting (of which Dunn was a member) for its 'tendency to promote strifes and divisions, and to endanger the peace of our Societies'. Among the reasons for the expulsion of Dunn and Griffith at the 1849 Conference was their refusal to discontinue its publication.

———

B. Gregory (1898) pp. 450–1, 458

JAV

Wesley Bible Union was founded in 1913 by a small group of WM ministers and laity in the aftermath of the controversy over G. *Jackson's *Fernley Lecture of 1912. Prominent among the laity were W.S. *Allen, J.W. *Laycock, R.W. *Perks The Union saw Jackson's lecture and his appointment to the staff of *Didsbury College as symptoms of a drift towards Modernism within WM. Through public meetings, pamphlets, a monthly journal, speeches in Synods and Conference, and disciplinary charges against alleged Modernists, it sought to enforce strict adherence to WM *doctrinal standards. Failure in this campaign and disillusionment with the proposed doctrinal clauses in the *Deed of Union led to secessions and to the rebirth of the WBU in 1931 as the non-denominational and ultra-conservative British Bible Union, which amalgamated in 1955 with the Bible Testimony Fellowship and later with the Advent Testimony and Preparation Movement.

MW

Wesley College, Bristol was formed in 1967 by the amalgamation of *Headingley College and *Didsbury College (which had moved from Manchester in 1951). Under its first Principal, R.E. *Davies, it fought for survival during the second round of cuts in theological colleges in the early 1970s and escaped closure by a close vote in Conference in 1972. It built up a strong reputation for biblical studies and church history through the contributions of K. *Grayston, W.D. *Stacey and R.E. *Davies and others to the Department of Theology in the University of Bristol. In 1993 links with the West of England Ministerial Training Course were formed and in 1994 a new BA degree was validated by the University of the West of England.

TSAM

Wesley College, Dublin was founded in 1845 as the WM Connexional School at St Stephen's Green. Among its notable pupils in the early days were Sir R. *Hart and George Bernard Shaw. In 1879 the College moved to a new site at St Stephen's Green, beside the Methodist Centenary Church. When girls were admitted in 1911 it became one of the few co-educational secondary schools at that time. In 1964 land was acquired at Ludford Park, an attractive 50-acre site at the foot of the Dublin Mountains. The school moved to this site in 1969 and Dundrum Methodist Church was built close by in 1978. The college enjoys a high reputation and with 840 pupils, including about 200 boarders, is one of the largest Protestant secondary schools in the Republic.

———

E. Armitage (1995)

NWT

Wesley College, Sheffield see **Sheffield**

Wesley Deaconess Order see **Deaconess Orders; Diaconate**

Wesley Fellowship, an inter-denominational society devoted to the understanding and interpretation of Wesleyan Arminian doctrine and devotion, was founded in 1985 by Dr H. McGonigle, Principal of the British Isles Nazarene Theological College and Drs A.S. *Wood and W. Parkes of the Methodist Church. It was conceived as a Wesleyan response to the *Calvinistic outlook of the Westminster Fellowship. Though not strictly either a theological or a historical society, it seeks to promote the total Wesleyan ethos within an evangelical affirmation. Its activities include residential conferences, a regular newsletter and other publishing. There is a special concern for an acceptable understanding and interpretation of entire *sanctification or 'perfect love'.

WP

Wesley Guild, a youth movement launched in 1896 by C.H. *Kelly and W.B. *Fitzgerald, who became its first connexional secretary. At the WM Conference that year opposition from conservatives such as D.T. *Young, who were suspicious of any suggestion of 'entertainment', was counterbalanced by the support of H.P. *Hughes and J.S. *Lidgett. The Guild was conceived as 'a Young People's Society, . . . holding weekly or periodical meetings for devotional, literary and social purposes', together with an emphasis on Christian service. Its motto was 'One heart, one way' and members renewed their vows annually in the light of the Guild Charter, which spoke of 'a wholehearted consecration of Body, Soul and Spirit to the Lord Jesus Christ' and of the 'diligent culture of the mind' in order to 'give God thoughtful and intelligent service.'

The Guild provided an effective means of recruiting and training *Sunday School teachers, *local preachers and other church officers. Fitzgerald's vigorous and enterprising leadership was effected through the *Guild Manual* and a monthly magazine. The wide range of its activities proved a winning attraction and in the first decade, reinforced by vigorous recruiting methods, local Guilds nose from 620 to 1,920 with a membership of 133,228. Guild Holidays began early in the new century; the first National Guild Conference was held in *Sheffield at Easter 1907. Other activities included a Christian Youth Campaign and a Pen and Camera Club. An important part of its commitment to service was its support of *medical missions in West Africa: Ilesha hospital, *Nigeria (built 1922 and completely rebuilt 1952); Ituk Mbang, *Côte d'Azure (1930); and Segbwema, *Sierra Leone, which developed from a dispensary into a fully equipped hospital in the 1930s. In 1943 the 'Methodist Guild Department' became part of the new Methodist Youth Department, but later reverted to its original title 'Wesley Guild'.

MR 25 May 1939; W. Leary (1995)

JAV

Wesley Historical Society Formed *c.* 1888 on the suggestion of G. *Stampe to R. *Green, the Society began as a small group of enthusiasts among whom a 'Manuscript Journal' was circulated. It was given a formal constitution and a wider membership in 1893 and held its first meeting during the 1894 WM Conference in *Birmingham. Other founding members included F.F. *Bretherton, C.H. *Crookshank, W.F. *Moulton, M. *Riggall, J.H. *Ritson, G.S. *Rowe, J. *Telford and T.E. *Westerdale. A spasmodic series of 'occasional publications' began in 1896. The quarterly (now triannual) *Proceedings* began publication in 1897. The first editor was the Rev. R. Waddy Moss. Despite its misleadingly restrictive name, one aim of the Society from the outset has been 'to promote the study of the History and Literature of Methodism', but only in recent years has it broken free of its Wesleyan moorings and encompassed non-WM and more recent Methodist history.

The first Annual Lecture was given during the Methodist Conference of 1934 by Dr H. *Bett on 'The Early Methodist Preachers'. The Society's Library, originating as a bequest of books and other material by Bretherton, was set up in the crypt of *Wesley's Chapel in 1959, moved temporarily to the nearby Epworth House in 1972, then to *Southlands College and in 1992 to *Westminster College, Oxford.

An autonomous Irish Branch, affiliated to the parent Society, was formed in 1926. The first of what became 16 'local branches' throughout England, Scotland and the Isle of Man, was organized in East Anglia in 1958. Each Branch is informally associated with the Society, arranges lectures and pilgrimages and publishes a journal or bulletin.

PWHS 6 pp. 64–6, 24 pp. 26–35, 41–4, 32 pp. 38–9, 37 pp. 33–6

JAV

Wesley House, Cambridge. In response to increasing numbers of ministerial students in WM after 1920, a house near Cheshunt College was rented and H.M. *Hughes was appointed Principal. Through the generosity of M. *Gutteridge and **William Greenhalgh**, Wesley House was built in Jesus Lane and opened in 1926, with special links to Jesus and Fitzwilliam Colleges within the University. Most students were entered for the theology tripos as part of their ministerial training. R.N. *Flew, tutor from 1928, succeeded as Principal in 1937 and was followed by W.F. *Flemington in 1955, E.G. *Rupp in 1967, M.J. *Skinner in 1974 and B.E. Beck in 1980. The college survived the cuts of the 1970s through its semi-independent character, protected by a special Trust Deed. It is now part of an ecumenical Federation of Theological Colleges in Cambridge.

W.B. Brash (1935) pp. 104–11; Frank Tice (1966) pp. 91–8; *PWHS* 49 pp. 44–54

TSAM

Wesley's Chapel, City Road, London, sometimes called 'the mother Church of World Methodism', but perhaps more plausibly, the 'cathedral of British Methodism'. After nearly 50 years at the *Foundery, in 1778 JW moved a short distance north-west and built his 'New Chapel' on what was then 'the Royal Row'. The site was allocated to him by the City authorities in 1776 and he launched a nationwide appeal to his followers in aid of a building fund. His architect was George Dance the Younger, surveyor to the City of London, who was at that time busy developing the Finsbury estate on part of Moorfields to the south. The builder was Samuel Tooth, a member of the *Foundery society. JW laid the foundation stone on 21 April 1777 and the chapel was opened on 1 November 1778. The following year he moved into the house he built on the south side of the forecourt. W described the chapel as 'perfectly neat, but not fine'; but the move from a multi-purpose building to a 'chapel' was symptomatic of Methodism's 'coming of age' and of the accelerating drift from the Church of England towards denominational independence.

Over the years there have been various changes, especially to the interior. The walls are now covered with memorials and the windows are of stained glass. The ships' masts that originally supported the gallery (said to have been the gift of King George III) were replaced in 1891 by pillars of French jasper, the gift of Methodist Churches overseas. Only the top section of the three-decker pulpit survives. The location of the original sanctuary in an apse behind the pulpit was common in the 'auditory' churches of the time, though swept away by the nineteenth century Oxford Movement. (This 'City Road arrangement' was copied in a number of early nineteenth-century WM churches, but survives only in Northbrook Street, Newbury.) The present sanctuary in front of the pulpit dates from the 1970s restoration. Following a serious fire in 1879, the Adam-style ceiling (reputed to have been the widest unsupported ceiling in England in its day) was replaced by a replica. Because of the swampy nature of the site the foundations had to be strengthened in 1891 and again in the 1970s. After major restoration, the Chapel was reopened on 1 November 1978 in the presence of HM Queen Elizabeth II and the Duke of Edinburgh.

JW is buried in the graveyard behind the Chapel, along with many of his followers. His house was converted to a museum and opened in 1898. The Museum of Methodism opened in the crypt in 1984. Among the many notable events in the Chapel's history are the inaugural meeting of the WMMS in 1818, the first Oecumenical (now World) Methodist Conference in 1881 and the opening service of the Uniting Conference at the time of *Methodist Union in 1932. On the first Sunday in September, at the beginning of the Methodist year, the *President of the Conference by tradition preaches in the Chapel and many *ordination services have been held there. Since 1989 its union with the *Leysian Mission has enhanced its continuing role as a centre of worship and service to the community.

MR(W) 1901 pp. 27–9; G.J. Stevenson (1872); J. Telford (n.d.); M.W. Woodward (1966)

JAV

Wesleyan Methodist Association, originally called the Wesleyan Association, was one of the smaller branches of Methodism which later became part of the *UMFC. It resulted from the *Warrenite controversy of 1834–35 over the establishment of a 'theological institution'. In 1833 the WM Conference appointed a committee, of which J. *Bunting was a member, to make proposals for the education of candidates for the ministry. This committee not only formulated a scheme, but nominated Bunting as 'President of the Theological Institution'. Bunting already held several offices and had twice been President of the Conference and many felt that too much authority was being concentrated in one man's hands. Dr S. *Warren, Superintendent of the *Manchester First Circuit, led the opposition and published his *Remarks on the Wesleyan Theological Institution*. For this he was suspended from his superintendency. The 1834 Conference approval of the scheme aroused opposition in the circuits, especially in the north. Eventually delegates of the dissidents met and called their first Annual Assembly in Manchester in 1836, having been joined the previous year by the *Protestant Methodists. The outlines of a constitution were worked out, including the principles of free representation in the Assembly and the independence of the circuits. The following year they reported 21,000 members. By the time they joined with the *Wesleyan Reformers in 1857 to form the UMFC, this figure had dropped to around 20,000.

See also **Eckett, Robert**

M. Baxter (1865)

OAB

'Wesleyan Quadrilateral', a term apparently coined by Albert C. Outler to describe the four interacting sources of authority in JW's theology. The term has become part of Methodist theological jargon, especially in America. W expanded the Anglican triad of *Scripture, reason and tradition by adding 'experience'. As *homo unius libri* he maintained the primacy of Scripture, but regularly linked it with reason (as a necessary tool of understanding and interpretation) and sometimes with tradition ('Christian antiquity' together with the accumulated wisdom of Anglicanism). To these he added, more explicitly than hitherto in Anglican theology, the role of experience in confirming scriptural truth or judging between rival interpretations. R.L. Maddox has described the quadrilateral as 'a unilateral *rule* of Scripture within a trilateral *hermeneutic* of reason, tradition, and experience'.

See also **'Experimental Religion'**

A.C. Outler (1991) pp. 21–37; R.L. Maddox (1994) pp. 36–47; B. Tabraham (1995) pp. 15–21; W.S. Gunter (1997)

JAV

Wesleyan Reform Union originated during the struggles for reform in WM in the mid-nineteenth century, brought to a head by the anonymous *Fly Sheets and the expulsion of J. *Everett and others in 1849. Wesleyan Reformers regard this as their year of origin, but 'Wesleyan Reform' was not, at that time, a new denomination, but an agenda for change within WM itself. Thus, at the Reformers' Delegate Meeting of 1852, a Declaration of Principles was drawn up, insisting that 'Christ is Head over all things to His Church' and that 'preachers of the Gospel are not 'lords over God's heritage'. To this was added a 'solemn demand' for 'the complete and immediate repeal of all rules and regulations whereby the rights and liberties of the People ... have been restricted or destroyed' and that 'all future deliberations affecting the interests of the Church ... be conducted in the presence of the people, who shall ... be fully and fairly represented.'

By 1859 hope of reform and reconciliation had waned and the Delegate Meeting of that year drew up a formal Constitution under the designation 'Wesleyan Reform Union', incorporating the 1852 Declaration and explicitly affirming the autonomy of the local church. It also provided for an annual Conference and an elected Executive Committee to act between Conferences. Initially a chairman was elected at the commencement of each Conference session, but from 1864 there was provision for an annual Presidency.

Nevertheless, it is clear from numerical returns that the Union had limited success in maintaining itself as a distinct movement without disintegration. As early as 1857 no fewer than 20,000 out of a membership of 46,000 amalgamated with the *WMA to form the *UMFC and within two years membership had further reduced to 17,000. By 1881 numbers were down to just over 7,000. Thereafter the decline was less rapid and the 1998 returns showed a membership of 2,279 meeting in 115 chapels. Theologically, the Union has strongly maintained its identity as an evangelical Methodist body and is a member of the Free Churches' Council and the Evangelical Alliance. Its headquarters are in *Sheffield.

Origin and History of the WRU (Sheffield, 1896); W.H. Jones (1952)

GDL

Wesleyan Reformers, a constituent part of the *UMFC which arose out of the expulsion of three WM ministers, J. *Everett, S. *Dunn and W. *Griffith, for their refusal to incriminate themselves on charges of having written the *Fly Sheets. This met with condemnation throughout the Connexion and, eventually, the loss of 100,000 members. In 1857 about half of them joined with the *WMA to form the *UMFC. The rest continued as the *Wesleyan Reform Union.

B. Gregory (1898) pp. 433–577; E.C. Urwin (1949); O.A. Beckerlegge (1957)

OAB

Wesleyan Takings sub-titled 'Centenary Sketches of Ministerial Character, as exhibited in the Wesleyan Connexion during the first hundred Years of its Existence', was published during the WM Conference at *Newcastle upon Tyne in 1840 and gave offence because of its highly critical nature. It consisted of a series of satirical biographical sketches, notably of J. *Bunting (placed first in the book but, unlike the rest, not named explicitly), who was depicted as intolerably autocratic, 'a monster of greatness'. A Preface added to the 3rd edition was condemned by the Conference of 1841 as 'unworthy of any person maintaining the Christian or ministerial character'. A second volume appeared in 1851, when the Conference was again in Newcastle. It contained a further attack on Bunting, reprinted from the *Wesleyan Times* Both volumes were published anonymously, but the main suspicion fell on J. *Everett, who, as he also did with regard to the *Fly Sheets, refused to incriminate himself before the 1841 Conference.

WL

Wesleyan Times was launched in January 1849 as an anti-Conference weekly newspaper, the successor to the debt-ridden *Wesleyan*. Within a few months it had published the letters of **Francis Pearson** which led to the formation of the *LPMAA and following the expulsion of J. *Everett, W. *Griffith and S. *Dunn it spearheaded the WR campaign, with countrywide reports of protest meetings. Published by John Kaye & Co. at 80 Fleet Street, by 1852 it claimed a sale double that of the *Watchman. G.J. *Stevenson was proprietor and editor 1861–67. Following a change of title to *Methodist Times* in 1867, it ceased publication in 1869.

PWHS 28 p. 37; G. Smith (1858–61) 3 pp. 503–4, 511–13, 515

EAR

Wesleyanism was a term used, at least occasionally, from as early as 1740 to distinguish the followers of JW from other Methodists such as 'Whitefieldites' and the *Countess of Huntingdon's Connexion. But it did not come into more general and formal use until early in the nineteenth century, when it served to differentiate the 'Original Connexion' from its offshoots (see below) and from *Welsh Calvinistic Methodism. Thus the 'new Kingswood' established in Yorkshire in 1811 was described as 'the Wesleyan Academy at *Woodhouse Grove'; in 1813 the first District Missionary Society (and in 1818 its connexional counterpart) was labelled 'Wesleyan Methodist'; and in 1822 'Wesleyan' was added to the title of the connexional *Methodist Magazine*. Throughout most of the century, however, the key phrase was 'Wesleyan Methodist Society'; not until 1891 did the Conference approved the change to 'Wesleyan Methodist Church', and this change was not reflected on the quarterly *class tickets until December 1893.

'Wesleyanism' was thus that part of JW's movement which stemmed most directly from his ministry and the provisions he made towards the end of his life (notably by the *Deed of Declaration in 1784) to perpetuate its fruits. But in 1791 the determination of the preachers in *Conference 'to follow strictly the plan which Mr Wesley left us at his death' proved too ambiguous a formula to guarantee unanimity. WM was divided into two camps, the 'Old Planners' who continued to see themselves as 'Methodist Anglicans' and the 'New Planners' who were eager to cut the umbilical cord by which they were still attached to Mother Church.

Inevitably, unresolved issues occupied the Conference and exercised the minds of both ministry and laity. The most contentious of these were the status and role of the *itinerant preachers (and the *pastoral office they fulfilled), their administration of the *Lord's Supper in the Methodist chapels and the timing of Methodist services in 'church hours'. Control of the chapels by the *Superintendents (representing the *Conference) rather than by the lay *trustees, was a vital factor in these issues. Although laymen held an increasing range of connexional offices, they were not admitted to the WM Conference until 1878.

During the Napoleonic period the WM hierarchy was desperately eager to demonstrate its patriotism to an administration fearful of any sign of radicalism, and both the leadership and much of the membership remained politically well to the right of the other Methodist bodies. One early result of the internal struggles after W's death was the formation of the *MNC in 1797. Other

secessions followed in the nineteenth century: notably the *Protestant Methodists (1827), the *Wesleyan Methodist Association (1835) and the *Wesleyan Reform movement, from which sprang the *United Methodist Free Churches (1857). In addition there were non-WM bodies which the old Wesleyan wineskins could not contain: *Primitive Methodism from 1811, the *Bible Christians from 1815, and the short-lived *Tent Methodism (from 1814). Although triggered by expulsions from WM, these were not secessions, but fresh outbursts of the evangelical fervour which had characterized Methodism's earliest days. Other smaller dissenting groups found their way into the *IM fold. This fissiparous tendency was partially reversed by the formation of the UMFC, and more fully by the successive *Methodist Unions of 1907 and 1932. Despite these developments, WM remained by far the largest of the Methodist denominations. It continued to cherish what it believed to be its special relationship with the Established Church and was slow to recognise its place in the Nonconformist camp, at least until the rise of Anglo-Catholicism. Nevertheless *Pusey's belated overtures in 1868 proved stillborn and were scornfully rejected.

In 1851 (the year of the *Religious Census) WM *membership was double that of all others combined, despite substantial losses during the recent Reform agitation. By 1932 the gap had narrowed, but WM membership in England was still 447,122 against a combined total of 338,568 from PM and the UM Church.

In America 'Wesleyan' is often used in phrases like 'Wesleyan theology', where it is synonymous with 'Methodist' in the sense of 'derived from or associated with the tradition originating with the Wesleys'. The Wesleyan Holiness Church, theologically conservative and evangelical in its stance, is of nineteenth century American origin, with a minimal presence in England.

R.E. Davies (1976) pp. 113–34; J.M. Turner (1985); B. Tabraham (1995) pp. 63–74

JAV

West Indies   Methodism was introduced into Antigua in 1760 by N. *Gilbert, when he began preaching to his slaves and formed a society which grew to 200 members during his lifetime. A Mulatto woman and a Negress kept it together until the shipwright J. *Baxter arrived in 1778 and took over the leadership. T. *Coke's missionary *Address* of 1786 included the West Indies among the four proposed mission fields and on Christmas morning that year he landed at St. John's, Antigua, with three missionary companions appointed by the British Conference. They were stationed in Antigua, St Vincent and St Christopher. On later visits he left missionaries in Dominica, Barbados, Nevis, Tortola and Jamaica. By the time of his fourth and last visit to the islands in 1792–93, membership had grown to 6,570 and there were twelve missionaries stationed in ten of the islands. The mission was extended to the Bahamas in 1803 and to Trinidad (ruled by the Spanish until 1797) in 1809. When Coke died in 1814, in spite of opposition from some of the plantation owners, who persecuted both missionaries and their converts, there were twelve Caribbean circuits with a membership of 17,000. Later developments included Haiti (1817) and Honduras (1825).

The West Indies were therefore British Methodism's earliest mission field, with the negro *slaves being its main concern and beneficiaries. An autonomous West Indies Conference was formed in 1885, divided in 1894 into Western and Eastern sections. But for financial reasons, in 1903 the WMMS resumed responsibility for the work. Finally, in 1967 the Methodist Church of the Caribbean and the Americas (MCCA) was inaugurated, with its headquarters in Antigua, bringing together six former Methodist Districts (Guyana, Honduras, Jamaica and Haiti, Leeward Islands, Panama and Costa Rice, and South Caribbean) with another (Bahamas) added in 1968. Methodism is a partner in the ecumenical United Theological College in Kingston, Jamaica; and in Antigua Methodists and Anglicans share in the work of the Gilbert Ecumenical Centre. In 1997 the MCCA reported a total membership of 189,295 and an estimated community of 440,600.

W. Moister (1871) pp. 109–54; F&H 2; J.A. Vickers (1969) pp. 149–72, 299–303

JAV

West Midland Counties (Glos, Herefords, Shropshire, Staffs, Warwicks, Worcs) These counties to the east of the Welsh border were still predominantly rural, especially in the south, with the largest and most rapidly growing population in Staffs to the north-east. The *Black Country, especially around *Wednesbury, was the scene of some of the earliest Methodist activity and anti-Methodist violence. Later in the eighteenth century, *Birmingham, the Black Country and the Potteries were affected by industrialization. (JW visited Matthew Boulton's Soho factory and saw the world's first cast-iron bridge being erected

over the Severn Gorge.) The extensive Staffordshire Circuit was in existence from 1749 and was gradually sub-divided until by 1851 the Birmingham and Shrewsbury WM District consisted of 22 circuits with 614 chapels.

PM was the only other branch of Methodism with a significant presence, predominantly in the rural areas. Its stronghold was in Herefordshire and Shropshire, where WM was most thinly scattered. (It was the *Shrewsbury Circuit which established the Brinkworth Mission from which much of PM in southern England stemmed.) It was weakest in Warwickshire. Even in Staffordshire, close to its origins, it had fewer chapels with only half the WM sittings in 1851, though it recorded two thirds of the WM attendances. Originally part of the Tunstall PM District, a separate West Midlands District, with 26 circuits, was not formed until 1873.

In 1851 the *Religious Census recorded 1,112 Methodist places of worship in this Division (including WM: 614; PM:446). By 1989 there were only 745 churches, half of them in the industrialized West Midlands and Staffs, the main centres of population. Total attendances reported in 1851 were 261,670 (12.3% of the population), with the PM figures rivalling the WM only in the afternoon. The evening services (usually the best attended, especially in WM) drew 116,110 worshippers (5.4% of the population). In 1989 adult worshippers totalled 48,600 (1.05%) and membership stood at 50,300 (1.1% of the population).

A.C. Pratt (1891); W.C. Sheldon (1903); *A Brief Sketch of the Rise of Methodism in the County and City of Hereford* (Hereford 1929)

JAV

West Street Chapel, London, was built in the late seventeenth century for a *Huguenot congregation and was rented by JW in 1743 as his base in West London, with the approval of the Archbishop and the Bishop of London. Until the building of his new chapel in City Road, it was usually referred to simply as 'the Chapel', distinguishing it from the *Foundery. CW conducted the first Methodist *Watchnight service there on 3 July 1747. J. *Fletcher hurried there from his ordination in March 1757 to assist JW in administering the *Lord's Supper and, as a consecrated building, it was the scene of regular sacramental services, prolonged by the large numbers of communicants. On 29 November 1759 services were held as part of the General Thanksgiving Day for Wolfe's capture of Quebec; and in 1779 B.B.

*Collins preached at a service inaugurating the Naval and Military Bible Society. In 1798 the society moved to a chapel in Great Queen Street, the forerunner of the Kingsway Hall; but the building still stands, marked by a plaque.

J. Telford (1886); J.C. Bowmer (1951)

JAV

Westbrook, Dr Francis Brotherton (1903–75; e.m. 1926), WM minister, born at Thornton Heath. Trained at *Didsbury College, he continued his musical studies after entering the circuit ministry and obtained a MusD. He was a fine pianist, a notable conductor and composer of anthems, cantatas, organ music and hymn tunes. He was ministerial secretary of the *MCMS for 26 years, Professor of harmony and Counterpoint at the London College of Music 1968–75 and the first Principal of the *Williams School of Church Music, Harpenden 1971–5 – a partial fulfilment of his conviction that there was a very real role for an ordained minister of music in the Methodist Church. He served on the editorial committees of the *School Hymn-book* (1950) and *Hymns and Songs* (1969) and edited *The Choir* magazine 1948–64. Some of his hymn tunes arc in *HP*.

MR 2 Oct. 1975; G.E. Radford (n.d.)

PLC

Westell, Thomas (c.1719–94), a Bristol carpenter who was one of the original members of the *society JW formed there on 4 April 1739. Though still based in Bristol, he was for many years 'half-itinerant', undertaking extensive preaching tours. In 1744, during an early venture into Cornwall, he was arrested while preaching at Camborne and imprisoned at Bodmin. He also faced a hostile mob at *Gwennap Pit. He was one of the first three lay preachers to assist JW and was present at the 1746 Conference. His tombstone at Portland Chapel, Bristol described him as 'a Pattern of Christian Simplicity and humble Love'.

C. Atmore (1801) pp. 86–7

JAV

Westgate (Weardale) *see* **Dales Circuit**

Westhill College, Birmingham, founded in 1907 as a 'training institute for Sunday School workers', was one of the founding members of the federation of Selly Oak Colleges. The Methodist Church was one of the founding trustees and still has a connection through what was formerly MYD. A connexional representative and the Chairman of the Birmingham District serve on the governing body. Successive heads of the Community and Youth Department were the Revs. B.H. *Reed (1946–52), D.S. *Hubery (1953–60) and F.W. *Milson (1960–77). The College is recognized by the Department of Education and Science for the training of teachers, youth leaders, community workers and others engaged in Christian education. Many students come on scholarships from overseas Churches. Its Christian Education Section is the lineal descendant of the original institute. In 1999 the College became a full partner with the University of Birmingham.

MR 29 Oct. & 19 Nov. 1998

EDG

Westminster Central Hall, a monument to Wesleyan triumphalism at the beginning of the twentieth century, was built with money from the *Twentieth Century Fund to house the connexional offices and provide a prestigious meeting place in central London. The site had been occupied by the Royal Westminster Aquarium and Winter Gardens, which closed in 1903 and was bought for over £300,000. A competition for the best design was won by A.B. Rickards, declared by John Betjeman to be 'the greatest exponent of the baroque style in Edwardian London'. The resulting 'Viennese baroque with Romanesque decoration', described by Pevsner as 'surprisingly worldly and surprisingly French' remains an imposing feature of the area, though the flanking towers of the original design and some exterior decoration were never carried out. The domed Great Hall has cantilevered galleries and originally seated 2,700. The Manning statue of JW now stands at the top of the Grand Staircase. The opening service was on 3 October 1912. The first ministers were J.E. *Wakerley (1912–14), D.T. *Young (1914–38), F.L. *Wiseman (1938–39) and W.E. *Sangster (1939–55). The inaugural meeting of the United Nations General Assembly was held there in 1946. The Conference Office moved to Marylebone in 1996, followed by other connexional offices between 1996 and 2000.

MR 26 Sept. 1912; J.V. Ellis (1982); P. Sangster (1982)

JAV

Westminster College was founded in 1851 in Horseferry Road, London, to train teachers for Methodist *day schools. Its buildings were designed by J. *Wilson. In 1872, on the opening of *Southlands College, it became an all-male establishment with some students accepting posts in the new Board Schools. Emphasis on higher education led to an increasing number of entrants qualified for university, so that by 1930 everyone followed a four-year course comprising a London University degree and professional training. In 1959 the college moved to North Hinksey, *Oxford, where it expanded and again admitted women students. Non-graduate trainees reverted to the Certificate course until 1967, when a minority were able to study for the BEd (Oxon) degree. It was one of the few colleges of education to survive the institutional closures of the 1970s without losing its individuality or straying far from its original purposes. It maintained its emphasis on education and theology and, through its centre at Saltley, *Birmingham, retained an interest in inner-city schooling. The campus also houses the Wesley and Methodist Study Centre, including the library of the *WHS. In 1997 it had 2,457 full and part-time students following professional and academic courses, at levels ranging from certificate to doctorate, validated by the University of Oxford and the Open University. It was later adversely affected by a reduction in the number of teacher training students and changes to the Government's funding system which led to consideration of its future as a free-standing college and a decision by the Conference of 1999 that it should be taken over by Oxford Brooks University.

_____

F.C. Pritchard (1951)

DBT

Weymouth (with the adjoining Melcombe Regis), formerly a busy port, was in decline in the early eighteenth century, but became a fashionable resort after 1789 under royal patronage. It was a stronghold of Dissent which, together with the isolation of southern Dorset, may have delayed the arrival of Methodism. (Portland to the south had been visited by CW in 1846 and a society was led by William Nelson – possibly a relative of J. *Nelson – until his death in 1770; Methodism was reintroduced by R.C. *Brackenbury in 1791.) A small society existed in Weymouth from c.1776, when JW preached in its 'new house' (probably the Assembly Room in the King's Head Yard). A chapel was built in Conygar Lane (later 'Lower Bond Street') in 1805, replaced by Maiden Street (designed by J. *Wilson) in 1867. Weymouth remained in the *Salisbury Circuit until 1794, when Blandford Circuit was formed (renamed Poole Circuit in 1797 and Weymouth Circuit in

1805). A short-lived WR society bought the Conygar Lane chapel in 1868, but sold it again in 1880.

A PM Mission, established in 1834 by the Sunderland Circuit, rented the Assembly Rooms, but a dispute between the two itinerants split the society and the mission was taken under the wing of the Manchester Circuit. A chapel was built in Hope Square in 1841. The mission continued small and isolated until revitalized during the ministry (1855–59) of Robert Pattinson (1826–66; e.m.1851). The St Leonard's Road church (1872) was badly damaged in World War II and the society united with Maiden Street in 1962.

_____

J.S. Simon (1870); E.M. Pearson (1967)

JAV

Whatcoat, Richard (1736–1806; e.m. 1769) WM itinerant and Bishop of the MEC, was born in Quinton, Glos. He was one of the two preachers ordained by JW in 1784 for the newly independent USA. As an Elder of the MEC he travelled widely, presiding over groups of circuits and administering the Sacrament. In 1787 the American preachers asserted their independence of JW's authority by declining to make Whatcoat a Bishop alongside *Asbury. In the 1790s he was so disheartened by the O'Kelly disruption that he seriously considered returning home. But in 1800 he was at length elected as Bishop and continued to travel widely, despite increasing physical weakness in his closing years.

See also **Ordination**

_____

WMM 1807 p. 423; W. Phoebus (1828); S.B. Bradley (1936)

JAV

Wheatley, James (d.1775) became a Methodist itinerant _c._ 1742/3 and attended the 1745 Conference. JW at first thought highly of him, but began to have doubts about 1749 and in 1751 in the face of evidence of immoral conduct at Bradford-on-Avon was forced to expel him. Wheatley quickly established himself as an independent preacher in *Norwich, where he proved a controversial figure, attracting both enthusiastic support and violent hostility. The 'Tabernacle' built for him in 1751 was badly damaged by the mob, but another was built in 1753. In 1754 he was charged in the Consistory Court with immorality, found guilty in 1756 and lost two appeals against the verdict. JW unwisely attempted to salvage the Tabernacle society but found its members ungovernable. The WM society in Norwich was compromised for some years by being associated with Wheatley in the public mind.

See also **Antinomianism**

C. Atmore (1801) pp. 488–91; E.J. Bellamy (1994)

JAV

Wheeldon, Elizabeth (*née* Hunt (1796–1841/44?) was a PM itinerant for one year (1822), before marrying Richard Wheeldon, a Belper *local preacher. On his death in 1826 she returned to the itinerancy in Darlaston, then in 1832 in Shefford Circuit, where she faced much persecution, being hit in the eye with a stone. In 1835 she married a fellow itinerant, Samuel West, and they virtually exercised a joint ministry.

PMM, 1827, 1835, 1867

EDG

Whitby By 1750 Methodists were meeting in Cappleman's Yard off Church Street. The arrival of a stonemason William Ripley, who was also a *local preacher, brought growth. JW made his first visit in 1761, preaching on the Abbey Plain and in 1762 an octagonal preaching house was built by Ripley on Henrietta Street, with a larger 7-storey building called Ebenezer added alongside it in 1769. Between 1761 and 1769 the 40 members had become 220, described by JW as the 'most affectionate in England'. He continued to visit every other year, preaching in the octagon, in Baxtergate and in the market place. In 1783 Whitby became a separate circuit. Ripley died in 1786. His daughter Dorothy *Ripley, who became a Quaker, was also a preacher who frequently crossed the Atlantic to campaign against slavery.

In 1787 the octagon chapel collapsed into the sea and a new chapel (later known as 'Wesley') on Church Street was opened by JW in 1788 (closed 1938 because of subsidence). In 1814 Brunswick Chapel was built on the west side of the river. Seating 900, it came to house the larger society. In 1823 a WM day school was built alongside, where the Sunday Schools also flourished. In 1890–91 an enlarged Brunswick, to accommodate summer visitors, was built on the site, together with the adjoining Brunswick Room, with its Dantzig oak panelling and Powell mosaics, financed by a local benefactor and solicitor R.E. Pannett (1834–1920) who was determined that the children should have the best.

W. *Clowes preached at the Town Hall in 1821 so effectively that the PM work 'broke forth like a torrent on the hillside', especially among the fishing community. Chapels were built on Church Street (1841; replaced 1911, closed 1968) and on the Fishburn Park estate (1867). The WM and PM circuits merged in 1944. Brunswick was sold in 1997 and the Whitby Methodists now meet in shared premises (as perhaps at the beginning).

A branch of *NCH was located at Larpool Hall from 1919 to 1966 and in 1955 Moorlands, a Methodist Guild Holiday hotel, opened on the West Cliff.

E.W. Dickinson (1925); S. Davis (1962); J. Marsland (1983); N. Vickers (1992)

JHL

White, John (1866–1933; e.m. 1892), WM missionary. After two years in Transvaal, he moved to Rhodesia, where work had begun in 1891, and served from 1894 to 1932, mainly in Mashonaland. His Shona NT was published in 1907. As District Chairman 1901–26 he travelled extensively, establishing new work north of the Zambezi and among uprooted Africans in the new mine compounds. At Nenguwo he established the Waddilove Institution and was for many years its Principal. Although he attacked brutal African and European practices alike with the same passion for justice, he was known, and in some white circles hated, as a friend of the voiceless, voteless African, notably in the 1896 Shona rebellion, the 1922 famine and the persistent arguments about African land rights. In spite of ill-health he was the acknowledged leader of the regular Missionary Conferences which were influential in the life of the colony.

MR 10 Aug. 1933; C.F. Andrews (1935); H. Davies (1951) pp. 169–80

JRP

White, Richard Henry (1853–1929), PM layman, born in *Redruth. In 1878 he emigrated to South *Australia to manage an engineering company. He and his wife Emily (née Wincey) strongly supported the evangelical campaigns of the Americans Chapman and Alexander in Adelaide and established the undenominational Australasian Chapman-Alexander Bible Institute along the lines of Moody's Chicago Institute, giving their home in Wayville for this purpose. Due to lack of numbers and in view of the strength of Methodism in South Australia, in 1926 White offered the Institute to the Conference and the following year the Methodist Theological Institute opened on the site. The income from a considerable sum of money that became available from

White's estate in 1950 still provides scholarships for lay and ministerial education.

DGH

White, William (b.1794; e.m. 1822), WM missionary, born at Ingleton, Co. Durham. He accompanied S. *Leigh to *New Zealand in 1823, where they established the mission at Wesleydale. Despite his inexperience, he assumed leadership on Leigh's departure at the end of 1823. The following year he made an exploratory visit to the Waikato, possibly the first European to have done so. He returned to England in 1825 in search of a wife, and in his absence the Mission at Whangaroa was sacked and the missionaries took refuge in Sydney. In 1830 he was appointed Superintendent of the new Mission at Mangungu on the Hokianga Harbour and was instrumental in founding several stations on the west coast of the North Island. But his intractable, sometimes choleric character led to soured relationships with his own and his CMS colleagues. His dismissal in 1838 was as much for his trading activities as for alleged improper relationships with Maori women. He continued in business in and around Auckland until his death.

DNZB; M.B. Gittos (1982); M.B. Gittos (1997)

MJF/DJP

Whitefield, George (1714–1770) Anglican clergyman and Methodist preacher, born at the Bell Inn, *Gloucester. He went to Pembroke College, Oxford, and was introduced to the *Holy Club by CW. Deeply moved by reading Scougal's *Life of God in the Soul of Man*, he found personal assurance of salvation in 1735. Ordained in 1736, he began preaching in *London with almost instant success and was attended everywhere by crowded congregations. It was the same when he commenced preaching in *Bristol in January 1737. Returning to *Bristol after his first visit to America, he began to preach out-of-doors in February 1739. He encouraged both JW and CW to this *'field preaching' that same year. On April 29 1739, now excluded from the London churches that had formerly welcomed him, he took his stand in the open space of Lower Moorfields. The huge crowd that attended was a harbinger of the vast congregations that flocked to his preaching in England, Scotland and America for the next thirty years.

Whitefield made seven visits to America, opened an orphanage near Savannah and witnessed amazing scenes of spiritual fervour during his revival preaching in New England. There he became firm friends with Jonathan Edwards and the Tennent brothers, a friendship that greatly strengthened his *Calvinistic convictions. This led to controversy and a break in friendship with the Wesley brothers, and eventually, after many years of uneasy tension, to Methodism dividing in the 1770s into Wesleyan (*Arminian) and Calvinistic branches. Despite this, when Whitefield died at Newburyport, Mass., on 30 September 1770, JW preached his funeral sermon in the London Tabernacle. Whitefield was a humble and sincere Christian, totally devoted to his Lord and his calling. A flaming evangelist with an unquenchable passion to bring men and women to Christ, he possessed extraordinary gifts of oratory and dramatic power to which the great David Garrick bore testimony and which captivated and convicted congregations for three decades. Throughout his life it was he, rather than the Wesleys, who was the archetypal Methodist in the public mind.

C. Atmore (1801) pp. 492–502; A.D. Belben in *LQHR* July 1954 pp. 217–22; H. Davies (1961) pp. 146–83; A. Dallimore (1970, 1980)

HMG

Whitehaven, despite its isolated location, became the most important centre of early Methodism in north-west England. JW paid 25 visits between 1749 and 1788, using the port for visits to *Ireland and the *Isle of Man, and also on journeys to and from the north-east of England and south-western Scotland. During his second visit, in September 1749, he was confronted by CW over his relationship with Grace *Murray. The first chapel was opened in Michael Street in 1761. J. *Cownley and J. *Rowell exercised influential ministries there. Originally in the *Newcastle Round and then in the *Haworth Round, it became the head of a circuit in 1769. The Whitehaven District lasted from 1791 to 1805, being replaced by the growing influence of Carlisle. The Lowther Street chapel was opened in 1877.

PM also had early success in the town, largely through W. *Clowes' preaching tour of 1823, leading to the formation of the Fox Lane society. The sea-going and mining communities were particularly receptive. A WMA chapel opened in Catherine Street in 1836.

J. Burgess (1980)

EL

Whitehead, Dr John (1740(?)-1804), JW's
personal physician and a *local preacher in
London. He joined the Methodists early in life,
became a Quaker and rejoined the Methodists in
1784. He studied medicine at Leiden and was
a physician to the London Dispensary. He was
present at JW's death and preached his funeral
sermon. As one of W's literary executors he was
appointed to write the official biography, but a
dispute over his remuneration led to disagreement
over the possession of W's papers, fuelled by
his distrust of the itinerants and the authority of
Conference. As a result, he was expelled from the
London pulpits and the other literary executors T.
*Coke and H. *Moore hastened to publish their
official biography in 1792. Whitehead's two volumes followed in 1793 and 1796. In 1798, after
he had restored W's papers to the Conference,
there was a reconciliation and Whitehead
composed the inscription for the memorial tablet
to JW in *Wesley's Chapel. The large crowds
attending his own funeral were proof of the respect
in which he was held.

L.F. Church (1949) pp. 40–1; R.P. Heitzenrater
(1984) 2 pp. 170–3; R.P. Heitzenrater (1995)
pp. 314–15

EWD

Whitehead, Silvester (1841–1917; e.m.
1865), WM missionary in *China from 1866 until
his return in 1876 because of his wife's health.
He remained one of the foremost missionary advocates, became Chairman of the Halifax and Bradford District in 1897 and was President of the
1904 Conference. From 1905 until his retirement
in 1910 he was Governor and Tutor in Pastoral
Theology at *Handsworth College.

MR 21 July 1904, 11 Jan. 1917

JAV

Whitelamb, Rev. John (1707–69), born of
poor parents at Wroote, Lincs, and educated at the
local charity school. He became the amanuensis
of Samuel Wesley Senr (*see* **Wesley Family**),
transcribed his *Dissertations on the Book of Job*
and helped with the maps and illustrations. On
one occasion he saved the rector's life. Samuel
helped him to go to Oxford, where JW was his
tutor at Lincoln College and thought highly of his
ability. He married Mary Wesley and her father
assigned the living at Wroote to him; but she died
in childbirth in 1734. A proposal that he should go
out to Georgia came to nothing and his remaining

years were spent at Wroote, where his association
with the Wesleys was minimal.

L. Tyerman (1878) pp. 374–86

JAV

Whiteley, John (1806–69; e.m. 1831), WM
missionary to *New Zealand who succeeded J.
*Hobbs at Mangungu in 1833, but also served on
the Kawhia station in the Waikato. Travelling
extensively, he gained the confidence and respect
of local tribes. In 1856 he took charge of the
work in the Taranaki area at a time of prolonged
disturbances over land ownership. He encouraged
the signing of the Treaty of Waitangi, but joined
his colleagues in 1846 in protesting against
governmental land policy, which he believed con-
travened Treaty principles. He was much in
demand as an interpreter and adviser and acted as
an unpaid commissioner for native lands, but then
became an advocate for settler land rights, which
hampered his work as a missionary. Following an
attack on a settlement north of New Plymouth, he
was caught up in an incident and killed. The shock
of his death caused the Maoris to take stock and
desist from further action.

DNZB; G. Brazendale (n.d.)

MJF/DJP

Whitham, Alfred Edward (1878–1938; e.m.
1902), a WM minister from a PM home, who
held leading pulpits, though never quite attaining
the influence of a *Weatherhead or *Sangster. His
sermons were characterized by a love of literature,
especially Browning; but he became known
chiefly for his catholic predilections, derived from
his desire in World War I to love his enemies and
fostered by his friendship with the evangelical S.
*Chadwick. In 1935 he became the first President
of the *Methodist Sacramental Fellowship. His
elegant journalism, inspired by his conviction that
the life of man is the vision of God, was collected
into three volumes after his death.

MR 27 Jan. & 3 Feb. 1938

GSW

Whitla, Sir William (1851–1933), one of
Ulster's most distinguished men of medicine, was
born into a Methodist family in Monaghan. He
studied pharmacy and then medicine at Queen's
University, Belfast, where after a period in private
practice he was called to the chair of pharma-
cology. His medical works, particularly his *Dictionary of Medical Treatment*, were in wide

demand and translated into many languages. Honoured by many universities, he was knighted in 1902. He was pro-Chancellor of QUB, represented the university in Parliament 1918–22, and was appointed physician to King George V. He left endowments to *Methodist College, Belfast, Queen's University and the Ulster Medical Society.

ICA 5 Jan. 1934

RPR

Whitlock, Ralph (1914–95), farmer, writer and broadcaster, was born and lived at Pitton, near *Salisbury. In addition to regular contributions to *The Field*, *Daily Telegraph* etc., he published over one hundred books on country matters. From 1946 to 1962 he broadcast his 'Cowleaze Farm' series on Children's Hour and was a regular panellist on 'Any Questions?' Retiring from farming in 1968, he spent five years travelling abroad as the MMS's agricultural consultant. His book collection is now in the local history library at Salisbury.

Times, 30 Nov. 1995; *MR* 2 Nov. 1995

JAV

Whittaker, Frank (1894–1961; e.m. 1920), one of three Methodists made CSI bishops in 1947 and Deputy Moderator 1950–52. He had worked in Hyderabad, especially in theological training and rural work, since 1922 and was a member of the Joint Committee preparing for church union from 1932. He was Secretary of the National Christian Council of *India 1938–43 and in 1943–47 Chairman of the Hyderabad District. On retiring as Bishop of Medak in 1960 he taught briefly at the Andhra United Theological College in Dornakal. His wife Dr **Constance Whittaker** (*née* Snowdon, 1897–1965) qualified at Manchester University Medical School, specializing in Ophthalmology and joined the staff of the Women's Work hospital at Karim Nagar, Hyderabad District, in 1922. After their marriage in 1925, as well as sharing fully in her husband's ministry, she made her own distinctive contribution as a doctor and became a deeply loved 'mother in God' to the women of the Medak Diocese. She was involved in the formation of the CSI Women's Fellowship in 1948, and after her husband's death continued to serve the Medak and Dornakal dioceses, despite crippling arthritis.

MR 21 Dec. 1961, 21 Oct. 1965

JRP/EMJ

Wigfield, Dr Dorothea (1895–1977), medical missionary in *India, was accepted as a Women's Auxiliary missionary while still training at the Royal Free Hospital. From 1921 she worked in the Karim Nagar area, Hyderabad District. Enormous resourcefulness, excellent health and good medical skills were called for in the busy round of teaching, working, touring and hospital administration which such an appointment required. She returned to England for family reasons in 1935, but resumed duties from 1945 to 1958 and was still able to serve in India as furlough relief in 1964.

MJF

Wigley Family   Albert John Wigley (1863–1941; e.m. 1888), PM minister and pacifist, served for 30 years on the British *Christian Endeavour Union's National Council. Two of his sons entered the PM ministry: **Henry Townsend Wigley** (1893–1970; e.m. 1917) served with the *Wesley Guild 1933–45 as Young Methodist Secretary (1933–39) and *Christian Endeavour Union President (1933–36), and as FCFC General Secretary, 1945–52; **Alfred Lanceley Wigley** (1901–85; e.m. 1928) was the father of **David L. Wigley** (b. 1932), Chief Executive for the *MHA from 1982 and a Secretary of the Division of *Social Responsibility.

MR 11 June 1970, 23 Jan. 1986

DCD

Wilkinson, Ellen (1891–1947) was associated with the National Union of Distributive and Allied Workers, then became MP for Middlesbrough East 1924–31 and for Jarrow from 1935. She was briefly Minister of Education in the Labour government of 1945. Noted for her hard work and fighting qualities, she had 'a passion for justice, especially for the under-privileged'.

Times 7 Feb. 1947

JAV

Wilkinson, Dr John Thomas, FRHS (1893–1980; e.m. 1917), PM minister and scholar, born in *Hull and educated at Manchester University and *Hartley College. After nearly 30 years in circuit, he was appointed tutor in Church History and English Literature at *Hartley Victoria College in 1946, becoming Principal in 1953. He edited the memorial volume (1958) to A.S. *Peake, whom he greatly admired and founded the Peake Memorial Lecture in 1954. His interest in seventeenth century *Puritanism led to editions of Richard Baxter's *Reformed Pastor* (1939) and *The Saints' Everlasting Rest* (1962). His other interests included the Cambridge Platonists and *Primitive Methodism and he wrote biographies of both W. *Clowes (1951) and H. *Bourne (1952). He was awarded the rare Manchester DD for his published works. His son Leonard served as a medical missionary and his younger son Alan became an Anglican priest and historian.

MR 27 Nov. 1980

JAV

Willey, Basil (1897–1978) came of combined Methodist and Anglican stock and took 1st class honours in the English Tripos at Cambridge in 1921, alongside F.R. Leavis and others. He lectured in English from 1923, was elected Fellow of Pembroke College in 1935 and succeeded Quiller-Coach in 1946 as King Edward VII Professor of English Literature. He gave the Hibbert Lectures in 1959 and the Warton Lecture, on Coleridge, in 1946 and was visiting professor at Columbia 1948–49 and at Cornell, 1953. He published a series of literary studies and his lectures in the Divinity Faculty appeared as *Christianity, Past and Present* in 1952. As literary adviser to the *Faith and Order Committee in the preparation of the 1975 *Methodist Service Book*, he rather deplored the use of the American RSV and the inclusion of the historic creeds. Two volumes of autobiography were published under the titles *Cambridge and Other Memories* (1959) and *Spots of Time . . . 1897–1920* (1965).

Times 5 Sept. 1978; *MR* 5 Oct.1978

JAV

Williams, Albert Hughes (1907–96) graduated at the University College, Bangor and became a schoolmaster and later an HMI in Wales. He was the author of standard historical textbooks, as well as works on Welsh Methodist history, notably his *Welsh Wesleyan Methodism 1800–1858* (1935), based on his MA thesis. In 1946 he was instrumental in founding the Historical Society of Welsh Methodism and its journal *Bathafarn*, which he edited until 1970. He was President of the Society from 1970 until his death.

Y Gwyliedydd, Oct-Nov. 1996 p. 3

OEE

Williams, Thomas (*c.* 1720–1787) was converted in 1741 during a visit by CW to his home at Llanishen near Cardiff and soon afterwards became one of JW's itinerant preachers. Having been involved in the conflicts with Anglican clergy in Darlaston and Walsall in 1743, he was criticized by JW for his 'inexcusable folly'. This led to an estrangement between him and the Wesleys, whom he is said to have deemed 'Papists, tyrants, enemies of the Church'. In 1744 his bid for episcopal ordination was foiled by CW and his resentment may account for his persistently accepting and publicizing scandalous rumours about CW's alleged immoral conduct. For this he was expelled by JW in August 1744, but by the end of the year he had recanted and been reinstated, though only as a probationer. In March 1746 he went, probably at JW's request, to *Dublin, where a small society had grown under the leadership of J. *Cennick into a flourishing *Moravian-type society. Arriving in August 1747 JW found there a Methodist society of some 280 members, the result of Williams' powerful preaching and enthusiastic leadership. This led A.H. *Williams to claim for him such titles as 'father' and 'pioneer' of Irish Methodism, though significantly another preacher was put in charge of the work. From 1749 on he was back in the English work, until finally expelled in 1755 for an unknown offence. He was later ordained into the Anglican ministry through the good offices of Lady *Huntingdon.

C. Atmore (1801) pp. 506–7; A.H. Williams in WHS(I) 2 part 3 (Summer 1992) pp. 15–30; O.E. Evans (1993) pp. 123–41

OEE

Williams, William of Pantycelyn (1717–1791), Anglican clergyman, author, poet, hymnwriter and pioneer of *Welsh Calvinistic Methodism. Williams was ordained deacon in 1740 and served as a curate in Breconshire until 1743. Refused ordination as a priest, he became an assistant to the Rev. D. *Rowland and began to concentrate on his literary work. He is particularly remembered for his hymns, which appeared in numerous collections between 1744 and 1790 and included works in English. Three of his hymns in English translation appear in *HP*, of which 'Guide me, O thou great Jehovah' has become a firm favourite. He also composed, in Welsh, two epic poems of over 1,000 stanzas. His numerous prose works were intended for the edification of the converts, and he is today regarded as one of the giants of Welsh literature.

W.J. Roberts in *LQHR* Oct. 1950 pp. 330–4; G.T. Hughes (1983); G.M. Roberts (1949, 1958); E. Evans (1996); D.Ll. Morgan (1988)

GT

Williams School of Church Music George H.T. Williams, for many years the organist at Bethnal Green Methodist church, left his home, The Bourne, Harpenden, complete with large music room, three-manual organ and Bechstein grand piano, to be used as an ecumenical (primarily nonconformist) school of church music. It opened in 1971 with F.B. *Westbrook as its first Principal and the participation of the *MCMS, chiefly through the devoted service of Edward Jones as clerk to the foundation. A Bourne orchestra and Bourne choir were among the activities. The second Principal was Clive Bright of the London College of Music. The School closed in the 1980s and the premises now house Musicale Holidays, which trains young instrumentalists. The organ from The Bourne is in High Street Methodist Church, Harpenden.

G.E. Radford (n.d.) pp. 113–17

JAV

Wilson, Benjamin (1824–97), *Chartist, born at Skircoat Green near *Halifax, noted for both its radicalism and its Methodism. In his autobiography *The Struggles of an Old Chartist* (1887) he recalled hearing William Thornton, a popular radical and Methodist preacher, lecture in the local Wesleyan School. He pursued a variety of occupations, including 'woollen weaver, comber, railway navvy and barer in the delph', finally becoming a gardener and horticultural expert. He later moved, via the co-operative and temperance movements, into Gladstonian Liberalism.

D. Vincent (1977)

JAH

Wilson, Gordon (1927–95), Irish Methodist businessman, was thrust into the limelight by the death of his daughter Marie in the 1987 IRA Remembrance Day bombing at *Enniskillen. Her dying words and his belief that peace and reconciliation were possible motivated the last eight years of his life. His own words of forgiveness, quoted in the Queen's Christmas broadcast, became a symbol of hope and in 1988 he received the World Methodist Peace award. In 1993 he accepted a seat in the Irish Senate and that year

made a personal appeal to the IRA. His son Peter's death in a car crash (1994) struck a blow that hastened his own death.

A. McCreary (1996)

RPR

Wilson, James (1816–1900), a prolific and versatile architect, known as 'Wilson of *Bath'. From 1839, with his partners (notably W.J. Willcox from 1865, who took over from him in 1886), he designed many buildings in Bath and the south-west, especially churches, chapels and schools. His Methodist commissions included *Richmond College (1843), *Queen's College, Taunton (1843), New King Street, *Bath (1847), *Westminster Training College (1851), Maiden Street, *Weymouth (1867) and *Headingley College (1869). He was instrumental in the decision to locate the new *Kingswood School in Bath and in obtaining its commanding site on the slopes of Lansdown, where he himself lived and worked.

Charles Robertson (1975); Neil Jackson (1991)

AMB

Wilson, John (1837–1915), *trade unionist, born at Greatham, Co. Durham. He received a sparse education at a dame school, but developed a growing appetite for reading. He began work at Stanhope quarries, but was subsequently employed in a number of pits. He took a leading part in the formation of the Durham Miners' Association in 1869 and about this time was converted, becoming a PM *local preacher in 1870. For a while he ran a stationer's shop, but returned to *Durham in 1882 and became successively agent and secretary of the Durham Miners' Association. After involvement in local politics he was elected Liberal MP for Houghton-le-Spring in 1885, but was defeated the following year. He was MP for Mid-Durham 1890–1915. He was also an alderman of Durham County Council and was awarded an honorary DCL by Durham University in 1906.

Times, 25 & 29 March 1915; R.F. Wearmouth (1959)

NADS

Wilson, John (1856–1918), born at Doddington, Northumberland. After a minimal education he began work at the age of 8 at Bideabout Pit and subsequently at a number of mines and collieries, ending at Cambois colliery. Here he became secretary of the Aged Mineworkers' Association and was also active in a variety of local and political roles, including membership of the Morpeth Board of Guardians and treasurer of the Morpeth Liberal Association. Converted in a local revival in the vicinity of Lowick, he was active as a PM *local preacher and Sunday School teacher.

DLB; R.F. Wearmouth (1957)

NADS

Wilson, Joseph (1833–1926), PM lay worker, born in *Bradford, Yorks. When he later established his own business and woollen mill, he introduced improved working conditions and a profit-sharing scheme. Somewhat eccentric, he was totally devoted to the *temperance movement, bought an old church and created a Gospel Temperance Mission Institute. He was ostracized by the PMs for his enthusiasm. He was a keen vegetarian and a Liberal councillor. A PM President said of him that 'he gave time and strength to reform movements every day for three quarters of a century.'

WHS(N. Lancs) Bulletin no.15 (1992)

EWD

Wilson, Thomas (1773–1858), WM layman, born in *Gateshead. He began life as a coalminer, but was sufficiently well educated by 19 to become a teacher and later a partner in a counting-house. He was one of the first town councillors in Gateshead. His poem *The Pitman's Pay* (1826), perhaps semi-autobiographical, shows a working-man's struggle for decency, self-sufficiency and respectability accomplished through thrift, frugality and co-operation between employer and employed, in contrast to the prevailing ideas of militant confrontation. He used working-class patois where appropriate to the characters. The enduring popularity of the poem was responsible for a dramatized version which toured Tyneside in the early twentieth century.

Northern Tribune, Jan-March 1855 pp. 52–4; R. Welford (1895) 3 pp. 650–53; M. Vicinus (1974)

CJS

Winchester As in other cathedral cities, Methodism found itself squeezed between the Church and Dissent. The first society was not formed until 1763 and remained small. Its leader, a local tradesman, Jasper Winscom, was a difficult character. JW paid the first of 18 visits in October 1766. The society suffered at the hands of the mob, but was supported by Methodist soldiers

quartered in the city and encouraged by a visit from Captain T. *Webb and R.C. *Brackenbury in 1783. The first preaching house on Silver Hill was opened by JW in November 1785, but they returned to their former premises in 1796, following a dispute with Winscom and moved to a new chapel at the junction of Parchment Street and St George's Street in 1816 (succeeded by the St Peter Street church in 1865). Winchester was briefly the head of a separate circuit 1816–18, but then reverted to Southampton Circuit until 1862.

Local support for the WMA led to division in 1835, with a number of members and some of the more able *local preachers setting up a separate society in Hyde Close and building a chapel in Upper Brook Street (c.1839). From there they moved to the east side of Parchment Street in 1874. The village chapels north and west of the city were all taken over by the WMA. PM reached the city from its base in Micheldever. An attempt in 1837 to mission the town met with violent opposition and was abandoned despite support from the authorities. A firmer start was made in 1852, when PM preachers held meetings in the Corn Exchange. A former Independent chapel in Parchment Street was taken in 1853. It was rebuilt in 1903 and amalgamated with St Peter Street in 1973 which, since 1974 has been part of a united Methodist/URC congregation.

E.R. Pillow (1985)

JAV

Winfield, Robert (1772–1850), born at Amberston, near Derby, and converted *c.* 1797. After three years with the MNC he returned to WM until expelled in 1814 for attending a *camp meeting. He was a PM itinerant until 1819, when he left to found a connexion of *Methodist Revivalists, which soon encompassed 12 circuits, 30 itinerant preachers and 4–5,000 members. Chapel debts and inexperienced preachers caused the Winfieldite movement to collapse after six years and Winfield to return to his Derbyshire farm. He joined the MNC in 1836 and remained a *local preacher in their *Derby Circuit until his death.

MNCM 1852 pp. 633–8

EAR

Winston, William Ripley (1847–1918; e.m. 1872), WM missionary. After 14 years in North Ceylon (*Sri Lanka) he launched the WM mission in Upper Burma (now *Myanmar) in 1886. His missionary strategy was learned under J. *Kilner and Edmund Rigg (1838–1906; e.m. 1865). He nurtured an indigenous ministry and opened schools in strategic centres as a means of evangelism. His social and philanthropic ventures included a home for lepers. He returned home in 1898 on health grounds and in 1912 was elected to the Legal Hundred. His son **Frederick Dyson Winston** (1880–1970; e.m. 1904) also served in Burma, from 1904 to 1913.

F&H 5 pp. 382–7; W.R. Winston (1892)

JAV

Wiseman, Caroline Meta (*née* Shum) (1834–1912), for over 30 years the dominant organizer of the Ladies' Auxiliary (later *Women's Work) of the WMMS. She was born in *Bath, where she became the first woman to be appointed to the School Board. In 1874 she married the widower L.H. *Wiseman, at that time Secretary of the WMMS. After his death nine months later, her home in Barnsbury became a headquarters for the work of the Auxiliary, which she transformed into a much larger organization, including *medical work, which began during her period in office. She travelled extensively overseas and energetically supervised and publicized the work of women missionaries.

MR 18 July & 8 Aug. 1912; L. Tyack (1915)

PMW

Wiseman, Dr Frederick Luke (1858–1944; e.m. 1881), WM minister, born at *York, the son of L.H. *Wiseman. The larger part of his ministry was in the *Birmingham Mission, where he served for 26 years. He was President of the WM Conference in 1912 and of the Methodist Conference in 1933. He had a keen interest in hymnody and served as Chairman of the committee preparing the *MHB* (1933), which included eleven tunes he himself had composed. Following publication, he travelled extensively throughout the Connexion, preaching and commending the new book. In 1931 he delivered the Drew Lectures on *Charles Wesley, Evangelist and Poet*. One of his sons, **Christopher Luke Wiseman** (1893–1987) was headmaster of *Queen's College, Taunton 1926–53; another, **Frederick Daniel Wiseman** (1894–1952) was editor of the *Methodist Recorder* 1934–52.

MR 13 July 1933, 20 & 27 Jan. 1944

PMW

Wiseman, Luke Holt (1822–75; e.m. 1840), WM minister, born in *Norwich. He was renowned as preacher and biblical scholar. A strong supporter of the Anti-Slavery Association and of the Bible Society, he became Secretary of the WMMS in 1868. He was one of the founders of the *Methodist Recorder* in 1861 and was elected President of the 1872 Conference.

MR 12 Feb. 1875; MR(W) 1893 pp. 70–1

PMW

Witness of the Spirit *see* **Assurance**

Wolff, George (1736–1828), a Danish merchant who later served as Danish Consul in London. He was a member at *Wesley's Chapel and a generous benefactor of Methodist causes. A man of great humility, his home in Balham was a favourite retreat of JW in the London area. It was from there that W was taken back to City Road a week before he died. He was one of the executors of JW's will.

WMM 1828 p. 286

JAV

Wolsingham (Weardale) *see* **Dales Circuit**

Wolverhampton, Viscount *see* **Fowler, H.H.**

Wolverhampton was a rapidly expanding industrial town, but had only one parish church, St Peter's, until St John's was built in 1760. A Whitefieldite preacher encountered a violent mob in 1745. *Whitefield himself followed in 1753, but JW did not visit the town until 1760, after a society had been formed by J. *Bennet. The first WM chapel (1762) was destroyed by a mob, but rebuilt at the expense of the instigator of the rioting. It was replaced by 'Noah's Ark Chapel' in 1787, when a Wolverhampton Circuit was formed. The first Darlington Street chapel, built in 1825, was replaced by the present church in 1901. Trinity, Compton Road (1862), whose trust deed provided for Morning Prayer to be used, became the head of a circuit in 1888. An extension scheme launched in 1885 provided new chapels in the suburbs.

The first *MNC chapel (1813) was replaced by Mount Zion chapel in Horsley Fields (1829, rebuilt 1867). In 1819 Sampson Turner missioned the area for the PMs. H. *Bourne preached there several times and a chapel and school were built in 1833. PM Chapels proliferated later in the century.

See also **Fowler, H.H.**

Conference Handbook 1966

JAV

Women have played an undeniably important, but not undisputed, role in Methodism ever since the days of JW. The organization of the early societies gave women ample opportunity to exercise their gifts as class leaders, teachers, carers and housekeepers. Though he placed restrictions on their preaching, W recognized that women had an 'extraordinary' ministry and permitted them to give brief addresses at what were to be called prayer meetings rather than preaching services.

After W's death the Conference of 1803 pronounced 'preaching by women both unnecessary and generally undesired' and ordered women preachers to address only those of their own sex. But this did not deter some 25 women already preaching publicly from continuing to do so, notably M. *Bosanquet (Mrs Fletcher) and M. *Taft who corresponded extensively with one another. Despite considerable opposition, a number of new women preachers emerged in WM during the first half of the nineteenth century. In the *PM and the *BC connexions, some women were accepted as full-time preachers and pastors.

By the end of the nineteenth century new roles were emerging for women. Several had gone overseas as missionaries, supported by the Women's Auxiliary movements (*see* Women's Work). In 1878 T.B. *Stephenson founded an Order of Sisters for work in the *NCH. In 1887 H.P. *Hughes and his wife Katherine recruited 'Sisters of the Poor' for work in the West London Mission, a pattern repeated in other city missions. In the same year a Female Evangelists' house was opened by G. *Clegg as part of the *Joyful News Mission. In 1890 the Wesley *Deaconess Order came into being. The number of women *local preachers grew considerably and the 1910 Conference lifted the ban that had restricted women to preaching only to their own sex. In 1911 the first women representatives to the WM Conference were appointed, including M.K. *Hughes. In 1918 women local preachers were accorded the same status as men, though they remained for some years heavily outnumbered among those on trial. The first woman candidate for the ministry, Minnie Burns, was nominated in 1920 in the Harrow Circuit, only to be vetoed by the District Chairman; she became a Deaconess in 1923. Shortly before the *Union of 1932, a joint committee was set up to discuss the *ordination of women. It reported to the Conference of 1933 that it could find no reason for disqualifying women from the same ministry as men. But the Conference of 1934 rejected a scheme for the ordination of women.

New proposals, brought to the Conference of 1938, were approved, but then delayed by the outbreak of war. The Conference of 1945 again declared its willingness to ordain women and referred the matter to the *Synods. But the Conference of 1948 declined to admit women to the ministry. The question was reopened in 1959, when a committee was appointed to consider the status of deaconesses and the admission of women to the ministry. It reported inconclusively to five successive Conferences. In 1965 its recommendation raising the status of deaconesses was accepted, but Conference resolved that, whilst accepting in principle the ordination of women, it would not take unilateral action during the *Anglican-Methodist negotiations. When these failed, Conference finally accepted the admission of women to the ministry and the first British Methodist ordinations took place in 1974. (The Rev. Peggy Hiscock had already been ordained in the United Church of *Zambia.)

The first woman to become *President of the Conference was Dr K.M. *Richardson in 1992. Meanwhile the role of lay women had been recognized in the election of Mrs M. *Lewis as the first woman *Vice-President in 1948, followed by an increasing number of others since. It is now generally accepted that all committees of the Methodist Church include women and all offices in the Church are open to women as well as men.

MR(W) 1895 pp. 65–9; G.T. Brake (1984) pp. 314–28; R.E. Davies in *PWHS* 48 pp. 105–12; J. Field-Bibb (1990); J.H. Lenton in R. Sykes (1998) pp. 58–86; D. Shorney in R.N. Swanson (1988) pp. 309–22

PMW

Women's Fellowship was formed in 1942. Mrs J. Oliver Hornabrook and Dr C. *Roberts convened a group of women under the auspices of *HM to discuss what could be done to train women for leadership, to co-ordinate the work of the various women's meetings around the country and to meet the social and pastoral needs of women whose lives had been disrupted by war. The Conference of 1944 approved the name and constitution of the Women's Fellowship as a branch of HM. Its first Chairman was Mrs H.B. *Rattenbury. The welfare work initiated by the WF included two Mother and Baby Homes for unmarried mothers and a hostel for young women working in London. Its main emphasis was on training, through connexional schools, District Councils and family holiday conferences. A Young Wives' movement was formed. The work continued until WF and *Women's Work amalgamated in 1987 to form Network.

———

M. Bielby (1965)

PMW

Women's Work originated as 'The Ladies' Committee for the Amelioration of the Condition of Women in Heathen Countries, Female Education etc.' (later the 'Ladies' Auxiliary for Female Education'). Formed in 1858 as an auxiliary movement within the WMMS, it undertook to train, equip and finance the sending of women missionaries overseas. In *Ireland, local Methodist Women's Associations began in 1865 and a Ladies' Committee in support of overseas missions first met in 1884. A similar BC Women's Missionary League was formed in 1892, to be followed by the Ladies' Missionary Auxiliary in the UMFC in 1897. PM co-ordinated its work supporting women overseas in a Women's Missionary Federation, formed in 1909. At *Methodist Union in 1932 these organizations combined under the title 'Women's Work'. This became a full partner in the work of the MMS, having its own headquarters administration and a connexional system of District, Circuit and local committees. Its work became fully amalgamated with the General Committee of the MCOD in 1970 and Women's Work itself joined with *Women's Fellowship to form Network in 1987.

———

Women's Work Annual Reports; P.M. Webb (1958); C. Davey & H. Thomas (1984)

PMW

Wood Family **James Wood** (1777–1849), partner in the cotton firm of Wood and *Westhead, was the first President of the *Manchester Chamber of Commerce. A friend of the young J. *Bunting, he was politically conservative and an opponent of free trade. He was a class leader and *local preacher, and one of the instigators of the *Watchman. As Treasurer of the *Centenary Fund, he strongly recommended the setting up of a Theological Institute as a fitting memorial of the occasion. His son Dr **Peter Wood** (1811–77) was a pioneer advocate of sea-bathing, had much to do with the early development of *Southport and was its first Mayor. In the next generation, his son, another **James Wood** (1844–99) was several times Mayor and was the father of the

children's writer Lucy M. Boston (1892–1990). The family was related by marriage to the *Heald and the *Garrett families.

———

E.A. Wood (1902); *HWM* 3, passim; W.R. Ward (1972) pp. 13, 18–19; L.M. Boston (1979)

JAV

Wood, Annie M. (d.1931), a teacher from *Cork, who was an educational missionary in Canton, 1885–1904. She used her considerable literary skills in several pamphlets describing everyday scenes and events in *China. After a period of furlough, she returned to China in 1892 accompanied by her 15-year-old sister, **Connie Wood**. Adventurous and high-spirited, she reported in 1894 that her work gave her 'great encouragement' amidst plague and riots. Another sister, **Fanny Wood**, qualified as a doctor in *Edinburgh in 1900 and served in *India.

———

N.W. Taggart (1986) pp. 64–6

NWT

Wood, Dr Arthur Skevington (1916–93; e.m. 1939), born at Ashbourne (Derbys), trained for the ministry at *Headingley College and received his doctorate at Edinburgh University for a thesis on T. *Haweis. He travelled widely while working for the Movement for World Evangelism 1962–70. He then joined the staff of *Cliff College, becoming Principal in 1977. He was a frequent speaker at the Keswick and *Southport Conventions. He gave the Drew Lectures in 1979 on Immortality and published a number of books on biblical and historical subjects, including studies of the Evangelical Revival *The Inextinguishable Blaze* (1960) and of JW's ministry, *The Burning Heart* (1967).

———

MR 4 March 1993

EDG

Wood, Enoch (1759–1840), Burslem potter for whom JW sat in March 1781. The resulting bust was considered by W himself (and later by A. *Clarke) to be the most faithful likeness of him ever achieved. In 1830, when Samuel Manning was working on a statue of W commissioned by J. *Butterworth, Clarke sent him two copies of the bust, one of them (now in the Museum of Methodism at *Wesley's Chapel) specially supplied by Wood himself from the original mould, as a model for the features. The statue, formerly at *Richmond College, is now at *Westminster

Central Hall. Wood also produced busts of G. *Whitefield and A. *Clarke.

See also **Ceramics**

F. Falkner (1912); A.D. Cummings (1962); R. Green in *PWHS* 6 pp. 17–23

DHR

Wood, Dr Enoch (1804–88; e.m. 1826), pioneer missionary in *Canada, was born in *Gainsborough. After three years in Montserrat, WI (1826–29) he transferred to New Brunswick, where he served for 18 years in urban churches. From 1847 to 1878 he was Superintendent, and later General Secretary, of the Canadian missions. He showed administrative ability and vision, launching a mission to Japan in 1873 despite the misgivings of colleagues. He was President of the Canada Conference 1851–8 and of the Toronto Conference in 1874.

F&H 1

JAV

Wood, Sir Howard Kingsley, MP (1881–1943), son of a WM minister, Arthur Wood (1853–1919; e.m. 1875). He practised as a solicitor until elected to the London County Council in 1911. He was elected Conservative MP for Woolwich West in 1918 and though no orator had an effective political career. He was appointed Privy Counsellor in 1928 and Lord Privy Seal in 1940. As Postmaster General 1931–35, he reformed the Post Office, saving it from privatization. Earlier experience of health insurance contributed to his service as Minister of Health, 1935–38; and as Secretary of State for Air (1938–40) he dramatically accelerated aircraft production. PAYE was introduced during his term as Chancellor of the Exchequer (1940–3). For many years he served as Treasurer at *Wesley's Chapel.

DNB; *Times* 22, 23 Sept. 1943; *MR* 23 Sept. 1943

JAV

Wood, Dr Joseph (1829–98; e.m. 1851), PM minister who served mainly in the Hull District. He was chiefly responsible for the establishment of the PM Sunday School Union (1874) and was its first Secretary 1875–82 and Agent 1878–81. He was President of the Conference in 1882 and Principal of *Hartley College 1889–93.

G.J. Stevenson (1884–86) 5 pp. 783–803

DCD

Woodcock, Henry (1829–1922; e.m. 1847), PM minister, born in Bridlington. He left school at 9 and entered a local printing office. Most of his ministry was spent in Yorkshire and Lincolnshire. He contributed a weekly article to the *Primitive Methodist*. His publications included *Popery Unmasked* (1862), *PM in the Yorkshire Wolds* (1889) and one on the origin and history of the Gypsies; and he collaborated with John Harrison on a *Student's Handbook to Scripture Doctrine*.

WL

Woodford, George Ernest (1873–1970; e.m. 1898), missionary in *India, born in Stone, Bucks. After training at *Richmond College, he served in Bengal 1898–1925 among the Santal tribes, campaigning against official corruption and the vicious system of land tenure and contributing to the McAlpine Report (1909) which mitigated the worst evils of the system. He strongly opposed drink and gambling, founded a boarding school and supported the hospital at Sarenga, but as Chairman was unhappy in administrative responsibilities. Physically robust and of great courage, he could be an obstinate and sometimes difficult colleague.

MR 23 July 1970

JAV

Woodhouse Grove School, Apperley Bridge, W. Yorks, opened in 1812 for the sons of Methodist preachers. It was reorganized in 1875 as the junior department of *Kingswood School, closed by *Conference eight years later and immediately reopened as a proprietary school for sons of middle-class Methodists and a few ministers' sons. With improved boarding accommodation, a house system and an extended curriculum, it established a sound academic reputation, broadened its intake and accepted public grants mainly in support of local elementary school boys. After the withdrawal of state support in 1976 it reverted to full independence. In 1997 it had 798 boarding and day pupils of both sexes, aged 3 to 18.

F.C. Pritchard (1978)

DBT

Woodward, Max Wakerley (1908–96; e.m. 1929), born in *Sunderland, the son of Alfred Woodward (1870–1956; e.m. 1892). He trained at *Handsworth College and in 1929 was posted to the South Ceylon District, where he married Margaret, daughter of A.S. *Beaty. Returning home in 1942, he was a naval chaplain until the end of the war. He was minister at *Wesley's Chapel, London 1958–63 and wrote its history, *One at London* (1966) He was British Secretary of the *WMC, 1964–71.

MR 9 May 1966

WL

Woon, William (1804–58; e.m. 1830), WM missionary and trained printer from Cornwall, who went to *Tonga in 1831. Discouraged in his work and concerned for his wife's health, he resigned in 1834 and travelled to *New Zealand, where he took charge of the mission press at Mangungu. Reinstated in 1837, he extended his usefulness both to the church and in the stations for which he was now available. Large in stature, his service was of equal worth whether as a layman or as a ministerial missionary. Of limited financial resources (unlike some of his colleagues) his – and his family's – service was sacrificial in many aspects.

MJF

Worcester   JW first visited the city in 1760, but did not preach there until 1768. A chapel was built in New Street in 1772, but when W preached in it in 1778 he found it already too small. The first Pump Street chapel, on the site of a former Independent chapel, was opened in 1795; rebuilt in 1813 and enlarged in 1874, it was replaced by a new church in 1902. This in turn was succeeded in 1968 by St Andrew's as part of a city-centre commercial redevelopment. Its second-floor sanctuary reflects the influence of the Liturgical Movement. Worcester was in the Gloucester Circuit until a Worcestershire Circuit was formed in 1788. There was also a *Countess of Huntingdon's Connexion chapel in Deansway.

In 1820 the PM boy preacher T. *Brownsword was arrested while preaching at Stourbridge and imprisoned with others in the county gaol at Worcester. At the court hearing, the case against him was dismissed and a mass meeting was held at the race course. The widespread publicity and popular support this engendered led to a PM society being formed, which at first was in the extensive Darlaston Circuit. The chapel built in George Street (1882) closed in 1963.

MR 15 Jan. 1903; *WMM* 1904 pp. 592–600

JAV

Workman, Dr Herbert Brook (1862–1951; e.m. 1885), WM minister and scholar, was born in Peckham, London and educated at *Kingswood School and Owen's College, Manchester, where he gained a first in Philosophy. He was Assistant Tutor at *Didsbury College 1885–88. After 15 years of circuit ministry, in 1903 he was appointed Principal of *Westminster Training College, a post he held until retirement in 1930. His tenure witnessed a great improvement in academic standards and closer relations with the University of London, of which he was a Senator. As Secretary of the *Education Committee 1919–40, he fostered the growth of *residential schools, notably *Hunmanby Hall and *Culford School, and oversaw the transfer of *Southlands College to Wimbledon. He was President of the Conference in 1930. As one of Methodism's greatest church historians, specializing in the Medieval and Reformation periods, his publications included *Christian Thought to the Reformation* (1900), *The Evolution of the Monastic Ideal* (1913) and widely acclaimed biographies of Wyclif and Hus. He gave the *Fernley Lecture in 1906 on *Persecution in the Early Church* and as one of the editors of the *New History of Methodism* (1909) contributed a chapter on 'The Place of Methodism in the Catholic Church'.

MR 30 Aug. 1951

TSAM

Worksop   In 1780 JW preached to 'only a small company of as stupid people as I ever saw'. From such a beginning things could only improve, though for some years the small society struggled to survive. However, by 1813 they had built a chapel on a prominent site in Bridge Street. PM missioned the town in 1818, but it was not until 1831 that they opened a small chapel in Newgate Street. The WM society suffered a secession to the WMA, which built its own chapel (later UMFC and UM) in Potter Street in 1837. During the second half of the century all three denominations either rebuilt or replaced their chapels, WM in 1863, UMFC in 1875 and PM in 1880. The present church was rebuilt in 1969 after the WM church had burned down.

R. Ledger (n.d.)

MJJ

World Methodism (until 1951 designated Oecumenical Methodism) was one of the first Christian World Communions, dating from 1881, when the Oecumenical Methodist Council was established to foster links between Methodist-related denominations throughout the world. The first Oecumenical Methodist Conference, held in

London that year, had 400 delegates from 30 Methodist bodies, mostly British and American. The Conference met every ten years until 1931 and from 1951 every five years. By 1996 there were 73 member Churches located in 108 different countries, representing a total reported membership of nearly 34 million and a community of over 70 million.

The World Methodist Council comprises 500 representatives of member Churches and meets every five years, operating in the intervals through a series of committees and an Executive Committee. Its headquarters are at Lake Junaluska NC, with a European office at Geneva. Its activities include a programme of World Evangelism, dialogue with other world communions, a Peace Award and a ministerial exchange programme. Affiliated organizations include the World Federation of Methodist Women, the *World Methodist Historical Society and the *Oxford Institute of Methodist Theological Studies.

WMC *Handbook of Information 1997–2001*

JAV

World Methodist Historical Society (originally the International Methodist Historical Society) was formed in 1947 to co-ordinate the activities of historical societies and individual historians throughout the world. The first issue of its news bulletin *World Parish* appeared in 1948 and its first quinquennial meeting was held during the World Methodist Conference in 1951. Dr M.L. *Edwards was elected President in 1966. At the World Methodist Conference in Denver in 1971, the Society was reorganized under its present title, and with a new Constitution. It held its first international conference at *Wesley College, Bristol in 1973.

The British Section's committee was appointed by Conference, with Dr F. *Baker as its first secretary, and was charged with the oversight of historic sites and the commemoration of significant events. The first British residential conference was held at *Kingsmead College, Selly Oak, in 1975; these are now run jointly with the *WHS. A publishing programme was launched in 1975. The British Section was involved in the organization of the first *Archives Centre in London and its Secretary is now a member of the connexional Archives and History Committee.

JAV

Worn Out Ministers' Fund *see* **Finance, Ministerial**

Worrall, Dr Stanley, OBE (1912–91), the son of Sidney Albert Worrall (1880–1978; e.m. 1904), had a distinguished academic and educational career, interrupted by World War II, during which he worked as a conscientious objector in the Yorkshire Coal-mines. He was appointed headmaster of *Methodist College, Belfast in 1961 and for 13 years led the school with unbroken success. He served the Irish Conference and the Irish Council of Churches, and after retirement was elected Chairman of the NI Arts Council. In 1974 with other churchmen he met with the IRA to persuade them to call a ceasefire.

See also **Young, F.M.**

Methodist Newsletter Jan. 1992

RPR

Worthington, Reginald T. (1880–1933; e.m. 1910), UM pioneer missionary in Meru, *Kenya, 1913–22 and 1928–33. He took a crash course in medicine before sailing and within months of arriving had opened a dispensary. He ran a boarding school which thrived in spite of a fire in 1914 in which five of the first twelve boys died. The first baptisms were in 1916. During an interval in home circuits he continued translating the Gospels into Kimeru. He supervised the opening of a hospital at Maua in 1928–29 and of a girls' boarding school at Kaaga in 1933.

MR 26 Oct. 1933

JRP

Wright, Dr Charles James (1888–1967; e.m. 1912), born in *Glasgow and descended from Isaac Watts. A protégé of T.H. *Barratt, he gained a London PhD for a thesis on *Miracle in History and in Modern Thought* (published 1930) and was tutor in Systematic Theology and Philosophy of Religion at *Didsbury College 1930–42. In 1937 he published *Modern Issues in Religious Thought*. The most liberal theologian Methodism ever produced, he broadened the outlook and liberated the minds of some students. He was well thought of by the philosopher Samuel Alexander. The Anglican *Modern Churchman* H.D.A. Major allocated the Fourth Gospel to him in the symposium *The Mission and Message of Jesus* (1937). During World War II he was much involved with the *Manchester Free Churches and the Religion and Life Campaigns. Frustrated in Methodism, he was ordained in the Church of England in 1944, but his time there was unhappy. He fell foul of Archbishop Fisher for his views on the Virgin Birth and suffered a severe nervous breakdown. He had welcomed Tillich, but was not capable of further serious theological work.

C.J. Wright (1944); A.M.G. Stephenson (1984) pp. 146, 191

GSW

Wright, Duncan (1736–1791), early itinerant, born in Perthshire. He enlisted in the army and while stationed in *Ireland came under Methodist influence, was converted and began preaching. He was greatly encouraged to recognize his calling when he heard JW and *T. Walsh preaching in Ireland. Leaving the army, he began travelling with JW in 1765 in English, Scottish and Irish circuits. He spent twenty eight years as an itinerant, being especially gifted in preaching in Gaelic in the Scottish Highlands.

EMP 2 pp. 107–30; C. Atmore (1801) pp. 510–12

HMG

Wright, John Gibbon (1822–1904; e.m. 1845), PM minister, born in Scoulthorpe, Norfolk. He served in five PM circuits before emigrating to South *Australia, where he was first stationed at Kooringa on the Burra Copper field. Because of the exodus to the Victorian gold fields, only two members were left, but he reopened the church and by vigorous evangelism had almost 200 members within three years. This was the first of eleven long and fruitful ministries in South Australia circuits, shaped by the PM tradition of *camp meetings, open-air preaching and prayers for revival. He was President of the PM South Australia Assembly nine times between 1857 and 1891.

DGH

Wright, Joseph (1818–85), PM architect who had an outstanding influence in the North East during a period of prolific chapel building from the 1860s on. Articled to Cuthbert Brodrick, a distinguished exponent of the Classical style, he practised in *Hull and *Leeds. His economical use of brick, often multi-coloured, in ornamental façades Italianate in style, was very inventive; and the elaborate and sometimes excessive touches of his chapels exhibited the joy characteristic of the worship inside. His Bourne Chapel, Hull (1871), spoken of as the PM cathedral, was one of the Connexion's first forays into Gothic.

BWB

Wright, Dr William David (1906–97), Professor of Applied Optics at Imperial College, London, where he spent most of his career, though his reputation was international. His pioneer work on the measurement of colour contributed to the development of colour TV and he did research into eyesight colour definition. He published five significant books on his special field and contributed to many other publications. He was one of those for whom science and religion were not opposed but complementary and he was for many years a member at The Bourne, Southgate, where he was Superintendent of the Sunday School.

MR 21 Aug. 1997

JAV

Yarm, a prosperous port and trading community in the eighteenth century and an important centre of early Methodism in the Cleveland area. JW's first visit on 16 August 1748 was on the invitation of several local men including G. *Merryweather, who was usually his host on his 18 visits. The chapel built in 1763–64 was one of the earliest octagons (*see* Architecture) and regarded by JW as a model. It was raised to include a gallery in 1815. Originally in the vast *Dales Circuit, in 1764 Yarm became the head of a new circuit, renamed the Stockton Circuit in 1793.

J. Wright (1949)

GEM

York was an early centre of Methodism, thanks to J. *Nelson who preached on Heworth Moor whilst quartered in York as an impressed militiaman in May 1744. He returned in the autumn and as a result a class led by Thomas Slaton began to meet at Acomb. In 1744 Slaton started a class in the city, in the house of Thomas Stodhart in the Bedern close by the minster. An intended visit by JW in 1747 was aborted after Nelson was almost killed by a mob, so his first visit was not until April 1752. Despite this inauspicious start, the cause grew rapidly. On his third visit in July 1757 W preached in the open air and a subscription was started for a chapel, which he opened in Peasholme Green on 15 July 1759. Though accommodating 400, galleries were added in 1775. A large chapel, opened in New Street in 1805, remained the circuit chapel for the next century. Further chapels were opened in Albion Street (1816) and in St George's parish, Walmgate (1826). The latter was replaced by the imposing Centenary Chapel (1840).

The MNC had little impact on York. A small society supported by R. *Oastler met in a former Calvinistic chapel in Grape Lane in 1799, but survived only until 1804. Until 1850 other branches of Methodism made little impact. W. *Clowes preached in York in 1819 and formed a small society, which moved into Grape Lane chapel in 1820. In 1830 a chapel of *Protestant Methodists was opened in Lady Peckett's Yard. Following the *Fly Sheets controversy a major split occurred in 1850; WM was set back by a decade and PM expanded, moving from Grape Lane to Ebenezer chapel in Little Stonegate in 1851. A mission led by W. *Booth re-established the MNC at Peckitt Street chapel in 1855. Other reformers joined with former *Protestant Methodists to open a UMFC chapel at Monk Bar in 1859. Wesley Chapel (replacing Albion Street, 1856) became the head of a second WM circuit west of the Ouse in 1867, and Centenary Circuit was created in 1888. The PM *Elmfield College opened in 1864. PM formed a Second Circuit in 1883, following the opening of Victoria Bar chapel (1880). They moved from Ebenezer to the John Petty Memorial Chapel in Monkgate in 1903. But numerically WM was never challenged and dominated the suburbs, with large chapels at Melbourne Terrace (1877), the Groves (1883), Southlands Road (1887) and Clifton (1909, replacing New Street). Following *Methodist Union in 1932 and numerical decline many chapels closed, especially in the city centre. In 1999 only Centenary remained within the city walls.

J. Lyth (1885); Conference Handbook 1926 (WM), 1956; E. Royle in C.H. Feinstein (1981); E. Royle (1985)

ER

Yorkshire provided fertile soil for Methodist expansion in the eighteenth and early nineteenth centuries. Archbishop Herring's Visitation Returns for 1743, which record that nearly half the 836 parishes in the huge diocese of York had non-resident clergy, reveal that Methodists were already active in 22 localities. In 1748 the first circuit *Quarterly Meeting was held near *Todmorden and in 1753 the first of JW's Conferences to be held in the North assembled at *Leeds. By 1764 the incumbents of no fewer than 108 Yorkshire benefices reported Methodists among their parishioners and among the surviving early preaching houses are the distinctive *octagon chapels at *Yarm and *Heptonstall. By 1785, when Yorkshire Methodists numbered over 15,000, many more chapels had been built across the county, especially in industrial parishes engaged in textile manufacture, coal mining and metallurgy. This remarkable religious revival, initially stimulated by itinerant evangelists (including B. *Ingham, W. *Darney, D. *Taylor, J. *Bennet and *CW), was reinforced by JW's frequent visits between 1742 and 1790. The revival was also supported by sympathetic clergymen, notably W. *Grimshaw of *Haworth and H. *Venn of *Huddersfield, and by energetic lay preachers such as J. *Nelson, W. *Shent and Francis Scott, the Wakefield joiner.

Between 1790 and 1795 the average annual rate of increase was 1,000 members, reaching a total of more than 21,000 by 1795. WM expansion was temporarily checked by the MNC secession at *Leeds in 1797, which won strong support from West Riding urban circuits such as Huddersfield, whose membership was almost halved. The secession of the *Protestant Methodists in 1827 was another setback. In 1836 they amalgamated with the WMA, which had a Yorkshire membership of c. 3,000 in 1837. PM also gained growing support after 1819, particularly in the North and East Ridings and at *Hull, where the first PM Conference was held in 1820 and which became the base for missions as far afield as Kent and Cornwall. The most damaging secession, as elsewhere, was that of the *WR movement, which cost the WM societies in the county over 15,000 members in 1850–51, almost halving the membership of the Bramley, Cleckheaton, Sheffield East and Wakefield Circuits, and which eventually established its headquarters in *Sheffield. Despite this, WM predominated in every Yorkshire borough in 1851 and only in *Halifax did the combined strength of the non-Wesleyan groups challenge the WM ascendancy. There were isolated pockets of support for the *BCs in the county, e.g. in *Bradford, where the Toller Lane congregation was formed by migrants from Somerset.

Expansion and secession had resulted in a proliferation of chapel accommodation in the county, which led to a process of amalgamation and closure following *Methodist Union in 1932, against a background of declining membership. For example, 38 of the 111 chapels in the city of Leeds in 1932 had been closed by 1956, a period which saw a membership decline of 2,500; and in 1961, four years after the formation of the West Yorkshire District, schemes of amalgamation were reported to be proceeding in no fewer than 16 circuits.

In 1851 the *Religious Census enumerated

1,855 Methodist places of worship in Yorkshire (including WM: 1,177; PM: 476; WR: 77; MNC: 73; WMA:52). By 1989 there were 1,082 Methodist churches in Yorkshire and Humberside. Total attendances reported in 1851 amounted to 426,787 (23.7% of the population), with evening services (usually the best attended) totalling 168,547 (9.4%). In 1989 Methodist worshippers totalled 65,400 (1.6% of the population) and Methodist members 69,700 (1.7%). In both 1851 and 1989, the proportion of the population attending Methodist worship was higher in the predominantly rural North and East of the county than in the urban conurbations of the West and South.

JAH

Young, David (1844–1913; e.m. 1868), Welsh WM minister from Pontlotyn, noted as a gifted and popular preacher in both English and Welsh and for his pastoral and administrative gifts. His social concern was born of his background in the Merthyr Tydfil area. In 1880, following a period of controversy over the amalgamation of the English and Welsh work, he was appointed, despite his youth, as Chairman of the South Wales District. He was the first Welsh Chairman to advocate the unsuccessful policy of 'amalgamation', with the backing of H.P. *Hughes. In 1888 he transferred to the English work and was stationed in *Cardiff, where he had a leading part in founding the new University College. A good historian, his continuing interest in Welsh Methodism resulted in his *Origin and History of Methodism in Wales* (1893).

EW 105 p. 358; *DWB*

EHG

Young, Dr Dinsdale Thomas (1861–1938; e.m. 1882) was born at Corbridge-on-Tyne. After training at *Headingley College, he began a ministerial career of great distinction, especially at Nicolson Square, *Edinburgh (1901–4) and *Wesley's Chapel (1906–14). He was President of the WM Conference in 1914 and from that year until 1938 was minister at *Westminster Central Hall. His gifts as a preacher (though avowedly fundamentalist) and as popular lecturer, advocate of good causes, writer and administrator were used to the full. He travelled some 10,000 miles a year, preaching and lecturing. He wrote biographies of P. *Mackenzie (1904) and R. *Newton (*c.* 1910) and an autobiography, *Stars of Retrospect* (1919).

MR 27 Jan. 1938, 30 Nov. 1961; H. Murray (1938)

JDB

Young, Prof. Frances Margaret (*née* *Worrall), (1939– ; e.m. 1980), grand-daughter of two ministers, a patristic and NT scholar, was briefly a Research Fellow at Clare Hall, Cambridge before moving to Birmingham University, becoming Edward Cadbury Professor of Theology in 1986. From 1988 to 1992 she was Head of the School of Philosophy and Theology and from 1995 to 1998 Dean of the Faculty of Arts. She has written both academic and semi-popular books, notably *From Nicaea to Chalcedon* (1983), *Meaning and Truth in 2 Corinthians* (with David Ford, 1987) and *Theology of the Pastoral Letters* (1994). She has served on the connexional *Faith and Order Committee and the Council of The *Queen's College, Birmingham. She led the Bible Studies at the 5th World Conference on Faith and Order at Santiago in 1993.

DJC

Young, Robert Newton (1829–98; e.m. 1851), WM minister, son of a missionary to Nova Scotia, **Robert Young** (1796–1865; e.m. 1820; President, 1856), was educated at *Woodhouse Grove School and became tutor in Biblical Literature and Classics at *Headingley College in 1876, then at *Handsworth College when it opened in 1881, becoming Governor 1892–97. In 1886, he became the only son of a former *President of the Conference to be elected President.

MR 11 Aug. 1898

JAV

Young Laymen's League *see* **Girls' League**

Younger, William (1869–1956; e.m. 1894), PM minister, trained at *Hartley College; Chairman of the Hull District, 1832–39. He preached in many European countries and in the USA and Canada. He delivered the *Hartley Lecture in 1924 on *The International Value of Christian Ethics*. He was President of the last PM Conference (1932) and being senior to the other two Presidents took the chair at the opening of the Uniting Conference. In due course he was elected President of the Methodist Conference in 1934.

MR 23 Feb. 1956

WL

Youth Missionary Association YMA) resulted in 1953 from a merger of the *Girls' and Young Men's Leagues with the aim of reaching all in Methodism's burgeoning work with young people, to make them aware of contemporary Methodism's missionary achievements and challenges. From its London headquarters and through its Conferences and the local activities of YMA secretaries and affiliated groups, it was hoped by study, activity and service to make young people more informed and supportive of all aspects of missionary work. When the *Divisions were instituted in the 1974 *restructuring, both MCOD and DEY were involved in what became the World Affairs Youth (WAY) programme, and later MAYC World Action.

MJF

Youth Work Methodism shares fully in the world-wide organizations (Girls' and Boys' Brigades, Guides and Scouts) which sprang up in the late nineteenth and early twentieth centuries. The *Wesley Guild began as a youth movement in 1896. *Christian Endeavour, which took root in PM, produced people articulate about their faith.

Government Circular 1486 *The Service of Youth* (1939) urged young people to join youth clubs and Methodists seized this opportunity for informal youth education. The Methodist Association of Youth Clubs (1945) became one of the largest church-based youth organizations in Europe. MAYC Charter Clubs committed themselves to seven principles: Create a group; grow real persons; encourage a sense of belonging; work towards wholeness; go for the best; live on a large map; take your place in the Church. MAYC London Weekends have brought together thousands of young people and their leaders, deepened awareness, provided an arena for local groups and celebrated the presence of Christ in youth culture. The gifts of young people in the performing arts are developed in the context of fellowship through the MAYC Choir and Orchestra, the Methodist Youth Brass Band and the annual event 'Youth Makes Music, Dance and Drama'. Following the Albemarle Report (1960), partnership with Government led to purpose-built youth centres and grant-aided staff. But the 1979–1997 Conservative Governments found the non-directive culture of parts of the Youth Service unacceptable and substantially reduced financial support.

The Methodist Youth Department, formed in 1943, brought together the *Sunday School Department and the *Wesley Guild (then known as the Methodist Guild Department) as a basis for new work with the 12–20 age group. From 1973 the Division of Education and Youth aimed to integrate formal and informal education. The Connexional Team (1996) brought further integration. From 1992 World Affairs Youth (formerly the *Youth Missionary Association) evolved into MAYC World Action, sharing with young people in imaginative campaigns on social and global issues. The review by Districts, *Now for the Nineties!* developed into *Charter 95*, the younger generation's vision of the Church which Conference accepted in 1995.

Methodist youth work, understood as Christ's mission among those between 13 and 25, shares established values with young people, even as it empowers them to realise their own potential. Since 1990 the emphasis has moved from participation, through empowerment, to a constitutional place for young people in the *Conference.

Annual Reports of the Connexional Sunday School Council, Youth Department and Division of Education and Youth

CHS

Yoxall, Sir James Henry, MP (1857–1925), a WM of the fourth generation, was an educationalist, a *local preacher and a *temperance advocate. From Redditch WM school he went as a pupil teacher at Bridgehouses WM school in *Sheffield, then to *Westminster College, where he won the commendation of Matthew Arnold. As a board school headmaster in Sheffield he fostered the appreciation of literature, music and art. From 1895 to 1919 he was Liberal MP for *Nottingham (West). He served on the Royal Commission on Secondary Education 1894–95, was President and then General Secretary of the NUT 1892–1925 and leader of the teachers' panel on the early Burnham Committee. His particular concern was for the education of the poor. He received honorary degrees from both Cambridge (1899) and Oxford (1907) and was the first elementary school teacher to be knighted (1911).

MR 5 Feb. 1925; *WM Committee of Education Report* (1924–5) pp. 125–7

JAV

Zambia In 1894 H. *Buckenham and a party of PM missionaries reached Lozi (then transcribed as Barotse) territory in what was to become Northern Rhodesia (now Zambia). After initial opposition four mission posts were established, but the first baptisms did not take place until 1906. WM work began in 1912, with urban missions in Lusaka and Kabwe and later a pioneering girls' school at Chipembi. In 1916 a training centre for teacher-evangelists at Kafue was opened jointly by WM, PM and the London Missionary Society. It moved to Livingstone in 1958. After coppermining began in the 1920s, a United Mission to the Copperbelt was launched in 1936, which in 1945 became the United Church of Central Africa. Elsewhere Methodist work continued independently until in January 1965, three months after Zambian independence, Methodist, Presbyterian and other evangelical Christians came together as the United Church of Zambia with the Methodist C.M. *Morris as its first President.

JRP

Zimbabwe WM work in Southern Rhodesia began as an outpost of the Transvaal District, when missionaries accompanied Rhodes' pioneer column in 1891. Black South African evangelists had a leading role, and some were murdered in the Shona uprising of 1896. The growth of the Church was accompanied by the founding of some notable educational institutions, including Waddilove and Thekwane. A Methodist minister Canaan Banana (1936–) was the country's first President. The restrictions placed on rural church life during Zimbabwe's war of independence in the 1970s did not prevent the District becoming an autonomous Conference in 1977 under the outstanding leadership of A. Ndhlela. In 1989 the title of President was changed to Bishop. Several American-related Methodist Churches (UMC, AMEZ, CME) also work in Zimbabwe, as does an African Methodist Church which broke away from British Methodism in 1947.

C. Thorpe (1951); C. Banana (1991)

JRP

Zinzendorf, Nikolaus Ludwig Graf von (1700–60), German count, was born in Dresden, studied at Wittenburg and in 1734 was ordained into the Lutheran ministry at Tübingen. Sympathizing with the Bohemian Brethren driven from their homeland by persecution, he offered them a site for a settlement called Herrnhut on his estate at Berthelsdorf, Saxony. He organized the 'Renewed Church of the United Brethren', better known as *Moravian Church, but alienated the authorities and was banished from Saxony in 1736. JW first met him at Marienborn near Frankfurt when on his way to Herrnhut in July 1738. Their relationship seems to have been problematical from the outset, partly because both were natural autocrats. They met again and conversed at some length in London in September 1741, by which time JW had begun to distance himself from the Moravians and had written a letter critical of some aspects of their community life at Herrnhut. Before he was allowed to return to Saxony in 1748, Zinzendorf had established further settlements in England and the Netherlands and had visited *America.

A.G. Spangenberg (1838); J.R. Weinlick (1956); A.J. Lewis (1962)

JAV

Abbreviations

ADB	*Australian Dictionary of Biography*
ADEB	*Australian Dictionary of Evangelical Biography*
AM	*Arminian Magazine*
AV	Authorized ['King James'] Version of the Bible
BC,	Bible Christian(s)
BCC	British Council of Churches
BCP	*Book of Common Prayer*
BFBS	British & Foreign Bible Society
CHP	*Companion to Hymns and Psalms*
CIM	China Inland Mission
CMS	Church Missionary Society
CofE	Church of England
CM	Calvinistic Methodism/Methodist(s)
CMHA	(Journal of the) Cornish Methodist Historical Society
CPD	*Constitutional Practice and Discipline of the Methodist Church*
CSI	Church of South India
CW	Charles Wesley
CWJ	Charles Wesley's Journal
DBR	*Dictionary of Business Biography*
DEB	*Dictionary of Evangelical Biography*
DEY	Division of Education and Youth
DHR	*Dublin Historical Record*
DLB	*Dictionary of Labour Biography*
DNB	*Dictionary of National Biography*
DNZB	*Dictionary of New Zealand Biography*
DWB	*Dictionary of Welsh Biography*
e.m.	entered the ministry
ER	*Epworth Review*
ERE	*Encyclopaedia of Religion and Ethics*
Ev. Mag.	*Evangelical Magazine*
EW	*Yr Eurgrawn Wesleyaidd*
F&H	G.G. Findlay and W.W. Holdsworth, *The History of the Wesleyan Methodist Missionary Society*
FCFC	Free Church Federal Council
HM	Home Mission(s)
HMGB	*History of the Methodist Church in Great Britain*
HP	*Hymns and Psalms*

ICA	*Irish Christian Advocate*
IM	Independent Methodism/Methodist(s)
IOM	Isle of Man
JW	John Wesley
JWJ	John Wesley's Journal
K-i-H	Kaisar-i-Hind Medal
Lincs FHS	Journal of the Lincolnshire Family History Society
LPMAA	Local Preachers' Mutual Aid Association
LQ(H)R	*London Quarterly (& Holborn) Review*
MCI	Methodist Church in Ireland
MCOD	Methodist Church Overseas Division
MEC	Methodist Episcopal Church [of America]
MH	*Methodist History* (American quarterly)
MHA	Methodist Homes for the Aged
MHB	*Methodist Hymn Book*
Minutes	*Minutes of Conference* (Wesleyan unless otherwise stated)
MMS	Methodist Missionary Society
MNC	Methodist New Connexion
MNCM	*Methodist New Connexion Magazine*
MR	*Methodist Recorder*
MR(W)	*Methodist Recorder, Winter Number(s)*
MYD	Methodist Youth Department
NCH(O)	National Children's Home (and Orphanage)
NHM	*A New History of Methodism*
Notes	John Wesley, *Explanatory Notes upon the New Testament*
NT	New Testament
OCLW	*Oxford Companion to the Literature of Wales*
ODCC	*Oxford Dictionary of the Christian Church*
OT	Old Testament
PM	Primitive Methodism/Methodist(s)
PMM	*Primitive Methodist Magazine*
PMQR	*Primitive Methodist Quarterly Review*
PWHS	*Proceedings* of the Wesley Historical Society
PWM	Primitive Wesleyan Methodism/Methodist(s)
QM	Quarterly Meeting
RC	Roman Catholic
SCH	*Studies in Church History*
SJ	*The Journal of John Wesley*, 'Standard Edition', ed. N. Curnock
SL	*Letters of John Wesley*, 'Standard Edition', ed. J. Telford
SO	Standing Orders
UM	United Methodism/Methodist(s)
UMFC	United Methodist Free Churches
UMM	*United Methodist Magazine*
VCH	*Victoria County History*
W	Wesley
WCC	World Council of Churches

WDO	Wesley Deaconess Order
WHS	Wesley Historical Society
WHS(B)	*Bulletin* of the Wesley Historical Society, Bristol Branch
WHS(EA)	*Bulletin* of the Wesley Historical Society, East Anglia Branch
WHS(I)	*Bulletin* of the Wesley Historical Society, Irish Branch
WHS(NE)	*Bulletin* of the Wesley Historical Society, North East Branch
WHS(NL)	*Bulletin* of the Wesley Historical Society, North Lancashire Branch
WHS(S)	*Journal* of the Wesley Historical Society, Scottish Branch
WJW	Bicentennial Edition of the *Works* of John Wesley
WM	Weslcyan Methodism/Methodist(s)
WMA	Wesleyan Methodist Association
WMC	World Methodist Council
WMM	(*Wesleyan*) *Methodist Magazine*
WMMS	Wesleyan Methodist Missionary Society
WR(U)	Wesleyan Reform (Union)
YBC	*Y Bywgraffiadur Cynweig*

Bibliography

Unless specified, place of publication is London or unknown

Addison, T. Powley (1964), *A Thousand Tongues, the History of Methodism in Inverness*
Airey, A. & J. (1979), *The Bainbridges of Newcastle* (Newcastle)
Allen, R. (1866), *The History of Methodism in Preston* (Preston)
Anderson, J.H. (1975), *The Tunstall Methodists 1783–1975* (Tunstall)
Anderson, Joan M. (1953), *Early Methodism in Bedford* (Bedford)
Andrews, C.F. (1935), *John White of Mashonaland*
Ankers, Arthur R. (1988), *The Pater: John Lockwood Kipling. His Life and Times* (Otford)
Anstey, Roger T. (1975), *The Atlantic Slave Trade and British Abolition 1760–1810*
Antliff, William (1872), *The Life of the Venerable Hugh Bourne* (revd edn 1892)
Armitage, Ernest (1995), *Wesley College, Dublin 1845–1995* (Dublin)
Armstrong, W.H. [1932], *John Alfred Sharp, a Memoir*
Arthur, William (1852), *The Successful Merchant: sketches of the life of Mr Samuel Budgett*
Arthur, William (1876), *The Life of Gideon Ouseley*
Articles of Religion prepared by order of the Conference of 1806 (1897)
Askew, E. (1899), *Free Methodist Manual*
Atkinson, J. Baines (ed.) (1945), *To the Uttermost: the Southport Holiness Convention*
Atkinson, John (1898), *Life of Rev. Colin C. McKechnie*
Atkinson, John (1976), *Doctors' Dilemmas*
Atmore, Charles (1801), *The Methodist Memorial* (Bristol)
Australian Dictionary of Biography, ed. Douglas Pike (Melbourne, 1966–1996) [*ADB*]
Australian Dictionary of Evangelical Biography, ed. Brian Dickey (Sydney, 1994) [*ADEB*]

Bainbridge, R.H. (1913), *Reminiscences*
Baker, Derek (1975), *Partnership in Excellence* (Cambridge)
Baker, Eric W. (1948), *A Herald of the Evangelical Revival*
Baker, Frank (1948), *Charles Wesley as Revealed by his Letters*
Baker, Frank (1957), *Methodism and the Love Feast*
Baker, Frank (1963), *William Grimshaw 1708–63*
Baker, Frank (1970), *John Wesley and the Church of England*
Baker, Frank (1976), *From Wesley to Asbury: Studies in Early American Methodism* (Durham NC)
Baker, Frank (1988a), *Charles Wesley's Verse: an Introduction* (revd edn)
Baker, Frank (1988b), *Sixty Years on the Wesley Trail* (Durham NC, 1988)
Baker, N. (1980), *Truro School 1880–1980*
Baldwin, A. (n.d.), *A Missionary Outpost in Central Africa*
Baldwin, A.W. (1960), *The Macdonald Sisters*
Balleine, G.R. (1948), *A Biographical Dictionary of Jersey*
Banana, C. (1991), *A Century of Methodism in Zimbabwe*
Banks, John (1977), *Here for Good* (Manchester)

Banks, John (1984), *Nancy, Nancy. The story of Ann Bolton* (Leeds)

Banks, John (1996), *Samuel Francis Collier* (Peterborough)

Barber, B.A. (1936), *The Art of Frank O. Salisbury* (Leigh-on-Sea)

Barber, W.T.A. (1898), *David Hill, Missionary and Saint*

Barclay, Wade Crawford (1949), *History of Methodist Missions* (New York)

Barger, B.D. (1965), *Lord Dartmouth and the American Revolution* (Columbia, SC)

Barker, Joseph (1880), *The Life of Joseph Barker, written by himself*

Barker, William (1928), *The Mother Church of Manchester Primitive Methodism* (Manchester)

Barratt, George (1866), *Recollections of Methodism and Methodists in the City of Lincoln* (Lincoln)

Barrett, Alfred (1852), *The Life of the Rev. John Hewgill Bumby*

Barrett, Alfred (1854), *The Ministry and Polity of the Christian Church*

Barritt, Gordon E. (1972), *The Edgworth Story*

Barritt, Gordon E. (1996), *Thomas Bowman Stephenson* (Peterborough)

Bartels, F.L. (1965), *The Roots of Ghana Methodism*

Bateman, T. (1870), *Memoir of the Life and Labours of John Wedgwood*

Bates, E. Ralph (1972), *The Rise of Methodism in the Vale of Aylesbury*

Bates, E. Ralph (1975), *Captain Thomas Webb, Anglo-American Methodist Hero*

Batty, Margaret (1985), *Bygone Reeth* (Reeth)

Batty, Margaret (1993a), *Stages in the Development and Control of Wesleyan Lay Leadership 1791–1878* (Peterborough)

Batty, Margaret (1993b), *The Story of the Methodist Church, Low Row*

Batty, Margaret (1998), *James Hamilton of Dunbar* (Peterborough)

Baxter, Matthew (1865), *Memorials of Free Methodism*

Baynes, B. (1995), *Other People Did the Work*

Beadle, Harold L. (1980), *The Beginning of Methodism in Upper Teesdale and the Story of Newbiggin Chapel*

Beadle, Harold L. (1984), *Methodism in Richmond 1750–1950* (Richmond, Yorks)

Beasley, John D. (1989), *The Bitter Cry Heard and Heeded*

Bebbington, D.W. (1982), *The Nonconformist Conscience*

Beckerlegge, Oliver A. (1957), *The United Methodist Free Churches*

Beckerlegge, Oliver A. (ed.) (1980), *The Lavington Correspondence* (Bunbury)

Beckerlegge, Oliver A. (1996), *The Three Expelled* (Peterborough)

Beckworth, William (1910), *A Book of Remembrance, being records of Leeds Primitive Methodism*

Beech, H. Eva [1999], *History of Wesley Methodist Church, Stoke, 1799–1999* (Stoke-on-Trent)

Beech, John H. (1883), *Centenary of the Burslem Wesleyan Circuit* (Burslem)

Bellamy, Elizabeth J. (1994), *James Wheatley and Norwich Methodism in the 1750s* (Peterborough)

Benham, Daniel (1865), *Life and Labours of John Gambold*

Bennett, G.V. & Walsh, J.D. (eds) (1966), *Essays in Modern Church History in memory of Norman Sykes*

Bennis, E. (1809), *Christian Correspondence* (Philadelphia)

Benson, Joseph (1804), *The Life of the Rev. John W. de la Fléchère*

Best, G. (1998), *The History of Kingswood School*

Bett, Henry (1937), *The Spirit of Methodism*

Bibb, J.F. (1991), *Women into Priesthood*

Bielby, Morwenna (1965), *A Great Host*

Biggs, Barry J. (1965), in *Souvenir of the 150th Anniversary of Bishop Street Methodist Chapel, Leicester 1815–1965* (Leicester)

Biggs, Barry J. (1970), *The Story of the Methodists of Retford and District*

Biggs, Barry J. (1987), *The Wesleys and the Early Dorset Methodists* (Gillingham)

Billington, R.J. (1969), *The Liturgical Movement and Methodism*

Birtwhistle, N. Allen (1950), *Thomas Birch Freeman, West African Pioneer*

Birtwhistle, N. Allen (1954), *In his Armour: the Life of John Hunt*

Birtwhistle, N. Allen (1966), *William Threlfall: A study in missionary vocation*

Bishop, John (1950), *Methodist Worship in relation to Free Church Worship*

Bissell, Don and Weetman, Barry (1997), *Bert Bissell, God's Mountaineer*

Blackburn, F. (1954), *George Tomlinson*

Blackwell, John (1838), *Life of the Rev. Alexander Kilham*

Blackwell Dictionary of Evangelical Biography 1730–1860, ed. Donald M. Lewis (Oxford 1995) [*DEB*]

Bland, E. (1911), *Southport Methodism. A Centenary and Jubilee Souvenir* (Southport)

Blanshard, Thomas W. (1870), *The Life of Samuel Bradburn, the Methodist Demosthenes*

Blatherwick, Douglas (1959), *A Layman Speaks*

Blatherwick, R. (n.d.), *Douglas Pursey Blatherwick*

Bleakley, D. (1980), *Sadie Patterson*

Bleby, Henry (1876), *A Missionary Father's Tales*

Bleby, Henry M. [1935], *The Fourth Generation: a Modern Sequel to A Missionary Father's Tales*

Boaden, Edward (1896), *Memoir of the Rev. Richard Chew*

Boahen, A.A. (1996), *Mfantsipim and the Making of Ghana* (Accra)

Body, A.H. (1936), *John Wesley and Education*

Bolitho, Paul (1987), *150 Glorious Years: Handbook of the 150th Celebration of the Leamington Methodist Circuit* (Leamington)

Bolton, A.J. (1994), *The Other Side': Opposition to Methodist Union 1913–1932* (Peterborough)

Boocock, N. (1912), *Our Fernandian Missions*

Booth, W. (1977), *Centenary History of Ashville College*

Borgen, Ole E. (1972), *John Wesley on the Sacraments* (Nashville)

Boston, Lucy M. (1979), *Perverse and Foolish*

Bourne, Frederick W. (1869), *Billy Bray, the King's Son*

Bourne, Frederick W. (1895), *The Centenary Life of James Thorne of Shebbear*

Bourne, Frederick W. (1905), *The Bible Christians*

Bowden, K.E. (1982), *Samuel Chadwick and Stacksteads*

Bowmer, John C. (1951), *The Sacrament of the Lord's Supper in Early Methodism*

Bowmer, John C. (1961), *The Lord's Supper in Methodism 1791–1960*

Bowmer, John C. (1963), 'The Local Preacher on Early Methodism' in *Local Preacher's Handbook* No.8, pp. 1–14

Bowmer, John C. (1975), *Pastor and People: A Study of Church and Ministry in Wesleyan Methodism 1791–1858*

Bowran, J.G. (1922), *Life of Arthur Thomas Guttery*

Boyce, W.B. (1874), *Memoir of the Rev. William Shaw*

Bradfield, William (1913), *The Life of Thomas Bowman Stephenson*

Bradford, N. (1984), *Robert Bradford*

Bradley, D.H. (1956), *History of the AME Zion Church* (Nashville)

Bradley, Sidney B. [1936], *The Life of Bishop Richard Whatcoat* (Louisville, Ky)

Brailsford, Dennis (1997), *British Sport: a Social History* (2nd edn)

Brailsford, E.J. (1906), *Richard Watson, Theologian and Missionary Advocate*

Brake, George Thompson (1984), *Policy and Politics in British Methodism 1932–1982*

Bramwell, W. (1796), *A Short Account of the Life and Death of Ann Cutler* (Sheffield)

Bramwell-Booth, C. (1970), *Catherine Booth, the story of her loves*

Brash, W. Bardsley (1935), *The Story of our Colleges 1835–1935*

Brash, W. Bardsley and Wright, C.J. (1942), *Didsbury College Centenary*

Brazendale, G. (n.d.), *John Whiteley – Land Sovereignty and the Land Wars of the Nineteenth Century* (New Zealand)

Bredon, Juliet (1909), *Sir Robert Hart: the Romance of a Great Career*

Bretherton, F.F. (1903), *Early Methodism in and around Chester* (Chester)

Brice, J.I. (1934), *The Crowd for Christ*

Bridges, Yseult (1962), *Poison and Adelaide Bartlett*

Broadbent, Samuel (1857), *The Missionary Martyr of Namaqualand. Memorials of the Rev. William Threlfall*

Brooks, Peter (ed.) (1975), *Christian Spirituality: essays in honour of Gordon Rupp*

Brown, Earl Kent (1983), *Women of Mr Wesley's Methodism* (New York)

Brown, James W.M. (1986), *The Story of St Andrew's Methodist Church, Sholing* (Southampton)

Brown, Kenneth D. (1988), *A Social History of the Nonconformist Ministry in England and Wales* (Oxford)

Brown-Lawson, A. (1994), *John Wesley and the Anglican Evangelicals of the Eighteenth Century* (Bishop Auckland)

Bucke, E.S. (ed.) (1964), *The History of American Methodism* (Nashville)

Bulmer, Agnes (1836), *Memoirs of Mrs Elizabeth Mortimer; with selections from her correspondence*

Bunting, T.P. and Rowe, G. Stringer (1887), *The Life of Jabez Bunting, DD*

Burdsall, Richard (1797), *Memoirs* (York)

Burge, Janet (1996), *Women Preachers in Community* (Peterborough)

Burgess, John (1980), *A History of Cumbrian Methodism* (Kendall)

Burgin, H. (1988), *An Illustrated History of Bondgate Methodist Church Darlington* (Darlington)

Burnett, R.G. (1932), *Chudleigh*

Burnett, R.G. (1945), *Through the Mill*

Burt, Thomas (1924), *Pitman and Privy Councillor; an autobiography*

Buss, F.H. & Burnett, R.G. (1949), *A Goodly Fellowship 1849–1949*

Butler, C. (1902), *William Butler*

Butler, David (1995), *Methodists and Papists*

Butler, P. (ed.) (1983), *Pusey Rediscovered*

Butler, Mrs Thomas (1924), *Missions as I Saw Them*

Butterworth, James (1970), *Clubland 1920–1970*

Calman, A.L. (1875), *Life and Labours of John Ashworth* (Manchester)

Calvert, David (ed.) (1992), *The Outside Church* (Manchester)

Campbell, Ted A. (1991), *John Wesley and Christian Antiquity* (Nashville)

Carter, David (1994), *James H. Rigg* (Peterborough)

Carter, E.R. (1980), *History of Bath Road Methodist Church, Swindon 1880–1980*

Carwardine, Richard (1978), *Transatlantic Revivalism: popular evangelicalism in Britain and America 1790–1865*

Casteras, Susan P. (1995), *James Smetham – Artist, Author, Pre-Raphaelite Associate*

Cathcart, B. (1992), *Nine Ulster Lives* (Belfast)

Chadwick, Owen (1966, 1970), *The Victorian Church*

Chambers, W.A. (1982), *Samuel Ironside in New Zealand 1839–1858* (Auckland)

Chambers, W.A. (1987), *Not Self – but Others: the Story of the New Zealand Methodist Deaconess Order* (Auckland)

Champness, Eliza M. (1907), *The Life-story of Thomas Champness*

Channon, H.J. (1957), *History of Queen's College, Taunton* (Taunton)

Chapels Society (1998), *Miscellany 1*

Chappel, John W. (1901), *In the Power of God* (Burslem)

Chapman, E.V. (1952), *John Wesley & Co. (Halifax)* (Halifax)

Chapman, E.V. (1982), *The Rev. Robert Aitken* (IOM)

Chapman, E.V. and Turner, G.A. (1964), *Heptonstall Octagon* (Heptonstall)

Chapman, Stanley (1974), *Jesse Boot of Boots the Chemist*

Cheeseman, Thomas F. (1910), *The Story of William Threlfall* (Capetown)

Chew, Richard (1875), *James Everett: A biography*

Chew, Richard (1885), *William Griffith, Memorials and Letters*

Chick, E. (1907), *A History of Methodism in Exeter and the Neighbourhood* (Exeter)

Chilcote, Paul Wesley (1991), *John Wesley and the Women Preachers of Early Methodism* (Metuchen, NJ)

Church, Frederick and Leslie F. (1914), *A Mender of Hearts: the story of Henry T. Meakin*

Church, Leslie F.(1948), *The Early Methodist People*

Church, Leslie F. (1949), *More About the Early Methodist People*

Church, R.W. (1895), *Pascal and Other Sermons*

Clancy, Eric G. (1972), *Silas Gill, A Giant for Jesus* (Sydney)

Clarke, Adam (1823), *Memoirs of the Wesley Family*

Clarke, W.K. Lowther (1944), *Eighteenth Century Piety*

Cliff, P.B. (1986), *The Rise and Development of the Sunday School Movement in England 1780–1980* (Redhill)

Cocking, Thomas (1836), *The History of Wesleyan Methodism in Grantham and its Vicinity* (Grantham)

Coke, Thomas (1816), *Extracts of the journals of the late Rev. Thomas Coke L.L.D.* (Dublin)

Coke, Thomas & Moore, Henry (1792), *The Life of the Rev. John Wesley, A.M.*

Cole, G.D.H. (1941), *Chartist Portraits*

Cole, R. Lee (1932), *History of Methodism in Dublin* (Dublin)

Cole, R. Lee (1938), *John Wesley's Journal: an appreciation*

Cole, R. Lee (1960), *History of Methodism in Ireland 1860–1960* (Belfast)

Coley, Samuel (1868), *The Life of the Rev. Thomas Collins*

Collier, R. (1965), *The General Next to God*

Collins, Kenneth (1989), *John Wesley on Salvation* (Grand Rapids)

Constitutional Practice and Discipline [CPD], various editions

Cook, V.C. (1914), *Thomas Cook, evangelist-saint*

Cooney, D.A.L. (1998), *Asses Colts and Loving People* (Carlow)

Cooper, W. Donald (1973), *Methodism in Portsmouth* (Portsmouth)

Coulson, John E. (1865), *The Peasant Preacher; Memorials of Mr. Charles Richardson*

Court, Lewis H. (1923), *These Hundred Years: The Story of the United Methodist Church in Brighton and Hove* (Brighton)

Court, Lewis H. (1935), *Ready, Aye Ready – the Story of a Romantic Career*

Cozens-Hardy, B. (1957), *The History of Letheringsett* (Norwich)

Cozens-Hardy, W.H. (1852), *A Report of the Proceedings in Chancery...*

Cragg, George G. (1947), *Grimshaw of Haworth, a Study in Eighteenth Century Evangelism*

Cragg, Gerald R. (ed.) (1975), *The Appeals to Men of Reason and Religion and Certain Related Open Letters* (*Works of John Wesley*, Bicentennial Edition, Oxford)

Crane, Dennis [1906], *James Flanagan, the story of a remarkable career*

Crane, Dennis (1909), *The Life-Story of Sir Robert W. Perks Bt, MP*

Crawford, Keith Early (1996), *Praise, People and Pipes* (Witney)

Cresswell, Amos S. (1983), *The Story of Cliff* (Sheffield)

Crofts, Bruce (ed.) (1990), *At Satan's Throne: the Story of Methodism in Bath* (Bristol)

Crookshank, C.H. (1882), *Memorable Women of Irish Methodism in the Last Century*

Crookshank, C.H. (1885–88), *A History of Methodism in Ireland* (Belfast)

Crowther, Jonathan (1815), *Life of the Rev. Thomas Coke, LL.D.* (Leeds)

Crutchley, G.W. (1921), *John Mackintosh, a Biography*

Cumbers, Frank H. (ed.) (1944), *Richmond College 1843–1943*

Cumbers, Frank H. (1956), *The Book Room*

Cumming, G.J. and Baker, D. (eds) (1972), *Popular Belief and Practice*

Cummings, Arthur D. (1962), *A Portrait in Pottery*

Cunningham, G.F. (1965), *The Divine Comedy in English: A Critical Biography 1782–1900*

Currie, Robert (1968), *Methodism Divided*

Currie, Robert, Gilbert, Alan and Horsley, Lee (1977), *Churches and Churchgoers* (Oxford)

Cutt, Margaret Nancy (1979), *Ministering Angels: a study of nineteenth-century evangelical writing for children* (Wormley)

Dallimore, Arnold (1970, 1980), *George Whitefield* (London & Edinburgh)

Davey, Cyril J. (1951), *The March of Methodism*

Davey, Cyril J. (1968), *A Man for All Children*

Davey, Cyril J. (1976), *Home from Home*

Davey, Cyril J. (1979), *The Glory Man*

Davey, Cyril J. (1983), *Home for Good*

Davey, Cyril J. (1988), *Changing Places*

Davey, Cyril J. (n.d.), *Rue Roquépine* (Paris)

Davey, Cyril and Thomas, Hugh (1984), *Together Travel On: A History of Women's Work*

Davey, T. Frank and Kathleen (n.d.), *Compassionate Years: a Medical Te Deum*

Davie, Donald (1978), *A Gathered Church: the Literature of the English Dissenting Interest, 1700–1930*

Davies, G.C.B. (1951), *The Early Cornish Evangelicals, 1735–1760: a Study of Samuel Walker of Truro and others*

Davies, Horton (1951), *Great South African Christians* (Cape Town)

Davies, Horton (1961), *Worship and Theology in England: From Watts and Wesley to Maurice, 1690–1850* (Princeton)

Davies, P. (1983), *E. Tegla Davies* (Cardiff)

Davies, Rupert E. (ed.) (1957), *John Scott Lidgett: a Symposium*

Davies, Rupert E. (1976), *Methodism* (revd edn)

Davies, Rupert E. (1979), *The Church in Our Times*

Davies, Rupert E. (1989), *The Methodist Societies: History, Nature and Design* (*Works of John Wesley*, Bicentennial Edition, Nashville)

Davies, Rupert E. (1993), *Methodism and Ministry* (Peterborough)

Davies, Rupert, George, A. Raymond and Rupp, Gordon (eds) (1965–1988), *A History of the Methodist Church in Great Britain* [*HMGB*]

Davies, S. (1877), *Gweithiau Y Parch. Thomas Aubrey*

Davies, T.R. (1908), *Eminent Welshmen*, Vol. 1 (Cardiff)

Davies, W. (1900), *John Bryan a'i amserau* (Bangor)

Davis, George W. (1995), *The Robert Dall Story* (Arbroath)

Davis, George W. (1996), *Arbroath Methodism* (Arbroath)

Davis, Samuel (1962), *Whitby's Brunswick Room* (Whitby)

Davison, J. (1840), *The Vessel of Beaten Gold* (Grimsby)

Dawson, Joseph (1896), *Peter Mackenzie, his Life and Labours*

Dawson, Joseph [1906], *William Morley Punshon, the orator of Methodism*

Deacon, Lois (1951), *So I Went my Way*

Deacon, M. (1980), *Philip Doddridge of Northampton 1702–51* (Northampton)

Dearing, Trevor (1966), *Wesleyan and Tractarian Worship*

Deschner, J.W. (1960), *Wesley's Christology: an interpretation* (Dallas)

Dews, D. Colin (ed.) (1982), *From Mow Cop to Peake 1807–1932* (Leeds)

Dews, D. Colin (ed.) (1987), *Preachers All* (Leeds)

Diack, C. (1901), *Sketch of Methodism in Aberdeen* (Aberdeen)

Dickinson, E.W. (1925), *John Wesley's Visits to Whitby and Robin Hood's Bay* (Whitby)

Dickson, Mora (1976), *The Inseparable Grief: Margaret Cargill of Fiji*

Dickson, Mora (1980), *The Powerful Bond: Hannah Kilham 1774–1832*

Dictionary of Business Biography ed. Leslie Hannah and David J. Jeremy (1984–6) [*DBB*]

Dictionary of Labour Biography ed. Joyce Bellamy and John Saville (1972–93) [*DLB*]

Dictionary of National Biography (1886–

Dictionary of New Zealand Biography ed. W.H. Oliver (1990–1998) (Wellington) [*DNZB*]

Dictionary of Welsh Biography [*DWB*]

Dieter, Melvin E. (1980), *The Holiness Revival of the Nineteenth Century*

Dimond, Sydney G. (1926), *The Psychology of the Methodist Revival*

Dinnick, J.Dunn [1890], *The Transfiguration of Christ, and other Sermons of Samuel Dunn, with a Biographical Sketch*

Dixon, Richard W. (1874), *The Life of James Dixon, Wesleyan Minister*

Dockray, K. and Laybourn, K. (eds.) (1999), *The Representation and Reality of War* (Stroud)

Dolan, J. (1996), *Peter's People* (Wigan)

Dolby, George W. (1964), *The Architectural Expression of Methodism: the first hundred years*

Doughty, W.L. (1944), *John Wesley: His Conferences and his Preachers*

Doughty, W.L. (1955), *John Wesley, Preacher*

Drew, Jacob H. (1834), *The Life, Character and Literary Labours of Samuel Drew, A.M.*

Drew, Samuel (1817), *Life of the Rev. Thomas Coke. LL.D.*

Driver, Cecil (1946), *Tory Radical: the Life of Richard Oastler* (New York)

Dunn, Samuel (1863), *The Life of Adam Clarke, LL.D.*

Dunning, Norman G. (1933), *Samuel Chadwick*

Dunstan, Alan and Peart-Binns, John S. (1977), *Cornish Bishop*

Dwyer, John (1875), *Christian Thoroughness; a memorial sketch of Thomas Averell Shillington* of Portadown

Dymond, G.P. [1913], *Thomas Ruddle of Shebbear, a North Devon Arnold*

Dyson, John B. (1865), *Methodism in the Isle of Wight* (Ventnor)

Eakins, David (1959), *Sugden of Queen's* (Melbourne)

Eayrs, George [1916], *William John Townsend, D.D., Methodist Preacher, Free Church Leader*

Ede, Janet and Virgoe, Norma (1998), *Religous Worship in Norfolk* (Norwich)

Ede, Janet, Virgoe, Norma and Williamson, Tom (1996), *Halls of Zion* (Norwich)

Edwards, E. (1980), *Yr Eglwys Fethodistaidd* (with Supplement 1987)

Edwards, John (1984), *Victory Purdy, 'the Kingswood Collier'* (Bristol)

Edwards, Maldwyn L. (1942), *Adam Clarke*

Edwards, Maldwyn L. (1949a), *Family Circle*

Edwards, Maldwyn L. (1949b) *John A. Broadbelt, Methodist Preacher*

Edwards, Maldwyn L. (1949c), *S.E. Keeble, Pioneer and Prophet*

Edwards, Maldwyn L. (1995), *The New Room* (revised edn., Peterborough)

Edwards, Maldwyn L., *My Dear Sister* (n.d.)

Edwards, Michael S. (1977), *S.E. Keeble, the Rejected Prophet*

Edwards, Michael S. (1994), *Purge This Realm: a Life of Joseph Rayner Stephens*

Edwards, N. (1998), *Ploughboy's Progress* (Norwich)

Elis, I.F. (ed.) (1956), *Edward Tegla Davies, Llenor a Phroffwyd*

Ellingworth, Paul (1995), *Thomas Birch Freeman* (Peterborough)

Ellis, John V. (1982), *Wesley's Centenary Memorial*

Entwisle, Joseph (1848), *Memoir of the Rev. Joseph Entwisle* (Bristol)

Epworth Review [ER]

Erhall, H. (1980), *Tegla*

Etheridge, J.W. (1858), *The Life of the Rev. Adam Clarke*

Etheridge, J.W. (1860), *The Life of the Rev. Thomas Coke, DCL*

Evangelical Magazine [Ev. Mag.]

Evans, A.W. (1932), *Warburton and the Warburtonians*

Evans, D.T. (1950), *Atgofion Cynnar* (Tywyn)

Evans, Eifion (1980), *Life of Humphrey Rowland Jones* (Bridgend)

Evans, Eifion (1985), *Daniel Rowland and the Great Awakening in Wales* (Edinburgh)

Evans, Eifion (1996), *Pursued by God* (Bridgend)

Evans, Owen E. (ed.) (1993), *Gwarchod y Gair* (Denbigh)

Evans, Seth (1912), *New Mills Wesleyanism* (New Mills)

Evans, W.H. (1888), *Cyfrol Goffadwriaethol Cynfaen* (Holywell)

Evens, Eunice (1946), *Through the Years with Romany*

Everett, James (1823), *Historical Sketches of Wesleyan Methodism in Sheffield* (Sheffield)

Everett, James (1827), *Wesleyan Methodism in Manchester* (Manchester)

Everett, James (1830), *The Village Blacksmith, or, Piety and unsefulness exemplified in a memoir of the life of Samuel Hick*

Everett, James (1839), *The Polemic Divine, or Memoirs of... the Rev. Daniel Isaac*

Everett, James (1842), *Memoir of William Dawson*

Everett, James (1866), *Adam Clarke Portrayed* (2nd edn)

Everson, F.H. (1947), *The Manchester Round* (Manchester)

Fairchild, A. (ed.) (1987), *A School Apart* (Shebbear)

Falkner, Frank (1912), *The Wood Family of Burslem*

Farndale, W.E. (1950), *The Secret of Mow Cop*

Farr, Nicholas (1921), *At the Heart of the City: A Methodist Mission in the Twentieth Century* (Sheffield)

Feinstein, C.H. (ed.) (1981), *York 1821–1981* (York)

Ferguson, F. (1876), *A History of the Evangelical Union* (Glasgow)

Fifield, A.C. (1927), *Salome Hocking Fifield* (Coulsdon)

Findlay, G.G. (1910), *William F. Moulton, the Methodist Scholar*

Findlay, G.G. & M.C. (1913), *Wesley's World Parish*

Findlay, G.G. and Holdsworth, W.W. (1924), *The History of the Wesleyan Methodist Missionary Society* [F&H]

Fletcher, Mary (1820), *Account of Sarah Lawrence*

Flew, R. Newton (1934), *The Idea of Perfection in Christian Theology*

Foot, Hugh (1964), *A Start in Freedom*

Foot, Sarah (1980), *My Grandfather Isaac Foot* (Bodmin)

Ford, J. (1968), *In the Steps of John Wesley: The Church of the Nazarene in Britain*

Forsaith, Peter S. (1994), *John Fletcher* (Peterborough)

Forward, Martin (1998), *A Bag of Needments: Geoffrey Parrinder and the Study of Religion*

Fowler, Edith Henrietta (1912), *The Life of Henry Hartley Fowler, first Viscount Wolverhampton*

Fraser, W. (1868), *Memoir of the Life of David Stow* (Edinburgh)

Freeman, John (1930), *Last Poems*

Frischauer, Willi (1971), *David Frost*

Frost, Brian (1996), *Goodwill on Fire*

Funnell, James A. (n.d.), *The Story of William Dinnick* (Brighton)

Fussell, G.E. (1948), *From Tolpuddle to TUC* (Slough)

Fyfe, Christopher (1962), *A History of Sierra Leone*

Gadd, Bernard (1964), *William Morley 1842–1926* (Auckland)

Gadd, Bernard (1966), *The Rev. James Buller 1812–1884* (Auckland)

Gailey, A. (1995), *Crying in the Wilderness: Jack Sayers* (Belfast)

Gallagher, R.D.E. (1989), *At Points of Need* (Belfast)

Gallagher, Robert H. (1960), *John Bredin* (Belfast)

Gallagher, Robert H. [1963], *Adam Clarke, saint and scholar: A Memoir* (Belfast)

Gallagher, Robert H. [1965], *Pioneer Preachers of Irish Methodism* (Belfast)

Gammie, A. (1909), *The Churches of Aberdeen* (Aberdeen)

Garlick, Kenneth B. (1983), *Garlick's Methodist Registry*

Garner, William (1857), *Jubilee of English Camp Meetings*

Garner, William (1868), *The Life of the Venerable William Clowes*

Garnett, Jane and Matthew, Colin (1993), *Revival and Religion since 1700*

Gee, Charles H. (1939), *Methodism in Heptonstall*

Gee, H.L. (1949), *The Spirit of Romany*

Gentry, Peter W. (1994), *The Countess of Huntingdon* (Peterborough)

Gibbins, Ronald C. (1995), *Methodist East Enders* (Peterborough)

Gibbs, John M. (1982), *The Morels of Cardiff* (Cardiff)

Gibbs, John M. (1989), *Methodist Residential Schools*

Giles, C. and Goodall, I.H. (1992), *Yorkshire Textile Mills, 1770–1930*

Gill, Frederick C. (1937), *The Romantic Movement and Methodism*

Gill, Frederick C. (1964), *Charles Wesley, the First Methodist*

Gittos, M.B. (1982), *Mana at Mangungu* (Auckland, NZ)

Gittos, M.B. (1997), *Give Us a Pakeha* (Auckland, NZ)

Goodwin, Charles H. (1993), *A Dismal Notoriety: the rise and progress of Methodism at Wednesbury* (Cannock)

Goodwin, Charles H. (1994), *Cries of Anguish, Shouts of Praise: the development of Methodist revivalism 1739–1818* (Cannock)

Gordon, Colin (1980), *By Gaslight: a Victorian family history through the magic lantern*

Goss, Edmund (1903), *Jeremy Taylor*

Gowland, David A. (1979), *Methodist Secessions: the Origins of Free Methodism in Three Lancashire Towns – Manchester, Rochdale, Liverpool* (Manchester)

Gowland, David and Roebuck, Stuart (1990), *Never Call Retreat – a Biography of Bill Gowland*

Graham, E. Dorothy (1989), *Chosen by God* (Bunbury)

Graham, E. Dorothy (1998), *Three Colleges: PM Secondary Ventures*

Green, J. Brazier (1945), *John Wesley and William Law*

Green, Richard (1902), *Anti-Methodist Publications*

Green, V.H.H. (1961), *The Young Mr. Wesley*

Greet, Kenneth G. (1960), *Moderate Drinkers and Total Abstainers*

Greet, Kenneth G. (1995), *Jabez Bunting* (Peterborough)

Greet, Kenneth G. (1997), *Fully Connected: A Volume of Memoirs* (Peterborough)

Gregory, Benjamin (1897), *Sidelights on the Conflicts of Methodism*

Gregory, Benjamin (1903), *Autobiographical Recollections*

Griffin, Ernest W. (1957), *A Pilgrim People: the Story of Methodism in Brighton, Hove and District, 1807–1957* (Hove)

Grist, W.A. (1920), *Samuel Pollard, Pioneer Missionary in China*

Groves, Reginald (1949), *Sharpen the Sickle*

Gruffydd, R.G. (1959), *Diwygiad 1859 yng Nghymru* (Port Talbot)

Gunter, W. Stephen (1989), *The Limits of Love Divine* (Nashville)

Gunter, W. Stephen *et al.* (1997), *Wesley and the Quadrilateral: renewing the conversation* (Nashville)

Guy, J. and Potter, W.S. (1893), *Jubilee Memorial Volume of Fifty Years of Primitive Methodism in New Zealand* (Wellington, NZ)

Gwyther, C. (1975), *Exploits of a Hundred Years* (Liverpool)

Haigh, E.A.H. (ed.) (1992), *Huddersfield, a most handsome town* (Huddersfield)

Haime, J.W. (1970), *The Haimes: A Dorset Family* (Gillingham)

Halévy, Elie (1961), *A History of the English People in the Nineteenth Century*

Haliburton, G. (1971), *The Prophet Harris*

Hall, C. (1918), *Calvert of Cannibal Fiji*

Hall, Ebenezer (1870), *The Earnest Preacher: memoirs of the Rev. Joseph Spoor*

Hall, James (1886), *Methodism in West Bromwich from 1742 to 1885*

Hall, Sir John (1927), *The Trial of Adelaide Bartlett*

Hames, E.W. (1967), *Walter Lawry and the Wesleyan Mission in the South Seas* (Auckland)

Hamilton, Mary A. (1938), *Arthur Henderson*

Hamlyn, F. (1930), *S. Parkes Cadman* (New York)

Hampson, John (1791), *Memoirs of the Late Rev. John Wesley, A.M.* (Sunderland)

Hanna, A.G. (1967), *Methodism in Enniskillen* (Enniskillen)

Hardcastle, Titus (1871), *Methodism in Armley* (Leeds)

Hargreaves, John A. (1994), *Sowerby Bridge in Old Photographs* (Otley)

Hargreaves, John A. (1999), *Halifax* (Edinburgh)

Harris, H. (1791), *A Brief Account of the Life of Howell Harris, Esq* (Trevecka)

Harris, Josiah (1871), *A Tear and a Floweret* (Truro)

Harris, Thomas R. (1963), *Samuel Dunn, Reformer* (Redruth)

Harris, Thomas R. (1968), *Dr. George Smith, 1800–1868, Wesleyan Methodist Layman* (Redruth)

Harrison, A.W. (1937), *Arminianism*

Harrison, A.W. (1945), *The Separation of Methodism from the Church of England*

Harrison, A.W. *et al.* (1932), *The Methodist Church: its Origins, Divisions and Reunion*

Harrison, G. Elsie (1935), *Methodist Good Companions*

Harrison, G. Elsie (1937a), *Haworth Parsonage*

Harrison, G. Elsie (1937b), *Son to Susanna*

Harrison, G. Elsie (1948), *The Clue to the Brontës*

Harvey, F. Brompton (1946), *Archibald Harrison; an appreciation*

Harvey, Wallace (1983), *Thomas Clarke of Canterbury* (Whitstable)

Harwood, G.H. (1872), *History of Wesleyan Methodism in Nottingham and it Vicinity* (Nottingham)

Haslam, J. (1886), *The History of Wesleyan Methodism in South Australia* (Adelaide)

Hastings, A.W. and E. (eds.) (1966), *Theologians of our Time*

Hatcher, Stephen (1999), *God is Building a House: from Mr Smith's kitchen to Vision 2000* (Englesea Brook)

Hay, A.M. (n.d.), *Charles Inwood*

Hayes, Alan J. (1976), *Edinburgh Methodism 1761–1975* (Edinburgh)

Hayes, Alan J. and Gowland, D.A. (eds) (1981), *Scottish Methodism in the early Victorian Period: The Scottish Correspondence of the Rev. Jabez Bunting, 1800–57* (Edinburgh)

Hayman, J.G.(1871), *Methodism in North Devon* (supplement, 1900)

Heald, C.A. (1994), *The Irish Palatinates in Ontario* (Gananoque, Ont.)

Heitzenrater, Richard P. (1984), *The Elusive Mr Wesley* (Nashville)

Heitzenrater, Richard P. (1989), *Mirror and Memory: Reflections on Early Methodism* (Nashville)

Heitzenrater, Richard P. (1995), *Wesley and the People Called Methodists* (Nashville)

Hempton, David (1984), *Methodism and Politics in British Society, 1750–1850*

Hempton, David (1996), *The Religion of the People: Methodism and popular religion c. 1750–1900*

Hempton, David and Hill, Myrtle (1992), *Evangelical Protestantism in Ulster Society 1740–1890*

Herod, George [1855], *Biographical Sketches of some of those Preachers... of the Primitive Methodist Connexion*

Hewitt, John H. (1991), *Collected Poems*

Hewlett, Maurice (1921), *Wiltshire Essays*

Heywood, M. and F. (1996), *A History of Todmorden* (Otley)

Heywood, Percy (1970), *Donald Hughes, Headmaster* (Colwyn Bay)

Hildebrandt, Franz (1951), *From Luther to Wesley*

Hildebrandt, Franz and Beckerlegge , Oliver A. (eds) (1983), *A Collection of Hymns for the Use of the People called Methodists* (*The Works of John Wesley*, Bicentennial Edition, Oxford)

Hill, A.W. (1958), *John Wesley among the Physicians*

Hindmarsh, D.B. (1996), *John Newton and the English Evangelical Tradition* (Oxford)

Hodgson, J.L. (1924), *The History of Aeronautics in Great Britain*

Hogg, J. (1987), *To Those in Need: the story of the Hull Methodist Mission, 1847–1946*

Holland, B.G. (1970), *Baptism in Early Methodism*

Holroyd, Michael (1964), *Hugh Kingsmill: a critical biography*

Honeyman, Katrina and Goodman, Jordan (1986), *Technology and Enterprise: Isaac Holden and the Mechanisation of Woolcombing in France, 1848–1914* (Aldershot)

Hopkins, H.E. (1977), *Charles Simeon of Cambridge*

Hopkins, J.K. (1982), *A Woman to Deliver her People* (Texas)

Horn, Pamela (1971), *Joseph Arch: the Farm Workers' Leader* (Kineton)

Horne, Melville (1799), *Works*

Howard, W.F. (ed.) (1938), *A.S. Peake: Recollections and Appreciations*

Howarth, David. H. (1983), *How Great a Flame: Samuel Chadwick, 50 years on* (Ilkeston)

Hubery, Douglas S. (1977), *The Methodist Contribution to Education in England 1738–1977*

Hudspeth, W.H. (1937), *Stone-Gateway and the Flowery Miao*

Hughes, Dorothea Price (1904), *The Life of Hugh Price Hughes*

Hughes, Glyn T. (ed.) (1979), *Thomas Olivers of Tregynon* (Tregynon)

Hughes, Glyn T. (1983), *Williams Pantycelyn* (Cardiff)

Hughes, H.J. (1892), *Life of Howell Harris* (Newport)

Hughes, H. Maldwyn (1915), *The Theology of Experience*

Hughes, H. Trevor (1960), *The Piety of Jeremy Taylor*

Hughes, H. Trevor (1979), *A Progress of Pilgrims*

Hughes, Katherine Price (1945), *The Story of My Life*

Hulme, Samuel (1881), *Memoir of the Rev. Thomas Allin*

Hulme, Samuel (1886), *Memoir of the Rev. William Cooke*

Humphries, A.L. and Barker, W. (1931), *The Story of Hartley Primitive Methodist College, Manchester, 1881–1931* (Manchester)

Hunston, Ramon (1981), *Order! Order! A biography of...George Thomas* (Basingstoke)

Hunt, A.D. (1977), *A Tall Cedar in our Lebanon* (Salisbury, NSW)

Hunt, J. (1846), *Memoir of the Rev. William Cross, Wesleyan Missionary to the Friendly Islands*

Hurd, F.H. (1872), *Earnest Men: Sketches of eminent Primitive Methodists, ministers and laymen*

Huston, Robert (1853), *The Earnest Minister, exemplified in the Life and Labours of Fossey Tackaberry*

Hyde, H. Montgomery (1964), *Norman Birkitt*

Hyde, R. (ed.) (1993), *The Streets of London 1880–1928: Evocative Watercolours by H.E. Tidmarsh*

'Impartial Hand' (1746), *A Brief Account of the Late Persecution and Barbarous Usage of the Methodists of Exeter and a Vindication of the Foregoing Discourse* (Exeter)

Ince, L. (1993), *The South Wales Iron Industry* (Cardiff)

Independent Methodist Magazine [*IM Magazine*]

Ingram, L.E. (1945), *Fifty Years for Youth*

Irish Christian Advocate [*ICA*]

Isaac, E. (1930), *Life of Humphrey Rowland Jones*

Ives, A.G. (1969), *Kingswood School in Wesley's Day and Since*

Jacka, Alan A. (1967), *The Story of the Children's Home*

Jackson, Annie (1949), *George Jackson: a Commemorative Volume*

Jackson, George [1923], *Collier of Manchester: A friend's tribute*

Jackson, Neil (1991), *Nineteenth-Century Bath: Architects and Architecture* (Bath)

Jackson, Thomas (1834), *Memoirs of the Life and Writings of the Rev. Richard Watson*

Jackson, Thomas (1841), *The Life of the Rev. Charles Wesley*

Jackson, Thomas (1855), *The Life of the Rev. Robert Newton, D.D.*

Jackson, Thomas (ed.) (1871–72), *The Lives of the Early Methodist Preachers, chiefly written by themselves* (4th edn) [*EMP*]

Jakes, Eileen (1988), *The Ely Methodists 1774–1932* (Ely)

James, David W. (1982), *Brothers in Ministry* (Bognor Regis)

James, Francis B. (1991), *For the Quiet Hour* (Peterborough)

James, Margaret (1986), *The Kent College Saga*

Jeffery, Frederick (1964), *Irish Methodism. An Historical Account of its Traditions, Theology and Influence* (Belfast)

Jenkins, David E. (1908), *Life of Thomas Charles* (Denbigh)

Jenkins, David E. (1911), *Calvinistic Methodist Holy Orders* (Carnarvon)

Jeremy, D.J. (ed.) (1988), *Business and Religion in Britain* (Aldershot)

Jessop, W. (1880), *Account of Methodism in Rossendale* (Manchester)

Jobson, Frederick J. (1850), *Chapel and School Architecture*

Jolly, Cyril (n.d.), *The Spreading Flame: The Coming of Methodism to Norfolk*

Jones, B. Alcwyn, (1981) *The Story of Halfords*

Jones, C.E. (1987), *Black Holiness* (Metuchen, NJ)

Jones, D.G. and H.M. Hughes (1904), *Cofiant Glanystwyth* (Bangor)

Jones, David (1902), *The Life and Times of Griffith Jones*

Jones, H. (1904), *Cofiant y Parch. Samuel Davies yr Ail* (Bangor)

Jones, H. (1911–13), *Hanes Wesleyaeth Gymreig* (Bangor)

Jones, J. (1883), *One Hundred Years Ago: Wesleyan Methodism in Derby* (Derby)

Jones, J.W. (1893), *Belfast Methodism 1756–1893* (Belfast)

Jones, R.T. (1979), *Thomas Charles o'r Bala* (Cardiff)

Jones, Scott J. (1995), *John Wesley's Conception and Use of Scripture* (Nashville)

Jones, T. Snell (1822), *Life of Lady Glenorchy* (Edinburgh)

Jones, William H. (1952), *History of the Wesleyan Reform Union*

Jones-Humphreys, T. (1990), *Methodistiaeth Wesleyaidd Cymreig* (Holywell)

Jutsum, H. (1876), *Jubilee Memorial of Tiviot Dale Wesleyan Church* (Stockport)

Keeling, Annie E. (1896), *What he did for Cannibals – Some Account of the Life and Work of the Rev. Samuel Leigh*

Kelly, Hugh (1825), *An Impartial History of Independent Methodism in the counties of Durham and Northumberland* (Newcastle)

Kendall, H.B.[1906], *The Origin and History of the Primitive Methodist Church*

Kendall, R. Elliott (1954), *Eyes of the Earth: The Diary of Samuel Pollard*

Kendall, R. Elliott (1978), *Charles New and the East Africa Mission* (Nairobi)

Kent, John (1956), *The Age of Disunity*

Kent, John (1978), *Holding the Fort: Studies in Victorian Revivalism*

Kilby, W.M. (1986), *Yonder Country is Ours* (2nd edn)

Kimbrough, S.T. (ed.) (1992), *Charles Wesley, Poet and Theologian* (Nashville)

Kimbrough, S.T., and Beckerlegge, Oliver A. (eds) (1988–92), *The Unpublished Poetry of Charles Wesley* (Nashville)

Kingscote-Greenhead, W. (1930), *Raymond Preston, British and Australian Evangelist*

Kirby, Gilbert W. (1990), *The Elect Lady*

Kirsop, Joseph (1885), *Historic Sketches of Free Methodism* (1885)

Kissack, R. (1960), *Methodists in Italy* (1960)

Knox, Ronald A. (1950), *Enthusiasm* (Oxford)

Koss, Stephen E. (1975), *Nonconformity in Modern British Politics*

Lambert, A.J. (1930), *The Chapel on the Hill* (Bristol)

Lambert, David W. (1954), *What Hath God Wrought; the story of Cliff College*

Lancaster, John (1821), *The Life of Darcy, Lady Maxwell, of Pollock*

Langford, Thomas A. (1998), *Methodist Theology*

Langham, James P. (*c.* 1910), *The Tunstall Book: a souvenir of one hundred years of grace*

Lapp, E.C. (1977), *To Their Heirs For Ever* (Belleville, Ont.)

Larkin, W. (1825), *A Concise History of the First Establishment of Wesleyan Methodism in the City of Norwich in the year 1754* (Norwich)

Laurenson, G.I. (1972), *Te Hahi Weteriana: three half centuries of the Methodist Maori Missions 1822–1972* (Auckland, NZ)

Lawson, Jack (1936), *Peter Lee*

Lawson, John (1946), *Notes on Wesley's Forty-four Sermons*

Lawton, George (1960), *Shropshire Saint: A Study in the Ministry and Spirituality of Fletcher of Madeley*

Lawton, George (1983), *Within the Rock of Ages: the Life and Work of Augustus Montague Toplady* (Cambridge)

Laycock, J.W. (1909), *Methodist Heroes of the Great Haworth Round 1734 to 1784* (Keighley)

Lazell, David (1997), *Gypsy from the Forest* (Bridgend)

Le Messurier, B. (1962), *A History of the Mint Methodist Church, Exeter* (Exeter)

Leary, William (1969), *Methodism in the City of Lincoln* (Lincoln)

Leary, William (1972), *Methodism in the Town of Boston* (Boston)

Leary, William (1988), *Lincolnshire Methodism* (Buckingham)

Leary, William (1995), *Wesley Guild: the first hundred years*

Leary, William (1996), *The Grimsby and Cleethorpes Circuit*

Leary, William and Robinson, D.N. (1981), *A History of Methodism in Louth*

Leask, G.A. (1909), *Peter Thompson: the Romance of the East End Mission*

Ledger, Richard (n.d.), *The Worksop Wesleyan Methodist Circuit, 1815–1915*

Lee, Helen (1987), *Ploughshares of Prayer: a memoir of the Lyth family of York in the Nineteenth Century* (Leeds)

Lee, Roger (1988), *Wesleyana and Methodist Pottery*

Léger, Augustin (1910), *Wesley's Last Love*

Leigh, Harvey (1855), '*Praying Johnny'; or the life and labours of John Oxtoby, Primitive Methodist minister*

Leitch, A. [1983], *Paisley Central Hall, a History*

Lenton, John H. (1995), *Harold Roberts* (Peterborough)

Lester, George (1890), *Grimsby Methodism (1743–1889)*

Lewis, A.J. (1962), *Zinzendorf, the Ecumenical Pioneer*

Liddon, H.P. (1893–97), *Life of Edward Bouverie Pusey*

Lidgett, J. Scott (1936), *My Guided Life*

Lightfoot, J. (1862), *The Power of Faith and Prayer exemplified in the Life and Labours of Mrs Mary Porteous*

Lightwood, J.T. (1935), *The Music of the Methodist Hymn-Book*

Lightwood, J.T. (1937), *Samuel Wesley*

Lindegaard, D.P. (1988), *The Budgetts of Kingswood Hill and their Bristol Family* (Bristol)

Lindstrom, H. (1946), *Wesley and Sanctification*

Local Preachers' Who's Who (1934)

Lockley, W.H. (1909), *The Story of the Stockport Circuit of the United Methodist Church* (Stockport)

Lockwood, J.F. (1868), *Memorials of the Life of Peter Böhler*

Lockwood, John P. (1881), *The Western Pioneers: or Memorials of the Lives and Labours of the Rev. Richard Boardman and the Rev. Joseph Pilmoor*

Lofthouse, W.F. *et al.* (1954), *Wilbert Howard, Appreciations of the Man*

London Mission Report (1985), *Going Places*

London Mission Report (1961), *London Century 1861–1961*

London Quarterly [and Holborn] Review [LQ(H)R]

Longworth, Allan (1996), *William Grimshaw* (Peterborough)

Loveridge, G. (1995), *Romany Returns*

Lowe, T. (1881), *The Norfolk Herald of the Cross*

Lowery, Ralph (1982), *Robert Wearmouth of Oxhill* (Newcastle upon Tyne)

Luckcock, Janet L. (1992), *Thomas of Tonga, 1797–1881: the Unlikely Pioneer* (Peterborough)

Luckcock, Janet L. (1998), *Thomas of Tonga* (Peterborough)

Luke, Sir Henry (1954), *Queen Salote and her Kingdom*

Lyth, J. (1885), *Glimpses of Early Methodism in York* (York)

McCallum, Colin A. (n.d.), *James Dredge, 1796–1846*

McClure, W. (1872), *Life and Labours of John McClure*

McConnell, H.O. (1976), *Haiti Diary*

McCrea, Alexander (1931), *Irish Methodism in the Twentieth Century* (Belfast)

McCreary, A. (1996), *Gordon Wilson*

McCullagh, H.H. (1909), *Thomas McCullagh, a short story of a long life*

McCullagh, T. (1881), *The Rev. W.M. Punshon*

McCullagh, T. (1891), *Sir William McArthur* (1891)

McCullagh, T. (1906), *Gideon Ouseley, the wonderful Irish Missionary*

Macdonald, Mrs R. (1908), *Life of Dr. Roderick Macdonald*

Macdonald, F.W. (1887), *Life of William Morley Punshon*

Macdonald, James (1822), *Memoirs of the Rev. Joseph Benson*

McGonigle, Herbert (1993), *John Wesley and the Moravians* (Ilkeston)

MacHardie, Elizabeth (1875), *James Turner or 'how to reach the masses'* (Aberdeen)

McKinney, J.W. and Sterling, W.S. (1972), *Gurteen College*

Mackintosh, Harold Vincent (1966), *By Faith and Work*

McLachlan, H. (1919), *The Methodist Unitarian Movement* (Manchester)

McLachlan, H. (1923), *The Story of a Nonconformist Library* (Manchester)

McLean, Isabel, *Joseph Foord 1714–1788 of Kirkby Moorside* (forthcoming)

McLeod, Hugh (1974), *Class and Religion in the Late Victorian City*

McMurray, Nigel (1999), *The Stained Glass of Wesley's Chapel* (2nd edn)

MacNab, G. (1993), *J. Arthur Rank and the British Film Industry*

Macpherson, James (1870), *The Life and Labours of the Rev. John Petty*

Macquiban, Timothy S.A. (ed.) (1996), *Issues in Education: some Methodist perspectives* (Oxford)

Macquiban, Timothy S.A. (1978), *Priory Place Methodist Church [Doncaster] 1832–1978*

Maddox, Randy L. (1990), *Aldersgate Reconsidered* (Nashville)

Maddox, Randy L. (1994), *Responsible Grace: John Wesley's Practical Theology* (Nashville)

Maitland, C. (1960), *Leslie Weatherhead*

Mallinson, Joel (1898), *History of Methodism in Huddersfield*, etc.

Mallinson, William (1936), *A Sketch of my Life*

Malmgreen, Gail (1985), *Silk Town:Industry and Culture in Macclesfield* (Hull)

Manders, F.W.D. (1973), *A History of Gateshead* (Gateshead)

Manning, Bernard, Lord (1942), *The Hymns of Wesley and Watts*

Marlowe, Joyce (1974), *The Tolpuddle Martyrs*

Marquardt, Manfred (1992), *John Wesley's Social Ethics: Praxis and Principles* (Nashville)

Marshall, Polly (1988), *Wesley Memorial Church, Epworth*

Marshall, Ronald (1968), *Methodist College, Belfast*

Marsland, John (1978), *Over Two Centuries of Methodism in Robin Hood's Bay 1747–1978* (Lincoln)

Marsland, John (1983), *Whitby Methodist Circuit Bicentenary 1783–1983* (Lincoln)

Martin, Bernard (1950), *An Ancient Mariner: A Biography of John Newton*

Martin, I. & W. (1969), *Some Memories of Mother and Father*

Martin, J. Henry (1946), *John Wesley's London Chapels*

Maser, Frederick E. (1988), *The Story of John Wesley's Sisters* (Rutland, Vt)

Maser, F.E. and Magg, H.E. (eds) (1969), *The Journal of Joseph Pilmore* (Philadelphia)

Mathews, H.F. (1949), *Methodism and the Education of the People 1791–1851*

Meadley, Thomas D. (1983), *Kindled by a Spark: the story of Thomas Champness* (Ilkeston)

Mee, Josiah (1906), *Thomas Champness as I Knew Him*

Methodist Insurance Company (1970), *Century of Service*

Mews, Stuart (ed.) (1993), *Modern Religious Rebels*

Milbank, D. (1972), *College in Crisis*

Milburn, Geoffrey E. (1977), *The Christian Lay Churches*

Milburn, Geoffrey E. (1982), *A School for the Prophets* (Manchester)

Milburn, Geoffrey E. (1987), *The Travelling Preacher: John Wesley in the North East 1742–1790*

Milburn, Geoffrey E. (1988), *St John's Ashbrooke: A church and its story 1888–1988* (Sunderland)

Milburn, Geoffrey E. (1990), *Unique in Methodism: 100 Years of Chapel Aid* (Englesea Brook)

Milburn, Geoffrey and Batty, Margaret (eds) (1995), *Workaday Preachers* (Peterborough)

Minutes of the [Wesleyan] Methodist Conference [Minutes]

Moister, William, (1871) *A History of Wesleyan Missions*

Monk, R.C. (1966), *John Wesley: His Puritan Heritage*

Moore, A.E. Clucas (n.d.), *What is The Voice of Methodism?* (Camborne)

Moore, Henry (1817), *The Life of Mrs Mary Fletcher*

Moore, Henry (1824–25), *The Life of the Rev. John Wesley, in which are included, the Life of his Brother, the Rev. Charles Wesley*

Moore, R.D. (1952), *Methodism in the Channel Islands*

Moore, Robert (1974), *Pitmen, Preachers and Politics* (Cambridge)

Morgan, Derec Ll. (1988), *The Great Awakening in Wales*

Morgan, James (1762), *Life of Thomas Walsh*

Morgan, Kenneth (1990), *John Wesley in Bristol* (Bristol)

Morgan, W.I.(1976), *Isaac Jenkins*

Morris, G.M. (1988), *The Story of Methodism in Doncaster and District 1743–1988*

Morris, W.E. (1961), *History of Methodism in Shrewsbury and District* (Shrewsbury)

Moss, R. Waddy [1909], *The Rev. W.B. Pope, D.D., theologian and saint*

Mossner, Ernest Campbell (1936), *Bishop Butler and the Age of Reason* (New York)

Moule, H.G.C. (1892), *Charles Simeon*

Moulton, J.E. (1921), *Moulton of Tonga*

Moulton, William Fiddian (1899), *William F. Moulton*

Moulton, William Fiddian (1919), *James Hope Moulton*

Moulton, William Fiddian (1926), *Richard Green Moulton*

Moulton, William Fiddian (1928), *The Story of Cliff*

Mounfield, A. (ed.) (1905), *A Short History of Independent Methodism* (Wigan)

Mounfield, A. (1924), *The Quaker Methodists* (Nelson)

Mudie-Smith, R. (1904), *The Religious Life of London*

Muir, Elizabeth G. (1991), *Petticoats in the Pulpit: the story of early nineteenth -century Methodist women preachers in Upper Canada* (Toronto)

Murray, A. Victor (1992), *A Northumberland Methodist Childhood* (Newcastle)

Murray, Harold (*c.* 1935), *Preachers Only*

Murray, Harold (1937), *Sixty Years an Evangelist*

Murray, Harold (1938), *Dinsdale Young, the Preacher*

Murray, James (1955), *Independent Methodist History 1905–1955* (Wigan)

Musgrave, J. (1865), *The Origin of Methodism in Bolton* (Bolton)

Nayler, J. (1938), *Charles Delamotte*

NCH Action for Children (1997), *The Cities: A Methodist Report*

Neave, David (1991), *The Lost Churches and Chapels of Hull*

Newton, John A. (1964), *Methodism and the Puritans*

Newton, John A. (1968), *Susanna Wesley and the Puritan Tradition in Methodism*

Newton, John A. (1984), *A Man for all Churches, Marcus Ward*

Newton, John A. (1989), *The Wesleys for Today*

Noble, Walter J. (1957), *Something to Remember*

Norman, Diana (1970), *The Road from Singapore*

Northcott, Michael (ed.) (1998), *Urban Theology: A Reader*
Northridge, W.L. (1952), *The Story of Edgehill College* (Belfast)
Northrup, L.W. (1988), *Ambassadors for Christ* (Indiana)
Norwood, Frederick A. (1974), *The Story of American Methodism* (Nashville)
Nthamburi, Z.J. (1982), *A History of the Methodist Church in Kenya*
Nuttall, Geoffrey F. (ed.) (1951), *Philip Doddidge 1702–51; his Contribution to English Religion*
Nuttall, Geoffrey F. (1965), *Howell Harris: the Last Enthusiast* (Cardiff)
Nuttall, Geoffrey F. (1967), *The Puritan Spirit*

O'Connor, P.J. (1989), *People Make Places* (Newcastle West)
Oldstone-Moore, Christopher (1999), *Hugh Price Hughes: Founder of a new Methodism, Conscience of a new Nonconformity* (Cardiff)
Olsen, G.W. (1990), *Religion and Revolution in England: The Halévy Thesis and its Critics* (Lanham, Md)
Outler, Albert C. (ed.) (1964), *John Wesley* (Oxford)
Outler, Albert C. (1984–87), *Sermons of John Wesley* (*Works of John Wesley*, Bicentennial Edition, Nashville)
Outler, Albert C. (1991), *The Wesleyan Theological Heritage* (Grand Rapids)
Owen, G.P. (1997), *Atgofion John Evans, Y Bala* (Caernarfon)
Owen, J.A. (1972), *A Short History of the Dowlais Ironwork, Merthyr Tydfil* (Merthyr Tydfil)
Owen, W.R. (1909), *Methodism in the Hartlepools*
Owens, John M.R. (1974), *Prophets in the Wilderness: the Wesleyan Mission to New Zealand* (Auckland)
Oxford Companion to the Literature of Wales ed. Meic Stephens (1986) (Oxford) [*OCLW*]
Oxford Dictionary of the Christian Church, ed. F.L. Cross and E.A. Livingstone (3rd edn, Oxford 1997)) [*ODCC*]

Packer, George (ed) (1897), *The Centenary of the Methodist New Connexion 1797–1897*
Parker, C.A. (1998), *Confidence in Mutual Aid* (Peterborough)
Parker, John (1839), *Memoir of Miss Hannah Ball* (revised edn)
Parker, T.L. (1867), *Methodism in Scotland* (Knottingley)
Parkes, William (1965), *Thomas Bryant – Independent Methodist* (Sheffield)
Parkes, William (1995), *The Arminian Methodists* (Cannock)
Parsons, R. K. (1985), *My Moving Tent, a biographical sketch of Lois Anna Thorne* Patterson, Arthur H. (1903), *From Hayloft to Temple: the Story of Primitive Methodism in [Great] Yarmouth*
Patterson, W.M. (1909), *Northern Primitive Methodism*
Pawlyn, J.S. (1877), *Bristol Methodism in John Wesley's Day* (Bristol)
Pawson, John (1994–95), *The Letters of John Pawson* (Peterborough)
Peake, A.S. (1926), *The Life of Sir William Hartley*
Peake, L.S. (1930), *Arthur Samuel Peake: A Memoir*
Pearce, J. (1935), *Burning and Shining Lights: a souvenir of Primitive Methodist radiant personalities* (Halesowen)
Pearce, John (1964), *The Wesleys in Cornwall* (Truro)
Pearson, Edith M. (1967), *Soli Deo Gloria: Maiden Street Methodist Church, Weymouth 1867–1967* (Weymouth)
Peck, Albert E. (1979), *200 Years of Methodism in Coventry* (Coventry)
Perdue, H. (1997), *Gurteen Agricultural College 1947–1997* (Ballingarry)
Perkins, E. Benson (1952), *Methodist Preaching Houses and the Law*
Perkins, E. Benson (1958), *Gambling in English Life*

Perkins, E. Benson and Hearne, Albert (1946), *The Methodist Church Builds Again*

Perks, R.W. (1936) *Sir Robert William Perks, Baronet*

Perry, George (1985), *Rupert, A Bear's Life*

Petty, John (1857), *Memoir of the Life and Labours of the Rev. Thomas Batty*

Petty, John (1880), *A History of the Primitive Methodist Connexion from its Origin to the Conference of 1860* (2nd edn)

Phillips, W. (1896), *Early Methodism in Shropshire* (Shrewsbury)

Phillipson, W. Oliver (1966a), *A Methodist Church Builder's Decalogue* (Manchester)

Phillipson, W. Oliver (1966b), *Performance and Promise: the work of the Trustees for Methodist Church Purposes 1866–1966*

Philpot, T. (1994), *NCH Action for Children*

Phoebus, W. (1828), *Richard Whatcoat*

Piggott, Sir Theodore Caro and Durley, Thomas (1921), *Life and Letters of Henry James Piggott*

Pilkington, W. (1890), *Makers of Wesleyan Methodism in Preston and the Relation of Methodism to the Temperance and Teetotal Movement* (Preston)

Pillow, E. Ronald (1985), *Two Centuries of Winchester Methodism* (Winchester)

Plummer, Alfred and Early, Richard E. (1969), *The Blanket Makers*

Pocklington, G.R. (1949), *The Story of W.H. Smith & Son* (revd edn)

Pocock, G. (1822), *The Life, Ministry and Writings of Victory Purdy*

Pocock, William Willmer (1885), *A History of Wesleyan Methodism in some of the Southern Counties of England*

Podmore, Colin (ed.) (1992), *The Fetter Lane Moravian Congregation, London 1742–1992*

Podmore, Colin (1998), *The Moravian Church in England, 1728–1760* (Oxford)

Pointon, A.G. (1982), *Methodism in West Somerset...1790–1980* (Minehead)

Pollock, John C. (1981), *John Newton*

Pool, P.A.S. (1986), *William Borlase* (Truro)

Pope, W.B. (1876), *Memoir of James Heald*

Potter, William (1929), *Thomas Jackson of Whitechapel*

Poultney, S.V. (1965), *Battle for the Big-Lips*

Pound, R. (1972), *The Fenwick Story*

Pratt, A.C. (1891), *Black Country Methodism*

Price, Lynn (1996), *Faithful Uncertainty*

Prickett, Barbara (*c.* 1960), *Island Base*

Pritchard, E. Cook (n.d.), *Under the Southern Cross*

Pritchard, Frank C. (1949), *Methodist Secondary Education*

Pritchard, Frank C. (1951), *The Story of Westminster College*

Pritchard, Frank C. (1978), *The Story of Woodhouse Grove School* (Apperley Bridge)

Pritchard, J. (1871), *Memoirs of the Life, Literary and Itinerant Labours of the Rev. Philip Pugh*

Proceedings of the Wesley Historical Society [*PWHS*]

Purcell, William (1983), *Donald Soper*

Pyke, Richard (1934), *Edgehill College 1884–1934*

Pyke, Richard (1941), *The Early Bible Christians*

Pyke, Richard (1953), *The Story of Shebbear College* (Shebbear)

Pyke, Richard (n.d.), *The Golden Chain: the Story of the Bible Christian Methodists*

Race, Steve (1979), *Musician at Large*

Race, Steve (1988), *The Two Worlds of Joseph Race*

Rack, Henry D. (1989), *Reasonable Enthusiast: John Wesley and the Rise of Methodism* (revd edn 1992)

Rack, Henry D. (1996), *How Primitive was Primitive Methodism?* (Englesea Brook)

Radford, G.E. (n.d.), *My Providential Way: A Biography of Francis Brotherton Westbrook*

Ranson, C.W. (1988), *A Missionary Pilgrimage*

Rattenbury, H.M. (1994), *Rat-Rhyme: A Screed* (Silverdale)

Rattenbury, H.O. (1884), *The Rev. John Rattenbury Memorials* (2nd edn)

Rattenbury, Harold B. (1949), *David Hill, Friend of China*

Rattenbury, J. Ernest (1938), *The Conversion of the Wesleys*

Rattenbury, J. Ernest (1941), *The Evangelical Doctrines of Charles Wesley's Hymns*

Rattenbury, J. Ernest (1948), *The Eucharistic Hymns of John and Charles Wesley*

Rattenbury, Owen (1931), *Flame of Freedom*

Raynes, John R. (1907), *History of Wesleyan Methodism in the Mansfield Circuit, 1807–1907* (Mansfield)

Ream, B. (1988), *Too Hot for Comfort*

Rhodes, I.C. (1986), *John Russell RA* (Guildford)

Richardson, W.F. (1976), *Preston Methodism's 200 Fascinating Years* (Preston)

Richie, M. (1839), *William Black*

Ridge, F.M. (1936), *Samuel Parkes Cadman*

Rigg, James H. (1905), *Jabez Bunting, a Great Methodist Leader*

Rigg, John (1848), *An Interesting Historical Sketch of the Rise and Progress of the Wesleyan Society in Bath* (Bath)

Ritson, J. (1926), *The Centenary of Glasgow Primitive Methodism 1826–1926* (Leominster)

Ritson, J.H. (1939), *The World is Our Parish*

Ritson, T. Nicholson (ed.) [1908], *The Story of a Century: the History of Wesleyan Methodism in the Ipswich Circuit*

Roberts, Colin A. (1945), *These Christian Commando Campaigns*

Roberts, G.M. (1949, 1958), *Y Per Ganiedydd* (Aberystwyth)

Roberts, G.M. (ed.) (1973, 1978), *Hanes Methodistiaeth Galfinaidd Cymru* (Caernarfon)

Roberts, Griffith T. (1951), *Howell Harris*

Roberts, J.P. and Hughes, T. (1903), *Cofiant y Parch. John Evans Eglwysbach* (Bangor)

Roberts, O.M. (1934), *Cofiant y Parch. Hugh Jones DD* (Bangor)

Roberts, T.R. (1908), *Dictionary of Eminent Welshmen*

Robertson, Charles (1975), *Bath, an Architectural Guide*

Robertson, E.H. (1992), *George*

Robinson, Arthur R.B. (1992), *The Counting House: Thomas Thompson of Hull 1754–1822 & his Family* (York)

Robson, W.J. (ed.) (1910), *Silsden Primitive Methodism: Records and Reminiscences* (Silsden)

Rodd, C.S. (ed.) (1987), *Foundation Documents of the Faith* (Edinburgh)

Roebuck, Stuart & Joan (1995), *The Happiest Days: Culford Hall and School through the Years* (Culford)

Rogers, Hester Ann (1796), *Experience and Spiritual Letters...written by herself* (Bristol)

Rose, E. Alan (1967, 1969), *Methodism in Ashton-under-Lyne* (Ashton)

Rose, J. (1951), *A Church Born to Suffer*

Routh, Francis (1973), *Early English Organ Music*

Routley, Erik (1968), *The Musical Wesleys*

Roux, Th. (1941), *Le Méthodisme en France* (Paris)

Row, W. (1794), Memoir in *Works* of A.M. Toplady

Rowe, G.S. (1870), *Memorials of the late Rev. William M. Bunting*

Rowlands, W. (1847), *Cofiant John Davies* (Llanidloes)

Royle, Edward (1985), *Nonconformity in Nineteenth-Century York* (York)

Royle, Edward (1994), *Queen Street Chapel and Mission, Huddersfield* (Huddersfield)
Ruddle, Thomas (1893), *S.T. Thorne, Minister of the Gospel*
Rule, William H. (1844), *Memoir of a Mission to Gibraltar and Spain*
Rule, William H. (1886), *Recollections of My Life and Work at home and abroad*
Rupp, E. Gordon (1954), *Thomas Jackson, Methodist Patriarch*
Rupp, E. Gordon (1986), *Religion in England, 1688–1791* (Oxford)
Rupp, E. Gordon (1994), *Wisdom and Wit* (Peterborough)
Russell, J. (1987), *James Starkey/Seumas O'Sullivan, a critical biography* (Toronto)
Russell, Kate Pyer (1865), *Memoirs of John Pyer*
Russell, R.W. (1920), *Life of James Flanagan, Preacher, Evangelist, Author*
Russell, Thomas (1879), *Records of Events in Primitive Methodism*
Ryan, Sarah (1763), *An Account of the Work of God in Leytonstone*

Sackett, A. Barrett (1972a), *James Rouquet and his Part in Early Methodism* (Broxton)
Sackett, A. Barrett (1972b), *John Jones – First after the Wesleys?* (Broxton)
Sackett, F.C. (1951), *Posnett of Medak*
Sadler, C. (ed.) (1967), *Never a Young Man* (Cape Town)
Salt, William (1822), *A Memorial of the Wesleyan Methodist New Connexion... from its formation in 1797 to the present time* (Nottingham)
Sampson, W. (1896), *Alexander M'Aulay, the Apostle of East London Methodism*
Sampson, William F. (1998), *'Affable and Humane': the gistory of the development and growth of Methodism in the King's Lynn Circuit*
Samuel, David (1993), *No Silver Spoon*
Sandall, R., Wiggins, R. & Coutts, F. (1947–86), *History of the Salvation Army*
Sanderson, William (1899), *Life and Labours* (Wigan)
Sangster, Paul (1962), *Doctor Sangster*
Sangster, Paul (1963), *Pity my Simplicity: the Evangelical Revival and the Religious Education of Children*
Sangster, Paul (ed.) (1982), *Eight Essays* [on Westminster Central Hall]
Sangster, William E. (1943), *The Path to Perfection*
Sargant,, N.C. and Ward, A.M. (1950), *Tomlinson of Mysore*
Schlenther, Boyd Stanley (1997), *Queen of the Methodists. The Countess of Huntingdon and the Eighteenth Century Crisis of Faith and Society* (Durham)
Schmidt, Martin (1962–73), *John Wesley, a theological biography*
Scholes, Percy A. (ed.) (1938), *The Oxford Companion to Music*
Scotland, Nigel (1981), *Methodism and the Revolt of the Field* (Gloucester)
Secker, Thomas, *Autobiography* (1988), (Lawrence, KS)
Seed, T. Alexander (1907), *History of Norfolk Street Chapel and Wesleyan Methodism in Sheffield*
Seeley, R.B. (1842), *Memoir of the Life and Writings of Michael Thomas Sadler*
Sellers, Ian (1971), *The Methodist Chapels and Preaching Places of Liverpool 1750–1971* (Warrington)
Sellers, Ian (1976), *The Methodist Chapels of the Warrington Circuit, 1750–1976* (Warrington)
Semmel, Bernard (1971), *The Birth of Methodism in England* (Chicago)
Semmel, Bernard (1974), *The Methodist Revolution*
Semmens, Bernard L. (1971), *The Conferences after Wesley* (Melbourne)
Senior, Geoffrey R. (1989), *For Love of the Chinese* (Plymouth)
Senior, Geoffrey R. (1994), *The China Experience* (Peterborough)
Senior, Geoffrey R. (1995), *Donald Braithwaite Childe* (Peterborough)
Senior, Geoffrey R. (1996), *Thomas Frank Davey* (Peterborough)

Senior, Geoffrey R. (1999), *Samuel Pollard* (Emsworth)

Sharp, Cuthbert (1851), *History of Hartlepool*, with supplement (Hartlepool)

Shaw, A.M. (1984), *When You were There: Edgehill College 1884–1984*

Shaw, Charles (1903), *When I was a Child*

Shaw, George (1894), *Life of John Oxtoby* (Hull)

Shaw, Thomas (1965), *The Bible Christians 1815–1907*

Shaw, Thomas (1967), *A History of Cornish Methodism* (Truro)

Shaw, Thomas (1969), *Richard Treffry, Senr.* (Truro)

Shaw, Thomas (1992), *Gwennap Pit* (Busveal)

Shiels, W.J. (ed.) (1984), *Persecution and Toleration* (Oxford)

Sheldon, W.C. (1903), *Early Methodism in Birmingham*

Shepherd, T.B. (1940), *Methodism and the Literature of the Eighteenth Century*

Short, Colin C. (1995), *Durham Colliers and West Country Methodists* (Kidderminster)

Shrewsbury, J.V.B. (1856), *Memorials of the Rev. William J. Shrewsbury, an Holy Man of God* (Manchester)

Sidney, Edwin (1834), *Life of the Rev. Rowland Hill*

Sidney, Edwin (1835), *The Life, Ministry [etc.] of the Rev. Samuel Walker*

Sidney, Edwin (1839), *The Life of Sir Richard Hill, Bart, MP*

Sigston, James (1820), *A Memoir of the Life and Ministry of Mr W. Bramwell*

Simeon, Charles (1838), *Works* edited by Richard Whittingham

Simon, John S. (1870), *Methodism in Dorset* (Weymouth)

Simon, John S. (1921), *John Wesley and the Religious Societies*

Simon, John S. (1923a), *John Wesley and the Methodist Societies*

Simon, John S. (1923b), *A Summary of Methodist Law and Discipline* (5th edn)

Simon, John S. (1925), *John Wesley and the Advance of Methodism*

Simon, John S. (1927), *John Wesley the Master Builder*

Simon, John S. (1934), *John Wesley, the Last Phase*

Small, Walter J.T. (ed.) (1964), *A History of the Methodist Church in Ceylon* (Colombo)

Smart, H.T. (1913), *The Life of Thomas Cook*

Smetham, James (1892), *Letters* edited by W. Davies and S. Smetham

Smith, B. (1985), *History of Methodism in Macclesfield*

Smith, Edward (1889), *Three Years in Central London*

Smith, George (1858–61), *A History of Wesleyan Methodism*

Smith, Henry (c. 1893), *Sketches of Eminent Methodist New Connexion Ministers*

Smith, Henry (1894), *Wesleyan Methodism in Portsmouth*

Smith, Henry [1913], *Ministering Women: the story of the UM Deaconess Institute*

Smith, Henry, Swallow, John Edward and Treffry, William (1932), *The Story of the United Methodist Church*

Smith, Henry and Beard, A.H. (1899), *Bethesda Chapel, Hanley* (Hanley)

Smith, John T. (1998), *Methodism and Education, 1849–1902: J.H. Rigg, Romanism and Wesleyan Schools* (Oxford)

Smith, Mrs Richard (1844), *The Life of the Rev. Mr. Henry Moore*

Smith, T. (1871), *Memoirs of the Rev. John Wesley Etheridge*

Smith, T.W. (1877), *History of the Methodist Church in Eastern British America*

Smyth, Charles (1940), *Simeon and Church Order*

Southey, Robert (1820), *The Life of Wesley and the Rise and Progress of Methodism*

Spangenberg, A.G. (1838), *Life of Nicholas Lewis Count Zinzendorf*

Spener, P.J. (1964), *Pia Desideria*

Spooner, W.A. (1901), *Bishop Butler*

Spurr, F.C. [1915], *Some Chaplains in Khaki*

Stacey, J. (1862), *A Prince in Israel or sketches of the life of John Ridgway*

Stacey, John (ed.) (1988), *John Wesley: Contemporary Perspectives*

Stamp, William W. (1841), *Historical Notices of Wesleyan Methodism in Bradford* (Bradford)

Stamp, William W. (1863), *The Orphan House of Wesley, with notices of early Methodism in Newcastle upon Tyne*

Statements of the Methodist Church on Faith and Order, 1933–1983 (1984)

Steele, Anthony (1857), *History of Methodism in Barnard Castle*

Stell, C.F. (1986), *Nonconformist Chapels and Meeting-houses in Central England* (London)

Stenton, M. and Lees, S. (eds) (1976–), *Who's Who of British Members of Parliament*

[Stephens, J.R.] (1838), *The Life and Opinions of Richard Oastler*

Stephens, W. Peter (1998), *Methodism in Europe*

Stephenson, Alan M.G. (1984), *The Rise and Decline of English Modernism*

Stephenson, T. Bowman (1907), *William Arthur*

Stevens, Abel (1864), *History of Methodism* (revd edn)

Stevenson, G.J. [1872], *City Road Chapel and its Associations*

Stevenson, G.J. [1876], *Memorials of the Wesley Family*

Stevenson, G.J. (1884–6), *Methodist Worthies*

Stevenson, Joan & Robin (1988), *John Wesley in Leicestershire*

Stewart, R.M.M. (1980), *Life and Labour*

Stirling, A.M.W. (1954), *Victorian Sidelights*

Stoddart, Anna M. (1908), *Life and Letters of Hannah E. Pipe*

Stovin, J. (ed.) (1982), *Journals of a Methodist Farmer*

Sturdy, W.A. (1932), *Methodist Finance Past, Present and Future*

Sugden, Edward H. (ed.) (1921), *Wesley's Standard Sermons*

Sugden, Mary Florence (1941), *Edward H Sugden* (Melbourne)

Sundkler, B. (1954), *The Church of South India*

Sunman, W.R. (1902), *The History of Free Methodism in and about Newcastle upon Tyne* (Newcastle)

Sutcliff, J. (1996), *Square Chapel* (Hebden Bridge)

Sutcliffe, Barry P. and Church, David C. (1988), *250 Years of Chiltern Methodism* (Ilkestone)

Sutherland, Alexander (1903), *Methodism in Canada: its work and its story*

Sutherland, J. (1988), *Longman Companion to Victorian Fiction*

Swain, Peter L. (1978), *Charles John Prescott* (Sydney)

Swanson, R.N. (ed.) (1998), *Gender and Christian Religion* (Woodbridge)

Swartz, H. (1980), *The French Prophets*

Swift, Rowland C. (1982), *Lively People: Methodism in Nottingham 1740–1979* (Nottingham)

Swift, Rowland C. (1987), *Methodism in Sussex*

Swift, Wesley F. (1947a), *Methodism in Scotland*

Swift, Wesley F. (1947b), *The Romance of Banffshire Methodism* (Banff)

Sykes, Norman H. (1926), *Edmund Gibson*

Sykes, Richard (ed.) (1998), *Beyond the Boundaries* (Oxford)

Symons, J.C. (1870), *Life of the Rev. Daniel James Draper*

Tabraham, Barrie (1995), *The Making of Methodism*

Taft, Mary (1827), *Memoirs*

Taft, Zechariah (1825, 1828), *Biographical Sketches of the Lives and Public Ministry of Various Holy Women*

Taggart, Norman W. (1986), *The Irish in World Methodism*
Taggart, Norman W. (1993), *William Arthur, First among Methodists*
Taylor, E.R. (1935), *Methodism and Politics 1791–1851*
Taylor, Ina (1987), *Victorian Sisters*
Taylor, John (1885), *The Apostles of Fylde Methodism*
Taylor, Paul (ed.) (1996), *Wesley Pieces*
Taylor, W.G. (1920), *The Life Story of an Australian Evangelist* (Sydney)
Telford, John (1886), *Two West End Chapels*
Telford, John (1900), *The Life of the Rev. Charles Wesley, MA* (revised edn)
Telford, John (1912), *James Harrison Rigg*
Telford, John (1927), *Sayings and Portraits of Charles Wesley*
Telford, John (n.d.), *A Short History of Wesleyan Methodist Foreign Missions*
Telford, John (n.d.), *Wesley's Chapel and Wesley's House*
Thomas, P.W. and Thomas, P. Wm (1992), *The Days of our Pilgrimage* (Indianapolis)
Thomis, Malcolm I. (1969), *Politics and Society in Nottingham 1785–1835* (Oxford)
Thompson, Dorothy (1984), *The Chartists* (Aldershot)
Thompson, Douglas W. (1962), *Beginning at Skegness*
Thompson, Douglas W. (1971), *Donald Soper*
Thompson, Edgar W. (1955), *The Methodist Missionary Society: its Origin and Name*
Thompson, Edgar W. (1960), *Nathaniel Gilbert, Lawyer and Evangelist*
Thompson, Edwin (1990), *Always Your Friend, a personal appreciation of H. Cecil Pawson* (Newcastle)
Thompson, Rosalie B. (1910), *Peter Thompson*
Thompson, W.H. (1895), *Early Chapters in Hull Methodism, 1746–1800* (Hull)
Thorne, James (1869), *Memoir of William Reed, Bible Christian Minister* (Shebbear)
Thorne, John (1873), *James Thorne of Shebbear: a memoir compiled from his diary and letters*
Thorne, R.F.S. (1978), *Hocking. The Works of Joseph, Silas and Salome*
Thorne, Samuel L. (1874), *Samuel Thorne, Printer*
Thorne, Samuel L. (1877), *The Converted Wrestler*; 3rd edn, *The Cornish Wrestler* (Launceston 1888)
Thorne, Samuel L. (1878), *William O'Bryan, Founder of the Bible Christians: the man and his work* (Plymouth)
Thorne, Samuel L. (1889), *The Maiden Preacher, Wife and Mother: Miss Mary O'Bryan – Mrs Thorne*
Thorpe, Clarence (1951), *Limpopo to Zambesi: Sixty Years of Methodism in Southern Rhodesia*
Thwaites, William (1909), *Wesleyan Methodism in Durham City*
Tice, Frank (1966), *The History of Methodism in Cambridge*
Tillyard, A. (1926), *Agnes E. Slack* (Cambridge)
Timmins, T.C.B. (1997), *Suffolk Returns from the Census of Religious Worship, 1851* (Woodbridge)
Told, Silas (1786), *The Life of Mr Silas Told Written by Himself*
Tomkins, D. (1997), *Mission Accomplished* (Peterborough)
Toplady, Augustus Montague (1778), *A Memoir of some Principal Circumstances in the Life and Death of A.M. Toplady*
Towlson, C.W. (1957), *Moravian and Methodist*
Townsend, W.J. [1890], *Alexander Kilham, the first Methodist reformer*
Townsend, W.J. (1891), *James Stacey DD, Reminiscences and Memorials*
Townsend, W.J., Workman, H.B. and Eayrs, George (eds) (1909), *A New History of Methodism* [*NHM*]
Tovey, David (1985), *W.H.Y. Titcombe, Artist of Many Parts* (Bushey)
Tracy, Clarence (1967), Introduction to reprint of Richard Graves, *The Spiritual Quixote* (Oxford)
Tracy, Clarence (1987), *A Portrait of Richard Graves* (Cambridge)
Travell, John C. (1999), *Doctor of Souls: Leslie D. Weatherhead 1893–1976*

Travis, James (1914), *Seventy Five Years*

Treffry, Richard sen. (1840), *Memoirs of the Life, Character and Labours of the Rev. Joseph Benson*

Treffry, Richard jun. (1832), *Life of John Smith*

Trinder, Barrie (1965), *History of Methodism in Banbury with special reference to the Centenary of Marlborough Road Church 1865–1965* (Banbury)

Trinder, Barrie (1973), *The Industrial Revolution in Shropshire* (Chichester)

Trinder, Barrie (1982), *Victorian Banbury* (Chichester)

Trinder, Barrie (1991), *Fletcher Memorial Church, 150th Anniversary*

Tripp, David H. (1969), *The Renewal of the Covenant in the Methodist Tradition*

Trotter, Robert (1913), *The Centenary of Bondgate Chapel* (Darlington)

Tucker, K.B. Westerfield (ed.) (1996), *The Sunday Service of the Methodists* (Nashville)

Turner, J.G. (1872), *The Pioneer Missionary: Life of the Rev. Nathaniel Turner* (Melbourne)

Turner, John Munsey (1985), *Conflict and Reconciliation: Studies in Methodism and Ecumenism in England 1740–1982*

Turner, John Munsey (1998), *Modern Methodism in England 1932–1998*

Tuttle, R.G. (1978), *John Wesley, his Life and Theology* (Grand Rapids)

Tyack, Lena (1915), *Caroline Meta Wiseman*

Tyerman, Luke (1866), *The Life and Times of the Rev. Samuel Wesley*

Tyerman, Luke (1873), *The Oxford Methodists*

Tyerman, Luke (1878), *The Life and Times of the Rev. John Wesley, MA, Founder of the Methodists* (4th edn)

Tyerman, Luke (1882), *Wesley's Designated Successor*

Tytler, Sarah (1907), *The Countess of Huntingdon and her Circle*

United Methodist Magazine [*UMM*]

Unwin, Mrs George & Telford, John (1930), *Mark Guy Pearse, Preacher, Author, Artist 1842–1930*

Urwin, E.C. (1943), *Methodism and Sobriety*

Urwin, E.C. (1949), *The Significance of 1849, Methodism's Greatest Upheaval*

Valentine, Simon Ross (1997), *John Bennet and the Origins of Methodism and the Evangelical Revival in England* (Lanham, MD)

Valenze, Deborah M. (1985), *Prophetic Sons and Daughters: Popular Religion and Social Change in England 1790–1850* (Princeton)

Vasey, Mary Jane (1874), *Life of Thomas Vasey... by his Widow*

Vaughan, C.M. (1975), *Pioneers of Welsh Steel*

Venn, H. (ed.) (1834), *Life and a Selection from the Letters of the late Rev. Henry Venn*

Vicinus, Martha (1974), *The Industrial Muse*

Vicinus, Martha (1984), *The Ambiguities of Self-Help*

Vickers, James (1920), *A History of Independent Methodism* (Wigan)

Vickers, John A. (1961), *The Story of Canterbury Methodism* (Canterbury)

Vickers, John A. (1969), *Thomas Coke, Apostle of Methodism*

Vickers, John A. (1990), *Charles Wesley* (Peterborough)

Vickers, John A. (1996), *The 1851 Religious Census*

Vickers, John A. and Hilary F. (1977), *Methodism in a Cathedral City* (Chichester)

Vickers, Noreen (1992), *Brunswick Methodist Church, Whitby, Centenary Year 1991/2* (Burton-on-Trent)

Vincent, D. (ed.) (1977), *Testaments of Radicalism: memoirs of working-class politicians 1790–1885*

Vincent, John J. (1984), *OK, Let's Be Methodists*

Virgoe, Norma & Williamson, Tom (1993), *Religious Dissent in East Anglia* (Norwich)

Waddy, Adeline (1878), *The Life of the Rev. Samuel D. Waddy DD*

Waddy, J. Leonard (1976), *The Bitter Sacred Cup: the Wednesbury Riots 1743–44*

Waddy, J. Leonard (1982), *The Waddy Family* (Bognor Regis)

Wainwright, Geoffrey (1995), *Methodists in Dialog* (Nashville)

Wakefield, E.S. (1904), *Thomas Wakefield, missionary and geographical pioneer in East Equatorial Africa*

Wakefield, Gordon S. (1971), *Robert Newton Flew, 1886–1962*

Wakefield, Gordon S. (1998), *An Outline of Christian Worship*

Wakefield, Gordon S. (2000), *T.S. Gregory* (Emsworth)

Wakelin, Mark (1996), *J. Arthur Rank, the man behind the gong* (Oxford)

Walford, John (1855–57), *The Memoirs of the Life and Labours of the late Venerable Hugh Bourne* (Burslem)

Walker, A. Keith (1973), *William Law, his life and work*

Walker, F. Deaville (1929), *Thomas Birch Freeman, the son of an African*

Walker, F. Deaville (1942), *A Hundred Years in Nigeria*

Walker, J.V. (1836), *History of Wesleyan Methodism in Halifax and its Vicinity* (Halifax)

Walker, W. (1863), *Records of Early Methodism in Bolton* (Bolton)

Waller, John (ed.) (1989), *A Methodist Pilgrimage in France: The Journal of Matthew Gallienne, 1877* (Loughborough)

Walls, Andrew F. (1973), *Some Personalities of Aberdeen Methodism*

Walpole, Cecil F. (1941), *Silver Streams*

Walpole, Cecil F. (1947), *Golden Links*

Walsh, John (ed.) (1979), *A.B. Sackett: a memoir*

Walters, Arthur (1907), *Hugh Price Hughes, Pioneer and Reformer*

Ward, J. (1902), *Notes on the Wesleyan Methodist Church and its growth in Longton*

Ward, John (1865), *Methodism in Swaledale and the Neighbourhood* (Bingley)

Ward, T. Humphry (ed.) (1884), *Humphry Sandwith: a memoir compiled from autobiographical notes*

Ward, W.R. (ed.) (1972a), *The Early Correspondence of Jabez Bunting 1820–1829*

Ward, W.R. (1972b), *Religion and Society in England, 1790–1850*

Ward, W.R. (ed.) (1976), *Early Victorian Methodism. The Correspondence of Jabez Bunting 1830–1858* (Oxford)

Ward, W. Reginald and Heitzenrater, Richard P. (1988–99), *Journal and Diaries [of John Wesley]* (*Works of John Wesley*, Bicentennial Edition, Nashville)

Warren, C. (1995), *History of the Lay Worker Movement in the Methodist Church*

Warren, Samuel (1827), *Chronicles of Wesleyan Methodism*

Warren, W.N. (1929), *Gilbert Warren of Hunan*

Watkins, O.S. [1906], *Soldiers and Preachers Too*

Watmough, Abraham (1826), *History of Methodism in the Town and Neighbourhood of Great Yarmouth*

Watmough, Abraham (1829), *History of Methodism in the Neighbourhood and City of Lincoln*

Watson, David L. (1985), *The Early Methodist Class Meeting* (Nashville)

Watson, F.E. (1980), *Culford School, The First Hundred Years 1881–1981* (Bury St Edmunds)

Watson, J.R. (1997), *The English Hymn: A Critical and Historical Study* (Oxford)

Watson, Nigel (1994), *In Hortis Reginae*

Watson, Philip S. (1959), *The Concept of Grace*

Watson, Richard and Trickett, Kenneth (eds) (1988), *Companion to* Hymns & Psalms (Peterborough) [*CHP*]

Watts, H.J. (1937), *Hill Top Methodist Church Centenary* (Burslem)

Watts, Michael (1978, 1995), *The Dissenters* (Oxford)

Waymark, J. (1986), *Farringtons School 1911–1986*

Wearmouth, Robert F. (1948), *Some Working-Class Movements of the Nineteenth Century*

Wearmouth, Robert F. (1954), *Methodism and the Struggle of the Working Classes 1850–1900*

Wearmouth, R.F. (1957), *The Social and Political Influence of Methodism in the Twentieth Century*

Wearmouth, Robert F. (1959), *Methodism and the Trade Unions*

Wearmouth, Robert F. (1972), *Methodism and the Working Class Movements of England 1800–1850*

Weatherhead, Kingsley (1975), *Leslie Weatherhead*

Weatherill, G.W. (1953), *The Story of Darlington Methodism 1753–1953* (Darlington)

Webb, Pauline M. (1958), *Women of our Company*

Webb, Pauline M. (1963), *Women of our Time*

Welch, Edwin (1990), *Cheshunt College: the Early Years* (Ware)

Welch, Edwin (1995), *Spiritual Pilgrim. A reassessment of the life of the Countess of Huntingdon* (Cardiff)

Welford, Richard (1895), *Men of Mark twixt Tyne and Tweed*

Werner, Julia S. (1984), *The Primitive Methodist Connexion: its background and early history* (Madison, Wis)

Wesley, John (1742), *The Character of a Methodist*

Wesley, John (1749), *A Short Account of the School in Kingswood*

Wesley, John (1786), *A Short Account of the Life and Death of the Revd. John Fletcher*

Wesley, John, *Journal* (Standard Edition, ed. Nehemiah Curnock, 1909–16) [SJ]

Wesley, John, *Letters* (Standard Edition, ed. John Telford, 1931) [SL]

Wesley, John, *Works* (Oxford/Bicentennial Edition): *see* Cragg, G.R.; Davies, R.E.; Hildebrandt, F.; Outler, A.C.; Ward, W.R.

West, Francis A. (1843), *Memoirs of Jonathan Saville of Halifax* (Leeds)

West, H.F. (ed.) (1959), *Autobiography of Robert Watchorn* (Oklahoma City)

Westoby, A. (1837), Memoir of the author in T. Adam, *Exposition of the Gospels*

White, Herbert W. (1988), *Wesley's Taunton* (Taunton)

White, J.F. (ed.) (1995), *John Wesley's Prayer Book* (Akron, Ohio)

Whitehead, John (1793–96), *The Life of the Rev. John Wesley, MA*

Whiteley, J.H. (1939), *Wesley's Anglican Contemporaries*

Whittingham, Richard (ed.) (1838), Memoir in *Works of Charles Simeon*

Whyle, I. (ed.) (1990), *Rev. John Bumby Commemoration* (Auckland, NZ)

Wickes, Michael J.L. (1985), *John Wesley in Devon* (Bideford)

Wickes, Michael J.L. (1987), *The West Country Preachers. A new history of the Bible Christian Church (1815–1907)* (Appledore)

Wigley, D.L. (1997), *The Person, Not the Problem*

Wilkes, A. and Lovatt, J. (1942), *Mow Cop and the Camp Meeting Movement* (Leominster)

Wilkinson, Alan (1998), *Christian Socialism: Scott Holland to Tony Blair*

Wilkinson, E. (1972), *The Story of Early Methodism in Aberdeen* (Aberdeen)

Wilkinson, John T. (1951), *William Clowes, 1780–1851*

Wilkinson, John T. (1952), *Hugh Bourne, 1772–1852*

Wilkinson, John T. (1963), *Samuel Drew* (CMHA)

Wilkinson, John T. (1971), *Arthur Samuel Peake*

Williams, A.H. (1935), *Welsh Wesleyan Methodism* (Bangor)

Williams, A.H. (1971), *John Wesley in Wales* (Cardiff)

Williams, Colin W. (1960), *John Wesley's Theology Today*

Williams, Eva (1972), *The History of Southlands College*

Williams, G.A. (1988), *The Merthyr Rising* (Cardiff)

Williams, Henry W. (1881), *The Constitution and Polity of Wesleyan Methodism*
Williams, Martha (1841), *Memoirs of Ann Carr*
Williamson, George C. (1894), *John Russell, RA*
Williment, T.M.I. (1985), *John Hobbs 1800–1883 Wesleyan Missionary* (Wellington, NZ)
Wilson, D. (1850), *Methodism in Scotland* (Aberdeen)
Wilson, D. Dunn (1969), *Many Waters Cannot Quench*
Wilson, Robert (1890), *Wesleyan Methodism in the North End of Darlington* (Darlington)
Winston, W.R. (1892), *Four Years in Upper Burma*
Wiseman, Frederick Luke (1932), *Charles Wesley, Evangelist and Poet*
Wollen, Roger A. (1993), *The Church and the Artist*
Wood, A.H. (1975, 1978), *Overseas Missions of the Australian Methodist Church* (Melbourne)
Wood, A. Skevington (1957), *Thomas Haweis, 1734–1820*
Wood, A. Skevington (1983), *On Fire for God*
Wood, A. Skevington (1985), *Let Us Go On* (Ilkeston)
Wood, A. Skevington (1987), *The Kindled Flame*
Wood, A. Skevington (1992), *Brothers in Arms: John Wesley's Early Clerical Associates*
Wood, Eliza A. (1902), *Memorials of James Wood*
Wood, Thomas (1820), *A Biographical Sketch of ... Mr James Bundy* (2nd edn)
Woodcock, H. (*c.* 1907), *The Romance of Reality*
Woodward, Max W. (1966), *One at London: the story of Wesley's Chapel*
Woolcock, J. (1897), *A History of the Bible Christian Churches on the Isle of Wight*
World Methodist Council (1997), *Handbook 1997–2001*
Wright, Charles J. (1944), 'My Reasons for Entering the Church of England' in *Modern Churchman*,
    Dec. 1944
Wright, Christopher (1985), *Kent College Canterbury Centenary Book*
Wright, Don and Clancy, Eric (1993), *The Methodists: A History of Methodism in New South Wales*
    (St Leonards, NSW)
Wright, E.P. (1968), *A Catalog of the Joanna Southcote Collection at the University of Texas* (Texas)
Wright, John (1949), *Early Methodism in Yarm* (Billingham)
Wright, Stanley F. (1950), *Hart and the Chinese Customs* (Belfast)
Wycherley, R.N. (1936), *The Pageantry of Methodist Union*
Wyman, Edward (1997), *Methodism in Robin Hood's Bay Old and New* (reprint)

Y Bywgraffiadur Cynweig [*YBC*]
Yates, A.S. (1952), *The Doctrine of Assurance*
Young, David (1893), *The Origins and History of Methodism in Wales*
Young, Dinsdale T. [1907], *Robert Newton, the Eloquent Divine*
Young, Hugo (1989), *One of Us: a biography of Margaret Thatcher*
Young, J. (ed.) (1923), *Memories* (Sunderland)
Young, John (1903), *After a Hundred Years* (Burslem)
Young, Robert (1923), *Timothy Hackworth and the Locomotive*
Young, R.F. and Jebanesan, S. (1995), *The Bible Trembled* (Vienna)